Royal Navy Officers of the Seven Years War provides detailed reference information on over 2,000 commissioned officers of the Royal Navy: all of those whose career as a commissioned officer included the Seven Years War (1756-1763). In addition, those officers commissioned during and after 1748 and who died before 1756 are included.

Sourced primarily from some 15,000 original source documents held in the National Archives, the individual entries include the officers' pre-commission postings and commissions to ships as well as other naval and civil appointments. Genealogical information such as dates of birth, death, and marriage, and the names and dates of the officer's immediate family are also included for most of the entries.

As the first published reference work since 1849 to include this level of detail for all the Royal Navy officers of the period, *Royal Navy Officers of the Seven Years War* provides unparalleled access to information previously unpublished.

Cy Harrison has been a military and naval history enthusiast from an early age. Having studied Classical Civilisation at college, he first worked for the wargames company Games Workshop, before changing direction and becoming a market trader and finally a software developer. Being an early adopter of the World Wide Web, he became an active member of a group of historians intent on expanding the availability of information on naval history. He is a contributor to several naval history sites and forums, which has led to him founding the naval history website 'Three Decks – Warships in the Age of Sail' (https://threedecks.org) in 2010. He remains the owner and editor-in-chief of the site, which now has contributors from around the globe.

Royal Navy Officers of the Seven Years War

A Biographical Dictionary of Commissioned Officers 1748–1763

Cy Harrison

Helion & Company Limited

Dedicated to

David Robert and Barbara Mae

Thanks

Helion & Company Limited
Unit 8 Amherst Business Centre
Budbrooke Road
Warwick
CV34 5WE
England
Tel. 01926 499619
Email: info@helion.co.uk
Website: www.helion.co.uk
Twitter: @helionbooks
Visit our blog at http://blog.helion.co.uk/

Published by Helion & Company 2019
Designed and typeset by Mary Woolley, Battlefield Design (www.battlefield-design.co.uk)
Cover designed by Paul Hewitt, Battlefield Design (www.battlefield-design.co.uk)

Text © Cy Harrison, 2019
Cover: Detail from Battle of Quiberon Bay by Richard Perret (public domain)

Every reasonable effort has been made to trace copyright holders and to obtain their permission for the use of copyright material. The author and publisher apologise for any errors or omissions in this work, and would be grateful if notified of any corrections that should be incorporated in future reprints or editions of this book.

ISBN 978-1-912866-68-7

British Library Cataloguing-in-Publication Data.

A catalogue record for this book is available from the British Library.
All rights reserved. No part of this publication may be reproduced, stored in a retrieval system, or transmitted, in any form, or by any means, electronic, mechanical, photocopying, recording or otherwise, without the express written consent of Helion & Company Limited.
For details of other military history titles published by Helion & Company Limited, contact the above address, or visit our website: http://www.helion.co.uk

We always welcome receiving book proposals from prospective authors.

Contents

Acknowledgments

All books have an effect on those people who share in the world occupied by the author. This one is no different and the following are those I am most indebted to.

Firstly to my wife Jayne. Without her understanding, support, never-ending patience, and acceptance of a slightly obsessed husband's random behavior, this book would never have even been started.

I also want to share my appreciation of my parents David and Barbara, who have not only supported me when necessary in all sorts of ways, but even resorted to diving into records and proofreading first drafts with apparent enthusiasm and enjoyment when asked.

It would be remiss of me not to mention my editor, Andrew Bamford, who has guided me through the process and even spent time photographing documents in the National Archives when asked.

There are numerous others, many of these are 'virtual' friends, who because of the danger of upsetting them by an error of omission, I will not attempt to name individually. They know who they are and will understand that I consider their support, thoughts and encouragement essential.

Finally, I would like to mention my great dependence on those people who have selflessly spent their time making available much previously unknown details on that great information resource known as the internet. Whether this is an individual researching his family history, an academic publishing papers, or those many researchers contributing to general interest and specialist websites, their efforts are making the world a better and more informed place. This book would not have been half as complete without their contributions.

Cy Harrison
2019

The Royal Navy and the Seven Years War

On 23 December 1754, two Royal Navy ships, the *Centurion* (60) and the *Norwich* (54), under the command of Commodore Augustus Keppel, sailed from Cork as escorts to several transports carrying Major General Edward Braddock and his troops to North America. It was the first aggressive act by the British against the French in what was to become known as the Seven Years War.

Braddock and his 1,500 troops were intended to assault the French encroachment into the Ohio territories. They were to fail after a disastrous defeat at the Battle of the Monongahela on the 9 July 1755. Among the dead at that battle was Lieutenant Charles Spendelowe RN, commanding a detachment of 32 Royal Navy seamen. His commission, dated 30 November 1754, including instructions 'to attend the troops in their marches in order to assist in making floats for their passing the rivers and also to take a draft of the country though which they pass'. It was the first time the British Army and Royal Navy would cooperate during the war, it would not be the last.

Initially both France and Great Britain attempted to prevent an escalation of the war in Europe. The situation in North America was growing more serious, however. In April 1755, the French had collected 14 ships of the line and 3,000 troops at Brest intended for North America, in response, the British Cabinet ordered the preparation of a British squadron to be stationed of Louisbourg with instructions to take French vessels carrying troops or armaments to Canada and to engage them if they resisted. This squadron was under the command of Vice Admiral Edward Boscawen and when it sailed on 27 April 1755, included 11 ships of the line. The French squadron, now numbering 19 ships of the line and six frigates, sailed on 5 May, and on 11 May, the British sent an additional six ships of the line under Rear Admiral Francis Holburne to reinforce Boscawen.

On 8 June 1755, the first naval engagement of the war took place when ships of Boscawen's squadron engaged three French vessels off the Grand Banks near the entrance to the Gulf of St. Lawrence, taking two of them. The French fleet had been scattered, but Boscawen was unable to prevent the rest from reaching Louisbourg and, on hearing the news of the action, the French severed diplomatic relations: war was now inevitable.

In home waters, the British Channel Fleet had put to sea under Vice Admiral Edward Hawke in July. On 23 August, he received orders to take any French warships, merchantmen, and privateers he found. After returning to port in September, the fleet returned to sea in October, this time commanded by Vice Admiral John Byng. During October and November, the squadron took more than 300 French vessels, including a 74-gun ship of the line, and captured over 6,000 French sailors, events which significantly reduced the number of trained seamen available to the French and exacerbated their already severe shortage of men for their navy.

Meanwhile the British were busily expanding their influence in the Indian sub-continent where troops and vessels of the East India company under Commodore James were supported by Royal Navy vessels under Rear Admiral Charles Watson. Other operations to reduce the influence of pirates on the Malabar coast took place and separate campaigns were fought by the East India company against several independent palaiyakkarars, or barons, who controlled districts of Madura, nominally in territory under the dominion of the Nawab of Arcot and at his request. These activities led the French Governor of Pondicherry to send troops into the territory of the Nawab at the request of the Mysore in Carnatic. When the East India Company threatened military action against these incursions, the French withdrew, but further hostilities were inevitable. In North America, British forces occupied Fort Beauséjour in May 1755. While there had been no formal declaration during 1755, the situation in North America, India, and at sea meant that war was now a reality in all but name.

The British strategy during the war was, in general, linked to the pursuit of three basic principles. First and foremost, to prevent a French invasion of the British Isles; secondly to prevent France from occupying Hanover, the home state of King George II and, from 1760 of King George III; finally, to gain British dominance in North America. These aims were complemented by the understanding that during the inevitable peace talks, bargaining tokens would be required, denying such to the French and obtaining them for Britain was thus also a consideration. It was within these operational parameters that the Royal Navy operated.

At the end of 1755, Britain was in negotiation with Russia, hoping to keep Russian troops on the Prussian border to secure Hanover from a potential Prussian threat. Getting wind of this Frederick II of Prussia, who had been a French ally up to this point, offered not only to not attack Hanover, but to actively defend it. At a stroke the secondary British objective in Europe could be achieved and the Treaty of Westminster was signed on 16 January 1756. In May the French and Austrians, who had been enemies, signed a defensive alliance and with Austria already having an extant defensive treaty, from 1746, with Russia the battle lines had been drawn for an extended conflict in Europe.

In early 1756, the Royal Navy was kept busy with preparations for war, as well as maintaining a blockade of the French coast. In March Hawke was at sea off Brest and Rochefort. In April Byng was dispatched to the Mediterranean to defend Minorca, Commodore Augustus Keppel was off Cherbourg with orders to destroy the landing barges being built there, Holburne had sailed for North America escorting troop transports, and preparations were underway to transport 18,000 Hanoverian and Hessian troops to Britain, they arrived in May.

In India, operations against the Indian pirates on the Malabar coast continued, this time with East India Company troops commanded by Robert Clive and a Royal Navy squadron commanded by Rear Admiral Watson in a combined operation against Gheriah, which was taken on 14 February.

In the Mediterranean, a French fleet of 12 ships of the line and five frigates left Toulon on 10 April 1756, escorting transports carrying 16,000 troops. they arrived off Minorca on 18 April, and began to land the troops. By 23 April they had begun to besiege the British garrison which had withdrawn to Fort St. Philip. Byng arrived on 20 May, and following the indecisive Battle of Minorca on the same day, withdrew to Gibraltar on 24 May, leaving the French to continue their siege without interference. Fort St Philip surrendered on 7 June. Byng was recalled and eventually executed on 14 March 1757, for his failure to protect the island.

Meanwhile Great Britain had declared war against France on 18 May 1756, signifying the formal commencement of hostilities between the two nations; France reciprocated on 9 June. It was the beginning of a war sometimes seen as the first truly global conflict, but this was only the case for the British, French, and – later –the Spanish. It encompassed conflict in Europe, North America, the Caribbean, Africa, and the Indian subcontinent.

During the remainder of 1756, the Royal Navy in Europe concentrated on blockading the French fleet in Brest and Rochefort with the Channel Fleet which at its peak contained

18 ships of the line, however the difficulty of maintaining the ships on station meant that on three occasions the French managed to put fleets to sea and reinforce their holdings in North America.

In the Channel the small war of the 'guerre de course' was at its peak with British and French privateers, cruisers and merchant vessels involved. During the war, France issued letters of marque to over 700 privateer vessels, while Britain issued over 1,600.

In India, the new Mughal nawab, Siraj Ud Daulah, began a campaign against the British which culminated in his capture of Calcutta in June. In October 1756, Vice Admiral Watson convoyed Company troops commanded by Clive on a mission of reprisal up the Hugli River. Watson's ships engaged the enemy at Fort William on 2 January 1757, while Clive recovered control of Calcutta. After a determined counter-attack by the Indian forces, a peace treaty with the nawab was signed in February.

During 1757, the British again tried to maintain a blockade of the French coast. Despite the presence of Hawke, the French managed to send a fleet consisting of 15 ships of the line, five frigates and 5,000 troops to the West Indies, and a fleet of nine ships of the line, four frigates and 1,200 troops to Louisbourg in May, as well as dispatching a fleet from Lorient for the East Indies.

In early 1757 the Hessian and Hanoverian troops were returned to Europe to aid the defence of Hanover. In March, the French began an invasion of Hanover, the British sent a small squadron under Captain Hyde Parker to support their forces there. He arrived too late to prevent the French taking Emden, the primary supply route into Hanover, but spent the rest of the year blockading the French-held coast and keeping the longer secondary supply route via Stade in the Elbe estuary open. Hanover was overrun and on 8 September, the Allied commander, the Duke of Cumberland, signed Cumberland signed the Convention of Kloster-Zeven ceding control to the French, but maintaining control of Stade.

On 5 April 1757, Rear Admiral Charles Saunders, Commander in Chief in the Mediterranean, intercepted a French squadron of six ships near Gibraltar, but was unable to prevent them from exiting the Mediterranean and sailing as reinforcements for Louisbourg.

In September 1757, the British commenced the first of their 'descents' on the French coast. This was a series of landings in force on the French coast intended to draw troops away from Hanover. The target was Rochefort and the British Fleet commanded by Sir Edward Hawke sailed on 8 September, carrying 7,000 troops. On 23 September, following a naval bombardment, British troops took the outlying Île-d'Aix, destroying the defensive works. No further landings were attempted though and on 1 October, the British sailed for home.

While a failure in every respect, this expedition did allow some valuable lessons to be learnt. Firstly, it was apparent that combined operations of this type could not rely on 'command by committee'. Henceforth the Royal Navy would command at sea, with the army only taking control once a landing had been completed. Secondly, and possibly more importantly, it was realised that trying to land troops in a motley assortment of ships boats, cutters, and launches caused difficulty in the actual landing of troops. This led to the development of specialist flat bottom landing barges, in two sizes, which were designed to carry troops much closer to the shore and were to be used in all future amphibious operations carried by ships of war and transports alike.

In North America, in addition to continued skirmishing in the Great Lakes, which generally went in favour of the French and led to them controlling all the lake and river routes into Canada, the British were preparing for an expedition to take the French fortress Louisbourg on Cape Breton island. This was seen as the linchpin of French possessions in North America, being able to intercept ships heading for the St. Lawrence, and taking it would open up access to the rest of Canada for the British now an invasion from New York via the Great Lakes was no longer possible. Accordingly, 90 transports, accompanied by Rear Admiral Charles Hardy with five vessels, were assembled at New York. These moved to Sandy Hook and then Halifax where the British fleet now consisted of 17 ships of the line, 14 frigates and sloops, two bomb ketches, and one fire ship escorting 179 transports carrying 16,000 troops commanded by Vice Admiral Francis Holburne.

On 10 August 1757 Holburne took part of his fleet to reconnoitre Louisbourg. On 20 August, he was close enough to receive some fire from the defending forts and to confirm that reports of the French strength, 18 ships of the line, were true. On 11 September, he returned to Halifax to repair and re-supply before returning to blockade Louisbourg. On 24 September, the fleet was struck by a gale, two ships, *Tilbury* (58) and *Ferret* (14), were lost and all the rest damaged and scattered. The attempt on Louisbourg was abandoned, although a strong squadron was left at Halifax in preparation for a further attempt in 1758.

Following the recovery of Calcutta, the British forces in India began a campaign against the French settlement of Chandernagore, 50 kilometres up the Hugli river from Calcutta. Supported by five Royal Navy and two Company vessels under Vice Admiral Watson, Chandernagore was taken on 23 March 1757. On 13 June, Clive began a further march upstream into Bengal, which culminated in his victory at the Battle of Plassey on 23 June, often seen as the start of British control in India.

In the West Indies there was an indecisive action between three British ships of the line under Commodore Arthur Forrest and four French ships of the line off Cap-Français, Haiti, on 21 October 1757. The British were attempting to intercept the convoy which the French were escorting. The French resistance and damage received meant the British had to withdraw to Jamaica. The French convoy eventually reached France unmolested.

By the beginning of 1758, the British strategy of blockading the French fleet in port had reduced the threat of a French invasion of the British Isles. However, the French invasion of Hanover in late 1757 had inevitably been followed by an Allied counter-offensive in late 1757, which had some success but failed in recovering Hanover. The offensive recommenced in January and by 4 February, eight British ships commanded by Rear Admiral Charles Holmes were operating in the Ems, Weser, and Elbe in its support. On 23 March, Holmes' squadron appeared off Emden and forced the withdrawal of the French garrison. Holme's landed a marine force to occupy the city, which was later replaced by a regiment of foot, the first British troops to land in Europe during the war.

In the Mediterranean, a French squadron of eight ships of the line and four frigates had sailed from Toulon in December 1757, bound for North America and the West Indies. They had been forced into Cartagena by the presence of the British Mediterranean Fleet under Admiral Henry Osborne and were still being blockaded in February 1758. On 28 February six French ships attempted to join the French in Cartagena so their combined strength would allow a breakout. Two ships of the line did get in, but two more ships of the line were taken and 1 more run ashore and destroyed by the British. The French frigate escaped. The French eventually escaped back to Toulon, but were prevented from leaving the Mediterranean.

In India, Vice Admiral George Pocock was now in command, and having been reinforced now commanded a squadron of seven ships of the line, one frigate and a store ship. On 28 April 1758 he sighted a French fleet putting in to the roadstead of the British controlled Fort Saint-David near Cuddalore. Two British frigates were in the roadstead and to avoid capture were run ashore and burnt, and the French landed troops and a siege train. On 29 April, the French came out and an indecisive action between seven British and nine French ships of the line ensued. The French lost one ship forced ashore, but the British had to withdraw to Madras to refit. This allowed the French to occupy Cuddalore and besiege Fort Saint-David, which capitulated on 2 June.

On 25 July Pocock sailed out of Madras in search of the French squadron. On 27 July, he arrived off Pondicherry where the French were seen at anchor. On 28 July, the French weighed and sailed Southwards pursued by the British. After several days of pursuit, the British, with seven ships of the line and one frigate, came up with the French, with eight ships of the line and one frigate, off Negapatam on 3 August 1758. The British had the better of the engagement which degenerated into a running fight as the French fled for Pondicherry, which they reached without loss.

Elsewhere two expeditions to Senegal on the West African coast had succeeded in taking the French possessions of Fort Louis on 1 May and the island of Goree on 29 December 1758. While not of major strategic importance these operations were an example of the British governments developing policy of 'economic warfare', denying income to the French and benefiting themselves.

As part of this policy the Royal Navy now embarked on its first major offensive operations in the West Indies. Prior to this the British forces had been primarily operating on a defensive footing maintaining the flow of goods to the British Isles and protecting British trade. A force of 11 ships of the line was collected, together with supporting vessels and 60 transports carrying 5,000 troops. The British fleet commanded by Commodore Richard Hughes sailed from Barbados on 3 January 1759, in an attempt on Martinique. Troops were landed unopposed on 16 January, but French opposition and the difficulties of moving around the island meant the British withdrew on 19 January. It was then decided to make an attempt on the island of Guadeloupe instead. Landings were undertaken on 22 January and on 1 May 1759, the island finally capitulated.

On the 5 June 1758, the British Channel Fleet of 24 ships of the line commanded by Admiral of the Fleet Lord Anson landed 13,000 troops in Cancale Bay, in the vicinity of Saint-Malo. Due to the inability to move its siege train the British did not take Saint-Malo, but inflicted significant damage on French shipping and trade, including the destruction of 20 privateers. The landing force was withdrawn and looked for further opportunities on the French coast. On two occasions, off Havre de Grace on 26 June, and off Cherbourg on 29 June, the landing boats were launched and troops embarked before the proposed landings were abandoned. The British withdrew and arrived at St. Helens on 1 July.

In July 1758, preparations for further landings in force began, this time with the target of Cherbourg. On 6 August 1758, a British fleet, of five ships of the line, eight frigates and various smaller vessels commanded by Commodore Richard Howe, escorted 140 transports into Cherbourg Bay. The troops landed on 8 and 9 August, and after some French resistance occupied Cherbourg and by 15 August the pier, docks, magazines, forts and defences of the harbour had been destroyed and several vessels destroyed or carried off. 150 pieces of captured artillery were taken back to Britain following which the entire force withdrew on 16 August and sailed for Britain.

On arrival at home, new orders were issued for the expedition to continue operations, this time against Saint-Malo. After various delays the British troops were landed in the Bay of Saint-Briac, west of Saint-Malo, without opposition, but in the face of strong French opposition achieved little and re-embarked at Saint-Cast bay in the face of French assaults on 11 September. The British lost 2,000 men killed, wounded and captured, including one general dead and three naval captains and a commander taken prisoner while they were supervising the re-embarkation. It was the last British attempt against mainland France during the conflict.

In North America, which was now the focus of British aggression, a major operation to take Louisbourg had started in May 1758, although preparations had begun immediately after the failed attempt in 1757. As soon as the weather permitted in early 1758, Rear Admiral Sir Charles Hardy had placed himself off Louisbourg in an attempt to blockade the harbour. an enterprise in which he was only partially successful, some French reinforcements succeeding in getting through and then sailing on to Quebec. On 1 June 1758, the British Fleet, commanded by Admiral Edward Boscawen, arrived in sight of Louisbourg having sailed from Halifax on 28 May. This fleet now consisted of 23 ships of the line and 18 frigates and escorted transports carrying 12,000 regular troops. After delays caused by fog and strong winds, the British force landed on 8 June, supported by fire from the frigates and under fire from French defenders.

For several days, communications between the troops and the fleet were interrupted by bad weather which meant that the siege train wasn't landed until 18 June and the siege began in earnest. The French surrendered on 18 July. Following this success, Rear Admiral Hardy was dispatched to destroy various French settlements on the shores of the St. Lawrence, Rear Admiral Philip Durell was left in North America with a squadron and Boscawen sailed for home, encountering a French squadron returning from Quebec on 27 October, but being unable to bring them to action succeeded only in retaking a captured East Indiaman.

Following this success, in 1759 the British tried to reduce Quebec, the main base of the French in Canada. The British dispatched a force of 9,000 men under Major General James Wolfe escorted by a fleet of 22 ships of the line, 13 frigates and 14 smaller vessels. This force sailed on 17 February 1759 and reached Louisbourg in May. On 1 June, the British started to leave Louisbourg with the last transport sailing on 6 June. In May 1759, Rear-Admiral Durell had been dispatched into the St. Lawrence to intercept French reinforcements, but had sailed too late to prevent a French flotilla of 22 ships from sailing to Quebec with supplies and troops. Durell did though take three small vessels that had straggled behind. and then remained in the St. Lawrence until the main fleet arrived.

On 26 June, the British anchored a few miles below Quebec and the following day landed the British army. On 28 June, the French launched a fireship attack against the British fleet. Despite causing some chaos in the British army camp, they failed to cause any damage as many were intercepted by Royal Navy sailors and dragged ashore and others ran aground.

Following the development of siege works and the moving of the *Sutherland* (50), 6 frigates, sloops and transports past Quebec on 18 July, and an unsuccessful assault on French positions at Beauport, the British decided on a landing below the Plains of Abraham on the night of 12 September. In the subsequent land battle the French were defeated and both commanding officers were killed. Following this action, which bypassed their main defences, the majority of the French force promptly departed, leaving Quebec with a small garrison which surrendered on 18 September. There were several further skirmishes between British and French vessels in the river until, on 24 November, the French attempted to force their way past the British, some six or seven vessels succeeded, while others were stranded and abandoned. One of these, the *Elisabeth*, later exploded killing some 40 British officers and crewmen.

In the hope of diverting the Royal Navy from its operations in North America and the East Indies, the French planned a series of invasions of the British Isles. This was to be a three-pronged assault, with forces intended to land in Ireland, Scotland and England. To this end, the fleet in Brest, of 21 ships of the line, was to be joined by the French Mediterranean Fleet of 12 ships of the line from Toulon. Flat bottom landing barges were being built in large numbers at Le Havre for the invasion of England and forces assembled at Dunkirk intended for Scotland and Vannes intended for Ireland.

However, Brest was blockaded by Admiral Hawke who, despite occasional small-scale attempts by the French, kept them in harbour until November. In July 1759, a British squadron sailed for Le Havre commanded by Rear Admiral George Brydges Rodney. As well as five small ships of the line and five frigates the squadron included six bomb-vessels. They arrived off Le Havre on 3 July and on the following day began a 52-hour bombardment of the town and harbour. The town and harbour were severely damaged and all the landing barges were destroyed. The British squadron then took position off the harbour and maintained a close blockade for the rest of the year.

In the Mediterranean, the fleet under Admiral Boscawen continued to blockade Toulon until August when the French attempted to breakout and sail to Brest. They sailed from Toulon with 12 ships of the line and three frigates on 5 August, and on 17 August passed the Straits of Gibraltar where they were sighted by a British frigate. Informed of the French presence Boscawen took the British fleet to sea to intercept.

On the morning of 18 August, five French ships had separated during the night and sailed to Cadiz. The British engaged the remainder in Lagos Bay, and in a decisive victory took three ships of the line, ran two more ashore and chased the survivors into Cadiz where they were blockaded. The French had failed to join their two fleets and now had to rely on the Brest Fleet getting to sea.

The French expedition for Scotland in Dunkirk, of six frigates carrying some 2,000 troops, was being blockaded by a squadron under Commodore William Boys. It was not until 15 October, with Boys off station due to a gale, that this force put to sea. Boys lost contact, but cruised off the coast of Scotland to prevent a landing there. The French though had sailed for Ostend and later moved to Bergen. They later briefly landed troops at Carrickfergus, Ireland in February 1760, before the surviving three French frigates were all forced to surrender by a British squadron commanded by Captain John Elliot on 28 February 1760.

Finally, on 14 November the French attempted to force their way out of Brest. They sailed with 21 ships of the line in an attempt to attack the squadron of Commodore Robert Duff, which was blockading the French transports in the Morbihan River. Hawke and the main squadron had been blown off station by a gale were now at Torbay. They also sailed on the same day and, having been informed off the French escape, also headed for Quiberon Bay.

On 20 November, the two fleets met in the bay. The weather was poor, with squalls, gales and poor visibility. The British had 26 ships of the line with seven frigates, the French 21 ships of the line and four frigates. By the end of the day the British had won a major victory in a battle often seen as of equal importance to Trafalgar in 1805. The British lost two ships, both by going aground, but the French fleet was shattered. One French ship of the line was captured, four more had been sunk or wrecked and the remainder scattered into several ports: two were later burnt and some of the survivors remained blockaded for the rest of the war.

In India Admiral Pocock, having refitted at Madras, sailed to engage the French squadron previously left at Pondicherry. He eventually found them off Ceylon on 3 September 1759. The French managed to evade him and sailed for Pondicherry, where on 10 September they were engaged. This time the British had nine ships of the line to the French 11 and the French managed to enter Pondicherry harbour. On 30 September, the French squadron quit Pondicherry and sailed for the Île de France. This left the Royal Navy complete master of the seas around India and directly led to the British capture of Pondicherry in January 1761.

The tide of war had swung decisively in favour of the British during 1759. The threat of an invasion of the British Isles had been entirely removed and the French fleet significantly damaged. The taking of Quebec, together with other land operations had set the scene for British dominance in Canada and Northern America. The successes of the East India Company and Royal Navy in India was laying the foundation for the British empire in India. it is not without reason that 1759 is sometimes referred to as the 'Annus mirabilis'.

Although it now appeared inevitable that Britain would prevail, the war was not yet over. In Canada French forces from Montreal attempted to retake Quebec. They travelled down the St. Lawrence during April 1760 in boats escorted by two frigates and two sloops. By 29 April they had begun siege operations outside Quebec, the sole British sloop having been sent to Halifax with a cry for help. On 15 May three British ships, including a ship of the line, arrived as relief and with their presence the French had withdrawn to Montreal by the end of the month. In July, escorted by two frigates, a sloop and a schooner, the British at Quebec began an advance on Montreal, which after a lengthy campaign which included action on the lakes of Champlain and Ontario resulted in the capitulation of Montreal on 8 September. With this the whole of Canada and all its dependencies passed to the British crown, remaining French forces were transferred back to France in British ships. Britain now controlled the whole of Northern America and one of its primary aims in the war had been accomplished.

On the coast of France, the Royal Navy maintained its blockades of Le Havre, Quiberon Bay, and Toulon. These blockades succeeded in keeping the weakened French navy in port and prevented supplies and reinforcements reaching North America or the West Indies. In India, the British squadron continued in its role of support to the East India Company.

In the West Indies, the French fleet had been so reduced as to pose little danger, the British continued their policy of defending the trade vessels and escorting convoys to Europe. There was little action of note, until on 16 October, a French convoy, with an escort of five frigates, put to sea from Cap-Francois in Cuba. These were intercepted by three British ships and during a running fight on 18 and 19 October all, but for one French frigate, were taken or destroyed.

At the start of 1761 the Royal Navy was maintaining squadrons and fleets in the Channel, Quiberon Bay, the Mediterranean, North America, Jamaica, the Leeward Islands, and the East Indies. There had been planned in 1760 an operation to take Mauritius which had been postponed. With the newly developing danger of the Spanish joining forces with the French it was thought to risky to send a large part of the Royal Navy into the Indian Ocean, instead an operation to occupy Belle-Isle was undertaken. This had the benefit of keeping the navy close to home, and, if as seemed likely, peace negotiations were in the offing, provide a major advantage in the British position at such talks.

Accordingly, an expedition sailed on 29 March 1761. The escorting fleet consisted of 10 ships of the line, eight frigates, three sloops, three bombs, and two fire ships commanded by Commodore Augustus Keppel, it was accompanied by 7,000 troops in 100 transports. They arrived off Belle-Isle on 6 April. A second squadron under Captain Matthew Buckle with 13 ships of the line and three frigates had meanwhile been dispatched to cruise of Brest and prevent any French interference from there.

The British landed on 22 April, and with support from Royal Navy which suppressed defending batteries succeeded and forced the French to withdraw into the fortress of Le Palais. By 31 April, Keppel had been reinforced with an additional six ships of the line and dispatched Captain Thomas Stanhope to blocked Rochefort where eight French ships of the line were being prepared, he maintained the blockade through the remainder of the year. Keppel was later to send five ships to join Captain Buckle off Brest where another seven French vessels were being readied for sea, all the while maintaining a squadron to support the British army's activities on the island. Belle-Isle itself resisted until 10 June, when the British occupied La Palais and began an occupation that would last for the remainder of the war.

In the West Indies, a squadron of four ships of the line and three frigates commanded by Commodore James Douglas escorted 1,500 troops transferred from North America in an expedition against Dominica. They sailed from Guadeloupe on 3 June 1761, landing troops on 6 June and accepting the French surrender on the following day.

At the start of 1762, a British force assembled throughout 1761 and commanded by Rear Admiral George Brydges Rodney had been prepared with the intention of occupying Martinique. Sailing from Barbados on 5 January, the fleet contained 17 ships of the line, 14 frigates and assorted supporting vessels and was escort to transports carrying 14,000 troops. Arriving off Martinique on 7 January, after several days spent deploying his forces and reconnoitring the island for landing places, the British forces finally began landed under cover of the fleet on 16 January. After reducing some French outlying defences, the British began operations against the main port of Fort Royal on 25 January. Fort Royal surrendered on 4 February and a detachment of ships was sent to land marines at La Trinité which also surrendered, signifying the end of operations on the island. Rodney then detached a small squadron under Captain Augustus John Hervey to occupy Saint Luca. the squadron, consisting of 4 ships and a bomb vessel arrived on the 24 February. The following day they entered the main harbour and the French surrendered without a fight.

Rodney then, on 28 February 1762, received orders to begin hostilities against the Spanish, Britain having declared war on 4 January, 1762. He spent the next couple of months consolidating his position. In March Rodney received orders to suspend further operations until the arrival of a fleet commanded by Admiral George Pocock and sent reinforcements to support the British squadron in Jamaica which were to join with Pocock when he arrived.

By 23 May, the various squadrons had combined and were now off Haiti. The combined force under Pocock now consisting of 21 ships of the line with 24 smaller warships and transports carrying 13,000 troops. On 6 June, the British approached Cuba and began landing troops to besiege Fort Morro across the bay from Havana itself. On 22 June, land batteries opened fire on the fort and siege works were begun. Eventually, on 30 July, a mine was detonated under the fort's walls and an assault secured control of the fort. Following the fall of Fort Morro, British attention turned to Havana, beginning a bombardment on 11 August, by the afternoon the Spanish began to sue for terms. The British entered the city on 14 August, and the Royal Navy took possession of nine Spanish ships of the line, three frigates, nine smaller vessels, as well as several privateers and merchant vessels.

There was only one further Royal Navy expedition of any size during the war. The British squadron in India, now commanded by Rear Admiral Samuel Cornish, with eight ships of the line and three frigates sailed on 1 August, escorting a transport fleet with 3,000 troops to attack Manilla. They arrived on 23 September, much to the surprise of the Spanish who did not know that war had started. When the Spanish refused an opportunity to surrender, troops were landed on the 24 and 25 September. Operations were begun to take the city, which included naval fire against the Spanish defences. A combined land and naval bombardment was begun on 4 October, and on 6 October the defences were stormed and Havana taken. On 31 October two British ships of the line took the Spanish Manila Galleon, having been specially detached for that purpose.

The taking of Manila was the last action of the Royal Navy during the war. They had supported British policy throughout the world, had enabled the conquest of North America, made significant gains in the West Indies, helped to secure British dominance in India, all while suppressing any threat from the French navy in Europe.

On 10 February 1763, the Treaty of Paris was signed, establishing peace between France, Great Britain, Hanover, and Spain. Five days later Austria, Prussia, and Saxony signed the Treaty of Hubertusburg and the Seven Years War was over.

As part of the peace agreement, Britain returned Manilla and Havana to Spain and Guadeloupe, Martinique, Saint Lucia and Gorée to France. In return, Britain regained Minorca and was formally recognised as holding sovereignty over Canada, Dominica and several other islands, as well as receiving large portions of French Louisiana. The Royal Navy's dominance had allowed Britain to come out of the conflict several steps ahead of its continental rivals.

Introduction to the Service Records

The following pages contain information on the careers of 2,025 Royal Navy commissioned officers. To qualify for inclusion in this volume an officer must have been first commissioned as a lieutenant after 18 October 1748, the date of the treaty of Aix-la-Chapelle which concluded the War of the Austrian Succession, and before 10 February 1763, the date of the Treaty of Paris which formally marked the conclusion the Seven Years War. Alternately, officers that do not qualify through the first date of commission are included if the officer was commissioned before the date of the Treaty of Aix-la-Chapelle and was either known to be still alive on 1 January 1755 or, where no date of death is known, had active service on or after 1 January1755.

QUALIFICATIONS FOR COMMISSIONING

To be commissioned in the Royal Navy, an officer was required to have fulfilled service requirements introduced in 1677 by Samuel Pepys as an attempt to provide the Royal Navy with a more professional officer class. The first requirement was that they had to be at least 20 years of age, although some officers managed to avoid this and be commissioned earlier. The second requirement was that they had at least three years sea service. Finally, they needed to have completed a minimum of one year's service as a midshipman or master's mate. This service was as a normal completed as a rating, an impermanent position on a ship to which a seaman was assigned by the captain and encompassing those crew members who did not hold a commission or a warrant. Occasionally an officer would have served in one of the 'warrant officer' positions or as an 'acting' commissioned officer as well. In 1703 the service time requirement was raised to four years with at least two as a midshipman or master's mate. In 1729 the total service time was again raised, this time to six years, although the requirement for two years as a midshipman or master's mate remained unchanged. These requirements were for service in Royal Navy vessels, but in 1745 service in the merchant navy was permitted to count for the four years of 'general' service although merchant service had occasionally been accepted prior to this date.

DATES

Throughout these records dates are presented in the format dd.mm.yyyy (day, month, year). Where an exact date is unknown the day and month may be omitted. Dates prior to 14 September 1752, the date the United Kingdom adopted the Gregorian calendar and switched the first day of the year to 1 January from 25 March, will also include a suffix indicating the Julian and Gregorian years for dates in the overlapping part of the year. For example, 1 March 1750 in the Julian Calendar will be displayed as 1.3.1750/51.

Dates may also include one of the prefixes noted below.

1. c. Circa, indicating the date is an approximation
2. bef. Before, indicating that the event occurred no later than the given date

SERVICE RECORDS

The officers service records are organised in alphabetical order on surname followed by forename. Each officer's record is split into three distinct areas.

DATES

A list of known events unrelated to the officer's naval career. These include dates of birth and death, baptism, probate of will and honours received. These are all shown with the date first, then the event, followed by a location if known and relevant.

FAMILY

These are restricted to immediate family; parents, siblings, spouses and children, legitimate or otherwise. Within these records surnames are omitted for siblings and children and those for mothers and wives are their maiden name when known. Daughters and sisters may include a married surname enclosed in brackets, e.g. [Smith], where known and all relatives may include dates of birth and death enclosed in parentheses, e.g. (1720-1810). Any relative with service in the Royal Navy is indicated by the suffix RN.

SERVICE

This section lists the known positions held by the officer, including those held prior to their first commission when available. These records consist of individual events with a start of service date, an end of service date where the service is not understood to have been sequential; the rating or rank held, the ship the position was held on, with the vessels type for unrated vessels and the vessels nominal armament indicated in parentheses.

The first commission given at a rank is highlighted in **bold** and is used to highlight progression in the Royal Navy hierarchy, from lieutenant, through commander, to captain and the various grades of admiral. Where they are not preceded by a date the commission is for the first ship immediately succeeding the commission. Where a commission is at a rank different to the officer's nominal substantive rank, e.g. as a commodore, this is indicated as normal, except that commanders, who in the early period hold the substantive rank of lieutenant, are indicated as commanders. To aid clarity, lieutenants commanding ships are shown as lieutenant-commanders even though the rank is anachronistic, being a Victorian innovation.

Dates within the service history may also include superscript notations. Where these appear on the first or only date of a service history event, they indicate that the commission was first issued overseas. The superscript element includes a short code for the location, see the list later in this introduction for details, and the date the commission was confirmed by the Admiralty. The entry 29.11.1756$^{\text{(ECH 12.11.1759)}}$ thus indicates a commission issued in the English Channel on 29 November 1756 and confirmed 12 November 1759.

Where they appear as a suffix to the second date of an event they give an indication of why that period of service terminated.

†	The officer died or was killed
P	Vessel was paid off
S	Vessel sank in action
C	Vessel was taken by the enemy or the officer was otherwise captured
W	Vessel was wrecked
F	Vessel foundered
R	The officer resigned his position
D	The officer was dismissed from his position

SC Vessel scuttled
B Vessel burnt
L The officer was granted leave
FE The fire ship being served on was expended

Where no reason has been appended to a second or end of service date the officer is assumed to have been superseded. Where an event has no second date then the officer is assumed to have had continuous service and taken up his subsequent position with little or no gap between. In some cases this will include a new or renewed commission to the same vessel.

Dates shown are generally the date that the commission was issued and as such do not necessarily correspond to the date the officer actually arrived on the ship. A delay of days, sometimes weeks or months, would have been common. Dates for service prior to the issue of the first commission are mostly taken from extant lieutenant's passing certificates. These, with a handful of exceptions, do not specify dates of service, but length of service only. In the absence of other information, the dates have been extrapolated by calculating backwards from the date the examination was passed, assuming that the records are sequential and in chronological order. Events such as ships being paid off or lost have been used to modify this process where possible.

ABBREVIATIONS

In order to save space most ranks and ratings are indicated in the service histories using an abbreviation. These are shown in the table of ratings and ranks below.

Ratings and ranks are shown with the abbreviation used in parentheses and a brief note on the position's role in the Royal Navy. Where no abbreviation is given the rating or rank is used as-is.

These lists do not include all Royal Navy ratings and ranks, but instead are restricted to those that are referenced in the service records. See Appendix xxx for a list of all official ratings and ranks used during the period.

RATINGS

Ratings for seamen and petty officers were normally assigned by the vessel's commanding officer in consultation with other senior officers and according to their skills and ability. Sometimes referred to as the ship's 'people'.

Able Seaman (Able)	Considered to be an experienced sailor.
Crew	The sailmaker (Sail Crew) and the carpenter (Carp Crew) both had several hands making their 'crew' to assist them in their duties.
Invalid	A sailor carried on board and part of the ship's company but incapable of work due to illness or infirmity.
Landsman (Land)	No sea experience at all.
Not Rated (NR)	A seaman serving on a vessel without having been rated by the captain.
Ordinary Seaman (Ord)	A useful seaman, but not of the standard to be rated 'Able'.
Quarter Gunner (QGnr)	There was one quarter-gunner for each four guns on a ship.
Retinue	A member of the retinue of a commodore (Com Ret) or admiral (Adm Ret) on a flag ship

Servants (Serv)	Servants are all identified by the abbreviation for the person they are serving, plus 'Serv'. E.g. a Captain's servant has the abbreviation (Capt Serv), a lieutenant's as (L. Serv). Occasionally the entry is as servant (Serv) alone.
Supernumerary (Supnum)	A person carried in excess of a ships normal complement
Unknown (Unk)	A record where the rating is not known, usually because it is not recorded. This is distinct from being not rated.
Volunteer (Vol)	A sailor serving in a voluntary role, often hoping for preferential treatment.

PETTY OFFICERS

Captain's Clerk (Clerk)	Typically hired by the captain to perform various administrative tasks.
Corporal (Cpl)	An assistant to the master-at-arms
Coxswain (Cox)	Commander of a barge, often the captain's or ship's boat
Master's Mate (Mate)	A senior petty officer assisting the ship's master in his duties and, on smaller vessels, capable of standing a watch. One of the positions with a service time requirement to qualify to take the lieutenant's examination.
Mate	Warrant officers generally had one or more mates to assist them in their duties. These are abbreviated by appending the word Mate to the abbreviation for the officer they assist
Midshipman (Mid)	A senior petty officer, sometimes considered as a trainee officer but often filled by young 'gentlemen'. One of the positions with a service time requirement to qualify to take the lieutenant's examination
Midshipman Ordinary (MidO)	Taking the position and role of a midshipman, but being paid as an able seaman
Midshipman Extra (MidE)	An officer who previously held a commission taking the position of a midshipman in the hope of being recommissioned.
Volunteer per Order (VpO)	A young candidate, of approximately 14 years of age, warranted by the Admiralty to serve on board ship in the place of a midshipman.
Yeoman of the Powder Room (YoP)	Responsible to the gunner and for the maintenance and care of the powder stores.
Yeoman of the Sheets (YoS)	Assistant to the Boatswain and responsible for the upkeep and care of the sail locker.

WARRANT OFFICERS

Warrant officers were appointed to the vessel by one of the various boards responsible to the navy. They were senior non-commissioned officers, generally with extensive experience in their role. The boatswain, gunner, and carpenter were 'standing officers' and remained with the ship even when not in commission.

Gunner (Gnr)	Examined by the Ordinance Board and responsible for the vessel's guns and ammunition.
Master	Responsible for the navigation of the ship. Appointed by warrant from the Navy Board. Also known as the 'Sailing Master'.
Purser	Warranted by the Admiralty. Responsible for all ship's stores.
Surgeon (Sur.)	Warranted by the Navy Board they had to pass an examination set by the Surgeon's Company

Boatswain (Bosun)	Warranted by the Admiralty and responsible for the sails and associated ropes and rigging.
Carpenter (Carp)	Warranted by the Admiralty and responsible for the ship's hull and masts
Cook	Often an older seaman incapable of normal duties.

COMMISSIONED OFFICERS

All commissions were nominally issued by the Lord Commissioners of the Admiralty. Many were instead issued on station by local commanders and later confirmed by the Admiralty. Commissions to a lieutenancy or command of a vessel would indicate the vessel the commission was for. Those for flag rank did not and neither did most commissions for service as a commodore, often referred to in the commission documents as 'on a particular service'.

Some positions were filled by officers holding temporary, or acting, appointments. Not usually commissioned, all such positions are prefixed with the word 'Act.' where they appear.

Lieutenant (L.)	The lowest of the commissioned ranks in the Royal Navy. Acting as assistants to the vessel's captain and as commanding officers of vessels too small for a commander or captain. Abbreviations preceded by a number, '1L', '2L' etc. indicate the relative seniority within the vessel. An officer with the rank of lieutenant is usually the only such officer onboard, but may indicate an officer whose relative seniority is unknown.
Commander	The commanding officer of an unrated vessel of less than 20 guns.
Post Captain (Captain)	The commanding officer of a rated vessel of 20 or more guns. The officer's seniority in the navy was reckoned from the date of his first commission to this rank.
Commodore	A senior Post Captain assigned to command a squadron of vessels. He may be allowed a captain to command his ship or may command himself in a dual role.

FLAG OFFICERS

The Royal Navy during the Seven Years War was nominally divided into three squadrons, Red, White, and Blue with the Red Squadron being the most senior and the Blue Squadron the most junior. At the start of the 18th Century each squadron had, in theory, only three flag officers, an Admiral who command the squadron and main division, a Vice Admiral who commanded the Vanguard and a Rear Admiral to command the Rearguard. There was no rank of Admiral of the Red Squadron before 1805 as that post was filled by the Admiral of the Fleet, the most senior officer in the Royal Navy. By 1753 it had become apparent that nine flag officers was too small a number and George II was persuaded to permit more than one holder of each grade.

Flag officers were commissioned in strict order of seniority, the most senior post captains being appointed first, and promotion within the grades was also by seniority. However, being commissioned did not guarantee an active posting and many flag officers never went to sea at all.

Some senior post captains were not actually promoted to flag rank as part of a squadron, but were instead commissioned 'to the Rank of Rear Admiral in his Majesty's Fleet'. Sometimes known as 'without the honour of a squadron' or a 'Yellow Admiral' this was a way of moving officers out of the way of more able juniors. These promotions are indicted as a promotion to 'Superannuated Rear Admiral'.

No abbreviations are used for Flag Ranks, all are included fully except that the word squadron is omitted.

List of all Flag Ranks in the Royal Navy in order of seniority.

- Superannuated Rear Admiral
- Rear Admiral of the Blue Squadron
- Rear Admiral of the White Squadron
- Rear Admiral of the Red Squadron
- Vice Admiral of the Blue Squadron
- Vice Admiral of the White Squadron
- Vice Admiral of the Red Squadron
- Admiral of the Blue Squadron
- Admiral of the White Squadron
- Admiral of the Red Squadron (from 1805 only).
- Admiral of the Fleet

Service Records A

ABBS, WILLIAM

Dates: c.1736 Born; 20.9.1799 Died Monkwearmouth, Sunderland.
Family: Wife Thomasin Usher (d.1800) married 20.12.1767; Son John (1768-?); Daughter Mary (1767-?).
Service: 20.10.1755 Able *Romney* (44); 28.7.1756 Able *Guernsey* (50); 5.4.1757 Action of April 5 1757; 24.6.1758 Mid *Guernsey* (50); 18.8.1759-19.8.1759 Battle of Lagos Bay; 3.6.1761 Passed; Lieutenant; 7.7.1762-8.2.1763P L. *Hawk* (10) Sloop; 6.12.1776 4L *Egmont* (74); 5.9.1777 3L *Egmont* (74); 27.7.1778 1st Battle of Ushant; 23.1.1779 2L *Egmont* (74); 8.6.1779-22.8.1781P 1L *Egmont* (74); 1793-20.9.1799 Impress Service at Sunderland.

ABDY, SIR WILLIAM (6TH BARONET OF FELIX HALL, ESSEX)

Dates: 1732 Born; 16.4.1775 6th Baronet of Felix Hall, Essex; 21.7.1803 Died Chobham, Surrey; 28.7.1803 Buried St Laurence, Chobham, Surrey; 4.8.1803 Will Probate.
Family: Father Sir William Abdy, 4th Bt. (1689-1750); Mother Mary Stotherd (d. 1743); Wife Mary Brebner-Gordon (d.1829) married 1776; Daughter Catherine Mary [Fellowes] (1776-1817); Son William, 7th bt. (1779–1868); Daughter Charlotte Anne [Caldwell] (1783-?); Daughter Harriet [Caldwell] (1786-?); Sister Charlotte Elizabeth [Rutherforth] (1715-1733); Brother Sir Anthony Thomas, 5th Bt. (1720-1775); Brother Rev. Stotherd (c.1728-1773); Sister Ann Hester (1734-?).
Service: 1.7.1748-19.1.1749P Capt Serv *Milford* (44); 25.12.1749-7.7.1752P Capt Serv *Windsor* (60); 8.7.1752 Able *Rainbow* (44); 1753-1754 Mid *True Briton* (22) HEIC; 1754-12.1755 Mate *Stafford* (26) HEIC; 30.12.1755 Mid *Weymouth* (60); 11.1.1757 Mid *Duke* (90); 2.1.1758 Passed; **Lieutenant**; 1.2.1758 3L *Dover* (44); 26.4.1758 2L *Venus* (36); 20.11.1759 Battle of Quiberon Bay; **Commander**; 19.5.1761 *Beaver* (14) Sloop; **Captain**; 24.6.1766-21.7.1766P *Actaeon* (28); 23.4.1773-20.6.1775 *Milford* (28).

ACTON, JOHN

Dates: c.1720 Born; 1.1.1761 Died Bay of Bengal; 22.3.1762 Will Probate.
Family: Mother Sarah.
Service: 15.8.1734 Capt Serv *Princess Louisa* (40); 5.4.1735 Ord. *Princess Louisa* (40); 21.5.1737 Ord. *Grampus* (6) Sloop; 26.6.1737 Cox *Grampus* (6) Sloop; 3.5.1739 Able *Grampus* (6) Sloop; 15.7.1739 Able *Greenwich* (50); 10.8.1740 Mid *Greenwich* (50); 19.5.1741 Mid *Woolwich* (50); 30.7.1742 Mate *Woolwich* (50); 21.9.1742 Passed; Lieutenant; 6.4.1744 4L *Lennox* (70); 9.9.1745(NA 2.9.1747) 3L *Pembroke* (60); 22.1.1745/46(NA 2.9.1747) 3L *Dorsetshire* (80); 22.3.1745/46(NA 2.9.1747) 2L *Dorsetshire* (80); 11.4.1746(NA 2.9.1747)-25.7.1746 1L *Kingston* (60).

ADAMS, SIR THOMAS (6TH BARONET OF LONDON)

Dates: c.2.1738 Born London; 17.2.1738 Baptised Old St. Pancras Church, London; 1754 6th Baronet of London; 12.4.1770 Died North America; 13.4.1770 Buried at sea, Virginia.
Family: Father Sir Robert Adams, 5th Bt. (d.1754); Mother Diana (d.1765); Brother William (d.c.1741);
Service: 1750-8.1753 Merchant Service; 14.8.1753 Capt Serv *Yarmouth* (64); 5.8.1754 Able *Yarmouth* (64); 27.10.1754 Able *Centurion* (50); 17.4.1755 Mid *Centurion* (50); 20.7.1755 Mid *Seahorse* (24); 3.9.1755 Mid *Swiftsure* (68); 9.2.1756 Mid *Torbay* (74); 17.5.1757 Passed; **Lieutenant**; 8.6.1757-24.5.1758 3L *Norwich* (50); 25.7.1758 3L *Panther* (60); 16.1.1759-19.1.1759 Attack on Martinique; 20.1.1759-1.5.1759 Capture of Guadeloupe; 12.5.1759(BLI 23.11.1759) 4L *Cambridge* (80); 12.7.1759(BLI 23.11.1759) 3L *Cambridge* (80); **Commander**; 12.11.1759 *Happy* (8) Sloop; **Captain**; 27.8.1760 *Terpsichore* (24); 24.5.1762-26.3.1763P *Boston* (32); 25.3.1763-29.11.1766 *Niger* (32); 23.8.1769-12.4.1770† *Boston* (32).

ADAMS, WILLIAM

Dates: 1716 Born; 3.2.1763 Died.
Family:
Service: 1741 Mid *Gosport* (44); 6.3.1749/50(EI 13.5.1752) 4L *Vigilant* (60); 26.3.1750 Passed; 26.3.1750 **Lieutenant**; 7.11.1751(EI 13.5.1752)-6.6.1752P 2L *Vigilant* (60); 6.2.1755-8.11.1756 4L *Yarmouth* (64); 15.11.1756 6L *Invincible* (74); 17.12.1756 6L *Royal George* (100); 6.5.1757 5L *Royal George* (100); 29.7.1757 4L *Royal George* (100); 24.12.1757 3L *Royal George* (100); 27.1.1758 3L *Namur* (90); 6.6.1758-27.7.1758 The Siege of Louisbourg; **Commander**; 2.8.1758(NA 13.2.1760) *Hunter* (10) Sloop; **Captain**; 22.9.1759 *Northumberland* (68); 22.9.1760(NA 14.2.1763)-25.1.1763P *Diana* (32).

ADAMSON, CUTHBERT

Dates: c.1737 Born Newcastle upon Tyne; 28.10.1804 Died.
Family: Wife Mary Huthwaite (1737-1804) married 21.8.1782; Son John (1787-1855).
Service: 1751-1756 Merchant Service; 13.2.1756 Able *Torbay* (74); 14.8.1756 Mid *Torbay* (74); 5.9.1757-6.10.1757 Raid on Rochefort; 5.6.1758-12.6.1758 Raid on Saint-Malo; 19.8.1758 Able *Torbay* (74); 29.12.1758 Capture of Goree; 11.4.1759 Passed; **Lieutenant**; 4.3.1760-24.2.1763P 3L *Sutherland* (50); 3.6.1761-7.6.1761 Occupation of Dominica; 7.1.1762-10.2.1762 Operations against Martinique; 6.6.1762-13.8.1762 Operations against Havana; 16.1.1770-12.11.1770 L. *Nautilus* (16) Sloop; 16.4.1773-21.3.1775 2L *Racehorse* (16) Sloop; 24.10.1775-24.10.1776 LCmdr *Swift* Hired Tender; 16.5.1790-20.1.1792 LCmdr *Busy* (14) Cutter.

ADSTON, JAMES

Dates: c.1734 Born; 3.11.1734 Baptised Saint Clement Danes, Westminster; 1771 Died; 21.10.1771 Will Probate.
Family: Father Mark Adston; Mother Dorothy; Wife Sarah Brace Thwaites (d.1797) married 1762; Son Mark; Daughter Sara Brace Thwaites [Barker]; Son James; Daughter Ann.
Service: 1750-1754 Merchant Service; 9.5.1754 Capt Serv *Amazon* (22); 11.3.1755 Capt Serv *Seahorse* (24); 8.4.1757 Able *Prince* (90); 20.6.1757 Mate *Raven* (14) Sloop; 7.11.1757 Passed; **Lieutenant**; 19.11.1757 3L *Penzance* (44); 28.8.1758-1.12.1762P 2L *Penzance* (44); 3.6.1761-7.6.1761 Occupation of Dominica; 7.1.1762-10.2.1762 Operations against Martinique; 24.2.1762-25.2.1762 Capture of Saint Lucia; 6.6.1762-13.8.1762 Operations against Havana; 11.5.1763-26.5.1766 3L *Yarmouth* (64); **Commander** (Royal Mail); 25.9.1769-1771† *Earl of Bossborough* Packet.

AFFLECK, SIR EDMUND (1ST BARONET OF DALHAM HALL)

Dates: 19.4.1725 Born Dalham Hall, Suffolk; 10.7.1782 1st Baronet of Dalham Hall; 19.11.1788 Died Colchester;

Family: Father Gilbert Affleck (1684?-1764); Mother Anna Dolben; Wife Mrs Esther Creffield née Ruth (d 1787); Wife Margaret Smithers née Burgess married 14.5.1788; Brother Philip, RN (1726-1799);

Service: 13.10.1740 Mid *Suffolk* (70); 4.3.1740/41-5.1741 Operations against Cartagena; 29.6.1742 Mid *Stirling Castle* Hulk; 30.4.1743 Mid *Victory* (100); 21.9.1743 Mid *Duke* (90); 18.3.1744 Mid *Victory* (100); 29.5.1744-10.4.1745 Mid *Cornwall* (80); 13.4.1745 Passed; **Lieutenant**; 25.7.1745[(JAM 3.7.1749)] 3L *Plymouth* (60); 23.10.1745[(JAM 3.7.1749)] 2L *Plymouth* (60); 30.5.1746[(JAM 3.7.1749)] 1L *Plymouth* (60); 3.8.1746 Action of August 3 1746; 25.3.1747 Action of March 25 1747; 10.5.1747-14.4.1748 3L *Lennox* (70); 9.4.1748 Battle of Santiago de Cuba; 23.7.1748[(JAM 3.7.1749)] 2L *Cornwall* (80); 12.10.1748 Battle of Havana; 1.11.1748[(JAM 3.7.1749)]-27.11.1748 1L *Cornwall* (80); 24.7.1755 1L *Newark* (80); 5.8.1755 1L *Winchester* (50); **Commander**; 5.6.1756 *Albany* (14) Sloop; **Captain**; 23.3.1757 *Mercury* (20); 9.7.1759-13.11.1762 *Launceston* (44); 29.3.1761-11.6.1761 Expedition against Belle-Isle; 25.10.1770-1.6.1771[P] *San Antonio* (64); 10.4.1778-5.5.1781 *Bedford* (74); 16.1.1780 Battle of Cape St. Vincent; 16.3.1781 Battle of Cape Henry; 5.5.1781-17.7.1783[P] Commodore *Bedford* (74); 5.9.1781 Battle of the Chesapeake; 25.1.1782-26.1.1782 Battle of Saint Kitts; 4.3.1782-19.11.1788 M.P. for Colchester; 12.4.1782 Battle of the Saintes; 10.2.1784 **Rear Admiral of the Blue**; 24.9.1787 **Rear Admiral of the Red.**

AFFLECK, PHILIP

Dates: 1726 Born Dalham Hall, Suffolk; 22.12.1799 Died Bath; 11.1.1800 Will Probate.

Family: Father Gilbert Affleck (1684?–1764); Mother Anna Dolben; Brother Sir Edmund (1st Baronet of Dalham Hall), RN (1725-1788).

Service: 1744-1748 Merchant Service; 29.10.1748 Able *Preston* (50) Hulk; 17.11.1748-23.11.1749[SC] Mid *Preston* (50) Hulk; 18.5.1751 Mid *Vigilant* (60); 9.4.1755 Passed; **Lieutenant**; 3.5.1755[(NA 19.12.1755)] 4L *Northumberland* (68); 9.11.1756 6L *Invincible* (74); 11.11.1756 5L *Invincible* (74); 15.11.1756 4L *Invincible* (74); 17.12.1756 4L *Royal George* (100); 6.5.1757 3L *Royal George* (100); 29.7.1757 2L *Royal George* (100); 24.12.1757 1L *Royal George* (100); 27.1.1758 1L *Namur* (90); 6.6.1758-27.7.1758 The Siege of Louisbourg; **Commander**; 1.8.1758[(NA 6.4.1759)] *Gramont* (18) Sloop; 1.8.1759 *Terror* (8) Bomb Vessel; **Captain**; 20.8.1759[(NA 19.9.1759)]-4.10.1759 *Namur* (90); 8.11.1759-30.4.1761 *Panther* (60); 3.5.1761[(EI 15.12.1764)] *Baleine* (20); 18.7.1763[(EI 6.10.1768)]-9.6.1767[P] *Argo* (28); 29.10.1778-13.5.1781 *Triumph* (74); 15.5.1780 Action of March 15 1780; 19.5.1780 Action of March 19 1780; 12.5.1781 First Captain; 2.10.1782 *Triumph* (74); 15.4.1783-11.9.1784 *Triumph* (74); 24.9.1787 **Rear Admiral of the Blue**; 11.2.1789-1793 CinC — Jamaica; 22.3.1789-27.7.1792[P] *Centurion* (50); 21.9.1790 **Rear Admiral of the White**; 1.2.1793 **Vice Admiral of the Blue**; 26.4.1793-6.3.1795 Lord Commissioner of the Admiralty; 12.4.1794 **Vice Admiral of the White**; 4.7.1794 **Vice Admiral of the Red**; 1.6.1795 **Admiral of the Blue**; 24.12.1798-c.10.9.1799[P] *Canopus* (80); 14.2.1799 **Admiral of the White.**

AFFLECK, WILLIAM

Dates: 1740 Born; 24.12.1791 Died West Indies.

Family: Father John Affleck; Mother Sarah Metcalfe; Wife Harriet Anne Crawley.

Service: **Lieutenant**; 27.10.1761[(EI 7.2.1766)]-2.6.1762 4L *Medway* (60); 26.5.1766-2.10.1769[P] 2L *Preston* (50); 3.11.1770 3L *San Antonio* (64); 21.5.1771 1L *Trident* (64); **Commander**;

7.4.1772(MED 11.11.1773) *Raven* (14) Sloop; **Captain**; 4.6.1774 *Medway* (60); 6.7.1779 Battle of Grenada; 17.4.1780 Battle of Martinique; 5.6.1780(BLI 13.9.1781) *Grafton* (74); 1.1.1781(JAM 3.1.1783)-23.11.1782P *Southampton* (32); 14.4.1783-25.5.1784P *Duc de Chartres* (18) Sloop; 24.1.1789-25.7.1792P *Blonde* (32).

AGNEW, ALEXANDER

Dates: c.1741 Born; 7.2.1792 Died.
Family:
Service: 7.5.1756 Capt Serv *Jersey* (60); 11.12.1757 Able *Royal Anne* (100); 4.5.1758 Able *Shannon* (28); 6.6.1758-27.7.1758 The Siege of Louisbourg; 14.5.1759 Mid *Shannon* (28); 5.8.1761 Passed; **Lieutenant**; 7.8.1761-5.2.1763P 5L *Cornwall* (74); 6.12.1763-12.12.1766 3L *Rippon* (60); 17.12.1770 4L *Northumberland* (68); 10.1.1771-29.1.1771 3L *Northumberland* (68); 5.3.1771-31.5.1774 3L *Asia* (64); 26.9.1774 1L *Pallas* (36); 27.9.1777 1L *Russell* (74); **Commander**; 20.11.1777 *Hazard* (8) Sloop; 1.2.1779-28.5.1781D *Fury* (16) Sloop; 30.4.1780 Action of 30th April 1780; 28.5.1781 Dismissed.

ALEXANDER, JOHN

Dates: 1785 Died.
Family: Wife Mary.
Service: **Lieutenant**; 17.3.1760(EI 1.6.1762) 4L *Sunderland* (60); 28.6.1760(EI 11.6.1762)-28.8.1761P 4L *Salisbury* (50); 9.6.1762-26.11.1762 L. *Nautilus* (16) Sloop; 30.11.1769-2.2.1771 L. *Cruizer* (8) Sloop; 13.5.1778-11.8.1780P LCmdr *Meredith* (10) Cutter.

ALLAN, GEORGE

Dates: c.1715 Born; 1757 Died.
Family:
Service: 18.3.1734/35-10.2.1735/36 Able Captain (70); 10.2.1735/36-28.4.1738 Mid Captain (70); 28.4.1738-3.7.1740 Mid Edinburgh (70); 4.7.1740-18.1.1740/41 Mate Scarborough (18) Hospital Ship; 19.1.1740/41-4.10.1741 Mate Marlborough (90); 5.10.1741-16.11.1741 Able Duke (90); 17.11.1741 Mate Duke (90); 5.5.1743 Passed; Lieutenant; 23.12.1743 L. Aetna (8) Fireship; 7.7.1744 3L Eltham (40); 6.6.1745(NA 24.9.1745) 2L Eltham (40); 24.6.1745(NA 24.9.1745)-12.6.1750P 1L Eltham (40); 9.1748-10.1748 Siege of Pondicherry; 26.5.1756 2L Saint George (90); 29.3.1757 1L Pembroke (60).

ALLAN, JAMES

Dates: c.1707 Born; 1768 Died.
Family:
Service: 16.10.1731 Ord. *Sunderland* (60); 26.12.1731 Able *Dreadnought* (60); 3.5.1733 Mid *Dreadnought* (60); 23.9.1733 Able *Flamborough* (20); 19.9.1735 Mid *Princess Caroline* (80); 5.7.1736 Able *Dunkirk* (60); 22.3.1736/37-23.9.1738P Mid *Dunkirk* (60); 12.4.1739 Passed; **Lieutenant**; 14.1.1743/44 2L *Roebuck* (44); 23.3.1743/44-18.12.1744 6L *Duke* (90); 8.1.1744/45 6L *Duke* (90); 21.10.1745 6L *Royal George* (100); 13.11.1745 5L *Royal George* (100); 23.1.1745/46-28.3.1747 3L *Royal George* (100); 28.3.1747-5.8.1748P 2L *Gloucester* (50); 14.10.1747 2nd Battle of Cape Finisterre; 26.5.1756 2L *Marlborough* (80); 5.7.1756-7.1.1757 2L *Terrible* (74); 26.4.1757-20.11.1759S 1L *Essex* (64); 5.6.1758-12.6.1758 Raid on Saint-Malo; 20.11.1759 Battle of Quiberon Bay; **Commander**; 24.7.1760-27.6.1761C *Speedwell* (8) Hired Cutter.

ALLEN, JAMES

Dates: c.1728 Born; 1771 Died.

Family:

Service: 31.10.1748 Able *Falmouth* (50); 2.5.1749 Mid *Falmouth* (50); 8.10.1750 Able *Falmouth* (50); 27.1.1751 Able *Dragon* (60); 23.5.1751-1.6.1753 Mid *Dragon* (60); 2.6.1753 Mid *Grampus* (14) Sloop; 6.8.1755 Passed; **Lieutenant**; 23.3.1759 L. *Fly* (8) Sloop; 27.8.1760-20.2.1763[P] 1L *Blonde* (32).

ALLEN, JOHN CARTER

Dates: 19.1.1724 Born; 2.10.1800 Died; 16.10.1800 Will Probate.

Family: Father Carter Allen; Mother Emma Hay; Wife Mrs. Caroline Addington married 20.6.1780; Wife Stella Frances Freeman married 29.6.1799; Son Thomas (1773-1852); Son John, RN (1774-1854); Daughter Charlotte.

Service: **Lieutenant**; 14.6.1745 L. *Mediator* (10) Sloop; 6.8.1745 L. *Sheerness* (24); 21.5.1746-10.9.1748[P] 2L *Ambuscade* (40); 3.5.1747 1st Battle of Cape Finisterre; 14.3.1750/51 L. *Swan* (14) Sloop; 6.4.1751-1.2.1751/52[P] 2L *Gosport* (44); 13.2.1751/52-26.4.1755[P] 2L *Jason* (44); 31.7.1755 3L *Hampshire* (50); 1.11.1755 4L *Princess Royal* (90); 19.12.1755-12.1.1757 3L *Princess Royal* (90); 12.1.1757 4L *Princess Royal* (90); **Commander**; 5.4.1757 *Grampus* (14) Sloop; **Captain**; 21.3.1758-23.5.1759[P] *Experiment* (24); 29.12.1758 Capture of Goree; 10.8.1759 *Repulse* (32); 3.6.1761-7.6.1761 Occupation of Dominica; 7.1.1762-10.2.1762 Operations against Martinique; 6.11.1762 *Rochester* (50); 18.1.1763[BLI 24.5.1764]-14.3.1764[P] *Vanguard* (68); 15.11.1769-26.5.1770[P] *Superb* (74); 23.5.1770-7.6.1771[P] *Ajax* (74); 27.10.1775-18.4.1778 *Albion* (74); 27.4.1778-8.3.1780 *Egmont* (74); 27.7.1778 1st Battle of Ushant; 20.3.1780-13.10.1780 *Gibraltar* (80); 22.1.1781-25.1.1781 *Formidable* (98); 6.5.1782-12.2.1783[P] *Royal William* (84); 20.10.1782 Battle of Cape Spartel; 24.9.1787 **Rear Admiral of the White**; 21.9.1790 **Rear Admiral of the Red**; 1.2.1793 **Vice Admiral of the White**; 12.4.1794 **Vice Admiral of the Red**; 1.6.1795 **Admiral of the Blue**; 14.2.1799 **Admiral of the White**.

ALLEN, NATHANIEL

Dates: c.1725 Born; 1771 Died; 23.4.1771 Will Probate.

Family: Son Nathaniel; Daughter Dorcus.

Service: 30.9.1739 Able *Newcastle* (50); 5.5.1741 Mid *Newcastle* (50); 11.4.1744 Mid *Chichester* (80); 21.10.1745-10.1.1746 Mid *Shrewsbury* (80); 10.1.1745/46 Passed; **Lieutenant**; 16.9.1746 L. *Porcupine* (16) Sloop; 5.5.1748-22.6.1748[P] 6L *Duke* (90); 6.2.1755 3L *Prince George* (80); 6.4.1756-3.11.1757 2L *Stirling Castle* (64); 21.11.1757 2L *Penzance* (44); 6.9.1758-2.7.1759 1L *Penzance* (44); 1.12.1768-11.4.1771[P] LCmdr *Winchelsea* (4) Cutter.

ALLEN, THOMAS

Dates: c.1738 Born; 1808 Died.

Family:

Service: 21.1.1750 Ord. *Saltash* (14) Sloop; 23.12.1751 Able *Devonshire* (66); 6.8.1752 Able *Deptford* (50); 20.5.1756 Battle of Minorca; 21.7.1756 Mid *Deptford* (50); 27.10.1756 Mid *Lancaster* (66); 6.6.1758-27.7.1758 The Siege of Louisbourg; 5.12.1758 Passed; **Lieutenant**; 22.2.1759-28.8.1765[P] 3L *York* (60); 8.4.1801 **Superannuated Commander**.

ALLEN, THOMAS

Dates: c.1733 Born; 23.1.1781 Died.

Family:

Service: 1753-1756 Merchant Service; 6.10.1755 Able *Torbay* (74); 15.1.1756 Mid *Torbay* (74); 26.10.1756 Able *Invincible* (74); 28.1.1757 Mate *Royal George* (100); 7.3.1758 Mate *Namur* (90); 6.6.1758-27.7.1758 The Siege of Louisbourg; 7.3.1759 Passed; **Lieutenant**; 23.3.1759-25.10.1763[P] 4L *Mars* (74); 20.11.1759 Battle of Quiberon Bay; 29.3.1761-11.6.1761 Expedition against Belle-Isle; 22.6.1764 LCmdr *Gaspe* (6) Schooner; 21.11.1770 3L *Intrepid* (64); 23.10.1771-22.4.1775[P] 2L *Intrepid* (64); 26.2.1776 2L *Resolution* (74); 14.11.1776 2L *Ardent* (64); 12.2.1778 1L *Courageux* (74); 27.7.1778 1st Battle of Ushant; **Commander**; 13.11.1778-22.12.1779[P] *Infernal* (8) Fireship; **Captain**; 7.6.1780-26.8.1780 *Britannia* (100).

ALLEN, WILLIAM

Dates: c.1724 Born; 1801 Died.

Family:

Service: 25.8.1743 Able *Anglesea* (40); 14.12.1744 Able *Sunderland* (60); 20.4.1747 Mate *Yarmouth* (64); 3.5.1747 1st Battle of Cape Finisterre; 14.10.1747 2nd Battle of Cape Finisterre; 27.12.1747 Mid *Yarmouth* (64); 1.6.1749 Mate *Yarmouth* (64); 15.6.1753 Mid *Somerset* (68); 5.7.1754 Passed; **Lieutenant**; 10.7.1755[(NA 15.7.1756)] 4L *Fougueux* (64); 22.7.1755[(NA 15.7.1756)] 3L *Fougueux* (64); 15.8.1755[(NA 15.7.1756)]-29.11.1756 L. *Siren* (20); 29.11.1756[(ECH 12.11.1759)]-28.4.1760[P] 2L *Princess Louisa* (60); 5.4.1757 Action of April 5 1757; 18.8.1759-19.8.1759 Battle of Lagos Bay; 16.1.1761-19.8.1763[P] 2L *Arrogant* (74).

ALLEN, WILLIAM

Dates: 1728 Born; 24.10.1804 Died Lambeth, London.

Family: Wife Catherine Douglas (1753-1802); Daughter Catherine Allen (1773-1833); Daughter Amelia Allen (1780-1834); Son William Edward Hughes, RN (1787-1856); Son Barnard Cuthbert Allen (1787-?).

Service: **Lieutenant**; 17.5.1756 4L *Orford* (68); 8.1757-10.1757 Louisbourg Expedition; 6.6.1758-27.7.1758 The Siege of Louisbourg; 24.9.1759-16.11.1761 3L *Orford* (68); **Commander**; 21.11.1761-bef.23.12.1762[P] *Pluto* (8) Fireship; **Captain**; 20.6.1765-9.6.1767 *Fowey* (24); 14.5.1767-12.5.1771[P] *Glasgow* (20); 16.5.1778-11.10.1780 *Chatham* (50); 2.6.1781-11.12.1781 *Sceptre* (64); 8.1.1782-1.6.1784[P] *Cumberland* (74); 20.6.1783 2nd Battle of Cuddalore; 1.2.1793 **Rear Admiral of the Blue**; 12.4.1794 **Rear Admiral of the Red**; 4.7.1794 **Vice Admiral of the Blue**; 1.6.1795 **Vice Admiral of the White**; 14.2.1799 **Admiral of the Blue**.

ALLISON, THOMAS

Dates: 22.3.1776 Died.

Family:

Service: 17.10.1728-22.2.1729/30 Able *Stirling Castle* (70); 22.2.1729/30-8.11.1730 Mate *Stirling Castle* (70); 8.11.1730-11.1.1730/31 Mid *Romney* (50); 11.1.1730/31-6.10.1731 Able *Captain* (70); 6.10.1731-27.1.1732/33 Able *Gibraltar* (20); 27.1.1732/33-18.4.1734 Mate *Gibraltar* (20); 18.4.1734-28.4.1734 Able *Dreadnought* (60); 28.4.1734 Mate *Dreadnought* (60); 2.3.1736/37 Passed; **Lieutenant**; 16.7.1740 L. *Success* (20); 20.12.1742 2L *Princess* (70); 11.2.1743/44-12.2.1743/44 Battle of Toulon; 3.6.1745[(MED 10.1.1748/49)]-7.2.1746/47 1L *Russell* (80); **Captain**; 9.2.1745/46[(MED 11.8.1746)]-20.11.1746 *Boyne* (80); 1770 **Superannuated Rear Admiral**.

ALLWRIGHT, THOMAS

Dates: c.1722 Born; 28.1.1803 Died Greenwich Hospital; 17.2.1803 Will Probate.
Family:
Service: 25.1.1732 Capt Serv *Otter* (6) Sloop; 8.4.1732 Capt Serv *Torrington* (44); 12.5.1733 Ord. *Torrington* (40); 31.1.1737 Able *Torrington* (40); 5.12.1737 Able *Charlotte* (8) Yacht; 24.12.1739 Able *Torrington* (40); 21.6.1740 Able *Berwick* (70); 25.12.1742 Able *Shrewsbury* (80); 26.3.1743 Able *Oxford* (50); 11.2.1743/44-12.2.1743/44 Battle of Toulon; 23.9.1744 Mid *Oxford* (50); 24.10.1746-6.10.1747 Mid *Shrewsbury* (80); 7.10.1747-20.11.1747 Able *Kent* (64); 14.10.1747 2nd Battle of Cape Finisterre; 20.11.1747 Passed; **Lieutenant**; 7.12.1747 3L *Penzance* (44); 3.5.1748-18.12.1748[P] 2L *Penzance* (44); 6.2.1755-19.8.1757 5L *Barfleur* (80); 13.10.1757-9.1.1759[P] 4L *Barfleur* (80); 5.6.1758-12.6.1758 Raid on Saint-Malo; 19.7.1759 1L *Monarch* (74); **Commander**; 21.9.1759-7.2.1760[P] *Broderick* Hired Armed vessel; 28.1.1765-14.12.1767[P] *Spy* (10) Sloop; 3.8.1768-10.8.1771 *Dispatch* (14) Sloop.

ALMS, JAMES

Dates: 15.7.1728 Born Gosport; 8.6.1791 Died Chichester; 14.6.1791 Buried Chichester Cathedral, Chichester.
Family: Father John Alms; Mother Mary; Son James, RN (d.1816); Son George Pigot, RN (d.1782).
Service: 25.3.1739 Capt Serv *Namur* (90); 5.8.1739 Capt Serv *Victory* (100); 1.2.1740/41 L. Serv *Cambridge* (80); 6.5.1742 Able *Winchester* (50); 7.6.1742 Able *Victory* (100); 27.10.1742 Able *Dragon* (60); 23.2.1742/43 Mid *Dragon* (60); 11.2.1743/44-12.2.1743/44 Battle of Toulon; 13.3.1744/45 Passed; 13.3.1744/45 Mid *Namur* (90); **Lieutenant**; 14.5.1749[(EI 13.6.1752)]-28.5.1752[P] L. *Siren* (20); 23.3.1759 1L *Mars* (74); 20.11.1759 Battle of Quiberon Bay; 29.3.1761-11.6.1761 Expedition against Belle-Isle; **Commander**; 10.7.1761-26.10.1761 *Flamborough Prize* (14) Sloop; 9.11.1761 *Ferret* (14) Sloop; 7.1.1762-10.2.1762 Operations against Martinique; 25.7.1762-11.7.1763[P] *Alarm* (32); 17.8.1762[(EI 2.8.1763)]-12.8.1763 *Cygnet* (18) Sloop; **Captain**; 20.6.1765-25.8.1766 *Levant* (28); 31.5.1770 *Montreal* (32); 8.12.1772[(MED 14.6.1773)]-25.6.1773 *Pallas* (36); 1776 Impress Service at Sussex; 25.9.1780-5.7.1784[P] *Monmouth* (64); 16.4.1781 Battle of Porto Praya; 17.2.1782 Battle of Sadras; 12.4.1782 Battle of Providien; 6.7.1782 2nd Battle of Negapatam; 3.9.1782 Battle of Trincomalee; 20.6.1783 2nd Battle of Cuddalore.

AMBROSE, JOHN

Dates: 25.3.1771 Died Bath.
Family:
Service: **Lieutenant**; 20.6.1728[(JAM 29.5.1728)]-6.6.1729[P] 4L *Lennox* (70); 9.6.1729 3L *Leopard* (50); 25.11.1729-22.12.1729[P] 2L *Leopard* (50); 13.1.1729/30-12.1.1732/33 L. *Solebay* (6) Bomb Vessel; **Captain**; 27.3.1734-4.4.1740 *Greyhound* (20); 12.9.1740-11.4.1745 *Rupert* (60); 11.2.1743/44-12.2.1743/44 Battle of Toulon; 7.11.1745 Dismissed; 17.4.1750 **Superannuated Rear Admiral**.

AMHERST, JOHN

Dates: 1718 Born Sevenoaks, Kent; 14.2.1778 Died Gosport.
Family: Father Jeffrey Amherst; Wife Anne Linzee; Wife Elizabeth Kerrill; Brother Lieutenant-General William Amherst; Brother Field Marshal Jeffery Amherst, 1st Baron Amherst.
Service: 1.9.1730-13.6.1732 Able *Success* (24); 13.6.1732-25.12.1734 Able *Dursley Galley* (20); 26.12.1734 Mate *Dursley Galley* (20); 6.1.1736/37 Passed; **Lieutenant**; 24.7.1739 3L *Dragon* (60); 24.7.1741 Action of 1741-07-24; 2.10.1741[(MED 28.1.1741/42)] 1L *Sunderland* (60); 20.2.1741/42-

26.2.1741/42 1L *Sutherland* (50); 27.2.1741/42 2L *Sutherland* (50); 6.4.1743 3L *Captain* (70); 28.10.1743 2L *Captain* (70); 9.6.1744 2L *Cornwall* (80); **Commander**; 30.8.1744 *Mortar* (10) Bomb Vessel; **Captain**; 29.12.1744 *Success* (20); 24.8.1745 *Southsea Castle* (44); 3.2.1745/46 *Princess Mary* (60); 5.4.1747[(EI 5.9.1749)]-23.11.1749[SC] *Preston* (50); 20.12.1750-14.11.1752[P] *Monarch* (74); 16.1.1753-24.6.1755[W] *Mars* (64); 1.1.1756 *Lancaster* (66); 22.3.1756-3.10.1756 *Deptford* (50); 20.5.1756 Battle of Minorca; 1.2.1757-19.11.1759 *Captain* (64); 8.1757-10.1757 Louisbourg Expedition; 6.6.1758-27.7.1758 The Siege of Louisbourg; 16.1.1761-19.8.1763[P] *Arrogant* (74); 23.5.1765 **Rear Admiral of the Blue**; 18.10.1770 **Rear Admiral of the White**; 24.10.1770 **Vice Admiral of the Blue**; 2.2.1774-14.2.1778 CinC — Plymouth; 7.12.1775 **Vice Admiral of the White**; 2.4.1776 **Vice Admiral of the Red**; 29.1.1778 **Admiral of the Blue**.

ANDERSON, MATHEW

Dates: c.1726 Born; 1776 Died.
Family:
Service: 12.7.1749 Able *Dover* (44); 22.4.1751 Mid *Dover* (44); 19.2.1753-5.5.1756 Mate *Renown* (30); 5.5.1756 Passed; **Lieutenant**; 12.5.1758[(BLI 31.1.1760)] 4L *Buckingham* (68); 16.1.1759-19.1.1759 Attack on Martinique; 20.1.1759-1.5.1759 Capture of Guadeloupe; 23.8.1759[(BLI 19.8.1760)] 2L *Buckingham* (68); 23.12.1760-2.3.1763[P] 3L *Superb* (74); 24.10.1766-26.10.1769 2L *Ramillies* (74); 30.11.1770 1L *Raisonable* (64); 25.8.1774 2L *Triumph* (74); 15.9.1774 1L *Triumph* (74); 19.1.1775 1L *Mars* (74); 9.6.1775-1.8.1775 2L *Mars* (74).

ANDREWS, ROBERT

Dates: c.1706 Born; c.1755 Died; 27.11.1755 Will Probate.
Family:
Service: 7.10.1722-23.5.1723[P] Ord. *Falmouth* (54); 23.3.1725/26 Able *Bredah* (70); 13.8.1726 Able *Scarborough* (20); 22.4.1731 QGnr *Torrington* (40); 15.9.1731-16.12.1732[P] Gnr Mate *Torrington* (40); 30.7.1735 Able *Torrington* (40); 15.8.1735 Mate *Torrington* (40); 25.11.1739 Able *Fly* (8) Sloop; 4.1.1739/40 Mate *Fly* (8) Sloop; 10.3.1741/42 ActL *Advice* (54); 3.9.1742 Master *Portland* (50); 5.5.1743 Passed; **Lieutenant**; 19.5.1747 4L *Yarmouth* (64); 14.10.1747 2nd Battle of Cape Finisterre; 21.10.1748-19.2.1748/49[P] L. *Solebay* (24); 4.12.1753[(EI 13.11.1756)]-6.4.1754 L. *Kingfisher* (14) Sloop.

ANDREWS, THOMAS

Dates: 20.5.1756 Died.
Family:
Service: **Lieutenant**; 17.4.1741[(JAM 1.4.1743)] L. *Alderney* (8) Bomb Vessel; 7.1741-10.1741 Operations against Santiago; 12.1.1741/42[(JAM 1.4.1743)] L. *Bonetta* (8) Sloop; 14.10.1742[(West Indies 1.4.1743)]-6.3.1742/43[P] 3L *Defiance* (60); 28.10.1743 L. *Portsmouth* (24) Storeship; 17.12.1743 5L *Duke* (90); 19.3.1743/44 4L *Duke* (90); 23.3.1743/44 2L *Roebuck* (44); 25.10.1744[(MED 17.1.1748/49)] 1L *Princess Caroline* (80); 14.1.1744/45[(MED 17.1.1748/49)]-24.2.1744/45 6L *Neptune* (90); **Commander**; 26.5.1745[(MED 17.2.1748/49)] *Postiillon* Xebec; **Captain**; 15.7.1745-27.12.1748[P] *Worcester* (58); 3.8.1746 Action of August 3 1746; 25.3.1747 Action of March 25 1747; 9.4.1748 Battle of Santiago de Cuba; 16.1.1753 *Cumberland* (66); 28.3.1754-26.8.1754[P] *Eagle* (60); 31.7.1754-20.5.1756 *Defiance* (60); 6.6.1755-8.6.1755 Action of 6-8 June 1755; 20.5.1756 Battle of Minorca.

ANGEL, HENRY

Dates: c.1714 Born; 1777 Died.
Family:
Service: 13.4.1732 Mid *Lennox* (70); 4.11.1732 Mid *Berwick* (70); 22.12.1732 Mid *Rye* (20); 7.6.1735 Mid *Rippon* (60); 25.5.1736 Mid *Oxford* (50); 21.8.1737 Able *Ipswich* (70); 1.5.1738 Mid *Ipswich* (70); 24.8.1738 Passed; **Lieutenant**; 25.6.1739 3L *Greenwich* (50); 2.2.1740/41 2L *Greenwich* (50); 13.4.1741 1L *Greenwich* (50); 20.11.1743(JAM 4.10.1744)-24.7.1745[P] 1L *Montagu* (60); **Commander**; 24.7.1755 *Swallow* (14) Sloop; **Captain**; 23.8.1756 *Deal Castle* (20); 18.10.1758-14.5.1762 *Stag* (32); 7.1.1762-10.2.1762 Operations against Martinique.

ANNINGSON, JOSEPH

Dates: 7.10.1733 Baptised Westow, Yorkshire; 1817 Died; 25.8.1818 Will Probate.
Family: Father Bushel Anningson (1699–1750); Mother Mary Luck; Wife Mary Preston(1736–1816); Son Bushell (1780–1846); Son Stamper (1786–1853); Daughter Mary Ann (c.1786-?).
Service: 1750-1756 Merchant Service; 27.1.1756 Able *Ambuscade* (40); 15.7.1756 Mate *Ambuscade* (40); 19.9.1756 Able *Ambuscade* (40); 5.11.1756 Mid *Ambuscade* (40); 10.2.1757 Mid *Coventry* (28); 28.6.1757-4.4.1759 Mate *Coventry* (28); 5.6.1758-12.6.1758 Raid on Saint-Malo; 4.4.1759 Passed; **Lieutenant**; 22.8.1759-23.8.1759 L. *Basilisk* (8) Bomb Vessel; 4.4.1781 3L *Victory* (100); 9.4.1781-24.4.1783[P] 1L *Artois* (40); 5.8.1781 Battle of Dogger Bank; 30.11.1803 **Superannuated Commander**.

ANSELL, WILLIAM

Dates: c.4.1722 Born; 1782 Died Greenwich Hospital.
Family:
Service: 31.5.1738 Able *Garland* (20); 28.4.1740 Mid *Garland* (20); 4.10.1741 Mid *Dragon* (60); 8.3.1743 Mid *Plymouth* (60); 15.8.1743-3.9.1744 Mid *Prince Frederick* (70); 3.9.1744 Passed; **Lieutenant**; 26.2.1744/45(EI 22.8.1749)-26.9.1745 3L *Medway* (60); 1774-1782 Lieutenant of Greenwich Hospital.

ANSON, LORD GEORGE (1ST BARON ANSON)

Dates: 23.4.1697 Born Colwich, Staffordshire; 13.6.1747 1st Baron Anson; 6.6.1762 Died Moor Park, Hertfordshire.
Family: Father William Anson (1656-1720); Mother Isabella Carrier; Wife Hon. Elizabeth Yorke (1725–1760) married 25.4.1748; Sister Janette [Adams] (c.1690-1771); Brother Thomas, MP (c.1695-1773);
Service: 2.1711 Vol. *Ruby* (54); 27.3.1711-30.6.1713[P] Mid *Monmouth* (64); **Lieutenant**; 19.5.1716(ECH 7.12.1716)-28.11.1717[P] 2L *Hampshire* (54); 17.3.1717/18 2L *Montagu* (60); 11.8.1718 Battle of Cape Passaro; 2.10.1719-17.11.1720[P] L. *Barfleur* (90); **Commander**; 19.6.1722-2.1.1723/24 *Weazle* (8) Sloop; **Captain**; 1.2.1723/24 *Scarborough* (20); 12.7.1728 *Garland* (20); 11.10.1728-17.7.1730[P] *Garland* (20); 19.5.1731-4.9.1731[P] *Diamond* (40); 24.1.1731/32-18.7.1735[P] *Squirrel* (20); 9.12.1737 *Centurion* (60); 18.9.1740 Commodore *Centurion* (60); 21.6.1743 Commodore *Centurion* (60); 23.6.1744 **Rear Admiral of the Blue**; 8.12.1744-1.7.1747 M.P. for Hedon; 27.12.1744-21.6.1751 Lord Commissioner of the Admiralty; 23.4.1745 **Rear Admiral of the White**; 29.4.1745-20.5.1745 CinC — River Medway and The Nore; 14.7.1746 **Vice Admiral of the Blue**; 31.7.1746-20.7.1747 CinC — English Channel; 9.8.1746 *Yarmouth* (64); 4.1747-23.11.1747 *Prince George* (90); 3.5.1747 1st Battle of Cape Finisterre; 15.7.1747 **Vice Admiral of the Red**; 12.5.1748 **Admiral of the Blue**; 14.7.1749-

6.6.1762 Vice Admiral of Great Britain; 22.6.1751-17.11.1756 1st Lord; 24.2.1757 **Admiral of the White**; 2.7.1757-6.6.1762 1st Lord; 1758-1759 *Royal George* (100); 13.5.1758 CinC — English Channel; 30.7.1761 **Admiral of the Fleet**; 8.1761-9.1761 *Royal Charlotte* (8) Yacht.

ANTROBUS, CHARLES

Dates: Buried Saint Paul's Anglican Church Cemetery, Falmouth, Saint Paul, Antigua; 1725 Born; 3.11.1769 Died West Indies.
Family:
Service: **Commander**; 15.11.1756 *Vesuvius* (14) Fireship; **Captain**; 17.2.1758 *Surprise* (24); 11.12.1759-14.2.1763[P] *Southampton* (32); 29.3.1761-11.6.1761 Expedition against Belle-Isle; 13.1.1763-8.2.1763 *Ludlow Castle* (24); 4.4.1763-28.8.1766[P] *Maidstone* (28); 3.2.1768-3.11.1769[†] *Jason* (32).

APPLEBY, THOMAS

Dates: 1790 Died.
Family:
Service: **Lieutenant**; 12.11.1761[(EI 24.7.1765)]-23.4.1762 2L *Seaford* (20); 27.10.1770-10.8.1771 2L *Prudent* (64).

ARBUTHNOT, MARRIOT

Dates: 1711 Born Weymouth; 6.3.1711/12 Baptised Wyke Regis, Weymouth; 31.1.1794 Died 13 Leicester Square, London; 19.2.1794 Buried Wyke Regis, Dorset.
Family: Father Robert Arbuthnot; Mother Sarah Bury; Wife Martha Taver married 25.7.1745; Son John Arbuthnot (d.1810); Son Charles Arbuthnot.
Service: 25.3.1731-24.4.1733[P] Vol. *Prince Frederick* (70); 25.4.1733 Mid *Princess Amelia* (80); 6.11.1733-29.12.1734 Mid *Princess Louisa* (40); 30.12.1734-28.8.1735[P] Mid *Winchelsea* (20); 1.3.1736/37 Mid *Lichfield* (50); 28.7.1737 Able *Lichfield* (50); 22.8.1737 Able *Argyll* (50); 9.9.1737 Mid *Argyll* (50); 30.7.1738-27.11.1738[P] ActL *Argyll* (50); 20.12.1738 Mid *Argyll* (50); 30.5.1739 Mate *Portland* (50); 18.8.1739 Passed; **Lieutenant**; 21.8.1739 3L *Tiger* (50); 6.8.1740 3L *Guernsey* (50); 28.12.1743[(MED 29.1.1744/45)] 4L *Somerset* (80); 11.2.1743/44-12.2.1743/44 Battle of Toulon; **Commander**; 25.6.1746 *Jamaica* (10) Sloop; **Captain**; 22.6.1747 *Triton* (20); 12.10.1749-7.12.1752[P] *Nightingale* (22); 5.6.1754-20.12.1757[P] *Garland* (24); 15.11.1758 *Portland* (50); 18.8.1759-19.8.1759 Battle of Lagos Bay; 20.11.1759 Battle of Quiberon Bay; 5.10.1761 *Modeste* (64); 11.11.1761-20.9.1763[P] *Orford* (68); 6.6.1762-13.8.1762 Operations against Havana; 20.10.1770-28.9.1773[P] *Terrible* (74); 15.8.1775-5.1776 Resident Commissioner at Halifax; 26.4.1776-6.1778 Gov. of Nova Scotia; 23.1.1778 **Rear Admiral of the White**; 22.2.1779-4.1781 CinC — North America; 19.3.1779 **Vice Admiral of the Blue**; 4.1780-1781 *Roebuck* (44); 26.9.1780 **Vice Admiral of the White**; 1781-6.1781 *Royal Oak* (74); 16.3.1781 Battle of Cape Henry; 24.9.1787 **Vice Admiral of the Red**; 1.2.1793 **Admiral of the Blue**.

ARCHER, JOHN

Dates: c.1723 Born; 1762 Died; 3.5.1762 Will Probate.
Family:
Service: 13.10.1746 Mid *Cornwall* (80); 10.7.1747 Mate *Cornwall* (80); 19.7.1747 Able *Vigilant* (60); 12.11.1747 Passed; **Lieutenant**; 14.1.1747/48-1.8.1748[P] L. *Raven* (10) Sloop; 11.3.1755-1.12.1757 2L *Falmouth* (50); 7.1760-6.1763[P] LCmdr *Delight* Hired Tender.

ARDESOIF, JOHN PLUMMER

Dates: 1737 Born London; 21.5.1790 Died London.

Family: Father Abraham Ardesoif; Mother Diana Plummer; Wife Marianne Dufour(1758–1778) married 1771; Wife Lucinda Mence married 11.1778; Wife Jane Windover (1748–1790) married 7.2.1790; Daughter Mary Anne Plummer Ardesoif(1772–1865); Son William Stratford, RN (d.1796).

Service: 1753-1756 Merchant Service; 9.2.1756 Ord. *Arundel* (24); 26.9.1756 Able *Arundel* (24); 18.2.1757 Mid *Arundel* (24); 28.11.1757 Mid *Penzance* (44); 20.1.1758 Mid *Tartar* (28); 5.6.1758-12.6.1758 Raid on Saint-Malo; 5.9.1759 Passed; 10.10.1759 **Lieutenant**; 5.1.1760-7.7.1762 4L *Torbay* (74); 29.3.1761-11.6.1761 Expedition against Belle-Isle; 16.9.1765 1L *Boreas* (28); 8.7.1767-11.1.1769 1L *Carysfort* (28); 31.10.1770 1L *Terrible* (74); 25.2.1772 2L *Terrible* (74); 24.3.1772 1L *Terrible* (74); 9.9.1773-21.9.1773 1L *Ramillies* (74); 21.1.1775 1L *Argo* (28); 10.8.1776[BLI 23.4.1779] LCmdr *Pelican* Hired Tender; 22.2.1779 2L *Europe* (64); **Commander**; 16.11.1779[NA 4.4.1780] *Loyalist* (14) Sloop; **Captain**; 5.5.1781[NA 3.10.1781]-1.10.1781 *Royal Oak* (74); 5.9.1781 Battle of the Chesapeake.

ARMIGER, JOHN

Dates: c.1709 Born; 1777 Died; 16.12.1777 Will Probate.

Family:

Service: 15.3.1727/28-11.6.1729 Vol-p-O *Kinsale* (40); 11.6.1729-28.3.1731 Vol-p-O *Oxford* (50); 29.3.1731 Mid *Salisbury* (50); 12.6.1734 Passed; **Lieutenant**; 19.1.1740/41[West Indies 1.6.1741] L. *Wolf* (8) Sloop; 12.6.1741 3L *Dartmouth* (50); 10.8.1741 3L *Advice* (54); 18.3.1741/42-4.4.1744[P] 2L *Advice* (54); 17.11.1744 4L *Royal George* (100); **Commander**; 28.1.1744/45-4.11.1745 *Baltimore* (14) Sloop.

ARNOLD, SAMPSON

Dates: c.1728 Born; 3.7.1765 Died.

Family:

Service: 1752-1754 Merchant Service; 7.5.1754 Ord. *Lynn* (44); 21.4.1755 Mid *Rye* (20); 8.1.1757 Able *Humber* (44); 3.6.1757-5.1.1758[P] Mid *Humber* (44); 6.1.1758 Mid *Norfolk* (74); 5.6.1758-12.6.1758 Raid on Saint-Malo; 11.10.1758 Passed; **Lieutenant**; 27.10.1758 3L *Torrington* (44); 26.1.1759 2L *Torrington* (44); 5.10.1761-8.1.1762 1L *Torrington* (44); 31.8.1762 3L *Terrible* (74); 4.12.1762-23.1.1763[P] 1L *Terrible* (74).

ARNOTT, ROBERT

Dates: 1760 Died; 18.8.1760 Will Probate.

Family:

Service: 16.6.1718-1.11.1718 Ord. *Phoenix* (24) Fireship; 2.11.1718-2.11.1720 Vol-p-O *Phoenix* (24) Fireship; 3.11.1720-15.10.1722 Mid *Phoenix* (24) Fireship; 16.10.1722-31.7.1723 Mid *Chatham* (14) Yacht; 1.8.1723-11.2.1725/26 Mid *Cumberland* (80); 11.1.1725/26 Passed; **Lieutenant**; 10.4.1740-11.5.1740 4L *Torbay* (80); 25.5.1741[West Indies 9.3.1741/42] 3L *Torbay* (80); 12.4.1742-21.1.1744/45 2L *Torbay* (80); 11.2.1743/44-12.2.1743/44 Battle of Toulon.

ARROWSMITH, JOSEPH

Dates: c.1723 Born; 1759 Died.

Family:

Service: 22.5.1747 Mid *Lark* (44); 23.7.1747-7.10.1747[S] Able *Dartmouth* (50); 16.3.1748/49 Mid *Kent* (64); 4.10.1750 QGnr *Berwick* (70); 9.4.1752-26.4.1755[P] Mate *Jason* (44); 6.6.1755

Mid *Prince George* (80); 16.6.1756 Mate *Monarch* (74); 4.4.1757 Passed; **Lieutenant**; 6.5.1757 3L *Windsor* (60); 10.5.1757-21.5.1759[P] L. *Beaver* (18) Sloop; 6.6.1758-27.7.1758 The Siege of Louisbourg; 12.8.1761-22.7.1763[P] 3L *Belleisle* (64); 6.6.1762-13.8.1762 Operations against Havana; 2.6.1765-20.7.1768 LCmdr *Grace* (6) Cutter; 21.12.1769-27.2.1771[P] 1L *Rippon* (60).

ARTHUR, DAVID

Dates: c.1736 Born; 1785 Died; 16.7.1785 Will Probate.
Family: Wife Susannah.
Service: 1751-1755 HEIC Service; 16.11.1755 Mid *Cambridge* (80); 13.4.1757 Mid *Lowestoffe* (28); 7.2.1758 Passed; **Lieutenant**; 11.10.1758 6L *Union* (90); 30.1.1759 6L *Royal William* (84); 22.2.1759 5L *Royal William* (84); 9.1.1760-23.2.1763[P] 4L *Royal William* (84); 29.3.1761-11.6.1761 Expedition against Belle-Isle; 2.1.1768-25.9.1769 1L *Seahorse* HEIC.

ARUNDELL, FRANCIS

Dates: c.1709 Born; c.1764 Died.
Family:
Service: 20.6.1729-20.1.1729/30 Ord. *Argyll* (50); 21.1.1729/30-28.9.1730 Able *Argyll* (50); 29.9.1730-8.6.1731 Mid *Argyll* (50); 9.6.1731-17.3.1731/32 Mid *Exeter* (60); 18.3.1731/32 Able *Exeter* (60); 19.3.1731/32-22.5.1732 Mid *Exeter* (60); 23.5.1732-3.7.1732 Able *Exeter* (60); 3.7.1732-13.2.1732/33 Mid *Saltash* (8) Sloop; 1.8.1733-15.1.1733/34 Able *Swallow* (60); 16.1.1733/34-21.3.1733/34 Mid *Swallow* (60); 22.3.1733/34-5.6.1734 Able *Revenge* (70); 6.6.1734-24.7.1735 Mid *Revenge* (70); 25.7.1735 Mid *Newark* (80); 4.12.1735 Passed; **Lieutenant**; 31.8.1739-10.11.1740 4L *Norfolk* (80); 25.2.1741/42 3L *Norfolk* (80); 24.9.1742[(MED 16.4.1746)] 4L *Marlborough* (90); 1.10.1742[(MED 16.4.1746)] 2L *Marlborough* (90); 24.3.1742/43[(MED 8.8.1743)] 2L *Pembroke* (60); 3.2.1743/44 1L *Princess Royal* (90); 29.3.1744-15.6.1744 2L *Exeter* (58); 23.6.1744-12.7.1745[P] LCmdr *James and Mary* (16) Hired Sloop.

ASHBURY, FRANCIS

Dates: c.1738 Born; 1766 Died.
Family:
Service: 16.12.1752 Capt Serv *Culloden* (74); 19.3.1753 Capt Serv *Unicorn* (24); 20.2.1756 Able *Yarmouth* (64); 22.3.1756 Mid *Yarmouth* (64); 31.1.1757-19.2.1758[W] Mid *Invincible* (74); 8.1757-10.1757 Louisbourg Expedition; 24.9.1758 Able *Dorsetshire* (68); 25.12.1758 Able *Fly* (8) Sloop; 19.3.1759 Mid *Mars* (74); 20.11.1759 Battle of Quiberon Bay; 12.3.1760 Passed; **Lieutenant**; 27.12.1762[(MED 22.4.1763)]-4.3.1763[P] 5L *Thunderer* (74); 1.2.1770-30.5.1770 L. *Ranger* (8) Sloop.

ASHINGTON, HENRY

Dates: 19.9.1729 Born Deal; 24.1.1807 Died; 16.4.1807 Will Probate.
Family: Father Robert Ashington (1700-1734); Mother Elizabeth Gammon (1707-?); Wife Jane Cattral married 17.5.1784; Daughter Elizabeth; Sister Mary (1724-?); Brother Robert Ashington (1727-1765); Brother John (1730-).
Service: 5.6.1751 L. Serv *Somerset* (68); 23.5.1752 Able *Vulture* (14) Sloop; 6.2.1753 Mid *Vulture* (14) Sloop; 17.8.1753 Mid *Ferret* (14) Sloop; 20.2.1755 Mate *Barfleur* (80); 17.4.1757 Mate *Invincible* (74); 8.1757-10.1757 Louisbourg Expedition; 5.12.1757 Passed; **Lieutenant**; 14.12.1757 L. *Lightning* (6) Hospital Ship; 6.6.1758-27.7.1758 The Siege of Louisbourg; 29.1.1759 3L *Rochester* (50); 20.11.1759 Battle of Quiberon Bay; 14.3.1760 2L *Rochester* (50); 7.1.1762-10.2.1762 Operations against Martinique; 1.5.1762[(EI 3.3.1763)]-29.11.1762[F] 3L

Marlborough (68); 6.6.1762-13.8.1762 Operations against Havana; 27.10.1770-28.10.1773 1L *Boyne* (68); 11.9.1777-30.6.1780[SC] 2L *Cornwall* (74); 6.7.1779 Battle of Grenada; 17.4.1780 Battle of Martinique; 15.5.1780 Action of March 15 1780; 19.5.1780 Action of March 19 1780; 3.10.1780 LCmdr *Lioness* (26) Convalescent Ship; 27.11.1780-1782 LCmdr *Mars* Prison Ship; 1.12.1797 **Superannuated Commander**.

ASKEW, ROBERT

Dates: 1756 Died; 1.6.1756 Will Probate.
Family: Wife Millicent married 21.12.1728; Daughter Millicent.
Service: 5.2.1720/21-18.7.1723 Vol-p-O *Faversham* (42); 19.7.1723-14.3.1727/28 Mid *Scarborough* (20); 14.3.1728/29 Passed; **Lieutenant**; 4.3.1739/40 3L *York* (60); 8.12.1741[JAM 2.10.1742]-22.1.1741/42 3L *Jersey* (60); 26.5.1742-31.5.1742 2L *Revenge* (70); 20.8.1742-19.9.1742 L. *Otter* (14) Sloop; 3.1.1742/43-31.5.1743 L. *Baltimore* (14) Sloop; 27.7.1743-28.9.1743 L. *Port Mahon* (20); 21.2.1743/44 L. *Merlin* (10) Sloop; 16.10.1744-31.1.1744/45 1L *Ipswich* (70); **Commander**; 12.7.1745-12.9.1746 *Serpent* (10) Bomb Vessel; **Captain**; 21.8.1747-27.12.1748[P] *Port Mahon* (24).

ATKINS, CHRISTOPHER

Dates: c.7.1728 Born; 17.7.1728 Baptised Saint Marys, Portsea; 21.1.1791 Died.
Family: Father Christopher.
Service: 31.5.1743 Able *Princess Amelia* (80); 12.11.1744 Able *Hampshire* (50); 5.8.1745 Able *Shrewsbury* (80); 1.9.1750 Mid *Surprise* (24); 4.7.1752 Mid *Jason* (44); 9.1.1754 Passed; **Lieutenant**; 6.4.1757 2L *Richmond* (32); 30.8.1757-28.2.1760 2L *Diana* (32); 6.6.1758-27.7.1758 The Siege of Louisbourg; 7.1763-1769 In the service of Kingdom of Sardinia; 7.1763 **Capitano di Vascello** (State Navy); 8.1763 Capitano di Vascello *Hermione* (34); **Commander**; 20.11.1763-22.11.1763 *Happy* (8) Sloop; 1766-1769 Capitano di Vascello *Asuncion* (44); 3.12.1771 *Scorpion* (14) Sloop; **Captain**; 18.9.1772[MED 15.2.1773] *Pallas* (36); 8.12.1772[MED 15.2.1773] *Montreal* (32); 19.6.1775-29.6.1776 *Actaeon* (28); 9.10.1776-4.10.1780 *Aeolus* (32).

ATKINS, JOHN

Dates: 1769 Died; 7.9.1769 Will Probate.
Family:
Service: 21.11.1735-12.1.1735/36 Able *Monmouth* (70); 28.2.1735/36-24.3.1736/37 Able *Torrington* (40); 28.4.1737 Able *Bridgewater* (32); 11.10.1737 Able *Aldborough* (20); 3.6.1738 Mid *Aldborough* (8) Fireship; 21.1.1741/42 Mid *Chatham* (50); 13.1.1743/44-6.9.1745 Mid *Bedford* (70); 11.2.1743/44-12.2.1743/44 Battle of Toulon; 7.9.1745 Passed; **Lieutenant**; 3.10.1745-8.6.1746 3L *Chatham* (50); 22.1.1746/47-3.11.1747 3L *Warwick* (60).

ATKINS, SAMUEL

Dates: 5.1.1765 Died Wickham, Southampton; 29.10.1765 Will Probate.
Family: Wife Elizabeth; Wife Sarah Shales (1703-1736) married 27.3.1722; Son George (1726–1773); Son John.
Service: **Lieutenant**; 17.1.1708/9[MED 7.12.1709] L. *Hunter* (24); 15.7.1709[MED 7.12.1709] 2L *Antelope* (54); 29.11.1709 5L *Royal Sovereign* (100); 9.5.1710 4L *Royal Sovereign* (100); 2.2.1710/11-21.6.1711[P] 5L *Marlborough* (90); 27.9.1711-8.2.1714/15 1L *Gloucester* (54); 5.3.1714/15-20.2.1716/17 2L *Cumberland* (80); **Commander**; 8.1.1717/18 *Basilisk* (4) Bomb Vessel; 17.3.1717/18 *Bedford Galley* (32); 24.3.1717/18 *Garland* (32); 11.8.1718 Battle of Cape Passaro; **Captain**; 3.12.1718[MED 24.3.1719/20]-19.3.1719/20[P] *Charles Galley* (42); 21.6.1720-15.5.1723[P]

Panther (54); 25.1.1725/26-3.11.1726 *Portland* (50); 7.9.1727-31.1.1727/28[P] *Captain* (70); 26.7.1728 *Falkland* (50); 1.2.1731/32-30.6.1738 *Port Mahon* (20); 27.9.1741-2.7.1742 *Sandwich* (90); 15.7.1747 **Superannuated Rear Admiral.**

ATKINSON, ANTHONY

Dates: 1775 Died.

Family:

Service: **Lieutenant**; 28.11.1741[(MED 16.9.1742)] 4L *Lancaster* (80); 19.10.1742 4L *Princess Amelia* (80); 27.3.1744 3L *Princess Amelia* (80); 14.7.1744 3L *Monmouth* (70); 2.9.1746 2L *Monmouth* (70); 19.1.1746/47-2.9.1748[P] 1L *Monmouth* (70); 3.5.1747 1st Battle of Cape Finisterre; 14.10.1747 2nd Battle of Cape Finisterre; 1756 Impress Service; 28.10.1757-18.9.1758 1L *Royal Sovereign* (104).

ATKINSON, EDWARD

Dates: 1786 Died; 2.6.1786 Will Probate.

Family: Wife Margaret; Daughter Elizabeth; Son Edward; Sister Margaret [Railton].

Service: 12.5.1759 **Lieutenant**; 12.11.1759[(BLI 12.11.1759)] 3L *Ludlow Castle* (44); 16.1.1760-22.12.1761 2L *Argo* (28); 6.4.1763-9.6.1766 LCmdr *Winchelsea* (4) Cutter; 2.2.1771-10.6.1771[P] 2L *Arrogant* (74).

ATKINSON, JOHN

Dates: 17.3.1782 Died.

Family:

Service: 22.12.1725-7.12.1726[P] Mid *Diamond* (40); 24.12.1726 Able *Adventure* (40); 27.3.1727 Mid *Royal Oak* (70); 27.3.1729 Mid *Grafton* (70); 10.7.1730 Able *Oxford* (50); 1.3.1730/31 Mid *Salisbury* (50); 10.6.1731 Able *Namur* (90); 16.1.1731/32 Able *Katherine* (8) Yacht; 8.5.1732 Passed; **Lieutenant**; 29.11.1745 6L *Duke* (90); 2.4.1748 5L *Duke* (90); 5.5.1748-22.6.1748[P] 4L *Duke* (90); 5.12.1748-16.11.1752[P] 2L *Kent* (64); 16.1.1753 2L *Culloden* (74); 20.2.1753 2L *Invincible* (74); 16.5.1753-22.5.1754 2L *Terrible* (74); 22.5.1754 3L *Terrible* (74); 25.2.1755 2L *Terrible* (74); 13.5.1755 2L *Ramillies* (90); 7.10.1755 1L *Kingston* (60); 24.12.1755 2L *Prince George* (80); 14.5.1756-3.7.1756 1L *Prince George* (80); 19.11.1767-26.5.1768 2L *Temeraire* (74); 30.11.1781-17.3.1782[W] LCmdr *Repulse* (12) Cutter.

AUGUSTUS, LORD EDWARD (PRINCE EDWARD)

Dates: 14.3.1739 Prince Edward; 14.3.1738/39 Born Norfolk House, St James's Square, London, London; 1.4.1760 Duke of York and Albany; 1.4.1760 Earl of Ulster; 17.9.1767 Died Monaco; 3.11.1767 Buried Westminster Abbey.

Family: Father Frederick Lewis, prince of Wales; Mother Princess Augusta of Saxe-Gotha (1719-1772);

Service: **Captain**; 14.6.1759-4.7.1759 *Phoenix* (44); 27.10.1760-17.9.1767 Privy Counsellor; 31.3.1761 **Rear Admiral of the Blue**; 22.6.1762-23.1.1763[P] *Princess Amelia* (80); 21.10.1762 **Vice Admiral of the Blue**; 11.1762 Resigned; 1766 **Admiral of the Blue.**

AYLMER, LORD HENRY (3RD BARON AYLMER)

Dates: 1718 Born; 21.5.1718 Baptised; 26.6.1754 3rd Baron Aylmer; 17.10.1766 Died.

Family: Father Henry, 2nd Baron Aylmer (d.1754); Mother Elizabeth Priestman (1690-1750); Wife Anne Pierce (d.1756); Son Henry Aylmer, 4th Baron Aylmer (d.1785); Daughter Anne;

Brother Matthew Aylmer (1717-1748); Brother Philip Aylmer (1721-1721); Brother Rev John Aylmer (1723-1793);
Service: **Lieutenant**; 14.6.1735[(Portugal 3.12.1736)]-16.10.1735 3L *Warwick* (60); 18.11.1737 L. *Bonetta* (8) Sloop; 28.2.1737/38 3L *Hector* (40); 4.1740-5.7.1740 Attack on St. Augustine; **Captain**; 18.9.1741-4.6.1744 *Port Mahon* (20).

AYSCOUGH, JAMES

Dates: c.7.1735 Born; 7.7.1735 Baptised Grantham, Lincolnshire; 1789 Died.
Family: Father William Ayscough; Mother Jane.
Service: 14.8.1747 Capt Serv *Jamaica* (10) Sloop; 4.10.1747 Able *Jamaica* (10) Sloop; 16.12.1747 Able *Surprise* (24); 5.11.1748 Mid *Surprise* (24); 1.9.1749 Able *Seahorse* (24); 26.9.1750 Mid *Seahorse* (24); 5.11.1752 Able *Nightingale* (22); 14.4.1753 Mid *Newark* (80); 5.1.1757 Passed; **Lieutenant**; 10.2.1757 L. *Port Royal* (12) Storeship; 14.4.1761[(JAM 28.7.1761)]-25.1.1762 1L *Enterprise* (44); 19.5.1762-18.12.1762[P] 5L *Royal George* (100); 14.12.1762-4.4.1763[P] 1L *Chester* (50); 14.4.1763 LCmdr *Alarm* (6) Cutter; 27.11.1763 LCmdr *Ferret* (6) Cutter; 3.2.1768 1L *Bellona* (74); 22.6.1768 2L *Bellona* (74); 6.1769-4.1.1770 LCmdr *Bellona* Hired Tender; 21.9.1770 3L *Bellona* (74); 3.10.1770-2.2.1771 2L *Bellona* (74); **Commander**; 10.1.1771-1.10.1778 *Swan* (14) Sloop; 2.7.1776-4.7.1776 Staten Island Landings.

Service Records B

BABB, WILLIAM

Dates: c.1730 Born; 21.5.1791 Died Camborne, Cornwall; 19.7.1791 Will Probate.
Family: Wife Julian Vivian (1738-1801) married 13.10.1770.
Service: 1749-1755 Merchant Service; 9.7.1755 Mid *Ramillies* (90); 20.5.1756 Battle of Minorca; 26.12.1756 Master *Captain* (64); 8.1757-10.1757 Louisbourg Expedition; 13.3.1758 Master *Maidstone* (28); 5.6.1758-12.6.1758 Raid on Saint-Malo; 1.8.1759 Passed; **Lieutenant**; 2.8.1759 3L *Launceston* (44); 11.1.1760 2L *Launceston* (44); 26.1.1761 3L *Launceston* (44); 29.3.1761-11.6.1761 Expedition against Belle-Isle; 7.8.1761-12.5.1763[P] 2L *Launceston* (44); 6.2.1771-23.5.1771[P] 3L *Cambridge* (80).

BACON, WILLIAM

Dates: c.1730 Born; 5.11.1790 Died.
Family:
Service: 1746-1748 HEIC Service; 14.11.1747 Able *Greenwich* (50); 16.3.1747/48-21.8.1749[P] Able *Winchester* (50); 11.10.1750 Able *Torrington* (44); 2.11.1750 Mid *Winchester* (50); 17.2.1750/51 Mid *Princess Louisa* (60); 27.11.1751 Able *Princess Louisa* (60); 10.12.1752 Able *Norwich* (50); 22.5.1753 Mid *Norwich* (50); 7.8.1754 Mate *Norwich* (50); 14.3.1755 Passed; **Lieutenant**; 27.10.1757 L. *Rye* (20); 9.3.1758-24.5.1758 Capture of Fort Louis; 16.1.1759-19.1.1759 Attack on Martinique; 20.1.1759-1.5.1759 Capture of Guadeloupe; 2.4.1762-22.12.1762[P] L. *Hazard* (8) Sloop; 29.11.1773-7.2.1776 1L *Torbay* (74); 7.2.1776-29.3.1776 L. *Ranger* (8) Sloop; 8.1776-1779 Impress Service at Waterford.

BAGSTER, JOHN

Dates: 1720 Born Cowes; 1792 Died Leeds; 30.3.1792 Buried Leeds, St Peter, Leeds; 26.6.1792 Will Probate.
Family: Wife Dorothy Hall married 8.6.1742; Daughter Henrietta (1746–1829).
Service: 12.12.1737 Able *Centurion* (60); 17.3.1737/38 Able *Princess Louisa* (60); 18.11.1738 Mid *Princess Louisa* (60); 21.11.1739 Attack on Puerto Bello; 20.4.1740 Mid *Cumberland* (80); 25.3.1741 Mate *Cumberland* (80); 26.10.1741 Master *Looe* (44); 27.11.1742 Master *Severn* (50); 27.7.1744 Passed; **Lieutenant**; 28.7.1744[BLI 22.8.1745] L. *Comet* (10) Bomb Vessel; 12.8.1744[BLI 22.8.1745] L. *Bien Aime* (18) Armed Storeship; 23.5.1745[22.8.1745]-22.6.1745 3L *Mermaid* (44); 21.8.1745 2L *Prince Edward* (44); 3.7.1746 2L *Bristol* (50); 3.5.1747 1st Battle of Cape Finisterre; 5.7.1747-30.9.1748[P] L. *Amazon* (22); 1.7.1756 2L *Berwick* (64); 24.9.1756 1L *Union* (90); 1.8.1757 1L *Neptune* (90); 5.9.1757-6.10.1757 Raid on Rochefort; 17.1.1759 1L *Shrewsbury* (74); 22.2.1760-5.10.1763[P] 1L *Dublin* (74); 15.7.1760-6.8.1761 LCmdr *Barbadoes* (14) Sloop; 7.1.1762-10.2.1762 Operations against Martinique; **Commander**; 14.5.1762-8.3.1763[P] *Escort* (14) Sloop; 6.6.1762-13.8.1762 Operations against Havana.

BAIKIE, HUGH

Dates: 1739 Born; 21.7.1816 Died Welwyn, Hertfordshire; 7.8.1816 Will Probate.
Family: Father Thomas; Mother Cecilia Graeme; Wife Mary Edwards (1749-1800) married 18.1.1780; Daughter Cecilia Mary (1793-1841); Brother Mungo (1735-?).
Service: 1752-1756 Merchant Service; 5.10.1756 Mid *Monarch* (74); 16.1.1757 Mate *Barbadoes* (14) Sloop; 27.8.1758 Mid *Amazon* (22); 16.1.1759-19.1.1759 Attack on Martinique; 20.1.1759-1.5.1759 Capture of Guadeloupe; 30.5.1760 Passed; **Lieutenant**; 22.1.1761-12.4.1763 2L *Maidstone* (28); 5.5.1763 L. *Pomona* (18) Sloop; 18.5.1763-23.7.1767 L. *Squirrel* (20); 23.2.1769-6.3.1772[P] 2L *Dunkirk* (60); 28.7.1772 1L *Alarm* (32); 4.1776-1777 Agent for Transports; 10.10.1777 1L *Europa* (64); **Commander**; 9.12.1777-9.12.1778 *Three Brothers* (20) Hired Armed Ship; 10.7.1779 *Fairy* (14) Sloop; **Captain**; 19.2.1780-29.1.1781 *Ranger* (30) Hired Armed Ship.

BAILLIE, ALEXANDER

Dates: c.1720 Born; 1764 Died; 13.9.1764 Will Probate.
Family:
Service: 12.10.1739 Able *Edinburgh* (70); 7.6.1740 Able *Torbay* (80); 10.10.1741 Able *Marlborough* (90); 29.12.1741 Gnr Mate *Marlborough* (90); 20.8.1743 Mid *Marlborough* (90); 11.2.1743/44-12.2.1743/44 Battle of Toulon; 22.8.1745 Mid *Chichester* (80); 18.11.1745 Mate *Ruby* (50); 11.9.1746 Passed; **Lieutenant**; 9.11.1756 4L *Northumberland* (68); 24.12.1756-19.2.1758[W] 5L *Invincible* (74); 8.1757-10.1757 Louisbourg Expedition; 18.4.1758 1L *Thames* (32); 7.8.1761 4L *Blenheim* (90); 17.6.1762[MED 9.8.1762]-18.1.1763[P] 3L *Neptune* (90).

BAILLIE, ALEXANDER FRANCIS

Dates: 1732 Born; 29.4.1822 Died London; 7.5.1822 Buried St Luke, Finsbury, London; 23.5.1822 Will Probate.
Family: Wife Ann Maxey married 11.8.1797; Wife Elizabeth Gordon married 17.8.1803.
Service: 1752-1754 Merchant Service; 17.1.1754 QGnr *Fowey* (24); 24.2.1756 Mid *Buckingham* (68); 20.5.1756 Battle of Minorca; 9.5.1758 Passed; **Lieutenant**; 24.4.1759 L. *Wolf* (8) Sloop; 3.7.1759 Bombardment of Le Havre; 25.9.1759 L. *Laurel* (12) Sloop; 3.10.1759-20.4.1761 L. *Wolf* (8) Sloop; 16.3.1764-24.3.1767 L. *Zephyr* (10) Sloop; 14.3.1769-16.5.1769 L. *Peggy* (8) Sloop; 30.11.1802 **Superannuated Commander**.

BAILLIE, THOMAS

Dates: 1725 Born Dublin; 13.12.1802 Died Chelsea, Middlesex; 18.12.1802 Will Probate.
Family: Father Robert Baillie; Daughter Phillippa; Daughter Eliza Baxter (1794–1853); Brother William Baillie (1723–1810).
Service: **Lieutenant**; 29.3.1745[MED 27.10.1746] 4L *Berwick* (70); 30.3.1747 2L *Mars* (64); 10.7.1747-5.8.1748[P] 3L *Gloucester* (50); 14.10.1747 2nd Battle of Cape Finisterre; 23.8.1748-30.9.1748 L. *Scorpion* (14) Sloop; 11.9.1751 3L *Culloden* (74); 3.6.1752-28.4.1756 3L *Deptford* (50); **Commander**; 10.11.1756 *Alderney* (10) Sloop; **Captain**; 30.3.1757-2.3.1760[W] *Tartar's Prize* (24); 1.1761-1774 Captain of Greenwich Hospital; 1774-8.1778 Lieutenant-governor of Greenwich Hospital at Greenwich Hospital; 1.3.1784-5.12.1802 Clerk of the Deliveries of the Ordnance.

BAINES, CUTHBERT

Dates: 1743 Born Layham, Suffolk; 25.12.1810 Died Duke st, Manchester sq., London; 15.1.1811 Will Probate.

Family: Father John Baines (1700–1776); Mother Elizabeth Johnson (1711–1804); Wife Lydia Veale (1747-1803) married 25.8.1774; Wife Mary Anne Mawby married 1808; Son James Johnson Baines (1778–1854).

Service: 25.9.1755 Capt Serv *Hampton Court* (64); 21.5.1756 Capt Serv *Prince George* (80); 2.7.1756 Capt Serv *Buckingham* (68); 29.10.1756 Ord. *Buckingham* (68); 6.6.1757 Mid *Intrepid* (64); 18.7.1757 Capt Serv *Intrepid* (60); 5.9.1757-6.10.1757 Raid on Rochefort; 24.10.1757-6.6.1758 Land. *Intrepid* (60); 4.3.1761 Passed; **Lieutenant**; 11.3.1761 L. *Alderney* (10) Sloop; 26.3.1761-7.8.1761 2L *Minerva* (32); 14.9.1761-6.11.1762 4L *Africa* (64); 4.4.1763-28.8.1766[P] 1L *Maidstone* (28); 11.12.1767 L. *Wolf* (8) Sloop; 30.10.1770-21.1.1771 6L *Namur* (90); **Commander**; 21.1.1771-29.7.1774[P] *Falcon* (14) Sloop; 7.1777-7.1780 Impress Service; 25.10.1809 **Superannuated Captain**.

BAIRD, JOHN

Dates: c.1732 Born; 1806 Died; 12.1.1806 Buried All Saints, Fulham, London; 8.2.1806 Will Probate.

Family: Wife Ann Hoult married 4.4.1774.

Service: 3.1.1746 Capt Serv *Hound* (10) Sloop; 26.5.1747 Mid *Anglesea* (44); 20.2.1749 MidO *Rainbow* (44); 22.4.1749 Able *Success* (20); 18.6.1750 Mid *Success* (20); 3.1.1753 Passed; **Lieutenant**; 12.8.1757-13.4.1758[B] 6L *Prince George* (80); 13.5.1758[(MED 31.10.1759)] 3L *Saint George* (90); 13.6.1758[(MED 8.4.1760)] 4L *Prince* (90); 18.8.1759-19.8.1759 Battle of Lagos Bay; 13.6.1760[(MED 8.4.1760)] 3L *Prince* (90); 20.10.1761 4L *Prince* (90); 6.9.1762-25.1.1763[P] 3L *Prince* (90); 7.1769-7.1772 LCmdr *Esther* (6) Cutter; 16.4.1773-14.10.1773[P] 1L *Carcass* (8) Bomb Vessel; 13.3.1776 1L *Richmond* (32); 17.1.1778-30.7.1783[P] 1L *America* (64); 27.7.1778 1st Battle of Ushant; 16.3.1781 Battle of Cape Henry; 5.9.1781 Battle of the Chesapeake; 25.1.1782-26.1.1782 Battle of Saint Kitts; 12.4.1782 Battle of the Saintes; 21.9.1796 **Superannuated Commander**.

BAIRD, PATRICK

Dates: 1700 Born Edinburgh; 1761 Died.

Family: Father Sir James Baird of Saughtonhall, 2nd Bt. (1658-1715); Mother Elizabeth Gibson (1665-?); Brother Charles Baird (c.1696-c.1778).

Service: **Lieutenant**; 29.11.1738-26.8.1740 1L *Roebuck* (40); 27.8.1740-16.8.1742[SC] 3L *Gloucester* (50); **Commander**; 12.7.1745-24.1.1746/47 *Fly* (8) Sloop; **Captain**; 27.5.1747-3.3.1748/49 *Rainbow* (44); 7.4.1749 *Shoreham* (24); 2.6.1749 *Surprise* (24); 5.6.1755-26.6.1756 *Portland* (50); 20.2.1756[(MED 19.2.1757)]-20.8.1756 *Defiance* (60); 20.5.1756 Battle of Minorca; 1.2.1757 *Defiance* (60); 8.1757-10.1757 Louisbourg Expedition; 6.6.1758-27.7.1758 The Siege of Louisbourg; 10.1.1759 *Duke* (90); 30.5.1759-16.4.1761 *Defiance* (60); 20.11.1759 Battle of Quiberon Bay.

BAIRD, SIR WILLIAM (5TH BARONET OF SAUGHTON HALL)

Dates: c.1727 Born; 1.7.1745 5th Baronet of Saughton Hall; 17.8.1771 Died Saughton Hall, Edinburgh;

Family: Father Sir Robert Baird (1690-1740), 3rd Bt; Mother Janet Baikie (d.1733); Wife Frances Gardiner (1729-1811) married 1750; Daughter Frances (1751-1842); Son Lt.-Col. Sir James Gardiner Baird (d.1830), 6th Bt; Brother Sir David Baird of Saughtonhall (1729-1745), 4th Bt.

Service: 1742-1744 Merchant Service; 4.8.1744 Able *Mermaid* (44); 18.8.1745 Mid *Vigilant* (60); 4.1.1747/48 Able *Royal George* (100); 23.3.1747/48 Able *Boyne* (80); 12.8.1748 Mid *Superb* (60); 2.6.1749 Passed; **Lieutenant**; 15.2.1757 L. *Hound* (14) Sloop; 23.2.1757 3L *Weymouth* (60); 25.3.1758[(EI 10.12.1760)] 5L *Yarmouth* (64); 29.4.1758 Battle of Cuddalore; 3.8.1758 Battle of Negapatam; **Captain**; 3.3.1759[(EI 24.5.1762)]-28.8.1761[P] *Salisbury* (50); 10.9.1759 Battle of Pondicherry.

BAKER, HENRY

Dates: c.1718 Born; 1785 Died.
Family:
Service: 1734-1740 Merchant Service; 24.10.1740 Able *Panther* (54); 26.3.1741 Mate *Roebuck* (40); 14.11.1742 Mate *Anglesea* (44); 21.4.1744 Mate *Sunderland* (60); 13.3.1745/46 Passed; **Lieutenant**; 5.7.1746 L. *Basilisk* (8) Bomb Vessel; 15.8.1746-27.6.1747[W] 3L *Maidstone* (50); 21.11.1747-5.12.1748[P] 3L *Intrepid* (64); 14.5.1756-5.9.1760 2L *Orford* (68); 8.1757-10.1757 Louisbourg Expedition; 6.6.1758-27.7.1758 The Siege of Louisbourg.

BAKER, JAMES

Dates: 31.3.1765 Died.
Family:
Service: **Lieutenant**; 3.9.1744[(MED 23.12.1748)] 4L *Chichester* (80); 1.6.1745[(MED 23.12.1748)]-14.7.1745 4L *Torbay* (80); 10.8.1745[(MED 23.12.1748)]-26.10.1748[P] 2L *Rupert* (60); 2.1.1751/52 L. *Vulture* (14) Sloop; 18.10.1755[(NA 11.12.1755)]-29.11.1756 2L *Defiance* (60); 20.5.1756 Battle of Minorca; **Commander**; 17.8.1757 *Fortune* (14) Sloop; **Captain**; 3.3.1758[(MED 6.9.1758)] *Saint Albans* (60); 6.11.1758[(JAM 14.8.1760)]-30.6.1760 *Lyme* (28); 18.8.1759-19.8.1759 Battle of Lagos Bay; 11.4.1763-31.3.1765[†] *Lowestoffe* (32).

BAKER, JAMES

Dates: c.1729 Born; 1811 Died.
Family:
Service: 14.11.1751 Carp Serv *Deptford* (60); 7.10.1752 Able *Augusta* (60); 14.6.1755-4.10.1755 Boy *Greyhound* (20); 5.10.1755 Mid *Greyhound* (20); 13.11.1755 Mate *Greyhound* (20); 10.4.1758 Passed; **Lieutenant**; 6.10.1758 L. *Kingfisher* (8) Bomb Vessel; 16.1.1759-19.1.1759 Attack on Martinique; 20.1.1759-1.5.1759 Capture of Guadeloupe; 12.6.1759-3.4.1760 5L *Sandwich* (90); 5.1.1767 1L *Edgar* (60); 8.1.1767 2L *Edgar* (60); 19.12.1768-1.2.1770 3L *Edgar* (60); 2.2.1771-25.1.1772 L. *Aldborough* (20); 10.7.1776-2.8.1776 2L *Culloden* (74); 2.8.1776 2L *Belleisle* (64); 10.8.1776-30.5.1778 1L *Belleisle* (64); 9.1.1779-15.9.1779 1L *Union* (90).

BAKER, SAMUEL

Dates: 13.11.1758 Died.
Family:
Service: **Lieutenant**; 30.3.1746[(BLI 8.10.1746)]-19.7.1746[C] L. *Albany* (10) Sloop; 2.12.1746 L. *Swift* (8) Sloop; 24.3.1746/47 3L *Thetis* (44); 5.1.1747/48-5.7.1748[P] 2L *Thetis* (44).

BAKER, THOMAS

Dates: c.1714 Born; 1762 Died.
Family:
Service: 15.9.1734 Mid *Tilbury* (60); 10.1.1734/35 Mid *Neptune* (90); 3.12.1736 Able *Shoreham* (20); 20.1.1737/38 Able *Torrington* (40); 2.2.1737/38 Passed; **Lieutenant**; 23.5.1738[(1.5.1740)] 4L

Edinburgh (70); 12.4.1739[1.5.1740]-30.5.1740[P] 3L *Edinburgh* (70); 25.8.1740-29.8.1740 2L *Grafton* (70); 22.12.1740 1L *Tiger* (50); 6.5.1741 6L *Royal George* (100); 21.1.1741/42 5L *Royal George* (100); 10.2.1741/42 4L *Royal George* (100); 27.2.1741/42-2.9.1742[P] 3L *Royal George* (100).

BAKER, WILLIAM

Dates: bef.9.12.1760 Died.
Family:
Service: c.10.1737 ActL *Drake* (8) Sloop; **Lieutenant**; 1.5.1738[2.8.1738]-23.9.1738[P] 3L *Dunkirk* (60); 9.5.1739-29.8.1739 L. *Trial* (8) Sloop; 30.8.1739-11.10.1740 2L *Rochester* (54); 12.10.1740-19.9.1744[P] 1L *Rochester* (54); 21.10.1745[MED 14.3.1747/48] 1L *Bedford* (70); 20.8.1747[MED 14.3.1747/48]-11.12.1747[P] 3L *Norfolk* (80); 10.1.1753-29.3.1753 1L *Northumberland* (68).

BALFOUR, DAVID

Dates: c.1731 Born; 1761 Died.
Family:
Service: 19.4.1750 Able *Porcupine* (16) Sloop; 29.11.1752 QGnr *Porcupine* (16) Sloop; 24.7.1754 QM *Porcupine* (16) Sloop; 28.12.1755 Mid *Firebrand* (6) Fireship; 9.2.1757 ActL *Firebrand* (6) Fireship; 3.5.1757 Mid *Medway* (60); 5.9.1757-6.10.1757 Raid on Rochefort; 30.1.1758 Passed; **Lieutenant**; 5.10.1758-26.3.1759 4L *Berwick* (64); 16.1.1759-19.1.1759 Attack on Martinique; 15.11.1759 3L *Cambridge* (80); 13.10.1760-10.8.1763[P] 4L *Temeraire* (74); 29.3.1761-11.6.1761 Expedition against Belle-Isle; 7.1.1762-10.2.1762 Operations against Martinique; 6.6.1762-13.8.1762 Operations against Havana.

BALFOUR, GEORGE

Dates: c.1720 Born; 28.6.1794 Died St. Georges' Square, Portsmouth; 9.7.1794 Will Probate.
Family: Wife Mary; Son George; Son Charles Edward; Daughter Cecilia; Son William Henry; Son Robert; Sister Hannah.
Service: 25.6.1738-28.1.1740/41 Able *Shoreham* (20); 29.1.1740/41-3.2.1741/42 Mid *Shoreham* (20); 7.1741-10.1741 Operations against Santiago; 4.2.1741/42-10.2.1741/42 Able *Prince Frederick* (70); 11.2.1741/42-11.6.1742 Mid *Prince Frederick* (70); 12.6.1742-26.8.1744 Mid *Dreadnought* (60); 27.8.1744 Mate *Dreadnought* (60); 7.2.1744/45 Passed; **Lieutenant**; 5.7.1745 3L *Falkland* (50); 11.1.1745/46 2L *Falkland* (50); 26.5.1746-30.8.1748[P] 2L *Defiance* (60); 3.5.1747 1st Battle of Cape Finisterre; 14.10.1747 2nd Battle of Cape Finisterre; 28.1.1755 4L *Torbay* (74); 6.6.1755-8.6.1755 Action of 6-8 June 1755; 2.8.1755[NA 9.12.1755] 3L *Torbay* (74); 31.1.1756 3L *Invincible* (74); 5.8.1756 2L *Invincible* (74); 11.11.1756 1L *Invincible* (74); **Commander**; 15.11.1756 *Aetna* (16) Fireship; **Captain**; 26.7.1758-15.8.1763[P] *Bienfaisant* (64); 12.10.1770 *Venus* (36); 14.2.1772-15.10.1773 *Royal Oak* (74); 10.7.1776-23.1.1781[W] *Culloden* (74); 4.5.1781-5.9.1783[P] *Conqueror* (74); 12.4.1782 Battle of the Saintes; 19.6.1788 **Superannuated Rear Admiral.**

BANDINEL, FRANCOIS

Dates: 1738 Born Jersey; 14.6.1738 Baptised St Saviour, Jersey; 1768 Died; 25.5.1768 Will Probate.
Family: Father George Bandinel (1700-1742); Mother Elizabeth Lempriere; Brother George (1732-?); Brother Thomas Bandinel (1734-); Half-brother Thomas (1727-); Half-sister Elizabeth (1728-); Brother James Bandinel (1733-); Sister Ann Elizabeth (1736-1824); Brother Thomas Bandinel (1734-); Sister Rachel Bandinel (1741-).

Service: **Lieutenant**; 10.8.1761[JAM 28.4.1762] 3L *Pembroke* (60); 29.9.1761[JAM 28.4.1762]-18.4.1763 L. *Merlin* (18) Frigate; 6.6.1762-13.8.1762 Operations against Havana; c.1764 CaptM *Mary and Ann* Mer.

BANDINEL, THOMAS

Dates: 1763 Died.
Family:
Service: **Lieutenant**; 13.9.1759[BLI 1.10.1760] 3L *Lion* (58); 11.5.1760[BLI 19.11.1760] 2L *Lion* (58); 23.12.1760[BLI 19.11.1760]-15.12.1762[P] 1L *Lion* (58); 29.3.1761-11.6.1761 Expedition against Belle-Isle.

BANKS, FRANCIS

Dates: c.1730 Born; 18.6.1777 Died Newport, Rhode Island.
Family:
Service: 27.10.1748 Able *Mary Galley* (44); 6.11.1749 Mid *Mary Galley* (44); 10.2.1752 Able *Rainbow* (44); 24.2.1753 Mid *Devonshire* (66); 14.3.1754 Able *Berwick* (70); 11.6.1754 Mid *Glory* (44); 6.5.1755 Passed; **Lieutenant**; 31.3.1756 4L *Devonshire* (66); 28.6.1756 3L *Devonshire* (70); **Commander**; 23.3.1757 *Proserpine* (8) Fireship; 5.9.1757-6.10.1757 Raid on Rochefort; 25.11.1757 *Viper* (10) Sloop; 14.12.1757-16.1.1758 *Granado* (8) Bomb Vessel; 3.1.1759 *Swallow* (14) Sloop; **Captain**; 14.4.1760-24.9.1761 *Rose* (20); 7.2.1762-20.5.1763[P] *Lizard* (28); 6.6.1762-13.8.1762 Operations against Havana; 6.12.1769 *Niger* (32); 7.8.1771[MED 3.4.1772]-6.3.1772[P] *Pembroke* (60); 21.7.1775-18.6.1777[†] *Renown* (50); 6.12.1776-8.12.1776 Occupation of Rhode Island.

BARBER, EDWARD

Dates: 4.4.1762 Died; 26.8.1762 Will Probate.
Family:
Service: 3.5.1721-5.10.1721[P] Able *Newcastle* (50); 14.12.1721-7.2.1721/22 Able *Windsor* (60); 8.2.1721/22-16.5.1723 MidO *Prince Frederick* (70); 17.5.1723-19.9.1724 MidO *Southampton* (40); 20.9.1724-14.11.1724 MidO *Stirling Castle* (70); 15.11.1724-19.11.1726 Mid *Stirling Castle* (70); 20.11.1726 Mate *Stirling Castle* (70); 26.7.1728 Passed; **Lieutenant**; 26.7.1728-31.7.1728 2L *Kent* (70); 1.8.1728-13.9.1729[P] 3L *Ludlow Castle* (40); 27.1.1729/30-5.4.1732 3L *Portland* (50); 6.4.1732-16.12.1732[P] 3L *Torrington* (40); 24.5.1734-29.5.1741 2L *Torrington* (40); 29.1.1741/42 1L *Advice* (54); 18.3.1741/42 2L *Cambridge* (80); 12.5.1742 1L *Cambridge* (80); 26.5.1742 1L *Revenge* (70); 2.3.1742/43 Sinking of the San Isidoro; 11.2.1743/44-12.2.1743/44 Battle of Toulon; 29.1.1744/45[MED 31.7.1745] 1L *Barfleur* (90); **Commander**; 18.5.1747-14.9.1748[P] *Princess Royal* (24) Storeship; 7.10.1755 *Peggy* (8) Sloop; **Captain**; 15.6.1756 *Princess Royal* (90); 18.10.1758-4.4.1762 *Princess* (70).

BARBER, ROBERT

Dates: c.1731 Born; 15.6.1782 Died Jamaica; 5.1783 Will Probate.
Family:
Service: 15.1.1744-20.4.1746 Ord. *Antelope* (50); 21.4.1746-11.9.1746[P] Mid *Aetna* (8) Fireship; 6.6.1748 Able *Nottingham* (60); 20.6.1749 Mid *Lyme* (24); 13.10.1751 Able *Lyme* (24); 21.5.1752 Mate *Lyme* (24); 6.6.1753 Passed; **Lieutenant**; 23.2.1756 6L *Royal George* (100); 4.3.1756 5L *Royal George* (100); 12.5.1756 2L *Lowestoffe* (24); 13.6.1757 1L *Lowestoffe* (28); 30.1.1758 4L *Royal George* (100); 22.5.1758 2L *Royal George* (100); **Commander**; 26.9.1758 *Postillion* (18) Sloop; **Captain**; 4.6.1759-25.7.1763[P] *Kennington* (20); 15.1.1779-31.8.1781[P] *Belleisle* (64);

25.9.1781 *Fame* (74); 12.4.1782 Battle of the Saintes; 19.4.1782 Battle of the Mona Passage; 19.4.1782[(BLI 24.10.1783)]-13.6.1782 *Alfred* (74).

BARFORD, FRANCIS

Dates: c.1739 Born; 1776 Died.
Family:
Service: 1751-1756 HEIC Service; 5.9.1756 Mid *Barfleur* (80); 16.3.1757-12.2.1758[W] Mid *Invincible* (74); 8.1757-10.1757 Louisbourg Expedition; 29.4.1758 Mid *Dorsetshire* (68); 30.8.1758 Able *Dorsetshire* (68); 21.9.1758 Mid *Dorsetshire* (68); 20.11.1759 Battle of Quiberon Bay; 15.2.1760 Passed; **Lieutenant**; 2.9.1760 4L *Essex* (64); 29.3.1761-11.6.1761 Expedition against Belle-Isle; 14.9.1762-17.9.1762 3L *Essex* (64).

BARGRAVE, CHARLES

Dates: 1686 Born Kent; 4.8.1755 Buried Eastchurch, Kent.
Family: Father Charles Bargrave (1651-1713); Mother Elizabeth Withwick (d.1732); Wife Sarah Austen married 22.9.1719; Daughter Phoebe (1721-?); Daughter Elizabeth (1723-?); Sister Elizabeth St. Leger (1678-?; Brother Isaac (1680-1727); Sister Honora Knowler (1682-1776); Sister Martha Pilcher (1684-1750); Sister Hester Bridges (1692-1741); Brother Robert (1695-1779); Sister Mary Denne (1697-?);
Service: 1701-5.12.1701 Vol-p-O *Swiftsure* (64); 6.12.1701-16.1.1704/5 Vol-p-O *Lennox* (70); 12.10.1702 Battle of Vigo; 21.7.1704-23.7.1704 Capture of Gibraltar; 13.8.1704 Battle of Malaga; 20.1.1704/5-10.7.1707 Mid *Lennox* (70); 10.1.1707/8 Passed; **Lieutenant**; 26.2.1707/8-2.11.1710 L. *Warspite* (64); 3.11.1710-2.1.1711/12 2L *Tiger* (48); 3.1.1711/12-21.11.1712[P] 2L *Falkland* (50); 2.2.1740/41 1L *Royal George* (100); **Captain**; 28.4.1741-24.2.1741/42 *Advice* (54); 24.2.1741/42 Dismissed.

BARGUS, RICHARD

Dates: 1723 Born; 1805 Died Fareham, Hampshire; 10.4.1805 Will Probate.
Family: Wife Anne Locke (1735-1814); Daughter Elizabeth (1760-1828); Daughter Charlotte (1761-1803); Daughter Sophia [Leeke] (1762-1847); Son John.
Service: **Lieutenant**; 24.9.1742[(MED 13.3.1745/46)]-23.8.1743 L. *Guarland's Prize* Xebec; 17.8.1743[(MED 13.3.1745/46)]-6.8.1744[C] L. *Solebay* (20); 21.9.1796 **Superannuated Commander**.

BARKER, JOHN

Dates: 23.1.1776 Died.
Family: Father William Barker (c.1668-1721); Mother Mary Harrington; Wife Mrs Ann Charlton, née Russell (1710-1788); Daughter Elizabeth (1743-?); Daughter Mary (1745-?); Daughter Lydia (1748-?); Daughter Frances Harriet; Son Lt-Col. John (1752-1804).
Service: 3.5.1725 Able *Rose* (28); 26.2.1725/26 MidO *Torbay* (80); 1.8.1727-26.4.1728[P] Mid *Torbay* (80); 14.7.1728 Mid *Princess Louisa* (40); 1.10.1728 Mid *Gibraltar* (20); 16.7.1731 Mate *Gibraltar* (20); 5.5.1732 Passed; **Lieutenant**; 5.5.1735-23.6.1739 L. *Solebay* (8) Fireship; 24.1.1739/40[(2.11.1742)] 2L *Nassau* (70); 30.11.1740[(15.1.1742/43)] 4L *Somerset* (80); 17.5.1741 3L *Somerset* (80); 24.11.1741 4L *Marlborough* (90); 7.4.1742 3L *Marlborough* (90); 27.5.1742[(2.11.1742)] 3L *Lancaster* (80); 8.10.1742 1L *Princess Mary* (60); **Commander**; 11.6.1744 *Saltash* (14) Sloop; **Captain**; 19.9.1745 *Gibraltar* (20); 11.11.1746-5.7.1748[P] *Thetis* (44); 24.7.1749-17.10.1754 *Wasp* (8) Sloop; 23.9.1755-10.2.1757 *Newark* (80); 12.3.1757-19.4.1757 *Prince* (90); 19.4.1757 *Royal Anne* (100); 3.8.1757 *Jersey* (60); 18.8.1759-19.8.1759 Battle of Lagos Bay; 20.8.1760[(MED

1.9.1760)-7.4.1763[P] *Culloden* (74); 6.6.1762-13.8.1762 Operations against Havana; 24.10.1770 **Rear Admiral of the White**; 31.3.1775 **Rear Admiral of the Red.**

BARKER, THOMAS

Dates: 1762 Died.

Family:

Service: **Lieutenant**; 2.6.1744(13.7.1745)-24.7.1745[P] 3L *Montagu* (60); 23.8.1745 L. *Grand Turk* (22); 7.11.1746-13.12.1747[P] 3L *Devonshire* (80); 30.1.1746/47-4.4.1747 2L *Devonshire* (66); 4.4.1747 2L *Chester* (50); 3.5.1747 1st Battle of Cape Finisterre; 29.7.1747-21.6.1748[P] 6L *Royal George* (100); 31.7.1755 1L *Chesterfield* (44); 20.5.1756 Battle of Minorca; 24.8.1757-31.7.1758 1L *Lancaster* (66); 6.6.1758-27.7.1758 The Siege of Louisbourg.

BARKER, THOMAS

Dates: c.1733 Born; 4.8.1779 Died.

Family:

Service: 25.4.1749 Able *Tilbury* (58); 16.7.1749 Able *Captain* (70); 23.5.1750 Ord. *Rainbow* (44); 4.8.1750 Capt Serv *Rainbow* (44); 1.9.1752 Able *Rainbow* (44); 25.7.1753 Able *Glory* (44); 18.8.1753 Mid *Glory* (44); 6.11.1754 Able *Experiment* (24); 4.6.1755 Mate *Experiment* (24); 20.11.1755-4.9.1756 Mate *Prince Edward* (44); 5.5.1756 Passed; **Lieutenant**; 6.5.1756 3L *Prince Edward* (44); 15.3.1757 3L *Preston* (50); 5.4.1757 2L *Preston* (50); 21.2.1759-20.8.1759 1L *Hero* (74); 6.4.1763-1.8.1766 LCmdr *Tartuffe* (6) Cutter; 10.6.1769-2.7.1770[P] LCmdr *Tartuffe* (6) Cutter; **Commander**; 22.4.1778(NA 7.12.1778) *Carcass* (8) Bomb Vessel.

BARKER, WILLIAM

Dates: c.1718 Born; 1763 Died.

Family:

Service: 4.11.1744 Mid *Royal Sovereign* (104); 17.2.1744/45 Able *Princess Louisa* (60); 20.6.1745 Mid *Princess Louisa* (60); 29.5.1746 Mid *Windsor* (60); 3.5.1747 1st Battle of Cape Finisterre; 10.6.1747 Passed; **Lieutenant**; 2.7.1747 3L *Chester* (50); 5.10.1747-21.6.1748[P] 6L *Saint George* (90); 6.4.1751 3L *Torrington* (44); 9.5.1751 2L *Torrington* (44); 19.9.1755 2L *Hampton Court* (64); 24.6.1757 2L *Princess Amelia* (80); 5.9.1757-6.10.1757 Raid on Rochefort; 25.11.1757 L. *Granado* (8) Bomb Vessel; 24.6.1758-11.4.1760 2L *Norwich* (50); 3.7.1759 Bombardment of Le Havre.

BARKLEY, ANDREW

Dates: c.1737 Born; 1.2.1790 Died London; 20.6.1807 Will Probate.

Family:

Service: 1752-1756 HEIC Service; 27.5.1756 Mid *Oxford* (50); 24.12.1757 Able *Prince* (90); 31.1.1758 Mid *Union* (90); 22.5.1758-6.10.1758 Mid *Royal Sovereign* (104); 6.10.1758 Passed; **Lieutenant**; 27.10.1758-22.5.1759 L. *Swan* (14) Sloop; 31.7.1759-11.1.1760 2L *Launceston* (44); 6.4.1763-1.1.1766 LCmdr *Hunter* (4) Cutter; **Commander**; 31.5.1766-7.6.1769 *Wolf* (8) Sloop; **Captain**; 30.5.1770-6.3.1772[P] *Salisbury* (50); 14.1.1773 *Portland* (50); 31.5.1773(BLI 23.11.1773)-24.9.1773[P] *Princess Amelia* (80); 8.10.1774-29.4.1779[P] *Scarborough* (20); 7.2.1779(NA 7.7.1784) *Blonde* (32); 24.7.1779-12.8.1779 Penobscot Expedition; 24.9.1781(NA 24.9.1783)-9.8.1783[P] *Prudent* (64); 25.1.1782-26.1.1782 Battle of Saint Kitts.

BARLOW, GEORGE

Dates: 21.2.1787 Died Acomb, Yorkshire; 15.3.1787 Will Probate.
Family:
Service: **Lieutenant**; 17.7.1761[(JAM 20.9.1763)]-3.3.1763 3L *Defiance* (60); 6.6.1762-13.8.1762 Operations against Havana; 1770 Impress Service; 3.11.1770-29.5.1771[P] 2L *Elizabeth* (74); 9.11.1776 6L *Queen* (90); 27.3.1778-20.4.1778 5L *Queen* (90).

BARNARD, ISAAC

Dates: 1758 Died.
Family:
Service: 29.7.1707 Vol-p-O *Cambridge* (80); 30.12.1708 Vol-p-O *Somerset* (80); 6.10.1709 Mid *Somerset* (80); 5.5.1710 Able *Somerset* (80); 26.3.1711-21.11.1711[P] Able *Leake* Hired Hospital Ship; 14.7.1712 Able *Guernsey* (54); 22.7.1712-11.12.1713 Mid *Guernsey* (54); 11.11.1713 Passed; **Lieutenant**; 4.4.1720 3L *Kingston* (60); 31.10.1720[(20.12.1720)]-30.10.1721 2L *Kingston* (60); 1.11.1721-1.5.1722 3L *Gloucester* (54); 2.5.1722-31.3.1723[P] 3L *Lynn* (42); 6.5.1730-8.6.1732[P] 1L *Gosport* (42); 23.11.1733-15.5.1738 1L *Orford* (70); 16.5.1738-27.11.1738 1L *Sunderland* (60); 21.6.1739-13.11.1739 1L *Sunderland* (60); **Commander**; 1.3.1739/40-4.5.1742[P] *Firebrand* (8) Fireship; 4.3.1740/41-5.1741 Operations against Cartagena.

BARNSLEY, HENRY

Dates: c.1715 Born; 25.9.1757 Died.
Family: Son William; Son John; Son Thomas; Daughter Lucy.
Service: 21.6.1729-18.9.1731[P] Able *Scarborough* (20); 20.9.1732 MidO *Flamborough* (20); 16.4.1733 Mid *Flamborough* (20); 20.9.1734 MidO *Flamborough* (20); 27.5.1735 Mid *Flamborough* (20); 15.6.1736 Able *Swallow* (60); 23.10.1736 Passed; **Lieutenant**; 1.8.1740 3L *Russell* (80); 6.8.1740 3L *Lichfield* (50); 26.8.1740-9.12.1744[P] 2L *Lichfield* (50); 4.3.1740/41-5.1741 Operations against Cartagena; **Commander**; 10.1.1745/46 *Dispatch* (10) Sloop; **Captain**; 7.5.1748-29.11.1750[P] *America* (44); 7.2.1757-25.9.1757[W] *Tilbury* (58).

BARNSLEY, JOHN

Dates: 1777 Died.
Family:
Service: **Lieutenant**; 13.8.1755[(NA 26.2.1757)]-22.12.1756 3L *Centurion* (50); 26.2.1757 2L *Centurion* (50); 29.3.1757-5.5.1763 1L *Centurion* (50); 6.6.1758-27.7.1758 The Siege of Louisbourg; 6.6.1762-13.8.1762 Operations against Havana.

BARNSLEY, SAMUEL

Dates: c.1734 Born; 24.1.1809 Died; 27.1.1809 Buried Saint Tudy, Cornwall.
Family: Wife Jane Bligh (1762-1855) married 2.3.1788.
Service: 9.2.1752 Able *Dispatch* (14) Sloop; 19.2.1753 Cox *Dispatch* (14) Sloop; 14.7.1754 Mid *America* (44); 1.8.1755 Mate *America* (44); 16.8.1756 Mid *Boston* (44); 18.2.1757 Mid *Tilbury* (58); 17.8.1757 Able *Newark* (80); 6.11.1757 Mid *Newark* (80); 9.6.1758 Passed; **Lieutenant**; 13.6.1758-28.5.1760 L. *Porcupine* (16) Sloop; 2.1.1762-9.3.1763[P] L. *Wolf* (8) Sloop.

BARON, JAMES

Dates: 1808 Died.

Family:

Service: **Lieutenant**; 9.11.1756 4L *Monmouth* (70); 14.2.1757-6.11.1757[P] 3L *Monmouth* (70); 10.1.1761-21.2.1763[P] 2L *Monmouth* (70); 29.3.1761-11.6.1761 Expedition against Belle-Isle; 11.5.1763-24.3.1764 1L *Fame* (74); 20.6.1769-30.6.1770[P] LCmdr *Fly* (4) Cutter; 21.9.1796 **Superannuated Commander.**

BARRINGTON, THE HON. SAMUEL

Dates: Honourable; 15.2.1729 Born Shrivenham, Berkshire; 16.8.1800 Died Bath.

Family: Father John Shute, 1st Viscount Barrington; Mother Anne Daines; Brother William Wildman Barrington-Shute, 2nd Viscount Barrington; Brother Daines Barrington; Brother Major-General Hon. John Barrington.

Service: 19.6.1740 Able *Adventure* (40); 20.12.1740 Able *Lark* (40); 21.7.1741 Able *Leopard* (50); 14.4.1742 Mid *Leopard* (50); 20.8.1744 Mid *Faversham* (44); 25.9.1745 Passed; **Lieutenant**; 13.10.1745[MED 8.9.1746]-3.5.1746 3L *Antelope* (50); **Commander**; 6.11.1746 *Weazle* (16) Sloop; **Captain**; 29.5.1747 *Bellona* (30); 21.11.1747 *Romney* (44); 4.11.1748-31.3.1753 *Seahorse* (24); 3.4.1753-20.8.1754[P] *Crown* (44); 21.8.1754 *Norwich* (50); 1.4.1757-21.8.1759 *Achilles* (60); 5.9.1757-6.10.1757 Raid on Rochefort; 3.7.1759 Bombardment of Le Havre; 22.6.1762-25.12.1762[P] *Hero* (74); 24.6.1768-28.10.1768 *Venus* (36); 14.3.1769-19.6.1770[P] *Venus* (36); 21.9.1770-20.9.1773 *Albion* (74); 29.10.1776 *Prince of Wales* (74); 23.1.1778 **Rear Admiral of the White**; 28.1.1778-8.2.1780[P] *Prince of Wales* (74); 29.1.1778 **Rear Admiral of the Red**; 30.1.1778 CinC — Barbados & the Leeward Islands; 14.12.1778-15.12.1778 Battle of St. Lucia; 19.3.1779 **Vice Admiral of the Blue**; 6.7.1779 Battle of Grenada; 7.2.1780-11.10.1780 *Barfleur* (98); 26.9.1780 **Vice Admiral of the White**; 1785-1799 Lieutenant-general of Marines; 24.9.1787 **Admiral of the Blue**; 1791-8.9.1791[P] *Barfleur* (98); 12.4.1794 **Admiral of the White**; 1799-16.8.1800 General of Marines.

BARRY, THE HON. RICHARD

Dates: 1720 Honourable; c.1721 Born Westminster; 23.11.1787 Died.

Family: Father James Barry, 4th Earl of Barrymore (1667-1748); Mother Lady Anne Chichester (d.1753)); Wife Jane Hyde (d.1751); Son Unknown (d.1751); Half-sister Penelope [Cholmondeley]; Half-sister Charlotte (d.1708); Half-sister Anne [Maule]; Sister Catherine (d.1738); Sister Anne [Taylor] (d.1758); Brother James, 5th Earl of Barrymore (1717-1751); Brother Arthur (1724-1770); Brother John [Smith-Barry] (1725-1784).

Service: 30.6.1733-1.7.1735 Vol-p-O *Edinburgh* (70); 2.7.1735-11.7.1736 Vol-p-O *Falkland* (50); 12.7.1736-7.10.1738 MidO *Falkland* (50); 8.10.1738 MidO *Pembroke* (60); 26.6.1740 Passed; **Lieutenant**; 27.9.1740 3L *Panther* (54); 21.2.1740/41 6L *Saint George* (90); 10.10.1741 5L *Saint George* (90); 3.4.1742 4L *Saint George* (90); 25.5.1742 3L *Saint George* (90); 20.10.1742-2.1.1745 LCmdr *Ursula* (16) Hired Tender; 29.3.1744 2L *Saint George* (90); 1.6.1744-8.1.1744/45 1L *Lark* (44); **Commander**; 11.4.1745-27.3.1746 *Trial* (10) Sloop; 17.4.1754-28.3.1761 M.P. for Wigan.

BARTER, JAMES

Dates: bef.2.1.1759 Died; 26.2.1759 Will Probate.

Family: Sister Anne.

Service: **Lieutenant**; 2.4.1757[EI 22.11.1757] 3L *Anson* (60); 1.4.1758-bef.2.1.1759† 2L *Liverpool* (28).

BARTON, MATTHEW

Dates: 2.8.1716 Born Rushton, Northamptonshire; 30.12.1795 Died Hampstead, London; 5.1.1796 Will Probate; 6.1.1796 Buried St Andrew, Holborn, London.

Family: Father Geoffrey Barton; Mother Elizabeth; Brother Cutts (d.1781).

Service: 31.8.1730-6.8.1732[P] Vol-p-O *Fox* (20); 21.7.1733 Able *Falmouth* (50); 30.7.1733 Mid *Falmouth* (50); 14.3.1735/36 Mid *Cornwall* (80); 18.11.1736 Able *Edinburgh* (70); 13.2.1736/37 Mid *Eltham* (40); 30.3.1739 Able *Somerset* (80); 22.8.1739 Mid *Somerset* (80); 2.1.1739/40 Passed; **Lieutenant**; 4.1.1739/40 4L *Lennox* (70); 8.4.1740 Capture of the Princesa; 27.9.1740-13.1.1740/41 4L *Princess Caroline* (80); 28.12.1741 3L *Nonsuch* (50); 3.4.1742 2L *Nonsuch* (50); 11.2.1743/44-12.2.1743/44 Battle of Toulon; 17.9.1744[MED 24.3.1747/48]-20.10.1744 6L *Marlborough* (90); 25.3.1745[JAM 24.11.1748] 4L *Neptune* (90); **Commander**; 28.5.1745[MED 24.11.1748] *Duke* (8) Fireship; **Captain**; 7.2.1746/47[MED 27.7.1747] *Antelope* (50); 14.3.1746/47[MED 25.10.1748]-23.8.1748[P] *Postillon* Xebec; 5.4.1755-29.11.1758[W] *Lichfield* (50); 9.10.1760 *Temeraire* (74); 29.3.1761-11.6.1761 Expedition against Belle-Isle; 7.1.1762-10.2.1762 Operations against Martinique; 6.6.1762-13.8.1762 Operations against Havana; 8.9.1762[EI 6.6.1763]-13.5.1763[P] *Devonshire* (70); 28.4.1777 **Rear Admiral of the Blue**; 23.1.1778 **Rear Admiral of the White**; 29.1.1778 **Rear Admiral of the Red**; 19.3.1779 **Vice Admiral of the Blue**; 26.9.1780 **Vice Admiral of the White**; 24.9.1787 **Admiral of the Blue**; 1.2.1789 **Admiral of the White.**

BASKERVILLE, PETER

Dates: 13.12.1728 Baptised Portsmouth; 13.12.1728 Born Portsmouth; 26.4.1814 Buried Cowes; 24.5.1814 Will Probate.

Family: Father William Baskerville (1697-1778); Mother Elizabeth Haswell (1704-1742); Wife Elizabeth Stevens (1737-?) married 15.9.1762; Son William; Daughter Sophia [Nagle]; Brother Robert (d.1734); Sister Mary (1721-1759); Brother William (1724-1776).

Service: 7.4.1745 Able *Swift* (8) Sloop; 24.7.1745 Able *Triton* (20); 12.3.1746 Able *Portland Prize* (50); 3.2.1747-28.6.1748[P] Mid *Portland Prize* (50); 3.2.1750 Mid *Triton* (20); 4.7.1755 Mate *Orford* (68); 7.1.1756 Passed; **Lieutenant**; 13.1.1758-27.6.1762[C] L. *Gramont* (18) Sloop; 6.6.1758-27.7.1758 The Siege of Louisbourg; 18.8.1759-19.8.1759 Battle of Lagos Bay; 23.6.1767-21.7.1769 1L *Aeolus* (32); 9.8.1770-29.5.1771[P] 1L *Dorsetshire* (68); 3.7.1776 2L *Hector* (74); 10.7.1776 1L *Hector* (74); 5.11.1777 2L *Sandwich* (90); 16.5.1778 1L *Sandwich* (90); 27.7.1778 1st Battle of Ushant; 10.3.1779 2L *Portland* (50); **Commander**; 24.10.1779[NF 12.1.1780]-19.6.1783 *Cygnet* (14) Sloop; 1803 *Medina* (6) Yacht; **Captain**; 25.10.1809-26.4.1814[†] *Medina* (6) Yacht.

BASSET, CHRISTOPHER

Dates: c.1724 Born; 18.5.1765 Died.

Family:

Service: 2.6.1740 Ord. *Orford* (70); 17.9.1740 Ord. *Chichester* (80); 10.1.1741 Able *Chichester* (80); 28.8.1742 Able *Princess Caroline* (80); 23.11.1742 Mid *Princess Caroline* (80); 11.2.1743/44-12.2.1743/44 Battle of Toulon; 28.6.1744 Mid *Faversham* (44); 21.8.1744-12.6.1745[P] Mid *Newcastle* (50); 30.7.1745 Mid *Neptune* (90); 21.11.1745 Passed; **Lieutenant**; 22.11.1745 3L *Southsea Castle* (44); 20.3.1745/46-7.10.1748[P] 2L *Southsea Castle* (44); 27.5.1755 1L *Colchester* (50); 7.10.1755-5.6.1756 2L *Ramillies* (90); 20.5.1756 Battle of Minorca; **Commander**; 26.6.1756[MED 1.2.1757]-9.9.1756 *Fortune* (14) Sloop; **Captain**; 23.3.1757 *Seahorse* (24); 19.4.1757 *Rainbow* (44); 11.8.1759[MED 25.3.1761]-8.4.1761[P] *Ambuscade* (40).

BASTARD, JOHN

Dates: 1776 Died.

Family:

Service: 18.1.1742/43 Passed; **Lieutenant**; 18.1.1743/44[MED 19.1.1746/47] L. *Firedrake* (8) Bomb Vessel; 6.2.1744/45[MED 19.1.1746/47] 2L *Hampshire* (50); 6.4.1748-2.8.1748[P] 1L *Hampshire* (50); 21.3.1755 3L *Essex* (64); 1.10.1756-13.1.1757 2L *Essex* (64); 13.5.1758 2L *Conqueror* (68); 22.3.1759-26.10.1760[W] 1L *Conqueror* (68); 18.8.1759-19.8.1759 Battle of Lagos Bay; 14.9.1761-3.2.1763[P] 1L *Minerva* (32); 29.11.1766-2.5.1770 1L *San Antonio* (64).

BATE, ELIAS

Dates: c.1715 Born; 18.7.1752 Died; 1.8.1754 Will Probate.

Family:

Service: 24.6.1732 Vol-p-O *Phoenix* (20); 9.7.1734 MidO *Phoenix* (20); 27.9.1734 Mid *Phoenix* (20); 18.2.1735 Mid *Pembroke* (60); 14.12.1737 Able *Dragon* (54); 3.5.1738 Able *Hampton Court* (70); 21.11.1739 Attack on Puerto Bello; 19.4.1740 Passed; **Lieutenant**; 27.9.1740 L. *Carcass* (8) Bomb Vessel; 26.4.1743[MED 4.10.1745] 2L *Russell* (80); 11.2.1743/44-12.2.1743/44 Battle of Toulon; 23.8.1744[MED 4.10.1745] 1L *Russell* (80); 3.5.1745[MED 5.7.1746]-6.7.1745 1L *Ipswich* (70); **Commander**; 25.6.1746 *Scorpion* (10) Sloop; **Captain**; 13.12.1750-18.7.1752[†] *Mermaid* (24).

BATEMAN, NATHANIEL

Dates: c.1723 Born; 1797 Died.

Family: Son Charles Philip Butler, RN (1776-?).

Service: 4.4.1741 Ord. *Chichester* (80); 6.10.1742 Able *Marlborough* (90); 11.2.1743/44-12.2.1743/44 Battle of Toulon; 17.9.1745 Mid *Burford* (70); 3.11.1745 Cox *Liverpool* (44); 7.4.1746 Able *Barfleur* (90); 26.4.1746-28.3.1750 Mid *Worcester* (58); 3.8.1746 Action of August 3 1746; 25.3.1747 Action of March 25 1747; 9.4.1748 Battle of Santiago de Cuba; 29.3.1750 Mid *Invincible* (74); 30.4.1753 Mate *Penzance* (44); 23.2.1754 Able *Penzance* (44); 19.3.1754 Mate *Raven* (14) Sloop; 21.3.1755 NR *Rye* (20); 4.6.1755 Passed; **Lieutenant**; 5.7.1756[ECH 25.8.1758] 6L *Prince George* (80); 3.10.1756[ECH 25.8.1758] 6L *Prince* (90). 27.10.1756[ECH 25.8.1758]-22.4.1757 5L *Prince* (90); 1.6.1757[MED 25.8.1758] 5L *Saint George* (90); 20.6.1757[MED 25.8.1758]-9.10.1758 4L *Saint George* (90); 15.1.1759 4L *Torbay* (74); **Commander**; 22.9.1759-31.3.1760 *Hunter* (10) Sloop; **Captain**; 31.3.1760[NA 18.11.1762]-26.6.1760[W] *Eurus* (24); 22.9.1760[NA 9.11.1762] *Northumberland* (68); 8.2.1763-18.7.1764[P] *Ludlow Castle* (24); 20.2.1776 *Winchelsea* (32); 22.7.1778-24.10.1780[D] *Yarmouth* (64); 6.7.1779 Battle of Grenada; 17.4.1780 Battle of Martinique; 15.5.1780 Action of March 15 1780; 19.5.1780 Action of March 19 1780; 24.10.1780 Dismissed; 13.11.1780 **Superannuated Commander**.

BATEMAN, THE HON. WILLIAM

Dates: Honourable; c.1723 Born Boxgrove, Sussex; 19.6.1783 Died.

Family: Father William Bateman, 1st Visct. (c.1695-1744); Wife Anne Maria Hedges married 17.2.1755; Brother John, 2nd Visct. (1721-1802).

Service: 5.2.1736/37 Capt Serv *Diamond* (40); 6.2.1738/39-15.8.1740[P] Mid *Diamond* (40); 23.3.1739/40 Attack on Chagres; 9.4.1741 Mid *Salisbury* (50); 17.5.1741 Mid *Nassau* (70); 29.10.1741 Mid *Winchester* (50); 25.1.1741/42 Able *Dragon* (60); 8.3.1741/42 Mid *Dragon* (60); 22.11.1742 Able *Plymouth*; 18.5.1743 Mid *Dreadnought* (60); 7.12.1743 ActL *Kinsale* (44); 30.1.1743/44 Passed; **Lieutenant**; 30.1.1743/44-24.12.1744 3L *Roebuck* (44); **Captain**; 27.12.1745 *Lys* (24); 11.8.1746-21.11.1747 *Romney* (44); 26.1.1748/49-7.7.1752[P] *Windsor*

(60); 5.5.1751 Resigned; 10.4.1752-16.4.1754 M.P. for Gatton; 14.6.1756-20.3.1761 Extra Commissioner of the Navy; 1761-19.6.1783 Comptroller of the Storekeeper's accounts.

BAYNE, WILLIAM

Dates: 4.11.1730 Born Edinburgh; 9.4.1782 Died of Wounds.
Family: Father Alexander Bayne (c.1684-1737); Mother Mary Carstairs (1695-1759).
Service: **Lieutenant**; 5.4.1749[EI 13.12.1750] 3L *Deptford* (60); 14.7.1749[EI 13.12.1750]-18.5.1750[P] 2L *Deptford* (60); 28.1.1755 3L *Torbay* (74); 6.6.1755-8.6.1755 Action of 6-8 June 1755; 2.8.1755[NA 9.12.1755] 2L *Torbay* (74); 31.1.1756 2L *Invincible* (74); 5.8.1756 1L *Invincible* (74); **Commander**; 10.11.1756-24.3.1760 *Spy* (10) Sloop; 16.1.1759-19.1.1759 Attack on Martinique; 20.1.1759-1.5.1759 Capture of Guadeloupe; **Captain**; 1.7.1760 *Woolwich* (44); 7.1.1762-10.2.1762 Operations against Martinique; 1.7.1762[BLI 24.5.1764]-14.5.1764[P] *Stag* (32); 21.10.1778-9.4.1782[†] *Alfred* (74); 17.4.1780 Battle of Martinique; 29.4.1781-30.4.1781 Battle of Fort Royal; 5.9.1781 Battle of the Chesapeake; 25.1.1782-26.1.1782 Battle of Saint Kitts.

BAYNES, HENRY

Dates: 1742 Born Leeds; 6.8.1810 Died Carmarthen, Wales.
Family:
Service: **Lieutenant**; 4.10.1760-1.2.1763 2L *Aquilon* (28); 29.3.1761-11.6.1761 Expedition against Belle-Isle.

BAYNES, ROBERT

Dates: 1714 Born; bef.21.9.1758 Died.
Family:
Service: 26.9.1729-1.9.1732 Vol-p-O *Dreadnought* (60); 2.9.1732-12.7.1736 MidO *Dursley Galley* (20); 13.7.1736 Mid *Dursley Galley* (20); 3.2.1736/37 Passed; **Lieutenant**; 31.8.1739 L. *Trial* (8) Sloop; 3.11.1740[Pacific Ocean 16.5.1746]-14.5.1741[W] L. *Wager* (28).

BAZELY, JOHN

Dates: 3.1741 Born Dover; 6.4.1809 Died Dover.
Family: Mother Margaret Barber; Wife Amelia Baker; Son Henry, RN; Son John, RN.
Service: 1753-1755 Merchant Service; 21.6.1755 L. Serv *Ambuscade* (40); 1.4.1756 Able *Hampshire* (50); 30.9.1756 Mid *Prince George* (80); 9.8.1757-7.4.1760 Mid *Somerset* (68); 6.6.1758-27.7.1758 The Siege of Louisbourg; 12.3.1760 Passed; **Lieutenant**; 7.4.1760 2L *Stag* (32); 5.2.1762[BLI 15.11.1762] L. *Basilisk* (8) Bomb Vessel; 24.2.1762-25.2.1762 Capture of Saint Lucia; 17.7.1762[EI 15.11.1762]-16.12.1762[P] 3L *Cambridge* (80); 17.11.1764-26.5.1768 L. *Cruizer* (8) Sloop; 18.1.1771 2L *Somerset* (68); 22.4.1773 3L *Somerset* (68); 12.7.1773-18.6.1776 LCmdr *Greyhound* (4) Cutter; **Commander**; 1.10.1777 *Alert* (10) Cutter; **Captain**; 15.4.1778 *Formidable* (98); 27.7.1778 1st Battle of Ushant; 8.5.1779 *Pegasus* (28); 17.4.1780 Battle of Martinique; 20.6.1780 *Apollo* (32); 19.12.1780-25.2.1784[P] *Amphion* (32); 23.2.1791-6.9.1791[P] *Marlborough* (74); 31.3.1792-13.11.1794[P] *Alfred* (74); 1.6.1794 Glorious 1st of June; 1.6.1795 **Rear Admiral of the White**; 14.2.1799 **Vice Admiral of the Blue**; 1.1.1801 **Vice Admiral of the White**; 23.4.1804 **Vice Admiral of the Red**.

BEALE, RICHARD

Dates: c.1717 Born; 1787 Died.

Family:

Service: 1738-1739 Merchant Service; 24.9.1739 Able *Tilbury* (60); 4.3.1740/41-5.1741 Operations against Cartagena; 12.5.1741 Mid *Rippon* (60); 27.8.1745 Passed; **Lieutenant**; 29.11.1756$^{\text{(ECH 12.6.1759)}}$-27.3.1759^{D} L. *Polacca* (12) Sloop; 27.3.1759 Dismissed; 2.2.1771-18.7.1772 L. *Seahorse* (24); 1775-29.4.1775^{D} LCmdr *Mercury* Hired Tender.

BEAMISH, WILLIAM

Dates: c.1714 Born; 1772 Died; 30.7.1772 Will Probate.

Family:

Service: 21.7.1734 Able *Plymouth*; 20.5.1738 Mid *Plymouth*; 9.9.1739 Able *Plymouth*; 16.10.1739 Able *Berwick* (70); 3.2.1739/40 Mid *Berwick* (70); 21.4.1740 Mid *Shrewsbury* (80); 12.2.1740/41 Mate *Shrewsbury* (80); 10.11.1741 Passed; **Lieutenant**; 7.8.1744-4.1.1745/46 3L *Dreadnought* (60); 2.9.1755-23.8.1756 L. *Brilliant* (16) Hired Unknown; 4.1758-11.1762 Impress Service at Cork; 1771-1772 Impress Service at Cork.

BEAUCLERK, LORD VERE (1ST BARON VERE, OF HANWORTH)

Dates: 14.7.1699 Honourable; 14.7.1699 Lord; 14.7.1699 Born; 1750 1st Baron Vere, of Hanworth; 21.10.1781 Died.

Family: Father Charles Beauclerk, 1st Duke of St Albans (1670-1726); Mother Lady Diana de Vere; Wife Mary Chambers (c.1714-1783) married 13.4.1736; Son Vere (1737–1739); Son Chambers (1738–1747); Son Sackville (1739–1739); Son Aubrey, 5th Duke of St Albans (1740–1802); Daughter Elizabeth (1742-1746); Daughter Mary [Spencer] (1743-1812); Brother Charles, 2nd Duke of St Albans (1696–1751); Sister Diana (c.1697); Brother William (1698–1733); Brother Henry (1701–1761); Brother Sidney (1703–1744); Brother George (1704–1768); Brother Seymour (1708–c.1709); Brother James (c.1709–1787); Brother Aubrey, RN (1710-1741); Sister Mary (c.1712-?); Sister Anne (c.1714-?).

Service: **Lieutenant**; 23.8.1717-19.9.1717 L. *Blandford* (20); 20.9.1717-2.12.1718 2L *Charles Galley* (42); 11.8.1718 Battle of Cape Passaro; 3.12.1718$^{\text{(11.7.1720)}}$-29.5.1721 2L *Rochester* (54); **Captain**; 30.5.1721-16.7.1727^{P} *Lyme* (20); 31.5.1726-28.4.1740 M.P. for Windsor; 11.1.1727/28-1.4.1729 *Kinsale* (40); 2.4.1729-31.12.1730^{P} *Oxford* (50); 19.5.1731-23.12.1731^{P} *Hampton Court* (70); 1732 Extra Commissioner of the Navy; 13.3.1738-18.3.1742 Lord Commissioner of the Admiralty; 11.5.1741-28.3.1750 M.P. for Plymouth; 27.12.1744-24.12.1749 Lord Commissioner of the Admiralty; 23.4.1745 **Rear Admiral of the Red**; 14.7.1746 **Vice Admiral of the Blue**; 15.7.1747 **Vice Admiral of the Red**; 12.5.1748 **Admiral of the Blue**; 1761-1771 Lord Lieutenant of Berkshire.

BECHER, JOHN

Dates: 1726 Born London; 1783 Died; 22.1.1784 Will Probate.

Family:

Service: **Lieutenant**; 21.1.1757$^{\text{(21.7.1757)}}$ L. *Mediterranean* (12) Xebec; 24.5.1757$^{\text{(21.7.1757)}}$-8.10.1758 3L *Jersey* (60); 8.10.1758$^{\text{(JAM 2.4.1761)}}$-8.4.1761^{P} 3L *Ambuscade* (40); 16.11.1776 1L *Saint Albans* (64); **Commander**; 1.2.1778$^{\text{(NA 5.5.1779)}}$-3.4.1779 *Nautilus* (16) Sloop.

BECHER, MICHAEL

Dates: 26.12.1760 Died.

Family:

Service: **Lieutenant**; 3.1.1754-26.4.1755[P] 3L *Jason* (44); 26.8.1755 4L *Swiftsure* (68); 19.2.1756 3L *Torbay* (74); 20.5.1756-15.1.1759 2L *Torbay* (74); 5.9.1757-6.10.1757 Raid on Rochefort; 5.6.1758-12.6.1758 Raid on Saint-Malo; 29.12.1758 Capture of Goree.

BECHINOE, BENJAMIN

Dates: 1735 Born Stepney, Middlesex; 24.4.1791 Died.

Family: Father Benjamin Bechinoe (d.1761); Mother Susannah Dix (d.1755); Wife Susannah (d.1804) married 1761; Daughter Annabella [Ashford]; Daughter Susannah [Williams]; Daughter Elizabeth (1765 - 1838); Daughter Mary [Bellenden - Ker/Manners] (1768 - 1805); Brother John (1727-?); Brother James (1729-?); Brother Benjamin (c.1731-1733); Brother Charles (1738-?); Brother Samuel (1744-?); Brother Richard (1749-?).

Service: **Lieutenant**; 29.3.1759[(NA 9.12.1760)]-20.3.1761 3L *Pembroke* (60); 30.11.1770-18.7.1771 1L *Crescent* (32) Frigate; c.8.1772-5.1775 LCmdr *Esther* (6) Cutter; 17.7.1776 LCmdr *Elephant* (10) Storeship; **Commander**; 30.4.1779-28.1.1781[P] *York* (14) Storeship.

BEDFORD, THOMAS

Dates: bef.5.8.1762 Died.

Family:

Service: 3.4.1719 MidO *Launceston* (42); 27.4.1719 Mid *Launceston* (42); 30.1.1719/20 Mid *Warwick* (54); 7.12.1721-12.2.1721/22[P] MidO *Worcester* (54); 28.1.1722/23 Mid *Deptford* (50); 23.2.1724/25 Passed; **Lieutenant**; 15.6.1731-5.2.1731/32[P] 3L *Lark* (40); 12.6.1739-14.3.1739/40 1L *Weymouth* (60).

BELITHA, WARREN

Dates: c.1696 Born; 1759 Died; 14.4.1759 Will Probate.

Family: Wife Jane Saunders married 21.9.1721.

Service: 1.2.1732/33 Able *Deptford* (60); 26.12.1733 Able *Assistance* (50); 3.9.1736 Mid *Mary* (8) Yacht; 11.3.1738/39 MidO *Colchester* (50); 4.10.1739 Passed; **Lieutenant**; 25.4.1740 L. *Fox* (20); 29.10.1740 2L *Panther* (54); 11.4.1741 1L *Panther* (54); 11.9.1742-5.2.1743/44[W] 1L *Looe* (44); 23.11.1744 5L *Royal Sovereign* (104); 29.8.1745 4L *Royal Sovereign* (104); 11.1.1745/46-22.1.1745/46 3L *Royal Sovereign* (104); **Commander**; 19.3.1745/46-12.1.1746/47[P] *Scipio* (8) Fireship; 20.9.1746-25.9.1746 Lorient Operations.

BELL, GEORGE

Dates: 1762 Died.

Family:

Service: **Lieutenant**; 27.4.1757[(3.8.1757)] L. *Gibraltar* (20); 18.8.1759-19.8.1759 Battle of Lagos Bay; 22.2.1760 3L *Dublin* (74); 4.8.1760[(BLI 11.9.1761)]-24.3.1761 2L *Defiance* (60); 16.6.1761[(JAM 11.9.1761)]-31.8.1761[P] L. *Port Antonio* (12) Storeship.

BELL, THOMAS

Dates: None Known.

Family:

Service: 6.1757-8.1758 Lieut *Liverpool* (22) PMW; 8.1758 CaptP *Liverpool* (22) PMW; **Lieutenant**; 10.1.1761-20.10.1761 2L *Prince* (90); 1779-5.1779 Master *Spitfire* (16) PMW.

BELL, WILLIAM

Dates: c.1738 Born; 21.1.1804 Died.

Family:

Service: 1750-1755 Merchant Service; 30.4.1755 Able *Buckingham* (68); 20.5.1756 Battle of Minorca; 24.5.1757 Mid *Buckingham* (68); 16.1.1759-19.1.1759 Attack on Martinique; 20.1.1759-1.5.1759 Capture of Guadeloupe; 8.4.1760 Mate *Buckingham* (68); **Lieutenant**; 6.9.1760(EI 31.12.1762) 2L *Southsea Castle* (28) Storeship; 22.10.1760 Passed; 10.7.1761(EI 31.12.1762)-13.3.1763 2L *Panther* (60); 24.9.1762-6.10.1762 Battle of Manilla; 1.5.1771-30.9.1772 3L *Boyne* (68).

BELLEW, HENRY

Dates: c.1729 Born; 18.4.1791 Died; 14.5.1791 Will Probate.

Family: Father Henry Bellew; Mother Frances Barbor; Wife Mrs Anne Wentworth.

Service: 24.12.1743 Ord. *Chichester* (80); 11.2.1743/44-12.2.1743/44 Battle of Toulon; 26.4.1744 Capt Serv *Lively* (20); 18.5.1744 Capt Serv *Weymouth* (60); 22.12.1744-16.2.1744/45[W] Ord. *Weymouth* (60); 17.4.1747 MidE *Launceston* (44); 28.8.1747 Able *Mermaid* (44); 30.10.1747 Able *Superb* (60); 8.4.1748 Mid *Expedition* (44); 24.10.1749 Mid *Dispatch* (14) Sloop; 11.4.1751-26.7.1751 Mid *Dispatch* (14) Sloop; 26.7.1751 Passed; **Lieutenant**; 23.6.1756(MED 16.2.1757) 3L *Defiance* (60); 12.4.1757(MED 16.2.1757)-2.11.1758 2L *Defiance* (60); 8.1757-10.1757 Louisbourg Expedition; 6.6.1758-27.7.1758 The Siege of Louisbourg; 8.10.1759-26.3.1761 1L *Minerva* (32); 20.11.1759 Battle of Quiberon Bay; 7.8.1761-2.5.1763[P] 1L *Africa* (64); 6.11.1762-20.3.1763[P] *Dispatch* (14) Sloop; 6.11.1764 **Commander**; 23.6.1767 *Beaver* (14) Sloop; **Captain**; 10.1.1771-11.1.1771 *Colchester* (50); 20.6.1775 *Solebay* (28) Frigate; 5.7.1775-11.2.1778[W] *Liverpool* (28); 21.10.1778-12.3.1779 *Licorne* (32).

BENNETT, WILLIAM

Dates: 1790 Died.

Family:

Service: **Lieutenant**; 25.3.1741(16.9.1741)-bef.1.12.1741[P] 4L *Hampton Court* (70); 11.1.1741/42 4L *Princess Amelia* (80); 20.4.1742 3L *Princess Amelia* (80); 24.6.1742 2L *Falmouth* (50); 6.1744 Bombardment of Porto Bello; 22.2.1744/45(JAM 8.10.1745)-24.11.1747 3L *Assistance* (50); 21.3.1747/48 1L *Fougueux* (64); 24.10.1749 2L *Fougueux* (64); 8.5.1751-16.11.1752[P] 1L *Fougueux* (64); 22.5.1754 1L *Terrible* (74); 6.2.1755 1L *Edinburgh* (64); 15.6.1756 1L *Namur* (90); 5.9.1757-6.10.1757 Raid on Rochefort; 19.1.1758 6L *Ramillies* (90); 26.4.1758 5L *Ramillies* (90); 5.6.1758-12.6.1758 Raid on Saint-Malo; 11.10.1758 4L *Ramillies* (90); **Commander**; 10.1.1759 *Terror* (8) Bomb Vessel; 31.7.1759 *Gramont* (18) Sloop; 18.8.1759-19.8.1759 Battle of Lagos Bay; **Captain**; 5.3.1760 *Royal George* (100); 10.1.1761-18.12.1762[P] *Royal George* (100); 12.12.1763-12.12.1766 *Rippon* (60); 9.6.1767-27.2.1772[P] *Aeolus* (32); 12.3.1773-18.6.1776[P] *Aldborough* (20); 17.6.1778-18.4.1783[P] *Lennox* (74); 20.10.1787 **Superannuated Rear Admiral**.

BENSLEY, JOHN

Dates: c.1735 Born; bef.8.1769 Died.

Family:

Service: 25.5.1749 Able *Gloucester* (50); 2.7.1750 Mid *Gloucester* (50); 7.4.1753 Able *Unicorn* (24); 25.5.1755 Mid *Unicorn* (24); 3.12.1755 Passed; **Lieutenant**; 23.4.1756(NA 21.11.1757) L. *Shoreham* (24); 21.5.1757(NA 19.2.1759)-19.7.1759 2L *Princess Mary* (60); 1.7.1760 LCmdr *Anson*

(10) Schooner; 2.9.1761 2L *Belleisle* (64); 6.6.1762-13.8.1762 Operations against Havana; 27.4.1763[JAM 30.7.1764]-24.6.1764[P] 5L *Grafton* (68); 29.11.1766-8.1769† 1L *Tweed* (32).

BENSLEY, SIR WILLIAM (1ST BARONET OF ST MARYLEBONE)

Dates: c.1737 Born; 24.6.1801 1st Baronet of St Marylebone; 17.12.1809 Died.
Family: Father Thomas Bensley; Mother Elizabeth Winter; Wife Mary Biscoe (1760-1830) married 12.6.1798.
Service: 29.6.1750 Able *Surprise* (24); 15.5.1753 Mid *Surprise* (24); 30.9.1754 Mid *Nightingale* (22); 16.4.1756 Mid *Barfleur* (80); 1.9.1756 Passed; **Lieutenant**; 6.4.1757 5L *Royal William* (84); 3.6.1757 L. *William and Ann* (20) Hired Armed Ship; 7.3.1758 3L *Deptford* (50); 5.4.1758 2L *Deptford* (50); 5.6.1758-12.6.1758 Raid on Saint-Malo; 3.7.1759 Bombardment of Le Havre; 9.7.1759-7.8.1761 1L *Deptford* (50); 26.12.1761-3.3.1763[P] 1L *Saint Florentine* (60); 1764-1777 HEIC Service; 1781-17.12.1809 East India Company Director; 21.9.1796 **Superannuated Commander**.

BENTINCK, JOHN ALBERT

Dates: 29.12.1737 Born; 23.9.1775 Died; 28.9.1775 Will Probate.
Family: Father Willem Bentinck van Rhoon, 1st Count Bentinck (1704–1774); Mother Charlotte Sophia Aldenburg; Wife Renira de Tuyll de Serooskerken married 17.7.1763; Son William, RN (1764-1813); Daughter Sophia Henrietta [Hawkins-Whitshed] (1765-1852); Daughter Charlotte Frances [Milnes] (1768-1850); Daughter Harriet Elizabeth [Martin] (1770-1806); Son John (1771-1804); Son Charles John (1773-1781); Son Henry Saville (d 1776); Brother Christian F. Anthony, 2nd Count Bentinck (1734-1768).
Service: **Lieutenant**; 21.7.1757[NA 18.11.1757] 3L *Arc-en-Ciel* (50); 9.8.1757[NA 18.11.1757] 3L *Nottingham* (60); 1.2.1758 4L *Dorsetshire* (68); **Commander**; 18.5.1758 *Fly* (8) Sloop; **Captain**; 17.10.1758 *Dover* (44); 27.10.1759-25.8.1762 *Niger* (32); 30.3.1761-16.3.1768 M.P. for Rye; 1.11.1762-29.3.1763[P] *Anson* (60); 6.5.1766-21.3.1769 *Dragon* (74); 25.10.1770-26.10.1773 *Centaur* (74).

BENTLEY, SIR JOHN

Dates: 1703 Born; 27.12.1703 Baptised St Leonard's, Deal; 9.1759 Knight Bachelor; 3.1.1772 Died; 19.2.1772 Will Probate.
Family: Father William Bentley (1660–1719); Mother Sarah Ballard (1666–1738); Brother Thomas Bentley (d.1739); Sister Elizabeth (d.1763); Sister Sarah (d.1769).
Service: 27.11.1718 L. Serv *Falmouth* (54); 16.5.1719 L. Serv *Antelope* (54); 16.5.1720 L. Serv *Dartmouth* (54); 4.12.1720-9.11.1721[P] MidO *Dartmouth* (54); 18.1.1723 Able *Ferret* (4) Sloop; 27.11.1724-23.11.1726 MidO *Plymouth* (60); 23.11.1726 Passed; **Lieutenant**; 28.3.1734 L. *Poole* (32); 31.1.1734/35-8.12.1738[P] L. *Seahorse* (20); 12.6.1739 2L *Superb* (60); 30.8.1739 1L *Superb* (60); 19.1.1739/40[13.3.1744/45]-8.3.1739/40 1L *Ipswich* (70); 17.5.1741[13.3.1744/45] 4L *Somerset* (80); 25.11.1741[13.3.1744/45] 4L *Marlborough* (90); 25.6.1743[13.3.1744/45] 6L *Namur* (90); 11.2.1743/44-12.2.1743/44 Battle of Toulon; **Commander**; 6.3.1743/44[MED 30.12.1745] *Sutherland* (54); **Captain**; 1.8.1744-19.8.1744 *Burford* (70); 13.9.1744[MED 30.12.1745] *Liverpool* (44); 14.2.1744/45[MED 30.12.1745] *Worcester* (58); 14.4.1746 *Duke* (90); 20.5.1747-30.8.1748[P] *Defiance* (60); 14.10.1747 2nd Battle of Cape Finisterre; 30.8.1748 *Invincible* (74); 7.2.1755 *Charlotte* (8) Yacht; 12.6.1756 *Barfleur* (80); 26.4.1757-19.2.1758[W] *Invincible* (74); 8.1757-10.1757 Louisbourg Expedition; 19.7.1758-7.5.1761 *Warspite* (74); 18.8.1759-19.8.1759 Battle of Lagos Bay; 20.11.1759 Battle of Quiberon Bay; 1761-28.12.1763 Extra Commissioner of the Navy; 21.10.1763 **Rear Admiral of the White**; 18.10.1770 **Vice Admiral of the Blue**; 24.10.1770 **Vice Admiral of the White**.

BERROW, EDWARD

Dates: 13.4.1778 Died.
Family:
Service: **Lieutenant**; 9.4.1760 5L *Centaur* (74); 7.5.1762[JAM 26.11.1762]-1.12.1762[P] 3L *Penzance* (44); 6.6.1762-13.8.1762 Operations against Havana.

BERTIE, THE HON. PEREGRINE

Dates: 13.3.1740/41 Born; 13.3.1741 Honourable; 20.8.1790 Died; 23.9.1790 Will Probate.
Family: Father Willoughby, 3rd Earl of Abingdon (1692-1760); Mother Anna Maria Collins; Wife Elizabeth Hutchins married 7.5.1790; Sister Elizabeth Peregrine [Gallini] (1728–1804); Sister Jane [Clifton] (c.1730–1791); Sister Bridget (1732–1760); Brother James, Lord Norreys (1735–1745); Sister Anne Eleanora [Wenman] (c.1737-1804); Brother Willoughby, 4th Earl of Abingdon (1739–1799); Sister Mary [Stapleton] (1746–1826); Sister Sophia (1748–1760).
Service: **Lieutenant**; 17.12.1759[JAM 9.2.1760]-30.8.1760 3L *Enterprise* (44); 1.6.1761 5L *Magnanime* (74); **Commander**; 1.1.1762 *Dispatch* (14) Sloop; **Captain**; 6.11.1762-1.2.1763 *Repulse* (32); 2.8.1763-20.9.1764 *Shannon* (28); 5.10.1774-20.8.1790 M.P. for Oxford; 4.12.1782-9.4.1783[P] *Fortitude* (74); 21.4.1786-1.5.1789 *Carnatic* (74).

BESSON, CHARLES

Dates: 20.9.1822 Died.
Family:
Service: 24.8.1755 Mid *Revenge* (64); 20.5.1756 Battle of Minorca; 28.2.1758 Battle of Cartagena; 4.10.1758 Passed; **Lieutenant**; 27.10.1758-28.10.1758 2L *Argo* (28); bef.1759-20.9.1822 Lieutenant of Greenwich Hospital.

BICKERTON, SIR RICHARD (1ST BARONET BICKERTON OF UPWOOD)

Dates: 23.6.1727 Born; 24.6.1773 Knight Bachelor; 29.5.1778 1st Baronet Bickerton of Upwood; 25.2.1792 Died London.
Family: Father Henry Bickerton (d.1746); Mother Mary Dowdall; Wife Mary Anne Hussey (d.1811) married 2.1.1758; Son Richard Hussey (2nd Baronet Bickerton of Upwood), RN (1759-1832).
Service: 15.1.1737/38 Capt Serv *Grafton* (70); 13.3.1739/40 Capt Serv *Buckingham* (70); 29.8.1740 Capt Serv *Suffolk* (70); 28.4.1741 Ord. *Suffolk* (70); 30.6.1741 Able *Suffolk* (70); 2.12.1742-12.5.1743 Able *Stirling Castle* (70); 13.5.1743 Mid *Stirling Castle* (70); 9.9.1743 Mid *Saint George* (90); 2.1.1744 Mid *Duke* (90); 16.6.1744 Mid *Victory* (100); 17.8.1744-25.8.1745 Mid *Cornwall* (80); 1.1.1745/46 Passed; **Lieutenant**; 8.2.1745/46[JAM 13.12.1748] 3L *Worcester* (58); 3.8.1746 Action of August 3 1746; 25.3.1747 Action of March 25 1747; 9.4.1748 Battle of Santiago de Cuba; 10.1.1753-6.2.1755 3L *Fougueux* (64); 6.2.1755-22.7.1755 3L *Fougueux* (64); 6.6.1755-8.6.1755 Action of 6-8 June 1755; 17.12.1756 5L *Royal George* (100); 6.5.1757 4L *Royal George* (100); 29.7.1757 3L *Royal George* (100); 24.12.1757 2L *Royal George* (100); 27.1.1758 2L *Namur* (90); 6.6.1758-27.7.1758 The Siege of Louisbourg; **Commander**; 2.8.1758[NA 5.2.1759] *Aetna* (8) Fireship; **Captain**; 21.8.1759[MED 21.9.1759] *Glasgow* (20); 4.5.1761[JAM 11.1.1762] *Lively* (20); 12.3.1762-22.3.1763[P] *Port Mahon* (24); 27.4.1762-2.7.1762 *Devonshire* (70); 6.6.1762-13.8.1762 Operations against Havana; 8.9.1762[EI 3.10.1763]-10.8.1763[P] *Temeraire* (74); 29.11.1766-26.5.1768 *Renown* (30); 26.5.1768-14.7.1768[P] *Ferret* (14) Sloop; 14.1.1771 *Marlborough* (74); 1.11.1773 *Augusta* (64); 29.10.1776-30.11.1779 *Terrible* (74); 27.7.1778 1st Battle of Ushant; 13.3.1780 *Fortitude* (74); 5.8.1781 Battle of Dogger Bank; 9.11.1781-8.1.1782 *Cumberland* (74); 8.1.1782-24.7.1784[P] Commodore *Gibraltar* (80); 20.6.1783 2nd Battle of

Cuddalore; 15.9.1786 CinC — Barbados & the Leeward Islands; 5.1.1787-12.12.1787 *Sibyl* (28); 24.9.1787 **Rear Admiral of the Blue**; 14.7.1789-22.1.1791 CinC — Plymouth; 19.6.1790-25.2.1792 M.P. for Rochester; 8.1790-1791 *Impregnable* (98); 21.9.1790 **Rear Admiral of the White**; 22.1.1791-25.9.1792 CinC — Plymouth; 24.3.1791-9.1791 *Cambridge* (80).

BIGGS, ROBERT

Dates: 11.7.1803 Died Catisfield, Hampshire; 30.7.1803 Buried Alverstoke, Hampshire; 25.8.1803 Will Probate.

Family:

Service: 19.2.1752 L. Serv *Monarch* (74); 17.3.1753 L. Serv *Berwick Hulk*; 8.7.1753 L. Serv *Captain* (64); 9.3.1755 Able *Monarch* (74); 28.5.1755 Able *Savage* (8) Sloop; 2.3.1756 Cox *Tartar* (24); 4.8.1756 Mid *Tartar* (24); 5.6.1758-12.6.1758 Raid on Saint-Malo; 30.9.1758-7.2.1759 Able *Chatham* (50); 17.2.1759 Passed; **Lieutenant**; 7.8.1761-13.8.1762 4L *Belleisle* (64); 6.6.1762-13.8.1762 Operations against Havana; 12.12.1766 2L *Rippon* (60); 27.1.1768-20.7.1768 LCmdr *Folkestone* (6) Cutter; 20.7.1768 LCmdr *Grace* (6) Cutter; **Commander**; 10.1.1771-10.8.1775 *Favorite* (16) Sloop; **Captain**; 18.3.1778-9.7.1778[C] *Lively* (20); 15.3.1780-28.7.1783[P] *Amphitrite* (24); 10.5.1795 *Commerce de Marseilles* (50); 1.6.1795 **Rear Admiral of the White**; 14.2.1799 **Vice Admiral of the Blue**; 1.1.1801 **Vice Admiral of the White**.

BINDLOSS, EDWARD

Dates: c.1728 Born; 1789 Died.

Family:

Service: 24.10.1751 Able *Greenwich* (50); 31.3.1753 Captain's Clerk *Viper* (14) Sloop; 10.12.1753 Captain's Clerk *Swift* (8) Sloop; 11.4.1754 Mid *Sutherland* (50); 4.7.1754 Purser *Glasgow* (20); 10.2.1755 Purser *Phoenix* (24); 13.11.1755 Purser *Flamborough* (20); 5.9.1757 Passed; 7.2.1758-5.9.1759 Mate *Princess Royal* (90); **Lieutenant**; 27.8.1760-17.10.1761 3L *Anson* (60).

BINKS, WILLIAM

Dates: 1761 Died; 18.6.1761 Will Probate.

Family:

Service: **Lieutenant**; 15.9.1744[(30.3.1745)]-20.10.1744[P] L. *Bonetta* (8) Sloop; 16.7.1745 3L *Nottingham* (60); 6.3.1746/47 2L *Nottingham* (60); 3.5.1747 1st Battle of Cape Finisterre; 14.10.1747 2nd Battle of Cape Finisterre; 3.12.1747-12.10.1748[P] 1L *Nottingham* (60); 31.1.1747/48 Action of 1748/01/31; 11.3.1755 2L *Newcastle* (50); 24.12.1755-30.6.1756 1L *Newcastle* (50); 30.1.1758-22.5.1758 1L *Royal George* (100).

BIRD, TIMOTHY

Dates: c.1734 Born; 26.11.1793 Died; 30.5.1794 Will Probate.

Family: Wife Mary Mitchell married 19.1.1768.

Service: 1752-1756 Merchant Service; 18.1.1756 QGnr *Intrepid* (64); 20.5.1756 Battle of Minorca; 3.11.1756 Mid *Intrepid* (64); 16.1.1757-9.9.1758[P] Mid *Monarch* (74); 28.2.1758 Battle of Cartagena; 14.9.1758 Mid *Panther* (60); 16.1.1759-19.1.1759 Attack on Martinique; 20.1.1759-1.5.1759 Capture of Guadeloupe; 7.11.1759 Passed; **Lieutenant**; 2.2.1761-3.6.1763[P] L. *Racehorse* (16) Sloop; 29.8.1763-18.4.1764 2L *Actaeon* (28); 30.11.1770 5L *Royal Oak* (74); 10.5.1771 4L *Royal Oak* (74); 25.6.1773-29.11.1773 3L *Royal Oak* (74); 6.6.1775-28.6.1777 1L *Exeter* (64); 10.10.1777-1.2.1779 1L *Exeter* (64); 27.7.1778 1st Battle of Ushant; 16.9.1779-1.10.1779[P] 2L *Sandwich* (90); 9.10.1779-25.5.1780 2L *Dublin* (74); 29.12.1780-28.2.1781 2L

Mars (32); 29.5.1790-4.1791 LCmdr *Vulture* (14) Storeship; 25.12.1792-26.11.1793[†] 1L *Royal William* (84).

BIRT, JOHN

Dates: c.1735 Born; 31.10.1764 Died; 22.5.1765 Will Probate.
Family: Sister Ann; Sister Elizabeth; Sister Sarah; Sister Mary.
Service: 12.11.1743 Ord. *Lion* (60); 5.6.1744 Capt Serv *Yarmouth* (64); 20.4.1745-28.9.1745[C] Mid *Falcon* (10) Sloop; 29.10.1747-7.10.1748[P] Mid *Bellona* (30); 11.9.1749 Able *Surprise* (24); 4.10.1750 MidO *Surprise* (24); 25.11.1751 Mid *Surprise* (24); 2.1.1754 Able *Surprise* (24); 23.10.1754 Able *Trial* (10) Sloop; 15.1.1755 Mid *Trial* (10) Sloop; 19.3.1756 Passed; **Lieutenant**; 20.3.1756-8.5.1757 4L *Captain* (64); 20.5.1756 Battle of Minorca; 17.11.1760 5L *Royal George* (100); 27.7.1761 3L *Royal George* (100); 19.5.1762-18.12.1762[P] 2L *Royal George* (100); 1.1764 LCmdr *Spy* (4) Cutter; 15.2.1764-31.10.1764 LCmdr *Lapwing* (6) Cutter.

BISHOP, THOMAS

Dates: c.1721 Born; 1788 Died; 3.12.1788 Will Probate.
Family: Wife Rebecca Monckton married 17.12.1777.
Service: 24.5.1741 Able *Roebuck* (40); 8.6.1742 Mid *Roebuck* (40); 29.12.1742 Mate *Anglesea* (44); 14.6.1744 Mate *Sunderland* (60); 24.8.1744 Mate *Sunderland* (60); 13.2.1744/45 Able *Sunderland* (60); 4.12.1746 Passed; **Lieutenant**; 31.12.1747-6.10.1748[P] L. *Vulcan* (8) Fireship; 6.4.1751 3L *Gosport* (44); 13.2.1751/52-22.4.1752 3L *Jason* (44); 16.1.1753 3L *Tiger* (60); 28.3.1754 3L *Bristol* (50); 31.7.1754 3L *Defiance* (60); 13.11.1754-18.10.1755 2L *Defiance* (60); 6.6.1755-8.6.1755 Action of 6-8 June 1755; 22.4.1757 1L *Dover* (44); **Commander**; 6.1.1758-9.5.1758[P] *Adventure* (18) Hired Armed Ship; 4.4.1763-15.9.1766[P] *Fortune* (14) Sloop; **Captain**; 26.5.1768 *Seahorse* (24); 6.9.1770-12.3.1771[P] *Hussar* (28); 26.1.1774-25.8.1777[P] *Lively* (20).

BLACKETT, SIR EDWARD (3RD BARONET BLACKETT OF NEWCASTLE)

Dates: 1683 Born; 23.4.1718 3rd Baronet Blackett of Newcastle; 1.3.1756 Died.
Family: Father Edward Blackett, 2nd Bt. (1649-1718); Mother Mary Yorke; Wife Mary Jekyll (d.1756).
Service: 6.2.1702/3 Vol-p-O *Somerset* (80); 20.3.1702/3 Vol-p-O *Kent* (70); 10.4.1704 Mid *Berwick* (70); 21.7.1704-23.7.1704 Capture of Gibraltar; 13.8.1704 Battle of Malaga; 1.3.1704/5 Mid *Torbay* (80); 31.3.1706 Mid *Barfleur* (90); 21.1.1706/7 Mid *Albemarle* (96); 2.5.1707 Passed; **Lieutenant**; 18.11.1707-20.11.1710 2L *Oxford* (54); **Commander**; 3.2.1710/11 *Phoenix* (20) Fireship; **Captain**; 17.6.1713-5.10.1715 *Phoenix* (24) Fireship.

BLADEN, JOHN

Dates: 11.1.1755 Died.
Family:
Service: 12.1.1737/38 Scholar *Royal Naval Academy*; 16.2.1739/40 Vol-p-O *Strafford* (60); 1.8.1740 Vol-p-O *Augusta* (60); 4.9.1740 Vol-p-O *Portland* (50); 17.11.1740 Mid *Portland* (50); 19.11.1741-17.3.1742/43[P] 3L *Portland* (50); 3.3.1742/43 Passed; **Lieutenant**; 1.6.1743 L. *Baltimore* (14) Sloop; 25.6.1743-14.10.1744[P] L. *Greyhound* (20); 20.11.1744 3L *Edinburgh* (64); 2.4.1746 2L *Edinburgh* (64); 14.10.1747 2nd Battle of Cape Finisterre; 23.12.1747-1.12.1748 1L *Devonshire* (66); 1.12.1748-14.11.1752[P] 1L *Monarch* (74); 16.1.1753 1L *Berwick* (70); 16.5.1753-2.1.1755 1L *Captain* (64).

BLADWELL, WILLIAM CLEMENT

Dates: 1703 Born Norfolk; 25.3.1783 Died; 4.1783 Buried St Mary's Church, Rickmansworth, Hertfordshire; 7.4.1783 Will Probate.

Family: Father John Bladwell (1665-?); Mother Elizabeth Dartinqueneve (1671-?); Wife Margaret Whitfield (c.1708-1777) married 6.8.1745; Brother Charles (1691-1764); Sister Henrietta (1693-?); Brother John (1699-1779); Brother Giles (1700-?); Brother Erasmus Giles (1701-?); Sister Elizabeth (1702-?); Brother Paston Howard (1704-?).

Service: 29.8.1718 Vol-p-O *Rupert* (60); 21.7.1720 Vol-p-O *Hampshire* (54); 17.12.1720 Mid *Hampshire* (54); 13.3.1721/22 Mid *Essex* (70); 10.5.1722 Able *Essex* (70); 29.5.1722 MidO *Essex* (70); 7.9.1722 Mid *Essex* (70); 21.2.1722/23 MidO *Essex* (70); 15.4.1723 Able *Dover* (40); 2.11.1724 Mid *Sandwich* (90); 8.3.1724/25 Passed; **Lieutenant**; 6.10.1727[(8.10.1728)] 3L *Diamond* (40); 22.6.1728[(8.10.1728)] 2L *Diamond* (40); 9.2.1728/29 4L *Cornwall* (80); 11.2.1728/29-27.12.1731[P] L. *Squirrel* (20); 13.1.1731/32-3.3.1731/32 2L *Kingston* (60); 23.2.1733/34-22.12.1735 2L *Yarmouth* (70); 23.12.1735 L. *Squirrel* (20); 4.1740-5.7.1740 Attack on St. Augustine; 10.1.1740/41 1L *Faversham* (44); 21.2.1740/41 1L *Essex* (70); 27.3.1741 1L *Barfleur* (90); **Commander**; 29.5.1741-24.6.1744 *Swift* (8) Sloop; **Captain**; 17.9.1745-19.8.1748[P] *Mercury* (20); 24.3.1748/49-25.6.1752[P] *Rose* (24) Ship; 5.11.1770 **Superannuated Rear Admiral.**

BLAIR, JAMES

Dates: 1770 Died.

Family:

Service: **Lieutenant**; 3.11.1741-10.12.1741[P] 2L *Colchester* (50); 12.5.1742-19.8.1744 4L *Cambridge* (80); 11.2.1743/44-12.2.1743/44 Battle of Toulon; 21.11.1744[(MED 21.11.1748)]-15.11.1748[P] 1L *Nonsuch* (50).

BLAIR, WILLIAM

Dates: 1741 Born Edinburgh; 12.4.1782 Died Battle of the Saintes; 23.7.1782 Will Probate.

Family: Father Daniel Blair.

Service: 1754-1755 Merchant Service; 27.7.1755 Surg Serv *Windsor* (60); 17.1.1757 Able *Firebrand* (6) Fireship; 13.6.1757 Able *Amazon* (22); 11.7.1757 Able *Alcide* (64); 15.8.1757 Able *Hussar* (28); 7.12.1757 Mid *Hussar* (28); 13.2.1759 Mid *Aeolus* (32); 20.11.1759 Battle of Quiberon Bay; 28.2.1760 Action of February 28 1760; 30.5.1760 Passed; **Lieutenant**; 9.10.1760 L. *Granado* (10) Sloop; 5.12.1760-2.3.1763[P] 4L *Superb* (74); 18.5.1763 2L *Centurion* (50); 20.6.1765-25.9.1766[P] 1L *Centurion* (50); 31.5.1770-6.3.1772[P] 2L *Salisbury* (50); 14.10.1777 1L *Grafton* (74); **Commander**; 6.12.1777 *Wasp* (8) Sloop; **Captain**; 18.4.1778 *Albion* (74); 4.5.1778 *Princess Royal* (98); 6.7.1779 Battle of Grenada; 31.8.1779[(JAM 3.5.1780)]-8.3.1780[P] *Nonsuch* (64); 2.3.1781 *Dolphin* (44); 5.8.1781 Battle of Dogger Bank; 23.8.1781-12.4.1782 *Anson* (64); 12.4.1782 Battle of the Saintes.

BLAKE, PETER

Dates: c.1736 Born; 3.1764 Died; 18.12.1764 Will Probate.

Family: Father Thomas Blake.

Service: 12.7.1753 Capt Serv *Arundel* (24); 2.5.1754 Able *Arundel* (24); 15.7.1754 Mid *Arundel* (24); 7.4.1755 Mid *Newcastle* (50); 4.4.1757 Passed; **Lieutenant**; 19.9.1757 2L *Southampton* (32); 6.2.1758-20.3.1761 1L *Southampton* (32); 5.6.1758-12.6.1758 Raid on Saint-Malo; **Commander**; 4.5.1761-3.1764[F] *Epreuve* (14) Sloop.

BLANCKLEY, GEORGE

Dates: c.1720 Born; 1759 Died.
Family:
Service: 26.6.1735 Ord. *Buckingham* (70); 24.11.1735 Able *Buckingham* (70); 1.7.1737 Able *Lancaster* (80); 25.7.1738 MidO *Hampton Court* (70); 10.2.1739 Mid *Hampton Court* (70); 3.10.1739 Able *Hampton Court* (70); 21.11.1739 Attack on Puerto Bello; 17.5.1740 Mid *Diamond* (40); 7.10.1740 Mid *Elizabeth* (70); 27.6.1741 Mid *Sandwich* (90); 18.10.1741 Mid *Norwich* (50); 7.12.1741-18.2.1742 Mid *Princess Amelia* (80); 18.2.1741/42 Passed; **Lieutenant**; 18.3.1741/42-4.4.1744[P] 3L *Advice* (54); 26.5.1744-27.6.1745 L. *Shoreham* (20); 6.7.1745 2L *Norwich* (50); 15.5.1746 2L *Royal George* (100); 9.10.1746 1L *Royal George* (100); **Commander**; 8.3.1747/48 *Deptford* (24) Storeship; 23.5.1748-22.1.1748/49[P] *Porcupine* (16) Sloop.

BLANKETT, JOHN

Dates: 1741 Born; 13.2.1740/41 Baptised Rotherhithe; 4.7.1801 Died Nr Mocha; 12.12.1801 Will Probate.
Family: Father Stephen Blankett; Mother Elizabeth Born.
Service: 1754-1756 Merchant Service; 1.1.1756 Capt Serv *Deal Castle* (20); 2.8.1756 Mid *Prince George* (26) HEIC; 7.7.1757 Mid *Somerset* (68); 6.6.1758-27.7.1758 The Siege of Louisbourg; 16.4.1760 Passed; 16.4.1761 **Lieutenant**; 5.9.1763-29.4.1766[P] 2L *Alarm* (32); 29.9.1766-24.1.1769 L. *Hind* (24); 21.9.1770 5L *Albion* (74); 15.1.1771-4.9.1773 4L *Albion* (74); 10.10.1777-20.2.1778 1L *Ruby* (64); 13.5.1778 4L *Victory* (100); 2.7.1778 3L *Victory* (100); 27.7.1778 1st Battle of Ushant; 17.9.1778 2L *Victory* (100); 20.11.1778 1L *Victory* (100); **Commander**; 30.1.1779 *Nymph* (14) Sloop; **Captain**; 23.1.1780[(EI 3.3.1781)]-3.5.1782 *Rippon* (60); 11.9.1782-2.5.1783[P] *Thetis* (38); 3.5.1783-17.5.1786[P] *Thetis* (38); 4.6.1790-24.9.1791[P] *Leopard* (50); 1.5.1794-19.8.1796 Commodore *America* (64); 1798-13.2.1799 Commodore *Leopard* (50); **Rear Admiral of the White**; 14.2.1799-31.12.1800 *Leopard* (50); **Rear Admiral of the Red**; 1.1.1801-4.7.1801 *Leopard* (50).

BLIGH, JOHN

Dates: 26.12.1735 Born Gosport; 1795 Died; 27.1.1795 Buried Alverstoke, Hampshire; 28.2.1795 Will Probate.
Family: Father Richard Bligh, RN (1713-1748); Mother Ann Worsley (1744-1797); Wife Elizabeth Titcher (1739-1822) married 20.7.1769; Son John, RN (1770-1831); Brother Sir Richard Rodney, RN (1737-1821); Sister Susanna (1739-?).
Service: 11.9.1759 **Lieutenant**; 14.9.1759[(EI 28.9.1761)] 4L *Newcastle* (50); 17.3.1760[(EI 28.9.1761)] 3L *Newcastle* (50); 24.7.1760[(EI 28.9.1761)]-1.1.1761[W] 2L *Newcastle* (50); 22.2.1762 3L *Saint Ann* (64); 8.6.1762-3.6.1763[P] 2L *Saint Ann* (64); 15.10.1770-17.3.1773[P] L. *Merlin* (18) Frigate; 10.5.1776 3L *Centaur* (74); 16.11.1776 2L *Centaur* (74); 13.5.1778-22.9.1779 1L *Centaur* (74); 27.7.1778 1st Battle of Ushant; 30.5.1780 8L *Barfleur* (98); 12.2.1781 1L *Flora* (36); 30.5.1781 Action of 1781-05-30; 30.5.1781-19.6.1781[C] LCmdr *Crescent* (28); 19.6.1781 Action of 1781-06-19; **Commander**; 1.12.1781 *Merchant* (20) Hired Armed Ship; 6.7.1782-22.3.1783[P] *Arundel* (74) Hospital Ship.

BLIGH, SIR RICHARD RODNEY

Dates: 8.11.1737 Born Gosport; 16.5.1820 Knight Bachelor; 30.4.1821 Died Belle Vue, Southampton.
Family: Father Richard Bligh, RN (1713-1748); Wife Ann Worsley (1744-1797) married 1765; Wife Mary Golightly (1745-1834) married 28.6.1800; Daughter Harriet Worsley [Ricketts]

(1767-?); Daughter Anne [Driffield] (1769-?); Daughter Elizabeth [Peard] (1771-?); Daughter Sophia Holmes [Carter] (1775-1817); Son George Miller, RN (1780-1834); Brother John, RN (1735-1795); Sister Susanna (1739-?).
Service: 1750 Mid *Rainbow* (44); 1756 Mid *Ramillies* (90); **Lieutenant**; 30.9.1757[NA 3.7.1759] L. *Nightingale* (22); 6.6.1758-27.7.1758 The Siege of Louisbourg; 5.2.1762[BLI 27.3.1764] 1L *Stag* (32); 17.3.1762[BLI 27.3.1764] 4L *Marlborough* (68); 1.5.1762[EI 27.3.1764] 3L *Rochester* (50); 8.6.1762[BLI 27.3.1764] 2L *Foudroyant* (80); **Commander**; 22.10.1762[BLI 9.7.1764]-11.5.1764[P] *Virgin* (12) Sloop; 27.10.1774 *Wasp* (8) Sloop; **Captain**; 6.12.1777 *Camel* (24); 31.12.1779 Affair of Fielding and Bylandt; 1.1.1780 *Nemesis* (28); 23.3.1782-3.4.1783[P] *Asia* (64); 20.10.1782 Battle of Cape Spartel; 24.9.1787-13.2.1788[P] *Pegase* (74); 24.8.1790-26.3.1791 *Dictator* (64); 20.3.1794 *Excellent* (74); 12.4.1794-6.11.1794[C] *Alexander* (74); 23.10.1794 **Rear Admiral of the Blue**; 6.11.1794 Taken Prisoner; 5.1795 Released from captivity; **Rear Admiral of the Red**; 1.6.1795 *Brunswick* (74); 16.6.1795-17.6.1795 First Battle of Groix; 8.1796-1799 Second in Command — Jamaica; 14.2.1799 **Vice Admiral of the White**; 10.1799 *Regulus* (44) Ship; 1.1.1801 **Vice Admiral of the Red**; 1803-23.4.1804 CinC — Leith; 11.1803-23.4.1804 *Roebuck* (44) Troop Ship; 23.4.1804 **Admiral of the Blue**; 28.4.1808 **Admiral of the White**; 4.12.1813 **Admiral of the Red**.

BLOMER, CHARLES

Dates: 1738 Born; 25.11.1738 Baptised Surrey; 1770 Died Bengal; 7.6.1770 Will Probate.
Family: Wife Mary Perreau married 3.3.1763; Sister Mary [White].
Service: **Lieutenant**; 12.3.1757[EI 21.12.1758]-1.4.1757 2L *Kingfisher* (14) Sloop; 9.5.1760-12.5.1763[P] 1L *Jersey* (60).

BLOOM, WILLIAM

Dates: c.1717 Born; 1777 Died King's Lynn; 10.4.1777 Will Probate.
Family: Brother John.
Service: 1738-1745 Merchant Service; 28.1.1745 Able *Kennington* (20); 13.12.1745-22.1.1746[P] Mate *Kennington* (20); 1746-1753 Merchant Service; 19.11.1753 Mate *Deptford* (24) Storeship; 4.5.1754 Mate *Essex* (64); 4.8.1756 Passed; **Lieutenant**; 15.11.1756-2.8.1758 L. *Aetna* (16) Fireship; 6.6.1758-27.7.1758 The Siege of Louisbourg; 13.2.1759 2L *Bienfaisant* (64); 2.4.1759 1L *Bienfaisant* (64); 11.6.1761[BLI 3.8.1761]-27.10.1761 L. *Arundel* (24).

BLYTE, GEORGE

Dates: c.1718 Born; 14.7.1797 Died.
Family:
Service: 9.4.1735 Able *Blandford* (20); 1.8.1739 Mid *Saint Albans* (50); 29.8.1740 Mate *Saint Albans* (50); 23.8.1741-3.9.1741 Mid *Barfleur* (90); 3.9.1741 Passed; **Lieutenant**; 22.6.1743 3L *Lynn* (44); 12.12.1744[27.5.1745] 2L *Lynn* (44); 2.3.1744/45[27.5.1745]-12.3.1744/45 1L *Launceston* (44); 28.12.1745-20.3.1745/46 1L *Eagle* (60); **Commander**; 3.11.1747[JAM 13.3.1749/50]-13.1.1747/48[P] *Achilles* (8) Schooner; 9.3.1747/48[MED 29.7.1748]-28.7.1748[P] *Drake* (14) Sloop; 2.9.1755-31.12.1756[P] *Maryland Planter* (16) Hired Armed Ship; 26.1.1757-16.5.1758 *Otter* (14) Sloop.

BODLEDGE, JOHN

Dates: c.1735 Born; 19.3.1735 Baptised Worcestershire; 1769 Died.
Family: Wife Catherine Riley married 19.1.1764; Son Edward (1765-?); Son John (1767-?).
Service: 6.5.1750 Capt Serv *Sphinx* (24); 26.1.1752 Able *Advice* (50); 23.3.1754 Mid *Advice* (50); 26.2.1756-22.5.1756[P] Mate *Advice* (50); 27.10.1756 Mid *Torbay* (74); 17.5.1757 Passed; **Lieutenant**; 8.6.1757-20.6.1758 3L *Rainbow* (44); 1.2.1760[(JAM 11.4.1760)]-31.5.1760[P] 3L *Saint Albans* (60); 4.6.1760-18.10.1760[W] 2L *Lyme* (28); 11.8.1761-8.2.1763[P] 1L *Revenge* (64); 3.2.1768-6.11.1771[P] 1L *Jason* (32).

BOGER, RICHARD

Dates: 25.7.1739 Born St Germans, Cornwall; 19.10.1822 Died Plymouth; 21.11.1822 Will Probate.
Family: Father Richard Boger; Mother Sarah; Wife Sarah Ellery (d.1804); Wife Mrs Maria Drake married 8.1806; Daughter Marie [Dupre]; Son Coryndon, RN (1777-1804).
Service: 28.11.1754 Capt Serv *Vanguard* (68); 30.5.1755 Ord. *Vanguard* (68); 18.7.1756 Able *Vanguard* (68); 20.4.1757 Able *America* (60); 5.9.1757-6.10.1757 Raid on Rochefort; 23.4.1758 Mid *Greyhound* (20); 26.8.1758 Mate *Greyhound* (20); 30.5.1760 Passed; 4.5.1761 L. *Hawk* (10) Sloop; 8.5.1761 **Lieutenant**; 6.7.1762-19.3.1763[P] 2L *Brilliant* (36); 25.4.1763-11.3.1766[P] 2L *Thames* (32); 22.6.1775 2L *Kent* (74); 9.8.1775 2L *Foudroyant* (80); 31.5.1776 3L *Foudroyant* (80); 22.11.1776 1L *Foudroyant* (80); 20.11.1778 5L *Victory* (100); 16.2.1779-23.3.1779 4L *Victory* (100); 29.5.1779-19.1.1781 1L *Foudroyant* (80); 24.3.1780 LCmdr *Pilote* (14) Cutter; 28.5.1781 7L *Britannia* (100); 12.12.1781 2nd Battle of Ushant; 13.3.1782 5L *Britannia* (100); **Commander**; 2.4.1782 *Ostrich* (14) Sloop; 11.4.1782 *Vesuvius* (8) Bomb Vessel; **Captain**; 6.7.1782-10.1.1783[P] *Ocean* (90); 20.10.1782 Battle of Cape Spartel; 18.3.1783-26.3.1783 *Winchelsea* (32); 2.5.1783-13.9.1784[P] *Blenheim* (90); 17.10.1787-12.12.1787[P] *Hannibal* (74); 26.12.1792-18.4.1799 *Cambridge* (80); 20.9.1793 **Commander**; 23.4.1804 **Rear Admiral of the Blue**; 9.11.1805 **Rear Admiral of the Red**; 28.4.1808 **Vice Admiral of the Blue**; 31.7.1810 **Vice Admiral of the White**; 12.8.1812 **Vice Admiral of the Red**; 4.6.1814 **Admiral of the Blue**.

BOLES, JOHN

Dates: 1761 Died; 19.8.1761 Will Probate.
Family: Father Richard Boles; Wife Jannet married 21.7.1752; Sister Catherine; Sister Jane; Brother Henry; Brother Lewis; Brother Arthur; Brother George.
Service: **Lieutenant**; 2.1.1744/45[(West Indies 24.3.1745/46)]-25.3.1746[P] L. *Basilisk* (8) Bomb Vessel; 2.9.1746 3L *Monmouth* (70); 3.5.1747 1st Battle of Cape Finisterre; 14.10.1747 2nd Battle of Cape Finisterre; **Commander**; 23.5.1748-19.11.1749[P] *Deptford* (24) Storeship; 11.1.1757-21.11.1760 *Weazle* (16) Sloop; 16.1.1759-19.1.1759 Attack on Martinique; 20.1.1759-1.5.1759 Capture of Guadeloupe.

BOLLARD, ROBERT

Dates: c.1706 Born; 16.1.1766 Died Gravesend; 6.5.1766 Will Probate.
Family: Wife Maria Alexander married 16.6.1759.
Service: 16.2.1734/35 Mid *Lowestoffe* (20); 21.11.1735 Mate *Falkland* (50); 16.10.1739 Able *Tiger* (50); 26.10.1740 Able *Victory* (100); 29.11.1740 Mid *Victory* (100); 18.3.1740/41 Mate *Victory* (100); 20.3.1741/42 Passed; **Lieutenant**; 23.4.1742[(MED 26.1.1747/48)]-9.11.1742 4L *Russell* (80); 31.1.1743/44[(MED 13.2.1747/48)]-19.12.1745 3L *Diamond* (44); 11.2.1743/44-12.2.1743/44 Battle of Toulon; 18.3.1746/47[(MED 13.2.1747/48)] 1L *Princess Caroline* (80); 3.9.1747[(MED 2.12.1748)]-17.11.1748[P]

2L *Revenge* (70); 24.10.1755 1L *Cambridge* (80); **Commander**; 27.3.1756-31.12.1756[P] *Brilliant* (16) Hired Unknown.

BOND, ROBERT

Dates: c.1722 Born; 1772 Died.
Family:
Service: 1738-1741 Merchant Service; 9.6.1741 Able *Saint George* (90); 4.1.1741/42 QGnr *Russell* (80); 7.3.1741/42 Mid *Russell* (80); 11.2.1743/44-12.2.1743/44 Battle of Toulon; 18.4.1744 Mid *Marlborough* (90); 6.9.1745 Mate *Marlborough* (90); 16.9.1745 Mate *Neptune* (90); 21.1.1745/46 Mate *Devonshire Hulk*; 9.4.1746 Able *Edinburgh* (64); 29.7.1746 Passed; **Lieutenant**; 13.3.1746/47 L. *Princess Royal* (24) Storeship; 13.1.1747/48-8.2.1747/48 3L *Tilbury* (58); 8.3.1747/48 2L *Humber* (44); 21.3.1748/49-10.12.1753[P] L. *Albany* (14) Sloop; 31.7.1754 L. *Port Mahon* (24); 9.12.1755-17.9.1756 4L *Vanguard* (68); 20.1.1757 L. *Scorpion* (14) Sloop; **Commander**; 7.2.1757 *Speedwell* (8) Sloop; 8.1757-10.1757 Louisbourg Expedition; **Captain**; 13.1.1758-19.5.1761 *Hind* (24); 6.6.1758-27.7.1758 The Siege of Louisbourg; 20.6.1770-14.2.1771 *Gibraltar* (20).

BONE, JOHN

Dates: 1762 Died; 2.7.1764 Will Probate.
Family:
Service: **Lieutenant**; 28.11.1757 L. *Swan* (14) Sloop; 30.12.1757 4L *Norfolk* (74); 5.6.1758-12.6.1758 Raid on Saint-Malo; 5.10.1758 3L *Norfolk* (74); 16.1.1759-19.1.1759 Attack on Martinique; 20.1.1759-1.5.1759 Capture of Guadeloupe; 20.11.1759 2L *Norfolk* (74); 19.12.1759 1L *Norfolk* (74); 1761-1762[†] 1L *Grafton* (68).

BONFOY, HUGH

Dates: c.1715 Born; 12.3.1762 Died Dublin.
Family: Wife Anna; Daughter Anna (d.1821).
Service: 26.6.1731 Vol-p-O *Diamond* (40); 7.11.1732 MidO *Rose* (20); 8.4.1733 MidO *Lowestoffe* (20); 20.1.1733/34 Mid *Lowestoffe* (20); 23.5.1735 Mid *Blenheim* (96); 18.12.1735 MidO *Portland* (50); 10.12.1736 Able *Ipswich* (70); 6.4.1738 Passed; **Lieutenant**; 22.10.1738[4.3.1739/40] 3L *Canterbury* (60); 15.9.1739[4.3.1739/40]-28.4.1740[P] 2L *Canterbury* (60); 12.5.1740-11.1.1740/41 L. *Lively* (20); 16.1.1740/41 6L *Saint George* (90); 21.2.1740/41-26.3.1741 3L *Essex* (70); 27.3.1741 2L *Essex* (70); 24.8.1743 2L *Duke* (90); 7.12.1743-12.1.1743/44 1L *Princess Royal* (90); **Commander**; 16.1.1743/44 *Ferret* (14) Sloop; **Captain**; 12.4.1745 *Greyhound* (20); 3.2.1745/46-8.12.1746 *Southsea Castle* (44); 5.6.1747-30.8.1748[P] *Augusta* (60); 1.12.1748-14.11.1752[P] *Berwick* (70); 1753-1754 Gov. of Newfoundland; 23.1.1753-11.2.1755 *Penzance* (44); 25.11.1755-12.3.1762 *Dorset* Yacht.

BONNYMAN, JONAS

Dates: 17.1.1713/14 Baptised St Nicholas, Deptford; bef.17.1.1713/14 Born; 4.10.1757 Will Probate; bef.4.10.1757 Died.
Family: Father Jos Bonnyman; Wife Elizabeth Crow (c.1725-?) married 8.4.1755.
Service: **Lieutenant**; 4.9.1741 4L *Chichester* (80); 11.1.1741/42 4L *Russell* (80); 18.1.1741/42-19.5.1744 4L *Princess Caroline* (80); 11.2.1743/44-12.2.1743/44 Battle of Toulon; 27.2.1744/45[MED 8.8.1745]-25.5.1745 6L *Barfleur* (90); 19.3.1747/48-25.6.1748[P] 1L *Greenwich* (50); 21.10.1755-19.9.1757 2L *Princess Royal* (90).

BOOG, DAVID

Dates: 6.10.1721 Born Burntisland, Fife; 27.2.1807 Died Burntisland.
Family: Father Thomas Boog; Mother Elizabeth Ross; Wife Agatha Cowe married 21.4.1767; Daughter Christian (1768–1829).
Service: 1736-1741 Merchant Service; 12.4.1741 Cox *Princess Royal* (18) Hospital Ship; 7.1741-10.1741 Operations against Santiago; 14.11.1743 Mid *Princess Royal* (18) Hospital Ship; 4.1.1743/44 Mid *Augusta* (60); 18.1.1745/46 Passed; **Lieutenant**; 3.4.1746-10.6.1746[P] 4L *Shrewsbury* (80); 19.9.1746-23.11.1748[P] 3L *Colchester* (50); 27.2.1755-10.7.1755 4L *Fougueux* (64); 6.6.1755-8.6.1755 Action of 6-8 June 1755; 29.12.1756 1L *Fougueux* (64); 17.6.1757 L. *Amazon* (22); 22.5.1758 1L *Pallas* (36); 5.6.1758-12.6.1758 Raid on Saint-Malo; 7.6.1759-14.1.1763[P] 1L *Windsor* (60); 12.7.1763-6.6.1766[P] LCmdr *Greyhound* (4) Cutter; 21.9.1796 **Superannuated Commander.**

BORWICK, HALLEY

Dates: c.1730 Born Scarborough; 23.4.1770 Died.
Family: Wife Ann Heath married 6.3.1756; Son James; Daughter Frances (1762-?).
Service: 1749-1750 HEIC Service; 9.1.1749/50 Capt Serv *Prince Edward* (44); 14.7.1750 Ord. *Prince Edward* (44); 18.7.1751 Able *Glasgow* (20); 5.11.1752-5.1.1755 Mid *Glasgow* (20); 5.11.1755 Passed; **Lieutenant**; 1.7.1756-5.10.1758 4L *Berwick* (64); 5.4.1757 Action of April 5 1757; 28.2.1758 Battle of Cartagena; 10.1.1761 4L *Prince* (90); 20.10.1761-17.6.1762 1L *Prince* (90); 21.6.1769-11.6.1770 LCmdr *Cholmondley* (4) Cutter.

BOSCAWEN, THE HON. EDWARD

Dates: 19.8.1711 Born Tregothnan, Cornwall; 19.8.1711 Honourable; 1761 Buried Hatchlands Park, Surrey; 10.1.1761 Died;
Family: Father Hugh Boscawen, 1st Visc. Falmouth (c.1680–1734); Mother Charlotte (d. 1754) daughter of Charles & Arabella Godfrey; Wife Frances Glanville (1719–1805) married 11.12.1742; Daughter Frances [Leveson-Gower] (1746-1813); Daughter Elizabeth [Somerset] (1747-1828); Son Unknown (c.1757-?); Son Unknown (c.1757-?); Son George Evelyn, 3rd Visc. Falmouth (1758-1808); Brother Hon. Hugh, MP (1707-82); Brother Hon. George, MP (1712-75); Brother Hon. John, MP (1714-67).
Service: 4.1.1725/26 Vol-p-O *Superb* (64); 26.8.1727 Mid *Superb* (64); 1.8.1728 MidO *Lowestoffe* (20); 8.11.1728 Mid *Canterbury* (60); 12.10.1730 Mid *Hector* (40); 26.7.1731 Mid *Namur* (90); 25.5.1732 Passed; **Lieutenant**; 14.6.1732 4L *Royal Oak* (70); 29.8.1732-16.12.1732[P] 3L *Hector* (40); 17.10.1735[(19.2.1736/37)]-3.3.1735/36 4L *Grafton* (70); 5.10.1736[(10.6.1737)] 3L *Britannia* (100); **Captain**; 12.3.1736/37-3.5.1737[P] *Leopard* (50); 13.6.1738 *Shoreham* (20); 25.3.1741[(18.10.1742)]-22.6.1742 *Prince Frederick* (70); 21.6.1742-10.1.1761 M.P. for Truro; 23.6.1742-12.2.1744/45 *Dreadnought* (60); 2.12.1745-30.5.1746 *Namur* (74); 11.2.1745/46-17.7.1746 CinC — River Medway and The Nore; 4.9.1746 *Namur* (74); 3.5.1747 1st Battle of Cape Finisterre; **Rear Admiral of the Blue**; 15.7.1747-13.4.1749[W] *Namur* (74); 1748-1750 CinC — East Indies; 12.5.1748 **Rear Admiral of the White**; 1751-10.1.1761 General of Marines; 1751 Elder Brother of Trinity House; 22.6.1751-10.1.1761 Lord Commissioner of the Admiralty; 1755-1761 Vice Admiral of the Coast , Cornwall; **Vice Admiral of the Blue**; 4.2.1755 *Torbay* (74); 6.6.1755-8.6.1755 Action of 6-8 June 1755; 8.1.1756-8.1756 *Invincible* (74); 8.1756 *Royal George* (100); 2.12.1756 **Vice Admiral of the White**; 24.2.1757 **Vice Admiral of the Red**; 18.5.1757 CinC — English Channel; 29.12.1757 CinC — North America; 31.1.1758 **Admiral of the Blue**; 8.2.1758 *Namur* (90); 6.6.1758-27.7.1758 The Siege of Louisbourg; 1.1759-10.1.1761 Privy Counsellor; 29.5.1759 CinC — The Mediterranean Sea; 18.8.1759-19.8.1759 Battle of Lagos

Bay; 10.1759 *Royal William* (84); 15.1.1760 CinC — English Channel; 2.1760-1.9.1760 *Namur* (90).

BOSTON, THOMAS

Dates: c.1735 Born; 5.7.1808 Died Windsor; 2.8.1808 Will Probate.
Family: Father John Boston; Wife Kitty Cockerell married 24.10.1783; Daughter Eleanora; Son Henry Scott (1790-?); Sister Katherine.
Service: 1755-1756 Merchant Service; 18.2.1756 Able *Porcupine* (16) Sloop; 17.11.1758 Able *Torrington* (44); 29.4.1759 Mid *Torrington* (40); 12.2.1762 Passed; **Lieutenant**; 9.6.1762-17.12.1762[P] L. *Carcass* (8) Bomb Vessel; 3.6.1763-4.4.1766[P] 2L *Juno* (32); 27.2.1768-1770 LCmdr *Spy* (4) Cutter; 17.11.1775-31.5.1776 2L *Ardent* (64); 23.4.1776 LCmdr *Three Brothers* Hired Tender; **Commander**; 30.7.1779 *Sulphur* (8) Fireship; **Captain**; 19.7.1781-2.3.1782 *Edgar* (74); 12.12.1781 2nd Battle of Ushant; 8.5.1783-13.7.1784 *Latona* (38); 24.10.1787-19.11.1787 *Ambuscade* (32); 1801 **Superannuated Rear Admiral**.

BOSWELL, ROBERT

Dates: 1777 Died.
Family:
Service: **Lieutenant**; 5.9.1759 4L *Essex* (64); 17.10.1759-20.11.1759[S] 3L *Essex* (64); 20.11.1759 Battle of Quiberon Bay; 29.2.1760-15.9.1760 3L *Falkland* (50); 4.5.1762[(EI 2.3.1763)]-29.11.1762[F] 4L *Marlborough* (68); 6.6.1762-13.8.1762 Operations against Havana; 30.10.1765-19.12.1768 3L *Edgar* (60); 8.12.1769 3L *Cornwall* (74); 18.9.1770-5.11.1770 4L *Cornwall* (74); 10.8.1776-18.4.1777 2L *Belleisle* (64).

BOTELER, PHILIP

Dates: c.1731 Born; 1787 Died; 10.7.1787 Will Probate.
Family: Wife Mary Farnley married 12.10.1753; Son John (1754-?).
Service: 13.7.1748 Capt Serv *Harwich* (50); 5.5.1749 Capt Serv *Harwich* (50); 21.8.1750 Able *Harwich* (50); 12.5.1753 Mid *Harwich* (50); 6.8.1755 Passed; **Lieutenant**; 23.2.1756 4L *Bedford* (64); 21.7.1757 3L *Bedford* (64); 8.1757-10.1757 Louisbourg Expedition; 30.1.1758 2L *Bedford* (64); 6.6.1758-27.7.1758 The Siege of Louisbourg; 29.3.1761-11.6.1761 Expedition against Belle-Isle; **Commander**; 16.6.1761 *Thunder* (14) Bomb Vessel; 7.1.1762-10.2.1762 Operations against Martinique; **Captain**; 26.3.1762[(BLI 6.12.1762)]-1.12.1762[P] *Penzance* (44); 6.6.1762-13.8.1762 Operations against Havana; 20.9.1764-30.10.1765 *Shannon* (28); 31.1.1778 *Actaeon* (44); 19.1.1779-16.4.1779 *Ajax* (74); 18.6.1779-17.8.1779[C] *Ardent* (64); 2.3.1780 Dismissed.

BOTTERELL, JOHN

Dates: c.1716 Born; 12.9.1793 Died; 18.9.1793 Will Probate.
Family: Daughter Isabella [Kirkland].
Service: 20.7.1731 Vol-p-O *Hampton Court* (70); 25.1.1731/32 Vol-p-O *Kingston* (60); 14.7.1733 MidO *Kingston* (60); 3.1.1734/35-5.9.1735[P] Mid *Kingston* (60); 26.12.1735 Mid *Dorsetshire* (80); 1.2.1735/36 MidO *Lowestoffe* (20); 6.6.1737 Mid *Lowestoffe* (20); 25.5.1741 Mate *Lowestoffe* (20); 3.9.1741 Passed; **Lieutenant**; 4.9.1742[(6.4.1744)] 3L *Rippon* (60); 2.8.1743[(12.6.1745)]-31.8.1745[P] 2L *Assistance* (50); 1.12.1748-14.11.1752[P] 2L *Berwick* (70); 8.5.1755 2L *Prince Frederick* (64); 14.6.1757 1L *Dunkirk* (60); 5.9.1757-6.10.1757 Raid on Rochefort; 5.6.1758-12.6.1758 Raid on Saint-Malo; 6.10.1758 5L *Royal George* (100); 23.2.1759 4L *Royal George* (100); 19.6.1759 3L *Royal George* (100); 5.9.1759 2L *Royal George* (100); 17.10.1759 1L *Royal George* (100); 20.11.1759 Battle of Quiberon Bay; **Commander**; 18.2.1760-26.3.1762

Granado (8) Bomb Vessel; 7.1.1762-10.2.1762 Operations against Martinique; **Captain**; 7.4.1762-18.2.1764[P] *Success* (20); 23.7.1767 *Squirrel* (20); 4.11.1769[(BLI 26.11.1771)]-6.11.1771[P] *Jason* (32).

BOUCHER, JAMES

Dates: c.1725 Born; 1757 Died; 16.2.1758 Will Probate.
Family:
Service: 21.10.1738 Able *Sunderland* (60); 13.4.1739 Able *Deal Castle* (20); 4.8.1739 Mid *Portland* (54); 28.9.1743 Mid *Boyne* (80); 11.2.1743/44-12.2.1743/44 Battle of Toulon; 12.3.1744/45 Passed; **Lieutenant**; 16.3.1744/45[(MED 18.5.1750)] L. *Maidstone* (54) Hospital Ship; 22.1.1747/48[(MED 7.1.1748/49)]-14.1.1748/49[P] L. *Seaford* (20) Ship; 25.4.1755 L. *Granado* (8) Bomb Vessel; 18.6.1755-20.11.1755 L. *Centaur* (20); 17.3.1756 1L *Anson* (60); 15.7.1756-3.4.1757 1L *Winchester* (50).

BOURGEOIS, LOUIS FREEMAN

Dates:
Family: Wife Katharine Lardner married 25.7.1765.
Service: **Lieutenant**; 27.11.1760[(EI 25.9.1765)] 5L *Grafton* (68); 7.5.1761[(EI 25.9.1765)] 4L *Panther* (60); 19.6.1761[(EI 25.9.1765)] 3L *Panther* (60); 24.9.1762-6.10.1762 Battle of Manilla; 13.6.1763[(EI 25.9.1765)]-27.6.1765[D] 2L *Panther* (60).

BOURKE, WILLIAM FRANCIS

Dates: c.1727 Born; 21.3.1802 Died.
Family:
Service: 19.6.1742-11.12.1743[P] Able *Southsea Castle* (40); 11.12.1743 Able *Warwick* (60); 11.2.1743/44-12.2.1743/44 Battle of Toulon; 23.2.1744/45-29.12.1748[P] Mid *Lennox* (70); 3.8.1746 Action of August 3 1746; 25.3.1747 Action of March 25 1747; 9.4.1748 Battle of Santiago de Cuba; 12.10.1748 Battle of Havana; 5.11.1756-c.1757 CaptP *Eltham* (12) PMW; 9.6.1758 Passed; **Lieutenant**; 10.6.1758 4L *Warspite* (74); 18.8.1759-19.8.1759 Battle of Lagos Bay; 21.9.1759 3L *Warspite* (74); 20.11.1759 Battle of Quiberon Bay; 11.2.1760 4L *Cambridge* (80); **Commander**; 24.7.1761[(JAM 9.4.1763)]-31.3.1763 *Merlin* (18) Frigate; 6.6.1762-13.8.1762 Operations against Havana.

BOURMASTER, JOHN

Dates: 1736 Born; 1807 Died Titchfield, Hampshire; 23.12.1807 Will Probate.
Family: Daughter Harriet [Dickson] (1781-1863).
Service: 1751-1756 Merchant Service; 23.4.1756 Able *Torbay* (74); 6.10.1756 YoS *Torbay* (74); 16.6.1757 Able *Torbay* (74); 19.7.1757 Mid *Torbay* (74); 5.9.1757-6.10.1757 Raid on Rochefort; 5.6.1758-12.6.1758 Raid on Saint-Malo; 29.12.1758 Capture of Goree; 30.12.1758-10.10.1759 Mate *Torbay* (74); 10.10.1759 Passed; **Lieutenant**; 19.10.1759 3L *Portland* (50); 20.11.1759 Battle of Quiberon Bay; 7.3.1760-12.7.1764[P] 5L *Valiant* (74); 29.3.1761-11.6.1761 Expedition against Belle-Isle; 6.6.1762-13.8.1762 Operations against Havana; 1.10.1766-19.10.1769 1L *Phoenix* (44); 3.1774-30.5.1776 Agent for Transports for Boston; **Commander**; 30.5.1776[(NA 8.1.1777)]-2.6.1776 *Albany* (16) Sloop; **Captain**; 9.9.1777[(NA 1.10.1778)] *Renown* (50); 26.11.1779-4.4.1782 *Royal George* (100); 16.1.1780 Battle of Cape St. Vincent; 8.4.1782 *Ocean* (90); 9.4.1782-19.4.1782 *Victory* (100); 26.11.1782-20.4.1783 *Bombay Castle* (74); 26.4.1786-1.5.1789[P] *Elizabeth* (74); 30.3.1791-8.9.1791[P] *Barfleur* (98); 7.7.1794 *Glory* (98); **Rear Admiral**

of the Blue; 23.10.1794 *Glory* (98); 1.6.1795 **Rear Admiral of the Red**; 14.2.1799 **Vice Admiral of the White**; 1.1.1801 **Vice Admiral of the Red**; 23.4.1804 **Admiral of the Blue**.

BOURN, GEORGE

Dates: c.14.1.1732 Born Elham, Kent; 29.6.1787 Died; 2.7.1787 Buried Kent; 27.7.1787 Will Probate;

Family: Father John Bourn; Mother Mary; Wife Elizabeth Granger married 5.5.1761; Son George (1761-?); Brother Bateman; Sister Ann; Sister Mary [Spears];

Service: 1752-1755 Merchant Service; 24.5.1755 Mate *Falmouth* (50); 13.6.1756 Acting Master *Ferret* (14) Sloop; 27.12.1756-14.2.1759 Mate *Falmouth* (50); 14.2.1759 Passed; **Lieutenant**; 23.8.1759 L. *Basilisk* (8) Bomb Vessel; 27.3.1760-27.11.1761 5L *Mars* (74); 29.3.1761-11.6.1761 Expedition against Belle-Isle.

BOVER, JOHN

Dates: 1714 Born Guernsey; 20.5.1782 Died Newcastle upon Tyne; 27.8.1782 Will Probate.

Family: Father M. de Beauvoir; Wife Mary Kenwright (1731-1793) married 29.9.1752; Son John (1753-1759); Son James (1753-1769); Daughter Sophia (1754-1757); Daughter Mary (1758-1810); Daughter Sophia [Dickinson] (1758-?); Son Peter (1762-1764); Son George (1763-1839); Daughter Ann [Hinchcliffe] (1768-1850); Son Henry (1769-?); Son William (1770-?); Son Peter Turner, RN (1772-1802).

Service: 2.6.1738 Able *Deal Castle* (20); 17.2.1740/41 Mate *Sapphire*; 18.4.1741 Mate *Dartmouth* (50); 3.6.1743-15.9.1744 Mate *Warwick* (60); 11.2.1743/44-12.2.1743/44 Battle of Toulon; 16.9.1744 Passed; **Lieutenant**; 19.9.1744(4.2.1743/44) 3L *Folkestone* (44); 4.2.1744/45 2L *Canterbury* (60); 30.9.1745(22.2.1745/46) 1L *Canterbury* (60); 22.8.1747(JAM 8.4.1748)-23.3.1748/49[P] 2L *Norwich* (50); 8.2.1755 1L *Buckingham* (68); 20.5.1756 Battle of Minorca; 25.11.1756 1L *Neptune* (90); **Commander**; 23.3.1757 *Pluto* (8) Fireship; 28.3.1757-20.7.1757 *Raven* (14) Sloop; **Captain**; 12.3.1762-7.4.1762 *Lively* (20); 29.8.1763 *Actaeon* (28); 22.5.1764(BLI 2.6.1766)-14.8.1766[P] *Princess Louisa* (60); 1771 Regulating Officer at Newcastle upon Tyne.

BOWEN, ESSEX

Dates: c.1735 Born; 7.1811 Died; 29.11.1811 Will Probate.

Family: Brother David; Brother James; Brother George.

Service: 5.3.1750/51 Able *Grampus* (14) Sloop; 2.5.1751 Mid *Grampus* (14) Sloop; 7.3.1752/53 Able *Penzance* (44); 29.11.1753 Mid *Penzance* (44); 3.4.1754 Able *Saltash* (14) Sloop; 12.12.1754 Mid *Saltash* (14) Sloop; 30.10.1755 Mate *Dover* (44); 21.6.1757-4.7.1757 Mid *Barfleur* (80); 4.7.1757 Passed; **Lieutenant**; 28.2.1758(NA 7.11.1758)-30.11.1758 4L *Lancaster* (66); 6.6.1758-27.7.1758 The Siege of Louisbourg; 21.2.1759 3L *Hero* (74); 20.8.1759-25.12.1762[P] 2L *Hero* (74); 20.11.1759 Battle of Quiberon Bay; 29.3.1761-11.6.1761 Expedition against Belle-Isle; 11.1.1771-26.4.1771 1L *Kent* (74); 11.8.1798 **Superannuated Commander**.

BOWEN, JOHN

Dates: c.1741 Born; c.1809 Died.

Family:

Service: 23.6.1756 Mid *Dublin* (74); 5.9.1757-6.10.1757 Raid on Rochefort; 8.3.1757/58 Mid *Dublin* (74); 9.3.1760/61 Able *Marlborough* (68); 18.7.1761 Able *Maidstone* (54) Hospital Ship; 30.8.1761-24.2.1762 Able *Foudroyant* (80); 7.1.1762-10.2.1762 Operations against Martinique; 24.2.1762 Passed; **Lieutenant**; 24.11.1762(BLI 13.3.1764) L. *Ferret* (14) Sloop; 7.5.1763(BLI 13.3.1764)-19.1.1764[P] 1L *Melampe* (36).

BOWER, EDMUND

Dates: 1811 Died; 9.8.1811 Buried Edmondsham, Dorset; 22.1.1812 Will Probate.
Family: Wife Elizabeth; Daughter Harriet; Daughter Philadelphia [Munro] (1769-?); Daughter Sophia; Daughter Jane; Daughter Caroline [Starr]; Daughter Ann [Robinson].
Service: **Lieutenant**; 14.10.1761[(BLI 13.4.1763)]-7.4.1763[P] 5L *Culloden* (74); 6.6.1762-13.8.1762 Operations against Havana.

BOWER, ROBERT

Dates: c.1734 Born; 1770 Died.
Family:
Service: 21.12.1746 Capt Serv *Jamaica* (10) Sloop; 9.5.1747 Able *Jamaica* (10) Sloop; 18.10.1747 Able *Surprise* (24); 21.12.1749 Mid *Surprise* (24); 5.6.1750 Able *Humber* (44); 2.3.1751/52 Able *Monarch* (74); 24.5.1753 Mid *Speedwell* (8) Sloop; 14.8.1754 Able *Speedwell* (8) Sloop; 22.9.1755 Mid *Antelope* (50); 18.12.1755-5.1.1757 Mate *Newark* (80); 5.1.1757 Passed; **Lieutenant**; 19.7.1757-24.9.1759 L. *Scorpion* (14) Sloop.

BOWERBANK, JOHN

Dates: c.1725 Born; 1777 Died.
Family:
Service: 4.10.1741 Able *Romney* (50); 4.8.1742 Able *Nassau* (70); 15.9.1742 Mid *Nassau* (70); 26.5.1743 Able *Nassau* (70); 11.2.1743/44-12.2.1743/44 Battle of Toulon; 15.3.1743/44 Mid *Burford* (70); 18.1.1744/45 Able *Marlborough* (90); 6.4.1745-4.10.1745 Able *Hector* (44); 5.10.1745 Able *Chester* (50); 3.5.1746 ActL *Louisburg* (8) Fireship; 3.11.1746-1.9.1747[F] ActL *Hind* (10) Sloop; **Lieutenant**; 14.4.1748[(JAM 26.10.1750)]-29.12.1748[P] 3L *Lennox* (70); 12.10.1748 Battle of Havana; 21.7.1749 Act3L *Cornwall* (80); 30.10.1749 Able *Canterbury* (60); 14.1.1749/50 Act2L *Canterbury* (60); 23.7.1750 Passed; 6.2.1755 4L *Grafton* (68); 5.1.1757-25.1.1757 2L *Grafton* (68); 19.7.1759 1L *Launceston* (44); **Commander**; 19.5.1761-11.6.1763[P] *Goree* (10) Sloop.

BOWERS, JOHN HOPE

Dates: c.1736 Born; 26.9.1783 Died.
Family: Wife Rachel How married 18.11.1764; Son John Bowers (1771-?); Daughter Mary Ann Bowers (1772-?); Daughter Amelia Bowers (1774-?); Son John Francis Bowers (1775-?); Daughter Leonora Wynch Bowers (1779-?).
Service: 1752-1756 HEIC Service; 13.10.1755 Capt Serv *Tiger* (60); 11.1.1756-14.1.1756 Capture of Geriah; 21.9.1756 Mid *Union* (90); 27.7.1757 Mid *Torbay* (74); 5.9.1757-6.10.1757 Raid on Rochefort; 5.6.1758-12.6.1758 Raid on Saint-Malo; 29.12.1758 Capture of Goree; 5.1.1759 Passed; **Lieutenant**; 2.9.1759[(MED 3.12.1760)]-3.7.1760 4L *Alcide* (64); 3.1.1769-10.8.1770[P] 1L *Neptune* HEIC; 15.2.1772-1.8.1773[P] 1L *Nassau* HEIC; 9.1.1776-23.7.1777[P] 1L *Nassau* HEIC; 11.6.1778 1L *Defiance* (64); 27.7.1778 1st Battle of Ushant; **Commander**; 15.5.1780[(NA 26.10.1780)]-11.8.1781[P] *Halifax* (14) Sloop; 24.6.1782-26.9.1783[†] *Orestes* (18) Sloop.

BOWYER, SIR GEORGE (5TH BARONET OF DENHAM COURT)

Dates: 1740 Born Denham, Buckinghamshire; 8.9.1794 1st Baronet of Radley; 4.1799 5th Baronet of Denham Court; 6.12.1800 Died Radley Hall.
Family: Father Sir William Bowyer, 3rd Baronet; Mother Anne Stonehouse; Wife Mrs Margaret Downing née Price (d.1778) married 11.11.1768; Wife Henrietta Brett married 4.6.1782;

Son Sir George, 6th Baronet; Daughter Unknown; Son Unknown; Daughter Unknown; Son Unknown;
Service: 6.7.1751 Capt Serv *Glory* (44); 16.7.1752 Ord. *Dolphin* (6) Fireship; 10.7.1755 Able *Dolphin* (6) Fireship; 30.10.1755 Mid *Princess Louisa* (60); 20.5.1756 Battle of Minorca; 12.11.1756 Mid *Lancaster* (66); 20.4.1757 Mid *Royal Anne* (100); 5.9.1757-6.10.1757 Raid on Rochefort; 6.2.1758 Passed; **Lieutenant**; 13.2.1758 3L *Nottingham* (60); 6.6.1758-27.7.1758 The Siege of Louisbourg; 25.8.1758[(NA 30.1.1759)] 2L *Nottingham* (60); 31.1.1760 4L *Magnanime* (74); **Commander**; 4.5.1761-30.6.1761[C] LCmdr *Swift* (10) Cutter; **Captain**; 28.10.1762-17.12.1763[P] *Sheerness* (24); 31.10.1776 *Burford* (68); 4.5.1778-24.12.1781[P] *Albion* (74); 6.7.1779 Battle of Grenada; 17.4.1780 Battle of Martinique; 15.5.1780 Action of March 15 1780; 19.5.1780 Action of March 19 1780; 20.3.1783-22.6.1785 Commodore *Irresistible* (74); 23.5.1783 CinC — River Medway and The Nore; 3.10.1787-7.12.1787[P] *Bellona* (74); 18.8.1790-10.1.1791[P] *Boyne* (98); 1.2.1793 **Rear Admiral of the White**; 10.3.1793 *Prince* (98); 7.1793-9.1794 *Brunswick* (74); 12.1793-8.1794 *Barfleur* (98); 12.4.1794 **Rear Admiral of the Red**; 1.6.1794 Glorious 1st of June; 1.7.1794 **Vice Admiral of the Blue**; 1.6.1795 **Vice Admiral of the Red**; 14.2.1799 **Admiral of the Blue**.

BOYCE, CRAWFORD

Dates: 3.1.1767 Died North Cotes Sands, Leith.
Family:
Service: 5.11.1755 Adm Serv *Saint George* (90); 3.8.1756 Mid *Gosport* (44); 11.9.1756 Mid *Experiment* (24); 17.9.1758 Mid *Sapphire* (32); 20.11.1759 Battle of Quiberon Bay; 13.2.1760 Passed; **Lieutenant**; 21.7.1761[(BLI 22.5.1765)]-5.11.1762 L. *Virgin* (12) Sloop; 7.1.1762-10.2.1762 Operations against Martinique.

BOYD, JAMES

Dates: c.1725 Born; 19.5.1800 Died; 21.9.1800 Will Probate.
Family:
Service: 7.11.1742-21.11.1746[P] Mid *Cambridge* (80); 11.2.1743/44-12.2.1743/44 Battle of Toulon; 24.4.1757 Mid *Devonshire Hulk*; 4.11.1757 Able *Devonshire Hulk*; 21.2.1758 Master *Tamar* (16) Sloop; 10.6.1758 Master *Greyhound* (20); 4.10.1758 Passed; **Lieutenant**; 27.10.1758 3L *Trident* (64); 1.10.1760[(NA 15.1.1763)]-24.2.1763[P] 1L *Sutherland* (50); 3.6.1761-7.6.1761 Occupation of Dominica; 7.1.1762-10.2.1762 Operations against Martinique; 6.6.1762-13.8.1762 Operations against Havana.

Boyd, John

DATES: C.1722 BORN; 1762 DIED.

Family:
Service: 1738-1741 Merchant Service; 14.10.1740 Able *Oxford* (50); 1.10.1741-5.6.1745 Mid *Oxford* (50); 11.2.1743/44-12.2.1743/44 Battle of Toulon; 5.6.1745 Passed; **Lieutenant**; 15.2.1745/46 L. *Pluto* (16) Sloop; 16.7.1746 L. *Experiment* (24); 31.5.1748-8.10.1749[P] L. *Swift* (8) Sloop; 9.1.1756-25.1.1757 1L *Gosport* (44); 6.5.1757-15.5.1758 1L *Enterprise* (44); 22.5.1758 1L *Cerberus* (28); 4.12.1758-12.9.1759 L. *Pelican* (8) Bomb Vessel; **Captain**; 5.11.1761-26.3.1762 *Penzance* (44); 7.1.1762-10.2.1762 Operations against Martinique; 24.2.1762-25.2.1762 Capture of Saint Lucia.

BOYLE, THE HON. ROBERT

Dates: 3.1736 Honourable; 3.1736 Born; 5.10.1780 Died off San Domingo.
Family: Father Henry Boyle, 1st Earl of Shannon (1682-1764); Mother Lady Henrietta Burlington; Wife Charlotte Hanbury Williams married 17.7.1759; Son Richard (1762-1788); Daughter Charlotte [FitzGerald], Baroness de Ros of Helmsley (1769-1831); Brother Henry (d.1757); Brother William (d.1748); Brother Charles (d.1758); Sister Juliana [Butler] (c.1728-1804); Brother Richard, 2nd Earl of Shannon (1728-1807);
Service: 22.1.1748 Ord. *Dublin* (12) Yacht; 3.6.1749 Able *Assurance* (44); 24.6.1751-24.4.1753[W] Mid *Assurance* (44); 24.9.1753 Mid *Cumberland* (74); 21.4.1754-6.11.1754 Mid *Anson* (60); 16.11.1754 Passed; **Lieutenant**; 23.3.1756 4L *Revenge* (64); 20.5.1756 Battle of Minorca; **Commander**; 16.2.1757 *Crown* (18) Storeship; 8.3.1757 *Badger* (10) Sloop; **Captain**; 15.6.1757 *Jason* (44); 3.8.1757-18.2.1760 *Boreas* (28); 14.2.1758-7.12.1761 M.P. for Knaresborough; 6.6.1758-27.7.1758 The Siege of Louisbourg; 3.7.1759 Bombardment of Le Havre; 20.2.1761-27.4.1762 *Modeste* (64); 7.12.1761-18.3.1768 M.P. for Fowey; 7.1.1762-10.2.1762 Operations against Martinique; 2.7.1762-7.2.1763[P] *Romney* (50); 18.3.1768-5.10.1780 M.P. for Knaresborough; 23.2.1778 *Thunderer* (74); 5.3.1778 FRS; 27.7.1778 1st Battle of Ushant; 31.12.1779 Affair of Fielding and Bylandt; 15.2.1780-5.10.1780[†] Commodore *Thunderer* (74).

BOYS, PEARSON

Dates: c.1739 Born; 7.2.1739/40 Baptised Deal; 11.6.1793 Died Sandwich; 24.7.1793 Will Probate.
Family: Father William Boys, RN (1700-1774); Mother Elizabeth Pearson; Wife Ann Fennell married 15.10.1781; Daughter Elizabeth (1783-?); Daughter Ann (1785-?); Daughter Jane (1790-?); Brother William (1735–1803); Sister Elizabeth [Harvey] (1740 - 1823); Sister Jane.
Service: 1752-1753 Merchant Service; 30.3.1753 Capt Serv *Pearl* (44); 5.5.1753 Able *Cruizer* (8) Sloop; 9.5.1755 Mid *Prince George* (80); 11.11.1755 Mate *Royal Sovereign* (104); 29.3.1757 Mid *Somerset* (68); 4.8.1757 Mate *Royal Sovereign* (104); 23.10.1758 Passed; **Lieutenant**; 27.10.1758 2L *Aurora* (38); 19.5.1759 2L *Argo* (28); 16.1.1760 1L *Argo* (28); 1.4.1760-15.1.1763[P] 6L *Princess Royal* (90); 1.11.1764-24.5.1765 LCmdr *Swift* (4) Cutter;

BOYS, WILLIAM

Dates: 25.6.1700 Born Deal; 4.3.1774 Died Deal.
Family: Father William Boys (d. 1756?); Mother Jane Laurence (d.c.1756); Wife Elizabeth Pearson; Son William (1735–1803); Daughter Jane; Son Pearson, RN (1739-1793); Daughter Elizabeth Harvey (1740 - 1823).
Service: 1717 Mid *Prince Frederick* (70); 1725-25.6.1727[B] Mate *Luxborough Galley* (26); 11.8.1728 Mid *Guernsey* (50); 6.1.1730 Mid *Shoreham* (20); 29.1.1732 Mate *Shoreham* (20); 2.10.1733 Able *Ludlow Castle* (40); 18.11.1733 Mid *Diamond* (40); 26.2.1734-8.5.1734 Able *Trial* (8) Sloop; 8.5.1734 Passed; **Lieutenant**; 5.5.1735-9.5.1737[P] L. *Looe* (42); 16.5.1738-6.8.1739 3L *Newcastle* (50); 7.8.1739-8.6.1741 2L *Dunkirk* (60); 7.1.1740/41 Action of January 7 1741; 4.3.1740/41-5.1741 Operations against Cartagena; **Commander**; 8.6.1741[(26.12.1740)] *Aetna* (8) Fireship; 18.12.1742 *Baltimore* (14) Sloop; **Captain**; 25.6.1743-14.10.1744[P] *Greyhound* (20); 11.12.1744 *Torrington* (44); 28.1.1744/45 *Princess Louisa* (60); 14.3.1745/46-1.9.1749[P] *Pearl* (44); 16.10.1755 *Royal Sovereign* (104); 16.3.1759 CinC — Thames, Medway and The Nore; 22.5.1759 CinC — The Downs; 22.5.1759-4.7.1761 Commodore *Preston* (50); 16.6.1760 CinC — Thames, Medway and The Nore; 4.7.1761-4.3.1774 Lieutenant-governor of Greenwich Hospital.

BRABAZON, LAMBERT

Dates: 1742 Born Louth, Ireland; 29.3.1811 Died; 20.6.1811 Will Probate.
Family: Father Wallop Brabazon (1698-1767); Mother Vincentia Townley (1704-1763); Wife Susanna Grey married 4.1796; Brother William (1732-1793); Brother Blayney (1736-1800); Brother Henry (1739-1811); Sister Vincentia (1747-1825); Sister Lucy (1744-1777).
Service: 1752-1756 Merchant Service; 30.3.1756 Mid *Tilbury* (58); 15.1.1757-24.9.1757[W] Mid *Tilbury* (58); 7.11.1757 Mate *Bedford* (64); 6.6.1758-27.7.1758 The Siege of Louisbourg; 4.10.1758 Passed; **Lieutenant**; 10.10.1758 4L *Temple* (68); 14.5.1759 3L *Temple* (68); 20.11.1759 Battle of Quiberon Bay; 7.1.1762-10.2.1762 Operations against Martinique; 3.3.1762-17.1.1764[P] L. *Weazle* (16) Sloop; 10.1.1771 1L *Triumph* (74); 28.8.1771-9.9.1772 2L *Triumph* (74); **Commander**; 25.12.1782[(BLI 11.8.1783)]-5.7.1783[P] *Princessa* (70); **Captain**; 12.5.1786-16.6.1789 *Porcupine* (24); 10.5.1804-4.4.1811[†] *Dorset* Yacht.

Bracey, Jay

DATES: C.1734 BORN; 4.8.1734 BAPTISED GREAT YARMOUTH; 6.10.1791 DIED GREAT YARMOUTH; 3.11.1791 WILL PROBATE.

Family: Father William Bracey (1697-1751); Mother Mary Jay (1701-?); Wife Mary Brown married 5.6.1770; Sister Isabella (1737-?).
Service: 1750-1754 Merchant Service; 26.5.1754 Able *Fortune* (14) Sloop; 10.3.1755 QGnr *Elizabeth* (70); 13.8.1755 Mid *Elizabeth* (70); 23.1.1757 Mid *Monarch* (74); 28.2.1758 Battle of Cartagena; 24.8.1758 Mid *Panther* Hired Tender; 1.7.1759 Mate *Panther* Hired Tender; 12.12.1759 Passed; **Lieutenant**; 9.1.1760-31.8.1762 L. *Vesuvius* (8) Fireship; 29.3.1761-11.6.1761 Expedition against Belle-Isle; 2.2.1771-21.6.1771[P] 5L *Namur* (90).

BRADBY, DANIEL

Dates: c.1740 Born; 1.3.1798 Died; 25.6.1798 Will Probate.
Family: Father Daniel Bradby; Wife Henrietta; Brother James, RN (d.1809).
Service: 1752-1755 Merchant Service; 23.4.1755 Mid *Chichester* (68); 1.7.1755 Mid *Chichester* (68); 8.9.1757 Able *Cambridge* (80); 1.1.1758 Mid *Cambridge* (80); 16.1.1759-19.1.1759 Attack on Martinique; 20.1.1759-1.5.1759 Capture of Guadeloupe; 17.4.1760 Mid *Dublin* (74); 6.6.1760 Passed; **Lieutenant**; 8.3.1762[(BLI 10.1.1763)]-3.5.1762 3L *Norwich* (50); 17.9.1770-7.6.1771[P] 5L *Ajax* (74); 1779-1781 Impress Service at Newhaven; 25.12.1792-16.4.1794[P] 3L *Royal William* (84).

BRADBY, JAMES

Dates: 1809 Died; 5.8.1809 Buried Hamble-le-Rice, Hampshire; 16.8.1809 Will Probate.
Family: Son Bonamy, RN (d.1795); Daughter Jane; Son James, RN (d.1801); Daughter Ann [Wright]; Son Mathew Barton, RN (d.1831); Brother Daniel, RN (1740-1798).
Service: **Lieutenant**; 30.9.1758[(NA 19.11.1759)] 4L *Prince Frederick* (64); 31.12.1760-17.8.1762 3L *Temeraire* (74); 29.3.1761-11.6.1761 Expedition against Belle-Isle; 7.1.1762-10.2.1762 Operations against Martinique; 6.6.1762-13.8.1762 Operations against Havana; 12.11.1766-15.11.1769[P] 3L *Superb* (74); 2.11.1776 2L *Valiant* (74); 26.1.1778 2L *Prince George* (98); 13.5.1778 1L *Victory* (100); **Commander**; 2.7.1778 *Pluto* (8) Fireship; 27.7.1778 1st Battle of Ushant; **Captain**; 26.8.1780-2.4.1782 *Britannia* (100); 12.12.1781 2nd Battle of Ushant; 11.9.1782 *Trusty* (50); 10.4.1783-13.12.1785[P] *Salisbury* (50); 2.3.1801-19.4.1802[P] *Ajax* (74).

BRADSHAW, JOHN

Dates: c.1738 Born; bef.20.3.1762 Died; 22.4.1762 Will Probate.
Family: Father William Bradshaw (1706-1784); Mother Mary Hill (1705-1779); Brother William (1735-1746); Sister Susannah; Sister Sarah (1741-?); Brother Cornelius (1745-1796); Sister Ann (1749-?).
Service: 9.10.1750 Scholar *Royal Naval Academy*; 19.5.1754 Able *Seahorse* (24); 3.8.1757 Mid *Queenborough* (24); 29.4.1758 Battle of Cuddalore; 3.8.1758 Battle of Negapatam; 5.9.1758 Mid *Union* (90); 5.9.1759 Passed; **Lieutenant**; 31.1.1760 3L *Nottingham* (60); 7.10.1760-20.3.1762[†] 2L *Nottingham* (60); 7.1.1762-10.2.1762 Operations against Martinique.

BRADSHAW, THOMAS

Dates: c.1735 Born; 1810 Died; 8.3.1810 Will Probate.
Family:
Service: 13.5.1750 Capt Serv *Surprise* (24); 25.7.1751 Able *Surprise* (24); 17.8.1752 Able *Surprise* (24); 2.6.1753 Able *Culloden* (74); 14.8.1753 Able *Surprise* (24); 9.3.1754 Mid *Surprise* (24); 10.3.1755 Mid *Gosport* (44); 7.4.1756 Passed; 21.6.1756-8.10.1756 Mate *Gosport* (44); **Lieutenant**; 9.11.1756 L. *Happy* (8) Sloop; 17.6.1757 2L *Jason* (44); 2.1.1758 1L *Jason* (30); 5.6.1758-12.6.1758 Raid on Saint-Malo; 28.1.1762-10.11.1762[P] 3L *Saint George* Prison Ship; 28.4.1763-27.3.1764 1L *Pearl* (32); 1787 Resigned.

BRADY, JAMES

Dates: c.1740 Born; 20.12.1778 Died; 1.12.1779 Will Probate.
Family: Wife Ann.
Service: 26.8.1753 Capt Serv *Arundel* (24); 16.2.1754 Mid *Arundel* (24); 30.3.1755 Mid *Newcastle* (50); 24.3.1757 Mid *Monarch* (74); 28.2.1758 Battle of Cartagena; 12.8.1758 Mid *Prince* (90); 18.8.1759-19.8.1759 Battle of Lagos Bay; 13.2.1760 Passed; **Lieutenant**; 4.4.1760-11.4.1760 5L *Monarch* (74); 9.7.1760-13.4.1761 L. *Hound* (14) Sloop; 16.12.1761-26.8.1763[P] 5L *Newark* (80); 5.1.1767-16.1.1770 2L *Dorsetshire* (68); 21.9.1770 2L *Centaur* (74); 7.11.1770 3L *Centaur* (74); 4.3.1773-21.9.1773 4L *Centaur* (74); 2.5.1775-5.4.1776 LCmdr *Meredith* (10) Cutter; 2.7.1778 **Commander**.

BRADY, MATTEATE

Dates: 23.12.1718 Born Hampshire; 1786 Died Portsmouth.
Family: Father Samuel Brady (1693–1747); Mother Anne Colby; Daughter Sarah; Daughter Jane.
Service: 18.12.1734 Scholar *Royal Naval Academy*; 31.1.1738 Vol-p-O *Falkland* (50); 19.2.1739 Mid *Worcester* (60); 16.3.1739 Mid *Superb* (60); 10.4.1739 MidO *Princess Charlotte* (8) Yacht; 8.7.1739 Able *Shoreham* (20); 15.10.1739 Mid *Kent* (70); 9.11.1739 Mid *Princess Amelia* (80); 7.11.1740 NR *Lively* (20); 11.2.1741 Mid *Saint George* (90); 22.7.1741-3.9.1741 Mid *Hound* (8) Sloop; 3.9.1741 Passed; **Lieutenant**; 8.2.1741/42 6L *Royal Sovereign* (104); 16.3.1741/42-23.1.1743/44 5L *Royal Sovereign* (104).

BRAITHWAITE, THOMAS PATRICKSON

Dates: 1732 Born; 7.4.1794 Died Falmouth; 12.6.1794 Will Probate.
Family: Wife Elizabeth; Wife Dinah Brutton married 20.12.1778; Son Thomas Patrickson (1767-?). Daughter Mary;
Service: 1750-1755 Merchant Service; 12.2.1755 Mate *Dunkirk* (60); 6.6.1755-8.6.1755 Action of 6-8 June 1755; 10.3.1757 Passed; **Lieutenant**; 11.7.1757-18.6.1759 5L *Magnanime* (74);

5.9.1757-6.10.1757 Raid on Rochefort; 5.6.1758-12.6.1758 Raid on Saint-Malo; 31.1.1760 3L *Magnanime* (74); 14.6.1762 2L *Magnanime* (74); 22.6.1762-23.1.1763[P] 2L *Princess Amelia* (80); **Commander**; 3.3.1763 *Hampden* Packet.

BRAND, ANDREW

Dates: c.1732 Born; 1788 Died; 26.8.1788 Will Probate.
Family:
Service: 28.1.1749 Able *Lyme* (24); 4.7.1751 Able *Swan* (14) Sloop; 29.6.1754 Mid *Swan* (14) Sloop; 9.11.1754 Mid *Siren* (20); 22.5.1755-14.6.1755 British attack on Fort Beauséjour; 3.9.1756 Mid *Namur* (90); 24.12.1756 Mate *Medway* (60); 5.9.1757-6.10.1757 Raid on Rochefort; 2.1.1758 Passed; 9.3.1758 **Lieutenant**; 3.9.1758-24.9.1759 4L *Shrewsbury* (74).

BRAND, ELLIS

Dates: 1681 Born; 22.10.1759 Died; 1.12.1759 Will Probate.
Family: Wife Mary Sayer married 30.6.1710; Son John; Son Ellis.
Service: 24.2.1695/96 Capt Serv *Mary Galley* (34); 20.2.1698/99-24.5.1699[P] Capt Serv *Burlington* (54); 17.6.1700 Able *Defiance* (64); 10.4.1701 Mid *Defiance* (64); 20.8.1702-24.8.1702 Benbow vs DuCasse; 20.4.1703 Passed; **Lieutenant**; 11.1.1706/7-15.6.1709 1L *Portland* (54); 28.5.1708 Wager's Action; 4.6.1709 Action of 1709-06-04; **Commander**; 5.2.1710/11-24.9.1712[P] *Cruizer* (14); 1.4.1713 *Suffolk* (6) Storeship; **Captain**; 19.10.1715 *Garland* (32); 19.2.1716/17-14.8.1719[P] *Lyme* (32); 10.4.1721 *Hector* (40); 1.6.1722-8.8.1728 *Winchelsea* (20); 25.4.1732-11.10.1732 *Success* (20); 18.12.1733-2.8.1736[P] *Newcastle* (50); 28.7.1738-9.7.1739 *Burford* (70); 25.3.1740-10.7.1740 *Buckingham* (70); 28.7.1747 **Superannuated Rear Admiral**.

BRAND, JOHN

Dates: 7.2.1764 Died Woodbridge, Suffolk; 21.3.1764 Will Probate.
Family: Wife Mary.
Service: **Lieutenant**; 7.4.1737-18.5.1737 3L *Gloucester* (50).

BRANDRETH, WILLIAM ALSTON

Dates: 5.1.1741/42 Baptised; 1742 Born Toddington, Bedfordshire; 1814 Died; 19.12.1814 Will Probate.
Family: Father Nehemiah Brandreth (1713-1753); Mother Frances Alston (d.1769); Wife Hannah Parker (d.1828) married 22.5.1779.
Service: **Lieutenant**; 26.7.1762[(MED 6.5.1763)]-7.5.1763[P] 4L *Dorsetshire* (68); 11.12.1770-28.2.1771 2L *Warwick* (50); 25.10.1809 **Commander**.

BRATHWAITE, RICHARD

Dates: c.1728 Born; 28.6.1805 Died Greenwich; 11.7.1805 Will Probate.
Family: Wife Ulrica Eleanora; Daughter Jane Maria; Daughter Georgina; Daughter Elizabeth [Christie].
Service: 30.6.1742 Able *Orford* (70); 30.3.1744-13.2.1745[W] Mid *Orford* (70); 18.3.1745-24.10.1746[P] Mid *Falmouth* (50); 5.12.1749 Mid *Dragon* (60); 10.9.1750 Mid *Captain* (70); 1.6.1752 Able *Humber* (44); 9.11.1752 Mate *Humber* (44); 16.1.1754 Passed; **Lieutenant**; 7.5.1755 6L *Saint George* (90); 11.11.1755 5L *Saint George* (90); 24.5.1756 5L *Namur* (90); 5.6.1756 5L *Ramillies* (90); **Commander**; 29.11.1756[(ECH 3.6.1760)] *Polacca* (12) Sloop; 6.1.1760[(JAM 27.7.1761)] *Saltash* (14) Sloop; **Captain**; 6.4.1761[(MED 9.7.1761)]-7.2.1763[P] *Shannon* (28); 30.10.1765-20.12.1765[P] *Shannon* (28); 13.2.1766 *Gibraltar* (20); 3.3.1767-2.3.1772[P] *Liverpool* (28);

20.6.1775 *Milford* (28); 14.7.1775 *Centurion* (50); 2.7.1776-4.7.1776 Staten Island Landings; 6.12.1776-8.12.1776 Occupation of Rhode Island; 14.12.1778-15.12.1778 Battle of St. Lucia; 17.4.1780 Battle of Martinique; 15.5.1780 Action of March 15 1780; 19.5.1780 Action of March 19 1780; 9.1.1781-2.3.1782 *Bienfaisant* (64); 5.8.1781 Battle of Dogger Bank; 21.9.1790 **Rear Admiral of the White**; 1.2.1793 **Vice Admiral of the Blue**; 12.4.1794 **Vice Admiral of the White**; 1.6.1795 **Vice Admiral of the Red**; 14.2.1799 **Admiral of the Blue**; 1.1.1801 **Admiral of the White**.

BRAY, JOHN

Dates: 1795 Died.
Family:
Service: **Lieutenant**; 28.8.1743[(11.12.1744)]-18.9.1744[P] L. *Guarland's Prize* Xebec; 11.5.1745-2.4.1748 4L *Duke* (90); 24.7.1755-5.11.1755 1L *Lynn* (44); 14.12.1756 4L *Neptune* (90); 6.4.1757 3L *Neptune* (90); **Commander**; 15.6.1757 *Adventure* (18) Hired Armed Ship; **Captain**; 6.1.1758 *Princess Amelia* (80); 6.6.1758-27.7.1758 The Siege of Louisbourg; 6.4.1761-15.12.1761 *Newark* (80); 5.6.1789 **Superannuated Rear Admiral.**

BREEDON, JOSEPH

Dates: c.1735 Born; 18.2.1792 Died.
Family: Son Joseph Sanders.
Service: 1752-1755 Merchant Service; 16.1.1755 QGnr *Saint George* (90); 10.4.1756 YoP *Namur* (90); 5.9.1757-6.10.1757 Raid on Rochefort; 13.1.1758 Mid *Royal George* (100); 2.10.1758 Mate *Royal George* (100); 20.11.1759 Battle of Quiberon Bay; 13.2.1760 Passed; **Lieutenant**; 4.4.1760 L. *Lightning* (6) Hospital Ship; 19.9.1760-24.6.1761 3L *Woolwich* (44); 26.7.1769-3.1770[L] L. *Hawk* (10) Sloop.

BREMER, JAMES

Dates: c.1723 Born; 9.7.1774 Died; 18.5.1775 Will Probate.
Family: Wife Marianne Gernier married 25.5.1764; Daughter Marianne Elizabeth (1767-?); Son James Hughes, RN (d.1835).
Service: 12.6.1744 Able *Faversham* (44); 27.2.1747 Mid *Faversham* (44); 8.5.1747-15.1.1747/48[P] Mid *Chatham* (50); 15.1.1751 YoP *Essex* (70); 6.7.1751 Mid *Essex* (70); 8.2.1752 Mate *Essex* (64); 21.4.1755 Passed; **Lieutenant**; 29.10.1755-21.1.1756 L. *Saltash* (14) Sloop; 6.2.1756 L. *Spy* (10) Sloop; 12.8.1756 2L *Harwich* (50); 24.12.1756 3L *Invincible* (74); 21.9.1757 1L *Montagu* (60); 28.2.1758 Battle of Cartagena; 13.1.1759 1L *Magnanime* (74); 20.11.1759 Battle of Quiberon Bay; **Commander**; 4.6.1762-15.6.1762 *Alderney* (10) Sloop; 4.7.1763 *Savage* (8) Sloop; 8.9.1763-18.1.1764[P] *Zephyr* (10) Sloop; 7.1.1764 *Ferret* (14) Sloop; **Captain**; 20.6.1765 *Seaford* (20); 25.8.1766-13.8.1767 *Solebay* (28) Frigate; 5.11.1771-13.1.1773[P] *Pearl* (32).

BRENT, ROBERT

Dates: 1757 Died.
Family:
Service: 1732-1741 Merchant Service; 10.4.1741 Mate *Bedford* (70); 6.2.1744-14.7.1745 Mid *Bedford* (70); 11.2.1743/44-12.2.1743/44 Battle of Toulon; 14.7.1745 Passed; **Lieutenant**; 18.7.1745[(MED 10.12.1747)]-27.6.1746 4L *Norfolk* (80); 20.8.1747[(MED 10.12.1747)]-22.1.1747/48[P] 2L *Bedford* (70); 21.6.1748-28.11.1748 L. *Falcon* (10) Bomb Vessel.

BRENTON, JAHLEEL

Dates: 1729 Born; 30.1.1802 Died Stafford Place, Pimlico, London.
Family: Father Jahleel Brenton (d.1766); Wife Henrietta Cowley (d.1820); Son James Wallace, RN (d.1799); Son Jahleel (1st Baronet), RN (1770-1844); Son Edward Pelham, RN (1774-1839).
Service: 30.11.1746 Able *Chester* (54); 24.7.1747 Able *Devonshire* (66); 14.10.1747 2nd Battle of Cape Finisterre; 19.11.1747 Able *Saint George* (90); 12.2.1748 Able *Vigilant* (60); 24.2.1747/48 Mid *Vigilant* (60); 4.10.1752 Able *Kent* (64); 6.12.1752 Passed; **Lieutenant**; 6.4.1757 3L *Royal William* (84); 3.6.1757 L. *Salamander* (16) Fireship; 5.6.1758-12.6.1758 Raid on Saint-Malo; 2.4.1759 2L *Bienfaisant* (64); 2.10.1761-15.8.1763[P] 1L *Bienfaisant* (64); 23.2.1776 1L *Winchelsea* (32); 18.5.1776 1L *Egmont* (74); 30.5.1776-18.11.1776[P] LCmdr *Pembroke* (60); **Commander**; 23.8.1777 *Tortoise* (26) Armed Storeship; 16.4.1779[(NA 13.7.1780)] *Strombolo* (8) Fireship; 19.9.1780 *Queen* (20) Hired Armed Ship; **Captain**; 3.9.1781-13.5.1782 *Termagant* (26); 1.1.1801 **Rear Admiral of the Blue.**

BRERETON, WILLIAM

Dates: 1728 Born Winchester, Hampshire; 1800 Died Wykeham, Hampshire.
Family:
Service: 29.12.1745 Ord. *Eagle* (60); 7.10.1747-14.8.1748[P] Able *Eagle* (60); 14.10.1747 2nd Battle of Cape Finisterre; 12.10.1748 Able *Mars* (74); 25.4.1749 Mid *Rainbow* (44); 26.7.1751-19.6.1752 Able *Rainbow* (44); 19.6.1752 Passed; 1754 Mid *Kent* (64); **Lieutenant**; 4.7.1755[(EI 21.11.1759)] 4L *Salisbury* (50); 11.1.1756-14.1.1756 Capture of Geriah; 16.1.1757[(EI 21.11.1759)] 5L *Kent* (64); 24.3.1757[(EI 21.11.1759)] 4L *Kent* (64); 1.4.1757[(EI 21.11.1759)]-1.8.1757 3L *Kent* (64); 1.8.1757[(EI 1.9.1761)] 3L *Cumberland* (66); 1.9.1757[(EI 1.9.1761)] 4L *Cumberland* (66); 24.3.1758[(EI 1.9.1761)] 3L *Cumberland* (66); **Captain**; 25.3.1758 *Queenborough* (24); 29.3.1758-7.6.1758 ActCapt *Cumberland* (66); 29.4.1758 Battle of Cuddalore; 28.6.1758 ActCapt *Cumberland* (66); 7.7.1758 *Salisbury* (50); 3.8.1758 Battle of Negapatam; 3.3.1759[(EI 5.1.1762)] *Tiger* (60); 10.9.1759 Battle of Pondicherry; 10.9.1760[(EI 28.2.1766)]-16.1.1765[P] *Falmouth* (50); 24.9.1762-6.10.1762 Battle of Manilla; 10.1762-1765 Gov. of Manila; 9.1.1770-27.5.1771[P] *Rippon* (60); 26.10.1773-26.10.1776 *Centaur* (74); 16.4.1778-29.10.1778 *Duke* (90); 27.7.1778 1st Battle of Ushant; 1786 **Superannuated Captain**.

BRETON, JOHN

Dates: None Known.
Family:
Service: **Lieutenant**; 30.1.1759-29.9.1761 L. *Merlin* (18) Frigate; 24.11.1763-5.6.1766[P] 1L *Tartar* (28); 26.7.1769-25.4.1772[P] 2L *Stag* (32); 23.11.1776 LCmdr *Adventure* Hired Tender; 10.3.1778 1L *Victory* (100); **Commander**; 29.4.1778 *Lynx* (16) Sloop; 3.8.1780 *Fortune* (16) Sloop; **Captain**; 18.4.1782-12.4.1783[P] *Portland* (50); 12.4.1804 **Superannuated Captain**.

BRETT, CHARLES

Dates: c.1715 Born; 10.2.1799 Died.
Family: Father Timothy Brett, RN (d.1739); Wife Elizabeth Hooker married 1753; Brother John, RN (d.1785); Brother Timothy.
Service: bef.1747 **Lieutenant**; 14.11.1751-26.9.1753 Storekeeper at Plymouth Dockyard; 1755-9.1763 Clerk of the Cheque at Portsmouth Dockyard; 7.4.1756 Agent for Prizes at Portsmouth Dockyard; 7.1766-1.1770 Paymaster of the Navy; 19.3.1768-28.11.1776 M.P. for Lostwithiel; 25.11.1776-11.9.1780 M.P. for Sandwich; 3.1782-4.1783 Lord Commissioner of the Admiralty; 16.4.1782-5.4.1784 M.P. for Dartmouth; 12.1783-7.1788 Lord Commissioner of the Admiralty; 1.4.1784-17.6.1790 M.P. for Sandwich.

BRETT, JOHN

Dates: 1785 Died.
Family: Father Timothy Brett, RN (d.1739); Brother Timothy; Brother Charles, RN (1715-1799).
Service: 28.12.1721 Capt Serv *Ferret* (4) Sloop; 4.5.1727 Vol-p-O *Deal Castle* (20); 18.2.1728/29 Mid *Cornwall* (80); 11.5.1729 Mid *Princess Amelia* (80); 21.7.1729 Mid *William and Mary* (10) Yacht; c.14.8.1732 Passed; **Lieutenant**; 2.3.1733/34 L. *Bridgewater* (32); 4.2.1734/35 4L *Cornwall* (80); 24.7.1735-31.1.1735/36^{P} 3L *Cornwall* (80); 2.11.1736-25.12.1738 2L *Eltham* (40); **Commander**; 17.1.1739/40$^{(16.9.1740)}$ *Grampus* (6) Sloop; **Captain**; 25.3.1741 *Roebuck* (40); 2.11.1742 *Anglesea* (44); 5.4.1744-15.9.1746 *Sunderland* (60); 4.2.1755 *Chichester* (68); 19.5.1756 *Saint George* (90); 29.1.1770 **Admiral**.

BRETT, SIR PIERCY

Dates: c.1710 Born; 2.1.1753 Knight Bachelor; 12.10.1781 Died.
Family: Father Piercy Brett (d.1752); Mother Ann Logan; Wife Henrietta Colby; Son Piercy Anson (1746-?); Daughter Henrietta [Bowyer]; Son Piercy (1748-?); Brother William, RN (1718-1769); Sister Ann (1715-?).
Service: 8.9.1723 Vol-p-O *Dorsetshire* (80); 3.5.1724 MidO *Lowestoffe* (20); 18.12.1724 Mid *Lowestoffe* (20); 29.12.1729 Passed; **Lieutenant**; 6.12.1734$^{(3.3.1734/35)}$-26.5.1736 3L *Falkland* (50); 27.5.1737-28.7.1738 2L *Falkland* (50); 28.7.1738-28.5.1739 2L *Pembroke* (60); 25.5.1739-4.7.1739 2L *Adventure* (40); 5.7.1739-14.3.1739/40 1L *Adventure* (40); 15.3.1739/40 1L *Gloucester* (50); 19.2.1740/41$^{(21.8.1744)}$ 2L *Centurion* (60); 21.6.1743$^{(21.8.1744)}$ 1L *Centurion* (60); **Captain**; 30.9.1743$^{(29.12.1744)}$-20.7.1744^{P} *Centurion* (60); 22.4.1745 *Lion* (58); 9.7.1745 Lion v L'Elizabeth; 11.8.1746-26.8.1747 *Yarmouth* (64); 3.5.1747 1st Battle of Cape Finisterre; 9.11.1747-26.8.1748^{P} *Yarmouth* (64); 25.11.1748-18.11.1752^{P} *Yarmouth* (64); 7.11.1753 *Royal Caroline* (8) Yacht; 13.4.1754-7.10.1774 M.P. for Queenborough; 22.10.1755 *Cambridge* (80); 5.11.1756 *Royal George* (100); 15.11.1756 *Royal Caroline* (8) Yacht; 29.12.1757 *Norfolk* (74); 5.6.1758-12.6.1758 Raid on Saint-Malo; 29.9.1758 Commodore *Duke* (90); 10.1759 Commodore *Isis* (50); 1760 Commodore *Saint George* (90); 2.12.1761 Second in Command — The Mediterranean Sea; 1762-10.1762 Commodore *Newark* (80); 21.10.1762 **Rear Admiral of the Red**; 4.11.1762 CinC — The Mediterranean Sea; 11.12.1766-27.2.1770 Lord Commissioner of the Admiralty; 18.10.1770 **Vice Admiral of the Blue**; 24.10.1770 **Vice Admiral of the White**; 31.3.1775 **Vice Admiral of the Red**; 29.1.1778 **Admiral of the Blue**.

BRETT, WILLIAM

Dates: c.1718 Born; 21.9.1718 Baptised Saint Dunstan, Stepney, London; 19.1.1769 Died.
Family: Father Piercy Brett (d.1752); Mother Ann Logan; Wife Frances Harvey (1733-1773) married 23.5.1754; Daughter Mary (d.1759); Son William Edward (d.1764); Sister Ann (1715-?); Brother Sir Piercy, RN (1710-1781).
Service: 7.3.1730/31 Able *Lowestoffe* (20); 29.1.1731/32 Vol-p-O *Lowestoffe* (20); 13.2.1733/34 Mid *Hampton Court* (70); 2.6.1734 Mid *Namur* (90); 27.12.1734 Able *Britannia* (100); 13.2.1735/36 Mid *Britannia* (100); 29.7.1737 Able *Falkland* (50); 18.10.1738 Mid *Pembroke* (60); 15.9.1739 Mate *Adventure* (40); 4.10.1739 Passed; **Lieutenant**; 3.3.1739/40 L. *Phaeton* (8) Fireship; 27.7.1740 3L *Augusta* (60); 7.1.1740/41 Action of January 7 1741; 7.1741-10.1741 Operations against Santiago; 26.1.1741/42$^{(24.5.1742)}$ 1L *Augusta* (60); 4.6.1742 1L *Leopard* (50); **Commander**; 10.4.1746 *Baltimore* (14) Sloop; 1.5.1746 Action of 1746-05-01; **Captain**; 18.7.1747-29.5.1752^{P} *Tartar* (20); 11.3.1755-21.2.1759 *Falmouth* (50); 21.8.1759 *Achilles* (60); 1.3.1760-4.2.1763^{P} *Torbay* (74); 29.3.1761-11.6.1761 Expedition against Belle-Isle.

BREWSE, HOBART

Dates: 1754 Died; 27.8.1754 Will Probate.
Family: Father John Brewse; Mother Anne; Brother John, RN (1715-1785).
Service: **Lieutenant**; 25.5.1749[EI 10.5.1750]-16.5.1750[P] 3L *Harwich* (50).

BREWSE, JOHN

Dates: c.1715 Born; 15.9.1785 Died Ipswich.
Family: Father John Brewse; Mother Anne; Wife Mary Chambers married 20.6.1767; Daughter Mary; Brother Hobart, RN (d.1754).
Service: 13.1.1733/34 Vol-p-O *Edinburgh* (70); 4.3.1733/34 Vol-p-O *Royal Oak* (70); 16.4.1736 Able *Dolphin* (20); 4.9.1737 MidO *Dolphin* (20); 12.9.1738 Mid *Berwick* (70); 19.4.1740 Passed; **Lieutenant**; 17.3.1741/42[30.6.1742]-17.8.1742[P] 3L *Chester* (54); 11.10.1742 3L *Cornwall* (80); 9.5.1743-18.9.1743[W] L. *Bridgewater* (20); 1745 **Lieutenant** (Corps of Engineers); 1757 **Captain-lieutenant** (Corps of Engineers); 1778 **Lieutenant-colonel** (Corps of Engineers); 1780 **Colonel** (Corps of Engineers).

BRICE, ROBERT

Dates: c.1730 Born Ireland; 23.11.1805 Died Hampshire.
Family: Father Charles Brice (1684–1748); Mother Jane Robinson; Wife Elizabeth Corry (1716–1783) married 8.2.1763.
Service: 28.8.1746 Able *Speedwell* (10) Sloop; 3.11.1746 Able *Flamborough* (20); 4.9.1748 Mid *Flamborough* (20); 27.4.1749 Able *Assurance* (44); 3.7.1749-5.7.1754 Mid *Blandford* (20); 5.7.1754 Passed; **Lieutenant**; 29.4.1756 L. *Aldborough* (20); 16.11.1756 1L *Enterprise* (44); 17.2.1757 1L *Coventry* (28); 5.6.1758-12.6.1758 Raid on Saint-Malo; 20.11.1759 Battle of Quiberon Bay; 10.3.1760 4L *Royal George* (100); 27.6.1760 3L *Royal George* (100); 17.11.1760 1L *Royal George* (100); **Commander**; 3.7.1761 *Swallow* (14) Sloop; 19.10.1761 *Basilisk* (8) Bomb Vessel; 7.1.1762-10.2.1762 Operations against Martinique; 24.2.1762-25.2.1762 Capture of Saint Lucia; 19.4.1762 *Guadaloupe* Sloop; **Captain**; 26.5.1762[BLI 6.12.1762]-4.11.1762[P] *Crescent* (32) Frigate; 9.3.1778-3.12.1778 *Vigilant* (64); 27.7.1778 1st Battle of Ushant; 15.12.1779-8.9.1780 M.P. for Yarmouth IOW; 17.10.1782-30.3.1783 *Elizabeth* (74); 30.3.1783-24.4.1786[P] *Elizabeth* (74); 5.4.1784-19.6.1790 M.P. for Tregony; 4.8.1790 *Duke* (98); 26.3.1791-29.8.1791 *Duke* (98); 1.2.1793 **Rear Admiral of the White**; 31.8.1793 CinC — Cork; 1794 *Swiftsure* (74); 12.4.1794 **Rear Admiral of the Red**; 4.7.1794 **Vice Admiral of the White**; 1.6.1795 **Vice Admiral of the Red**; 1796-1800 *Polyphemus* (64); 12.1797 *Comeet* (14) Brig-Corvette; 1799 CinC; 14.2.1799 **Admiral of the Blue**; 23.4.1804 **Admiral of the White**; 9.11.1805 **Admiral of the Red**.

BRISBANE, JOHN

Dates: 10.12.1807 Died Southampton.
Family: Father Thomas Brisbane; Mother Isabel Nicholson; Wife Mary Young married 11.6.1759; Son Lt. Col. Thomas Stewart (d.1795); Son John Douglas, RN (d.1782); Son Charles, RN (1769-1829); Son James, RN (1774-1826); Son William Henry, RN (d.1795).
Service: **Lieutenant**; 5.8.1757[NA 8.8.1758]-13.1.1758 3L *Windsor* (60); 9.1.1760 2L *Windsor* (60); 22.2.1760 4L *Dublin* (74); **Commander**; 17.10.1760[BLI 21.5.1762] *Virgin* (12) Sloop; **Captain**; 24.9.1761[BLI 14.4.1762] *Lizard* (28); 7.2.1762[BLI 14.4.1762] *Nightingale* (22); 20.8.1762-5.6.1763[P] *Echo* (24); 4.10.1769 *Cruizer* (8) Sloop; 25.9.1770-5.10.1772 *Cerberus* (28); 4.12.1775-7.8.1778[SC] *Flora* (32); 7.7.1777 Action of 7th July 1777; 15.7.1779-14.11.1780 *Alcide* (74); 12.6.1781-24.12.1781 *Hercules* (74); 21.9.1790 **Rear Admiral of the Blue**; 1.2.1793 **Rear Admiral of**

the Red; 12.4.1794 **Vice Admiral of the Blue**; 4.7.1794 **Vice Admiral of the White**; 1.6.1795 **Vice Admiral of the Red**; 14.2.1799 **Admiral of the Blue**; 1.1.1801 **Admiral of the White**; 9.11.1805 **Admiral of the Red**.

BRISBANE, STEWART

Dates: c.1735 Born; 1762 Died.
Family:
Service: 1752-1754 Merchant Service; 5.1.1754 Capt Serv *Seahorse* (24); 26.6.1754 Ord. *Seahorse* (24); 16.4.1755 Able *Seahorse* (24); 2.9.1755 Mid *Bedford* (64); 3.3.1756/57 Mid *Harwich* (50); 29.6.1757-7.11.1757 Mid *Royal Anne* (100); 5.9.1757-6.10.1757 Raid on Rochefort; 7.11.1757 Passed; **Lieutenant**; 24.1.1758 2L *Active* (28); 5.6.1758-12.6.1758 Raid on Saint-Malo; 22.2.1759-4.4.1760 3L *Montagu* (60); 20.11.1759 Battle of Quiberon Bay.

BROADLEY, HOUSMAN

Dates: c.1722 Born; 29.1.1759 Died.
Family:
Service: 30.4.1738 L. Serv *Romney* (50); 9.6.1738 Able *Romney* (50); 18.3.1740/41 Mid *Blaze* (8) Fireship; 1.3.1741/42 Mid *Chatham* (50); 19.5.1742 Mid *Terrible* (6) Bomb Vessel; 25.6.1744 Able *Winchelsea* (20); 17.10.1744 Mid *Winchelsea* (20); 7.2.1744/45 Passed; **Lieutenant**; 18.5.1745-28.9.1745[C] L. *Falcon* (10) Sloop; 30.12.1745 L. *Falcon* (10) Bomb Vessel; 3.5.1747 1st Battle of Cape Finisterre; 2.9.1747 3L *Anson* (60); 23.12.1747 2L *Anson* (60); 26.8.1748-16.9.1752[P] 2L *Centurion* (50); 2.10.1754-25.5.1755 2L *Centurion* (50); **Commander**; 28.4.1755[(MED 20.12.1756)] *Oswego* (5) Sloop; 22.7.1756 *Jamaica* (10) Sloop; 8.1.1757 *Hawke* (8) Sloop; 8.1757-10.1757 Louisbourg Expedition; 14.12.1757-29.1.1759[†] *Viper* (10) Sloop.

BROCK, JOHN

Dates: c.1722 Born; 1786 Died.
Family:
Service: 18.9.1739 Able *Norfolk* (80); 26.3.1740 Able *Mary Galley* (40); 26.3.1742 Able *Bedford* (70); 24.5.1742 Able *Bridgewater* (20); 5.8.1742-7.1.1742/43[P] Mid *Bridgewater* (20); 11.1.1742/43 Mid *Bridgewater* (20); 14.3.1742/43 Mate *Bridgewater* (20); 30.9.1743 Mid *Princess Mary* (60); 21.3.1743/44 Mate *Princess Mary* (60); 18.10.1744 Mate *Royal Sovereign* (104); 1.3.1744/45 Mate *Pearl* (40) PMW; 2.6.1745-26.8.1745 ActL *Wolf* (14) Sloop; 27.8.1745 Passed; **Lieutenant**; 2.9.1745 L. *Winchelsea* (20); 5.9.1745 2L *Hastings* (44); 20.9.1746-25.9.1746 Lorient Operations; 9.4.1747 1L *Hastings* (44); 13.5.1747-15.8.1748[P] 2L *Advice* (50); 29.1.1756 3L *Revenge* (64); 23.3.1756-2.4.1759 2L *Revenge* (64); 20.5.1756 Battle of Minorca; 28.2.1758 Battle of Cartagena; 30.11.1770-18.4.1771 1L *Cambridge* (80).

BRODIE, DAVID

Dates: 1709 Born; 1787 Buried Abbey Church, Bath; 11.8.1787 Will Probate.
Family: Father Joseph Brodie (1671-1717); Mother Margaret Hume (1686-?); Wife Mary Aston (1706-1756) married 31.5.1753; Son William (1749-1812); Half-brother James (1695-1777); Sister Margaret (1710-?); Brother Hugh (1715-?).
Service: 23.12.1716 Able *Chatham* (14) Yacht; 18.5.1717 Mid *Chatham* (14) Yacht; 13.4.1720 Mid *Buckingham* (70); 9.6.1720-5.11.1721[P] Able *Buckingham* (70); 8.2.1729/30 Mate *James of Banff* Mer; 16.7.1733 Master *Margarett* Mer; 9.2.1733/34 Passed; 5.10.1736 **Lieutenant**; 16.5.1738-6.6.1739 3L *Princess Louisa* (60); 7.6.1739-27.11.1739 3L *Princess Louisa* (60); 21.11.1739 Attack on Puerto Bello; 14.6.1741[(12.3.1741/42)] 1L *Worcester* (60); 7.1741-10.1741

Operations against Santiago; 11.11.1743 1L *Monmouth* (70); **Commander**; 6.6.1744 *Aetna* (8) Fireship; 16.10.1744-11.9.1747 *Merlin* (10) Sloop; **Captain**; 9.3.1747/48[JAM 17.8.1749]-7.7.1749[P] *Strafford* (58); 9.4.1748 Battle of Santiago de Cuba; 12.10.1748 Battle of Havana; 1753 **Superannuated Captain**.

BRODRICK, THOMAS

Dates: 1704 Born; 1.1.1769 Died; 19.1.1769 Will Probate.
Family: Father William Brodrick, attorney-general of Jamaica; Wife Mary Robins (d. 1760) married 29.5.1728; Son Edward; Sister Catherine [Ward].
Service: 13.1.1723/24 Vol-p-O *Mermaid* (36); 4.4.1725 Able *Launceston* (42); 2.10.1725 Able *Falkland* (50); 5.7.1726 Mid *Falkland* (50); 2.11.1726 Able *Spence* (8) Sloop; 28.12.1726 MidO *Diamond* (40); 9.7.1727 Mid *Superb* (64); 10.10.1727 Mid *Spence* (8) Sloop; 10.1.1727/28 Passed; **Lieutenant**; 11.1.1727/28 L. *Rye* (20); 2.9.1729 4L *Nassau* (70); 6.5.1730-8.6.1732[P] 3L *Gosport* (42); 20.11.1733-30.7.1736 3L *Diamond* (40); 13.6.1738-13.12.1738[P] L. *Alderney* (8) Bomb Vessel; 16.7.1739 1L *Strafford* (60); 21.11.1739 Attack on Puerto Bello; **Commander**; 23.9.1740[22.4.1743] *Cumberland* (8) Fireship; 4.3.1740/41-5.1741 Operations against Cartagena; **Captain**; 25.3.1741[28.3.1742]-11.5.1743[P] *Shoreham* (20); 7.1741-10.1741 Operations against Santiago; 27.7.1743 *Phoenix* (20); 14.3.1743/44 *Exeter* (58); 23.11.1744-10.2.1744/45 *Ipswich* (70); 12.2.1744/45-8.9.1748[P] *Dreadnought* (60); 30.1.1755 CinC — Jamaica; 10.7.1755 *Hampton Court* (64); 15.5.1756 *Prince George* (80); 4.6.1756 **Rear Admiral of the Blue**; 24.2.1757 **Rear Admiral of the White**; 6.1757-10.1757 *Princess Amelia* (80); 10.1757-13.4.1758 *Prince George* (80); 1759 *Prince* (90); 14.2.1759 **Vice Admiral of the Blue**; 21.10.1762 **Vice Admiral of the White**; 5.8.1767 **Vice Admiral of the Red.**

BROGRAVE, WILLIAM

Dates: c.1730 Born; 10.2.1784 Died Shipdham, Norfolk; 18.2.1784 Will Probate;.
Family: Mistress Rebecca Trousou; Mistress Frances Cliffin; Illegitimate Son Thomas Trousou; Illegitimate Daughter Mary Trousou; Illegitimate Son Henry Trousou; Illegitimate Son George Trousou; Illegitimate Son Edward Cliffin (1782-?); Illegitimate Daughter Frances Cliffin.
Service: 8.4.1746 Able *Royal Sovereign* (104); 14.9.1746 Capt Serv *Dragon* (60); 25.10.1747 Ord. *Dragon* (60); 4.12.1748 Able *Intrepid* (64); 22.2.1748/49 Mid *Rainbow* (44); 11.6.1751 Able *Rainbow* (44); 28.4.1752 Able *Intrepid* (64); 19.6.1752 Passed; **Lieutenant**; 19.8.1753-6.9.1753[P] 3L *Glory* (44); 20.2.1755-9.12.1755 4L *Vanguard* (68); 18.1.1757-23.4.1757 2L *Monarch* (74); **Commander**; 13.10.1760-18.2.1762 *Albany* (14) Sloop.

BROME, HENRY

Dates: 1729 Born; 16.11.1729 Baptised St Mary Magdalene, Woolwich; 1785 Died; 26.2.1785 Will Probate.
Family: Father John Brome; Mother Elizabeth; Wife Ann (1725-1810).
Service: 10.5.1745 Able *Prince George* (90); 29.1.1746/47 Able *Windsor* (60); 3.5.1747 1st Battle of Cape Finisterre; 18.8.1747-18.8.1748[P] QM *Windsor* (60); 14.10.1747 2nd Battle of Cape Finisterre; 25.11.1748 Able *Garland* (24); 15.3.1748/49 Mid *Somerset* (68); 24.11.1750 Mid *Amazon* (22); 3.2.1751/52 Passed; 9.11.1756 **Lieutenant**; 21.11.1756 L. *Sarah* (16) Hired Armed Ship; 24.10.1758-6.2.1761 L. *Garland* (24); 12.11.1776-17.7.1777[P] LCmdr *Lively* Hired Tender; 13.5.1779-11.9.1779 L. *Pandora* (24).

BROMEDGE, HUGH

Dates: c.1714 Born Worcestershire; 18.8.1792 Died Bristol.
Family: Wife Mary Franklin (d.1794) married 17.7.1733; Son John, RN (1733-1779).
Service: 1744 CaptP *Vulture* PMW; 6.11.1745-30.6.1748 Mate *Folkestone* (44); 1748-1756 Merchant Service; 4.8.1756 Passed; **Lieutenant**; 21.9.1756 L. *Swift* (8) Sloop; 9.11.1756-17.12.1756 4L *Royal George* (100); **Commander**; 3.4.1759 *Wolf* (8) Sloop; 3.7.1759 Bombardment of Le Havre; 25.9.1759 *Laurel* (12) Sloop; 3.10.1759-25.2.1760 *Wolf* (8) Sloop; 27.8.1760-9.4.1763 *Happy* (8) Sloop; 22.11.1763-14.9.1766[W] *Happy* (8) Sloop; 6.3.1772-16.9.1776[W] *Savage* (8) Sloop; 28.3.1777 *Buffalo* (50); **Captain**; 29.4.1778-6.5.1780 *Buffalo* (50); 31.12.1779 Affair of Fielding and Bylandt; 14.6.1781-27.11.1782[P] *Princess Caroline* (44).

BROMEDGE, JOHN

Dates: 1733 Born Worcestershire; 1779 Died; 25.8.1779 Will Probate.
Family: Father Hugh Bromedge, RN (1714-1792); Mother Mary Franklin (d.1794); Wife Sarah Leath (1738–?) married 29.8.1762; Daughter Mary Anne (1767–1809); Daughter Harriet (1771–1795).
Service: 1753-1756 Merchant Service; 10.4.1756 Mid *Devonshire* (66); 11.2.1758 Mid *Rye* (20); 9.3.1758-24.5.1758 Capture of Fort Louis; 12.6.1758 Mate *Rye* (20); 16.1.1759-19.1.1759 Attack on Martinique; 17.2.1759 Mate *Woolwich* (2); 1.8.1759 Passed; **Lieutenant**; 3.9.1759-17.12.1759 L. *Cygnet* (18) Sloop; 1.6.1769-29.6.1772 L. *Alderney* (10) Sloop; 1774-1775 CaptM *Polly and Sally* Mer.

BROMFIELD, GEORGE

Dates: c.1717 Born; 1758 Died.
Family:
Service: 30.9.1734 Ord. *York* (60); 10.4.1735 Vol-p-O *Captain* (70); 27.5.1735 Able *Captain* (70); 12.1.1735/36 Vol-p-O *Romney* (50); 6.3.1736/37 Able *Torrington* (40); 21.3.1736/37 Mid *Torrington* (40); 8.4.1738 Mid *Deptford* (24) Storeship; 5.8.1739 Able *Seaford* (20); 1.5.1740 Able *Mary Galley* (40); 12.5.1741 Passed; **Lieutenant**; 26.5.1741 3L *Assistance* (50); 10.8.1742 2L *Assistance* (50); 18.7.1743[(JAM 5.3.1747/48)] L. *Bonetta* (8) Sloop; 22.2.1743/44[(11.9.1744)]-25.9.1744[P] 2L *Grafton* (70); 28.1.1744/45 2L *Princess Louisa* (60); 7.9.1745-27.1.1745/46 1L *Princess Louisa* (60); 12.4.1746-10.6.1746 1L *Portland Prize* (50); 1.7.1746-30.11.1746 LCmdr *Panther* Hired Tender.

BROOKE, WILLIAM

Dates: 10.7.1735 Born Leamington, Warwickshire; 25.7.1735 Baptised; 1787 Died; 24.9.1792 Will Probate;
Family: Father Matthew Brookes; Mother Mary; Wife Susanna Hill (1750-?) married 13.10.1771; Sister Ann; Brother David.
Service: 1753-1755 Merchant Service; 15.1.1755 QGnr *Princess Charlotte* (8) Yacht; 18.8.1755 Mid *Princess Charlotte* (8) Yacht; 5.6.1756 Mid *Saint George* (90); 9.6.1757 Mid *Culloden* (74); 21.6.1758 Mid *Revenge* (64); 22.2.1759-2.1.1760 Mate *Hussar* (28); 2.1.1760 Passed; **Lieutenant**; 4.4.1760-11.9.1761 L. *Proserpine* (8) Fireship; 5.11.1761 L. *Hazard* (8) Sloop; 22.3.1762-5.5.1763 L. *Lively* (20); 3.11.1770 3L *Boyne* (68); 18.12.1775-18.6.1776[P] L. *Aldborough* (20); 14.11.1776 2L *Boyne* (68); 4.12.1776-19.2.1777 3L *Boyne* (68).

BROOKES, JOHN

Dates: c.1721 Born; 8.7.1791 Died; 20.7.1791 Will Probate.
Family: Wife Elizabeth; Son Gustavus William (1749-1808).
Service: 21.9.1739 Mst Serv *Shoreham* (20); 23.9.1740 Mid *Southsea Castle* (40); 18.3.1741/42-23.1.1744/45[P] Mid *Namur* (90); 11.2.1743/44-12.2.1743/44 Battle of Toulon; 5.4.1745 Mid *Poole* (44); 1.8.1745 Mid *Poole* (44); 20.9.1746-25.9.1746 Lorient Operations; 1.10.1746 Action of 1746-10-01; 9.3.1746/47 Passed; **Lieutenant**; 9.7.1747 2L *Severn* (50); 31.7.1748[(MED 18.10.1748)]-22.11.1748[P] 4L *Princess* (70); 20.3.1748/49 L. *Shark* (8) Sloop; 7.7.1749[(BLI 8.11.1752)] 3L *Tavistock* (50); 30.1.1749/50[(BLI 24.3.1751/52)]-2.10.1752[P] L. *Shark* (8) Sloop; 6.2.1755-28.10.1755 L. *Blandford* (20); 11.12.1755 2L *Hampshire* (50); 10.3.1757 3L *Princess Amelia* (80); 4.5.1757-8.5.1758 L. *Seahorse* (24); **Commander**; 26.5.1758-21.11.1760 *Peregrine* (20) Sloop; 24.3.1761 *Pomona* (18) Sloop; **Captain**; 24.9.1762-22.12.1762[P] *Captain* (64); 27.3.1763-9.12.1765 *Fly* (8) Sloop; 25.9.1770-3.10.1774[P] *Minerva* (32); 1.8.1776-15.1.1779 *Belleisle* (64).

BROOKING, PETER FRANKLIN

Dates: c.1707 Born; 1757 Died.
Family:
Service: 20.11.1732 Mst Serv *Bideford* (20); 30.12.1734 Able *Shark* (8) Sloop; 18.9.1735 Mid *Shark* (8) Sloop; 23.10.1739 Mate *Colchester* (50); 28.1.1739/40 Mid *Colchester* (50); 5.4.1740 Mate *Colchester* (50); 18.2.1740/41 Master *Colchester* (50); 5.3.1740/41 Passed; **Lieutenant**; 13.3.1740/41-22.7.1741 L. *Blaze* (8) Fireship.

BROOKS, JOHN

Dates: c.1739 Born.
Family:
Service: 1.3.1755 Capt Serv *Dunkirk* (60); 6.6.1755-8.6.1755 Action of 6-8 June 1755; 2.5.1757 Able *Dunkirk* (60); 10.7.1757 Mid *Magnanime* (74); 5.9.1757-6.10.1757 Raid on Rochefort; 5.6.1758-12.6.1758 Raid on Saint-Malo; 20.11.1759 Battle of Quiberon Bay; 29.12.1760 Passed; **Lieutenant**; 7.8.1761 L. *Carcass* (14) Bomb Vessel; 28.11.1761-27.12.1762 4L *Belliqueux* (64); 6.12.1763-21.2.1764 3L *Achilles* (60); 15.2.1764-26.2.1767[P] LCmdr *Spy* (4) Cutter; 19.1.1771-1.6.1775[P] 3L *Orford* (68); 1.11.1776 3L *Sandwich* (90); 15.11.1776-15.2.1777 5L *Sandwich* (90).

BROUGHTON, FRANCIS

Dates: 1786 Died.
Family:
Service: **Lieutenant**; 20.9.1759[(JAM 3.4.1760)] 4L *Conqueror* (68); 6.1.1760[(JAM 3.4.1760)] 6L *Prince* (90); 2.12.1763-1.12.1766 1L *Cornwall* (74); 23.12.1767-4.9.1771 1L *Montreal* (32).

BROWN, ALEXANDER

Dates: c.1716 Born; 1794 Died; 23.12.1794 Buried St George in the East, Tower Hamlets, Middlesex; 2.1.1795 Will Probate.
Family: Brother John; Sister Allison.
Service: 4.3.1736/37 Mid *Aldborough* (20); 8.5.1738 Able *Kennington* (20); 27.5.1739 Able *Salisbury* (50); 20.8.1741 Mid *Saint George* (90); 7.6.1744 Passed; **Lieutenant**; 29.1.1747/48[(JAM 1.12.1749)] 3L *Enterprise* (44); 1.8.1748[(JAM 1.12.1749)]-11.4.1749[P] 4L *Elizabeth* (70); 4.11.1748[(JAM 1.12.1749)]-12.12.1749[P] 3L *Rippon* (54); 5.8.1755 L. *Sheerness* (24); 24.9.1756 4L *Union* (90); 1.8.1757 4L *Neptune* (90); 5.9.1757-6.10.1757 Raid on Rochefort; 20.10.1757 3L *Neptune* (90); 12.2.1759-

20.11.1759[S] 2L *Resolution* (74); 20.11.1759 Battle of Quiberon Bay; 8.11.1776-27.6.1777 LCmdr *Nightingale* (22) Hospital Ship.

BROWN, ANNESLEY

Dates: 1766 Died.
Family:
Service: **Lieutenant**; 24.7.1760[(EI 14.2.1763)]-1.1.1761[F] 2L *Queenborough* (24); 4.1.1764-27.6.1765[D] 1L *Panther* (60); 27.6.1765 Dismissed.

BROWN, DAVID

Dates: c.1712 Born; 1774 Died.
Family:
Service: 29.3.1739 Able *Torbay* (80); 10.2.1739/40 MidO *Torbay* (80); 25.5.1741 Able *Elizabeth* (70); 28.11.1741 Mid *Elizabeth* (70); 11.2.1743/44-12.2.1743/44 Battle of Toulon; 18.1.1745/46 NR *Amazon* (22); 6.6.1746 Passed; **Lieutenant**; 14.6.1760[(EI 30.7.1764)]-12.5.1761 5L *Grafton* (68); 2.11.1770-1774[†] 3L *Buckingham* (68).

BROWN, JAMES

Dates: c.1734 Born; 1757 Died.
Family:
Service: 17.12.1749 Capt Serv *Humber* (44); 18.12.1750 Ord. *Humber* (44); 26.6.1751 Able *Gosport* (44); 9.5.1752-21.12.1754 Mid *Advice* (50); 22.12.1754 Able *Trial* (10) Sloop; 3.12.1755-4.2.1756 ActL *Badger* (10) Sloop; 4.2.1756 Passed; **Lieutenant**; 28.4.1756-25.6.1756 3L *Deptford* (50); 20.5.1756 Battle of Minorca.

BROWN, JOHN

Dates: c.1707 Born; 1755 Died.
Family:
Service: 21.4.1729 Able *Yarmouth* (70); 27.5.1731 Mid *Anglesea* (40); 3.12.1733 Mid *Hampton Court* (70); 17.6.1735 Passed; **Lieutenant**; 31.8.1739 3L *Lichfield* (50); 30.11.1739-5.8.1740 3L *Cumberland* (80); 6.8.1740-7.6.1741 2L *Cumberland* (80); 13.10.1741-22.8.1744 1L *Russell* (80); 11.2.1743/44-12.2.1743/44 Battle of Toulon.

BROWN, JOHN

Dates: c.1725 Born; 1782 Died.
Family:
Service: 28.5.1741 Ord. *Ruby* (54); 30.10.1741-9.9.1743[P] Able *Ruby* (54); 9.4.1746-14.9.1747[P] Able *Mermaid* (44); 11.1.1747/48 Mid *Severn* (50); 24.10.1749 Mid *Saint Albans* (60); 24.10.1750 Passed; **Lieutenant**; 2.5.1755[(NA 11.12.1755)] 3L *Nottingham* (60); 2.3.1756 2L *Nottingham* (60); 6.6.1758-27.7.1758 The Siege of Louisbourg; 25.8.1758[(NA 30.1.1759)] 1L *Nottingham* (60); 15.9.1761 4L *Newark* (80); 16.12.1761-26.8.1763[P] 3L *Newark* (80).

BROWN, JOHN

Dates: c.1732 Born; 14.11.1793 Died.
Family:
Service: 20.2.1750 Able *Falcon* (10) Bomb Vessel; 13.7.1750 Mid *Falcon* (10) Bomb Vessel; 9.10.1751 Able *Lyme* (20); 5.11.1752 Mate *Lyme* (24); 1.12.1753 Able *Somerset* (68); 3.3.1754 Mid *Somerset* (68); 27.2.1755 Mate *Somerset* (68); 27.3.1755 Mate *Barfleur* (80); 14.2.1757

Passed; **Lieutenant**; 6.4.1757 L. *Peggy* (8) Sloop; 27.8.1759[EI 5.1.1762] 1L *Active* (28); **Commander**; 27.10.1761-19.7.1762[P] *London Buss* Storeship; 8.6.1763-14.2.1767[P] *Hawk* (10) Sloop.

BROWN, JOHN

Dates: c.1734 Born.

Family:

Service: 29.12.1747 Capt Serv *Looe* (44); 9.7.1748 Ord. *Looe* (44); 17.12.1748 Ord. *Queenborough* (24); 12.6.1749 Capt Serv *Garland* (24); 23.12.1750 Able *Garland* (24); 26.9.1753 Mid *Garland* (24); 19.1.1757 Mate *Garland* (24); 4.4.1757 Passed; **Lieutenant**; 16.4.1757 L. *Bonetta* (10) Sloop; 13.5.1758 3L *Conqueror* (68); 22.3.1759 2L *Conqueror* (68); 30.3.1759 3L *Conqueror* (68); 24.7.1759-29.11.1762[P] 1L *Woolwich* (44); 7.1.1762-10.2.1762 Operations against Martinique.

BROWN, JOHNSON

Dates: 14.3.1735/36 Born; 6.4.1736 Baptised Berwick-upon-Tweed; 1760 Died; 25.7.1760 Will Probate.

Family: Father William Brown; Sister Isabella.

Service: 6.5.1751 Capt Serv *Gosport* (44); 15.1.1752 Capt Serv *Advice* (50); 30.7.1753 Able *Advice* (50); 31.7.1754 Mid *Advice* (50); 24.4.1756 Mid *Duke* (90); 13.6.1756 QM *Aldborough* (20); 29.7.1756 Mid *Aldborough* (20); 24.11.1756 Mid *Enterprise* (44); 12.11.1757 Able *Enterprise* (44); 18.1.1758 Mid *Enterprise* (44); 13.4.1758 ActL *Enterprise* (44); 9.6.1758 Passed; **Lieutenant**; 15.6.1758-17.12.1759 3L *Enterprise* (44).

BROWN, JOSEPH

Dates: c.1740 Born.

Family:

Service: 26.2.1755 Ord. *Prince George* (80); 11.3.1756 Ord. *Monarch* (74); 8.3.1757 Able *Dublin* (74); 5.9.1757-6.10.1757 Raid on Rochefort; 26.1.1758 Mid *Dublin* (74); 30.8.1758 Mid *Defiance* (60); 7.9.1758 Mid *Dublin* (74); 21.1.1759 Able *Namur* (90); 26.7.1759 Mid *Namur* (90); 18.8.1759-19.8.1759 Battle of Lagos Bay; 20.11.1759 Battle of Quiberon Bay; 3.2.1761 Mid *Marlborough* (68); 28.9.1761 Passed; **Lieutenant**; 17.1.1762[BLI 20.7.1763]-10.8.1763[P] 5L *Temeraire* (74); 6.6.1762-13.8.1762 Operations against Havana; 25.8.1766-4.8.1769 2L *Levant* (28); 11.12.1770-19.3.1771 1L *Warwick* (50); 26.4.1771-21.1.1773 2L *Achilles* (60); 8.11.1773 4L *Centaur* (74); 24.1.1774 4L *Lennox* (74); 13.6.1774 3L *Lennox* (74); 19.1.1775 3L *Exeter* (64); 28.2.1775 2L *Exeter* (64); 28.3.1776 1L *Flora* (32); 7.7.1777 Action of 7th July 1777; **Commander**; 1.12.1777-21.9.1779[C] *Hope* (14) Sloop; 3.10.1780-12.2.1781 *Fairy* (14) Sloop.

BROWN, RICHARD

Dates: c.1718 Born; 1756 Died; 24.8.1756 Will Probate.

Family: Wife Susannah.

Service: 23.4.1730 Ord. *Drake* (8) Sloop; 21.5.1730 Able *Drake* (8) Sloop; 28.12.1735 Cox *Seahorse* (20); 4.7.1738 Mid *Seahorse* (20); 13.10.1739 Mate *Seahorse* (20); 19.1.1739/40 Mate *Oxford* (50); 27.11.1740 Passed; **Lieutenant**; 21.2.1740/41 2L *Faversham* (44); 11.5.1741-5.7.1741 6L *Marlborough* (90); 30.4.1744-6.7.1744 1L *Winchester* (50); 17.8.1745 2L *Prince George* (90); 3.2.1745/46-21.6.1748[P] 1L *Prince George* (90); 3.5.1747 1st Battle of Cape Finisterre; 1.12.1748-14.11.1752[P] 1L *Berwick* (70); 16.1.1753-28.1.1755 1L *Monarch* (74); 6.2.1755-7.1.1756 1L *Monarch* (74).

BROWN, WILLIAM

Dates: 1774 Died Middlesex; 7.3.1775 Will Probate.

Family:

Service: **Commander**; 2.6.1746-7.6.1747[W] *Shoreham Prize* (10) Sloop; 25.4.1755 *Swan* (14) Sloop; **Captain**; 17.6.1755-5.1.1759[P] *Centaur* (20).

BROWN, WILLIAM

Dates: c.1725 Born; 23.11.1790 Died.

Family:

Service: 30.3.1748 Able *Elizabeth* (70); 6.4.1748 Mid *Elizabeth* (70); 9.4.1748 Battle of Santiago de Cuba; 29.5.1752 Able *Royal George* (100); 16.6.1752 Mid *Royal George* (100); 1.3.1752/53 Mate *Royal George* (100); 18.2.1755 Able *Princess Charlotte* (8) Yacht; 7.4.1755 Mid *Augusta* (60); 17.6.1755-3.11.1756 Mate *Augusta* (60); 3.11.1756 Passed; **Lieutenant**; 9.11.1756-17.12.1756 5L *Royal George* (100); 2.5.1758 3L *Antelope* (50); 30.4.1759 2L *Antelope* (50); 1.4.1763-4.4.1764[P] 1L *Antelope* (50); 10.11.1770-21.5.1771 1L *Trident* (64); 19.12.1775 1L *Blonde* (32); 9.1.1777 1L *Apollo* (32); **Commander**; 20.3.1779-3.4.1781 *Drake* (14) Sloop.

BRUCE, ALEXANDER

Dates: c.1736 Born; 1.12.1765 Died.

Family:

Service: 1749-1753 Merchant Service; 23.8.1753 L. Serv *Looe Hulk* (44); 4.5.1754 Able *Success* (20); 5.2.1755 Mid *Success* (20); 22.5.1755-14.6.1755 British attack on Fort Beauséjour; 8.1757-10.1757 Louisbourg Expedition; 11.10.1757 Able *Newark* (80); 28.11.1757 Mid *Newark* (80); 6.3.1757/58-27.3.1758 Mate *Newark* (80); 27.3.1758 Passed; **Lieutenant**; 18.4.1758-21.4.1758 2L *Melampe* (36).

BRUDENELL, RICHARD

Dates: c.1737 Born; 1762 Died.

Family:

Service: 16.1.1751 Bosun Serv *Unicorn* (24); 20.3.1751 Capt Serv *Unicorn* (24); 13.6.1753 Able *Falcon* (10) Bomb Vessel; 23.10.1753 Mid *Falcon* (10) Bomb Vessel; 2.3.1754 Mid *Assistance* (50); 12.1.1755 Mid *Experiment* (24); 28.4.1755 Able *Centurion* (50); 12.6.1755 Mid *Centurion* (50); 8.3.1757 Passed; **Lieutenant**; 10.3.1757 4L *Princess Amelia* (80); 5.9.1757-6.10.1757 Raid on Rochefort; 17.1.1758 3L *Princess Amelia* (80); 6.6.1758-27.7.1758 The Siege of Louisbourg; 21.3.1759[(NA 21.5.1760)]-26.9.1761[P] 3L *Bedford* (64); 29.3.1761-11.6.1761 Expedition against Belle-Isle; **Commander**; 15.6.1762-3.11.1762 *Alderney* (10) Sloop.

BRUSTIS, PAUL

Dates: c.1727 Born; 1798 Died Stoke Damerell, Devon; 7.6.1798 Will Probate.

Family: Wife Mary Rawlings (d.1818) married 21.9.1764.

Service: 18.8.1746 QGnr *Lichfield* (50); 13.7.1747 QGnr *Superb* (60); 14.10.1747 Mid *Superb* (60); 17.9.1748 Mate *Princess* (70); 19.1.1749 Mid *Nightingale* (22); 14.1.1750 Mate *Triton* (20); 2.7.1755 Passed; **Lieutenant**; 13.7.1756-16.11.1757 3L *Roebuck* (44); 19.10.1759[(JAM 16.3.1761)] 6L *Marlborough* (80); 23.2.1760[(JAM 16.3.1761)] 5L *Marlborough* (80); 20.5.1760[(JAM 16.3.1761)]-30.9.1760[P] 4L *Marlborough* (80); 8.5.1761-21.3.1763[P] 2L *Ocean* (90); 25.10.1763 1L *Belleisle* (64); 30.8.1764-24.10.1766 2L *Belleisle* (64); 20.7.1768 1L *Burford* (68); 21.9.1769 **Superannuated Commander**; 22.2.1770-29.5.1771[P] 1L *Defence* (74); 10.7.1771-25.8.1774 1L *Somerset* (68);

31.5.1776 1L *Raisonable* (64); 10.3.1777-5.2.1780[P] 2L *Blenheim* (90); 25.2.1780 2L *Cambridge* (80); 17.3.1780-14.3.1781 1L *Cambridge* (80).

BRYANT, GEORGE

Dates: c.1722 Born; 1770 Died.
Family:
Service: 23.3.1737/38 Able *Salisbury* (50); 10.6.1738 Mid *Salisbury* (50); 25.6.1740 Mid *Pearl* (40); 3.1.1740/41 ActL *Pearl* (40); 29.1.1740/41 Mid *Pearl* (40); 5.2.1742/43 Mid *Princess Mary* (60); 7.1.1743/44 Mate *Princess Mary* (60); 18.7.1744 Passed; **Lieutenant**; 29.8.1744-4.10.1744 L. *Lively* (20); 17.10.1744 L. *Bridgewater* (20); 3.7.1745 Action of 1745-07-03; 16.7.1745 LCmdr *York* (16) Hired Armed vessel; 15.5.1748-24.8.1748[P] LCmdr *Boyne* Hired Tender.

BRYNE, HENRY

Dates: c.1741 Born; 11.10.1780 Died.
Family: Wife Maria Byrne; Sister Judith Thompson.
Service: 10.1754-12.1755 Merchant Service; 25.12.1755 Mid *Colchester* (50); 17.5.1756 Action of 17th May 1756; 19.9.1758 Mid *Monmouth* (70); 20.6.1759 Able *Cumberland* (66); 10.9.1759 Battle of Pondicherry; 21.3.1760 Able *Cambridge* (80); 16.11.1761 ActL *Trent* (28); 5.2.1762 ActL *Pembroke* (60); 4.4.1762 Mid *Princess Royal* (90); 13.9.1762 Passed; **Lieutenant**; 14.9.1762 4L *Essex* (64); 29.3.1763-6.6.1763 2L *Pearl* (32); 14.7.1763-16.12.1766[P] 2L *Dreadnought* (60); 15.1.1771 2L *Dreadnought* (60); **Commander**; 21.1.1771-17.8.1773[P] *Pomona* (18) Sloop; 21.1.1775 *Pomona* (18) Sloop; **Captain**; 20.11.1775[(BLI 14.8.1777)]-5.9.1777 *Hind* (24); 5.9.1777-11.10.1780[F] *Andromeda* (28); 27.7.1778 1st Battle of Ushant; 17.4.1780 Battle of Martinique; 15.5.1780 Action of March 15 1780; 19.5.1780 Action of March 19 1780.

BUCHANAN, JOHN

Dates: c.1735 Born; 13.1.1791 Died; 18.1.1791 Buried St Luke, Chelsea, Kensington and Chelsea, Middlesex; 10.2.1791 Will Probate.
Family: Wife Esther Robinson married 16.11.1789; Daughter Mary.
Service: 2.9.1752 Able *Surprise* (24); 6.7.1754 QGnr *Gosport* (44); 29.4.1756 Mid *Gosport* (44); 27.1.1757 Mate *Gosport* (44); 7.2.1759 Passed; **Lieutenant**; 22.8.1759-23.8.1759 L. *Proserpine* (8) Fireship; 16.6.1760 4L *Chichester* (68); 29.3.1761-11.6.1761 Expedition against Belle-Isle; 22.10.1761-5.4.1763[P] 3L *Chichester* (68); 17.11.1764 2L *San Antonio* (64); 29.11.1766-3.2.1768 3L *San Antonio* (64); 10.7.1770-10.7.1772[P] LCmdr *Goodwill* (4) Cutter; 10.7.1776 3L *Culloden* (74); 2.8.1776 1L *Culloden* (74); 28.1.1778 4L *Sandwich* (90); 16.5.1778 3L *Sandwich* (90); 27.7.1778 1st Battle of Ushant; 13.3.1779 3L *Portland* (50); 31.12.1779 Affair of Fielding and Bylandt; 10.2.1780 1L *Portland* (50); **Commander**; 17.7.1780[(NF 20.12.1780)]-22.10.1781 *Proteus* (26); 6.1.1783 *Fortune* (16) Sloop; **Captain**; 18.1.1783-20.1.1783 *Danae* (32).

BUCKINGHAM, JAMES

Dates: c.1731 Born; 1779 Died; 20.2.1779 Will Probate.
Family: Wife Elizabeth; Sister Mary [Quin]; Sister Ann.
Service: 18.5.1747-28.6.1748[P] Able *Portland Prize* (50); 1748-1752 Merchant Service; 6.5.1752 Able *Monmouth* (70); 22.12.1752 Able *Centurion* (50); 10.5.1754 Mid *Centurion* (50); 11.3.1755 Mid *Torbay* (74); 6.6.1755-8.6.1755 Action of 6-8 June 1755; 12.1.1756-19.11.1756 Mid *Invincible* (74); 19.11.1756 Passed; **Lieutenant**; 5.4.1757 3L *Preston* (50); 15.4.1761 6L *Namur* (90); 28.10.1761-1.2.1762 5L *Namur* (90); 27.2.1762 5L *Royal Sovereign* (104); 24.5.1762-27.12.1762[P] 4L *Royal Sovereign* (104); 8.3.1766 1L *Fame* (74); 24.3.1767 2L

Fame (74); 30.11.1770 3L *Torbay* (74); 18.12.1770 2L *Torbay* (74); 28.5.1771 1L *Torbay* (74); 7.7.1772 2L *Torbay* (74); 3.11.1773-29.11.1773 1L *Torbay* (74); 22.10.1776 *Anna Teresa* Packet; 30.7.1778-1779 *Weymouth* Packet.

BUCKLE, MATHEW

Dates: 1716 Born; 9.7.1784 Died; 17.7.1784 Will Probate.

Family: Wife Hannah Hughes married 6.6.1768; Son Mathew, RN (1770-1855).

Service: 2.12.1731 Vol-p-O *Edinburgh* (70); 23.7.1732 Vol-p-O *Buckingham* (70); 5.9.1732 Able *Buckingham* (70); 31.10.1732 MidO *Fly* (8) Sloop; 7.7.1733 Mid *Pearl* (40); 10.4.1734 Mate *Pearl* (40); 16.4.1736 Mid *Newcastle* (50); 14.10.1736 Able *Nottingham* (60); 20.11.1736 Mid *Greenwich* (50); 9.4.1738 Mate *Greenwich* (50); 5.12.1738 Passed; **Lieutenant**; 14.6.1739-29.1.1741/42 L. *Tartar* (20); 4.1740-5.7.1740 Attack on St. Augustine; 6.5.1742-27.8.1743 2L *Norfolk* (80); **Commander**; 16.7.1744[MED 17.9.1746] *Spence* (8) Sloop; **Captain**; 29.5.1745[MED 25.5.1748]-4.6.1748[P] *Russell* (80); 7.10.1747 Action of 1747-10-07; 21.12.1748 *Assistance* (50); 9.12.1749 *Culloden* (74); 2.3.1749/50 *Assistance* (50); 22.7.1752-15.11.1752[P] *Culloden* (74); 10.1.1753 *Unicorn* (24); 8.1.1756 *Swiftsure* (68); 30.6.1756 *Invincible* (74); 11.11.1756 *Namur* (90); 17.12.1756 *Royal George* (100); 27.1.1758-20.8.1759 *Namur* (90); 6.6.1758-27.7.1758 The Siege of Louisbourg; 18.8.1759-19.8.1759 Battle of Lagos Bay; 4.10.1759-11.2.1762 *Namur* (90); 20.11.1759 Battle of Quiberon Bay; 29.3.1761-11.6.1761 Expedition against Belle-Isle; 18.10.1770 **Rear Admiral of the White**; 24.10.1770 **Rear Admiral of the Red**; 31.3.1775 **Vice Admiral of the Blue**; 7.12.1775 **Vice Admiral of the White**; 29.1.1778 **Vice Admiral of the Red**; 26.3.1778 CinC — The Downs; 29.4.1778 *Buffalo* (50); 26.9.1780 **Admiral of the Blue**.

BUCKNALL, JOSEPH

Dates: c.1717 Born; 1773 Died; 25.6.1773 Will Probate.

Family: Brother James.

Service: 29.8.1734 Mid *Montagu* (60); 10.10.1735 Ord. *Royal Oak* (70); 22.9.1736 Able *Rippon* (60); 11.10.1737 Able *Alderney* (8) Bomb Vessel; 4.10.1738 Mid *Plymouth* (60); 6.10.1741 Passed; **Lieutenant**; 29.1.1742/43 L. *Scipio* (8) Fireship; 15.2.1742/43 L. *Shark* (8) Sloop; 14.3.1742/43-30.3.1743 L. *Portsmouth* (24) Storeship; 31.5.1743[MED 12.9.1745]-18.3.1743/44 3L *Torbay* (80); 11.2.1743/44-12.2.1743/44 Battle of Toulon; 22.1.1744/45[MED 21.6.1745]-12.6.1745[P] 2L *Newcastle* (50); 7.5.1755-20.5.1755 2L *Trident* (64); 20.5.1755-5.8.1755 3L *Trident* (64); 26.4.1757 1L *Invincible* (74); 8.1757-10.1757 Louisbourg Expedition; 6.2.1758-19.2.1758[W] 1L *Invincible* (74).

BUCKNER, CHARLES

Dates: 1.1736 Born Sussex; 12.1.1735/36 Baptised Boxgrove, Sussex; c.2.1811 Buried St Giles in The Fields, Camden, London; 11.3.1811 Will Probate.

Family: Father Richard Buckner (1699-1777); Mother Mary Saunders (1700-1772); Wife Mary Stepney married 18.8.1763; Wife Anne Frewen (1743-1825) married 30.5.1798; Son Charles (1770-?); Daughter Mary (1771-?); Son Richard (1773-?).

Service: 18.6.1750 Capt Serv *Humber* (44); 10.11.1750 Able *Humber* (44); 11.12.1751 Able *Centurion* (50); 26.1.1753 Mid *Centurion* (50); 8.5.1753 Mid *Deptford* (50); 20.5.1756 Battle of Minorca; **Lieutenant**; 6.6.1756 6L *Ramillies* (90); 26.8.1756 Passed; 30.3.1757 4L *Lancaster* (66); 28.2.1758[NA 5.12.1758] 3L *Lancaster* (66); 1.7.1758[NA 5.12.1758] 2L *Lancaster* (66); 6.7.1759[BLI 20.11.1759] 1L *Cambridge* (80); 12.12.1759 2L *Dublin* (74); **Commander**; 26.9.1761-22.10.1762 *Virgin* (12) Sloop; 7.1.1762-10.2.1762 Operations against Martinique; 22.12.1762-4.7.1763 *Savage* (8) Sloop; **Captain**; 17.2.1766-16.8.1766 *Lark* (32); 16.8.1766[BLI 23.12.1767]-3.8.1768

Chatham (50); 25.3.1780 *Prothee* (64); 12.4.1782 Battle of the Saintes; 10.5.1782-6.6.1783[P] *Royal Oak* (74); 22.12.1786-1792 *William and Mary* (10) Yacht; 1.2.1793 **Rear Admiral of the Blue**; 12.4.1794 **Rear Admiral of the White**; 4.7.1794 **Vice Admiral of the Blue**; 2.3.1795-1797 CinC — River Medway and The Nore; 1.6.1795 **Vice Admiral of the White**; 8.1795-7.1797 *Sandwich* (90); 14.2.1799 **Admiral of the Blue**; 9.11.1805 **Admiral of the White**; 28.4.1808 **Admiral of the Red.**

BUCKWORTH, FRANCIS

Dates: c.1734 Born; c.8.1759 Died; 2.11.1759 Will Probate.
Family:
Service: 30.3.1753 Capt Serv *Centurion* (50); 7.8.1753 Mid *Wager* (24); 20.3.1753/54 Able *Ferret* (14) Sloop; 5.7.1754 Mid *Fougueux* (64); 17.9.1754 Mid *Jason* (44); 27.11.1755 Mid *Edinburgh* (64); 18.1.1757 Able *Medway* (60); 6.7.1757-26.1.1758 Mid *Medway* (60); 5.9.1757-6.10.1757 Raid on Rochefort; 26.1.1758 Passed; **Lieutenant**; 27.10.1758 L. *Pluto* (8) Fireship; 30.1.1759-8.1759† 3L *Edgar* (60).

BUDWORTH, WILLIAM

Dates:
Family:
Service: 1754-1756 HEIC Service; 24.1.1756 Able *Ambuscade* (40); 9.3.1755/56 Mid *Ambuscade* (40); 14.7.1758 Mate *Ambuscade* (40); 28.9.1758 Mid *Ambuscade* (40); 8.11.1758-1.4.1761 Mate *Ambuscade* (40); 1.4.1761 Passed; **Lieutenant**; 9.8.1762-6.4.1763 L. *Sardoine* (14) Sloop; 24.10.1775 2L *Fox* (28); 7.6.1777 Action of 7th June 1777; 7.4.1778-19.4.1779 1L *Romney* (50); 8.6.1779-7.12.1779 2L *Egmont* (74); 25.3.1780-23.11.1781 1L *Prothee* (64).

BULTEELE, JAMES

Dates: 1764 Died.
Family:
Service: **Lieutenant**; 2.8.1748[(MED 8.11.1748)]-18.11.1748[P] 4L *Royal Oak* (70); 30.1.1753 3L *Yarmouth* (64); 8.11.1756-17.1.1757 2L *Yarmouth* (64); 17.1.1757-15.2.1757 4L *Yarmouth* (64); 17.2.1757 3L *Yarmouth* (64); 23.2.1757-25.3.1758 2L *Yarmouth* (64); 25.3.1758-25.3.1761[P] 2L *Cumberland* (66); 29.4.1758 Battle of Cuddalore; 3.8.1758 Battle of Negapatam; 10.9.1759 Battle of Pondicherry.

BUNYAN, WILLIAM

Dates: c.1723 Born; 24.10.1777 Died Westminster; 20.12.1777 Will Probate.
Family:
Service: 27.1.1733/34 Bosun Serv *Somerset* (80); 24.12.1734 Bosun Serv *Nottingham* (60); 1.1.1735/36 Bosun Serv *Somerset* (80); 15.3.1737/38 Bosun Serv *Grafton* (70); 9.2.1739/40 Able *Grafton* (70); 22.6.1740-25.9.1744[P] Mid *Grafton* (70); 11.1.1744/45 Passed; **Lieutenant**; 1.1.1748/49[(EI 10.5.1750)]-14.5.1750[P] 3L *York* (60); 28.1.1755 2L *Torbay* (74); 5.4.1755 L. *Gibraltar* (20); 9.11.1756 2L *Sunderland* (60); 2.8.1757[(NA 19.11.1757)]-25.8.1758 1L *Nottingham* (60); 6.6.1758-27.7.1758 The Siege of Louisbourg.

BURDON, GEORGE

Dates: 24.4.1778 Died; 15.8.1778 Will Probate.
Family: Wife Rachael Hannah; Daughter Maria Ann; Daughter Susanna; Son George; Daughter Sophia.

Service: **Lieutenant**; 12.5.1756-16.11.1757 L. *Flamborough* (20); **Commander**; 24.8.1762-17.5.1763[P] *Jamaica* (10) Sloop; 28.3.1777-24.4.1778 *Drake* (14) Sloop.

BURFORD, SAMUEL

Dates: c.1735 Born; 1774 Died; 22.12.1774 Will Probate.
Family:
Service: 1752-1756 HEIC Service; 2.2.1756 Able *Wolf* (8) Sloop; 7.4.1756 Mid *Weymouth* (60); 4.2.1757 Mate *Duke* (90); 5.6.1758-12.6.1758 Raid on Saint-Malo; 25.3.1759-11.4.1759 Supnum *Royal Anne* (100); 11.4.1759 Passed; **Lieutenant**; 2.5.1759 4L *Belliqueux* (64); 2.10.1761-23.11.1761 2L *Belliqueux* (64).

BURNABY, SIR WILLIAM (1ST BARONET BURNABY OF BROUGHTON HALL)

Dates: 1710 Born; 9.4.1754 Knight Bachelor; 31.10.1767 1st Baronet Burnaby of Broughton Hall; 1776 Died;
Family: Father John Burnaby (d.c.1718); Mother Clara Wood; Wife Mrs. Margaret Donovan (d.1757); Wife Grace Ottley (c.1739-1823) married 6.10.1757; Son Sir William Chaloner (2nd Baronet Burnaby of Broughton Hall), RN (1746-1794); Son Edward Augustus Caesar, RN.
Service: 10.7.1722 Vol-p-O *Torbay* (80); 18.1.1722/23 Vol-p-O *Nonsuch* (50); 23.4.1723 Able *Nonsuch* (50); 18.10.1724 MidO *Superb* (60); 19.4.1725 Mid *Argyll* (50); 20.3.1726/27 Passed; **Lieutenant**; 16.12.1732[(25.7.1734)] L. *Deal Castle* (20); 2.3.1733/34[(18.11.1735)]-3.11.1735[P] 2L *Rupert* (60); 9.12.1737-7.4.1739 2L *Falmouth* (50); 10.1.1740/41 3L *Duke* (90); **Commander**; 7.9.1741-8.10.1742 *Thunder* (8) Bomb Vessel; **Captain**; 9.12.1742[(28.3.1744)] *Lark Hulk*; 1.5.1743[(22.11.1745)] *Thunder* (8) Bomb Vessel; 19.7.1743[(28.3.1744)] *Lichfield* (50); 11.11.1743[(23.7.1745)]-13.9.1745 *Cumberland* (80); 1755-1756 High Sheriff for Oxfordshire; 15.10.1755 *Jersey* (60); 20.8.1756-29.11.1756 *Hampton Court* (64); 3.8.1757-18.12.1760[P] *Royal Anne* (100); 5.9.1757-6.10.1757 Raid on Rochefort; 5.6.1758-12.6.1758 Raid on Saint-Malo; 21.10.1762 **Rear Admiral of the Red**; 14.7.1763-25.11.1766 CinC — Jamaica; 19.7.1763-25.11.1766 *Dreadnought* (60); 18.10.1770 **Vice Admiral of the White**; 24.10.1770 **Vice Admiral of the Red**.

BURNETT, JAMES

Dates: c.1733 Born; 1779 Died; 9.9.1779 Will Probate.
Family: Wife Ann Hobbs married 10.12.1750.
Service: 22.8.1747 Able *Launceston* (44); 5.11.1748 Able *Seahorse* (20); 13.11.1749 Able *Triton* (20); 14.6.1750-2.7.1755 Mate *Triton* (20); 2.7.1755 Passed; **Lieutenant**; 12.3.1757[(JAM 12.7.1758)] 3L *Humber* (44); 15.7.1757[(JAM 26.12.1758)] L. *Wager* (24); 25.8.1758[(JAM 14.2.1759)]-4.3.1759[P] 3L *Eagle* (60); 26.3.1759 2L *Mars* (74); 20.11.1759 Battle of Quiberon Bay; 17.11.1760 6L *Royal George* (100); 27.7.1761 4L *Royal George* (100); 19.5.1762-18.12.1762[P] 3L *Royal George* (100).

BURNETT, THOMAS

Dates: 1724 Born; 4.6.1783 Died; 27.6.1783 Will Probate.
Family: Wife Mary; Daughter Ann (b.1765); Sister Sarah.
Service: 4.10.1736 Able *Tartar* (20); 8.12.1738-19.1.1738/39 Able *Strafford* (60); 19.1.1738/39 Able *Tartar* (20); 4.1740-5.7.1740 Attack on St. Augustine; 23.1.1741/42 Mid *Chatham* (50); 3.3.1741/42 Passed; 11.3.1742/43 Supnum *Namur* (90); 25.3.1743 Mid *Chatham* (50); **Lieutenant**; 20.8.1744[(17.5.1746)] 4L *Cambridge* (80); 27.7.1745[(17.5.1746)]-8.2.1745/46 2L *Worcester* (58); 19.3.1747/48-29.7.1748[P] 2L *Berwick* (70); 2.3.1753-11.2.1755 1L *Penzance* (44); 13.2.1756 1L *Royal George* (100); **Commander**; 12.5.1756 *Happy* (8) Sloop; **Captain**; 5.5.1757 *Cambridge* (80); 16.1.1759-19.1.1759 Attack on Martinique; 20.1.1759-1.5.1759 Capture of Guadeloupe;

5.3.1760 *Rochester* (50); 7.1.1762-10.2.1762 Operations against Martinique; 1.5.1762[(EI 17.3.1763)]-29.11.1762[F] *Marlborough* (68); 6.6.1762-13.8.1762 Operations against Havana; 20.10.1770-21.10.1773 *Boyne* (68); 7.6.1779-24.9.1781 *Prudent* (64); 16.3.1781 Battle of Cape Henry; 1.10.1781-10.5.1782 *Royal Oak* (74); 12.4.1782 Battle of the Saintes; 5.1782 Resigned.

BURNETT, WILLIAM

Dates: c.1741 Born.
Family:
Service: 1.9.1755 Capt Serv *Triton* (20); 25.5.1757-28.4.1758[B] Able *Triton* (20); 7.1.1759 Able *Yarmouth* (64); 10.9.1759 Battle of Pondicherry; 21.11.1759-19.12.1760[P] Mid *Yarmouth* (64); 22.1.1761 Mid *Charlotte* (8) Yacht; 14.7.1761 Mid *Mars* (74); 9.1.1762 Mid *Orford* (68); 25.1.1762 Passed; **Lieutenant**; 5.5.1762 3L *Rippon* (60); 31.7.1762-13.3.1763[P] 2L *Rippon* (60); 20.12.1763-5.1.1767 3L *Dorsetshire* (68).

BURR, DANIEL

Dates: c.1732 Born; 13.5.1802 Died Pembrokeshire; 22.5.1802 Will Probate.
Family:
Service: 7.1.1748/49 Capt Serv *Anson* (60); 25.10.1749 Ord. *Centurion* (50); 10.6.1750 Able *Centurion* (50); 8.6.1751 Mid *Centurion* (50); 17.9.1753 Able *Centurion* (50); 31.12.1753 Mid *Saint Albans* (60); 21.4.1755 Passed; **Lieutenant**; 19.2.1756 L. *Wager* HEIC; 15.7.1757[(JAM 1.4.1758)]-5.1.1758[P] 3L *Humber* (44); 11.4.1758-21.5.1759[P] 3L *Fougueux* (64); 29.12.1758 Capture of Goree; 29.3.1762-22.6.1763[P] 1L *Unicorn* (28); 14.3.1764-14.5.1766 1L *Guernsey* (50); 21.2.1795 **Superannuated Commander**.

BURR, JOHN

Dates: c.1725 Born; 1776 Died; 18.4.1778 Will Probate.
Family: Wife Jane; Brother William, RN (1718-1769).
Service: 15.2.1740/41 Capt Serv *Barfleur* (90); 10.11.1741 Able *Hastings* (44); 21.5.1745 Mid *Scarborough* (20); 10.6.1745 Mid *Jamaica* (10) Sloop; 27.12.1746 Mid *Royal George* (100); 10.7.1747 Passed; **Lieutenant**; 23.6.1758[(JAM 11.4.1760)] 3L *Saint Albans* (60); 18.8.1759-19.8.1759 Battle of Lagos Bay; 30.11.1759[(JAM 11.4.1760)]-31.5.1760[P] 2L *Saint Albans* (60); 7.7.1760-3.4.1763[P] L. *Otter* (14) Sloop; 26.5.1766 1L *Dragon* (74); 24.9.1766 2L *Dragon* (74); 21.3.1769 L. *Merlin* (18) Frigate; **Commander**; 13.9.1769-3.9.1773[P] *Hound* (14) Sloop; 1771-1772 Gov. of Falkland Islands; **Captain**; 15.10.1773 *Hussar* (28); 6.10.1775-16.1.1777 *Milford* (28); 6.6.1776 Milford vs Yankee Hero.

BURR, WILLIAM

Dates: c.1718 Born; 1769 Died.
Family: Son Richard; Brother John, RN (1725-1776).
Service: 16.8.1733 Ord. *Namur* (90); 9.4.1734 Ord. *Berwick* (70); 27.4.1737 Able *Gloucester* (50); 6.10.1738 Mid *Gloucester* (50); 9.5.1740 Mid *Prince Frederick* (70); 20.11.1740 Passed; **Lieutenant**; 21.2.1740/41 3L *Hastings* (44); 17.5.1742-26.10.1742 2L *Hastings* (44); 1.3.1742/43-6.11.1748[P] 2L *Antelope* (50); 19.2.1755 2L *Royal George* (100); 9.1755 LCmdr *Elizabeth* Hired Tender; 17.1.1756 2L *Royal Anne* (100); 19.4.1757-10.8.1757 1L *Royal Anne* (100).

BURRISH, GEORGE

Dates: 1770 Died; 20.7.1770 Will Probate.
Family:
Service: 27.1.1718/19 Vol-p-O *Assistance* (54); 28.9.1719 Vol-p-O *Gloucester* (54); 1.10.1720 MidO *Faversham* (42); 18.6.1721 Mid *Faversham* (42); 23.2.1722/23 Able *Lynn* (32); 10.3.1722/23 Mid *Lynn* (32); 21.3.1722/23-8.3.1723/24 ActL *Lynn* (42); 8.3.1724/25 Passed; **Lieutenant**; 25.1.1725/26-21.2.1727/28 3L *Swallow* (50); 22.2.1727/28[(20.6.1728)]-8.2.1728/29 3L *Advice* (54); 9.2.1728/29-21.2.1728/29 3L *Kent* (70); 22.2.1728/29-1.4.1729 4L *Princess Amelia* (80); 2.4.1729-25.5.1730 3L *Berwick* (70); 26.5.1730-15.9.1731[P] 2L *Enterprise* (42); **Captain**; 7.5.1733-13.12.1740[P] *Blandford* (20); 10.1.1740/41 *Dover* (44); 28.1.1742/43-12.4.1745 *Dorsetshire* (80); 11.2.1743/44-12.2.1743/44 Battle of Toulon; 9.10.1745 Dismissed.

BURROWS, JOHN

Dates: c.1734 Born; bef.1777 Died.
Family:
Service: 1750-1755 Merchant Service; 3.4.1755 Mid *Buckingham* (68); 20.5.1756 Battle of Minorca; 13.9.1756 Mid *Saint George* (90); 22.12.1756-1.8.1757 Mid *Torbay* (74); 1.8.1757 Passed; **Lieutenant**; 27.10.1758 4L *Terrible* (74); 30.4.1760-2.6.1760 2L *Milford* (28); 22.7.1760-7.6.1761 4L *Stirling Castle* (64); 3.6.1761-7.6.1761 Occupation of Dominica.

BURROWS, JOHN

Dates: 1738 Born; 25.6.1818 Died Oreston, Plymouth; 25.9.1818 Will Probate.
Family:
Service: 31.10.1754 Able *Peregrine* (20) Sloop; 27.11.1755 Able *Barrington* Tender; 9.3.1757/58 Able *Venus* (36); 13.9.1758-2.9.1761 Mid *Venus* (36); 20.11.1759 Battle of Quiberon Bay; 2.9.1760 Passed; **Lieutenant**; 24.5.1762 6L *Duke* (90); 14.6.1762-19.2.1763[P] 5L *Duke* (90); 3.11.1770 5L *Fame* (74); 4.9.1771 4L *Saint Albans* (64); 27.7.1772 3L *Saint Albans* (64); 9.9.1773 3L *Ardent* (64); 21.9.1773-6.9.1774 2L *Ardent* (64); 1.1.1777 1L *Somerset* (68); 3.9.1777 LCmdr *Trelandvean* Hired Tender; 29.6.1778-10.1779 LCmdr *Aurora* Hired Tender; 12.1792-5.12.1800[P] LCmdr *Myrmidon* (22).

BURROWS, RICHARD

Dates: c.1722 Born; 1763 Died; 7.6.1763 Will Probate.
Family: Wife Edy.
Service: 15.4.1740 Able *Princess Amelia* (80); 4.11.1740 Able *Romney* (50); 25.2.1742/43 Mid *Saint George* (90); 29.7.1746 Passed; **Lieutenant**; 5.11.1746-26.1.1746/47[C] L. *Hornet* (10) Sloop; 2.11.1747-12.8.1748[P] 3L *Falkland* (50); 22.12.1748 3L *Saint Albans* (60); 12.11.1751 2L *Saint Albans* (60); 5.8.1752 1L *Saint Albans* (60); 4.10.1752-20.11.1752[P] 3L *Mars* (64); 25.1.1753-2.3.1753 1L *Penzance* (44); 2.3.1753-13.2.1755 2L *Penzance* (44); 26.5.1757-28.4.1758 5L *Duke* (90); 1758 LCmdr *Devonshire* Hired Tender.

BURSLEM, FRANCIS

Dates: 1.1723 Born Packington, Leicestershire; 15.1.1723 Baptised; 11.12.1801 Died Youghal, Ireland; 21.5.1802 Will Probate.
Family: Father James Burslem (Bef 1695-1765); Mother Elizabeth Godolphin (1688-1767); Wife Mary (d.1815); Daughter Elizabeth (c.1776-1846); Son James Godolphin (c.1780-1861); Son Thomas (c.1779-c.1826); Daughter Frances (c.1780-?); Daughter Margaret (c.1781-?).

Service: 26.6.1735 Scholar *Royal Naval Academy*; 24.10.1738 Vol-p-O *Ipswich* (70); 20.11.1740 Mid *Ipswich* (70); 2.3.1742/43 Sinking of the San Isidoro; 5.5.1743 Passed; **Lieutenant**; 17.9.1743 L. *Scipio* (8) Fireship; 27.3.1744 4L *Princess Amelia* (80); 26.5.1744 2L *Lark* (44); 18.6.1746-20.4.1749[P] 1L *Lynn* (44); 23.1.1753 L. *Raven* (10) Sloop; 4.12.1753 L. *Rye* (20); 13.5.1755 1L *Ambuscade* (40); 24.1.1756 1L *Harwich* (50); 5.8.1756 4L *Invincible* (74); 11.11.1756 3L *Invincible* (74); 15.11.1756 2L *Invincible* (74); 17.12.1756 2L *Royal George* (100); 6.5.1757 1L *Royal George* (100); **Commander**; 24.6.1757-27.9.1758 *Racehorse* (18) Sloop; 18.10.1758 *Badger* (10) Sloop; **Captain**; 4.10.1759-13.10.1760 *Coventry* (28); 20.11.1759 Battle of Quiberon Bay.

BURSTALL, JOHN

Dates: c.1736 Born; 21.10.1736 Baptised Kingston upon Hull; c.2.1807 Died Yorkshire; 8.2.1807 Buried Hedon, York; 3.3.1807 Will Probate.
Family: Father William Burstall; Mother Catherine Thompson(1709–1785); Wife Elizabeth (1744-?) married c.1764; Wife Lydia Teesdale (1749-1822); Son John (1765–1831); Daughter Elizabeth [Burton] (1767–); Son William (1769–1771); Son William (1771–1780); Son Samuel (1772–1775); Daughter Ann (1773–1777); Son Samuel (1776–1841); Daughter Ann (1778–1857); Daughter Kitty [Stubbing] (1775–1808); Brother William, RN (1730-1813).
Service: 6.6.1756 Able *Prince George* (80); 23.6.1756 Mid *Prince George* (80); 8.9.1756 Able *Prince* (90); 13.11.1756 Able *Culloden* (74); 6.1.1757 Mid *Culloden* (74); 5.4.1757 Action of April 5 1757; 25.5.1757 Mid *Saint George* (90); 6.6.1758 Able *Montagu* (60); 25.7.1758 Able *Ramillies* (90); 2.3.1758/59 Able *Neptune* (90); 25.4.1759-9.1.1760 Mid *Neptune* (90); 9.1.1760 Passed; **Lieutenant**; 2.4.1760-17.3.1762 4L *Devonshire* (70); 7.1.1762-10.2.1762 Operations against Martinique; 1.4.1762[(BLI 19.5.1763)]-30.5.1763[P] 1L *Repulse* (32); 1807 **Superannuated Lieutenant.**

BURSTALL, WILLIAM

Dates: c.1730 Born Kingston upon Hull; 15.10.1730 Baptised Holy Trinity, Kingston upon Hull; 24.3.1813 Died Acomb, Yorkshire; 22.4.1813 Will Probate.
Family: Father William Burstall; Mother Catherine Thompson(1709–1785); Wife Mary Collinson(d.1787) married 21.8.1764; Brother John, RN (1736-1807).
Service: 4.7.1755 Mid *Prince* (90); 8.1.1756 Mate *Prince* (90); 9.9.1756 Able *Prince George* (80); 28.9.1756 Mid *Prince George* (80); 7.1.1757 Mate *Prince* (90); 8.3.1756/57 Mate *Culloden* (74); 5.4.1757 Action of April 5 1757; 25.9.1757-6.10.1758 Mate *Saint George* (90); 6.10.1758 Passed; **Lieutenant**; 27.10.1758 2L *Levant* (28); 2.5.1759-2.9.1763[P] 1L *Levant* (28); 7.1.1762-10.2.1762 Operations against Martinique; 6.4.1765-6.1769 LCmdr *Morning Star* (4) Cutter; 16.10.1770 2L *Pallas* (36); 3.11.1770-25.3.1771 1L *Pallas* (36); 9.1780 LCmdr *Charming Betsey* (6) Hired Tender; 5.11.1800 **Superannuated Commander.**

BURTON, JOHN

Dates: c.1716 Born; 1757 Died; 19.2.1757 Buried Boughton Aluph, Kent; 14.4.1757 Will Probate.
Family: Wife Judith Thomas married 16.1.1749.
Service: 10.1.1738/39 Able *Princess Caroline* (80); 7.1.1739/40 Able *Rippon* (60); 14.12.1740-26.2.1741/42[P] Able *Alderney* (8) Bomb Vessel; 4.3.1740/41-5.1741 Operations against Cartagena; 7.1741-10.1741 Operations against Santiago; 13.4.1742 Cox *Falkland* (50); 15.5.1743 Mid *Falkland* (50); 5.3.1743/44 Able *Falkland* (50); 24.6.1744 Able *Cambridge* (80); 19.7.1744 Mid *Cambridge* (80); 6.12.1744 Mate *Neptune* (90); 24.3.1744/45 Mate *Swift* (8)

Sloop; 21.5.1745 Mid *Terrible* (6) Bomb Vessel; 31.7.1745-22.4.1746[P] Mate *Trelawney* (14) Armed Storeship; 15.9.1747 Passed; **Lieutenant**; 16.7.1749[(EI 18.5.1750)] L. *Swallow* (14) Sloop; 19.9.1749[(EI 18.5.1750)]-14.5.1750[P] 3L *Chester* (50); 23.10.1754 3L *Anson* (60); 13.11.1754-24.4.1755 3L *Defiance* (60).

BUTCHART, JOHN

Dates: 1796 Died; 26.8.1796 Will Probate.
Family: Wife Janet Galletry married 14.6.1784.
Service: **Lieutenant**; 3.9.1760[(EI 6.12.1763)]-2.6.1761 4L *America* (60); 14.3.1769 2L *Carysfort* (28); 11.1.1770 1L *Carysfort* (28); 29.1.1770-27.2.1772[P] 1L *Aeolus* (32); 14.10.1773 2L *Thames* (32); 31.5.1774-4.7.1775[P] 1L *Thames* (32); 20.6.1775 1L *Arethusa* (32); 18.4.1778 4L *Albion* (74); 4.5.1778 4L *Princess Royal* (98); **Commander**; 1.12.1778[(NA 1.2.1779)]-24.3.1779 *Star* (10) Brig; 24.3.1779[(NA 6.7.1780)] *Tobago* (16) Sloop; **Captain**; 15.6.1779[(NA 2.11.1779)] *Fame* (74); 6.7.1779 Battle of Grenada; 31.5.1781-20.3.1783 *Argo* (44); 17.2.1783 Action of 1783-02-17.

BUTLER, DANIEL

Dates: c.1731 Born.
Family:
Service: 25.2.1743/44 Capt Serv *Medway* Receiving Ship; 25.6.1746 1st Battle of Negapatam; 29.2.1747/48-19.10.1748[P] Mid *Medway* (60); 25.3.1751 Ord. *Pearl* (44); 5.3.1751/52 Able *Wager* (24); 19.8.1752 Cpl *Wager* (24); 31.7.1753 Mid *Wager* (24); 6.8.1755 Passed; **Lieutenant**; 22.3.1757 L. *Firedrake* (10) Bomb Vessel; 5.9.1757-6.10.1757 Raid on Rochefort; 21.10.1757-16.1.1759 3L *Prince Edward* (44); 29.12.1758 Capture of Goree; 16.7.1767-13.9.1768[D] L. *Bonetta* (10) Sloop; 13.9.1768 Dismissed; 1782-27.11.1783[P] LCmdr *Union* Hired Tender.

BUTLER, JACOB

Dates: c.1731 Born; 1770 Died; 20.4.1770 Will Probate.
Family: Father Thomas Butler; Mother Elizabeth.
Service: 1754-1755 Merchant Service; 28.11.1755 Mid *Prince Edward* (44); 11.12.1758 Able *Duke* (90); 15.1.1759 Able *Vengeance* (28); 23.9.1759 Able *Duke* (90); 13.10.1759 Mid *Duke* (90); 20.11.1759 Battle of Quiberon Bay; 4.2.1761 Passed; **Lieutenant**; 31.8.1762-23.2.1763[P] L. *Vesuvius* (8) Fireship.

BUTLER, JAMES

Dates: c.1718 Born; 1759 Died; 16.5.1759 Will Probate.
Family: Wife Mary Viney.
Service: 7.5.1735 Able *Devonshire* (80); 26.2.1735/36 Capt Serv *Falkland* (50); 1.9.1736 Able *Falkland* (50); 25.6.1738 Able *Pembroke* (60); 9.9.1738 Able *Dursley Galley* (20); 12.11.1738 Mate *Dursley Galley* (20); 3.8.1740 Mid *Dursley Galley* (20); 4.11.1740 Mid *Garland* (20); 23.8.1741 Able *Port Mahon* (20); 6.10.1741 Passed; **Lieutenant**; 25.2.1741/42 L. *Spy* (8) Sloop; 7.4.1742-14.5.1744 3L *Leopard* (50); 12.6.1744 2L *Princess Mary* (60); 14.10.1744-24.10.1745 3L *Prince Frederick* (70); **Commander**; 11.11.1746-11.5.1748 *Vulture* (10) Sloop; 9.4.1748 Battle of Santiago de Cuba; **Captain**; 27.2.1753-3.4.1753 *Mermaid* (24).

BYAM, EDWARD

Dates: 19.9.1782 Died.
Family:
Service: **Lieutenant**; 26.10.1762[(BLI 4.6.1763)]-30.10.1762[P] L. *Guadaloupe* Sloop; 2.12.1763-17.12.1764 3L *Cornwall* (74); 21.11.1770-8.12.1772 4L *Intrepid* (64); 21.8.1778 LCmdr *Charming Molly* Hired Tender; 1.12.1778-1779 LCmdr *Charming Betsey* (6) Hired Tender; 1780-2.1780 LCmdr *Sweepstakes* Hired Tender; 15.4.1780 LCmdr *Repulse* (12) Cutter; 30.11.1781-19.9.1782[†] L. *Ville de Paris* (104).

BYNG, HENRY

Dates: c.1721 Born; 1812 Died; 14.8.1812 Will Probate.
Family: Wife Elizabeth Nixon married 2.4.1745; Daughter Penelope Banks (1750-?).
Service: 4.6.1736 Able *Torrington* (40); 28.6.1740 Able *Hampton Court* (70); 13.12.1740 Mid *Hampton Court* (70); 2.6.1741 Mid *Sandwich* (90); 7.8.1741 Mate *Rupert's Prize* (8); 3.3.1742/43 Passed; **Lieutenant**; 17.4.1744-4.10.1744 L. *Sheerness* (20); 19.12.1744-7.1.1744/45 6L *Duke* (90); 28.2.1745/46 2L *Canterbury* (60); 15.10.1746[(NA 11.4.1747)]-26.2.1746/47[P] 2L *Kingston* (60); 10.2.1755-15.2.1757 L. *Hound* (14) Sloop; 27.8.1759 6L *Royal Anne* (100); 11.1.1760-18.12.1760[P] 5L *Royal Anne* (100); 21.9.1796 **Superannuated Commander.**

BYNG, THE HON. JOHN

Dates: 10.1704 Born Southhill, Bedfordshire; 10.1704 Honourable; 14.3.1757 Died *Monarch*;
Family: Father George Byng (1st Viscount Torrington of Devon), RN (1664-1733); Mother Margaret Master (1670–1756); Brother Hon. Pattee, MP (1699-1747); Brother The Hon. Robert (1703-1740);
Service: 8.3.1717/18-29.2.1719/20[P] Mid *Superb* (64); 11.8.1718 Battle of Cape Passaro; 29.2.1719/20 Mid *Dover* (40); 31.12.1722 Passed; **Lieutenant**; 9.4.1723-20.2.1723/24 L. *Solebay* (42); 9.4.1724 2L *Superb* (64); 19.11.1725-30.3.1726 3L *Superb* (64); 19.4.1726-27.5.1727 4L *Burford* (70); **Captain**; 8.8.1727 *Gibraltar* (20); 29.7.1728 *Princess Louisa* (40); 7.7.1730-31.5.1735[P] *Falmouth* (50); 16.5.1738 *Augusta* (60); 13.4.1739 *Portland* (50); 30.7.1739 *Sunderland* (60); 20.2.1741/42 *Sutherland* (50); 16.6.1742 Gov. of Newfoundland; 4.4.1743 *Captain* (70); 28.10.1743-15.6.1744 *Saint George* (90); 29.6.1744-6.11.1744 *Winchester* (50); 9.8.1745 **Rear Admiral of the Blue**; 9.1745-1746 *Kinsale* (44); 1746-7.1746 *Princess Caroline* (80); 9.1.1745/46-11.2.1745/46 CinC — North Sea; 1747 *Superb* (60); 15.7.1747 **Vice Admiral of the Blue**; 9.1747 *Boyne* (80); 15.9.1747-8.8.1748 CinC — The Mediterranean Sea; 10.1747 *Princess* (70); 12.5.1748 **Vice Admiral of the Red**; 23.1.1750/51-14.3.1757 M.P. for Rochester; 28.9.1755-7.1756 *Ramillies* (90); 10.1755-11.1755 CinC — English Channel; 17.3.1756 **Admiral of the Blue**; 2.4.1756-3.7.1756 CinC — The Mediterranean Sea; 20.5.1756 Battle of Minorca.

BYRON, JOHN

Dates: 8.11.1723 Born; 10.4.1786 Died London.
Family: Father William Byron, 4th Baron (1669-1736); Mother Frances Berkeley; Wife Sophia Trevanion married 8.9.1748; Son George Anson, RN (d.1793); Brother Lord William (5th Baron Byron), RN (1722-1798).
Service: **Lieutenant**; 22.3.1745/46 6L *Saint George* (90); **Commander**; 21.4.1746-10.11.1746 *Vulture* (10) Sloop; **Captain**; 30.12.1746 *Siren* (20); 23.10.1747-9.8.1748[P] *Falkland* (50); 22.12.1748-26.8.1752 *Saint Albans* (60); 16.1.1753 *Augusta* (60); 17.10.1753 *Vanguard* (68); 5.4.1757 *America* (60); 5.9.1757-6.10.1757 Raid on Rochefort; 16.2.1759-29.1.1763[P] *Fame*

(74); 29.3.1761-11.6.1761 Expedition against Belle-Isle; 26.3.1764 *Dolphin* (24); 18.6.1764 CinC — East Indies; 14.2.1769 CinC — Newfoundland; 14.2.1769-19.2.1771[P] Commodore *Antelope* (50); 8.1.1771-14.2.1772 Commodore *Panther* (60); 31.3.1775 **Rear Admiral of the Blue**; 28.4.1777 **Rear Admiral of the White**; 23.1.1778 **Rear Admiral of the Red**; 29.1.1778 **Vice Admiral of the Blue**; 4.5.1778-1.1780 *Princess Royal* (98); 6.11.1778-1779 CinC — North America; 6.7.1779 Battle of Grenada; 26.9.1780 **Vice Admiral of the White.**

BYRON, LORD WILLIAM (5TH BARON BYRON)

Dates: 5.11.1722 Born; 8.8.1736 5th Baron Byron; 19.5.1798 Died.

Family: Father William Byron, 4th Baron (1669-1736); Mother Frances Berkeley; Wife Elizabeth Shaw married 28.3.1747; Brother John, RN (1723-1786).

Service: 17.11.1733 Ord. *Dorsetshire* (80); 4.1.1733/34 Ord. *Norfolk* (80); 22.11.1735 Able *Greyhound* (20); 19.1.1735/36 Able *Lyme* (20); 3.11.1736 Mid *Falkland* (50); 18.3.1737/38 Able *Superb* (60); 11.4.1738 Able *Norwich* (50); 1.11.1738 Mid *Ruby* (54); 3.3.1738/39 Mid *Assistance* (50); 14.9.1739 Mid *Oxford* (50); 19.2.1739/40 Mid *Dover* (44); 26.3.1740 Passed; **Lieutenant**; 27.3.1741 3L *Dartmouth* (50); 12.6.1741 6L *Victory* (100); 21.9.1741 4L *Victory* (100); 16.3.1741/42 3L *Victory* (100); 13.7.1742-7.2.1743/44 2L *Victory* (100).

Service Records C

CAESAR, CHARLES

Dates: c.1726 Born; 1782 Died King's Lynn; 2.1782 Will Probate.
Family:
Service: 27.9.1748 Able *Hampshire* (50); 13.5.1750 Mid *Revenge* (70); 14.11.1753 Able *Monarch* (74); 23.4.1754 Mid *Mermaid* (24); 24.5.1754 Mid *Kent* (64); 21.11.1754 Able *Kent* (64); 10.3.1755 Passed; **Lieutenant**; 16.4.1756^(MED 16.2.1757) 3L *Trident* (64); 20.5.1756 Battle of Minorca; 26.2.1757 5L *Prince George* (80); 4.4.1757 4L *Prince George* (80); 29.7.1757 3L *Prince George* (80); 4.8.1757 2L *Dover* (44); 1.2.1758 1L *Dover* (44); 7.11.1759-12.12.1760 1L *Niger* (32); 22.7.1761-2.5.1763 1L *Juno* (32); 3.1.1765-26.5.1766 1L *Dragon* (74); 19.6.1766-18.6.1767 LCmdr *Anson* (6) Cutter; 18.9.1770-27.5.1771^P 1L *Cornwall* (74); 29.6.1771-28.8.1772 2L *Resolution* (74); 18.1.1773-7.4.1774 L. *Ferret* (14) Sloop; 30.5.1776-18.5.1777 2L *Rippon* (60); 1777-1782 Impress Service.

CALDER, PATRICK

Dates: 16.11.1790 Died Yarm, Yorkshire.
Family:
Service: **Lieutenant**; 6.11.1747^(JAM 6.5.1748)-23.7.1748 3L *Norwich* (50); 4.12.1753 L. *Experiment* (24); 6.2.1755 4L *Barfleur* (80); 5.9.1757-6.10.1757 Raid on Rochefort; 13.10.1757-1.12.1758 1L *Trent* (28); 6.6.1758-27.7.1758 The Siege of Louisbourg; 4.9.1764-14.9.1767 LCmdr *Prince George* (4) Cutter.

CALDER, SIR ROBERT KCB, (1ST BARONET OF SOUTHWICK)

Dates: 2.7.1745 Born Park Place, Kent; 3.3.1797 Order of the Bath; 22.8.1798 1st Baronet of Southwick; 1.9.1818 Died Holt, Hampshire.
Family: Father Sir James Calder, 3rd Bt. (1712-1774); Mother Alice Hughes (d.1768); Wife Amelia Mitchell; Brother Thomas (1739-1774); Brother Henry, 4th Bt. (1740-1792).
Service: 4.1.1756 Capt Serv *Princess Royal* (90); 27.4.1757 Capt Serv *Nassau* (64); 8.1757-10.1757 Louisbourg Expedition; 17.5.1758 Mid *Nassau* (64); 26.12.1758 Mid *Nassau* (64); 29.12.1758 Capture of Goree; 18.1.1761 Mid *Superb* (74); 22.6.1761 Mid *Dublin* (74); 7.1.1762-10.2.1762 Operations against Martinique; 2.6.1762 Passed; **Lieutenant**; 31.8.1762-14.2.1763^P L. *Speedwell* (8) Sloop; 25.5.1763 L. *Diligence* (10) Sloop; 6.5.1766 1L *Launceston* (44); 3.11.1766 3L *Launceston* (44); 8.11.1767-16.7.1769 LCmdr *Magdalen* (6) Schooner; 20.12.1776 4L *Terrible* (74); 5.3.1778 3L *Terrible* (74); 2.7.1778 6L *Victory* (100); 27.7.1778 1st Battle of Ushant; 17.9.1778 4L *Victory* (100); 20.11.1778 3L *Victory* (100); 16.2.1779-23.3.1779 2L *Victory* (100); **Commander**; 27.8.1779 *Lightning* (8) Fireship; **Captain**; 27.8.1780-28.8.1780 *Buffalo* (50); 30.4.1782 *Diana* (32); 12.11.1782-16.4.1783^P *Thalia* (36); 1.5.1789-30.9.1789 *Barfleur* (98); 28.9.1790 *Stately* (64); 30.8.1791-7.6.1792 *Duke* (98); 4.11.1793-2.10.1795 *Theseus* (74); 2.10.1795-4.12.1795 1Capt. *Victory* (100); 13.2.1797-30.6.1798 *Ville de Paris* (110); 14.2.1799 **Rear Admiral of the Blue**; 7.1800-1806 *Prince of Wales* (98); 1.1.1801 **Rear**

Admiral of the White; 29.4.1802 **Rear Admiral of the Red**; 6.1803-5.1804 *Princess Royal* (98); 23.4.1804 **Vice Admiral of the Blue**; 22.7.1805 3rd Battle of Cape Finisterre; 19.11.1805 **Vice Admiral of the White**; 28.4.1808 **Vice Admiral of the Red**; 10.6.1810-1813 CinC — Plymouth; 17.7.1810 *Salvador del Mundo* (112); 31.7.1810 **Admiral of the Blue**; 4.12.1813 **Admiral of the White.**

CALDWELL, SIR BENJAMIN

Dates: 31.1.1739 Born Liverpool; 16.5.1820 Knight Bachelor; 1.11.1820 Died Farleigh House, near Basingstoke.
Family: Father Charles Caldwell,; Mother Elizabeth Heywood; Wife Charlotte Osbourne.
Service: 22.8.1753 Scholar *Royal Naval Academy*; 22.11.1756 Able *Isis* (50); 17.12.1756 Able *Royal Naval Academy*; 22.2.1757-20.2.1759 Mid *Isis* (50); 20.2.1759 Able *Namur* (90); 18.3.1759 Mid *Namur* (90); 18.8.1759-19.8.1759 Battle of Lagos Bay; 20.11.1759 Battle of Quiberon Bay; 6.2.1760 Passed; **Lieutenant**; 25.3.1760 3L *Achilles* (60); 29.3.1761-11.6.1761 Expedition against Belle-Isle; **Commander**; 24.5.1762-4.6.1763[P] *Martin* (14) Sloop; 22.6.1763 *Martin* (14) Sloop; **Captain**; 1.4.1765[(BLI 5.6.1766)]-3.11.1766[P] *Milford* (28); 19.4.1768-15.11.1771 *Rose* (20); 22.11.1775-5.7.1779[P] *Emerald* (32); 25.12.1779 *Hannibal* (50); 28.3.1781-10.6.1783[P] *Agamemnon* (64); 12.12.1781 2nd Battle of Ushant; 12.4.1782 Battle of the Saintes; 3.10.1787-13.2.1788[P] *Alcide* (74); 28.8.1790-25.1.1793 *Berwick* (74); 1.2.1793 **Rear Admiral of the White**; c.22.9.1793-c.9.8.1796[P] *Impregnable* (98); 10.1793-8.1794 *Cumberland* (74); 12.4.1794 **Rear Admiral of the Red**; 1.6.1794 Glorious 1st of June; 4.7.1794 **Vice Admiral of the Blue**; 1.1795-1796 *Majestic* (74); 1.6.1795 **Vice Admiral of the Red**; 14.2.1799 **Admiral of the Blue**; 23.4.1804 **Admiral of the White**; 9.11.1805 **Admiral of the Red**.

CALDWELL, CHARLES

Dates: c.1734 Born; bef.6.12.1776 Died.
Family:
Service: c.13.3.1750 Able *Mermaid* (24); c.14.5.1753 Mid *Mermaid* (24); c.2.4.1754 Mid *Terrible* (74); 13.6.1754 Mid *Experiment* (24); 2.7.1755 Passed; **Lieutenant**; 11.11.1756-8.9.1757 L. *Saint Anne* (18) Hired Armed Ship; 3.11.1757-22.7.1760 3L *Stirling Castle* (64); 1.2.1762-22.5.1763[P] 2L *Phoenix* (44); 26.8.1763 1L *Prince Edward* (44); 6.5.1766-28.8.1767 1L *Emerald* (32); 30.10.1770 1L *Fame* (74); 7.11.1771-31.1.1772 1L *Dublin* (74); 26.5.1775 2L *Barfleur* (90); 20.8.1776-6.12.1776† 1L *Barfleur* (90).

CALLIS, SMITH

Dates: 1709 Born Rivenhall, Essex; 15.10.1761 Died; 18.10.1761 Buried Abbey Church, Bath; 20.10.1761 Will Probate.
Family: Father Robert Callis; Brother RIchard; Sister Ann [Western] (d.1776);
Service: **Lieutenant**; 1.9.1731[(9.6.1732)]-7.6.1732[P] L. *Tartar* (32); 21.5.1733-27.4.1738 2L *Pearl* (40); 28.4.1738-12.10.1738 2L *Assistance* (50); 13.10.1738[(3.4.1739)]-13.7.1740 1L *Salisbury* (50); 14.7.1740 2L *Dragon* (60); **Commander**; 30.11.1740[(10.7.1742)]-14.6.1742[FE] *Duke* (8) Fireship; 14.6.1742 Duke's attack at St Tropez; **Captain**; 9.8.1742-31.8.1745[P] *Assistance* (50); 14.9.1745-18.12.1747 *Oxford* (50); 27.1.1757-23.3.1757 *Fougueux* (64); 1.6.1757[(MED 21.2.1760)] *Culloden* (74); 19.5.1759 **Rear Admiral of the Blue**; 18.8.1759-19.8.1759 Battle of Lagos Bay; 21.8.1759-20.8.1760 *Culloden* (74).

CALMADY, WARWICK

Dates: 1711 Born; 19.1.1788 Died Westminster; 29.1.1788 Buried South cloister, Westminster Abbey;

Family: Father Francis Calmady (d.1747); Mother Cecilia Pollexfen; Brother Francis Vincent Calmady (d.1767).

Service: 3.5.1726 Vol-p-O *Dunkirk* (50); 6.8.1728 MidO *Phoenix* (20); 17.9.1729 Mid *Assistance* (50); 31.8.1731 Mid *Norfolk* (80); 18.12.1731 Able *Norfolk* (80); 28.4.1732 Mid *Experiment* (20); 21.6.1732 Able *Experiment* (20); 16.10.1734 Passed; **Lieutenant**; 3.7.1739-13.8.1739 L. *Cumberland* (8) Fireship; 14.8.1739 3L *Advice* (54); 10.8.1741 2L *Advice* (54); 18.3.1741/42 1L *Advice* (54); 30.4.1743[(West Indies 1.4.1747)] 1L *Suffolk* (70); **Commander**; 22.6.1743[(BLI 27.10.1746)] *Otter* (14) Sloop; **Captain**; 30.9.1743-9.6.1744[P] *Lively* (20); 26.5.1744-15.10.1744 *Weymouth* (60); 20.2.1744/45[(BLI 27.10.1746)] *Launceston* (44); 22.6.1745[(BLI 27.10.1746)] *Mermaid* (44); 6.7.1745[(BLI 27.10.1746)]-25.3.1746 *Superb* (60); 2.2.1757 Resigned.

CAM, JOSEPH

Dates: c.1725 Born; 5.7.1767 Died; 10.7.1767 Buried St George the Martyr, Southwark, Surrey.

Family:

Service: 17.8.1751 Ord. *Berwick* (70); 7.1.1755 Able *Sunderland* (60); 28.7.1755 Mid *Sunderland* (60); 14.5.1757 Able *Hampton Court* (64); 18.5.1757-6.12.1758 Mid *Hampton Court* (64); 28.2.1758 Battle of Cartagena; 6.12.1758 Passed; **Lieutenant**; 22.1.1759 L. *Terror* (8) Bomb Vessel; 20.4.1761[(MED 23.6.1762)]-15.3.1762[P] L. *Polacca* (12) Sloop.

CAMPBELL, ALEXANDER

Dates: 17.11.1758 Died.

Family: Wife Unknown;

Service: **Lieutenant**; 25.8.1740[(22.4.1743)]-24.3.1740/41 4L *Hampton Court* (70); 27.4.1741[(22.4.1743)]-11.5.1743[P] L. *Shoreham* (20); 7.1741-10.1741 Operations against Santiago; 31.3.1744-3.9.1744 2L *Strafford* (58); 4.9.1744 1L *Strafford* (58); 1.7.1745[(JAM 4.2.1746/47)] 1L *Adventure* (44); 11.1.1745/46 1L *Captain* (70); **Commander**; 28.4.1747[(BLI 21.12.1747)] *Saxon* (16) Ship; 23.2.1747/48-27.2.1747/48[W] *Lizard* (14) Sloop; 5.3.1747/48-6.5.1752[P] *Fortune* (14) Sloop; 29.10.1755 *Macclesfield* (16) Hired Armed Ship; 1.11.1755 *Porcupine* (16) Sloop; **Captain**; 4.4.1757-8.4.1757 *Port Mahon* (24); 25.10.1757-17.11.1758[†] *Rye* (20); 9.3.1758-24.5.1758 Capture of Fort Louis.

CAMPBELL, ANDREW

Dates: c.1739 Born; 1766 Died.

Family:

Service: 31.10.1754 Capt Serv *Siren* (20); 22.5.1755-14.6.1755 British attack on Fort Beauséjour; 13.8.1756 Able *Namur* (90); 3.12.1756 MidO *Medway* (60); 5.9.1757-6.10.1757 Raid on Rochefort; 23.12.1757 Mid *Medway* (60); 12.2.1760 Mid *Royal Anne* (100); 14.1.1761 Passed; **Lieutenant**; 31.7.1761-20.6.1762 3L *Winchester* (50).

CAMPBELL, DUNCAN

Dates: c.1733 Born; 1801 Died.

Family:

Service: 23.8.1749 Ord. *Nottingham* (60); 19.3.1751 Able *Tavistock* (50); 4.11.1752 Mid *Tavistock* (50); 27.2.1755 NR *Winchester* (50); 6.8.1755 Passed; **Lieutenant**; 2.12.1755[(BLI 10.4.1758)]-11.3.1756[C] 3L *Warwick* (60); 25.7.1758 2L *Panther* (60); 16.1.1759-19.1.1759 Attack on Martinique; 20.1.1759-1.5.1759 Capture of Guadeloupe; 26.11.1759-23.3.1763[P] L. *Infernal* (8) Bomb Vessel; 29.3.1761-11.6.1761 Expedition against Belle-Isle; 7.1.1762-10.2.1762 Operations against Martinique; 5.5.1763-21.2.1765[P] L. *Lively* (20); 21.9.1786 **Superannuated Commander.**

CAMPBELL, JAMES

Dates: c.1714 Born.

Family:

Service: 28.3.1735 Able *Captain* (70); 15.3.1736/37 Able *Gibraltar* (20); 22.12.1738 Able *Edinburgh* (70); 31.12.1738 Mid *Edinburgh* (70); 24.6.1740 Able *Boyne* (80); 20.8.1740 Mid *Suffolk* (70); 4.3.1740/41-5.1741 Operations against Cartagena; 6.5.1742 Passed; **Lieutenant**; 19.7.1742 L. *Granado* (8) Bomb Vessel; 4.4.1743-1.7.1744 3L *Superb* (60); 4.9.1744 **Commander**; 4.9.1745[(West Indies 24.3.1745/46)] *Fame* (12) Sloop; 29.1.1747/48-11.8.1748[P] *Badger* (10) Sloop; 25.1.1748/49-16.7.1749[P] *Chesterfield* (44); 26.1.1748/49 **Captain**; 29.4.1756 *Nightingale* (22); 8.1757-10.1757 Louisbourg Expedition; 6.6.1758-27.7.1758 The Siege of Louisbourg; 7.2.1762[(BLI 19.6.1765)]-19.2.1762 *Echo* (24); 20.3.1762[(BLI 19.6.1765)]-17.8.1762 *Stirling Castle* (64); 6.6.1762-13.8.1762 Operations against Havana; 16.8.1762 Dismissed.

CAMPBELL, JOHN

Dates: 1719 Born Kirkbean, near Dumfries, Scotland; 16.12.1790 Died Charles Street, Berkeley Square, London; 3.2.1791 Will Probate.

Family: Father John Campbell (d. 1733); Wife Unknown.

Service: 23.11.1737 Able *Blenheim* (96); 25.11.1738 Able *Torbay* (80); 9.11.1739 Able *Russell* (80); 26.11.1740 Mid *Centurion* (60); 1.4.1741 Mate *Centurion* (60); 6.12.1743 Master *Centurion* (60); 8.1.1744/45 Passed; **Lieutenant**; 16.1.1744/45 L. *Scipio* (8) Fireship; 22.4.1745 2L *Lion* (58); 9.7.1745 Lion v L'Elizabeth; 6.8.1745 1L *Lion* (58); 11.8.1746 1L *Yarmouth* (64); 3.5.1747 1st Battle of Cape Finisterre; **Commander**; 27.5.1747 *Falcon* (10) Bomb Vessel; **Captain**; 23.11.1747-7.10.1748[P] *Bellona* (30); 23.6.1749 *Mermaid* (24); 24.7.1749 *Kent* (64); 10.1.1749/50-3.5.1750 *Mermaid* (24); 20.12.1750 *Charlotte* (8) Yacht; 10.7.1751 *Mary* (8) Yacht; 19.9.1755 *Assistance* (50); 25.11.1755 *Prince* (90); 12.5.1756 *Royal George* (100); 5.11.1756 *Essex* (64); 5.6.1758-12.6.1758 Raid on Saint-Malo; 4.6.1759 *Royal George* (100); 20.11.1759 Battle of Quiberon Bay; 21.2.1760-7.5.1763[P] *Dorsetshire* (68); 14.12.1763 *Mary* (8) Yacht; 17.5.1764 FRS; 18.10.1770 *Royal Charlotte* (8) Yacht; 23.1.1778 **Rear Admiral of the Blue**; 29.1.1778 **Rear Admiral of the White**; 3.2.1778 CinC — River Medway and The Nore; 16.5.1778-18.10.1778 *Victory* (100); 27.7.1778 1st Battle of Ushant; 19.3.1779 **Vice Admiral of the Blue**; 26.9.1780 **Vice Admiral of the White**; 4.1782-12.4.1783[P] *Portland* (50); 2.4.1782-1.3.1785/86 CinC — Newfoundland; 3.1783-12.1785 *Winchelsea* (32); 10.4.1783-13.12.1785[P] *Salisbury* (50); 24.9.1787 **Vice Admiral of the Red.**

CAMPBELL, WILLIAM

Dates: 27.10.1755 Died.

Family:

Service: 8.4.1716 Ord. *Kinsale* (36); 9.4.1717 Able *Kinsale* (36); 7.12.1717 Able *Ludlow Castle* (42); 27.7.1718-8.12.1720[P] MidO *Ludlow Castle* (42); 1.5.1721 MidO *Winchester* (50); 6.5.1723 Passed; **Lieutenant**; 6.3.1727/28-24.2.1728/29 L. *Dursley Galley* (20); 25.2.1728/29[(JAM 29.5.1729)]-26.1.1729/30 2L *Lark* (40); 11.8.1729-18.8.1729 MidE *Lion* (60); 19.8.1729-18.5.1731 4L *Royal Oak* (70); 19.5.1731-31.12.1731 2L *York* (60); 1.1.1731/32-2.3.1732/33 2L *York*

(60); 23.2.1733/34-8.4.1736[P] 5L *Namur* (90); **Commander**; 10.12.1739-12.4.1741 *Scipio* (8) Fireship; **Captain**; 16.4.1741-10.2.1741/42 *Sapphire* (44); 10.2.1741/42 Dismissed.

CAMPBELL, WILLIAM

Dates: c.1737 Born; 1770 Died.
Family:
Service: 13.12.1750 Scholar *Royal Naval Academy*; 10.5.1752 Capt Serv *Deptford* (60); 30.4.1754 Able *Port Mahon* (24); 28.2.1755 Mid *Port Mahon* (24); 26.4.1756 Mid *Terrible* (74); 22.7.1756-6.9.1758 Mid *Berwick* (64); 5.4.1757 Action of April 5 1757; 28.2.1758 Battle of Cartagena; 6.9.1758 Passed; 22.3.1759 **Lieutenant**; 23.3.1759 L. *Lightning* (6) Hospital Ship; 24.7.1759 3L *Woolwich* (44); 19.9.1760-5.7.1762 2L *Woolwich* (44); 7.1.1762-10.2.1762 Operations against Martinique.

CAMPBELL, LORD WILLIAM

Dates: 1730 Born Southampton; 1730 Lord; 3.9.1778 Died.
Family: Father John Campbell, 4th Duke of Argyll (d.1770); Mother Mary Drummond Ker; Wife Sarah Izard married 17.4.1763; Daughter Unknown; Son Unknown; Son Unknown; Sister Lady Caroline (1721-1803); Brother Lord John, 5th Duke of Argyll (1723-1806); Brother Lord Frederick (1729-1816);
Service: 23.3.1752/53 Able *Penzance* (44); 13.9.1753 Mid *Penzance* (44); 10.1.1754 Mid *Tiger* (60); 6.3.1753/54 Able *Tiger* (60); 11.1.1756-14.1.1756 Capture of Geriah; 25.2.1757 Mid *Tiger* (60); 7.3.1757-1.4.1757 Expedition against Chandernagore; 29.4.1758 Battle of Cuddalore; 3.8.1758 Battle of Negapatam; 14.3.1758/59-3.12.1760 Mid *Yarmouth* (64); 10.9.1759 Battle of Pondicherry; 3.12.1760 Passed; **Lieutenant**; 5.12.1760 5L *Superb* (74); **Commander**; 28.1.1762 *Carcass* (14) Bomb Vessel; **Captain**; 20.8.1762-26.8.1763[P] *Nightingale* (22); 17.1.1764-7.1766 M.P. for Argyllshire; 19.3.1764 *Achilles* (60); 17.5.1765-22.7.1766 *Bellona* (74); 7.1766-10.1773 Gov. of Nova Scotia; 21.2.1775-29.7.1775 *Scorpion* (14) Sloop; 18.6.1775-15.9.1775 Gov. of South Carolina; 16.5.1778-3.9.1778[†] *Lion* (64).

CANDLER, JOHN

Dates: c.1720 Born; 1772 Died; 6.8.1772 Buried Poole; 31.10.1772 Will Probate.
Family: Wife Elizabeth Fiddeman married 1.12.1755; Sister Ann [Barber]; Sister Frances [Carpendale]; Sister Jane.
Service: 12.9.1735 Able *Centurion* (60); 13.6.1736 Able *Lancaster* (80); 7.6.1738 Able *Romney* (50); 16.6.1741 Mid *Nassau* (70); 8.3.1741/42 Mid *Princess Amelia* (80); 29.5.1742 Mid *Kinsale* (44); 14.4.1743 Mid *Augusta* (60); 10.10.1743 Passed; **Lieutenant**; 15.6.1744 4L *Suffolk* (70); 26.1.1745/46[NA 29.12.1746]-11.9.1746 3L *Hampshire* (50); 6.4.1748-2.8.1748[P] 2L *Hampshire* (50); 11.3.1755 1L *Falmouth* (50); 26.4.1757-8.6.1757 5L *Royal Anne* (100); 20.7.1757 5L *Royal Anne* (100); 5.9.1757-6.10.1757 Raid on Rochefort; 17.1.1758-18.12.1760[P] 4L *Royal Anne* (100); 5.6.1758-12.6.1758 Raid on Saint-Malo; 28.12.1763-4.10.1765 LCmdr *Hope* (6) Schooner.

CANNON, RICHARD

Dates: 1769 Died.
Family:
Service: 1751-1755 HEIC Service; 31.1.1755 Mate *Winchester* (50); 5.8.1755 Mate *Hampton Court* (64); 20.6.1756 Mate *Prince George* (80); 7.12.1756 Mid *Deptford* (50); 8.2.1757 Mid *Torbay* (74); 11.4.1757 Passed; **Lieutenant**; 25.8.1758[JAM 20.9.1759]-30.1.1760 3L *Guernsey* (50);

18.8.1759-19.8.1759 Battle of Lagos Bay; 30.1.1760(JAM 21.4.1760)-26.10.1760[W] 4L *Conqueror* (68); 2.4.1762 L. *Success* (20); 9.4.1762-28.3.1763[P] 2L *Kent* (74).

CAREY, JOHN

Dates: c.1715 Born; 1782 Died.
Family:
Service: 13.11.1729 Able *Seahorse* (20); 23.5.1731 MidO *Seahorse* (20); 15.5.1732 Able *Buckingham* (70); 19.5.1733 Mid *Buckingham* (70); 27.7.1733 Able *Buckingham* (70); 2.9.1733 Able *Hound* (8) Sloop; 16.6.1734 Carp *Hound* (8) Sloop; 10.8.1735 Mid *Hound* (8) Sloop; 17.9.1740 Mid *Suffolk* (70); 4.3.1740/41-5.1741 Operations against Cartagena; 6.10.1741-20.3.1742 Mate *Suffolk* (70); 20.3.1741/42 Passed; **Lieutenant**; 6.3.1743/44(MED 17.4.1746) 4L *Princess* (70); 10.7.1745(MED 17.4.1746) 3L *Princess* (70); 2.8.1746-18.4.1747[P] 5L *Sandwich* (90); 24.8.1747-26.5.1749[P] 1L *Crown* (44); 17.1.1757 2L *Weymouth* (60); 29.4.1758 Battle of Cuddalore; 3.8.1758 Battle of Negapatam; 10.9.1759 Battle of Pondicherry; 1.2.1762-14.6.1762 1L *Namur* (90); **Commander**; 14.6.1762(EI 21.2.1764)-29.6.1762 *Lurcher* (6) Cutter; 2.7.1762(EI 18.1.1764)-6.2.1764[P] *Bonetta* (10) Sloop.

CARKETT, JOHN

Dates: c.2.1716 Born; 23.2.1715/16 Baptised Saint Johns, Cornwall; 1774 Died.
Family: Father John Carkett; Mother Mary; Wife Jane.
Service: 19.7.1735 Ord. *York* (60); 5.1.1736/37 Able *York* (60); 14.1.1737/38 Able *Torrington* (40); 5.1.1738/39 Mid *Torrington* (40); 5.11.1741 Passed; **Lieutenant**; 11.3.1741/42 L. *Terror* (8) Bomb Vessel; 28.10.1743 4L *Captain* (70); 15.6.1744 1L *Captain* (70); 11.1.1745/46 4L *Royal Sovereign* (104); 23.1.1745/46-10.5.1747 3L *Royal Sovereign* (104); 27.9.1748-29.11.1748[P] 2L *Tiger* (60).

CARKETT, ROBERT

Dates: c.1719 Born; 5.10.1780 Died Sliver Key Reef, off San Domingo.
Family: Father Robert Carkett; Son Robert.
Service: 16.4.1734 Able *Exeter* (60); 25.6.1736 Able *Grampus* (6) Sloop; 11.7.1737 Able *Alderney* (8) Bomb Vessel; 16.7.1738 Mid *Plymouth* (60); 24.8.1739 Able *Plymouth* (60); 15.2.1739/40 Mid *Plymouth* (60); 4.6.1742 Mate *Plymouth* (60); 18.7.1743 Passed; **Lieutenant**; 26.2.1744/45(29.8.1746) 3L *Preston* (50); 1.2.1745/46(24.9.1746)-25.9.1746[P] 3L *Deptford* (60); 28.4.1747-3.2.1748/49[P] L. *Surprise* (24); 6.2.1755 2L *Vanguard* (68); 6.3.1755 1L *Monmouth* (70); 28.2.1758 Battle of Cartagena; 28.2.1758 ActCapt *Foudroyant* (80); **Captain**; 12.3.1758 *Royal Caroline* (8) Yacht; 26.12.1758-23.5.1762[C] *Hussar* (28); 2.8.1763-8.6.1767[P] *Active* (28); 15.6.1769-12.5.1773[P] *Lowestoffe* (32); 30.10.1778-5.10.1780[†] *Stirling Castle* (64); 6.7.1779 Battle of Grenada; 21.12.1779-22.12.1779 Action of 1779-12-21; 17.4.1780 Battle of Martinique; 15.5.1780 Action of March 15 1780; 19.5.1780 Action of March 19 1780.

CARNEGIE, LORD GEORGE (6TH EARL OF NORTHESK)

Dates: 2.8.1716 Born; 24.6.1741 6th Earl of Northesk; 22.1.1792 Died.
Family: Father David Carnegie, 4th Earl of Northesk (1675-1729); Mother Margaret Wemyss, Countess of Wemyss (1677-1763); Wife Anne Leslie (d.1779) married 30.4.1738; Daughter Mary Anne [Kemp] (d.1798); Son David, Lord Rosehill (1749-1788); Daughter Lady Elizabeth [Hope-Johnstone] (1751-1793); Son William (7th Earl Northesk), RN (1756-1831); Son Lt.-Col. George (1773-1839); Daughter Margaret [Watson] (1779-1793); Sister Elizabeth [Elphinstone] (1699–1767); Brother David, 5th Earl of Northesk (1749-1788); Sister Margaret

[Leslie] (1702–1722); Sister Anne [Hope] (1700-1733); Sister Christian (1703-1787); Brother James (1705-?); Sister Mary (1712-1798); Sister Henrietta (1714-?).
Service: **Lieutenant**; 6.4.1737[29.4.1737]-8.12.1737 3L *Windsor* (60); 15.3.1737/38-23.7.1739 3L *Dragon* (60); 24.7.1739[7.5.1740]-30.5.1740[P] 2L *Edinburgh* (70); 2.2.1740/41 4L *Marlborough* (90); 20.3.1740/41-5.7.1741 2L *Marlborough* (90); **Captain**; 25.8.1741 *Bideford* (20); 4.1.1741/42 *Looe* (44); 8.9.1742-5.4.1747 *Preston* (50); 24.1.1744/45 Straits of Banca; 25.6.1746 1st Battle of Negapatam; 6.3.1755-5.4.1755 *Orford* (68); 4.6.1756 **Rear Admiral of the Blue**; 13.7.1758 **Rear Admiral of the White**; 14.2.1759 **Vice Admiral of the Blue**; 21.10.1762 **Vice Admiral of the White**; 18.10.1770 **Admiral of the Blue**; 29.1.1778 **Admiral of the White**.

CARPENTER, ROBERT

Dates: c.1734 Born; 14.2.1773 Died.
Family:
Service: 11.12.1746 Capt Serv *Captain* (70); 20.10.1747-9.9.1748[P] Capt Serv *Sutherland* (50); 25.9.1749 Able *Sheerness* (24); 20.6.1750 Mid *Sheerness* (24); 17.3.1750/51 Mid *Kent* (64); 26.6.1751 Mid *Torrington* (44); 10.12.1752 Able *Torrington* (44); 5.6.1754 Passed; **Lieutenant**; 28.4.1755[ECH 19.5.1757]-14.8.1756[C] L. *Ontario* (12) Sloop; 27.5.1757 L. *Scarborough* (20); 6.6.1758-27.7.1758 The Siege of Louisbourg; 16.11.1758[NA 16.11.1758] 2L *Prince Frederick* (64); **Commander**; 9.2.1759 *Baltimore* (8) Bomb Vessel; **Captain**; 3.1.1760 *Aldborough* (20); 21.11.1760-19.3.1763[P] *Coventry* (28); 5.1.1767-11.1.1770 *Edgar* (60).

CARR, JOHN

Dates: c.1738 Born; 1772 Died; 2.12.1772 Will Probate.
Family:
Service: 4.11.1753 Capt Serv *Bridgewater* (24); 5.6.1755 Ord. *Bridgewater* (24); 13.1.1756 Able *Salisbury* (50); 28.5.1756 Mid *Salisbury* (50); 7.3.1757-1.4.1757 Expedition against Chandernagore; 19.3.1758 Mid *Cumberland* (66); 29.4.1758 Battle of Cuddalore; 3.8.1758 Battle of Negapatam; 22.3.1759 Mid *Yarmouth* (64); 10.9.1759 Battle of Pondicherry; 29.12.1760 Passed; **Lieutenant**; 24.3.1762[EI 3.3.1763] 4L *Hampton Court* (64); 17.7.1762[EI 15.9.1763]-27.9.1763[P] 2L *Cerberus* (28); 25.10.1763-16.3.1764 3L *Superb* (74); 18.5.1768 3L *Arrogant* (74); 24.5.1769-23.11.1769 3L *Achilles* (60).

CARRE, ROBERT

Dates: c.1724 Born; 8.10.1778 Died; 3.4.1779 Will Probate.
Family: Father John Carre; Sister Agnes.
Service: 19.1.1739/40 Ord. *Dolphin* (20); 7.5.1740 Able *Dolphin* (20); 30.7.1741 Mid *Dolphin* (20); 8.6.1743 Mid *Argyll* (50); 11.11.1745 Able *Pembroke* (60); 26.11.1745 Mid *Pembroke* (60); 17.2.1745/46-12.8.1746[P] Mid *Argyll* (50); 2.10.1746 Passed; **Lieutenant**; 23.6.1748[JAM 14.6.1750] 3L *Lark* (44); 18.8.1749[NA 14.6.1750]-23.6.1750[P] 2L *Lark* (44); 15.3.1757 3L *Prince George* (80); 29.7.1757 2L *Prince George* (80); 20.10.1757 2L *Princess Amelia* (80); **Commander**; 13.1.1758-17.4.1758[P] *Gibraltar's Prize* (14) Tender; 20.6.1759-21.4.1763[P] *Hound* (14) Sloop.

CARTER, ROBERT

Dates: c.1741 Born; 7.4.1741 Baptised Paignton, Devon; 23.4.1818 Died; 7.7.1818 Will Probate.
Family: Father Elias Carter; Mother Jane; Wife Ann; Son Robert; Son Thomas; Son Gilbert; Daughter Ann; Son Rawden; Son John; Son Charles; Daughter Jane; Daughter Phillippa; Daughter Catherine; Sister Catherine (1743-?); Brother Burrington (1747-?); Brother William (1750-?).

Service: 13.7.1753 Able *Saltash* (14) Sloop; 2.12.1755 Able *Dover* (44); 12.7.1756 Mid *Dover* (44); 20.8.1758 Able *Dover* (44); 16.1.1759 Mid *Dover* (44); 3.10.1759 Passed; **Lieutenant**; 27.8.1760 L. *Terpsichore* (24); 20.4.1761 3L *Winchester* (50); 19.5.1761 2L *Winchester* (50); 31.7.1761-3.7.1764[P] 1L *Winchester* (50); 28.8.1767 1L *Emerald* (32); 18.12.1770 4L *Torbay* (74); 28.5.1771 3L *Torbay* (74); 28.6.1771 4L *Torbay* (74); 29.11.1771 3L *Torbay* (74); 2.5.1772 2L *Torbay* (74); 7.7.1772 3L *Torbay* (74); 3.11.1773-2.8.1774 2L *Torbay* (74); 30.12.1775-7.8.1778 1L *Juno* (32); 23.1.1779-12.11.1779 2L *Intrepid* (64); 3.11.1807 **Superannuated Commander**.

CARTERET, JAMES

Dates: 1789 Died.
Family:
Service: **Lieutenant**; 28.3.1758-21.10.1762 3L *Weymouth* (60); 29.4.1758 Battle of Cuddalore; 3.8.1758 Battle of Negapatam; 10.9.1759 Battle of Pondicherry; 24.9.1762-6.10.1762 Battle of Manilla; 28.8.1778-24.3.1779 2L *Britannia* (100).

CARTERET, JOHN

Dates: c.1730 Born.
Family:
Service: 7.1.1743/44 Capt Serv *Dolphin* (20); 22.4.1744 Capt Serv *Harwich* (50); 25.5.1745 Able *Harwich* (50); 25.6.1746 1st Battle of Negapatam; 28.6.1746 Mid *Harwich* (50); 21.11.1748 Able *Vigilant* (60); 27.8.1749 Mid *Vigilant* (60); 2.9.1752 Passed; **Lieutenant**; 27.2.1755-13.5.1755 3L *Ambuscade* (40); 6.3.1761-8.4.1761[P] 2L *Ambuscade* (40); 7.4.1777-2.8.1778 1L *Yarmouth* (64); 7.3.1778 Action of 1778-03-07.

CARTERET, PETER

Dates: c.1722 Born; 4.9.1777 Died.
Family:
Service: 30.11.1734 Capt Serv *Ipswich* (70); 18.3.1734/35 Adm Serv *Ipswich* (70); 8.4.1735 Adm Serv *Blenheim* (96); 4.2.1736/37 Able *Somerset* (80); 11.2.1737/38 Mid *Somerset* (80); 29.10.1740 Mid *Marlborough* (90); 9.9.1741 Mate *Winchester* (50); 3.3.1742/43 Passed; **Lieutenant**; 20.4.1744 L. *Lightning* (8) Bomb Vessel; 6.6.1744 3L *Pearl* (44); 6.10.1744 2L *Pearl* (44); 2.4.1746 1L *Pearl* (44); 12.9.1748[EI 5.9.1749]-22.8.1749[P] 3L *Princess Mary* (60); 6.2.1755 1L *Elizabeth* (70); 24.10.1755 3L *Royal Sovereign* (104); 27.11.1756 2L *Royal Sovereign* (104); 13.12.1756-5.5.1757 1L *Royal Sovereign* (104); **Commander**; 5.5.1757-6.8.1758[C] *Stork* (10) Sloop; 25.9.1776-4.9.1777[†] *Druid* (16) Sloop; 4.9.1777 Action of 1777-09-04.

CARTERET, PHILIP

Dates: 22.1.1732/33 Born Trinity Manor, Jersey; 21.7.1796 Died Southampton; 18.8.1796 Will Probate.
Family: Father Charles de Carteret; Mother Françoise Marie St Paul; Wife Marie Rachel (d. 1797); Son Sir Philip (2nd Baronet Silvester), RN (1777-1828).
Service: 27.12.1747 Capt Serv *Salisbury* (50) Hulk; 31.3.1749 Able *Monmouth* (70); 17.3.1751/52 Mid *Saint Albans* (60); 22.2.1753 Mid *Augusta* (60); 20.10.1753 Able *Vanguard* (68); 26.2.1754 Mid *Vanguard* (68); 13.4.1754 Able *Vanguard* (68); 31.10.1754 Mid *Vanguard* (68); 6.8.1755 Passed; **Lieutenant**; 14.6.1757 3L *Guernsey* (50); 18.3.1758[NA 27.12.1758] 3L *Hampshire* (50); 27.12.1758-13.6.1760 2L *Hampshire* (50); 1.6.1766-9.9.1767 1L *Tamar* (16) Sloop; **Commander**; 1.7.1766-12.4.1769[P] *Swallow* (14) Sloop; **Captain**; 10.1.1771-1.6.1772[P]

Flamborough (20); 24.8.1779-31.8.1781[P] *Endymion* (44); 29.4.1794 **Superannuated Rear Admiral**.

CARTERET, RICHARD

Dates: c.1716 Born; 1780 Died.
Family:
Service: 3.5.1738 Able *Anglesea* (40); 14.8.1739 Mid *Strafford* (60); 21.11.1739 Attack on Puerto Bello; 5.5.1742 Able *Cumberland* (80); 19.5.1743-15.9.1744[P] ActL *Kent* (70); 2.11.1744 Passed; **Lieutenant**; 15.11.1744 L. *Falcon* (10) Sloop; **Commander**; 18.5.1745-28.9.1745[C] *Falcon* (10) Sloop; 5.5.1757 *Racehorse* (18) Sloop; 24.6.1757-16.4.1761 *Merlin* (18) Frigate; **Captain**; 16.4.1761[(JAM 18.2.1763)] *Lively* (20); 11.5.1761 *Glasgow* (20); 2.7.1762 *Devonshire* (70); 29.7.1762-16.12.1762[P] *Cambridge* (80).

CARTWRIGHT, CHARLES

Dates: 1807 Died.
Family:
Service: **Lieutenant**; 1.2.1763[(BLI 14.9.1763)]-18.9.1763[P] 2L *Aquilon* (28); 31.5.1781 1L *Argo* (44); 28.11.1782 1L *Diadem* (64); 28.3.1783 1L *Diadem* (64).

CARTWRIGHT, JOHN

Dates: c.1741 Born; 23.9.1824 Died.
Family:
Service: 1753-1758 Merchant Service; 29.7.1758 Able *Magnanime* (74); 4.9.1759 Mid *Magnanime* (74); 20.11.1759 Battle of Quiberon Bay; 15.1.1762 Passed; **Lieutenant**; 15.9.1762-20.2.1763[P] L. *Wasp* (8) Sloop; 19.4.1763-1.1764 LCmdr *Spy* (4) Cutter; 7.12.1763-31.12.1765 LCmdr *Sherborne* (6) Cutter; 14.5.1766-5.1.1769[P] 1L *Guernsey* (50); 21.2.1769 1L *Antelope* (50); 7.12.1770-28.6.1771 4L *Barfleur* (90); 25.10.1809 **Commander**.

CARY, EBENEZER

Dates: 1756 Died; 6.11.1756 Will Probate.
Family: Wife Ann married 24.1.1753.
Service: **Lieutenant**; 7.11.1751[(EI 27.5.1752)]-6.6.1752[P] 4L *Vigilant* (60).

Cary, John
Dates: c.1708 Born; 11.7.1795 Died.
Family:
Service: 8.8.1726 Ord. *Grafton* (70); 19.6.1727 Able *Cornwall* (80); 16.11.1727 Able *Grafton* (70); 13.4.1728 MidO *Grafton* (70); 29.8.1728 Able *Grafton* (70); 17.3.1728/29 Mid *Grafton* (70); 2.1.1729/30 Able *Grafton* (70); 23.7.1731 Mid *Grafton* (70); 5.11.1731 Schoolmaster *Grafton* (70); 29.3.1732 Able *Grafton* (70); 31.8.1732 Mid *Grafton* (70); 9.11.1732 Able *Grafton* (70); 7.12.1732 Mid *Grafton* (70); 11.7.1734 Mid *Britannia* (100); 11.1.1734/35 Passed; **Lieutenant**; 24.10.1744-20.11.1744 L. *Vulture* (10) Sloop; 4.7.1745-20.5.1746 3L *Saint George* (90).

CASE, JAMES

Dates: c.1.3.1732 Born Great Fansham, Norfolk; 31.3.1732 Baptised; 16.7.1795 Died King's Lynn, Norfolk; 31.7.1795 Will Probate.
Family: Father Thomas Case (1695-1760); Mother Blanche Lee (1704-1737); Brother Thomas (1731-1793); Sister Blanche (1734-1734); Brother Edward (1735-1781).

Service: c.1754-c.1757 Merchant Service; 22.1.1757 Mate *Preston* (50); 28.3.1757 Mate *Magnanime* (74); 18.6.1757-3.9.1760 Mate *Royal William* (84); 5.9.1757-6.10.1757 Raid on Rochefort; 6.6.1758-27.7.1758 The Siege of Louisbourg; 3.9.1760 Passed; **Lieutenant**; 7.8.1761-8.2.1763[P] 4L *Revenge* (64); 10.6.1766-30.5.1769 LCmdr *Hector* (4) Cutter; 2.2.1771-1.10.1773[P] 3L *Saint Albans* (64); 12.11.1776 3L *Egmont* (74); 5.9.1777-24.11.1777 2L *Egmont* (74).

CATFORD, CHARLES

Dates: 24.9.1756 Died; 16.12.1756 Will Probate.
Family: Sister Jane [Percy].
Service: 14.9.1714 Vol-p-O *Speedwell* (42); 30.3.1716 Vol-p-O *Ludlow Castle* (42); 1.7.1717 Able *Swallow* (50); 2.10.1718 Ord. *Ludlow Castle* (42); 20.11.1719-21.11.1720[W] MidO *Speedwell* (8) Bomb Vessel; 1.7.1723 Mid *Bredah* (70); 18.1.1724/25 Passed; **Lieutenant**; 29.7.1727[(25.4.1728)]-22.12.1727 3L *Dunkirk* (50); 9.2.1728/29-7.5.1731 3L *Sunderland* (60); 6.3.1732/33-12.3.1733/34 3L *Romney* (50); 13.3.1733/34-11.11.1736 2L *Romney* (50); 12.11.1736-18.6.1739 1L *Greenwich* (50); 19.6.1739-31.7.1740 2L *Russell* (80); 1.8.1740-2.10.1740 1L *Russell* (80); 3.10.1740 1L *Grafton* (70); 22.11.1740 2L *Buckingham* (70); 30.1.1740/41 1L *Royal Sovereign* (104); **Commander**; 5.2.1741/42-13.8.1743 *Deptford Prize* (8) Sloop; **Captain**; 12.10.1743-7.6.1745 *Lyme* (20); 17.12.1745-3.6.1746 *Lynn* (44); 16.1.1753 *Berwick* (70); 16.5.1753 *Captain* (64); 20.5.1756 Battle of Minorca.

CAULDWELL, EDWARD

Dates: 1773 Died.
Family:
Service: **Lieutenant**; 9.7.1762[(MED 7.4.1763)]-4.4.1763[P] L. *Terror* (8) Bomb Vessel; 25.10.1763 3L *Belleisle* (64); 18.8.1764 4L *Essex* (64); **Commander**; 20.6.1765 *Weazle* (16) Sloop; 13.8.1766 *Vulture* (14) Sloop; **Captain**; 4.11.1769[(BLI 16.5.1770)]-15.1.1772[P] *Squirrel* (20).

Caulfield, Tobias

Dates: c.1739 Born; 31.1.1781 Died Port Royal, Jamaica; 23.6.1781 Will Probate.
Family:
Service: 15.3.1753 Capt Serv *Otter* (14) Sloop; 2.5.1754 Able *Otter* (14) Sloop; 8.4.1755 Able *Captain* (64); 30.3.1756 Mid *Captain* (64); 20.5.1756 Battle of Minorca; 18.10.1756 Mid *Lancaster* (66); 6.6.1758-27.7.1758 The Siege of Louisbourg; 15.12.1758 Mid *Royal Sovereign* (104); 24.2.1759 Mid *Royal Oak* (70); 27.3.1759 Mid *Kennington* (20); 22.4.1759 Mid *Hero* (74); 13.6.1759 Passed; **Lieutenant**; 20.7.1759 3L *Torrington* (44); 11.3.1761-22.5.1763[P] 3L *Phoenix* (44); 26.7.1764 2L *Montreal* (32); 20.6.1765-23.12.1767 1L *Montreal* (32); 23.10.1770-10.6.1771[P] 3L *Arrogant* (74); 16.5.1772 3L *Lennox* (74); 22.4.1773 4L *Lennox* (74); 27.5.1773 3L *Lennox* (74); 17.12.1773 3L *Barfleur* (90); 14.7.1774 2L *Barfleur* (90); 11.4.1775-26.5.1775 3L *Barfleur* (90); 13.10.1775-25.4.1777 2L *Bristol* (50); **Commander**; 5.7.1776[(NA 7.10.1777)] *Thunder* (8) Bomb Vessel; **Captain**; 6.7.1776[(NA 7.10.1777)]-6.9.1776 *Bristol* (50); 6.9.1776 *Chatham* (50); 6.12.1776-8.12.1776 Occupation of Rhode Island; 25.12.1777-31.1.1781 *Bristol* (50); 20.3.1780 1st Action off Monti Christi; 20.6.1780 Action off Monti Christi.

CAVE, JOSEPH

Dates: 7.11.1720 Born Edinburgh; 1781 Died; 8.2.1781 Will Probate.
Family: Father Joseph Cave; Mother Mary Chieslie; Wife Susanna married 18.10.1777; Sister Christian.
Service: 23.11.1738 Able *Seahorse* (20); 29.8.1739 Able *Lichfield* (50); 26.10.1739 Able *Assistance* (50); c.23.12.1739 Mid *Lichfield* (50); c.24.12.1740 Mid *Princess Louisa* (60);

4.3.1740/41-5.1741 Operations against Cartagena; c.25.12.1741 Mid *Worcester* (54); 16.5.1742 Mid *Chichester* (80); 7.11.1743 Able *Saint George* (90); 28.1.1743/44-5.3.1743/44 Mid *Neptune* (94); c.4.1744-c.1745 Merchant Service; 8.7.1745 Passed; **Lieutenant**; 10.7.1745[MED 24.1.1748/49] 4L *Princess* (70); 4.1.1745/46[NA 3.2.1748/49] 3L *Dreadnought* (60); 26.1.1745/46[NA 3.2.1748/49] 2L *Dreadnought* (60); 19.5.1747[3.2.1748/49]-18.2.1748/49[P] 3L *Ludlow Castle* (44); 8.3.1755 3L *Monmouth* (70); 19.4.1755 2L *Monmouth* (70); 9.11.1756 1L *Harwich* (50); 9.3.1758-24.5.1758 Capture of Fort Louis; **Commander**; 10.8.1758-27.10.1761 *London Buss* Storeship.

CAYLEY, WILLIAM

Dates: 5.5.1742 Born York; 3.1.1801 Died Chatham; 10.1.1801 Will Probate.

Family: Father George Cayley, 4th Bt. (1707-1791); Mother Philadelphia Digby (1709-1765); Mistress Mary Leiberwood; Wife Martha Ward married 30.4.1781; Mistress Elizabeth Miller; Illegitimate Son Thomas Allen; Daughter Sarah Martha; Illegitimate Daughter Frances Leiberwood; Illegitimate Daughter Caroline Leiberwood; Illegitimate Son William Miller; Illegitimate Son William Leiberwood; Daughter Philadelphia (1739-1739); Brother Thomas, 5th Bt. (1732-1792); Sister Everilda (1734-1741); Brother George (1736-1801); Sister Philadelphia (1737-1741); Sister Frances [Cayley] (1738-1814); Brother Arthur (1739-1818); Sister Dorothy (1737-1739); Sister Mary (1740-1741); Brother John (1741-1818); Brother William (1742-1801); Sister Rebecca (1743-?); Brother Rev. Digby (1745-1798); Brother Edward (1746-?).

Service: **Lieutenant**; 26.7.1762[MED 23.3.1763] 5L *Hercules* (74); 17.6.1763 3L *Phoenix* (44); 27.8.1764-1.10.1766 2L *Phoenix* (44); 8.11.1770 4L *Trident* (64); 21.12.1770-21.5.1771 3L *Trident* (64); 10.5.1776 3L *Mars* (74); 14.12.1776-5.2.1778[P] 2L *Mars* (74); 31.1.1778 1L *Actaeon* (44); 24.3.1779-19.1.1780 1L *Britannia* (100); **Commander**; 14.2.1781 *Harpy* (18) Sloop; **Captain**; 1.5.1782-31.3.1783[P] *Edgar* (74); 20.10.1782 Battle of Cape Spartel; 18.7.1794 *Unicorn* (32); 10.7.1795 *Juste* (80); 18.10.1795-3.1.1801[†] *Invincible* (74); 16.2.1797-17.2.1797 Capture of Trinidad; 11.8.1799-20.8.1799 Surrender of Surinam.

CHADS, HENRY

Dates: c.1737 Born; 10.10.1799 Died Chichester; 29.10.1799 Will Probate.

Family: Father Henry Chads (1710-1752); Mother Anne Robins (1709-1760); Wife Eleanor (1739-1779); Wife Susannah Cornell (1757-1795) married 15.7.1783; Daughter Mary Cornell [Barney] (1785-1832); Daughter Caroline (1786-1824); Son Henry Ducie, RN (1788-1868); Son William Catherwood (1789-1873); Son Thomas (1790-1804); Son John Cornell (1793-1854).

Service: 5.7.1752 Capt Serv *Surprise* (24); 31.8.1752 Able *Surprise* (24); 22.12.1753 MidO *Surprise* (24); 6.8.1754 Able *Anson* (60); 29.11.1754 Mid *Anson* (60); 26.7.1757 Mid *Magnanime* (74); 5.9.1757-6.10.1757 Raid on Rochefort; 11.5.1758 Mid *Essex* (64); 5.6.1758-12.6.1758 Raid on Saint-Malo; 27.7.1758 ActL *Swallow* (14) Sloop; 11.10.1758 Passed; **Lieutenant**; 7.3.1759-7.4.1761 L. *Swallow* (14) Sloop; 9.7.1761 L. *Spy* (10) Sloop; 22.12.1761-9.6.1767[P] 2L *Argo* (28); 24.9.1762-6.10.1762 Battle of Manilla; 15.6.1769-10.8.1772[P] 1L *Quebec* (32); 1773-1781 Agent for Transports; **Commander**; 18.9.1779[NA 6.12.1779] *Victor* (14) Sloop; **Captain**; 14.4.1783[NA 8.9.1783]-15.4.1783 *Chatham* (50).

CHADS, JAMES

Dates: c.1724 Born; 1781 Died; 5.2.1781 Buried Greenwich; 13.2.1781 Will Probate.

Family: Father Henry Chads; Wife Eleanor Townsend (d.1795); Son Thomas Townsend (1754-1793).

Service: 8.2.1739/40 Able *Advice* (54); 13.1.1741/42 Mid *Greenwich* (50); 6.12.1742 Able *Phaeton* (8) Fireship; 20.12.1742-7.3.1742/43[P] Mid *Phaeton* (8) Fireship; 27.9.1743 Mid *Experiment* (20); 17.12.1745 Mid *Rippon* (60); **Lieutenant**; 17.5.1746-21.8.1751 4L *Monmouth* (70); 9.8.1746 Passed; 3.5.1747 1st Battle of Cape Finisterre; 14.10.1747 2nd Battle of Cape Finisterre; 21.8.1751-6.2.1756 L. *Surprise* (24); 8.6.1757 2L *Magnanime* (74); 5.9.1757-6.10.1757 Raid on Rochefort; 29.3.1758 1L *Magnanime* (74); 5.6.1758-12.6.1758 Raid on Saint-Malo; **Commander**; 18.10.1758-23.2.1763[P] *Vesuvius* (8) Fireship; 29.3.1761-11.6.1761 Expedition against Belle-Isle; 9.12.1765 *Fly* (8) Sloop; **Captain**; 2.4.1766 *Launceston* (44); 6.5.1766-5.1.1769[P] *Guernsey* (50); 16.12.1771-25.1.1773[P] *Glory* (32); 29.11.1773-2.3.1774[P] *Hind* (24); 20.4.1774-8.10.1774 *Scarborough* (20); 3.12.1774 *Cerberus* (28); 25.7.1775-18.10.1775 *Deal Castle* (20); 30.10.1775-13.2.1776 *Conquestador* (60).

CHADS, WILLIAM

Dates: 1769 Died.
Family: Father Henry Chads; Wife Mary Reeves married 1745; Daughter Eleanor (1739-1779); Son James (1751-1769); Son Thomas (1754-1793).
Service: **Lieutenant**; 6.3.1740/41[JAM 17.7.1745]-19.6.1741 L. *Cumberland* (8) Fireship; 4.10.1742[JAM 17.7.1745] 2L *Rippon* (60); 14.10.1742[JAM 17.7.1745]-4.11.1746 1L *Rippon* (60); 10.7.1755-22.7.1755 1L *Princess Mary* (60); 28.5.1756 1L *Marlborough* (80); 5.7.1756 1L *Terrible* (74); 8.1757-10.1757 Louisbourg Expedition; 6.6.1758-27.7.1758 The Siege of Louisbourg; 21.5.1760-3.8.1763[P] 1L *Intrepid* (60).

CHALONER, EDWARD

Dates: 1689 Born; 10.3.1766 Died Buckinghamshire; 9.4.1766 Will Probate.
Family: Father William Chaloner (1643-1719); Mother Christiana Freeston; Wife Elizabeth (d.1752); Brother Charles (d.1727); Brother John (d.1710); Brother William (1676-1736).
Service: 9.1.1706 Vol-p-O *Dunkirk* (50); 16.8.1709 Mid *Dunkirk* (50); 31.12.1711 Passed; **Lieutenant**; 22.4.1723-10.5.1723[P] 1L *Swallow* (50); 25.1.1725/26 2L *Advice* (54); 11.8.1727-10.4.1729 2L *Advice* (54); 11.4.1729 3L *Burford* (70); 19.5.1731 3L *Edinburgh* (70); 14.6.1732-15.2.1732/33 3L *Edinburgh* (70); 23.2.1733/34 2L *Deptford* (60); 23.3.1733/34-19.7.1736[P] 1L *Deptford* (60); 28.7.1738-31.8.1738 1L *Saint Albans* (50); 4.3.1739/40-11.3.1739/40 2L *Cambridge* (80).

CHAMPERNOWNE, RAWLIN

Dates: 1726 Born Paignton, Devon; 1774 Died; 25.2.1774 Will Probate.
Family: Father John Champernowne (1682-1732); Mother Margaret Mallock (1703-1736); Wife Agnes Hore Trist married 1770; Mistress Joan Philips; Mistress Grace Barnes; Daughter Margaret (1772-1860); Daughter Elizabeth Philips; Son Humphrey Barnes; Sister Margaret [Whitsell] (1722-?); Brother Richard (1727-?); Sister Ann (1729-?)); Brother Henry (1730-1774).
Service: **Captain**; 16.11.1756-7.2.1763[P] L. *Solebay* (24).

CHANDLER, DAVID

Dates: 1789 Died.
Family:
Service: **Lieutenant**; 20.3.1758-18.9.1761 L. *Dolphin* (24).

CHAPLEN, JAMES

Dates: c.1724 Born; 4.2.1766 Died; 10.11.1766 Will Probate.
Family:
Service: 24.4.1735 Able *Terrible* (6) Bomb Vessel; 25.11.1737 Mid *Cornwall* (80); 26.5.1738 Mid *Lion* (60); 27.3.1739 Mate *Worcester* (60); 21.11.1739 Attack on Puerto Bello; 12.4.1740 ActL *Princess Caroline* (80); 8.5.1740 ActL *Walpole* HEIC; 9.9.1742 Mate *Albany and Friendship* Mer; **Lieutenant**; 8.11.1744[MED 28.10.1748] L. *Nazareth* (8) Fireship; 9.11.1744 Passed; 1.6.1745[MED 28.10.1748] 3L *Essex* (70); 9.4.1748[MED 28.10.1748]-25.10.1748[P] 2L *Essex* (70); 9.7.1755 2L *Princess Mary* (60); 19.5.1757[JAM 11.9.1759] 2L *Roebuck* (44); 8.11.1757 1L *Stirling Castle* (64); 25.1.1758 1L *Deptford* (50); 5.6.1758-12.6.1758 Raid on Saint-Malo; 3.7.1759 Bombardment of Le Havre; **Commander**; 9.7.1759-12.7.1762[P] *Furnace* (8) Bomb Vessel; 29.3.1761-11.6.1761 Expedition against Belle-Isle.

CHAPMAN, JOHN

Dates: c.1734 Born.
Family:
Service: 28.9.1747 Ord. *Kingfisher* (10) Sloop; 26.3.1748 Mid *Kingfisher* (14) Sloop; 22.1.1749/50 Able *Kingfisher* (14) Sloop; 11.3.1749/50 Mid *Kingfisher* (14) Sloop; 15.4.1751 Able *Kingfisher* (14) Sloop; 8.5.1752 Mid *Torrington* (44); 12.2.1753 Mate *Falcon* (10) Bomb Vessel; 2.9.1753 Mate *Assistance* (50); 6.4.1754-7.8.1754 ActL *Assistance* (50); 7.8.1754 Passed; **Lieutenant**; 16.10.1755 3L *Gosport* (44); 25.4.1757 2L *Gosport* (44); 8.5.1759 1L *Gosport* (44); 20.3.1760-2.10.1761 1L *Belliqueux* (64); **Commander**; 26.5.1768 *Crown* (18) Storeship; 10.3.1769-10.12.1770 *Nautilus* (16) Sloop; 12.3.1776 *Shark* (16) Sloop; **Captain**; 13.7.1778-8.5.1779 *Dunkirk* (60); 1.10.1783-13.5.1784 *Trimmer* (14) Cutter.

CHARLEY, ISAAC

Dates: 1720 Born Faversham; 16.3.1719/20 Baptised; 1784 Died; 2.8.1784 Will Probate.
Family: Father Isaac Charley; Mother Elizabeth; Wife Ann Rayer married 19.4.1743.
Service: 1750-1753 HEIC Service; 16.3.1752/53 Mid *Ludlow Castle* (44); 4.12.1753 Mate *Eagle* (60); 14.7.1756-1.12.1756 Mate *Monarch* (74); 1.12.1756 Passed; **Lieutenant**; 6.4.1757 4L *Dublin* (74); 5.9.1757-6.10.1757 Raid on Rochefort; 23.1.1759-8.4.1760 2L *Sapphire* (32); 20.11.1759 Battle of Quiberon Bay; 14.5.1762-19.3.1763[P] 1L *Emerald* (32); 2.2.1771-24.5.1771[P] 2L *Bellona* (74).

CHENOWETH, MICHAEL

Dates: c.1762 Died.
Family:
Service: **Lieutenant**; 31.3.1756 L. *Viper* (10) Sloop; 29.11.1757 L. *Firedrake* (8) Bomb Vessel; 7.12.1757-23.1.1762[†] 2L *Falmouth* (50).

CHILD, SMITH

Dates: 1729 Born; 21.1.1813 Died.
Family:
Service: 21.2.1753 Mid *Unicorn* (24); 16.4.1754 Mate *Unicorn* (24); 2.5.1755-5.11.1755 Mid *Prince* (90); 5.11.1755 Passed; **Lieutenant**; 7.11.1755 6L *Princess Royal* (90); 4.4.1757 5L *Princess Royal* (90); 24.5.1757 4L *Devonshire* (70); 8.6.1757 3L *Devonshire* (70); 6.6.1758-27.7.1758 The Siege of Louisbourg; 3.11.1758-25.7.1763[P] L. *Kennington* (20); 7.4.1777 2L *Yarmouth* (64); 27.6.1777 LCmdr *Nightingale* (22) Hospital Ship; **Commander**; 30.10.1777

Pacific (26) Storeship; **Captain**; 15.5.1780[NA 25.12.1780]-29.8.1780 *Raisonable* (64); 29.8.1780[NA 27.3.1782]-4.3.1782[P] *Europe* (64); 16.3.1781 Battle of Cape Henry; 5.9.1781 Battle of the Chesapeake; 10.9.1795-16.3.1796[P] *Commerce de Marseilles* (50); 14.2.1799 **Rear Admiral of the White**; 1.1.1801 **Rear Admiral of the Red**; 23.4.1804 **Vice Admiral of the Blue**; 9.11.1805 **Vice Admiral of the White**; 31.7.1810 **Admiral of the Blue.**

CHINNERY, SAINT JOHN

Dates: c.1730 Born; c.1.1787 Died; 3.1.1787 Buried Clifton, Gloucestershire; 28.3.1787 Will Probate.
Family: Brother Broderick.
Service: 18.8.1745 Land. *Terror* (8) Bomb Vessel; 21.3.1745/46 Able *Terror* (8) Bomb Vessel; 1.5.1746 Action of 1746-05-01; 14.3.1746/47 Mid *Anglesea* (40); 27.9.1747 Able *Anglesea* (44); 17.1.1748/49 Able *Assurance* (44); 14.10.1752-24.4.1753[W] Mid *Assurance* (44); 23.1.1754-27.2.1755 Mid *Culloden* (74); 10.3.1755 Passed; **Lieutenant**; 19.6.1756[MED 8.3.1759]-26.6.1756 4L *Hampton Court* (64); 1.4.1758[MED 29.4.1760] 1L *Monmouth* (70); 20.6.1758[JAM 29.4.1760]-10.1.1761 1L *Prince* (90); 18.8.1759-19.8.1759 Battle of Lagos Bay; **Commander**; 6.4.1761[MED 3.5.1763]-4.4.1763[P] *Terror* (8) Bomb Vessel; 26.10.1771 *Racehorse* (16) Sloop; 13.4.1773 *Wasp* (8) Sloop; **Captain**; 25.6.1773 *Pallas* (36); 26.6.1773-27.10.1774 *Wasp* (8) Sloop; 20.3.1776-15.3.1780 *Daphne* (20).

CHRISTIAN, EDWARD

Dates: 1758 Died.
Family:
Service: **Captain**; 28.7.1749[EI 11.10.1749]-23.8.1749[P] *Medway Prize* (30).

CHRISTIAN, JOHN

Dates: c.1711 Born; 1758 Died.
Family:
Service: 1.1.1723/24 Vol-p-O *Lyme* (20); 11.1.1726/27 Ord. *Lyme* (20); 10.3.1728/29 Able *Kinsale* (40); 5.6.1730 Able *Oxford* (50); 16.9.1731 MidO *Salisbury* (50); 24.3.1731/32 Mid *Salisbury* (50); 5.6.1733 Mid *Romney* (50); 9.3.1733/34 Passed; 10.6.1740-6.1742 Purser *Lively* (20); 6.1742-19.2.1742/43 ActL *Lively* (20); 18.2.1742/43 Attack on La Guaira; **Lieutenant**; 28.4.1747[BLI 18.4.1749] 4L *Suffolk* (70); 19.5.1747[BLI 28.4.1749] 2L *Ludlow Castle* (44); 7.12.1748[BLI 28.4.1749]-16.7.1749[P] 1L *Chesterfield* (44); 9.5.1757-bef.4.4.1758[†] LCmdr *Princess Caroline* (80) Hospital Ship.

CHUBB, JOHN FHOEDRA

Dates: c.1725 Born; 1786 Died; 3.3.1786 Will Probate.
Family: Wife Sarah married 5.11.1777.
Service: 1748-1755 Merchant Service; 4.8.1755 Mate *Greyhound* (20); 19.1.1756-9.11.1758 Master *Greyhound* (20); 9.11.1758 Passed; **Lieutenant**; 27.8.1759[JAM 27.5.1760] 3L *Conqueror* (68); 20.9.1759[JAM 27.5.1760]-26.10.1760[W] 2L *Conqueror* (68); 18.6.1761-12.4.1763 1L *Lowestoffe* (32); 13.10.1775 4L *Barfleur* (90); 2.8.1776 3L *Barfleur* (90); 6.12.1776 2L *Barfleur* (90); 5.4.1777 2L *Princess Royal* (90); 4.5.1778-24.12.1781[P] 2L *Albion* (74); 6.7.1779 Battle of Grenada; 17.4.1780 Battle of Martinique; 15.5.1780 Action of March 15 1780; 19.5.1780 Action of March 19 1780.

CHURCHILL, THOMAS

Dates: c.1708 Born; 1757 Died; 14.6.1757 Will Probate.

Family: Wife Eleanor Hunt married 26.2.1745/46.
Service: 1.11.1734 Mid *Kent* (70); 28.11.1736 Mate *Eltham* (40); 26.4.1737 Mid *Eltham* (40); 1.2.1737/38-5.3.1740/41 Mate *Eltham* (40); 5.3.1739/40 Passed; 12.3.1740/41 **Lieutenant**; 13.3.1740/41 L. *Hawk* (8) Sloop; 16.2.1743/44 2L *Ruby* (44); 26.5.1744 2L *Mermaid* (44); 14.4.1746-28.8.1746 1L *Mermaid* (44); 7.5.1755-20.5.1755 1L *Trident* (64); 20.5.1755-31.12.1755 2L *Trident* (64); **Commander**; 15.11.1756-10.6.1757 *Canterbury* (6).

CLAPP, JOHN
Dates: 1760 Died Dover; 20.8.1760 Will Probate.
Family: Wife Mary Ellet married 16.7.1741.
Service: 12.10.1744 Passed; **Lieutenant**; 8.3.1744/45[BLI 31.1.1746/47] 3L *Woolwich* (50); 7.7.1745[BLI 31.1.1746/47]-20.4.1747[P] 2L *Woolwich* (50); 10.8.1746 Action of 1746-10-18.

CLARK, ARCHIBALD
Dates: c.1735 Born; 3.1800 Died; 23.3.1800 Buried St Pancras Old Church, Camden, Middlesex; 10.10.1800 Will Probate.
Family: Son George.
Service: 31.12.1748 Able *Lyme* (24); 18.6.1752 Mid *Lyme* (24); 10.1.1753 Able *Northumberland* (68); 19.1.1755 Mid *Northumberland* (68); 29.4.1755 Mid *Yarmouth* (64); 12.8.1756 Passed; **Lieutenant**; 23.2.1757-18.11.1761 L. *Weazle* (16) Sloop; 16.1.1759-19.1.1759 Attack on Martinique; 20.1.1759-1.5.1759 Capture of Guadeloupe; 23.3.1762-8.3.1763[P] L. *Escort* (14) Sloop; 25.10.1763 2L *Belleisle* (64); 30.8.1764-24.10.1766[P] 3L *Belleisle* (64); 30.11.1770-29.11.1773 L. *Hind* (24); 21.9.1796 **Superannuated Commander**.

CLARK, EDWARD
Dates: c.1718 Born; 3.1764 Died; 19.10.1764 Will Probate.
Family: Sister Jane [Hamilton]; Sister Elizabeth.
Service: 25.6.1737 Able *Salisbury* (50); 6.8.1738 Able *Somerset* (80); 14.7.1739 Mid *Princess Caroline* (80); 20.9.1740 Mate *Princess Caroline* (80); 13.1.1740/41 Mate *Burford* (70); 24.1.1741/42 Able *Neptune* (90); 16.4.1742 Mid *Neptune* (90); 11.2.1743/44-12.2.1743/44 Battle of Toulon; 29.4.1744 Mid *Salisbury* (50); 18.7.1744 Passed; **Lieutenant**; 29.8.1744 3L *Ludlow Castle* (44); 12.2.1744/45 5L *Sandwich* (90); 2.8.1746 3L *Princess* (70); 19.1.1746/47 5L *Royal Sovereign* (104); 2.3.1746/47-14.8.1748[P] 2L *Eagle* (60); 14.10.1747 2nd Battle of Cape Finisterre; 11.3.1755 2L *Prince George* (80); 7.10.1755-5.6.1756 5L *Ramillies* (90); 20.5.1756 Battle of Minorca; 19.4.1757 1L *Prince* (90); **Commander**; 3.3.1758[MED 5.2.1759] *Fortune* (14) Sloop; 13.3.1758-21.3.1758 *Sapphire* (32); 21.3.1758 **Captain**; 12.5.1759[BLI 16.12.1760]-22.1.1760[P] *Bristol* (50); 30.8.1762-3.1764[†] *Liverpool* (28).

CLARK, HENRY
Dates: c.1738 Born; 1773 Died.
Family:
Service: 2.8.1747 Capt Serv *Canterbury* (60); 9.4.1748 Battle of Santiago de Cuba; 17.7.1748-19.1.1748/49[P] Capt Serv *Milford* (44); 19.11.1752 Able *Lyme* (24); 21.11.1754 Capt Serv *Lyme* (24); 6.4.1756 Able *Lyme* (24); 17.5.1756 Action of 17th May 1756; 26.10.1756 Able *Penzance* (44); 9.10.1757 Mid *Somerset* (68); 6.6.1758-27.7.1758 The Siege of Louisbourg; 18.2.1759 Mid *Newark* (80); 3.7.1759-6.2.1760 Mid *Royal Sovereign* (104); 6.2.1760 Passed; **Lieutenant**; 5.12.1760-23.3.1762 L. *Escort* (14) Sloop; 29.3.1761-11.6.1761 Expedition against Belle-Isle; 11.5.1762-4.12.1762 2L *Chester* (50).

Clark, John

***DATES:* C.1712 BORN; 1789 DIED; 19.3.1789 WILL PROBATE.**
Family: Daughter Joanna.
Service: 7.5.1728 Ord. *Berwick* (70); 25.10.1730 Ord. *Rose* (20); 26.6.1731 Able *Rose* (20); 28.8.1733 QGnr *Gibraltar* (20); 1.12.1734 Cpl *Gibraltar* (20); 12.2.1734/35 Mid *Dreadnought* (60); 9.7.1737 Able *Dreadnought* (60); 28.10.1737 Mid *Dreadnought* (60); 29.12.1737 Mate *Romney* (50); 4.1.1738/39 Mid *Romney* (50); 26.4.1739 Mate *Romney* (54); 14.4.1740 Passed; **Lieutenant**; 21.2.1740/41 3L *Kingston* (60); 11.2.1743/44-12.2.1743/44 Battle of Toulon; 8.12.1744[(MED 18.3.1745/46)]-1.5.1745 3L *Antelope* (50); 16.10.1745[(25.8.1746)] 3L *Marlborough* (90); 15.4.1746-13.6.1746[P] 2L *Marlborough* (90); 3.7.1746 1L *Chichester* (80); 21.8.1746 1L *Lion* (58); 14.10.1747 2nd Battle of Cape Finisterre; 1.2.1747/48-5.8.1748[P] 1L *Princess Louisa* (60); 1.12.1748-15.11.1752[P] 1L *Culloden* (74); 30.1.1753 1L *Yarmouth* (64); 28.1.1755 2L *Prince* (90); 22.4.1755 1L *Prince* (90); **Commander**; 14.10.1755 *Firebrand* (6) Fireship; 31.12.1755 *Bonetta* (10) Sloop; **Captain**; 19.1.1758-28.10.1762 *Sheerness* (24); 30.11.1771-7.7.1774 *Prudent* (64); 12.7.1774[(EI 8.2.1777)]-22.2.1776 *Dolphin* (24).

CLARK, WILLIAM

Dates: c.1734 Born; 1778 Died.
Family:
Service: 6.12.1748 Able *Kingfisher* (14) Sloop; 12.4.1749 Mid *Kingfisher* (14) Sloop; 16.1.1749/50 Able *Kingfisher* (14) Sloop; 10.12.1751 Mid *Kingfisher* (14) Sloop; 12.3.1751/52 Able *Mars* (64); 26.6.1752 Mid *Eagle* (60); 22.9.1752 Able *Mars* (64); 23.10.1752 Able *Falcon* (10) Bomb Vessel; 11.5.1753 Mid *Falcon* (10) Bomb Vessel; 1.2.1755 Able *Jason* (44); 4.2.1755 Mid *Jason* (44); 3.5.1755 Mid *Saint George* (90); 3.12.1755 Passed; **Lieutenant**; 9.12.1755 L. *Port Mahon* (24); 8.1757-10.1757 Louisbourg Expedition; 6.6.1758-27.7.1758 The Siege of Louisbourg; 26.4.1759 3L *Hercules* (74); 20.11.1759 Battle of Quiberon Bay; 8.3.1763-26.3.1763[P] 2L *Hercules* (74); 6.9.1763-19.4.1766[P] 2L *Kent* (74).

CLARK, WILLIAM

Dates: c.1737 Born.
Family:
Service: 11.5.1754 Capt Serv *Norwich* (50); 14.4.1755 Able *Norwich* (50); 27.7.1755 Able *Terrible* (74); 6.8.1755 Mid *Terrible* (74); 24.5.1756 Mid *Marlborough* (80); 29.12.1756 Able *Newark* (80); 3.2.1757 Mid *Newark* (80); 8.1757-10.1757 Louisbourg Expedition; 5.6.1758-12.6.1758 Raid on Saint-Malo; 5.1.1759 Passed; **Lieutenant**; 21.3.1759 L. *Happy* (8) Sloop; 2.5.1759-8.6.1762 2L *Levant* (28); 7.1.1762-10.2.1762 Operations against Martinique; 19.6.1766-19.5.1768[P] 1L *Dolphin* (24).

CLARKE, ARTHUR

Dates: c.1733 Born; 1766 Died.
Family:
Service: 24.11.1745 Mid *Woolwich* (44); 2.8.1748 Capt Serv *Garland* (24); 7.9.1748-30.12.1748 Capt Serv *Princess Royal* (90); 1753-1756 Merchant Service; 7.3.1759 Passed; **Lieutenant**; 9.3.1759 L. *Deal Castle* (20); 11.1.1760-6.10.1760[P] 4L *Monarch* (74); 22.1.1761-2.3.1763[P] 2L *Buckingham* (68); 29.3.1761-11.6.1761 Expedition against Belle-Isle; 24.12.1763-30.10.1765 3L *Edgar* (60).

CLARKE, CHARLES

Dates: c.1739 Born; 1798 Died.
Family:
Service: 21.10.1748 Scholar *Royal Naval Academy*; 25.9.1755 Mid *Experiment* (24); 20.5.1756 Battle of Minorca; 30.5.1757 Able *Experiment* (24); 17.9.1757 Mid *Experiment* (24); 29.6.1758 Able *Experiment* (24); 14.10.1758 Able *Phoenix* (20); 31.1.1759 Passed; **Lieutenant**; 30.4.1759-8.12.1759 3L *Antelope* (50); 15.12.1761-4.11.1762 3L *Assistance* (50); 20.2.1779 **Captain**.

CLARKE, EDWARD

Dates: c.1708 Born; 1779 Died.
Family:
Service: 7.4.1727 Vol-p-O *Stirling Castle* (70); 3.4.1729 Able *Gibraltar* (20); 12.4.1729 Mid *Gibraltar* (20); 8.10.1732 Able *Salisbury* (50); 16.11.1733 Passed; **Lieutenant**; 18.4.1735-16.2.1735/36[P] 4L *Yarmouth* (70); 12.5.1738 3L *Ipswich* (70); 2.3.1742/43 Sinking of the San Isidoro; **Commander**; 14.4.1744 *Drake* (14) Sloop; 3.8.1746 Action of August 3 1746; **Captain**; 11.9.1747 *Milford* (44); 1.8.1748[(JAM 24.7.1749)]-9.5.1749[P] *Canterbury* (60); 12.10.1748 Battle of Havana; 13.12.1753-19.1.1755 *Jason* (44); 25.6.1756-12.5.1759 *Ludlow Castle* (44); 16.1.1759-19.1.1759 Attack on Martinique; 20.1.1759-1.5.1759 Capture of Guadeloupe; 4.2.1778 **Superannuated Rear Admiral**.

CLARKE, FRANCIS

Dates: c.1721 Born; c.1758 Died; 21.6.1758 Will Probate.
Family: Wife Elizabeth.
Service: 12.7.1734-3.5.1738 Scholar *Royal Naval Academy*; 4.8.1738-29.6.1740 Vol-p-O *Plymouth*; 30.6.1740-13.4.1741 Mid *Plymouth*; 14.4.1741 Mid *Plymouth*; 5.5.1743 Passed; **Lieutenant**; 16.6.1743 L. *Granado* (8) Bomb Vessel; 29.12.1743-8.5.1744[C] 4L *Northumberland* (64); 13.2.1744/45 2L *Ludlow Castle* (44); 17.7.1745-22.9.1745 1L *Ludlow Castle* (44); 22.9.1746-10.5.1747 4L *Royal Sovereign* (104); 29.1.1757-20.3.1758 L. *Dolphin* (24).

CLARKE, PETER

Dates: c.1735 Born; 1773 Died.
Family:
Service: 1750-1751 Merchant Service; 1.1.1750/51 Scholar *Royal Naval Academy*; 2.1.1754 Able *Seahorse* (24); 11.2.1754 Able *Dolphin* (24); 28.3.1754 Mid *Dolphin* (24); 12.3.1755/56-19.11.1756 Mid *Dunkirk* (60); 19.11.1756 Passed; **Lieutenant**; 29.7.1757[(NA 4.2.1758)] 3L *Sunderland* (60); 8.1757-10.1757 Louisbourg Expedition; 10.9.1759 Battle of Pondicherry; 17.3.1760[(EI 23.12.1760)]-19.12.1760[P] 3L *Yarmouth* (64); 1.2.1762 3L *Namur* (90); **Commander**; 2.7.1762[(EI 13.9.1763)] *Lurcher* (6) Cutter; 25.7.1762[(EI 13.9.1763)] *Ferret* (14) Sloop; **Captain**; 5.5.1763[(BLI 1.11.1763)]-19.1.1764[P] *Melampe* (36); 20.6.1770-6.6.1772 *Kennington* (20).

CLAYTON, SAMUEL WITTEWRONGE

Dates: 5.2.1734 Born Barbados; 10.1795 Died Peckham.
Family: Father Samuel Clayton (d. 1735); Mother Thomasine Wittewonge; Wife Mary Walker married 21.5.1765; Son Thomas Wittewronge Whitewell, RN (1766-1806).
Service: 16.1.1744/45 Capt Serv *Cornwall* (80); 22.11.1746 L. Serv *Cornwall* (80); 9.4.1748 Battle of Santiago de Cuba; 12.10.1748 Battle of Havana; 31.10.1748-6.5.1749[P] Able *Weazle* (16) Sloop; 29.1.1749/50 Able *Triton* (20); 7.12.1750 Mid *Triton* (20); 17.9.1755 Mid *Buckingham* (68); 7.1.1756 Passed; **Lieutenant**; 29.11.1756[(ECH 5.4.1757)]-12.4.1757 2L *Defiance*

(60); 12.4.1757 3L *Defiance* (60); 8.1757-10.1757 Louisbourg Expedition; 6.6.1758-27.7.1758 The Siege of Louisbourg; 2.11.1758 2L *Defiance* (60); 31.5.1759-9.11.1759 LCmdr *Barrington* Tender; 18.7.1762[EI 6.4.1763]-7.4.1763[P] 1L *Culloden* (74); 20.12.1763 1L *Dorsetshire* (68); 12.1.1764 2L *Dorsetshire* (68); 27.3.1764-29.10.1767 2L *Augusta* (64); 20.9.1770 2L *Augusta* (64); 13.11.1770-29.6.1771 1L *Egmont* (74); 1.11.1772-16.10.1774[P] LCmdr *Penguin*; 1773-1776 Gov. of Falkland Islands; 20.5.1776 L. *Camilla* (20); **Commander**; 1.8.1776 *Strombolo* (8) Fireship; **Captain**; 23.4.1778[NA 1.2.1779] *Iris* (28); 18.9.1778[NA 3.3.1779]-11.6.1779[P] *Ardent* (64); 5.5.1780 *Victory* (100); 29.3.1781 *Centurion* (50); 1.12.1782[NA 18.3.1783]-28.2.1783[P] *Warwick* (50); 8.6.1795 **Superannuated Rear Admiral**.

CLEAR, HENRY

Dates: c.1736 Born; 12.4.1765 Died.
Family:
Service: 6.10.1751 Able *Intrepid* (64); 17.10.1752 Able *Fowey* (24); 29.10.1754 Mid *Fowey* (24); 16.10.1756 Able *Edinburgh* (64); 26.12.1756 Mid *Edinburgh* (64); 28.1.1757 Cox *Surprise* (24); 19.4.1757 Mate *Surprise* (24); 9.7.1757-2.1.1758 Mid *Winchester* (50); 2.1.1758 Passed; **Lieutenant**; 22.5.1758 2L *Renown* (30); 5.6.1758-12.6.1758 Raid on Saint-Malo; 16.1.1759-19.1.1759 Attack on Martinique; 20.1.1759-1.5.1759 Capture of Guadeloupe; 4.8.1759[JAM 2.10.1761]-25.8.1764[P] 1L *Renown* (30).

CLELAND, JOHN

Dates: 24.6.1795 Died Portsmouth; 10.7.1795 Will Probate.
Family: Wife Mary Amelia (d.1798); Daughter Jane Montague (d.1786); Daughter Susanna Elizabeth (d.1784).
Service: 7.5.1740 Mid *Seahorse* (20); 15.7.1740 Capt Serv *Lichfield* (50); 4.8.1740 Mid *Assistance* (50); 1.10.1740 Mid *Lichfield* (50); 17.4.1741 Mid *Princess Louisa* (60); 6.6.1741 Mid *Worcester* (60); 7.1741-10.1741 Operations against Santiago; 11.2.1742/43 Mid *Stirling Castle* (70); 1.9.1743 Mid *Dunkirk* (60); 11.2.1743/44-12.2.1743/44 Battle of Toulon; 23.3.1743/44 Able *Namur* (90); 4.2.1744/45 Passed; **Lieutenant**; 5.2.1744/45[MED 2.12.1748] 4L *Princess Caroline* (80); 24.5.1745[MED 2.12.1748]-22.8.1747 3L *Jersey* (60); 6.11.1754 2L *Culloden* (74); 28.1.1755 4L *Prince* (90); 14.10.1755 3L *Prince* (90); 12.11.1755 2L *Prince* (90); 7.4.1756 1L *Prince* (90); 12.5.1756 1L *Royal George* (100); **Commander**; 10.6.1756-19.4.1757[C] *Merlin* (10) Sloop; 9.1.1758 *Scorpion* (14) Sloop; **Captain**; 12.5.1759-26.9.1760[P] *Squirrel* (20); 26.9.1762[MED 10.8.1763]-24.5.1763[P] *Montagu* (60); 22.7.1779-13.8.1780[P] *Arrogant* (74); 28.8.1780 *Buffalo* (50); 25.1.1781-9.11.1781 *Formidable* (98); 6.3.1782-8.4.1782 *Ocean* (90); 6.10.1787 **Superannuated Rear Admiral.**

CLELAND, THOMAS

Dates: 1759 Died.
Family:
Service: **Lieutenant**; 17.9.1735 3L *Princess Louisa* (40); 1.10.1736-30.12.1736 2L *Princess Louisa* (40); 4.2.1736/37-5.12.1739 2L *Diamond* (40); 17.4.1740-25.7.1744 L. *Experiment* (20); 4.3.1740/41-5.1741 Operations against Cartagena; 7.1741-10.1741 Operations against Santiago; **Commander**; 20.2.1744/45-22.4.1745 *Scipio* (8) Fireship.

CLEMENTS, MICHAEL

Dates: 1735 Born Colwich, Staffordshire; 1797 Died Weybridge, Surrey; 4.7.1797 Will Probate.
Family: Father Rev. John Clements; Wife Ann; Son Michael; Daughter Mary Ann.

Service: 27.1.1748 Mid *Yarmouth* (64); 7.8.1748 Able *Siren* (20); 26.7.1751-28.5.1752[P] Mid *Siren* (20); 30.4.1753 Mid *Unicorn* (24); 1.11.1755 ActL *Unicorn* (24); 3.12.1755 Passed; **Lieutenant**; 4.12.1755 L. *Unicorn* (24); 24.9.1756 1L *Unicorn* (28); **Commander**; 25.5.1757 *London* (6) Storeship; **Captain**; 29.9.1757 *Actaeon* (28); 5.6.1758-12.6.1758 Raid on Saint-Malo; 4.6.1759-14.1.1764[P] *Pallas* (36); 28.2.1760 Action of February 28 1760; 4.10.1769-29.5.1771[P] *Dorsetshire* (68); 9.3.1778-10.2.1779 *Vengeance* (74); 27.7.1778 1st Battle of Ushant; 12.11.1788 **Superannuated Rear Admiral**.

CLEMENTS, RICHARD

Dates: c.1714 Born; 1775 Died.
Family:
Service: 31.10.1734 Gnr Serv *Salisbury* (50); 28.8.1737 Able *Plymouth* (60); 3.4.1738 Mid *Berwick* (70); 20.4.1740 Mid *Shrewsbury* (80); 29.6.1741-14.12.1741 Mate *Shrewsbury* (80); 14.12.1741 Passed; **Lieutenant**; 12.4.1744 6L *Saint George* (90); 21.6.1744 5L *Saint George* (90); 11.12.1744 2L *Dreadnought* (60); 18.2.1744/45 3L *Shrewsbury* (80); 4.12.1745-13.4.1749[W] 2L *Namur* (74); 3.5.1747 1st Battle of Cape Finisterre; **Captain**; 29.9.1748[(EI 29.8.1749)]-9.10.1748 *Harwich* (50); 1775 Captain of Greenwich Hospital.

CLERK, JOHN

Dates: 22.8.1741 Born; 1780 Died.
Family:
Service: **Lieutenant**; 10.6.1761[(BLI 10.6.1761)]-2.11.1761 4L *Temple* (68); 19.1.1771-28.5.1771 5L *Ocean* (90); 17.4.1778 1L *Janus* (44); 21.10.1778-1780[†] 1L *Alfred* (74).

CLERKE, SIR JOHN

Dates: 31.1.1772 Knight Bachelor; 1775 Died.
Family: Brother Charles, RN (1743-1779).
Service: **Lieutenant**; 19.3.1756[(EI 21.11.1758)]-23.7.1756 2L *Bridgewater* (24); **Commander**; 9.3.1759 *Basilisk* (8) Bomb Vessel; 3.7.1759 Bombardment of Le Havre; **Captain**; 26.5.1761-5.5.1763 *Melampe* (36).

CLEVELAND, ARCHIBALD

Dates: 6.1766 Died.
Family:
Service: **Lieutenant**; 28.4.1755[(MED 4.6.1756)]-25.5.1755 3L *Norwich* (50); 14.6.1755[(MED 15.10.1756)] L. *Jamaica* (10) Sloop; 17.10.1755[(NA 15.10.1756)] 3L *Fougueux* (64); **Commander**; 28.9.1756 *Stork* (10) Sloop; **Captain**; 5.11.1756 *Gibraltar* (20); 17.8.1757 *Pallas* (36); 5.6.1758-12.6.1758 Raid on Saint-Malo; 4.6.1759 *Windsor* (60); 17.6.1763-6.1766[†] *Phoenix* (44).

CLIFFORD, NICHOLAS

Dates: c.1728 Born; 1794 Died; 25.4.1794 Will Probate.
Family:
Service: 27.4.1747 Able *Prince George* (90); 3.5.1747 1st Battle of Cape Finisterre; 4.2.1748 Able *Rainbow* (44); 30.9.1748 Mid *Rainbow* (44); 15.9.1749 Cox *Sphinx* (24); 17.12.1750 Mid *Savage* (8) Sloop; 23.3.1755 Mate *Prince George* (90); 14.6.1756 Mate *Monarch* (74); 6.6.1757 Passed; **Lieutenant**; 6.8.1759[(NA 25.5.1761)]-20.4.1761 L. *Polacca* (12) Sloop; 18.3.1762 L. *Raven* (8) Fireship; 13.9.1762-27.3.1764 2L *Achilles* (60); 30.11.1770 L. *Nautilus* (16) Sloop; 11.12.1770 4L *Royal Oak* (74); 9.1.1771 3L *Royal Oak* (74); 10.5.1771 2L *Royal Oak* (74); 23.10.1771 3L

Intrepid (64); 1.4.1772-29.11.1773 2L *Raisonable* (64); 6.9.1776 3L *Ocean* (90); 30.8.1777 2L *Ocean* (90); 25.10.1777 3L *Ocean* (90); 13.5.1778-2.9.1779 2L *Ocean* (90); 27.7.1778 1st Battle of Ushant.

CLINTON, THE HON. GEORGE

Dates: 1686 Born Stourton Parva, Lincolnshire; 10.7.1761 Died.
Family: Father Francis Clinton, 6th Earl of Lincoln (1635-1693); Mother Susan Penniston; Wife Anne Carle; Son died in infancy; Daughter Lucy Mary [Roddam]; Daughter Died in infancy; Son General Sir Henry Clinton; Daughter died in infancy; Son died in infancy.
Service: **Lieutenant**; 22.11.1712(6.1.1712/13)-13.5.1713 2L *Nottingham* (60); 14.5.1713(6.1.1713/14)-13.8.1714[P] 4L *Blenheim* (96); **Captain**; 25.6.1716-29.3.1717 Capt&M *Speedwell* (42); 30.3.1717(21.6.1717) *Fox* (24); 21.6.1717-8.2.1719/20 *Success* (20); 9.2.1719/20-24.11.1720 *Monck* (50); 31.1.1720/21-14.3.1721/22 *Nottingham* (60); 15.3.1721/22-1.12.1727[P] *Colchester* (50); 26.7.1728-21.2.1728/29 *Sunderland* (60); 1731-1737 Gov. of Newfoundland; 4.2.1730/31-17.4.1732 *Salisbury* (50); 18.4.1732-14.4.1734 *Namur* (90); 15.4.1734-6.4.1737 *Berwick* (70); 7.4.1737 CinC — The Mediterranean Sea; 7.4.1737 *Gloucester* (50); 28.2.1739/40-15.9.1740 *Prince Frederick* (70); 16.9.1740 *Nassau* (70); 29.1.1740/41-4.6.1741 *Barfleur* (90); 9.1743-1753 Gov. of New York; 7.12.1743 **Rear Admiral of the Red**; 19.6.1744 **Vice Admiral of the White**; 23.4.1745 **Vice Admiral of the Red**; 15.7.1747 **Admiral of the White**; 1754-10.7.1761 M.P. for Saltash; 3.1757 **Admiral of the Fleet**.

CLIVE, BENJAMIN

Dates: 1764 Died.
Family: Brother Rev. Robert; Sister Judith.
Service: **Lieutenant**; 16.3.1745/46(MED 28.6.1749) 4L *Boyne* (80); 28.8.1746(MED 28.6.1749) 3L *Liverpool* (44); 3.1.1748/49(MED 28.6.1749)-10.7.1749[P] 2L *Liverpool* (44); **Commander**; 22.7.1756-14.8.1756[C] *Oswego* (5) Sloop; 5.5.1757 *Cormorant* (18) Sloop; **Captain**; 22.5.1758 *Rose* (20); 5.6.1758-12.6.1758 Raid on Saint-Malo; 14.4.1760-1.10.1760 *Sutherland* (50); 24.11.1760-13.12.1762[P] *Trident* (64); 29.3.1761-11.6.1761 Expedition against Belle-Isle.

COALKE, WILLIAM

Dates: c.1726 Born; 11.9.1766 Died.
Family:
Service: 13.10.1737 Capt Serv *Plymouth*; 15.5.1738-30.5.1740[P] Gnr Serv *Edinburgh* (70); 9.11.1742 L. Serv *Russell* (80); 29.1.1743 L. Serv *Grafton* (70); 7.4.1743 L. Serv *Buckingham* (70); 16.6.1743 L. Serv *Royal Sovereign* (104); 27.6.1744 Clerk *Deptford Prize* (8) Sloop; 17.9.1744 Mid *Shrewsbury* (80); 15.5.1745 Able *Kingston* (60); 20.7.1746-3.6.1748[P] Mid *Folkestone* (44); 1748-1757 Merchant Service; 4.4.1757 Passed; **Lieutenant**; 29.5.1758(NA 19.12.1758)-18.10.1758 L. *Kennington* (20); 6.6.1758-27.7.1758 The Siege of Louisbourg.

COARD, WILLIAM

Dates: c.1713 Born; 1758 Died; 4.3.1758 Will Probate.
Family: Brother George; Sister Christian; Sister Alice; Sister Elizabeth; Sister Margaret; Sister Mary.
Service: 6.10.1728 Ord. *Gosport* (42); 25.4.1730 Able *Gosport* (42); 20.10.1730-8.6.1732[P] QGnr *Gosport* (42); 22.4.1734 Mid *Norfolk* (80); 3.6.1734 Able *Rose* (20); 12.12.1734 Mate *Lowestoffe* (20); 4.12.1735 Able *Pembroke* (60); 18.12.1735 Mate *Pembroke* (60); 1.3.1738/39 Passed; **Lieutenant**; 20.2.1741/42(13.6.1745) 3L *Ludlow Castle* (40); 15.6.1744(JAM 29.7.1745) 4L *Cumberland*

(80); 31.3.1745[JAM 29.7.1745] 3L *Cumberland* (80); 18.9.1745 2L *London* (100); 11.6.1746-28.6.1748[P] 1L *Portland Prize* (50); 1.12.1748-14.11.1752[P] 2L *Eagle* (60); 3.1.1754-28.4.1758[SC] L. *Bridgewater* (24); 11.1.1756-14.1.1756 Capture of Geriah; 7.3.1757-1.4.1757 Expedition against Chandernagore.

COATES, THOMAS

Dates: 4.6.1712 Born; 16.7.1767 Died.
Family: Father John Cotes; Mother Lady Dorothy Shirley; Wife Mrs. Mary Kendal (d. 1754); Wife Miss Ryder.
Service: 15.4.1726 Vol-p-O *Superb* (64); 27.10.1726 Vol-p-O *Bredah* (70); 16.7.1728 Mid *Lion* (60); 1.10.1728 Mid *Plymouth* (60); 9.10.1730 Mid *Falmouth* (50); 17.10.1732 Passed; **Lieutenant**; 2.3.1733/34 4L *Somerset* (80); 13.3.1733/34 3L *Somerset* (80); 2.8.1734-19.7.1736[P] 2L *Deptford* (60); **Commander**; 26.7.1738-1.5.1740 *Cruizer* (8) Sloop; **Captain**; 12.5.1740-17.7.1740 *Lively* (20); 18.7.1740 *York* (60); 20.2.1744/45-7.3.1746/47 *Edinburgh* (64); 11.7.1747-9.8.1748[P] *Edinburgh* (64); 14.10.1747 2nd Battle of Cape Finisterre; 9.1.1751/52 Commodore *Severn* (50); 14.1.1751/52 CinC — Jamaica; 5.1755 **Rear Admiral of the Blue**; 4.6.1755-1756 *Severn* (50); 4.6.1756 **Rear Admiral of the White**; 1.1757-1760 *Marlborough* (80); 24.2.1757 **Rear Admiral of the Red**; 7.1757-1760 CinC — Jamaica; 31.1.1758 **Vice Admiral of the Blue**; 14.2.1759 **Vice Admiral of the White**; 26.3.1761-16.7.1767 M.P. for Great Bedwyn; 21.10.1762 **Vice Admiral of the Red.**

COBBY, THOMAS

Dates: 1711 Born; 1789 Died.
Family:
Service: 28.8.1739 Mid *Rochester* (54); 11.4.1741 Mate *Tiger* (50); 7.1741-10.1741 Operations against Santiago; 26.1.1741/42 Able *Lion* (60); 16.5.1742 Mate *Lion* (60); 9.12.1743 Mid *Dolphin* (20); 17.2.1743/44 Mid *Chester* (54); **Lieutenant**; 4.3.1745/46[ECH 15.5.1747]-16.10.1747 2L *Vigilant* (60); 14.5.1747 Passed; 1.11.1755-23.4.1757 2L *Dover* (44).

COCK, WILLIAM

Dates: 1757 Died.
Family:
Service: **Lieutenant**; 24.12.1743[BLI 15.10.1745]-24.5.1744 3L *Launceston* (44); 2.3.1744/45[BLI 15.10.1745]-18.10.1745[P] 2L *Lynn* (44); 19.12.1745[MED 3.6.1748] 3L *Boyne* (80); 6.5.1747[MED 3.6.1748]-4.6.1748[P] 2L *Russell* (80); 7.10.1747 Action of 1747-10-07.

COCK, WILLIAM

Dates: 1766 Died.
Family:
Service: 16.4.1736 Able *Pearl* (40); 6.1.1738/39 Mid *Pearl* (40); 28.7.1739 Mid *Squirrel* (20); 4.1740-5.7.1740 Attack on St. Augustine; 4.3.1740/41-5.1741 Operations against Cartagena; 31.5.1743 Mid *Launceston* (44); 1.6.1744 Passed; **Lieutenant**; 20.2.1745/46[MED 23.5.1749] L. *Conqueror* (8) Fireship; 29.8.1746[MED 23.5.1749]-9.1.1748/49[P] L. *Enterprise* Sloop; 24.12.1755-4.3.1761[P] 1L *Kingston* (60); 20.5.1756 Battle of Minorca; 8.1757-10.1757 Louisbourg Expedition; 6.6.1758-27.7.1758 The Siege of Louisbourg; 20.11.1759 Battle of Quiberon Bay.

COCKBURNE, ANDREW

Dates: c.1709 Born; 1768 Died Holborn, London; 18.2.1769 Will Probate.
Family: Daughter Susanna Johanna; Daughter Helen.
Service: 24.5.1728 Able *Dursley Galley* (20); 7.4.1732 MidO *Kingston* (60); 24.5.1732 Able *Hector* (40); 9.4.1733 Mid *Hector* (40); 4.11.1734 Mid *Devonshire* (80); 5.4.1735 Passed; **Lieutenant**; 11.6.1741 3L *Prince Frederick* (70); 25.6.1742 3L *Dreadnought* (60); 11.2.1743/44 2L *Dreadnought* (60); 7.8.1744 1L *Dreadnought* (60); 22.2.1744/45-1.11.1745 1L *Edinburgh* (64); 4.12.1745 1L *Namur* (74); 3.5.1747 1st Battle of Cape Finisterre; **Commander**; 9.10.1748[EI 23.5.1751] *Swallow* (14) Sloop; 1.9.1749[EI 23.5.1751] *Basilisk* (8) Bomb Vessel; **Captain**; 16.1.1749/50[EI 11.5.1750]-14.5.1750[P] *York* (60); 13.2.1751/52-14.2.1755 *Weazle* (16) Sloop.

COCKBURNE, GEORGE

Dates: c.1717 Born; 1770 Died.
Family: Father John Cockburn (c.1679-1758); Mother Arabella Rowe; Wife Lady Caroline Forrester (d.1784); Daughter Anna Maria (d.1808); Daughter Mary Shuttleworth [Holden] (d.1777).
Service: 18.11.1721 Vol-p-O *Cornwall* (80); 3.8.1722 Able *Dolphin* (20); 1.12.1724 MidO *Dolphin* (20); 23.10.1725 Mid *Newark* (80); 1.1.1725/26 Mid *Captain* (70); 13.1.1727/28-23.5.1728 Able *Berwick* (70); 12.1.1737/38 Passed; **Lieutenant**; 15.3.1737/38-22.5.1738 4L *Edinburgh* (70); 1.9.1739-11.11.1739 3L *Lichfield* (50); **Commander**; 25.3.1741 *Drake* (8) Sloop; **Captain**; 11.6.1741 *Gibraltar* (20); 24.5.1742 *Medway* (60); 20.5.1752-6.9.1753[P] *Glory* (44); 6.9.1753-16.1.1755 *Yarmouth* (64); 4.2.1755-8.5.1756 *Nassau* (64); 29.12.1756-6.8.1770 Comptroller of the Navy.

COCKFIELD, SAMUEL

Dates: c.1725 Born; 1766 Died; 1.12.1766 Will Probate.
Family: Wife Elizabeth Fossick married 26.5.1748; Daughter Hannah (1749-1749).
Service: **Lieutenant**; 9.7.1756 3L *Windsor* (60); 8.12.1756-9.1.1760 2L *Windsor* (60); 8.1757-10.1757 Louisbourg Expedition; 23.2.1760 1L *Dorsetshire* (68); **Commander**; 24.11.1761-4.4.1763 *Fortune* (14) Sloop.

COCKS, REGINALD

Dates: c.1705 Born; 1790 Died; 2.11.1790 Will Probate.
Family: Daughter Caroline; Son Thomas, RN.
Service: 6.1.1727/28 Able *Rippon* (60); 12.9.1730 Able *Assistance* (50); 26.11.1730 QGnr *Portland* (50); 9.6.1732 Able *Grampus* (6) Sloop; 23.9.1733 QGnr *Swallow* (60); 5.1.1733/34 YoS *Swallow* (60); 24.11.1735 QM *Swallow* (60); 21.10.1737 Mid *Swallow* (60); 8.1.1738/39 Mid *Princess Louisa* (60); 27.3.1739 Mate *Norfolk* (80); 6.10.1739 Mid *Namur* (90); 12.4.1740 Mate *Victory* (100); 20.1.1740/41 Passed; **Lieutenant**; 13.4.1741 6L *Sandwich* (90); 23.11.1741-28.4.1742 4L *Lennox* (70); 15.3.1742/43 3L *Jersey* (60); 8.2.1743/44 2L *Jersey* (60); 30.4.1744 2L *Prince Frederick* (70); 7.12.1744 1L *Prince Frederick* (70); 3.5.1747 1st Battle of Cape Finisterre; 1.12.1748-21.11.1752[P] 1L *Somerset* (68); 6.2.1755 1L *Somerset* (68); 11.2.1755 1L *Penzance* (44); 7.2.1757 1L *Royal Anne* (100); 19.4.1757 2L *Prince* (90); **Commander**; 12.3.1758[MED 5.2.1759]-15.10.1759 *Fortune* (14) Sloop.

COCKS, THOMAS

Dates:
Family: Father Reginald Cocks, RN (1705-1790).
Service: **Lieutenant**; 20.7.1759-28.9.1760[P] 3L *Princess Mary* (60); 30.11.1770-6.2.1771 3L *Cambridge* (80).

CODRINGTON, CHRISTOPHER

Dates: c.1729 Born; 1772 Died.
Family:
Service: 23.10.1743 Capt Serv *Sheerness* (20); 28.3.1744 Capt Serv *Falkland* (50); 27.6.1746 Able *Defiance* (60); 30.6.1747 Mid *Defiance* (60); 1.8.1748 Able *Captain*; 14.12.1748-28.7.1749[P] Mid *Richmond* (24); 21.9.1749 Mid *Invincible* (74); 27.4.1750 Passed; **Lieutenant**; 2.8.1755[(NA 29.3.1756)] 2L *Augusta* (60); 1.6.1756 4L *Chichester* (68); 8.6.1756-3.7.1756 3L *Antelope* (50); **Commander**; 17.1.1757-17.4.1758 *Antigua* (14) Sloop; **Captain**; 16.10.1758-7.12.1758 *Garland* (24); 4.7.1759-29.11.1762 *Phoenix* (44).

COE, FYFIELD

Dates: 1763 Died; 24.1.1763 Will Probate.
Family: Wife Mary; Daughter Mary.
Service: 19.1.1716/17 Ord. *Saint Albans* (54); 2.10.1718 Ord. *Ipswich* (70); 21.9.1719-11.11.1719 Expedition to Vigo; 25.1.1719/20 Able *Woolwich* (54); 22.6.1720 Mid *Oxford* (54); 26.5.1722 Mate *Centurion* (54); 14.10.1722 Mid *Centurion* (54); 15.3.1722/23 Passed; **Lieutenant**; 4.5.1727-12.11.1731[P] L. *Deal Castle* (20); 23.2.1733/34-8.4.1736[P] 4L *Namur* (90); 28.7.1738 2L *Falkland* (50); 16.9.1740-5.10.1740 1L *Rupert* (60); 10.1.1740/41 2L *Duke* (90); 27.3.1741-23.8.1743 1L *Duke* (90); **Commander**; 16.8.1743-25.10.1744[P] *Deptford Prize* (8) Sloop.

COLBY, CHARLES

Dates: c.1701 Born; 28.12.1771 Died Gunton Hall, Lowestoft; 9.3.1772 Will Probate.
Family: Daughter Mary [Lewis] (d. 1774).
Service: 21.5.1718 Capt Serv *Dragon* (54); 26.2.1719/20 Able *Dragon* (54); 24.5.1721 Mid *Dragon* (54); 11.6.1724 Mid *Argyll* (50); 7.11.1725 Able *Argyll* (50); 7.12.1725 Mid *Argyll* (50); 23.2.1725/26 Passed; **Lieutenant**; 19.6.1727 3L *Chatham* (50); 16.1.1727/28-30.6.1730[P] 2L *Chatham* (50); 31.1.1733/34 3L *Grafton* (70); 5.5.1735-13.4.1736[P] 2L *Grafton* (70); 16.5.1738-13.7.1738 2L *Worcester* (60); 28.7.1738-23.11.1738[P] 1L *Superb* (60); 12.6.1739 1L *Superb* (60); 13.7.1739 2L *Burford* (70); 21.11.1739 Attack on Puerto Bello; **Commander**; 11.2.1739/40[(22.10.1741)]-11.1.1740/41 *Eleanor* (8) Fireship; 23.3.1739/40 Attack on Chagres; **Captain**; 12.1.1740/41 *Boyne* (80); 8.6.1741[(22.10.1741)]-3.1.1741/42 *Princess Caroline* (80); 4.1.1741/42-7.1.1741/42 *Bideford* (20); 24.6.1742 *Falmouth* (50); 6.1744 Bombardment of Porto Bello; 29.1.1744/45[(13.8.1745)] *Seahorse* (20); 4.3.1744/45[(13.8.1745)]-8.7.1745[P] *Experiment* (20); 14.9.1745 *London* (100); 28.1.1755 *Torbay* (74); 6.6.1755-8.6.1755 Action of 6-8 June 1755; 8.1.1756-30.6.1756 *Invincible* (74); 7.1756-1763 Resident Commissioner at Gibraltar; 8.1.1762-1763 CinC — Gibraltar.

COLBY, STEPHEN

Dates: c.1720 Born; 1779 Died.
Family:
Service: 7.11.1735 Ord. *Warwick* (60); 22.2.1736/37 Able *Warwick* (60); 12.3.1737/38 Able *Ipswich* (70); 21.4.1738 Mid *Ipswich* (70); 1.2.1739/40 Mid *Berwick* (70); 26.3.1740 Mid *Shrewsbury* (80); 23.9.1740 Mid *Victory* (100); 18.2.1741/42 Passed; **Lieutenant**; 11.3.1741/42 L. *Serpent* (8) Bomb Vessel; 26.5.1742-11.1.1743/44 L. *Gibraltar* (20); 16.1.1743/44 3L *Eltham* (40); 7.7.1744-23.6.1745 2L *Eltham* (40); **Commander**; 30.3.1746[(BLI 3.10.1746)]-19.7.1746[C] *Albany* (10) Sloop; 27.5.1748-20.5.1752[P] *Grampus* (14) Sloop; **Captain**; 20.8.1756 *Deal Castle* (20); 23.8.1756 *Yarmouth* (64); 11.11.1756 *Invincible* (74); 26.4.1757 *Barfleur* (80); 5.9.1757-6.10.1757 Raid on Rochefort; 19.10.1757-2.12.1757 *Prince George* (80); 17.4.1758 *Thames* (32); 21.11.1760-30.6.1761 *Intrepid* (60); 8.1.1771-7.5.1772 *Kent* (74); 20.9.1777-15.6.1779 *Fame* (74).

COLE, JOHN SUTTON

Dates: 9.9.1740 Baptised St Botolph Without Aldgate, London; 9.9.1740 Born London; 1778 Died.
Family: Father Richard Cole; Mother Mary.
Service: 12.4.1757 Capt Serv *Lichfield* (50); 5.7.1757 Capt Serv *Orford* (68); 8.1757-10.1757 Louisbourg Expedition; 6.6.1758-27.7.1758 The Siege of Louisbourg; 6.5.1759 Able *Speedwell* (8) Sloop; 21.6.1759 Mid *Speedwell* (8) Sloop; 18.4.1760 Mid *Hind* (24); 15.3.1762 Able *Lowestoffe* (32); 7.7.1762 Passed; **Lieutenant**; 23.8.1762 L. *Barbadoes* (14) Sloop; 23.12.1762-2.8.1763 2L *Liverpool* (28); 3.11.1770-29.5.1771[P] 3L *Elizabeth* (74).

COLE, MARTIN

Dates: c.1728 Born; 1803 Died; 23.12.1803 Will Probate.
Family: Wife Sarah; Daughter Sarah (1775-?).
Service: 17.9.1742-12.6.1745[P] Capt Serv *Newcastle* (50); 25.11.1746 Able *Chichester* (68); 28.11.1747-5.6.1748[P] Mid *Chichester* (80); 5.12.1751 Able *Tilbury* (58); 13.9.1752 Mid *Captain*; 5.4.1755 Mate *Ramillies* (90); 13.5.1755 Mid *Terrible* (74); 8.7.1756 Passed; **Lieutenant**; 8.5.1757[(NA 30.8.1759)]-21.3.1760[P] 4L *Captain* (64); 8.1757-10.1757 Louisbourg Expedition; 6.6.1758-27.7.1758 The Siege of Louisbourg; 16.1.1761-19.8.1763[P] 3L *Arrogant* (74); 31.1.1775 2L *Ocean* (90); 7.7.1775 1L *Ocean* (90); 28.8.1777 1L *Sultan* (74); 25.10.1777 1L *Ocean* (90); **Commander**; 13.5.1778-7.4.1781[P] *Wolf* (8) Sloop; 31.12.1779 Affair of Fielding and Byland.

COLES, CHRISTOPHER

Dates: c.1720 Born; 1757 Died.
Family:
Service: 10.5.1735-28.6.1736 Serv *Success* (24) Hulk; 29.6.1736-14.11.1737 Capt Serv *Pearl* (40); 15.11.1737-11.9.1739 Capt Serv *Newcastle* (50); 12.9.1739-13.11.1739 Ord. *Augusta* (60); 14.11.1739-21.2.1740/41 Able *Augusta* (60); 7.1.1740/41 Action of January 7 1741; 22.2.1740/41-2.9.1741 Able *Deptford Prize* (8) Sloop; 3.9.1741 Mid *Lynn* (44); 20.2.1743/44 Passed; **Lieutenant**; 31.3.1744 4L *Prince Frederick* (70); 25.10.1745 3L *Prince Frederick* (70); 3.5.1747 1st Battle of Cape Finisterre; 7.3.1747/48-6.12.1748[P] 2L *Prince Frederick* (70).

COLINS, HENRY

Dates: 3.1791 Died West Indies.

Family:

Service: **Lieutenant**; 2.11.1761-18.12.1762[F] 4L *Temple* (68); 7.1.1762-10.2.1762 Operations against Martinique; 6.6.1762-13.8.1762 Operations against Havana; 17.7.1769-15.8.1775 LCmdr *Magdalen* (6) Schooner; 7.5.1777 L. *Fowey* (24); **Commander**; 23.8.1777-26.9.1777 *Zebra* (14) Sloop; **Captain**; 20.3.1779 *Victory* (100); 27.4.1780 *Aurora* (28); 18.1.1782-14.4.1783 *Aeolus* (32); 25.6.1789-19.3.1791 *Culloden* (74).

COLLEY, WILLIAM

Dates: c.1738 Born; bef.8.3.1766 Died; 3.5.1766 Will Probate.

Family: Wife Priscilla Tressions married 19.9.1759; Son William John (1765-?); Son Hugh (1765-?).

Service: 1752-1756 Merchant Service; 6.6.1756 Mid *Windsor* (60); 8.1757-10.1757 Louisbourg Expedition; 13.6.1759 Able *Windsor* (60); 6.11.1759-6.2.1760 Mid *Fame* (74); 6.2.1760 Passed; **Lieutenant**; 1.4.1760-25.6.1760 5L *Thunderer* (74); 5.12.1760-15.12.1761 3L *Assistance* (50); 25.8.1762 2L *Torrington* (44); 11.5.1763 2L *Fame* (74); 24.3.1764-bef.8.3.1766[†] 1L *Fame* (74).

COLLIER, SIR GEORGE

Dates: 11.5.1738 Born London; 27.1.1775 Knight Bachelor; 6.4.1795 Died London; 28.4.1795 Will Probate.

Family: Father George Collier (1720-?); Mother Henrietta Louisa Sophia Ralph (1715-1768); Wife Christiana Gwyn (1749-?) married 3.9.1763; Wife Elizabeth Fryer (1745-1830) married 19.7.1781; Daughter Unknown (1765-?); Son William George (1769-1832); Son George (1783-1814); Daughter Louisa Elizabeth (1784-?); Son Francis Augustus, RN (1785-1849); Son Henry Theodosius, RN (1780-1872); Daughter Georgina (1790-?); Son Charles (1790-1818); Daughter Georgina Emma Maria [Aide] (1792-1875).

Service: 7.5.1747-17.6.1747[W] Capt Serv *Maidstone* (50); 5.10.1748 Capt Serv *Anson* (60); 2.8.1749 Ord. *Centurion* (50); 18.3.1750 Able *Centurion* (50); 15.3.1751 Mid *Centurion* (50); 4.11.1752 Able *Nightingale* (22); 9.3.1753 Mid *Nightingale* (22); 14.6.1753 Mid *Otter* (14) Sloop; 9.1.1754 Passed; **Lieutenant**; 3.7.1754[(EI 16.11.1759)] 4L *Salisbury* (50); 4.12.1754[(EI 16.11.1759)]-10.9.1759 3L *Salisbury* (50); 11.1.1756-14.1.1756 Capture of Geriah; 7.3.1757-1.4.1757 Expedition against Chandernagore; 29.4.1758 Battle of Cuddalore; 3.8.1758 Battle of Negapatam; 10.9.1759 Battle of Pondicherry; **Commander**; 6.8.1761 *Wasp* (8) Sloop; **Captain**; 12.7.1762-7.3.1763[P] *Boulogne* (32); 19.12.1763-5.1.1767 *Edgar* (60); 2.2.1770 *Tweed* (32); 8.8.1771 *Levant* (28); 10.10.1771-19.2.1773[P] *Flora* (32); 27.12.1775 *Rainbow* (44); 7.7.1777 Action of 7th July 1777; 1.2.1778-24.5.1780[P] Commodore *Camilla* (20); 3.4.1779-4.12.1779 Commodore *Raisonable* (64); 24.7.1779-12.8.1779 Penobscot Expedition; 1.1780-5.1780 Operations against Charleston; 28.1.1780-23.6.1781 *Canada* (74); 2.4.1784-25.6.1790 M.P. for Honiton; 1.2.1785-30.1.1787[P] *Hector* (74); 21.7.1790-20.12.1790[P] *Saint George* (98); 1.2.1793 **Rear Admiral of the White**; 12.4.1794 **Rear Admiral of the Red**; 4.7.1794 **Vice Admiral of the Blue**; 10.2.1795-2.3.1795 CinC — River Medway and The Nore.

COLLIER, THOMAS

Dates: c.1736 Born; 10.10.1761 Died.

Family:

Service: 19.4.1753 Able *Gloucester* (50); 17.9.1756 Able *Severn* (50); 23.9.1757 Mid *Severn* (50); 20.10.1758 Mid *Monarch* (74); 28.1.1759 Mid *Royal Anne* (100); 24.4.1759 Mid *Edgar*

(60); 18.8.1759-19.8.1759 Battle of Lagos Bay; 19.9.1759 Mid *Firedrake* (8) Bomb Vessel; 12.10.1759 Mate *Firedrake* (8) Bomb Vessel; 13.2.1760 Passed; **Lieutenant**; 3.7.1760 L. *Raven* (14) Sloop; 8.6.1761-10.10.1761[F] L. *Pheasant* (14) Sloop.

COLLINGWOOD, GEORGE

Dates: 26.4.1732 Born Lincolnshire; 1796 Died Morpeth, Northumberland; 6.12.1796 Will Probate.
Family: Father John Collingwood; Mother Elizabeth; Sister Ann.
Service: 4.4.1749 Able *Sunderland* (60); 21.7.1750 Mid *Sunderland* (60); 23.10.1751 Able *Peggy* (8) Sloop; 12.2.1753 Mid *Peggy* (8) Sloop; 13.4.1754 Able *Peggy* (8) Sloop; 8.1.1756 Passed; **Lieutenant**; 4.7.1756[(ECH 26.4.1757)] 3L *Isis* (50); 16.5.1757[(ECH 26.4.1757)]-15.3.1763 2L *Isis* (50); 3.7.1759 Bombardment of Le Havre.

COLLINGWOOD, JOHN TREVOR

Dates: c.6.1738 Born Piddinghoe, Sussex; 12.6.1738 Baptised St. Alfege, Kent; 29.9.1796 Died Piddinghoe, Sussex.
Family: Father Edward Collingwood (1694-1779); Mother Jane Carlton (1714-1791); Wife Sarah Arlward (1752-1823) married 9.4.1779; Illegitimate Daughter Jane Collingwood Arlward (1775-?); Son Thomas (1787-1865); Daughter Sarah (1789-?); Brother William (1739-1740); Sister Jane (1740-1815); Brother Edward, RN (1743-1809); Brother Francis, RN (1745-1799); Sister Susannah (1748-1818); Brother Carlton (1749-1749); Brother Carlton (1752-1828).
Service: 19.9.1749 Capt Serv *Devonshire* (66); 13.11.1752 Mid *Culloden* (74); 23.11.1753 Able *Culloden* (74); 1.3.1754 Able *Penzance* (44); 30.1.1755 Mid *Yarmouth* (64); 23.9.1756 Mid *Somerset* (68); 6.6.1758-27.7.1758 The Siege of Louisbourg; 27.8.1758 Mid *Namur* (90); 31.1.1759 Passed; **Lieutenant**; 22.2.1759 3L *Anson* (60); 25.7.1760-21.11.1762 2L *Anson* (60); 9.5.1765-6.12.1766 L. *Hazard* (8) Sloop; 29.11.1766-29.1.1770 L. *Speedwell* (8) Sloop; 21.2.1771 2L *Intrepid* (64); 23.10.1771 2L *Royal Oak* (74); 25.6.1773 1L *Royal Oak* (74); 10.1.1774-1.3.1774 2L *Royal Oak* (74); 21.8.1776-2.3.1780 LCmdr *Union* Hired Unknown.

COLLINGWOOD, THOMAS

Dates: 2.6.1780 Died.
Family: Wife Mary Hughes (d.1824).
Service: **Lieutenant**; 28.10.1750[(NA 18.11.1751)]-2.3.1750/51 L. *Queenborough* (24); 28.1.1755 6L *Saint George* (90); 7.5.1755 4L *Saint George* (90); 11.11.1755 3L *Saint George* (90); 24.5.1756 3L *Namur* (90); 5.6.1756 3L *Ramillies* (90); **Commander**; 9.9.1756[(ECH 20.3.1758)]-19.11.1756 *Fortune* (14) Sloop; **Captain**; 29.11.1756[(ECH 23.6.1758)]-19.6.1758[P] *Siren* (20); 18.10.1758-26.5.1762 *Crescent* (32) Frigate; 7.1.1762-10.2.1762 Operations against Martinique; 25.3.1762-10.9.1762 *Nottingham* (60); 6.6.1762-13.8.1762 Operations against Havana; 10.9.1762-18.12.1762[F] *Temple* (68); 29.11.1766-2.2.1770 *Tweed* (32); 27.11.1771-28.9.1774[P] *Rainbow* (44); 26.1.1778 *Monmouth* (64); 27.2.1779[(NA 21.11.1780)] *Fame* (74); 6.7.1779 Battle of Grenada; 14.7.1779[(NA 21.11.1780)] *Grafton* (74); 30.7.1779-2.6.1780 Commodore *Grafton* (74); 17.4.1780 Battle of Martinique; 15.5.1780 Action of March 15 1780; 19.5.1780 Action of March 19 1780.

COLLINS, DAVID

Dates: c.1734 Born; 12.5.1787 Died.
Family:
Service: 19.2.1744 Able *Grampus* (14) Sloop; 6.4.1744-30.9.1744[C] Clerk *Grampus* (14) Sloop; 25.4.1746 Clerk *Grampus* (10) Sloop; 17.6.1746 Able *Gibraltar* (20); 21.6.1746 Clerk *Gibraltar*

(20); 17.9.1746 Mid *Dover* (44); 5.2.1749 Mid *Centurion* (50); 19.12.1751 Mate *Assistance* (50); 1.11.1752 Mate *Culloden* (74); 20.12.1752 Mate *Unicorn* (24); 8.1.1756 Passed; **Lieutenant**; 15.11.1756-4.5.1757 L. *Seahorse* (24); 14.5.1757 3L *Princess Amelia* (80); 17.1.1758 2L *Princess Amelia* (80); 6.6.1758-27.7.1758 The Siege of Louisbourg; 24.12.1760 1L *Princess Amelia* (80); 29.3.1761-11.6.1761 Expedition against Belle-Isle; 22.6.1762-14.1.1763[P] 1L *Magnanime* (74); 29.10.1767 2L *Augusta* (64); 14.12.1768 1L *Augusta* (64); 8.11.1770 2L *Barfleur* (90); 7.12.1770 2L *Resolution* (74); 29.6.1771-3.10.1771 3L *Resolution* (74); 20.2.1778 1L *Invincible* (74); **Commander**; 15.5.1778-16.5.1778 *Diligence* (10) Sloop; 13.7.1778 *Shark* (16) Sloop; 15.10.1778-8.8.1782[P] *Alfred* (20) Armed Ship.

COLLINS, HENRY

Dates: c.1725 Born.
Family:
Service: 28.8.1742 Able *Shrewsbury* (80); 31.7.1743 Mid *Shrewsbury* (80); 14.11.1743 Mid *Antelope* (50); 25.8.1745 Able *Portsmouth* (24) Storeship; 19.3.1745/46 Mid *Folkestone* (44); 9.4.1747 Able *Lynn* (44); 16.6.1747 Mid *Lynn* (44); 2.2.1749/50 Passed; **Lieutenant**; 6.4.1754[(EI 19.7.1759)]-3.7.1754 L. *Kingfisher* (14) Sloop; 3.7.1754[(EI 20.7.1759)] 5L *Kent* (64); 30.1.1755[(EI 20.7.1759)]-1.4.1757 3L *Tiger* (60); 11.1.1756-14.1.1756 Capture of Geriah; 7.3.1757-1.4.1757 Expedition against Chandernagore; 6.7.1761-15.11.1763[P] 1L *Brune* (32).

COLLINS, SIR JOHN

Dates: c.1734 Born; 4.7.1783 Knight Bachelor; 1794 Died; 23.6.1794 Will Probate.
Family: Wife Sarah (d.1827); Son Augustus Leveson Rogers, RN (1782-1808); Daughter Elizabeth [Conolly].
Service: 22.3.1751 Able *Monarch* (74); 28.7.1752 Able *Dolphin* (6) Fireship; 24.8.1754 Able *Mars* (64); 27.12.1754 Mid *Mars* (64); 3.7.1755 Mid *Torbay* (74); 13.2.1756 Mid *Invincible* (74); 8.3.1757 Passed; **Lieutenant**; 15.6.1757 L. *Flamborough Prize* (14) Sloop; 16.11.1757-28.11.1757 2L *Roebuck* (44); 1.12.1757 L. *Penquin* (20); 1.5.1758-15.7.1758 3L *Dover* (44); 28.9.1758-18.11.1758 4L *Nassau* (64); 5.1.1760-12.7.1764[P] 3L *Valiant* (74); 29.3.1761-11.6.1761 Expedition against Belle-Isle; 6.6.1762-13.8.1762 Operations against Havana; 12.11.1766-15.11.1769 1L *Superb* (74); **Commander**; 10.1.1771-1.8.1774[P] *Infernal* (14) Bomb Vessel; 8.2.1775 *Nautilus* (16) Sloop; **Captain**; 1.2.1778[(NA 3.5.1780)]-24.5.1780[P] *Camilla* (20); 24.7.1779-12.8.1779 Penobscot Expedition; 1.1780-5.1780 Operations against Charleston; 23.7.1782-25.6.1783[P] *Ruby* (64); 20.10.1782 Battle of Cape Spartel; 6.12.1782 Ruby v La Solitaire; 24.1.1784-1.2.1785 *Hector* (74); 25.9.1790 *Rose* (28); 25.1.1793-28.1.1794 *Berwick* (74).

COLLINS, JOHN

Dates:
Family:
Service: **Lieutenant**; 17.1.1758-18.10.1758 3L *Prince of Orange* (60); 6.6.1758-27.7.1758 The Siege of Louisbourg.

COLLINS, RICHARD

Dates: 1779 Died.
Family:
Service: 30.12.1720 Vol-p-O *Gosport* (42); 13.1.1723 MidO *Gosport* (42); 28.6.1723 Mid *Gosport* (42); 30.9.1723 Mid *Essex* (70); 21.4.1724 Mid *Solebay* (42); 30.3.1725-16.7.1725 Mid *Plymouth* (60); 16.7.1725 Passed; **Lieutenant**; 11.11.1729[(19.3.1729/30)]-13.6.1732 3L *Sapphire*

(42); 14.6.1732-1.3.1732/33 3L *Sunderland* (60); 2.3.1732/33-27.8.1733 2L *Suffolk* (70); 28.8.1733-27.7.1738 L. *Shark* (8) Sloop; 28.7.1738-31.8.1738 2L *Saint Albans* (50); 1.9.1738-12.6.1739 1L *Saint Albans* (50); 13.6.1739 1L *Warwick* (60); 30.7.1741[(12.9.1743)] L. *Port Mahon* (20); **Commander**; 27.7.1743-31.3.1744 *Grampus* (14) Sloop; 17.5.1744 *Grampus* (14) Sloop; **Captain**; 7.7.1744 *Gibraltar* (20); 2.10.1744-24.1.1746/47 *Dover* (44); 22.1.1747/48-8.2.1747/48 *Tilbury* (58); 1.12.1748-14.11.1752[P] *Eagle* (60); 17.10.1755-15.6.1756 *Princess Royal* (90); 28.6.1756-19.11.1759 *Terrible* (74); 8.1757-10.1757 Louisbourg Expedition; 6.6.1758-27.7.1758 The Siege of Louisbourg; 13.1.1762 **Superannuated Rear Admiral**.

COLLINS, RICHARD

Dates: c.1730 Born; c.1766 Died.

Family:

Service: 4.1.1742 L. Serv *Saint Albans* (50); 13.5.1742 Able *Warwick* (60); 11.2.1743/44-12.2.1743/44 Battle of Toulon; 27.6.1744 Clerk *Port Mahon* (20); 19.11.1744 Mid *Port Mahon* (20); 17.7.1746 Mid *Grampus* (10) Sloop; 21.4.1747 Mid *Gibraltar* (20); 12.7.1747 Mid *Warwick* (60); 23.9.1747 Able *Warwick* (60); 30.9.1747-21.6.1748[P] Mid *Saint George* (90); 14.4.1749 Able *Gibraltar* (20); 10.7.1749 Mid *Invincible* (74); 16.1.1750 Mate *Eagle* (60); 7.11.1753 Able *Assistance* (50); 23.2.1754 Mid *Assistance* (50); 7.8.1754 Passed; **Lieutenant**; 11.3.1755 3L *Rochester* (50); 20.1.1757 2L *Rochester* (50); 1.2.1758 1L *Rochester* (50); 5.6.1758-12.6.1758 Raid on Saint-Malo; 20.11.1759 Battle of Quiberon Bay; 7.1.1762-10.2.1762 Operations against Martinique; 1.5.1762[(EI 17.3.1763)]-29.11.1762[F] 2L *Marlborough* (68); 6.6.1762-13.8.1762 Operations against Havana.

COLLINS, RICHARD

Dates: c.1735 Born; 1780 Died; 7.10.1780 Will Probate.

Family: Wife Anna.

Service: 24.7.1747 Ord. *Romney* (44); 2.8.1748 Ord. *Windsor* (60); 20.5.1749 Mid *Sphinx* (24); 27.8.1749 Able *Sphinx* (24); 19.8.1752 Mid *Assistance* (50); 5.8.1753 Able *Assistance* (50); 12.8.1753 Mid *Assistance* (50); 6.11.1754 Passed; **Lieutenant**; 7.4.1756 LCmdr *Hunter* (10) Hired Cutter; 22.12.1756-1.10.1758 L. *Queenborough* (24); 29.4.1758 Battle of Cuddalore; 3.8.1758 Battle of Negapatam; **Captain**; 11.9.1759[(EI 7.8.1765)] *Queenborough* (24); 1.1.1760[(EI 7.8.1765)]-1.1.1761[W] *Newcastle* (50); 18.2.1761[(EI 15.1.1766)]-19.7.1765[P] *Weymouth* (60); 24.9.1762-6.10.1762 Battle of Manilla; 9.4.1771 *Achilles* (60); 18.1.1773[(BLI 15.4.1774)] *Diana* (32); 31.8.1773[(JAM 26.5.1775)]-4.5.1775[P] *Seaford* (20); 25.8.1778-16.5.1780[P] *Warwick* (50).

COLLINS, WILLIAM

Dates: c.1770 Died.

Family:

Service: 1.4.1710 Vol-p-O *Ruby* (54); 12.4.1715 Vol-p-O *Windsor* (60); 17.2.1715/16-10.11.1716[W] Vol-p-O *August* (60); 24.9.1719 MidO *Dartmouth* (54); 14.1.1719/20-21.7.1720 Mid *Dartmouth* (54); 22.7.1720-29.1.1720/21 Mid *Enterprise* (42); 30.1.1720/21-24.9.1722 Mid *Weymouth* (50); 25.9.1722 Mate *Weymouth* (50); 18.5.1724 Passed; **Lieutenant**; 2.3.1733/34-31.7.1737[P] 3L *Nottingham* (60); 12.7.1739 2L *Warwick* (60); 10.1.1740/41-4.2.1740/41 1L *Dover* (44).

COLMER, JOHN

Dates: c.1730 Born.
Family:
Service: 7.2.1747 Capt Serv *Warwick* (60); 22.9.1747 Ord. *Fowey* (44); 25.12.1747 Able *Warwick* (60); 9.4.1748 Battle of Santiago de Cuba; 12.10.1748 Battle of Havana; 9.1.1749 Able *Intrepid* (64); 15.8.1750 Mid *Intrepid* (64); 18.12.1751 Mid *Severn* (50); 21.10.1752-24.4.1753[W] Mid *Assurance* (44); 11.7.1753 Passed; **Lieutenant**; 10.9.1756-1.10.1756 L. *Badger* (10) Sloop; 22.11.1756-15.5.1758 2L *Enterprise* (44).

COLPOYS, JOHN CB,

Dates: 1742 Born Dublin; 14.2.1798 Order of the Bath; 2.1.1815 Order of the Bath; 2.1815 Royal Guelphic Order; 4.4.1821 Died.
Family: Father John Colpoys; Mother Miss Madden.
Service: 1755-1757 Merchant Service; 12.4.1757 Able *Badger* (10) Sloop; 20.4.1757 Mid *Badger* (10) Sloop; 7.10.1757-31.3.1760 Mid *Boreas* (28); 6.6.1758-27.7.1758 The Siege of Louisbourg; 3.7.1759 Bombardment of Le Havre; 1.4.1760 Mid *Dragon* (60); 3.4.1761 Mid *Modeste* (64); 7.5.1761 ActL *Modeste* (64); 28.9.1761 Passed; **Lieutenant**; 22.10.1762[(BLI 23.2.1764)]-14.3.1764[P] 4L *Modeste* (64); 17.11.1764-31.12.1765 2L *Lowestoffe* (32); 28.10.1767-13.10.1768 3L *Phoenix* (44); 15.6.1769 2L *Quebec* (32); 29.1.1771 3L *Northumberland* (68); **Commander**; 30.7.1773[(EI 14.9.1774)] *Swallow* (14) Sloop; **Captain**; 25.8.1773[(EI 14.9.1774)] *Northumberland* (68); 9.11.1775 *Seaford* (20); 19.11.1778-7.10.1779 *Royal George* (100); 27.10.1779 *Mercury* (28); 1.1.1780-21.10.1782 *Orpheus* (32); 14.4.1781 Action of 1781-04-14; 5.9.1781 Battle of the Chesapeake; 29.4.1783-26.8.1785 *Phaeton* (38); 10.5.1790 *Hannibal* (74); 31.8.1791-27.3.1794[P] *Hannibal* (74); 12.4.1794 **Rear Admiral of the Blue**; 4.7.1794 **Rear Admiral of the White**; 8.1794-14.5.1795 *London* (90); 1.6.1795 **Vice Admiral of the Blue**; 23.4.1798-1802 *Northumberland* (74); 12.2.1799 **Vice Admiral of the Red**; 18.2.1800 Capture of the Généreux; 1.1.1801 **Admiral of the Blue**; 24.3.1803-14.10.1804 *Salvador del Mundo* (112); 6.1803-5.1804 CinC — Plymouth; 5.1804-5.1805 Lord Commissioner of the Admiralty; 9.11.1805 **Admiral of the White**; 25.10.1809 **Admiral of the Red**; 1816-4.4.1821 Governor of Greenwich Hospital.

COLTHEART, WALTER

Dates: c.10.1721 Born; 20.10.1721 Baptised Saint Paul Covent Garden, Westminster; 1783 Died; 25.9.1783 Buried Portsea.
Family: Father Peter Coltheart; Mother Elizabeth; Brother Walter (1712-?); Brother Peter (1713-?); Sister Martha (1715-?); Sister Sarah (1717-?); Sister Eleanor (1718-?).
Service: 30.10.1740 Ord. *Sandwich* (90); 26.10.1741 Able *Sandwich* (90); 19.6.1742 Able *Royal Caroline* (8) Yacht; 25.10.1742 Able *Peregrine Prize* (8) Sloop; 2.3.1742/43 Able *Saltash* (14) Sloop; 19.10.1744-15.2.1744/45[P] Mid *Princess Amelia* (80); 23.6.1745 Able *Chester* (50); 8.9.1745 Able *Tilbury* (58); 8.4.1746 Mid *Tilbury* (58); 20.9.1746-25.9.1746 Lorient Operations; 14.10.1747 2nd Battle of Cape Finisterre; 10.12.1747 Passed; **Lieutenant**; 25.10.1758 L. *Fortune* (14) Sloop; 28.2.1759-17.3.1762 1L *Aquilon* (28); 29.3.1761-11.6.1761 Expedition against Belle-Isle; 18.7.1770 2L *Tweed* (32); 10.8.1771 2L *Levant* (28); 24.10.1771 2L *Asia* (64); 13.1.1772-21.9.1773 1L *Asia* (64).

COLTON, CALEB

Dates: c.1738 Born; 25.4.1738 Baptised Shrivenham, Berkshire; 13.1.1791 Died Saltash.
Family: Father Caleb Colton (1694-1785); Mother Adrey Barfoot (1708-1765); Wife Juliana (1740-1814); Son Barfoot (1764-?); Daughter Adrey Barfoot (1768-1810).

Service: 31.5.1751-1.2.1751/52[P] Capt Serv *Gosport* (44); 8.5.1752 Capt Serv *Advice* (50); 11.2.1754 MidO *Advice* (50); 29.11.1755-1.7.1756[P] Mid *Advice* (50); 17.11.1756 Mid *Kennington* (20); 11.7.1757 Able *Winchester* (50); 29.11.1757-7.2.1759 Mid *Winchester* (50); 16.1.1759-19.1.1759 Attack on Martinique; 7.2.1759 Passed; **Lieutenant**; 9.3.1759 3L *Firm* (74); bef.29.12.1760-13.5.1763[P] 2L *Firm* (74); 2.8.1763-20.12.1765[P] 1L *Shannon* (28); 12.11.1767 1L *Belleisle* (64); 10.11.1769 2L *Belleisle* (64); 29.3.1770-6.5.1771[P] 3L *Belleisle* (64); 30.11.1773 1L *Boyne* (68); 18.3.1777-5.2.1780[P] 3L *Blenheim* (90).

COLUMBINE, EDWARD

Dates: 1788 Died.
Family: Wife Sarah Thorneloe married 1760; Son Edward Henry, RN (1763-1811); Daughter Sarah [Dorington].
Service: **Lieutenant**; 2.4.1757 3L *Pembroke* (60); 6.6.1758-27.7.1758 The Siege of Louisbourg; 30.1.1759 2L *Edgar* (60); 18.8.1759-19.8.1759 Battle of Lagos Bay; 6.6.1762-13.8.1762 Operations against Havana; 7.6.1763-5.3.1768[P] L. *Hornet* (10) Sloop; 30.7.1771-12.7.1774 LCmdr *Wells* (6) Cutter.

COLVILLE, LORD ALEXANDER (7TH VISCOUNT COLVILLE OF CULROSS)

Dates: 28.2.1717 Born; 20.4.1741 7th Viscount Colville of Culross; 21.5.1770 Died Drumsheugh, Scotland.
Family: Father John Colville, 6th Viscount Colville of Culross (1690-1741); Mother Elizabeth Johnston (1701-1748); Mistress Elizabeth Greene; Wife Elizabeth Macfarlane (c.1735 - 1794) married 1768; Son Charles (1750-?); Son James Alexander (1759-?)); Daughter Sophia Green (1765-?); Brother Charles; Brother George; Brother John, 8th Viscount Colville of Culross (1725-1811); Brother Charles (1726 - 1761); Sister Mary (d.1731); Brother James, RN (d.1761); Sister Margaret [Castleman]; Sister Elizabeth [Petrie].
Service: 26.10.1732 Vol-p-O *Lyme* (20); 27.10.1734 MidO *Lyme* (20); 17.5.1737 Mid *Lyme* (20); 8.11.1737 Mid *Phoenix* (20); 18.7.1738 Able *Rose* (20); 16.12.1738 Mid *Rose* (20); 25.1.1738/39 Passed; **Lieutenant**; 31.8.1739-16.4.1741 L. *Alderney* (8) Bomb Vessel; 23.3.1739/40 Attack on Chagres; 3.4.1742-25.4.1743 2L *Russell* (80); **Commander**; 25.6.1743[(MED 18.12.1745)] *Sutherland* (54); 11.2.1743/44-12.2.1743/44 Battle of Toulon; **Captain**; 6.3.1743/44 *Dursley Galley* (20); 21.9.1744[(MED 27.1.1748/49)]-30.10.1748[P] *Leopard* (50); 11.3.1748/49 *Shoreham* (24); 24.3.1748/49-9.12.1752[P] *Success* (20); 10.1.1753-19.12.1757 *Northumberland* (68); 8.1757-10.1757 Louisbourg Expedition; 7.2.1758-22.9.1759 *Northumberland* (68); 6.6.1758-27.7.1758 The Siege of Louisbourg; 11.1759-10.1762 CinC — North America; 21.10.1762 **Rear Admiral of the White**; 1.1763-6.1763 CinC — Plymouth; 6.6.1763-16.10.1766[P] *Romney* (50); 8.6.1763-1766 CinC — North America.

COLVILLE, JAMES

Dates: 1.1.1761 Died Pondicherry.
Family: Father John Colville, 6th Viscount Colville of Culross (1690-1741); Mother Elizabeth Johnston (d.1748); Brother Charles; Brother Lord Alexander (7th Viscount Colville of Culross), RN (1717-1770); Brother George; Brother John, 8th Viscount Colville of Culross (1725-1811); Brother Charles (1726 - 1761); Sister Mary (d.1731); Sister Margaret [Castleman]; Sister Elizabeth [Petrie].
Service: **Captain**; 17.10.1758 *Newcastle* (50); 22.2.1759-1.1.1761[†] *Sunderland* (60); 10.9.1759 Battle of Pondicherry;

COMBS, JAMES

Dates: c.1709 Born; 1785 Died; 27.2.1785 Buried Chew Magna, Somerset; 10.5.1785 Will Probate.
Family: Wife Alison Barber.
Service: 6.2.1736/37 Able *Orford* (70); 7.3.1736/37 QGnr *Orford* (70); 28.6.1739 Mid *Prince of Orange* (70); 11.10.1739 Able *Superb* (60); 7.8.1740 Mid *Superb* (60); 16.8.1740 Mate *Superb* (60); 24.6.1742 Able *Duke* (90); 24.8.1742 Mate *Duke* (90); 11.2.1745/46 Passed; **Lieutenant**; 23.11.1747-15.7.1748[P] L. *Mortar* (8) Bomb Vessel; 23.8.1756 L. *Queenborough* (24); 22.12.1756 L. *Scarborough* (20); 27.5.1757-2.9.1762 L. *Crown* (18) Storeship.

COODE, NICHOLAS

Dates: c.1722 Born; 1765 Died.
Family:
Service: 2.4.1737 Capt Serv *Diamond* (40); 4.4.1739 MidE *Diamond* (40); 23.3.1739/40 Attack on Chagres; 19.11.1740 Mid *Salisbury* (50); 18.11.1741 MidO *Deal Castle* (20); 29.1.1741/42 Mate *Diamond* (40); 23.10.1742 Mid *Diamond* (40); 7.11.1742 Mid *Princess Mary* (60); 13.1.1742/43 Mate *Princess Mary* (60); 20.5.1743 Able *Princess Mary* (60); 7.6.1744 Passed; **Lieutenant**; 27.7.1744-27.11.1744[W] L. *Rye* (20); 21.2.1744/45 6L *Prince George* (90); 7.8.1746 5L *Prince George* (90); 9.2.1746/47-14.5.1750[P] 1L *York* (60).

COOK, ANDREW

Dates: 1710 Born; 1777 Died; 26.7.1777 Will Probate.
Family:
Service: 1737-1741 Merchant Service; 30.8.1741 Mid *Buckingham* (70); 15.5.1742 Mid *Neptune* (90); 11.2.1743/44-12.2.1743/44 Battle of Toulon; 12.9.1745 Passed; **Lieutenant**; 14.11.1746-27.9.1747 3L *Superb* (60); 3.1.1748/49[MED 28.6.1749]-10.7.1749[P] 3L *Liverpool* (44).

COOK, JAMES

Dates: c.1733 Born; 1800 Died.
Family:
Service: 1754-1757 Merchant Service; 28.1.1757 Able *Royal George* (100); 9.1.1758 Mid *Royal George* (100); 9.2.1758-20.2.1760 Mid *Namur* (90); 6.6.1758-27.7.1758 The Siege of Louisbourg; 18.8.1759-19.8.1759 Battle of Lagos Bay; 20.11.1759 Battle of Quiberon Bay; 20.2.1760 Passed; **Lieutenant**; 1.4.1760-11.3.1763[P] 3L *Gosport* (44); 19.5.1763 L. *Hazard* (8) Sloop; 30.8.1764-11.12.1767 L. *Wolf* (8) Sloop; 30.1.1773 L. *Speedwell* (8) Sloop; 2.8.1776-5.9.1777 2L *Egmont* (74); 1778 LCmdr *Wells* (6) Cutter; 1.6.1779-12.7.1786[P] LCmdr *Griffin* (10) Cutter.

COOKE, JOHN

Dates: 1762 Died.
Family:
Service: 31.3.1720 Able *Worcester* (54); 10.5.1720-11.5.1720 Bombardment of Donan Castle; 5.2.1721/22 Able *Royal Oak* (70); 25.2.1721/22 Able *Devonshire* (80); 20.5.1722 MidO *Preston* (50); 11.2.1722/23 Mid *Preston* (50); 14.7.1723 Mid *Weymouth* (50); 10.3.1723/24 Mid *Deptford* (50); 17.10.1727 Mid *Seahorse* (20); 5.12.1727 Passed; **Lieutenant**; 7.5.1728-2.4.1729 3L *Looe* (42); 31.1.1733/34-29.3.1734 4L *Lennox* (70); **Commander**; 8.11.1734-10.8.1739 *Swift* (6) Sloop.

COOKSON, THOMAS

Dates: c.1711 Born; 18.11.1775 Died.
Family:
Service: 12.12.1730 L. Serv *Ludlow Castle* (40); 22.12.1731 Able *Kent* (70); 25.8.1732 Able *Gosport* (42); 8.9.1734 Mid *Hampton Court* (70); 2.3.1736/37 Passed; **Lieutenant**; 16.11.1739 3L *Lark* (40); 31.3.1740-18.2.1740/41 3L *Eltham* (40); 27.3.1741-12.4.1741 2L *Fowey* (40); 10.12.1744 3L *Sandwich* (90); 12.1.1744/45 2L *Sandwich* (90); 9.5.1745 3L *Sandwich* (90); 20.5.1745 2L *Sandwich* (90); 1.7.1745 1L *Sandwich* (90); **Commander**; 24.1.1746/47-2.8.1748[P] *Fly* (8) Sloop; 26.11.1757-19.11.1761 *Trial* (10) Sloop; 16.7.1767 *Bonetta* (10) Sloop; 6.8.1767-1.3.1769 *Senegal* (14) Sloop.

COOPER, THOMAS

Dates: 1760 Died; 19.8.1760 Will Probate.
Family: Wife Elizabeth.
Service: 19.5.1712 MidO *Crown* (50); 21.8.1715 Able *Blandford* (20); 26.10.1715 Mid *Exeter* (60); 14.1.1716/17 Mid *Shrewsbury* (80); 7.10.1717 Mid *Royal Oak* (70); 7.3.1717/18 Passed; 27.2.1718/19[(3.1.1720/21)]-8.1.1720/21[P] 2L *Dunkirk* (50); 15.3.1721/22-17.7.1724[P] 2L *Nonsuch* (50); 23.12.1727[(17.5.1728)]-18.5.1728[P] 2L *Dunkirk* (50); 2.4.1729-24.12.1731[P] 1L *Grafton* (70); 14.6.1732-27.6.1732 6L *Namur* (90); 28.6.1732-20.1.1733/34 5L *Namur* (90); 21.2.1733/34-25.7.1734 3L *Britannia* (100); 26.7.1734-4.5.1735 2L *Britannia* (100); **Commander**; 5.5.1735 *Solebay* (8) Fireship; **Captain**; 14.11.1738[(28.12.1739)] *Solebay* (20); 24.6.1739[(13.2.1739/40)] *Chester* (54); 12.10.1740 *Dunkirk* (60); 7.1.1740/41 Action of January 7 1741; 4.3.1740/41-5.1741 Operations against Cartagena; 4.8.1743[(MED 5.12.1746)]-2.12.1745 *Stirling Castle* (70); 11.2.1743/44-12.2.1743/44 Battle of Toulon.

COOPER, WILLIAM

Dates: c.1717 Born; bef.7.1758 Died; 11.9.1758 Will Probate.
Family: Wife Elizabeth.
Service: 14.5.1733 Com Ret *Kingston* (60); 15.11.1733 Ord. *Kingston* (60); 20.6.1734 Vol-p-O *Spence* (8) Sloop; 29.6.1736 Mid *Newcastle* (50); 23.4.1737 Able *Seaford* (20); 25.6.1738 Mid *Seaford* (20); 17.4.1740 Passed; **Lieutenant**; 11.7.1740 L. *Shark* (8) Sloop; 4.2.1742/43 3L *Torrington* (44); 11.11.1743-7.9.1744 2L *Torrington* (44); 8.9.1744 4L *Sandwich* (90); 12.1.1744/45-11.2.1744/45 3L *Sandwich* (90); 11.2.1744/45-6.7.1745 2L *Ipswich* (70); 3.5.1745[(MED 16.5.1749)] 2L *Russell* (80); **Commander**; 20.2.1745/46[(MED 8.11.1748)] *Conqueror* (8) Fireship; 29.8.1746[(MED 5.5.1749)]-9.1.1748/49[P] *Enterprise* Sloop; 22.5.1756-8.1.1757 *Hawke* (8) Sloop; c.6.5.1757-31.5.1758[†] *Postillion* (18) Sloop.

COPE, JOHN

Dates: c.1726 Born; 1793 Died.
Family:
Service: 14.8.1742 Ord. *Woolwich* (50); 31.12.1742 Mid *Monmouth* (70); 29.12.1743 Able *Monmouth* (70); 18.7.1744 Mid *Lennox* (70); 24.7.1745 Mid *Duke* (90); 14.9.1746 Mid *Kent* (70); 3.4.1747 Passed; **Lieutenant**; 16.4.1748[(JAM 3.2.1748/49)]-17.2.1748/49[P] 3L *Warwick* (60); 12.10.1748 Battle of Havana.

CORBETT, WALTER

Dates: c.1723 Born; 1778 Died.
Family:
Service: 18.4.1741 Mid *Marlborough* (90); 16.1.1741/42 Mid *Somerset* (80); 11.2.1743/44-12.2.1743/44 Battle of Toulon; 17.3.1744/45 Mid *Saint George* (90); 16.5.1746 Passed; **Lieutenant**; 22.11.1757 3L *Harwich* (50); 9.3.1758-24.5.1758 Capture of Fort Louis; **Commander**; 1.5.1759-22.11.1760[P] *Union* Hired Galliot.

CORMACK, JOHN

Dates: c.1712 Born; 1758 Died.
Family:
Service: 10.5.1737 Able *Superb* (60); 30.7.1737 Able *Solebay* (20); 10.5.1738 2Mst *Spy* (8) Sloop; 19.6.1739 Mid *Spy* (8) Sloop; 18.7.1743 Passed; **Lieutenant**; 20.11.1744 L. *Greyhound* (20); 1.5.1746 Action of 1746-05-01; 18.5.1748-21.5.1748[P] L. *Salamander* (8) Fireship; 1.12.1748-14.11.1752[P] 3L *Berwick* (70); 5.2.1754 1L *Bristol* (50); 28.3.1754-1.8.1757 1L *Tiger* (60); 11.1.1756-14.1.1756 Capture of Geriah; 7.3.1757-1.4.1757 Expedition against Chandernagore.

CORNER, JOHN

Dates: c.1727 Born; 1.11.1772 Died; 3.2.1773 Will Probate.
Family:
Service: 29.11.1740 Able *Leopard* (50); 23.10.1743-14.12.1744[P] Able *Dursley Galley* (20); 11.2.1743/44-12.2.1743/44 Battle of Toulon; 9.2.1744/45 Mid *Defiance* (60); 22.9.1746 Able *Defiance* (60); 22.10.1746 Mid *Defiance* (60); 3.5.1747 1st Battle of Cape Finisterre; 14.10.1747 2nd Battle of Cape Finisterre; 4.2.1747/48 Passed; **Lieutenant**; 15.2.1757-20.3.1757 4L *Yarmouth* (64); 6.10.1758 L. *Pelican* (8) Bomb Vessel; 4.12.1758-16.10.1759 2L *Cerberus* (28); 6.4.1763 1L *Rainbow* (44); **Commander**; 9.5.1765 *Lynx* (10) Sloop; **Captain**; 20.6.1765 *Liverpool* (28); 14.12.1765-1.7.1766 *Coventry* (28); 24.2.1767 *Romney* (50); 9.5.1769[(NA 5.9.1770)]-6.9.1770 *Hussar* (28); 29.6.1771-1.11.1772[†] *Crescent* (32) Frigate.

CORNEWALL, FREDERICK

Dates: 1706 Born; 3.8.1706 Baptised; 4.8.1786 Died Delbury Hall, Shropshire.
Family: Father Rev. Frederick Cornewall (d.1748); Mother Elizabeth Trice; Wife Mary Herbert married 2.5.1746; Son Henry James (1747-1747); Son Frederick, MP (1752-1783); Son Folliott, Bishop of Bristol (1753-1831).
Service: 8.11.1718-21.5.1721[P] Vol-p-O *Falmouth* (54); 10.3.1722/23-7.5.1723[P] Vol-p-O *Falmouth* (54); 7.5.1724 MidO *Sheerness* (20); 11.5.1727 Mid *Sheerness* (20); 2.9.1728 Passed; **Lieutenant**; 13.3.1733/34-13.4.1735 3L *Centurion* (60); 14.4.1735-4.5.1735 2L *Centurion* (60); 5.5.1735-19.7.1736[P] 3L *Deptford* (60); 12.11.1736-13.6.1739 2L *Greenwich* (50); 14.6.1739-15.7.1739 2L *Pearl* (40); 16.7.1739-3.3.1739/40 3L *Saint Albans* (50); 5.3.1740/41-19.2.1741/42 2L *Bedford* (70); 11.2.1743/44-12.2.1743/44 Battle of Toulon; **Captain**; 11.2.1743/44[(26.5.1744)]-21.2.1743/44 *Marlborough* (90); 20.7.1744-21.10.1744[W] *Colchester* (50); 23.11.1744-19.2.1744/45 *Hector* (44); 15.3.1744/45-1.4.1746 *Hector* (44); 16.9.1746-22.2.1748/49[P] *Sunderland* (60); 21.5.1755-11.8.1756 *Revenge* (64); 20.5.1756 Battle of Minorca; 15.6.1771-10.10.1774 M.P. for Montgomery Boroughs.

CORNISH, SIR SAMUEL (1ST BARONET OF SHARNBROOK)

Dates: 1715 Born; 1.2.1766 1st Baronet of Sharnbrook; 30.10.1770 Died.
Family: Wife Susan Gambler.
Service: 8.2.1727/28 Vol-p-O *Anglesea* (40); 1.10.1730 Mid *Anglesea* (40); 13.6.1731 Able *Romney* (50); 17.9.1731 Mid *Edinburgh* (70); 21.3.1731/32 Able *Kingston* (60); 14.2.1732/33 Mid *Spence* (8) Sloop; 8.3.1733/34 Mate *Phoenix* (20); 4.9.1734 Passed; **Lieutenant**; 12.11.1739 3L *Lichfield* (50); 6.8.1740 2L *Lichfield* (50); 26.8.1740 1L *Lichfield* (50); 31.10.1740(2.2.1742/43) 1L *Weymouth* (60); 7.1.1740/41 Action of January 7 1741; 4.3.1740/41-5.1741 Operations against Cartagena; **Commander**; 25.2.1741/42 *Mortar* (8) Bomb Vessel; **Captain**; 12.3.1741/42 *Namur* (90); 21.9.1742(MED 31.10.1748)-22.8.1748[P] *Guernsey* (50); 11.2.1743/44-12.2.1743/44 Battle of Toulon; 1.7.1755 *Stirling Castle* (64); 28.12.1758-30.1.1759 *Union* (90); **Rear Admiral of the Blue**; 20.3.1759 *Lennox* (74); 19.5.1759 **Rear Admiral of the White**; 1761-1763 CinC — East Indies; 17.5.1761-29.7.1764[P] *Norfolk* (74); 24.9.1762-6.10.1762 Battle of Manilla; 21.10.1762 **Vice Admiral of the Blue**; 23.12.1765-30.10.1770 M.P. for New Shoreham; 18.10.1770 **Vice Admiral of the Red.**

CORNWALL, THOMAS

Dates: 4.7.1796 Died.
Family:
Service: **Lieutenant**; 13.6.1749(JAM 6.10.1749)-7.7.1749[P] 3L *Strafford* (58); 6.4.1750 MidE *Rainbow* (44); 6.2.1755 3L *Somerset* (68); 10.7.1755(NA 9.12.1755) 6L *Torbay* (74); 2.8.1755(NA 9.12.1755) 5L *Torbay* (74); 15.1.1756-5.8.1756 5L *Invincible* (74); **Commander**; 6.8.1756 *Speedwell* (8) Sloop; **Captain**; 7.2.1757-18.1.1758 *Grafton* (68); 8.1757-10.1757 Louisbourg Expedition; 17.4.1758-15.7.1760 *Emerald* (28); 25.8.1762-17.3.1763[P] *Niger* (32).

CORNWALLIS, WILLIAM GCB,

Dates: 20.2.1744 Born; 2.1.1815 Order of the Bath; 5.7.1819 Died.
Family: Father Charles, 1st Earl Cornwallis (1700-1762); Mother Elizabeth Townshend; Sister Mary [Whitbread] (1736-1770); Brother Charles KG PC, 1st Marquess Cornwallis (1738-1805); Brother Hon. Henry (1740-61); Brother James, 4th Earl Cornwallis (1743-1824); Sister Elizabeth [Southwell] (d.1796); Sister Charlotte [Madan] (d.1794).
Service: 1755-1757 Mid *Newark* (80); 1758 Mid *Kingston* (60); 1759-12.1760 Mid *Dunkirk* (60); 20.11.1759 Battle of Quiberon Bay; 12.1760 Mid *Neptune* (90); **Lieutenant**; 6.4.1761(MED 12.7.1762) 5L *Thunderer* (74); **Commander**; 12.7.1762 *Wasp* (8) Sloop; 14.10.1762-22.11.1764 *Swift* (14) Sloop; **Captain**; 20.4.1765-29.5.1766[P] *Prince Edward* (44); 27.6.1766-24.10.1768[P] *Guadeloupe* (28); 18.3.1768-22.3.1774 M.P. for Eye; 17.1.1769-29.9.1773[P] *Guadeloupe* (28); 26.9.1774 *Pallas* (36); 21.12.1776 *Isis* (50); 7.12.1777(NA 1.6.1778) *Bristol* (50); 25.12.1777(NA 1.6.1778) *Chatham* (50); 16.5.1778-22.7.1778 *Medea* (28); 23.9.1778 *Lion* (64); 6.7.1779 Battle of Grenada; 20.3.1780 1st Action off Monti Christi; 20.6.1780 Action off Monti Christi; 23.6.1781-28.10.1782[P] *Canada* (76); 25.1.1782-26.1.1782 Battle of Saint Kitts; 3.4.1782-2.4.1784 M.P. for Eye; 12.4.1782 Battle of the Saintes; 30.12.1782 *Foudroyant* (80); 14.1.1783 *Ganges* (74); 13.3.1783 *Royal Charlotte* (8) Yacht; 1.4.1784-19.6.1790 M.P. for Portsmouth; 3.10.1787-8.12.1787[P] *Robust* (74); 10.11.1788-1794 CinC — East Indies; 10.11.1788-11.1790 Commodore *Crown* (64); 6.11.1792-12.1.1807 M.P. for Eye; **Rear Admiral of the White**; 1.2.1793-26.5.1794[P] *Minerva* (38); 12.4.1794 **Rear Admiral of the Red**; 3.6.1794 *Excellent* (74); 4.7.1794 **Vice Admiral of the Blue**; 8.1794 *Caesar* (80); 12.1794-7.1795 *Royal Sovereign* (100); 1.6.1795 **Vice Admiral of the Red**; 16.6.1795-17.6.1795 First Battle of Groix; 10.2.1796 CinC — Barbados & the Leeward Islands; 3.1796-1.1.1801 Rear Admiral of Great Britain; 14.2.1799 **Admiral of the**

Blue; 10.1800-4.1802 *Belleisle* (74); 1801 *Ville de Paris* (110); 1.1.1801-14.5.1814 Rear Admiral of the United Kingdom; 1803-1806 CinC — English Channel; 5.1803-9.7.1803 *Dreadnought* (98); 9.7.1803-1805 *Ville de Paris* (110); 23.4.1804 **Admiral of the White**; 9.11.1805 **Admiral of the Red**; 14.5.1815-5.7.1819 Vice Admiral of the United Kingdom.

COSBY, PHILIPS

Dates: 1729 Born Nova Scotia; 10.1.1808 Died Bath.
Family: Father Colonel Alexander Cosby; Mother Anne Winnard; Wife Mrs. Eliza Hurst, nee Gunthorpe.
Service: 7.8.1739 Passed; 21.8.1745 Able *Mermaid* (44); 11.9.1745-14.9.1747[P] Mid *Mermaid* (44); 8.8.1749 Mid *Severn* (50); 30.4.1751 Able *Blandford* (20); 2.9.1751 Mate *Blandford* (20); 21.9.1752 Mid *Torrington* (44); 23.2.1753 Able *Centaur* (20); 18.8.1753-7.8.1754 Mid *Centaur* (20); **Lieutenant**; 28.1.1755-6.2.1755 4L *Monarch* (74); 22.3.1755 4L *Orford* (68); 14.5.1756 3L *Orford* (68); 8.1757-10.1757 Louisbourg Expedition; 6.6.1758-27.7.1758 The Siege of Louisbourg; **Commander**; 2.6.1760 *Laurel* (12) Sloop; 11.2.1761 *Beaver* (14) Sloop; **Captain**; 19.5.1761 *Hind* (24); 11.8.1762-14.5.1763[P] *Isis* (50); 6.3.1766 *Montreal* (32); 23.12.1767-31.5.1770 *Montreal* (32); 14.2.1778 *Centaur* (74); 27.7.1778 1st Battle of Ushant; 31.3.1779-24.9.1782[P] *Robust* (74); 16.3.1781 Battle of Cape Henry; 22.7.1785-1789 CinC — The Mediterranean Sea; 10.1785-1.1789 Commodore *Trusty* (50); 23.7.1790 CinC — Cork; 21.9.1790 **Rear Admiral of the White**; 1791-c.10.9.1791[P] *Impregnable* (98); 22.3.1792-6.8.1793 CinC — Plymouth; 12.1792-1794 *Windsor Castle* (98); 1.2.1793 **Vice Admiral of the Blue**; 12.4.1794 **Vice Admiral of the White**; 10.1794-11.1794 *Alcide* (74); 1.6.1795 **Vice Admiral of the Red**; 14.2.1799 **Admiral of the Blue**; 9.11.1805 **Admiral of the Red**.

COSTOBADIE, HENRY

Dates: c.1725 Born; 1811 Died; 21.6.1811 Will Probate.
Family:
Service: 1.1.1737/38 Able *Kennington* (20); 16.7.1740-1.7.1742 Able *Lancaster* (80); 1.8.1742-14.5.1743 Mid *Essex* (70); 16.7.1744-21.1.1745/46 Mid *Essex* (70); 11.2.1745/46 Passed; 12.2.1746 **Lieutenant**; 12.2.1745/46[MED 13.12.1748]-16.3.1745/46 4L *Boyne* (80); 16.3.1746/47[MED 3.2.1748/49]-27.10.1748[P] 3L *Roebuck* (44); 6.2.1755 3L *Edinburgh* (64); 31.12.1755-16.1.1761[P] 2L *Edinburgh* (64); 21.10.1757 Forrest's Action; 1777 Regulating Officer at Greenock; 21.9.1796 **Superannuated Commander**.

COTES, JOHN

Dates: 1772 Died.
Family:
Service: **Lieutenant**; 13.6.1760[JAM 14.10.1761] 2L *Renown* (30); 24.2.1761[JAM 30.8.1763] 3L *Defiance* (60); 6.6.1762-13.8.1762 Operations against Havana; 3.3.1763[JAM 30.8.1763]-10.8.1763[P] 2L *Defiance* (60).

COTTON, ROWLAND

Dates: c.1740 Born Cheshire; 30.11.1794 Died; 30.12.1794 Will Probate.
Family: Father Lynch Salusbury Cotton (1705-1775); Mother Elizabeth Abigail (1711-1777); Wife Elizabeth Aston (1741-1795); Daughter Sidney Arabella [Moore] (1778-1848); Son Willoughby (1783-1860); Brother Henry Calverley (1755-1837); Brother George (1742-1805).
Service: 1.5.1753-c.1756 Scholar *Royal Naval Academy*; **Lieutenant**; 31.1.1760[BLI 6.10.1760]-5.1760[C] L. *Virgin* (12) Sloop; 28.1.1762 6L *Saint George* Prison Ship; **Commander**;

25.8.1762-20.12.1762[P] *Druid* (10) Sloop; 2.4.1763 *Druid* (10) Sloop; **Captain**; 7.5.1764[JAM 3.7.1764]-29.4.1766[P] *Alarm* (32); 24.12.1776-19.1.1778 *Pallas* (36); 6.5.1780-27.8.1780 *Buffalo* (50); 28.8.1780-14.12.1781 *Inflexible* (64); 23.12.1782 *Vengeance* (74); 9.4.1783-10.9.1783[P] *Vengeance* (74); 16.8.1783-11.6.1786 *Culloden* (74); 6.7.1790-16.9.1791[P] *Robust* (74); 1.2.1793 **Rear Admiral of the White**; 6.8.1793 CinC — Plymouth; 1794 *Cambridge* (80); 12.4.1794 **Rear Admiral of the Red**; 4.7.1794 **Vice Admiral of the Blue**.

COUCHMAN, THOMAS

Dates: c.1738 Born; 1776 Died.

Family:

Service: 20.4.1747-14.9.1747[P] Mid *Mermaid* (44); 3.7.1748 Mid *Tavistock* (50); 18.7.1749 Mid *Yarmouth* (64); 18.6.1753 Mid *Culloden* (74); 9.7.1754 Mid *Bridgewater* (24); 11.1.1756-14.1.1756 Capture of Geriah; 24.5.1756 Mate *Bridgewater* (24); 7.3.1757-1.4.1757 Expedition against Chandernagore; 24.6.1757 Mid *Kent* (64); 14.12.1757 Mid *Cumberland* (66); 29.4.1758 Battle of Cuddalore; 6.5.1758 Passed; **Lieutenant**; 6.5.1758[EI 20.4.1761]-25.3.1761[P] 5L *Cumberland* (66); 3.8.1758 Battle of Negapatam; 10.9.1759 Battle of Pondicherry; 2.4.1762-9.6.1762 L. *Nautilus* (16) Sloop.

COULTAS, JEREMIAH

Dates: c.1723 Born; 1757 Died; 15.12.1757 Will Probate.

Family: Wife Dorothy Lister married 19.8.1751.

Service: 21.9.1738 Able *Grafton* (70); 22.1.1738/39 Able *Chester* (54); 29.1.1739/40 Mid *Plymouth* (60); 27.10.1741 Mid *Plymouth* (60); 11.4.1743 Able *Dragon* (60); 13.4.1743 Mid *Dragon* (60); 11.2.1743/44-12.2.1743/44 Battle of Toulon; 25.3.1745 Passed; **Lieutenant**; 7.6.1745 3L *Sapphire* (44); 13.11.1745 2L *Sapphire* (44); 23.1.1745/46 2L *Salisbury* (50); 16.11.1747-5.7.1748 L. *Shoreham* (24); 29.5.1755-1757[†] 2L *Humber* (44).

COVELL, ISAAC

Dates: 1781 Died.

Family:

Service: **Lieutenant**; 3.6.1746-1.8.1746 4L *Princess* (70); 16.9.1746 3L *Centurion* (50); 18.2.1746/47 6L *Royal Sovereign* (104); 10.6.1747 4L *Royal Sovereign* (104); 9.10.1747-7.6.1748[P] 4L *Barfleur* (90); 5.8.1755 3L *Trident* (64); 31.12.1755 2L *Trident* (64); 20.5.1756 Battle of Minorca; 4.8.1756-4.7.1757 L. *Diligence* (10) Sloop; 1.2.1759-4.6.1759 L. *Solebay* (24).

COWE, JOHN

Dates: c.1736 Born.

Family:

Service: 23.4.1751 Able *Porcupine* (16) Sloop; 14.5.1752 Able *Fowey* (24); 10.3.1755 Mid *Fowey* (24); 23.5.1756 Mate *Namur* (90); 2.5.1757 Passed; **Lieutenant**; 17.6.1757-26.11.1757 3L *Jason* (44); 19.1.1758 4L *Grafton* (68); 2.2.1758 3L *Grafton* (68); 20.7.1759[EI 9.8.1764] 3L *Elizabeth* (64); 10.9.1759 Battle of Pondicherry; 24.9.1762-6.10.1762 Battle of Manilla; 9.12.1762[EI 9.8.1764]-30.7.1764[P] 2L *Elizabeth* (64); 21.9.1796 **Superannuated Commander**.

COWE, PETER

Dates: c.1701 Born; 1773 Died; 4.11.1773 Will Probate.
Family: Daughter Christian Ann.
Service: 27.5.1731-16.4.1732 Mid *Terrible* (6) Bomb Vessel; 16.4.1732 Mate *Terrible* (6) Bomb Vessel; 12.4.1739 Passed; **Lieutenant**; 1.11.1739[(6.12.1740)] L. *Solebay* (20); 16.1.1739/40[(29.6.1741)] 3L *Jersey* (60); 19.1.1739/40[(29.6.1741)] 1L *Superb* (60); 27.7.1740[(29.6.1741)] 3L *Falkland* (50); 13.4.1741 2L *Falkland* (50); 11.9.1741 L. *Bideford* (20); 11.5.1742 1L *Looe* (44); 11.9.1742 2L *Preston* (50); 24.1.1744/45 Straits of Banca; 26.2.1744/45[(EI 10.11.1749)]-21.7.1745[SP] 1L *Deptford* (60); 21.7.1745[(EI 10.11.1749)]-20.12.1745 2L *Deptford* (60); 1.2.1745/46[(EI 10.11.1749)]-25.5.1749 1L *Harwich* (50); 25.6.1746 1st Battle of Negapatam; **Commander**; 10.9.1756-21.7.1758[P] *Princess of Wales* (18) Hired Armed Ship.

COWELL, HENRY

Dates: c.1721 Born; 12.4.1765 Died.
Family:
Service: 15.6.1731 Capt Serv *Chatham* (50); 26.12.1731 Capt Serv *Romney* (50); 26.5.1732 Capt Serv *Buckingham* (70); 2.4.1736 Clerk *Buckingham* (70); 8.12.1736 Able *Nottingham* (60); 24.8.1737 Able *Dragon* (54); 11.1.1737/38 Able *Hampton Court* (70); 21.11.1739 Attack on Puerto Bello; 8.3.1739/40 Mid *Hampton Court* (70); 9.10.1741 Mid *Sandwich* (90); 6.5.1742 Passed; **Lieutenant**; 31.5.1744[(JAM 24.8.1744)]-25.9.1744[P] 4L *Grafton* (70); 3.10.1744-8.7.1748[P] 2L *Portland* (50); 14.10.1747 2nd Battle of Cape Finisterre; 31.1.1747/48 Action of 1748/01/31; 21.4.1756 2L *Orford* (68); 14.5.1756 1L *Orford* (68); 3.2.1757 1L *Elizabeth* (64); 29.4.1758 Battle of Cuddalore; 3.8.1758 Battle of Negapatam; 10.9.1759 Battle of Pondicherry; **Commander**; 27.11.1760[(EI 14.10.1765)] *Southsea Castle* (28) Storeship; **Captain**; 1.2.1761[(EI 15.8.1765)]-28.8.1765[P] *York* (60).

COWLING, JOHN

Dates: 1792 Died.
Family:
Service: **Lieutenant**; 8.9.1758[(BLI 30.5.1760)]-14.12.1762 L. *Amazon* (22); 16.1.1759-19.1.1759 Attack on Martinique; 20.1.1759-1.5.1759 Capture of Guadeloupe; 27.9.1770 1L *Prince of Wales* (74); 24.1.1771 4L *Princess Amelia* (80); 26.8.1771-8.6.1772 LCmdr *Sir Edward Hawke* (8) Schooner; **Commander**; 3.6.1779[(JAM 29.12.1780)] *Port Royal* (18) Sloop; **Captain**; 13.1.1780[(JAM 9.8.1780)]-27.2.1781 *Ruby* (64); 20.3.1780 1st Action off Monti Christi; 20.6.1780 Action off Monti Christi; 27.2.1781[(JAM 23.10.1782)] *Ramillies* (74); 28.2.1782[(JAM 5.11.1782)]-10.10.1782 *Sandwich* (90).

COX, HENRY

Dates: c.1734 Born; 25.11.1759 Died Quebec.
Family:
Service: 1751-1752 Merchant Service; 21.5.1752 Able *Triton* (20); 19.10.1755 Mid *Triton* (20); 15.11.1755 Mid *Roebuck* (44); 10.1.1758 Mid *Princess Amelia* (80); 6.3.1758 Passed; **Lieutenant**; 7.11.1758-bef.25.11.1759[†] L. *Racehorse* (8) Bomb Vessel.

COZENTINE, EZEKIEL

Dates: 1783 Died; 9.7.1783 Will Probate.
Family: Wife Jane Penton married 16.3.1757; Sister Ann.
Service: **Lieutenant**; 26.5.1742-5.10.1743 L. *Serpent* (8) Bomb Vessel; 15.6.1744 3L *Captain* (70); 11.1.1745/46 2L *Captain* (70); 23.12.1746-12.7.1748[P] 2L *Launceston* (44); 6.2.1755 1L *Weymouth* (60); 16.7.1755-23.2.1757 1L *Tilbury* (58).

CRAIG, ROBERT

Dates: 1715 Born; 20.5.1769 Died.
Family:
Service: 27.9.1734 Able *Kent* (70); 26.5.1735 Able *Kent* (70); 1.11.1736 Able *William and Mary* (10) Yacht; 4.6.1738 Mid *William and Mary* (10) Yacht; 20.9.1739 Mid *Charlotte* (8) Yacht; 23.2.1739/40 Mate *Deptford* (24) Storeship; 18.11.1740 Passed; **Lieutenant**; 27.2.1740/41 3L *Faversham* (44); 27.3.1741 3L *Tiger* (50); 12.5.1741 2L *Tiger* (50); 7.1741-10.1741 Operations against Santiago; 11.11.1743-2.7.1746 3L *Chichester* (80); 11.2.1743/44-12.2.1743/44 Battle of Toulon; 6.3.1746/47 1L *Lark* (44); **Commander**; 23.6.1748[(JAM 19.6.1749)]-24.1.1750/51 *Vulture* (14) Sloop; **Captain**; 4.1.1757-18.10.1758 *Solebay* (24).

CRANSTON, JAMES

Dates: c.1733 Born; 31.7.1790 Died Lewes; 19.9.1790 Will Probate.
Family: Wife Catherine; Daughter Mary.
Service: 20.2.1746/47 Capt Serv *Warwick* (60); 15.6.1747 Ord. *Warwick* (60); 13.9.1747 Capt Serv *Canterbury* (60); 9.4.1748 Battle of Santiago de Cuba; 2.8.1748-19.1.1748/49[P] Mid *Milford* (44); 24.6.1749 Mid *Amazon* (22); 2.4.1751 Able *Amazon* (22); 21.10.1752 Mid *Culloden* (74); 22.12.1752 Mid *Culloden* (74); 7.2.1753 Passed; **Lieutenant**; 21.3.1755 4L *Essex* (64); 1.10.1756 3L *Essex* (64); 13.1.1757 2L *Essex* (64); 5.6.1758-12.6.1758 Raid on Saint-Malo; 5.9.1759 6L *Royal George* (100); 17.10.1759 5L *Royal George* (100); 20.11.1759 Battle of Quiberon Bay; 10.3.1760 3L *Royal George* (100); 27.6.1760 2L *Royal George* (100); **Commander**; 27.8.1760-3.7.1761 *Swallow* (14) Sloop; **Captain**; 7.4.1762 *Squirrel* (20); 26.9.1762[(MED 20.6.1763)]-18.5.1763 *Squirrel* (20); 20.10.1770 *Ocean* (90); 17.6.1771-22.4.1775[P] *Intrepid* (64); 12.6.1778-8.1.1782 *Defence* (74); 16.1.1780 Battle of Cape St. Vincent; 30.5.1782-26.11.1782 *Bombay Castle* (74).

CRAVEN, THOMAS

Dates: c.1715 Born; 14.12.1772 Died.
Family: Father John Craven; Wife Maria Rebecca Green; Brother William, MP (1705-69).
Service: 22.9.1730 Able *Success* (20); 12.6.1732 Able *Dursley Galley* (20); 27.8.1733 Mid *Dursley Galley* (20); 6.9.1735 Able *Dursley Galley* (20); 23.7.1736 Mid *Salisbury* (50); 4.9.1736 Mid *Sheerness* (20); 9.10.1736 Passed; 20.11.1739 **Lieutenant**; 28.11.1739[(26.5.1743)] 3L *Princess Louisa* (60); 4.3.1740/41-5.1741 Operations against Cartagena; 26.6.1741[(23.5.1743)] 2L *Princess Louisa* (60); 6.1.1741/42[(23.5.1743)] 1L *Strafford* (60); 24.8.1743 2L *Boyne* (80); 23.9.1743-8.5.1744[C] 1L *Northumberland* (64); 15.2.1744/45 1L *Pembroke* (60); **Commander**; 14.5.1745 *Weazle* (16) Sloop; **Captain**; 8.2.1745/46 *Rye* (20); 9.12.1746-7.10.1748[P] *Southsea Castle* (44); 1.7.1755-5.7.1759 *Princess Mary* (60); 2.4.1766-14.12.1772 M.P. for Berkshire; 18.10.1770 **Rear Admiral of the Blue**.

CRESPIN, ABRAHAM

Dates: c.1741 Born; 1786 Died; 10.11.1786 Will Probate.
Family: Father William Crespin; Wife Martha Legassicke.
Service: 28.2.1755 Able *Elizabeth* (70); 29.11.1756 Mid *Elizabeth* (64); 7.2.1757 Mid *Monarch* (74); 28.2.1758 Battle of Cartagena; 23.9.1758 Supnum *Royal Sovereign* (104); 6.2.1759 Supnum *Royal Anne* (100); 25.2.1759 Mid *Raisonnable* (64); 18.7.1759 Mid *Panther* (60); 27.11.1759 Mid *Terrible* (74); 20.4.1760 Supnum *Thunderer* (74); 29.4.1760 Mid *Newark* (80); 4.3.1761 Passed; **Lieutenant**; 20.1.1762-21.3.1763[P] 6L *Ocean* (90); 11.5.1763-26.2.1768[P] 3L *Fame* (74); 3.10.1770 3L *Bellona* (74); 7.11.1770-10.4.1773 LCmdr *Halifax* (6) Schooner; 18.1.1771 4L *Sandwich* (90); 22.6.1775 3L *Kent* (74); 9.8.1775 3L *Foudroyant* (80); 28.2.1776 L. *Martin* (14) Sloop; 11.10.1776 3L *Romney* (50); 7.4.1778 1L *Europe* (64); **Commander**; 13.5.1778-14.5.1778 *Diligence* (10) Sloop; 19.5.1778 *Vesuvius* (8) Bomb Vessel; **Captain**; 17.1.1780[(EI 14.9.1780)]-13.10.1781[P] *Suffolk* (74); 17.4.1780 Battle of Martinique; 15.5.1780 Action of March 15 1780; 19.5.1780 Action of March 19 1780.

CREWS, JOHN

Dates: c.1731 Born; 7.3.1811 Died.
Family:
Service: 14.5.1747 Capt Serv *Canterbury* (60); 9.4.1748 Battle of Santiago de Cuba; 12.10.1748 Battle of Havana; 3.12.1748 Able *Canterbury* (60); 10.10.1749 Mid *Canterbury* (60); 20.7.1750 Able *Scorpion* (14) Sloop; 29.1.1750/51 Mate *Mermaid* (24); 11.10.1752 Mid *Hornet* (10) Sloop; 1.8.1753 Passed; **Lieutenant**; 13.11.1756 4L *Elizabeth* (64); 29.4.1758 Battle of Cuddalore; 3.8.1758 Battle of Negapatam; 10.9.1759 Battle of Pondicherry; 24.2.1761-6.12.1762 L. *Martin* (14) Sloop.

CRICKETT, EDWARD

Dates: c.1709 Born; 1769 Died; 30.5.1770 Will Probate.
Family: Wife Mary.
Service: 21.10.1730-6.6.1731 Able *Elizabeth* (70); 6.6.1731-25.12.1731 Able *Medway* (60); 24.12.1731-28.7.1733 Able *Sunderland Hulk* (60); 28.7.1733-11.6.1734 Able *Garland* (20); 11.6.1734-23.6.1736 Mid *Garland* (20); 24.6.1736-4.1.1736/37 Able *Suffolk* (70); 5.1.1736/37-11.8.1737 Mid *Burford* (70); 11.8.1737-4.1.1737/38 Mid *Somerset* (80); 4.1.1737/38-16.4.1738 Mate *Somerset* (80); 16.4.1738-17.4.1738 Able *Somerset* (80); 18.4.1738 Mate *Somerset* (80); 6.3.1739/40 Passed; **Lieutenant**; 29.10.1740 4L *Kent* (70); 21.11.1740 4L *Buckingham* (70); 22.12.1740 3L *Buckingham* (70); 2.2.1740/41-19.1.1744/45[P] 2L *Buckingham* (70); 11.2.1743/44-12.2.1743/44 Battle of Toulon; **Commander**; 22.6.1747-26.5.1748[P] *Dolphin* (6) Fireship; 12.5.1756-3.4.1759 *Wolf* (8) Sloop; 30.8.1769-4.10.1769 *Cruizer* (8) Sloop.

CRISPO, JOHN

Dates: c.1706 Born; 12.1784 Died; 31.12.1784 Buried St. Mary's, Lambeth, Surrey; 14.1.1785 Will Probate.
Family: Wife Margaret Barret married 19.8.1758.
Service: 27.5.1734 Cox *Edinburgh* (70); 21.5.1735 Mate *Edinburgh* (70); 9.8.1736 2Mst *Edinburgh* (70); 30.3.1738-3.5.1740[P] Mate *Edinburgh* (70); 30.5.1740-3.10.1741 Gnr *Cruizer* (8) Sloop; 4.3.1740/41-5.1741 Operations against Cartagena; **Lieutenant**; 26.12.1743[(BLI 6.7.1744)]-9.6.1744[P] L. *Lively* (20); 5.7.1744 Passed; 9.7.1744 2L *Weymouth* (60); 6.7.1745 3L *Norwich* (50); 2.4.1746 3L *Edinburgh* (64); 20.3.1746/47-19.11.1748 2L *Lark* (44); 19.11.1748[(JAM 14.2.1748/49)]-19.2.1748/49[P] L. *Bideford* (20); 10.7.1755-16.5.1757[P] 2L *Oxford* (50); 20.5.1757

2L *Prince Frederick* (64); 17.6.1757 1L *Prince Frederick* (64); 1758 Impress Service at North Shields; 17.1.1758 5L *Princess Royal* (90); 3.4.1759-29.5.1759 4L *Princess Royal* (90); 10.11.1769 1L *Hero* (74); 23.11.1769-1.4.1771P 1L *Firm* (74); 26.4.1771-25.10.1771 1L *Kent* (74); 1785 **Superannuated Lieutenant**.

CROMWELL, HENRY

Dates: c.1739 Born; 1814 Died.
Family:
Service: 3.11.1756 Able *Success* (20); 9.6.1757 Mid *Arc-en-Ciel* (50); 19.8.1757 Able *Orford* (68); 21.10.1757 Mid *Orford* (68); 6.6.1758-27.7.1758 The Siege of Louisbourg; 20.5.1761 Passed; **Lieutenant**; 6.7.1761-22.1.1763P 2L *Flora* (32); 10.5.1763-19.11.1764 L. *Senegal* (14) Sloop; 24.11.1777 2L *Egmont* (74); 27.7.1778 1st Battle of Ushant; 23.1.1779 1L *Egmont* (74); **Commander**; 18.5.1779-3.9.1781P *Cabot* (14) Sloop; 5.8.1781 Battle of Dogger Bank; **Captain**; 14.11.1781 *Victory* (100); 12.12.1781 2nd Battle of Ushant; 4.4.1782-6.4.1782 *Royal George* (100); 1.1.1801 **Rear Admiral of the Blue**; 23.4.1804 **Rear Admiral of the White**; 9.11.1805 **Rear Admiral of the Red**; 13.12.1806 **Vice Admiral of the Blue**; 25.10.1809 **Vice Admiral of the White**; 31.7.1810 **Vice Admiral of the Red**.

CROOKE, CHARLES CUNNINGHAM

Dates: c.1739 Born; 1806 Died.
Family:
Service: 16.7.1756 Able *Elizabeth* (64); 11.3.1757 Mid *Namur* (90); 5.9.1757-6.10.1757 Raid on Rochefort; 14.3.1758 Mid *Royal George* (100); 5.5.1758 Mate *Dorsetshire* (68); 25.6.1758 Mid *Dorsetshire* (68); 20.11.1759 Battle of Quiberon Bay; 9.1.1760 ActL *Intrepid* (60); 30.5.1760 Passed; **Lieutenant**; 4.12.1761 L. *Carcass* (14) Bomb Vessel; 7.1.1762 5L *Bellona* (74); 24.5.1762-19.1.1763P 4L *Bellona* (74); 16.10.1770-20.2.1772P 1L *Juno* (32); 7.1.1782-28.4.1783P LCmdr *Expedition* (10) Cutter.

CROOKE, PETER THOMAS

Dates: c.1719 Born; 5.8.1760 Died Quiberon Bay.
Family: Wife Henrietta A. Crooke.
Service: 13.9.1742 Able *Centurion* (60); 27.2.1742/43 Mid *Sapphire* (44); 2.11.1743 Able *Sapphire* (44); 10.12.1743 Mid *Cambridge* (80); 11.2.1743/44-12.2.1743/44 Battle of Toulon; 23.9.1746 Mid *Elizabeth* (70); 6.11.1746 Passed; **Lieutenant**; 9.11.1747-24.1.1748/49 L. *Jamaica* (10) Sloop; 7.4.1749 L. *Shoreham* (24); 2.6.1749-21.8.1751 L. *Surprise* (24); 14.5.1756 2L *Rainbow* (44); 2.6.1756 1L *Rainbow* (44); 27.10.1757-3.2.1758 1L *Brilliant* (36); 8.3.1758-4.12.1758 1L *Duc d'Aquitaine* (64); 5.6.1758-12.6.1758 Raid on Saint-Malo; 1760-5.8.1760 Lieutenant *Hawke* Hired Cutter.

CROOKS, WILLIAM

Dates: c.1732 Born; 1768 Died.
Family:
Service: 30.4.1755 Mid *Royal George* (100); 17.5.1757 Mid *Prince* (90); 8.7.1758 Mid *Saint George* (90); 4.11.1758-11.4.1759 Mid *Royal Sovereign* (104); 11.4.1759 Passed; **Lieutenant**; 11.4.1760 5L *Torbay* (74); 29.3.1761-11.6.1761 Expedition against Belle-Isle; 7.7.1762-23.8.1762 4L *Torbay* (74).

CROOKSHANKS, JOHN

Dates: 1708 Born; 20.2.1795 Died London.
Family:
Service: 9.2.1725/26 Vol-p-O *Torbay* (80); 28.1.1727/28 MidO *Gibraltar* (20); 20.9.1728 MidO *Princess Louisa* (40); 8.7.1730 Mid *Falmouth* (50); 23.8.1732 Passed; **Lieutenant**; 2.3.1733/34 3L *Montagu* (60); 13.12.1734 L. *Rose* (20); 13.6.1739 2L *Orford* (70); 14.9.1739 1L *Greenwich* (50); 2.2.1740/41 6L *Royal George* (100); 6.5.1741 5L *Royal George* (100); 21.1.1741/42 4L *Royal George* (100); 10.2.1741/42 3L *Royal George* (100); 27.2.1741/42 2L *Royal George* (100); **Captain**; 3.7.1742-24.12.1744 *Lowestoffe* (20); 24.12.1744[(18.10.1746)] *Dartmouth* (50); 28.12.1745[(18.10.1746)]-29.1.1745/46 *Deptford* (24) Storeship; 22.1.1746/47-6.2.1747/48 *Lark* (44); 1.2.1747/48 Dismissed.

CROSBE, WILLIAM

Dates: c.1730 Born; 1807 Died.
Family: Son William, RN.
Service: 19.8.1745 L. Serv *Falkland* (50); 31.5.1746 L. Serv *Defiance* (60); 3.5.1747 1st Battle of Cape Finisterre; 14.10.1747 2nd Battle of Cape Finisterre; 21.1.1747/48-30.8.1748[P] Able *Defiance* (60); 8.6.1749 Capt Serv *Assurance* (44); 19.8.1749 Able *Assurance* (44); 3.1.1753 Mid *Sphinx* (24); 5.2.1755 Passed; **Lieutenant**; 20.3.1758 4L *Chichester* (68); 22.5.1758 3L *Chichester* (68); 5.6.1758-12.6.1758 Raid on Saint-Malo; 20.11.1759 Battle of Quiberon Bay; 16.6.1760 2L *Chichester* (68); 29.3.1761-11.6.1761 Expedition against Belle-Isle; 22.10.1761-5.4.1763[P] 1L *Chichester* (68); 8.1.1767 1L *Edgar* (60); 19.12.1768 2L *Edgar* (60); 17.1.1770-18.3.1770[P] LCmdr *Boscawen* (4) Cutter; 18.11.1772 1L *Saint Albans* (64); 9.9.1773 1L *Ardent* (64); 21.9.1773 1L *Asia* (64); 27.10.1774 2L *Lennox* (74); 19.1.1775-28.2.1775 2L *Exeter* (64); 30.5.1776 1L *Egmont* (74); 13.5.1778 1L *Princess Amelia* (80); 5.8.1781 Battle of Dogger Bank; 22.9.1781-22.3.1783[P] 1L *Arundel* (74) Hospital Ship; 28.9.1798 **Superannuated Commander**.

CROSBY, NATHANIEL

Dates: c.1720 Born; 1780 Died.
Family:
Service: 31.1.1740/41 Able *Russell* (80); 20.9.1741 Able *Folkestone* (44); 19.12.1741 Mid *Folkestone* (44); 3.8.1745 Mid *Pembroke* (60); 3.5.1747 1st Battle of Cape Finisterre; 20.11.1747 Passed; **Lieutenant**; 15.11.1756 L. *Rose* (20); 21.1.1757-20.5.1759 L. *Rose* (20); 5.6.1758-12.6.1758 Raid on Saint-Malo; 13.1.1767-9.11.1768 1L *Dorsetshire* (68); 5.7.1769-26.4.1771 1L *Achilles* (60); 1.1.1777 2L *Princess Amelia* (80); 10.1.1777 1L *Princess Amelia* (80); **Commander**; 19.11.1777-8.10.1778[D] *Heart of Oak* (20) Hired Armed Ship; 8.10.1778 Dismissed.

CROSS, JOHN

Dates: c.1739 Born; 1774 Died; 28.2.1774 Will Probate.
Family: Father William Crosse.
Service: 9.8.1756 Able *Tartar* (24); 5.6.1758-12.6.1758 Raid on Saint-Malo; 30.11.1758 Mid *Chatham* (50); 3.7.1759 Bombardment of Le Havre; 20.11.1759 Battle of Quiberon Bay; 20.5.1760 Mid *Bedford* (64); 3.12.1760 Passed; **Lieutenant**; 19.5.1761-30.3.1763[P] 2L *Venus* (36); 9.6.1766-17.6.1768 LCmdr *Hornet* (6) Cutter; 22.2.1771 1L *Captain* (64); **Commander**; 18.3.1773[(NA 9.9.1773)]-11.9.1773 *Tamar* (16) Sloop.

CROUCH, ISAAC

Dates: 11.1788 Died; 11.11.1788 Buried Brading, Hampshire; 7.1.1789 Will Probate;
Family: Sister Cornelia [Kelly]; Brother John;
Service: **Lieutenant**; 5.2.1746/47[EI 17.8.1749] 3L *Medway* (60); 19.10.1748[EI 17.8.1749]-21.8.1749[P] 3L *Winchester* (50); 11.3.1755-18.3.1757[C] 2L *Greenwich* (50); 27.9.1759-1762 LCmdr *Phoenix* (20).

CROW, WILLIAM

Dates: c.1722 Born; 1780 Died.
Family:
Service: 7.9.1740 Able *Cumberland* (8) Fireship; 4.3.1740/41-5.1741 Operations against Cartagena; 1.7.1741 Cox *Phaeton* (8) Fireship; 28.9.1741-7.3.1743[P] Mid *Phaeton* (8) Fireship; 4.4.1743 Mid *Augusta* (60); 5.4.1745-10.7.1747 Mate *Augusta* (60); 10.7.1747 Passed; **Lieutenant**; 15.4.1748 4L *Vanguard* (68); 26.7.1748 3L *Vanguard* (68); 20.9.1752-24.8.1753 3L *Saint Albans* (60); 6.2.1755-30.11.1758 3L *Lancaster* (66); 20.5.1756 Battle of Minorca; 6.6.1758-27.7.1758 The Siege of Louisbourg.

CROWCHER, JAMES

Dates: c.1724 Born; 1783 Died.
Family:
Service: 26.7.1740 Serv *Panther* (54); 21.12.1740 Able *Kent* (70); 6.11.1742 Mid *Cruizer* (8) Sloop; 27.11.1744 Mid *Sandwich* (90); 13.3.1744/45 Mid *Ipswich* (70); 30.5.1745 Mid *Russell* (80); 18.2.1745/46 Passed; **Lieutenant**; 14.8.1746[MED 26.1.1747/48] 4L *Stirling Castle* (70); 7.3.1747/48-23.3.1749/50 L. *Trial* (10) Sloop.

Crowley, William
Dates: c.1724 Born; 1767 Died; 15.12.1767 Will Probate.
Family: Father John Crowley; Mother Christian; Wife Ann; Son John; Brother Thomas.
Service: 8.10.1744 QGnr *Princess Royal* (90); 21.4.1745 Able *Alderney* (20); 15.9.1745 Mid *Alderney* (20); 5.9.1748-15.9.1748[P] Able *Alderney* (20); 7.10.1750 Able *Warwick* (60); 27.1.1750/51 Mid *Warwick* (60); 22.9.1751 Mate *Warwick* (60); 2.9.1752 Passed; **Lieutenant**; 22.5.1758-19.2.1759 2L *Aquilon* (28); 28.3.1759 3L *Mars* (74); 20.11.1759 Battle of Quiberon Bay; 29.3.1761-11.6.1761 Expedition against Belle-Isle; 6.9.1762-12.3.1763[P] 2L *Prince Frederick* (64).

CRYMBLE, MURRAY

Dates: 1762 Died.
Family:
Service: **Lieutenant**; 6.8.1748[JAM 27.12.1748]-19.1.1748/49[P] 3L *Milford* (44).

Cuckow, Trevor
Dates: 1736 Born; 1792 Died.
Family:
Service: 23.2.1749/50 Able *Vanguard* (68); 5.12.1750 Mid *Vanguard* (68); 22.10.1753 Able *Torrington* (44); 25.5.1754 Mid *Vulture* (14) Sloop; 12.6.1756-21.3.1756/57 Mid *Yarmouth* (64); 21.3.1757 Passed; **Lieutenant**; 21.6.1757 L. *London* (18) Hired Armed vessel; 25.3.1758 4L *Lennox* (74); 5.6.1758-12.6.1758 Raid on Saint-Malo; 22.2.1759-20.11.1759[S] 4L *Resolution* (74); 20.11.1759 Battle of Quiberon Bay; 3.4.1760 4L *Sandwich* (90); 29.3.1761-11.6.1761 Expedition against Belle-Isle; 30.7.1762 3L *Sandwich* (90); 27.9.1762-22.1.1763[P] 2L *Sandwich* (90); 2.2.1771-19.2.1771 L. *Cruizer* (8) Sloop.

CUMBY, DAVID PRYCE

Dates: 17.8.1814 Died; 2.12.1814 Will Probate.
Family: Wife Susanna Marsh married 1.9.1783; Son William Pryce, RN (1771-1837); Son Charles, RN (1779-?).
Service: **Lieutenant**; 24.9.1759[(NA 17.3.1760)]-22.2.1760 4L *Dublin* (74); 21.3.1760 5L *Foudroyant* (80); 1.4.1760-28.9.1760 4L *Foudroyant* (80); 5.2.1762[(BLI 28.4.1762)] L. *Nightingale* (22); 5.10.1762 1L *Torrington* (44); 13.4.1763-4.9.1766 2L *Milford* (28); 1769-4.1771[P] LCmdr *Endeavour* (4) Cutter; 25.10.1775 1L *Greyhound* (28); 2.7.1776-4.7.1776 Staten Island Landings; 17.3.1777-11.9.1777 2L *Cornwall* (74); 1790-1791 LCmdr *Sheerness* (4); 6.5.1805 **Superannuated Commander**.

CUMINE, JOHN

Dates: c.1738 Born; 1760 Died.
Family:
Service: 1.8.1752 Capt Serv *Deptford* (50); 25.3.1755 Able *Deptford* (50); 20.5.1756 Battle of Minorca; 10.10.1756-6.12.1758 Mid *Lancaster* (66); 6.6.1758-27.7.1758 The Siege of Louisbourg; 6.12.1758 Passed; **Lieutenant**; 31.3.1759-13.9.1759 2L *Crescent* (32) Frigate.

CUMING, PENHALLOW

Dates: c.1715 Born.
Family:
Service: 13.9.1732 Ord. *Lyme* (20); 30.6.1733 Able *Lyme* (20); 21.11.1735-30.9.1737[P] Mid *Lyme* (20); 19.2.1737/38 Mid *Phoenix* (20); 27.4.1738 Able *Hampton Court* (70); 20.12.1738 Mid *Hampton Court* (70); 6.10.1739 Passed; **Lieutenant**; 4.3.1739/40 3L *Chatham* (50); 12.3.1741/42-18.9.1744 2L *Chatham* (50); 9.5.1743 LCmdr *Friends Adventure* Hired Tender; 18.9.1744[(MED 1.5.1747)]-2.5.1746 L. *Alderney* (20); 3.11.1747[(JAM 18.4.1749)] 1L *Canterbury* (60); **Commander**; 8.4.1748[(JAM 14.3.1748/49)]-31.10.1748[P] *Barrington* Sloop; 28.10.1755 *Saltash* (14) Sloop; **Captain**; 23.8.1756 *Saltash* (14) Sloop; 28.3.1757-26.12.1758 *Blandford* (20); 9.3.1759 Dismissed.

CUMMING, JAMES

Dates: 1766 Died.
Family: Wife Anne Hills; Son James, RN (1738-1808); Son William, RN (1731-1795).
Service: **Lieutenant**; 14.7.1740-20.3.1742/43 3L *Salisbury* (50); 14.11.1744-24.1.1745/46 1L *Princess Mary* (60); 8.2.1747/48-5.5.1748 1L *Tilbury* (58); 7.2.1748/49-16.2.1748/49[P] 1L *Captain* (70); 16.1.1753-6.11.1754 1L *Culloden* (74).

CUMMING, JAMES

Dates: 16.4.1738 Born Sandwich; 1808 Died; 19.8.1808 Buried St Lukes, Greenwich.
Family: Father James Cumming, RN (d.1766); Mother Anne Hills; Brother William, RN (1731-1795).
Service: 1.8.1751-c.1754 Scholar *Royal Naval Academy*; **Lieutenant**; 7.4.1758[(MED 29.1.1758)]-23.9.1758[W] L. *Mediterranean* (12) Xebec; 19.2.1759 3L *Fame* (74); 15.3.1759-29.1.1763[P] 2L *Fame* (74); 29.3.1761-11.6.1761 Expedition against Belle-Isle; 29.3.1763-17.5.1763 1L *Lark* (32); 25.10.1763 3L *Augusta* (64); 26.3.1764 L. *Dolphin* (24); **Commander**; 28.4.1765[(EI 28.7.1766)]-9.9.1767 *Tamar* (16) Sloop; 25.8.1766-30.8.1769 *Wasp* (8) Sloop; 24.6.1771 *Cruizer* (8) Sloop; **Captain**; 30.7.1772-25.7.1775 *Deal Castle* (20); 28.6.1777 *Aurora* (28); 14.12.1778-15.12.1778 Battle of St. Lucia; 27.4.1780 *Assurance* (44); 7.5.1781[(NA 6.11.1781)]-21.9.1781[P] *Confederate* (36);

19.7.1793 *Resolution* (74); 12.4.1794 **Rear Admiral of the Blue**; 4.7.1794 **Rear Admiral of the White**; 1.6.1795 **Vice Admiral of the Blue**; 14.2.1799 **Vice Admiral of the Red**; 1.1.1801 **Admiral of the Blue**; 9.11.1805 **Admiral of the White.**

CUMMING, WILLIAM

Dates: c.1731 Born; 1795 Died.
Family: Father James Cumming, RN (d.1766); Brother James, RN (1738-1808).
Service: 22.1.1746/47 Able *Princess Mary* (60); 5.4.1748 Vol-p-O *Captain* (70); 7.8.1748 Mid *Captain* (70); 26.3.1749 Mid *Mercury* (20); 21.1.1750/51-16.1.1751/52[P] Mid *Boston* (24); 9.3.1752 Mate *Winchelsea* (20); 6.6.1753 Passed; **Lieutenant**; 21.10.1755 L. *Firebrand* (6) Fireship; 31.12.1755 L. *Bonetta* (10) Sloop; 16.11.1756 L. *Aldborough* (20); 17.6.1757 6L *Royal William* (84); 5.9.1757-6.10.1757 Raid on Rochefort; 6.6.1758-27.7.1758 The Siege of Louisbourg; 30.1.1759 6L *Union* (90); 20.11.1759 Battle of Quiberon Bay; 8.5.1761 5L *Union* (90); 5.8.1761-25.2.1763[P] 4L *Union* (90); 5.3.1766-20.6.1769 LCmdr *Lord Howe* (6) Cutter; 2.11.1770 1L *Barfleur* (90); 7.12.1770-2.11.1773 1L *Resolution* (74); **Commander**; 6.11.1777 *Supply* (26) Armed Storeship; **Captain**; 27.2.1779[(NA 27.10.1779)] *Monmouth* (64); 8.4.1779-9.10.1780 *Carysfort* (28); 15.6.1795 **Superannuated Rear Admiral.**

CUNDALL, GEORGE

Dates: c.1734 Born; 1773 Died.
Family:
Service: 19.10.1747 Capt Serv *Prince Edward* (44); 27.2.1748 Capt Serv *Edinburgh* (64); 3.7.1748 Capt Serv *Tavistock* (50); 28.6.1749 Com Ret *Gloucester* (50); 13.7.1752 Able *Gloucester* (50); 17.4.1753 Mid *Swift* (8) Sloop; 29.4.1755 Mid *Weymouth* (60); 4.6.1755 Passed; **Lieutenant**; 21.7.1756[(JAM 24.10.1759)]-30.4.1757 L. *Rye* (20); 8.4.1760-6.12.1763[P] 2L *Centaur* (74); 6.6.1762-13.8.1762 Operations against Havana.

CUNNINGHAM, ALEXANDER

Dates: 12.1.1799 Died Anstruther, Scotland.
Family:
Service: **Lieutenant**; 7.4.1759[(JAM 21.9.1759)] 3L *America* (60); 18.8.1759-19.8.1759 Battle of Lagos Bay; 18.10.1759 2L *America* (60); 24.9.1762-6.10.1762 Battle of Manilla; 21.10.1762[(EI 25.6.1764)]-20.6.1764[P] 1L *Lennox* (74); 19.1.1771 1L *Saint Albans* (64); 18.11.1772 2L *Saint Albans* (64); 9.9.1773 2L *Ardent* (64); 21.9.1773-20.1.1774 1L *Ardent* (64); 17.3.1777 1L *Stirling Castle* (64); 27.7.1778 1st Battle of Ushant; 6.7.1779 Battle of Grenada; 21.12.1779-22.12.1779 Action of 1779-12-21; 19.1.1780[(NA 19.10.1780)] 1L *Britannia* (100); **Commander**; 20.9.1781 *Royal Charlotte* (8) Yacht; **Captain**; 18.12.1783-19.4.1784 *Daphne* (20).

CUNNINGHAM, JAMES

Dates: c.1716 Born; 1781 Died Deal; 4.4.1781 Buried Deal; 23.4.1781 Will Probate.
Family: Son Peter; Daughter Elizabeth.
Service: 4.9.1732 Able *Drake* (8) Sloop; 16.7.1735 Able *Seahorse* (20); 30.9.1735 Mid *Seahorse* (20); 7.7.1739 Mid *Garland* (20); 12.3.1739/40 Passed; **Lieutenant**; 22.2.1743/44[(MED 7.11.1745)]-6.3.1744/45 L. *Sutherland* (54); 2.8.1745[(MED 12.11.1745)] 2L *Neptune* (90); 30.4.1746 L. *Centaur* (20); 16.2.1746/47 L. *Fortune* (10) Sloop; 27.9.1748[(BLI 17.2.1748/49)]-23.12.1748[P] 3L *Poole* (44);

10.7.1755 1L *Isis* (50); 3.7.1759 Bombardment of Le Havre; **Commander**; 19.11.1761-4.4.1763 *Trial* (10) Sloop.

CUNNINGHAM, THOMAS

Dates: 1764 Died.
Family:
Service: **Lieutenant**; 6.10.1744 3L *Hector* (44); 12.12.1747-28.8.1748[P] 2L *Centurion* (50); 24.6.1755-5.3.1756 3L *Princess Louisa* (60); 22.5.1758-11.6.1761 L. *Arundel* (24).

CUNNINGHAM, THOMAS

Dates: 1772 Died.
Family:
Service: 16.2.1746/47 **Lieutenant**; 16.1.1753 3L *Berwick* (70); 16.5.1753-16.1.1755 3L *Captain* (64); 16.1.1755 4L *Captain* (64); 20.3.1756 3L *Captain* (64); 20.5.1756 Battle of Minorca; 26.2.1757 3L *Prince George* (80); 15.3.1757-8.5.1757 3L *Northumberland* (68); 13.10.1757-1.3.1760 L. *Surprise* (24); 18.5.1759 Dismissed; 17.5.1762-23.12.1762[P] 2L *Princess Mary* (60).

CUNNINGHAM, WILLIAM

Dates: c.1740 Born; 1771 Died.
Family:
Service: 1754-1757 Merchant Service; 14.11.1757 Capt Serv *Montagu* (60); 28.2.1758 Battle of Cartagena; 3.11.1758 Able *Montagu* (60); 29.9.1759 Mid *Montagu* (60); 20.11.1759 Battle of Quiberon Bay; 7.10.1761 Passed; **Lieutenant**; 5.6.1762[(West Indies 23.2.1763)] 2L *Boreas* (28); 6.6.1762-13.8.1762 Operations against Havana; 31.8.1762 5L *Terrible* (74); 7.10.1762 4L *Terrible* (74); 12.4.1763-30.4.1763[D] L. *Pomona* (18) Sloop; 30.4.1763 Dismissed.

CURLE, NICHOLAS WILSON

Dates: 1773 Died.
Family:
Service: **Lieutenant**; 8.6.1758[(JAM 10.4.1759)] 3L *Eagle* (60); 22.8.1758 3L *Princess Mary* (60); 7.6.1759-3.4.1760 4L *Sandwich* (90); 19.4.1760 3L *Modeste* (64); 10.1.1761 2L *Modeste* (64); 11.3.1761 3L *Bellona* (74); 7.1.1762-19.1.1763[P] 2L *Bellona* (74).

CURRY, ROBERT

Dates: c.1734 Born; 8.11.1812 Died St Marylebone, Middlesex; 20.11.1812 Will Probate.
Family:
Service: 30.11.1749 Able *Princess* (70); 24.3.1750 Able *Superb* (60); 6.9.1750 Able *Liverpool* (44); 18.12.1750 Able *Assurance* (44); 13.8.1751 Able *Garland* (24); 30.1.1754 Mid *Rye* (20); 20.5.1755 Mid *Ambuscade* (40); 4.2.1756 Passed; **Lieutenant**; 8.11.1756 L. *Stork* (10) Sloop; 24.12.1756-19.2.1758[W] 6L *Invincible* (74); 8.1757-10.1757 Louisbourg Expedition; 29.3.1758-22.8.1758 3L *Eagle* (60); 25.8.1758[(JAM 4.3.1760)] L. *Wager* (24); 6.5.1760 2L *Dunkirk* (60); 1.4.1763-11.4.1763[P] 1L *Dunkirk* (60); 21.9.1796 **Superannuated Commander**.

CURTISS, HYDE

Dates: c.1728 Born; 1810 Died; 9.3.1810 Buried Creech St Michael, Somerset.
Family: Wife Mary Gerrard (d.1809) married 3.9.1773.
Service: 6.10.1744 Able *Nassau* (70); 19.7.1745 Able *Winchester* (50); 9.1.1746 Able *Chichester* (80); 23.11.1746 Mid *Revenge* (70); 17.10.1750 Mid *Experiment* (24); 5.12.1750 Mid

Nightingale (22); 25.1.1751 Able *Fougueux* (64); 12.8.1751 Mid *Fougueux* (64); 23.6.1752 Able *Berwick Hulk*; 2.8.1753 Mid *Terrible* (74); 16.7.1755 Mate *Ramillies* (90); 3.12.1755 Passed; **Lieutenant**; 20.6.1758[(BLI 24.10.1760)] 3L *Rainbow* (44); 1.2.1760[(BLI 24.10.1760)]-22.12.1760[P] 2L *Rainbow* (44); 23.7.1762-2.3.1763[P] 2L *Shrewsbury* (74); 26.11.1799 **Superannuated Commander**.

Service Records D

DALRYMPLE, HUGH
Dates: c.1730 Born; 11.12.1784 Died; 17.2.1785 Will Probate.
Family: Father Sir James Dalrymple 2nd Baronet of Hailes (1692-1751)); Mother Lady Christian Hamilton (d/1770); Wife Helen Wemyss married 2.5.1754; Brother Sir David 3rd Bt. of Hailes (1762-1792); Brother Lt-Col. James (d.1791); Brother John, Lord provost of Edinburgh (d.1779).
Service: 12.9.1744 Ord. *Princess Mary* (60); 9.2.1744/45 Ord. *Royal Sovereign* (104); 27.5.1746 Able *Exeter* (60); 5.8.1746 Able *Eltham* (40); 13.12.1746 Able *Bridgewater* (24); 23.2.1746/47 Able *Scarborough* (20); 17.6.1747 Able *Warwick* (60); 9.4.1748 Battle of Santiago de Cuba; 12.10.1748 Battle of Havana; 29.10.1748 Mid *Milford* (44); 14.3.1748/49 Able *Grampus* (14) Sloop; 16.5.1749 Mid *Shoreham* (24); 30.6.1749 Mid *Surprise* (24); 28.1.1750/51 Able *Surprise* (24); 26.10.1751 Mid *Surprise* (24); 5.2.1751/52 Passed; **Lieutenant**; 28.2.1756[JAM 3.9.1756] L. *Falcon* (10) Bomb Vessel; 5.4.1756[JAM 5.1.1759] L. *Sphinx* (24); 22.11.1758-19.3.1759 1L *Vestal* (32); **Commander**; 18.4.1759-4.10.1759 *Medway* (6) Storeship; 3.12.1759-17.2.1763[P] *Postillion* (18) Sloop; 25.5.1763 *Diligence* (10) Sloop; **Captain**; 24.11.1763[NA 14.4.1764]-19.2.1764[P] *Arundel* (24); 23.4.1771-5.5.1772[P] *Emerald* (32); 5.10.1772-3.12.1774 *Cerberus* (28); 1.12.1775-7.8.1778 *Juno* (32); 22.2.1779-28.12.1779 *Canada* (74).

DALRYMPLE, JAMES
Dates: 1773 Died.
Family:
Service: **Lieutenant**; 17.1.1762[BLI 14.1.1763]-17.3.1762 4L *Marlborough* (68); **Commander**; 26.5.1762[BLI 1.9.1763]-30.10.1762[P] *Guadaloupe* Sloop.

DALRYMPLE, JOHN
Dates: 1722 Born; 10.10.1798 Died Manchester Square, London; 2.11.1798 Will Probate.
Family: Father Robert Dalrymple; Wife Eleanor Howard married 1765; Daughter Frances Jane Pryllmead (1783-1862); Son Robert.
Service: 9.7.1740 Capt Serv *Dolphin* (20); 20.2.1741/42 Capt Serv *Dolphin* (20); 29.7.1743 Capt Serv *Argyll* (50); 21.9.1743 Able *Argyll* (50); 9.9.1744 Mid *Argyll* (50); 2.10.1746 Passed; 28.2.1756 **Lieutenant**; 12.3.1757 3L *Prince* (90); **Commander**; 23.3.1757-10.8.1757[P] *Hazard's Prize* (8) Sloop; 17.8.1757 *Albany* (14) Sloop; **Captain**; 18.10.1758 *Solebay* (24); 3.7.1761-3.7.1764[P] *Winchester* (50); 26.3.1779-15.11.1782 *Union* (90); 12.12.1781 2nd Battle of Ushant; 20.10.1782 Battle of Cape Spartel; 24.9.1787 **Rear Admiral of the White**; 8.5.1790-25.12.1790 CinC — River Medway and The Nore; 12.5.1790-24.2.1791[P] *Sandwich* (90); 21.9.1790 **Rear Admiral of the Red**; 28.3.1791-19.9.1791 CinC — River Medway and The Nore; 4.1791-9.1791 *Dictator* (64); 1.2.1793 **Vice Admiral of the White**; 4.2.1793 CinC — River Medway and The Nore; 3.1793-8.1795 *Sandwich* (90); 12.4.1794 **Vice Admiral of the Red**; 1.6.1795 **Admiral of the Blue**; 23.5.1796-10.10.1798 FRS.

DALRYMPLE, PRIMROSE

Dates: 1737 Born Dysart, Fife; 1767 Died; 17.5.1767 Buried St Mary, Islington, Middlesex; 28.7.1773 Will Probate.

Family: Father Robert Dalrymple (1688–1765); Mother Anne Kennedy; Brother Hugh Dalrymple (1699–1774); Sister Elizabeth Dalrymple(1724–1829); Sister Margaret Dalrymple(1723–1811); Brother Cathcart Dalrymple (1729–1763).

Service: 1750-1755 Merchant Service; 27.11.1755 Mate *Assistance* (50); 23.2.1756 Mid *Assistance* (50); 22.4.1756 Mid *Dunkirk* (60); 27.8.1757-27.3.1758 Mate *Magnanime* (74); 5.9.1757-6.10.1757 Raid on Rochefort; 27.3.1758 Passed; **Lieutenant**; 28.3.1760-30.9.1761 2L *Coventry* (28); 8.3.1762-2.6.1763[P] L. *Surprise* (24).

DALRYMPLE, ROBERT

Dates: c.1720 Born; 1763 Died.

Family:

Service: 6.6.1740 Able *Suffolk* (70); 4.3.1740/41-5.1741 Operations against Cartagena; 13.6.1742 Able *Stirling Castle* (70); 15.1.1742/43 Mid *Stirling Castle* (70); 11.2.1743/44-12.2.1743/44 Battle of Toulon; 30.3.1746 Mate *Stirling Castle* (70); 4.2.1747/48 Passed; **Lieutenant**; 6.4.1757 6L *Saint George* (90); 1.6.1757[(MED 5.6.1760)] 6L *Culloden* (74); 27.10.1757[(MED 5.6.1760)] 5L *Culloden* (74); 6.8.1759[(MED 21.5.1760)] 4L *Culloden* (74); 18.8.1759-19.8.1759 Battle of Lagos Bay; 20.8.1759[(MED 21.5.1760)] 3L *Culloden* (74); 15.8.1760-1763[†] 2L *Culloden* (74); 6.6.1762-13.8.1762 Operations against Havana.

DALSTON, SIR GEORGE (4TH BARONET DALSTON OF DALSTON)

Dates: 1718 Born; 5.3.1723 4th Baronet Dalston of Dalston; 7.3.1765 Died.

Family: Father Charles Dalston, 3rd Baronet Dalston of Dalston (d.1723); Mother Susan Blake; Wife Anne Huxley married 28.10.1742.

Service: 1.5.1735 Scholar *Royal Naval Academy*; 29.7.1737 Vol-p-O *Gloucester* (50); 17.9.1737 Mid *Dursley Galley* (20); 12.10.1737 Vol-p-O *Gloucester* (50); 20.10.1738 Mid *Gloucester* (50); 17.3.1739/40 Mid *Chester* (54); 10.4.1740 Mid *Prince Frederick* (70); 3.10.1740 Mid *Nassau* (70); 6.5.1741 Passed; **Lieutenant**; 20.1.1741/42-23.4.1742 4L *Russell* (80); 25.4.1754-14.6.1759 M.P. for Westmorland.

DALYELL, THOMAS

Dates: 19.4.1728 Born Abercorn, West Lothian, Scotland; 1767 Died; 3.10.1767 Will Probate.

Family: Father James Dalyell, 3rd Bt. (1691-1747); Mother Helen Campbell (d.1774); Sister Katherine (1724-?); Brother Robert 4th Bt. (1726-1791); Sister Magdalane [Stewart] (1735-?).

Service: 1750-1755 HEIC Service; 5.9.1755 Mid *Essex* (64); 15.9.1756-9.11.1758 Mate *Essex* (64); 5.6.1758-12.6.1758 Raid on Saint-Malo; 9.11.1758 Passed; **Lieutenant**; 22.8.1759-5.1.1760 3L *Valiant* (74); 24.7.1760-23.4.1763[P] L. *Seahorse* (24); 24.9.1762-6.10.1762 Battle of Manilla.

DANIEL, THOMAS

Dates: c.1730 Born; 1.1.1761 Died Off Pondicherry; 8.7.1763 Will Probate.

Family: Father Thomas Daniel; Mother Mary; Brother John; Brother Edward; Sister Mary [Crosbie].

Service: 1745-1747 Merchant Service; 13.7.1747 Able *Vigilant* (60); 3.6.1749-19.6.1752 Mid *Vigilant* (60); 19.6.1752 Passed; **Lieutenant**; 3.5.1755[(NA 27.1.1756)] 6L *Monarch* (74); 14.5.1756

4L *Monarch* (74); 2.6.1756 3L *Monarch* (74); 23.2.1757-8.5.1757 3L *Yarmouth* (64); **Captain**; 1.1.1760(EI 1.12.1764)-1.1.1761F *Queenborough* (24).

DANIEL, WILLIAM

Dates: 21.2.1800 Died.

Family: Wife Mary Dawson married 4.5.1762; Son Robert Savage, RN (1760-1798); Son William Henry, RN (1763-1838).

Service: 19.10.1750 Capt Serv *Winchester* (50); 4.6.1755 Mid *Trident* (64); 26.10.1755 Mid *Duke* (90); 30.6.1756 Mid *Duke* (90); 16.10.1756-4.7.1757 Mid *Magnanime* (74); 4.7.1757 Passed; **Lieutenant**; 27.10.1758-5.1.1759P L. *Centaur* (20); 11.4.1759-8.1.1762P 3L *Raisonnable* (64); 1.12.1766-8.12.1769 2L *Cornwall* (74); 22.4.1773 3L *Dublin* (74); 12.5.1773 2L *Dublin* (74); 12.7.1773-24.2.1776P 1L *Dublin* (74); 25.2.1776-3.5.1776 1L *Raisonable* (64); 4.11.1776 2L *Sandwich* (90); 15.11.1776-22.10.1777 3L *Sandwich* (90); 27.8.1778 4L *Britannia* (100); 19.10.1778-26.3.1779 3L *Britannia* (100); **Commander**; 14.7.1779 *Greenwich* (22) Storeship; **Captain**; 15.9.1781-10.3.1783P *Greenwich* (22) Storeship; 1787.9.24-1787.11.29P Conqueror (74).

DARBY, GEORGE

Dates: c.1720 Born Ireland; 26.3.1790 Died.

Family: Father Jonathon Darby; Mother Anna Marie Frend; Wife Mary St Quentin (1735-1772) married 1768; Wife Mrs Anne Bridges, née Jackson (d.1790) married 19.12.1774; Son William Thomas (1769-1805); Son Matthew Chitty Darby-Griffith (1772-1823).

Service: **Lieutenant**; 7.9.1742 4L *Suffolk* (70); 18.2.1742/43 Attack on La Guaira; 15.4.1743-24.4.1743 Attack on Porto Cabello; 22.6.1743(16.8.1743)-4.11.1743 2L *Suffolk* (70); 29.11.1743 3L *Harwich* (50); 13.1.1743/44 6L *Princess Royal* (90); 1.6.1744 3L *Edinburgh* (64); 20.11.1744-1.4.1746 2L *Edinburgh* (64); 3.4.1746 3L *Norwich* (50); 22.8.1747(JAM 24.7.1749) 1L *Warwick* (60); **Captain**; 12.9.1747(JAM 23.6.1749) *Warwick* (60); 3.11.1747(JAM 23.6.1749)-12.7.1749P *Aldborough* (20); 18.9.1755-6.6.1756 *Seahorse* (24); 2.5.1757 *Norwich* (50); 3.7.1759 Bombardment of Le Havre; 5.3.1760-27.4.1762 *Devonshire* (70); 7.1.1762-10.2.1762 Operations against Martinique; 23.1.1778 **Rear Admiral of the White**; 19.3.1779 **Vice Admiral of the Blue**; 4.1779-9.1779 *Britannia* (100); 6.1779-8.1779 *Royal George* (100); 8.9.1780-3.1782 CinC — English Channel; 8.9.1780-13.3.1783P *Britannia* (100); 12.9.1780-7.4.1784 M.P. for Plymouth; 22.9.1780-31.3.1782 Lord Commissioner of the Admiralty; 26.9.1780 **Vice Admiral of the White**; 6.11.1781-26.3.1790 Rear Admiral of Great Britain; 12.12.1781 2nd Battle of Ushant; 20.10.1782 Battle of Cape Spartel; 24.9.1787 **Vice Admiral of the Red.**

DARE, WILLIAM

Dates: c.1735 Born; 1771 Died.

Family:

Service: 19.4.1754 Mid *Culloden* (74); 14.2.1755 Mid *Culloden* (74); 10.1.1756 Able *Culloden* (74); 20.5.1756 Battle of Minorca; 4.7.1756 Mid *Culloden* (74); 4.12.1756 Mid *Prince* (90); 26.4.1757 Able *Royal Anne* (100); 11.6.1757 Mid *Royal Sovereign* (104); 9.3.1758 Mate *Royal Sovereign* (104); 5.1.1759 Passed; **Lieutenant**; 22.2.1759-2.8.1763 2L *Active* (28).

DARROCK, ARCHIBALD

Dates: 15.2.1760 Died.

Family:

Service: **Lieutenant**; 9.9.1741 4L *Shrewsbury* (80); 28.11.1743 3L *Burford* (70); 7.3.1744/45[MED 14.2.1745/46] 4L *Marlborough* (90); 2.8.1745[MED 14.11.1745] 4L *Neptune* (90); 15.2.1745/46-19.1.1748/49[P] 1L *Milford* (44); 3.8.1746 Action of August 3 1746; 31.7.1755 1L *Hampshire* (50); 11.12.1755 L. *Blandford* (20); 27.2.1757[EI 7.9.1757]-20.2.1759 1L *Anson* (60); 14.5.1759 6L *Ramillies* (90); 18.10.1759-15.2.1760[W] 5L *Ramillies* (90).

DAVERS, HENRY
Dates: c.1736 Born.
Family:
Service: 4.5.1750 Capt Serv *Humber* (44); 13.4.1751 Ord. *Humber* (44); 18.10.1751 Able *Gosport* (44); 6.8.1752 Mid *Advice* (50); 28.2.1755 ActL *Badger* (10) Sloop; 3.1.1756 ActL *Prince* (90); 3.3.1756 Passed; **Lieutenant**; 2.6.1756-30.11.1756 6L *Prince* (90); 15.1.1759-5.1.1760 3L *Torbay* (74); 20.11.1759 Battle of Quiberon Bay.

DAVIDS, CHARLES
Dates: 23.11.1786 Died Brecon.
Family:
Service: **Lieutenant**; 14.8.1739-7.7.1740 3L *Dunkirk* (60); 27.2.1741/42-2.9.1742[P] 4L *Royal George* (100); 3.11.1742 1L *Roebuck* (40); 29.12.1742 2L *Dorsetshire* (80); 11.2.1743/44-12.2.1743/44 Battle of Toulon; 27.2.1744/45[MED 7.2.1745/46]-29.5.1745 1L *Torbay* (80); 16.12.1748-5.11.1751 L. *Sphinx* (24); 1754 **Superannuated Lieutenant**.

DAVIDSON, WILLIAM
Dates: 1779 Died France; 27.4.1779 Will Probate.
Family: Father James Davidson; Mother Margarite; Brother John Davidson; Sister Mary; Sister Catherine; Sister Jannet; Sister Margarite.
Service: **Lieutenant**; 16.10.1762[BLI 28.2.1764]-12.12.1763 4L *Vanguard* (68).

DAVIES, LEWIS
Dates: c.1717 Born; 1794 Died; 31.7.1794 Will Probate.
Family: Wife Elizabeth; Son William.
Service: 16.6.1739 Able *Prince of Orange* (70); 17.5.1740 Mid *Lancaster* (80); 5.11.1740 Mid *Lancaster* (80); 14.10.1742-13.2.1744/45[W] Mid *Orford* (70); 22.4.1745 Able *Cumberland* (80); 14.8.1745 Mid *Prince George* (90); 5.12.1745 Passed; **Lieutenant**; 2.4.1746-13.9.1748 3L *Pearl* (44); 30.1.1755 5L *Torbay* (74); 6.6.1755-8.6.1755 Action of 6-8 June 1755; 2.8.1755[NA 9.12.1755] 4L *Torbay* (74); 31.1.1756-5.8.1756 4L *Invincible* (74); 13.11.1756 2L *Elizabeth* (64); 3.2.1757-15.2.1757 1L *Lichfield* (50); 15.2.1757 2L *Bedford* (64); 8.1757-10.1757 Louisbourg Expedition; 30.1.1758-26.9.1761[P] 1L *Bedford* (64); 6.6.1758-27.7.1758 The Siege of Louisbourg; 29.3.1761-11.6.1761 Expedition against Belle-Isle; 28.1.1762-10.11.1762[P] 1L *Saint George* Prison Ship; 11.5.1763 2L *Prince of Orange* (60); 6.6.1763 2L *Bellona* (74); 6.9.1763-13.6.1766 1L *Bellona* (74); 10.1.1774-14.6.1775 1L *Royal Oak* (74); 1794 **Superannuated Lieutenant**.

DAVIES, WILLIAM
Dates: 16.2.1759 Died.
Family:
Service: **Lieutenant**; 29.1.1706/7[5.5.1707] L. *Hunter* (8); 14.3.1707/8[26.4.1708] 1L *Salisbury Prize* (50); 7.8.1711 Capture of the San Joaquín; **Commander**; 26.2.1712/13[16.6.1713] *Trial* (10) Sloop; 14.12.1714-13.8.1716 *Trial* (10) Sloop; 26.2.1716/17-17.3.1717/18 *Bedford Galley* (32);

Captain; 30.6.1719 *Experiment* (20); 10.4.1721-17.12.1722[P] *Jersey* (54); 25.1.1725/26 *Tiger* (50); 12.4.1729-16.12.1729[P] *Princess Amelia* (80); 3.7.1731 *Suffolk* (70); 15.2.1732/33 *Edinburgh* (70); 7.5.1734-31.3.1736[P] *Kent* (70); 12.6.1739-24.9.1740 *Prince of Orange* (70); 2.3.1743/44-17.7.1744 *Royal Sovereign* (104); 22.4.1744-27.10.1744 CinC — River Medway and The Nore.

DAVIS, FRANCIS

Dates: c.1720 Born; 1770 Died; 29.10.1770 Will Probate.

Family: Wife Elizabeth Garr married 9.3.1755.

Service: 30.12.1733-1.5.1734 Capt Serv *Grafton* (70); 2.5.1734-28.4.1736 Ord. *Namur* (90); 29.4.1736-19.2.1737/38 Able *Shoreham* (20); 20.2.1737/38-9.7.1739 Able *Chatham* (50); 10.7.1739-25.3.1740 Mid *Orford* (70); 26.3.1740 Mid *Chichester* (80); 5.11.1741 Passed; **Lieutenant**; 1.6.1742[(4.11.1745)]-10.8.1743 6L *Marlborough* (90); 21.4.1747[(MED 25.11.1748)]-17.11.1748[P] 1L *Revenge* (70); 31.8.1757 1L *Richmond* (32); **Commander**; 16.5.1758-3.4.1763[P] *Otter* (14) Sloop; 8.9.1763-24.10.1766 *Savage* (8) Sloop; 26.10.1769-18.9.1770 *Pomona* (18) Sloop.

DAVIS, HENRY

Dates: c.1732 Born; 12.1776 Died off Bermuda, West Indies; 9.10.1777 Will Probate.

Family: Wife Elizabeth married 6.4.1772.

Service: 11.3.1748 Capt Serv *Triton* (20); 20.6.1750 Ord. *Nightingale* (22); 3.11.1750 Able *Nightingale* (22); 6.5.1752 Mate *Nightingale* (22); 4.7.1753 Mid *Captain* (64); 13.11.1754 Passed; **Lieutenant**; 24.9.1756 2L *Unicorn* (28); 8.4.1757 6L *Magnanime* (74); 3.6.1757 6L *Royal William* (84); 15.6.1757 5L *Royal William* (84); 17.6.1757 4L *Royal William* (84); 5.9.1757-6.10.1757 Raid on Rochefort; 6.6.1758-27.7.1758 The Siege of Louisbourg; 30.1.1759 4L *Union* (90); 20.11.1759 Battle of Quiberon Bay; 16.3.1761 2L *Hampton Court* (64); 22.5.1761-19.9.1763[P] 1L *Hampton Court* (64); 24.3.1762-12.7.1764[P] L. *Valiant* (74); 6.6.1762-13.8.1762 Operations against Havana; **Commander**; 20.6.1765 *Lynx* (10) Sloop; 13.8.1766 *Hunter* (10) Sloop; **Captain**; 26.5.1768 *Sphinx* (24); 7.8.1771 *Seaford* (20); 31.8.1773[(BLI 23.12.1773)]-17.12.1773[P] *Diana* (32); 18.12.1775-12.1776[F] *Repulse* (32).

DAVIS, HENRY

Dates: c.1736 Born; 1773 Died; 14.7.1773 Will Probate.

Family: Sister Alice; Sister Ester [Beveaus].

Service: 4.6.1749 Mst Serv *Tiger* (60); 5.5.1753 Able *Seahorse* (24); 15.9.1755 Mid *Seahorse* (24); 25.4.1757 Mate *Seahorse* (24); 20.5.1757-9.6.1758 Mid *Norwich* (50); 9.6.1758 Passed; **Lieutenant**; 8.5.1759 3L *Gosport* (44); 1.4.1760-11.3.1763[P] 2L *Gosport* (44).

DAVIS, NATHANIEL

Dates: 18.5.1765 Died; 21.5.1765 Will Probate.

Family: Wife Mary.

Service: **Lieutenant**; 30.5.1744[(West Indies 3.2.1748/49)]-22.6.1745[F] L. *Fame* (12) Sloop; 31.10.1745[(NA 3.2.1748/49)] 2L *Lennox* (70); 11.11.1745[(NA 3.2.1748/49)]-10.5.1747[P] 1L *Lennox* (70); 3.8.1746 Action of August 3 1746; 25.3.1747 Action of March 25 1747; 18.10.1756-3.5.1758 L. *Lively* (20).

DAVIS, RICHARD

Dates: 1768 Died.

Family:

Service: 2.5.1718-14.2.1718/19[W] Able *Burford* (70); 11.8.1718 Battle of Cape Passaro; 11.3.1719/20 Able *Buckingham* (70); 29.4.1721 Able *Medway* (60); 1.8.1721 Mid *Advice* (54);

26.3.1722 Mate *Advice* (54); 18.10.1722 Mid *Dorsetshire* (80); 28.8.1723 Mate *Guernsey* (50); 3.7.1724 Mid *Guernsey* (50); 26.11.1724 Mid *Adventure* (42); 14.3.1725/26 Mate *Cumberland* (80); 10.3.1726/27 Mate *Cornwall* (80); 13.10.1727 Passed; **Lieutenant**; 31.8.1739-14.11.1739 3L *Bristol* (54); 15.11.1739-12.1.1739/40 2L *Sunderland* (60); 21.11.1743 1L *Burford* (70); 3.10.1744 L. *Dursley Galley* (20); 5.12.1744 1L *Defiance* (60); 26.5.1746-12.11.1746 1L *Falkland* (50); 18.1.1757-15.3.1757 1L *Ludlow Castle* (44).

DAWNAY, GEORGE

Dates: 16.11.1766 Died.
Family:
Service: 26.12.1712 Vol-p-O *Deptford* (48); 30.8.1714 Vol-p-O *Cumberland* (80); 29.12.1714 MidO *Elizabeth* (70); 31.3.1715-31.12.1716[P] Mid *Elizabeth* (70); 29.1.1716/17 Passed; **Lieutenant**; 11.1.1719/20 3L *Revenge* (70); 4.4.1720-28.10.1721[P] 4L *Revenge* (70); 4.3.1723/24-26.4.1725 3L *Argyll* (50); 14.2.1726/27-10.4.1727 4L *Revenge* (70); 11.4.1727-21.8.1727 3L *Revenge* (70); 16.1.1727/28-13.6.1732 3L *Medway* (60); 14.6.1732-22.2.1733/34 2L *Suffolk* (70); 23.2.1733/34-5.1.1735/36 2L *Lancaster* (80); 16.5.1738-26.11.1738[P] 1L *Prince of Orange* (70); 13.6.1739-3.3.1739/40 1L *Orford* (70); **Captain**; 8.1.1741/42-23.8.1742 *Bideford* (20); 29.12.1742-11.10.1743 *Lyme* (20).

DAWS, JOHN

Dates: c.1728 Born; bef.30.7.1763 Died; 28.9.1763 Will Probate.
Family: Father Matthew Daws; Stepmother Sarah; Brother James.
Service: 9.1.1750/51 Capt Serv *Bridgewater* (24); 18.12.1751 Able *Superb* (60); 2.2.1753 Mid *Superb* (60); 27.4.1753 Able *Superb* (60); 17.6.1754 Mid *Superb* (60); 10.10.1754 Mid *Superb* (60); 30.9.1755 Mid *Launceston* (44) Hulk; 8.7.1756 Mate *Launceston* (44) Hulk; 7.2.1757 Passed; **Lieutenant**; 17.6.1757-21.5.1759[P] 4L *Fougueux* (64); 29.12.1758 Capture of Goree; 2.7.1759-30.7.1763 L. *Rose* (20); 7.1.1762-10.2.1762 Operations against Martinique; 6.6.1762-13.8.1762 Operations against Havana.

DAWSON, GEORGE

Dates: c.1739 Born.
Family:
Service: 22.6.1755 Capt Serv *Saint George* (90); 18.7.1756 Adm Serv *Ramillies* (90); 21.11.1756 Able *Fortune* (14) Sloop; 2.1.1757 Able *Siren* (20); 23.4.1758 Mid *Revenge* (64); 20.11.1759 Battle of Quiberon Bay; 1.4.1760 Mid *Dragon* (74); 2.7.1760 Mid *Monmouth* (70); 6.2.1761 Able *Royal George* (100); 1.4.1761 Mid *Royal George* (100); 1.7.1761 Passed; **Lieutenant**; 9.8.1762-18.11.1763[P] 2L *Aeolus* (32); 2.1.1767 3L *Guernsey* (50); 31.3.1768-14.12.1775[P] LCmdr *Hope* (6) Schooner; **Commander**; 13.5.1776[NA 13.12.1777]-16.5.1776 LCmdr *Hope* (14) Sloop; 19.6.1777 ActCapt *Renown* (50); **Captain**; 9.9.1777[NA 23.11.1779]-6.12.1780 *Renown* (50); 1.8.1780[NA 17.4.1782]-11.9.1781[C] *Iris* (32); 16.3.1781 Battle of Cape Henry; 26.8.1785 *Phaeton* (38); 20.9.1786-20.11.1788 *Phaeton* (38); 20.11.1788 Dismissed.

DAY, BUNBURY

Dates: 10.3.1762 Died.
Family:
Service: **Lieutenant**; 23.6.1760[EI 16.8.1764] 4L *Grafton* (68); 27.11.1760[EI 16.8.1764]-10.3.1762[†] 3L *Grafton* (68).

DAY, CHRISTOPHER

Dates: c.1731 Born; 4.11.1800 Died; 10.11.1800 Buried Wyke-Regis, Dorset; 9.3.1801 Will Probate.
Family: Wife Catherine.
Service: 1752-1755 Merchant Service; 21.6.1755 Mid *Essex* (64); 5.6.1758-12.6.1758 Raid on Saint-Malo; 22.8.1758 Mate *Conqueror* (68); 18.8.1759-19.8.1759 Battle of Lagos Bay; 5.10.1759 Mate *Princess Louisa* (60); 5.12.1759 Passed; **Lieutenant**; 7.10.1762[(MED 12.5.1763)]-14.5.1763[P] 3L *Isis* (50).

DAY, GEORGE

Dates: c.1731 Born; 3.2.1791 Died; 11.3.1791 Will Probate.
Family: Wife Mary; Son Robert Pynsent Wright; Son George Major, RN (1768-?); Daughter Mary.
Service: 28.5.1746 Capt Serv *Monmouth* (70); 3.5.1747 1st Battle of Cape Finisterre; 7.6.1747 Able *Monmouth* (70); 14.10.1747 2nd Battle of Cape Finisterre; 29.12.1748 Able *Badger* (10) Sloop; 25.2.1751 Mid *Badger* (10) Sloop; 12.2.1752 Mate *Badger* (10) Sloop; 24.3.1753 Able *Badger* (10) Sloop; 10.1.1754 Mate *Advice* (50); 5.11.1755 Passed; **Lieutenant**; 9.7.1762[(MED 20.9.1763)]-26.9.1763[P] L. *Gibraltar* (20); 30.7.1765-5.8.1768 3L *Augusta* (64); 10.11.1769 3L *Hero* (74); 29.9.1770-20.5.1771[P] 4L *Hero* (74); 25.6.1771-17.8.1773[P] L. *Pomona* (18) Sloop; 29.11.1773 2L *Raisonable* (64); 25.8.1775-1.4.1780 2L *Nonsuch* (64); 14.12.1778-15.12.1778 Battle of St. Lucia; 6.7.1779 Battle of Grenada; **Commander**; 31.12.1779[(North Sea 17.5.1780)] *Star* (10) Brig; 23.1.1780-14.4.1782 *Surprise* (18) Cutter.

DAY, THOMAS

Dates: c.1728 Born; 20.6.1803 Died.
Family:
Service: 8.1.1747 Capt Serv *Hector* (44); 1.5.1748 Capt Serv *Exeter* (60); 2.3.1749 Ord. *Exeter* (60); 18.12.1749-3.5.1750[P] Able *Exeter* (60); 29.9.1754 Mid *Deptford* (50); 20.5.1756 Battle of Minorca; 5.9.1757 Passed; **Lieutenant**; 16.11.1757 L. *Flamborough* (20); 3.5.1758-18.5.1759[P] L. *Roman Emperor* (8) Fireship; 29.12.1758 Capture of Goree; 20.9.1759-8.4.1762 1L *Milford* (28).

DE HAVILLAND, JAMES

Dates: 1785 Died.
Family:
Service: **Lieutenant**; 12.1.1759[(NA 18.1.1760)] 4L *Devonshire* (70); 2.4.1760[(NA 18.1.1760)] 3L *Devonshire* (70); 7.1.1762-10.2.1762 Operations against Martinique; 3.4.1762[(JAM 3.5.1763)]-13.5.1763[P] 2L *Devonshire* (70); 6.6.1762-13.8.1762 Operations against Havana; 7.1765-1769 In the service of Kingdom of Sardinia; 7.1765 **Capitano di Pavillione** (State Navy); 1766-1769 Capitano di Fregata *San Vittorio* (34).

DEACON, RICHARD

Dates: 17.4.1780 Died.
Family: Mother Ann.
Service: 1753 Unk *Jamaica* (10) Sloop; **Lieutenant**; 31.3.1759[(JAM 25.10.1759)] L. *Polacca* (12) Sloop; 5.8.1759[(NA 3.10.1763)]-1.10.1763[P] L. *Valeur* (28); 24.3.1767-15.12.1767[P] L. *Zephyr* (10) Sloop; 10.3.1769-16.1.1770 L. *Nautilus* (16) Sloop; 19.10.1770 4L *Ajax* (74); 4.12.1770-7.6.1771[P] 3L *Ajax* (74); 17.12.1773 3L *Lennox* (74); 13.6.1774 L. *Ranger* (8) Sloop; 7.2.1776-29.5.1778[P] 1L

Torbay (74); 31.5.1778 1L *Egmont* (74); 27.7.1778 1st Battle of Ushant; 23.1.1779-6.9.1782[P] 1L *Intrepid* (64); 17.4.1780 Battle of Martinique; 15.5.1780 Action of March 15 1780; 19.5.1780 Action of March 19 1780; 29.4.1781-30.4.1781 Battle of Fort Royal; 5.9.1781 Battle of the Chesapeake; 25.1.1782-26.1.1782 Battle of Saint Kitts.

DEACON, SABINE

Dates: c.1717 Born; 27.7.1759 Died.

Family:

Service: 15.11.1736 Able *Greyhound* (20); 8.5.1740-13.11.1740[P] Mid *Greyhound* (20); 12.5.1741 Mid *Rupert* (60); 13.7.1742 Mate *Rupert* (60); 11.2.1743/44-12.2.1743/44 Battle of Toulon; 24.11.1745 Passed; **Lieutenant**; 2.1.1745/46-4.5.1749[P] L. *Swan* (10) Sloop; 23.4.1753 L. *Saltash* (14) Sloop; 28.10.1755 1L *Dover* (44); 23.4.1757 2L *Monarch* (74); 28.2.1758 Battle of Cartagena; 5.4.1758 3L *Royal George* (100); **Commander**; 27.9.1758-27.7.1759[†] *Kingfisher* (8) Bomb Vessel; 16.1.1759-19.1.1759 Attack on Martinique; 20.1.1759-1.5.1759 Capture of Guadeloupe.

DEANE, EDWARD

Dates: c.1733 Born; 1760 Died.

Family:

Service: 25.11.1746 Capt Serv *Boyne* Hired Tender; 27.4.1747 Ord. *Boyne* Hired Tender; 25.7.1747 Ord. *Nottingham* (60); 4.9.1747 Ord. *Gloucester* (50); 14.10.1747 2nd Battle of Cape Finisterre; 10.1.1748/49 Able *Greyhound* (20); 22.3.1748/49 Mid *Greyhound* (20); 16.3.1751/52 Mate *Wager* (24); 2.7.1755 Passed; **Lieutenant**; 22.10.1755[(EI 29.9.1756)] 3L *Winchester* (50); 9.11.1756-5.9.1757 2L *Winchester* (50).

DEANE, JOSEPH

Dates: c.1731 Born; 1779 Died; 31.7.1780 Will Probate.

Family: Son Charles; Brother Charles;

Service: 18.2.1746 Able *Princess Mary* (60); 4.9.1747 Mid *Princess Mary* (60); 26.8.1749 Able *Anson* (60); 9.6.1750 Able *Mercury* (20); 19.1.1751 Able *Boston* (24); 2.10.1751-15.1.1752[P] Mid *Boston* (24); 16.1.1752-19.4.1752[P] Able *Winchelsea* (20); 8.7.1752 Able *Winchelsea* (20); 6.6.1753 Passed; **Lieutenant**; 29.4.1755[(MED 19.5.1757)]-14.8.1756[C] L. *Oswego* (5) Sloop; 18.7.1757 1L *Hussar* (28); **Commander**; 23.2.1758 *Vesuvius* (14) Fireship; **Captain**; 17.10.1758 *Eurus* (24); 10.1.1759-19.5.1760[W] *Lowestoffe* (28); 7.4.1762 *Pearl* (32); 7.4.1763-31.12.1767[P] *Mermaid* (28); 9.1766-11.1766 CinC — North America; 26.7.1769-25.4.1772[P] *Stag* (32); 15.10.1773-1.11.1775 *Royal Oak* (74); 19.9.1777-4.1779[†] *Ruby* (64).

DEARDS, JOHN

Dates: c.1721 Born; c.1755 Died; 7.2.1755 Will Probate.

Family:

Service: 18.1.1737/38 Ord. *Hector* (40); 12.5.1738-13.4.1742[P] Able *Hector* (40); 4.1740-5.7.1740 Attack on St. Augustine; 25.9.1742 Able *Medway* (60); 21.12.1742 Mid *Medway* (60); 19.7.1744 Mid *Strafford* (58); 29.10.1745 Mid *Adventure* (44); 15.5.1746 Passed; **Lieutenant**; 3.7.1746-12.9.1748[P] 3L *Prince Edward* (44).

DEBAT, PETER

Dates: c.1733 Born; 22.3.1733 Baptised St James, Paddington, Middlesex; c.1761 Died; 6.10.1761 Will Probate.
Family: Father Rev. Daniel Debat; Mother Jane; Sister Clementia; Sister Jane.
Service: **Lieutenant**; 10.3.1759(JAM 9.9.1760) L. *Port Antonio* (12) Storeship; 25.2.1760(JAM 25.6.1760) 3L *Harwich* (50); 21.5.1760(JAM 25.6.1760)-4.10.1760[W] 2L *Harwich* (50); 21.8.1761-9.1761† 2L *Deptford* (50).

DENIS, SIR PETER (1ST BARONET OF ST MARY'S)

Dates: c.1713 Born; 28.10.1767 1st Baronet of St Mary's; 10.6.1778 Died.
Family: Father Rev. Jacob Denis; Mother Martha Leach; Wife Elizabeth Pappet (d.1765) married 2.9.1750; Brother Charles.
Service: 27.6.1725 Chap Serv *Success* (24); 18.9.1728 Capt Serv *Grafton* (70); 17.10.1728 Able *Tartar* (32); 2.7.1730 MidO *Tartar* (32); 27.12.1730-7.6.1732[P] Mid *Tartar* (32); 25.11.1732 Mid *York* (60); 8.5.1733 Able *Hound* (8) Sloop; 2.7.1734 Mate *Hound* (8) Sloop; 16.10.1734 Passed; 1739 Mid *Centurion* (60); **Lieutenant**; 12.11.1739-27.12.1739 3L *Centurion* (60); 28.12.1739 L. *Wager* (28); 3.11.1740(7.9.1744)-20.6.1743 3L *Centurion* (60); **Commander**; 25.6.1744-2.8.1744 *Swift* (8) Sloop; **Captain**; 9.2.1744/45 *Greyhound* (20); 1.7.1745-7.2.1745/46 *Folkestone* (44); 14.2.1746/47-27.8.1748[P] *Centurion* (50); 3.5.1747 1st Battle of Cape Finisterre; 18.4.1754-19.3.1768 M.P. for Hedon; 30.1.1755 *Medway* (60); 15.11.1756 *Royal George* (100); 17.12.1756-27.1.1758 *Namur* (90); 5.9.1757-6.10.1757 Raid on Rochefort; 27.1.1758-21.2.1760 *Dorsetshire* (68); 20.11.1759 Battle of Quiberon Bay; 25.2.1760-21.11.1760 *Bellona* (74); 5.1762-2.1763 Commodore *Bellona* (74); 10.5.1762 CinC — Basque Roads; 14.12.1763 *Royal Charlotte* (8) Yacht; 18.10.1770 **Rear Admiral of the Blue**; 24.10.1770 **Rear Admiral of the Red**; 7.12.1770-6.1771 CinC — River Medway and The Nore; 26.5.1771-24.9.1774[P] *Trident* (64); 24.6.1771 CinC — The Mediterranean Sea; 31.3.1775 **Vice Admiral of the Blue**; 7.12.1775 **Vice Admiral of the White**; 29.1.1778 **Vice Admiral of the Red.**

DENNE, WILLIAM

Dates: c.1733 Born; 28.12.1791 Died; 7.2.1792 Will Probate.
Family: Wife Ann.
Service: 22.3.1748 Able *Assistance* (50); 15.12.1748 Able *Bristol* (50); 25.6.1751 Mid *Vulture* (14) Sloop; 23.10.1753 Able *Torrington* (44); 1.5.1754 Passed; **Lieutenant**; 31.5.1756 L. *Hawke* (8) Sloop; 8.5.1757 3L *Northumberland* (68); 8.1757-10.1757 Louisbourg Expedition; 6.6.1758-27.7.1758 The Siege of Louisbourg; 7.6.1763-16.10.1766[P] 2L *Romney* (50); 2.11.1776 1L *Prince George* (90); **Commander**; 16.9.1777 *Speedwell* (8) Sloop; 12.5.1778 *Nymph* (14) Sloop; 14.10.1779 *Dromedary* (30) Armed Storeship; **Captain**; 20.10.1779 *Dromedary* (30) Armed Storeship; 23.8.1781-27.9.1781 *Yarmouth* (64).

DENNIS, HENRY

Dates: 29.9.1757 Died.
Family:
Service: **Lieutenant**; 29.7.1727(25.10.1728) L. *Happy* (10) Sloop; 21.9.1727(25.10.1728) L. *Spence* (8) Sloop; 2.7.1728(25.10.1728)-25.10.1728[P] 3L *Dragon* (54); 9.2.1728/29-6.1.1731/32[P] 3L *Dreadnought* (60); 14.6.1732 3L *Dreadnought* (60); 31.8.1732 L. *Shark* (8) Sloop; 19.5.1734(10.11.1735)-3.11.1735[P] 1L *Rupert* (60); 6.1.1735/36 L. *Blandford* (20); 11.2.1739/40(4.11.1741) 4L *Burford* (70); 25.8.1740(4.11.1741) 3L *Burford* (70); 30.9.1740(4.11.1741) 2L *Burford* (70); 30.12.1740(4.11.1741) 1L *Burford* (70); **Commander**; 12.1.1740/41(4.11.1741) *Eleanor* (8) Fireship; 4.3.1740/41-

5.1741 Operations against Cartagena; **Captain**; 6.6.1741 *Experiment* (20); 7.1741-10.1741 Operations against Santiago; 4.3.1744/45[23.9.1746]-25.10.1746[P] *Seahorse* (20); 3.8.1746 Action of August 3 1746; 9.1.1751/52 *Severn* (50); 26.2.1756[JAM 21.9.1757]-11.1.1757 *Sphinx* (24); 2.9.1757 **Superannuated Rear Admiral.**

DENT, COTTON

Dates: 28.1.1761 Died.
Family: Father Digby Dent, RN (d.1737); Wife Catherine Bowerbank; Son Sir Digby, RN (1739-1817); Brother Digby, RN (1710-1761).
Service: **Lieutenant**; 18.5.1735[8.8.1738] 3L *Antelope* (54); 7.5.1736[8.8.1738] 2L *Antelope* (54); 21.4.1737[8.8.1738]-5.8.1737 3L *Kinsale* (40); 6.8.1737[8.8.1738]-30.4.1738 3L *Dunkirk* (60); 13.6.1739 3L *Augusta* (60); 2.9.1740 4L *Boyne* (80); 27.9.1740-12.10.1740 4L *Kent* (70); 13.10.1740 4L *Elizabeth* (70); 30.1.1740/41 4L *Sandwich* (90); 13.4.1741 3L *Sandwich* (90); 5.10.1741-22.1.1741/42 L. *Lightning* (8) Bomb Vessel; **Commander**; 28.12.1743[25.6.1745] *Thunder* (8) Bomb Vessel; **Captain**; 23.1.1745/46 *Kennington* (20); 20.11.1746[MED 5.5.1749]-16.8.1748 *Nonsuch* (50); 30.3.1747[MED 4.6.1748]-10.11.1748[P] *Boyne* (80); 3.5.1750-22.7.1752 *Culloden* (74).

DENT, DIGBY

Dates: 1710 Born; 5.6.1761 Died; 9.7.1761 Will Probate.
Family: Father Digby Dent, RN (d.1737); Wife Sophia Pitt Drake (d.1767); Brother Cotton, RN (d.1761).
Service: 20.10.1726 Ord. *Lennox* (70); 26.10.1726 Vol-p-O *Lennox* (70); 8.5.1729 Able *Carolina* (20) Yacht; 25.9.1729 Mid *Princess Louisa* (40); 20.9.1730 Able *Dreadnought* (60); 11.3.1730/31 Able *Captain* (70); 23.5.1731 Mid *Captain* (70); 14.7.1732 Mid *Edinburgh* (70); 19.1.1733/34 Passed; **Lieutenant**; 2.3.1733/34-7.11.1734 4L *Ipswich* (70); 8.11.1734-5.6.1737 3L *Dunkirk* (60); **Commander**; 6.8.1737 *Drake* (8) Sloop; **Captain**; 9.6.1738[8.6.1742] *Kinsale* (40); 11.8.1738 *Hampton Court* (70); 21.11.1739 Attack on Puerto Bello; 2.5.1741[29.3.1743] *Tilbury* (60); 7.1741-10.1741 Operations against Santiago; 20.11.1741[29.3.1743]-15.7.1742[P] *Jersey* (60); 8.9.1742 *Looe* (44); 4.4.1743 *Shrewsbury* (80); 19.9.1743-11.12.1743 *Boyne* (80); 20.12.1743-28.7.1748[P] *Plymouth* (60); 3.8.1746 Action of August 3 1746; 1747 CinC — Jamaica; 25.3.1747 Action of March 25 1747; 9.4.1748 Battle of Santiago de Cuba; 24.6.1756-29.12.1756 Comptroller of the Navy.

DENT, SIR DIGBY

Dates: 16.11.1739 Born Portsmouth; 8.5.1778 Knight Bachelor; 15.3.1817 Died nr. Dublin; 23.7.1823 Will Probate.
Family: Father Cotton Dent, RN (d.1761); Mother Catherine Bowerbank; Wife Elizabeth Greentree (d.1786); Wife Susanna; Wife Elizabeth; Son Digby, RN (d.1798).
Service: **Lieutenant**; 4.2.1758[EI 11.2.1760] 5L *Cumberland* (66); 25.3.1758[EI 11.2.1760] 2L *Yarmouth* (64); 29.4.1758 Battle of Cuddalore; **Captain**; 7.7.1758[EI 19.2.1760] *Queenborough* (24); 3.8.1758 Battle of Negapatam; 10.9.1759 Battle of Pondicherry; 11.9.1759[EI 14.7.1762] *Newcastle* (50); 1.1.1760[NA 14.7.1762] *Falmouth* (50); 10.9.1760[EI 14.7.1762]-10.7.1761[P] *Tiger* (60); 10.5.1763-24.7.1766[P] *Deal Castle* (20); 4.5.1768-22.2.1769[P] *Boreas* (28); 10.4.1770-23.3.1771 *Dolphin* (24); 23.4.1773-26.4.1773[P] *Seahorse* (24); 20.6.1775 *Arethusa* (32); 26.12.1776 *Princess Amelia* (80); 3.12.1778 *Vigilant* (64); 6.7.1779 Battle of Grenada; 27.8.1779[NA 29.12.1780]-4.12.1779 *Royal Oak* (74); 29.8.1780[NA 19.1.1781] *Raisonable* (64); 23.11.1780-9.11.1781 *Repulse* (64); 5.5.1788 **Superannuated Rear Admiral.**

DERING, DANIEL

Dates: c.1734 Born; 29.5.1760 Died.
Family:
Service: 17.11.1749-16.9.1752[P] Capt Serv *Centurion* (50); 13.4.1753 Able *Centurion* (50); 19.9.1753 Mid *Centurion* (50); 26.12.1753 Mid *Saint Albans* (60); 14.4.1755 Mid *Kent* (64); 11.1.1756-14.1.1756 Capture of Geriah; 26.1.1757 Passed; **Lieutenant**; 26.1.1757-1.4.1757 3L *Achilles* (60); 6.4.1757 2L *Norwich* (50); 16.4.1757 4L *Devonshire* (70); 12.5.1757 4L *Cambridge* (80); **Commander**; 17.4.1758 *Antigua* (14) Sloop; **Captain**; 18.11.1758[BLI 15.6.1759] *Rye* (20); 16.1.1759-19.1.1759 Attack on Martinique; 29.1.1759[BLI 11.7.1759]-29.5.1760[†] *Woolwich* (44).

DEWEY, THOMAS

Dates: 1810 Died.
Family: Daughter Anna [Box].
Service: 7.10.1752 Scholar *Royal Naval Academy*; 8.10.1755 Vol. *Seaford* (20); 22.5.1756 Mid *Seaford* (20); 13.7.1758-7.3.1758/59 Able *Duc d'Aquitaine* (64); 1759 **Lieutenant**; 7.3.1759 Passed; 27.9.1759-14.3.1763[P] L. *George* (30) Hired Armed vessel; 29.1.1770-15.12.1778 L. *Swan* (14) Sloop; 2.7.1776-4.7.1776 Staten Island Landings; 3.4.1780-16.1.1781 1L *Cumberland* (74); 6.5.1788 1L *Carnatic* (74); **Commander**; 26.8.1789-29.5.1790 *Vulture* (14) Sloop; 1793-1798 Impress Service at Exeter.

DICKENS, WILLIAM

Dates: 1794 Died.
Family:
Service: **Lieutenant**; 16.11.1756 L. *Bonetta* (10) Sloop; 9.5.1757-20.7.1758 L. *Raven* (14) Sloop; 9.12.1758-6.8.1759 L. *Postillion* (18) Sloop; 14.4.1762-23.3.1763[P] 2L *Milford* (28).

DICKENSON, JAMES

Dates: c.1734 Born; 24.1.1794 Died Portsea; 2.7.1794 Will Probate.
Family: Wife Hannah; Sister Ann [Cornhill].
Service: 1752-1755 Merchant Service; 6.7.1755 Able *Eagle* (60); 31.8.1755 Mid *Eagle* (60); 8.8.1757-11.4.1759 Mate *Eagle* (60); 11.4.1759 Passed; **Lieutenant**; 24.8.1759 L. *Tamar* (16) Sloop; 20.8.1763 1L *Solebay* (28) Frigate; 15.6.1769-6.5.1771[P] LCmdr *Greyhound* (4) Cutter; 11.1772-1775 Agent for Transports; 24.2.1778 2L *Formidable* (98); 27.7.1778 1st Battle of Ushant; 27.11.1778-29.5.1779 1L *Formidable* (98); **Commander**; 19.6.1779 *Mackworth* (18) Hired Armed vessel; 9.4.1781-24.2.1783[P] *Lady Mackworth* Hired Armed Ship; 30.7.1789 *Savage* (14) Sloop; **Captain**; 21.9.1790 *Thetis* (38); 1.2.1793 *Amphitrite* (24); 20.5.1793-24.1.1794[†] *Thisbe* (28).

DICKSON, SIR ARCHIBALD (1ST BARONET OF HARDINGHAM HALL)

Dates: c.1739 Born; 21.9.1802 1st Baronet of Hardingham Hall; 1803 Died.
Family: Father Archibald Dickson; Wife Elizabeth Porter (d. 1779); Wife Frances Anne Willis married 1800; Daughter Elizabeth [Dickson] (d.1856); Brother William, RN (1728-1803); Brother John; Sister Mary [Smith]; Sister Elizabeth [Ball].
Service: 1752-1755 Merchant Service; 12.7.1755 Mid *Isis* (50); 8.6.1758 Mate *Isis* (50); 7.2.1759 Passed; **Lieutenant**; 19.9.1759 2L *Milford* (28); 19.4.1760 4L *Modeste* (64); 10.1.1761 3L *Modeste* (64); 8.4.1761 4L *Modeste* (64); 5.10.1761-22.10.1762 3L *Modeste* (64); 7.1.1762-10.2.1762 Operations against Martinique; 14.3.1764-20.3.1765 3L *Guernsey* (50); 1.4.1765 LCmdr *Egmont* (10) Schooner; 17.10.1765 2L *Superb* (74); 12.11.1766-3.2.1768 2L *Bellona*

(74); 15.11.1769-26.5.1770[P] 3L *Superb* (74); 23.5.1770 3L *Ajax* (74); 17.9.1770-19.10.1770 4L *Ajax* (74); **Commander**; 10.1.1771 *Thunder* (8) Bomb Vessel; **Captain**; 31.1.1774-7.9.1774 *Antelope* (50); 21.10.1775-25.9.1779 *Greyhound* (28); 2.7.1776-4.7.1776 Staten Island Landings; 24.7.1779-12.8.1779 Penobscot Expedition; 2.1.1781-19.2.1783[P] *Dublin* (74); 20.10.1782 Battle of Cape Spartel; 9.8.1786-18.9.1789 *Goliath* (74); 28.6.1790-3.12.1790[P] *Captain* (74); 1.1.1793 *Egmont* (74); 12.4.1794 **Rear Admiral of the Blue**; 4.7.1794 **Rear Admiral of the White**; 1.6.1795 **Vice Admiral of the Blue**; 6.1798-1799 *Veteran* (64); 1.1799-3.1799 *Monmouth* (64); 14.2.1799 **Vice Admiral of the Red**; 5.1799-6.1799 *Monarch* (74); 1800-1802 CinC — North Sea; **Admiral of the Blue**; 1.1.1801-15.12.1802 *Blenheim* (74).

DICKSON, WILLIAM

Dates: c.1728 Born; 5.1803 Died.

Family: Father Archibald Dickson; Wife Jane Collingwood; Wife Elizabeth Charteris married 1786; Son James; Son William (d.1795); Son Sir Archibald Collingwood, RN (1772-1827); Son Alexander; Daughter Jane [Dickson]; Daughter Eleanor; Son James; Son David John, RN; Daughter Mary Anne; Son Rowland; Son Robert; Daughter Louisa; Brother Sir Archibald (1st Baronet of Hardingham Hall), RN (1739-1803); Brother John; Sister Mary [Smith]; Sister Elizabeth [Ball].

Service: 16.6.1745 Clerk *Faversham* (44); 2.7.1746 Ord. *Saint George* (90); 17.12.1746 Able *Surprise* (24); 31.7.1747 Cox *Grampus* (10) Sloop; 7.2.1748/49 Mid *Grampus* (14) Sloop; 19.2.1750/51 NR *Boston* (24); 6.12.1751 Passed; **Lieutenant**; 31.12.1755 L. *Firebrand* (6) Fireship; 29.12.1756 3L *Fougueux* (64); 17.6.1757-21.5.1759[P] 2L *Fougueux* (64); 29.12.1758 Capture of Goree; 7.8.1759 1L *Phoenix* (44); 1.2.1762-25.2.1763[P] 5L *Namur* (90); 6.6.1762-13.8.1762 Operations against Havana; **Commander**; 10.5.1765-20.6.1765 *Swallow* (14) Sloop; **Captain**; 2.5.1766-20.12.1769[P] *Jersey* (60); 25.9.1779 *Greyhound* (28); 17.4.1780 Battle of Martinique; 18.4.1780[(BLI 14.3.1781)] *Terrible* (74); 16.6.1780[(BLI 25.12.1780)]-6.2.1781[P] *Conqueror* (74); 25.4.1781-15.1.1782 *Sampson* (64); 26.9.1782 *Standard* (64); 18.4.1783-26.6.1786 *Standard* (64); 6.10.1790 *Gibraltar* (80); 1.2.1793 **Rear Admiral of the Blue**; 12.4.1794 **Rear Admiral of the White**; 4.7.1794 **Vice Admiral of the Blue**; 1.6.1795 **Vice Admiral of the White**; 14.2.1799 **Admiral of the Blue**.

DICKSON, WILLIAM

Dates: c.1737 Born; c.1800 Died; 21.5.1800 Will Probate/

Family: Brother John; Brother James; Brother Connelly; Brother Harry; Sister Edwina; Sister Elizabeth [Allingham]/

Service: 1754-1757 Merchant Service; 21.1.1757 Able *Torbay* (74); 30.5.1757 Mid *Torbay* (74); 5.9.1757-6.10.1757 Raid on Rochefort; 5.6.1758-12.6.1758 Raid on Saint-Malo; 29.12.1758 Capture of Goree; 23.9.1759-20.2.1760 Able *Torbay* (74); 20.11.1759 Battle of Quiberon Bay; 20.2.1760 Passed; **Lieutenant**; 15.11.1762[(JAM 31.1.1763)]-29.3.1763 3L *Deptford* (50)/

DIGBY, ROBERT

Dates: 20.12.1732 Born; 25.2.1815 Died.

Family: Father Edward Digby, MP; Mother Charlotte Fox; Wife Mrs Eleanor Jauncey, née Elliot married 19.8.1784; Brother Edward, 6th Baron Digby (1730-57); Brother Henry, 7th Baron Digby (1731-93).

Service: **Lieutenant**; 29.10.1752[(JAM 29.10.1755)] 3L *Severn* (50); **Commander**; 14.2.1755[(JAM 6.1.1756)] *Weazle* (16) Sloop; **Captain**; 5.8.1755-7.10.1755 *Solebay* (24); 11.2.1756-15.11.1756 *Bideford* (20); 15.11.1756-22.2.1757 *Achilles* (60); 13.6.1757-11.4.1763[P] *Dunkirk* (60); 5.9.1757-

6.10.1757 Raid on Rochefort; 15.12.1757-27.3.1761 M.P. for Wells; 5.6.1758-12.6.1758 Raid on Saint-Malo; 29.12.1758 Capture of Goree; 20.11.1759 Battle of Quiberon Bay; 18.3.1777 *Trident* (64); 29.4.1777-31.3.1779 *Ramillies* (74); 27.7.1778 1st Battle of Ushant; **Rear Admiral of the Blue**; 19.3.1779-24.7.1783[P] *Prince George* (98); 16.1.1780 Battle of Cape St. Vincent; 26.9.1780 **Rear Admiral of the Red**; 13.6.1781-1783 CinC — North America; 1782-1783 *Lion* (64); 25.1.1782-26.1.1782 Battle of Saint Kitts; 12.4.1782 Battle of the Saintes; 24.9.1787 **Vice Admiral of the Blue**; 21.9.1790 **Vice Admiral of the White**; 1.2.1793 **Vice Admiral of the Red**; 12.4.1794 **Admiral of the Blue**; 1.6.1795 **Admiral of the White**; 9.11.1805 **Admiral of the Red**.

DIGGES, DUDLEY

Dates: 27.9.1779 Died; 5.10.1779 Buried Saint Mary's.
Family:
Service: 9.6.1739 Unk *Prince of Orange* (70); 9.10.1741 Unk *Chichester* (80); 27.2.1741/42 Mid *Chatham* (50); 25.2.1743/44 Mid *Bedford* (70); 12.7.1745 Passed; **Lieutenant**; 13.7.1745[MED 29.11.1748] 3L *Guernsey* (50); 9.4.1748[MED 29.11.1748] 4L *Essex* (70); 5.8.1748[MED 29.11.1748]-16.8.1748 4L *Boyne* (80); 14.3.1750/51 1L *Glory* (44); **Commander**; 23.4.1752 *Swan* (14) Sloop; **Captain**; 18.12.1753-16.8.1754[P] *Centaur* (20); 2.10.1754 *Nightingale* (22); 27.3.1756-4.1.1758 *Kennington* (20); 8.1757-10.1757 Louisbourg Expedition; 27.1.1758 *Maidstone* (28); 5.6.1758-12.6.1758 Raid on Saint-Malo; 20.11.1759 Battle of Quiberon Bay; 5.8.1761-27.4.1763 *Deptford* (50); 6.6.1762-13.8.1762 Operations against Havana.

DILKE, WILLIAM

Dates: 30.5.1756 Died.
Family: Father Sir Thomas Dilkes, RN (d.1706); Mother Mary O'Brien; Brother Lt. Gen. Michael O'Brien (d.1774).
Service: **Lieutenant**; 23.5.1717 L. *Griffin* (8); 15.8.1717 2L *Dartmouth* (54); 17.3.1717/18 3L *Royal Oak* (70); 4.4.1718-27.4.1718 3L *Hampton Court* (70); 26.11.1718 2L *Defiance* (60); 31.12.1718-24.10.1721[P] 1L *Defiance* (60); 4.12.1721 3L *Nassau* (70); 15.3.1721/22 1L *Leopard* (50); 10.7.1722 4L *Essex* (70); 21.7.1722-18.12.1722[P] 3L *Essex* (70); 1.5.1723-13.3.1726/27 1L *Prince Frederick* (70); 14.3.1726/27-31.1.1727/28[P] 2L *Captain* (70); 16.7.1728-6.3.1732/33 1L *Romney* (50); 23.11.1733 2L *Ipswich* (70); 27.2.1733/34-17.2.1735/36[P] 2L *Blenheim* (96); 7.4.1737 1L *Berwick* (70); 22.5.1738 2L *Princess Amelia* (80); **Commander**; 26.7.1738-15.12.1740 *Hound* (8) Sloop; 12.1.1740/41 *Saint George* (90); 16.1.1740/41 **Captain**; 26.11.1741 *Nassau* (70); 13.9.1742[3.3.1742/43]-4.3.1742/43[P] *Winchester* (50); 16.8.1743 *Boyne* (80); 19.9.1743 *Shrewsbury* (80); 12.12.1743 *Chichester* (80); 11.2.1743/44-12.2.1743/44 Battle of Toulon; 6.3.1743/44[8.1.1744/45] *Namur* (90); 16.8.1744[MED 30.6.1746]-28.5.1745 *Revenge* (70); 5.12.1745 Dismissed.

DILKES, JOHN

Dates: c.1742 Born; 25.2.1827 Died Exeter.
Family: Father Lt. Gen. Michael O'Brien Dilkes (d.1774); Mother Anne Cummin; Wife Miss Epworth married 1804; Brother William Thomas; Brother Thomas.
Service: 28.11.1756 Scholar *Royal Naval Academy*; 29.11.1759 Mid *Boreas* (28); 18.10.1760 Action off Cuba; 4.3.1761 Able *Valiant* (74); 29.3.1761-11.6.1761 Expedition against Belle-Isle; 3.11.1761 Mid *Valiant* (74); 6.6.1762-13.8.1762 Operations against Havana; 31.7.1762[EI 11.5.1763]-13.3.1763[P] 3L *Rippon* (60); 31.7.1762 **Lieutenant**; 13.12.1762 Passed; 12.10.1770-1.4.1771 2L *Tartar* (28); 23.2.1778 3L *Thunderer* (74); 27.7.1778 1st Battle of Ushant; 24.12.1778 2L

Thunderer (74); 22.7.1779-9.5.1780 1L *Alcide* (74); 25.4.1782 1L *Blenheim* (90); **Commander**; 1.8.1782-19.3.1783^{P} *Lisburne* (14) Sloop; 8.7.1790 *Shark* (16) Sloop; **Captain**; 21.9.1790-24.5.1793 *Santa Margarita* (36); 15.8.1795-14.1.1801 *Madras* (56); 21.1.1801-25.4.1802^{P} *Raisonable* (64); 2.4.1801 Battle of Copenhagen; 25.7.1803-25.4.1805 *Salvador del Mundo* (112); 28.4.1808 **Rear Admiral of the Blue**; 25.10.1809 **Rear Admiral of the White**; 12.8.1812 **Vice Admiral of the Blue**; 4.6.1814 **Vice Admiral of the White**.

DISHER, JAMES

Dates: 4.3.1721/22 Born; 3.1795 Died; 26.3.1795 Buried St Mary, Rotherhithe; 4.4.1795 Will Probate.

Family: Father Walter Disher; Mother Catherine Bell; Wife Hannah Bungy married 17.2.1746; Sister Catherine (1716-?); Sister Christian (1719-?).

Service: 26.3.1734 Vol. *Royal Oak* (70); 16.10.1734 Able *Kingston* (60); 7.11.1734 Mid *Kingston* (60); 21.4.1735-5.9.1735^{P} Able *Kingston* (60); 4.3.1738/39 Mid *Somerset* (80); 23.12.1740 Able *Somerset* (80); 20.2.1740/41 Mid *Somerset* (80); 16.5.1741 Able *Somerset* (80); 28.1.1741/42 Mid *Somerset* (80); 27.10.1742 Mate *Somerset* (80); 7.1.1742/43 Mate *Grafton* (70); 29.3.1743 Able *Cambridge* (80); 9.9.1743 Mid *Cambridge* (80); 24.11.1743 Mid *Neptune* (90); 11.2.1743/44-12.2.1743/44 Battle of Toulon; 7.6.1746 Passed; 31.8.1757 **Lieutenant**; 24.5.1758 3L *Norwich* (50); 3.7.1759 Bombardment of Le Havre; 11.4.1760-24.9.1762^{P} 2L *Norwich* (50); 3.6.1761-7.6.1761 Occupation of Dominica; 7.1.1762-10.2.1762 Operations against Martinique; 2.5.1777-1782 LCmdr *Union* Hired Tender.

DISHINGTON, ANDREW

Dates: c.1714 Born Kirkwall; 1780 Died; 30.9.1780 Will Probate.

Family: Father Andrew Dishington; Wife Jane (d.1796); Daughter Catherine (1768-1803).

Service: 5.1.1733/34-2.8.1736^{P} Able *Newcastle* (50); 6.12.1743 Mid *Princess Amelia* (80); 28.4.1744 Mate *Princess Amelia* (80); 17.7.1744 Mate *Princess Royal* (90); 11.7.1745 Passed; **Lieutenant**; 5.11.1745 L. *Scipio* (8) Fireship; 1.1.1745/46-19.8.1747 L. *Kingfisher* (10) Sloop; 30.12.1747-1.9.1748^{P} L. *Gibraltar* (20); 6.9.1755-19.5.1757 3L *Dreadnought* (60); 17.10.1777-28.10.1780 LCmdr *Jane* Hired Tender.

DISNEY, DANIEL

Dates: c.1734 Born; 11.3.1792 Died.

Family:

Service: 1752-1755 Merchant Service; 21.11.1755 Mate *Solebay* (24); 25.5.1756 Mid *Porcupine* (16) Sloop; 19.8.1757 Acting Master *Porcupine* (16) Sloop; 30.9.1758-12.3.1760 Acting Master *Lizard* (28); 12.2.1760 Passed; **Lieutenant**; 11.10.1760 5L *Temeraire* (74); 18.3.1761-12.5.1763^{P} L. *Mortar* (14) Bomb Vessel; 14.7.1775-17.7.1778 L. *Alderney* (10) Sloop.

DOAKE, JAMES

Dates: c.1721 Born; 26.8.1761 Died; 19.5.1762 Will Probate.

Family:

Service: 23.2.1740/41 QGnr *Panther* (54); 27.7.1741 YoP *Panther* (54); 4.2.1743/44 Mid *Plymouth* (60); 7.4.1744 Mid *Sapphire* (44); 26.6.1745 Mate *Gloucester* (50); 3.4.1747 Passed; **Lieutenant**; 24.11.1747-25.12.1747 3L *Assistance* (50); 25.12.1747 3L *Tiger* (60); 16.9.1748-1.5.1752 L. *Garland* (24); 16.1.1753 3L *Monarch* (74); 19.3.1754 2L *Anson* (60); 23.7.1754 3L *Monarch* (74); 28.1.1755 6L *Prince* (90); 14.10.1755 5L *Prince* (90); 12.11.1755 4L *Prince* (90); 7.4.1756 3L *Prince* (90); 12.5.1756 3L *Royal George* (100); 6.8.1756-9.11.1756 1L *Royal George*

(100); **Commander**; 12.10.1756 *Hound* (14) Sloop; **Captain**; 18.10.1758-26.8.1761† *Lizard* (28); 3.6.1761-7.6.1761 Occupation of Dominica.

DOBSON, CHARLES

Dates: 2.6.1798 Died.
Family:
Service: **Lieutenant**; 30.7.1758(NA 13.11.1759) 4L *Prince Frederick* (64); 30.9.1758(NA 13.11.1759)-12.3.1763P 3L *Prince Frederick* (64); 29.3.1761-11.6.1761 Expedition against Belle-Isle.

DOD, THOMAS

Dates: 1777 Died; 10.10.1777 Will Probate.
Family:
Service: **Lieutenant**; 9.8.1745(MED 9.5.1748)-4.12.1747P L. *Firedrake* (8) Bomb Vessel; 13.5.1748-3.8.1748P L. *Flamborough* (20); 29.5.1754-18.7.1757 L. *Fortune* (14) Sloop; 20.5.1756 Battle of Minorca; 18.4.1758-27.8.1761 1L *Melampe* (36); 29.3.1761-11.6.1761 Expedition against Belle-Isle; 2.5.1776-17.10.1783P LCmdr *Sandwich* Hired Tender.

DODD, EDMUND

Dates: 1734 Born; 18.12.1815 Died.
Family:
Service: **Lieutenant**; 26.2.1760(JAM 24.2.1763)-1.4.1763P 3L *Hampshire* (50); 18.10.1760 Action off Cuba; 6.6.1762-13.8.1762 Operations against Havana; 26.8.1763-29.4.1764 2L *Prince Edward* (44); 18.8.1766-2.5.1767 L. *Wasp* (8) Sloop; 24.7.1775-8.2.1781 1L *Renown* (50); 24.12.1775-17.5.1777W LCmdr *Diligent* (10) Schooner; 6.12.1776-8.12.1776 Occupation of Rhode Island; 3.6.1777 LCmdr *Cabot* (14) Sloop; **Commander**; 12.11.1778 *Cabot* (14) Sloop; **Captain**; 18.5.1779-23.11.1780 *Siren* (24); 23.11.1780-12.9.1782P *Lizard* (28); 29.4.1781-30.4.1781 Battle of Fort Royal; 25.1.1782-26.1.1782 Battle of Saint Kitts; 12.4.1782 Battle of the Saintes; 6.10.1787 *Lowestoffe* (28); 15.10.1790 *Director* (64); 10.9.1792 *Charon* (44); 24.9.1793 *Dictator* (64); 20.3.1795-27.2.1797 *Atlas* (98); 20.2.1797 **Rear Admiral of the Blue**; 14.2.1799 **Rear Admiral of the Red**; 1.1.1801 **Vice Admiral of the Blue**; 23.4.1804 **Vice Admiral of the White**; 9.11.1805 **Vice Admiral of the Red**; 28.4.1808 **Admiral of the Blue**; 31.7.1810 **Admiral of the White.**

DODD, EDWARD

Dates: 1763 Died.
Family:
Service: 27.8.1704 Vol-p-O *Folkestone* (42); 3.6.1707 Mid *Folkestone* (42); 13.11.1711 Passed; **Lieutenant**; 4.4.1720-3.5.1723 3L *Nottingham* (60); 4.5.1723-1.9.1727P 2L *Edinburgh* (70); 23.2.1733/34-31.7.1737P 2L *Nottingham* (60); 15.7.1737-27.4.1740 2L *Dragon* (60); 28.4.1740 1L *Dragon* (60); 24.7.1741 Action of 1741-07-24; **Captain**; 25.1.1742/43-7.10.1748P *Blandford* (20).

DODD, HENRY

Dates: c.1733 Born; 1797 Died; 31.1.1797 Will Probate.
Family: Wife Martha Crapp née Pyne married 1.7.1783.
Service: 5.3.1749/50 Capt Serv *Gloucester* (50); 13.7.1750 Able *Gloucester* (50); 11.5.1753 Mid *Gloucester* (50); 29.10.1753 Able *Crown* (44); 13.11.1754 Able *Port Mahon* (24); 28.6.1755 Mid *Port Mahon* (24); 9.8.1756 Mid *Berwick* (64); 5.4.1757 Action of April 5 1757; 28.2.1758 Battle

of Cartagena; 5.3.1758 Passed; **Lieutenant**; 22.5.1758 3L *Chatham* (50); 30.3.1759-18.7.1763 2L *Chatham* (50); 3.7.1759 Bombardment of Le Havre; 20.11.1759 Battle of Quiberon Bay; 21.3.1777 2L *Trident* (64); 29.4.1777-5.9.1781[P] 1L *Trident* (64); 6.7.1779 Battle of Grenada; 17.4.1780 Battle of Martinique; 15.5.1780 Action of March 15 1780; 19.5.1780 Action of March 19 1780.

DOHERTY, JOHN

Dates: c.1719 Born; 1788 Died.
Family:
Service: 24.4.1741 Able *Flamborough* (20); 2.8.1742 Able *Pearl* (40); 16.4.1743 Clerk *Furnace* (8) Bomb Vessel; 15.2.1744/45 Clerk *Gibraltar* (20); 5.1.1745/46 Mid *Looe* (44); 7.1.1747/48 Passed; **Lieutenant**; 10.5.1757 L. *Cormorant* (18) Sloop; 22.5.1758-31.12.1762[P] LCmdr *Jane and Barbara* Hired Tender.

DON, WILLIAM

Dates: 30.6.1816 Died Whitehaven; 15.8.1816 Will Probate.
Family: Father John Don; Mother Anna Seton; Brother Gen. George Don (1756-1782).
Service: **Lieutenant**; 2.8.1758[(NA 13.2.1759)]-11.1.1760 L. *Aetna* (8) Fireship; 21.9.1773 LCmdr *Ferret* (6) Cutter; 13.3.1776 L. *Unicorn* (20); 7.4.1777 3L *Yarmouth* (64); 28.6.1777 2L *Yarmouth* (64); 7.3.1778 Action of 1778-03-07; 5.8.1778 1L *Dunkirk* (60); **Commander**; 25.12.1782-3.3.1783[P] *Mackworth* (18) Hired Armed vessel; 25.10.1809 **Captain**.

DONALDSON, JAMES

Dates: c.1713 Born; 1765 Died.
Family:
Service: 15.2.1733/34 Able *Lark* (40); 22.2.1733/34 QGnr *Lark* (40); 6.10.1734 Able *Edinburgh* (70); 7.10.1735 Mid *Edinburgh* (70); 16.6.1736 Able *Edinburgh* (70); 25.6.1736 Mid *Cruizer* (8) Sloop; 11.11.1738 Mid *Buckingham* (70); 10.2.1738/39-22.8.1739[P] Mid *Port Mahon* (20); 10.9.1739 Mid *Severn* (50); 15.4.1740 Passed; **Lieutenant**; 2.9.1740[(15.10.1740)]-19.10.1740 L. *Blaze* (8) Fireship; 20.10.1740 2L *Argyll* (50); 18.9.1742 1L *Argyll* (50); 8.2.1742/43 L. *Aldborough* (20); 22.10.1744 1L *Harwich* (50); 20.12.1745[(2.10.1746)]-25.9.1746[P] 2L *Deptford* (60); 29.5.1747 3L *Yarmouth* (64); 14.10.1747 2nd Battle of Cape Finisterre; 5.12.1747-26.8.1748[P] 1L *Yarmouth* (64); 30.1.1748/49-3.4.1754[P] L. *Amazon* (22); 12.6.1754-14.2.1757 L. *Garland* (24); 5.5.1757-13.9.1757 1L *Royal Sovereign* (104).

DONKLEY, JOHN

Dates: c.1713 Born; 17.3.1758 Died; 3.3.1759 Will Probate.
Family: Wife Jane.
Service: 13.10.1729 Able *Princess Louisa* (40); 21.7.1730 Able *Falmouth* (50); 24.11.1732 Mid *Falmouth* (50); 18.7.1735 Able *Cornwall* (80); 8.1.1735/36 Passed; **Lieutenant**; 12.10.1739[(8.12.1744)] L. *Dursley Galley* (20); 25.9.1743[(MED 29.10.1747)] 1L *Faversham* (44); 11.2.1743/44-12.2.1743/44 Battle of Toulon; 6.3.1743/44[(MED 7.11.1745)]-26.2.1744/45 2L *Dragon* (60); 24.2.1744/45[(MED 26.10.1745)]-2.8.1745 6L *Neptune* (90); **Commander**; 5.7.1745[(MED 4.11.1748)]-1.11.1748[P] *Spence* (8) Sloop; 2.9.1755 *Brilliant* (16) Hired Unknown; **Captain**; 27.3.1756 *Nightingale* (22); 29.4.1756 *Aldborough* (20); 10.11.1756-17.3.1758[†] *Enterprise* (44).

DORRILL, RICHARD

Dates: 1762 Died.
Family:
Service: **Lieutenant**; 12.9.1739-3.3.1739/40 4L *Cumberland* (80); 4.3.1739/40 2L *Saint Albans* (50); 21.8.1741-16.9.1742 3L *Royal Oak* (70); 18.9.1744[17.1.1743/44]-23.1.1744/45[P] 5L *Namur* (90); 16.7.1745 1L *Nottingham* (60); **Commander**; 2.3.1746/47 *Dolphin* (8) Storeship; 22.6.1747-23.9.1747 *Jamaica* (10) Sloop; **Captain**; 11.2.1755-12.2.1756[P] *Penzance* (44); 13.2.1756 *Royal George* (100); 12.5.1756-8.4.1757 *Lowestoffe* (24); 27.1.1758-4.6.1759 *Royal George* (100).

DOUGLAS, SIR CHARLES (1ST BARONET CARR)

Dates: 8.2.1726/27 Born Kinglassie, Fife; 16.2.1727 Baptised Kinglassic, Fife; 1777 1st Baronet Carr; 10.3.1789 Died Edinburgh.
Family: Father Master Charles Ayton Douglas (1700–1744); Mother Christian Hepburn (1700–1788); Wife Uranie Lidie Marteilhe (1732–1769) married 23.6.1760; Wife Sarah Wood (1744–1779) married 1.1.1771; Wife Jane Baillie married 10.11.1781; Son William Henry, RN (1763-1809); Daughter Lidie Marie Anne (1769-?); Daughter Chistiana (1772-1773); Son Charles, RN (1774-1809); Daughter Sarah (1775-?); Son Howard, 3rd Bt. (1776-1861); Daughter Ann Irwin (1777-1815); Son Frederick (1779-1779); Brother Robert (1726-?); Brother Sholto (1730-?); Sister Helena (1730-1800); Sister Jean (1731-?).
Service: **Lieutenant**; 4.12.1753 L. *Raven* (14) Sloop; 5.11.1755 3L *Lynn* (44); 8.2.1757 2L *Somerset* (68); 23.5.1758 4L *Newark* (80); 5.6.1758-12.6.1758 Raid on Saint-Malo; **Commander**; 14.2.1759 *Rodney* Hired Armed vessel; **Captain**; 13.3.1761 *Siren* (20); 25.12.1762-19.3.1764 *Tweed* (32); 1764-1765 In the service of Russia; 2.5.1766-16.8.1769 *Emerald* (32); 11.1.1771-1.10.1773[P] *Saint Albans* (64); 9.9.1773-11.1.1774 *Ardent* (64); 17.10.1775-21.12.1776 *Isis* (50); 17.3.1777 *Stirling Castle* (64); 27.7.1778 1st Battle of Ushant; 29.10.1778-24.11.1781 *Duke* (90); 24.11.1781-13.4.1782 1Capt. *Formidable* (98); 12.4.1782 Battle of the Saintes; 16.8.1783-1785 CinC — Nova Scotia; 15.9.1783-1.1784 Commodore *Assistance* (50); 24.9.1787 **Rear Admiral of the Blue**; 11.2.1789 CinC — Nova Scotia.

DOUGLAS, SIR JAMES (1ST BARONET DOUGLAS)

Dates: 1703 Born; 16.10.1759 Knight Bachelor; 26.7.1786 1st Baronet Douglas; 2.11.1787 Died.
Family: Father George Douglas; Mother Elizabeth Scott; Wife Helen Brisbane (d.1766) married 1753; Wife Lady Helen Boyle married 25.9.1768; Son George, 2nd Bt. (1754-1821); Son James, RN (1755-1839); Son Unknown; Son Unknown; Daughter Unknown; Daughter Unknown; Daughter Unknown.
Service: **Lieutenant**; 1.7.1732[28.5.1734]-1.1.1732/33 L. *Shoreham* (20); 2.1.1732/33[20.5.1734]-26.9.1734 L. *Spence* (8) Sloop; 27.9.1734-14.3.1737/38 3L *Ipswich* (70); 28.7.1738-25.11.1738 2L *Tiger* (50); 8.6.1739-29.8.1739 L. *Salamander* (6) Bomb Vessel; 30.8.1739-26.5.1740 2L *Tilbury* (60); 27.5.1740 1L *Tilbury* (60); 24.2.1740/41[28.4.1743] 4L *Princess Caroline* (80); 25.3.1741[28.4.1743] 3L *Princess Caroline* (80); 17.4.1741[28.4.1743] 2L *Princess Caroline* (80); 23.4.1741[28.4.1743] 1L *Princess Caroline* (80); **Commander**; 5.5.1741[2.2.1741/42] *Princess Royal* (18) Hospital Ship; 7.1741-10.1741 Operations against Santiago; 2.9.1743 *Ferret* (14) Sloop; **Captain**; 19.3.1743/44 *Ruby* (44); 26.5.1744-22.5.1745 *Mermaid* (44); 23.5.1745[BLI 1.5.1747]-23.9.1747 *Vigilant* (60); 18.3.1747/48-29.7.1748[P] *Berwick* (70); 15.5.1754-6.5.1768 M.P. for Orkney and Shetland; 14.2.1755 *Fougueux* (64); 26.3.1755 *Bedford* (64); 4.4.1757-22.9.1759 *Alcide* (64); 5.6.1758-12.6.1758 Raid on Saint-Malo; 18.2.1760 CinC — Barbados & the Leeward Islands; 18.2.1760 Commodore *Stirling Castle* (64); 3.6.1761-7.6.1761 Occupation of Dominica; 1762

CinC — Jamaica; 7.1.1762-10.2.1762 Operations against Martinique; 18.2.1762-5.10.1763^{P} Commodore *Dublin* (74); 6.6.1762-13.8.1762 Operations against Havana; 21.10.1762 **Rear Admiral of the White**; 18.10.1770 **Vice Admiral of the Blue**; 24.10.1770 **Vice Admiral of the White**; 1.11.1773-25.7.1776 *Marlborough* (74); 18.5.1774-1777 CinC — Portsmouth; 7.12.1775 **Vice Admiral of the Red**; 29.1.1778 **Admiral of the Blue**; 8.4.1782 **Admiral of the White.**

DOUGLAS, JOHN

Dates: 1787 Died.
Family:
Service: 13.2.1722/23 Vol-p-O *Kingston* (60); 24.1.1723/24 Vol-p-O *Winchester* (50); 3.6.1725 MidO *Winchester* (50); 29.3.1726 Mid *Nottingham* (60); 17.1.1726/27 Mid *Poole* (32); 16.2.1726/27 Mid *Burford* (70); 19.3.1728/29 Passed; **Lieutenant**; 16.6.1730 3L *Hector* (40); 29.8.1732-16.12.1732^{P} 2L *Hector* (40); 10.1.1735/36-8.3.1735/36^{P} 2L *Hector* (40); **Commander**; 12.4.1745 *Ferret* (14) Sloop; **Captain**; 22.4.1746-20.4.1748 *Squirrel* (20).

DOUGLAS, JOHN LEIGH

Dates: 1741 Born; 13.11.1810 Died Montague Square, London; 4.2.1811 Will Probate.
Family: Father Rev. Alexander Douglas; Mother Isabel Houston; Wife Charlotte Douglas (1750-1840).
Service: **Lieutenant**; 17.6.1760$^{(BLI\ 11.11.1761)}$-26.10.1761^{P} 2L *Emerald* (28); 2.3.1762 4L *Lancaster* (66); 16.6.1762 3L *Lancaster* (66); 31.1.1763-18.7.1764^{P} L. *Ludlow Castle* (24); 20.6.1777 2L *Torbay* (74); 15.8.1777 3L *Prince George* (90); **Commander**; 19.9.1777 *Cameleon* (14) Sloop; 24.2.1779 *Delight* (14) Sloop; **Captain**; 5.4.1779-5.5.1779 *America* (64); 30.11.1779 *Terrible* (74); 16.1.1780 Battle of Cape St. Vincent; 17.4.1780 Battle of Martinique; 18.4.1780 *Venus* (36); 15.5.1780 Action of March 15 1780; 19.5.1780 Action of March 19 1780; 18.1.1782-19.12.1782 *Vigilant* (64); 20.10.1782 Battle of Cape Spartel; 9.12.1794-26.12.1794 *Irresistible* (74); 1.6.1795 **Rear Admiral of the Blue**; 14.2.1799 **Rear Admiral of the Red**; 1.1.1801 **Vice Admiral of the Blue**; 23.4.1804 **Vice Admiral of the White**; 1805-1806 Second in Command — English Channel; 10.1805-5.2.1806 *Hibernia* (110); 9.11.1805 **Vice Admiral of the Red**; 28.4.1808 **Admiral of the Blue**; 31.7.1810 **Admiral of the White.**

DOUGLAS, RICHARD

Dates: c.1728 Born Edinburgh; 1803 Died; 21.10.1803 Buried Edinburgh.
Family: Wife Mary Campbell (1742-1801); Son Richard (1755-?).
Service: c.1751-1755 Merchant Service; 8.4.1755 Mid *Torbay* (74); 6.6.1755-8.6.1755 Action of 6-8 June 1755; 13.2.1756 Mid *Invincible* (74); 3.1.1757-11.4.1757 Mid *Royal Anne* (100); 11.4.1757 Passed; **Lieutenant**; 27.11.1760$^{(EI\ 14.10.1765)}$-25.8.1764^{P} 2L *Baleine* (20); 10.3.1778 2L *Victory* (100); 29.4.1778 1L *Victory* (100); 13.5.1778 1L *Prince George* (98); 27.7.1778 1st Battle of Ushant; 13.5.1779-30.5.1780 1L *Ramillies* (74).

DOUGLAS, STAIR

Dates: c.1735 Born Richmond, Yorkshire; 8.4.1789 Died.
Family: Father Sir John Douglas; Mother Christian Cunningham.
Service: 2.6.1749 Scholar *Royal Naval Academy*; 26.6.1753 Able *Fowey* (24); 2.6.1754 MidO *Fowey* (24); 9.10.1754 Mate *Fowey* (24); 12.4.1756 Mid *Barfleur* (80); 3.11.1756 Passed; 8.12.1756 3L *Windsor* (60); 13.12.1756 **Lieutenant**; 25.4.1757 3L *Gosport* (44); 3.2.1758 1L *Brilliant* (36); 5.6.1758-12.6.1758 Raid on Saint-Malo; 3.7.1759 Bombardment of Le Havre;

28.2.1760 Action of February 28 1760; 10.3.1760 6L *Royal George* (100); 27.6.1760 5L *Royal George* (100); 17.11.1760 3L *Royal George* (100); **Commander**; 7.7.1761-26.3.1762 *Sardoine* (14) Sloop; 26.3.1762[BLI 3.11.1764] *Granado* (8) Bomb Vessel; **Captain**; 29.6.1762[EI 30.7.1764]-3.4.1763 *Glasgow* (20); 3.4.1763[JAM 6.9.1764]-25.6.1764[P] *Richmond* (32); 15.11.1769-29.10.1770 *Seaford* (20); 21.11.1770[JAM 21.4.1772]-6.3.1772[P] *Dunkirk* (60); 1.11.1773-9.5.1777 *Squirrel* (20); 29.11.1777-21.1.1780[P] *Montreal* (32); 1.4.1780 *Prince William* (64); 29.4.1781-30.4.1781 Battle of Fort Royal; 13.5.1781[BLI 18.3.1782]-17.12.1781[P] *Triumph* (74); 2.11.1782 *Grafton* (74); 30.12.1782-22.4.1783[P] *Cambridge* (80).

DOUTHWAITE, GEORGE

Dates: c.1717 Born; 1766 Died; 9.7.1766 Will Probate.
Family:
Service: 3.10.1739 Able *Argyll* (50); 5.6.1740 YoP *Argyll* (50); 2.5.1741 Able *Kingston* (60); 21.9.1741 Cox *Kingston* (60); 28.3.1742 Mid *Kingston* (60); 19.7.1743 Mate *Essex* (70); 11.2.1743/44-12.2.1743/44 Battle of Toulon; 20.9.1744 Able *Marlborough* (90); 6.2.1745-12.6.1745[P] Able *Newcastle* (50); 16.7.1745-6.3.1746 Mate *Milford* (44); 6.3.1745/46 Passed; 8.1746 Unk *Windsor* (60); 3.5.1747 1st Battle of Cape Finisterre; 14.10.1747 2nd Battle of Cape Finisterre; **Lieutenant**; 23.11.1747-18.8.1748[P] 3L *Windsor* (60); 6.2.1755 3L *Weymouth* (60); 7.10.1755 2L *Weymouth* (60); 24.12.1756 2L *Invincible* (74); 6.4.1757-29.7.1757 5L *Neptune* (90); 1.8.1757 4L *Union* (90); 27.1.1758 2L *Dorsetshire* (68); 26.4.1758 1L *Dorsetshire* (68); 19.6.1759 6L *Royal George* (100); 5.9.1759 5L *Royal George* (100); 17.10.1759 4L *Royal George* (100); 20.11.1759 Battle of Quiberon Bay; 10.3.1760 2L *Royal George* (100); **Commander**; 2.6.1760-18.1.1762[P] *Ranger* (8) Sloop.

DOVE, JONATHAN

Dates: 1808 Died; 4.7.1808 Will Probate.
Family: Daughter Ester [Westerdale]; Daughter Elizabeth [Sissons]; Son John.
Service: **Lieutenant**; 31.8.1761[EI 9.10.1764] 2L *Seahorse* (24); 27.10.1761[EI 9.10.1764]-12.12.1762 3L *Medway* (60); 8.9.1763[EI 9.10.1764]-11.8.1764[P] 4L *America* (60); 8.11.1770-5.10.1772 L. *Weazle* (16) Sloop; 17.11.1775-19.3.1777 1L *Carysfort* (28); 14.8.1777-10.3.1783[P] LCmdr *Dorothy and Ann* Hired Tender.

DOVE, THOMAS

Dates: 1767 Died.
Family: Wife Hannah Artis married 26.8.1734.
Service: 20.7.1720[23.6.1767] Ord. *Jersey* (54); 18.5.1721 Ord. *Essex* (70); 23.6.1722 Able *Essex* (70); 5.2.1722/23 Able *Yarmouth* (70); 12.8.1723 Mid *Deptford* (50); 29.3.1724 MidO *Dover* (40); 3.3.1724/25 MidO *Plymouth* (60); 10.12.1725 Passed; **Lieutenant**; 16.12.1727[30.4.1728] 4L *Stirling Castle* (70); 11.4.1729-19.5.1731 4L *Berwick* (70); 19.5.1731 3L *Orford* (70); 7.6.1731 3L *Buckingham* (70); 14.6.1732 3L *Grafton* (70); 31.1.1733/34-22.2.1733/34 3L *Revenge* (70); 13.3.1733/34-13.7.1738 2L *Portland* (50); 14.6.1739 2L *Deptford* (60); 12.3.1739/40-19.11.1741 1L *Deptford* (60); 4.3.1740/41-5.1741 Operations against Cartagena; 3.2.1743/44 1L *Sandwich* (90); **Commander**; 18.5.1745-9.12.1752[P] *Hound* (10) Sloop.

DOW, ARCHIBALD

Dates: 1815 Died; 19.1.1815 Will Probate.
Family: Daughter Margaret; Son John; Son Edward.
Service: **Lieutenant**; 26.1.1762-26.1.1763[P] L. *Dolphin* (24); 28.1.1765-10.2.1768 L. *Dispatch* (14) Sloop; 29.6.1768 2L *Emerald* (32); 6.6.1770-27.6.1771 1L *Emerald* (32); 9.10.1776 3L *Ramillies* (74); 7.4.1777-20.1.1778 2L *Ramillies* (74); 25.10.1809 **Commander**.

DOWN, EDWARD

Dates: 1743 Born Devon; 23.6.1806 Died; 4.9.1806 Will Probate.
Family: Wife Mary Sommers married 12.10.1767.
Service: 17.2.1755 Capt Serv *Torbay* (74); 6.6.1755-8.6.1755 Action of 6-8 June 1755; 20.1.1756 Capt Serv *Invincible* (74); 17.8.1756 Adm Ret *Invincible* (74); 1.1.1757 Adm Ret *Royal Anne* (100); 5.9.1757-6.10.1757 Raid on Rochefort; 8.2.1758 Adm Ret *Namur* (90); 29.8.1758 Capt Serv *Shannon* (28); 8.1.1759 Able *Shannon* (28); 10.4.1759 Mid *Shannon* (28); 23.5.1761 Able *Shannon* (28); 7.10.1761 Passed; **Lieutenant**; 12.10.1761 3L *Montagu* (60); 20.11.1761-24.5.1763[P] 2L *Montagu* (60); 11.9.1764 LCmdr *Kite* (4) Cutter; 3.1.1765-27.1.1768 LCmdr *Folkestone* (6) Cutter; 31.10.1770-13.11.1771 3L *Terrible* (74); 9.1.1777-21.5.1782[W] 1L *Blonde* (32); 24.7.1779-12.8.1779 Penobscot Expedition.

DOWNING, DENNIS

Dates: 1763 Died.
Family:
Service: 16.1.1744/45 **Lieutenant**; 28.12.1745-2.3.1746/47 2L *Eagle* (60); 29.12.1747-23.12.1748[P] 3L *Saint Albans* (60); 5.6.1755 2L *Portland* (50); 20.5.1756 Battle of Minorca; 5.4.1757 Action of April 5 1757; 5.6.1758-12.6.1758 Raid on Saint-Malo; **Commander**; 18.10.1758-11.12.1759 *Fly* (8) Sloop.

DOWNS, JONATHON

Dates: c.1737 Baptised; 1761 Died.
Family:
Service: 20.1.1752 Mst Serv *Otter* (14) Sloop; 26.7.1755-16.5.1757[P] Mid *Oxford* (50); 9.6.1757 Mid *Pembroke* (60); 27.3.1758 Passed; **Lieutenant**; 5.2.1759[(BLI 19.10.1759)]-19.8.1761[P] 4L *Lancaster* (66).

DOWSON, CHARLES

Dates: c.1727 Born; c.1776 Died; 28.3.1776 Will Probate.
Family: Sister Mary; Sister Dorothy.
Service: 27.8.1740 Ord. *Terrible* (6) Bomb Vessel; 4.3.1740/41-5.1741 Operations against Cartagena; 21.6.1742 Able *Terrible* (6) Bomb Vessel; 15.5.1743 Mid *Terrible* (6) Bomb Vessel; 13.1.1744/45 Able *Terrible* (6) Bomb Vessel; 27.2.1744/45 Mid *Oxford* (50); 27.12.1746-5.6.1748 Mate *Chichester* (80); 3.1.1758 Passed; **Lieutenant**; 28.4.1759[(NA 19.5.1761)]-9.4.1761[D] 2L *Thetis* (32); 9.4.1761 Dismissed.

DRAKE, SIR FRANCIS SAMUEL (1ST BARONET DRAKE)

Dates: 1729 Born; 12.8.1782 1st Baronet Drake; 19.10.1789 Died.
Family: Father Sir Francis Henry Drake, 4th Bt (d.1740); Mother Anne Heathcote; Wife Pooley Onslow married 1788; Sister Anne Pollexfen [Eliott]; Brother Francis William, RN (1724-1787); Brother Sir Francis Henry, 5th Bt. (1723-94).

Service: **Lieutenant**; 21.8.1749[EI 10.1.1750/51]-22.8.1749[P] L. *Lively* (24); 9.5.1751 3L *Torrington* (44); 12.6.1754 L. *Otter* (14) Sloop; 21.5.1755 2L *Windsor* (60); **Commander**; 30.3.1756 *Viper* (10) Sloop; **Captain**; 15.11.1756 *Bideford* (20); 11.3.1757-11.11.1762[P] *Falkland* (50); 20.11.1759 Battle of Quiberon Bay; 3.6.1761-7.6.1761 Occupation of Dominica; 7.1.1762-10.2.1762 Operations against Martinique; 6.11.1762 *Vanguard* (68); 18.1.1763-2.4.1764[P] *Rochester* (50); 6.5.1766-3.3.1767[P] *Burford* (68); 4.4.1772 *Torbay* (74); 14.1.1778-17.6.1780 *Russell* (74); 17.6.1780 Commodore *Russell* (74); **Rear Admiral of the Blue**; 26.9.1780 *Gibraltar* (80); 29.4.1781-30.4.1781 Battle of Fort Royal; 13.5.1781-5.7.1783[P] *Princessa* (70); 5.9.1781 Battle of the Chesapeake; 25.1.1782-26.1.1782 Battle of Saint Kitts; 12.4.1782 Battle of the Saintes; **Rear Admiral of the Red**; 24.9.1787 *Ganges* (74); 12.8.1789-19.10.1789 Lord Commissioner of the Admiralty.

DRAKE, FRANCIS WILLIAM

Dates: 1724 Born; 22.8.1724 Baptised; 12.1787 Died.
Family: Father Sir Francis Henry Drake, 4th Bt (d.1740); Wife Elizabeth Heathcote married 3.11.1763; Daughter Marianne; Daughter Sophia [de Salis] (1765-1803); Sister Anne Pollexfen [Eliott]; Brother Sir Francis Samuel (1st Baronet Drake), RN (1729-1789); Brother Sir Francis Henry, 5th Bt. (1723-94).
Service: 28.11.1737 Ord. *Priscilla* Mer; 10.2.1739/40 Mid *Centurion* (60); 20.7.1744 Mid *Princess Royal* (90); 1.3.1744/45 Mid *Suffolk* (70); 27.5.1745 Passed; **Lieutenant**; 26.1.1745/46[NA 7.3.1748/49]-21.5.1746 3L *Suffolk* (70); **Commander**; 28.4.1747[BLI 7.3.1748/49]-15.1.1747/48 *Dreadnought Prize* (12) Sloop; **Captain**; 29.1.1747/48[JAM 7.3.1748/49]-27.6.1748[W] *Fowey* (44); 7.3.1748/49-31.1.1750/51[P] *Mercury* (20); 24.1.1750/51 *Boston* (24); 16.1.1751/52-6.5.1753[P] *Winchelsea* (20); 2.10.1754 *Winchelsea* (20); 7.10.1755-11.3.1757 *Falkland* (50); 18.10.1758 *Aurora* (38); 13.12.1758-23.9.1763[P] *Edgar* (60); 18.8.1759-19.8.1759 Battle of Lagos Bay; 6.6.1762-13.8.1762 Operations against Havana; 29.1.1771-8.10.1774 M.P. for Bere Alston; 23.1.1778 **Rear Admiral of the Blue**; 20.1.1779 CinC — The Downs; 19.3.1779 **Rear Admiral of the Red**; 7.1779-11.1779 *Dunkirk* (60); 11.1779-1781 *Dromedary* (30) Armed Storeship; **Vice Admiral of the Blue**; 26.9.1780-29.12.1780 *Victory* (100); 3.5.1782-3.5.1783[P] *Rippon* (56); 28.6.1782-1783 *Panther* (60); 20.10.1782 Battle of Cape Spartel; 24.9.1787 **Vice Admiral of the Red**.

DRING, ROBERT

Dates: c.1734 Born; 1789 Died; 25.5.1789 Buried Hammersmith, London.
Family:
Service: **Lieutenant**; 24.9.1757[EI 3.8.1761]-28.4.1758[B] 2L *Triton* (20); 10.9.1759 Battle of Pondicherry; 10.9.1759[EI 3.8.1761]-28.6.1760 3L *Salisbury* (50); 20.10.1761 5L *Prince* (90); 6.9.1762-25.1.1763[P] 4L *Prince* (90); 4.3.1766 1L *Lark* (32); **Commander**; 3.8.1768 *Lynx* (10) Sloop; 4.11.1769[BLI 30.1.1770]-28.12.1770 *Vulture* (14) Sloop; 21.11.1775-1.2.1777 *Carcass* (8) Bomb Vessel.

DRUMMOND, CHARLES

Dates: 1771 Died; 29.11.1771 Will Probate.
Family: Father James Drummond; Mother Isabella Murray; Brother Gavin.
Service: 1694-1704 Merchant Service; 28.5.1704 Able *Lightning* (28); 13.8.1704 Battle of Malaga; 9.3.1704/5 Mid *Terrible* (26); 2.3.1705/6 Mate *Experiment* (32); 15.11.1706 Mid *Sunderland* (60); 13.1.1706/7 Mate *Sunderland* (60); 9.5.1708 Mid *Resolution* (70); 14.7.1708 Passed; **Lieutenant**; 23.5.1711 L. *Discovery* (10); 4.2.1711/12 L. *Seahorse* (24); 14.12.1714-

27.6.1716[P] L. *Seahorse* (20); 17.3.1717/18 3L *Shrewsbury* (80); 11.8.1718 Battle of Cape Passaro; 14.2.1718/19 2L *Shrewsbury* (80); 6.3.1718/19 2L *Monmouth* (70); 13.5.1719-15.11.1721 L. *Rye* (32); 4.5.1725-10.1.1726/27 1L *Kinsale* (40); **Commander**; 2.11.1732-10.9.1735 *Hawk* (8) Sloop; **Captain**; 12.1.1735/36 *Lowestoffe* (20); 24.5.1742-29.5.1745 *Cambridge* (80); 11.2.1743/44-12.2.1743/44 Battle of Toulon; 21.7.1747 **Superannuated Rear Admiral**.

DRUMMOND, JOHN

Dates: c.1704 Born; 1763 Died.
Family: Wife Mary Patoun married 4.5.1745.
Service: 20.3.1717 Capt Serv *Charles Galley* (42); 11.8.1718 Battle of Cape Passaro; 30.1.1719-19.3.1720[P] Ord. *Charles Galley* (42); 19.2.1748 Master *Hornet* (10) Sloop; 16.8.1752 ActL *Hornet* (10) Sloop; 6.6.1753 Passed; 7.5.1755 Master *Humber* (44); **Lieutenant**; 5.1.1757-12.3.1757 3L *Humber* (44); 31.1.1758-7.3.1758 3L *Deptford* (50); 22.5.1758-23.12.1760 L. *Peregrine* (20) Sloop.

DRUMMOND, PATRICK

Dates: 31.8.1792 Died.
Family: Father Patrick Drummond; Half-brother Adam (1720-1792).
Service: 1735-1740 Merchant Service; 28.2.1739/40 Mid *Chichester* (80); 3.1.1742 Mate *Hastings* (44); 16.1.1744-2.9.1744 ActL *Otter* (14) Sloop; 2.9.1744 Passed; **Lieutenant**; 4.9.1744[West Indies 4.8.1746]-5.12.1744 L. *Otter* (14) Sloop; 16.12.1744[BLI 4.8.1746] 3L *Argyll* (50); 5.7.1745[BLI 4.8.1746]-12.8.1746[P] 2L *Argyll* (50); 25.12.1747 2L *Tiger* (60); 27.9.1748-6.10.1752[P] 2L *Tavistock* (50); 7.10.1755-29.3.1756 1L *Assistance* (50); 10.2.1757 3L *Newark* (80); 8.1757-10.1757 Louisbourg Expedition; 5.6.1758-12.6.1758 Raid on Saint-Malo; 18.8.1759-19.8.1759 Battle of Lagos Bay; 9.1.1760 4L *Namur* (90); 2.4.1761-1.2.1762 1L *Namur* (90); **Captain**; 22.10.1762[BLI 3.3.1763] *Greyhound* (20); 10.4.1766-2.3.1768 *Pearl* (32); 23.4.1773-20.2.1776 *Lark* (32).

DUANE, ABRAHAM

Dates: 1718 Born; c.1767 Died; 28.8.1767 Will Probate.
Family: Father Anthony Duane (1670-1722); Mother Eva Benson (1692-1722); Brother Richard (d.1740); Brother Cornelius.
Service: **Lieutenant**; 26.11.1756 3L *Revenge* (64); 28.2.1758 Battle of Cartagena; 2.4.1759 2L *Revenge* (64); 27.7.1759-21.3.1760 3L *Foudroyant* (80); 31.3.1761 L. *Pomona* (18) Sloop; 12.4.1763 1L *Coventry* (28); 7.6.1763 3L *Princess Louisa* (60); 2.11.1764 LCmdr *Lowestoffe* (32); 31.3.1765-1.11.1765 3L *Princess Louisa* (60); **Commander**; 19.8.1766-23.6.1767 *Beaver* (14) Sloop.

DUBOIS, HENRY RICHARD

Dates: 4.2.1723/24 Born Westminster; 1.3.1723/24 Baptised St Martin in the Fields, Westminster; 12.1792 Died.
Family: Father Nicholas Dubois; Mother Anne; Wife Rebecca Price married 21.2.1743/44; Son Finch (1746-?).
Service: 29.9.1737 Capt Serv *Eltham* (40); 21.6.1740 Mid *Orford* (70); 7.1.1740/41 Action of January 7 1741; 31.7.1742 Mid *Russell* (80); 11.2.1743/44-12.2.1743/44 Battle of Toulon; 5.7.1744 Passed; **Lieutenant**; 7.7.1744 3L *Princess Louisa* (60); 27.7.1744 2L *Princess Louisa* (60); 28.1.1744/45-11.8.1745 5L *Royal George* (100); 8.3.1745/46-6.8.1746 5L *Prince George* (90); 6.8.1747 2L *Saint George* (90); 5.10.1747-10.2.1748/49 3L *Chester* (50); 6.4.1751-20.4.1752[P] 1L *Rainbow* (44); 10.1.1753 2L *Northumberland* (68); 3.5.1753-31.5.1755 L.

Baltimore (14) Sloop; 6.1.1756 LCmdr *Princess Caroline* (80) Hospital Ship; **Commander**; 2.5.1757-14.12.1763 *Fubbs* (12) Yacht.

DUCKITT, PETER

Dates: 1767 Died.
Family:
Service: **Lieutenant**; 21.5.1760[JAM 26.11.1762]-4.10.1760[W] 3L *Harwich* (50); 22.1.1761[JAM 26.11.1762]-2.7.1763[P] L. *Glasgow* (20); 6.6.1762-13.8.1762 Operations against Havana; 15.7.1763-29.9.1767 L. *Greyhound* (20).

DUDDINGSTON, WILLIAM

Dates: 11.1740 Born Kilconquhar, Fife; 20.11.1740 Baptised Kilconquhar, Fife; 27.10.1817 Died Earlsferry, Fife.
Family: Father James Duddingston 1695–1794); Mother Margaret Gillespie(d.1752); Wife Antonia Steuart-Barclay married 7.11.1802.
Service: 1752-1755 Merchant Service; 6.1.1755 Adm Serv *Saint George* (90); 5.8.1756 Mid *Gosport* (44); 10.9.1756 Mid *Buckingham* (68); 5.1.1757 Mid *Trident* (64); 3.3.1759 Mid *Ramillies* (90); 13.6.1759 Passed; 10.10.1759 **Lieutenant**; 8.5.1762 2L *Rainbow* (44); 18.4.1763-3.10.1766[P] 2L *Rainbow* (44); 12.9.1771-10.6.1772[B] LCmdr *Gaspe* (6) Schooner; **Commander**; 28.8.1772 *Bonetta* (10) Sloop; 18.1.1775-11.7.1776 *Senegal* (14) Sloop; 2.7.1776-4.7.1776 Staten Island Landings; 21.3.1777 *Cameleon* (14) Sloop; **Captain**; 19.9.1777-18.7.1782[P] *Boston* (28); 12.11.1794 **Superannuated Captain.**

DUDLEY, O'BRIEN

Dates: 26.8.1759 Died.
Family:
Service: **Lieutenant**; 1.11.1741[JAM 31.7.1745] 4L *Grafton* (70); 5.12.1743[16.7.1746] 4L *Cumberland* (80); 28.12.1743[16.7.1746] 3L *Cumberland* (80); 18.4.1744[16.7.1746] 2L *Cumberland* (80); 12.5.1744[16.7.1746] 1L *Cumberland* (80); 1.3.1744/45 **Commander**; 26.3.1745-25.3.1746[P] *Basilisk* (8) Bomb Vessel; **Captain**; 11.8.1746 *Rose* (24) Ship; 23.11.1747-25.1.1748/49 *Chesterfield* (44).

DUFF, ROBERT

Dates: 1721 Born; 6.6.1787 Died.
Family: Father Robert Duff; Mother Anne Innes; Wife Helen Duff married 1764.
Service: 9.3.1738/39 Passed; 9.3.1738/39[15.4.1743] 4L *Ipswich* (70); 9.4.1739 **Lieutenant**; 2.3.1742/43 Sinking of the San Isidoro; 29.3.1744 1L *Exeter* (58); 14.7.1744 1L *Saint George* (90); **Commander**; 4.12.1744 *Terror* (8) Bomb Vessel; 1.5.1746 Action of 1746-05-01; 23.10.1746 **Captain**; 24.10.1746-4.8.1748[P] *Anglesea* (44); 21.3.1748/49-18.7.1755 *Queenborough* (24); 11.3.1755 *Rochester* (50); 5.6.1758-12.6.1758 Raid on Saint-Malo; 20.11.1759 Battle of Quiberon Bay; 5.3.1760-8.6.1762 *Foudroyant* (80); 7.1.1762-10.2.1762 Operations against Martinique; 27.2.1775 CinC — Newfoundland; 31.3.1775 **Rear Admiral of the Blue**; 4.1775-4.1776 *Romney* (50); 7.12.1775 **Rear Admiral of the Red**; 16.9.1777 CinC — The Mediterranean Sea; 16.9.1777-1779 *Panther* (60); 29.1.1778 **Vice Admiral of the Blue**; 26.9.1780 **Vice Admiral of the Red.**

DUFF, WILLIAM

Dates: c.1730 Born; 1762 Died.
Family:
Service: 16.4.1746 Able *Chesterfield* (44); 19.5.1748 Mid *Assistance* (50); 21.3.1748/49 Mid *Tavistock* (50); 19.6.1752 Mate *Tavistock* (50); 7.3.1753 Passed; **Lieutenant**; 16.4.1756[(MED 22.2.1757)]-1.3.1758 4L *Trident* (64); 20.5.1756 Battle of Minorca; 27.10.1758 1L *Trident* (64); 22.7.1760-14.9.1762[P] 2L *Stirling Castle* (64); 3.6.1761-7.6.1761 Occupation of Dominica; 7.1.1762-10.2.1762 Operations against Martinique; 6.6.1762-13.8.1762 Operations against Havana.

DUGDALE, ROBERT

Dates: 4.9.1791 Died; 13.9.1791 Will Probate.
Family: Wife Sarah.
Service: **Lieutenant**; 21.4.1747[(MED 19.6.1749)]-6.5.1747 4L *Boyne* (80); 13.5.1747[(MED 19.6.1749)]-23.6.1749[P] 3L *Lichfield* (50); 6.1.1756-8.3.1757 L. *Porcupine* (16) Sloop; 31.8.1757 2L *Richmond* (32); 16.5.1758-25.6.1764[P] 1L *Richmond* (32); 5.6.1758-12.6.1758 Raid on Saint-Malo; 6.6.1762-13.8.1762 Operations against Havana; 28.12.1763-17.11.1764[D] LCmdr *Magdalen* (6) Schooner; 17.11.1764 Dismissed.

DUMARESQ, GEORGE

Dates: 1783 Died.
Family:
Service: **Lieutenant**; 17.12.1761[(BLI 11.5.1764)]-3.7.1762 L. *Granado* (8) Bomb Vessel; 7.1.1762-10.2.1762 Operations against Martinique; 4.9.1766-29.5.1767[P] L. *Glasgow* (20); 1.12.1775-20.3.1776 2L *Juno* (32); 6.6.1778 1L *Lion* (64); 23.9.1778-18.2.1779 1L *Medea* (28); 20.10.1778 Action of 1778-10-20.

DUMARESQ, THOMAS

Dates: 1729 Born; 23.7.1729 Baptised Saint Helier; 18.7.1802 Died.
Family: Father Jean Dumaresq; Mother Anne Bockinham; Son William; Brother William; Sister Ann; Sister Elizabeth.
Service: 25.1.1741/42 Capt Serv *Elizabeth* (70); 5.4.1743 Ord. *Elizabeth* (70); 11.2.1743/44-12.2.1743/44 Battle of Toulon; 6.5.1744-20.12.1745[P] Mid *Dragon's Prize* Xebec; 2.7.1747 Mid *Liverpool* (44); 14.2.1749/50 Mid *Boyne* (80) Prison Ship; 19.1.1750/51 Mid *Boyne* (80) Prison Ship; 2.5.1751-6.5.1752[SC] Able *Gloucester* (50); 6.5.1752 Able *Queenborough* (6) Yacht; 5.10.1752 Mid *Queenborough* (6) Yacht; 16.12.1753 Mate *Queenborough* (6) Yacht; 1.10.1754 Able *Gloucester* (50); 4.6.1755 Passed; **Lieutenant**; 23.10.1755[(EI 28.7.1757)] L. *Trial* (10) Sloop; 15.7.1756[(EI 28.7.1757)] 1L *Humber* (44); 12.3.1757[(NA 28.7.1757)]-19.5.1757 4L *Edinburgh* (64); 20.3.1758-30.3.1763[P] 1L *Venus* (36); 20.11.1759 Battle of Quiberon Bay; 28.4.1763-30.6.1766 LCmdr *Esther* (6) Cutter; 7.3.1772 1L *Chatham* (50); **Commander**; 2.11.1772[(Leeward Islands 30.6.1773)]-25.6.1773 *Spy* (10) Sloop; **Captain**; 23.1.1775-10.3.1779 *Portland* (50); 7.5.1779 *Ulysses* (44); 15.11.1780[(JAM 4.12.1781)]-5.9.1781[P] *Trident* (64); 22.11.1781 *Repulse* (64); 12.4.1782 Battle of the Saintes; 13.6.1782[(BLI 11.9.1783)]-26.7.1783[P] *Alfred* (74); 12.4.1794 **Rear Admiral of the Blue**; 4.7.1794 **Rear Admiral of the White**; 1.6.1795 **Vice Admiral of the Blue**; 14.2.1799 **Vice Admiral of the Red**; 1.1.1801 **Admiral of the Blue**.

DUMARESQUE, PHILIP

Dates: 1764 Died.

Family:

Service: 26.4.1699 MidE *Lizard* (24); 22.12.1700 Ord. *Lizard* (24); 8.5.1701 Able *Hastings* (32); 28.6.1702 Mid *Pembroke* (60); 12.10.1702 Battle of Vigo; 10.5.1703 Mid *Deptford* (48); 24.11.1704 Passed; **Lieutenant**; 31.1.1705/6 2L *Crown* (50); 24.12.1706 1L *Crown* (50); 14.3.1708/9 5L *Royal Sovereign* (100); 4.10.1709 3L *Russell* (80); 13.2.1710/11-18.4.1711 3L *Cumberland* (80); 1.4.1712-12.2.1712/13[P] 1L *Bedford* (70); 10.3.1712/13-5.3.1714/15 1L *Cumberland* (80).

DUMARESQUE, WILLIAM

Dates: c.1720 Born; 22.9.1813 Died.

Family:

Service: 20.12.1736 Able *Otter* (6) Sloop; 5.8.1738 Able *Strafford* (60); 6.5.1739 Mid *Tartar* (20); 4.1740-5.7.1740 Attack on St. Augustine; 12.4.1742 Mate *Tartar* (20); 10.10.1743 Passed; **Lieutenant**; 29.3.1744 6L *Saint George* (90); 12.4.1744 5L *Saint George* (90); 21.6.1744-28.3.1745 4L *Saint George* (90); 14.2.1744/45-3.9.1747 2L *Jersey* (60); 5.9.1746[MED 8.11.1748] L. *Conqueror* (8) Fireship; 3.9.1747[MED 8.11.1748] 2L *Burford* (70); 9.12.1747[MED 8.11.1748]-7.11.1748[P] L. *Terrible* (6) Bomb Vessel; 30.4.1755 2L *Warwick* (60); 23.2.1756 1L *Bedford* (64); 8.1757-10.1757 Louisbourg Expedition; 30.1.1758 1L *Royal William* (84); 6.6.1758-27.7.1758 The Siege of Louisbourg; 30.1.1759-25.2.1763[P] 1L *Union* (90); 20.11.1759 Battle of Quiberon Bay; 29.3.1761-11.6.1761 Expedition against Belle-Isle; 10.4.1779 **Superannuated Lieutenant**; 21.9.1796 **Superannuated Commander.**

DUNCAN, LORD ADAM (1ST VISCOUNT DUNCAN OF CAMPERDOWN)

Dates: 1.7.1731 Born Dundee; 21.10.1797 1st Viscount Duncan of Camperdown; 21.10.1797 1st Baron Duncan of Lundie; 4.8.1804 Died Edinburgh;

Family: Father Alexander Duncan; Mother Helen Haldane; Son Henry, RN (1786-1835);

Service: 5.8.1746 Mid *Trial* (10) Sloop; 4.4.1748 Mid *Shoreham* (24); 16.6.1748 Mate *Shoreham* (24); 21.1.1748/49 Mid *Centurion* (50); 28.7.1749-4.10.1752 Able *Centurion* (50); 4.10.1752 Passed; **Lieutenant**; 10.1.1755 3L *Norwich* (50); 28.4.1755 3L *Centurion* (50); 22.12.1756 5L *Torbay* (74); 3.1.1757-15.1.1759 3L *Torbay* (74); 5.9.1757-6.10.1757 Raid on Rochefort; 5.6.1758-12.6.1758 Raid on Saint-Malo; 29.12.1758 Capture of Goree; **Commander**; 21.9.1759 *Royal Exchange* (22) Hired Armed Ship; **Captain**; 25.2.1761-12.7.1764[P] *Valiant* (74); 29.3.1761-11.6.1761 Expedition against Belle-Isle; 6.6.1762-13.8.1762 Operations against Havana; 12.5.1778 *Suffolk* (74); 8.12.1778-20.9.1780 *Monarch* (74); 16.1.1780 Battle of Cape St. Vincent; 11.4.1782-23.12.1782 *Blenheim* (90); 20.10.1782 Battle of Cape Spartel; 15.1.1783 *Foudroyant* (80); 2.4.1783-9.8.1786[P] *Edgar* (74); 24.9.1787 **Rear Admiral of the Blue**; 21.9.1790 **Rear Admiral of the White**; 1.2.1793 **Vice Admiral of the Blue**; 12.4.1794 **Vice Admiral of the White**; 11.10.1794-8.1795 *Prince George* (98); 11.3.1795-1799 CinC — North Sea; 6.1795-11.1797 *Venerable* (74); 1.6.1795 **Admiral of the Blue**; 23.6.1795 Action of Ile Groix; 11.10.1797 Battle of Camperdown; 4.1798-1802 *Kent* (74); 8.1798 *Belliqueux* (64); 14.2.1799 **Admiral of the White.**

DUNCAN, HENRY

Dates: 1735 Born Scotland; 7.10.1814 Died Dartmouth.

Family: Wife Mary French married 21.11.1761; Daughter Isabella (1764-?); Son Arthur French Duncan (1769-?); Son Henry, RN (d.1802).

Service: 10.5.1755 Able *Nassau* (64); 1756 Mid *Nassau* (64); 8.1757-10.1757 Louisbourg Expedition; 9.3.1758-24.5.1758 Capture of Fort Louis; 29.12.1758 Capture of Goree; 3.1.1759 Passed; 23.3.1759 ActL *America* (60); 7.4.1759 Mid *Prince* (90); 18.8.1759-19.8.1759 Battle of Lagos Bay; 20.8.1759 Able *Namur* (90); **Lieutenant**; 21.9.1759 6L *Barfleur* (80); 24.9.1759 5L *Barfleur* (80); 28.11.1760-24.3.1762 4L *Hampton Court* (64); 29.3.1761-11.6.1761 Expedition against Belle-Isle; 17.8.1762[EI 15.9.1763]-10.8.1763[P] 3L *Temeraire* (74); **Commander**; 26.5.1768 *Terror* (8) Bomb Vessel; 30.8.1769-21.10.1772 *Wasp* (8) Sloop; **Captain**; 7.2.1776-30.4.1777 *Eagle* (64); 20.9.1780 *Medea* (28); 16.3.1781 Battle of Cape Henry; 5.9.1781 Battle of the Chesapeake; 25.10.1781-15.4.1782 *Ambuscade* (32); 10.4.1782-6.12.1782 *Victory* (100); 20.10.1782 Battle of Cape Spartel; 3.1783-1799 Resident Commissioner at Halifax; 1800-1.1801 Resident Commissioner at Sheerness; 1.1801-1806 Deputy Controller of the Navy.

DUNCOMB, ABRAHAM

Dates: c.3.1778 Died; 27.3.1778 Will Probate.
Family: Wife Isabella Harris married 10.6.1738.
Service: 1.6.1711 Vol-p-O *Greenwich* (54); 27.11.1711-24.8.1713[P] Vol-p-O *Nottingham* (60); 27.3.1715 Mid *Gloucester* (54); 9.5.1717 Passed; **Lieutenant**; 13.5.1720[26.9.1721]-5.10.1721[P] 3L *Newcastle* (50); 24.1.1725/26 4L *Ipswich* (70); 31.1.1725/26 4L *Monmouth* (70); 7.9.1727-13.4.1728[P] 3L *Monmouth* (70); 26.7.1728 2L *Assistance* (50); 9.2.1728/29 2L *Falkland* (50); 10.5.1731 3L *Kent* (70); 14.6.1732 2L *Captain* (70); 31.1.1733/34-4.5.1737[P] 2L *Captain* (70); 14.7.1738 2L *Lennox* (70); 4.1.1739/40 1L *Lennox* (70); 8.4.1740 Capture of the Princesa; 27.9.1740-18.2.1740/41 1L *Princess Caroline* (80); **Commander**; 11.3.1741/42-25.2.1742/43 *Terror* (8) Bomb Vessel.

DUNDAS, ADAM

Dates: c.1740 Born; 1773 Died.
Family:
Service: 1754-1756 Merchant Service; 21.3.1756 Capt Serv *Torbay* (74); 5.9.1757-6.10.1757 Raid on Rochefort; 5.6.1758-12.6.1758 Raid on Saint-Malo; 12.7.1758 Mid *Torbay* (74); 29.12.1758 Capture of Goree; 20.11.1759 Battle of Quiberon Bay; 10.2.1760 Mid *Valiant* (74); 4.2.1761 Passed; **Lieutenant**; 25.11.1761 L. *Trial* (10) Sloop; 25.3.1763 2L *Emerald* (32); 20.6.1765-6.6.1770 1L *Emerald* (32).

DUNDAS, CHARLES

Dates: 1772 Died.
Family:
Service: **Lieutenant**; 31.3.1758[EI 12.4.1762] 4L *Tiger* (60); 29.4.1758 Battle of Cuddalore; 3.8.1758 Battle of Negapatam; 1.10.1758[EI 12.4.1762] 3L *Tiger* (60); 3.3.1759[EI 12.4.1762] 2L *Tiger* (60); 10.9.1759 Battle of Pondicherry; 11.9.1759[EI 12.4.1762]-10.7.1761[P] 1L *Tiger* (60).

DUNDAS, RALPH

Dates: c.1730 Born; 11.6.1787 Died.
Family: Father Ralph Dundas (1709-1789); Mother Mary Ferguson.
Service: 3.9.1748 Capt Serv *Wager* HEIC; 16.12.1748 Able *Gloucester* (50); 12.10.1750-23.12.1752[P] Mid *Gloucester* (50); 15.10.1754 Able *Weazle* (16) Sloop; 7.10.1755 Able *Greenwich* (50); 21.12.1755 Mid *Greenwich* (50); 16.4.1756 Mid *Rye* (20); 4.7.1756 Mate *Rye* (20); 3.10.1757 Passed; **Lieutenant**; 1.11.1757-31.8.1759 L. *Zephyr* (10) Sloop; 1.3.1760 L. *Surprise* (24); 30.9.1761 2L *Coventry* (28); 4.11.1762-19.3.1763[P] 1L *Coventry* (28); 17.6.1764-

26.7.1766 LCmdr *Saint Lawrence* (6) Schooner; 21.7.1767-28.1.1775[P] LCmdr *Saint Lawrence* (6) Schooner; **Commander**; 3.4.1779-14.1.1782 *Bonetta* (14) Sloop; 12.12.1782-19.1.1787[P] *Calypso* (16) Sloop; 1788 **Captain (HEIC)** (East India Company).

DUNDAS, ROBERT

Dates: 1760 Died.
Family:
Service: **Lieutenant**; 14.5.1744[(MED 31.10.1748)]-4.3.1745/46 3L *Leopard* (50); 8.4.1755 2L *Romney* (44); 5.7.1756 2L *Guernsey* (50); 29.9.1756 1L *Guernsey* (50); 5.4.1757 Action of April 5 1757; **Commander**; 14.6.1757-20.7.1758[P] *Dolphins Prize* (12) Sloop.

DUNKLEY, JOHN

Dates: c.1713 Born; 1765 Died; 11.3.1765 Will Probate.
Family: Wife Mary Tublay married 24.2.1745/46; Brother Francis.
Service: 20.10.1726 Surg Serv *Torbay* (80); 18.11.1726-26.4.1728[P] Capt Serv *Torbay* (80); 16.8.1728 Mst Serv *Diamond* (40); 30.5.1732 Mid *Grafton* (70); 7.1.1732/33 Able *Grafton* (70); 16.5.1733 Mid *Grafton* (70); 20.7.1733 Able *Grafton* (70); 30.7.1733 Able *Spy* (8) Sloop; 4.8.1734 Able *Revenge* (70); 14.9.1734 Mate *Somerset* (80); 19.3.1734/35-16.2.1735/36[P] Mid *Dorsetshire* (80); 19.1.1741/42 Passed; **Lieutenant**; 2.7.1742[(8.1.1743/44)]-17.1.1743/44[B] L. *Astrea* (20) Armed Storeship; 3.6.1744[(8.1.1744/45)] 2L *York* (60); 18.5.1745-29.4.1746 3L *Duke* (90).

DUNN, GEORGE

Dates: c.1714 Born; 1755 Died.
Family:
Service: 5.10.1741 Mid *Success* (20); 2.1.1741/42 Mate *Panther* (54); 31.10.1742 Mid *Bonetta* (8) Sloop; 31.10.1743 Mid *Berwick* (70); 27.12.1743 Able *Sandwich* (90); 24.1.1743/44 Mid *Sandwich* (90); 4.6.1744 Mate *Sandwich* (90); 13.3.1745/46 Passed; **Lieutenant**; 30.4.1746-22.1.1750/51 L. *Vulture* (10) Sloop; 9.4.1748 Battle of Santiago de Cuba.

DUPRE, MICHAEL

Dates: c.1732 Born; 2.8.1768 Died.
Family:
Service: 12.12.1746 Capt Serv *Fox* (20); 1.4.1748 Able *Fox* (20); 26.7.1748 Able *Renown* (30); 21.4.1750-25.6.1752 Mid *Glasgow* (20); 1.10.1755 Passed; **Lieutenant**; 1.5.1759[(NA 24.11.1760)]-10.3.1763[P] 3L *Prince of Orange* (60); 29.3.1761-11.6.1761 Expedition against Belle-Isle.

DURELL, PHILIP

Dates: 1707 Born Jersey; 6.8.1766 Died North America; 16.11.1766 Will Probate.
Family: Father Jean Durell?; Mother Elizabeth Corbet; Wife Madelaine de Sausmarez (1711-?); Wife ? Skey; Wife Mrs Catherine Taylor nee Vincent (1737-1803) married 1761; Daughter Ann (1733-?); Brother George Charles, RN (1714-1754); Brother Thomas (1717-1741).
Service: 28.5.1722 Ord. *Seahorse* (20); 24.3.1722/23 Able *Seahorse* (20); 23.2.1723/24 MidO *Seahorse* (20); 30.11.1725 Able *Ludlow Castle* (40); 30.6.1727 Able *Kent* (70); 9.7.1727 Mate *Kent* (70); 30.7.1727 Able *Lion* (60); 2.8.1727 Mid *Lion* (60); 22.3.1727/28 Mid *Plymouth* (60); 11.1.1728/29 Mid *Solebay* (6) Bomb Vessel; 12.1.1729/30 Passed; **Lieutenant**; 30.6.1731-13.6.1732 3L *Assistance* (50); 14.6.1732-30.1.1732/33 4L *Suffolk* (70); 31.1.1733/34-4.5.1735 4L *Grafton* (70); 5.5.1735-13.4.1736[P] 3L *Grafton* (70); 16.5.1738 2L *Strafford* (60); 27.10.1739[(5.7.1743)] 1L *Strafford* (60); 21.11.1739 Attack on Puerto Bello; 14.1.1740/41[(5.7.1743)] 4L *Princess Caroline*

(80); 19.2.1740/41(5.7.1743) 3L *Princess Caroline* (80); 24.2.1740/41(5.7.1743) 2L *Princess Caroline* (80); 25.3.1741(5.7.1743) 1L *Princess Caroline* (80); **Commander**; 17.4.1741(5.7.1743) *Success* (8) Fireship; 9.6.1741(5.7.1743) *Strombolo* (8) Fireship; 12.9.1741 *Vesuvius* (8) Fireship; **Captain**; 6.2.1741/42(5.7.1743) *Seahorse* (20); 4.10.1742(5.7.1743) *Gibraltar* (20); 16.1.1743/44-23.6.1745 *Eltham* (40); 6.7.1745(BLI 23.9.1746)-23.9.1745 *Chester* (50); 4.2.1746/47-5.12.1747 *Gloucester* (50); 14.10.1747 2nd Battle of Cape Finisterre; 10.2.1755 *Terrible* (74); 13.5.1755 *Ramillies* (90); 23.9.1755 *Trident* (64); 20.5.1756 Battle of Minorca; 3.10.1756(ECH 1.2.1757) *Prince George* (80); 19.10.1757-6.1.1758 *Princess Amelia* (80); 9.1.1758 Second in Command — North America; 9.1.1758 Commodore *Diana* (32); 6.7.1758 **Rear Admiral of the Blue**; 8.7.1758 *Princess Amelia* (80); 19.2.1759 **Rear Admiral of the Red**; 29.3.1761-11.6.1761 Expedition against Belle-Isle; 6.1761-1.1763 CinC — Plymouth; 21.10.1762 **Vice Admiral of the Blue**; 1.11.1762-19.2.1763[P] *Duke* (90); 18.1.1766-6.11.1769[P] *Launceston* (44); 2.4.1766-6.8.1766 CinC — North America.

DURELL, PHILIP

Dates: c.1734 Born; 27.3.1772 Died Mediterranean Sea.
Family:
Service: 25.4.1748-5.8.1748[P] Capt Serv *Gloucester* (50); 24.8.1749 Capt Serv *Berwick* (70); 27.11.1749 Able *Gloucester* (50); 17.12.1751 Mid *Gloucester* (50); 15.9.1753 Able *Wager* (24); 23.2.1754-5.11.1755 Mid *Wager* (24); 5.11.1755 Passed; **Lieutenant**; 18.6.1757 6L *Prince George* (80); 29.7.1757-13.4.1758[B] 4L *Prince George* (80); 10.1.1761 1L *Prince* (90); 20.10.1761 3L *Prince* (90); 6.9.1762-19.2.1763[P] 4L *Duke* (90); 13.2.1764-13.2.1765 LCmdr *Laurel* (6) Cutter; **Commander**; 20.6.1765-14.7.1768[P] *Cygnet* (18) Sloop; **Captain**; 14.3.1769 *Pembroke* (60); 7.8.1771(MED 19.8.1772)-27.3.1772[†] *Niger* (32).

DURELL, THOMAS PIKE

Dates: c.1736 Born; 16.2.1784 Will Probate; 29.1.1804 Died Poole.
Family: Wife Susanna Green married 15.2.1769; Daughter Susannah Pike [Ledgard] (1776-1862).
Service: 1749-1755 Merchant Service; 16.8.1755 Mate *Ramillies* (90); 18.12.1755-5.9.1757 Mate *Trident* (64); 20.5.1756 Battle of Minorca; 5.9.1757 Passed; **Lieutenant**; 27.9.1757 L. *Adventure* (18) Hired Armed Ship; 17.1.1758 4L *Princess Amelia* (80); 6.6.1758-27.7.1758 The Siege of Louisbourg; 21.3.1759 3L *Princess Amelia* (80); 24.12.1760 2L *Princess Amelia* (80); 29.3.1761-11.6.1761 Expedition against Belle-Isle; 22.6.1762-14.1.1763[P] 2L *Magnanime* (74); 7.11.1776 2L *Bienfaisant* (64); 18.7.1777 1L *Bienfaisant* (64); 7.4.1778 3L *Europe* (64); **Commander**; 28.10.1778(NF 29.6.1780) *Martin* (14) Sloop; 23.11.1780-4.4.1781 *Snake* (14) Slop Ship; **Captain**; 3.5.1782-3.5.1783[P] *Rippon* (56).

DYSON, THOMAS

Dates: 1736 Born; 18.4.1798 Died.
Family:
Service: 1750-1755 Merchant Service; 5.11.1755 Mid *Monarch* (74); 3.1.1757-30.1.1758 Mid *Magnanime* (74); 5.9.1757-6.10.1757 Raid on Rochefort; 30.1.1758 Passed; **Lieutenant**; 24.9.1759-23.2.1760 L. *Scorpion* (14) Sloop; 22.5.1760 L. *Albany* (14) Sloop; 8.1.1761-15.7.1763 L. *Greyhound* (20); 7.1.1762-10.2.1762 Operations against Martinique; 16.5.1769-2.2.1771 2L *Glory* (32); 17.3.1777-16.12.1777 1L *Conqueror* (74); 3.11.1780-23.11.1780 LCmdr *Snake* (14) Slop Ship; 1.5.1781-20.10.1781[P] LCmdr *Advice* (10) Cutter; **Commander**; 25.3.1782-15.8.1782[P] *Helena* (14) Schooner.

DYVE, HENRY
Dates: 1779 Died.
Family:
Service: **Lieutenant**; 12.5.1734(8.12.1735)-3.11.1735[P] 3L *Rupert* (60); 9.12.1737-3.4.1740 2L *Windsor* (60); 28.8.1740(25.6.1741)-13.12.1740[P] L. *Blandford* (20); 29.6.1741 2L *Advice* (54); **Commander**; 10.8.1741-23.2.1741/42 *Rupert's Prize* (8); **Captain**; 2.9.1745-2.7.1748[P] *Winchelsea* (20); 5.11.1770 **Superannuated Rear Admiral**.

Service Records E

EASTWOOD, JENNINGS
Dates: c.1726 Born; 1760 Died.
Family:
Service: 26.6.1740 Capt Serv *Orford* (70); 7.1.1740/41 Action of January 7 1741; 10.3.1740/41 Capt Serv *Chichester* (80); 12.10.1741 Able *Duke* (90); 14.3.1741/42 Able *Sandwich* (90); 7.1.1742/43 Mid *Antelope* (50); 1.3.1745/46 Able *Chichester* (80); 22.5.1746 Mid *Vulture* (10) Sloop; 29.7.1746 Passed; 14.2.1755 **Lieutenant**; 19.2.1755[(JAM 12.7.1756)] L. *Weazle* (16) Sloop; 12.10.1755[(JAM 12.7.1756)] 3L *Severn* (50); 23.4.1756[(NA 12.7.1756)] 2L *Severn* (50); 11.1.1757-19.10.1759 4L *Marlborough* (80).

EASTWOOD, JOSEPH
Dates: 1762 Died; 13.12.1762 Will Probate;.
Family: Wife Mary; Son Joseph; Son Richard.
Service: **Lieutenant**; 16.5.1743[(MED 26.8.1748)] 3L *Guernsey* (50); 11.2.1743/44-12.2.1743/44 Battle of Toulon; 3.8.1745[(MED 26.8.1748)]-22.8.1748[P] 1L *Guernsey* (50); 3.6.1752-19.6.1756 L. *Dolphin* (24); 20.5.1756 Battle of Minorca; 8.6.1757 1L *Magnanime* (74); 5.9.1757-6.10.1757 Raid on Rochefort; **Commander**; 1.11.1757 *Peggy* (8) Sloop; 13.5.1758-1.3.1760 *Diligence* (10) Sloop; 5.6.1758-12.6.1758 Raid on Saint-Malo.

EASTWOOD, THOMAS
Dates: c.1732 Born; 7.9.1776 Died West Indies.
Family: Wife Ann.
Service: 11.1.1745/46 Ord. *Duke* (90); 25.2.1746/47 Able *Portland Prize* (50); 10.3.1747/48 Mid *Duke* (90); 15.1.1748/49-9.5.1749[P] Mid *Squirrel* (20); 28.3.1752 Able *Yarmouth* (64); 19.7.1752 Mid *Yarmouth* (64); 28.11.1752 Able *Rainbow* (44); 9.12.1753 Able *Penzance* (44); 5.4.1754 Mate *Penzance* (44); 3.9.1754 Able *Captain*; 27.11.1754 Mid *Captain* (64); 4.6.1755 Passed; **Lieutenant**; 9.11.1756 L. *Ranger* (8) Sloop; 22.5.1758-21.3.1759 L. *Happy* (8) Sloop; 4.5.1759 3L *Gosport* (44); 8.5.1759 2L *Gosport* (44); 1.4.1760-11.3.1763[P] 1L *Gosport* (44); 18.10.1763-24.10.1766 2L *Ramillies* (74); 18.1.1771 2L *Sandwich* (90); 23.1.1775 1L *Portland* (50); 20.11.1775 LCmdr *Pomona* (18) Sloop; **Commander**; 19.2.1776-7.9.1776[†] *Pomona* (18) Sloop.

EDGAR, ALEXANDER
Dates: 17.8.1736 Born Westruther, Berwick-upon-Tweed; 20.2.1817 Died; 24.2.1817 Buried St George the Martyr, Camden, London; 11.3.1817 Will Probate.
Family: Wife Margaretta Sophia Johnston (d.1807) married 1.5.1783; Daughter Maria Bethia [Campbell] (1784-1856).
Service: 29.12.1747 Ord. *Siren* (20); 30.8.1748 Able *Siren* (20); 1.8.1753 Able *Arundel* (24); 13.4.1754 Mid *Arundel* (24); 3.5.1755 Mid *Newcastle* (50); 8.3.1757 Passed; **Lieutenant**;

20.12.1757 L. *Firedrake* (10) Bomb Vessel; 6.5.1758 L. *Vesuvius* (8) Fireship; 29.8.1759[MED 1.11.1759]-19.5.1760[W] 2L *Lowestoffe* (28); 3.7.1760-9.5.1763[P] 1L *Quebec* (32); 6.12.1763-30.11.1765[P] 1L *Africa* (64); 6.1.1766-23.6.1767 1L *Aeolus* (32); 9.11.1768-9.8.1770 1L *Dorsetshire* (68); 3.11.1770 5L *Ocean* (90); 19.1.1771 4L *Ocean* (90); 25.6.1773 3L *Ocean* (90); 14.8.1773-3.11.1773 2L *Ocean* (90); 1.1.1777 3L *Princess Amelia* (80); 10.1.1777 2L *Princess Amelia* (80); 29.11.1777 1L *Valiant* (74); 26.1.1778 3L *Prince George* (98); 13.5.1778 2L *Victory* (100); 2.7.1778 1L *Victory* (100); 27.7.1778 1st Battle of Ushant; **Commander**; 27.8.1778 *Vulcan* (8) Fireship; **Captain**; 30.11.1780[NA 10.3.1781] *Royal Oak* (74); 14.1.1781[NA 15.5.1781]-11.4.1781[P] *Clinton* (32); 11.1.1782-21.4.1783[P] *Medway* (60); 18.4.1783-24.11.1785[P] *Leocadia* (36); 27.9.1787-10.12.1787[P] *Prince George* (98); 10.5.1790-25.10.1790 *Illustrious* (74); 20.2.1799 **Superannuated Rear Admiral.**

EDGCOMBE, ROBERT

Dates: 1781 Died.
Family:
Service: **Lieutenant**; 18.5.1747-4.7.1747 L. *Carcass* (6) Sloop; 17.9.1755-12.3.1760 2L *Swiftsure* (68); 28.2.1758 Battle of Cartagena; 18.8.1759-19.8.1759 Battle of Lagos Bay; 20.11.1759 Battle of Quiberon Bay; 6.6.1766-21.6.1769 LCmdr *Cholmondley* (4) Cutter; 3.11.1770 2L *Ocean* (90); 25.6.1773-14.8.1773 1L *Ocean* (90); 19.9.1780-3.11.1780 LCmdr *Snake* (14) Slop Ship.

EDGCUMBE, LORD GEORGE (1ST EARL OF MOUNT EDGCUMBE)

Dates: 3.3.1720 Born; 5.5.1721 Baptised St Martin-in-the-Fields, London; 10.5.1761 3rd Baron Edgcumbe; 1781 1st Viscount of Mount Edgcumbe and Valletort; 31.8.1789 1st Earl of Mount Edgcumbe; 4.2.1795 Died Grosvenor Street, London; 1795 Buried Maker, Cornwall.
Family: Father Richard Edgcumbe, 1st Baron Edgcumbe (1680-1758); Mother Matilda Furnese (1698/9–1721); Wife Emma Gilbert (1729–1807) married 16.8.1761; Son Richard Edgcumbe, 2nd Earl (1764–1839); Brother Richard Edgcumbe, 2nd Baron (1716–1761).
Service: 14.8.1733 Scholar *Royal Naval Academy*; 5.8.1735 Able *York* (60); 14.12.1735 Mid *York* (60); 26.6.1737 Able *Pembroke* (60); 16.8.1737 Mid *Lyme* (20); 5.11.1737 Mid *Phoenix* (20); 3.3.1737/38 Mid *Romney* (50); 10.7.1739 Mid *Princess Caroline* (80); 4.10.1739 Passed; **Lieutenant**; 5.10.1739-18.1.1739/40 3L *Superb* (60); 19.1.1739/40[17.9.1740]-18.9.1740 3L *Jersey* (60); 19.9.1740-26.9.1740 3L *Rupert* (60); 27.9.1740 3L *Kingston* (60); 2.2.1740/41 4L *Royal Sovereign* (104); 13.3.1740/41 2L *Nassau* (70); **Commander**; 3.6.1743[MED 19.2.1746/47] *Terrible* (6) Bomb Vessel; **Captain**; 19.8.1744[MED 23.9.1745] *Kennington* (20); 22.1.1745/46-3.1.1748/49[P] *Salisbury* (50); 30.7.1746-17.12.1761 M.P. for Fowey; 1.12.1748-31.5.1752[P] *Monmouth* (70); 3.6.1752 *Deptford* (50); 19.8.1752 CinC — The Mediterranean Sea; 22.3.1756-31.7.1758 *Lancaster* (66); 20.5.1756 Battle of Minorca; 6.6.1758-27.7.1758 The Siege of Louisbourg; 21.2.1759-4.5.1761 *Hero* (74); 20.11.1759 Battle of Quiberon Bay; 18.6.1761-4.2.1795 Lord Lieutenant of Cornwall; 21.10.1762 **Rear Admiral of the Blue**; 1766-1771 CinC — Plymouth; 18.10.1770 **Rear Admiral of the Red**; 24.10.1770 **Vice Admiral of the Blue**; 7.11.1771 *Dublin* (74); 25.6.1773 **Vice Admiral of the White**; 7.12.1775 **Vice Admiral of the Red**; 29.1.1778 **Admiral of the Blue**; 1782-4.2.1795 Vice Admiral of the Coast , Cornwall; 8.4.1782 **Admiral of the White.**

EDGCUMBE, ROBERT

Dates: 1763 Died.
Family:
Service: **Lieutenant**; 8.7.1758[(NA 3.12.1759)] 4L *Vanguard* (68); 10.12.1759[(NA 3.12.1759)] 3L *Vanguard* (68); 3.10.1761[(MED 3.12.1759)]-1763† 2L *Vanguard* (68); 7.1.1762-10.2.1762 Operations against Martinique.

EDWARDS, ARTHUR

Dates: c.1730 Born; 30.3.1805 Died.
Family:
Service: 18.6.1748 Capt Serv *Portland* (50); 6.11.1749 MidO *Portland* (50); 14.6.1750 Mid *Portland* (50); 20.1.1750/51 Able *Prince Henry* (44); 19.3.1754 Mate *Prince Henry* (44); 31.10.1754 Master *Prince Henry* (44); 4.3.1755 Master *Scorpion* (14) Sloop; 4.2.1756 Passed; **Lieutenant**; 13.6.1759 L. *Carcass* (14) Bomb Vessel; 3.7.1759 Bombardment of Le Havre; 17.1.1761 2L *Nassau* (64); 6.12.1763-12.12.1766 2L *Rippon* (60); 21.5.1771-24.9.1774[P] 3L *Trident* (64).

EDWARDS, CHARLES

Dates: c.1740 Born; 1762 Died.
Family:
Service: 26.4.1755 Mid *Somerset* (68); 6.6.1758-27.7.1758 The Siege of Louisbourg; 7.2.1759 Able *Namur* (90); 18.8.1759-19.8.1759 Battle of Lagos Bay; 7.9.1759 Mid *Namur* (90); 20.11.1759 Battle of Quiberon Bay; 23.5.1760 ActL *Foudroyant* (80); 28.9.1761 Passed; **Lieutenant**; 28.9.1761-8.6.1762 5L *Foudroyant* (80); 7.1.1762-10.2.1762 Operations against Martinique.

EDWARDS, CHARLES TURNER

Dates: c.1757 Died; 11.5.1757 Will Probate.
Family: Wife Mary Mockett married 13.11.1746.
Service: **Lieutenant**; 6.6.1745[(NA 24.9.1745)] 3L *Eltham* (40); 9.10.1746 2L *Centurion* (50); 3.5.1747 1st Battle of Cape Finisterre; 12.12.1747 3L *Hector* (44); 31.12.1747-9.3.1747/48 2L *Hector* (44); 10.1.1753 3L *Eagle* (60); 2.4.1754-1757† 3L *Cumberland* (66); 11.1.1756-14.1.1756 Capture of Geriah.

EDWARDS, DAVID

Dates: c.1718 Born; 1781 Died.
Family: Son Thomas.
Service: 12.11.1734 Vol-p-O *Princess Amelia* (80); 26.12.1734 Able *Gibraltar* (20); 14.1.1735/36 Vol-p-O *Princess Amelia* (80); 5.4.1738 Mid *Greenwich* (50); 27.3.1740 MidO *Torbay* (80); 2.8.1740 Mid *Victory* (100); 18.11.1740 Passed; **Lieutenant**; 2.2.1740/41 3L *Faversham* (44); 21.2.1740/41 2L *Gosport* (44); 1.9.1741 1L *Gosport* (44); 24.8.1743 4L *Boyne* (80); 3.9.1743-22.9.1744 3L *Boyne* (80); 11.2.1743/44-12.2.1743/44 Battle of Toulon; 10.2.1745/46[(MED 29.11.1748)] 4L *Russell* (80); **Commander**; 29.8.1746[(MED 11.11.1748)]-7.11.1748[P] *Conqueror* (8) Fireship; 18.2.1755 *Dispatch* (14) Sloop; **Captain**; 24.9.1756 *Seaford* (20); 6.6.1758[(JAM 27.5.1760)]-30.6.1760[P] *Assistance* (50); 9.10.1780 **Superannuated Rear Admiral**.

EDWARDS, EDWARD

Dates: c.1728 Born; 13.4.1815 Died Stamford; 13.6.1815 Will Probate.
Family: Father Richard Edwards; Mother Mary Fuller; Brother Samuel.
Service: 30.4.1746 Able *Leopard* (50); 19.1.1747/48 Clerk *Leopard* (50); 25.5.1750 Mid *Deptford* (24) Storeship; 31.3.1751 Mid *Tavistock* (28) Mer; 14.3.1755 Passed; 31.8.1757 CaptP *Viscount Falmouth* (24) PMW; **Lieutenant**; 7.9.1759-16.1.1761 4L *Nassau* (64); 17.6.1761-25.4.1763 2L *Lowestoffe* (32); 1.11.1763 L. *Zephyr* (10) Sloop; 7.1.1764-16.1.1768 L. *Ferret* (14) Sloop; 16.3.1769 3L *Pembroke* (60); 19.1.1771-3.12.1771 2L *Pembroke* (60); 15.11.1776-23.10.1777[S] 1L *Augusta* (64); **Commander**; 22.4.1778[(NA 4.4.1780)] *Carcass* (8) Bomb Vessel; 14.12.1778-15.12.1778 Battle of St. Lucia; 17.6.1780 *Hornet* (14) Sloop; **Captain**; 25.4.1781-27.3.1784[P] *Narcissus* (20); 6.8.1790-28.8.1791 *Pandora* (24); c.1793 Regulating Officer at Argyllshire; 14.2.1799 **Rear Admiral of the Blue**; 1.1.1801 **Rear Admiral of the White**; 23.4.1804 **Rear Admiral of the Red**; 9.11.1805 **Vice Admiral of the Blue**; 28.4.1808 **Vice Admiral of the White**; 31.7.1810 **Admiral of the Blue**; 4.6.1814 **Admiral of the White.**

EDWARDS, OWEN

Dates: c.1719 Born; 1762 Died.
Family:
Service: 20.4.1734 Scholar *Royal Naval Academy*; 26.7.1737 Able *Centurion* (60); 22.1.1738/39 Able *Plymouth* (60); 10.2.1739/40 Mid *Plymouth* (60); 15.9.1740 Able *Plymouth* (60); 9.3.1740/41 Mid *Plymouth* (60); 18.7.1743 Passed; **Lieutenant**; 14.3.1743/44-28.11.1745 L. *Fly* (8) Sloop; **Commander**; 6.4.1757-17.5.1758[P] *Firedrake* (10) Bomb Vessel; 5.9.1757-6.10.1757 Raid on Rochefort.

EDWARDS, RICE

Dates: 14.1.1779 Died Aberystwith, Wales; 20.2.1779 Will Probate.
Family:
Service: 1.7.1719-17.11.1720[P] Adm Serv *Barfleur* (90); 5.4.1721 Able *Rippon* (60); 22.10.1721 Able *Dunkirk* (50); 10.7.1722 MidO *Dolphin* (20); 26.6.1723 Able *Nonsuch* (50); 31.3.1724 MidO *Nonsuch* (50); 16.6.1724 Mid *Nonsuch* (50); 22.1.1724/25 Passed; **Lieutenant**; 6.2.1728/29[(16.9.1729)]-9.9.1729[P] 3L *Faversham* (42); 31.1.1733/34-5.3.1735/36 4L *Captain* (70); 16.7.1739 L. *Deptford* (24) Storeship; 14.8.1739 2L *Panther* (54); 17.3.1739/40 1L *Montagu* (60); 25.2.1741/42 2L *Norfolk* (80); 6.5.1742 1L *Norfolk* (80); 11.2.1743/44-12.2.1743/44 Battle of Toulon; 14.7.1745[(MED 16.11.1745)]-26.11.1745[P] 4L *Torbay* (80).

EDWARDS, RICHARD

Dates: 16.6.1773 Died.
Family:
Service: 20.8.1712 Vol-p-O *Mary Galley* (42); 11.7.1713 Vol-p-O *Kent* (70); 11.5.1714 Able *Romney* (54); 7.7.1717 MidO *York* (60); 4.2.1717/18 Mid *York* (60); 15.6.1718 Mid *Burford* (70); 11.8.1718 Battle of Cape Passaro; 19.10.1718 Mid *Barfleur* (90); 26.11.1718 MidO *Flamborough* (24); 16.7.1719 Passed; 19.10.1727 **Lieutenant**; 11.1.1727/28-21.11.1728 3L *Kinsale* (40); 4.4.1729-31.12.1730[P] 2L *Oxford* (50); 19.5.1731-23.12.1731[P] 3L *Hampton Court* (70); 31.12.1733-25.1.1735/36[P] L. *Garland* (20); 9.2.1735/36-14.2.1739/40 L. *Dolphin* (20); **Commander**; 16.6.1740-7.11.1740[P] *Swift* (6) Sloop; **Captain**; 4.11.1740-12.11.1742 *Fox* (20); 4.2.1742/43 *Torrington* (44); 7.11.1744 *Princess Mary* (60); 16.12.1745 Capt&M *Charlotte* (8) Yacht; 20.12.1750 *Fubbs* (12) Yacht; 2.5.1757-30.5.1757 *Princess Amelia* (80); 21.6.1757 **Superannuated Rear Admiral.**

EDWARDS, RICHARD

Dates: 1715 Born; 3.2.1795 Died; 13.3.1795 Will Probate.
Family: Wife Julia Pike.
Service: **Lieutenant**; 30.11.1740(28.1.1741/42) L. *Salamander* (6) Bomb Vessel; 14.5.1744 1L *Pearl* (40); 28.6.1745-31.3.1747 L. *Shoreham* (24); **Commander**; 3.8.1747-24.1.1751/52[P] *Kingfisher* (10) Sloop; 10.6.1752 *Falcon* (10) Bomb Vessel; **Captain**; 27.12.1753 *Assistance* (50); 29.8.1754 *Gosport* (44); 1757-1759 Gov. of Newfoundland; 5.3.1760-13.8.1763[P] *Belliqueux* (64); 19.11.1767 *Ramillies* (74); 18.10.1770-1.11.1776 *Mary* (8) Yacht; 1.11.1776-9.3.1779[P] *Sandwich* (90); 27.7.1778 1st Battle of Ushant; 1779-1781 Gov. of Newfoundland; 4.3.1779-2.4.1782 CinC — Newfoundland; 19.3.1779 **Rear Admiral of the Blue**; 1780-23.2.1781 *Portland* (50); 26.9.1780 **Rear Admiral of the Red**; 24.9.1787 **Vice Admiral of the White**; 26.9.1787-23.8.1788 CinC — River Medway and The Nore; 1.2.1793 **Vice Admiral of the Red**; 12.4.1794 **Admiral of the Blue.**

EDWARDS, THOMAS

Dates: 1804 Died.
Family:
Service: **Lieutenant**; 19.9.1759(EI 29.7.1761) 2L *Queenborough* (24); 24.7.1760(EI 8.2.1763)-1.1.1761[W] 3L *Newcastle* (50); 11.9.1761 L. *Proserpine* (8) Fireship; 26.1.1762 3L *Prince Edward* (44); 15.4.1762(MED 27.5.1763)-1.5.1763[P] 2L *Vestal* (32); 6.9.1763 2L *Thunderer* (74); 2.5.1766-20.12.1769[P] 2L *Jersey* (60); 3.11.1770 4L *Fame* (74); 6.2.1771-18.4.1771 4L *Cambridge* (80).

EDWARDS, TIMOTHY

Dates: 1731 Born Nanhoran, North Wales; 12.7.1780 Died At sea.
Family: Father Reverend William Edwards; Mother Frances Williams; Wife Catherine Browning; Son John Browning, RN.
Service: 13.4.1747-27.2.1748/49 Serv *Chesterfield* (44); 28.2.1748/49 Mid *Assistance* (50); 18.3.1749/50-18.3.1751/52 Mid *Sphinx* (24); 19.3.1751/52 Able *Sphinx* (24); 19.6.1752 Passed; **Lieutenant**; 6.2.1755 6L *Ramillies* (90); 13.5.1755 4L *Terrible* (74); 16.8.1756 1L *Tartar* (24); **Commander**; 16.11.1757 *Favorite* (16) Sloop; **Captain**; 5.8.1759(NA 19.2.1760)-1.4.1761 *Valeur* (28); 14.5.1762-19.3.1763[P] *Emerald* (32); 19.9.1777 *Europa* (64); 23.1.1778-30.6.1780[SC] *Cornwall* (74); 6.7.1779 Battle of Grenada; 17.4.1780 Battle of Martinique; 15.5.1780 Action of March 15 1780; 19.5.1780 Action of March 19 1780; 30.6.1780-12.7.1780 Capt *Actaeon* (44).

EELES, JOHN

Dates: 1755 Died.
Family:
Service: **Lieutenant**; 14.8.1739 3L *Portland* (50); 28.1.1742/43 1L *Portland* (50); 17.12.1743-22.6.1748[P] 1L *Duke* (90); 1754 **Superannuated Lieutenant**.

ELIOT, JOHN

Dates: 2.6.1742 Born Cornwall; 2.5.1769 Died.
Family: Father Richard Eliot (d.1749); Mother Harriet Craggs; Brother Edward, M.P. 1st Baron Eliot (1727-1804); Sister Ann [Bonfoy] (1729-1810); Sister Harriot (1731-1776).
Service: 18.2.1752 Mid *Penzance* (44); 12.6.1752-19.3.1753 Able *Penzance* (44); 12.5.1753-8.7.1754 Mid *Penzance* (44); 10.11.1754-9.2.1757 Mid *Vanguard* (68); 14.2.1757 Mid *Marlborough* (80); **Lieutenant**; 25.10.1757(JAM 6.8.1759) 3L *Augusta* (60); 31.7.1758(JAM 4.9.1759) L. *Viper* (10) Sloop; 5.4.1759 L. *Hornet* (10) Sloop; **Commander**; 4.9.1759-9.12.1759[C] *Hawke*

(8) Sloop; **Captain**; 25.4.1760 *Gosport* (44); 13.10.1760 *Coventry* (28); 21.11.1760-11.3.1766[P] *Thames* (32); 24.10.1766-20.5.1767 *Firm* (74); 2.4.1769-2.5.1769 Gov. of West Florida.

ELLERKER, WILLIAM

Dates: 1771 Died.
Family: Brother John.
Service: 21.2.1706 Vol-p-O *Yarmouth* (70); 2.9.1706 Vol-p-O *Cornwall* (80); 28.7.1708 Mid *Cornwall* (80); 18.11.1708 Mid *Warspite* (64); 27.10.1709 Mid *Ramillies* (96); 24.7.1710-22.1.1712 Mid *Deptford* (48); 22.1.1711/12 Passed; **Lieutenant**; 26.10.1714-15.4.1716[P] 2L *Greenwich* (54); 19.5.1731-23.12.1731[P] 1L *Cornwall* (80); 23.2.1733/34-17.6.1734 1L *Falkland* (50); 18.6.1734-31.3.1736[P] 1L *Kent* (70).

ELLERY, GEORGE

Dates: c.1734 Born; 1783 Died; 11.11.1783 Will Probate.
Family: Wife Hester.
Service: 1732-1734 Merchant Service; 1.12.1739 Able *Tilbury* (60); 8.1.1739/40-22.9.1742[B] Mid *Tilbury* (60); 4.3.1740/41-5.1741 Operations against Cartagena; 7.1741-10.1741 Operations against Santiago; 6.10.1742 Mid *Montagu* (60); 9.8.1745 Passed; **Lieutenant**; 11.9.1747-21.6.1748 L. *Falcon* (10) Bomb Vessel.

ELLETSON, WILLIAM

Dates: c.1731 Born; c.1818 Will Probate.
Family:
Service: 4.12.1752 Mid *Hazard* (8) Sloop; 21.6.1753 Able *Fougueux* (64); 6.11.1753 Mid *Fougueux* (64); 25.11.1753 Able *Fougueux* (64); 22.6.1754 Able *Berwick* (70); 14.10.1754 Able *Captain* (64); 21.11.1754-10.7.1755 Mid *Captain* (64); 11.7.1755 Able *Nottingham* (60); 29.11.1755 Mid *Nottingham* (60); 2.3.1756-15.9.1758[P] Mid *Nottingham* (60); 6.6.1758-27.7.1758 The Siege of Louisbourg; 15.9.1758 Able *Namur* (90); 13.12.1758 Passed; **Lieutenant**; 20.8.1759[NA 19.9.1759] 4L *Namur* (90); 25.10.1759 2L *Valiant* (74); 5.1.1760-4.2.1763[P] 2L *Torbay* (74); 29.3.1761-11.6.1761 Expedition against Belle-Isle; 17.12.1770 4L *Lennox* (74); 22.4.1773 5L *Lennox* (74); 27.5.1773-24.1.1774 4L *Lennox* (74); 6.10.1774 3L *Asia* (64); 2.7.1776-4.7.1776 Staten Island Landings; 29.4.1777-17.2.1778 1L *Asia* (64); 19.3.1778-17.8.1781[P] 2L *Vengeance* (74); 27.7.1778 1st Battle of Ushant; 21.12.1779-22.12.1779 Action of 1779-12-21; 17.4.1780 Battle of Martinique; 15.5.1780 Action of March 15 1780; 19.5.1780 Action of March 19 1780; 15.8.1803 **Superannuated Commander**.

ELLIOT, BENJAMIN

Dates: c.1733 Born; 10.9.1759 Died; 7.3.1761 Will Probate.
Family: Father James Elliot.
Service: 10.12.1746 Able *Royal George* (100); 21.10.1747 Capt Serv *Namur* (74); 13.12.1748 Clerk *Swallow* (14) Sloop; 31.8.1749-8.5.1750[P] Clerk *Basilisk* (8) Bomb Vessel; 19.2.1752 Able *Badger* (10) Sloop; 16.6.1752 Cox *Badger* (10) Sloop; 2.4.1753 Mid *Badger* (10) Sloop; 17.1.1754 Able *Jason* (44); 5.7.1754 Mid *Jason* (44); 24.5.1755 Mid *Nassau* (64); 5.11.1755 Passed; **Lieutenant**; 19.8.1757-9.1.1759[P] 6L *Barfleur* (80); 5.9.1757-6.10.1757 Raid on Rochefort; 5.6.1758-12.6.1758 Raid on Saint-Malo.

ELLIOT, JOHN

Dates: 4.1732 Born Scotland; 20.9.1808 Died; 31.12.1808 Will Probate.

Family: Father Sir Gilbert Elliot, 2nd Bt. (1693-1766); Mother Helen Steaurt; Brother Sir Gilbert, MP, 3rd Bt. (1722-1777); Sister Jean (1727-1805); Brother Andrew (1728-1797).

Service: 3.7.1746 Capt Serv *Augusta* (60); 29.6.1748 Able *Chesterfield* (44); 9.1.1748/49 Mid *Assistance* (50); 26.1.1749/50 Mid *Peggy* (8) Sloop; 1.5.1752 Passed; 1.5.1752 Mid *Penzance* (44); **Lieutenant**; 30.4.1756 L. *Scarborough* (20); 25.11.1756 5L *Neptune* (90); **Commander**; 21.1.1757 *Mediterranean* (12) Xebec; 23.3.1757 *Albany* (14) Sloop; **Captain**; 5.4.1757-3.6.1757 *Royal William* (84); 18.7.1757 *Hussar* (28); 30.11.1758 *Aeolus* (32); 20.11.1759 Battle of Quiberon Bay; 28.2.1760 Action of February 28 1760; 8.5.1761-5.4.1763[P] *Chichester* (68); 6.5.1763 *Prince of Orange* (60); 6.6.1763-17.5.1765 *Bellona* (74); 9.1.1767-28.3.1768 M.P. for Cockermouth; 25.9.1770-7.8.1771 *Portland* (50); 1.1776-20.9.1808 FRS; 29.4.1777-11.4.1778 *Trident* (64); 11.4.1778-22.5.1779 Commodore *Trident* (64); 22.5.1779-19.2.1780 *Edgar* (74); 16.1.1780 Battle of Cape St. Vincent; 17.5.1780-19.7.1781 *Edgar* (74); 19.7.1781-8.1781 Commodore *Victory* (100); 1.3.1785/86-11.1788 CinC — Newfoundland; 8.3.1786-24.9.1787 Commodore *Salisbury* (50); **Rear Admiral of the Red**; 24.9.1787-28.11.1788[P] *Salisbury* (50); 1790 *Barfleur* (98); 21.9.1790 **Vice Admiral of the Blue**; 1.2.1793 **Vice Admiral of the White**; 12.4.1794 **Vice Admiral of the Red**; 14.2.1799 **Admiral of the White**; 9.11.1805 **Admiral of the Red.**

ELLIOTT, GEORGE

Dates: c.1714 Born; 5.8.1795 Died Copford, Essex; 10.10.1795 Will Probate.

Family: Wife Susan; Daughter Thomasin Ann; Son John; Son Luther Gilbert.

Service: 4.8.1730-12.2.1730/31 Ord. *Burford* (70); 13.2.1730/31-30.3.1731 Ord. *Exeter* (60); 31.3.1731-26.1.1731/32 Mid *Edinburgh* (70); 27.1.1731/32-7.9.1732 Able *Kingston* (60); 8.9.1732-31.8.1735 Mid *Kingston* (60); 1.9.1735 Mid *Blenheim* (96); 3.1.1735/36 Passed; **Lieutenant**; 20.10.1740-26.4.1741 3L *Superb* (60); 8.6.1741[JAM 4.2.1745/46] 3L *York* (60); 2.5.1743[JAM 4.2.1745/46] 4L *Cumberland* (80); 19.7.1743[JAM 4.2.1745/46] 3L *Cumberland* (80); 5.12.1743[JAM 4.2.1745/46] 2L *Cumberland* (80); 20.12.1743[JAM 4.2.1745/46]-11.5.1744 1L *Cumberland* (80); **Commander**; 18.4.1744 *Blast* (8) Bomb Vessel; **Captain**; 12.5.1744 *Rippon's Prize* (20); 11.9.1744-22.10.1744[W] *Bonetta* (8) Sloop; 14.9.1745-23.11.1747 *Assistance* (50); 6.12.1762 **Superannuated Rear Admiral.**

ELLIS, THOMAS

Dates: c.1732 Born; 1764 Died; 1.2.1765 Will Probate.

Family: Wife Mary Shaw married 14.7.1755.

Service: 9.6.1743 Able *Guernsey* (50); 11.2.1743/44-12.2.1743/44 Battle of Toulon; 4.11.1746 Mid *Guernsey* (50); 7.1.1750/51 Passed; **Lieutenant**; 13.11.1756 L. *Hind* (24); 6.6.1758-27.7.1758 The Siege of Louisbourg; 9.9.1758[NA 9.11.1758] 3L *York* (60); 7.2.1759[NA 9.11.1758] 2L *York* (60); 26.2.1759[NA 9.11.1758]-c.1764[†] 1L *York* (60).

ELLISTON, EDMUND

Dates: c.1734 Born; 1804 Died; 18.12.1804 Will Probate.

Family: Father William Elliston (1709-1767); Mother Mary Gray (1704–1777); Wife Sarah Wintle (1752-?) married 7.8.1782; Sister Sarah [Rawston].

Service: 1750-1755 HEIC Service; 17.10.1755 Mid *Hampshire* (50); 14.2.1759 Passed; **Lieutenant**; 30.3.1759-18.1.1761 3L *Chatham* (50); 3.7.1759 Bombardment of Le Havre; 20.11.1759 Battle of Quiberon Bay; 25.10.1790 LCmdr *Chatham* (50).

ELLYS, CHARLES

Dates: c.1730 Born; 1794 Died.
Family:
Service: 18.10.1745 Capt Serv *Folkestone* (44); 11.5.1746 Capt Serv *Windsor* (60); 14.2.1746/47 Capt Serv *Centurion* (50); 3.5.1747 1st Battle of Cape Finisterre; 5.1.1747/48 Able *Centurion* (50); 30.4.1748-27.8.1748[P] Mid *Centurion* (50); 6.9.1748 Mid *Prince Henry* (44); 7.11.1750 Mate *Prince Henry* (44); 2.7.1752-9.9.1752[P] ActL *Prince Henry* (44); 1.11.1752 Passed; **Lieutenant**; 1.3.1753 L. *Shoreham* (24); 23.4.1756[(NA 30.7.1756)] L. *Falcon* (10) Bomb Vessel; 1.9.1756 4L *Namur* (90); 9.11.1756 3L *Namur* (90); 15.11.1756-17.12.1756 1L *Royal George* (100); 4.1.1757 3L *Namur* (90); 5.9.1757-6.10.1757 Raid on Rochefort; 27.1.1758 3L *Dorsetshire* (68); 26.4.1758 2L *Dorsetshire* (68); 19.6.1759 1L *Dorsetshire* (68); 20.11.1759 Battle of Quiberon Bay; 23.2.1760 1L *Bellona* (74); **Commander**; 21.11.1760 *Escort* (14) Sloop; 29.3.1761-11.6.1761 Expedition against Belle-Isle; **Captain**; 10.5.1762-19.1.1763[P] *Bellona* (74); 21.5.1771-24.9.1774[P] *Trident* (64).

ELMY, BENJAMIN

Dates: 1770 Died.
Family:
Service: **Lieutenant**; 6.10.1741[(7.10.1743)]-24.10.1743[P] 3L *Lion* (60); 16.1.1743/44 2L *Eltham* (40); 7.7.1744-23.6.1745 1L *Eltham* (40); 15.4.1746-13.6.1746[P] 3L *Marlborough* (90); 3.7.1746 2L *Chichester* (80); 21.8.1746 1L *Chichester* (80); 23.2.1746/47-14.5.1750[P] 2L *York* (60); 10.7.1755-2.12.1755 1L *Dreadnought* (60); 24.3.1756-27.11.1756 1L *Royal Sovereign* (104).

ELPHINSTONE, JOHN

Dates: 1722 Born Lopness, Orkney Islands; 28.2.1785 Died London; 9.3.1785 Will Probate.
Family: Father John Elphinston RN; Mother Anne Williams; Wife Amelia Warburton (d. 1786) married 23.10.1750; Son Samuel William, RN (1758-1789); Son Molyneux Rowley; Son Lt.-Gen. Sir Howard, 1st Bt. (1773-1846); Son Thomas, RN; Daughter Anne Charlotte Maria (d. 1809); Daughter Jane Alice Amelia (d. 1856); Daughter Catherine Sarah.
Service: 1739-1743 Merchant Service; 25.7.1742 Able *Torbay* (80); 15.4.1743 Mid *Torbay* (80); 11.2.1743/44-12.2.1743/44 Battle of Toulon; 4.9.1744 Mid *Barfleur* (90); 11.7.1745 Passed; **Lieutenant**; 23.8.1746-12.1.1746/47[P] L. *Scipio* (8) Fireship; 20.9.1746-25.9.1746 Lorient Operations; 19.1.1746/47-4.3.1748/49[P] 3L *Oxford* (50); 12.10.1748 Battle of Havana; 16.1.1753-2.4.1754 2L *Cumberland* (66); 27.11.1756 5L *Royal Sovereign* (104); **Commander**; 5.5.1757 *London* (6) Storeship; 23.5.1757-11.8.1758[C] *Salamander* (16) Fireship; 5.6.1758-12.6.1758 Raid on Saint-Malo; **Captain**; 1.2.1759-31.3.1760 *Eurus* (24); 24.6.1760 *Richmond* (32); 6.6.1762-13.8.1762 Operations against Havana; 15.9.1762-24.4.1763[P] *Infanta* (74); 6.10.1763-24.10.1766 *Firm* (74); 2.3.1768-5.12.1768[P] *Pearl* (32); 1770-1774 In the service of Russia; 1770 **Admiral** (Imperial Russian Navy); 7.1.1774-27.4.1778 *Egmont* (74); 2.7.1778-14.11.1781 *Magnificent* (74); 6.7.1779 Battle of Grenada; 21.12.1779-22.12.1779 Action of 1779-12-21; 17.4.1780 Battle of Martinique; 15.5.1780 Action of March 15 1780; 19.5.1780 Action of March 19 1780; 12.4.1781-25.6.1781[P] *Cambridge* (80); 16.12.1782-25.3.1783[P] *Atlas* (98).

ELWALL, EBER

Dates: c.1715 Born; c.1756 Died; 26.3.1756 Will Probate.
Family: Sister India; Sister Ann.
Service: 15.9.1731 Adm Serv *Namur* (90); 3.4.1732 Able *Scarborough* (20); 29.9.1736 Mate *Scarborough* (20); 22.11.1736 Mid *Eltham* (40); 8.1.1739/40 Passed; **Lieutenant**; 23.6.1740 L. *Vulcan* (8) Fireship; 27.9.1740 2L *Superb* (60); 20.10.1740 1L *Superb* (60); 2.10.1741 3L *Sutherland* (50); 16.10.1741-23.6.1742 3L *Falmouth* (50); 29.10.1744-6.2.1745/46 L. *Mortar* (10) Bomb Vessel; 3.7.1746-17.10.1746 1L *Prince Edward* (44).

EMERY, CHARLES

Dates: c.1739 Born; 1780 Died.
Family:
Service: 19.5.1753 Mate *Raven* (14) Sloop; 6.3.1753/54 Capt Serv *Rye* (20); 28.7.1754 Able *Rye* (20); 9.6.1755 Able *Ambuscade* (40); 8.10.1755 Mid *Hazard* (8) Sloop; 16.7.1757 Mid *Harwich* (50); 26.10.1757 Mid *Montagu* (60); 10.1.1758 Mid *Mercury* (20); 17.8.1759 Mid *Launceston* (44); 21.2.1760-13.8.1760 Mate *Launceston* (44); 13.8.1760 Passed; **Lieutenant**; 3.12.1761[(EI 22.12.1763)]-25.6.1762 2L *Alderney* (10) Sloop; 28.12.1763 2L *Tweed* (32); 2.4.1764-7.4.1767 3L *Ramillies* (74); 16.1.1771-25.5.1771 1L *Worcester* (64).

EPWORTH, FARMERY

Dates: c.1738 Born; 1804 Died; 10.11.1804 Will Probate.
Family: Father Farmery Epworth; Mother ? Gillson; Wife Jane Cumin (1744-?); Son Farmery Predam, RN (1766-1826); Daughter Mary Jane Harriot (1768-?); Son Christopher (1778-?); Daughter Elizabeth (1774-).
Service: 1754-1756 Merchant Service; 1.6.1756 Able *Torbay* (74); 25.7.1757-5.3.1759/60 Mid *Torbay* (74); 5.9.1757-6.10.1757 Raid on Rochefort; 5.6.1758-12.6.1758 Raid on Saint-Malo; 29.12.1758 Capture of Goree; 20.11.1759 Battle of Quiberon Bay; 5.3.1760 Passed; **Lieutenant**; 24.12.1762[(JAM 13.12.1763)] L. *Lurcher* (6) Cutter; 29.3.1763[(JAM 13.12.1763)] 3L *Deptford* (50); 27.4.1763[(JAM 13.12.1763)]-6.12.1763[P] 5L *Centaur* (74); 10.1772-26.12.1775 LCmdr *Lurcher* (6) Cutter; 6.12.1776-26.2.1777 3L *Albion* (74); 27.9.1777-28.2.1778 1L *Fame* (74); **Commander**; 8.5.1778 *Alert* (10) Hired Cutter; **Captain**; 13.5.1778-20.5.1778[P] *Antelope* (50); 17.12.1778-19.4.1780 *Squirrel* (20); 19.6.1795 **Superannuated Rear Admiral**.

ERICKS, JAMES

Dates: c.1716 Born; bef.24.3.1756 Died.
Family:
Service: 11.4.1733 Vol-p-O *Sunderland* (60); 7.12.1733 Able *Garland* (20); 27.9.1734 Mid *Garland* (20); 11.9.1736 Mid *Ipswich* (70); 3.1.1736/37 Mid *Blenheim* (96); 2.11.1738 Mid *Greenwich* (50); 11.8.1740 Mid *Namur* (90); 20.1.1740/41 Passed; **Lieutenant**; 27.3.1741 6L *Neptune* (90); 1.5.1741 5L *Neptune* (90); 11.2.1743/44-12.2.1743/44 Battle of Toulon; 19.3.1743/44[(24.4.1745)]-26.2.1744/45 5L *Barfleur* (90); 1.12.1748-14.11.1752[P] 1L *Tiger* (60); 16.10.1755-bef.24.3.1756[†] 1L *Royal Sovereign* (104).

ERSKINE, ROBERT

Dates: 7.11.1766 Died.
Family: Wife Mary; Daughter Mary.
Service: 31.1.1714/15 Ord. *Fowey* (40); 28.5.1716 Able *Monck* (64); 30.4.1717 Able *Panther* (54); 12.3.1717/18 QGnr *Dorsetshire* (80); 11.8.1718 Battle of Cape Passaro; 28.12.1718-

16.4.1723[P] Mid *Winchester* (50); 19.4.1725 Passed; **Lieutenant**; 2.4.1729 L. *Drake* (8) Sloop; 20.9.1734 L. *Rose* (20); 13.12.1734 3L *Montagu* (60); 10.6.1735-12.2.1735/36[P] 2L *Montagu* (60); **Commander**; 3.3.1737/38 *Royal Escape* Smack; 26.12.1739-4.1.1739/40 *Trial* (8) Sloop; **Captain**; 13.11.1742-17.4.1744 *Fox* (20); 14.9.1745 *Warwick* (60); 12.9.1747[(JAM 28.2.1748/49)] *Canterbury* (60); 9.4.1748 Battle of Santiago de Cuba; 1.8.1748[(JAM 28.12.1749)]-19.1.1748/49[P] *Milford* (44); 6.12.1762 **Superannuated Rear Admiral.**

ESSINGTON, CLAPHAMSON

Dates: 1725 Born; 18.10.1725 Baptised; 1755 Died.
Family: Father John Essington M.P. (1689-1729); Mother Elizabeth Claphamson; Wife Mary; Wife Ann Hill (1729 - 1774) married 1.5.1750; Son Torin Archer (1747-?); Daughter Anne (1751-?); Daughter Margarate Jane (1752-1752); Son William (1753-?).
Service: **Lieutenant**; 8.4.1748[(JAM 13.4.1749)]-31.10.1748[P] L. *Barrington* Sloop.

EVANS, HENRY FRANCIS

Dates: c.18.2.1742 Born Westminster; 24.2.1742 Baptised Westminster; 21.7.1781 Died North America; 4.3.1782 Will Probate.
Family: Father Robert Evans; Mother Elizabeth; Sister Unknown [Teasdale]; Sister Mary; Sister Rebecca.
Service: 8.6.1756 Ord. *Monmouth* (70); 27.12.1757 Adm Serv *Neptune* (90); 29.8.1758 Supnum *Royal Anne* (100); 3.9.1758 Adm Ret *Neptune* (90); 12.2.1759 Able *Isis* (50); 2.4.1759 Mid *Isis* (50); 3.7.1759 Bombardment of Le Havre; 27.6.1762 Mid *Active* (28); 1.9.1762 Passed; **Lieutenant**; 27.9.1762 L. *Laurel* (12) Sloop; 29.3.1763 L. *Spy* (10) Sloop; 27.3.1764-1.5.1765 3L *Achilles* (60); 4.1767 Agent for Transports; **Commander**; 12.11.1777-21.4.1778 *Countess of Scarborough* (20) Hired Armed Ship; **Captain**; 29.4.1778-2.5.1778[P] *Royal Oak* (74); 4.12.1779-15.5.1780 *Raisonable* (64); 15.5.1780-21.7.1781[†] *Charlestown* (28); 21.7.1781 Action of 1781-07-21.

EVANS, JOHN

Dates: 1717 Born; 15.7.1794 Died Feltham, Middlesex.
Family:
Service: 21.5.1733 Able *Revenge* (70); 4.6.1734 Able *Dunkirk* (60); 29.7.1736-17.7.1737 MidO *Dunkirk* (60); 18.7.1738 Able *Hampton Court* (70); 7.7.1739 Mid *Saint Albans* (54); 24.5.1740 Passed; **Lieutenant**; 16.9.1740-18.9.1740 3L *Rupert* (60); 19.9.1740 3L *Jersey* (60); 4.3.1740/41-5.1741 Operations against Cartagena; 8.12.1741[(JAM 13.8.1745)]-25.7.1745 2L *York* (60); 31.3.1745[(10.7.1745)] 2L *Cumberland* (80); 18.9.1745 1L *London* (100); **Commander**; 20.8.1746-9.4.1748 *Granado* (8) Bomb Vessel; **Captain**; 20.4.1748-23.4.1748 *Flamborough* (20); 18.11.1748-25.6.1752[P] *Glasgow* (20); 4.12.1753 *Experiment* (24); 18.7.1755 *Prince Edward* (44); 18.1.1757-6.5.1763[P] *Preston* (50); 24.10.1766-26.10.1769 *Augusta* (64); 1778-4.1779 Commodore *Romney* (50); 23.1.1778-2.5.1778 *Invincible* (74); 5.1778 Commodore *Invincible* (74); 19.3.1779 **Rear Admiral of the White**; 1780-1781 *Dromedary* (30) Armed Storeship; 26.9.1780 **Vice Admiral of the Blue**; 1781-1782 *Diligent* (70); 24.9.1787 **Vice Admiral of the White**; 21.9.1790 **Vice Admiral of the Red**; 1.2.1793 **Admiral of the Blue**.

EVANS, JOHN

Dates: c.1716 Born; 2.5.1763 Will Probate; bef.2.5.1763 Died.

Family:

Service: 21.5.1736 Ord. *Burford* (70); 29.11.1736 Able *Burford* (70); 4.8.1739 Able *Oxford* (50); 6.8.1743 Mid *Oxford* (50); 11.2.1743/44-12.2.1743/44 Battle of Toulon; 18.2.1744/45 Mid *Shrewsbury* (80); 12.9.1745 Passed; **Lieutenant**; 14.4.1746-5.8.1748[P] 3L *Princess Louisa* (60); 3.5.1747 1st Battle of Cape Finisterre; 14.10.1747 2nd Battle of Cape Finisterre; 27.11.1755 5L *Princess Royal* (90); 11.1.1757-10.3.1759 5L *Marlborough* (80); 7.8.1761-bef.20.5.1763[†] 1L *Belleisle* (64); 6.6.1762-13.8.1762 Operations against Havana.

EVANS, ROBERT

Dates: c.1739 Born; 1777 Died; 6.5.1777 Will Probate.

Family: Mother Elizabeth; Sister Sarah; Sister Susan.

Service: 1753-1755 HEIC Service; 9.1.1755 Able *Tiger* (60); 4.3.1754/55 Ord. *Tiger* (60); 13.3.1754/55 Able *Tiger* (60); 11.1.1756-14.1.1756 Capture of Geriah; 5.8.1756-2.1.1760 Mid *Tiger* (60); 7.3.1757-1.4.1757 Expedition against Chandernagore; 29.4.1758 Battle of Cuddalore; 3.8.1758 Battle of Negapatam; 10.9.1759 Battle of Pondicherry; 2.1.1760 Passed; **Lieutenant**; 11.1.1760 3L *Launceston* (44); 26.1.1761-12.3.1763[P] 3L *Nassau* (64).

EVANS, THOMAS

Dates: 1775 Died.

Family:

Service: **Lieutenant**; 25.9.1743[(2.9.1745)]-10.8.1745 2L *Rupert* (60); 11.2.1743/44-12.2.1743/44 Battle of Toulon; 28.12.1745 L. *Lys* (24); 12.8.1746 2L *Romney* (44); 23.11.1747-18.8.1748[P] 1L *Windsor* (60); 1.12.1748-19.8.1749 2L *Cumberland* (66); 19.8.1749-17.11.1752[P] 3L *Cumberland* (66); 30.1.1755 1L *Yarmouth* (64); 9.12.1755 6L *Prince* (90); 7.4.1756 5L *Prince* (90); 12.5.1756 5L *Royal George* (100); 3.7.1756[(ECH 20.3.1758)] 1L *Prince George* (80); 3.10.1756[(ECH 20.3.1758)]-29.11.1756 1L *Prince* (90); **Commander**; 12.7.1757-9.1.1758 *Scorpion* (14) Sloop; **Captain**; 30.1.1758 *Royal William* (84); 6.6.1758-27.7.1758 The Siege of Louisbourg; 30.1.1759-25.2.1763[P] *Union* (90); 20.11.1759 Battle of Quiberon Bay; 29.3.1761-11.6.1761 Expedition against Belle-Isle; 23.10.1770-7.11.1770[P] *Augusta* (64); 15.9.1773-11.3.1775 *Ramillies* (74).

EVERITT, MICHAEL

Dates: 1716 Born; 17.10.1776 Will Probate; bef.17.10.1776 Died.

Family: Wife Elizabeth Gayton; Son Charles Holmes, RN; Son Michael John, RN (d.1779).

Service: 2.5.1732 Able *Dursley Galley* (20); 29.4.1736 Mid *Dursley Galley* (20); 5.3.1737/38 Able *Gibraltar* (20); 15.3.1738/39 Able *Dursley Galley* (20); 1.11.1740 Mate *Dursley Galley* (20); 24.2.1741/42 Mate *Romney* (50); 21.4.1743-5.8.1743[P] Mate *Garland* (20); 10.10.1743 Passed; **Lieutenant**; 15.6.1744 3L *Weymouth* (60); 13.3.1744/45[(BLI 11.5.1747)] 2L *Superb* (60); **Commander**; 1.10.1745[(BLI 2.1.1746/47)]-4.3.1745/46 *Louisburg* (8) Fireship; **Captain**; 23.12.1747-30.9.1748[P] *Amazon* (22); 8.2.1755-7.6.1756 *Buckingham* (68); 20.5.1756 Battle of Minorca; 25.11.1756 *Neptune* (90); 1.8.1757 *Union* (90); 5.6.1758-12.6.1758 Raid on Saint-Malo; 28.12.1758 *Stirling Castle* (64); 3.6.1761-7.6.1761 Occupation of Dominica; 7.1.1762-10.2.1762 Operations against Martinique; 3.3.1762[(BLI 3.3.1763)]-24.2.1763[P] *Sutherland* (50); 6.6.1762-13.8.1762 Operations against Havana; 22.7.1766-26.7.1769 *Bellona* (74); 24.7.1776-19.9.1776 *Bedford* (74).

EVERY, DENNIS

Dates: c.1710 Born; 1777 Died; 23.4.1777 Will Probate.
Family: Wife Anna Maria Coulson.
Service: 24.7.1724 Ord. *Essex* (70); 2.4.1726 Ord. *Elizabeth* (70); 6.7.1726-31.8.1727^{P} Able *Elizabeth* (70); 2.10.1737 MidO *Medway* (60); 28.9.1738 Able *Ludlow Castle* (40); 20.5.1739 Able *Shoreham* (20); 13.10.1739 Mid *Shoreham* (20); 3.3.1739/40 Mid *Britannia* (100); 16.7.1741 Passed; **Lieutenant**; 2.9.1741 3L *Lynn* (44); 12.12.1741$^{(22.1.1741/42)}$ 2L *Lynn* (44); 28.10.1742 L. *Scipio* (8) Fireship; 29.1.1742/43 3L *Dover* (44); 14.5.1744-5.10.1744 2L *Pearl* (44); 6.11.1745-14.2.1745/46 1L *Milford* (44); 21.3.1745/46 1L *Eagle* (60); 27.8.1746 2L *Sunderland* (60); 30.9.1746-22.2.1748/49^{P} 1L *Sunderland* (60); 10.8.1757 1L *Jersey* (60); 18.8.1759-19.8.1759 Battle of Lagos Bay; **Commander**; 31.8.1762-22.12.1762^{P} *Hazard* (8) Sloop; 9.4.1763-17.11.1763^{D} *Happy* (8) Sloop; 17.11.1763 Dismissed.

EXTON, FRANCIS

Dates: c.1737 Born; 1784 Died; 19.10.1784 Will Probate.
Family: Father Francis Exton; Mother Mary Bull; Wife Mary Neale married 7.1.1772; Brother Thomas; Sister Jane [Lee].
Service: 14.2.1752 Ord. *Grampus* (14) Sloop; 25.11.1752 Able *Grampus* (14) Sloop; 14.2.1753 Able *Porcupine* (16) Sloop; 12.8.1755 Mid *Winchelsea* (20); 3.6.1756 Mid *Falkland* (50); 30.10.1757 Mid *Barfleur* (80); 10.4.1758 Passed; **Lieutenant**; 17.5.1758 4L *Warspite* (74); 10.6.1758 3L *Warspite* (74); 18.8.1759-19.8.1759 Battle of Lagos Bay; 21.9.1759-5.5.1763^{P} 2L *Warspite* (74); 20.11.1759 Battle of Quiberon Bay; 17.12.1770 2L *Northumberland* (68); 5.3.1771-24.10.1771 2L *Asia* (64).

Service Records F

FABIAN, WILLIAM

Dates: c.1718 Born; 1762 Died; 27.5.1762 Will Probate.

Family: Wife Elizabeth Martin married 20.9.1758.

Service: 17.3.1735/36-6.4.1737[P] Able *Royal Oak* (70); 29.12.1740 Able *Guernsey* (50); 2.12.1742 QM *Guernsey* (50); 14.3.1742/43 Mid *Guernsey* (50); 11.2.1743/44-12.2.1743/44 Battle of Toulon; 6.5.1747-15.1.1747/48[P] Mid *Chatham* (50); 4.2.1747/48 Passed; **Lieutenant**; 10.2.1757 L. *Barbadoes* (14) Sloop; 28.5.1758[(BLI 5.1.1759)]-27.10.1758 4L *Trident* (64); 8.2.1759-18.10.1759 3L *Jason* (30).

FACEY, JOHN

Dates: 1767 Died; 19.12.1767 Will Probate.

Family: Mistress Elizabeth Battow; Daughter Mary Battow.

Service: **Lieutenant**; 10.11.1741-18.11.1741[P] 3L *Falkland* (50); 28.12.1741 3L *Diamond* (44); 8.3.1741/42-bef.18.12.1744[P] 2L *Diamond* (44); 11.2.1743/44-12.2.1743/44 Battle of Toulon; 27.10.1746-10.7.1755 LCmdr *Blenheim* (96); 21.2.1757-2.1.1760 LCmdr *Blenheim* (96).

FAIRFAX, SIR WILLIAM GEORGE

Dates: 8.3.1739 Born Bagshot, Surrey; 1797 Knight Bachelor; 17.11.1813 Died Edinburgh.

Family: Father Joseph Fairfax; Mother Mary Anne; Wife Margaret Charters; Wife Hannah Spears (d.1770).

Service: 15.7.1750 Ord. *Centurion* (50); 23.2.1750/51 Able *Centurion* (50); 28.2.1753 Able *Mars* (64); 1.5.1754 Mid *Garland* (24); 5.12.1757 Passed; **Lieutenant**; 20.12.1757 6L *Duke* (90); 5.6.1758-12.6.1758 Raid on Saint-Malo; 27.10.1758-26.6.1760[W] L. *Eurus* (24); 23.6.1766-15.6.1769[SP] LCmdr *Greyhound* (4) Cutter; 2.8.1776-25.11.1777 L. *Hazard* (8) Sloop; 26.11.1777 2L *Sultan* (74); 26.1.1778 1L *Prince George* (98); 15.4.1778 LCmdr *Alert* (10) Cutter; **Commander**; 13.5.1778-17.7.1778[C] *Alert* (10) Cutter; **Captain**; 12.1.1782-25.10.1785[P] *Tartar* (28); 30.10.1793 *Sheerness* (44); 1.5.1795-13.9.1796 *Repulse* (64); 14.9.1796-14.3.1798[P] *Venerable* (74); 11.10.1797 Battle of Camperdown; 14.3.1798 *Quebec* (32); 30.1.1799-7.1.1801 *Venerable* (74); 14.2.1799-17.11.1813 Colonel of Marines; 2.7.1799 Attack on Aix Roads; 1.1.1801 **Rear Admiral of the Blue**; 23.4.1804 **Rear Admiral of the White**; 9.11.1805 **Rear Admiral of the Red**; 25.10.1809 **Vice Admiral of the White**; 31.7.1810 **Vice Admiral of the Red**.

FAIRLIE, GILBERT

Dates: c.1797 Died; 7.1.1797 Will Probate.

Family: Wife Elizabeth Fish married 20.7.1763; Daughter Elizabeth (1764-?); Daughter Mary (1765-?); Daughter Susan Key (1768-?); Daughter Rosella Day (1773-?); Daughter Amelia Day (1775-?).

Service: **Lieutenant**; 18.6.1759 L. *Mortar* (8) Bomb Vessel; 3.7.1759 Bombardment of Le Havre; 18.3.1761-15.12.1761 5L *Temeraire* (74); 29.3.1761-11.6.1761 Expedition against Belle-Isle; 25.3.1762-9.6.1762 4L *Princess Amelia* (80); 18.5.1768-10.6.1769 L. *Alderney* (10) Sloop; 30.5.1769-7.7.1771[P] LCmdr *Hector* (4) Cutter.

FALCONER, GEORGE

Dates: c.1725 Born; 1780 Died.

Family:

Service: 7.1.1738/39 Able *Edinburgh* (70); 25.1.1739/40 Able *Ipswich* (70); 1.1.1740/41 Mid *Ipswich* (70); 2.3.1742/43 Sinking of the San Isidoro; 8.2.1743/44 Able *Sandwich* (90); 17.6.1744 Able *Saint George* (90); 22.6.1744 Mid *Saint George* (90); 11.1.1744/45 Passed; **Lieutenant**; 12.2.1744/45 3L *Ludlow Castle* (44); 17.7.1745-19.5.1747 2L *Ludlow Castle* (44); 8.2.1747/48 4L *Suffolk* (70); 19.3.1747/48-29.7.1748[P] 3L *Berwick* (70); 1.12.1748-18.11.1752[P] 2L *Yarmouth* (64); 16.1.1755 1L *Winchester* (50); 5.8.1755 2L *Newark* (80); 7.10.1755 2L *Intrepid* (64); 20.5.1756 Battle of Minorca; 3.7.1756[(ECH 21.10.1756)] 3L *Antelope* (50); **Commander**; 10.11.1756 *Katherine* (8) Yacht; 23.3.1757-1.11.1757 *Diligence* (10) Sloop; **Captain**; 27.4.1762 *Captain* (64); 24.9.1762 *Juno* (32); 26.12.1763-22.7.1766[P] *Essex* (64); 1.12.1773-21.1.1775[P] *Triumph* (74); 19.1.1775-5.2.1778[P] *Mars* (74); 29.10.1778 *Diana* (32); 21.3.1780-2.5.1780 *Invincible* (74).

FALKINGHAM, EDWARD

Dates: c.1679 Born; 18.9.1757 Died; 23.9.1757 Buried St Alfege, Greenwich; 30.9.1757 Will Probate.

Family: Son Edward, RN (d.1783); Son John, RN (d.1777).

Service: 1695-1698 HEIC Service; 8.3.1697/98-11.12.1698[P] Ord. *Gloucester* (60); 28.9.1698 Capt Serv *Devonshire* (80); 17.5.1701 Mid *Suffolk* (70); 21.11.1701 Mid *Monmouth* (64); 21.3.1701/2 Mid *Russell* (80); 17.4.1702 Passed; **Lieutenant**; 24.8.1702 5L *Britannia* (100); 12.9.1702 3L *Royal Oak* (70); 6.1.1702/3 2L *Royal Oak* (70); 13.8.1704 Battle of Malaga; 16.12.1704-6.2.1707/8 1L *Revenge* (70); 10.3.1704/5 Battle of Marbella; 7.2.1707/8-20.9.1709 2L *Monmouth* (64); 15.8.1710 1L *Defiance* (64); **Commander**; 28.8.1711[(8.1.1713/14)] *Trial* (10) Sloop; **Captain**; 26.2.1712/13[(24.12.1714)] *Weymouth* (50); 13.6.1713-7.2.1714/15 *Shoreham* (32); 17.2.1714/15-3.1.1716/17[P] Capt&M *Gibraltar* (20); 23.1.1716/17 *Dartmouth* (54); 14.3.1717/18 *Orford* (70); 11.8.1718 Battle of Cape Passaro; 4.6.1720[(11.10.1721)]-5.10.1721[P] *Newcastle* (50); 29.4.1723-13.4.1728[P] *Prince Frederick* (70); 26.7.1728 *Monmouth* (70); 2.4.1729 *Princess Amelia* (80); 12.4.1729 *Cornwall* (80); 14.10.1729 *Monmouth* (70); 29.4.1730 *Cornwall* (80); 19.5.1731 *Namur* (90); 2.1.1731/32 *Namur* (90); 18.4.1732-25.7.1736 *Salisbury* (50); 5.5.1732 CinC — Newfoundland; 16.5.1738-9.10.1740 *Elizabeth* (70); 2.2.1740/41-2.9.1742[P] *Royal George* (100); 10.1742-6.1744 Resident Commissioner at Port Mahon; 1745-1746 Resident Commissioner at Woolwich Dockyard; 28.2.1755-25.11.1755 Comptroller of the Navy.

FALKINGHAM, EDWARD

Dates: 1783 Died; 8.11.1783 Buried St. Michael's, Southampton; 6.3.1784 Will Probate.

Family: Father Edward Falkingham, RN (1679-1757); Wife Eleanor; Brother John, RN (d.1777).

Service: 17.9.1726 Able *Kinsale* (40); 27.8.1727 Vol-p-O *Prince Frederick* (70); 29.7.1728 MidO *Canterbury* (60); 28.8.1729 Mid *Canterbury* (60); 12.1.1729/30 MidO *Canterbury* (60); 23.8.1730-27.12.1731[P] Mid *Canterbury* (60); 2.5.1732 Mid *Salisbury* (50); 23.4.1733 Passed; **Lieutenant**; 7.6.1734 L. *Bonetta* (8) Sloop; 17.10.1735[(13.3.1735/36)]-9.12.1735 3L *Hector* (40); 16.5.1738-4.12.1738[P] 3L *Deptford* (60); 7.6.1739-1.10.1739 3L *Elizabeth* (70); 2.10.1739-

2.10.1740 2L *Elizabeth* (70); 3.10.1740 2L *Russell* (80); 4.9.1741[JAM 4.9.1745]-19.12.1743 1L *Cumberland* (80); **Commander**; 2.5.1743-23.6.1743 *Basilisk* (8) Bomb Vessel; **Captain**; 26.3.1746-21.1.1746/47[P] *Success* (20); 8.10.1755-12.5.1758 *Sutherland* (50); 8.1757-10.1757 Louisbourg Expedition; 5.11.1770 **Superannuated Rear Admiral**.

FALKINGHAM, JOHN

Dates: 1777 Died; 8.12.1777 Buried St Olave, London.
Family: Father Edward Falkingham, RN (1679-1757); Brother Edward, RN (d.1783).
Service: **Lieutenant**; 20.2.1742/43[5.11.1745] L. *Lively* (20); 15.4.1743-24.4.1743 Attack on Porto Cabello; 27.7.1744[5.11.1745] 2L *Woolwich* (50); 11.2.1745/46 2L *Princess Mary* (60); **Commander**; 5.4.1747[30.11.1748]-5.1747[P] *Fogo* Fireship; 20.3.1748/49-2.10.1752[P] *Shark* (8) Sloop; 26.3.1754-26.11.1757 *Trial* (10) Sloop; **Captain**; 18.10.1758-15.1.1763[P] *Princess Royal* (90); 2.4.1766-16.8.1766 *Chatham* (50); 16.8.1766[BLI 22.6.1768]-31.8.1769[P] *Lark* (32); 20.12.1770-20.5.1771[P] *Conquestador* (60).

FANSHAWE, CHARLES

Dates: 15.2.1757 Died.
Family: Wife Elizabeth Rogers; Son Robert, RN (1740-1823).
Service: 12.1.1714/15 Vol-p-O *Warwick* (54); 20.5.1717 MidO *Hampshire* (54); 25.2.1717/18 Able *Preston* (50); 21.3.1718/19 Mid *Preston* (50); 9.4.1719 Able *Salisbury* (50); 15.5.1719-24.6.1720 Mid *Salisbury* (50); 20.6.1720 Passed; **Lieutenant**; 27.9.1720-8.4.1723 3L *Weymouth* (50); 22.4.1723-31.1.1723/24 2L *Weymouth* (50); 1.2.1723/24-1.4.1729 L. *Scarborough* (20); 2.4.1729-24.7.1729 2L *Kingston* (60); 25.7.1729-8.9.1731[P] L. *Scarborough* (20); **Commander**; 13.1.1731/32-1.11.1732 *Hawk* (8) Sloop; **Captain**; 11.1.1732/33-2.4.1734[P] *Solebay* (6) Bomb Vessel; 7.5.1734 *Lyme* (20); 6.9.1737-23.4.1742[P] *Phoenix* (20); 4.1740-5.7.1740 Attack on St. Augustine; 15.7.1747 **Superannuated Rear Admiral**.

FANSHAWE, ROBERT

Dates: 4.1.1740 Born; 4.2.1823 Died Stonehall, Stonehouse, Plymouth.
Family: Father Charles Fanshawe, RN (d.1757); Mother Elizabeth Rogers; Wife Christiana Gennys; Son Robert, RN (d.1804); Son Edward; Son Sir Arthur, RN (1795-1864).
Service: 1753-11.9.1759 Mid *Salisbury* (50); 11.1.1756-14.1.1756 Capture of Geriah; 7.3.1757-1.4.1757 Expedition against Chandernagore; 29.4.1758 Battle of Cuddalore; 3.8.1758 Battle of Negapatam; 10.9.1759 Battle of Pondicherry; **Lieutenant**; 11.9.1759[EI 30.6.1762] 4L *Tiger* (60); 1.2.1761[EI 30.6.1762]-10.7.1761[P] 3L *Tiger* (60); **Commander**; 23.8.1762-17.12.1762[P] *Carcass* (8) Bomb Vessel; 8.6.1763-16.9.1766[P] *Speedwell* (8) Sloop; **Captain**; 25.5.1768 *Sheerness* (24); 27.4.1769-10.12.1770 *Lively* (20); 13.11.1775 *Carysfort* (28); 8.4.1779[NA 24.12.1779]-13.11.1779[P] *Monmouth* (64); 6.7.1779 Battle of Grenada; 8.3.1780-22.8.1781[P] *Egmont* (74); 18.12.1781-6.6.1783[P] *Namur* (90); 12.4.1782 Battle of the Saintes; 7.4.1784-1.2.1790 M.P. for Plymouth; 26.1.1785-3.2.1785[P] *Bombay Castle* (74); 28.2.1787-3.2.1789 *Bombay Castle* (74); 13.11.1789-12.12.1815 Resident Commissioner at Plymouth Dockyard.

FARMAR, ROBERT

Dates: c.1715 Born; c.1758 Died Philadelphia; 12.4.1758 Will Probate.
Family: Father Samuel Farmar; Mother Mary Wilkinson (1696-1726); Brother Richard; Brother Samuel.
Service: 23.12.1734-19.1.1735/36 Able *Dolphin* (20); 19.1.1735/36-24.9.1738 Able *Dursley Galley* (20); 24.9.1738-11.1.1738/39 Mid *Deptford* (60); 11.1.1738/39-12.11.1740 Mid *Princess*

Louisa (60); 21.11.1739 Attack on Puerto Bello; 12.11.1740-18.9.1742 Mate *Princess Louisa* (60); 4.3.1740/41-5.1741 Operations against Cartagena; 18.9.1742 ActL *Chester* (54); 21.9.1742 Passed; **Lieutenant**; 2.4.1744 3L *Princess Mary* (60); 14.11.1744-5.2.1745/46 2L *Princess Mary* (60); 1.6.1756-22.4.1760[P] 2L *Augusta* (60); 21.10.1757 Forrest's Action.

FARMER, GEORGE

Dates: c.1732 Born Youghal, Cork; 6.10.1779 Died; 2.11.1779 Will Probate.
Family: Father John Farmer (d.1740); Mother Alphra Grade (c.1710-?); Wife Rebecca Fleming (d.1782) married 15.12.1761; Son Sir George William (1st Baronet of Mount Pleasant), RN (1763-1814); Daughter Emily Broomfield [Power] (1773-1855).
Service: 1752-1755 Merchant Service; 27.9.1755 Mid *Dreadnought* (60); 6.2.1756 Able *Dreadnought* (60); 28.7.1756 Mid *Dreadnought* (60); 17.7.1757 Able *Roebuck* (44); 14.9.1757 Able *Achilles* (60); 16.10.1757 Mid *Achilles* (60); 9.8.1758 Passed; **Lieutenant**; 23.5.1759-16.1.1761[P] 2L *Aurora* (38); **Commander**; 26.5.1768-14.3.1769 *Weazle* (16) Sloop; 27.9.1769-13.3.1770 *Swift* (14) Sloop; 1770 Gov. of Falkland Islands; 3.10.1770 *Tamar* (16) Sloop; **Captain**; 10.1.1771 *Launceston* (44); 25.8.1773-26.6.1777 *Seahorse* (24); 10.3.1778-6.10.1779[†] *Quebec* (32); 6.10.1779 Quebec vs Surveillante.

FARMER, THE HON. WILLIAM

Dates: c.1722 Born; 9.1758 Died.
Family:
Service: 11.7.1736 Able *Dolphin* (20); 16.11.1738 MidO *Dolphin* (20); 30.12.1739 Mid *Dolphin* (20); 12.2.1739/40 Able *Gloucester* (50); 6.6.1740 Able *Prince Frederick* (70); 26.6.1740 Able *Weymouth* (60); 24.11.1740 Mid *Prince Frederick* (70); 7.1.1740/41 Action of January 7 1741; 4.3.1740/41-5.1741 Operations against Cartagena; 10.6.1741 Mid *Oxford* (50); 5.8.1741 Able *Torrington* (40); 20.12.1741 Mid *Barfleur* (90); 12.6.1742 Mid *Rochester* (54); 3.8.1742 Passed; **Lieutenant**; 16.8.1742 4L *Orford* (70); 9.2.1742/43 6L *Sandwich* (90); 15.6.1743-5.2.1743/44[W] 3L *Looe* (44); **Captain**; 12.1.1744/45[(MED 4.2.1744/45)] *Torbay* (80); 1.5.1745[(MED 20.11.1746)] *Roebuck* (44); 9.11.1745[(MED 20.11.1746)] *Dunkirk* (60); 2.1.1745/46[(MED 4.2.1745/46)]-13.6.1746 *Chatham* (50); 15.1.1746/47 *Experiment* (24); 1.11.1748-12.10.1749 *Nightingale* (22).

FARR, WALKER

Dates: 31.10.1756 Died; 13.9.1757 Will Probate.
Family: Wife Mary Bowdler married 21.1.1751/52.
Service: 1746 Passed; **Lieutenant**; 28.11.1747-7.10.1748[P] L. *Blandford* (20); 5.5.1749-29.11.1750[P] 3L *America* (44); 21.1.1751/52-20.11.1752[P] 3L *Bristol* (50); 3.5.1753-19.1.1755 L. *Weazle* (16) Sloop; **Commander**; 5.4.1756 *Falcon* (10) Bomb Vessel; 13.7.1756-31.10.1756[W] *Swift* (8) Sloop.

FAULKNOR, JONATHON

Dates: c.1729 Born; 24.6.1795 Died London; 1.7.1795 Buried Alverstoke, Hampshire; 23.7.1795 Will Probate.
Family: Father Samuel Faulknor, RN (d.1744); Mother Fanny; Wife Mary Curry married 27.8.1754; Son Jonathon, RN (d.1809); Son Jonathon, RN (d.1809); Son Richard, RN; Daughter Mary; Brother Robert, RN (1721-1769); Brother Samuel, RN (1719-1759).
Service: 28.11.1743 Scholar *Royal Naval Academy*; 15.11.1746 Mid *Amazon* (22); 15.3.1747 Able *Advice* (50); 28.6.1747 Mid *Advice* (50); 18.1.1748 Able *Advice* (50); 23.3.1748 Mid *Advice* (50); 27.2.1749 Mid *Centurion* (50); 13.11.1749 Able *Centurion* (50); 5.6.1752 Mate

Centurion (50); 4.10.1752 Passed; **Lieutenant**; 24.8.1753(JAM 15.1.1754)-11.2.1754[P] 3L *Saint Albans* (60); 16.1.1755 L. *Albany* (14) Sloop; 20.3.1755 5L *Prince George* (80); 30.9.1755 3L *Swiftsure* (68); 19.2.1756 2L *Torbay* (74); 20.5.1756 1L *Torbay* (74); 5.9.1757-6.10.1757 Raid on Rochefort; 5.6.1758-12.6.1758 Raid on Saint-Malo; **Commander**; 28.9.1758 *Furnace* (8) Bomb Vessel; 29.12.1758 Capture of Goree; 3.7.1759 Bombardment of Le Havre; **Captain**; 9.7.1759-5.11.1761 *Mercury* (20); 12.10.1766-15.11.1769 *Superb* (74); 24.10.1776 *Royal Oak* (74); 26.1.1778-13.5.1778 *Prince George* (98); 13.5.1778 *Victory* (100); 27.7.1778 1st Battle of Ushant; 30.5.1782-11.4.1783 *Princess Royal* (98); 20.10.1782 Battle of Cape Spartel; 14.4.1783 *Princess Royal* (98); 8.9.1784-3.4.1786[P] *Triumph* (74); 24.9.1787 **Rear Admiral of the White**; 21.9.1790 **Rear Admiral of the Red**; 1791-9.1791 *Barfleur* (98); 1.2.1793 **Vice Admiral of the Blue**; 12.4.1794 **Vice Admiral of the White**; 4.7.1794 **Vice Admiral of the Red**; 1.6.1795 **Admiral of the Blue**.

FAULKNOR, ROBERT

Dates: 1721 Born; 9.5.1769 Died Dijon, France.

Family: Father Samuel Faulknor, RN (d.1744); Mother Fanny; Wife Elizabeth; Son Robert, RN (1763-1795); Son William Humphry, RN; Son Edward; Brother Jonathon, RN (1729-1795); Brother Samuel, RN (1719-1759).

Service: 3.12.1731 Vol-p-O *Berwick* (70); 10.6.1732 Able *Berwick* (70); 3.9.1733 Vol-p-O *Norfolk* (80); 20.10.1733 Able *Romney* (50); 7.9.1734 Vol-p-O *Leopard* (50); 19.9.1737 Able *Britannia* (100); 21.9.1737 Mid *Britannia* (100); 5.11.1737 MidO *Sheerness* (20); 4.6.1740 Mid *Sheerness* (20); 22.10.1740 Mid *Princess Louisa* (60); 4.3.1740/41-5.1741 Operations against Cartagena; 9.5.1741 Mid *Chichester* (80); 1.10.1741 Passed; **Lieutenant**; 5.10.1741 4L *Cambridge* (80); 12.5.1742 3L *Cambridge* (80); 11.2.1743/44-12.2.1743/44 Battle of Toulon; 18.8.1744(MED 14.11.1745)-19.11.1745[P] 1L *Elizabeth* (70); 4.5.1746 L. *Amazon* (22); 5.7.1747-15.4.1748 2L *Bristol* (50); 21.10.1748-13.6.1751 1L *Bristol* (50); 14.10.1755 6L *Prince* (90); 12.11.1755 5L *Prince* (90); 7.4.1756 4L *Prince* (90); 12.5.1756 4L *Royal George* (100); 6.8.1756 2L *Royal George* (100); **Commander**; 5.11.1756-10.1.1757 *Stork* (10) Sloop; **Captain**; 19.1.1757 *Marlborough* (80); 6.6.1758(JAM 6.5.1760) *Seaford* (20); 21.11.1760 *Bellona* (74); 7.4.1762-28.3.1763[P] *Kent* (74).

FAULKNOR, SAMUEL

Dates: c.1719 Born; 28.5.1759 Died.

Family: Father Samuel Faulknor, RN (d.1744); Mother Fanny; Brother Robert, RN (1721-1769); Brother Jonathon, RN (1729-1795).

Service: 19.10.1729 Vol-p-O *Grafton* (70); 29.4.1731 Able *Kingston* (60); 1.1.1731/32 Able *Berwick* (70); 17.2.1731/32 Able *Leopard* (50); 25.8.1732 Able *Advice* (54); 27.1.1733/34 Vol-p-O *Advice* (54); 16.5.1734 Capt Serv *Hound* (8) Sloop; 14.11.1735 Vol-p-O *Argyll* (50); 5.3.1737/38 Mid *Gloucester* (50); 6.3.1739/40 Passed; **Lieutenant**; 30.6.1740 3L *Severn* (50); 13.8.1742 3L *Orford* (70); 28.12.1743(JAM 12.8.1746) 4L *Cumberland* (80); 18.4.1744(JAM 12.8.1746) 3L *Cumberland* (80); 12.5.1744(JAM 12.8.1746) 2L *Cumberland* (80); 31.3.1745(JAM 12.8.1746) 1L *Cumberland* (80); **Commander**; 2.9.1745 *Vulture* (10) Sloop; **Captain**; 21.4.1746 *Amazon* (22); 22.12.1747-5.8.1748[P] *Gloucester* (50); 30.9.1748-11.9.1751[W] *Fox* (20); 26.8.1752-11.2.1754[P] *Saint Albans* (60); 16.1.1755 *Lyme* (24); 21.5.1755-28.5.1759 *Windsor* (60); 8.1757-10.1757 Louisbourg Expedition.

FAWLER, JOHN

Dates: 1777 Died.
Family:
Service: 30.5.1724 Ord. *Spy* (8) Sloop; 10.2.1725/26 Mid *Spy* (8) Sloop; 15.8.1726-13.5.1728[P] Mid *Swallow* (50); 5.8.1728 Able *Ludlow Castle* (40); 7.10.1729 Able *Looe* (42); 14.12.1730 Mid *Looe* (42); 19.5.1732 Mid *Tiger* (50); 1.8.1733 Passed; **Lieutenant**; 13.3.1733/34 4L *Revenge* (70); 4.11.1734 3L *Revenge* (70); 15.3.1734/35-17.2.1735/36[P] 3L *Newark* (80); 16.5.1738-26.11.1738[P] 3L *Prince of Orange* (70); 12.6.1739 2L *Lion* (60); 4.3.1740/41-5.1741 Operations against Cartagena; 6.10.1741[(9.7.1743)] 4L *Boyne* (80); 15.10.1741[(9.7.1743)] 3L *Boyne* (80); 6.2.1741/42[(9.7.1743)] 2L *Boyne* (80); 26.6.1742[(9.7.1743)] 1L *Boyne* (80); **Commander**; 23.8.1742[(14.6.1743)] *Deptford* (24) Storeship; **Captain**; 2.12.1745-22.1.1745/46 *Stirling Castle* (70).

FEATTUS, JAMES

Dates: c.1728 Born; 1784 Died.
Family: Wife Lydia Inglefield married 20.1.1755.
Service: 25.1.1746 Able *Mark and Rebecca* Hired Tender; 14.6.1746-11.5.1748[P] Mate *Mark and Rebecca* Hired Tender; 17.9.1752 Able *Penzance* (44); 28.9.1754 QM *Trial* (10) Sloop; 29.11.1754 Mate *Trial* (10) Sloop; 11.8.1755 Mid *Lichfield* (50); 4.5.1756 Mate *Lichfield* (50); 8.3.1757 Passed; **Lieutenant**; 23.3.1757-7.2.1760 2L *Lizard* (28); 7.2.1760 1L *Juno* (32); **Commander**; 7.7.1761-31.12.1763[P] *Crown* (18) Storeship; 18.1.1770-26.1.1773 *Speedwell* (8) Sloop; 18.5.1776 *Cormorant* (14) Sloop; 13.6.1776-14.11.1778[D] *Vulture* (14) Sloop; 14.11.1778 Dismissed.

FEILD, THOMAS

Dates: c.1736 Born; 1766 Died.
Family:
Service: 12.7.1749 Capt Serv *Trial* (10) Sloop; 2.4.1752 Capt Serv *Advice* (50); 10.5.1754 Able *Advice* (50); 7.11.1754 Mid *Advice* (50); 13.7.1756 Mid *Seaford* (20); 29.11.1756 Mid *Seaford* (20); 7.11.1757 Passed; **Lieutenant**; 27.10.1758-27.6.1759 6L *Duke* (90); 9.9.1763-21.7.1766[P] 1L *Actaeon* (28).

FENWICK, BARNABAS

Dates: c.1731 Born; 1795 Died; 6.11.1795 Will Probate.
Family: Wife Ann; Daughter Elizabeth; Daughter Penelope; Son Barnabas.
Service: 19.12.1747 Ord. *Prince Edward* (44); 29.5.1749 Able *Garland* (24); 10.3.1751/52 Mid *Garland* (24); 29.5.1753 Mid *Peggy* (8) Sloop; 1.10.1755 Passed; **Lieutenant**; 23.2.1757 L. *Firebrand* (6) Fireship; 27.6.1757 3L *Dunkirk* (60); 5.9.1757-6.10.1757 Raid on Rochefort; 5.6.1758-12.6.1758 Raid on Saint-Malo; 6.10.1758-17.3.1760 2L *Dunkirk* (60); 29.12.1758 Capture of Goree; 20.11.1759 Battle of Quiberon Bay; 12.4.1762-18.2.1764[P] L. *Success* (20).

FENWICK, BENJAMIN

Dates: 14.3.1757 Died.
Family:
Service: **Lieutenant**; 10.1.1705/6[(10.3.1706/7)]-24.4.1709[C] 2L *Bristol* (50); 9.5.1709[(6.6.1709)] L. *Sweepstakes* (42); 1.1.1711/12 2L *Reserve* (54); 29.1.1713/14-18.11.1714[P] 1L *Reserve* (54); 12.4.1717 L. *Seahorse* (20); 17.1.1717/18-9.10.1718 1L *Guernsey* (50); 23.2.1733/34-16.2.1735/36[P] 1L *Devonshire* (80); 30.8.1739 1L *Princess Amelia* (80); **Commander**;

1.3.1739/40 *Aetna* (8) Fireship; 4.3.1740/41-5.1741 Operations against Cartagena; 8.6.1741 **Captain**; 8.6.1741(24.5.1742)-16.7.1742[P] *Bristol* (54).

FERGUSON, JAMES

Dates: 1723 Born; 14.2.1793 Died; 7.3.1793 Will Probate.
Family: Illegitimate Son Walter Meldrum; Sister Margaret [Robertson]; Sister Janet [Dorf]; Sister Mary [Bowry].
Service: 19.8.1742 Able *Leopard* (50); 25.7.1743 Mid *Leopard* (50); 10.3.1747/48 Mate *Leopard* (50); 20.10.1749 Mate *Success* (20); 8.6.1753-19.12.1755 Mate *Northumberland* (68); 19.12.1755 Passed; **Lieutenant**; 15.11.1756 L. *Amazon* (22); 29.12.1756 4L *Northumberland* (68); 8.1757-10.1757 Louisbourg Expedition; 6.6.1758-27.7.1758 The Siege of Louisbourg; 22.9.1759 **Commander**; 31.3.1760(NA 9.11.1762) *Hunter* (10) Sloop; 4.4.1763 *Peggy* (8) Sloop; **Captain**; 6.6.1763-16.10.1766[P] *Romney* (50); 30.12.1775 *Brune* (32); 6.12.1776-8.12.1776 Occupation of Rhode Island; 18.9.1778(NA 7.7.1780) *Venus* (36); 14.12.1778-15.12.1778 Battle of St. Lucia; 17.4.1780 Battle of Martinique; 18.4.1780(BLI 22.3.1781)-23.7.1780 *Intrepid* (64); 15.5.1780 Action of March 15 1780; 19.5.1780 Action of March 19 1780; 23.7.1780(BLI 28.12.1782)-16.6.1781 *Terrible* (74); 29.4.1781-30.4.1781 Battle of Fort Royal; 17.8.1782-10.1.1783 *Egmont* (74); 20.10.1782 Battle of Cape Spartel; 1784-14.2.1793 Lieutenant-governor of Greenwich Hospital at Greenwich Hospital.

FERGUSON, JOHN

Dates: c.1708 Born; 13.6.1767 Died.
Family: Wife Lydia Cumber; Son John, RN (1731-1818).
Service: 10.8.1727 Able *Chatham* (50); 23.3.1727/28 Mid *Chatham* (50); 30.4.1728 Able *Chatham* (50); 12.11.1728 MidO *Portland* (50); 20.2.1728/29-6.1.1731/32[P] Mid *Dreadnought* (60); 27.12.1734 Mid *Dreadnought* (60); 21.2.1734/35 Able *Britannia* (100); 27.7.1736 Mid *Britannia* (100); 6.4.1738 Passed; **Lieutenant**; 2.10.1739 L. *Seahorse* (20); 6.6.1740 2L *Adventure* (40); 7.7.1740 2L *Lark* (40); 20.10.1741-6.4.1742 2L *Leopard* (50); 3.7.1742 L. *Lowestoffe* (20); 23.11.1744 3L *Royal Sovereign* (104); 3.1.1744/45 LCmdr *Ursula* (16) Hired Tender; 3.7.1745 Action of 1745-07-03; 29.8.1745 3L *Royal Sovereign* (104); **Commander**; 12.11.1745 *Furnace* (8) Bomb Vessel; **Captain**; 6.10.1746-5.10.1748[P] *Nightingale* (22); 3.5.1750 *Porcupine* (16) Sloop; 7.10.1755-4.1.1757 *Solebay* (24); 22.3.1757 *Prince of Orange* (60); 6.6.1758-27.7.1758 The Siege of Louisbourg; 30.9.1758(NA 2.1.1759) *Port Mahon* (24); 15.2.1759-13.5.1763[P] *Firm* (74).

FERGUSON, JOHN

Dates: c.1731 Born; 4.4.1818 Died Southampton.
Family: Father John Ferguson, RN (1708-1767); Mother Lydia Cumber.
Service: 19.3.1748/49 Able *Bristol* (50); 30.11.1749 Mid *Bristol* (50); 27.4.1752 Mid *Saint Albans* (60); 25.6.1754 Able *Northumberland* (68); 1.4.1755 NR *Vanguard* (68); 19.12.1755 Passed; **Lieutenant**; 17.9.1756 4L *Vanguard* (68); 5.4.1757 3L *America* (60); 5.9.1757-6.10.1757 Raid on Rochefort; 15.2.1759 2L *America* (60); 8.3.1759 1L *America* (60); 15.3.1759-29.1.1763[P] 1L *Fame* (74); 29.3.1761-11.6.1761 Expedition against Belle-Isle; 8.12.1770 1L *Antelope* (50); 8.1.1771-25.2.1772 1L *Panther* (60); 16.1.1775-16.4.1777[P] LCmdr *Cherokee* (6); **Commander**; 5.9.1777-27.8.1779 *Sylph* (14) Sloop; 12.10.1780 *Dragon* (74) Receiving Ship; **Captain**; 21.3.1781 *Berwick* (74); 5.8.1781 Battle of Dogger Bank; 6.3.1782-15.1.1783 *Surprise* (28); 14.2.1799 **Rear Admiral of the Blue**; 1.1.1801 **Rear Admiral of the White**; 23.4.1804 **Rear Admiral of the Red**; 9.11.1805 **Vice Admiral of the Blue**; 28.4.1808 **Vice Admiral of the White**; 31.7.1810 **Admiral of the Blue**; 4.6.1814 **Admiral of the White**.

FERGUSON, PATRICK

Dates: c.1736 Born; c.1761 Died; 1.12.1761 Will Probate.
Family:
Service: 15.9.1752 Able *Porcupine* (16) Sloop; 1.4.1756 Mid *Solebay* (24); 21.2.1757 Mid *Vanguard* (68); 31.5.1757-9.8.1758 Mid *America* (60); 5.9.1757-6.10.1757 Raid on Rochefort; 9.8.1758 Passed; **Lieutenant**; 27.10.1758 2L *Griffin* (28); 7.5.1760-29.12.1760 1L *Firm* (74).

FERRIOR, SAMUEL

Dates: 2.10.1732 Born Haverfordwest, Pembrokeshire; 10.10.1732 Baptised; 1774 Died; 27.5.1774 Will Probate.
Family: Father Rev. Benjamin Ferrier (1705-1763); Mother Martha Purser (?-1739); Sister Martha [Booth] (1731-1802); Sister Elizabeth (1735-?); Brother Benjamin (1737-?).
Service: 25.8.1747-3.6.1748[P] Able *Intrepid* (18) Hired Advice Boat; 5.4.1750 Able *Nightingale* (22); 1.1.1750/51 Cox *Nightingale* (22); 8.4.1751 Able *Nightingale* (22); 24.11.1752 Mid *Nightingale* (22); 21.4.1754 Mate *Port Mahon* (24); 5.9.1755 Passed; **Lieutenant**; 2.8.1758[(NA 20.3.1761)]-31.3.1760 L. *Hunter* (10) Sloop.

FIELD, JOHN

Dates: c.1736 Born; 5.10.1768 Died English Channel.
Family:
Service: 20.4.1750 Capt Serv *Scorpion* (14) Sloop; 13.12.1750 Capt Serv *Mermaid* (24); 21.2.1752 Able *Mermaid* (24); 19.6.1753 Able *Saltash* (14) Sloop; 29.6.1755 Mid *Vanguard* (68); 4.7.1757 Passed; **Lieutenant**; 27.10.1758 1L *Vengeance* (28); 14.5.1759-24.5.1761[P] 2L *Vengeance* (28); 20.11.1759 Battle of Quiberon Bay; 6.9.1763 3L *Kent* (74); 19.4.1766-5.10.1768[F] LCmdr *Duke William* (4) Cutter.

FIELDING, BASIL

Dates: 8.1777 Died.
Family:
Service: **Lieutenant**; 28.8.1754[(BLI 26.11.1754)]-22.5.1756[P] 3L *Advice* (50); 22.9.1757 2L *Vanguard* (68); 6.6.1758-27.7.1758 The Siege of Louisbourg; **Commander**; 19.11.1759-20.1.1761 *Grampus* (14) Sloop.

FIELDING, CHARLES

Dates: 2.7.1738 Born; 11.1.1783 Died.
Family: Father Lt-Col Hon. Charles Fielding (1717-1746); Mother Mrs Anne Bridges, née Palmer; Wife Sophia Finch married 29.2.1772; Daughter Augustus Sophia; Son Charles, RN (1780-1837); Daughter Matilda; Daughter Sophia Charlotte; Sister Elizabeth.
Service: 26.10.1756-1757 CaptP *Tartar* (32) PMW; **Lieutenant**; 19.5.1757[(JAM 1.5.1759)] 4L *Edinburgh* (64); 21.10.1757 Forrest's Action; 1.5.1759 4L *Sandwich* (90); 7.6.1759-3.4.1760 3L *Sandwich* (90); **Commander**; 14.4.1760 *Swallow* (14) Sloop; **Captain**; 27.8.1760-4.11.1760 *Flamborough* (20); 19.5.1761-22.6.1763[P] *Unicorn* (28); 21.6.1769 *Achilles* (60); 16.8.1770-27.11.1771 *Rainbow* (44); 7.5.1772-8.5.1775 *Kent* (74); 20.2.1776 *Diamond* (32); 14.11.1778[(NA 13.5.1780)] *Sultan* (74); 14.4.1779-8.3.1780 *Namur* (90); 31.12.1779 Affair of Fielding and Bylandt; 13.4.1780-9.11.1781 *Minerva* (38); 16.3.1782-11.1.1783[P] *Ganges* (74); 20.10.1782 Battle of Cape Spartel.

FIELDING, WILLIAM

Dates: 23.9.1773 Died.
Family: Father Sir John Fielding (d.1715); Mother Susan Booth (d.1715); Wife Mary Cormack; Daughter Sarah [Farrell]; Brother Charles, R.M. (d.1746).
Service: 26.8.1717 Ord. *Rye* (32); 16.2.1717/18 Ord. *Rye* (32); 20.5.1718 Vol-p-O *Guernsey* (50); 1.4.1719 Vol-p-O *Defiance* (60); 23.9.1719 Mid *Defiance* (60); 5.3.1721/22 Passed; **Lieutenant**; 3.12.1724[(26.4.1726)]-18.3.1725/26[P] 2L *Falkland* (50); 27.4.1726-7.5.1728 L. *Drake* (14) Sloop; 13.9.1728 L. *Lowestoffe* (20); 25.11.1729 2L *Portland* (50); 22.8.1732 L. *Spy* (8) Sloop; 14.8.1739 1L *Advice* (54); 17.6.1741-10.8.1745 1L *Nassau* (70); 28.2.1741/42 *Fly* (8) Sloop; **Captain**; 11.1.1742/43-18.9.1743[W] *Bridgewater* (20); 11.2.1743/44-12.2.1743/44 Battle of Toulon; 11.5.1744 *Pearl* (44); 20.2.1744/45-31.3.1747 *Saint George* (90); 20.5.1752-19.2.1756 *Fly* (8) Sloop; 28.10.1762 **Superannuated Rear Admiral.**

FIELDING, WILLIAM CARR

Dates: c.1740 Born; 23.12.1765 Died Gosport.
Family: Father Charles Fielding, R.M. (d.1746); Mother Maria Johnson; Sister Maria; Brother Charles John Johnson.
Service: 1753-1755 Merchant Service; 17.5.1755 Ord. *Romney* (44); 7.6.1756 Mid *Romney* (44); 6.7.1756 Mid *Guernsey* (50); 21.10.1756-1.4.1761 Mid *Guernsey* (50); 5.4.1757 Action of April 5 1757; 18.8.1759-19.8.1759 Battle of Lagos Bay; 1.4.1761 Passed; **Lieutenant**; 11.6.1761 L. *Cruizer* (8) Sloop; 12.11.1761-21.11.1762 4L *Bienfaisant* (64); 2.8.1763-9.9.1765 2L *Active* (28).

FITZHERBERT, THOMAS

Dates: 1727 Born; 13.9.1794 Died Stoke Damerel, Plymouth.
Family: Wife Margaret Langford (d.1793); Son Thomas; Daughter Anna Alicia [Salt].
Service: 30.4.1739-4.10.1741[SC] Purs Serv *Trial* (8) Sloop; 5.10.1741 Purs Serv *Trial Prize* (8); 30.4.1742 Purs Serv *Gloucester* (50); 1.6.1742 Purs Serv *Centurion* (60); 31.12.1746 Capt Serv *Princess Royal* (90); 2.11.1747 Mid *Captain* (70); 19.2.1749/50 Able *Sutherland* (50); 27.6.1750 Able *Gloucester* (50); 23.6.1751 Mid *Gosport* (44); 25.3.1752 Passed; **Lieutenant**; 20.2.1755 3L *York* (60); 1.6.1756 2L *York* (60); 23.1.1758-29.1.1759[P] 1L *York* (60); 6.6.1758-27.7.1758 The Siege of Louisbourg; 23.2.1759 6L *Royal George* (100); 19.6.1759 5L *Royal George* (100); 5.9.1759 4L *Royal George* (100); 17.10.1759 3L *Royal George* (100); 20.11.1759 Battle of Quiberon Bay; **Commander**; 14.3.1760 *Speedwell* (8) Sloop; 11.2.1761 *Senegal* (14) Sloop; **Captain**; 10.7.1761-14.3.1763[P] *Wager* (24); 2.4.1766-1.9.1769 *Adventure* (32); 1.9.1769[(JAM 6.9.1770)]-31.7.1770[P] *Renown* (30); 21.4.1773 *Conquestador* (60); 9.11.1773-24.2.1776[P] *Dublin* (74); 25.2.1776 *Raisonable* (64); 4.12.1779[(NA 22.12.1779)] *Royal Oak* (74); 11.5.1780 *Belliqueux* (64); 29.4.1781-30.4.1781 Battle of Fort Royal; 5.9.1781 Battle of the Chesapeake; 25.1.1782-26.1.1782 Battle of Saint Kitts; 12.4.1782 Battle of the Saintes; 19.4.1782 Battle of the Mona Passage; 19.12.1782-11.4.1783[P] *Alexander* (74); 22.4.1783-22.5.1786 *Powerful* (74); 21.9.1790 **Rear Admiral of the Blue**; 1.2.1793 **Rear Admiral of the Red**; 12.4.1794 **Vice Admiral of the Blue**; 4.7.1794 **Vice Admiral of the White**.

FLEMING, WILLIAM

Dates: c.1728 Born; 1780 Died.
Family:
Service: 9.12.1749 Able *Lichfield* (50); 15.3.1751 Mid *Lichfield* (50); 11.5.1752 Able *Lyme* (24); 28.11.1752 Able *Unicorn* (24); 14.12.1753 Mid *Unicorn* (24); 19.9.1754 Mid *Unicorn*

(24); 6.1.1755 Mid *Assistance* (50); 3.3.1755 Able *Severn* (50); 16.5.1755 Mid *Severn* (50); 5.9.1756 Mid *Dreadnought* (60); 3.10.1757 Passed; **Lieutenant**; 21.10.1757 L. *Firedrake* (8) Bomb Vessel; 29.11.1757 L. *Viper* (10) Sloop; 31.7.1758[JAM 28.11.1759]-22.4.1760[P] 3L *Augusta* (60); 24.3.1761[JAM 18.8.1763] 2L *Defiance* (60); 6.6.1762-13.8.1762 Operations against Havana; 3.3.1763[JAM 18.8.1763]-10.8.1763[P] 1L *Defiance* (60); 17.12.1776-11.4.1780 LCmdr *Admiral Spry* Hired Tender; 24.1.1777 LCmdr *Swallow* Hired Tender.

FLEMING, WILLIAM HENRY

Dates: 18.5.1771 Died.
Family: Wife Sophie Johns married 27.1.1731/32; Daughter Rebecca [Farmer].
Service: 9.7.1702 Vol-p-O *Monck* (64); 10.11.1702 Vol-p-O *Medway* (60); 8.4.1706 Mid *Milford* (36); 19.3.1706/7-20.3.1706/7 Loss of the Resolution; 14.4.1708 Passed; **Lieutenant**; 26.8.1709-25.2.1710/11 L. *Monck Prize* (16); 26.2.1710/11-23.12.1712[P] 3L *Swiftsure* (64); 4.3.1714/15-9.1.1717/18 2L *Plymouth* (60); 10.1.1717/18-3.4.1718 2L *Hampton Court* (70); 4.4.1718-5.9.1720 2L *Royal Oak* (70); 11.8.1718 Battle of Cape Passaro; 6.9.1720-9.4.1721 2L *Nassau* (70); **Captain**; 26.7.1728-12.8.1728 *Severn* (54); 19.2.1740/41 *Tiger* (50); 25.3.1741-15.7.1743 *Greenwich* (50).

FLETCHER, LOWTHER

Dates: 1758 Died.
Family:
Service: **Lieutenant**; 23.4.1748[EI 8.9.1749] 2L *Medway Prize* (30); 5.7.1748[EI 8.9.1749] 3L *Princess Mary* (60); 3.8.1748[EI 8.9.1749] 2L *Princess Mary* (60); 12.9.1748[EI 8.9.1749]-22.8.1749[P] 1L *Princess Mary* (60); 6.11.1754 4L *Captain* (64); 16.1.1755 3L *Winchester* (50); 22.10.1755[EI 15.10.1756] 2L *Winchester* (50); 8.11.1756 4L *Monmouth* (70); 9.11.1756-14.2.1757 3L *Monmouth* (70).

FLETCHER, PHILIP

Dates: c.1737 Born; 1763 Died.
Family:
Service: 1751-1755 Merchant Service; 24.4.1755 Able *Nassau* (64); 8.1757-10.1757 Louisbourg Expedition; 14.1.1758 Mid *Nassau* (64); 9.3.1758-24.5.1758 Capture of Fort Louis; 29.12.1758 Capture of Goree; 12.11.1760 Passed; **Lieutenant**; 16.1.1761-12.3.1763[P] 4L *Nassau* (64).

FOLEY, THOMAS

Dates: 2.5.1755 Died.
Family: Brother John;
Service: **Lieutenant**; 19.2.1740/41[30.3.1744]-16.8.1742[SC] 3L *Gloucester* (50); 9.2.1742/43 3L *Kinsale* (44); 7.12.1743 2L *Kinsale* (44); 7.11.1744 3L *Princess Royal* (90); 3.2.1745/46 3L *Prince George* (90); 4.6.1746 1L *Panther* (50); 15.1.1746/47 2L *Prince George* (90); 3.5.1747 1st Battle of Cape Finisterre; **Commander**; 3.5.1748 *Merlin* (10) Sloop; 23.3.1749/50 *Savage* (8) Sloop; **Captain**; 2.4.1754 *Fougueux* (64); 6.4.1754-22.4.1755 *Savage* (8) Sloop.

FOLEY, THOMAS

Dates: 8.1772 Died.
Family: Father John Foley, a landowner of Ridgeway, Narberth.
Service: **Lieutenant**; 18.6.1741[1.3.1741/42] L. *Vesuvius* (8) Fireship; 7.1741-10.1741 Operations against Santiago; 20.11.1741[1.3.1741/42] 2L *Deptford* (60); 20.4.1742-18.10.1742 4L *Princess Amelia* (80); 11.5.1745 5L *Prince George* (90); 6.2.1745/46-10.2.1745/46 2L *Princess Mary*

(60); 3.4.1746-17.6.1746 1L *Lark* (44); 25.6.1755 2L *Princess Louisa* (60); 20.5.1756 Battle of Minorca; **Commander**; 6.8.1756-28.3.1757 *Raven* (14) Sloop; 20.8.1763-14.8.1767[P] *Escort* (14) Sloop.

FORBES, LORD GEORGE (3RD EARL OF GRANARD)

Dates: 21.10.1685 Born Ireland; 24.8.1734 3rd Earl of Granard; 19.6.1765 Died Dublin.
Family: Father Arthur Forbes, 2nd Earl of Granard (c.1656–1734); Mother Mary Rawdon (1661–1724); Wife Mrs Mary Preston née Stewart (1673–1758) married 1709; Son George, 4th Earl of Granard (1710–1769); Son John, RN (1714-1796); Daughter Mary (d. 1797).
Service: **Lieutenant of Marines** (Royal Marines); 1702 Lieutenant of Marines *Saint George* (96); 15.7.1703 Vol-p-O *Britannia* (100); 14.9.1703 Vol-p-O *Torbay* (80); 16.3.1703/4 Mid *Torbay* (80); 13.8.1704 Battle of Malaga; 12.1.1704/5 Passed; **Lieutenant**; 16.1.1704/5 5L *Royal Anne* (100); 15.8.1705 2L *Triton* (42); 29.12.1705 4L *Saint George* (96); 31.1.1705/6 2L *Triton* (42); **Captain**; 16.7.1706 *Lynn* (32); 3.1.1706/7 *Leopard* (54); 5.3.1706/7 *Gosport* (42); 8.1.1707/8 Captain *Seaford* (24); 18.5.1708-21.5.1709 *Sunderland* (60); 22.7.1709-2.12.1710 *Grafton* (70); 21.8.1712-15.4.1716[P] *Greenwich* (54); 1718 Gov. of Minorca; 1719-1721 In the service of Austrian Empire; 19.3.1722/23-19.8.1727 M.P. for Queenborough; 13.4.1726-25.4.1728[P] *Canterbury* (60); 1729-1731 Gov. of Leeward Islands; 19.5.1731-23.12.1731[P] *Cornwall* (80); 1733-1734 Envoy Extraordinary to Russia; 4.5.1734 **Rear Admiral of the White**; 16.12.1734 **Rear Admiral of the Red**; 2.3.1735/36 **Vice Admiral of the Blue**; 28.5.1741-22.7.1747 M.P. for Ayr Burghs; 31.12.1742 Resigned.

FORBES, JOHN

Dates: 17.7.1714 Born Minorca; 10.3.1796 Died.
Family: Father Lord George Forbes (3rd Earl of Granard), RN (1685-1765); Mother Mary Stewart (1672–1758); Wife Lady Mary Capel (1722–1782).
Service: 31.5.1726-1727 Vol. *Burford* (70); 1729-13.1.1732/33 Mid *Lion* (60); **Lieutenant**; 16.3.1730/31[(25.5.1731)]-17.6.1731 L. *Trial* (10) Sloop; 18.6.1731-27.12.1731[P] 3L *Canterbury* (60); 13.1.1731/32-14.2.1732/33 3L *Kingston* (60); 15.2.1732/33-20.2.1733/34 4L *Edinburgh* (70); 21.2.1733/34-24.7.1734 6L *Britannia* (100); 26.7.1734-4.5.1735 5L *Britannia* (100); 5.5.1735-4.10.1736 3L *Britannia* (100); **Captain**; 3.10.1738 *Port Mahon* (20); 10.8.1739 *Severn* (50); 30.6.1740 *Tiger* (50); 6.8.1740 *Guernsey* (50); 21.9.1742[(MED 21.10.1745)]-19.8.1744 *Norfolk* (80); 11.2.1743/44-12.2.1743/44 Battle of Toulon; 15.7.1747 **Rear Admiral of the Blue**; 12.5.1748 **Rear Admiral of the White**; 12.7.1748-12.1748 CinC — The Mediterranean Sea; 1751-1766 M.P.P.I.; 4.2.1755 **Vice Admiral of the Blue**; 8.12.1756 **Vice Admiral of the White**; 13.12.1756-5.4.1757 Lord Commissioner of the Admiralty; 24.2.1757 **Vice Admiral of the Red**; 2.7.1757-20.4.1763 Lord Commissioner of the Admiralty; 31.1.1758 **Admiral of the Blue**; 1.5.1763-10.3.1796 General of Marines; 18.10.1770 **Admiral of the White**; 24.10.1781 **Admiral of the Fleet**.

FORBES, PETER

Dates: c.1730 Born.
Family:
Service: 3.3.1715-1.6.1715[P] Capt Serv *Lowestoffe* (32); 17.9.1716 Capt Serv *Dartmouth* (54); 24.1.1717 Ord. *Dartmouth* (54); 28.5.1717 Able *Dartmouth* (54); 29.7.1717 Mid *Dartmouth* (54); 29.9.1717 Mid *Marlborough* (90); 11.3.1718-21.7.1720[P] Mid *Kent* (70); 11.8.1718 Battle of Cape Passaro; 12.7.1725 Mid *Dunkirk* (50); 6.2.1726 Able *Dunkirk* (50); 1.6.1726-8.3.1727 Mid *Dunkirk* (50); 8.3.1757 Passed; **Lieutenant**; 4.4.1757 6L *Prince George* (80); 18.6.1757 5L

Prince George (80); 18.7.1757 2L *Hussar* (28); 5.5.1758 1L *Hussar* (28); 26.12.1758-25.4.1760 1L *Aeolus* (32); 20.11.1759 Battle of Quiberon Bay; 28.2.1760 Action of February 28 1760; **Commander**; 2.6.1760 *Cruizer* (8) Sloop; 30.3.1762-21.5.1763 *Nautilus* (16) Sloop.

FORD, FRANCIS

Dates: c.1737 Born; 1789 Died Bengal; 30.4.1789 Will Probate.
Family: Mistress Davinda; Illegitimate Daughter Sarah; Illegitimate Son Francis.
Service: 1752-1755 Merchant Service; 25.10.1755 Able *Woolwich* (44); 30.12.1755 Mid *Woolwich* (44); 4.10.1758 Passed; **Lieutenant**; 16.7.1759-15.8.1759 3L *Phoenix* (44); 5.9.1759-4.10.1759 4L *Barfleur* (80).

FORD, JOHN

Dates: c.1738 Born; 17.12.1738 Baptised Shropshire; 14.9.1796 Died Kensington, London; 16.9.1796 Will Probate.
Family: Father Edmund Ford; Mother Jane; Brother Edmund; Brother George; Brother Kirkland; Sister Elizabeth [Hovenden]; Sister Mary.
Service: 22.5.1753 Capt Serv *Fougueux* (64); 30.3.1754 Able *Fougueux* (64); 3.3.1755 Mid *Fougueux* (64); 6.6.1755-8.6.1755 Action of 6-8 June 1755; 11.8.1757 Able *Royal George* (100); 31.10.1757 Mid *Royal George* (100); 9.2.1758 Mid *Namur* (90); 6.6.1758-27.7.1758 The Siege of Louisbourg; 18.8.1759-19.8.1759 Battle of Lagos Bay; 3.10.1759 Passed; **Lieutenant**; 7.4.1761-1.7.1766 L. *Swallow* (14) Sloop; 12.10.1770 2L *Venus* (36); 21.1.1771-21.4.1772[P] 1L *Venus* (36); 6.6.1772-16.7.1772 1L *Winchelsea* (32); **Commander**; 28.10.1772 *Hazard* (8) Sloop; **Captain**; 25.6.1773 *Venus* (36); 26.6.1773-24.11.1775 *Hazard* (8) Sloop; 13.3.1776-10.7.1779 *Unicorn* (20); 27.9.1778 Capture of the Raleigh; 10.7.1779-19.10.1780 *Brilliant* (28); 23.11.1780 *Nymphe* (36); 5.9.1781 Battle of the Chesapeake; 12.4.1782 Battle of the Saintes; 25.12.1782[NA 13.11.1783]-27.6.1783[P] *Polyphemus* (64); 1.5.1789 *Carnatic* (74); 28.8.1791-30.8.1792[P] *Carnatic* (74); 10.9.1792 Commodore *Europa* (50); 5.10.1792-1795 CinC — Jamaica; 19.9.1793 Capture of Jeremie; **Rear Admiral of the Blue**; 12.4.1794-14.9.1795[P] *Europa* (50); 4.6.1794 **Rear Admiral of the White**; 1.6.1795 **Vice Admiral of the Blue**.

FORD, THOMAS

Dates: c.1720 Born; 12.9.1757 Died; 22.9.1757 Will Probate.
Family: Wife Elizabeth.
Service: 9.11.1739 Able *Solebay* (20); 26.2.1741/42 Mid *Bideford* (20); 29.9.1742 Mid *Royal Sovereign* (104); 9.5.1744 Gnr *Exeter* (58); 1.7.1745-13.12.1747[P] Mid *Devonshire* (80); 3.5.1747 1st Battle of Cape Finisterre; 4.2.1747/48 Passed; **Lieutenant**; 5.4.1757-12.9.1757[†] 2L *Southampton* (32).

FORDYCE, ALEXANDER

Dates: 1783 Died.
Family:
Service: **Lieutenant**; 30.3.1761 5L *Foudroyant* (80); 28.9.1761-21.9.1763[P] 4L *Foudroyant* (80); 7.1.1762-10.2.1762 Operations against Martinique; 13.4.1763-10.11.1765 L. *Aldborough* (20); 6.11.1777-5.8.1778 1L *Shrewsbury* (74); 27.7.1778 1st Battle of Ushant.

FORFORD, WILLIAM

Dates: 1772 Died.
Family:
Service: **Lieutenant**; 29.1.1747/48(JAM 7.4.1749) 3L *Milford* (44); 25.12.1748(JAM 7.4.1749)-9.5.1749[P] 2L *Canterbury* (60); 28.10.1755 L. *Badger* (10) Sloop; 9.12.1755 3L *Anson* (60); 3.4.1757(BLI 15.1.1759) 1L *Bristol* (50); 5.7.1758(BLI 15.1.1759)-27.10.1758 2L *Trident* (64); 16.2.1759-26.2.1759 1L *York* (60).

FORREST, ARTHUR

Dates: c.1716 Born; 26.5.1770 Died Jamaica; 9.8.1770 Will Probate.
Family: Wife Frederica Marina Cecilia Lynch (d.1802); Daughter Bridget [Byng] (d.1823).
Service: 1740-1741 Merchant Service; **Commander**; 25.5.1741-26.2.1741/42[P] *Alderney* (8) Bomb Vessel; 7.1741-10.1741 Operations against Santiago; 8.4.1743 *Hawk* (8) Sloop; **Captain**; 9.3.1744/45-23.6.1748[P] *Wager* (20); 9.5.1755 *Rye* (20); 13.4.1757(NA 26.6.1760) *Augusta* (60); 21.10.1757 Forrest's Action; 8.4.1760-6.12.1763[P] *Centaur* (74); 6.6.1762-13.8.1762 Operations against Havana; 21.2.1769-26.5.1770 Commodore *Dunkirk* (60); 16.5.1769-26.5.1770 CinC — Jamaica.

FORREST, DIGORY

Dates: c.1733 Born; 20.4.1733 Baptised Plymouth; 12.4.1766 Died; 24.4.1767 Will Probate.
Family: Father Austin Forrest; Mother Honour; Wife Ann.
Service: 30.5.1746-1.9.1749[P] Capt Serv *Pearl* (44); 29.10.1753 Mid *Saint Albans* (60); 28.9.1754 Able *Augusta* (60); 5.6.1755 Mate *Monmouth* (70); 13.2.1757-10.4.1758 Mid *Greyhound* (20); 10.4.1758 Passed; **Lieutenant**; 27.9.1759-23.4.1760 L. *Royal Exchange* (22) Hired Armed Ship; 23.4.1760-1.10.1760 1L *Sutherland* (50); 27.4.1761-13.12.1762[P] 4L *Trident* (64).

FORRESTER, LORD WILLIAM

Dates: c.1736 Born; 26.6.1748 7th Lord Forrester of Corstorphine; 11.1763 Died.
Family: Father John Forrester, RN (d.1737); Mother Elizabeth Tyrrel; Wife Hannah (1741-1825).
Service: 4.4.1750 Able *Seahorse* (24); 8.2.1753 Mid *Seahorse* (24); 8.6.1754 Mid *Crown* (44); 24.10.1755 Mid *Enterprise* (44); 19.2.1756 Mid *Monarch* (74); **Lieutenant**; 2.4.1756-12.5.1757 4L *Cambridge* (80); 3.5.1756 Passed.

FORSTER, JOHN

Dates: c.1730 Born; 1784 Died.
Family:
Service: 5.7.1755 Able *Culloden* (74); 21.10.1755 Able *Isis* (50); 21.8.1756 Mid *Isis* (50); 3.7.1759 Bombardment of Le Havre; 5.3.1760 Passed; **Lieutenant**; 30.10.1761-21.12.1762[P] LCmdr *Princess Caroline* (80) Hospital Ship; 18.4.1771-22.4.1773 5L *Lennox* (74).

FORSTER, WILLIAM

Dates: c.1724 Born; 13.8.1780 Died.
Family:
Service: 1.4.1738 Able *Torrington* (40); 17.8.1742 Mid *Hampshire* (50); 18.4.1745 Passed; **Lieutenant**; 26.4.1745 L. *Scipio* (8) Fireship; 5.11.1745-16.7.1749[P] 2L *Chesterfield* (44); 31.7.1755 2L *Hampshire* (50); 11.12.1755 1L *Hampshire* (50); 25.4.1758 2L *Duke* (90); 5.6.1758-12.6.1758 Raid on Saint-Malo; 20.11.1759 Battle of Quiberon Bay; **Commander**; 24.5.1762

Senegal (14) Sloop; 25.3.1763-26.3.1764 *Tamar* (16) Sloop; 9.6.1767 *Viper* (10) Sloop; **Captain**; 26.5.1768 *Flamborough* (20); 9.12.1779-1.11.1781 *Diamond* (32).

FORTESCUE, FAITHFUL ADRIAN

Dates: 1732 Born; 1773 Died; 1.1.1774 Will Probate.
Family: Wife Catherine Stirling (1736-?) married 21.7.1763; Son Faithful Adrian (1767-1796); Daughter Catherine (1770-?); Son Patrick Sterling (1771-?).
Service: 1755-1756 Merchant Service; 12.11.1756 Able *Vanguard* (68); 10.11.1757 Able *America* (60); 10.1.1758 Mid *Prince Edward* (44); 29.12.1758 Capture of Goree; 6.5.1761 Passed; **Lieutenant**; 24.5.1762-22.12.1762[P] 4L *Captain* (64); 1766 CaptM *Martha Bray* Mer; 30.11.1770 4L *Raisonable* (64); 7.9.1771-23.4.1774 L. *Glasgow* (20).

FORTESCUE, JOHN

Dates: c.1722 Born; 1808 Died; 17.10.1808 Will Probate.
Family: Father John Fortescue; Mother Theodora Braune; Son John.
Service: 11.5.1738 Able *Centurion* (60); 19.9.1739 Mid *Centurion* (60); 13.2.1740 Able *Centurion* (60); 6.5.1740 Mid *Centurion* (60); 5.10.1743-24.11.1744 Sailmaker's Mate *Centurion* (60); 23.11.1744 L. *Speedwell* (10) Sloop; 24.11.1744 Passed; 24.11.1744 **Lieutenant**; 12.7.1745 3L *Kinsale* (44); 11.4.1746[NA 3.10.1746]-1.9.1746[P] 2L *Dorsetshire* (80); 6.1.1746/47[BLI 13.9.1748]-20.6.1748 4L *Captain* (70); 16.5.1750-5.8.1752 3L *Tiger* (60); 5.6.1755 1L *Roebuck* (44); **Commander**; 30.6.1756 *Katherine* (8) Yacht; 24.8.1756-14.12.1757 *Granado* (8) Bomb Vessel; **Captain**; 4.9.1759-16.12.1760[P] *Barfleur* (80).

FORTESCUE, WILLIAM

Dates: 21.10.1775 Died.
Family:
Service: **Lieutenant**; 5.11.1740[15.1.1744/45] L. *Salamander* (6) Bomb Vessel; 30.11.1740[15.1.1743/44] 3L *Oxford* (50); 29.4.1741[15.1.1743/44]-14.3.1744/45[P] 2L *Oxford* (50); 11.2.1743/44-12.2.1743/44 Battle of Toulon; **Commander**; 8.2.1745/46 *Aetna* (8) Fireship; 17.4.1746-14.1.1746/47 *Swift* (8) Sloop; **Captain**; 4.1.1757-4.5.1761 *Prince Edward* (44); 29.12.1758 Capture of Goree; 4.5.1761 *Hero* (74); 22.6.1762-5.12.1763 *Achilles* (60).

FORTH, JOHN

Dates: c.1731 Born; 22.3.1790 Died.
Family:
Service: 15.4.1742-17.12.1742[P] Ord. *Royal Escape* Smack; 30.9.1756 Ord. *Royal Anne* (100); 14.11.1756 Mate *York* (60); 6.6.1758-27.7.1758 The Siege of Louisbourg; 16.8.1758 Able *Namur* (90); 14.10.1758 Mid *Namur* (90); 14.2.1759 Passed; **Lieutenant**; 5.8.1759[MED 12.2.1761]-4.8.1760 2L *Valeur* (28); 14.7.1763-16.12.1766[P] 1L *Dreadnought* (60); 2.1765-7.1765 ActM&C *Druid* (10) Sloop; 2.9.1766 HEIC Service.

FORTYE, ANTHONY

Dates: c.1722 Born; 16.3.1803 Died Greenwich Hospital; 23.3.1803 Buried Greenwich.
Family:
Service: 14.8.1737 Ord. *Alderney* (8) Bomb Vessel; 17.8.1738 Able *Deal Castle* (20); 21.9.1738 Adm Serv *Norfolk* (80); 27.12.1738 Capt Serv *Princess Louisa* (60); 12.7.1739 Able *Romney* (50); 29.4.1740 Mid *Romney* (50); 21.4.1743-5.8.1743[P] Able *Garland* (20); 28.9.1743-10.10.1743 NR *Northumberland* (64); 17.11.1743 Passed; **Lieutenant**; 6.6.1744 L. *Lightning* (8) Bomb Vessel;

29.1.1744/45[MED 4.12.1747] 3L *Nonsuch* (50); 24.4.1747[MED 4.12.1747]-11.12.1747[P] 4L *Norfolk* (80); 19.9.1755 L. *Solebay* (24); 4.11.1755 4L *Royal Sovereign* (104); 27.11.1756 3L *Royal Sovereign* (104); 13.12.1756-13.3.1759[P] 2L *Royal Sovereign* (104).

FOSS, JOSEPH
Dates: c.1707 Born; 1776 Died.
Family: Father Samuel Foss; Sister Hannah [Sparke].
Service: 17.3.1737/38 Able *Windsor* (60); 25.11.1739 Mid *Ludlow Castle* (40); 25.9.1741 Able *Defiance* (60); 10.6.1742-6.3.1742/43[P] Mid *Defiance* (60); 2.3.1743/44 Able *Boyne* (80); 1.4.1744 Mid *Shrewsbury* (80); 23.6.1744 Mid *Chichester* (80); 5.12.1745 Passed; **Lieutenant**; 7.2.1745/46 L. *Mortar* (8) Bomb Vessel; 20.9.1746-25.9.1746 Lorient Operations; 23.11.1747-18.8.1748[P] 2L *Windsor* (60); 14.10.1755 5L *Duke* (90); 14.7.1756 4L *Duke* (90); 26.5.1757-5.5.1758 3L *Duke* (90).

FOSTER, WILLIAM
Dates: 1723 Born; 10.1.1803 Died.
Family:
Service: 28.2.1740/41 QGnr *Scarborough* (20); 10.8.1741 Able *Victory* (100); 22.10.1742 Cox *Squirrel* (20); 14.4.1744 Cox *Dolphin* (20); 2.7.1744 Mid *Chester* (54); 14.10.1745 Mid *Royal Sovereign* (104); 3.7.1746 Passed; 26.8.1746 **Lieutenant**.

FOTHERINGHAM, PATRICK
Dates: c.1739 Born; 1784 Died.
Family:
Service: 1754-1757 Merchant Service; 24.4.1757 Gnr Serv *Tartar* (28); 3.4.1758-7.5.1760 Mid *Chatham* (50); 3.7.1759 Bombardment of Le Havre; 20.11.1759 Battle of Quiberon Bay; 7.5.1760 Passed; **Lieutenant**; 13.12.1760 L. *Happy* (8) Sloop; 23.4.1762-18.4.1763 3L *Rainbow* (44); 2.5.1763-3.6.1763 1L *Juno* (32); 7.6.1763 1L *Princess Louisa* (60); **Commander**; 1.4.1765[BLI 14.4.1766]-1.4.1767[P] *Martin* (14) Sloop; 26.1.1771-17.3.1773[P] *Merlin* (18) Frigate; **Captain**; 9.10.1773-8.7.1774[P] *Garland* (24); 21.10.1775-7.6.1777 *Fox* (28); 7.6.1777 Action of 7th June 1777; 24.7.1778 *Resource* (28); 27.2.1781[JAM 29.12.1781]-20.5.1781 *Ruby* (64).

FOULKES, PETER
Dates: c.1725 Born; 1782 Died; 11.7.1782 Will Probate.
Family: Sister Elizabeth; Sister Frances; Sister Jane;
Service: 20.5.1739 Able *Salisbury* (50); 22.5.1741 Mid *Prince of Orange* (70); 13.6.1741 Mid *Chichester* (80); 13.1.1741/42-15.2.1744/45 Mid *Princess Caroline* (80); 11.2.1743/44-12.2.1743/44 Battle of Toulon; 18.2.1744/45 Passed; **Lieutenant**; 29.3.1745[MED 14.5.1748]-12.2.1745/46 4L *Boyne* (80); 21.8.1747[MED 3.1.1748/49]-19.3.1747/48 3L *Princess* (70); 9.4.1748[MED 3.1.1748/49]-29.12.1748[P] L. *Phoenix* (24); 11.3.1748/49-4.2.1750/51[P] L. *Fly* (8) Sloop; 24.1.1750/51 L. *Vulture* (14) Sloop; 2.1.1751/52-16.4.1756 L. *Phoenix* (24); 24.12.1756 1L *Invincible* (74); 22.4.1757-12.3.1758 5L *Prince* (90); 18.10.1758 2L *Saint George* (90); 23.10.1758 1L *Saint George* (90); 16.1.1759-19.1.1759 Attack on Martinique; 20.1.1759-1.5.1759 Capture of Guadeloupe; 27.11.1759-6.3.1760[P] 1L *Monmouth* (70); 22.5.1760-15.12.1762[P] 1L *Dragon* (74); 29.3.1761-11.6.1761 Expedition against Belle-Isle; 7.1.1762-10.2.1762 Operations against Martinique; 24.2.1762-25.2.1762 Capture of Saint Lucia; 6.6.1762-13.8.1762 Operations against Havana; 6.10.1763-24.10.1766 1L *Hero* (74); 10.11.1769 1L *Belleisle* (64); 29.3.1770-

6.5.1771[P] 2L *Belleisle* (64); 27.6.1776 1L *Albion* (74); 4.11.1776 1L *Queen* (90); **Commander**; 15.12.1777-1.2.1780 *Satisfaction* (20) Hired Armed Ship.

FOWKE, THORPE

Dates: 14.3.1784 Died.
Family: Wife Margaret Simons married 2.1751.
Service: 13.9.1718 Vol-p-O *Dover* (40); 24.3.1721 MidO *Dover* (40); 13.3.1722 Mid *Leopard* (50); 29.10.1724-16.3.1725 Mid *Bedford* (70); 16.3.1724/25 Passed; **Lieutenant**; 20.9.1730(3.1.1731/32)-5.5.1732 L. *Dursley Galley* (20); 22.8.1732-18.6.1735 L. *Salamander* (6) Bomb Vessel; 19.6.1735-16.2.1735/36[P] 2L *Northumberland* (70); 16.5.1738-2.12.1738[P] 3L *Princess Amelia* (80); 12.6.1739-10.9.1739 3L *Princess Caroline* (80); 11.9.1739-20.4.1740 2L *Princess Caroline* (80); 21.4.1740-26.9.1740 1L *Princess Caroline* (80); 27.9.1740 1L *Lennox* (70); 16.1.1740/41 1L *Saint George* (90); **Captain**; 24.5.1742 *Gibraltar* (20); 4.10.1742(12.10.1744) *Seahorse* (20); 19.2.1743/44(27.8.1744)-15.9.1744[P] *Kent* (70); 7.11.1744-10.12.1744 *Torrington* (44); 2.11.1745 *Sapphire* (44); 26.3.1746 *Superb* (60); 1.8.1748(MED 18.10.1748)-22.11.1748[P] *Princess* (70); 10.7.1755-7.2.1757 *Tilbury* (58); 15.2.1757-17.12.1759[P] *Bedford* (64); 8.1757-10.1757 Louisbourg Expedition; 6.6.1758-27.7.1758 The Siege of Louisbourg; 30.6.1760 **Superannuated Rear Admiral.**

FOWLER, ANDREW

Dates: c.1721 Born; 1770 Died.
Family:
Service: 27.11.1751 Able *Russell* (80); 14.5.1755 Mid *Russell* (80); 20.10.1755 Mid *Diamond* (40); 1.8.1759 Passed; **Lieutenant**; 15.8.1759-11.3.1761 3L *Phoenix* (44).

FOWLER, RICHARD

Dates: c.1740 Born; 1797 Died; 5.9.1797 Will Probate.
Family: Wife Ann.
Service: 27.3.1756 Capt Serv *Hampton Court* (64); 12.8.1756 Capt Serv *Prince George* (80); 25.9.1756 Capt Serv *Buckingham* (68); 21.1.1757 Ord. *Buckingham* (68); 23.8.1757 Ord. *Princess Amelia* (80); 22.9.1757 Capt Serv *Intrepid* (60); 7.7.1758 Land. *Intrepid* (60); 22.9.1758 Mid *Intrepid* (60); 18.8.1759-19.8.1759 Battle of Lagos Bay; 20.11.1759 Battle of Quiberon Bay; 16.2.1761 Mid *Prince Frederick* (64); 29.3.1761-11.6.1761 Expedition against Belle-Isle; 7.7.1762 Passed; **Lieutenant**; 29.9.1762-21.4.1763[P] L. *Hound* (14) Sloop; 9.2.1769 L. *Merlin* (18) Frigate; 21.3.1769 3L *Dragon* (74); 11.10.1769 2L *Dragon* (74); 28.3.1770 2L *Centaur* (74); 21.9.1770-4.3.1773 4L *Centaur* (74); 16.12.1775-22.8.1776 LCmdr *Union* Hired Unknown.

FOX, THOMAS

Dates: 2.1763 Died; 21.2.1763 Will Probate.
Family: Wife Elizabeth.
Service: 26.3.1713 Able *Ormonde* (54); 25.7.1715 QGnr *Fox* (24); 25.6.1716 Cox *Fox* (24); 8.3.1717 Mid *Fox* (24); 26.7.1717 Mid *Speedwell* (42); 29.3.1719 Able *Dursley Galley* (20); 21.4.1719 Mid *Dursley Galley* (20); 27.7.1720-8.3.1721 Mate *Dursley Galley* (20); 8.3.1720/21 Passed; **Lieutenant**; 4.6.1728(13.8.1728)-22.8.1728[P] 4L *Bredah* (70); 9.2.1728/29 3L *Assistance* (50); 8.5.1731 4L *Cornwall* (80); 19.5.1731-1.1.1731/32[P] 6L *Namur* (90); 14.6.1732 5L *Namur* (90); 28.6.1732 4L *Namur* (90); 9.5.1733-23.2.1733/34 2L *Namur* (90); **Commander**; 30.12.1734 *Griffin* (8); 18.4.1735 *Drake* (8) Sloop; **Captain**; 6.8.1737(3.1.1737/38)-23.9.1738[P] *Dunkirk* (60); 7.8.1739 *Newcastle* (50); 6.3.1743/44(20.7.1745)-11.4.1745 *Chichester* (80); 14.2.1746/47-

25.12.1747 *Kent* (64); 3.5.1747 1st Battle of Cape Finisterre; 14.10.1747 2nd Battle of Cape Finisterre; 1.7.1749 **Superannuated Rear Admiral.**

FOX, WILLIAM

Dates: c.1734 Born; 1810 Died; 10.1.1811 Will Probate.
Family:
Service: 1751-1755 Merchant Service; 3.9.1755 Mid *Falmouth* (50); 13.6.1758 Mate *Falmouth* (50); 4.4.1759 Passed; **Lieutenant**; 22.8.1759 4L *Valiant* (74); 5.1.1760-4.2.1763[P] 3L *Torbay* (74); 29.3.1761-11.6.1761 Expedition against Belle-Isle; 30.5.1776 1L *Ramillies* (74); 27.7.1778 1st Battle of Ushant; 13.5.1779 1L *Prince George* (98); 4.12.1779 2L *Prince George* (98); 16.1.1780 Battle of Cape St. Vincent; 15.2.1780[(BLI 3.5.1780)]-19.4.1780 *Monarca* (68); 23.5.1780-31.12.1780 *Prince George* (98); 15.12.1780 **Captain**; 10.7.1781-16.8.1781[W] *Greyhound* (28); 11.1.1782 *Vestal* (28); 25.4.1783[(NA 15.8.1783)]-30.7.1783[P] *Jason* (32); 21.2.1799 **Superannuated Rear Admiral.**

FRAINE, JOSEPH

Dates: 3.1802 Died; 25.3.1802 Buried Walcot St Swithin, Somerset; 1.4.1802 Will Probate.
Family: Wife Catherine.
Service: 28.2.1742/43 Able *Lichfield* (50); 22.9.1743-16.2.1744/45[W] Mid *Weymouth* (60); 19.11.1745 Passed; **Lieutenant**; 2.12.1745[(MED 21.10.1746)] L. *Phoenix* (24); 22.8.1746[(MED 25.11.1746)] L. *Princess Royal* (24) Storeship; 13.3.1746/47-12.9.1748[P] 2L *Prince Edward* (44); 13.3.1752-2.9.1755 Mid *Stirling Çastle* (64); **Commander**; 13.1.1758-2.3.1759 *Speedwell* (8) Sloop; 5.6.1758-12.6.1758 Raid on Saint-Malo; **Captain**; 11.12.1759-2.6.1763[P] *Surprise* (24).

FRANCIS, THOMAS

Dates: c.1718 Born; 21.10.1762 Died; 21.1.1763 Will Probate.
Family: Wife Molly; Daughter Molly (1753-?).
Service: 28.5.1740 Able *Rose* (20); 27.11.1740 QGnr *Weymouth* (60); 7.1.1740/41 Action of January 7 1741; 4.3.1740/41-5.1741 Operations against Cartagena; 4.2.1741/42 Mid *Prince Frederick* Packet; 8.2.1742/43 Mid *Lark Hulk*; 22.6.1743 Able *Success* (24) Hulk; 29.7.1744 Mid *Pearl* (44); 11.7.1745 Passed; **Lieutenant**; 27.8.1745 3L *Pearl* (44); 2.4.1746-9.4.1746 2L *Pearl* (44); 18.12.1747-6.7.1748[P] 2L *Ranger* (28); 16.1.1753-24.6.1755[W] 1L *Mars* (64); 3.2.1756 LCmdr *Barrington* Tender; 11.4.1757 LCmdr *Devonshire* Hired Tender; **Commander**; 1.11.1757-5.6.1758[P] *Macclesfield* (16) Hired Armed Ship; **Captain**; 12.11.1759-21.10.1762[†] *Greyhound* (20); 7.1.1762-10.2.1762 Operations against Martinique.

FRANKLAND, ROBERT

Dates: c.1725 Born; 25.12.1757 Died Bombay; 26.1.1759 Will Probate.
Family: Father Henry Frankland (1690–1738); Brother Charles, 4th Bt.; Brother Sir Thomas (5th Baronet), RN (1718-1781).
Service: 27.4.1739 Able *Romney* (50); 7.3.1740/41 Mid *Nassau* (70); 22.9.1742-4.3.1742/43[P] Mid *Winchester* (50); 15.3.1742/43 Able *Torrington* (44); 25.3.1743 Able *Sandwich* (90); 21.10.1743 Mid *Jersey* (60); 16.5.1744 Mid *Prince Frederick* (70); 14.3.1744/45 Mid *Saint George* (90); 9.5.1745 Passed; **Lieutenant**; 18.5.1745 3L *Poole* (44); 15.1.1745/46-19.1.1745/46 2L *Windsor* (60); 18.2.1746/47 4L *Prince Frederick* (70); 3.5.1747 1st Battle of Cape Finisterre; 12.1.1747/48 4L *Invincible* (74); 3.3.1748/49-6.4.1751 1L *Rainbow* (44); **Commander**; 7.4.1756 *Macclesfield* (16) Hired Armed Ship; **Captain**; 15.11.1756-25.12.1757[†] *Yarmouth* (64).

FRANKLAND, SIR THOMAS (5TH BARONET)

Dates: 26.6.1718 Born India; 1768 5th Baronet; 21.11.1781 Died Bath.
Family: Father Henry Frankland (d. 1738); Mother Mary Cross (d. 1783); Wife Sarah Rhett (1724-1808); Son Sir Thomas Frankland, 6th Baronet (1750–1831); Son Roger Frankland (d. 1826); Daughter Mary Frankland; Daughter Anne Frankland (d. 1842); Daughter Dinah Frankland (Mrs. William Bowles); Daughter Catharine Frankland (Mrs. Thomas Whinyates); Daughter Charlotte Frankland; Daughter Grace Frankland (d. 1801); Son William Frankland (d. 1816); Brother Charles, 4th Bt.; Brother Robert, RN (1725-1757).
Service: 11.5.1731 Vol. *York* (60); 1732 Mid *Scarborough* (20); 1737 Mid *Oxford* (50); 3.11.1737 Passed; **Lieutenant**; 23.2.1737/38 3L *Chatham* (50); 24.2.1737/38[(13.6.1739)] 2L *Chatham* (50); 4.3.1739/40 2L *Cumberland* (80); 15.7.1740-14.1.1745/46 *Rose* (20) Ship; 14.8.1740 **Captain**; 22.2.1745/46-8.9.1748[P] *Dragon* (60); 12.5.1747-12.9.1780 M.P. for Thirsk; 5.1755 **Rear Admiral of the Blue**; 24.7.1755 *Newark* (80); 31.7.1755-10.1757 CinC — Barbados & the Leeward Islands; 31.7.1755-10.1757 *Winchester* (50); 4.6.1756 **Rear Admiral of the White**; 24.2.1757 **Rear Admiral of the Red**; 14.2.1759 **Vice Admiral of the White**; 21.10.1762 **Vice Admiral of the Red**; 18.10.1770 **Admiral of the Blue**; 31.3.1775 **Admiral of the White**; 3.4.1784-21.11.1784 M.P. for Thirsk.

FRANKS, JACOB

Dates: c.1731 Born; c.1761 Died; 13.6.1761 Will Probate.
Family: Sister Mary [Blatter].
Service: 27.3.1745 Capt Serv *Princess Louisa* (60); 3.5.1747 1st Battle of Cape Finisterre; 23.9.1747 Ord. *Princess Louisa* (60); 14.10.1747 2nd Battle of Cape Finisterre; 8.2.1747/48 Able *Romney* (44); 9.1.1748/49 Mid *Romney* (44); 12.2.1748/49 Mid *Seahorse* (24); 6.6.1753 Passed; **Lieutenant**; 19.2.1756-24.9.1757 L. *Triton* (20).

FRASER, JOHN

Dates: c.1711 Born; 1779 Died; 18.9.1779 Will Probate.
Family: Wife Sarah.
Service: 12.4.1726 Vol-p-O *Grafton* (70); 13.4.1728 MidO *Grafton* (70); 17.8.1728 MidO *Rose* (20); 5.12.1728-30.6.1730[P] MidO *Dover* (40); 3.6.1733 Mid *Grafton* (70); 14.1.1733/34 Able *Kingston* (60); 18.7.1734 Able *Experiment* (20); 28.12.1734 Able *Flamborough* (20); 23.5.1735 Able *Captain* (70); 7.10.1736-4.5.1737[P] Mid *Captain* (70); 13.2.1738/39 Mid *Greenwich* (50); 9.4.1740 Passed; **Lieutenant**; 3.8.1748[(EI 17.8.1749)] 3L *Princess Mary* (60); 12.9.1748[(EI 17.8.1749)]-22.8.1749[P] 2L *Princess Mary* (60); 13.5.1755-16.1.1763[P] LCmdr *Rupert* (60) Hospital Ship; 10.5.1766-3.3.1767[P] 1L *Burford* (68).

FRASER, THOMAS

Dates: c.1718 Born; 1775 Died; 22.7.1775 Will Probate.
Family: Wife Sophia Shepherd; Daughter Margaret; Daughter Elizabeth.
Service: 25.2.1734/35 Able *Dreadnought* (60); 20.8.1735 Able *Kinsale* (40); 15.8.1737 Mid *Kinsale* (40); 30.10.1739 Able *Falmouth* (50); 5.3.1740/41 Passed; **Lieutenant**; 6.3.1740/41-29.6.1741 4L *Bedford* (70); 18.9.1744[(MED 8.12.1746)] 2L *Burford* (70); 17.12.1745[(MED 24.11.1746)] 4L *Cambridge* (80); 11.1.1745/46[(MED 24.11.1746)]-21.11.1746[P] 3L *Cambridge* (80); 26.4.1755 L. *Swan* (14) Sloop; 20.5.1755-16.4.1756 1L *Trident* (64); 9.11.1756 1L *Sunderland* (60); 8.1757-10.1757 Louisbourg Expedition; 19.1.1758 1L *Sunderland* (60); 3.3.1759[(EI 12.12.1760)] 5L *Yarmouth* (64); 10.9.1759 Battle of Pondicherry; 11.9.1759[(EI 12.12.1760)] 4L *Yarmouth* (64); 17.3.1760[(EI 12.12.1760)]-

19.12.1760[P] 2L *Yarmouth* (64); 1.2.1762 2L *Namur* (90); **Commander**; 29.6.1762[(EI 4.7.1763)] *Lurcher* (6) Cutter; 2.7.1762[(EI 4.7.1763)]-6.1763[P] *Granado* (8) Bomb Vessel.

FRENCH, GEORGE

Dates: c.1734 Born.
Family:
Service: 29.3.1750 Capt Serv *Salisbury* (50); 23.8.1751 Ord. *Salisbury* (50); 13.9.1753 Able *Jersey* (60); 2.10.1753 Able *Gloucester* (50); 8.12.1753 Mid *Gloucester* (50); 18.10.1755 Mid *Royal Sovereign* (104); 8.4.1756 Passed; **Lieutenant**; 9.11.1756 L. *Fly* (8) Sloop; 17.6.1757 4L *Prince Frederick* (64); 17.1.1758-30.9.1758 3L *Prince Frederick* (64); 6.6.1758-27.7.1758 The Siege of Louisbourg; 10.1.1761 2L *Prince Frederick* (64); 29.3.1761-11.6.1761 Expedition against Belle-Isle; 25.8.1762-12.3.1763[P] 1L *Prince Frederick* (64).

FRENCH, WILDY

Dates: c.1720 Born; c.1791 Died; 17.10.1791 Will Probate.
Family: Wife Mary Hewson married 13.12.1753.
Service: 26.1.1734/35 Mid *Nottingham* (60); 17.1.1735/36-31.7.1737[P] Able *Nottingham* (60); 4.8.1738 Able *Dragon* (60); 18.3.1738/39 Mid *Dragon* (60); 24.7.1741 Action of 1741-07-24; 23.3.1742/43 Mate *Dragon* (60); 16.11.1743 Mate *Plymouth* (60); 9.4.1744 Passed; **Lieutenant**; 18.4.1744 L. *Dolphin* (20); 26.2.1744/45[(EI 29.8.1749)]-23.8.1749[P] 1L *Medway Prize* (30); 25.6.1746 1st Battle of Negapatam.

FRENO, ZACHARIAH

Dates: c.1767 Died; 6.1767 Will Probate.
Family:
Service: **Lieutenant**; 27.3.1748[(EI 3.5.1750)] 3L *Preston* (50); 3.8.1748[(EI 3.5.1750)] 3L *Harwich* (50); 14.8.1748[(EI 3.5.1750)] 2L *Harwich* (50); 25.5.1749[(EI 3.5.1750)]-16.5.1750[P] 1L *Harwich* (50); 9.10.1755 LCmdr *Royal Oak* (70).

FRIEND, BRAVIL

Dates: c.1739 Born; 1.2.1739 Baptised Melcombe Regis, Dorset; 9.1792 Died Melcombe Regis, Dorset; 14.9.1792 Buried Melcombe Regis, Dorset; 17.4.1793 Will Probate.
Family: Father John Friend; Mother Elizabeth; Wife Mary Elizabeth Wood married 30.7.1761; Daughter Susannah Edwards (1778-?); Son Bravel (1776-?).
Service: 18.12.1756 Able *Granado* (8) Bomb Vessel; 25.1.1757 Mid *Granado* (8) Bomb Vessel; 15.7.1757 Mid *Swiftsure* (68); 24.9.1757 Mid *Torbay* (74); 31.3.1758 Mate *Aldborough* (20); 30.7.1759 Mid *Phoenix* (20); 6.2.1760 Passed; 19.4.1760 L. *Salamander* (8) Fireship; 21.4.1760 **Lieutenant**; 10.6.1762 3L *Prince Edward* (44); 4.12.1762-24.12.1762 2L *Chester* (50); 29.3.1763-9.7.1766 L. *Swift* (14) Sloop; 3.2.1768 2L *San Antonio* (64); 13.10.1768-1.7.1771[P] LCmdr *Lion* (4) Cutter; 1.4.1772-2.5.1775 LCmdr *Meredith* (10) Cutter.

FRODSHAM, JOHN

Dates: c.1736 Born; 28.5.1791 Died; 9.7.1791 Will Probate.
Family: Wife Ann Leigh married 9.10.1780.
Service: 2.7.1752 Capt Serv *Penzance* (44); 22.8.1752 Mid *Penzance* (44); 29.8.1754 Able *Penzance* (44); 22.5.1755 Mid *Prince* (90); 5.7.1756 Able *Prince George* (80); 3.8.1756 Mid *Prince George* (80); 4.11.1756 Mid *Prince* (90); 31.12.1756 Mid *Culloden* (74); 5.4.1757 Action of April 5 1757; 4.7.1757 Mid *Saint George* (90); 17.6.1758 Mid *Montagu* (60); 9.8.1758 Passed;

Lieutenant; 11.10.1758 3L *Winchester* (50); 20.4.1761-17.1.1763 L. *Terpsichore* (24); 21.8.1778 1L *Yarmouth* (64); 6.7.1779 Battle of Grenada; **Commander**; 30.7.1779(NA 10.11.1779)-25.8.1779 *Aetna* (8) Bomb Vessel; 25.8.1779(NA 15.12.1779)-4.11.1779 *Tortoise* (26) Armed Storeship; 14.9.1780-26.6.1782[C] *Alligator* (14) Sloop; **Captain**; 10.10.1782-15.1.1783 *Sandwich* (90).

FROUDE, JAMES

Dates: c.1704 Born; 1770 Died.
Family:
Service: 22.9.1734-7.5.1737[P] Able *Defiance* (60); 24.12.1740 Able *Augusta* (60); 7.1.1740/41 Action of January 7 1741; 2.7.1741 Mid *Marlborough* (90); 6.4.1742 Mid *Somerset* (80); 11.2.1743/44-12.2.1743/44 Battle of Toulon; 1.3.1744/45 Mate *Somerset* (80); 7.6.1745 Mate *Edinburgh* (64); 10.1.1745/46 Passed; **Lieutenant**; 14.5.1746-30.7.1747 L. *Lizard* (10) Sloop; 19.10.1747-19.8.1748[P] L. *Mercury* (20); 6.2.1755-5.1.1757 3L *Grafton* (68).

FURNEAUX, ABRAHAM

Dates: 20.2.1737/38 Born Plymouth; 18.11.1773 Died Devon.
Family: Father William Furneaux(1696–1748); Mother Sarah Wilcocks (1698-1775); Brother Tobias, RN (1735-1781); Brother James, RN (d.1783); Brother William (1723-1749).
Service: 8.8.1749 Capt Serv *Eagle* (60); 19.11.1752 Mid *Eagle* (60); 14.3.1753 Capt Serv *Unicorn* (24); 8.10.1755 Able *Unicorn* (24); 12.4.1756 Mid *Swiftsure* (68); 4.8.1756 Mid *Invincible* (74); 10.1.1757 Mid *Royal Anne* (100); 5.9.1757-6.10.1757 Raid on Rochefort; 2.1.1758 Passed; **Lieutenant**; 2.8.1758(NA 19.3.1759)-9.12.1759[C] L. *Hawke* (8) Sloop; 15.8.1760-4.4.1763 4L *Culloden* (74); 6.6.1762-13.8.1762 Operations against Havana; 28.3.1763-7.4.1763[P] 3L *Culloden* (74); 24.10.1766-10.11.1769 2L *Hero* (74); 3.11.1770-7.11.1771 3L *Fame* (74); 7.11.1771-16.12.1772 3L *Dublin* (74).

FURNEAUX, JAMES

Dates: 1783 Died.
Family: Father William Furneaux(1696–1748); Mother Sarah Wilcocks (1698-1775); Brother Tobias, RN (1735-1781); Brother Brother William (1723-1749); Brother Abraham, RN (1738-1773).
Service: **Lieutenant**; 15.10.1744(MED 18.12.1747)-8.3.1744/45 4L *Burford* (70); 3.9.1747(MED 19.12.1747)-9.12.1747[P] 1L *Princess Caroline* (80); 6.3.1755 2L *Vanguard* (68); 16.11.1756 1L *Vanguard* (68); 5.4.1757-8.3.1759 1L *America* (60); 5.9.1757-6.10.1757 Raid on Rochefort.

FURNEAUX, TOBIAS

Dates: 21.8.1735 Born Swilly, Plymouth; 19.9.1781 Died Swilly, Plymouth.
Family: Father William Furneaux(1696–1748); Mother Sarah Wilcocks (1698-1775); Brother James, RN (d.1783); Brother Brother William (1723-1749); Brother Abraham, RN (1738-1773).
Service: **Lieutenant**; 19.10.1759(JAM 2.12.1760) 4L *Edinburgh* (64); 3.12.1760-25.10.1763 2L *Melampe* (36); 29.3.1761-11.6.1761 Expedition against Belle-Isle; 16.7.1766-19.5.1768[P] 2L *Dolphin* (24); 3.11.1770 3L *Trident* (64); 30.11.1770 4L *Torbay* (74); 18.12.1770 3L *Torbay* (74); 28.5.1771 2L *Torbay* (74); **Commander**; 28.11.1771-19.11.1772[P] *Raleigh* (10); **Captain**; 10.8.1775-6.11.1777[S] *Siren* (28); 4.1778-1779 Vol. *Isis* (50); 14.12.1778-15.12.1778 Battle of St. Lucia.

Service Records G

GABORIAN, JAMES

Dates: c.1731 Born; 18.2.1730/31 Baptised Saltash; 1811 Died Saltash, Cornwall; 18.8.1811 Will Probate.

Family: Father John Gaborian (1710-1747); Mother Jane Davies; Sister Mary; Brother Thomas, RN (1736-1795); Sister Ann (1744-?).

Service: 9.2.1749 Mid *Tavistock* (28) Mer; 23.10.1749 Mid *Assistance* (50); 20.5.1753 Mid *Bristol* (50); 15.5.1754 Able *Arundel* (24); 5.5.1755 Mid *Newcastle* (50); 10.3.1757 Passed; **Lieutenant**; 27.2.1759 L. *Sphinx* (24); 20.4.1761-7.4.1763 1L *Mermaid* (28); 6.10.1763-24.10.1766[P] 3L *Hero* (74); 16.5.1769 2L *Firm* (74); 24.1.1771-20.5.1771[P] 2L *Hero* (74); 29.11.1771-3.12.1774 1L *Cerberus* (28); 7.11.1776 3L *Bienfaisant* (64); 18.7.1777-10.11.1778 2L *Bienfaisant* (64); 27.7.1778 1st Battle of Ushant; 12.10.1787 1L *Cumberland* (74); 26.8.1801 **Superannuated Commander**.

GABORIAN, THOMAS

Dates: 1736 Born Saltash; 24.7.1736 Baptised Saltash; c.1795 Died Saltash, Cornwall; 17.8.1795 Will Probate.

Family: Father John Gaborian (1710-1747); Mother Jane Davies; Sister Ann (1744-?); Sister Mary; Brother James, RN (1731-1811).

Service: 1759 Passed; **Lieutenant**; 4.1.1759-14.1.1759[P] L. *Blandford* (20); 12.2.1759-25.4.1763 2L *Thames* (32); 20.12.1763 2L *Edgar* (60); 19.1.1768 1L *Burford* (68); 20.7.1768 LCmdr *Folkestone* (6) Cutter; 15.1.1771 2L *Kent* (74); 4.6.1775 LCmdr *Sherborne* (6) Cutter; **Commander**; 17.9.1777 *Wolf* (8) Sloop; **Captain**; 13.5.1778-15.3.1780 *Amphitrite* (24); 15.6.1795 **Superannuated Rear Admiral.**

GAGE, JOSEPH

Dates: 1713 Born Old Catton, Norfolk; 16.8.1713 Baptised; 1.8.1755 Died; 26.2.1756 Will Probate.

Family: Father Joseph Gage; Mother Sarah Gage; Brother Thomas; Sister Catherine.

Service: 1742 Mid *Otter* (14); **Lieutenant**; 22.6.1743[(11.8.1743)] 4L *Suffolk* (70); 12.12.1743 3L *Sapphire* (44); 7.6.1745 2L *Sapphire* (44); 13.11.1745-29.4.1746 1L *Sapphire* (44); 13.5.1746-10.9.1748[P] 1L *Ambuscade* (40); 3.5.1747 1st Battle of Cape Finisterre.

GAINES, FRANCIS

Dates: c.1701 Born; 1767 Died; 14.5.1767 Buried Penistone, Yorkshire.

Family:

Service: 29.11.1728 Able *Dover* (40); 3.8.1729-30.6.1730[P] Mid *Dover* (40); 21.5.1736 Mid *Tartar* (20); 10.6.1737 Mate *Tartar* (20); 26.8.1739-2.3.1740/41[P] Mid *Wolf* (8) Sloop; 4.1740-5.7.1740 Attack on St. Augustine; 16.7.1741 Passed; **Lieutenant**; 31.10.1741-6.12.1743[P] 3L

Southsea Castle (40); 3.2.1743/44 4L *Princess Royal* (90); 31.8.1744-24.12.1748[P] 1L *Mary Galley* (44); **Commander**; 10.2.1755-12.10.1756 *Hound* (14) Sloop.

GALBRAITH, JAMES

Dates: c.1717 Born; 1782 Died; 4.7.1782 Will Probate.
Family: Wife Elizabeth; Son Francis James; Sister Margaret; Brother William.
Service: 25.1.1732/33 Vol-p-O *Ludlow Castle* (40); 30.3.1735-14.8.1739[P] Mid *Kinsale* (40); 17.4.1740 Passed; **Lieutenant**; 22.12.1740-1.2.1740/41 3L *Tiger* (50); 27.3.1741 2L *Dartmouth* (50); 18.4.1741-26.10.1741 1L *Sapphire* (44); 18.11.1741 L. *Scipio* (8) Fireship; 8.9.1742 1L *Sapphire* (44); 29.4.1743 3L *Severn* (50); 1.7.1744[(JAM 12.5.1747)] 1L *Severn* (50); 28.10.1744[(West Indies 12.5.1747)]-13.3.1744/45 3L *Superb* (60); **Commander**; 13.3.1744/45[(5.11.1745)]-14.5.1745 *Comet* (10) Bomb Vessel; 23.9.1747-9.5.1750[P] *Jamaica* (10) Sloop; 7.10.1755-1.11.1755 *Porcupine* (16) Sloop; **Captain**; 6.2.1756 *Unicorn* (24); 24.9.1756 *Union* (90); 1.8.1757 *Neptune* (90); 5.9.1757-6.10.1757 Raid on Rochefort; 18.10.1758 *Alarm* (32); 16.6.1760-2.12.1762[P] *Centurion* (50); 6.6.1762-13.8.1762 Operations against Havana; 24.5.1779 **Superannuated Rear Admiral**.

GALBRAITH, JOHN

Dates: c.1735 Born; 1789 Died; 9.10.1789 Will Probate.
Family:
Service: 2.7.1750 Able *Jamaica* (10) Sloop; 25.5.1751 Able *Prince Henry* (44); 8.9.1752 Able *Ferret* (14) Sloop; 13.7.1753 Mid *Ferret* (14) Sloop; 9.3.1754 Able *Captain* (64); 22.11.1754 Mid *Captain* (64); 4.2.1755 Able *Captain* (64); 20.2.1755 Mid *Experiment* (24); 20.5.1756 Battle of Minorca; 5.6.1756 Gnr Mate *Experiment* (24); 28.11.1756 Able *Experiment* (24); 10.1.1757 Passed; **Lieutenant**; 21.9.1758 6L *Torbay* (74); 27.10.1758-11.7.1763[P] 2L *Alarm* (32); 6.6.1762-13.8.1762 Operations against Havana; 16.1.1770-7.7.1772 1L *Solebay* (28) Frigate; 28.4.1773 1L *Lark* (32); 14.10.1773 1L *Thames* (32); 31.5.1774-29.4.1777 2L *Asia* (64); 2.7.1776-4.7.1776 Staten Island Landings; 7.9.1780 1L *Saint Albans* (64); 9.12.1780 1L *Magnanime* (64); 12.4.1782 Battle of Providien; 20.6.1782-27.6.1783[P] 1L *Polyphemus* (64); 12.8.1782-25.8.1782[P] LCmdr *Terror* (8) Bomb Vessel; 20.10.1782 Battle of Cape Spartel.

GALLOWAY, WILLIAM

Dates: c.1710 Born; 1769 Died.
Family:
Service: 1.1.1726/27 Vol-p-O *Hampshire* (54); 6.10.1728 MidO *Adventure* (40); 19.9.1729 Able *Seaford* (20); 10.11.1729 MidO *Trial* (10) Sloop; 10.1.1729/30 MidO *Success* (20); 15.5.1730 Able *Diamond* (40); 28.4.1731 Mid *Exeter* (60); 11.11.1731 Mid *Scarborough* (20); 7.1.1731/32 MidO *York* (60); 7.2.1731/32-1.3.1732/33 Mid *Swift* (6) Sloop; 1.3.1733/34 Passed; **Lieutenant**; 2.3.1733/34-23.5.1738 4L *Lancaster* (80).

GAMBIER, JAMES

Dates: 1723 Born; 28.1.1789 Died Burlington Street, Bath.
Family: Father James Gambier, warden of the Fleet prison; Mother Mary Mead; Wife Mary Ruck (d.1763); Wife Jane Montpeson (d. c1785); Wife Sarah Newcombe; Son Samuel John, RN (d.1789).
Service: **Lieutenant**; 6.3.1743/44[(24.9.1745)] 4L *Buckingham* (70); 24.5.1744[(MED 23.5.1749)] 3L *Guernsey* (50); 3.8.1745[(MED 19.5.1749)]-2.12.1745 5L *Marlborough* (90); **Commander**; 3.4.1746 *Speedwell* (10) Sloop; **Captain**; 5.12.1747 *Flamborough* (20); 20.4.1748-9.5.1749[P] *Squirrel* (20); 19.4.1755 *Sphinx* (24); 17.8.1756 *Namur* (90); 20.8.1756 *Defiance* (60); 31.8.1756[(JAM 31.8.1756)] *Severn*

(50); 8.4.1757-15.4.1757 *Lowestoffe* (28); 4.2.1758-6.5.1763 *Burford* (68); 6.6.1758-27.7.1758 The Siege of Louisbourg; 16.1.1759-19.1.1759 Attack on Martinique; 20.1.1759-1.5.1759 Capture of Guadeloupe; 20.11.1759 Battle of Quiberon Bay; 29.3.1761-11.6.1761 Expedition against Belle-Isle; 12.10.1766-15.11.1769 *Yarmouth* (64); 2.12.1767 CinC — River Medway and The Nore; 11.7.1770-8.1771 CinC — North America; 11.7.1770-6.3.1772[P] Commodore *Salisbury* (50); 1773 Comptroller of the Victualling Accounts; 25.8.1773-26.1.1778 Resident Commissioner at Portsmouth Dockyard; 25.8.1773 Gov. of Royal Naval Academy; **Rear Admiral of the Blue**; 23.1.1778-11.6.1779[P] *Ardent* (64); 26.1.1778-10.1778 CinC — North America; 19.3.1779 **Rear Admiral of the Red**; 26.9.1780 **Vice Admiral of the Blue**; 14.8.1783-12.2.1784 CinC — Jamaica; 6.11.1783-12.2.1784 *Europa* (50); 24.9.1787 **Vice Admiral of the Red.**

GAMBIER, SAMUEL

Dates: c.1726 Born; 19.7.1726 Baptised London.
Family: Father James Gambier; Mother Mary.
Service: 1748-1752 HEIC Service; 23.4.1752 Mid *Adventure* (44); **Lieutenant**; 10.2.1754 3L *Adventure* (44); 6.11.1754 Passed; 10.2.1757-16.3.1757[D] L. *Port Antonio* (12) Storeship; 16.3.1757 Dismissed.

GARDINER, ARTHUR

Dates: c.1716 Born; 28.2.1758 Died; 5.9.1758 Will Probate.
Family: Sister Jane; Sister Ann; Sister Elizabeth.
Service: 23.8.1731 Vol-p-O *Falmouth* (50); 30.5.1734 MidO *Falmouth* (50); 1.6.1736 Mid *Falmouth* (50); 4.7.1736 MidO *Newark* (80); 24.1.1736/37-10.10.1737[P] Mid *Bridgewater* (32); 3.11.1737 Passed; **Lieutenant**; 4.7.1738[(22.9.1741)] 3L *Falmouth* (50); 8.4.1739[(22.9.1741)]-23.10.1739 2L *Falmouth* (50); 2.10.1741 2L *Sutherland* (50); 27.2.1741/42 1L *Sutherland* (50); 6.4.1743 2L *Captain* (70); 28.10.1743 1L *Captain* (70); **Commander**; 6.6.1744 *Lightning* (8) Bomb Vessel; 4.4.1745[(MED 3.2.1748/49)] *Postillon* Xebec; 17.5.1745 **Captain**; 27.5.1745[(MED 4.2.1746/47)] *Neptune* (90); 3.8.1745[(MED 4.2.1746/47)]-1.10.1745 *Marlborough* (90); 1.10.1746[(MED 15.11.1748)]-7.11.1748[P] *Faversham* (44); 30.1.1748/49-3.4.1754[P] *Amazon* (22); 27.5.1755 *Colchester* (50); 23.9.1755-5.6.1756 *Ramillies* (90); 20.5.1756 Battle of Minorca; 17.2.1757-28.2.1758[†] *Monmouth* (70); 28.2.1758 Battle of Cartagena.

GARDINER, JOHN

Dates: c.1714 Born; 1782 Died; 6.7.1782 Will Probate.
Family:
Service: 11.8.1733 Capt Serv *Looe* (42); 10.11.1734 Ord. *Montagu* (60); 20.8.1736 Able *Montagu* (60); 4.7.1737 Able *Ipswich* (70); 2.4.1738 MidO *Spy* (8) Sloop; 1.8.1739-3.9.1741 MidO *Prince Frederick* (70); 7.1.1740/41 Action of January 7 1741; 4.3.1740/41-5.1741 Operations against Cartagena; 8.9.1741 Passed; **Lieutenant**; 29.5.1742[(24.2.1743/44)] 4L *Somerset* (80); 28.8.1743[(MED 7.12.1747)] 4L *Norfolk* (80); 11.2.1743/44-12.2.1743/44 Battle of Toulon; 20.8.1744[(MED 7.12.1747)]-18.7.1745 3L *Norfolk* (80); 18.7.1745[(MED 7.12.1747)]-11.12.1747[P] 2L *Norfolk* (80); 5.11.1751-11.5.1754 L. *Sphinx* (24).

GARDNER, LORD ALAN (1ST BARON GARDNER OF UTTOXETER)

Dates: 12.2.1742 Born Uttoxeter; 1806 1st Baron Gardner of Uttoxeter; 1.1.1809 Died Bath.
Family: Father Lt. Col. William Gardner; Mother Elizabeth Farrington; Wife Mrs. Susannah Hyde Turner, née Gale (d.1823) married 20.5.1769; Son Valentine, RN (d.1820); Son William Henry; Son Alan Hyde (2nd Baron Gardner of Uttoxeter), RN (1770-1815); Son Bon, RN.
Service: 16.10.1755 Capt Serv *Medway* (60); 17.4.1757 Able *Medway* (60); 7.5.1757 MidO *Medway* (60); 5.9.1757-6.10.1757 Raid on Rochefort; 29.11.1757 Mid *Medway* (60); 2.3.1758 Mid *Dorsetshire* (68); 20.11.1759 Battle of Quiberon Bay; 15.2.1760 Passed; **Lieutenant**; 7.3.1760 5L *Bellona* (74); 23.12.1760 4L *Bellona* (74); 11.3.1761 5L *Bellona* (74); 7.1.1762 4L *Bellona* (74); **Commander**; 12.4.1762-24.2.1763[P] *Raven* (8) Fireship; **Captain**; 19.5.1766 *Preston* (50); 11.5.1769[(13.6.1770)]-30.5.1770[P] *Levant* (28); 19.1.1774-27.7.1779 *Maidstone* (28); 22.7.1778 Encounter at Sandy Hook; 17.3.1779[(NA 7.12.1779)]-9.5.1781 *Sultan* (74); 6.7.1779 Battle of Grenada; 20.6.1780 Action off Monti Christi; 24.12.1781-9.6.1783[P] *Duke* (90); 12.4.1782 Battle of the Saintes; 8.9.1785-1789 CinC — Jamaica; 23.1.1786-29.11.1788 Commodore *Expedition* (44); 10.1786-14.9.1789[P] *Europa* (50); 19.1.1790-6.3.1795 Lord Commissioner of the Admiralty; 1.2.1790-25.5.1796 M.P. for Plymouth; 10.5.1790 *Courageux* (74); 16.2.1791-10.9.1791[P] *Courageux* (74); **Rear Admiral of the Blue**; 1.2.1793-8.1796 *Queen* (90); 20.2.1793-11.1793 CinC — Barbados & the Leeward Islands; 12.4.1794 **Rear Admiral of the White**; 1.6.1794 Glorious 1st of June; 4.7.1794 **Vice Admiral of the Blue**; 23.6.1795 Action of Ile Groix; 10.60.1795 **Vice Admiral of the White**; 6.1796-3.1797 *Royal Sovereign* (100); 13.6.1796-19.11.1806 M.P. for Westminster; 14.2.1799 **Admiral of the Blue**; 1803-1804 *Trent* (36); 3.1803-6.1803 CinC — Portsmouth; 3.4.1805-1808 CinC — English Channel; 3.4.1805-10.1805 *Hibernia* (110); 9.11.1805 **Admiral of the White**; 1806 *Trent* (36) Hospital Ship; 1807-11.1807 *Hibernia* (110); 5.1807-1808 *Ville de Paris* (110); 28.4.1808 **Admiral of the Red**; 6.1808 *Bellerophon* (74).

GARDNER, JAMES

Dates: c.1707 Born; 1755 Died.
Family:
Service: 18.10.1727 MidO *Faversham* (42); 15.11.1728 Mid *Faversham* (42); 25.7.1731 Able *Hector* (40); 21.4.1733 Able *Royal Oak* (70); 27.7.1733 Mid *Royal Oak* (70); 22.9.1733 Able *Royal Oak* (70); 31.1.1735-6.4.1737[P] Mid *Royal Oak* (70); 1.3.1738 Mid *Berwick* (70); 6.11.1738 Mid *Garland* (20); 27.9.1741 Mate *Garland* (20); 27.5.1742 Able *Victory* (100); 1.8.1742 Mate *Squirrel* (20); 16.1.1744 Mate *Suffolk* (70); 6.3.1744 Act3L *Jersey* (60); 7.6.1744 Passed; **Lieutenant**; 8.6.1744 3L *Jersey* (60); 17.7.1744 4L *Hampton Court* (64); 8.1.1744/45 Action of 1745-01-08; 27.3.1745-25.8.1745 3L *Chester* (50); 7.9.1747-1.12.1748 3L *Culloden* (74); 16.1.1753 2L *Berwick* (70); 16.5.1753-1755[†] 2L *Captain* (64).

GARENCIERES, CHARLES

Dates: 1770 Died.
Family:
Service: **Lieutenant**; 12.10.1741[(22.1.1741/42)] 3L *Lynn* (44); 28.10.1742 2L *Lynn* (44); 22.6.1743[(9.8.1743)] 3L *Burford* (70); 28.11.1743 4L *Shrewsbury* (80); 3.2.1743/44 3L *Shrewsbury* (80); 22.10.1744 2L *Defiance* (60); 26.5.1746 2L *Falkland* (50); 13.11.1746-30.10.1747 1L *Falkland* (50); 3.5.1747 1st Battle of Cape Finisterre; 8.3.1747/48-21.6.1748[P] 1L *Royal George* (100); 22.5.1754 L. *Peregrine* (20) Sloop; 1.11.1755-12.11.1755 3L *Duke* (90); 12.11.1755 4L *Duke* (90); 18.5.1756 3L *Duke* (90); 26.5.1757 2L *Duke* (90); 25.4.1758-19.2.1763[P] 1L *Duke* (90); 5.6.1758-12.6.1758

Raid on Saint-Malo; 20.11.1759 Battle of Quiberon Bay; 6.4.1763-10.6.1766 LCmdr *Hector* (4) Cutter.

GARNER, WILLIAM
Dates: 20.3.1787 Died.
Family:
Service: 22.12.1748-c.1751 Scholar *Royal Naval Academy*; **Lieutenant**; 23.9.1757-8.7.1758 4L *Vanguard* (68); 10.12.1759 2L *Vanguard* (68); 3.10.1761 1L *Vanguard* (68); 7.1.1762-10.2.1762 Operations against Martinique; **Commander**; 1.2.1763[(BLI 30.8.1763)]-13.8.1764[P] *Lynx* (10) Sloop; 11.10.1764-12.12.1765 *Hound* (14) Sloop; 29.9.1766 *Lynx* (10) Sloop; **Captain**; 3.8.1768 *Chatham* (50); 20.3.1769[(BLI 28.2.1772)]-17.1.1772[P] *Scarborough* (20); 6.6.1772-30.9.1773[P] *Kennington* (20); 25.8.1774 *Hind* (24); 20.11.1775[(BLI 30.11.1776)]-26.10.1776[P] *Argo* (28); 17.10.1776-31.12.1780 *Southampton* (32); 26.12.1778-5.4.1779 *America* (64); 1.1.1781[(JAM 6.12.1781)]-10.9.1781[P] *Grafton* (74).

GARROW, JOSEPH
Dates: 1800 Died.
Family:
Service: **Lieutenant**; 19.6.1761[(EI 24.7.1765)] 4L *Panther* (60); 24.9.1762-6.10.1762 Battle of Manilla; 3.6.1763[(EI 24.7.1765)]-20.6.1765 3L *Panther* (60); 16.11.1770-20.5.1771[P] 3L *Conquestador* (60).

GASCOIGNE, EDWARD
Dates: c.1712 Born; 14.12.1764 Died; 10.1.1765 Will Probate.
Family: Sister Elizabeth [Maris]; Sister Mary [Stubbs].
Service: 7.1.1731/32 QGnr *Hampton Court* (70); 15.8.1732 Able *Seaford* (20); 27.11.1735 Able *Dreadnought* (60); 26.1.1737/38 QM *Dreadnought* (60); 24.3.1737/38 QM *Romney* (50); 30.7.1739 Mid *Romney* (50); 7.2.1740/41 Mate *Romney* (54); 7.6.1741 Mate *Nassau* (70); 1.10.1741 Passed; **Lieutenant**; 30.3.1742 L. *Comet* (8) Bomb Vessel; 18.2.1742/43 Attack on La Guaira; 3.9.1743-5.3.1743/44 4L *Boyne* (80); 11.2.1743/44-12.2.1743/44 Battle of Toulon; 24.12.1744[(MED 25.5.1748)] 3L *Roebuck* (44); 29.11.1745[(MED 13.5.1748)]-27.1.1745/46 2L *Dunkirk* (60); 23.1.1751/52-19.1.1755 L. *Wager* (24); **Commander**; 11.10.1755[(JAM 27.9.1756)]-11.1.1757 *Weazle* (16) Sloop; 5.5.1757 *Postillion* (18) Sloop; 6.5.1757-21.5.1759[P] *Beaver* (18) Sloop; 6.6.1758-27.7.1758 The Siege of Louisbourg; **Captain**; 18.2.1760-5.10.1763[P] *Dublin* (74); 7.1.1762-10.2.1762 Operations against Martinique; 6.6.1762-13.8.1762 Operations against Havana.

GASCOIGNE, JAMES
Dates: 1763 Died.
Family:
Service: **Lieutenant**; 16.12.1727[(5.8.1729)]-28.8.1728 3L *Nottingham* (60); 4.11.1734 1L *Warwick* (60); 18.4.1735-22.8.1735 L. *Aldborough* (20); **Commander**; 26.9.1735-14.3.1738/39 *Hawk* (8) Sloop.

GASCOIGNE, JAMES
Dates: 1765 Died.
Family:
Service: **Lieutenant**; 25.3.1757 4L *Nassau* (64); 8.1757-10.1757 Louisbourg Expedition; 9.3.1758-24.5.1758 Capture of Fort Louis; 28.9.1758-2.1.1759 3L *Nassau* (64); 29.12.1758 Capture of Goree; 20.6.1759 3L *Foudroyant* (80); 27.7.1759 4L *Foudroyant* (80); 21.3.1760

3L *Foudroyant* (80); 1.4.1760-8.6.1762 2L *Foudroyant* (80); 7.1.1762-10.2.1762 Operations against Martinique; 1.11.1765[(BLI 20.11.1766)]-25.1.1766 2L *Princess Louisa* (60).

GASPEY, WILLIAM

Dates: c.1725 Born; 15.9.1791 Died.
Family:
Service: 31.5.1746 Mid *Boyne* (80); 19.2.1749/50 Mid *Russell* (80); 21.3.1750/51 Able *Gloucester* (50); 25.8.1751 Mid *Mars* (64); 4.11.1751 Mid *Mars* (64); 24.6.1753 Able *Mars* (64); 22.7.1753 Able *Vanguard* (68); 11.7.1754-19.7.1754 Able *Eagle* (60); 20.7.1754 Able *Eagle* (60); 27.10.1754 Mid *Eagle* (60); 8.11.1754 Mid *Monarch* (74); 19.1.1755 Able *Monarch* (74); 23.7.1755 Mid *Monarch* (74); 12.8.1755 Able *Monarch* (74); 24.10.1755 Mid *Prince George* (80); 3.3.1756 Passed; **Lieutenant**; 18.10.1759 3L *Portland* (50); 19.10.1759-23.10.1760 2L *Portland* (50); 20.11.1759 Battle of Quiberon Bay.

GAUNTLETT, JOHN

Dates: c.1736 Born; 1783 Died; 14.10.1783 Will Probate.
Family:
Service: 3.2.1749/50 Scholar *Royal Naval Academy*; 12.7.1753 Vol-p-O *Crown* (44); 3.7.1754 MidO *Crown* (44); 10.9.1754 Mid *Norwich* (50); 8.3.1757 Passed; **Lieutenant**; 10.3.1757 L. *Hazard's Prize* (8) Sloop; 23.3.1757-22.1.1761 L. *Glasgow* (20); 22.2.1762-22.6.1763 2L *Dreadnought* (60); 22.6.1763-1.4.1767[P] L. *Martin* (14) Sloop; 24.6.1766-21.3.1767[P] ActM&C *Beaver* (14) Sloop; 6.12.1776-14.6.1780[P] LCmdr *Hope* Hired Tender; 1.10.1780-1.12.1781 LCmdr *Weymouth* Hired Tender.

GAVEN, WILLIAM

Dates: c.1737 Born; 1777 Died.
Family:
Service: 5.8.1747-30.9.1748[P] Capt Serv *Amazon* (22); 7.2.1751 Capt Serv *Amazon* (22); 25.1.1754-3.4.1754[P] Able *Amazon* (22); 7.5.1754 Mid *Rye* (20); 15.6.1755 Mid *Colchester* (50); 17.10.1755 Mid *Ramillies* (90); 20.5.1756 Battle of Minorca; 8.3.1757 Passed; **Lieutenant**; 6.4.1757 L. *Infernal* (8) Bomb Vessel; 5.9.1757-6.10.1757 Raid on Rochefort; 19.1.1758 3L *Grafton* (68); 2.2.1758-20.2.1759 2L *Grafton* (68); 29.9.1770-17.4.1771 1L *Minerva* (32); 4.12.1776-30.4.1777 LCmdr *Sally* Hired Tender.

GAYDON, JOHN

Dates: c.1738 Born; 1805 Died Devon; 2.5.1805 Will Probate.
Family: Sister Mary.
Service: 1753-1756 Merchant Service; 2.6.1756 Able *Vanguard* (68); 18.3.1756/57 Able *Monmouth* (70); 14.11.1757 Mid *Greyhound* (20); 26.11.1758 Able *Porcupine* (16) Sloop; 2.2.1759 Mid *Venus* (36); 28.4.1759-5.3.1759/60 Mid *Venus* (36); 20.11.1759 Battle of Quiberon Bay; 5.3.1760 Passed; **Lieutenant**; 7.8.1761-12.5.1763[P] 3L *Launceston* (44); 2.2.1771-25.1.1773[P] 2L *Glory* (32).

GAYTON, CLARK

Dates: 4.1712 Born Portsmouth; 1787 Died.
Family: Father John Gayton (d 1737); Mother Eleanor Clark (d1750); Wife Elizabeth Legge; Wife Judith Rawlins; Son George Clark Gayton (1751-1800); Brother George, RN (1724-1797).

Service: 14.4.1723 Ord. *Solebay* (42); 23.12.1723 Capt Serv *Solebay* (42); 6.1.1724/25 Able *Colchester* (50); 5.9.1728 Able *Dursley Galley* (20); 18.11.1728 Ord. *Sunderland* (60); 24.12.1729 Able *Kinsale* (40); 26.8.1731 Mid *Romney* (50); 11.10.1731 Able *Looe* (42); 13.6.1732 Able *Tiger* (50); 30.1.1732/33 Mid *Tiger* (50); 10.8.1733 Able *Princess Caroline* (80); 16.2.1733/34 Mid *Princess Caroline* (80); 23.3.1733/34 Mid *Blenheim* (96); 11.7.1735 Passed; **Lieutenant**; 11.3.1741/42-23.12.1743 3L *Launceston* (44); **Commander**; 12.8.1744-18.6.1745 *Bien Aime* (18) Armed Storeship; **Captain**; 6.7.1745-14.9.1747[P] *Mermaid* (44); 21.5.1755 *Antelope* (50); 4.6.1756 *Prince* (90); 30.6.1756 *Royal Anne* (100); 19.4.1757 *Prince* (90); 13.6.1758[25.8.1758]-27.12.1760[P] *Saint George* (90); 16.1.1759-19.1.1759 Attack on Martinique; 20.1.1759-1.5.1759 Capture of Guadeloupe; 16.5.1769 *San Antonio* (64); 24.10.1770 **Rear Admiral of the White**; 31.1.1774-20.5.1778[P] *Antelope* (50); 29.3.1774 CinC — Jamaica; 31.3.1775 **Rear Admiral of the Red**; 7.12.1775 **Vice Admiral of the White**; 29.1.1778 **Vice Admiral of the Red**; 8.4.1782 **Admiral of the Blue.**

GAYTON, GEORGE

Dates: 1724 Born; 23.9.1797 Died Portsmouth.

Family: Father John Gayton (d 1737); Mother Eleanor Clark (d 1750); Wife Mary Hunt (d.1785); Wife Anna Maria Palmer married 27.10.1787; Brother Clark, RN (1712-1787).

Service: **Lieutenant**; 6.3.1743/44[MED 22.7.1746]-8.11.1744 L. *Nazareth* (8) Fireship; 2.8.1745[MED 4.11.1748] 3L *Burford* (70); 17.12.1745[MED 4.11.1748] 2L *Burford* (70); 3.9.1747[MED 4.11.1748]-25.11.1748[P] 1L *Burford* (70); 16.1.1753-16.5.1753[P] 1L *Invincible* (74); 16.5.1753-22.5.1754 1L *Terrible* (74); 22.5.1754 2L *Terrible* (74); 25.2.1755 1L *Terrible* (74); 13.5.1755 1L *Ramillies* (90); 7.10.1755 3L *Newark* (80); 18.1.1757-10.2.1757 2L *Newark* (80); 12.3.1757-19.4.1757 2L *Prince* (90); 19.4.1757 4L *Prince* (90); 9.10.1758-23.10.1758 1L *Saint George* (90); 8.3.1759 6L *Royal Anne* (100); 22.5.1759 5L *Royal Anne* (100); **Commander**; 11.12.1759-27.3.1763 *Fly* (8) Sloop; 29.3.1761-11.6.1761 Expedition against Belle-Isle; **Captain**; 26.5.1768 *Nightingale* (22); 21.2.1769 *Antelope* (50); 8.1.1771-22.2.1772 *Panther* (60); 1.12.1777-19.2.1781[C] *Romulus* (44); 12.5.1790-16.9.1791[P] *Royal William* (84); 25.12.1792-16.4.1794[P] *Royal William* (84); 12.4.1794 **Rear Admiral of the White**; 4.7.1794 **Rear Admiral of the Red**; 1.6.1795 **Vice Admiral of the White.**

GEARY, SIR FRANCIS (1ST BARONET OF OXENHEATH)

Dates: 1709 Born; 3.8.1782 1st Baronet of Oxenheath; 7.2.1796 Died.

Family: Wife Mary Bartholomew married 5.1748; Son Francis (d.1776); Son William, 2nd Bt.;

Service: **Lieutenant**; 19.3.1733/34-11.6.1735 4L *Stirling Castle* (70); 12.6.1735-15.4.1736 L. *Gibraltar* (20); 25.5.1739-3.7.1739 1L *Adventure* (40); 4.7.1739-2.3.1739/40 6L *Namur* (90); 3.3.1739/40-16.4.1740[P] 4L *Namur* (90); 14.4.1740 4L *Victory* (100); 12.6.1741 3L *Victory* (100); 21.9.1741 1L *Victory* (100); **Captain**; 30.6.1742 *Squirrel* (20); 24.12.1743 *Dolphin* (20); 17.2.1743/44-5.7.1745 *Chester* (50); 14.9.1745 *Namur* (74); 3.5.1747 1st Battle of Cape Finisterre; 7.9.1747-25.11.1748 *Culloden* (74); 4.2.1755-5.7.1757 *Somerset* (68); 7.9.1757-1758 CinC — Thames, Medway and The Nore; 14.3.1758-9.2.1759 *Lennox* (74); 5.6.1758-12.6.1758 Raid on Saint-Malo; 9.2.1759-21.5.1759 *Resolution* (74); 14.2.1759 **Rear Admiral of the Blue**; 19.5.1759 **Rear Admiral of the White**; 21.5.1759-4.6.1759 Commodore *Resolution* (74); 5.6.1759 *Resolution* (74); 7.7.1759 *Sandwich* (90); 29.8.1759-9.1759 *Royal George* (100); 9.1759 *Sandwich* (90); 10.1760 *Royal Sovereign* (104); 1761-1763 CinC — Portsmouth; 21.10.1762 **Vice Admiral of the Blue**; 1769-1771 CinC — Portsmouth; 18.10.1770 **Vice Admiral of the Red**; 31.3.1775 **Admiral of the Blue**; 29.1.1778 **Admiral of the White**; 22.5.1780-27.8.1780 CinC — English Channel; 24.5.1780-27.8.1780[R] *Victory* (100).

GEARY, THOMAS

Dates: c.1734 Born; 5.2.1805 Died Isle of Wight; 9.3.1805 Will Probate.
Family: Son William; Daughter Ann.
Service: 1753-1756 HEIC Service; 23.11.1756 Able *Somerset* (68); 6.12.1756 Mid *Somerset* (68); 2.4.1757 Mate *Somerset* (68); 6.6.1758-27.7.1758 The Siege of Louisbourg; 20.2.1760 Passed; **Lieutenant**; 12.6.1760[(23.3.1760)] L. *Viper* (10) Sloop; 30.8.1760[(JAM 23.7.1761)]-21.1.1761 3L *Enterprise* (44); 6.12.1763-30.11.1765[P] 2L *Africa* (64); 21.3.1769 2L *Dragon* (74); 11.10.1769 1L *Dragon* (74); 28.3.1770 1L *Centaur* (74); 21.9.1770 3L *Centaur* (74); 30.10.1770-21.6.1771[P] 1L *Namur* (90); 15.11.1776 4L *Sandwich* (90); 28.1.1778 5L *Sandwich* (90); 16.5.1778-9.3.1779[P] 4L *Sandwich* (90); 27.7.1778 1st Battle of Ushant; 25.5.1780 1L *Victory* (100); **Commander**; 26.8.1780-30.11.1780[C] *Pluto* (8) Fireship.

GED, DOUGALDUS

Dates: c.1733 Born; 29.7.1765 Died Midlothian.
Family: Wife Margery Thomas married 2.3.1763.
Service: 1753-1757 Merchant Service; 12.3.1757 Mid *Buckingham* (68); 23.4.1758 Able *Buckingham* (68); 24.7.1758 Mid *Buckingham* (68); 16.1.1759-19.1.1759 Attack on Martinique; 20.1.1759-1.5.1759 Capture of Guadeloupe; 19.7.1759 Mate *Spy* (10) Sloop; 21.3.1760 ActL *Porcupine* (16) Sloop; 14.5.1760 Passed; **Lieutenant**; 21.5.1760-3.8.1763[P] 3L *Intrepid* (60).

GELL, JOHN

Dates: 1806 Died.
Family:
Service: **Lieutenant**; 6.1.1760[(JAM 23.3.1760)] 4L *Conqueror* (68); 30.1.1760[(JAM 23.3.1760)]-26.10.1760[W] 3L *Conqueror* (68); **Commander**; 14.10.1762-26.11.1762[P] *Grampus* (8) Fireship; **Captain**; 4.3.1766 *Guernsey* (50); 6.5.1766-6.11.1769[P] *Launceston* (44); 30.10.1777-21.9.1779 *Thetis* (32); 3.5.1780-9.6.1784[P] *Monarca* (68); 17.2.1782 Battle of Sadras; 12.4.1782 Battle of Providien; 6.7.1782 2nd Battle of Negapatam; 3.9.1782 Battle of Trincomalee; 20.6.1783 2nd Battle of Cuddalore; 30.7.1790-9.12.1790[P] *Excellent* (74); 1.2.1793 **Rear Admiral of the Blue**; 22.2.1794-28.2.1795 *Saint George* (98); 12.4.1794 **Rear Admiral of the White**; 4.7.1794 **Vice Admiral of the Blue**; 1.6.1795 **Vice Admiral of the White**; 14.2.1799 **Admiral of the Blue**; 9.11.1805 **Admiral of the White**.

GELLIE, LEWIS

Dates: c.1723 Born; 31.7.1812 Died.
Family:
Service: 7.11.1748 Able *Princess Caroline* (80); 12.8.1750 Cox *Princess Caroline* (80); 1.9.1751 Mid *Princess Caroline* (80); 29.10.1751 Mid *Shark* (8) Sloop; 27.11.1751 Mid *Phoenix* (24); 16.2.1751/52 Able *Phoenix* (24); 20.8.1753 Mate *Phoenix* (24); 30.11.1754 Mate *Princess* (70); 3.3.1755 Mate *Superb* (60); 3.12.1755 Passed; **Lieutenant**; 9.11.1756 L. *Speedwell* (8) Sloop; 21.9.1757-2.8.1758 2L *Juno* (32); 6.6.1758-27.7.1758 The Siege of Louisbourg; 9.1.1760 2L *Namur* (90); 2.4.1761 4L *Namur* (90); 28.10.1761-1.2.1762 3L *Namur* (90); 11.2.1762-25.2.1763[P] 6L *Namur* (90); 6.6.1762-13.8.1762 Operations against Havana; 14.4.1763-14.6.1766 LCmdr *Charlotte* (4) Cutter; 6.1769-2.7.1770[P] LCmdr *Charlotte* (4) Cutter; 21.9.1796 **Superannuated Commander**.

GENTIL, GEORGE

Dates: 20.4.1724 Born; 26.4.1724 Baptised Westminster; 1770 Died; 15.5.1770 Buried Southwark, Surrey; 26.11.1770 Will Probate.

Family: Father Thomas Gentil; Mother Mary; Wife Frances Sawkins; Son Thomas; Daughter Elizabeth.

Service: 24.3.1735/36 Merchant Service; 20.10.1740 Capt Serv *Elizabeth* (70); 24.9.1741 Able *Elizabeth* (70); 1.1.1743 Mid *Elizabeth* (70); 11.2.1743/44-12.2.1743/44 Battle of Toulon; 4.3.1745-19.5.1745 Mid *Roebuck* (44); **Lieutenant**; 12.5.1745(MED 16.5.1746) 3L *Dorsetshire* (80); 19.5.1745 Passed; 6.7.1745(MED 16.5.1746)-13.7.1746[P] 4L *Ipswich* (70); 20.3.1746/47-26.8.1748 3L *Prince Henry* (44); 23.7.1755 1L *Prince Edward* (44); 1.1.1756 L. *Queenborough* (24); 23.8.1756-12.4.1758 2L *Lynn* (44); 5.5.1758-4.9.1759 3L *Duke* (90); 5.6.1758-12.6.1758 Raid on Saint-Malo.

GEORGE, JAMES

Dates: c.1729 Born; 1809 Died Sandwich; 20.7.1809 Will Probate.

Family: Wife Ann.

Service: 1753-1755 Merchant Service; 5.8.1755 YoP *Bristol* (50); 24.6.1757 Mid *Bristol* (50); 16.1.1759-19.1.1759 Attack on Martinique; 11.2.1759 Mid *Woolwich* (44); 5.12.1759 Passed; **Lieutenant**; 24.6.1761(BLI 24.9.1762)-29.11.1762[P] 3L *Woolwich* (44); 7.1.1762-10.2.1762 Operations against Martinique; 2.2.1771-15.2.1771 3L *Bellona* (74); 29.6.1778-11.7.1783 LCmdr *Rambler* (10) Cutter; 6.10.1779 Quebec vs Surveillante.

GEST, JAMES

Dates: c.4.1736 Born; 30.4.1736 Baptised Kingston, Devon; 1772 Died.

Family: Father Thomas Gest; Mother Joan.

Service: 12.11.1754 MidO *Gosport* (44); 30.10.1755 Mid *Gosport* (44); 25.3.1756 Able *Gosport* (44); 16.7.1756 Mid *Gosport* (44); 13.5.1759 Mate *Gosport* (44); 16.3.1760 Able *Belliqueux* (64); 31.3.1760 Mid *Belliqueux* (64); 10.9.1760 Mate *Belliqueux* (64); 18.11.1761 Passed; **Lieutenant**; 27.12.1762(MED 2.8.1763)-13.8.1763[P] 4L *Belliqueux* (64); 29.9.1770-20.5.1771[P] 5L *Hero* (74).

GIBBES, ANTHONY

Dates: 1738 Born; 1815 Died; 3.2.1815 Will Probate.

Family: Wife Frances Jennings (c.1754-?) married 5.2.1784; Son John James (1785-?); Daughter Lucy (1786-?); Son Robert, RN.

Service: 22.9.1752 Able *Jason* (44); 3.9.1755 Able *Augusta* (60); 19.9.1755 Mid *Buckingham* (68); 20.5.1756 Battle of Minorca; 6.11.1757 Mid *Neptune* (90); 24.12.1757 Mid *Ramillies* (90); 5.6.1758-12.6.1758 Raid on Saint-Malo; 9.11.1758 Passed; **Lieutenant**; 2.6.1759(NA 7.1.1760) 4L *Dublin* (74); 24.9.1759(NA 7.1.1760)-22.2.1760 3L *Dublin* (74); 7.3.1760-5.3.1762 4L *Dorsetshire* (68); 3.11.1766 1L *Levant* (28); 10.2.1770(JAM 31.3.1772) LCmdr *Earl of Northampton*; 11.3.1771(JAM 31.3.1772)-26.8.1771[D] LCmdr *Sir Edward Hawke* (8) Schooner; 26.8.1771 Dismissed; 13.1.1778-3.4.1780 1L *Cumberland* (74); 27.7.1778 1st Battle of Ushant; 16.1.1780 Battle of Cape St. Vincent; 3.4.1781-20.12.1781 1L *Dolphin* (44); 5.8.1781 Battle of Dogger Bank; **Commander**; 11.7.1782(BLI 13.6.1783)-18.4.1783 *Arrow* (14) Sloop; 1800-1802 Regulating Officer at Swansea.

GIBSON, JOHN

Dates: c.1740 Born; 30.6.1824 Died Somerset; 23.9.1824 Will Probate.
Family: Wife Elizabeth; Son John Sanderson, RN (1774-1831).
Service: 12.2.1756 Capt Serv *Edinburgh* (64); 16.8.1756 Capt Serv *Swiftsure* (68); 28.1.1758 MidO *Swiftsure* (68); 28.2.1758 Battle of Cartagena; 29.7.1758 Mid *Swiftsure* (68); 18.8.1759-19.8.1759 Battle of Lagos Bay; 20.11.1759 Battle of Quiberon Bay; 5.11.1760 Passed; **Lieutenant**; 10.12.1760-20.1.1763[P] 4L *Swiftsure* (68); 29.3.1761-11.6.1761 Expedition against Belle-Isle; 13.9.1764 4L *Thunderer* (74); 20.3.1765-19.4.1768 L. *Fly* (8) Sloop; 4.12.1770-7.6.1771[P] 4L *Ajax* (74); 17.4.1776 LCmdr *Rose* Hired Tender; 12.11.1778-15.12.1779[C] LCmdr *Jackall* (10) Cutter; 12.8.1780 LCmdr *Speedwell* (14) Cutter; **Commander**; 21.3.1782 *Speedwell* (14) Cutter; **Captain**; 23.12.1782-9.1.1784[P] *Brilliant* (28); 8.5.1787-15.3.1791 *Perseus* (20); 23.4.1804 **Superannuated Captain.**

GIDEON, HENRY

Dates: 1781 Died; 5.10.1781 Will Probate.
Family:
Service: 7.3.1744/45 **Lieutenant.**

GIDEON, SOLOMON

Dates: 3.9.1756 Died.
Family:
Service: **Lieutenant**; 17.9.1706[(11.11.1706)]-26.10.1710[P] L. *Kinsale* (36); 23.5.1711-11.7.1711 L. *Sapphire* (42); 12.7.1711-19.10.1715 L. *Kinsale* (36); 23.2.1733/34-3.5.1737[P] 1L *Leopard* (50); 30.8.1739-29.2.1739/40 1L *Norfolk* (80); **Commander**; 1.3.1739/40-24.4.1740 *Blaze* (8) Fireship; **Captain**; 6.9.1740-18.10.1743[P] *Panther* (54); 10.11.1743 *Chichester* (80); 12.12.1743-10.6.1746[P] *Shrewsbury* (80); 21.6.1756 **Superannuated Rear Admiral.**

GIDOIN, JOHN LEWIS

Dates: c.1727 Born; 2.1796 Died Modbury, Devon.
Family: Wife Mary Legassicke married 15.11.1763.
Service: 28.6.1742 Capt Serv *Deptford* (60); 14.12.1743 Capt Serv *Suffolk* (70); 2.4.1744 Capt Serv *Hampton Court* (64); 8.1.1744/45 Action of 1745-01-08; 5.9.1745 Able *Hampton Court* (64); 18.9.1746 Mid *Hampton Court* (64); 11.10.1748 Passed; **Lieutenant**; 19.1.1755[(JAM 17.8.1756)] L. *Weazle* (16) Sloop; 14.2.1755 3L *Severn* (50); 12.10.1755 2L *Severn* (50); 23.4.1756 1L *Severn* (50); 11.1.1757 3L *Marlborough* (80); **Commander**; 9.3.1759 *Port Royal* (12) Storeship; 20.3.1759[(JAM 26.6.1761)]-22.7.1761 *Port Antonio* (12) Storeship; 3.5.1762 *Zephyr* (10) Sloop; 15.7.1763-11.2.1767[P] *Jamaica* (10) Sloop; **Captain**; 26.5.1768 *Surprise* (24); 13.3.1776-22.7.1779 *Richmond* (32); 11.8.1778 Howe's encounter with d'Estaing; 25.12.1779-17.3.1783 *Torbay* (74); 17.4.1780 Battle of Martinique; 29.4.1781-30.4.1781 Battle of Fort Royal; 25.1.1782-26.1.1782 Battle of Saint Kitts; 12.4.1782 Battle of the Saintes; 12.4.1794 **Rear Admiral of the White**; 4.7.1794 **Rear Admiral of the Red**; 1.6.1795 **Vice Admiral of the White.**

GILCHRIST, JAMES

Dates: 1777 Died Hunsfield, Lanarkshire.
Family: Wife Ann.
Service: 21.1.1728/29-24.2.1731/32 Able *Dursley Galley* (20); 24.2.1731/32-28.7.1732 Able *Kingston* (60); 29.4.1732 Mid *Hector* (40); 14.6.1734 Passed; **Lieutenant**; 28.8.1741 L. *Blast* (8) Bomb Vessel; 14.8.1742[(JAM 3.10.1745)]-4.11.1746 2L *Rippon* (60); 13.10.1747-12.4.1749[P] L.

Apollo (14) Storeship; **Commander**; 16.1.1749/50[(EI 11.5.1750)]-8.5.1750[P] *Basilisk* (8) Bomb Vessel; **Captain**; 18.7.1755-26.6.1756 *Experiment* (24); 20.5.1756 Battle of Minorca; 4.4.1757-11.12.1759 *Southampton* (32); 5.6.1758-12.6.1758 Raid on Saint-Malo.

GILL, THOMAS

Dates: c.1733 Born.

Family:

Service: 10.3.1746 Capt Serv *Falkland* (50); 3.5.1747 1st Battle of Cape Finisterre; 26.6.1747 Capt Serv *Falkland* (50); 3.12.1747 Capt Serv *Defiance* (60); 26.7.1748 Capt Serv *Weazle* (16) Sloop; 18.3.1749 Able *Tilbury* (58); 1.1.1750 MidO *Surprise* (24); 16.9.1750 Able *Humber* (44); 28.7.1751 Mid *Glory* (44); 14.1.1752 Mate *Swan* (14) Sloop; 9.5.1752 Able *Glory* (44); 8.6.1752 Mid *Glory* (44); 30.9.1752 Able *Glory* (44); 4.10.1752 Mate *Glory* (44); 9.1.1754 Passed; **Lieutenant**; 15.1.1756-20.3.1756 L. *Albany* (14) Sloop.

GILLAM, THOMAS

Dates: c.1723 Born; 1759 Died; 20.3.1759 Will Probate.

Family: Wife Jane Saunders married 13.3.1749.

Service: 1740-1746 Merchant Service; 11.1.1745/46 Mid *Chesterfield* (44); 10.3.1746/47 Mate *Chesterfield* (44); 29.4.1748 Mid *Chesterfield* (44); 14.9.1749 Passed; **Lieutenant**; 5.12.1749-17.11.1752[P] 3L *Anson* (60); 14.10.1755-1759[†] 2L *Sutherland* (50); 8.1757-10.1757 Louisbourg Expedition; 6.6.1758-27.7.1758 The Siege of Louisbourg.

GILLINGHAM, ROBERT

Dates: c.1735 Born.

Family:

Service: 24.4.1756 Able *Yarmouth* (64); 28.8.1756 Able *Yarmouth* (64); 12.12.1756 QM *Invincible* (74); 8.1757-10.1757 Louisbourg Expedition; 13.1.1758-19.2.1758[P] Mid *Invincible* (74); 22.3.1758 Mid *Royal George* (100); 24.10.1758 Mate *Royal Anne* (100); 20.2.1760 Passed; **Lieutenant**; 4.4.1760 5L *Princess Amelia* (80); 29.3.1761-11.6.1761 Expedition against Belle-Isle; 9.6.1762 4L *Princess Amelia* (80); 22.6.1762-14.1.1763[P] 4L *Magnanime* (74); 30.11.1770 3L *Trident* (64); 21.12.1770-21.5.1771 2L *Trident* (64); 18.11.1775 4L *Royal Oak* (74); 3.2.1777 3L *Royal Oak* (74); 6.9.1777-26.1.1778 2L *Royal Oak* (74); 29.4.1778-8.1.1781[P] 1L *Elizabeth* (74); 27.7.1778 1st Battle of Ushant; 6.7.1779 Battle of Grenada; 18.12.1779 Combat de la Martinique; 17.4.1780 Battle of Martinique; 15.5.1780 Action of March 15 1780; 19.5.1780 Action of March 19 1780.

GILLIS, JOHN

Dates: c.1712 Born; 25.9.1712 Baptised; 1773 Died Greenwich; 24.4.1773 Will Probate.

Family: Father Thomas Gillis; Brother Archibald; Sister Janet; Sister Ann; Sister Elizabeth.

Service: 23.11.1733 Able *Deptford* (60); 12.10.1735-31.3.1736[P] Able *Kent* (70); 13.12.1739 Able *Kent* (70); 6.2.1739/40 Mid *Kent* (70); 8.4.1740 Capture of the Princesa; 5.4.1744-15.9.1744[P] Mate *Kent* (70); 11.10.1744 Passed; **Lieutenant**; 19.12.1744 L. *Jamaica* (10) Sloop; 21.10.1747 3L *Tavistock* (50); 23.9.1748 3L *Anson* (60); 5.12.1749-17.11.1752[P] 2L *Anson* (60); 5.6.1755-19.10.1759 1L *Portland* (50); 20.5.1756 Battle of Minorca; 5.4.1757 Action of April 5 1757; 5.6.1758-12.6.1758 Raid on Saint-Malo; 18.8.1759-19.8.1759 Battle of Lagos Bay.

GIRLING, JOHN

Dates: 1794 Died Ipswich; 3.4.1794 Will Probate.
Family: Daughter Anna Maria.
Service: **Lieutenant**; 30.11.1759[JAM 27.10.1760] 3L *Saint Albans* (60); 1.2.1760[JAM 27.10.1760]-22.12.1760[P] 3L *Rainbow* (44); 13.8.1761-8.2.1763[P] 3L *Revenge* (64); 25.3.1763-1.12.1766 2L *Niger* (32).

GLASFORD, JAMES

Dates: c.1736 Born; 1796 Died Saltash; 27.8.1796 Will Probate.
Family: Wife Jane.
Service: 28.5.1750 Capt Serv *Mermaid* (24); 20.4.1753 Able *Mermaid* (24); 6.6.1753 Mid *Mermaid* (24); 13.9.1753 Able *Arundel* (24); 3.4.1755 Mid *Newcastle* (50); 10.3.1757 Passed; **Lieutenant**; 1.10.1758[EI 30.10.1765]-4.3.1759 4L *Tiger* (60); 1.5.1766-16.12.1767[P] L. *Favorite* (16) Sloop; 23.8.1769 1L *Boston* (32); 15.1.1771-11.5.1771[P] 1L *Royal William* (84); 25.10.1771 1L *Kent* (74); 7.7.1775 2L *Ocean* (90); 30.8.1777 1L *Ocean* (90); 25.10.1777 2L *Ocean* (90); 13.5.1778 1L *Ocean* (90); 27.7.1778 1st Battle of Ushant; 2.9.1779-3.10.1780 1L *Ocean* (90); 2.10.1780-30.11.1782 LCmdr *Monkey* (12) Cutter; **Commander**; 25.12.1782-31.3.1783[P] *Alderney* (12) Sloop; 5.11.1783-17.4.1786 *Otter* (14) Sloop; **Captain**; 22.11.1790-3.12.1792 *Orpheus* (32).

GLOVER, BONOVIER

Dates: 23.3.1780 Died; 16.8.1780 Will Probate.
Family:
Service: **Lieutenant**; 8.12.1760[NA 3.6.1761] 4L *Thunderer* (74); **Commander**; 6.8.1762-2.4.1763[P] *Favorite* (16) Sloop; **Captain**; 20.6.1765-10.1.1771 *Unicorn* (28); 4.10.1770-21.3.1771 *Tartar* (28); 15.4.1778-23.3.1780 *Janus* (44); 20.3.1780 1st Action off Monti Christi.

GLOVER, JOHN

Dates: c.1721 Born; 20.8.1778 Died.
Family:
Service: 5.2.1739/40 Mid *Rochester* (54); 4.1.1740/41-19.1.1744/45[P] Mid *Buckingham* (70); 11.2.1743/44-12.2.1743/44 Battle of Toulon; 30.5.1745 Mid *Shrewsbury* (80); 3.7.1746 Passed; **Lieutenant**; 20.6.1757 L. *Adventure* (18) Hired Armed Ship; 21.9.1757 3L *Montagu* (60); 28.2.1758 Battle of Cartagena; 22.2.1759 2L *Montagu* (60); 20.11.1759 Battle of Quiberon Bay; 2.10.1761-20.11.1761 1L *Montagu* (60); 19.4.1768-24.4.1771[P] LCmdr *Friendship* (4) Cutter; 11.1772-29.8.1775[P] LCmdr *Folkestone* (6) Cutter.

GOARD, JOHN

Dates: 1719 Born; 19.4.1719 Baptised East Looe, Cornwall; c.7.1755 Died; 3.7.1755 Buried Pembury, Kent; 4.12.1755 Will Probate.
Family: Father John Goard; Mother Mary Strong; Wife Ann.
Service: 18.5.1735 Capt Serv *York* (60); 11.3.1738 Able *Torrington* (40); 17.11.1741 Mid *Hampshire* (50); 17.11.1743 Passed; **Lieutenant**; 16.1.1744/45 L. *Aetna* (8) Fireship; 26.7.1745 2L *York* (60); 23.2.1746/47-5.6.1748[P] 2L *Chichester* (80); 30.9.1748 L. *Lyme* (24); 27.12.1750-18.11.1752[P] 2L *Vanguard* (68); 6.2.1755-c.7.1755† 1L *Ipswich* (64).

GODDARD, SAMUEL

Dates: 27.9.1762 Died Warwickshire; 29.9.1762 Buried Warwickshire.
Family:
Service: 10.11.1718 Vol-p-O *Mermaid* (36); 22.4.1721 MidO *Mermaid* (36); 9.9.1722 Mid *Mermaid* (36); 11.1.1723/24-31.12.1724[P] MidO *Bredah* (70); 11.3.1725/26 Passed; **Lieutenant**; 23.12.1727[(5.9.1728)]-4.9.1728[P] 3L *Leopard* (50); 9.2.1728/29-14.12.1729[P] 3L *Kingston* (60); 8.5.1731-24.12.1731[P] 3L *Grafton* (70); 1.1.1731/32-13.6.1732 2L *Grafton* (70); 14.6.1732-4.9.1732 4L *Grafton* (70); 5.9.1732-9.8.1739 L. *Cruizer* (8) Sloop; 14.8.1739-15.1.1740/41 1L *Ruby* (54); **Commander**; 22.1.1740/41 *Shark* (8) Sloop; **Captain**; 1.2.1742/43 *Deal Castle* (20); 4.9.1744[(West Indies 15.10.1745)]-18.10.1745[P] *Lynn* (44); 3.1744/45 Dismissed.

GODFREY, ANDREW

Dates: c.1727 Born; 23.8.1798 Died.
Family:
Service: 1754-1757 HEIC Service; 2.4.1757 Able *Ramillies* (90); 18.7.1757 Mid *Ramillies* (90); 5.9.1757-6.10.1757 Raid on Rochefort; 20.1.1758 Mid *Bideford* (20); 7.4.1758 Mate *Bideford* (20); 1.6.1758 Mate *Vestal* (32); 17.5.1759 Able *Vestal* (32); 23.5.1759 Mate *Duke* (90); 20.11.1759 Battle of Quiberon Bay; 14.5.1760 Passed; **Lieutenant**; 24.6.1761 6L *Marlborough* (68); 3.10.1761 5L *Marlborough* (68); 28.10.1761 6L *Marlborough* (68); 7.1.1762-10.2.1762 Operations against Martinique; 17.3.1762[(BLI 2.5.1763)]-13.5.1763[P] 4L *Devonshire* (70); 6.6.1762-13.8.1762 Operations against Havana; 5.11.1776-6.10.1778 3L *Saint Albans* (64).

GODFREY, JOHN

Dates: c.1734 Born; 1767 Died.
Family:
Service: 25.9.1750 Ord. *Warwick* (60); 23.1.1751 Able *Warwick* (60); 20.10.1752 Able *Assistance* (50); 13.1.1754 Able *Culloden*; 29.3.1754 Mid *Mermaid* (24); 22.5.1755-14.6.1755 British attack on Fort Beauséjour; 21.4.1756 Able *Hornet* (10) Sloop; 1.12.1756 Passed; **Lieutenant**; 15.3.1757 3L *Ludlow Castle* (44); 30.9.1758-16.1.1760[P] 2L *Ludlow Castle* (44); 16.1.1759-19.1.1759 Attack on Martinique; 20.1.1759-1.5.1759 Capture of Guadeloupe.

GODSALVE, HENRY

Dates: c.1713 Born; 1.12.1765 Died; 10.12.1765 Buried Great Baddow, Essex.
Family: Wife Honoria Hawker married 3.2.1758.
Service: 29.4.1728-22.8.1728[P] Vol-p-O *Bredah* (70); 6.11.1728 Vol-p-O *Nottingham* (60); 15.7.1731 Mid *Grafton* (70); 9.2.1731/32 MidO *Grafton* (70); 31.7.1732 Mid *Grafton* (70); 4.10.1732 MidO *Grafton* (70); 26.3.1734 Mid *Grafton* (70); 24.5.1734 Mid *Britannia* (100); 18.1.1734/35 Passed; **Lieutenant**; 23.5.1738 4L *Berwick* (70); 14.6.1739 3L *Pembroke* (60); 1.11.1739[(MED 2.5.1746)] 4L *Somerset* (80); 17.1.1739/40[(MED 2.5.1746)] 2L *Somerset* (80); **Commander**; 4.4.1740[(14.7.1743)]-6.5.1741 *Salamander* (6) Bomb Vessel; **Captain**; 17.5.1741[(MED 15.1.1744/45)] *Garland* (20); 4.4.1743[(MED 15.1.1744/45)]-10.8.1746 *Romney* (50); 11.2.1743/44-12.2.1743/44 Battle of Toulon; 13.7.1756 **Superannuated Rear Admiral**.

GODWIN, JAMES

Dates: c.1740 Born; 1811 Died; 20.12.1811 Will Probate.
Family:
Service: 7.7.1757 Able *Southampton* (32); 5.6.1758-12.6.1758 Raid on Saint-Malo; 16.10.1758 Mid *Southampton* (32); 4.10.1759 Able *Southampton* (32); 28.11.1759 Mid *Barfleur* (80);

19.4.1760 Mid *Fame* (74); 11.2.1761 Passed; **Lieutenant**; 7.10.1762-23.1.1763[P] 5L *Terrible* (74); 11.6.1767-9.10.1770 L. *Martin* (14) Sloop; 10.3.1777 1L *Venus* (36); 11.8.1778 Howe's encounter with d'Estaing; 14.12.1778-15.12.1778 Battle of St. Lucia; 17.4.1780 Battle of Martinique; 15.5.1780 Action of March 15 1780; 19.5.1780 Action of March 19 1780; 24.7.1781-3.3.1783[P] LCmdr *Basilisk* (14) Sloop.

GOOD, JOHN

Dates: c.1736 Born; 8.10.1769 Buried Bridport.
Family:
Service: 1754-1757 Merchant Service; 26.1.1757 QM *Sunderland* (60); 27.4.1757 Mid *Sunderland* (60); 31.5.1757 Sail Crew *Saint Albans* (60); 2.6.1758 Mid *Hampton Court* (64); 3.5.1759 Supnum *Duke* (90); 21.6.1759 Mid *Hero* (74); 20.11.1759 Battle of Quiberon Bay; 8.6.1760 Mate *Hero* (74); 11.2.1761 Passed; **Lieutenant**; 7.7.1762 3L *Chester* (50); 24.12.1762-4.4.1763[P] 2L *Chester* (50); 18.6.1767-bef.8.10.1769[†] LCmdr *Anson* (6) Cutter.

GOODALL, SAMUEL GRANSTON

Dates: 21.4.1801 Died Teignmouth.
Family:
Service: **Lieutenant**; 1.9.1756 6L *Namur* (90); 9.11.1756-27.1.1758 5L *Namur* (90); 5.9.1757-6.10.1757 Raid on Rochefort; **Commander**; 2.6.1760 *Hazard* (8) Sloop; **Captain**; 13.1.1762-30.3.1764[P] *Mercury* (20); 6.6.1762-13.8.1762 Operations against Havana; 23.2.1769-17.4.1772 *Winchelsea* (32); 18.2.1778 *Defiance* (64); 27.7.1778 1st Battle of Ushant; 20.3.1779-14.7.1783[P] *Valiant* (74); 31.12.1779 Affair of Fielding and Bylandt; 12.12.1781 2nd Battle of Ushant; 12.4.1782 Battle of the Saintes; 19.4.1782 Battle of the Mona Passage; 20.7.1789 CinC — English Channel; 19.5.1790 *Gibraltar* (80); 21.9.1790 **Rear Admiral of the Blue**; 3.1792-3.1793 *Romney* (50); 10.3.1792 CinC — The Mediterranean Sea; 1.1793-12.4.1794 *Princess Royal* (98); 1.2.1793 **Rear Admiral of the Red; Vice Admiral of the Blue**; 12.4.1794-1795 *Princess Royal* (98); 4.7.1794 **Vice Admiral of the White**; 1.6.1795 **Vice Admiral of the Red**; 14.2.1799 **Admiral of the Blue**; 1.1.1801 **Admiral of the White.**

GOODING, JOHN

Dates: c.1735 Born; 1763 Died; 19.5.1763 Will Probate.
Family:
Service: 1754-1756 Merchant Service; 22.4.1756 Able *Winchelsea* (20); 25.1.1757 Mid *Winchelsea* (20); 8.1757-10.1757 Louisbourg Expedition; 22.10.1757-10.10.1758[C] Mate *Winchelsea* (20); 22.6.1759 Able *Royal George* (100); 3.9.1759 Mid *Royal George* (100); 20.11.1759 Battle of Quiberon Bay; 20.2.1760 Passed; **Lieutenant**; 11.4.1760-23.9.1762[W] L. *Scorpion* (14) Sloop.

GOODING, NATHANIEL

Dates: 1811 Died; 18.4.1811 Will Probate.
Family:
Service: **Lieutenant**; 23.11.1759[EI 27.4.1763] 4L *Falmouth* (50); 7.6.1761[EI 27.4.1763] 3L *Falmouth* (50); 26.1.1762[EI 27.4.1763]-8.11.1762 2L *Falmouth* (50); 24.9.1762-6.10.1762 Battle of Manilla.

GOOSTREY, WILLIAM
Dates: 1.7.1762 Died.
Family:
Service: **Lieutenant**; 5.6.1744[14.2.1746/47] 6L *Marlborough* (90); 17.9.1744[MED 21.11.1748] 3L *Nonsuch* (50); 29.1.1744/45[MED 21.11.1748]-15.11.1748[P] 2L *Nonsuch* (50); 6.2.1755 1L *Ramillies* (90); 13.5.1755 1L *Terrible* (74); 5.7.1756 2L *Marlborough* (80); 16.11.1756-11.1.1757 1L *Marlborough* (80); 10.2.1757 1L *Newark* (80); 8.1757-10.1757 Louisbourg Expedition; **Commander**; 12.12.1757 *Lightning* (6) Hospital Ship; 6.6.1758-27.7.1758 The Siege of Louisbourg; **Captain**; 23.1.1759 *Dublin* (74); 12.12.1759-1.7.1762† *Cambridge* (80); 6.1.1761[JAM 24.1.1763]-22.1.1761 *Hampshire* (50).

GORDON, ALEXANDER
Dates: c.1712 Born; 1783 Died; 8.12.1783 Will Probate.
Family:
Service: 29.5.1733 Able *Burford* (70); 16.12.1733 Able *Guernsey* (50); 21.1.1733/34 Able *Lark* (40); 6.6.1735 Mid *Lark* (40); 1.2.1735/36 Able *Dursley Galley* (20); 17.2.1736/37 Mid *Greyhound* (20); 25.12.1737 Mid *Deptford* (60); 17.4.1740 Passed; **Lieutenant**; 25.2.1741/42 L. *Mortar* (8) Bomb Vessel; 16.6.1744 4L *Princess Amelia* (80); 14.7.1744-15.2.1744/45[P] 3L *Princess Amelia* (80); 17.5.1745 2L *Shrewsbury* (80); 26.4.1746-10.6.1746[P] 1L *Shrewsbury* (80); 1760-1783 Lieutenant of Greenwich Hospital.

GORDON, JAMES
Dates: c.1732 Born; 15.4.1776 Died; 3.7.1776 Will Probate.
Family: Wife Jane.
Service: 28.10.1747 Capt Serv *Trial* (10) Sloop; 28.6.1748 Capt Serv *Siren* (20); 4.11.1748 Capt Serv *Eagle* (60); 29.3.1751 Able *Success* (20); 19.5.1752 Mid *Success* (20); 13.11.1754 Passed; **Lieutenant**; 19.2.1756 L. *Bideford* (20); 13.3.1756-12.5.1758 3L *Sutherland* (50); 8.1757-10.1757 Louisbourg Expedition; 10.3.1761-23.6.1761 L. *Lightning* (6) Hospital Ship; 27.11.1763-27.11.1765 LCmdr *Alarm* (6) Cutter.

GORDON, JAMES
Dates: c.1721 Born; 20.10.1781 Died Greenwich; 21.10.1781 Buried St Alfege, Greenwich.
Family:
Service: 6.9.1743 Able *Salisbury* (50); 11.2.1743/44-12.2.1743/44 Battle of Toulon; 13.6.1744 Able *Princess* (70); 26.10.1746-29.12.1747[P] Mid *Sapphire* (44); 1748-1756 Merchant Service; 1.8.1756 Mate *Berwick* (64); 30.12.1756 Mid *Cambridge* (80); 26.5.1757 Mate *Devonshire* (70); 14.12.1757 Passed; **Lieutenant**; 24.1.1758 L. *Gibraltar's Prize* (14) Tender; 10.4.1758 L. *London* (18) Hired Armed vessel; 22.2.1759 L. *Lightning* (6) Hospital Ship; 22.3.1759 4L *Conqueror* (68); 18.8.1759-19.8.1759 Battle of Lagos Bay; 20.9.1759[JAM 26.5.1760] 2L *Lynn* (44); 23.12.1760-17.12.1761 L. *Granado* (10) Sloop; 17.8.1762[EI 29.7.1763]-10.8.1763[P] 2L *Temeraire* (74); 29.9.1770-29.5.1771[P] 3L *Defence* (74); 8.8.1771-15.9.1773[P] LCmdr *Endeavour* (6) Discovery Vessel; 28.11.1773-22.10.1774[P] LCmdr *Endeavour* (6) Storeship; 20.4.1776-24.12.1778[P] LCmdr *Boulogne* (32); 6.8.1778-10.4.1779 1L *Lennox* (74).

GORDON, JOHN

Dates: c.1718 Born; 6.4.1762 Died; 11.5.1762 Will Probate.

Family:

Service: 12.12.1733 Capt Serv *Kingston* (60); 23.1.1733/34 Capt Serv *Hector* (40); 22.1.1737/38-13.4.1742[P] Able *Hector* (40); 4.1740-5.7.1740 Attack on St. Augustine; 3.6.1742-20.8.1744[P] Mid *Hound* (8) Sloop; 6.9.1744 Passed; **Lieutenant**; 6.10.1744 3L *Maidstone* (50); 15.8.1746 3L *Romney* (44); 30.11.1747-4.11.1748[P] 2L *Romney* (44); 11.3.1755 2L *Warwick* (60); 30.4.1755 L. *Seaford* (20); 14.8.1755-16.5.1757[P] 3L *Oxford* (50); 20.5.1757 3L *Prince Frederick* (64); 17.6.1757 2L *Prince Frederick* (64); 17.1.1758-6.4.1762[†] 1L *Prince Frederick* (64); 6.6.1758-27.7.1758 The Siege of Louisbourg; 29.3.1761-11.6.1761 Expedition against Belle-Isle.

GORDON, LEWIS

Dates: c.1733 Born; 5.1758 Died.

Family:

Service: 1750-1755 Merchant Service; 18.3.1755 Mid *Medway* (60); 29.7.1756 Mate *Medway* (60); 21.12.1756 Mate *Royal George* (100); 27.1.1757 Mate *Namur* (90); 2.5.1757 Passed; **Lieutenant**; 15.6.1757-10.10.1757 L. *Roman Emperor* (16) Sloop; 4.2.1758-29.5.1758 L. *Kennington* (20).

GORDON, ROBERT

Dates: c.1716 Born; 1782 Died; 23.1.1782 Will Probate.

Family:

Service: 18.7.1738 Able *Deptford* (24) Storeship; 9.9.1739 Mate *Deptford* (24) Storeship; 11.11.1739 Mid *Deptford* (24) Storeship; 26.9.1740 Able *Deptford* (24) Storeship; 12.1.1740/41 Mid *Carcass* (8) Bomb Vessel; 19.5.1742 Mid *Looe* (44); 1.12.1742 Mid *Preston* (50); 17.7.1744 Mid *Wager* (20); 2.8.1744 Passed; **Lieutenant**; 1.3.1744/45 L. *Tavistock* (28) Mer; 14.10.1747 L. *Portsmouth* (24) Storeship; 6.4.1748-2.8.1748[P] 3L *Hampshire* (50); 7.10.1755 L. *Ferret* (14) Sloop; 11.6.1756 3L *Saint George* (90); 30.3.1757 2L *Saint George* (90); 6.4.1757 1L *Saint George* (90); 1.6.1757[(9.6.1760)]-15.8.1760 1L *Culloden* (74); 18.8.1759-19.8.1759 Battle of Lagos Bay.

GORDON, THOMAS

Dates: 31.12.1761 Died.

Family: Wife Ann.

Service: **Lieutenant**; 26.12.1743[(BLI 17.2.1748/49)]-1.5.1745 L. *Scarborough* (20); 26.8.1746[(JAM 4.4.1749)] 3L *Cornwall* (80); 9.4.1748 Battle of Santiago de Cuba; 23.7.1748[(JAM 4.4.1749)]-29.12.1748[P] 2L *Lennox* (70); 12.10.1748 Battle of Havana; 21.5.1755-12.5.1756 1L *Antelope* (50); **Commander**; 23.5.1757-17.4.1758[P] *William and Ann* (20) Hired Armed Ship; 1759-1.1761 Impress Service at Bristol; 2.7.1761 ActCapt *Alarm* (32); **Captain**; 10.9.1761-31.12.1761[W] *Bideford* (20).

GORDON, WILLIAM

Dates: 1705 Born Elgin, Moray; 25.4.1769 Died Banff, Aberdeenshire.

Family: Wife Elizabeth Forbes; Son William (1753-1772); Daughter Margaret [Forbes] (1755-1841); Son John (1756-1759).

Service: 2.5.1727 Mid *Berwick* (70); 3.7.1729 Mate *Berwick* (70); 24.10.1729 MidO *Winchelsea* (20); 1.9.1730 Mate *Princess Louisa* (40); 21.8.1731 Mid *Captain* (70); 2.8.1732 Mate *Captain* (70); 27.9.1732 Mid *Captain* (70); 2.8.1733 Mate *Captain* (70); 23.3.1733/34 Passed; **Lieutenant**; 1.5.1735[(2.8.1738)] 2L *Dunkirk* (60); 26.12.1735[(2.8.1738)]-10.1737 L. *Drake* (8) Sloop; 3.7.1739-6.1.1739/40 L. *Mercury* (8) Fireship; 30.1.1740/41 5L *Sandwich* (90);

27.3.1741 1L *Greenwich* (50); 13.4.1741 4L *Sandwich* (90); 5.10.1741-2.4.1742 3L *Sandwich* (90); **Commander**; 22.5.1742 *Hound* (8) Sloop; **Captain**; 26.5.1744-6.7.1744 *Gosport* (44); 4.8.1744-11.7.1745 *Sheerness* (20); 3.7.1745 Action of 1745-07-03; 20.7.1745-18.9.1745 *Looe* (44); 2.11.1745 *Chesterfield* (44); 23.11.1747-20.12.1748[P] *Assistance* (50); 18.9.1755 *Saint Albans* (60); 5.11.1756 *Cambridge* (80); 5.5.1757-5.3.1760 *Devonshire* (70); 6.6.1758-27.7.1758 The Siege of Louisbourg; 5.8.1761-26.9.1762 *Blenheim* (90); 8.4.1762-1765 CinC — Thames, Medway and The Nore; 21.10.1762 **Rear Admiral of the White.**

GORE, HAMILTON

Dates: 1719 Born; 10.1777 Died.
Family: Father William Gore (1680-1731); Mother Honora Prittie ((1687-1767); Brother William (d.1784); Brother Henry (d.1787); Brother Frederick (d.1764); Brother Ralph; Sister Catherine [Clements] (1705-1781); Sister Elizabeth [Brereton] (d.1765).
Service: 31.8.1734 Vol-p-O *Swallow* (60); 31.3.1737-30.9.1739 Able *Seaford* (20); 8.10.1739 Able *Seaford* (20); 29.11.1739-5.5.1740[P] Mid *Seaford* (20); 16.6.1740 Mid *Cambridge* (80); 6.5.1742 Passed; **Lieutenant**; 2.4.1743[(MED 6.12.1745)] 4L *Essex* (70); 4.6.1743[(MED 6.12.1745)] 3L *Essex* (70); 11.2.1743/44-12.2.1743/44 Battle of Toulon; 11.8.1746-4.11.1748[P] 1L *Romney* (44); 31.5.1750-8.6.1754[P] L. *Blandford* (20); 7.5.1755-4.3.1759[P] 1L *Eagle* (60); 30.3.1759 1L *Hercules* (74); 20.11.1759 Battle of Quiberon Bay; 23.12.1762[(MED 23.5.1763)]-10.5.1763[P] 1L *Blenheim* (90); **Commander**; 20.6.1765-1.7.1766 *Swift* (14) Sloop; 9.12.1776-10.1777[F] *Pegasus* (14) Sloop.

GOUGH, JOHN

Dates: c.1737 Born; 1771 Died.
Family:
Service: 26.11.1753 Able *Hazard* (8) Sloop; 30.4.1755 Mid *Somerset* (68); 23.7.1757 Able *Somerset* (68); 2.3.1758 Mid *Somerset* (68); 6.6.1758-27.7.1758 The Siege of Louisbourg; 12.3.1759 Mate *Somerset* (68); 5.3.1760 Passed; **Lieutenant**; 27.9.1762-22.1.1763[P] 6L *Sandwich* (90); 18.8.1766-3.6.1768 L. *Peggy* (8) Sloop; 3.6.1768 Dismissed.

GOUGH, WILLIAM

Dates: c.1722 Born; 1760 Died.
Family:
Service: 16.2.1738 Capt Serv *Falmouth* (50); 5.8.1740 Mid *Falmouth* (50); 4.3.1740/41-5.1741 Operations against Cartagena; 26.12.1741 Mid *Sutherland* (50); 26.4.1742 Able *Sutherland* (50); 3.5.1742 Mid *Sutherland* (50); 27.11.1743-7.6.1744 Mid *Hampshire* (50); 7.6.1744 Passed; **Lieutenant**; 10.7.1744 L. *Swift* (8) Sloop; 11.1.1744/45 3L *Torrington* (44); 6.3.1744/45-13.2.1746/47[P] 2L *Torrington* (44); 1.12.1748 3L *Fougueux* (64); 8.5.1751-16.11.1752[P] 2L *Fougueux* (64); 22.2.1755 2L *Kingston* (60); 30.9.1755 1L *Kingston* (60); 7.10.1755 1L *Ramillies* (90); 20.5.1756 Battle of Minorca; **Commander**; 6.6.1756[(MED 15.2.1757)] *Seahorse* (24); **Captain**; 26.6.1756[(MED 15.2.1757)]-4.7.1756 *Experiment* (24); 31.8.1758-5.11.1761 *Penzance* (44); 3.6.1761-7.6.1761 Occupation of Dominica.

GOULD, ABRAHAM

Dates: 1764 Died.
Family:
Service: 8.9.1721 Ord. *Orford* (70); 3.7.1722 Able *Shrewsbury* (80); 27.6.1723 MidO *Colchester* (50); 2.7.1724 Mid *Colchester* (50); 3.4.1725 Mid *Monmouth* (70); 5.12.1727 Passed; **Lieutenant**; 18.1.1727/28-4.4.1729 3L *Mary Galley* (40); 31.1.1733/34 4L *Revenge* (70); 23.2.1733/34 3L

Burford (70); 12.3.1733/34 2L *Burford* (70); 20.5.1735-30.4.1737[P] 1L *Burford* (70); 12.11.1739-5.8.1740 1L *Lichfield* (50); **Commander**; 17.12.1740-22.8.1742 *Deptford* (24) Storeship.

GOWER, THE HON. JOHN LEVESON
Dates: 11.7.1740 Born Wokingham, Berkshire; 15.8.1792 Died.
Family: Father John, 1st Earl Gower; Mother Mary Tufton (1701-1785); Wife Francis Boscawen married 5.7.1773; Son Augustus, RN (1782-1802); Son Edward, RN (1776-1853); Half-sister Gertrude [Russell] (1715-1794); Half-sister Mary [Wrottesley] (1717-1778); Half-sister Frances [Sackville] (1720-1788); Half-brother Granville, Visct. Trentham (1721-1803); Half-sister Elizabeth [Waldegrave] (1724-1784); Half-sister Evelyn [FitzPatrick/Vernon] (1725-1763); Brother Thomas (1738-c.1738).
Service: **Lieutenant**; 18.11.1758[(Africa 19.3.0017)]-2.2.1759 5L *Torbay* (74); 29.12.1758 Capture of Goree; 5.1.1760 4L *Valiant* (74); **Commander**; 6.2.1760 *Kingfisher* (8) Bomb Vessel; **Captain**; 30.6.1760 *Flamborough* (20); 23.8.1760-9.5.1763[P] *Quebec* (32); 6.9.1764-30.11.1765[P] *Africa* (64); 6.1.1766-9.6.1767 *Aeolus* (32); 19.1.1769-10.12.1770 *Pearl* (32); 20.9.1773-27.10.1775 *Albion* (74); 2.10.1776-20.3.1779 *Valiant* (74); 27.7.1778 1st Battle of Ushant; 10.4.1782-14.11.1782 1Capt. *Victory* (100); 20.10.1782 Battle of Cape Spartel; 30.1.1783-9.4.1783 Lord Commissioner of the Admiralty; 31.12.1783-11.8.1789 Lord Commissioner of the Admiralty; 9.4.1784-5.7.1790 M.P. for Appleby; 23.5.1785-7.10.1785[P] Commodore *Hebe* (38); 11.6.1787 CinC — English Channel; **Rear Admiral of the Blue**; 24.9.1787 *Edgar* (74); 22.5.1788 CinC — English Channel; 5.1790-10.1790 *Queen Charlotte* (100); 5.7.1790-15.8.1792 M.P. for Newcastle under Lyme; 8.7.1790 First Captain; 21.9.1790 **Rear Admiral of the White**; 3.1791-9.1791 *Formidable* (98).

GRAEME, ALEXANDER
Dates: 9.12.1741 Born Graemeshall, Holm, on the Orkney Islands; 5.8.1818 Died Edinburgh.
Family: Father Mungo Graeme; Mother Jean Chancellor.
Service: **Lieutenant**; 24.8.1760[(BLI 9.3.1763)]-13.3.1762 5L *Dublin* (74); 7.1.1762-10.2.1762 Operations against Martinique; 17.3.1762-18.9.1763[P] 1L *Aquilon* (28); 13.9.1764-1.3.1765 3L *Thunderer* (74); 20.3.1765 3L *Superb* (74); 17.10.1765-2.2.1771 LCmdr *Egmont* (10) Schooner; 26.1.1774 2L *Preston* (50); 14.11.1775 *Kingfisher* (14) Sloop; 15.11.1775 **Commander**; 6.12.1776-8.12.1776 Occupation of Rhode Island; **Captain**; 24.1.1778[(NA 28.10.1778)] *Sphinx* (20); 11.8.1778 Howe's encounter with d'Estaing; 24.11.1778[(NA 25.5.1779)] *Diamond* (32); 9.1.1779[(NA 25.5.1779)]-13.4.1779[P] *Pearl* (32); 14.7.1779 *Tartar* (28); 13.3.1781-13.8.1781 *Preston* (50); 5.8.1781 Battle of Dogger Bank; 5.1.1795 *Glory* (98); 1.6.1795 **Rear Admiral of the White**; 20.2.1797 **Rear Admiral of the Red**; 14.2.1799 **Vice Admiral of the White**; 8.1799-4.1803 CinC — The Nore; 8.1799-4.1803 *Zealand* (64); 29.4.1802 **Vice Admiral of the Red**; 23.4.1804 **Admiral of the Blue**; 28.4.1808 **Admiral of the White**; 4.12.1813 **Admiral of the Red.**

GRAHAM, EDMUND
Dates: c.1731 Born; 1762 Died.
Family:
Service: 18.10.1747 Able *Mars* (64); 22.4.1748 Able *Fox* (20); 3.9.1749-11.9.1751[W] Mid *Fox* (20); 23.6.1752 Mid *Advice* (50); 15.12.1753 Mate *Advice* (50); 2.7.1755 Passed; **Lieutenant**; 23.3.1756-22.3.1757 L. *Merlin* (10) Sloop; 25.4.1757 3L *Norwich* (50); 8.6.1757-24.5.1758 2L *Norwich* (50); 7.11.1758-1762[†] L. *Saltash* (14) Sloop; 29.12.1758 Capture of Goree.

GRAHAM, MITCHELL

Dates: c.1734 Born; 1795 Died.

Family: Father Sir Reginald Graham, 4th Bt. (1704-1755); Mother Jacoba Catherina Graham (d.1764); Wife Miss Jackman; Wife Maria Rebecca Bowater; Son John Bellingham, RM; Daughter Maria; Brother Bellingham, 5th Bt (1729-1790); Brother Reginald, RM; Sister Frances [Graham] (d.1801).

Service: 15.2.1748 Capt Serv *Tiger* (60); 22.11.1748 Capt Serv *Tavistock* (50); 28.8.1750 Able *Tavistock* (50); 18.1.1752-6.10.1752[P] Mid *Tavistock* (50); 26.4.1753 **Lieutenant**; 12.9.1753 Mid *Baltimore* (14) Sloop; 24.8.1754 Able *Shoreham* (24); 6.9.1754 Mid *Shoreham* (24); 14.3.1755 Passed; 26.4.1755 4L *Prince Frederick* (64); 16.6.1757-27.1.1758 4L *Namur* (90); 5.9.1757-6.10.1757 Raid on Rochefort; **Commander**; 9.2.1759 *Lightning* (6) Hospital Ship; **Captain**; 21.11.1760-9.4.1763 *Aldborough* (20); 29.3.1761-11.6.1761 Expedition against Belle-Isle; 4.4.1769-25.4.1772[P] *Fly* (8) Sloop; 6.10.1775 *Sphinx* (20); 24.10.1775-30.10.1777 *Thetis* (32); 16.10.1787 **Superannuated Rear Admiral**.

GRANT, CHARLES CATHCART

Dates: 3.4.1723 Born; 11.2.1772 Died.

Family: Father James Grant of Grant, 6th Bt. (1679-1747); Mother Anne Colquhoun (1685-1725); Sister Anne Drummouda [Innes] (d.1771); Sister Penuel [Grant]; Sister Clementina [Dunbar] (d.1765); Sister Jean [Duff] (1705-1788); Brother Ludovick, 7th Bt. (1707-1773); Brother James, 1st Bt. of Luss (1714-1786); Brother Lt.-Gen. Francis (1717-1781).

Service: 19.5.1737 Able *Torrington* (40); 20.8.1740-15.10.1741[P] Mid *Torrington* (40); 3.12.1741 Mid *Hampshire* (50); 18.7.1743 Passed; **Lieutenant**; 12.1.1743/44 L. *Gibraltar* (20); 25.11.1747-20.12.1748[P] 2L *Assistance* (50); 21.3.1755 2L *Essex* (64); 1.10.1756 1L *Essex* (64); **Commander**; 23.3.1757-23.9.1758[W] *Mediterranean* (12) Xebec; **Captain**; 17.1.1761 *Seahorse* (24); 24.9.1762-6.10.1762 Battle of Manilla; 21.10.1762[(EI 30.7.1764)]-20.6.1764[P] *Lennox* (74).

GRANT, FRANCIS

Dates: 1730 Born; 11.9.1803 Died.

Family: Father William Grant; Mother Barbara Gordon; Wife Miss Anston married 18.9.1770; Son Henry, RN; Son Charles; Son James Willoughby.

Service: 3.9.1746 Capt Serv *Squirrel* (20); 30.12.1746 Able *Squirrel* (20); 20.2.1747 Mid *Squirrel* (20); 11.6.1747 Able *Squirrel* (20); 2.1.1748-9.5.1749[P] Mid *Squirrel* (20); 3.12.1749 Able *Kent* (64); 27.12.1749 Mid *Mermaid* (24); 13.7.1750 Able *Mermaid* (24); 14.10.1751 ActL *Mermaid* (24); 29.6.1753-27.7.1753[P] L. *Mermaid* (24); 29.6.1753 **Lieutenant**; 1.8.1753 Passed; 11.2.1755 L. *Scorpion* (14) Sloop; 18.12.1756 3L *Tilbury* (58); 23.2.1757-1.8.1758 3L *Bedford* (64); 8.1757-10.1757 Louisbourg Expedition; 6.6.1758-27.7.1758 The Siege of Louisbourg; 13.2.1759-2.4.1759 1L *Bienfaisant* (64); 2.4.1759 L. *Salamander* (8) Fireship; 3.4.1760 3L *Sandwich* (90); 29.3.1761-11.6.1761 Expedition against Belle-Isle; 30.7.1762 2L *Sandwich* (90); **Commander**; 24.9.1762-19.2.1763[P] *Laurel* (12) Sloop; 31.3.1763-20.6.1765 *Merlin* (18) Frigate; **Captain**; 11.7.1765-2.2.1768[P] *Greyhound* (20); 21.1.1775-20.11.1776[D] *Argo* (28); 20.11.1775 Dismissed.

GRANT, MURDO

Dates: c.1716 Born; 1759 Died.

Family:

Service: 19.7.1738 Able *Anglesea* (40); 12.2.1740/41 Cox *Anglesea* (40); 4.3.1740/41-5.1741 Operations against Cartagena; 19.12.1741 Mid *Anglesea* (40); 17.3.1741/42 Mid *Sandwich*

(90); 5.7.1742 Mate *Sandwich* (90); 5.7.1744 Passed; **Lieutenant**; 29.1.1747/48[(JAM 11.4.1749)]-6.5.1749[P] L. *Weazle* (16) Sloop; 1759 Impress Service at Scotland.

GRANT, ROBERT

Dates: c.1719 Born; 1758 Died; 2.8.1760 Will Probate.

Family: Brother Andrew.

Service: 7.2.1733/34 Able *Edinburgh* (70); 14.4.1734 Able *Greyhound* (20); 1.6.1736 Mid *Greyhound* (20); 3.5.1738 Able *Greyhound* (20); 22.12.1738 Mid *Greyhound* (20); 23.12.1739 Mid *Rupert* (60); 9.4.1740 Passed; **Lieutenant**; 13.4.1741 3L *Mary Galley* (40); 26.5.1741-12.3.1742/43[P] 2L *Mary Galley* (40); 25.6.1743 2L *Cornwall* (80); 25.11.1743-26.7.1745 2L *Worcester* (58); 2.8.1745[(4.12.1745)]-19.11.1745[P] 4L *Elizabeth* (70); 3.7.1746 **Commander**; 10.7.1746-20.5.1749[P] *Hazard* (10) Sloop; 27.3.1755-6.12.1756[P] *Firedrake* (8) Bomb Vessel; **Captain**; 27.1.1758 *Jason* (30); 31.1.1758-bef.22.2.1759[†] *Sunderland* (60).

GRANT, WILLIAM

Dates: c.1728 Born; 1790 Died; 29.3.1790 Will Probate.

Family:

Service: 2.3.1742 Able *York* (60); 27.2.1745 Able *Canterbury* (60); 9.4.1748 Battle of Santiago de Cuba; 9.8.1748 Mid *Milford* (44); 12.11.1748-19.1.1748/49[P] Mate *Milford* (44); 1.3.1753 Mid *Shoreham* (24); 25.3.1753 Able *Surprise* (24); 18.6.1753 Mid *Surprise* (24); 22.7.1755 Able *Surprise* (24); 3.9.1755 Mid *Surprise* (24); 8.1.1756 Passed; **Lieutenant**; 9.11.1756 3L *Sunderland* (60); 29.7.1757[(12.6.1759)]-10.10.1758[C] L. *Winchelsea* (20); 8.1757-10.1757 Louisbourg Expedition; 20.6.1759 2L *Phoenix* (44); 1.2.1762-22.5.1763[P] 1L *Phoenix* (44); 10.2.1768-26.5.1768 L. *Gibraltar* (20); 19.10.1769-7.11.1770[P] 1L *Phoenix* (44); 1.7.1773-15.2.1777[P] LCmdr *Saint John* (6) Schooner; **Commander**; 24.10.1777-13.3.1780[P] *Lioness* (26) Storeship; 26.8.1780 *Arundel* (74); **Captain**; 18.5.1781-24.9.1781 *Hannibal* (50).

GRANT, WILLIAM

Dates: c.1738 Born; 3.1764 Died.

Family:

Service: 24.2.1754 Able *Salisbury* (50); 11.1.1756-14.1.1756 Capture of Geriah; 19.2.1757 Mid *Salisbury* (50); 7.3.1757-1.4.1757 Expedition against Chandernagore; 12.4.1758 Mid *Cumberland* (66); 29.4.1758 Battle of Cuddalore; 3.8.1758 Battle of Negapatam; 10.9.1759 Battle of Pondicherry; 14.10.1759 Mid *Yarmouth* (64); 5.11.1760 Passed; **Lieutenant**; 13.4.1761 L. *Hound* (14) Sloop; 16.7.1761 L. *Sardoine* (14) Sloop; 9.8.1762-3.1764[F] L. *Epreuve* (14) Sloop.

GRAPE, SAMUEL

Dates: c.1715 Born; 1775 Died.

Family:

Service: 8.9.1735-6.4.1736[P] Vol-p-O *Hampton Court* (70); 9.12.1736 Able *Squirrel* (20); 3.6.1739 Mid *Squirrel* (20); 4.5.1740 Mid *Dolphin* (20); 25.5.1744 Mid *Berwick* (70); 3.10.1746 Passed; **Lieutenant**; 24.10.1746-16.6.1748[P] L. *Shark* (8) Sloop; 28.10.1748-21.3.1748/49 L. *Viper* (14) Sloop; 17.1.1757-17.2.1757 2L *Yarmouth* (64).

GRAVES, JOHN

Dates: c.1741 Born; 6.5.1811 Died.

Family: Father Reverend John Graves (1709-1770); Mother Jane Hudson (d.1788); Brother Richard, RN (1758-1836); Brother Samuel, RN; Brother Thomas, RN (1747-1814).

Service: 6.4.1755 Able *Hazard* (8) Sloop; 21.4.1755 Able *Sheerness* (24); 2.12.1757 Mid *Unicorn* (28); 25.2.1759 Mid *Lennox* (74); 22.4.1762 Passed; **Lieutenant**; 13.7.1762-7.3.1763[P] 2L *Boulogne* (32); 1.4.1763-4.4.1764[P] 3L *Antelope* (50); 17.6.1768-1.1771 LCmdr *Hornet* (6) Cutter; 28.10.1773 1L *Boyne* (68); 30.11.1773 2L *Boyne* (68); 20.1.1774-4.12.1776 3L *Boyne* (68); 7.5.1775-22.12.1776 LCmdr *Saint Lawrence* (10) Schooner; 30.8.1777 5L *Prince George* (90); 19.9.1777 4L *Prince George* (90); 1.10.1777 3L *Prince George* (90); 26.1.1778 5L *Prince George* (98); 14.2.1778 2L *Albion* (74); 20.3.1778-18.4.1778 1L *Albion* (74); **Commander**; 11.4.1778-15.3.1779 *Savage* (14) Sloop; 11.10.1782 2L *Dunkirk* (60); **Captain**; 21.1.1783-3.3.1783[P] *Sandwich* (90); 30.12.1805 **Superannuated Rear Admiral.**

GRAVES, SAMUEL

Dates: 17.4.1713 Born; 8.3.1787 Died Honiton, Devon.
Family: Father Samuel Graves (1674-1727); Wife Margaret Spinkes; Wife Elizabeth Sedgwick (d. 1767); Brother Rev. John Graves (1709-1770).
Service: 6.10.1739 Passed; **Lieutenant**; 3.3.1739/40 L. *Aetna* (8) Fireship; 10.11.1740[JAM 24.3.1748/49] 4L *Norfolk* (80); 6.2.1741/42[17.1.1748/49]-2.5.1743 4L *Cumberland* (80); 19.7.1743[17.1.1748/49]-20.12.1743 1L *Cumberland* (80); **Commander**; 5.12.1743[17.1.1748/49] *Bonetta* (8) Sloop; **Captain**; 11.9.1744[18.11.1748]-10.5.1747[P] *Rippon's Prize* (20); 15.6.1756 *Duke* (90); 17.11.1756-17.1.1757 *Weymouth* (60); 18.6.1757 *Princess Amelia* (80); 5.9.1757-6.10.1757 Raid on Rochefort; 19.10.1757-9.1.1759[P] *Barfleur* (80); 5.6.1758-12.6.1758 Raid on Saint-Malo; 30.5.1759 *Duke* (90); 20.11.1759 Battle of Quiberon Bay; 21.10.1762 **Rear Admiral of the Blue**; 18.10.1770 **Rear Admiral of the Red**; 24.10.1770 **Vice Admiral of the Blue**; 1.1774-2.1776 *Preston* (50); 28.3.1774-27.1.1776 CinC — North America; 31.3.1775 **Vice Admiral of the White**; 7.12.1775 **Vice Admiral of the Red**; 10.9.1777-16.5.1783 CinC — Plymouth; 29.1.1778 **Admiral of the Blue**; 8.4.1782 **Admiral of the White.**

GRAVES, THOMAS

Dates: 1.12.1755 Died.
Family: Wife Elizabeth Budgell; Son William, MP (c.1724-1801); Son Thomas (1st Baron of Gravesend in the County of Londonderry), RN (1725-1802); Brother Samuel (1674-1727).
Service: **Lieutenant**; 3.11.1702[15.12.1702] L. *Vulcan* (28); 14.1.1702/3 L. *Vulcan* (28); 13.8.1704 Battle of Malaga; 19.8.1704[13.11.1704] 3L *Shrewsbury* (80); 27.9.1705[25.7.1706] 2L *Expedition* (70); 10.9.1706 2L *Chichester* (80); 28.3.1707[17.12.1707] 2L *Torbay* (80); 8.1.1707/8 2L *Ranelagh* (80); 1.4.1708[6.5.1709] 1L *Ranelagh* (80); **Commander**; 27.4.1709-28.9.1710[P] *Phoenix* (8) Fireship; 23.6.1711 *Dunwich* (24); **Captain**; 17.6.1713-16.9.1714[P] Capt&M *Dunwich* (24); 23.11.1733-2.5.1737[P] *Swallow* (60); 16.5.1738-27.7.1738 *Princess Louisa* (60); 28.7.1738-3.12.1738[P] *Norfolk* (80); 30.8.1739-21.9.1742 *Norfolk* (80); 21.9.1742[30.3.1745]-12.1.1743/44 *Marlborough* (90); 15.7.1747 **Superannuated Rear Admiral.**

GRAVES, THOMAS CB, (1ST BARON OF GRAVESEND IN THE COUNTY OF LONDONDERRY)

Dates: 23.10.1725 Born Thanckes, Cornwall; 24.10.1794 1st Baron of Gravesend in the County of Londonderry; 14.5.1801 Order of the Bath; 9.2.1802 Died Thanckes, Cornwall; 22.7.1802 Will Probate;
Family: Father Thomas Graves, RN (d.1755); Mother Elizabeth Budgell; Wife Elizabeth Peere-Williams (d.1827) married 22.6.1771; Daughter Anne Elizabeth [Hare] (d.1823); Son Peter William (d.1804); Daughter Elizabeth Anne [Bagwell] (); Son Thomas North, 2nd Baron (1775-1835); Daughter Margaret Anne [Nesham] (d.1808); Brother William, MP (c.1724-1801).

Service: 1741 Mid *Norfolk* (80); **Lieutenant**; 25.6.1743(24.1.1743/44)-5.2.1743/44 3L *Romney* (50); 2.8.1746 2L *Princess* (70); 19.1.1746/47-2.9.1748[P] 2L *Monmouth* (70); 3.5.1747 1st Battle of Cape Finisterre; 14.10.1747 2nd Battle of Cape Finisterre; 21.12.1748 1L *Assistance* (50); **Commander**; 12.3.1754 *Hazard* (8) Sloop; **Captain**; 8.7.1755 *Sheerness* (24); 18.5.1757 *Unicorn* (28); 3.7.1759 Bombardment of Le Havre; 1761-1764 Gov. of Newfoundland; 15.5.1761-4.4.1764[P] *Antelope* (50); 14.11.1764-19.11.1767 *Temeraire* (74); 17.11.1770-23.5.1771[P] *Cambridge* (80); 14.1.1773 *Raisonable* (64); 2.1.1775-5.1775 M.P. for East Looe; 25.8.1775-31.1.1776 *Nonsuch* (64); 17.3.1777-17.10.1778 *Conqueror* (74); 17.10.1778 Commodore *Conqueror* (74); **Rear Admiral of the Blue**; 19.3.1779-1782 *London* (90); 19.3.1780 **Rear Admiral of the White**; 26.9.1780 **Rear Admiral of the Red**; 1781 CinC — North America; 16.3.1781 Battle of Cape Henry; 5.9.1781 Battle of the Chesapeake; 7.1782-21.9.1782 *Ramillies* (74); 5.1786-1788 *Powerful* (74); 3.6.1786-14.7.1789 CinC — Plymouth; 24.9.1787 **Vice Admiral of the Blue**; 1788-1790 *Impregnable* (98); 12.5.1790-24.3.1791 *Cambridge* (80); 21.9.1790 **Vice Admiral of the White**; 1793 *Cambridge* (80); 2.1793-1794 *Royal Sovereign* (100); 1.2.1793 **Vice Admiral of the Red**; 12.4.1794 **Admiral of the Blue**; 1.6.1795 **Admiral of the White**; 1802-4.1802 *London* (90).

GREEN, JOHN

Dates: c.1732 Born; 1768 Died.
Family:
Service: 1752-1755 HEIC Service; 24.9.1755 Mid *Essex* (64); 5.6.1758-12.6.1758 Raid on Saint-Malo; 31.1.1759 Passed; **Lieutenant**; 9.3.1759 3L *Lynn* (44); 11.4.1759-20.9.1759 2L *Lynn* (44).

GREENFIELD, JOHN

Dates: c.1723 Born; 1774 Died.
Family:
Service: 2.5.1749 Able *Lynn* (44); 2.2.1751/52 Mid *Severn* (50); 4.8.1756 Passed; **Lieutenant**; 3.7.1757(JAM 2.9.1760) L. *Port Antonio* (12) Storeship; 10.3.1759(JAM 2.9.1760)-19.11.1760[P] 2L *Dreadnought* (60); 7.8.1761 1L *Thames* (32); 1.1.1766-1.6.1769 LCmdr *Hunter* (4) Cutter.

GREENWOOD, WILLIAM

Dates: c.1720 Born; 1796 Died.
Family:
Service: 28.6.1739 Able *Lady Lucy* Hired Tender; 26.1.1739/40 QM *Montagu* (60); 2.10.1740 Mid *Montagu* (60); 15.8.1745 Passed; **Lieutenant**; 7.9.1745 3L *Princess Louisa* (60); 8.4.1746(EI 21.9.1749) 2L *Pearl* (44); 10.4.1746-1.9.1749[P] 2L *Pearl* (44); 12.9.1748(EI 21.9.1749)-1.9.1749[P] 1L *Pearl* (44); 23.9.1755-15.11.1756 2L *Saint Albans* (60); **Commander**; 15.11.1756 *Macclesfield* (16) Hired Armed Ship; 1.11.1757-3.5.1762 *Zephyr* (10) Sloop; 7.1.1762-10.2.1762 Operations against Martinique; **Captain**; 26.5.1768-25.9.1770 *Cerberus* (28).

GREGORY, ROBERT

Dates: c.1734 Born; 18.2.1774 Died.
Family: Daughter ? [Stapyton] (c1765-1840).
Service: 29.1.1748/49 Able *Oxford* (50); 30.9.1749 Capt Serv *Vanguard* (68); 14.11.1749 Capt Serv *Centurion* (50); 11.2.1749/50 Ord. *Centurion* (50); 9.11.1751 Able *Centurion* (50); 10.7.1752 Mid *Centurion* (50); 16.7.1753 Mid *Crown* (44); 7.10.1754 Mid *Norwich* (50); 21.11.1754 Mid *Centurion* (50); 16.3.1755 Able *Centurion* (50); 11.6.1755 Mid *Centurion* (50); 5.9.1755 Passed; **Lieutenant**; 19.2.1756 5L *Torbay* (74); 20.5.1756-3.1.1757 4L *Torbay* (74);

3.1.1757-21.9.1758 5L *Torbay* (74); 5.9.1757-6.10.1757 Raid on Rochefort; 5.6.1758-12.6.1758 Raid on Saint-Malo; 5.1.1760-28.1.1762 2L *Valiant* (74); 29.3.1761-11.6.1761 Expedition against Belle-Isle; **Captain**; 27.4.1763[JAM 3.11.1763]-1.12.1763[P] *Siren* (20); 29.11.1766 *Scarborough* (20); 20.3.1769[BLI 1.2.1770]-28.8.1769[P] *Chatham* (50).

GREIG, SAMUEL (SAMUIL KARLOVICH GREIG)
Dates: 30.11.1735 Born; 2.12.1735 Baptised Inverkeithing , Fife; 19.7.1776 Order of Saint Alexander Nevsky; 7.1788 Order of Saint Vladimir; 26.10.1788 Died.
Family: Father Charles Greig; Mother Jean Charters; Wife Sarah Cook (1752-1793) married 1.9.1768; Son Aleksey Samuilovich (1775-1845); Son John (1776-1792); Son Samuel (1778-1807); Daughter Jean [Paterson] (1783-1820); Son Charles (1785-1817).
Service: 26.12.1758 Mate *Firedrake* (8) Bomb Vessel; 29.12.1758 Capture of Goree; 3.7.1759 Bombardment of Le Havre; 18.8.1759 Mid *Royal George* (100); 20.11.1759 Battle of Quiberon Bay; 23.12.1759 Mate *Royal George* (100); 1.10.1760 Able *Neptune* (90); 6.2.1761 Mid *Royal Sovereign* (104); 6.3.1761-1.2.1762[P] ActL *Albemarle* Hired Armed Troopship; 25.1.1762 Passed; **Lieutenant**; 4.2.1762-6.2.1762[F] L. *Laurel* (12) Sloop; 16.4.1764 Resigned; 1.5.1764-1788 In the service of Russia; 1.5.1764 **Leitenant** (Imperial Russian Navy); c.1768 **Captain** (Imperial Russian Navy); c.8.1769-1770 Captain *Trekh Ierarkhov* (66); 1772-1774 *Pobeda* (66); 21.10.1773-1774 *Sviatoi Velikomuchenik Isidor* (74); 21.7.1775 **Vice Admiral** (Imperial Russian Navy); 23.6.1788-26.10.1788[†] *Rostislav* (100); 17.7.1788 Battle of Hogland.

GRENFELL, WILLIAM
Dates:
Family:
Service: **Lieutenant**; 9.2.1757[EI 3.11.1758] L. *Speaker* (10) Sloop; 11.1.1759-9.4.1762 3L *Shrewsbury* (74).

GRESLEY, SIR NIGEL (6TH BARONET GRESLEY)
Dates: 11.1.1725/26 Born Drakelow Hall; 29.1.1725/26 Baptised; 23.12.1753 6th Baronet Gresley; 17.4.1787 Died Bath; 21.4.1787 Buried Bath Abbey, Bath.
Family: Father Sir Thomas Gresley, 4th Baronet (1699-1746); Mother Dorothy Bowyer (d.1736); Wife Elizabeth Wynn (1700-c1792) married 18.5.1752; Son Nigel Bowyer Gresley, 7th Baronet (1753-c1808); Daughter Dorothy (1754-1755); Daughter Anne [Heathcote] (1755-1797); Daughter Elizabeth (1756-1839); Daughter Frances (1757-1836); Daughter Louisa Jane [Gresley] (1759-1806); Daughter Harriet [Jelly] (1761-1832); Daughter Mary Susanna [Proby] (1762-1820); Brother William (1719-1724); Brother Thomas, 5th Baronet (1722-1753); Sister Dorothy (1725-1729); Brother John (1727-1730); Brother Charles (1728-1729); Sister Selina (1729-1738); Brother William (1730-1731).
Service: 21.2.1740/41-c.1744 Scholar *Royal Naval Academy*; **Lieutenant**; 22.4.1748-14.11.1748[P] L. *Inverness* (22).

GREY, HENRY
Dates: c.1737 Born; 1759 Died.
Family:
Service: 21.4.1755 Adm Serv *Monarch* (74); 10.5.1756 Able *Magnanime* (74); 25.10.1756 Mid *Magnanime* (74); 25.6.1757 Mid *Royal William* (84); 5.9.1757-6.10.1757 Raid on Rochefort; 3.11.1757 Mid *Pallas* (36); 5.6.1758-12.6.1758 Raid on Saint-Malo; 23.10.1758 Passed; **Lieutenant**; 27.10.1758 2L *Crescent* (32) Frigate; 31.3.1759 1L *Crescent* (32) Frigate.

GRIERSON, JAMES

Dates: c.1738 Born; 1.4.1810 Died.
Family:
Service: 1751-1754 Merchant Service; 3.5.1754 Mid *Bedford* (70); 17.8.1757 Able *Namur* (90); 5.9.1757-6.10.1757 Raid on Rochefort; 31.3.1758-10.10.1758 Mid *Namur* (90); 6.6.1758-27.7.1758 The Siege of Louisbourg; 10.10.1759 Passed; **Lieutenant**; 19.6.1760-5.11.1761 L. *Hazard* (8) Sloop; 23.11.1761-7.2.1763[P] L. *Solebay* (24); 29.11.1768-16.12.1771 L. *Hazard* (8) Sloop; 12.1807 **Superannuated Commander.**

GRIEVE, WILLIAM

Dates: c.1732 Born; 1810 Died.
Family:
Service: 1753-1757 Merchant Service; 13.1.1757 Able *Union* (90); 13.8.1757 Mid *Medway* (6) Storeship; 21.6.1759 Mid *Sandwich* (90); 7.7.1759 Mate *Sandwich* (90); 29.3.1761-11.6.1761 Expedition against Belle-Isle; 12.2.1762 Passed; **Lieutenant**; 18.3.1762-23.2.1763[P] L. *Roman Emperor* (8) Fireship; 25.10.1809 **Superannuated Commander.**

GRIFFIES, SAMUEL

Dates: c.1723 Born; 31.10.1756 Died; 14.10.1757 Will Probate.
Family:
Service: 6.8.1738 Capt Serv *Lennox* (70); 20.1.1739/40 Ord. *Newcastle* (50); 17.7.1741 Able *Newcastle* (50); 6.3.1741/42 QM *Newcastle* (50); 10.12.1742 Mid *Newcastle* (50); 26.3.1745-26.11.1745 Mid *Torbay* (80); 11.2.1745/46 Passed; **Lieutenant**; 11.6.1746 3L *Panther* (50); 7.3.1746/47-8.5.1750[P] L. *Basilisk* (8) Bomb Vessel; 4.8.1756-21.9.1756 L. *Swift* (8) Sloop.

GRIFFIN, THOMAS

Dates: 1692 Born; 1771 Died.
Family: Wife Elizabeth (1709-1781).
Service: 1709-1711 Merchant Service; 14.2.1710/11 Able *Weymouth* (50); 7.8.1711 Capture of the San Joaquín; 16.8.1712 Mid *Weymouth* (50); 25.4.1713 Mid *Centurion* (54); 3.1.1714/15 Mate *Centurion* (54); 4.8.1715 Passed; **Lieutenant**; 28.10.1718[(2.12.1720)]-14.2.1726/27 3L *Orford* (70); 8.8.1727 L. *Gibraltar* (20); 29.7.1728 1L *Princess Louisa* (40); 7.7.1730-28.8.1730 1L *Falmouth* (50); **Captain**; 1.4.1731-29.10.1733 *Shoreham* (20); 27.2.1733/34-17.2.1735/36[P] *Blenheim* (96); 16.5.1738-11.6.1739 *Oxford* (50); 12.6.1739-13.1.1740/41 *Princess Caroline* (80); 23.11.1741 *Nassau* (70); 26.11.1741 *Saint George* (90); 14.1.1741/42[(23.3.1741/42)]-2.7.1742 *Burford* (70); 28.10.1743 *Captain* (70); 15.1.1746-7.1748 CinC — East Indies; 15.3.1745/46-15.7.1747 Commodore *Princess Mary* (60); **Rear Admiral of the Red**; 15.7.1747-22.8.1749[P] *Princess Mary* (60); 12.5.1748 **Vice Admiral of the Blue**; 22.8.1749-3.5.1750[P] *Exeter* (60); 15.4.1754-26.3.1761 M.P. for Arundel; 4.2.1755 **Vice Admiral of the White**; 8.12.1756 **Vice Admiral of the Red**; 24.2.1757 **Admiral of the Blue**; 21.10.1762 **Admiral of the White.**

GRIFFITH, WALTER

Dates: 15.5.1727 Born; 18.12.1779 Died.
Family: Father Walter Griffith; Mother Prudence Trevor; Wife Mrs Mary Bentinck, nee Davies.
Service: 27.11.1745 Able *Duke* (90); 7.11.1747 Able *Duke* (90); 7.2.1747/48-22.6.1748[P] Mid *Duke* (90); 15.1.1748/49 Mid *Hector* (44); 27.6.1750 Mid *Fougueux* (64); 12.8.1751 Able *Gloucester* (50); 23.12.1751 ActL *Renown* (30); 10.3.1752/53-30.4.1755 Able *Gloucester* (50);

30.4.1755 Passed; **Lieutenant**; 7.5.1755 3L *Eagle* (60); 29.3.1758 5L *Royal George* (100); 5.10.1758 2L *Royal George* (100); 23.2.1759 1L *Royal George* (100); **Commander**; 4.6.1759 *Postillion* (18) Sloop; 5.9.1759 *Gibraltar* (20); **Captain**; 11.12.1759-26.9.1763[P] *Gibraltar* (20); 23.10.1770-21.6.1771[P] *Namur* (90); 31.1.1776-1.2.1778 *Nonsuch* (64); 31.8.1779[(West Indies 17.2.1781)]-18.12.1779[†] *Conqueror* (74); 18.12.1779 Combat de la Martinique.

GRIFFITHS, DELANOY

Dates: c.1736 Born; 1765 Died.
Family:
Service: 1753-1757 Merchant Service; 26.3.1757 Able *Experiment* (24); 13.5.1757 Mid *Experiment* (24); 28.3.1758 Mid *Chesterfield* (44); 3.12.1760 Passed; **Lieutenant**; 24.5.1762-19.1.1763[P] 5L *Bellona* (74).

GRIFFITHS, JOSEPH

Dates: c.1727 Born; 1775 Died.
Family:
Service: 1740-1741 Merchant Service; 12.11.1741 Able *Neptune* (90); 22.1.1742/43 Able *Revenge* (70); 2.3.1742/43 Sinking of the San Isidoro; 16.3.1742/43 Mid *Revenge* (70); 21.6.1743 Mid *Nassau* (70); 11.2.1743/44-12.2.1743/44 Battle of Toulon; 4.5.1747 Passed; **Lieutenant**; 6.2.1755-3.7.1756 4L *Ipswich* (64).

GRIGG, ARTHUR

Dates: c.1715 Born; c.1756 Died; 1.10.1756 Will Probate.
Family:
Service: 1736-1741 Merchant Service; 6.3.1740/41 QM Mate *Royal George* (100); 11.9.1741 QM *Royal George* (100); 1.12.1741 Mid *Royal George* (100); 30.7.1742-13.2.1744/45[W] Mid *Orford* (70); 15.4.1745 Mid *Cumberland* (80); 15.8.1745 Passed; **Lieutenant**; 20.3.1745/46-7.10.1748[P] 3L *Southsea Castle* (44); 25.6.1755-bef.1.10.1756[†] 3L *Humber* (44).

GROAT, ROBERT

Dates: c.1735 Born; 1773 Died.
Family:
Service: 22.3.1749/50 Capt Serv *Edinburgh* (64); 6.9.1752 Able *Swan* (14) Sloop; 14.1.1753 Gnr Mate *Swan* (14) Sloop; 17.12.1755 Mid *Tilbury* (58); 10.3.1756-25.9.1757[W] Mate *Tilbury* (58); 3.2.1758 Mid *Norfolk* (74); 9.5.1758 Passed; **Lieutenant**; 10.5.1758 L. *Diligence* (10) Sloop; 5.6.1758-12.6.1758 Raid on Saint-Malo; 15.9.1761-29.8.1763 1L *Actaeon* (28); 7.1.1762-10.2.1762 Operations against Martinique; 17.11.1764-19.11.1767 2L *Temeraire* (74).

GROVE, THOMAS SAUNDERS

Dates: c.1737 Born; 1814 Died.
Family:
Service: 18.7.1747 Capt Serv *Tartar* (20); 19.12.1751-29.5.1752[P] Mid *Tartar* (20); 16.11.1754 Mid *Winchelsea* (20); 21.12.1755-6.9.1758 Mid *Falkland* (50); 6.9.1758 Passed; **Lieutenant**; 21.11.1762[(MED 9.5.1763)]-29.3.1763[P] 3L *Anson* (60); 3.1.1770-4.4.1773[P] L. *Wasp* (8) Sloop; 15.4.1775 L. *Viper* (10) Sloop; 7.11.1776 2L *Blonde* (32); 9.1.1777-1.11.1777 2L *Apollo* (32); 22.3.1779-1.4.1780 1L *Apollo* (32); 16.1.1780 Battle of Cape St. Vincent; 12.12.1780-2.3.1784[P] LCmdr *Pondicherry* (18); 20.6.1783 2nd Battle of Cuddalore; 25.10.1809 **Commander**.

GUGELMAN, CHARLES

Dates: c.1704 Born; 1760 Died; 21.10.1760 Will Probate.
Family: Brother John Gugelman.
Service: 2.1.1716/17 Vol-p-O *Dunkirk* (50); 11.8.1718 Battle of Cape Passaro; 22.9.1719-31.10.1721[P] Vol-p-O *Gloucester* (54); 27.8.1725 Able *Lion* (60); 13.3.1726/27 Mid *Lion* (60); 3.12.1727 Mate *Lion* (60); 3.3.1728/29 Mid *Preston* (50); 25.6.1731 Mid *Torrington* (40); 26.2.1732/33 Mate *Torrington* (40); 13.3.1734/35 Passed; **Lieutenant**; 25.5.1742 L. *Aetna* (8) Fireship; 23.11.1742 6L *Princess Royal* (90); 13.1.1743/44 5L *Princess Royal* (90); 18.2.1745/46 4L *Princess Royal* (90); 20.5.1746-17.2.1746/47[P] 3L *Princess Royal* (90).

GUILLAUME, PETER

Dates: c.1740 Born; 1764 Died.
Family:
Service: 18.1.1756 L. Serv *Newark* (80); 2.4.1757 L. Serv *Prince* (90); 9.5.1757 L. Serv *Royal Anne* (100); 12.6.1757 Able *Canterbury* (60); 20.2.1758 Mid *Canterbury* (60); 29.3.1759 Mid *Port Mahon* (24); 20.8.1760 Passed; **Lieutenant**; 18.6.1762-12.2.1763[P] L. *Garland* (24).

GUILLIARD, JOHN

Dates: 1772 Died.
Family:
Service: **Lieutenant**; 4.3.1742/43[(MED 4.2.1745/46)]-20.12.1745[P] L. *Dragon's Prize* Xebec; 17.11.1755-4.7.1756 L. *Experiment* (24); 20.5.1756 Battle of Minorca; 20.5.1757-27.5.1757 1L *Devonshire* (70).

GUNMAN, JAMES

Dates: 1677 Born; 30.6.1756 Died.
Family: Father Christopher Gunman, RN (1634-1685).
Service: 4.6.1696 **Lieutenant**; 21.9.1696 3L *Warspite* (64); 23.11.1696 3L *Cumberland* (80); 13.3.1698/99 3L *Montagu* (60); 19.3.1699/0-28.12.1702 3L *Eagle* (70); 14.1.1702/3 3L *Saint Michael* (90); 30.7.1703 3L *Royal Katherine* (96); 26.8.1703-11.2.1703/4 3L *Royal Sovereign* (100); 27.12.1704 5L *Britannia* (100); 14.1.1705/6 1L *Britannia* (100); **Commander**; 24.9.1706[(22.11.1707)]-16.1.1707/8 *Weazle* (10) Sloop; 20.12.1708 **Captain**; 22.12.1708-13.10.1713[P] *Lyme* (32); 22.2.1733/34-16.2.1735/36[P] *Northumberland* (70).

GWENNAP, WALTER

Dates: 27.5.1798 Died; 13.9.1798 Will Probate.
Family:
Service: **Lieutenant**; 6.9.1760[(EI 9.8.1763)]-27.10.1761 4L *Medway* (60); 27.1.1766-3.2.1767 LCmdr *Boscawen* (4) Cutter; 7.2.1777 3L *Invincible* (74); 28.6.1777-7.2.1778 2L *Invincible* (74); 26.5.1778 2L *Namur* (90); 23.7.1778-26.10.1780 1L *Namur* (90); 31.12.1779 Affair of Fielding and Bylandt; 9.2.1781 8L *Prince George* (98); 25.1.1782-26.1.1782 Battle of Saint Kitts; 12.4.1782 Battle of the Saintes; **Commander**; 29.4.1782[(NA 8.10.1783)]-27.11.1783[SC] *Jersey* (60) Prison Ship; 7.6.1783[(NA 17.10.1783)]-20.11.1783[P] *Volcano* (8) Fireship; 8.9.1789-16.8.1790[P] *Termagant* (18) Sloop; **Captain**; 21.9.1790-22.11.1790 *Orpheus* (32).

GWYN, RICHARD

Dates: 2.12.1766 Died; 6.12.1766 Buried Bath.
Family:
Service: 24.11.1704 Vol-p-O *Seaford* (24); 4.1.1706/7 Mid *Royal Anne* (100); 25.4.1707 Mid *Royal Anne* (100); 31.5.1707 Mid *Windsor* (60); 18.10.1707-2.2.1707/8[P] Able *Kent* (70); 17.7.1709 Able *Kent* (70); 5.8.1709 Mid *Kent* (70); 13.12.1710 Mid *Triumph* (90); 22.3.1710/11 Passed; **Lieutenant**; 27.9.1711-26.9.1712[P] L. *Drake* (14) Sloop.

GWYNN, RICHARD

Dates: 10.12.1766 Died.
Family: Wife Elizabeth Townsend (c.1726-?) married c.1746; Daughter Elizabeth Jane Fenuel (1749-?); Daughter Alica Abigail (1753-?); Son Richard (1754-?); Daughter Henrietta Anna Margaretta (1756-?); Daughter Helena (1757-?).
Service: **Lieutenant**; 14.8.1739 L. *Hound* (8) Sloop; 21.2.1740/41 1L *Hastings* (44); 20.3.1740/41 3L *Marlborough* (90); 6.7.1741 2L *Marlborough* (90); 25.11.1741[29.1.1744/45] 2L *Somerset* (80); 11.2.1743/44-12.2.1743/44 Battle of Toulon; **Commander**; 27.12.1745 *Falcon* (10) Bomb Vessel; 3.5.1747 1st Battle of Cape Finisterre; **Captain**; 27.5.1747-10.9.1748[P] *Ambuscade* (40); 24.1.1756 *Ambuscade* (40); 11.8.1759[NA 12.3.1761]-22.12.1760[P] *Rainbow* (44).

GYDE, JAMES

Dates: c.1727 Born; 1766 Died.
Family:
Service: 13.8.1746 Capt Serv *Chatham* (50); 14.9.1746 Able *Chatham* (50); 30.3.1747 Mid *Drake* (14) Sloop; 8.10.1747 Able *Phoenix* (24); 14.10.1747 Mid *Phoenix* (24); 18.10.1751 Able *Boyne* (80) Prison Ship; 24.3.1751/52 Mid *Boyne* (80) Prison Ship; 6.6.1752 Able *Gloucester* (50); 15.7.1754 Able *Ferret* (14) Sloop; 24.12.1755 Able *Gloucester* (50); 5.5.1756 Passed; **Lieutenant**; 12.5.1756 3L *Rainbow* (44); 19.2.1757 2L *Coventry* (28); 5.6.1758-12.6.1758 Raid on Saint-Malo; 20.11.1759 Battle of Quiberon Bay; 28.3.1760 1L *Coventry* (28); **Commander**; 1.11.1762-8.2.1763[P] *Hawk* (10) Sloop.

Service Records H

HACKMAN, JAMES
Dates: c.1714 Born; 23.7.1763 Will Probate; 1764 Died.
Family:
Service: 15.12.1733 Able *Shoreham* (20); 1.4.1737 Gnr Mate *Shoreham* (20); 28.2.1737/38-4.3.1739/40[P] Mid *Berwick* (70); 8.5.1740 Passed; **Lieutenant**; 21.2.1740/41 L. *Deal Castle* (20); 28.12.1741 3L *Kinsale* (44); 9.2.1742/43 3L *Augusta* (60); 4.12.1745 2L *Augusta* (60); 21.4.1746 1L *Augusta* (60); **Commander**; 9.7.1747-7.10.1748[P] *Viper* (10) Sloop; 10.7.1755-3.5.1758[P] *Hazard* (8) Sloop; **Captain**; 18.10.1758-6.1.1760[W] *Mermaid* (24); 13.11.1762-12.5.1763[P] *Launceston* (44).

HACKMAN, WILLIAM
Dates: c.1716 Born; 1757 Died.
Family: Wife Mary; Son James (1752-1779).
Service: 10.5.1734 Able *Romney* (50); 29.7.1735-16.2.1735/36[P] Mid *Yarmouth* (70); 7.5.1736 Able *Swift* (6) Sloop; 14.9.1737 Mid *Swift* (6) Sloop; 4.10.1739 Passed; **Lieutenant**; 18.2.1739/40 L. *Cruizer* (8) Sloop; 4.3.1740/41-5.1741 Operations against Cartagena; 26.4.1743[(4.7.1744)]-6.2.1743/44 L. *Carcass* (8) Bomb Vessel; 8.9.1744 3L *Torrington* (44); 11.1.1744/45-13.2.1746/47[P] 2L *Torrington* (44); 24.10.1749-8.5.1751 1L *Fougueux* (64).

HALDANE, JAMES
Dates: 30.6.1768 Died; 22.7.1768 Will Probate.
Family: Father Lt.-Col. James Haldane (d.1742); Mother Margaret Pye; Wife Katherine Duncan; Son Robert (1764–1842); Daughter Helen (1765-1766); Son James Alexander (1768–1851).
Service: **Lieutenant**; 29.10.1747[(MED 14.4.1749)]-20.4.1749[P] 3L *Lynn* (44); 14.8.1755-13.10.1756 L. *Seaford* (20).

HALDANE, ROBERT
Dates: 22.8.1761 Died Madras.
Family: Father John Haldane (1693-1726); Mother Helen Scott (d.1738); Brother John (d.1739); Brother David (d.1753).
Service: **Lieutenant**; 25.5.1741[(26.4.1743)]-21.8.1741 3L *Bristol* (54); 2.8.1743[(11.9.1744)]-25.9.1744[P] 1L *Grafton* (70); **Commander**; 28.3.1746 *Trial* (10) Sloop; **Captain**; 24.2.1747/48-13.9.1748[P] *Shoreham* (24); 11.2.1756-21.6.1756 *Triton* (20); 15.4.1757-10.1.1759 *Lowestoffe* (28); 5.6.1758-12.6.1758 Raid on Saint-Malo; 28.12.1759-22.8.1761[†] *America* (60).

HALE, JOHN

Dates: c.1718 Born; 1791 Died; 24.1.1792 Will Probate.
Family:
Service: 27.5.1734 Able *Gibraltar* (20); 30.8.1736 Capt Serv *Dreadnought* (60); 5.11.1737 Able *Dreadnought* (60); 23.2.1738/39 Mid *Princess Louisa* (60); 3.6.1739 Mid *Norfolk* (80); 12.9.1739 Able *Jersey* (60); 13.10.1739 Mid *Jersey* (60); 4.3.1739/40 Mid *Anne Galley* (8) Fireship; 12.5.1741 Passed; **Lieutenant**; 26.5.1741 3L *Mary Galley* (40); 1.10.1742[(MED 4.11.1745)] 4L *Marlborough* (90); 15.8.1743[(MED 4.11.1745)] 3L *Marlborough* (90); 11.2.1743/44-12.2.1743/44 Battle of Toulon; 6.3.1743/44[(MED 4.11.1745)]-6.3.1744/45 2L *Marlborough* (90); 27.2.1744/45[(MED 4.10.1745)]-6.6.1745 2L *Dragon* (60); 20.3.1746/47 2L *Prince Henry* (44); **Commander**; 27.5.1747-5.10.1748[P] *Brave* (3) Storeship; 5.11.1752 *Badger* (10) Sloop; **Captain**; 7.10.1755-10.10.1758[C] *Winchelsea* (20); 8.1757-10.1757 Louisbourg Expedition; 3.4.1760-3.7.1761 *Winchester* (50); 30.6.1761-3.8.1763[P] *Intrepid* (60); 12.5.1779 **Superannuated Rear Admiral.**

HALL, JOHN

Dates: 1791 Died; 23.7.1791 Will Probate.
Family:
Service: 25.1.1745/46 Passed; **Lieutenant**; 26.1.1745/46[(NA 4.7.1746)]-13.4.1746 2L *Pembroke* (60); 5.11.1746-4.11.1748 3L *Rippon* (54); 21.7.1756-11.1.1757 4L *Marlborough* (80); 10.2.1757-23.5.1758 4L *Newark* (80); 8.1757-10.1757 Louisbourg Expedition; 3.4.1760 2L *Royal Sovereign* (104); 6.2.1761 1L *Royal Sovereign* (104).

HALL, WILLIAM

Dates: c.1718 Born; 1798 Died; 7.7.1798 Will Probate.
Family:
Service: 4.8.1738 Able *Strafford* (60); 6.7.1739 Mid *Strafford* (60); 21.11.1739 Attack on Puerto Bello; 21.4.1742 Mate *Strafford* (60); 24.6.1742 Mid *Prince of Orange* (70); 14.10.1742 Master *Prince of Orange* (70); 15.1.1742/43 Master *Fowey* (40); 6.9.1743 Master *Dover* (44); 12.12.1744 Act3L *Dover* (44); **Lieutenant**; 21.4.1746[(BLI 2.5.1747)] 3L *Dover* (44); 15.1.1746/47-17.8.1748[P] 2L *Dover* (44); 1.2.1746/47 Passed; 18.6.1755 L. *Granado* (8) Bomb Vessel; 18.5.1756 4L *Prince* (90); 22.6.1756 3L *Prince* (90); 26.2.1757 2L *Prince George* (80); 29.7.1757 1L *Prince George* (80); 20.10.1757 1L *Princess Amelia* (80); 6.6.1758-27.7.1758 The Siege of Louisbourg; 20.3.1760-2.3.1763[P] 1L *Shrewsbury* (74).

HALLAM, JOHN

Dates: c.1721 Born; 25.11.1794 Died.
Family:
Service: 20.10.1737 Able *Falmouth* (50); 18.5.1738-15.8.1740[P] Able *Diamond* (40); 23.3.1739/40 Attack on Chagres; 11.2.1740/41 Mid *Saint George* (90); 2.11.1744 Passed; **Lieutenant**; 26.2.1744/45 6L *Saint George* (90); 29.3.1745 5L *Saint George* (90); 23.5.1745 4L *Saint George* (90); 4.9.1745 2L *Hastings* (44); 22.3.1745/46-28.4.1747 L. *Surprise* (24); 2.9.1747-12.11.1748[P] 3L *Assurance* (44); 17.1.1757-1.10.1758 1L *Yarmouth* (64); 29.4.1758 Battle of Cuddalore; 3.8.1758 Battle of Negapatam; 21.9.1795 **Superannuated Commander**.

HALLUM, JOHN

Dates: c.1739 Born; c.1792 Died; 12.5.1792 Will Probate.
Family:
Service: 27.8.1758 Able *Achilles* (60); 20.10.1758 Able *Enterprise* (44); 1.1.1759 Mid *Norwich* (50); 3.7.1759 Bombardment of Le Havre; 2.9.1760 Mid *Anson* (60); 3.4.1761-9.12.1761 Mate *Anson* (60); 9.12.1761 Passed; **Lieutenant**; 7.7.1762-15.3.1763[P] 3L *Lynn* (44); 6.4.1763 L. *Peggy* (8) Sloop; 3.6.1763-22.2.1768[P] L. *Garland* (24); 22.6.1769 3L *Bellona* (74); 21.9.1770 4L *Bellona* (74); 17.4.1771-3.10.1774[P] 1L *Minerva* (32); 8.3.1775-24.11.1777 LCmdr *Adventure* (10) Storeship; 17.4.1778-8.8.1778 1L *Duke* (90); 27.7.1778 1st Battle of Ushant; 17.3.1780-25.5.1781[D] 2L *Cambridge* (80); 25.5.1781 Dismissed.

HALLUM, THOMAS

Dates: 1721 Baptised St Clements, Ipswich; 1804 Buried St Margaret's, Ipswich; c.1804 Died Ipswich; 16.4.1804 Will Probate.
Family: Father William Hallum; Mother Mary Bowell; Wife Lydia Strutt (1733-1797) married 1751; Daughter Lydia (1752-1728); Son Thomas (1755-1831); Son Edward (1765-1837); Son James (1770-1831).
Service: **Lieutenant**; 6.1.1741/42[(18.6.1745)] L. *Strombolo* (8) Fireship; 17.2.1742/43[(18.6.1745)]-20.10.1744[W] 3L *Saint Albans* (50); 6.1744 Bombardment of Porto Bello; 5.9.1745 L. *Winchelsea* (20); 2.12.1746-20.5.1749[P] 1L *Adventure* (44); 21.3.1755-1.10.1755 1L *Essex* (64); 13.5.1758-22.3.1759 1L *Conqueror* (68); **Commander**; 10.8.1759 *Albany* (14) Sloop; 11.2.1760 *Scorpion* (14) Sloop; **Captain**; 24.5.1762-13.1.1763 *Ludlow Castle* (24); 1763 Regulating Officer at Yarmouth IOW; 13.7.1778 *Royal George* (100); 19.11.1778-17.12.1778 *Convert* (32); 11.2.1793 **Superannuated Rear Admiral.**

HALSTEAD, WILLIAM ANTHONY

Dates: 11.2.1730 Born Padbury, Buckinghamshire; 2.3.1730 Baptised Padbury, Buckinghamshire; 16.5.1778 Died New York.
Family: Wife Mary Frankland married 28.5.1762; Son Charles (1763-1780); Son Sir Lawrence William, RN; Son John (1766-1830); Daughter Caroline (1768-1830); Daughter Amelia (1771-?); Son George (1774-1846).
Service: 13.11.1746 Capt Serv *Falkland* (50); 24.12.1746 L. Serv *Falkland* (50); 3.5.1747 1st Battle of Cape Finisterre; 4.3.1748-8.7.1748[P] Capt Serv *Falkland* (50); 11.7.1749 Capt Serv *Defiance* (60); 12.12.1750 Able *Defiance* (60); 13.6.1751-28.5.1752 Able *Centurion* (50); 29.5.1752 Mid *Centurion* (50); 31.8.1754 Able *Centurion* (50); 7.12.1754 Mid *Centurion* (50); 14.11.1755 Mid *Torbay* (74); 19.12.1755 Passed; **Lieutenant**; 20.5.1756 5L *Torbay* (74); 22.12.1756-10.2.1757 3L *Centurion* (50); 23.3.1757-7.2.1760 1L *Lizard* (28); 14.5.1762-20.12.1762[P] 2L *Bedford* (64); 12.1.1764-13.1.1767 1L *Dorsetshire* (68); 21.9.1770 2L *Bellona* (74); 3.10.1770-24.5.1771[P] 1L *Bellona* (74); 2.6.1772 1L *Barfleur* (90); **Commander**; 25.6.1773-18.1.1775 *Merlin* (18) Frigate; 22.11.1775-16.5.1778[†] *Jersey* (20) Hospital Ship.

HAMAR, JOSEPH

Dates: c.1712 Born; 14.6.1773 Died; 12.3.1774 Will Probate.
Family: Wife Elizabeth Limeburner married 5.7.1753; Wife Mrs Ann Berry; Daughter Margaret Elizabeth [Arden] (1754-1842); Stepson William Berry.
Service: 9.11.1727 Able *Otter* (6) Sloop; 18.4.1729 Able *Dolphin* (20); 8.7.1729 Able *Deal Castle* (20); 12.12.1730 Mid *Deal Castle* (20); 11.9.1732 Able *Deal Castle* (20); 2.1.1732/33 Mate *Deal Castle* (20); 16.6.1733-27.1.1733/34[P] Able *Suffolk* (70); 9.2.1733/34 Passed;

Lieutenant; 5.5.1735-7.5.1737[P] L. *Deptford* (24) Storeship; 17.4.1739 L. *Royal Escape* Smack; **Commander**; 10.6.1740 *Royal Escape* Smack; **Captain**; 22.10.1741 *Flamborough* (20); 17.12.1745 *Flamborough* (20); 3.4.1746 *Deal Castle* (20); 13.8.1746-20.5.1749[P] *Adventure* (44); 7.5.1755-17.9.1755 *Eagle* (60); 1.11.1758 **Superannuated Rear Admiral.**

HAMILTON, GEORGE

Dates: c.1725 Born; 4.1760 Died Halifax; 12.7.1760 Will Probate.
Family:
Service: 27.6.1741 Ord. *Romney* (50); 22.11.1741 Able *Romney* (50); 13.1.1743 Mid *Romney* (50); 25.6.1743 Mid *Princess Mary* (60); 26.12.1744 Mate *Royal Sovereign* (104); 17.9.1745 ActL *Poole* (44); 13.5.1746-3.10.1746 Mid *Fox* (20); 3.10.1746 Passed; **Lieutenant**; 25.10.1746 L. *Grampus* (10) Sloop; 23.3.1747/48-6.12.1748[P] 4L *Prince Frederick* (70); 2.6.1749 2L *Vanguard* (68); 27.12.1750-23.1.1753[P] L. *Lyme* (24); 6.2.1755 2L *Lancaster* (66); 20.5.1756 Battle of Minorca; 18.1.1757-10.2.1757 4L *Newark* (80); 12.3.1757 4L *Prince* (90); 19.4.1757-17.1.1758 4L *Royal Anne* (100); 5.9.1757-6.10.1757 Raid on Rochefort; **Commander**; 21.8.1758 *Porcupine* (16) Sloop; **Captain**; 22.9.1759[(NA 20.10.1760)]-24.6.1760 *Richmond* (32).

HAMILTON, JAMES

Dates: 1756 Died.
Family:
Service: 20.1.1703 Vol-p-O *Eagle* (70); 21.7.1704-23.7.1704 Capture of Gibraltar; 13.8.1704 Battle of Malaga; 30.9.1704 Mid *Eagle* (70); 20.8.1705-8.5.1706[P] Mid *Royal Katherine* (96); 4.12.1706 Mid *Royal Katherine* (96); 3.12.1707 Passed; **Lieutenant**; 11.3.1708/9-16.9.1713[P] 2L *Dartmouth* (54); 23.2.1733/34-12.4.1734 2L *Medway* (60); 1743 **Superannuated Lieutenant**.

HAMILTON, JAMES

Dates: 19.2.1816 Died; 30.3.1816 Will Probate.
Family:
Service: **Lieutenant**; 5.1.1760[(JAM 4.8.1760)]-2.3.1760[W] L. *Tartar's Prize* (24); 4.10.1760-17.3.1763[P] L. *Kingfisher* (14) Sloop; 2.6.1805 **Superannuated Commander**.

HAMILTON, JAMES

Dates: c.1735 Born; 24.9.1806 Died.
Family:
Service: 1754-1757 HEIC Service; 24.1.1757 Mid *Union* (90); 12.8.1757 Mid *Neptune* (90); 5.9.1757-6.10.1757 Raid on Rochefort; 21.10.1759 Mate *Neptune* (90); 6.2.1760 Passed; **Lieutenant**; 25.6.1760 5L *Thunderer* (74); 6.4.1761-4.3.1763[P] 4L *Thunderer* (74); 14.2.1763-4.3.1763[P] 3L *Thunderer* (74).

HAMILTON, THE HON. JOHN

Dates: 2.3.1713/14 Born; 18.12.1755 Died Portsmouth; 15.1.1756 Will Probate.
Family: Father James Hamilton, 7th Earl of Abercorn (1686–1744); Mother Anne Plumer (1690-1776); Wife Mrs Harriet Eliot née Craggs (c.1713-1769) married 13.10.1749; Daughter Jane [Allingham] (d.1839); Daughter Anne (c.1750-1764); Son John James, 1st Marquess of Abercorn (1756-1818); Brother James, 8th Earl of Abercorn (1712-1789); Brother William (c.1715-1717); Sister Anne [Mackworth] (1715-1792); Brother Rev. George (1718-1787); Brother Plumer (1720-?); Brother The Hon. William, RN (1722-1744); Sister Unknown (1736-?).

Service: **Lieutenant**; 4.3.1735/36(29.4.1736)-2.4.1736[P] 4L *Norfolk* (80); 1.10.1736-29.12.1736 3L *Princess Louisa* (40); 4.2.1736/37-3.7.1738 3L *Diamond* (40); 3.3.1739/40-16.4.1740[P] 6L *Namur* (90); 14.4.1740 6L *Victory* (100); **Captain**; 19.2.1740/41 *Deal Castle* (20); 28.12.1741 *Kinsale* (44); 25.1.1742/43 *Augusta* (60); 31.3.1748-12.11.1751 *Vanguard* (68); 4.2.1755-18.12.1755[†] *Lancaster* (66).

HAMILTON, SIR JOHN (1ST BARONET OF TREBINSHUN HOUSE)

Dates: 21.2.1726 Born; 6.7.1776 1st Baronet of Trebinshun House; 24.1.1784 Died.
Family: Father John Hamilton (1690-1733); Mother Mary Wright; Wife Cassandra Agnes Chamberlayne married 4.10.1763; Son Charles (2nd Baronet of Trebinshun House), RN (1767-1849); Son Edward Joseph, (1st Baronet of Marlborough House), RN (1772-1851); Sister Mary [Atcheson] (1728-?).
Service: 22.9.1740 Capt Serv *Rippon* (60); 7.1.1740/41 Action of January 7 1741; 4.3.1740/41-5.1741 Operations against Cartagena; 4.7.1741 Able *Alderney* (8) Bomb Vessel; 10.10.1741 Able *Success* (24) Hulk; 14.10.1742 Mid *Success* (24) Hulk; 8.5.1743 QGnr *Princess Royal* (90); 9.12.1743 NR *Bideford* (20); 16.5.1744 Mid *Tartar* (20); 5.1.1745/46 ActL *Tartar* (20); **Lieutenant**; 11.1.1746/47 L. *Tartar* (20); 6.2.1746/47 Passed; 1.2.1747/48-21.8.1749[P] 2L *Winchester* (50); 6.2.1755 3L *Ramillies* (90); 7.10.1755 1L *Colchester* (50); 17.5.1756 Action of 17th May 1756; 25.1.1760 1L *Prince Edward* (44); 26.1.1762 2L *Royal William* (84); **Commander**; 7.4.1762-13.12.1762[P] *Cormorant* (8) Fireship; 11.4.1764 *Zephyr* (10) Sloop; 8.2.1766 *Merlin* (18) Frigate; **Captain**; 26.5.1768-21.3.1771 *Active* (28); 20.6.1775-12.6.1776 *Lizard* (28); 3.7.1776 *Hector* (74); 27.7.1778 1st Battle of Ushant; 20.6.1780 Action off Monti Christi; 27.12.1782-4.4.1783[P] *Grafton* (74); 5.4.1783-22.1.1784 *Hector* (74).

HAMILTON, LORD RICHARD (4TH VISCOUNT BOYNE)

Dates: 24.3.1723/24 Born; 2.1.1772 4th Viscount Boyne; 30.7.1789 Died.
Family: Father Hon. Gustavus Hamilton (1685-1735); Mother Dorothea Bellew; Wife Georgiana Bury; Daughter Sophia [Lowe]; Son Gustavus, 5th Viscount Boyne (1749-1816); Daughter Catherine [Lyons]; Brother Frederick, 3rd Viscount Boyne (1718-1772).
Service: **Lieutenant**; 2.6.1748(MED 30.6.1748)-4.6.1748[P] 3L *Russell* (80); 1755-1761 M.P.P.I. at Navan; 8.6.1757-11.7.1757 3L *Magnanime* (74).

HAMILTON, WILLIAM

Dates: 10.4.1790 Died.
Family:
Service: **Lieutenant**; 6.2.1743/44(MED 4.11.1748) L. *Carcass* (8) Bomb Vessel; 5.3.1744/45(MED 4.11.1748)-8.11.1748[P] L. *Lowestoffe* (24); 11.3.1755 1L *Newcastle* (50); 24.12.1755 1L *Prince George* (80); 14.5.1756 1L *Monarch* (74); **Commander**; 17.1.1757 *Barbadoes* (14) Sloop; 14.7.1758(BLI 11.9.1764)-4.8.1758[P] *Speaker* (10) Sloop; 4.4.1763-16.12.1767[P] *Favorite* (16) Sloop; **Captain**; 10.1.1771-15.10.1773 *Success* (20).

HAMMETT, JOHN

Dates: c.1722 Born; 1785 Died.
Family:
Service: 30.6.1743 Able *Dorsetshire* (80); 11.2.1743/44-12.2.1743/44 Battle of Toulon; 11.4.1744 Gnr Mate *Nazareth* (8) Fireship; 30.7.1744 Able *Marlborough* (90); 23.11.1744 Invalid *Deptford* (24) Storeship; 11.1.1744/45 Mid *Pembroke* (60); 3.5.1747 1st Battle of Cape Finisterre; 12.11.1747 Passed; **Lieutenant**; 29.9.1757 L. *Dolphins Prize* (12) Sloop; 31.7.1758

2L *Adventure* (32); 4.11.1760 1L *Adventure* (32); 19.11.1760-16.1.1761[P] 3L *Edinburgh* (64); 13.4.1761-21.3.1763[P] 3L *Ocean* (90).

HAMMICK, STEPHEN

Dates: c.1715 Born; 1782 Died.
Family: Son Stephen.
Service: 31.10.1735 Able *York* (60); 28.12.1735 Ord. *Otter* (6) Sloop; 25.6.1736 Able *Otter* (6) Sloop; 11.5.1738 Able *Grampus* (6) Sloop; 30.12.1738 Able *Argyll* (50); 6.8.1739 QGnr *Assistance* (50); 27.8.1740 QGnr *Jersey* (60); 4.3.1740/41-5.1741 Operations against Cartagena; 11.7.1742 Mid *Jersey* (60); 17.1.1742/43-18.9.1743[P] Mid *Bridgewater* (20); 27.9.1743 Mid *Dover* (44); 15.6.1744 Mate *Dover* (44); 11.1.1744/45 Passed; **Lieutenant**; 25.10.1745 4L *Prince Frederick* (70); 2.4.1746 4L *Elizabeth* (70); 13.4.1747 6L *Saint George* (90); 27.5.1747-1.2.1747/48 2L *Princess Louisa* (60); 14.10.1747 2nd Battle of Cape Finisterre; 1.12.1748 2L *Somerset* (68); 30.12.1748-14.11.1752[P] 3L *Eagle* (60); 19.4.1755 3L *Monmouth* (70); 9.11.1756-6.11.1757[P] 2L *Monmouth* (70); **Commander**; 30.10.1761-6.12.1762[P] *Baltimore* (14) Sloop.

HAMMOND, THOMAS

Dates: 1759 Died.
Family:
Service: **Lieutenant**; 4.9.1744[(West Indies 18.12.1745)]-12.12.1745[P] L. *Deal Castle* (20); 2.5.1746 2L *Mermaid* (44); 29.8.1746 1L *Mermaid* (44); 22.4.1747[(JAM 2.5.1749)] L. *Shirley* (10) Sloop; 28.6.1747[(JAM 2.5.1749)] 3L *Nonsuch* (50); 12.9.1747[(JAM 2.5.1749)] 1L *Warwick* (60); 3.11.1747[(JAM 2.5.1749)]-29.1.1747/48 3L *Canterbury* (60); **Commander**; 11.5.1748[(JAM 6.3.1749/50)]-25.11.1748[P] *Vanqueur* Sloop.

HAMMOND, WILLIAM

Dates: 16.11.1778 Died.
Family:
Service: **Lieutenant**; 21.4.1747[(MED 15.11.1748)] 4L *Royal Oak* (70); 4.7.1747[(MED 15.11.1748)]-18.11.1748[P] 3L *Royal Oak* (70); 5.11.1755 L. *Raven* (14) Sloop; 5.5.1757 5L *Royal Sovereign* (104); 10.10.1757-13.3.1759[P] 4L *Royal Sovereign* (104).

HAMOND, SIR ANDREW SNAPE (1ST BARONET OF HOLLY GROVE)

Dates: 17.12.1738 Born Blackheath, London; 15.1.1779 Knight Bachelor; 10.12.1783 1st Baronet of Holly Grove; 12.10.1828 Died Lynn.
Family: Father Robert Hamond; Mother Susannah Snape; Wife Cecilia Sutherland married 11.4.1763; Wife Anne Graeme (d.1838) married 7.3.1779; Son Graham Eden, RN (1779-1862); Daughter Caroline [Hood];
Service: 13.5.1753 Capt Serv *Speedwell* (8) Sloop; 28.2.1755 Mid *Speedwell* (8) Sloop; 16.5.1756 Mid *Speedwell* (8) Sloop; 31.8.1756 Clerk *Speedwell* (8) Sloop; 16.11.1756 Mid *Sunderland* (60); 15.3.1756/57 Mate *Saint Albans* (60); 8.4.1758-6.9.1758 Mate *Hampton Court* (64); 6.9.1758 Passed; **Lieutenant**; 18.6.1759 5L *Magnanime* (74); 20.11.1759 Battle of Quiberon Bay; 1.6.1761 4L *Magnanime* (74); 14.6.1762 3L *Magnanime* (74); 22.6.1762-23.1.1763[P] 3L *Princess Amelia* (80); 12.4.1763-3.6.1765 LCmdr *Grace* (6) Cutter; **Commander**; 20.6.1765-3.7.1765 *Merlin* (18) Frigate; 24.10.1766 *Savage* (8) Sloop; **Captain**; 7.12.1770-25.5.1771 *Barfleur* (90); 25.5.1771-29.11.1773[P] *Arethusa* (32); 4.7.1775-2.7.1781 *Roebuck* (44); 22.7.1778 Encounter at Sandy Hook; 11.8.1778 Howe's encounter with d'Estaing; 1.1780-5.1780 Operations against Charleston; 1781-3.10.1782 Lieutenant Governor of Nova Scotia; 14.4.1781 Action of 1781-

04-14; 1.5.1781 CinC — Halifax; 1785-1788 CinC — River Medway and The Nore; 22.6.1785-28.3.1788[P] *Irresistible* (74); 22.6.1790-14.9.1791[P] *Vanguard* (74); 31.8.1791 *Bedford* (74); 29.12.1792-1.2.1793 *Duke* (98); 25.9.1794-3.3.1806 Comptroller of the Navy; 1796-1806 M.P. for Ipswich.

HANBURY, THOMAS

Dates: 4.11.1722 Born Pontypool, Monmouthshire; 13.12.1788 Died Île de Ré.
Family: Father John Hanbury MP (1664-1734); Mother Bridget Ayscough (1672-1741); Brother John (1705-1739); Brother Capel MP (1707-1765); Brother Charles (1709-1759).
Service: 24.1.1736/37 Capt Serv *Diamond* (40); 26.1.1738/39 Able *Diamond* (40); 10.3.1738/39-15.7.1740[P] MidO *Diamond* (40); 23.3.1739/40 Attack on Chagres; 15.3.1740/41 MidO *Lichfield* (50); 8.5.1741-8.5.1742[P] Mid *Weymouth* (60); 28.7.1742 Mid *Vanqueur* Sloop; 29.1.1742/43 Acting Fourth Lieutenant *Bedford* (70); **Lieutenant**; 28.8.1743[(26.11.1744)] 3L *Bedford* (70); 11.2.1743/44-12.2.1743/44 Battle of Toulon; 24.11.1744 Passed; 27.11.1744-9.9.1745 3L *Pembroke* (60); 25.1.1745/46[(NA 17.11.1746)]-1.9.1746[P] 1L *Dorsetshire* (80); **Commander**; 23.10.1747 *Salamander* (10) Bomb Vessel; 23.5.1748-1.9.1748[W] *Serpent* (10) Bomb Vessel; 11.10.1749-31.1.1753[P] *Hazard* (8) Sloop; 5.3.1754 Dismissed.

HANBY, JOSEPH

Dates: c.1732 Born; 26.5.1797 Died.
Family:
Service: 1749-1752 Merchant Service; 1.7.1752 Able *Penzance* (44); 21.1.1753 Mid *Penzance* (44); 4.6.1755 Passed; **Lieutenant**; 14.5.1756-26.2.1757 6L *Prince George* (80); 2.4.1759 1L *Revenge* (64); 20.11.1759 Battle of Quiberon Bay; 7.3.1760 1L *Dragon* (74); 22.5.1760-21.2.1763[P] 1L *Monmouth* (70); 29.3.1761-11.6.1761 Expedition against Belle-Isle; 21.9.1796 **Superannuated Commander**.

HANKERSON, THOMAS

Dates: c.1712 Born; 24.2.1780 Died Plymouth; 11.3.1780 Will Probate.
Family: Wife Elizabeth Bewes (d.1782).
Service: 3.3.1726/27-7.3.1727/28 Ord. *Dursley Galley* (20); 8.3.1727/28 Capt Serv *York* (60); 6.9.1728-1.11.1729 Ord. *Gibraltar* (20); 2.11.1729 Ord. *Princess Louisa* (40); 23.3.1730/31 Able *Drake* (8) Sloop; 10.5.1731 QGnr *Drake* (8) Sloop; 13.7.1731-1.9.1734 Mid *Drake* (8) Sloop; 4.9.1734 Passed; **Lieutenant**; 21.2.1740/41 2L *Sapphire* (44); 5.10.1741 3L *Rupert* (60); 10.12.1741 2L *Rupert* (60); 25.9.1743[(MED 1.4.1746)]-2.10.1744 L. *Dursley Galley* (20); 11.2.1743/44-12.2.1743/44 Battle of Toulon; 3.8.1745 6L *Marlborough* (90); 16.10.1745[(5.6.1746)] 2L *Marlborough* (90); 2.12.1745[(5.6.1746)]-13.6.1746[P] 1L *Marlborough* (90); **Commander**; 26.8.1748-5.11.1752 *Badger* (10) Sloop; 13.2.1753 *Swift* (8) Sloop; **Captain**; 11.3.1755 *Arundel* (24); 31.8.1757 *Richmond* (32); 5.6.1758-12.6.1758 Raid on Saint-Malo; 22.9.1759[(NA 27.1.1760)]-7.9.1763[P] *Alcide* (64); 7.1.1762-10.2.1762 Operations against Martinique; 6.6.1762-13.8.1762 Operations against Havana.

HANSFORD, WILLIAM

Dates: c.1719 Born; 1799 Died; 8.8.1799 Will Probate.
Family:
Service: 16.6.1740 Able *Eleanor* (8) Fireship; 8.9.1740-11.12.1741[P] Gnr Mate *Eleanor* (8) Fireship; 4.3.1740/41-5.1741 Operations against Cartagena; 11.12.1741 QM *Advice* (54); 11.7.1743 Mid *Advice* (54); 1.4.1746 Mid *Norwich* (50); 1.12.1746 Able *Norwich* (50);

30.12.1746 Mid *Sapphire* (44); 24.2.1748-30.6.1748[P] Mid *Folkestone* (44); 21.4.1749-13.6.1749 Able *Intrepid* (18) Hired Advice Boat; 14.6.1749 Mid *Intrepid* (64); 25.11.1751 Mate *Fougueux* (64); 24.1.1753 Mate *Berwick* (70); 25.5.1753 Mate *Captain* (64); 2.7.1755 Passed; **Lieutenant**; 6.1.1757[(ECH 24.1.1756)]-4.3.1761[P] 3L *Kingston* (60); 8.1757-10.1757 Louisbourg Expedition; 6.6.1758-27.7.1758 The Siege of Louisbourg; 20.11.1759 Battle of Quiberon Bay; 21.9.1796 **Superannuated Commander**.

HANWAY, THOMAS

Dates: c.1715 Born; 1.10.1772 Died.
Family:
Service: 24.8.1731-29.12.1733 Able *Kinsale* (40); 30.12.1733-14.2.1733/34 Able *Princess Amelia* (80); 15.2.1733/34-15.2.1734/35 Mid *Princess Amelia* (80); 16.2.1734/35-8.10.1735 Able *Rose* (20); 9.10.1735-27.1.1736/37 Mid *Rose* (20); 28.1.1736/37 Mid *Princess Amelia* (80); 4.5.1738 Passed; **Lieutenant**; 14.8.1739-13.2.1739/40 L. *Cruizer* (8) Sloop; 14.2.1739/40-31.7.1740 4L *Russell* (80); 6.12.1740 2L *Grafton* (70); 30.1.1740/41 3L *Royal Sovereign* (104); 21.9.1741 2L *Royal Sovereign* (104); 8.2.1741/42 1L *Royal Sovereign* (104); **Commander**; 20.2.1741/42 *Success* (8) Fireship; 15.9.1742 *Mortar* (10) Bomb Vessel; **Captain**; 5.4.1744 *Shoreham* (20); 18.7.1744 *Royal Sovereign* (104); 18.6.1745-9.1.1745/46 *Milford* (44); 10.1.1745/46-18.8.1748[P] *Windsor* (60); 3.5.1747 1st Battle of Cape Finisterre; 14.10.1747 2nd Battle of Cape Finisterre; 4.2.1755 *Weymouth* (60); 17.11.1756-10.1.1759 *Duke* (90); 5.6.1758-12.6.1758 Raid on Saint-Malo; 21.12.1758 CinC — Cork; 15.8.1759 Second in Command — Plymouth.

HARDY, SIR CHARLES

Dates: 1716 Born Portsmouth; 1755 Knight Bachelor; 18.5.1780 Died.
Family: Father Sir Charles Hardy, RN (1680-1744); Father Sir Charles Hardy, RN (1680-1744); Father Sir Charles Hardy, RN (1680-1744); Mother Elizabeth Burchett; Wife Mary Tate (d.1750); Wife Catherine Stanyan (d.1801); Son Charles (d.1781); Son Charles Temple, RN (1765-1714); Brother John, RN (1720-1796).
Service: 4.2.1730/31-1732 Vol. *Salisbury* (50); **Lieutenant**; 26.3.1737[(2.5.1737)]-2.5.1737[P] 3L *Swallow* (60); 16.5.1738 3L *Augusta* (60); 18.8.1738 2L *Augusta* (60); 13.4.1739 2L *Portland* (50); 14.9.1739 3L *Kent* (70); 7.12.1739 2L *Kent* (70); 8.4.1740 Capture of the Princesa; 27.9.1740 2L *Boyne* (80); 6.10.1740 1L *Rupert* (60); **Commander**; 9.6.1741 *Rupert's Prize* (8); **Captain**; 10.8.1741-12.4.1744[P] *Rye* (20); 1744 Gov. of Newfoundland; 30.4.1744-31.5.1748[P] *Jersey* (60); 1755-1757 Gov. of New York; 4.6.1756 **Rear Admiral of the Blue**; 6.1757 *Sutherland* (50); 7.1757 *Invincible* (74); 31.1.1758 **Rear Admiral of the White**; 6.1758-10.1758 *Royal William* (84); 6.6.1758-27.7.1758 The Siege of Louisbourg; 14.2.1759 **Vice Admiral of the Blue**; 6.1759-10.1759 *Foudroyant* (80); 1762-25.2.1763[P] *Union* (90); 9.1762-25.12.1762 *Hero* (74); 21.10.1762 **Vice Admiral of the White**; 1764-1768 M.P. for Rochester; 18.10.1770 **Admiral of the Blue**; 7.1771-3.1779 Governor of Greenwich Hospital at Greenwich Hospital; 29.1.1778 **Admiral of the White**; 19.3.1779-18.5.1780 CinC — English Channel; 19.3.1779-14.5.1780 *Victory* (100).

HARDY, JOHN

Dates: c.1720 Born; 5.1796 Died.
Family: Father Sir Charles Hardy, RN (1680-1744); Brother Sir Charles, RN (1716-1780).
Service: 2.12.1731-18.7.1732 Vol-p-O *Exeter* (60); 19.7.1732-7.12.1733 Able *Scarborough* (20); 8.12.1733-23.4.1736 Vol-p-O *Scarborough* (20); 24.4.1736-17.3.1736/37 Mid *Scarborough* (20); 18.3.1736/37-30.8.1737 Mate *Royal Caroline* (8) Yacht; 31.8.1737-7.2.1738/39 Mid

Gloucester (50); 8.2.1738/39-1.4.1740 Able *Gloucester* (50); 1.3.1739/40 Passed; **Lieutenant**; 4.3.1739/40 3L *Gloucester* (50); 15.3.1739/40 2L *Adventure* (40); 6.6.1740 L. *Seahorse* (20); 31.10.1740(19.3.1741/42)-7.6.1741 1L *Superb* (60); 8.10.1742 2L *Princess Mary* (60); 22.3.1742/43-2.2.1743/44 2L *Shrewsbury* (80); **Commander**; 14.3.1743/44 *Drake* (14) Sloop; 2.4.1744 *Vulture* (10) Sloop; **Captain**; 17.10.1744 *Bridgewater* (20); 28.1.1744/45-13.2.1746/47[P] *Torrington* (44); 6.12.1762 **Superannuated Rear Admiral.**

HARDY, THOMAS

Dates: c.1736 Born.
Family:
Service: 27.12.1744 Capt Serv *Liverpool* (44); 22.8.1746 Capt Serv *Mary Galley* (44); 27.1.1747 Capt Serv *Mary Galley* (44); 28.10.1749 Capt Serv *Blandford* (20); 27.1.1752 Able *Blandford* (20); 17.3.1754 Mid *Blandford* (20); 6.10.1754 Mid *Gosport* (44); 7.2.1757 Passed; **Lieutenant**; 22.6.1762(BLI 19.5.1764) 3L *Rochester* (50); 16.10.1762-14.3.1764[P] 3L *Vanguard* (68).

HARLAND, SIR ROBERT (1ST BARONET OF SPROUGHTON)

Dates: c.1715 Born; 1771 1st Baronet of Sproughton; 28.2.1783 Died.
Family: Father Robert Harland, RN (1685-1751); Mother Frances Clyatt (1690-?); Wife Susanna Reynold (1730-1805) married 1749; Daughter Marianne Dorothy [Dalrymple] (1759-1785); Daughter Susanna Edith [Rowley] (1763-1850); Son Robert, 2nd Bt. (1765-1848).
Service: 4.7.1729 Vol-p-O *Falkland* (50); 9.3.1729/30 Able *Dreadnought* (60); 7.5.1732 Able *Suffolk* (70); 30.7.1732 Able *Hector* (40); 5.2.1732/33 Mate *Hector* (40); 20.2.1733/34 Able *Greyhound* (20); 7.4.1734 MidO *Romney* (50); 11.7.1735 Passed; **Lieutenant**; 25.2.1741/42-8.5.1742[P] 3L *Weymouth* (60); 22.7.1742 3L *Princess* (70); 11.2.1743/44-12.2.1743/44 Battle of Toulon; 6.3.1743/44(21.2.1744/45) 4L *Namur* (90); 1.8.1744(21.2.1744/45) 2L *Namur* (90); 18.8.1744(21.2.1744/45)-20.8.1744 1L *Namur* (90); **Commander**; 4.1.1745/46 *Scipio* (8) Fireship; **Captain**; 19.3.1745/46-29.12.1747 *Tilbury* (58); 20.9.1746-25.9.1746 Lorient Operations; 14.10.1747 2nd Battle of Cape Finisterre; 29.12.1747 *Nottingham* (60); 31.1.1747/48 Action of 1748/01/31; 30.9.1748-17.1.1748/49 *Lyme* (24); 25.4.1749-20.12.1750 *Monarch* (74); 20.3.1755-5.11.1756 *Essex* (64); 13.5.1758 *Conqueror* (68); 13.8.1759(NA 7.5.1760)-28.4.1760[P] *Princess Louisa* (60); 18.8.1759-19.8.1759 Battle of Lagos Bay; 18.10.1770 **Rear Admiral of the Blue**; 21.1.1771-1775 CinC — East Indies; 3.1771-1774 *Northumberland* (68); 31.3.1775 **Rear Admiral of the Red**; 7.12.1775 **Vice Admiral of the Blue**; 2.4.1776 **Vice Admiral of the White**; 4.11.1776-8.1778 *Queen* (90); 12.5.1778 **Vice Admiral of the Red**; 27.7.1778 1st Battle of Ushant; 11.1778-6.1779 *Royal George* (100); 1.4.1782-29.1.1783 Lord Commissioner of the Admiralty; 8.4.1782 **Admiral of the Blue.**

HARMAN, WILLIAM

Dates: c.1719 Born; 19.1.1766 Died.
Family:
Service: 31.12.1733 Capt Serv *Pearl* (40); 6.6.1736 Able *Pearl* (40); 30.12.1736 Able *Somerset* (80); 19.3.1737/38 Mid *Prince of Orange* (70); 8.1.1739/40 Mid *Russell* (80); 27.11.1740 Passed; **Lieutenant**; 2.2.1740/41-30.9.1741 3L *Folkestone* (44); 24.7.1741 Action of 1741-07-24; 7.12.1744 2L *Pembroke* (60); 16.7.1745 *Kinsale* (44); 9.9.1745(NA 19.2.1746/47) 2L *Dorsetshire* (80); 6.12.1745(NA 19.2.1746/47)-25.1.1745/46 1L *Dorsetshire* (80); **Captain**; 26.1.1745/46(NA 19.2.1746/47) *Richmond* (24); 2.3.1745/46(NA 19.2.1746/47)-16.3.1746/47[P] *Kinsale* (44); 1.7.1755 *Oxford* (50); 12.5.1757-6.1.1758 *Prince Frederick* (64); 29.9.1758-5.8.1760[P] *Berwick* (64); 16.1.1759-

19.1.1759 Attack on Martinique; 20.1.1759-1.5.1759 Capture of Guadeloupe; 22.2.1762-3.6.1763[P] *Saint Ann* (64).

HARMER, BURWARD

Dates: 1742 Born; 16.3.1742 Baptised Watersfield, Suffolk; 1767 Died.
Family: Father Thomas Harmer (1714-1788); Mother Catherine (1720-?).
Service: 19.6.1755 Capt Serv *Prince Frederick* (64); 3.2.1757 Mid *Enterprise* (44); 11.3.1756/57 Mid *Coventry* (28); 13.7.1757 Able *Coventry* (28); 6.8.1757 Mid *Coventry* (28); 5.6.1758-12.6.1758 Raid on Saint-Malo; 20.11.1759 Battle of Quiberon Bay; 30.10.1760-1.7.1761 Mid *Royal George* (100); 1.7.1761 Passed; **Lieutenant**; 17.6.1762[MED 17.8.1762]-18.1.1763[P] 6L *Neptune* (90); 9.12.1765-14.7.1766 3L *Achilles* (60).

HARMER, JEREMIAH

Dates: c.1758 Died; 3.5.1758 Will Probate.
Family:
Service: **Lieutenant**; 25.4.1743[11.8.1743] 4L *Suffolk* (70); 22.6.1743[11.8.1743]-2.11.1743 3L *Suffolk* (70); 3.11.1743 4L *Suffolk* (70); 14.12.1743 3L *Deptford* (60); 18.4.1744 3L *Suffolk* (70); 12.6.1744 2L *Suffolk* (70); 28.4.1745[23.4.1747]-18.10.1746[C] 1L *Severn* (50); 10.8.1746 Action of 1746-10-18; 16.10.1747-6.6.1752[P] 1L *Vigilant* (60); 11.3.1755-1.2.1758 1L *Rochester* (50).

HARMOOD, HARRY

Dates: 1739 Born Sailsbury, Wiltshire; 2.1809 Died Mount St, Grosvenor Sq, London; 14.2.1809 Buried St. Mary, Paddington Green, Westminster; 13.3.1809 Will Probate.
Family: Son d'Oyley; Daughter Fanny; Daughter Susannah Dawes Harmood; Son Harry Harmood; Brother James, RN (1713-1773).
Service: 16.1.1751/52-c.1755 Scholar *Royal Naval Academy*; **Lieutenant**; 19.2.1759-4.10.1760 2L *Aquilon* (28); 25.3.1771-29.8.1771 1L *Arethusa* (32); 7.2.1776 3L *Eagle* (64); **Commander**; 16.2.1777[NA 30.3.1778] *Falcon* (14) Sloop; **Captain**; 17.10.1778[NA 20.4.1779] *Conqueror* (74); 6.7.1779 Battle of Grenada; 31.8.1779[NA 19.10.1780] *Princess Royal* (98); 17.4.1780 Battle of Martinique; 15.5.1780 Action of March 15 1780; 19.5.1780 Action of March 19 1780; 5.6.1780[BLI 30.10.1780]-11.1.1782 *Medway* (60); 12.12.1781 2nd Battle of Ushant; 22.3.1783-11.3.1786[P] *Ardent* (64); 1793-1796 Commissioner of the Navy; 1796-5.1801 Resident Commissioner at Sheerness Dockyard; 5.1801-6.1806 Resident Commissioner at Chatham Dockyard; 23.11.1801-2.1809 Commissioner of the Navy; 18.6.1806-2.1809 Governor of Greenwich Hospital.

HARMOOD, JAMES

Dates: c.1713 Born; bef.23.1.1773 Died; 24.1.1773 Buried Salisbury, Wiltshire; 25.6.1773 Will Probate.
Family: Brother Harry, RN (1739-1809); Sister Elizabeth [Anderson]; Sister Ann.
Service: **Lieutenant**; 9.9.1747[MED 4.11.1748] L. *Conqueror* (8) Fireship; 9.12.1747[MED 4.11.1748] 4L *Burford* (70); 9.1.1747/48[MED 4.11.1748]-25.11.1748[P] 3L *Burford* (70); 10.1.1753-15.3.1757 3L *Northumberland* (68); **Commander**; 15.5.1760 *Racehorse* (16) Sloop; 3.7.1760[NA 4.3.1763]-22.2.1763[P] *Porcupine* (16) Sloop; 6.6.1762-13.8.1762 Operations against Havana.

HARRINGTON, JOSEPH

Dates: 13.8.1781 Buried Deal; bef.13.8.1781 Died.

Family:

Service: **Lieutenant**; 12.5.1761(EI 6.6.1763) 5L *Grafton* (68); 12.11.1761(EI 26.6.1764) 4L *Grafton* (68); 24.9.1762-6.10.1762 Battle of Manilla; 21.10.1762(EI 26.6.1764)-20.6.1764[P] 3L *Lennox* (74); 18.1.1776-31.10.1778 2L *Emerald* (32); 24.8.1779 2L *Ajax* (74); 7.10.1779 1L *Ajax* (74); 16.1.1780 Battle of Cape St. Vincent; 17.4.1780 Battle of Martinique; 15.5.1780 Action of March 15 1780; 19.5.1780 Action of March 19 1780; 4.4.1781 5L *Victory* (100); 28.4.1781-bef.13.8.1781[†] 3L *Victory* (100).

HARRIS, GEORGE

Dates: c.1727 Born; 1761 Died.

Family:

Service: 17.6.1752 Able *Nottingham* (60); 10.11.1753 Mid *Nottingham* (60); 26.1.1754-18.8.1754 Able *Nottingham* (60); 19.8.1754 Gnr Mate *Nottingham* (60); 31.5.1755 Able *Nottingham* (60); 6.9.1755 Able *Centurion* (50); 1.11.1755 Mid *Eagle* (60); 9.11.1756-5.9.1757 Mid *Eagle* (60); 5.9.1757 Passed; **Lieutenant**; 22.5.1758-10.9.1759 L. *Jamaica* (10) Sloop.

HARRIS, JOHN

Dates: c.1723 Born; 26.9.1791 Died.

Family:

Service: 16.9.1741 Able *Chester* (54); 9.3.1742 Mid *Chester* (54); 17.11.1742 Able *Dreadnought* (60); 24.3.1743 Mid *Dreadnought* (60); 29.4.1743-8.9.1748[P] Mid *Dreadnought* (60); 1.10.1751-28.2.1752 Mate *Torrington* (44); 8.2.1751/52 Passed; **Lieutenant**; 3.7.1754(26.11.1761) 1L *Kingfisher* (14) Sloop; 11.1.1756-14.1.1756 Capture of Geriah; 25.2.1756(26.11.1761)-25.3.1761 1L *Salisbury* (50); 7.3.1757-1.4.1757 Expedition against Chandernagore; 29.4.1758 Battle of Cuddalore; 3.8.1758 Battle of Negapatam; 10.9.1759 Battle of Pondicherry; 30.11.1770 2L *Cambridge* (80); 18.4.1771-23.5.1771[P] 1L *Cambridge* (80).

HARRIS, STEPHEN

Dates: c.1739 Born; 1790 Died.

Family:

Service: 1753-1757 Merchant Service; 30.8.1757 Mid *Princess Mary* (60); 15.5.1759 Mid *Hercules* (74); 20.11.1759 Battle of Quiberon Bay; 20.7.1760 Mid *Barfleur* (80); 10.9.1760 Passed; **Lieutenant**; 18.3.1761(JAM 2.3.1763)-22.3.1763[P] L. *Port Mahon* (24); 6.6.1762-13.8.1762 Operations against Havana; 18.1.1766-3.2.1767 1L *Aquilon* (28); 29.9.1770-10.8.1771 2L *Portland* (50).

HARRIS, WILLIAM

Dates: c.1723 Born; 14.11.1766 Died.

Family:

Service: 4.5.1736 Capt Serv *Exeter* (60); 10.5.1737-12.1.1737/38 Able *Torrington* (40); 17.1.1737/38-15.10.1741[P] Able *Torrington* (40); 15.11.1741 Mid *Hampshire* (50); 10.12.1743 Passed; **Lieutenant**; 2.2.1743/44 L. *Terror* (8) Bomb Vessel; 14.3.1743/44 3L *Falkland* (50); 4.2.1744/45 3L *Saint George* (90); 18.5.1745 L. *Glasgow* (20); 24.1.1746/47 1L *Warwick* (60); 22.8.1747(JAM 29.4.1748) 1L *Norwich* (50); 13.8.1748(24.1.1748/49)-17.2.1748/49[P] 3L *Panther* (50); 13.2.1751/52-26.4.1755[P] 1L *Jason* (44); 19.9.1755 1L *Saint Albans* (60); **Commander**; 6.4.1756-

15.8.1756[C] *Mohawk* (12) Sloop; 18.10.1758 *Albany* (14) Sloop; **Captain**; 30.7.1759-28.3.1760 *Penquin* (20); 9.4.1763-23.7.1766[P] *Aldborough* (20).

HARRISON, HENRY

Dates: 13.3.1759 Died; 2.5.1759 Will Probate.

Family: Wife Mrs. Mary Arundell; Son Thomas, RN (1725-1768); Daughter Jane Trigge; Stepson Philip Arundell; Son John.

Service: **Lieutenant**; 19.1.1705/6-16.9.1714[P] L. *Dunwich* (24); 2.1.1733/34 1L *Swallow* (60); 1.5.1736[(16.7.1736)]-19.7.1736[P] 1L *Warwick* (60); 16.5.1738 1L *Princess Louisa* (60); **Commander**; 26.7.1738-13.12.1738 *Salamander* (6) Bomb Vessel; 7.6.1739 *Salamander* (6) Bomb Vessel; **Captain**; 28.2.1739/40 *Mary Galley* (40); 25.3.1741-24.12.1742 *Argyll* (50); 14.3.1742/43 *Superb* (60); 28.9.1743 *Chichester* (80); 9.11.1743-2.9.1748[P] *Monmouth* (70); 3.5.1747 1st Battle of Cape Finisterre; 14.10.1747 2nd Battle of Cape Finisterre; 6.3.1755-25.6.1756 *Monmouth* (70); 4.6.1756 **Rear Admiral of the White**; 17.11.1756-29.9.1758 *Duke* (90); 24.2.1757 **Rear Admiral of the Red**; 31.1.1758 **Vice Admiral of the Blue**; 5.6.1758-12.6.1758 Raid on Saint-Malo; 14.2.1759 **Vice Admiral of the Red.**

HARRISON, JAMES

Dates: c.1738 Born; 1767 Died; 2.6.1767 Will Probate.

Family:

Service: 29.10.1756 Able *Dolphin* (24); 5.12.1756 Capt Serv *Dolphin* (24); 2.3.1757 Mid *Medway* (6) Storeship; 8.8.1757 Mid *Norwich* (50); 3.7.1759 Bombardment of Le Havre; 12.3.1760 Passed; **Lieutenant**; 9.7.1762[(BLI 7.10.1762)]-11.11.1762[P] 3L *Falkland* (50).

HARRISON, JOHN

Dates: c.1720 Born; 15.10.1791 Died; 2.11.1791 Will Probate.

Family: Father Robert Harrison, RN (d.1739); Wife Margery; Sister Eleanor [Wall].

Service: 2.5.1732 Vol-p-O *Tiger* (50); 4.6.1734 Vol-p-O *Roebuck* (40); 17.8.1738 Mid *Roebuck* (40); 27.11.1740 Passed; **Lieutenant**; 2.2.1740/41 6L *Neptune* (90); 27.3.1741 2L *Roebuck* (40); 2.11.1742 2L *Anglesea* (44); 20.4.1744 2L *Sunderland* (60); 27.8.1746-14.8.1748[P] 1L *Eagle* (60); 14.10.1747 2nd Battle of Cape Finisterre; 11.3.1748/49 L. *Mercury* (20); 24.1.1750/51-28.11.1751 L. *Boston* (24); 16.1.1753 1L *Kent* (64); **Commander**; 17.2.1755[(27.1.1757)] *Kingfisher* (14) Sloop; **Captain**; 4.7.1755[(29.1.1760)] *Cumberland* (66); 11.1.1756-14.1.1756 Capture of Geriah; 7.3.1757-1.4.1757 Expedition against Chandernagore; 2.3.1758[(EI 16.3.1760)]-19.12.1760[P] *Yarmouth* (64); 29.4.1758 Battle of Cuddalore; 3.8.1758 Battle of Negapatam; 10.9.1759 Battle of Pondicherry; 11.2.1762-24.2.1763[P] *Namur* (90); 6.6.1762-13.8.1762 Operations against Havana; 27.3.1779 **Superannuated Rear Admiral.**

HARRISON, THOMAS

Dates: 1725 Born; 1.2.1768 Died.

Family: Father Henry Harrison, RN (d.1759).

Service: 6.3.1739/40-28.4.1740[P] Capt Serv *Canterbury* (60); 6.5.1740 Clerk *Mary Galley* (40); 6.6.1741 Clerk *Argyll* (50); 25.3.1742 Mid *Argyll* (50); 5.4.1743-6.5.1743[P] Able *Princess Amelia* (80); 7.5.1743 Mid *Superb* (60); 23.11.1743 Mid *Chichester* (80); 11.1.1743/44 Mid *Monmouth* (70); 21.10.1746 Mate *Monmouth* (70); 3.5.1747 1st Battle of Cape Finisterre; 14.10.1747 2nd Battle of Cape Finisterre; **Lieutenant**; 3.12.1747-12.10.1748[P] 3L *Nottingham* (60); 9.12.1747 Passed; 31.1.1747/48 Action of 1748/01/31; 12.11.1751 3L *Saint Albans* (60); 20.9.1752-18.11.1752[P] 3L *Vanguard* (68); 19.4.1753-9.4.1754 3L *Augusta* (60); 6.3.1754/55 4L

Monmouth (70); **Commander**; 1.11.1756 *Otter* (14) Sloop; **Captain**; 17.1.1757 *Greyhound* (20); 31.3.1758-30.3.1763[P] *Venus* (36); 20.11.1759 Battle of Quiberon Bay; 7.9.1763 CinC — The Mediterranean Sea; 7.9.1763-25.9.1766[P] *Centurion* (50).

HART, HENRY HARE

Dates: c.1726 Born; 26.2.1793 Died.
Family:
Service: 27.9.1742 Mid *Falmouth* (50); 6.1744 Bombardment of Porto Bello; 11.6.1746-8.9.1748[P] Mid *Dragon* (60); 28.7.1753 Mid *Shoreham* (24); 20.9.1754 Mate *Shoreham* (24); 14.3.1755 Mid *Shoreham* (24); 3.6.1755 Mate *Shoreham* (24); 22.9.1756 Passed; **Lieutenant**; 13.11.1756 L. *Hazard's Prize* (8) Sloop; 15.2.1757-6.12.1757 3L *Lynn* (44); 27.10.1758 2L *Lynn* (44); 5.12.1758 2L *Rochester* (50); 20.11.1759 Battle of Quiberon Bay; 14.3.1760 2L *Foudroyant* (80); 1.4.1760 1L *Foudroyant* (80); 22.7.1761-25.10.1763[P] 1L *Mars* (74); 22.4.1766-20.12.1769[P] 1L *Jersey* (60).

HARTWELL, BRODERICK

Dates: c.1714 Born Castle Connel, Cork; 15.3.1784 Died Greenwich Hospital.
Family: Father Barry Hartwell (1685-1741); Mother Mary Spierin (1700-?); Wife Rebecca Collins (1710-1770); Son Broderick (1740–1789); Daughter Mary (1748–?); Daughter Susanna (1750–?); Son George (1750–1842); Son James (1754–?); Son George (1757–1806); Son Sir Francis John (1st Baronet of Dale Hall, Essex), RN (1757-1831); Brother Samuel (1736-?); Sister Mary.
Service: 2.1.1730/31 Ord. *Kent* (70); 21.5.1731 Able *Kent* (70); 10.1.1731/32 Able *Rupert* (60); 31.12.1732 Mid *Rupert* (60); 25.7.1738 Able *Dorsetshire* (80); 17.10.1738-13.12.1740[P] Able *Blandford* (20); 12.5.1741 Passed; **Lieutenant**; 12.6.1741 3L *Ruby* (54); 31.7.1742-9.9.1743[P] 2L *Ruby* (54); 23.9.1743-8.5.1744[C] 2L *Northumberland* (64); 25.3.1745 2L *Gloucester* (50); 30.5.1745 1L *Gloucester* (50); 28.3.1747 3L *Royal George* (100); 25.12.1747-29.11.1748[P] 1L *Tiger* (60); 22.12.1748 2L *Saint Albans* (60); 12.11.1751 1L *Saint Albans* (60); 29.7.1752-20.11.1752[P] 2L *Devonshire* (66); 31.3.1756 1L *Devonshire* (66); **Commander**; 13.5.1757 *Cruizer* (8) Sloop; 16.11.1757-21.8.1758 *Porcupine* (16) Sloop; **Captain**; 18.10.1758-26.1.1763[P] *Neptune* (90); 21.10.1763-24.10.1766 *Belleisle* (64); 20.10.1770-21.5.1771 *Trident* (64); 21.10.1773-17.10.1776 *Boyne* (68); 10.3.1777-5.2.1780[P] *Blenheim* (90); 21.2.1780-12.4.1781 *Cambridge* (80); 1781-14.3.1784 Lieutenant-governor of Greenwich Hospital at Greenwich Hospital.

HARVEY, HENRY CB

Dates: 7.1737 Born Elmton, Kent; 8.1.1800 Order of the Bath; 28.12.1810 Died Walmer, Kent.
Family: Father Richard Harvey of Eastry, Kent; Mother Elizabeth Nichols; Wife Elizabeth Boys (1740 - 1823); Son Richard Harvey; Son Henry Harvey; Brother John, RN (1740-1794).
Service: 25.8.1751 Mid *Centaur* (20); 25.10.1752 Able *Centaur* (20); 12.4.1753 Mid *Centaur* (20); 2.11.1754 Mid *Nightingale* (22); 3.9.1755 Mate *Nightingale* (22); 23.4.1756 Mid *Devonshire* (66); 8.3.1757 Passed; **Lieutenant**; 10.3.1757 3L *Hampshire* (50); 18.3.1758[NA 15.1.1759]-1.4.1763[P] 1L *Hampshire* (50); 18.10.1760 Action off Cuba; 23.3.1762-23.5.1762[C] 1L *Hussar* (28); 6.6.1762-13.8.1762 Operations against Havana; 7.4.1763 1L *Mermaid* (28); 19.11.1764-7.11.1767 LCmdr *Magdalen* (6) Schooner; 7.4.1767-26.5.1768 2L *Launceston* (44); 18.8.1769-27.4.1771[P] LCmdr *Swift* (4) Cutter; 16.4.1773 1L *Racehorse* (16) Sloop; **Commander**; 15.10.1773-21.1.1775 *Racehorse* (16) Sloop; 31.1.1776 *Martin* (14) Sloop; **Captain**; 9.5.1777[NF 7.11.1777] *Squirrel* (20); 17.12.1778-13.9.1782[P] *Convert* (32); 25.1.1782-26.1.1782 Battle of Saint Kitts; 12.4.1782 Battle of the Saintes; 4.12.1782-15.4.1783[P] *Cleopatra* (32); 9.3.1786-16.1.1789

Rose (28); 24.6.1790 *Alfred* (74); 15.10.1790-17.9.1791[P] *Colossus* (74); 6.2.1793 *Ramillies* (74); 1.6.1794 Glorious 1st of June; 4.7.1794 **Rear Admiral of the Blue**; 6.8.1794 CinC — North Sea; 1.1795-1.6.1795 *Prince of Wales* (98); **Rear Admiral of the Red**; 1.6.1795-2.1799 *Prince of Wales* (98); 23.6.1795 Action of Ile Groix; 13.4.1796-1799 CinC — Barbados & the Leeward Islands; 16.2.1797-17.2.1797 Capture of Trinidad; 14.2.1799 **Vice Admiral of the White**; 1800-1802 *Royal Sovereign* (100); 1.1.1801 **Vice Admiral of the Red**; 23.4.1804 **Admiral of the Blue**; 9.11.1805 **Admiral of the White**.

HARVEY, JOHN

Dates: 1740 Born; 30.6.1794 Died Portsmouth.
Family: Son John, RN (d.1837); Brother Henry, RN (1737-1810).
Service: 1753-1755 Merchant Service; 22.4.1755 Capt Serv *Falmouth* (50); 27.3.1756 Able *Falmouth* (50); 30.6.1756 Mid *Falmouth* (50); 7.2.1759 Passed; **Lieutenant**; 18.9.1759-1.6.1763[P] L. *Hornet* (10) Sloop; 29.11.1765-27.6.1770 LCmdr *Alarm* (6) Cutter; **Commander**; 26.5.1768-26.10.1771 *Racehorse* (16) Sloop; 26.1.1776 *Speedwell* (8) Sloop; **Captain**; 16.9.1777 *Panther* (60); 15.1.1782-10.1.1783 *Sampson* (64); 20.10.1782 Battle of Cape Spartel; 21.2.1788-15.9.1791[P] *Arrogant* (74); 7.1.1793-30.6.1794[†] *Brunswick* (74); 1.6.1794 Glorious 1st of June.

HASLEDEN, THOMAS

Dates: c.1739 Born; 1763 Died.
Family:
Service: 8.11.1752 Scholar *Royal Naval Academy*; 7.4.1755 Vol-p-O *Arundel* (24); 2.2.1756 Mid *Gibraltar* (20); 20.9.1757 Mid *Pallas* (36); 5.6.1758-12.6.1758 Raid on Saint-Malo; 7.2.1759 Passed; **Lieutenant**; 19.6.1760-4.8.1762 L. *Bonetta* (10) Sloop.

HASWELL, ROBERT

Dates: c.1724 Born; 1801 Died.
Family:
Service: 17.5.1737 Unk *Bosphorus* Mer; 23.4.1738 Capt Serv *Gloucester* (50); 2.4.1739 Able *Somerset* (80); 20.7.1741 Mid *Somerset* (80); 20.11.1741 Mid *Marlborough* (90); 27.5.1743 Mate *Romney* (50); 11.2.1743/44-12.2.1743/44 Battle of Toulon; 13.3.1743/44 Able *Namur* (90); 23.4.1744 Passed; **Lieutenant**; 8.7.1744[(MED 26.1.1747/48)] 3L *Faversham* (44); 27.2.1744/45[(MED 27.1.1747/48)] 3L *Worcester* (58); 10.7.1745[(MED 27.1.1747/48)] L. *Firedrake* (8) Bomb Vessel; 9.8.1745[(MED 27.1.1747/48)]-28.3.1746 3L *Berwick* (70); 19.3.1747/48[(MED 24.11.1748)] 3L *Revenge* (70); 11.10.1748[(MED 6.3.1750/51)]-22.11.1748[P] 1L *Princess* (70); 11.2.1755-27.2.1755 2L *Ambuscade* (40); 24.1.1756 2L *Harwich* (50); 12.8.1756 1L *Harwich* (50); 5.5.1757-23.1.1759 2L *Dublin* (74); 5.9.1757-6.10.1757 Raid on Rochefort; 29.1.1759 1L *Northumberland* (68); 23.12.1760-1.5.1762 2L *Marlborough* (68); 7.1.1762-10.2.1762 Operations against Martinique; **Commander**; 26.3.1762[(BLI 30.8.1763)]-24.2.1763[P] *Thunder* (8) Bomb Vessel; 6.6.1762-13.8.1762 Operations against Havana; 20.3.1776 *Hornet* (14) Sloop; **Captain**; 17.6.1780[(BLI 4.8.1781)]-31.1.1781 *Russell* (74).

HASWELL, WILLIAM

Dates: c.1735 Born; 1796 Died.
Family:
Service: 26.11.1749 Mst Serv *Deptford* (24) Storeship; 28.10.1752 Mid *Berwick* (70); 16.11.1753 Able *Fougueux* (64); 20.11.1754 Mid *Port Mahon* (24); 7.1.1756 Passed; **Lieutenant**; 1.12.1756[(ECH 6.5.1757)] 3L *Guernsey* (50); 5.4.1757 Action of April 5 1757; 14.6.1757[(ECH 6.5.1757)]-

24.12.1762[P] 2L *Guernsey* (50); 18.8.1759-19.8.1759 Battle of Lagos Bay; 6.4.1763-15.9.1766[P] L. *Fortune* (14) Sloop; 2.12.1778 1L *London* (90); 11.9.1779-1.10.1779 1L *Sandwich* (90); 9.10.1779-25.5.1780 1L *Dublin* (74); 21.9.1796 **Superannuated Commander**.

HATCH, JOHN

Dates: c.1738 Born; 7.1.1792 Died.
Family:
Service: 26.9.1734 Able *Britannia* (100); 7.6.1735 Able *Leopard* (50); 23.3.1735/36 Able *Bonetta* (8) Sloop; 21.4.1738 Mid *Romney* (50); 2.2.1740/41 Passed; **Lieutenant**; 21.2.1740/41 3L *Liverpool* (44); 13.12.1742 2L *Liverpool* (44); 19.9.1743-15.7.1744[P] 1L *Liverpool* (44); 24.10.1746 2L *Anglesea* (44); 15.3.1747/48-4.8.1748[P] 1L *Anglesea* (44); 28.1.1755 1L *Monarch* (74); 6.2.1755 1L *Prince George* (80); 7.10.1755-26.5.1757 1L *Duke* (90); **Commander**; 14.6.1757-3.5.1758[P] *Flamborough Prize* (14) Sloop.

HATHORN, ROBERT

Dates: c.1719 Born; 28.4.1788 Will Probate; 1789 Died.
Family:
Service: 8.10.1736-2.12.1739 Able *Kinsale* (40); 3.12.1739 Mid *Ruby* (54); 20.12.1743-8.5.1744[C] Mid *Northumberland* (64); 25.3.1745 Passed; **Lieutenant**; 1.7.1745 L. *Hornet* (10) Sloop; 5.11.1746-12.12.1749[P] 1L *Rippon* (54); 6.2.1755 2L *Ramillies* (90); 13.5.1755 2L *Terrible* (74); 5.7.1756-17.9.1756 3L *Marlborough* (80); 16.11.1756-5.2.1757 2L *Marlborough* (80); 10.2.1757 2L *Newark* (80); 8.1757-10.1757 Louisbourg Expedition; **Commander**; 18.1.1758-23.12.1758 *Hawke* (8) Sloop; 6.6.1758-27.7.1758 The Siege of Louisbourg; **Captain**; 27.10.1759-27.12.1762[P] *Royal Sovereign* (104); 21.10.1763-12.10.1766 *Superb* (74).

HAVEN, ARTHUR

Dates: 2.1.1756 Buried Minster, Kent; c.2.1.1756 Died; 7.1.1756 Will Probate.
Family: Wife Mary; Sister Mary [Russen]; Sister Elizabeth.
Service: **Lieutenant**; 14.4.1744 3L *Winchester* (50); 7.7.1744-6.11.1744 2L *Winchester* (50); 7.11.1744 4L *Shrewsbury* (80); 12.12.1744-23.6.1748[P] L. *Terror* (8) Bomb Vessel; 1.5.1746 Action of 1746-05-01; 11.3.1755 1L *Warwick* (60); 5.8.1755-2.1.1756[†] LCmdr *Princess Caroline* (80) Hospital Ship.

HAVEN, JOHN

Dates: c.1730 Born.
Family:
Service: 1751-1755 Merchant Service; 8.10.1755-16.11.1757 Mid *Hampshire* (50); 16.11.1757 Passed; **Lieutenant**; 18.4.1758-12.2.1759 2L *Thames* (32); 28.1.1762-2.3.1762 L. *Proserpine* (8) Fireship.

HAWFORD, JOHN

Dates: 1760 Died.
Family:
Service: 6.11.1732 Ord. *Lyme* (20); 3.6.1733 Able *Lyme* (20); 22.1.1733/34 QGnr *Dreadnought* (60); 14.3.1733/34 Gnr Mate *Dreadnought* (60); 6.10.1738 Gnr Mate *Oxford* (50); 8.12.1739 Mid *Oxford* (50); 5.11.1740 Mate *Assistance* (50); 24.12.1740 Mid *Assistance* (50); 3.9.1741 Mate *Assistance* (50); 28.4.1742-31.8.1745[P] Mate *Assistance* (50); 12.9.1745 Passed; **Lieutenant**; 28.1.1745/46-6.7.1746 3L *Poole* (44); 7.7.1746-23.12.1748[P] 2L *Poole* (44); 20.9.1746-25.9.1746

Lorient Operations; 1.10.1746 Action of 1746-10-01; 10.7.1755 3L *Tilbury* (58); 25.5.1756-18.12.1756 2L *Tilbury* (58); 4.5.1757-9.10.1758 2L *Saint George* (90).

HAWKE, LORD EDWARD CB, (1ST BARON HAWKE OF TOWTON)

Dates: 21.2.1704/5 Born; 14.11.1747 Order of the Bath; 20.5.1776 1st Baron Hawke of Towton; 17.10.1781 Died Sunbury-on-Thames.
Family: Father Edward Hawke (d. 1718); Mother Elizabeth Bladen; Wife Catharine Brooke (1720-1756).; Son Chaloner (d 1777); Daughter Catharine; Son Lieutenant-colonel Edward Hawke (d 1773); Son Martin Bladen Hawke (1744-1805).
Service: 13.5.1720 Vol-p-O *Seahorse* (20); 14.5.1722 MidO *Seahorse* (20); 13.7.1723 Mid *Seahorse* (20); 2.6.1725 Passed; 2.6.1725-12.7.1727 Mid *Kinsale* (40); **Lieutenant**; 11.4.1729-24.11.1729 3L *Portland* (50); 25.11.1729-22.12.1729[P] 3L *Leopard* (50); 29.5.1731-27.12.1731 4L *Edinburgh* (70); 15.1.1731/32-6.9.1732 L. *Scarborough* (20); 10.11.1732-24.12.1732 L. *Flamborough* (20); 24.12.1732-12.4.1733 1L *Kingston* (60); **Commander**; 13.4.1733-19.3.1733/34 *Wolf* (8) Sloop; **Captain**; 20.3.1733/34[(26.8.1735)]-5.9.1735[P] *Flamborough* (20); 30.7.1739-17.3.1742/43[P] *Portland* (50); 14.6.1743 *Berwick* (70); 11.2.1743/44-12.2.1743/44 Battle of Toulon; 3.8.1745[(MED 1.3.1745/46)]-25.5.1746[P] *Neptune* (90); 30.3.1747-22.7.1747 *Mars* (64); 15.7.1747 **Rear Admiral of the White**; 9.8.1747-27.9.1747 *Windsor* (60); 27.9.1747-11.1747 *Devonshire* (66); 14.10.1747 2nd Battle of Cape Finisterre; 28.12.1747-20.5.1776 M.P. for Portsmouth; 1748-11.1748 *Kent* (64); 12.5.1748 **Vice Admiral of the Blue**; 1755-6.1756 CinC — English Channel; 6.1.1755-10.1755 *Saint George* (90); 4.2.1755 **Vice Admiral of the White**; 24.2.1757 **Admiral of the Blue**; 3.7.1757-3.1758 CinC — The Mediterranean Sea; 8.1757-1758 *Ramillies* (90); 5.9.1757-6.10.1757 Raid on Rochefort; 5.3.1758 CinC — English Channel; 11.1758-c.23.11.1759[P] *Ramillies* (90); 14.11.1759-11.3.1761 *Royal George* (100); 20.11.1759 Battle of Quiberon Bay; 8.4.1762 CinC — English Channel; 27.4.1762-3.9.1762 *Royal George* (100); 21.10.1762 **Admiral of the White**; 4.1.1763-5.11.1765 Rear Admiral of Great Britain; 5.1766-1767 *Triumph* (74); 10.12.1766-17.10.1781 Privy Counsellor; 11.12.1766-11.1.1771 1st Lord; 15.1.1768 **Admiral of the Fleet**; 1.1771 Resigned.

HAWKER, EDMUND

Dates: c.1739 Born.
Family:
Service: 14.2.1753 Scholar *Royal Naval Academy*; 22.8.1755 Vol-p-O *Princess Mary* (60); 14.10.1755-2.5.1759 Mid *Princess Mary* (60); 2.5.1759 Passed; 12.10.1759 **Lieutenant**; 17.7.1761-22.1.1763[P] 1L *Flora* (32); 16.1.1778 Resigned.

HAWKER, JAMES

Dates: c.1731 Born; 24.4.1786 Will Probate; 1787 Died.
Family: Daughter Unknown [Osborne]; Daughter Unknown [Boyles]; Son Unknown; Son Unknown; Daughter Unknown [Seymour]; Daughter Unknown; Daughter Unknown [Knighton]; Son Edward, RN (d.1860).
Service: 3.11.1744 L. Serv *Shrewsbury* (80); 19.9.1745 MidO *Portsmouth* (24) Storeship; 8.3.1745/46 MidO *Sheerness* (24); 17.9.1746 MidO *Ambuscade* (40); 8.11.1746 Mate *Colchester* (50); 20.1.1747/48 Mid *Colchester* (50); 27.2.1748/49 Mate *Sheerness* (24); 2.4.1749 Mate *Queenborough* (24); 25.6.1749 Mate *Unicorn* (24); 9.10.1752 Able *Peggy* (8) Sloop; 4.6.1755 Passed; **Lieutenant**; 31.12.1755 3L *Colchester* (50); 17.5.1756 Action of 17th May 1756; 25.1.1760-22.12.1760[P] 2L *Colchester* (50); **Commander**; 6.8.1761-9.2.1763[P] *Barbadoes* (14) Sloop; 7.1.1762-10.2.1762 Operations against Martinique; 6.6.1762-13.8.1762 Operations

against Havana; 4.4.1763-7.3.1768[P] *Sardoine* (14) Sloop; **Captain**; 26.5.1768 *Echo* (24); 1.3.1770-12.3.1773 *Aldborough* (20); 8.4.1776-8.7.1778[W] *Mermaid* (28); 5.7.1779 *Iris* (28); 1.8.1780[(12.6.1781)] *Renown* (50); 10.11.1780-23.7.1781 *Hero* (74); 16.4.1781 Battle of Porto Praya.

HAWKER, THOMAS

Dates: c.1734 Born; 30.11.1806 Died; 20.11.1807 Will Probate.
Family:
Service: 20.6.1750 Able *Peggy* (8) Sloop; 2.5.1756 Mid *Colchester* (50); 17.5.1756 Action of 17th May 1756; 8.9.1756 Mid *Royal Anne* (100); 9.12.1756 Mid *Colchester* (50); 22.3.1758 Mid *Hussar* (28); 9.8.1758 Passed; **Lieutenant**; 11.4.1759 3L *Lynn* (44); 7.1.1761-11.2.1762 1L *Sapphire* (32); 4.11.1762 3L *Assistance* (50); 4.12.1764 1L *San Antonio* (64); 29.11.1766-3.2.1768 2L *San Antonio* (64); 24.6.1768-19.6.1770[P] 2L *Venus* (36); 9.8.1770-29.5.1771[P] 2L *Dorsetshire* (68); 11.5.1776 2L *Centaur* (74); 4.11.1776 2L *Terrible* (74); 5.3.1778-29.6.1779 1L *Terrible* (74); 27.7.1778 1st Battle of Ushant; 14.7.1779 **Commander**; **Captain**; 21.9.1790-22.11.1790 *Brilliant* (28); 1799 Superintendent of Gun Vessels at Plymouth.

HAWKINS, JOHN

Dates: c.1725 Born; 1.1.1761 Died Pondicherry.
Family:
Service: 23.12.1743-26.11.1745[P] Able *Torbay* (80); 11.2.1743/44-12.2.1743/44 Battle of Toulon; 19.2.1746/47 Able *Barfleur* (90); 3.3.1746/47 Mid *Barfleur* (90); 17.1.1747/48-7.6.1748[P] Able *Barfleur* (90); 22.5.1751 Mid *Devonshire* (66); 15.6.1754 Mate *Mermaid* (24); 25.4.1755 Mid *Mermaid* (24); 22.5.1755-14.6.1755 British attack on Fort Beauséjour; 8.3.1757 Passed; **Lieutenant**; 10.5.1757 L. *Postillion* (18) Sloop; 4.12.1758 2L *Duc d'Aquitaine* (64); 3.4.1759-1.1.1761[W] 1L *Duc d'Aquitaine* (64).

HAWKINS, JOSEPH

Dates: c.1726 Born; 1775 Died.
Family:
Service: 29.3.1752 Able *Blandford* (20); 11.10.1753 Mid *Blandford* (20); 15.8.1755 Mid *Bristol* (50); 24.10.1756-9.9.1757 Able *Bristol* (50); 10.9.1757 Mid *Saint Albans* (50); 28.4.1758 Mate *Hampton Court* (64); 5.1.1759 Passed; **Lieutenant**; 4.4.1760 3L *Montagu* (60); 12.10.1761 2L *Montagu* (60); 20.11.1761-24.5.1763[P] 1L *Montagu* (60); 30.11.1770-6.2.1771 4L *Cambridge* (80).

HAY, CHARLES

Dates: bef.18.3.1773 Died; 10.12.1773 Will Probate.
Family:
Service: **Lieutenant**; 13.3.1759-11.2.1760 2L *Minerva* (32); 20.11.1759 Battle of Quiberon Bay; 19.5.1762-18.12.1762[P] 6L *Royal George* (100); 11.5.1763 3L *Dragon* (74); 13.10.1763 2L *Dragon* (74); 12.12.1766-10.8.1768 1L *Rippon* (60); 13.10.1768 2L *San Antonio* (64); 17.9.1770 3L *San Antonio* (64); 30.10.1770 5L *Namur* (90); **Commander**; 19.1.1771-bef.18.3.1773[†] *Tamar* (16) Sloop.

HAY, DAVID

Dates: c.1715 Born; 1788 Died; 21.4.1788 Will Probate.

Family:

Service: 30.6.1735 Vol-p-O *Tartar* (20); 24.5.1737 Able *Defiance* (60); 16.12.1739 Able *Blandford* (20); 16.1.1740/41 Able *Dover* (44); 20.2.1740/41 Mid *Marlborough* (90); 3.10.1741 Mid *Duke* (90); 12.12.1741 Mate *Bideford* (20); 26.1.1741/42 Mate *Looe* (44); 21.9.1742 Mate *Preston* (50); 12.2.1742/43 Mid *Duke* (90); 3.3.1742/43 Passed; **Lieutenant**; 4.4.1743 L. *Deptford Prize* (8) Sloop; 10.10.1743 3L *Hector* (44); 14.1.1743/44 2L *Hector* (44); 31.12.1747-12.8.1750[P] 1L *Hector* (44); 4.11.1755 L. *Solebay* (24); **Commander**; 10.11.1756-20.7.1758[P] *Saint Anne* (18) Hired Armed Ship.

HAY, JOHN

Dates: 1781 Died; 1.12.1781 Will Probate.

Family:

Service: **Lieutenant**; 13.2.1759 3L *Bienfaisant* (64); 21.2.1759 4L *Hero* (74); 20.8.1759 3L *Hero* (74); 20.11.1759 Battle of Quiberon Bay; **Commander**; 4.5.1761-25.2.1763[P] *Blast* (8) Bomb Vessel; 4.4.1763-31.5.1766 *Wolf* (8) Sloop.

HAY, ROBERT

Dates: 30.12.1789 Died; 30.3.1790 Will Probate.

Family:

Service: **Lieutenant**; 24.4.1747-8.9.1748[P] 3L *Dragon* (60); 30.7.1763-18.12.1763[P] LCmdr *Adventure* (6) Cutter.

HAY, WILLIAM

Dates: c.1734 Born; 1801 Died.

Family:

Service: 30.8.1749 Ord. *Rainbow* (44); 22.9.1749 Capt Serv *Rainbow* (44); 20.10.1751 Able *Rainbow* (44); 19.8.1752 Able *Deptford* (50); 3.7.1753 Mid *Deptford* (50); 4.8.1755-6.11.1755 Able *Deptford* (50); 5.11.1755 Passed; **Lieutenant**; 1.6.1756 3L *York* (60); 6.6.1758-27.7.1758 The Siege of Louisbourg; 1.8.1758[(NA 19.12.1758)] 2L *York* (60); 7.2.1759 5L *Royal William* (84); 19.2.1759 1L *Echo* (24); 20.6.1759 2L *Foudroyant* (80); 14.3.1760-1.4.1760 1L *Foudroyant* (80); **Commander**; 21.11.1760 *Peregrine* (20) Sloop; 20.1.1761 *Grampus* (14) Sloop; 18.2.1762 *Senegal* (14) Sloop; **Captain**; 12.4.1762 *Humber* (44); 14.4.1762-4.4.1763[P] *Chester* (50); 20.8.1763-25.8.1766 *Solebay* (28) Frigate; 24.1.1770-26.7.1773[P] *Carysfort* (28); 31.5.1776-30.5.1777 *Alarm* (32); 1779 Regulating Officer at Hastings; 6.2.1793 **Superannuated Rear Admiral.**

HAYES, FREDERICK

Dates: bef.15.8.1777 Died.

Family:

Service: **Lieutenant**; 30.3.1758[(EI 27.2.1760)]-19.9.1759 2L *Queenborough* (24); 29.4.1758 Battle of Cuddalore; 3.8.1758 Battle of Negapatam; 10.9.1759 Battle of Pondicherry; 28.10.1761-11.2.1762 6L *Namur* (90); 22.2.1762-14.7.1763 3L *Dreadnought* (60); 10.5.1766-25.7.1766[P] 2L *Thunderer* (74); 24.10.1766-10.11.1769 1L *Hero* (74); 17.9.1770 2L *San Antonio* (64); 31.10.1770-27.2.1771 1L *Buckingham* (68); 9.9.1772 3L *Resolution* (74); 3.12.1774-6.10.1775 2L *Resolution* (74); 2.11.1776-15.8.1777 2L *Prince George* (90).

HAYES, MATTHEW

Dates: c.1727 Born; c.1763 Died; 3.6.1763 Will Probate.

Family:

Service: 1752-1755 Merchant Service; 9.7.1755-20.8.1755 Able *Ipswich* (64); 21.8.1755 Mate *Ipswich* (64); 18.6.1757 Mid *Duke* (90); 5.1.1758 Mate *Duke* (90); 5.6.1758-12.6.1758 Raid on Saint-Malo; 5.1.1759 Passed; **Lieutenant**; 26.3.1759-17.6.1761 L. *Speedwell* (8) Sloop; 5.10.1761-25.8.1762 2L *Torrington* (44).

HAYGARTH, WILLIAM

Dates: bef.1789 Died Kendal.

Family:

Service: **Lieutenant**; 6.4.1757 2L *Vestal* (32); 10.10.1758-22.11.1758 1L *Vestal* (32); 14.12.1758 2L *Temple* (68); 30.4.1759 2L *Belliqueux* (64); 2.10.1761-13.8.1763[P] 1L *Belliqueux* (64); 19.12.1768 1L *Edgar* (60); 17.1.1770-22.5.1771[P] 2L *Edgar* (60); 21.5.1778-11.3.1779 1L *Jason* (28).

HAYNE, ARTHUR

Dates: 1797 Died.

Family:

Service: **Lieutenant**; 22.11.1757-27.10.1758 L. *Saltash* (14) Sloop; 5.6.1758-12.6.1758 Raid on Saint-Malo; 27.6.1759 5L *Duke* (90); 4.9.1759 4L *Duke* (90); 20.11.1759 Battle of Quiberon Bay; 16.1.1761-29.3.1762 2L *Unicorn* (28); 29.3.1761-11.6.1761 Expedition against Belle-Isle; 11.4.1763-31.5.1766 L. *Happy* (8) Sloop; 9.9.1773 2L *Centaur* (74); 25.8.1774-6.11.1775 1L *Centaur* (74); 24.10.1775-2.12.1777[P] LCmdr *Adventure* Hired Tender; 5.12.1777 LCmdr *Charming Molly* Hired Tender; 17.5.1778-31.12.1779[P] LCmdr *Sherborne* (6) Cutter; 7.1780-7.1783[P] LCmdr *Cruizer* (14) Cutter; 26.5.1797 **Superannuated Commander**.

HAYNES, THOMAS

Dates: c.1732 Born; 1789 Died; 12.1.1789 Will Probate.

Family:

Service: 17.6.1745 Able *Poole* (44); 20.9.1746-25.9.1746 Lorient Operations; 1.10.1746 Action of 1746-10-01; 23.5.1748 Mid *Tilbury* (58); 12.10.1748 Battle of Havana; 20.3.1748/49 Able *Ferret* (14) Sloop; 25.3.1749 Mid *Ferret* (14) Sloop; 3.11.1752-24.4.1753[W] Able *Assurance* (44); 6.11.1754 Passed; **Lieutenant**; 1.11.1755 4L *Cambridge* (80); 2.4.1756 3L *Cambridge* (80); 15.11.1756-26.2.1757 2L *Saint Albans* (60); 19.8.1757 5L *Barfleur* (80); 5.9.1757-6.10.1757 Raid on Rochefort; 13.10.1757 1L *Actaeon* (28); 5.6.1758-12.6.1758 Raid on Saint-Malo; 3.10.1759 1L *Arethusa* (32); 25.3.1763 1L *Emerald* (32); 6.12.1763-2.4.1764 1L *Achilles* (60); 2.4.1764-7.4.1767 1L *Ramillies* (74); 23.7.1767-19.2.1769 L. *Squirrel* (20); **Commander**; 9.4.1777-3.9.1778 *Porpoise* (16) Sloop; 2.10.1778-23.1.1779 *Nymphe* (36); 23.1.1779 **Captain**; 30.1.1779-24.3.1779 *Ambuscade* (32); 5.1.1780-1.11.1780 *Pelican* (24); 1.11.1780[JAM 28.1.1782] *Lowestoffe* (28); 20.5.1781[JAM 28.1.1782]-6.7.1782 *Ruby* (64); 30.7.1782-5.3.1783[P] *Belleisle* (64).

HAYTER, SAMUEL

Dates: 1800 Died.

Family:

Service: **Lieutenant**; 28.8.1761[EI 21.8.1764] 2L *Seaford* (20); 12.11.1761[EI 21.8.1764] 5L *Grafton* (68); 24.9.1762-6.10.1762 Battle of Manilla; 21.10.1762[EI 21.8.1764] 4L *Grafton* (68); 18.8.1763[EI 21.8.1764]-24.6.1764[P] 3L *Grafton* (68); 18.12.1770 L. *Favorite* (16) Sloop; 2.2.1771 3L *Modeste*

(64); 18.3.1771-16.10.1772[P] 2L *Modeste* (64); 2.11.1776-7.2.1777 3L *Invincible* (74); 2.9.1779 2L *Sandwich* (90); 16.9.1779-1.10.1779 3L *Sandwich* (90); 25.12.1792-16.4.1794[P] 2L *Royal William* (84); 14.2.1795-10.1795 LCmdr *Gladiator* (44) Convalescent Ship.

HAYWARD, THOMAS

Dates: 1775 Died; 19.9.1775 Will Probate.
Family:
Service: 3.3.1756 Passed; **Lieutenant**; 26.3.1758[(JAM 17.9.1759)]-5.4.1759 L. *Hornet* (10) Sloop; 26.2.1760[(JAM 12.2.1761)] 6L *Marlborough* (80); 20.5.1760[(JAM 12.2.1761)]-30.9.1760[P] 5L *Marlborough* (80); 3.11.1760 3L *Superb* (74); 23.12.1760-23.3.1761 2L *Superb* (74); **Commander**; 9.11.1761-21.1.1763[P] *Spy* (10) Sloop; 10.5.1763-10.2.1767[P] *Senegal* (14) Sloop; 11.6.1767-26.12.1771[P] *Martin* (14) Sloop; 3.6.1774-18.9.1775 *Wolf* (8) Sloop.

HAYWARD, THOMAS

Dates: c.1734 Born; 9.1795 Died.
Family:
Service: 1752-1757 Merchant Service; 20.10.1756 Able *Lowestoffe* (28); 24.4.1757 Mid *Lowestoffe* (28); 19.7.1757 Mid *Neptune* (90); 5.9.1757-6.10.1757 Raid on Rochefort; 1.11.1757 Mid *Union* (90); 5.6.1758-12.6.1758 Raid on Saint-Malo; 20.11.1759 Battle of Quiberon Bay; 20.2.1760 Passed; 1.10.1760 Mid *Union* (90); 29.3.1761-11.6.1761 Expedition against Belle-Isle; 9.7.1761 Mate *Union* (90); **Lieutenant**; 6.11.1762 6L *Blenheim* (90); 3.3.1763[(JAM 18.8.1763)]-10.8.1763[P] 3L *Defiance* (60); 30.10.1770-11.9.1771 3L *Prudent* (64); 1.1.1778-3.7.1778 1L *Robust* (74).

HEATHCOTE, GEORGE

Dates: c.1736 Born; 1771 Died.
Family:
Service: 9.6.1750 Able *Mercury* (20); 4.3.1750/51 Mid *America* (44); 28.2.1751/52-6.5.1753[P] Mid *Winchelsea* (20); 14.9.1754 Mid *Success* (20); 22.5.1755-14.6.1755 British attack on Fort Beauséjour; 12.10.1755 ActL *Vulture* (14) Sloop; 6.12.1755 Able *Torbay* (74); 23.2.1756 ActL *Jamaica* (10) Sloop; 16.2.1757 ActL *Nottingham* (60); 17.12.1757 ActL *Newark* (80); 9.5.1758 Passed; **Lieutenant**; 17.5.1758 4L *Conqueror* (68); 22.3.1759 3L *Conqueror* (68); 30.3.1759-26.4.1759 4L *Hercules* (74).

HEBDEN, BAKER

Dates: c.1712 Born; bef.20.1.1763 Died.
Family:
Service: 15.2.1731/32 Able *Port Mahon* (20); 12.4.1732 Mid *Port Mahon* (20); 14.6.1734 Mid *Yarmouth* (70); 25.1.1734/35 Able *Rose* (20); 19.10.1735 Mid *Rose* (20); 31.12.1737-15.12.1738[P] Mate *Rose* (20); 25.1.1738/39 Passed; **Lieutenant**; 22.1.1739/40 3L *Mary Galley* (40); 13.4.1741 2L *Mary Galley* (40); 26.5.1741 1L *Mary Galley* (40); 16.6:1741-14.2.1742/43 1L *Woolwich* (50); 17.6.1743 2L *Prince of Orange* (70); 25.6.1743-4.7.1745 2L *Argyll* (50).

HEMMINGS, WILLIAM

Dates: c.1734 Born; 1795 Died; 4.3.1795 Will Probate.
Family:
Service: 1753-1755 Merchant Service; 2.4.1755 Mid *Ramillies* (90); 12.10.1755-28.2.1756 Able *Ramillies* (90); 29.2.1756-11.4.1759 Mid *Ramillies* (90); 20.5.1756 Battle of Minorca; 5.9.1757-

6.10.1757 Raid on Rochefort; 5.6.1758-12.6.1758 Raid on Saint-Malo; 11.4.1759 Passed; 10.10.1759 **Lieutenant**; 23.10.1759 4L *Monarch* (74); 11.1.1760-2.2.1763[P] L. *Deal Castle* (20); 17.6.1767 1L *Carysfort* (28); 8.7.1767 2L *Boreas* (28); 14.3.1769 L. *Weazle* (16) Sloop; 10.4.1770 2L *Ramillies* (74); 24.4.1770 3L *Arrogant* (74); 25.9.1770-10.6.1771[P] 4L *Arrogant* (74); 24.10.1771-3.4.1775 2L *Levant* (28); 20.6.1775 1L *Solebay* (28) Frigate; 5.7.1775-7.5.1777 1L *Liverpool* (28).

HEMMINGTON, HENRY

Dates: c.1718 Born; 1763 Died.
Family:
Service: 9.3.1733/34-1.10.1734 Able *Dorsetshire* (80); 2.10.1734-25.12.1735 Mid *Dorsetshire* (80); 26.12.1735-7.4.1738 Mid *Blandford* (20); 8.4.1738-3.11.1738 Mate *Princess Amelia* (80); 4.11.1738-7.4.1739 Able *Lennox* (70); 8.4.1739-16.6.1739 Mid *Princess Charlotte* (8) Yacht; 17.6.1739 Mate *Princess Charlotte* (8) Yacht; 23.4.1740-15.5.1740 Able *Falkland* (50); 16.5.1740-26.6.1740 Able *Tiger* (50); 25.6.1740 Passed; **Lieutenant**; 8.8.1740[(25.8.1740)]-10.1.1741/42 4L *Princess Amelia* (80); 20.4.1742 2L *Princess Amelia* (80).

HEMMINGTON, JOHN

Dates: 26.12.1757 Died.
Family:
Service: 1695 Vol-p-O *Berkeley Castle* (46) Hired Ship; 14.1.1695/96 Vol-p-O *Monck* (58); **Lieutenant**; 30.6.1701 3L *Royal Oak* (70); 25.9.1701 2L *Severn* (54); 22.10.1702 1L *Prompt Prize* (70); 23.1.1702/3 2L *Burlington* (54); 21.12.1704-1.1.1705/6 2L *Russell* (80); 1.1.1705/6 2L *Newark* (80); **Commander**; 16.3.1707/8 *Carcass* (4) Bomb Vessel; 17.8.1708 *Fox* (24); **Captain**; 12.11.1708-5.3.1710/11 *Experiment* (32); 17.5.1711 *Bristol* (54); 14.12.1714-12.1.1714/15[P] *Bristol* (54); 21.5.1734-16.2.1735/36[P] *Dorsetshire* (80); 16.5.1738-2.12.1738[P] *Princess Amelia* (80); 30.8.1739-2.7.1742 *Princess Amelia* (80); 15.7.1747 **Superannuated Rear Admiral**.

HENDERSON, JOHN

Dates: c.1734 Born; 1762 Died.
Family:
Service: 24.6.1747 Capt Serv *Deal Castle* (20); 8.7.1748 Able *Deal Castle* (20); 28.6.1749 Able *Eltham* (40); 12.8.1749 Mid *Eltham* (40); 4.3.1750/51 Mid *Peregrine* (20) Sloop; 23.11.1751 Able *Peregrine* (20) Sloop; 28.5.1753 Able *Terrible* (74); 24.1.1755 Mid *Terrible* (74); 6.4.1755 Mid *Saint George* (90); 3.3.1756 Passed; **Lieutenant**; 5.7.1756[(ECH 5.4.1757)] 4L *Buckingham* (68); 28.4.1757-20.5.1757 3L *Buckingham* (68); 20.5.1757-12.5.1758 4L *Buckingham* (68).

HENDERSON, ROBERT

Dates: c.1739 Born; 1778 Died; 1.12.1778 Will Probate.
Family:
Service: 1754-1757 Merchant Service; 19.6.1757 Able *Shannon* (28); 27.2.1758 Mid *Shannon* (28); 6.6.1758-27.7.1758 The Siege of Louisbourg; 21.12.1758 Mid *Swan* (14) Sloop; 10.6.1759-9.7.1760 Mid *Princess Royal* (90); 9.7.1760 Passed; **Lieutenant**; 11.12.1760 2L *Arethusa* (32); 11.5.1763-22.7.1766[P] 3L *Essex* (64); 16.12.1771-1.1.1773 L. *Hazard* (8) Sloop.

HENDERSON, WILLIAM

Dates: c.1734 Born; 9.12.1797 Died.
Family:
Service: 24.11.1749 QGnr *Porcupine* (16) Sloop; 11.5.1751 Cox *Porcupine* (16) Sloop; 22.2.1751/52 Able *Porcupine* (16) Sloop; 20.5.1755 Mid *Porcupine* (16) Sloop; 29.10.1755 Mid *Solebay* (24); 18.11.1756-13.4.1758[B] Mid *Prince George* (80); 5.1.1759 Passed; **Lieutenant**; 22.5.1759 L. *Swan* (14) Sloop; 13.4.1763-3.11.1766[P] 1L *Milford* (28).

HENLEY, CHARLES

Dates: 1777 Died; 16.10.1777 Will Probate.
Family:
Service: **Lieutenant**; 27.7.1745-4.4.1746 L. *Flamborough* (20); 2.12.1746-20.5.1749[P] 2L *Adventure* (44); 26.3.1754 L. *Trial* (10) Sloop; 22.10.1755[(EI 12.5.1756)]-22.5.1756[P] 2L *Advice* (50); 1.7.1756 3L *Berwick* (64); 28.9.1756-5.8.1760[P] 2L *Berwick* (64); 5.4.1757 Action of April 5 1757; 28.2.1758 Battle of Cartagena; 16.1.1759-19.1.1759 Attack on Martinique; 20.1.1759-1.5.1759 Capture of Guadeloupe.

HENRY, JOHN

Dates: 28.9.1731 Born Anglesey; 6.8.1829 Died Rolvenden.
Family:
Service: **Lieutenant**; 27.4.1757[(JAM 31.10.1759)]-30.1.1759 3L *Assistance* (50); 22.5.1761-19.9.1763[P] 2L *Hampton Court* (64); 6.6.1762-13.8.1762 Operations against Havana; 27.10.1770-17.6.1771[P] 2L *Ramillies* (74); **Commander**; 16.4.1777[(NA 23.12.1778)] *Vigilant* (22); **Captain**; 22.11.1777[(NA 26.10.1780)]-15.5.1780 *Fowey* (24); 9.9.1779-18.10.1779 Seige of Savannah; 16.5.1780[(NA 26.3.1781)] *Providence* (32); 6.12.1780-4.8.1784[P] *Renown* (50); 12.12.1781 2nd Battle of Ushant; 26.4.1793-3.5.1794 *Irresistible* (74); 23.10.1794 **Rear Admiral of the Blue**; 1.6.1795 **Rear Admiral of the Red**; 14.2.1799 **Vice Admiral of the White**; 1.1.1801 **Vice Admiral of the Red**; 23.4.1804 **Admiral of the Blue**; 28.4.1808 **Admiral of the White**; 12.8.1812 **Admiral of the Red**.

HENSHAW, JOHN

Dates: 1780 Died; 21.4.1780 Will Probate.
Family:
Service: **Lieutenant**; 1.4.1758[(2.8.1758)]-5.3.1759[P] 4L *Hampton Court* (64); 23.2.1760 3L *Dorsetshire* (68); **Commander**; 24.5.1762-23.9.1762[W] *Scorpion* (14) Sloop; 4.4.1763-13.8.1766 *Hunter* (10) Sloop; 23.6.1768-1.7.1771 *Hunter* (10) Sloop; 3.6.1773-8.3.1776 *Ranger* (8) Sloop.

HERBERT, CHARLES

Dates: 1743 Born; 28.5.1743 Baptised; 5.9.1816 Died.
Family: Father Hon. William Herbert, MP (c.1696-1757); Wife Lady Caroline Montagu married 13.7.1775; Brother Henry, MP (1741-1811).
Service: **Lieutenant**; 5.9.1761[(MED 21.12.1762)]-12.5.1763[P] 3L *Jersey* (60); 7.6.1763 2L *Princess Louisa* (60); **Commander**; 3.7.1765-15.7.1765[P] *Merlin* (18) Frigate; **Captain**; 26.5.1768-4.10.1770 *Tartar* (28); 20.2.1775-11.9.1780 M.P. for Wilton; 1776 Resigned; 18.6.1777-5.9.1816 Groom of the bedchamber; 8.5.1807-5.9.1816 M.P. for Wilton.

HERBERT, THOMAS

Dates: c.1720 Born; 1784 Died; 1.9.1784 Will Probate.
Family:
Service: 25.9.1742 Mate *Mortar* (10) Bomb Vessel; 14.6.1744 Mid *Shoreham* (20); 8.8.1744 Mid *Royal Sovereign* (104); 28.9.1745 Mate *Royal Sovereign* (104); 26.3.1746 Able *Exeter* (60); 4.6.1746 Able *Eltham* (40); 11.10.1746-13.10.1747[P] Mid *Royal Sovereign* (104); 4.2.1747/48 Passed; **Lieutenant**; 21.2.1759[JAM 20.9.1759] 3L *Portland* (50); 18.8.1759-19.8.1759 Battle of Lagos Bay; 18.10.1759[JAM 20.9.1759] 2L *Portland* (50); 19.10.1759[JAM 20.9.1759]-6.12.1762[P] 1L *Portland* (50); 20.11.1759 Battle of Quiberon Bay.

HERNE, HANOVER

Dates: c.1713 Born; bef.17.10.1760 Died.
Family:
Service: 6.2.1726/27 Vol-p-O *Captain* (70); 26.12.1728 MidO *Kinsale* (40); 16.1.1729/30 Mid *Oxford* (50); 13.10.1731 Able *Squirrel* (20); 8.1.1731/32 Mid *Squirrel* (20); 26.9.1732 Mid *Edinburgh* (70); 22.5.1733-27.1.1733/34[P] Mid *Suffolk* (70); 4.9.1734 Passed; **Lieutenant**; 3.7.1739 L. *Anne Galley* (8) Fireship; 30.7.1741[12.1.1743/44]-24.1.1746/47 1L *Warwick* (60); 11.2.1743/44-12.2.1743/44 Battle of Toulon.

HERON, BENJAMIN

Dates: c.1722 Born; 1771 Died.
Family:
Service: 4.4.1735 Capt Serv *Captain* (70); 31.8.1735 Ord. *Captain* (70); 1.1.1735/36-4.5.1737[P] Capt Serv *Captain* (70); 15.4.1738-18.6.1739 Able *Garland* (20); 19.6.1739 Able *Deal Castle* (20); 31.12.1739 Mid *Deal Castle* (20); 15.4.1741 Mid *Sapphire*; 5.5.1741 Mid *Dreadnought* (60); 25.10.1741 MidO *Sunderland* (60); 9.12.1741 Mid *Cambridge* (80); 20.3.1741/42 Passed; **Lieutenant**; 3.10.1743-5.7.1745 L. *Bideford* (20); 31.8.1747 2L *Tavistock* (50); 23.9.1748-5.12.1749 2L *Anson* (60).

HERON, HARRY

Dates: 1743 Born; 1817 Died; 28.6.1817 Buried; 4.7.1817 Will Probate.
Family:
Service: 1755-1759 Merchant Service; 20.5.1758 Able *Magnanime* (74); 5.6.1758-12.6.1758 Raid on Saint-Malo; 8.1.1759-7.10.1761 Mid *Magnanime* (74); 20.11.1759 Battle of Quiberon Bay; 7.10.1761 Passed; **Lieutenant**; 2.1.1762 5L *Magnanime* (74); 14.6.1762 4L *Magnanime* (74); 21.6.1762 3L *Achilles* (60); 18.4.1763-20.9.1765 L. *Druid* (10) Sloop; 29.11.1766 1L *Hussar* (28); 29.6.1768-10.1.1771 2L *Hussar* (28); **Commander**; 1.12.1777-1.12.1781 *Merchant* (20) Hired Armed Ship; **Captain**; 23.3.1782-25.3.1782 *Nemesis* (28); 23.3.1804 **Superannuated Captain**.

HERON, WILLIAM

Dates: c.1740 Born; c.1766 Died; 15.9.1766 Will Probate.
Family:
Service: 1754-1755 Merchant Service; 1.4.1755 Able *Kent* (64); 11.1.1756-14.1.1756 Capture of Geriah; 23.10.1756 Able *Cumberland* (66); 7.3.1757-1.4.1757 Expedition against Chandernagore; 29.4.1758 Battle of Cuddalore; 9.7.1758 Mid *Cumberland* (66); 3.8.1758 Battle of Negapatam; 6.5.1759 Mid *Yarmouth* (64); 1.9.1759 Mid *Preston* (50); 13.3.1759/60 Mid *Princess Royal* (90); 9.4.1760-9.7.1760 Mid *Hornet* (10) Sloop; 9.7.1760 Passed; **Lieutenant**;

5.12.1760 L. *Seaford* (20); 24.9.1762-6.10.1762 Battle of Manilla; 2.1763-5.1763 L. *Panther* (60); 18.7.1763-19.9.1763[P] *Manilla* (14) Storeship.

HERVEY, LORD AUGUSTUS JOHN (3RD EARL OF BRISTOL)

Dates: 19.5.1724 Born; 18.3.1775 3rd Earl of Bristol; 23.12.1779 Died St James's Square, London; 28.12.1779 Buried Ickworth.

Family: Father John Hervey, Baron Hervey of Ickworth (1696–1743); Mother Mary Lepell (1699/1700–1768); Wife Elizabeth Chudleigh (c.1720–1788) married 4.8.1744; Mistress Mary Nesbitt (1743–1825); Brother George William, 2nd Earl of Bristol (1721-1775); Brother Frederick Augustus (1730–1803);

Service: 5.1735 Capt Serv *Pembroke* (60); 1740-30.10.1740 Mid *Superb* (60); **Lieutenant**; 31.10.1740(18.3.1741/42) 4L *Shrewsbury* (80); 24.2.1740/41(18.3.1741/42) 3L *Tilbury* (60); 4.3.1740/41-5.1741 Operations against Cartagena; 21.9.1741(18.3.1741/42)-8.5.1742[P] 2L *Superb* (60); 15.3.1742/43 2L *Superb* (60); 4.4.1743 4L *Captain* (70); 28.10.1743 3L *Captain* (70); 15.6.1744 3L *Cornwall* (80); 30.8.1744 2L *Cornwall* (80); **Commander**; 16.9.1746-24.12.1746 *Porcupine* (16) Sloop; **Captain**; 15.1.1746/47 *Princess* (70); 30.4.1748(MED 6.1.1748/49)-29.12.1748[P] *Phoenix* (24); 2.1.1751/52-8.5.1756 *Phoenix* (24); 15.5.1756 *Hampton Court* (64); 23.5.1756(MED 11.1.1759)-20.8.1756 *Defiance* (60); 1.2.1757-1.3.1758 *Hampton Court* (64); 28.2.1758 Battle of Cartagena; 29.3.1758(26.4.1759)-6.3.1760[P] *Monmouth* (70); 7.3.1760-15.12.1762[P] *Dragon* (74); 29.3.1761-11.6.1761 Expedition against Belle-Isle; 7.1.1762-10.2.1762 Operations against Martinique; 24.2.1762-25.2.1762 Capture of Saint Lucia; 6.6.1762-13.8.1762 Operations against Havana; 4.5.1763 CinC — The Mediterranean Sea; 4.5.1763-7.9.1763 *Centurion* (50); 2.2.1771-11.4.1775 Lord Commissioner of the Admiralty; 23.4.1773 Second in Command — The Mediterranean Sea; 31.3.1775 **Rear Admiral of the Blue**; 28.4.1777 **Rear Admiral of the White**; 23.1.1778 **Rear Admiral of the Red**; 29.1.1778 **Vice Admiral of the Blue.**

HERVEY, PYNSENT

Dates: 1778 Died.

Family: Father Edward Hervey; Mother Helen Chernocke; Sister Helen [Bayle]; Brother Edward;

Service: **Lieutenant**; 3.1.1748/49(EI 10.5.1750) 3L *Harwich* (50); 25.5.1749(EI 10.5.1750)-16.5.1750[P] 2L *Harwich* (50); 12.8.1755 4L *Newark* (80); 7.10.1755-7.7.1756 4L *Intrepid* (64); 20.5.1756 Battle of Minorca; 6.4.1757-29.9.1758 3L *Burford* (68); 5.9.1757-6.10.1757 Raid on Rochefort; 6.6.1758-27.7.1758 The Siege of Louisbourg; 28.1.1762-10.11.1762[P] 2L *Saint George* Prison Ship.

HESLOPP, ROBERT

Dates: c.1731 Born; 24.9.1757 Died.

Family:

Service: 27.2.1748/49 Able *Warwick* (60); 4.1.1750/51 Mid *Rose* (24) Ship; 3.12.1751 Mate *Rose* (24) Ship; 13.3.1754 Mate *Shoreham* (24); 30.4.1755 Passed; **Lieutenant**; 10.6.1756-24.9.1757[W] L. *Ferret* (14) Sloop.

HEWETT, SIR WILLIAM (5TH BARONET OF HEADLEY HALL)

Dates: c.1724 Born; 22.5.1749 5th Baronet of Headley Hall; 1.1.1761 Died;

Family: Father Sir William Hewett (4th Baronet of Headley Hall), RN (d.1749); Mother Elizabeth Levemore; Sister Elizabeth; Brother Herbert; Brother Levemore (d.1761).

Service: 20.4.1741 Scholar *Royal Naval Academy*; 9.7.1741 Mid *Sandwich* (90); c.1742-4.3.1742/43[P] Mid *Winchester* (50); 16.8.1743 Mid *Princess Louisa* (60); 29.10.1744 Mid *Dreadnought* (60) Receiving Ship; 18.2.1744/45 Mid *Ipswich* (70); c.5.1745 Mid *Russell* (80); 28.8.1745 ActL *Nassau* (70); 13.12.1745 Passed; **Lieutenant**; 17.12.1745(MED 20.1.1747/48)-14.5.1746 4L *Nassau* (70); 16.1.1753-5.2.1754 2L *Kent* (64); 5.2.1754 3L *Kent* (64); 11.1.1756-14.1.1756 Capture of Geriah; **Commander**; 25.2.1756(Geriah 6.11.1756)-11.3.1756 *Kingfisher* (14) Sloop; 24.12.1756 *Hunter* (10) Sloop; 8.1757-10.1757 Louisbourg Expedition; 22.5.1758 *Jamaica* (10) Sloop; **Captain**; 10.1.1759-5.2.1759[P] *Sphinx* (24); 29.1.1759-1.1.1761[F] *Duc d'Aquitaine* (64).

HEY, RAWLINS

Dates: c.1734 Born; 1.4.1757 Died India.
Family:
Service: 12.11.1747 Ord. *Saint George* (90); 5.9.1748 Able *Bristol* (50); 2.12.1748 Able *Kent* (64); 20.2.1748/49 Mid *Kent* (64); 16.6.1749 Mid *Devonshire Hulk*; 12.8.1749 Mid *Assurance* (44); 26.8.1751 Able *Centurion* (50); 23.11.1752 Able *Devonshire* (66); 21.1.1753 Able *Penzance* (44); 10.4.1753 Mid *Penzance* (44); 16.1.1754 Passed; **Lieutenant**; 11.3.1757(21.11.1759)-1.4.1757[†] 3L *Kent* (64).

HICKES, JOHN

Dates: c.1726 Born; c.1764 Died; 3.3.1764 Will Probate.
Family:
Service: 12.2.1739/40 Steward *Bonetta* (8) Sloop; 4.4.1741 Able *Mary Galley* (40); 9.6.1741 Ord. *Argyll* (50); 17.9.1741-19.10.1741 Able *Winchester* (50); 20.10.1741 Able *Argyll* (50); 7.2.1742/43 Mid *Woolwich* (50); 4.3.1742/43 Mid *Dolphin* (20); 6.11.1744 Mid *Maidstone* (50); 21.11.1745 Able *Maidstone* (50); 6.6.1746 Passed; **Lieutenant**; 10.6.1746-9.6.1747 L. *Port Mahon* (20); 12.6.1747-19.12.1747 3L *Deptford* (60); 7.5.1748-22.1.1748/49[P] 3L *Hastings* (44); 30.1.1748/49 3L *Assurance* (44); 11.9.1751-16.11.1752[P] 3L *Kent* (64); 9.4.1754 3L *Augusta* (60); 10.7.1755 2L *Bristol* (50); 31.3.1756 1L *Bristol* (50); 3.4.1757(EI 15.9.1757) 2L *Anson* (60); 27.1.1758 1L *Maidstone* (28); 5.6.1758-12.6.1758 Raid on Saint-Malo; **Commander**; 10.8.1759-19.5.1761 *Goree* (10) Sloop.

HICKES, THOMAS

Dates: 22.4.1731 Born; 9.5.1801 Died; 8.6.1801 Will Probate.
Family:
Service: 27.1.1744-13.6.1746[P] Capt Serv *Marlborough* (90); 11.2.1743/44-12.2.1743/44 Battle of Toulon; 12.11.1752-5.6.1754 Able *Monmouth* (70); 6.6.1754 Mid *Bristol* (50); 2.4.1755 Mid *Hazard* (8) Sloop; 17.10.1755 Mid *Sheerness* (24); 1.12.1756 Passed; **Lieutenant**; 3.5.1758(JAM 4.8.1761)-22.3.1762 L. *Lively* (20); 18.10.1760 Action off Cuba; 9.4.1762-28.3.1763[P] 1L *Kent* (74); 20.6.1775-29.6.1776 1L *Actaeon* (28); 9.10.1776 1L *Aeolus* (32); 30.10.1776-21.2.1778 1L *Terrible* (74); 20.4.1778 L. *Princess Augusta* (6) Yacht; **Commander**; 13.5.1778-16.9.1778[C] *Helena* (14) Brig; **Captain**; 10.11.1781-24.7.1784[P] *Gibraltar* (80); 20.6.1783 2nd Battle of Cuddalore; 16.8.1786-10.2.1787 *Jupiter* (50); 24.3.1791-3.9.1791 *Cambridge* (80); 3.9.1791 *Saint George* (98); 1.12.1792-4.12.1793 *Powerful* (74); 1.1.1801 **Rear Admiral of the Blue**.

HIGGS, RICHARD

Dates: c.1713 Born; 22.8.1782 Died.

Family:

Service: 3.3.1725/26-21.1.1726/27[P] Capt Serv *Cumberland* (80); 9.9.1731 Mst Serv *Shoreham* (20); 8.9.1733-14.9.1735 Able *Hawk* (8) Sloop; 15.9.1735 Mid *Hawk* (8) Sloop; 10.1.1735/36 QGnr *Lowestoffe* (20); 8.12.1736 Mid *Lowestoffe* (20); 29.6.1739 Able *Lowestoffe* (20); 18.2.1739/40 Mate *Lowestoffe* (20); 2.5.1741 Mate *Portland* (50); 26.6.1741 Master *Portland* (50); 28.7.1742-17.3.1742/43[P] ActL *Portland* (50); 3.3.1742/43 Passed; **Lieutenant**; 10.10.1743 3L *Medway* (60); 31.3.1744 3L *Strafford* (58); 1.7.1745[(JAM 30.12.1745)] 3L *Adventure* (44); 11.1.1745/46-7.2.1746/47[D] 3L *Captain* (70); 7.2.1746 Dismissed; 30.10.1747-12.8.1748[P] 1L *Falkland* (50); 8.2.1755 2L *Buckingham* (68); 20.5.1756 Battle of Minorca; 25.11.1756 2L *Neptune* (90); 6.4.1757 1L *Neptune* (90); **Commander**; 20.7.1757-19.10.1757 *Portsmouth* (6) Storeship.

HILDESLEY, JOHN

Dates: 13.2.1771 Died.

Family:

Service: 22.5.1702 Vol-p-O *Burlington* (54); 21.9.1704 Mid *Dorsetshire* (80); 5.9.1705 Mid *Barfleur* (90); 30.8.1706 Mid *Milford* (36); 9.10.1706 Passed; **Lieutenant**; 17.12.1707-21.1.1707/8 3L *Bedford* (70); 29.11.1709-7.7.1710 3L *Norfolk* (80); 3.8.1710[(21.8.1710)]-10.1710 5L *Royal Sovereign* (100); **Commander**; 20.12.1711-7.2.1714/15 LCmdr *Swift* (10) Sloop; **Captain**; 14.9.1716-7.10.1721[P] *Flamborough* (24); 10.5.1720-11.5.1720 Bombardment of Donan Castle; 22.2.1733/34-12.2.1735/36[P] *Montagu* (60); 14.7.1738-4.12.1738[P] *Lion* (60); 12.10.1739-6.9.1740 *Grafton* (70); 29.12.1742-27.1.1742/43 *Dorsetshire* (80); 24.6.1743-19.12.1743 *Cornwall* (80); 24.7.1747 **Superannuated Rear Admiral**.

HILGROVE, JAMES

Dates: c.1734 Born; c.1814 Died; 10.3.1814 Will Probate.

Family:

Service: 2.12.1748 Capt Serv *Superb* (60); 22.6.1750 Able *Superb* (60); 22.1.1750/51 Able *Princess* (70); 16.5.1751 Capt Serv *Gloucester* (50); 11.4.1753 Able *Gloucester* (50); 28.8.1754 Mid *Gloucester* (50); 28.2.1755 Able *Arundel* (24); 14.4.1755 Mid *Terrible* (74); 29.5.1755 Mid *Ramillies* (90); 12.10.1755 Mid *Newark* (80); 10.1.1757 Passed; **Lieutenant**; 5.4.1758 3L *Deptford* (50); 5.6.1758-12.6.1758 Raid on Saint-Malo; 3.7.1759 Bombardment of Le Havre; 9.7.1759-21.8.1761 2L *Deptford* (50); 27.10.1761-27.12.1762 5L *Blenheim* (90); 7.4.1777-17.11.1780[P] 1L *Boyne* (68); 14.12.1778-15.12.1778 Battle of St. Lucia; 6.7.1779 Battle of Grenada; 2.5.1799 **Superannuated Commander**.

HILL, BENJAMIN

Dates: c.1736 Born; 9.9.1785 Died.

Family:

Service: 1750-1756 HEIC Service; 31.7.1756-9.1.1760 Mid *Sutherland* (50); 8.1757-10.1757 Louisbourg Expedition; 6.6.1758-27.7.1758 The Siege of Louisbourg; 9.1.1760 Passed; **Lieutenant**; 31.3.1760-7.8.1761 3L *Deptford* (50); 8.4.1762 2L *Pearl* (32); 17.2.1763 1L *Tweed* (32); 2.4.1764 2L *Achilles* (60); 1.5.1765-9.12.1765 3L *Achilles* (60); 21.9.1770 4L *Albion* (74); 15.1.1771-20.9.1773 3L *Albion* (74); **Commander**; 18.3.1777-11.1777[F] *Bute* Hired Unknown; **Captain**; 28.1.1778 *Prince of Wales* (74); 14.12.1778-15.12.1778 Battle of St. Lucia; 6.7.1779

Battle of Grenada; 7.2.1780-11.10.1780 *Barfleur* (98); 2.4.1782-13.3.1783[P] *Britannia* (100); 20.10.1782 Battle of Cape Spartel.

HILL, CHRISTOPHER

Dates: c.1716 Born; 11.7.1778 Died.
Family:
Service: 17.10.1731 Vol-p-O *Norfolk* (80); 3.2.1731/32 Able *Gosport* (42); 22.10.1732 Vol-p-O *Norfolk* (80); 17.12.1732 Able *Norfolk* (80); 2.7.1733 Able *Exeter* (60); 26.7.1733 MidO *Swallow* (60); 18.3.1733/34 Mid *Saltash* (8) Sloop; 16.8.1734 Mid *Norfolk* (80); 5.8.1736 Able *Canterbury* (60); 20.8.1738 Mid *Canterbury* (60); 6.2.1739/40 Able *Somerset* (80); 6.3.1739/40 Passed; **Lieutenant**; 17.3.1739/40-26.9.1740 3L *Panther* (54); 27.9.1740-28.10.1740 2L *Panther* (54); 29.10.1740 L. *Fox* (20); 4.2.1742/43-10.1.1744/45 1L *Torrington* (44); **Commander**; 29.1.1745/46-18.5.1747 *Princess Royal* (24) Storeship; 18.7.1747 *Baltimore* (14) Sloop; **Captain**; 5.12.1747-10.2.1748/49[P] *Bridgewater* (24); 23.4.1753 *Saltash* (14) Sloop; 28.10.1755-23.4.1757 *Dover* (44); 11.9.1759-15.12.1760 *Saint Florentine* (60); 26.10.1769 *Augusta* (64); 9.1.1770-1771 CinC — River Medway and The Nore; 9.1.1770 Commodore *Augusta* (64); 23.10.1770-7.12.1770 *Barfleur* (90); 23.1.1778 **Rear Admiral of the Blue**; 29.1.1778 **Rear Admiral of the White**.

HILL, EDWARD

Dates: 1814 Died.
Family:
Service: **Lieutenant**; 5.3.1756[(28.3.1757)]-28.4.1760[P] 3L *Princess Louisa* (60); 20.5.1756 Battle of Minorca; 5.4.1757 Action of April 5 1757; 18.8.1759-19.8.1759 Battle of Lagos Bay; 7.5.1760-14.3.1763[P] L. *Wager* (24); 21.9.1796 **Superannuated Commander**.

HILL, GEORGE

Dates: c.1708 Born; 1766 Died.
Family:
Service: 5.5.1727-22.8.1728[P] Vol-p-O *Bredah* (70); 9.8.1730-23.1.1730/31 Mid *Hector* (40); 24.1.1730/31 MidO *Hector* (40); 8.4.1732-24.10.1732 Able *Hector* (40); 25.10.1732 Mid *Hector* (40); 25.4.1733 Able *Hector* (40); 17.6.1735 Passed; **Lieutenant**; 25.6.1739-1.4.1740 3L *Argyll* (50); 2.4.1740-2.10.1740 3L *Grafton* (70); 3.10.1740 2L *Rippon* (60); 7.1.1740/41 Action of January 7 1741; 24.2.1740/41-17.5.1741 L. *Terrible* (6) Bomb Vessel; 4.3.1740/41-5.1741 Operations against Cartagena; 3.4.1742 3L *Sandwich* (90); 4.6.1742-30.7.1742 2L *Sandwich* (90); 31.7.1742 3L *Sandwich* (90); 13.9.1742 2L *Sandwich* (90); 10.12.1744 1L *Exeter* (58); 30.4.1746 1L *Sapphire* (44); 20.9.1746-25.9.1746 Lorient Operations; 1.12.1748-22.11.1752[P] 1L *Intrepid* (64).

HILL, JAMES

Dates: 1784 Died.
Family:
Service: **Lieutenant**; 1.3.1759-7.5.1759[P] 3L *Arc-en-Ciel* (50); 10.8.1759-29.9.1763[P] 2L *Danae* (38); 21.11.1770-21.2.1771 2L *Intrepid* (64).

HILL, JOHN
Dates: c.1722 Born; 8.3.1773 Died.
Family:
Service: 18.4.1727 Vol-p-O *Leopard* (50); 16.4.1729 MidO *Leopard* (50); 26.10.1729 Mid *Grafton* (70); 2.7.1730 MidO *Advice* (54); 10.4.1731 Mid *Diamond* (40); 9.2.1732 Mid *Romney* (50); 25.5.1732 Able *Berwick* (70); 2.2.1733 Mid *Gibraltar* (20); 18.7.1733 Able *Gibraltar* (20); 25.8.1734-11.1.1735 Able *Gibraltar* (20); 11.1.1734/35 Passed; **Lieutenant**; 18.4.1735-13.6.1735 3L *Warwick* (60); 14.6.1735$^{(22.7.1736)}$-19.7.1736^{P} 2L *Warwick* (60); 28.2.1737/38-13.4.1742^{P} 2L *Hector* (40); 4.1740-5.7.1740 Attack on St. Augustine; 13.7.1742 6L *Victory* (100); 8.2.1743/44 4L *Victory* (100); 16.6.1744 2L *Shrewsbury* (80); **Commander**; 3.8.1744 *Swift* (8) Sloop; **Captain**; 26.8.1745 *Triton* (20); 10.4.1746-27.6.1748^{P} *Portland Prize* (50); 1770 **Superannuated Rear Admiral.**

HILL, LIONEL
Dates: c.1733 Born; 1800 Died; 4.10.1800 Will Probate.
Family:
Service: 28.10.1748 Mst Serv *Hector* (44); 14.5.1751 Able *Monmouth* (70); 14.10.1752 Able *Deptford* (50); 17.6.1754 Mid *Deptford* (50); 20.5.1756 Battle of Minorca; 11.2.1757-2.5.1757 Mate *Deptford* (50); 2.5.1757 Passed; **Lieutenant**; 31.1.1759-23.5.1763^{P} 3L *Somerset* (68); 10.5.1766-3.3.1767^{P} 2L *Burford* (68); 8.10.1770 2L *Hero* (74); 18.1.1771-6.7.1771^{D} 1L *Somerset* (68); 6.7.1771 Dismissed; 19.9.1780 1L *Arundel* (74) Hospital Ship; 22.9.1781-22.3.1783^{P} 2L *Arundel* (74) Hospital Ship; 7.1793-1800 LCmdr *Chatham* (50).

HILL, THOMAS
Dates: 1765 Died.
Family:
Service: 13.4.1723 Able *Elizabeth* (70); 2.2.1723/24 Ord. *Ludlow Castle* (40); 12.4.1724-7.10.1724 Able *Ludlow Castle* (40); 8.10.1724 Able *Lyme* (20); 11.6.1727 MidO *Rye* (20); 28.1.1728/29 Mid *Rye* (20); 12.1.1729/30 Passed; **Lieutenant**; 2.3.1733/34 4L *Devonshire* (80); 30.3.1734 3L *Devonshire* (80); 20.8.1734-3.5.1737^{P} 2L *Leopard* (50); 23.6.1738 L. *Deptford* (24) Storeship; 9.9.1738 1L *Eltham* (40); 18.2.1742/43 Attack on La Guaira; 9.4.1743-10.11.1743 1L *Sutherland* (50); 7.7.1744 1L *Princess Louisa* (60); **Commander**; 23.11.1744-24.11.1745^{C} *Hazard* (10) Sloop.

HILL, THOMAS
Dates: 20.12.1789 Died.
Family:
Service: **Lieutenant**; 8.11.1760$^{(BLI\ 2.8.1762)}$-17.10.1761^{W} 2L *Griffin* (28); 17.9.1762-27.1.1763^{P} 3L *Essex* (64); 5.6.1764-11.9.1768 LCmdr *Saint John* (6) Schooner; 10.1.1777 4L *Princess Amelia* (80); 8.12.1777-22.7.1778 2L *Princess Amelia* (80).

HILLS, WILLIAM
Dates: 23.12.1777 Died Off Guernsey, The Channel Islands.
Family: Wife Lydia.
Service: **Lieutenant**; 21.9.1759 4L *Warspite* (74); 20.11.1759 Battle of Quiberon Bay; 11.2.1760-5.5.1763^{P} 3L *Warspite* (74); 6.12.1763 2L *Achilles* (60); 21.2.1764 3L *Achilles* (60); 27.3.1764 2L *Achilles* (60); 2.4.1764 1L *Achilles* (60); 1.5.1765 2L *Achilles* (60); 1.7.1766-6.12.1766 3L *Achilles*

(60); 15.6.1769-31.3.1772[P] LCmdr *Mecklenburgh* (6) Cutter; 27.6.1775-1777 LCmdr *Wells* (6) Cutter; 9.1777-23.12.1777 LCmdr *Sprightly* (10) Cutter.

HINDE, RICHARD
Dates: c.1682 Born; c.1762 Died; 19.1762 Will Probate.
Family:
Service: 29.4.1720-23.2.1721/22 Able *Exeter* (60); 24.2.1721/22 QGnr *Exeter* (60); 14.3.1725/26-7.4.1726 Able *Ramillies* (96); 8.4.1726 Mate *Poole* (32); 1.9.1726 Mid *Poole* (32); 11.2.1728/29-5.6.1732[P] Mate *Lion* (60); 15.11.1740-3.11.1742 Master *Montagu* (60); 4.11.1742 Master *Prince Frederick* (70); 23.3.1742/43 Master *Dreadnought* (60) Receiving Ship; 12.1.1743/44 Passed; **Lieutenant**; 14.1.1743/44 4L *Suffolk* (70); 11.4.1744 4L *Hampton Court* (64); 21.4.1744-26.2.1744/45 3L *Medway* (60).

HINDMAN, MICHAEL
Dates: c.1739 Born; 1.5.1791 Died.
Family:
Service: 1753-1755 Merchant Service; 1.8.1755 Able *Firedrake* (10) Bomb Vessel; 14.8.1756 Mid *Unicorn* (24); 1.6.1757 Mid *Unicorn* (28); 4.4.1759 Passed; **Lieutenant**; 27.10.1761-3.12.1761 L. *Arundel* (24); 27.3.1764 1L *Tamar* (16) Sloop; 1.6.1766-9.9.1767 2L *Tamar* (16) Sloop; 30.12.1775-24.8.1781[P] 1L *Rainbow* (44); 14.1.1776-1778 LCmdr *Hope* (6) Schooner; 1777-1.12.1777 LCmdr *Hope* (14) Sloop; 7.7.1777 Action of 7 July 1777.

HINXMAN, JOHN
Dates: c.1711 Born; c.1764 Died; 16.4.1764 Will Probate.
Family:
Service: **Lieutenant**; 6.2.1741/42[(24.6.1745)]-24.7.1745[P] 2L *Montagu* (60); 2.11.1745-9.8.1748[P] 1L *Edinburgh* (64); 14.10.1747 2nd Battle of Cape Finisterre; 11.1.1757 1L *Marlborough* (80); **Commander**; 30.1.1759[(JAM 23.3.1761)]-22.2.1759 *Port Mahon* (24); 20.3.1759[(JAM 20.5.1763)] *Port Royal* (12) Storeship.

HOBBS, JAMES
Dates: c.1711 Born; 14.5.1770 Died.
Family:
Service: 16.11.1728 Able *Captain* (70); 5.10.1729 Able *Adventure* (40); 7.2.1732/33 Able *Royal Oak* (70); 31.12.1734 Mid *Royal Oak* (70); 18.2.1734/35 Mid *Blenheim* (96); 15.12.1736 Able *Rippon* (60); 20.12.1736 Mid *Rippon* (60); 2.3.1737/38 Mid *Anglesea* (40); 4.9.1740 Passed; **Lieutenant**; 16.1.1740/41 4L *Lennox* (70); 2.2.1740/41 3L *Lennox* (70); 16.6.1743-27.3.1746 3L *Berwick* (70); 11.2.1743/44-12.2.1743/44 Battle of Toulon; 30.3.1747 1L *Mars* (64); 23.12.1747-1.12.1748 2L *Devonshire* (66); 1.12.1748-14.11.1752[P] 2L *Monarch* (74); 28.1.1755 1L *Saint George* (90); 14.10.1755-5.5.1756 *Lightning* (8) Fireship; 14.10.1755 **Commander**; **Captain**; 19.5.1756 *Namur* (90); 5.6.1756 *Ramillies* (90); 5.9.1757-6.10.1757 Raid on Rochefort; 15.2.1758-3.3.1759[P] *Eagle* (60).

HODDER, EDWARD
Dates: c.1729 Born; c.1765 Died; 3.4.1765 Will Probate.
Family:
Service: 8.3.1745/46 Land. *Augusta* (60); 8.11.1746 Ord. *Augusta* (60); 30.1.1747/48 Able *Augusta* (60); 13.3.1748/49 Mid *Augusta* (60); 17.4.1749 MidO *Lyme* (24); 4.3.1749/50 Mid

Lyme (24); 1.4.1752 Able *Lyme* (24); 7.3.1753 Passed; **Lieutenant**; 14.10.1756 L. *Lightning* (6) Hospital Ship; 29.1.1757 5L *Terrible* (74); 8.1757-10.1757 Louisbourg Expedition; 6.6.1758-27.7.1758 The Siege of Louisbourg; 15.1.1759-23.3.1762 1L *Hussar* (28).

HODGES, JOHN

Dates: 1772 Died.
Family:
Service: **Lieutenant**; 8.9.1744[MED 24.2.1746/47]-18.7.1745 4L *Norfolk* (80); 18.6.1747 2L *Expedition* (44); 2.9.1747-3.1.1748/49[P] 1L *Expedition* (44); 24.9.1755 L. *Dispatch* (14) Sloop; **Commander**; 21.10.1756-1.1.1762 *Dispatch* (14) Sloop.

HODGSON, CONNOLLY

Dates: c.1733 Born.
Family:
Service: 1749-1753 HEIC Service; 28.12.1753 Mid *Assistance* (50); 2.5.1754 Mate *Assistance* (50); 8.6.1754 Mid *Vanguard* (68); 10.12.1754 Mid *Gosport* (44); 15.10.1755 Mid *Falcon* (10) Bomb Vessel; 16.6.1756 Mate *Hind* (24); 1.12.1756 Passed; **Lieutenant**; 23.2.1757 3L *Rainbow* (44); 8.6.1757 2L *Rainbow* (44); 10.8.1759[NA 7.5.1760]-18.10.1760[W] 1L *Lyme* (28); 18.8.1759-19.8.1759 Battle of Lagos Bay; 30.1.1761-12.2.1763[P] L. *Albany* (14) Sloop; 19.5.1763-16.5.1765[P] 1L *Venus* (36); 4.4.1768-20.1.1771 1L *Mermaid* (28); 14.5.1771-19.9.1771 1L *Active* (28); 25.5.1776-1.1777 LCmdr *Swallow* Hired Tender.

HOEY, WILLIAM PARSONS

Dates: c.1728 Born; c.1807 Died Wicklow.
Family: Wife Wilhelmina Bonham married 9.7.1761; Son George Bonham (1762-?); Daughter Susannah (1763-?); Son John Parsons (1765-?).
Service: 25.3.1747 Able *Deal Castle* (20); 25.6.1747 Mid *Deal Castle* (20); 18.10.1748 Mid *Lynn* (42); 13.6.1749 Able *Lynn* (44); 9.12.1749 Mid *Princess* (70); 12.6.1750 Able *Boyne* (80) Prison Ship; 14.6.1751 Mid *Boyne* (80) Prison Ship; 5.9.1751 Mid *Gosport* (44); 6.6.1752 Able *Advice* (50); 26.6.1753 Mate *Advice* (50); 16.1.1754 Passed; **Lieutenant**; 14.4.1756 L. *Macclesfield* (16) Hired Armed Ship; 17.4.1758 2L *Shrewsbury* (74); 5.6.1758-12.6.1758 Raid on Saint-Malo; 19.2.1760-3.7.1760 3L *Barfleur* (80); 21.9.1796 **Superannuated Commander**.

HOLBURNE, SIR ALEXANDER (3RD BARONET OF MENSTRIE)

Dates: c.1737 Born; 1758 3rd Baronet of Menstrie; 22.1.1772 Died;
Family: Father Sir James Holburn, 2nd Bt.; Mother Jean Spital; Brother James, RN (d.1756).
Service: 6.12.1753 Capt Serv *Triton* (20); 22.1.1754 Ord. *Triton* (20); 15.8.1755 Mid *Isis* (50); 10.11.1756 Mate *Isis* (50); 25.12.1756 Able *Ramillies* (90); 16.1.1757 ActL *Culloden*; **Lieutenant**; 20.7.1757[2.2.1759] 6L *Saint George* (90); 20.6.1758[2.2.1759] 2L *Monmouth* (70); 31.1.1759 Passed; 2.2.1759-11.4.1760 5L *Torbay* (74); 20.11.1759 Battle of Quiberon Bay; **Commander**; 6.4.1761[MED 12.11.1761] *Polacca* (12) Sloop; 15.3.1762 *Lynx* (10) Sloop; **Captain**; 1.2.1763[BLI 9.5.1763]-30.5.1763[P] *Repulse* (32).

HOLBURNE, FRANCIS

Dates: 1704 Born; 15.7.1771 Died.
Family: Father Sir James Holburne, 1st Bt. of Menstrie (d.1737); Mother Jean Spittal; Wife Mrs Frances Lascelles née Ball married c.1750; Stepson Edward Lascelles, MP (1740-1820); Son

Sir Alexander (3rd Baronet of Menstrie), RN (1737-1772); Daughter Jane [Sheldon] (d.1812); Daughter Unknown; Brother James, 2nd Bt. of Menstrie (d.1758).
Service: 17.7.1721 Vol-p-O *Saint Albans* (50); 2.4.1723 Vol-p-O *Essex* (70); 29.5.1723 Able *Guernsey* (50); 9.4.1724 Mid *Guernsey* (50); 3.9.1724 MidO *Southampton* (40); 4.11.1724 MidO *Southsea Castle* (40); 5.10.1725 Able *Hector* (40); 28.1.1725/26 Passed; **Lieutenant**; 12.12.1727(5.9.1728) 2L *Dunkirk* (50); 23.12.1727(5.9.1728)-4.9.1728[P] 2L *Leopard* (50); 9.2.1728/29-4.1.1729/30[P] 3L *Guernsey* (50); 6.5.1730-8.6.1732[P] 2L *Gosport* (42); 29.6.1732-21.8.1732 4L *Princess Amelia* (80); 22.8.1732-17.3.1733/34 L. *Terrible* (6) Bomb Vessel; 18.3.1733/34 1L *Kinsale* (40); 6.6.1737(15.9.1738)-5.8.1737 3L *Dunkirk* (60); **Commander**; 10.8.1739-3.1.1739/40 *Swift* (6) Sloop; 4.1.1739/40-14.2.1739/40 *Trial* (8) Sloop; **Captain**; 15.2.1739/40-9.5.1742 *Dolphin* (20); 25.6.1743 *Argyll* (50); 6.12.1745 *Pembroke* (60); 13.3.1745/46(NA 11.10.1746)-12.8.1746[P] *Argyll* (50); 4.11.1746-11.9.1747 *Rippon* (54); 25.12.1747 *Kent* (64); 13.9.1748 *Bristol* (50); 23.9.1748-6.10.1752[P] Commodore *Tavistock* (50); 28.10.1748 CinC — Barbados & the Leeward Islands; 4.2.1755-5.2.1755 *Ramillies* (90); **Rear Admiral of the Blue**; 8.5.1755-6.1756 *Terrible* (74); 9.1755-1756 *Edinburgh* (64); 4.6.1756 **Rear Admiral of the Red**; 11.1756-1.1757 *Marlborough* (80); 1757-1760 *Newark* (80); 24.2.1757 **Vice Admiral of the Blue**; 24.2.1757 CinC — North America; 8.1757-10.1757 Louisbourg Expedition; 12.1757-1766 CinC — Portsmouth; 31.1.1758 **Vice Admiral of the White**; 5.6.1758-12.6.1758 Raid on Saint-Malo; 14.2.1759 **Vice Admiral of the Red**; 18.8.1759-19.8.1759 Battle of Lagos Bay; 20.4.1761-11.4.1768 M.P. for Stirling Burghs; 1763-9.1763 *Royal Sovereign* (104); 5.8.1767 **Admiral of the Blue**; 18.3.1768-15.7.1771 M.P. for Plymouth; 28.2.1770-1.2.1771 Lord Commissioner of the Admiralty; 10.1770-14.7.1771 Rear Admiral of Great Britain; 18.10.1770 **Admiral of the White**; 1.1771-15.7.1771 Governor of Greenwich Hospital.

HOLBURNE, JAMES

Dates: 7.10.1756 Died.
Family: Brother Sir Alexander (3rd Baronet of Menstrie), RN (1737-1772).
Service: 11.1.1737 App *Providence* Mer; 5.6.1739 Ord. *Dolphin* (20); 13.1.1741 Able *Dolphin* (20); 9.5.1743-6.7.1745 Mid *Argyll* (50); 6.7.1745 Passed; **Lieutenant**; 7.7.1745(BLI 17.2.1748/49) 3L *Woolwich* (50); 26.1.1745/46(NA 17.7.1749) 3L *Dreadnought* (60); 28.5.1747(BLI 17.7.1749) 2L *Sutherland* (50); 24.5.1748(JAM 24.7.1749)-25.12.1748 3L *Canterbury* (60); 12.10.1748 Battle of Havana; 10.7.1755 1L *Hampton Court* (64); 18.5.1756 4L *Duke* (90); 5.7.1756 1L *Marlborough* (80); **Commander**; 24.8.1756 *Katherine* (8) Yacht; 24.9.1756-7.10.1756 *Dispatch* (14) Sloop.

HOLBURNE, WILLIAM

Dates: c.1711 Born; 1.4.1760 Died.
Family:
Service: 17.3.1726 Capt Serv *Bredah* (70); 12.9.1726-4.2.1729 Vol. *Nottingham* (60); 5.2.1729 Mid *Guernsey* (50); 11.12.1729 Mid *Lark* (40); 12.12.1730 Able *Lark* (40); 16.3.1731 Mid *Lark* (40); 1.5.1731-5.9.1731[P] Mid *Shark* (10) Sloop; 4.7.1732 Mid *Lyme* (20); 30.11.1732 Able *Garland* (20); 13.2.1733 Mid *Garland* (20); 2.9.1733-23.3.1734 Mate *Garland* (20); 23.3.1733/34 Passed; **Lieutenant**; 15.11.1739 4L *Prince of Orange* (70); 3.10.1740 3L *Prince of Orange* (70); 26.2.1741/42-11.8.1742[P] 2L *Prince of Orange* (70); 11.10.1742 2L *Cornwall* (80); 25.6.1743-30.8.1743 2L *Prince of Orange* (70); **Commander**; 21.4.1747-27.5.1747 *Brave* (3) Storeship; **Captain**; 15.4.1748-10.9.1748 *Prince Frederick* (70); 11.3.1755 *Greenwich* (50); 13.5.1755 *Terrible* (74); 28.6.1756 *Marlborough* (80); 10.2.1757-14.4.1760 *Newark* (80); 8.1757-10.1757 Louisbourg Expedition; 5.6.1758-12.6.1758 Raid on Saint-Malo; 18.8.1759-19.8.1759 Battle of Lagos Bay.

HOLCOMBE, ESSEX

Dates: c.1708 Born; 29.1.1770 Died; 12.2.1770 Will Probate.
Family:
Service: 4.2.1720/21 Vol-p-O *Bedford* (70); 29.11.1722 MidO *Ipswich* (70); 20.3.1722/23 Mid *Ipswich* (70); 6.6.1723 MidO *Ipswich* (70); 1.10.1723 MidO *Falkland* (50); 6.9.1724 Mid *Falkland* (50); 4.7.1726 Mid *Canterbury* (60); 20.6.1728 Passed; **Lieutenant**; 24.5.1730[(2.1.1730/31)]-5.3.1732/33 3L *Romney* (50); 31.1.1733/34 4L *Berwick* (70); 23.2.1733/34 3L *Warwick* (60); 29.4.1734 2L *Warwick* (60); 21.4.1735-14.6.1736 1L *Warwick* (60); **Commander**; 25.4.1740 *Blaze* (8) Fireship; **Captain**; 12.10.1740 *Winchelsea* (20); 3.6.1743[(MED 11.11.1748)] *Dartmouth* (50); 8.11.1744[(MED 24.11.1748)]-14.11.1748[P] *Nassau* (70); 9.7.1756 **Superannuated Rear Admiral**.

HOLL, JAMES

Dates: c.1735 Born; 1789 Died.
Family:
Service: 1752-1757 HEIC Service; 6.6.1757 Mid *Royal William* (84); 5.9.1757-6.10.1757 Raid on Rochefort; 6.6.1758-27.7.1758 The Siege of Louisbourg; 29.7.1758-8.9.1758 Able *Namur* (90); 9.9.1758 Mid *Namur* (90); 18.8.1759-19.8.1759 Battle of Lagos Bay; 20.11.1759 Battle of Quiberon Bay; 6.3.1759/60-19.5.1760[W] ActL *Lowestoffe* (28); 20.5.1760-25.6.1760 Supnum *Hunter* (10) Sloop; 2.7.1760 Passed; **Lieutenant**; 2.7.1760-3.7.1760 2L *Quebec* (32); 20.3.1761-14.2.1763[P] 2L *Southampton* (32); 29.3.1761-11.6.1761 Expedition against Belle-Isle; 29.11.1763-30.4.1764[P] L. *Dispatch* (14) Sloop; 1765-1767 Agent for Transports; 15.2.1771-24.5.1771[P] 3L *Bellona* (74); 28.8.1778-20.1.1779 5L *Britannia* (100).

HOLLINGWORTH, THOMAS

Dates: c.1732 Born; 1799 Died; 30.3.1799 Will Probate.
Family:
Service: 14.7.1747 Carp Serv *Dragon* (60); 5.4.1748 Ord. *Dragon* (60); 8.10.1749-24.4.1753[W] Mid *Assurance* (44); 13.2.1756-31.8.1756 Mate *Royal George* (100); 3.11.1756 Passed; **Lieutenant**; 6.11.1756-2.5.1758 3L *Antelope* (50); 14.11.1759 6L *Princess Royal* (90); 1.4.1760-18.12.1760[P] 6L *Royal Anne* (100); 21.4.1761 4L *Burford* (68); 14.10.1761-11.5.1763 3L *Burford* (68); 10.12.1776-10.1783 LCmdr *Prosperity* Hired Tender; 21.9.1796 **Superannuated Commander**.

HOLLWALL, JOHN

Dates: c.1723 Born; 13.7.1775 Died; 15.7.1775 Buried Catherington, Hampshire.
Family: Wife Sarah Linzee (1730-1796) married 4.9.1749.
Service: 30.1.1737/38 Capt Serv *Falmouth* (50); 4.3.1740/41-5.1741 Operations against Cartagena; 29.11.1741 Mid *Sutherland* (50); 10.4.1742 Mid *Antelope* (50); 22.3.1743/44 Passed; **Lieutenant**; 20.4.1744 4L *Suffolk* (70); 12.6.1744-26.1.1745/46 3L *Suffolk* (70); **Commander**; 4.4.1747[(BLI 13.7.1747)] *Dreadnought Prize* (12) Sloop; 11.12.1747-26.3.1753[P] *Hornet* (10) Sloop; **Captain**; 30.6.1753-27.7.1753[P] *Mermaid* (24); 26.3.1755 *Gibraltar* (20); 5.11.1756-1.11.1757 *Roebuck* (44); 25.1.1758 *Deptford* (50); 5.6.1758-12.6.1758 Raid on Saint-Malo; 3.7.1759 Bombardment of Le Havre; 21.4.1761 *Marlborough* (68); 7.1.1762-10.2.1762 Operations against Martinique; 27.4.1762-14.3.1764[P] *Modeste* (64); 12.12.1766 *Dorsetshire* (68); 16.9.1767 *Phoenix* (44); 7.10.1768 *San Antonio* (64); 16.5.1769-24.5.1770 *Glory* (32); 26.9.1770-28.5.1771[P] *Prince of Wales* (74); 7.12.1773-13.7.1775[†] *Resolution* (74).

HOLMES, CHARLES

Dates: 1711 Born; 19.9.1711 Baptised Yarmouth IOW; 21.11.1761 Died.
Family: Father Henry Holmes; Mother Mary; Brother Thomas, MP 1st Baron (1699-1764).
Service: 18.6.1734 Passed; **Lieutenant**; 18.6.1734-31.1.1735/36[P] 3L *Canterbury* (60); 16.5.1738-27.11.1738 2L *Sunderland* (60); 29.5.1739-16.1.1739/40 2L *Pembroke* (60); 26.3.1740 3L *Buckingham* (70); 27.5.1740 2L *Tilbury* (60); 30.9.1740[(3.5.1743)] 4L *Burford* (70); 30.12.1740[(3.5.1743)] 3L *Burford* (70); 14.1.1740/41[(3.5.1743)] 2L *Princess Caroline* (80); 19.2.1740/41[(3.5.1743)] 1L *Princess Caroline* (80); **Commander**; 24.2.1740/41 *Strombolo* (8) Fireship; 4.3.1740/41-5.1741 Operations against Cartagena; 9.6.1741 *Success* (8) Fireship; **Captain**; 20.2.1741/42 *Sapphire* (44); 20.12.1743 *Cornwall* (80); 30.5.1744-13.12.1748[P] *Enterprise* (50); 11.5.1747-29.12.1748[P] *Lennox* (70); 9.4.1748 Battle of Santiago de Cuba; 12.10.1748 Battle of Havana; 10.1.1753 *Anson* (60); 4.2.1755-7.2.1757 Commodore *Grafton* (68); 7.2.1757 Second in Command — North America; 3.2.1758 CinC — Weser, Elbe and Ems; 15.5.1758-19.7.1758 *Warspite* (74); 1.6.1758-21.11.1761 M.P. for Newport IOW; 6.7.1758 **Rear Admiral of the Blue**; 23.1.1759-18.2.1760 *Dublin* (74); 19.5.1759 **Rear Admiral of the White**; 14.1.1760-21.11.1761 *Cambridge* (80); 24.1.1760-20.11.1761 CinC — Jamaica.

HOLMES, LANCELOT

Dates: c.1729 Born; 1785 Died.
Family:
Service: 22.7.1747 Mid *Prince George* (90); 10.1.1749/50-22.11.1752[P] Mid *Intrepid* (64); 18.2.1753 Mate *Culloden* (74); 14.3.1755 Passed; **Lieutenant**; 26.6.1756[(MED 16.2.1757)]-1.4.1758 4L *Hampton Court* (64); 28.2.1758 Battle of Cartagena; 12.3.1758 5L *Prince* (90); 9.10.1758 4L *Saint George* (90); 18.10.1758 3L *Saint George* (90); 23.10.1758 2L *Saint George* (90); 16.1.1759-19.1.1759 Attack on Martinique; 20.1.1759-1.5.1759 Capture of Guadeloupe; **Commander**; 2.6.1760 *Bonetta* (10) Sloop; **Captain**; 2.7.1762[(EI 22.4.1763)]-26.2.1763[P] *Dover* (44).

HOLTON, FREDERICK

Dates: c.1722 Born; 1767 Died.
Family:
Service: 16.7.1742 Land. *Woolwich* (50); 13.12.1743-20.4.1747[P] Mid *Woolwich* (50); 10.8.1746 Action of 1746-10-18; 23.9.1752 Mid *Princess* (70); 10.1.1754 Mid *Elizabeth* (70); 21.10.1754 Mid *Strafford* (58); 22.4.1755 Mid *Cornwall* Prison Ship; 6.8.1755 Passed; **Lieutenant**; 28.6.1756 6L *Namur* (90); 1.9.1756 5L *Namur* (90); 9.11.1756 4L *Namur* (90); 16.6.1757 4L *Prince Frederick* (64); 17.6.1757 3L *Prince Frederick* (64); 17.1.1758-1.8.1758 2L *Prince Frederick* (64); 6.6.1758-27.7.1758 The Siege of Louisbourg; 17.12.1759-1.7.1761 L. *Cygnet* (18) Sloop.

HOME, GEORGE

Dates: c.1735 Born; 1769 Died.
Family:
Service: 27.9.1755 Able *Experiment* (24); 13.3.1756 QM *Experiment* (24); 20.5.1756 Battle of Minorca; 22.8.1756 Mid *Gosport* (44); 4.9.1757 Able *Gosport* (44); 12.10.1757 Mid *Gosport* (44); 1.9.1758 Mid *Royal George* (100); 4.10.1758 Passed; **Lieutenant**; 6.10.1758-22.1.1759 L. *Baltimore* (8) Bomb Vessel; 20.2.1759-25.7.1760 2L *Anson* (60).

HOME, SIR GEORGE (7TH BARONET OF BLACKADDER)

Dates: 1740 Born; 28.3.1755 7th Baronet of Blackadder; bef.2.5.1803 Buried Greyfriars Kirkyard, Edinburgh; 2.5.1803 Died Darnhall, Cheshire.
Family: Father James Home, 6th Bt. (d.1755); Mother Catherine Livington (d.1788); Wife Hemen Buchanan (d.1824) married 13.9.1785; Son George; Daughter Catherine; Son James, 8th Bt. (1790-1836); Daughter Helen (1795-1858).
Service: **Lieutenant**; 23.11.1759(EI 7.5.1762) 5L *Lennox* (74); 8.6.1761(EI 17.5.1762)-27.10.1761 3L *Medway* (60); 3.12.1761(EI 17.5.1762) L. *Arundel* (24); 8.7.1762 2L *Romney* (50); 25.3.1763 1L *Pearl* (32); 19.4.1763-28.12.1763 1L *Boreas* (28); 7.4.1767 3L *Ramillies* (74); 26.10.1769-10.4.1770 2L *Ramillies* (74); 21.9.1770 3L *Albion* (74); 15.1.1771-20.9.1773 2L *Albion* (74); 4.11.1776 2L *Prince of Wales* (74); 5.5.1778 1L *Prince of Wales* (74); **Commander**; 1.8.1778(BLI 17.8.1779) *Barbadoes* (14) Sloop; 9.4.1779(NA 10.11.1779)-21.7.1779 *Rover* (16) Sloop; **Captain**; 21.7.1779(NA 10.11.1779) *Royal Oak* (74); 27.8.1779(NA 26.3.1781)-18.1.1782 *Vigilant* (64); 17.4.1780 Battle of Martinique; 15.5.1780 Action of March 15 1780; 19.5.1780 Action of March 19 1780; 7.6.1782-31.12.1782 *Suffolk* (74); 20.10.1782 Battle of Cape Spartel; 17.6.1795 *Defiance* (74); 22.3.1796-24.2.1797 *Glory* (98); 20.2.1797 **Rear Admiral of the Blue**; 14.2.1799 **Rear Admiral of the Red**; 29.4.1802 **Vice Admiral of the Blue.**

HOOD, ALEXANDER ARTHUR CB (1ST VISCOUNT BRIDPORT)

Dates: 2.12.1726 Born; 7.5.1788 Order of the Bath; 14.11.1794 1st Baron Bridport; 13.6.1796 1st Baron Briport [GB]; 1800 1st Viscount Bridport; 2.5.1814 Died.
Family: Father Rev. Samuel Hood (d.1777); Mother Mary Hoskins; Wife Mary (Molly) West (d.1786) married 21.8.1758; Wife Mary Sophia Bray married 26.6.1788; Brother Samuel (1st Viscount Hood of Whitley), RN (1724-1816).
Service: 19.1.1740/41-22.4.1743 Capt Serv *Romney* (50); 22.4.1743-12.1744 Mid *Princess Mary* (60); 12.1744-3.1744/45 Mid *Royal Sovereign* (104); 3.1744/45-5.1746 Mid *Exeter* (60); 5.1746-2.12.1746 Mid *Hawk* (8) Sloop; **Lieutenant**; 2.12.1746-10.2.1748/49[P] L. *Bridgewater* (24); 28.1.1755 3L *Prince* (90); 14.10.1755 2L *Prince* (90); 12.11.1755 1L *Prince* (90); **Commander**; 23.3.1756 *Merlin* (10) Sloop; **Captain**; 10.6.1756 *Prince George* (80); 3.10.1756(ECH 6.9.1758) *Prince* (90); 29.11.1756(ECH 6.9.1758) *Culloden* (74); 5.4.1757 Action of April 5 1757; 1.6.1757(6.9.1758)-14.5.1758 *Saint George* (90); 5.1.1759 *Minerva* (32); 20.11.1759 Battle of Quiberon Bay; 5.8.1761-2.5.1763[P] *Africa* (64); 14.12.1763-31.12.1777[P] *Katherine* (8) Yacht; 27.12.1777-31.3.1779 *Robust* (74); 27.7.1778 1st Battle of Ushant; 26.9.1780 **Rear Admiral of the White**; 5.4.1784-19.6.1790 M.P. for Bridgwater; 24.9.1787 **Vice Admiral of the Blue**; 6.4.1790-3.1796 Rear Admiral of Great Britain; 5.1790-11.1790 *London* (90); 21.9.1790 **Vice Admiral of the White**; 20.12.1790-25.5.1796 M.P. for Buckingham; 1793-1795 CinC — English Channel; 2.1793-1796 *Royal George* (100); 1.2.1793 **Vice Admiral of the Red**; 6.5.1793-15.12.1794 *Victory* (100); 12.4.1794 **Admiral of the Blue**; 1.6.1794 Glorious 1st of June; 1.6.1795 **Admiral of the White**; 23.6.1795 Action of Ile Groix; 28.7.1795 *London* (90); 3.1796-1.1.1801 Vice Admiral of Great Britain; 8.12.1796 *Royal George* (100); 10.4.1797-1799 CinC — English Channel; 1.1.1801-2.5.1814 Vice Admiral of the United Kingdom; 9.11.1805 **Admiral of the Red.**

HOOD, SAMUEL GCB (1ST VISCOUNT HOOD OF WHITLEY)

Dates: 12.12.1724 Born Butleigh, Somerset; 20.5.1778 1st Baronet Hood; 12.9.1782 1st Baron Hood; 1.6.1796 1st Viscount Hood of Whitley; 2.1.1815 Order of the Bath; 27.1.1816 Died 5 Quen's Square, Bath;

Family: Father Rev. Samuel Hood (d.1777); Mother Mary Hoskins; Wife Susannah Linzee (1726 - 1806) married 25.8.1749; Son Samuel (1727?- 1751); Brother Lord Alexander Arthur (1st Viscount Bridport), RN (1726-1814).

Service: 6.5.1741-4.1743 Capt Serv *Romney* (50); 4.1743-11.1743 Capt Serv *Garland* (20); 11.1743-1744 Mid *Sheerness* (20); 1744-23.1.1745/46 Mid *Ludlow Castle* (44); **Lieutenant**; 17.6.1746 L. *Winchelsea* (20); 19.3.1747/48 3L *Greenwich* (50); 18.5.1748 3L *Lion* (58); 23.7.1748[16.12.1748] 1L *Lion* (58); 13.8.1748[16.12.1748]-17.2.1748/49[P] 1L *Panther* (50); 16.1.1753 3L *Invincible* (74); 16.5.1753 3L *Terrible* (74); **Commander**; 10.5.1754 *Jamaica* (10) Sloop; **Captain**; 22.7.1756 *Lively* (20); 14.6.1757 *Bideford* (20); 7.2.1758-1.5.1763[P] *Vestal* (32); 3.7.1759 Bombardment of Le Havre; 6.9.1763-25.7.1766[P] *Thunderer* (74); 24.2.1767 Commodore *Romney* (50); 9.4.1767-3.8.1768 CinC — North America; 3.8.1768 CinC — North America; 16.12.1768-1770 CinC — North America; 8.1.1771-11.5.1771[P] *Royal William* (84); 1.11.1773 *Marlborough* (74); 25.7.1776-7.2.1778 *Courageux* (74); 26.1.1778-30.9.1780 Resident Commissioner at Portsmouth Dockyard; **Rear Admiral of the Blue**; 26.9.1780-5.1783 *Barfleur* (98); 29.4.1781-30.4.1781 Battle of Fort Royal; 5.9.1781 Battle of the Chesapeake; 25.1.1782-26.1.1782 Battle of Saint Kitts; 12.4.1782 Battle of the Saintes; 19.4.1782 Battle of the Mona Passage; 9.1782-2.1783 *Queen* (90); 20.10.1782 Battle of Cape Spartel; 14.3.1785-16.7.1788 M.P. for Westminster; 4.1786-10.1787 *Triumph* (74); 24.4.1786-1789 CinC — Portsmouth; 24.9.1787 **Vice Admiral of the Blue**; 10.1787-1788 *Barfleur* (98); 16.7.1788-6.3.1795 Lord Commissioner of the Admiralty; 18.8.1789-19.6.1790 M.P. for Reigate; 2.7.1790-13.6.1796 M.P. for Westminster; 9.1790-11.1790 *Royal Sovereign* (100); 1.9.1790 CinC — North Sea; 1792-8.11.1793 *Duke* (98); 14.6.1792-13.3.1793 CinC — Portsmouth; 1.2.1793 **Vice Admiral of the Red**; 13.3.1793-10.1794 CinC — The Mediterranean Sea; 12.4.1794 **Admiral of the Blue**; 1796-1816 Governor of Greenwich Hospital; 14.2.1799 **Admiral of the White**; 9.11.1805 **Admiral of the Red.**

HOOLEY, JOSEPH

Dates: 1785 Died.

Family:

Service: **Lieutenant**; 13.8.1761[MED 24.3.1763] 5L *Hercules* (74); 26.7.1762[MED 24.3.1763] L. *Experiment* (24); 8.9.1763-30.10.1765 2L *Shannon* (28); 25.7.1776-1.8.1777 L. *Favorite* (16) Sloop.

HOOPER, EDWARD

Dates: c.1717 Born; 1763 Died; 25.5.1763 Will Probate.

Family:

Service: 10.6.1738 Able *Torrington* (40); 27.9.1738 Able *Shoreham* (20); 19.10.1740 Mid *Shoreham* (20); 25.4.1741 Clerk *Prince Frederick* (70); 20.11.1741 Mid *Prince Frederick* (70); 30.7.1742 Mid *Dreadnought* (60); 7.2.1744/45 Passed; **Lieutenant**; 28.9.1745-19.10.1747 L. *Mercury* (20).

HOOPER, EDWARD

Dates: c.1729 Born.
Family:
Service: 29.4.1747 Able *Guernsey* (50); 21.2.1747/48 QM Mate *Guernsey* (50); 2.4.1749 QM *Guernsey* (50); 22.6.1749 Mid *Guernsey* (50); 26.4.1752 Mate *Guernsey* (50); 17.3.1755 Passed; **Lieutenant**; 23.11.1757-9.12.1757[P] L. *Jamaica* (10) Sloop; 2.1.1758 3L *Norfolk* (74); 5.6.1758-12.6.1758 Raid on Saint-Malo; 5.10.1758-20.11.1759 2L *Norfolk* (74); 16.1.1759-19.1.1759 Attack on Martinique; 20.1.1759-1.5.1759 Capture of Guadeloupe.

HOPE, SIR WILLIAM (3RD BARONET HOPE OF KIRKLISTON)

Dates: c.1726 Born; 20.11.1729 3rd Baronet Hope of Kirkliston; 1763 Died Bengal.
Family: Father Sir George Hope, 2nd Bt.; Mother Anne Mackenzie;.
Service: **Lieutenant**; 14.7.1749[(EI 10.5.1750)]-18.5.1750[P] 3L *Deptford* (60).

HOPKINS, BENJAMIN

Dates: c.1735 Born; 1761 Died.
Family:
Service: 30.3.1750 Capt Serv *Rainbow* (44); 30.9.1752 Able *Deptford* (50); 24.3.1753 Able *Deptford* (50); 8.5.1754 Able *Fougueux* (64); 29.3.1755 Mid *Fougueux* (64); 6.6.1755-8.6.1755 Action of 6-8 June 1755; 20.2.1757 Mid *Orford* (68); 19.3.1757 Mid *Invincible* (74); 11.4.1757 Passed; **Lieutenant**; 13.10.1757 2L *Actaeon* (28); 5.6.1758-12.6.1758 Raid on Saint-Malo; 25.1.1760-22.12.1760[P] 3L *Colchester* (50); 18.9.1761-26.1.1762 L. *Dolphin* (24).

HOPKINS, TIMOTHY

Dates: c.1722 Born.
Family:
Service: 18.6.1741 Ord. *Duke* (90); 25.3.1742 Able *Duke* (90); 9.7.1744 Mid *Duke* (90); 15.6.1747 Mid *Lion* (58); 14.10.1747 2nd Battle of Cape Finisterre; 4.2.1747/48 Passed; **Lieutenant**; 19.6.1760-20.3.1763[P] L. *Dispatch* (14) Sloop; 28.2.1771 2L *Warwick* (50); 19.3.1771-28.2.1775[P] 1L *Warwick* (50).

HORE, DANIEL

Dates: 25.6.1762 Died.
Family:
Service: 15.6.1722 Vol-p-O *Mary* (60); 29.7.1723 Mid *Prince Frederick* (70); 18.6.1724 Able *Leopard* (50); 28.2.1725/26 Mid *Prince Frederick* (70); 8.5.1728 Passed; 29.5.1729 **Lieutenant**; 8.5.1731-17.2.1731/32 3L *Sunderland* (60); 18.2.1731/32-14.2.1732/33 2L *Sunderland* (60); 15.2.1732/33-29.7.1734 3L *Sunderland* (60); 28.2.1734/35-14.3.1737/38 2L *Somerset* (80); 15.3.1737/38 1L *Jersey* (60); 11.2.1739/40[(8.4.1743)] 1L *Burford* (70); **Commander**; 28.7.1740[(8.4.1742)] *Success* (8) Fireship; 15.4.1741-16.4.1741[S] *Galicia* (70); **Captain**; 17.4.1741[(8.4.1742)] *Ludlow Castle* (40); 12.10.1741[(8.4.1743)]-6.3.1742/43[P] *Defiance* (60); 29.1.1744/45-12.9.1747 *Canterbury* (60); 27.2.1762 **Superannuated Rear Admiral.**

HORNE, CHARLES

Dates: c.1735 Born; 1771 Died.
Family:
Service: 24.8.1750 Capt Serv *Anson* (60); 26.4.1751 Ord. *Centurion* (50); 11.9.1753 Mid *Centurion* (50); 15.5.1755 Mid *Mary* (8) Yacht; 5.10.1755 Able *Cruizer* (8) Sloop; 26.8.1756

Passed; **Lieutenant**; 9.11.1756-17.12.1756 6L *Royal George* (100); 13.1.1757 4L *Essex* (64); 5.6.1758-12.6.1758 Raid on Saint-Malo; 5.9.1759 3L *Essex* (64); 17.10.1759-20.11.1759[S] 2L *Essex* (64); 20.11.1759 Battle of Quiberon Bay; 23.2.1760-26.7.1762 2L *Dorsetshire* (68).

HORNE, EDMUND

Dates: 23.5.1764 Died.
Family:
Service: **Lieutenant**; 20.10.1740-3.9.1741 4L *Chichester* (80); 10.10.1741 3L *Chichester* (80); 16.1.1741/42-10.3.1741/42 2L *Launceston* (44); **Commander**; 11.3.1741/42-11.9.1743 *Serpent* (8) Bomb Vessel; **Captain**; 22.2.1744/45-14.3.1744/45 *Hector* (44); 12.4.1745-26.10.1748[P] *Rupert* (60).

HORTON, WILLIAM

Dates: c.1731 Born; 1762 Died.
Family:
Service: 1752-1756 HEIC Service; 5.5.1756 Able *Vanguard* (68); 31.10.1756-6.3.1757 Able *Fly* (8) Sloop; 7.3.1757 Able *Vulture* (14) Sloop; 8.1757-10.1757 Louisbourg Expedition; 23.1.1758 Mid *Pallas* (36); 5.6.1758-12.6.1758 Raid on Saint-Malo; 30.11.1758 Mid *Pallas* (36); 9.6.1759 Mate *Pallas* (36); 6.2.1760 Passed; **Lieutenant**; 1.4.1760-9.7.1762 L. *Gibraltar* (20).

HOSKINS, HENRY

Dates: 1763 Died.
Family:
Service: **Lieutenant**; 1.4.1757[(19.9.1757)] 2L *Kingfisher* (14) Sloop; 5.4.1758 3L *Rippon* (60); 16.1.1759-19.1.1759 Attack on Martinique; 19.3.1759-15.4.1762 1L *Vestal* (32); 3.7.1759 Bombardment of Le Havre.

HOTHAM, SIR WILLIAM (1ST BARON HOTHAM)

Dates: 8.4.1736 Born; 7.3.1797 1st Baron Hotham; 18.7.1811 11th Baronet Hotham; 2.5.1813 Died South Dalton Hall;
Family: Father Sir Beaumont Hotham, 7th Baronet (1698-1771); Mother Frances Thompson; Brother Beaumont Hotham (1737-1814).
Service: 7.8.1754 Passed; 28.1.1755 **Lieutenant**; 7.5.1755 5L *Saint George* (90); 11.11.1755 4L *Saint George* (90); 24.5.1756 4L *Namur* (90); 5.6.1756 4L *Ramillies* (90); **Commander**; 19.11.1756[(ECH 5.4.1757)] *Fortune* (14) Sloop; **Captain**; 17.8.1757-1.11.1757 *Gibraltar* (20); 17.4.1758 *Melampe* (36); 4.5.1761-18.11.1763[P] *Aeolus* (32); 24.10.1766-1.11.1769 *Hero* (74); 7.12.1770-7.12.1773 *Resolution* (74); 4.1776-1780 Commodore *Preston* (50); 6.12.1776-8.12.1776 Occupation of Rhode Island; 14.12.1778-15.12.1778 Battle of St. Lucia; 17.1.1780-17.8.1781[P] Commodore *Vengeance* (74); 17.4.1780 Battle of Martinique; 15.5.1780 Action of March 15 1780; 19.5.1780 Action of March 19 1780; 1.5.1782-31.3.1783[P] Commodore *Edgar* (74); 20.10.1782 Battle of Cape Spartel; 24.9.1787 **Rear Admiral of the Red**; 16.5.1790-9.9.1791[P] *Princess Royal* (98); 21.9.1790 **Vice Admiral of the Blue**; 1.1793-1.1796 *Britannia* (100); 1.2.1793 **Vice Admiral of the White**; 12.4.1794 **Vice Admiral of the Red**; 14.3.1795 Action off Genoa; 4.5.1795-11.1795 CinC — The Mediterranean Sea; 13.7.1795 Battle of Hyeres; 14.2.1799 **Admiral of the White**; 9.11.1805 **Admiral of the Red**.

HOULTON, JOHN

Dates: c.1728 Born; 1.1791 Died; 27.3.1791 Will Probate.
Family: Father Joseph Houton (d.1731); Brother Robert (d.1785); Brother Joseph (d.1771).
Service: 5.6.1744 Capt Serv *Tartar* (20); 11.1.1746 Able *Tartar* (20); 21.9.1746 Mid *Tartar* (20); 27.9.1747 Mid *Salisbury* (50); 26.7.1749 Able *Kent* (64); 31.8.1749 Mid *Mermaid* (24); 8.11.1749 Mate *Mermaid* (24); 21.2.1750-20.6.1750 Mid *Kent* (64); 20.6.1750 Passed; **Lieutenant**; 28.6.1756 4L *Devonshire* (70); 16.4.1757 3L *Devonshire* (70); 12.5.1757-21.12.1758 3L *Cambridge* (80); **Commander**; 29.1.1759[(BLI 16.8.1759)]-2.8.1759[P] *Bonetta* (10) Sloop; **Captain**; 5.11.1761 *Mercury* (20); 13.1.1762-26.1.1764[P] *Enterprise* (44); 24.2.1762-25.2.1762 Capture of Saint Lucia; 6.6.1762-13.8.1762 Operations against Havana; 17.8.1779-21.7.1781 *Montagu* (74); 16.1.1780 Battle of Cape St. Vincent; 17.4.1780 Battle of Martinique; 15.5.1780 Action of March 15 1780; 19.5.1780 Action of March 19 1780; 29.4.1781-30.4.1781 Battle of Fort Royal; 28.8.1790 *Royal Sovereign* (100); 21.9.1790 **Rear Admiral of the Blue.**

HOVELL, JAMES

Dates: c.1712 Born; 18.2.1757 Will Probate; bef.18.2.1757 Died.
Family:
Service: 4.10.1722 Capt Serv *Salisbury* (50); 26.7.1724 Capt Serv *Exeter* (60); 24.6.1725 Gnr Serv *Sheerness* (20); 7.11.1729 Able *Looe* (42); 23.3.1729/30 QGnr *Guernsey* (50); 29.1.1730/31 QGnr *Lark* (40); 25.8.1732 Gnr Mate *Lark* (40); 9.2.1732/33 Able *Torrington* (40); 1.10.1733 QGnr *Torrington* (40); 23.5.1734 Gnr Mate *Torrington* (40); 11.10.1738 Mate *Augusta* (60); 4.5.1739 Mid *Augusta* (60); 9.8.1739 Mate *Portland* (50); 26.11.1739 Mate *Sunderland* (60); 24.4.1741-19.2.1741/42[P] Mid *Sunderland* (60); 30.5.1742-1.2.1743 Mate *Garland* (20); 1.2.1742/43 Passed; **Lieutenant**; 31.1.1744/45[(21.6.1745)] 3L *Rippon* (60); 4.9.1745-13.4.1746 L. *Squirrel* (20); 3.7.1746 3L *Chichester* (80); 21.8.1746-3.1.1746/47 2L *Chichester* (80); 3.1.1746/47-13.5.1747 3L *Lichfield* (50); 21.10.1755 3L *Princess Royal* (90); 18.11.1755-bef.18.2.1757[†] 1L *Jersey* (60).

HOW, JOHN

Dates: c.1720 Born; 1758 Died.
Family:
Service: 1736-1741 Merchant Service; 2.3.1740/41 Able *Fox* (20); 15.4.1743 QM *Fox* (20); 3.9.1743 Mid *Fox* (20); 3.7.1745-27.7.1745 Able *Lion* (58); 9.7.1745 Lion v L'Elizabeth; 28.7.1745 Mid *Lion* (58); 21.11.1745 Passed; **Lieutenant**; 22.11.1745 L. *Salamander* (8) Fireship; 18.5.1748-30.9.1751[P] L. *Greyhound* (20); 31.7.1755-23.9.1756 2L *Chesterfield* (44); 20.5.1756 Battle of Minorca.

HOWARD, PHILLIP

Dates: c.1740 Born; 1778 Died.
Family:
Service: 8.3.1756 Capt Serv *Dover* (44); 13.5.1757 Ord. *Southampton* (32); 21.9.1757 Able *Southampton* (32); 9.11.1757 Mid *Southampton* (32); 5.6.1758-12.6.1758 Raid on Saint-Malo; 7.5.1760 Passed; **Lieutenant**; 23.12.1762[(JAM 20.12.1763)]-19.9.1763[P] 4L *Hampton Court* (64); 30.8.1764-11.1765[P] 4L *Africa* (64); 6.1.1766 2L *Aeolus* (32); 21.7.1769-20.1.1770 1L *Aeolus* (32); 29.9.1770-29.5.1771[P] 4L *Defence* (74).

HOWE, RICHARD (1ST EARL HOWE)

Dates: 19.3.1725/26 Born London; 6.7.1758 4th Viscount Howe; 1788 1st Baron Howe; 1788 1st Earl Howe; 5.8.1799 Died Grafton Street, London;
Family: Father Emanuel Scrope Howe, 2nd Visc. (1699-1735); Mother Mary Sophia Charlotte von Kielmansegg (1703-1782); Wife Mary Hartopp (1732-1800) married 16.2.1758; Brother General William (1729-1814); Brother Brigadier General George Augustus (1724-1758);
Service: 1736-7.1739 Merchant Service; 14.7.1739 Mid *Pearl* (40); 30.6.1740 Mid *Severn* (50); 18.10.1743 Mid *Suffolk* (70); 14.12.1743-24.5.1744 Mid *Superb* (60); 24.5.1744 Passed; **Lieutenant**; 12.8.1745 5L *Royal George* (100); **Commander**; 5.11.1745 *Baltimore* (14) Sloop; **Captain**; 10.4.1746-11.9.1747 *Triton* (20); 11.9.1747 *Rippon* (54); 29.10.1748-12.7.1749[P] *Cornwall* (80); 14.3.1750/51-20.5.1752 *Glory* (44); 3.6.1752-21.8.1754 *Dolphin* (24); 20.1.1755 *Dunkirk* (60); 6.6.1755-8.6.1755 Action of 6-8 June 1755; 13.6.1757 *Magnanime* (74); 5.9.1757-6.10.1757 Raid on Rochefort; 1.6.1758-4.7.1758 Commodore *Essex* (64); 5.6.1758-12.6.1758 Raid on Saint-Malo; 7.8.1758 Commodore *Pallas* (36); 27.1.1762 CinC — Basque Roads; 27.1.1762-14.1.1763[P] Commodore *Magnanime* (74); 22.6.1762-23.1.1763[P] *Princess Amelia* (80); 20.4.1763-30.7.1765 Lord Commissioner of the Admiralty; 1765-5.8.1799 Privy Counsellor; 18.10.1770 **Rear Admiral of the Blue**; 26.11.1770-1776 CinC — The Mediterranean Sea; 31.3.1775 **Rear Admiral of the White**; 7.12.1775 **Vice Admiral of the Blue**; 2.1776-12.1778 *Eagle* (64); 15.2.1776-9.1778 CinC — North America; 2.4.1776 **Vice Admiral of the White**; 12.5.1778 **Vice Admiral of the Red**; 14.8.1778 *Centurion* (50); 2.4.1782-1783 CinC — English Channel; 8.4.1782 **Admiral of the Blue**; 20.4.1782-14.11.1782 *Victory* (100); 20.10.1782 Battle of Cape Spartel; 30.1.1783-9.4.1783 1st Lord; 31.12.1783-15.7.1788 1st Lord; 24.9.1787 **Admiral of the White**; 5.1790-10.1790 *Queen Charlotte* (100); 13.5.1790 CinC — English Channel; 23.7.1790 CinC — English Channel; 23.3.1791 *Victory* (100); 9.6.1792-3.1796 Vice Admiral of Great Britain; 1.2.1793-1795 CinC — English Channel; 7.2.1793-1799 *Queen Charlotte* (100); 1.6.1794 Glorious 1st of June; 23.6.1795 Action of Ile Groix; 1796-1797 *Royal George* (100); 12.3.1796 **Admiral of the Fleet**.

HOWE, WILLIAM

Dates: c.1736 Born; 6.1.1764 Died.
Family:
Service: 25.9.1750 Able *Invincible* (74); 23.1.1753-14.5.1753 Able *Penzance* (44); 15.5.1753 Able *Otter* (14) Sloop; 29.11.1753 Mid *Otter* (14) Sloop; 22.2.1755 Mid *Winchester* (50); 12.11.1756 Passed; **Lieutenant**; 12.11.1756 3L *Winchester* (50); 11.10.1758 6L *Royal George* (100); 23.2.1759 5L *Royal George* (100); 19.6.1759 4L *Royal George* (100); 5.9.1759 3L *Royal George* (100); 17.10.1759 2L *Royal George* (100); 20.11.1759 Battle of Quiberon Bay; 24.11.1759 *Fortune* (14) Sloop; **Commander**; 18.2.1760 *Jamaica* (10) Sloop; **Captain**; 1.7.1760 *Bideford* (20); 10.9.1761-22.6.1764[P] *Montreal* (32); 23.6.1764 *Montreal* (32).

HOWORTH, EDWARD

Dates: c.1727 Born; 1797 Died.
Family:
Service: 12.4.1747 Able *Rupert* (60); 9.4.1748 Mid *Rupert* (60); 20.10.1749 Mate *Rupert* (60); 17.1.1750/51 Able *Boyne* (80) Prison Ship; 29.5.1751 Mid *Boyne* (80) Prison Ship; 12.8.1751 Mate *Humber* (44); 10.4.1753 Mate *Gosport* (44); 15.1.1754 Mate *Advice* (50); 7.8.1754 Passed; **Lieutenant**; 21.5.1755 3L *Windsor* (60); 14.4.1756 2L *Windsor* (60); 9.7.1756 1L *Windsor* (60); 8.1757-10.1757 Louisbourg Expedition; 21.2.1759-16.1.1765[P] 1L *Falmouth* (50); 24.9.1762-

6.10.1762 Battle of Manilla; 22.2.1772 2L *Lennox* (74); 27.5.1773-21.4.1774 1L *Lennox* (74); 10.5.1790-26.3.1791 LCmdr *Enterprise* (28); 21.9.1796 **Superannuated Commander**.

HOWORTH, JOHN

Dates: c.1729 Born; 1801 Died.
Family:
Service: 5.1.1741/42 Capt Serv *Montagu* (60); 30.5.1742-16.7.1742[P] Capt Serv *Bristol* (54); 2.3.1743/44-16.10.1746 Capt Serv *Kingston* (60); 17.10.1746 Capt Serv *Essex* (70); 18.12.1747 Capt Serv *Rupert* (60); 3.10.1748 Able *Rupert* (60); 7.7.1749 Mid *Rupert* (60); 1.5.1752 Passed; **Lieutenant**; 4.1.1757[(11.5.1763)] L. *Racehorse* (18) Sloop; 29.1.1757[(10.5.1763)]-5.9.1757 2L *Bridgewater* (24); 7.3.1757-1.4.1757 Expedition against Chandernagore; 7.12.1770 2L *Barfleur* (90); 25.6.1773-7.12.1773 1L *Barfleur* (90); 7.2.1776 2L *Eagle* (64); **Commander**; 1.2.1777[(NA 27.5.1777)]-22.4.1778 *Carcass* (8) Bomb Vessel; **Captain**; 4.4.1781-23.11.1781 *Victory* (100); 2.3.1782-4.3.1783[P] *Bienfaisant* (64); 20.10.1782 Battle of Cape Spartel; 1799 **Superannuated Captain**.

HOY, ISAAC

Dates: c.1717 Born; bef.1780 Died.
Family:
Service: 1.12.1732-21.11.1734 Able *Spy* (8) Sloop; 22.11.1734-3.4.1736 Ord. *Spy* (8) Sloop; 4.4.1736-22.12.1736 Able *Spy* (8) Sloop; 24.12.1738-30.1.1740/41 Mate *Ludlow Castle* (40); 31.1.1740/41-1.10.1741 Mid *Defiance* (60); 4.3.1740/41-5.1741 Operations against Cartagena; 2.10.1741-19.7.1742 Mate *Phaeton* (8) Fireship; 5.5.1743 Passed; **Lieutenant**; 6.10.1744 3L *Pearl* (44); 27.8.1745-21.1.1746/47[P] L. *Success* (20); 6.5.1747-28.4.1749[P] L. *Margate* (24); 9.10.1755-23.4.1760 1L *Sutherland* (50); 8.1757-10.1757 Louisbourg Expedition; 6.6.1758-27.7.1758 The Siege of Louisbourg; 21.4.1774 1L *Lennox* (74); 19.1.1775-6.6.1775 1L *Exeter* (64); 23.2.1778 1L *Thunderer* (74); 27.7.1778 1st Battle of Ushant; 21.9.1778[(JAM 19.6.1780)]-1780[†] L. *Ostrich* (14) Sloop.

HUDSON, CHARLES

Dates: Buried St. Mary's Newington, Southwark, London; c.1733 Born; 26.2.1803 Died London; 19.3.1803 Will Probate.
Family: Wife Margaret.
Service: 17.7.1746 Able *Triton* (20); 19.5.1747-12.12.1749[P] Able *Rippon* (54); 4.4.1751 Able *Porcupine* (16) Sloop; 31.12.1751 Mid *Porcupine* (16) Sloop; 1.9.1756 Passed; **Lieutenant**; 27.6.1757 L. *Dolphins Prize* (12) Sloop; 19.9.1757 3L *Prince of Orange* (60); 17.1.1758 2L *Prince of Orange* (60); 6.6.1758-27.7.1758 The Siege of Louisbourg; 29.3.1761-11.6.1761 Expedition against Belle-Isle; **Commander**; 24.8.1762-4.4.1763 *Peggy* (8) Sloop; 18.5.1763 *Vulture* (14) Sloop; **Captain**; 20.6.1765-13.7.1765 *Panther* (60); 25.7.1775 *Orpheus* (32); 5.8.1778 *Foudroyant* (80); 22.7.1779-31.3.1781[P] *Richmond* (32); 28.3.1783-3.6.1786[P] *Venus* (36); 11.4.1793 **Superannuated Rear Admiral**.

HUDSON, GEORGE

Dates: c.1719 Born; 1785 Died.
Family:
Service: 20.7.1733-6.7.1736 Vol-p-O *Edinburgh* (70); 7.7.1736-29.5.1737 Able *Torrington* (40); 30.5.1737-9.5.1738 Mid *Torrington* (40); 10.5.1738-2.6.1738 Mid *Edinburgh* (70); 3.6.1738 MidO *Edinburgh* (70); 4.12.1739 Passed; **Lieutenant**; 3.3.1739/40-5.1.1741/42 L. *Strombolo* (8) Fireship; 4.3.1740/41-5.1741 Operations against Cartagena; 7.1741-10.1741 Operations

against Santiago; 6.2.1741/42[24.5.1742]-16.7.1742[P] 1L *Bristol* (54); 31.8.1742-28.4.1743 2L *Suffolk* (70); 18.2.1742/43 Attack on La Guaira; 15.4.1743-24.4.1743 Attack on Porto Cabello; 30.4.1743[10.5.1744]-4.4.1744[P] 1L *Advice* (54); **Commander**; 16.2.1747/48-23.6.1748[P] *Terror* (8) Bomb Vessel; 2.9.1755-6.4.1756 *Roehampton* (16) Hired Armed Ship.

HUDSON, THOMAS

Dates: 2.2.1792 Died.
Family:
Service: **Lieutenant**; 29.10.1750[NA 5.8.1752] 1L *Renown* (30); 26.1.1750/51[NA 15.11.1752] 3L *Gloucester* (50); 2.3.1750/51[NA 2.9.1752] L. *Queenborough* (24); 21.10.1755 6L *Royal Sovereign* (104); 10.10.1757-13.3.1759[P] 5L *Royal Sovereign* (104); 17.12.1770-27.5.1773 1L *Lennox* (74).

HUE, PHILIP

Dates: 1812 Died; 2.4.1812 Will Probate.
Family:
Service: **Lieutenant**; 22.9.1759[NA 13.11.1759]-18.5.1763 3L *Centurion* (50); 6.6.1762-13.8.1762 Operations against Havana; 30.11.1770-4.10.1771 L. *Swallow* (14) Sloop; 31.5.1776 2L *Ardent* (64); 14.11.1776 3L *Prince George* (90); 15.8.1777 2L *Prince George* (90); 1.10.1777 1L *Prince George* (90); 26.1.1778-31.5.1781 1L *Sultan* (74); 6.7.1779 Battle of Grenada; 1780 LCmdr *Charming Betsey* (6) Hired Tender; 20.6.1780 Action off Monti Christi; 2.1797-1799 LCmdr *Argonaut* (64) Hospital Ship; **Commander**; 17.4.1799-11.4.1802[P] *Actaeon* (44) Receiving Ship.

HUGHES, EDWARD CB,

Dates: 1720 Born Hertfordshire; 27.10.1773 Knight Bachelor; 11.4.1777 Order of the Bath; 17.1.1794 Died Luxborough House nr Chigwell, Essex.
Family: Wife Ruth Morgan (1731-1800).
Service: 4.1.1734/35 Mid *Dunkirk* (60); 9.1736 Mid *Kinsale* (40); 7.1738 Mid *Diamond* (40); 2.1740 Mid *Burford* (70); **Lieutenant**; 25.8.1740[26.2.1741/42] L. *Cumberland* (8) Fireship; 6.3.1740/41[11.4.1743] 4L *Suffolk* (70); 9.6.1741 2L *Dunkirk* (60); 25.2.1741/42 1L *Dunkirk* (60); 11.2.1743/44-12.2.1743/44 Battle of Toulon; 1.8.1744[MED 1.4.1746]-1.5.1745 3L *Stirling Castle* (70); 18.10.1745[MED 1.4.1746] 3L *Marlborough* (90); 2.12.1745[MED 1.4.1746]-14.4.1746 2L *Marlborough* (90); **Captain**; 6.2.1747/48-23.6.1750[P] *Lark* (44); 26.1.1756-20.8.1756 *Deal Castle* (20); 20.8.1756-18.6.1757 *Intrepid* (64); 5.7.1757 *Somerset* (68); 6.6.1758-27.7.1758 The Siege of Louisbourg; 26.9.1762[MED 27.6.1763]-10.5.1763[P] *Blenheim* (90); 8.1.1771 *Somerset* (68); 2.9.1773-1777 CinC — East Indies; 2.9.1773 Commodore *Salisbury* (50); 23.1.1778 **Rear Admiral of the Blue**; 9.7.1778-15.11.1783[W] *Superb* (74); 10.7.1778-1784 CinC — East Indies; 19.3.1779 **Rear Admiral of the Red**; 26.9.1780 **Vice Admiral of the Blue**; 17.2.1782 Battle of Sadras; 12.4.1782 Battle of Providien; 6.7.1782 2nd Battle of Negapatam; 3.9.1782 Battle of Trincomalee; 20.6.1783 2nd Battle of Cuddalore; 1784-1.6.1785[P] *Sultan* (74); 24.9.1787 **Vice Admiral of the White**; 21.9.1790 **Vice Admiral of the Red**; 1.2.1793 **Admiral of the Blue**.

HUGHES, JOHN

Dates: c.1733 Born; 1787 Died.
Family:
Service: 16.12.1738 Able *Deptford* (60); 10.5.1739-6.7.1740 Able *Princess Louisa* (60); 21.11.1739 Attack on Puerto Bello; 7.7.1740 Mid *Princess Louisa* (40); 26.10.1740-3.7.1741 Able *Princess Louisa* (60); 4.3.1740/41-5.1741 Operations against Cartagena; 4.7.1741 Mid *Princess Louisa* (60); 25.7.1742-18.12.1742[P] Mate *Princess Louisa* (60); 17.4.1743 Mid *Jersey*

Hulk Hulk; 23.5.1744 Mid *Prince Frederick* (70); 11.4.1745 NR *Sunderland* (60); 3.5.1745 Mid *Prince George* (90); 9.5.1745 Passed; **Lieutenant**; 7.6.1745 L. *Shark* (8) Sloop; 24.10.1746-4.8.1748[P] 3L *Anglesea* (44); 1.12.1748-31.5.1752[P] 3L *Monmouth* (70); 31.3.1753 L. *Seahorse* (24); 28.4.1755[NA 27.11.1755] 1L *Norwich* (50); 25.5.1755[NA 25.11.1755] 2L *Centurion* (50); 19.2.1756 1L *Torbay* (74); 20.5.1756 6L *Royal George* (100); 6.8.1756 3L *Royal George* (100); 9.11.1756 1L *Royal George* (100); **Commander**; 15.11.1756-13.5.1757 *Cruizer* (8) Sloop; 13.1.1758 *Tamar* (16) Sloop; **Captain**; 21.11.1760-1.12.1761 *Seaford* (20).

HUGHES, RICHARD

Dates: 1670 Born Titchfield, Hampshire; 12.11.1756 Died Deptford.
Family: Wife Mary Loader; Son Sir Richard (1st Baronet of East Bergholt), RN (1708-1779); Son Robert, RN (d.1774); Brother Robert, RN (d.1729).
Service: 23.3.1688/89 Capt Serv *Phoenix* (42); 27.3.1690 Vol. *Phoenix* (42); 2.11.1691 Able *Elizabeth* (70); 19.5.1692 Battle of Barfleur; 15.6.1692-4.7.1693 Mid *Elizabeth* (70); 10.1.1692/93 Passed; 4.7.1693 **Lieutenant**; 7.5.1695 3L *London* (96); 3.9.1695 4L *Queen* (100); 26.3.1698 L. *Griffin* (28); 1.4.1699 2L *Romney* (54); 9.5.1699-14.3.1699/0 1L *Revenge* (70); 27.2.1700/1 2L *Somerset* (80); 7.3.1700/1 2L *Triumph* (90); 16.1.1701/2 1L *Royal Sovereign* (100); **Captain**; 19.6.1702[25.11.1702] 2Capt *Triumph* (90); 7.9.1702[11.11.1702]-20.1.1702/3 Capt&M *Newport* (24); 22.2.1702/3 *Hector* (42); 2.3.1702/3 2Capt *Association* (90); 26.7.1703[11.2.1703/4] *Poole* (32); 24.1.1704/5 *Dunkirk* (50); 8.3.1704/5 2Capt *Royal Anne* (100); 17.10.1705 *Chatham* (54); 22.3.1709/10[6.8.1713] *Somerset* (80); 5.11.1710[6.8.1713] *Stirling Castle* (70); 2.3.1714/15-27.3.1716 *Plymouth* (60); 23.2.1716/17 *Devonshire* (80); 24.3.1716/17 *Royal Oak* (70); 3.4.1717[26.11.1717] *Shrewsbury* (80); 6.7.1717-13.3.1717/18 *Royal Oak* (70); 28.7.1719 *Monck* (50); 12.1.1719/20 *Nottingham* (60); 27.1.1720/21-24.10.1721[P] *Chichester* (80); 22.4.1723-1.9.1727[P] *Edinburgh* (70); 26.7.1728-12.4.1729 *Cornwall* (80); 5.5.1729-12.2.1754 Resident Commissioner at Portsmouth Dockyard; 26.6.1733-1754 Gov. of Royal Naval Academy.

HUGHES, SIR RICHARD (1ST BARONET OF EAST BERGHOLT)

Dates: 1708 Born Deptford; 17.7.1773 1st Baronet of East Bergholt; 1779 Died Southampton;
Family: Father Richard Hughes, RN (1670-1756); Mother Mary Loader; Wife Joanne Collyer; Daughter Mary [Collingwood] (d.1824); Daughter Sarah; Son Sir Richard (2nd Baronet of East Bergholt), RN (1724-1812); Son Rev. Robert (1739-1814), 3rd Bt.; Brother Robert, RN (d.1774).
Service: 26.8.1721 Vol-p-O *Nottingham* (60); 20.9.1721 Vol-p-O *Chichester* (80); 23.6.1722 Able *Leopard* (50); 13.7.1723 Mid *Edinburgh* (70); 18.12.1725 Passed; **Lieutenant**; 28.7.1726[14.11.1726]-19.4.1727 4L *Grafton* (70); 20.4.1727-25.7.1728 3L *Grafton* (70); 26.7.1728-8.2.1728/29 2L *Cornwall* (80); 9.2.1728/29-10.4.1729 3L *Cornwall* (80); 12.4.1729-16.12.1729[P] 4L *Princess Amelia* (80); 4.2.1730/31-8.5.1732 2L *Salisbury* (50); 9.5.1732-14.2.1732/33 1L *Sunderland* (60); 15.2.1732/33-6.5.1735 2L *Sunderland* (60); 7.5.1735-16.10.1735 6L *Britannia* (100); 12.6.1739-2.7.1739 1L *Namur* (90); **Commander**; 3.7.1739 *Anne Galley* (8) Fireship; **Captain**; 24.10.1740[24.1.1742/43]-23.7.1742 *Dursley Galley* (20); 10.7.1741 CinC — Portsmouth; 25.7.1742-12.1.1743/44 *Faversham* (44); 1.4.1744-31.8.1744 *Chatham* (50); 18.8.1744[MED 23.2.1747/48]-25.10.1748[P] *Essex* (70); 10.1.1753-2.4.1754 *Fougueux* (64); 12.2.1754-25.8.1773 Resident Commissioner at Portsmouth Dockyard.

HUGHES, SIR RICHARD (2ND BARONET OF EAST BERGHOLT)

Dates: c.1724 Born; 1779 2nd Baronet of East Bergholt; 4.1.1812 Died.

Family: Father Sir Richard Hughes (1st Baronet of East Bergholt), RN (1708-1779); Mother Joanne Collyer; Wife Jane Sloane; Daughter Rose Mary [Browne]; Sister Mary [Collingwood] (d.1824); Sister Sarah; Brother Rev. Robert (1739-1814), 3rd Bt.

Service: 7.4.1739 Scholar *Royal Naval Academy*; 8.4.1742 Mid *Faversham* (44); 16.6.1743 Able *Sunderland* (60); 27.1.1743/44 Mid *Chatham* (50); 28.8.1744 Mid *Essex* (70); 15.11.1744 Mid *Dragon* (60); 15.2.1744/45 ActL *Burford* (70); 1.4.1745 Passed; **Lieutenant**; 2.4.1745(MED 25.3.1748)-18.10.1745 4L *Stirling Castle* (70); 9.1.1747/48(MED 18.4.1749) 4L *Boyne* (80); 5.8.1748(MED 18.4.1749)-1.5.1749[P] 2L *Superb* (60); 4.2.1751/52 2L *Advice* (50); 26.8.1755 1L *Swiftsure* (68); **Commander**; 6.2.1756 *Spy* (10) Sloop; **Captain**; 10.11.1756 *Hind* (24); 13.1.1758 *Active* (28); 5.6.1758-12.6.1758 Raid on Saint-Malo; 21.2.1759 *Falmouth* (50); 1.1.1760(EI 12.8.1761)-1.2.1761 *York* (60); 11.11.1761-6.12.1762[P] *Portland* (50); 4.4.1763-25.8.1766 *Boreas* (28); 20.5.1767-24.5.1770 *Firm* (74); 8.1.1771-8.1.1774 *Worcester* (64); 26.10.1776-14.2.1778 *Centaur* (74); 1778 Resident Commissioner at Halifax Dockyard; 1778-1781 Lieutenant Governor of Nova Scotia; 26.9.1780 **Rear Admiral of the Blue**; 1782-1783 *Princess Amelia* (80); 20.10.1782 Battle of Cape Spartel; 12.6.1783 CinC — Barbados & the Leeward Islands; 9.1783-c.10.4.1784[P] *Leander* (52); 1784-1786 *Adamant* (50); 24.9.1787 **Rear Admiral of the Red**; 10.2.1789-1.1792 *Adamant* (50); 10.4.1789-1792 CinC — Nova Scotia; 21.9.1790 **Vice Admiral of the Blue**; 1.2.1793 **Vice Admiral of the White**; 12.4.1794 **Vice Admiral of the Red**; 14.2.1799 **Admiral of the White**; 9.11.1805 **Admiral of the Red**.

HUGHES, ROBERT

Dates: 19.1.1774 Died.

Family: Father Richard Hughes, RN (1670-1756); Mother Mary Loader; Wife Sarah; Brother Sir Richard (1st Baronet of East Bergholt), RN (1708-1779).

Service: 18.6.1712 Vol-p-O *Newcastle* (50); 9.3.1714/15-8.11.1716 Able *Windsor* (60); 9.11.1716 Mid *Orford* (70); 2.8.1717 Mid *Burford* (70); 6.12.1717 Mid *Barfleur* (90); 5.5.1718 MidO *Dragon* (54); 26.2.1718/19 Mid *Dragon* (54); 13.8.1720 Mid *Barfleur* (90); 30.12.1720 Passed; **Lieutenant**; 14.7.1738(14.12.1739) 3L *Eltham* (40); 26.12.1738 2L *Eltham* (40); 4.3.1739/40 2L *Gloucester* (50); 18.3.1739/40 4L *Prince Frederick* (70); 8.5.1740 3L *Prince Frederick* (70); 30.6.1740 2L *Prince Frederick* (70); 7.1.1740/41 Action of January 7 1741; 4.3.1740/41-5.1741 Operations against Cartagena; 13.6.1741(27.5.1742) 1L *Prince Frederick* (70); 25.6.1742 1L *Dreadnought* (60); 8.2.1743/44 6L *Victory* (100); **Commander**; 14.7.1744 *Jamaica* (10) Sloop; 18.7.1744 *Shark* (8) Sloop; **Captain**; 2.4.1745(MED 5.2.1746/47)-26.2.1746/47[P] *Kingston* (60); 8.2.1747/48 *Tilbury* (58); 5.5.1748(3.2.1748/49)-16.2.1748/49[P] *Captain* (70); 24.1.1754-9.4.1756 *Port Mahon* (24); 9.4.1756 *Augusta* (60); 30.6.1756 *Berwick* (64); 5.4.1757 Action of April 5 1757; 28.2.1758 Battle of Cartagena; 29.9.1758-15.11.1759 *Norfolk* (74); 16.1.1759-19.1.1759 Attack on Martinique; 20.1.1759-1.5.1759 Capture of Guadeloupe; 5.12.1763 *Rippon* (60); 12.12.1763-12.12.1766 *Dorsetshire* (68); 21.3.1769-2.4.1770[P] *Dragon* (74); 28.3.1770-25.10.1770 *Centaur* (74); 24.10.1770 **Rear Admiral of the Red**.

HUISH, HENRY

Dates: c.1714 Born; 26.2.1763 Died.

Family:

Service: 10.2.1726/27 Able *Portland* (50); 27.11.1727 Ord. *Torbay* (80); 19.4.1728 Vol-p-O *Poole* (32); 14.12.1729 Vol-p-O *Kinsale* (40); 5.12.1731 Mid *Kinsale* (40); 6.7.1732 Mid *Royal Oak* (70); 5.5.1733 Mid *Romney* (50); 6.5.1734 Passed; **Lieutenant**; 5.5.1735-3.3.1735/36 4L

Princess Caroline (80); 6.3.1735/36[(29.4.1737)]-4.5.1737[P] 4L *Captain* (70); 16.5.1738-27.11.1738 3L *Sunderland* (60); 21.6.1739-24.6.1739 2L *Sunderland* (60); 25.6.1739 2L *Oxford* (50); 30.11.1740[(8.12.1742)]-12.11.1742[P] 2L *Lancaster* (80); 29.12.1742 1L *Severn* (50); 2.5.1743 2L *Boyne* (80); 3.5.1743 1L *Chichester* (80); 11.2.1743/44-12.2.1743/44 Battle of Toulon; 1.8.1744[(MED 3.10.1745)]-22.7.1745[P] 2L *Barfleur* (90); **Commander**; 2.11.1745 LCmdr *Pluto* (16) Sloop; **Captain**; 12.7.1746-14.1.1746/47 *Experiment* (24).

HULKE, BENJAMIN

Dates: 11.8.1708 Born Deal, Kent, Deal; 10.2.1757 Died.
Family: Son Thomas Manley, RN (1750-1787); Son Benjamin, RN (1754-1799).
Service: 1737-1742 HEIC Service; 29.6.1742 Mid *Ludlow Castle* (40); 21.5.1743 Mate *Ludlow Castle* (40); 5.7.1743-1.11.1744[P] Mate *Cruizer* (8) Sloop; 19.5.1746-6.4.1748 Mid *Norfolk* (80); 5.9.1755 Passed; **Lieutenant**; 16.11.1756-23.2.1757 3L *Dunkirk* (60).

HUME, JAMES

Dates: c.1717 Born; 7.4.1758 Died; 7.7.1759 Will Probate.
Family:
Service: 30.11.1732 Able *Shark* (8) Sloop; 28.11.1734 Mid *Squirrel* (20); 7.9.1735 Mid *Roebuck* (40); **Lieutenant**; 25.7.1740 3L *Pearl* (40); 17.11.1740 Passed; 21.2.1740/41 2L *Hastings* (44); 17.5.1742 1L *Hastings* (44); 13.7.1745 1L *Tilbury* (58); 20.9.1746-25.9.1746 Lorient Operations; 14.10.1747 2nd Battle of Cape Finisterre; 13.1.1747/48-7.6.1748[P] 3L *Barfleur* (90); 1.12.1748-17.11.1752[P] 1L *Cumberland* (66); 10.7.1755 1L *Stirling Castle* (64); **Commander**; 29.9.1757-7.4.1758[†] *Pluto* (8) Fireship.

HUME, JOHN

Dates: 16.11.1759 Died.
Family:
Service: 27.5.1721 Able *Chichester* (80); 15.2.1721/22 MidO *Ipswich* (70); 29.3.1722 MidO *Leopard* (50); 16.6.1723 MidO *Hawk* (8) Sloop; 24.5.1725 QGnr *Kinsale* (40); 19.7.1727 Passed; **Lieutenant**; 7.2.1731/32-28.8.1735[P] L. *Winchelsea* (20); 12.1.1735/36 L. *Lowestoffe* (20); **Commander**; 12.3.1741/42-14.9.1742 *Mortar* (8) Bomb Vessel; **Captain**; 20.7.1745-18.4.1747[P] *Sandwich* (90).

HUMPHRIS, THOMAS

Dates: 1.1.1761 Died Pondicherry; 8.12.1761 Will Probate.
Family:
Service: **Lieutenant**; 20.1.1746/47[(MED 25.11.1748)] 3L *Royal Oak* (70); 4.7.1747[(MED 25.11.1748)]-31.10.1748[P] L. *Carcass* (6) Sloop; 30.9.1755 3L *Newcastle* (50); 30.6.1756 2L *Newcastle* (50); 20.1.1757 1L *Newcastle* (50); 29.4.1758 Battle of Cuddalore; 3.8.1758 Battle of Negapatam; 10.9.1759 Battle of Pondicherry; 28.6.1760[(EI 1.2.1763)]-1.1.1761[†] 4L *Sunderland* (60).

HUNT, ANTHONY

Dates: c.1734 Born; 1796 Died; 26.1.1796 Will Probate.
Family:
Service: 7.1.1743/44 Capt Serv *Argyll* (50); 1.11.1746 Capt Serv *Bristol* (50); 8.12.1746 Capt Serv *Grand Turk* (22); 19.12.1747-1.7.1748[P] Able *Ranger* (28); 29.5.1751 Able *Greyhound* (20); 4.12.1751 Mate *Greyhound* (20); 8.8.1754 Able *Amazon* (22); 10.3.1755 Passed; **Lieutenant**; 2.4.1757-28.7.1757 L. *Pluto* (8) Fireship; 15.2.1758 3L *Gosport* (44); 14.4.1758-29.1.1759 3L

Rochester (50); 5.6.1758-12.6.1758 Raid on Saint-Malo; 4.10.1759-16.12.1760[P] 4L *Barfleur* (80); 6.9.1762-10.11.1762[P] 6L *Saint George* Prison Ship; 20.12.1763-5.1.1767 1L *Edgar* (60); 24.3.1767 1L *Fame* (74); **Commander**; 16.10.1767-29.6.1770[P] *Tamar* (16) Sloop; 1769-1770 Gov. of Falkland Islands; **Captain**; 10.1.1771-6.1771[P] *Ludlow Castle* (24); 25.10.1775-5.7.1776 *Sphinx* (20); 10.3.1779-8.4.1780 *Portland* (50); 31.12.1779 Affair of Fielding and Bylandt; 19.4.1780-25.11.1782 *Diligent* (70).

HUNT, EDMUND

Dates: c.1705 Born; c.1764 Died; 12.5.1764 Will Probate.
Family:
Service: 10.9.1731 Able *Exeter* (60); 21.4.1732 Able *Scarborough* (20); 18.12.1733-22.11.1736[P] Mid *Scarborough* (20); 28.8.1740 Mid *Scarborough* (20); 30.3.1741 NR *Elizabeth* (70); 6.10.1741 Passed; **Lieutenant**; 16.3.1741/42-14.4.1742[P] 6L *Royal Sovereign* (104); 3.12.1742-6.12.1743 3L *Anglesea* (44); 3.2.1743/44 6L *Sandwich* (90); 12.1.1744/45 5L *Sandwich* (90); 12.2.1744/45 3L *Sandwich* (90); 9.5.1745 4L *Sandwich* (90); 14.2.1746/47-18.4.1747[P] 3L *Sandwich* (90).

HUNT, JOSEPH

Dates: c.1733 Born; 8.1.1761 Died.
Family:
Service: 30.6.1741-1.11.1742[P] Capt Serv *Roebuck* (40); 23.8.1743 Capt Serv *Anglesea* (44); 17.1.1745 Capt Serv *Sunderland* (60); 12.1.1746 Able *Panther* (50); 5.1.1748 Mid *Panther* (50); 28.1.1748 Able *Lion* (58); 6.6.1748-11.9.1751[W] Mid *Fox* (20); 12.12.1752 Mid *Saint Albans* (60); 14.8.1753-11.2.1754 Mate *Saint Albans* (60); 1.5.1754 Passed; **Lieutenant**; 2.6.1756 5L *Monarch* (74); 4.4.1757-23.1.1759 3L *Dublin* (74); 5.9.1757-6.10.1757 Raid on Rochefort; **Commander**; 18.6.1759-15.1.1761 *Mortar* (8) Bomb Vessel; 3.7.1759 Bombardment of Le Havre; 1761 **Captain**.

HUNTER, CHARLES

Dates: c.1739 Born; 1803 Died.
Family:
Service: 19.7.1756 Capt Serv *Devonshire* (70); 18.6.1757 Able *Cambridge* (80); 10.1.1758 Mid *Cambridge* (80); 16.1.1759-19.1.1759 Attack on Martinique; 20.1.1759-1.5.1759 Capture of Guadeloupe; 2.2.1760 Able *Bedford* (64); 3.3.1760 Mid *Bedford* (64); 29.4.1760 Mid *Rochester* (50); 1.6.1760 Mid *Swiftsure* (68); 3.9.1760 Passed; **Lieutenant**; 6.7.1761 2L *Brune* (32); 4.1.1763[(MED 10.3.1763)]-28.2.1763[P] L. *Firedrake* (8) Bomb Vessel.

HUNTER, WILLIAM

Dates: c.1730 Born; 17.2.1810 Died.
Family:
Service: 1.8.1755 Able *Bedford* (64); 8.8.1755 Mid *Bedford* (64); 8.1757-10.1757 Louisbourg Expedition; 15.4.1758 Mate *Bedford* (64); 6.6.1758-27.7.1758 The Siege of Louisbourg; 8.2.1759 Mid *Princess Amelia* (80); 12.12.1759 Passed; **Lieutenant**; 24.1.1760 3L *Sutherland* (50); 4.3.1760-24.2.1763[P] 2L *Sutherland* (50); 3.6.1761-7.6.1761 Occupation of Dominica; 7.1.1762-10.2.1762 Operations against Martinique; 6.6.1762-13.8.1762 Operations against Havana; 18.10.1763 3L *Ramillies* (74); 2.4.1764 2L *Tweed* (32); 1.4.1765 2L *Aquilon* (28); 18.1.1766 2L *Launceston* (44); 6.5.1766 3L *Launceston* (44); 3.11.1766 2L *Launceston* (44); 7.4.1767 3L *Launceston* (44); 26.5.1768-6.11.1769[P] 2L *Launceston* (44); 16.11.1770-20.5.1771[P] 2L *Conquestador* (60); 23.7.1771 2L *Lizard* (28); 9.1.1773[(NA 17.1.1778)]-23.11.1775[C] LCmdr *Gaspe*

(6) Sloop; 7.1.1778-16.10.1779 2L *Cumberland* (74); 27.7.1778 1st Battle of Ushant; 1787-1810 Lieutenant of Greenwich Hospital.

HURT, CHRISTOPHER JARVIS

Dates: bef.1763 Died.
Family: Wife Mary Hooper married 1749.
Service: **Lieutenant**; 14.11.1745(MED 29.11.1746)-30.4.1747 2L *Royal Oak* (70); 13.6.1747-24.1.1748/49 2L *Deptford* (60).

HUTCHENSON, THOMAS HOWARD

Dates: c.1714 Born; 1758 Died; 12.5.1760 Will Probate.
Family:
Service: 5.6.1732 Vol-p-O *Nassau* (70); 27.12.1732 Able *Kingston* (60); 30.10.1733 Able *Hector* (40); 9.6.1735 Mid *Hector* (44); 23.2.1736 MidO *Centurion* (60); 9.7.1736 Mate *Montagu* (60); 5.11.1736 Mid *Berwick* (70); 2.11.1737 Able *Plymouth* (60); 5.5.1738 Mid *Plymouth* (60); 14.8.1739-6.3.1740 Mid *Berwick* (70); 6.3.1739/40 Passed; **Lieutenant**; 27.9.1740 3L *Argyll* (50); 18.9.1742-24.6.1743 2L *Argyll* (50); 1.3.1742/43 2L *Stirling Castle* (70); 11.2.1743/44-12.2.1743/44 Battle of Toulon; 25.3.1745(MED 5.2.1745/46)-4.4.1745 6L *Neptune* (90); 29.5.1745(MED 5.2.1745/46)-12.1745[P] *Nazareth* (8) Fireship; **Captain**; 23.11.1747-18.8.1748[P] *Rose* (24) Ship; 6.4.1751 *Torrington* (44); 27.1.1757-25.3.1758[†] *Newcastle* (50).

HUTCHINGS, EDWARD

Dates: 1760 Died.
Family:
Service: **Lieutenant**; 9.12.1747(MED 8.11.1748)-7.11.1748[P] L. *Conqueror* (8) Fireship; 30.9.1755-26.11.1755 2L *Ipswich* (64); 26.11.1755-1.3.1757[P] 3L *Ipswich* (64); 4.5.1757 4L *Saint George* (90); 1.6.1757(24.3.1760) 4L *Culloden* (74); 27.10.1757(24.3.1760)-1.4.1758 3L *Hampton Court* (64); 28.2.1758 Battle of Cartagena; 1.4.1758(22.7.1760) 2L *Monmouth* (70); 20.6.1758(22.7.1760) 1L *Monmouth* (70); 27.11.1759-4.3.1760 1L *Saint George* (90).

HYDE, BOYLE

Dates: c.1716 Born; 1776 Died.
Family:
Service: 19.4.1733 Capt Serv *Lyme* (20); 27.5.1733 Able *Lyme* (20); 6.9.1735-1.2.1735/36[P] Able *Canterbury* (60); 16.3.1737/38 Able *Canterbury* (60); 3.11.1739-28.4.1740[P] Mid *Canterbury* (60); 1.5.1741 Mid *Orford* (70); 1.2.1742/43 Passed; **Lieutenant**; 19.7.1745 L. *Raven* (10) Sloop; 8.12.1747-1.12.1748 1L *Intrepid* (64); 6.4.1751-26.4.1755 L. *Swan* (14) Sloop; 16.11.1756 2L *Vanguard* (68); 19.8.1757 3L *Barfleur* (80); 5.9.1757-6.10.1757 Raid on Rochefort; 5.6.1758-12.6.1758 Raid on Saint-Malo; 27.10.1758-9.1.1759[P] 2L *Barfleur* (80).

HYDE, FREDERICK

Dates: 21.5.1763 Died.
Family:
Service: **Commander**; 3.2.1743/44(19.6.1746) 6L *Marlborough* (90); 11.2.1743/44-12.2.1743/44 Battle of Toulon; 7.3.1744/45(25.6.1745)-15.3.1744/45[P] L. *Sutherland* (54); **Commander**; 5.3.1745/46 *Hawk* (8) Sloop; **Captain**; 11.11.1746-1.9.1748[P] *Gibraltar* (20).

Service Records I

I'ANSON, HENRY
Dates: 25.10.1734 Born Kent; 29.10.1767 Died; 6.2.1768 Will Probate.
Family: Father Sir Thomas Bankes I'Anson, 4th baronet of Bassetbury (c.1701–1764); Mother Mary Bankes (1693-1774); Wife Margaret Bazely (1737-1824) married 2.6.1764; Brother Rev. Sir Thomas Bankes I'Anson, 5th Baronet of Bassetbury (d.1799).
Service: 10.2.1748/49 YoS *Port Mahon* (24); 14.9.1749 Clerk *Port Mahon* (24); 5.2.1749/50 Able *Kent* (64); 19.3.1749/50 Able *Mermaid* (24); 12.6.1751 Mid *Mermaid* (24); 24.6.1753 Able *Mermaid* (24); 1.10.1753 Able *Cruizer* (8) Sloop; 19.2.1755 Mid *Torbay* (74); 14.3.1755 Passed; **Lieutenant**; 5.5.1755[NA 11.12.1755]-9.12.1755 3L *Anson* (60); 20.12.1756 2L *Achilles* (60); 17.1.1757-1.4.1757 2L *Achilles* (60); 7.3.1760-7.4.1760 1L *Achilles* (60); 28.11.1760 1L *Achilles* (60); 29.3.1761-11.6.1761 Expedition against Belle-Isle; 6.9.1762-25.12.1762[P] 1L *Hero* (74); 16.4.1763-15.6.1766 LCmdr *Mecklenburgh* (6) Cutter; **Commander**; 9.9.1767-16.10.1767 *Tamar* (16) Sloop.

IGGULDEN, EDWARD
Dates: 1742 Born; 27.12.1742 Baptised Deal; 24.9.1819 Died Deal.
Family: Father John Iggulden; Mother Elizabeth Warman; Sister Sarah.
Service: **Lieutenant**; 7.6.1761[EI 19.6.1765] 4L *Falmouth* (50); 26.1.1762[EI 19.6.1765] 3L *Falmouth* (50); 24.9.1762-6.10.1762 Battle of Manilla; 8.11.1762[EI 19.6.1765]-16.1.1765[P] 2L *Falmouth* (50); 26.10.1768 3L *Phoenix* (44); 8.11.1769-7.11.1770[P] 2L *Phoenix* (44); 10.1.1771-19.2.1773[P] 1L *Flora* (32); 20.1.1774 2L *Boyne* (68); 4.11.1776 4L *Queen* (90); 27.3.1778-20.4.1778 3L *Queen* (90); 23.7.1778 1L *Royal George* (100); 19.11.1778 1L *Queen* (90); 2.12.1779-5.4.1780 6L *Royal George* (100); 16.1.1780 Battle of Cape St. Vincent; **Commander**; 5.12.1780[BLI 22.12.1781]-5.12.1781[P] *Aetna* (8) Bomb Vessel; **Captain**; 18.1.1783-20.1.1783 *Buffalo* (50); 23.4.1804 **Superannuated Captain.**

INGLIS, CHARLES
Dates: c.1731 Born; 10.10.1791 Died.
Family: Father Sir John Inglis (1683-1771); Mother Anne Cockburn (d.1772); Illegitimate Son Charles, RN (d.1833); Brother Adam, 3rd Bt. (1714–1772); Brother John, 4th Bt. (c.1716–1799); Brother Patrick.
Service: 14.3.1744/45 Capt Serv *Ludlow Castle* (44); 3.12.1745 Able *Eagle* (60); 8.4.1747-14.8.1748[P] Mid *Eagle* (60); 14.10.1747 2nd Battle of Cape Finisterre; 17.12.1749 Mid *Albany* (14) Sloop; 22.8.1751 Mate *Albany* (14) Sloop; 24.3.1753-10.12.1753[P] Act3L *Albany* (14) Sloop; 5.2.1755 Passed; **Lieutenant**; 6.2.1755 5L *Monarch* (74); 16.4.1756 5L *Magnanime* (74); 26.8.1756 4L *Magnanime* (74); 8.4.1757 3L *Magnanime* (74); 3.6.1757 3L *Royal William* (84); **Commander**; 17.6.1757 *Escort* (14) Sloop; 12.6.1759 *Carcass* (14) Bomb Vessel; 3.7.1759 Bombardment of Le Havre; **Captain**; 15.12.1761-26.8.1763[P] *Newark* (80); 11.10.1770-17.12.1773[P] *Lizard* (28); 7.8.1778-4.9.1780[P] *Salisbury* (50); 20.6.1780 Action off Monti Christi;

11.10.1780-28.7.1783[P] *Saint Albans* (64); 25.1.1782-26.1.1782 Battle of Saint Kitts; 12.4.1782 Battle of the Saintes; 21.9.1790 **Rear Admiral of the Blue.**

INGLIS, JOHN

Dates: c.1733 Born; 1790 Died; 12.6.1790 Will Probate.
Family: Wife Anne Spens.
Service: 15.1.1745/46-24.1.1746/47[P] Able *Happy Jennet* (20) Hired Ship; 25.3.1753 Capt Serv *Nightingale* (22); 7.9.1754 Able *Nightingale* (22); 14.3.1754/55 Mate *Adventure* (44); 12.6.1756-4.4.1757 Mid *Devonshire* (70); 4.4.1757 Passed; **Lieutenant**; 7.8.1761-5.11.1762 3L *Deptford* (50); 6.6.1762-13.8.1762 Operations against Havana; 15.11.1762[(JAM 10.6.1763)]-3.6.1763[P] 4L *Saint Ann* (64); 15.7.1768-7.12.1772[P] LCmdr *Sultana* Schooner; 26.9.1770-29.11.1771 1L *Cerberus* (28); **Commander**; 11.4.1778-14.8.1778[C] *Senegal* (14) Sloop; 22.5.1779 *Delight* (14) Sloop; **Captain**; 28.3.1781-28.9.1783[P] *Pandora* (24).

INGLIS, JOHN

Dates: c.1741 Born Philadelphia; 11.3.1807 Died Edinburgh.
Family: Father John Inglis; Mother Catherine McCall; Wife Barbara Inglis; Daughter Jane [Crawford]; Son George, RN (1787-1849); Son Archibald.
Service: 1755-1758 HEIC Service; 2.5.1758 Able *Garland* (24); 3.8.1758 Able *Hussar* (28); 4.1.1759 Able *Eagle* (60); 7.4.1759 Mid *Eagle* (60); 6.5.1761 Passed; **Lieutenant**; 22.10.1761-5.3.1762 4L *Chichester* (68); 29.4.1777 4L *Trident* (64); 6.6.1778 LCmdr *Griffin* (10) Cutter; **Commander**; 1.6.1779-2.4.1781 *Zephyr* (14) Sloop; **Captain**; 23.8.1781-17.7.1782[P] *Squirrel* (20); 16.6.1795-12.6.1796[P] *Coromandel* (54); 20.5.1796-30.6.1797 *Belliqueux* (64); 1.10.1798-10.3.1799 *Belliqueux* (64); 1.1.1801 **Rear Admiral of the Blue**; 23.4.1804 **Rear Admiral of the White**; 9.11.1805 **Vice Admiral of the Blue.**

INNES, ALEXANDER

Dates: c.1713 Born; 21.1.1786 Died.
Family: Wife Susannah; Daughter Susannah; Daughter Margaret.
Service: 17.1.1732/33 Able *Dreadnought* (60); 14.2.1732/33 YoS *Dreadnought* (60); 12.4.1733 Able *Dreadnought* (60); 15.4.1733 Able *Terrible* (6) Bomb Vessel; 4.9.1733 Carp *Terrible* (6) Bomb Vessel; 16.11.1734 Mid *Kinsale* (40); 23.11.1738 Mid *Kinsale* (40); 30.1.1738/39 Passed; **Lieutenant**; 26.7.1739[(11.9.1739)] 4L *Lennox* (70); 14.9.1739 3L *Lennox* (70); 4.1.1739/40 2L *Lennox* (70); 8.4.1740 Capture of the Princesa; 8.7.1740 2L *Severn* (50); 11.5.1742 1L *Severn* (50); 13.8.1742-12.5.1744 2L *Orford* (70); 22.3.1745/46 1L *Elizabeth* (70); 23.4.1747 2L *Saint George* (90); 6.8.1747 1L *Saint George* (90); 1.4.1748 5L *Invincible* (74); 9.1.1751/52 1L *Severn* (50); **Commander**; 14.11.1752-17.7.1753[P] *Ferret* (14) Sloop; 16.1.1755 *Dispatch* (14) Sloop; 18.2.1755 *Otter* (14) Sloop; **Captain**; 25.6.1756 *Monmouth* (70); 8.11.1756 *Mermaid* (24); 7.4.1758 *Enterprise* (44); 13.1.1762-19.9.1763[P] *Hampton Court* (64); 6.6.1762-13.8.1762 Operations against Havana; 19.11.1778-3.10.1780 *Queen* (90); 26.9.1780 **Rear Admiral of the White**; 12.2.1784-21.1.1786 *Europa* (50); 26.8.1784-1786 CinC — Jamaica.

INNES, JAMES

Dates: c.1726 Born; 1779 Died.
Family: Father James Innes, Bt. (d.1723); Brother Robert (d.1757); Brother Charles, bt.; Brother Walter; Brother William.
Service: 24.2.1739/40 Able *Weymouth* (60); 7.1.1740/41 Action of January 7 1741; 4.3.1740/41-5.1741 Operations against Cartagena; 16.6.1742 Able *Norfolk* (80); 5.8.1743 Mid *Marlborough*

(90); 11.2.1743/44-12.2.1743/44 Battle of Toulon; 14.12.1744 Able *Somerset* (80); 3.2.1744/45 Mid *Pembroke* (60); 19.8.1745 Mid *Dorsetshire* (80); 24.1.1745/46 Passed; **Lieutenant**; 26.1.1745/46[(NA 26.12.1746)] 3L *Pembroke* (60).14.4.1746[(NA 26.12.1746)] 2L *Pembroke* (60); 25.7.1746[(NA 26.12.1746)]-26.2.1746/47[P] 3L *Kingston* (60); 1.9.1747 4L *Edinburgh* (64); 14.10.1747 2nd Battle of Cape Finisterre; 23.12.1747-9.8.1748[P] 3L *Edinburgh* (64); 6.2.1755 2L *Ipswich* (64); 30.9.1755-1.3.1757[P] 1L *Ipswich* (64); 20.5.1757-23.8.1759 1L *Buckingham* (68); 16.1.1759-19.1.1759 Attack on Martinique; 20.1.1759-1.5.1759 Capture of Guadeloupe; 24.5.1759-15.7.1760 *Antigua* (14) Sloop; **Captain**; 6.8.1761-9.2.1763[P] *Rye* (20).

IRVINE, ALEXANDER

Dates: c.1716 Born; 1795 Died.
Family:
Service: 2.5.1737 Able *Terrible* (6) Bomb Vessel; 4.1.1739/40 Gnr Mate *Scipio* (8) Fireship; 22.7.1741 Mate *Sapphire* (44); 4.5.1742 Mid *Sapphire* (44); 27.5.1742 Mid *Sapphire* (44); 6.3.1743/44 Mate *Cornwall* (80); 20.6.1744 Passed; **Lieutenant**; 21.6.1744 4L *Princess Amelia* (80); 15.11.1744-17.4.1745 4L *Hampton Court* (64); 8.1.1744/45 Action of 1745-01-08; 31.5.1745 3L *Hampton Court* (64); 10.1.1753 2L *Fougueux* (64); 6.2.1755 2L *Monarch* (74); 7.1.1756 1L *Monarch* (74); 16.4.1756 1L *Magnanime* (74); **Commander**; 23.8.1756-15.10.1756 *Charlotte* (8) Yacht; 17.1.1757-26.1.1757 *Otter* (14) Sloop; **Captain**; 10.1.1771 *Weymouth* (60).

IRWIN, JOHN

Dates: c.1724 Born; 19.2.1765 Will Probate; bef.19.2.1765 Died.
Family: Wife Jane Donald married 21.8.1756.
Service: 20.11.1751 Mid *Princess Louisa* (60); 5.7.1752 Able *Amazon* (22); 11.12.1754 Mate *Amazon* (22); 12.1.1756 Able *Rye* (20); 1.2.1757 Mate *Rye* (20); 20.2.1757 Mid *Colchester* (50); 29.4.1757 Mate *Ramillies* (90); 5.9.1757-6.10.1757 Raid on Rochefort; 25.12.1757-23.5.1759[P] Master *Experiment* (24); 29.12.1758 Capture of Goree; 5.8.1761 Passed; **Lieutenant**; 24.9.1761-20.12.1762[P] L. *Druid* (10) Sloop.

Service Records J

JACKSON, HENRY
Dates: 1794 Died Hampshire; 29.4.1794 Will Probate.
Family: Wife Elizabeth; Son Henry.
Service: **Lieutenant**; 28.12.1758(JAM 29.4.1760) L. *Thetis* (32); 25.10.1761(17.2.1762) 3L *Prince Edward* (44); 26.1.1762-27.1.1763[P] 2L *Prince Edward* (44); 30.11.1770 2L *Orford* (68); 19.1.1771-28.8.1771 2L *Triumph* (74); 5.11.1776 2L *Saint Albans* (64); 29.5.1779-25.6.1779 1L *Formidable* (98).

JACKSON, JOHN
Dates: c.1726 Born; 1778 Died; 6.4.1778 Will Probate.
Family: Wife Margaret Evans married 1.5.1767.
Service: 24.9.1743 Capt Serv *Rose* (20) Ship; 10.5.1747 Able *Defiance* (60); 14.10.1747 2nd Battle of Cape Finisterre; 21.8.1748 Mid *Defiance* (60); 13.6.1749 Mid *Somerset* (68); 2.7.1751 Able *Somerset* (68); 19.10.1752 Mate *Falcon* (10) Bomb Vessel; 20.2.1753 Able *Falcon* (10) Bomb Vessel; 22.8.1753 Mid *Falcon* (10) Bomb Vessel; 25.8.1753 Mate *Falcon* (10) Bomb Vessel; 27.4.1755 Able *Jason* (44); 30.4.1755 Mid *Jason* (44); 22.7.1755 Mid *Saint George* (90); 20.10.1755 Mate *Saint George* (90); 8.1.1756 Passed; **Lieutenant**; 26.7.1756(ECH 26.6.1758) L. *Polacca* (12) Sloop; 29.11.1756(ECH 26.6.1758)-19.6.1758[P] L. *Siren* (20); 15.7.1758 3L *Dover* (44); 19.7.1758 2L *Dover* (44); 24.1.1759 1L *Argo* (28); 11.1.1760-23.8.1765[P] 2L *Medway* (60); **Commander**; 22.1.1767 *Fortune* (14) Sloop; 3.12.1767 *Druid* (10) Sloop; **Captain**; 29.10.1770-17.11.1770 *Seaford* (20); 10.7.1777-1.2.1778 *Ariel* (20).

JACKSON, JOSEPH
Dates:
Family:
Service: **Lieutenant**; 24.9.1757(EI 18.10.1759)-28.4.1758[B] 1L *Triton* (20); 2.9.1760 2L *Essex* (64); 26.1.1761-14.9.1762 1L *Essex* (64); 29.3.1761-11.6.1761 Expedition against Belle-Isle; 26.5.1797 **Superannuated Commander**.

JACKSON, MICHAEL
Dates: c.1739 Born; 1794 Died.
Family:
Service: 1753-1758 Merchant Service; 21.9.1757 Mid *Rose* (20); 5.6.1758-12.6.1758 Raid on Saint-Malo; 30.12.1758 Mate *Rose* (20); 17.12.1759 Mate *Firm* (70); 3.12.1760-27.12.1760[P] Supnum *Saint George* (90); 6.5.1761 Passed; **Lieutenant**; 24.5.1762-26.3.1763[P] 2L *Boston* (32).

JACOBS, MAXIMILIAN

Dates: c.1731 Born; 1780 Died.
Family:
Service: 14.4.1751 Capt Serv *Hampton Court* (64); 20.11.1752 Passed; **Lieutenant**; 22.11.1752-7.12.1752[P] L. *Nightingale* (22); 10.1.1753 L. *Unicorn* (24); 30.7.1753 Able *Hampton Court* (64); 26.10.1753 Mid *Hampton Court* (64); 18.6.1754 Able *Centurion* (50); 29.8.1754-16.10.1755 3L *Gosport* (44); 20.12.1754 Mid *Centurion* (50); 29.10.1755 2L *Gosport* (44); 3.5.1756 6L *Magnanime* (74); 26.8.1756 5L *Magnanime* (74); 21.12.1756-28.1.1758 Able *Centurion* (50); 8.4.1757-8.6.1757 4L *Magnanime* (74); **Commander**; 13.6.1757 *Escort* (14) Sloop; 16.6.1757 *Alderney* (10) Sloop; **Captain**; 4.1.1758 *Kennington* (20); 6.6.1758-27.7.1758 The Siege of Louisbourg; 4.6.1759-11.12.1759 *Actaeon* (28); 1.3.1768-30.7.1772 *Deal Castle* (20); 7.2.1776 *Amazon* (32); 20.3.1779-15.2.1780[W] *Defiance* (64); 19.5.1780 Dismissed.

JACOBS, WILLIAM

Dates: c.1708 Born; 1758 Died.
Family:
Service: 4.12.1734 Mate *Britannia* (100); 5.4.1735 Mid *Argyll* (50); 12.5.1735 Mid *Hound* (8) Sloop; 17.7.1739 Mid *Portland* (50); 16.9.1739 Mate *Argyll* (50); 20.1.1740/41 Passed; **Lieutenant**; 13.4.1741-22.1.1747/48 L. *Seaford* (20) Ship; 1.2.1747/48[(9.12.1748)]-18.11.1748[P] 1L *Royal Oak* (70); 26.3.1754-14.2.1756 L. *Success* (20); 22.5.1755-14.6.1755 British attack on Fort Beauséjour.

JAGO, RICHARD

Dates: c.1725 Born; 1808 Died; 19.10.1808 Will Probate.
Family: Wife Elizabeth.
Service: 12.10.1742 Capt Serv *Seaford* (20) Ship; 21.7.1743 Ord. *Seaford* (20) Ship; 15.10.1743 Able *Seaford* (20) Ship; 30.11.1746-14.1.1749[P] Mid *Seaford* (20) Ship; 13.9.1752 Able *Dispatch* (14) Sloop; 5.11.1752 Mid *Dispatch* (14) Sloop; 13.2.1753-21.5.1753[P] Mid *Dispatch* (14) Sloop; 12.10.1754 Able *Ranger* (8) Sloop; 30.7.1755 Mate *Ranger* (8) Sloop; 13.12.1758 Passed; **Lieutenant**; 6.11.1762-2.5.1763[P] 4L *Africa* (64).

JAMES, JOHN

Dates: 1790 Died.
Family:
Service: **Lieutenant**; 12.5.1758[(NA 17.7.1760)] 3L *Sutherland* (50); 7.6.1763-3.2.1767 1L *Coventry* (28); 25.8.1769 2L *Tweed* (32); 29.1.1770 1L *Tweed* (32); 10.8.1771-1.5.1775 1L *Levant* (28).

JARDEN, JOHN

Dates: 1775 Died.
Family:
Service: **Lieutenant**; 6.4.1757 2L *Prince of Orange* (60); 17.1.1758-10.3.1763[P] 1L *Prince of Orange* (60); 6.6.1758-27.7.1758 The Siege of Louisbourg; 29.3.1761-11.6.1761 Expedition against Belle-Isle; 7.12.1770 3L *Barfleur* (90); 25.6.1773-7.12.1773 2L *Barfleur* (90).

JARDINE, GEORGE
Dates: c.1729 Born; 1801 Died; 28.7.1801 Will Probate.
Family:
Service: 1748-1751 Merchant Service; 11.6.1751 Capt Serv *Augusta* (60); 7.6.1752 Ord. *Augusta* (60); 24.4.1754 Mid *Augusta* (60); 29.10.1755 Mid *Newark* (80); 11.1.1756 Mate *Newark* (80); 5.5.1756 Passed; **Lieutenant**; 6.4.1757-5.1.1760 L. *Tartar's Prize* (24); 10.1796-11.1796 LCmdr *Wolf* (4) Gun-brig; 29.6.1799 **Commander**; 20.8.1799-6.8.1801 *Woolwich* (24) Storeship.

JARVIS, DANIEL
Dates: c.1719 Born; 1779 Died; 19.1.1779 Will Probate.
Family:
Service: 13.8.1735 Capt Serv *Windsor* (60); 20.11.1736 Ord. *Windsor* (60); 23.9.1738 Able *Newcastle* (50); 12.11.1739 Mid *Lion* (60); 26.12.1740 Able *Boyne* (80); 12.2.1740/41 Able *Elizabeth* (70); 1.4.1741 Mid *Sandwich* (90); 23.7.1741 Mid *Duke* (90); 3.8.1742 Passed; 6.10.1743 L. *Serpent* (10) Bomb Vessel; 7.10.1743 **Lieutenant**; 23.4.1744 L. *Squirrel* (20); 4.9.1745 1L *Hastings* (44); 20.9.1746-25.9.1746 Lorient Operations; 30.10.1746-21.6.1748[P] 2L *Royal George* (100).

JARVIS, JOHN
Dates: c.1735 Born; 25.8.1789 Died.
Family:
Service: 1752-1753 Merchant Service; 26.6.1753 Capt Serv *Hastings* (44); 22.1.1754 Capt Serv *Royal George* (100); 10.12.1754 Able *Royal George* (100); 26.6.1755 Mid *Rochester* (50); 5.6.1758-12.6.1758 Raid on Saint-Malo; 11.11.1758 Passed; **Lieutenant**; 3.9.1759-19.9.1759 2L *Milford* (28); 30.11.1761 2L *Essex* (64); 14.9.1762-27.1.1763[P] 1L *Essex* (64); 27.10.1770 1L *Prudent* (64); 10.8.1771 2L *Prudent* (64); 11.9.1771 3L *Prudent* (64); 25.2.1772-26.5.1775[P] 2L *Prudent* (64).

JASPER, RICHARD
Dates: 11.4.1761 Died.
Family:
Service: **Lieutenant**; 9.3.1738/39 3L *Chester* (54); 4.3.1739/40 2L *Chester* (54); 30.9.1740-10.6.1741 3L *Prince Frederick* (70); 7.1.1740/41 Action of January 7 1741; 4.3.1740/41-5.1741 Operations against Cartagena; 6.7.1742[(10.8.1743)] 3L *Strafford* (60); 3.1.1743/44[(MED 15.2.1745/46)] 6L *Namur* (90); 13.1.1743/44[(MED 15.2.1745/46)] 5L *Namur* (90); 11.2.1743/44-12.2.1743/44 Battle of Toulon; 6.3.1743/44[(MED 13.2.1745/46)]-19.8.1744 2L *Namur* (90); **Commander**; 1.8.1744 *Sutherland* (54); **Captain**; 13.2.1744/45[(MED 13.2.1745/46)] *Princess Caroline* (80); 2.4.1745[(MED 13.2.1745/46)] *Shark* (8) Sloop; 1.5.1745[(MED 13.2.1745/46)]-5.7.1745 *Phoenix* (24); 20.3.1746/47-19.9.1752[P] *Prince Henry* (44); 1753 Dismissed.

JEFFERSON, DAVID
Dates: c.1730 Born; 18.8.1789 Died.
Family:
Service: bef.1754-1756 Merchant Service; 13.9.1756-19.4.1757[C] Master *Merlin* (10) Sloop; 2.8.1757 Master *Hussar* (28); 16.1.1759 Master *Aeolus* (32); 20.11.1759 Battle of Quiberon Bay; 28.2.1760 Action of February 28 1760; 2.4.1760 Passed; **Lieutenant**; 25.4.1760 2L *Aeolus* (32); 9.8.1762-18.11.1763[P] 1L *Aeolus* (32); 14.1.1771-22.1.1774 1L *Marlborough* (74).

JEFFERYS, ROBERT

Dates: c.1709 Born; 1780 Died.

Family:

Service: 20.11.1726 MidO *Superb* (64); 21.10.1727 Mid *Superb* (64); 27.11.1727-30.8.1728[P] MidO *Rippon* (60); 16.10.1730 Able *Dreadnought* (60); 3.2.1730/31 Able *Looe* (42); 17.5.1731 Mid *Looe* (42); 2.7.1732 Mid *Tiger* (50); 14.9.1733 Passed; **Lieutenant**; 13.3.1733/34-7.8.1735 4L *Norfolk* (80); 28.7.1738-3.12.1738[P] 2L *Norfolk* (80); 14.6.1739 3L *Deptford* (60); 30.8.1739-3.3.1739/40 2L *York* (60); 28.7.1743[(3.7.1744)] 1L *Ludlow Castle* (40); **Commander**; 18.7.1744 *Jamaica* (10) Sloop; **Captain**; 1.5.1745-7.11.1748[P] *Scarborough* (20); 5.11.1770 **Superannuated Rear Admiral**.

JEKYLL, EDWARD

Dates: 19.6.1776 Died.

Family:

Service: **Lieutenant**; 30.10.1742[(MED 31.12.1745)] 4L *Essex* (70); 2.4.1743[(MED 31.12.1745)] 3L *Essex* (70); 4.6.1743[(MED 31.12.1745)] 2L *Essex* (70); 11.2.1743/44-12.2.1743/44 Battle of Toulon; **Commander**; 21.4.1746 *Fortune* (10) Sloop; **Captain**; 5.3.1747/48-23.12.1748[P] *Lion* (58); 23.7.1754 *Happy* (8) Sloop; 12.5.1756-3.3.1758 *Flamborough* (20); 7.3.1758-13.3.1763[P] *Rippon* (60); 16.1.1759-19.1.1759 Attack on Martinique; 20.1.1759-1.5.1759 Capture of Guadeloupe; 29.3.1761-11.6.1761 Expedition against Belle-Isle; 6.6.1762-13.8.1762 Operations against Havana; 3.1.1771-7.1.1774 *Egmont* (74).

JELFE, ANDREW

Dates: 14.3.1765 Died.

Family:

Service: **Lieutenant**; 25.8.1735[(23.5.1737)] 4L *Buckingham* (70); 30.5.1736[(23.5.1737)] 3L *Sunderland* (60); 5.10.1736[(23.5.1737)] 2L *Sunderland* (60); 26.3.1737[(23.5.1737)]-15.5.1738 1L *Sunderland* (60); 28.7.1738-25.11.1738 3L *Tiger* (50); 7.6.1739 4L *Lennox* (70); 5.7.1739 3L *Adventure* (40); 15.3.1739/40 3L *Gloucester* (50); 27.8.1740 2L *Gloucester* (50); 19.2.1740/41 6L *Victory* (100); 12.6.1741 5L *Victory* (100); 21.9.1741 3L *Victory* (100); 16.3.1741/42 2L *Victory* (100); 13.7.1742 1L *Victory* (100); **Commander**; 3.2.1743/44-24.12.1744[W] *Swallow* (10) Sloop; **Captain**; 12.4.1746 *Port Mahon* (20); 19.8.1747-12.11.1748[P] *Assurance* (44); 22.2.1757 ActCapt *Achilles* (60); 4.4.1757-9.12.1758 *Trident* (64).

JENKINS, WILLIAM

Dates: c.1740 Born; 1769 Died.

Family:

Service: 8.5.1756 Capt Serv *Nassau* (64); 8.1757-10.1757 Louisbourg Expedition; 17.3.1758 Mid *Nassau* (64); 29.12.1758 Capture of Goree; 28.10.1760 Mid *Superb* (74); 7.7.1762 Passed; **Lieutenant**; 6.8.1762-27.12.1762 5L *Thunderer* (74); 12.4.1763-28.8.1766[P] 2L *Maidstone* (28); 29.10.1767-13.9.1769 L. *Hound* (14) Sloop.

JERVIS, JOHN CB (1ST EARL ST. VINCENT)

Dates: 9.1.1734/35 Born; 29.5.1782 Order of the Bath; 23.6.1797 1st Earl St. Vincent; 1801 Viscount St Vincent; 2.1.1815 Order of the Bath; 14.3.1823 Died.

Family: Father Swynfen Jervis (1700–1771); Mother Elizabeth Parker (1700–1770); Wife Martha Parker married 5.6.1783.

Service: 6.1.1748/49 Able *Gloucester* (50); 30.6.1752 Able *Severn* (50); 9.8.1752 Mid *Severn* (50); 6.8.1754 Mid *Sphinx* (24); 15.11.1754 Supnum *Seaford* (20); 29.12.1754-5.2.1755 Able *Mary* (8) Yacht; 22.1.1755 Passed; **Lieutenant**; 19.2.1755 6L *Royal George* (100); 11.3.1755 3L *Nottingham* (60); 2.5.1755[(MED 11.12.1755)]-2.3.1756 2L *Nottingham* (60); 31.3.1756 3L *Devonshire* (66); 22.6.1756-12.3.1757 4L *Prince* (90); 15.1.1759 1L *Torbay* (74); **Commander**; 15.5.1759[(19.12.1759)]-11.2.1760 *Scorpion* (14) Sloop; 22.5.1760 *Albany* (14) Sloop; **Captain**; 13.10.1760-11.3.1763[P] *Gosport* (44); 21.2.1769-29.6.1772 *Alarm* (32); 8.5.1775-31.8.1775[P] *Kent* (74); 9.8.1775-5.8.1778 *Foudroyant* (80); 27.7.1778 1st Battle of Ushant; 22.7.1779 *Foudroyant* (80); 21.4.1782 Pégase vs Foudroyant; 20.10.1782 Battle of Cape Spartel; 26.12.1782-14.1.1783 Commodore *Salisbury* (50); 31.1.1783-5.4.1784 M.P. for Launceston; 3.4.1784-18.6.1790 M.P. for Great Yarmouth; **Rear Admiral of the Blue**; 24.9.1787-11.1787 *Carnatic* (74); 18.6.1790 First Captain; 19.6.1790-1.1794 M.P. for Chipping Wycombe; 6.8.1790-8.12.1790[P] *Prince* (98); 21.9.1790 **Rear Admiral of the White**; 1.2.1793 **Vice Admiral of the Blue**; 24.9.1793 CinC — Barbados & the Leeward Islands; 5.11.1793-1.5.1795 *Boyne* (98); 12.4.1794 **Vice Admiral of the White**; 1.6.1795 **Admiral of the Blue**; 2.10.1795-1799 CinC — The Mediterranean Sea; 3.12.1795-30.3.1797 *Victory* (100); 14.2.1797 2nd Battle of Cape St Vincent; 6.1797-6.1799[R] *Ville de Paris* (110); 14.2.1799 **Admiral of the White**; 1800-1803 CinC — English Channel; 4.1800-4.1801 *Ville de Paris* (110); 19.2.1801-15.5.1804 1st Lord; 20.2.1801-14.3.1823 Privy Counsellor; 29.4.1802-7.1802 *Robust* (74); 9.11.1805 **Admiral of the Red**; 1806-1807 CinC — English Channel; 17.2.1806-6.7.1806 *Hibernia* (110).

JOASS, JOHN

Dates: c.1734 Born; 1761 Died.

Family:

Service: 27.10.1749 Capt Serv *Queenborough* (24); 10.5.1750 Able *Queenborough* (24); 11.9.1751 Mid *Queenborough* (24); 9.5.1753 Able *Unicorn* (24); 23.6.1754 Mid *Unicorn* (24); 17.8.1755-3.12.1755 Mate *Unicorn* (24); 3.12.1755 Passed; **Lieutenant**; 18.3.1756-10.8.1756[C] L. *London* (18) Brigantine; 7.1.1757-16.11.1757 2L *Roebuck* (44); 28.11.1760 1L *Assistance* (50); 5.12.1760-22.5.1761 1L *Hampton Court* (64).

JOCELYN, ROBERT

Dates: c.1806 Died Stanstead Bury, Hertfordshire; 2.8.1806 Will Probate.

Family: Wife Elizabeth; Daughter Caroline; Son Robert Sainsbury Joselyn.

Service: **Lieutenant**; 21.7.1746[(BLI 17.12.1747)] 3L *Gosport* (44); 27.10.1746[(BLI 17.12.1747)]-8.2.1747/48[P] 2L *Gosport* (44); 29.3.1748-2.4.1748 L. *Scorpion* (14) Sloop; 11.4.1749 MidE *Shark* (8) Sloop; 5.3.1751/52-17.5.1756[P] L. *Fowey* (24); 16.6.1756 5L *Namur* (90); 1.9.1756 3L *Namur* (90); 9.11.1756-27.1.1758 2L *Namur* (90); 5.9.1757-6.10.1757 Raid on Rochefort; 16.2.1758 2L *Royal George* (100); 22.5.1758 1L *Royal George* (100); **Commander**; 21.9.1758 *Baltimore* (8) Bomb Vessel; **Captain**; 9.2.1759 *Lennox* (74); 24.9.1762-6.10.1762 Battle of Manilla; 21.10.1762[(EI 24.8.1763)]-23.4.1763[P] *Seahorse* (24).

JOHN, SAMUEL

Dates: c.1737 Born; 1818 Died; 29.8.1818 Will Probate.

Family:

Service: 1752-1755 Merchant Service; 17.12.1755 Able *Happy* (8) Sloop; 27.6.1756 Mid *Flamborough* (20); 4.4.1758-5.12.1759 Mate *Rippon* (60); 16.1.1759-19.1.1759 Attack on Martinique; 20.1.1759-1.5.1759 Capture of Guadeloupe; 5.12.1759 Passed; **Lieutenant**;

10.12.1760-20.1.1763[P] 3L *Swiftsure* (68); 29.3.1761-11.6.1761 Expedition against Belle-Isle; 24.12.1808 **Superannuated Commander.**

JOHNSTON, GEORGE

Dates: 1730 Born Dumfriesshire, Scotland; 24.5.1787 Died Hotwells, Bristol.
Family: Father Sir James Johnstone, 3rd Bt. of Westerhall; Mother Barbara Murray; Mistress Martha Ford; Wife Deborah Charlotte Dee married 31.1.1782; Son John Lowther; Illegitimate Son George Johnstone, MP (1764–1813); Brother Sir James, 4th Bt. (1726-94); Brother William [Pultney] (1729-1805); Brother John (1734-95).
Service: 1744 Merchant Service; 27.12.1744 Able *Hampshire* (50); 20.5.1745 Mid *Hampshire* (50); 26.8.1745 Mid *Revenge* (70); 2.12.1745 Mid *Dartmouth* (50); 24.3.1745/46 Able *Deptford* (24) Storeship; 28.3.1746 Mid *Deptford* (24) Storeship; 30.5.1746 Capt Serv *Edinburgh* (64); 16.6.1746 Mid *Sunderland* (60); 7.12.1746 Able *Hampton Court* (64); 16.5.1747 Mid *Lark* (44); 28.4.1748 Able *Canterbury* (60); 4.6.1748 Mid *Canterbury* (60); 12.10.1748 Battle of Havana; 5.2.1748/49 Mid *Cornwall* (80); 7.10.1749 NR *Intrepid* (64); 2.2.1749/50 Passed; **Lieutenant**; 9.10.1755 3L *Sutherland* (50); 13.3.1756 L. *Bideford* (20); 23.2.1757[(JAM 26.4.1759)] 2L *Dreadnought* (60); 19.5.1757[(JAM 26.4.1759)] 3L *Dreadnought* (60); 5.10.1757[(JAM 26.4.1759)] 1L *Augusta* (60); 21.10.1757 Forrest's Action; 8.8.1758[(JAM 26.4.1759)] L. *Trial* (10) Sloop; **Commander**; 6.2.1760 *Hornet* (10) Sloop; **Captain**; 11.8.1762-8.12.1762 *Hind* (24); 1763-1766 Gov. of West Florida; 24.5.1768-15.10.1774 M.P. for Cockermouth; 15.10.1775-18.9.1780 M.P. for Appleby; 6.5.1779 CinC — Portugal; 6.5.1779-11.1780 Commodore *Romney* (50); 25.6.1779 Commodore *Romney* (50); 1.12.1780-8.4.1784 M.P. for Lostwithiel; 19.1.1781 Commodore *Romney* (50); 16.4.1781 Battle of Porto Praya; 7.1781-1782 Commodore *Isis* (50); 1784-1786 East India Company Director; 22.2.1786-2.1787 M.P. for Ilchester.

JOHNSTON, JAMES

Dates: c.1711 Born; 12.10.1780 Died Near St Lucia.
Family:
Service: 3.9.1727 Able *Aldborough* (20); 21.5.1732 Mid *Aldborough* (20); 19.7.1733 Able *Northumberland* (70); 3.11.1733 Mid *Northumberland* (70); 7.3.1733/34-18.3.1735/36[F] Mid *Bideford* (20); 23.10.1741 Mid *Southsea Castle* (40); 12.4.1742-6.12.1743 Mate *Southsea Castle* (40); 12.1.1743/44 Passed; **Lieutenant**; 25.7.1744 L. *Mortar* (10) Bomb Vessel; 1.10.1744 L. *Vulture* (10) Sloop; 5.10.1744-21.7.1745 L. *Lively* (20); 26.9.1745[(EI 14.9.1749)]-19.10.1748[P] 1L *Medway* (60); 19.9.1755-24.9.1755 L. *Experiment* (24); 14.10.1755 4L *Duke* (90); 11.11.1755 6L *Saint George* (90); 24.5.1756 6L *Namur* (90); 5.6.1756-6.6.1756 6L *Ramillies* (90); **Commander**; 19.4.1758-21.11.1761 *Pluto* (8) Fireship; 5.6.1758-12.6.1758 Raid on Saint-Malo; 20.11.1759 Battle of Quiberon Bay; 11.9.1779-17.1.1780 *Cameleon* (14) Sloop; 20.1.1783-27.1.1783 *Shark* (16) Sloop.

JOHNSTON, SAMUEL

Dates: c.1716 Born; c.1772 Died; 27.8.1772 Will Probate.
Family:
Service: 1739-1741 Merchant Service; 19.12.1741 Able *Neptune* (90); 7.2.1743/44 Mid *Torbay* (80); 11.2.1743/44-12.2.1743/44 Battle of Toulon; 27.4.1745-26.11.1745[P] Mate *Torbay* (80); 3.7.1746 Passed; **Lieutenant**; 12.8.1757 6L *Union* (90); 5.6.1758-12.6.1758 Raid on Saint-Malo; 11.10.1758 5L *Union* (90); 20.11.1758 4L *Union* (90); 30.1.1759-9.1.1760 4L *Royal William* (84).

JOHNSTON, SIR WILLIAM

Dates: Knight Bachelor; c.1719 Born; 1772 Died.
Family:
Service: 20.6.1735 Able *Dreadnought* (60); 28.12.1735 Able *Sheerness* (20); 22.2.1735/36 Mid *Sheerness* (20); 28.8.1736 Able *Sheerness* (20); 15.2.1737/38 Mid *Sheerness* (20); 17.11.1740 Mid *Princess Louisa* (60); 4.3.1740/41-5.1741 Operations against Cartagena; 4.6.1741 Mid *Chichester* (80); 5.11.1741 Passed; **Lieutenant**; 25.2.1741/42 L. *Wolf* (14) Sloop; 21.2.1743/44 3L *Chester* (50); 14.3.1743/44-27.6.1745 2L *Chester* (50).

JOHNSTON, WILLIAM

Dates: 1779 Died.
Family:
Service: **Lieutenant**; 28.5.1760[(NA 14.3.1763)] L. *Porcupine* (16) Sloop; 6.6.1762-13.8.1762 Operations against Havana; 5.9.1763-29.4.1766[P] 1L *Alarm* (32); 19.4.1768 L. *Fly* (8) Sloop; 10.1.1771 1L *Arethusa* (32); 25.3.1771-3.6.1773[P] 1L *Pallas* (36); 21.9.1773 2L *Ramillies* (74); 17.12.1773 1L *Ramillies* (74); 30.5.1776-11.8.1778 3L *Rippon* (60); 10.8.1778 Second Battle of Pondicherry.

JOHNSTONE, GIDEON

Dates: 24.6.1739 Born Westerkirk, Scotland; 12.5.1788 Died; 4.7.1788 Will Probate.
Family: Father James Johnstone of Westerhall, 3rd Bt. (d.1772); Mother Barbara Murray (1698-1773); Wife Fanny Colquitt married 10.3.1780; Sister Barbara [Kinnaird] (1723-1765); Sister Margaret [Ogilvy] (1724-1757); Brother Alexander (1727-1783); Brother George (1730-1787); Sister Charlotte [Balmain] (1732-1773); Brother Patrick (1737-1756).
Service: 1752-1755 Merchant Service; 26.8.1755-4.10.1758 Mid *Revenge* (28); 4.10.1758 Passed; **Lieutenant**; 26.12.1758-23.5.1762[C] 2L *Hussar* (28); 26.7.1769 1L *Stag* (32); **Commander**; 23.3.1771[(EI 14.5.1772)] *Hawk* (10) Sloop; **Captain**; 2.6.1772[(EI 19.5.1775)] *Dolphin* (24); 7.7.1774[(30.6.1775)]-26.5.1775[P] *Prudent* (64); 3.11.1779-25.9.1781 *Adamant* (50); 16.3.1781 Battle of Cape Henry.

JOLLIFFE, JOHN

Dates: c.1740 Born; 28.12.1761 Died.
Family:
Service: 19.8.1754 Scholar *Royal Naval Academy*; 25.8.1757 Able *Terrible* (74); 30.11.1757 Mid *Hind* (24); 6.6.1758-27.7.1758 The Siege of Louisbourg; 4.8.1758 Able *Hind* (24); 9.12.1758 Mid *Active* (28); 17.8.1759 Mate *Active* (28); 7.2.1760-3.9.1760 Mate *Minerva* (32); 3.9.1760 Passed; **Lieutenant**; 23.12.1760-28.12.1761[F] L. *Peregrine* (20) Sloop.

JONES, AMBROSE

Dates: c.1725 Born; 1765 Died; 10.6.1765 Will Probate.
Family:
Service: 1739-1741 Merchant Service; 23.2.1740/41 Mid *Lyme* (20); 15.9.1742 Mid *Cambridge* (80); 30.12.1742 Mid *Revenge* (70); 23.2.1742/43 Mid *Namur* (90); 8.9.1744 Mid *Neptune* (90); 31.1.1744/45 Mid *Dunkirk* (60); 25.8.1745 Passed; **Lieutenant**; 27.1.1745/46[(MED 25.10.1748)] 3L *Roebuck* (44); 16.3.1745/46[(MED 25.10.1748)]-27.10.1748[P] 1L *Roebuck* (44); 29.3.1756 1L *Assistance* (50); 30.1.1759[(JAM 10.11.1760)] 6L *Marlborough* (80); 10.3.1759[(JAM 10.11.1760)] 5L *Marlborough* (80); 19.10.1759[(JAM 10.11.1760)] 4L *Marlborough* (80); 23.2.1760[(JAM 10.11.1760)] 3L *Marlborough* (80); 20.5.1760[(JAM 10.11.1760)]-30.9.1760[P] 2L *Marlborough* (80).

JONES, ANTHONY

Dates: c.1739 Born; 1793 Died; 17.4.1793 Will Probate.
Family:
Service: 1750-1756 Merchant Service; 12.8.1756 Able *Ambuscade* (40); 14.1.1757 QGnr *Ambuscade* (40); 20.11.1757 Mid *Ambuscade* (40); 22.8.1759-7.1.1760 Mate *Rainbow* (44); 7.1.1760 Passed; **Lieutenant**; 1.7.1761[(11.4.1763)] L. *Cygnet* (18) Sloop; 17.10.1761[(11.4.1763)] 3L *Anson* (60); 21.11.1762[(11.4.1763)]-29.3.1763[P] 2L *Anson* (60); 3.6.1768-29.11.1768 L. *Peggy* (8) Sloop.

JONES, JAMES

Dates: 11.10.1780 Died.
Family: Wife Eleanor;
Service: **Lieutenant**; 15.3.1743/44[(MED 20.5.1747)]-11.12.1746[P] 3L *Dartmouth* (50); 2.11.1746[(MED 28.5.1747)]-3.6.1747 L. *Portsmouth* (24) Storeship; 12.1.1747/48 L. *Scorpion* (14) Sloop; 28.3.1748-3.1.1748/49[P] 3L *Salisbury* (50); 8.7.1752-8.7.1753 L. *Hind* (24); 15.6.1756-23.2.1757 1L *Edinburgh* (64); 24.6.1757 2L *Dunkirk* (60); 5.9.1757-6.10.1757 Raid on Rochefort; 5.6.1758-12.6.1758 Raid on Saint-Malo; 6.10.1758-6.5.1760 1L *Dunkirk* (60); 29.12.1758 Capture of Goree; 20.11.1759 Battle of Quiberon Bay; 11.9.1761 1L *Blenheim* (90); 17.6.1762[(9.8.1762)]-18.1.1763[P] 1L *Neptune* (90); **Commander**; 20.6.1765 *Swallow* (14) Sloop; 2.4.1766-4.4.1769 *Fly* (8) Sloop; 30.5.1770-3.6.1773 *Ranger* (8) Sloop; 5.9.1776 *Beaver* (14) Sloop; **Captain**; 2.8.1777-23.8.1777 *Fowey* (24); 29.5.1778-11.10.1780[F] *Penelope* (24).

JONES, JAMES HOWELL

Dates: 22.2.1791 Died.
Family:
Service: **Lieutenant**; 27.11.1760[(16.12.1763)]-7.5.1761 1L *Baleine* (20); 6.4.1763 LCmdr *Prince George* (4) Cutter; 4.9.1764-27.6.1765 LCmdr *Wells* (6) Cutter; 10.5.1766-3.3.1767[P] 3L *Burford* (68); **Commander**; 26.5.1768 *Mortar* (14) Bomb Vessel; 10.12.1770-29.11.1773[P] *Nautilus* (16) Sloop; 2.8.1777-2.1.1778 *Beaver* (14) Sloop.

JONES, JOHN

Dates: c.1735 Born; 1764 Died.
Family:
Service: 1754-1756 Merchant Service; 30.8.1756 Able *Princess Louisa* (60); 5.4.1757 Action of April 5 1757; 25.11.1757 Able *Macclesfield* (16) Hired Armed Ship; 13.4.1758 Mid *Juno* (32); 6.6.1758-27.7.1758 The Siege of Louisbourg; 21.3.1759 Mate *Solebay* (24); 14.5.1760 Passed; **Lieutenant**; 19.5.1761 3L *Winchester* (50); 31.7.1761-3.7.1764[P] 2L *Winchester* (50).

JONES, MORGAN

Dates: c.1724 Born; 1780 Died; 23.5.1780 Will Probate.
Family:
Service: 12.2.1738/39 Able *Norfolk* (80); 25.5.1739 Able *Bonetta* (8) Sloop; 10.1.1739/40 Able *Norfolk* (80); 3.7.1740 Mid *Mary Galley* (40); 3.8.1741 Mid *Argyll* (50); 21.8.1741 Mate *Scipio* (8) Fireship; 8.11.1741 Clerk *Scipio* (8) Fireship; 16.11.1741 Mate *Blandford* (20); 9.3.1742/43 Mate *Kinsale* (44); 22.5.1743 Master *Kinsale* (44); 14.10.1743 Act3L *Kinsale* (44); 13.12.1743 Act2L *Kinsale* (44); 2.2.1743/44 Mid *Kinsale* (44); 18.6.1744 Mate *Kinsale* (44); 9.5.1745 Passed; **Lieutenant**; 23.5.1745 6L *Saint George* (90); 22.3.1745/46 5L *Saint George* (90); 14.4.1746 3L *Mermaid* (44); 29.8.1746-14.9.1747[P] 2L *Mermaid* (44).

JONES, ROGER

Dates: c.1712 Born; 1770 Died.
Family:
Service: 14.10.1728 Vol-p-O *Elizabeth* (70); 4.3.1728/29 Vol-p-O *Chatham* (50); 3.1.1730/31 Mid *Chatham* (50); 28.6.1731 Able *Salisbury* (50); 2.10.1731 MidO *Salisbury* (50); 5.10.1734-11.1.1735 Mid *Salisbury* (50); 11.1.1734/35 Passed; **Lieutenant**; 4.3.1739/40-9.4.1740 3L *Torbay* (80); 10.4.1740 2L *Torbay* (80); 12.4.1742 1L *Torbay* (80); 2.6.1743[(22.1.1743/44)]-10.8.1746 1L *Romney* (50); 11.2.1743/44-12.2.1743/44 Battle of Toulon.

JONES, THOMAS

Dates: c.1706 Born; 1769 Died.
Family:
Service: 20.1.1737/38 Able *Ludlow Castle* (40); 7.1.1740/41 Mid *Ludlow Castle* (40); 4.12.1741 Able *Lion* (60); 2.4.1742 Mid *Plymouth* (60); 5.12.1742 Able *Centurion* (60); 30.7.1743 Mid *Captain*; 12.1.1743/44 Passed; **Lieutenant**; 20.4.1744-17.7.1744 L. *Vulture* (10) Sloop; 5.10.1744-5.8.1745 L. *Sheerness* (20); 3.7.1745 Action of 1745-07-03; 2.11.1745-24.11.1747 1L *Chesterfield* (44); 24.6.1748-15.4.1751[P] MidE *Renown* (30); 5.5.1757 L. *Crown* (18) Storeship; 12.5.1757-12.5.1759 1L *Cambridge* (80); 16.1.1759-19.1.1759 Attack on Martinique; 20.1.1759-1.5.1759 Capture of Guadeloupe.

JONES, WILLIAM

Dates: c.1733 Born; 1758 Died; 23.1.1759 Will Probate.
Family: Father Rev. Lewis Jones.
Service: 23.7.1746 Scholar *Royal Naval Academy*; 18.5.1749 Mst Serv *Shark* (8) Sloop; 17.1.1751/52 Gnr Serv *Princess* (70); 21.4.1752 Ord. *Princess* (70); 19.5.1753-3.12.1755 Mid *America* (44); 3.12.1755 Passed; **Lieutenant;** 24.9.1756 4L *Essex* (64); 8.10.1756 L. *Hornet* (10) Sloop; 12.4.1758[(JAM 4.9.1760)]-19.11.1760[P] 3L *Dreadnought* (60).

JONES, WILLIAM

Dates: c.1731 Born; 1763 Died.
Family:
Service: 18.9.1748 Ord. *Ferret* (14) Sloop; 8.1.1748/49-9.5.1749[P] Ord. *Squirrel* (20); 26.5.1750 Capt Serv *Dolphin* (6) Fireship; 28.12.1750 Able *Dolphin* (6) Fireship; 25.3.1751 Mid *Deptford* (60); 12.9.1752 Mid *Captain* (70); 29.1.1754 Mid *Speedwell* (8) Sloop; 12.1.1755 Able *Speedwell* (8) Sloop; 6.2.1755 Mid *Speedwell* (8) Sloop; 7.4.1756 Passed; **Lieutenant**; 6.12.1757[(JAM 4.9.1760)] 3L *Lynn* (44); 27.8.1761 1L *Melampe* (36); **Commander**; 25.10.1762-17.4.1764 *Goree* (10).

JONES, WILLIAM

Dates: c.1731 Born; 27.11.1779 Died.
Family:
Service: 10.3.1758-23.11.1759 Mate *Ramillies* (90); 5.6.1758-12.6.1758 Raid on Saint-Malo; **Lieutenant**; 14.3.1759 2L *Prince Edward* (44); 19.3.1759-13.3.1761 3L *Prince Edward* (44); 12.12.1759 Passed; 20.8.1761-13.12.1762[P] L. *Cormorant* (8) Fireship; 29.6.1768-12.3.1771[P] 1L *Hussar* (28); 13.3.1771-26.5.1775[P] 1L *Buckingham* (68); 25.8.1775 1L *Boreas* (28); 11.11.1776-6.12.1776[C] LCmdr *Racehorse* (10) Schooner; 28.10.1778-27.11.1779[†] LCmdr *Nimble* (10) Cutter.

JORDAN, THOMAS

Dates: c.1737 Born; c.1779 Died; 13.9.1779 Will Probate.
Family:
Service: 1752-1754 Merchant Service; 21.7.1754 Able *Garland* (24); 9.7.1756 Mid *Garland* (24); 23.1.1758 Mate *Norfolk* (74); 5.6.1758-12.6.1758 Raid on Saint-Malo; 4.10.1758 Passed; **Lieutenant**; 27.10.1758-27.4.1761 4L *Trident* (64); 29.8.1765 1L *Jason* (32); **Commander**; 11.9.1766 *Carcass* (8) Bomb Vessel; 25.9.1770 *Cruizer* (8) Sloop; 24.6.1771 *Kingfisher* (14) Sloop; **Captain**; 7.7.1772(6.10.1772)-15.4.1774 *Fowey* (24); 20.3.1776-1.5.1779 *Galatea* (20).

JUDD, WILLIAM

Dates: c.1737 Born; 1783 Died.
Family:
Service: 31.10.1751 Able *Lyme* (24); 13.12.1753 Capt Serv *Lyme* (24); 18.12.1754 Able *Lyme* (24); 23.10.1755 Able *Experiment* (24); 4.5.1756 Mid *Defiance* (60); 20.5.1756 Battle of Minorca; 7.7.1756 Able *Yarmouth* (64); 10.12.1756 Mid *Defiance* (60); 24.5.1757 Able *Medway* (60); 20.7.1757 Mid *Medway* (60); 5.9.1757-6.10.1757 Raid on Rochefort; 3.1.1759 Passed; **Lieutenant**; 20.2.1759 4L *Raisonnable* (64); 14.7.1759(BLI 23.11.1761)-19.6.1761 3L *Panther* (60); 12.4.1763 L. *Garland* (24); 3.6.1763-18.8.1766 L. *Peggy* (8) Sloop; 14.9.1767 LCmdr *Prince George* (4) Cutter; 24.1.1771 1L *Princess Amelia* (80); **Commander**; 13.3.1773(2.7.1773) *Ferret* (14) Sloop; **Captain**; 7.9.1774-28.7.1777[C] *Antelope* (50); 28.7.1777 Taken Prisoner.

JURD, WILLIAM

Dates: c.1717 Born; 1756 Died; 20.10.1756 Will Probate.
Family: Wife Roberta.
Service: 3.11.1733 Able *Plymouth* (60); 23.11.1736 Able *Sheerness* (20); 9.8.1737 QGnr *Sheerness* (20); 4.11.1739 Cox *Sheerness* (20); 10.5.1740 Cox *Princess Louisa* (60); 4.3.1740/41-5.1741 Operations against Cartagena; 7.7.1741 Mid *Chichester* (80); 3.9.1741 Mid *Prince of Orange* (70); 3.11.1742 Mid *Burford* (70); 17.1.1742/43 Mate *Burford* (70); 26.10.1744 Mid *Marlborough* (90); 12.1.1744/45 Mate *Marlborough* (90); 22.10.1745 Able *Russell* (80); 2.6.1746 Mate *Russell* (80); **Lieutenant**; 30.8.1746(MED 21.11.1747)-26.8.1747[P] L. *Guernsey's Prize* Unknown; 20.11.1747 Passed; 14.1.1747/48-14.9.1748[P] L. *Princess Royal* (24) Storeship.

Service Records K

KATON, EDWARD
Dates: c.1732 Born; 1779 Died; 12.6.1779 Will Probate.
Family: Wife Sarah Knaller married 27.1.1758; Son William Brereton; Son Edward (1759-?); Son George (1761-?); Daughter Sarah (1763-?); Daughter Catherine (1766-?); Daughter Ann (1767-?); Son James, RN (1770-1845); Daughter Sophia (1772-?).
Service: 30.7.1746 Mid *Scorpion* (10) Sloop; 23.12.1747 Mid *Princess Amelia* (66); 29.3.1748 Able *Vanguard* (68); 4.9.1748 Able *Berwick* (70); 13.5.1749 Mid *Berwick* (70); 7.2.1749/50 Able *Berwick* (70); 7.10.1750 Mid *Berwick* (70); 6.5.1752 Able *Monarch* (74); 16.9.1753 Able *Penzance* (44); 17.1.1754 Mate *Penzance* (44); 4.6.1755 Passed; **Lieutenant**; 13.3.1759 L. *Basilisk* (8) Bomb Vessel; 3.7.1759 Bombardment of Le Havre; 20.8.1759 4L *Hero* (74); 20.11.1759 Battle of Quiberon Bay; 29.3.1761-11.6.1761 Expedition against Belle-Isle; 25.6.1761-25.12.1762[P] 3L *Hero* (74); 6.9.1763 3L *Augusta* (64); 25.10.1763-12.11.1766 1L *Superb* (74); 10.8.1768 1L *Rippon* (60); 21.12.1769-27.5.1771[P] 2L *Rippon* (60); 10.8.1771 1L *Prudent* (64); 11.9.1771 2L *Prudent* (64); 25.2.1772 1L *Terrible* (74); 24.3.1772 4L *Barfleur* (90); 25.6.1773 3L *Barfleur* (90); 7.12.1773 2L *Barfleur* (90); 14.7.1774-25.8.1774 1L *Barfleur* (90).

KEARNY, MICHAEL
Dates: 6.1797 Died.
Family:
Service: **Lieutenant**; 6.2.1743/44[(17.2.1744/45)]-14.8.1746 3L *Romney* (50); 11.2.1743/44-12.2.1743/44 Battle of Toulon; 30.10.1746-23.4.1753 L. *Arundel* (24); 22.6.1756-3.10.1756 1L *Prince* (90); 29.7.1757 6L *Royal George* (100); 24.12.1757 5L *Royal George* (100); 27.1.1758 5L *Namur* (90); 6.6.1758-27.7.1758 The Siege of Louisbourg; 18.8.1759-19.8.1759 Battle of Lagos Bay; **Commander**; 20.8.1759[(MED 3.5.1762)] *Terror* (8) Bomb Vessel; 6.4.1761[(10.12.1762)]-11.12.1762[P] *Saltash* (14) Sloop.

KEATING, CHRISTOPHER
Dates: c.1729 Born; 1764 Died; 7.11.1764 Will Probate.
Family: Brother William Cooper.
Service: 28.6.1745 Able *Princess Royal* (90); 17.11.1745 Able *Folkestone* (44); 4.3.1746/47 Able *Prince Edward* (44); 28.6.1747 Mid *Prince Edward* (44); 29.12.1748 Mid *Sheerness* (24); 2.3.1748/49 Mate *Sheerness* (24); 22.7.1749 Mid *Sheerness* (24); 3.10.1749 Able *Vigilant* (60); 19.1.1751/52 Passed; 9.2.1751/52-19.6.1752 Mid *Vigilant* (60); **Lieutenant**; 31.3.1756 3L *Bristol* (50); 21.12.1758[(BLI 10.9.1759)] 1L *Roebuck* (44); 16.1.1759-19.1.1759 Attack on Martinique; 20.1.1759-1.5.1759 Capture of Guadeloupe; 10.8.1759 2L *Royal Sovereign* (104); 7.11.1759 1L *Dover* (44); 23.3.1761-2.3.1763[P] 1L *Superb* (74).

KEELER, ROBERT

Dates: c.1735 Born; c.1811 Died Faversham; 18.2.1811 Will Probate.
Family: Daughter Judith [Simpson, Timms].
Service: 14.6.1749 Capt Serv *Berwick* (70); 20.10.1750 Able *Surprise* (24); 13.12.1751 Able *Invincible* (74); 9.6.1752 Mid *Invincible* (74); 27.2.1753 Mid *Monarch* (74); 5.2.1755 Mate *Monarch* (74); 7.1.1756 Passed; **Lieutenant**; 26.8.1756 6L *Magnanime* (74); 8.4.1757 5L *Magnanime* (74); 3.6.1757 5L *Royal William* (84); 15.6.1757 4L *Royal William* (84); 17.6.1757 3L *Royal William* (84); 5.9.1757-6.10.1757 Raid on Rochefort; 6.2.1758-19.2.1758[W] 2L *Invincible* (74); 29.3.1758 6L *Royal George* (100); 5.10.1758 3L *Royal George* (100); 23.2.1759 2L *Royal George* (100); 19.6.1759 1L *Royal George* (100); **Commander**; 4.9.1759 *Proserpine* (8) Fireship; 20.11.1759 Battle of Quiberon Bay; **Captain**; 19.5.1761 *Success* (20); 5.8.1761-26.1.1763[P] *Dolphin* (24); 13.8.1766-30.8.1769 *Cruizer* (8) Sloop; 22.8.1770-2.10.1773[P] *Mercury* (20); 14.7.1775-25.4.1776 *Experiment* (50); 15.2.1776[(BLI 10.7.1776)]-17.6.1776[P] *Lynx* (10) Sloop; 25.1.1779-26.10.1780[P] *Actaeon* (44); 22.9.1790 **Superannuated Rear Admiral.**

KEIR, FRANCIS

Dates: 27.5.1733 Baptised; 26.6.1733 Born; 15.9.1795 Died Edinburgh.
Family: Father John Keir (1686-1743); Mother Magdalene Lind; Brother George (1713-1737); Sister Grisel (1716-1788); Brother William.
Service: **Lieutenant**; 26.2.1760[(JAM 3.5.1762)]-16.6.1761 L. *Port Antonio* (12) Storeship; 17.12.1770-27.5.1771[P] 3L *Cornwall* (74); 6.11.1776 3L *Monarch* (74); 4.12.1776 2L *Monarch* (74); 27.7.1778 1st Battle of Ushant; 8.12.1778 2L *Suffolk* (74); 6.7.1779 Battle of Grenada; 21.12.1779-22.12.1779 Action of 1779-12-21; 6.1.1780-22.8.1780 1L *Conqueror* (74); 17.4.1780 Battle of Martinique; 15.5.1780 Action of March 15 1780; 19.5.1780 Action of March 19 1780.

KEITH, ALEXANDER

Dates: 1786 Died; 13.12.1786 Will Probate.
Family: Wife ?; Wife Isabel; Daughter Mary; Daughter Elizabeth; Son James; Son David; Son George; Daughter Isabel Frazer.
Service: **Lieutenant**; 24.5.1748[(JAM 30.6.1749)]-31.10.1748[P] L. *Saint Luke* Fireship; 26.1.1756-9.3.1759 L. *Deal Castle* (20).

KEITH, SIR BASIL

Dates: c.1734 Born; 10.6.1772 Knight Bachelor; 15.11.1777 Died Jamaica.
Family: Father Robert Keith (d. 1774); Mother Margaret Cunningham; Brother Lt. Gen. Sir Robert Murray (1730-1795).
Service: 5.10.1747 Capt Serv *Defiance* (60); 14.10.1747 2nd Battle of Cape Finisterre; 16.1.1748/49 Mid *Culloden* (74); 6.10.1749 Mid *Berwick* (70); 13.1.1749/50 MidO *Humber* (44); 17.8.1750 Mid *Humber* (44); 16.7.1751 Able *Cumberland* (66); 18.11.1751 Mid *Glory* (44); 3.1.1753 Mid *Culloden* (74); 13.2.1753 Able *Penzance* (44); 16.1.1754 Passed; **Lieutenant**; 13.11.1756[(23.11.1758)] 3L *Enterprise* (44); 28.10.1757 4L *Terrible* (74); **Commander**; 18.10.1758 *Medway* (6) Storeship; 18.4.1759-5.9.1759 *Badger* (10) Sloop; **Captain**; 11.4.1760 *Dover* (44); 21.7.1760-3.9.1763[P] *Amazon* (22); 25.8.1766 *Levant* (28); 11.5.1769[(18.10.1769)]-2.10.1769[P] *Preston* (50); 10.12.1770-5.11.1771 *Pearl* (32); 1.1774-15.11.1777 Gov. of Jamaica.

KELLY, CHARLES

Dates: c.1728 Born; 20.10.1800 Died.
Family:
Service: 7.5.1751 Able *Charlotte* (8) Yacht; 9.2.1757 Able *Ramillies* (90); 8.5.1757 Mid *Ramillies* (90); 5.9.1757-6.10.1757 Raid on Rochefort; 23.5.1758 Mate *Ramillies* (90); 5.6.1758-12.6.1758 Raid on Saint-Malo; 10.10.1759 Passed; **Lieutenant**; 15.11.1759 4L *Cambridge* (80); 11.2.1760-5.5.1763[P] 4L *Warspite* (74); 1.1771-1.7.1771[P] LCmdr *Hornet* (6) Cutter.

KELLY, TIMOTHY

Dates: c.1740 Born; 1788 Died.
Family:
Service: 1755-1757 Merchant Service; 1.3.1757 Ord. *Guernsey* (50); 5.4.1757 Action of April 5 1757; 10.9.1758 Able *Guernsey* (50); 12.3.1759 Mid *Guernsey* (50); 18.8.1759-19.8.1759 Battle of Lagos Bay; 5.8.1761 Passed; **Lieutenant**; 17.7.1762[(EI 12.10.1763)] 4L *Hampton Court* (64); 23.12.1762[(EI 12.10.1763)]-19.9.1763[P] 3L *Hampton Court* (64); 26.7.1775-13.9.1780 1L *Solebay* (28) Frigate; **Commander**; 13.1.1780[(JAM 17.9.1781)]-8.5.1781[C] *Port Royal* (18) Sloop; 16.3.1782-12.5.1783[P] *Fly* (14) Sloop.

KEMP, RICHARD

Dates: c.1737 Born; 12.1.1820 Died Ramsgate, Kent; 1.2.1820 Will Probate.
Family: Father William Kemp (1681-1729); Mother Elizabeth Egleston; Wife Mary; Daughter Mary.
Service: 26.12.1754 Able *Yarmouth* (64); 15.8.1755 Mid *Yarmouth* (64); 11.7.1757 Mid *Invincible* (74); 8.1757-10.1757 Louisbourg Expedition; 15.11.1757 Mid *Barfleur* (80); 5.6.1758-12.6.1758 Raid on Saint-Malo; 4.4.1759 Passed; **Lieutenant**; 6.8.1759 L. *Lightning* (6) Hospital Ship; 24.3.1760 4L *Thunderer* (74); 14.2.1763-4.3.1763[P] 2L *Thunderer* (74); 21.5.1803 **Superannuated Commander.**

KEMPENFELT, RICHARD

Dates: 1715 Born; 29.8.1782 Died Spithead.
Family: Father Magnus Kempenfelt; Mother Anne Hunt; Brother Gustavus.
Service: 24.3.1728 Vol-p-O *Lyme* (20); 21.4.1731 MidO *Lyme* (20); 16.3.1732 Mid *Lyme* (20); 12.11.1732 MidO *Lyme* (20); 27.1.1733 Mid *Lyme* (20); 6.5.1736-6.9.1737[P] Mate *Lyme* (20); 6.5.1737 Passed; **Lieutenant**; 14.1.1740/41[(JAM 8.9.1746)] 3L *Strafford* (60); 8.6.1741[(JAM 8.9.1746)] 1L *Superb* (60); 31.10.1741[(JAM 8.9.1746)]-25.10.1746[P] L. *Seahorse* (20); 3.8.1746 Action of August 3 1746; 25.8.1747 1L *Tavistock* (50); 23.9.1748-17.11.1752[P] 1L *Anson* (60); 10.1.1753 1L *Anson* (60); 16.1.1755 1L *Lichfield* (50); 5.4.1755 1L *Orford* (68); **Commander**; 5.5.1756 *Lightning* (8) Fireship; **Captain**; 17.1.1757 *Elizabeth* (64); 29.4.1758 Battle of Cuddalore; 3.8.1758 Battle of Negapatam; 20.2.1759[(EI 16.5.1763)] *Grafton* (68); 10.9.1759 Battle of Pondicherry; 23.6.1760[(16.5.1763)]-10.11.1762 *Norfolk* (74); 24.9.1762-6.10.1762 Battle of Manilla; 20.10.1770-19.2.1771 *Buckingham* (68); 2.10.1778 *Alexander* (74); 24.3.1779-5.5.1780 1Capt. *Victory* (100); 22.5.1780 1Capt. *Victory* (100); 8.9.1780 1Capt. *Britannia* (100); 26.9.1780 **Rear Admiral of the Blue**; 10.9.1781 *Victory* (100); 12.12.1781 2nd Battle of Ushant; 11.3.1782-29.8.1782[†] *Royal George* (100).

KEMPTHORNE, JAMES

Dates: 25.7.1737 Born Cury, nr. Helston, Cornwall; 9.6.1808 Died Helston, Cornwall.
Family: Father Edward Kempthorne; Mother Margaret Tregidgeon; Wife Eleanor Sandys married 4.5.1773; Son John (1775-1838); Son James (1777-1851); Son Thomas Warren (1779-1797); Daughter Eleanor (1789-1869); Brother Pascal?; Brother Robert; Brother Samuel.
Service: 30.11.1755 Able *Torbay* (74); 15.9.1756 Able *Invincible* (74); 7.6.1757 Able *Royal Anne* (100); 5.9.1757-6.10.1757 Raid on Rochefort; 17.2.1758 Able *Torbay* (74); 5.5.1758 Mid *Torbay* (74); 5.6.1758-12.6.1758 Raid on Saint-Malo; 29.12.1758 Capture of Goree; 20.11.1759 Battle of Quiberon Bay; 15.7.1760 Mid *Valiant* (74); 14.11.1760 Able *Valiant* (74); 25.12.1760 Mid *Valiant* (74); 29.3.1761-11.6.1761 Expedition against Belle-Isle; 5.8.1761 Passed; **Lieutenant**; 6.8.1761 L. *Aetna* (8) Fireship; 27.11.1762 L. *Lynx* (10) Sloop; 17.1.1763-27.2.1764[P] L. *Terpsichore* (24); 19.3.1764-24.10.1768[P] 1L *Guadeloupe* (28); 16.8.1769 L. *Hind* (24); 30.11.1770-25.1.1773[P] 1L *Glory* (32); 18.12.1773 1L *Raisonable* (64); 25.8.1775 1L *Nonsuch* (64); 14.12.1778-15.12.1778 Battle of St. Lucia; 26.1.1779 1L *Monarch* (74); 16.1.1780 Battle of Cape St. Vincent; 4.2.1780 1L *London* (90); 16.3.1781 Battle of Cape Henry; **Commander**; 29.7.1781[(NA 4.3.1782)] *Cormorant* (18) Sloop; **Captain**; 25.9.1781[(NA 20.4.1782)]-20.7.1783[P] *London* (90); 17.10.1782 Action of 1782-10-17; 18.10.1782 Action of 18 October 1782; 3.11.1790-14.12.1791[P] *Africa* (64); 1.1.1801 **Rear Admiral of the Blue**; 23.4.1804 **Rear Admiral of the White**; 9.11.1805 **Rear Admiral of the Red.**

KENDALL, CHARLES

Dates: c.1740 Born; 7.5.1806 Died.
Family: Wife Mary married 19.1.1790.
Service: 22.11.1755 Mid *Duke* (90); 10.6.1756 Able *Marlborough* (80); 18.11.1756 Mid *Sphinx* (24); 11.10.1757 Mid *Marlborough* (80); 3.9.1758 Mid *Dreadnought* (60); 27.12.1759 Mid *Marlborough* (80); 16.10.1760 Mid *Temeraire* (74); 21.2.1761 Mid *Royal Sovereign* (104); 30.4.1761 Mid *Nassau* (64); 20.3.1762 Mid *Princess Amelia* (80); 7.7.1762 Passed; **Lieutenant**; 1.2.1763[(30.11.1763)] L. *Lynx* (10) Sloop; 16.3.1764-30.8.1764 3L *Bellona* (74); 2.7.1766-2.10.1769[P] 3L *Preston* (50); 5.11.1770 5L *Cornwall* (74); 18.1.1771 5L *Sandwich* (90); 25.3.1771-15.4.1774 3L *Captain* (64); 30.5.1777-10.9.1777 2L *Burford* (68).

KENNEDY, LORD ARCHIBALD (11TH EARL OF CASSILIS)

Dates: 1720 Born; 18.12.1792 13th Lord Kennedy; 18.12.1792 11th Earl of Cassilis; 30.12.1794 Died.
Family: Father Archibald Kennedy; Wife Katherine Schuyler; Wife Anne Watts married 27.4.1769; Son Archibald, 1st Marquess of Ailsa (1770–1846); Son John (1771–1859); Son Robert (1773–1843).
Service: 11.12.1744 Passed; **Lieutenant**; 16.12.1744[(BLI 8.2.1745/46)]-29.2.1747/48 L. *Otter* (14) Sloop; 6.4.1751-16.8.1754[P] L. *Centaur* (20); **Commander**; 13.3.1756-14.8.1756[C] *Halifax* (18) Sloop; **Captain**; 4.4.1757-10.6.1757 *Vestal* (32); 3.3.1758 *Flamborough* (20); 5.6.1758-12.6.1758 Raid on Saint-Malo; 30.6.1760-23.8.1760 *Quebec* (32); 27.8.1760-20.2.1763[P] *Blonde* (32); 9.4.1763-14.12.1765 *Coventry* (28); 1.7.1766-15.2.1768[P] *Coventry* (28); 11.1766-7.1767 CinC — North America.

KENNEDY, SILVESTER

Dates: 1756 Died; 9.4.1756 Will Probate.
Family:
Service: 1697-1704 Merchant Service; 1.3.1703/4 Schoolmaster *Russell* (80); 3.3.1704/5 Mid *Sunderland* (60); 31.1.1706/7 Mid *Bredah* (70); 12.4.1708 Passed; **Lieutenant**; 30.4.1708 L. *Seaford* (24); 4.5.1711 L. *Seaford* (24); 16.5.1711 1L *Bristol* (54); 14.12.1714-12.1.1714/15[P] 1L *Bristol* (54); 16.5.1719 2L *Norwich* (50); 25.1.1725/26 2L *Hampton Court* (70); 23.2.1725/26 1L *Hampton Court* (70); 11.4.1729 1L *Nassau* (70); 23.2.1733/34-31.7.1737[P] 1L *Nottingham* (60); **Commander**; 28.4.1740 *Phaeton* (8) Fireship; 4.3.1740/41-5.1741 Operations against Cartagena; 12.6.1741-15.3.1741/42[P] *Cumberland* (8) Fireship.

KENT, JOHN

Dates: c.1734 Born; 1786 Died; 11.5.1786 Will Probate.
Family: Brother William George Carlisle, RN (1788-?).
Service: 1750-1757 Merchant Service; 7.9.1757 Mid *Royal William* (84); 6.6.1758-27.7.1758 The Siege of Louisbourg; 4.2.1760-3.6.1761 Mate *Royal William* (84); 3.6.1761 Passed; **Lieutenant**; 31.5.1762 L. *Hound* (14) Sloop; 28.7.1762-3.12.1762[P] L. *Salamander* (8) Fireship; 6.12.1763-30.11.1765[P] 3L *Africa* (64); 19.1.1769-3.1.1770 1L *Pearl* (32); 13.3.1777-2.10.1783[P] LCmdr *Phipps* Hired Tender.

KEPPEL, LORD AUGUSTUS (1ST VISCOUNT KEPPEL)

Dates: 2.4.1725 Born; 10.4.1782 1st Viscount Keppel; 2.10.1786 Died.
Family: Father William Anne Keppel, 2nd Earl of Albemarle (1702–1754); Mother Anne Lennox (1703–1789); Brother George, Visct. Bury (1724-72); Brother Hon. William, MP (1727-82); Sister Elizabeth [Russel].
Service: 21.6.1743[(27.7.1744)]-30.9.1743 3L *Centurion* (60); 21.3.1743/44 **Lieutenant**; 25.7.1744 Passed; 4.8.1744 2L *Dreadnought* (60); **Commander**; 7.11.1744 *Wolf* (14) Sloop; **Captain**; 11.12.1744-8.2.1744/45 *Greyhound* (20); 11.2.1744/45 *Sapphire* (44); 26.10.1745-27.6.1747[W] *Maidstone* (50); 2.11.1747 *Anson* (60); 26.8.1748-16.9.1752[P] *Centurion* (50); 11.3.1748/49-1751 CinC — The Mediterranean Sea; 9.10.1754-1755 CinC — North America; 9.10.1754 Commodore *Centurion* (50); 15.1.1755-25.3.1761 M.P. for Chichester; 26.7.1755-22.8.1755 Commodore *Seahorse* (24); 26.8.1755 *Swiftsure* (68); 8.1.1756 *Torbay* (74); 5.9.1757-6.10.1757 Raid on Rochefort; 5.6.1758-12.6.1758 Raid on Saint-Malo; 28.9.1758 Commodore *Torbay* (74); 29.12.1758 Capture of Goree; 19.4.1759 *Torbay* (74); 21.8.1759 *Valiant* (74); 25.2.1761-12.7.1764[P] Commodore *Valiant* (74); 25.3.1761-8.9.1780 M.P. for Windsor; 29.3.1761-11.6.1761 Expedition against Belle-Isle; 1762-1764 CinC — Jamaica; 6.6.1762-13.8.1762 Operations against Havana; 21.10.1762 **Rear Admiral of the Blue**; 31.7.1765-10.12.1766 Lord Commissioner of the Admiralty; 18.10.1770 **Rear Admiral of the Red**; 24.10.1770 **Vice Admiral of the Blue**; 31.3.1775 **Vice Admiral of the White**; 7.12.1775 **Vice Admiral of the Red**; 26.1.1778 *Prince George* (98); 29.1.1778 **Admiral of the Blue**; 9.3.1778-16.5.1778 *Victory* (100); 18.3.1778-1779 CinC — English Channel; 27.9.1780-22.4.1782 M.P. for Surrey; 27.3.1782-2.10.1786 Privy Counsellor; 1.4.1782-29.1.1783 1st Lord; 8.4.1782 **Admiral of the White**; 10.4.1783-30.12.1783 1st Lord.

KER, WILLIAM

Dates: 1770 Died.
Family:
Service: **Lieutenant**; 31.3.1760[(NA 6.11.1762)]-6.4.1763[P] L. *Hunter* (10) Sloop.

KERLY, ANTHONY

Dates: c.1714 Born Maker, Cornwall; 19.8.1714 Baptised Maker, Cornwall; 17.3.1764 Died Plymouth; 25.4.1764 Buried Plymouth; 25.12.1765 Will Probate.
Family: Father John Kerley (d.1763); Mother Hannah Downing (d.1767); Sister Sara (1705-?); Brother Joseph (1707-1774); Brother John (1707-1774); Sister Mary [Manley] (1711-1790); Sister Ann (1717-?); Sister Margaret [Hunt].
Service: 26.11.1727 Ord. *Seahorse* (20); 29.11.1727 Vol-p-O *Seahorse* (20); 1.12.1729 Mid *Seahorse* (20); 15.8.1730 MidO *Hector* (40); 30.9.1731 Mid *Hector* (40); 7.6.1734 Passed; **Lieutenant**; 5.6.1741(22.3.1741/42) 3L *Superb* (60); 2.11.1741(2.6.1743) 2L *Lion* (60); 28.8.1742(2.6.1743) 2L *Worcester* (60); 19.7.1743 3L *Argyll* (50); 4.9.1744(JAM 18.4.1747)-13.3.1744/45 3L *Superb* (60); 8.5.1745-10.5.1745 3L *Duke* (90); 8.8.1745 1L *Devonshire* (80); **Commander**; 8.2.1745/46 *Weazle* (16) Sloop; **Captain**; 2.7.1746 *Grand Turk* (22); 5.12.1747-6.7.1748[P] *Ranger* (24).

KERLY, JOSEPH

Dates: 1765 Died.
Family:
Service: **Lieutenant**; 12.12.1740 L. *Grampus* (6) Sloop; 2.6.1741 3L *Elizabeth* (70); 2.11.1742 1L *Anglesea* (44); 20.4.1744-29.9.1746 1L *Sunderland* (60).

KERR, ROBERT

Dates: 1764 Died.
Family:
Service: 12.10.1722 Vol-p-O *Dartmouth* (54); 9.10.1724 Mid *Dartmouth* (54); 9.6.1725 MidO *Kinsale* (40); 2.8.1727 Passed; **Lieutenant**; 30.3.1734-16.2.1735/36[P] 4L *Devonshire* (80); 28.7.1738-7.12.1738[P] 2L *Tilbury* (60); 19.6.1739-15.1.1739/40 3L *Jersey* (60); 7.9.1742-10.11.1743 1L *Monmouth* (70).

KERR, ROBERT

Dates: 15.3.1804 Died.
Family:
Service: **Lieutenant**; 9.1.1747/48(28.10.1748) 3L *Superb* (60); 5.8.1748(28.10.1748)-25.10.1748[P] 4L *Essex* (70); 29.5.1755-14.10.1755 3L *Woolwich* (44); 14.2.1756 3L *Saint Albans* (60); 15.11.1756 3L *Cambridge* (80); 12.5.1757 3L *Devonshire* (70); 6.6.1758-27.7.1758 The Siege of Louisbourg; 12.1.1759(NA 29.12.1759) 1L *Devonshire* (70); 7.1.1762-10.2.1762 Operations against Martinique; 14.3.1762(10.12.1762) 1L *Stag* (32); 5.7.1762(10.12.1762)-29.11.1762[P] 2L *Woolwich* (44); 18.10.1763 1L *Ramillies* (74); 2.4.1764 1L *Tweed* (32); 1.4.1765 1L *Aquilon* (28); 18.1.1766-2.4.1766 1L *Launceston* (44); 1797 Lieutenant of Greenwich Hospital.

KERSWELL, EDWARD

Dates: c.1724 Born; 1780 Died; 19.2.1780 Will Probate.
Family:
Service: 15.10.1742 Capt Serv *Norfolk* (80); 15.9.1743 Capt Serv *Marlborough* (90); 11.2.1743/44-12.2.1743/44 Battle of Toulon; 23.2.1743/44 Able *Marlborough* (90); 12.10.1745 Mid *Torrington* (44); 6.5.1747 Mate *Torrington* (44); 24.9.1747 Mate *Nottingham* (60); 14.10.1747 2nd Battle of Cape Finisterre; 31.1.1747/48 Action of 1748/01/31; 4.5.1749 Passed; **Lieutenant**; 7.12.1756 4L *Fougueux* (64); 17.6.1757 3L *Fougueux* (64); 27.1.1758 2L *Maidstone* (28); 5.6.1758-12.6.1758 Raid on Saint-Malo; 20.11.1759 Battle of Quiberon Bay; 22.1.1761 1L

Maidstone (28); 10.9.1761-22.6.1764[P] 1L *Montreal* (32); 23.6.1764 1L *Montreal* (32); 20.6.1765-25.9.1766[P] 3L *Centurion* (50); 3.11.1770-19.1.1771 4L *Ocean* (90).

KESTELL, JOHN

Dates: 1755 Died.
Family:
Service: **Lieutenant**; 10.2.1748/49 3L *Chester* (50); 19.9.1749-22.1.1753[P] L. *Swallow* (14) Sloop.

KIDD, DANDY

Dates: c.1736 Born; 1772 Died; 4.4.1772 Will Probate.
Family:
Service: 1753-1755 Merchant Service; 16.2.1755 Mid *Medway* (60); 20.10.1756 Able *Medway* (60); 30.12.1756-14.2.1759 Mid *Medway* (60); 5.9.1757-6.10.1757 Raid on Rochefort; 14.2.1759 Passed; **Lieutenant**; 11.4.1759 4L *Revenge* (64); 2.11.1759 3L *Revenge* (64); 20.11.1759 Battle of Quiberon Bay; 7.3.1760-15.12.1762[P] 3L *Dragon* (74); 29.3.1761-11.6.1761 Expedition against Belle-Isle; 7.1.1762-10.2.1762 Operations against Martinique; 24.2.1762-25.2.1762 Capture of Saint Lucia; 6.6.1762-13.8.1762 Operations against Havana.

KING, ISAAC

Dates: c.1729 Born; 1759 Died; 22.12.1759 Will Probate.
Family: Wife Mary;
Service: 8.3.1744/45 Ord. *Canterbury* (60); 16.5.1745 Able *Canterbury* (60); 27.6.1746-4.1.1746/47[C] Mid *Louisburg* (8) Fireship; 16.7.1751 Mid *Tartar* (20); 10.7.1755-13.5.1756 Mid *Dunkirk* (60); 13.5.1756 Passed; **Lieutenant**; 27.7.1757 L. *Fly* (8) Sloop; 2.5.1758 L. *Furnace* (8) Bomb Vessel; 18.11.1758[(Africa 19.3.1759)] 4L *Nassau* (64); 29.12.1758 Capture of Goree; 2.1.1759[(Africa 19.3.1759)]-7.9.1759[†] 3L *Nassau* (64).

KING, SIR RICHARD (1ST BARONET OF BELLEVUE)

Dates: 10.8.1730 Born Gosport; 2.6.1784 Knight Bachelor; 1792 1st Baronet of Bellevue; 7.11.1806 Died.
Family: Father Curtis King (d. 1745); Mother Mary (fl. c.1700–c.1750), daughter of Lieutenant Benjamin Barnett RN (d. 1703); Wife Susannah Margaretta Coker; Son Richard (2nd Baronet of Bellevue), RN (1774-1834).
Service: 28.6.1738-8.11.1742 Able *Dragon* (60); 24.7.1741 Action of 1741-07-24; 3.4.1743-23.4.1744 Mid *Prince Frederick* (70); 25.1.1744/45-20.12.1745 Mid *Deptford* (60); 1.2.1745/46 Passed; **Lieutenant**; 1.2.1745/46[(EI 17.8.1749)] 3L *Preston* (50); 25.6.1746 1st Battle of Negapatam; 24.3.1747/48[(EI 17.8.1749)]-23.11.1749[SC] 2L *Preston* (50); 23.4.1753 L. *Arundel* (24); 19.2.1754 2L *Bristol* (50); 28.3.1754 2L *Tiger* (60); 11.1.1756-14.1.1756 Capture of Geriah; **Commander**; 23.7.1756 *Kingfisher* (14) Sloop; 19.1.1758 *Bonetta* (10) Sloop; 16.1.1759-19.1.1759 Attack on Martinique; **Captain**; 29.1.1759[(BLI 25.10.1759)] *Rye* (20); 12.5.1759[(BLI 22.7.1760)]-16.1.1760[P] *Ludlow Castle* (44); 11.1.1760 *Argo* (28); 24.9.1762-6.10.1762 Battle of Manilla; 18.7.1763[(EI 6.8.1764)]-24.6.1764[P] *Grafton* (68); 7.12.1770 *Northumberland* (68); 28.1.1771 *Ardent* (64); 5.3.1771-7.12.1773 *Asia* (64); 5.1.1778 *Monmouth* (64); 19.1.1778 *Pallas* (36); 14.9.1778 Occupation of Saint-Pierre and Miquelon; 15.10.1778[(NF 30.11.1778)] *Europe* (64); 25.1.1779-25.1.1780 *Exeter* (64); 1.1782-8.1782 Commodore *Exeter* (64); 17.2.1782 Battle of Sadras; 12.4.1782 Battle of Providien; 6.7.1782 2nd Battle of Negapatam; 8.1782-6.1784 Commodore *Hero* (74); 3.9.1782 Battle of Trincomalee; 20.6.1783 2nd Battle of Cuddalore; 24.9.1787 **Rear Admiral of the White**; 29.6.1790 CinC — The Downs; 29.6.1790 *Adventure* (44); 23.8.1790 *Dictator*

(64); 21.9.1790 **Rear Admiral of the Red**; 29.3.1791-2.9.1791[P] *Saint George* (98); 4.9.1791-13.2.1793 *Saint George* (98); 11.4.1792-1793 Gov. of Newfoundland; 11.4.1792-21.5.1794 CinC — Newfoundland; 8.1792-1.1793 *Assistance* (50); 1.2.1793 **Vice Admiral of the Blue**; 11.2.1793-1794 *Stately* (64); 12.4.1794 **Vice Admiral of the White**; 4.7.1794 **Vice Admiral of the Red**; 3.12.1794-1796 CinC — Plymouth; 1.1795-1799 *Cambridge* (80); 1.6.1795 **Admiral of the Blue**; 14.2.1799 **Admiral of the White**; 9.11.1805 **Admiral of the Red.**

KINLOCH, DAVID

Dates: 1736 Born Perth, Scotland; 17.6.1818 Died Gourdie, Dundee; 2.1.1819 Will Probate.
Family: Father Charles Kinloch; Mother Margaret Nairne; Wife Isabella Mylne married 14.12.1786.
Service: 1751-1755 Merchant Service; 2.3.1754/55 Mid *Saint George* (90); 12.6.1756 Able *Ramillies* (90); 5.7.1756-2.5.1757 Mid *Ramillies* (90); 2.5.1757 Passed; **Lieutenant**; 22.5.1758-22.2.1759 L. *Cormorant* (8) Fireship; 5.6.1758-12.6.1758 Raid on Saint-Malo; 3.4.1759-1.1.1761[F] 4L *Duc d'Aquitaine* (64); 1.8.1799 **Superannuated Commander.**

KINNEER, JAMES

Dates: 19.4.1811 Died.
Family:
Service: **Lieutenant**; 7.8.1759-5.1.1762 4L *Somerset* (68); 17.11.1764-19.11.1767 3L *Temeraire* (74); 10.2.1768 L. *Dispatch* (14) Sloop; 16.1.1770 2L *Solebay* (28) Frigate; 7.7.1772 1L *Solebay* (28) Frigate; 4.3.1773-22.6.1775 3L *Kent* (74); 9.8.1775-16.3.1776 1L *Foudroyant* (80); 6.9.1776 2L *Albion* (74); 14.2.1778 1L *Albion* (74); 24.2.1778 1L *Formidable* (98); 27.7.1778 1st Battle of Ushant; **Commander**; 19.11.1778-21.9.1779 *Salamander* (8) Fireship; 22.2.1780-4.6.1782[P] *Lord Amherst* Hired Armed Ship; 30.3.1787-8.9.1789 *Wasp* (14) Sloop; **Captain**; 26.8.1789-4.12.1789 *Diana* (32); 10.5.1790 *Daphne* (20); 11.11.1790 *Hyaena* (24); 30.10.1791-16.4.1792 *Hyaena* (24); 6.5.1808 **Superannuated Rear Admiral.**

KINSEY, WILLIAM

Dates: 30.5.1755 Died; 27.2.1756 Will Probate.
Family: Sister Margaret;
Service: **Lieutenant**; 29.5.1741-1.2.1741/42 6L *Barfleur* (90); **Commander**; 13.2.1744/45[MED 4.2.1745/46] *Enterprise* Sloop; 8.2.1745/46-25.5.1746[P] 4L *Neptune* (90); 10.12.1751-30.5.1755[†] *Vulture* (14) Sloop.

KIRBY, ANTHONY

Dates: 1770 Died.
Family:
Service: **Lieutenant**; 17.7.1761[29.9.1763] 2L *Cerberus* (28); 17.7.1762[EI 29.9.1763]-27.9.1763[P] 1L *Cerberus* (28); 26.5.1769-15.6.1769 3L *Yarmouth* (64); 28.6.1769-1770[†] 1L *Lowestoffe* (32).

KIRBY, MATHEW

Dates: c.1717 Born; 1781 Died.
Family:
Service: 18.5.1730-24.1.1731/32[P] Capt Serv *Lark* (40); 25.11.1733 Capt Serv *Salisbury* (50); 22.6.1737 QGnr *Gloucester* (50); 9.4.1738 Mid *Flamborough* (20); 18.5.1740 Mate *Flamborough* (20); 25.9.1740 Mid *Flamborough* (20); 3.9.1741 Passed; **Lieutenant**; 31.10.1753-1.6.1757 4L

Culloden (74); 20.5.1756 Battle of Minorca; 5.4.1757 Action of April 5 1757; 10.9.1759 5L *Princess Royal* (90); 12.10.1762-15.1.1763[P] 4L *Princess Royal* (90).

KIRK, JAMES

Dates: c.1721 Born; 10.1787 Died.

Family:

Service: 5.7.1742 Passed; **Lieutenant**; 29.1.1742/43 L. *Furnace* (8) Bomb Vessel; 6.6.1744-15.4.1745 3L *Gosport* (44); 29.9.1746 2L *Dragon* (60); **Commander**; 29.1.1747/48[(JAM 16.3.1749/50)] *Vanqueur* Sloop; 11.5.1748[(JAM 12.5.1749)] *Vulture* (14) Sloop; **Captain**; 23.6.1748[(JAM 12.5.1749)]-11.4.1749[P] *Elizabeth* (70); 24.7.1755 *Lynn* (44); 10.1.1759-29.1.1759 *Duc d'Aquitaine* (64); 20.2.1759-28.12.1759 *America* (60); 18.8.1759-19.8.1759 Battle of Lagos Bay; 1777-10.1787 Commissioner of the Victualling Board.

KIRK, ROBERT

Dates: c.1731 Born; 1798 Died.

Family:

Service: 21.4.1744 Gnr Serv *Hampton Court* (64); 8.1.1744/45 Action of 1745-01-08; 18.4.1748 Able *Hampton Court* (64); 30.11.1748 Able *Centurion* (50); 25.6.1749 Mid *Centurion* (50); 18.6.1752 Able *Centurion* (50); 4.10.1752 Passed; **Lieutenant**; 15.2.1755[(24.5.1762)] 2L *Kingfisher* (14) Sloop; 11.1.1756-14.1.1756 Capture of Geriah; 25.2.1756[(24.5.1762)] 1L *Kingfisher* (14) Sloop; 23.7.1756[(24.5.1762)] 2L *Bridgewater* (24); 29.1.1757[(24.5.1762)] 1L *Bridgewater* (24); 11.3.1757[(1.6.1762)] 5L *Cumberland* (66); 1.4.1757[(1.6.1762)] 5L *Kent* (64); 1.8.1757[(1.6.1762)] 5L *Cumberland* (66); 4.9.1757[(EI 1.6.1762)]-13.10.1757 3L *Tiger* (60); 25.3.1758[(EI 7.6.1762)]-17.3.1760 3L *Yarmouth* (64); 29.4.1758 Battle of Cuddalore; 3.8.1758 Battle of Negapatam; 10.1758 **Commander**; **Captain**; 1.10.1758[(EI 24.5.1762)]-2.11.1760 *Cumberland* (66); 10.9.1759 Battle of Pondicherry.

KIRKWOOD, ALEXANDER

Dates: c.1735 Born; 29.12.1792 Died.

Family:

Service: 13.11.1752 Able *Nightingale* (22); 18.9.1755 Able *Prince George* (80); 25.11.1755 Mid *Prince George* (80); 10.11.1756 Able *Prince George* (80); 11.2.1757 Mid *Prince George* (80); 22.7.1757 Mate *Gibraltar* (20); 21.5.1758 Mate *Gramont* (18) Sloop; 6.6.1758-27.7.1758 The Siege of Louisbourg; 27.12.1758 ActL *Scarborough* (20); 11.8.1759 Mate *Scarborough* (20); 15.2.1760 Passed; **Lieutenant**; 26.7.1762[(14.2.1763)]-5.1763[P] L. *Charming Polly* Hired Transport; 2.5.1767 L. *Wasp* (8) Sloop; 17.1.1769-30.3.1770[D] 1L *Guadeloupe* (28); 30.3.1770 Dismissed; 29.9.1770 L. *Kingfisher* (14) Sloop; 18.9.1771-11.5.1775 L. *Raven* (14) Sloop; 26.7.1777-12.6.1780 1L *Hussar* (28); 19.1.1781-19.1.1782 1L *Raisonable* (64); 9.3.1782-24.6.1782 1L *Crown* (64); 29.7.1783 1L *Grampus* (50).

KITE, WILLIAM

Dates: c.1719 Born; 25.6.1792 Died.

Family:

Service: 25.6.1741 QGnr *Lion* (60); 29.10.1741 Mid *Lichfield* (50); 22.8.1742 Able *Guernsey* (50); 24.7.1743 Able *Port Mahon* (20); 10.10.1743 Mid *Lynn* (44); 10.6.1745 Mid *Dover* (44); 10.1.1745/46 Passed; **Lieutenant**; 7.3.1745/46-6.7.1749 L. *Swallow* (10) Sloop; 9.6.1746-26.6.1747[W] Mid *Maidstone* (50); 16.7.1749[(EI 31.5.1750)]-12.6.1750[P] 2L *Eltham* (40); 16.1.1753 2L *Mars* (64); 22.4.1755-24.6.1755[W] 2L *Mars* (64); 26.5.1756 3L *Marlborough* (80); 5.7.1756-

15.1.1759 3L *Terrible* (74); 8.1757-10.1757 Louisbourg Expedition; 6.6.1758-27.7.1758 The Siege of Louisbourg; **Commander**; 4.3.1761-14.2.1763[P] *Speedwell* (8) Sloop.

KNACKSTON, THOMAS

Dates: 1710 Born; 1788 Died.
Family:
Service: 7.10.1735 Passed; **Lieutenant**; 15.12.1738[(6.12.1740)] 3L *Windsor* (60); 4.4.1740[(6.12.1740)] 2L *Windsor* (60); 27.3.1741 3L *Duke* (90); 7.9.1741 2L *Duke* (90); 30.9.1741 1L *Marlborough* (90); 25.11.1741[(19.1.1743/44)] 1L *Somerset* (80); 11.2.1743/44-12.2.1743/44 Battle of Toulon; **Commander**; 12.7.1745-1.9.1745 *Vulture* (10) Sloop; 22.4.1746-23.10.1747 *Ferret* (14) Sloop; 23.4.1753 *Grampus* (14) Sloop; **Captain**; 5.4.1757-21.9.1757 *Vanguard* (68).

KNIGHT, GEORGE

Dates: c.1733 Born; 2.7.1768 Died.
Family:
Service: 3.9.1747 QM Mate *Saltash* (10) Sloop; 15.1.1748/49 Mid *Saltash* (14) Sloop; 27.12.1750 Able *Saltash* (14) Sloop; 5.8.1752 Mid *Phoenix* (24); 14.3.1755 Passed; **Lieutenant**; 1.4.1758[(30.9.1758)] 2L *Hampton Court* (64); 2.2.1759 4L *Monmouth* (70).

KNIGHT, JAMES

Dates: c.1733 Born; 29.9.1765 Died.
Family:
Service: 1.1.1742/43 Able *Cumberland* (80); 2.10.1743 Mid *Cumberland* (80); 5.11.1743 Mid *Centurion* (60); 7.3.1743/44 Mid *Defiance* (60); 30.3.1747-2.9.1747 Able *Namur* (90); 14.2.1759 Passed; **Lieutenant**; 9.1.1760 5L *Royal William* (84); 3.11.1760 6L *Royal William* (84); 16.2.1761-23.2.1763[P] 5L *Royal William* (84); 29.3.1761-11.6.1761 Expedition against Belle-Isle.

KNIGHT, JAMES

Dates: c.1739 Born; 1762 Died.
Family:
Service: 1753-1754 Merchant Service; 28.8.1754 Mid *Wolf* (8) Sloop; 12.5.1756 Mid *Hampton Court* (64); 21.6.1756 Mate *Phoenix* (24); 21.2.1757 Mate *Medway* (60); 5.9.1757-6.10.1757 Raid on Rochefort; 1.12.1757 Mate *Penzance* (44); 6.4.1758 Able *Tartar* (28); 7.6.1758 Mate *Tartar* (28); 2.5.1759 Passed; **Lieutenant**; 4.4.1760 L. *Cormorant* (8) Fireship; 1.7.1760-9.9.1763[P] 2L *Trent* (28); 6.6.1762-13.8.1762 Operations against Havana.

KNIGHT, JOHN

Dates: c.1712 Born; 1788 Died.
Family: Wife Jean Hay; Son John, RN (1747-1831).
Service: 16.2.1726/27 Able *Dursley Galley* (20); 24.6.1730 YoS *Dursley Galley* (20); 6.12.1730 Able *Rye* (20); 17.7.1731-16.12.1732[P] Gnr Mate *Rye* (20); 4.3.1737/38 Mid *Rippon* (60); 24.1.1738/39 Mid *Oxford* (50); 16.4.1740 Passed; **Lieutenant**; 18.7.1740 L. *Gibraltar* (20); 25.5.1742-9.10.1743 1L *Medway* (60); **Commander**; 3.4.1746-19.10.1746 *Happy Jennet* (20) Hired Ship; 27.10.1746-1.7.1752[P] *Saltash* (10) Sloop; 23.7.1754 *Wolf* (8) Sloop; **Captain**; 8.5.1756-21.5.1756 *Phoenix* (24); 20.5.1756 Battle of Minorca; 14.2.1757 *Arundel* (24); 18.11.1757 *Penzance* (44); 13.1.1758 *Tartar* (28); 5.6.1758-12.6.1758 Raid on Saint-Malo;

31.8.1762-15.12.1762[P] *Lion* (58); 25.3.1763-2.5.1766 *Emerald* (32); 4.11.1780 **Superannuated Rear Admiral.**

KNIGHT, SIR JOSEPH

Dates: c.1708 Born; 24.6.1773 Knight Bachelor; 18.7.1775 Died; 14.10.1775 Will Probate.
Family:
Service: 28.11.1727 Mid *Hampton Court* (70); 30.4.1729 Mid *Pearl* (40); 23.4.1730 ActL *Pearl* (40); 7.6.1730 Mid *Pearl* (40); 14.1.1731/32 Mid *Advice* (54); 10.3.1731/32 Able *Gosport* (42); 2.5.1732 Able *Rupert* (60); 10.10.1732 Mate *Experiment* (20); 13.7.1734 Mate *Deal Castle* (20); 2.10.1735 Passed; **Lieutenant**; 11.2.1739/40(9.5.1741)-28.8.1740 L. *Blandford* (20); 28.8.1741(19.11.1741) 1L *Windsor* (60); 28.12.1741 1L *Cambridge* (80); 16.4.1742(13.2.1743/44) 3L *Russell* (80); 24.7.1742(13.2.1743/44) 6L *Namur* (90); 4.10.1742(13.2.1743/44) 5L *Namur* (90); 13.11.1742(13.2.1743/44) 3L *Namur* (90); 17.3.1742/43(13.2.1744/45)-13.8.1743 2L *Namur* (90); **Commander**; 2.6.1743(11.12.1744)-18.9.1744[P] *Guarland's Prize* Xebec; **Captain**; 31.7.1746-29.5.1752[P] *Ruby* (50); 20.9.1746-25.9.1746 Lorient Operations; 12.5.1756 *Rainbow* (44); 23.3.1757-21.5.1759[P] *Fougueux* (64); 29.12.1758 Capture of Goree; 5.7.1759 *Princess Mary* (60); 5.8.1761-22.7.1763[P] *Belleisle* (64); 6.6.1762-13.8.1762 Operations against Havana; 23.10.1770-17.6.1771[P] *Ramillies* (74); 18.6.1771-1.11.1773 *Ocean* (90); 31.3.1775 **Rear Admiral of the White.**

KNIGHT, RICHARD

Dates: 1798 Died; 6.11.1798 Will Probate.
Family:
Service: 27.2.1741/42(MED 28.6.1746) 6L *Marlborough* (90); 27.5.1742 **Lieutenant**; 1.6.1742(MED 18.6.1746) 5L *Marlborough* (90); 1.9.1742(MED 18.6.1746) 4L *Nassau* (70); 11.9.1742(MED 18.6.1746) 4L *Marlborough* (90); 11.2.1743/44-12.2.1743/44 Battle of Toulon; 8.11.1744(MED 18.6.1746)-14.1.1744/45 6L *Neptune* (90); 24.2.1744/45(MED 18.6.1746) 2L *Neptune* (90); 25.3.1745(MED 18.6.1746) 1L *Neptune* (90); **Commander**; 4.4.1745(MED 11.7.1746)-16.6.1746[F] *Lightning* (8) Bomb Vessel; **Captain**; 5.2.1756 *Surprise* (24); 17.2.1758-30.8.1762 *Liverpool* (28); 20.4.1779 **Superannuated Rear Admiral.**

KNOLLYS, THE HON. CYPRIAN

Dates: 8.9.1734 Baptised Burford, Oxfordshire; 10.4.1760 Died.
Family: Father Rev. Charles Knollis, 4th Earl of Banbury (1703-1771); Mother Martha; Brother William, 5th Earl (d.1776); Brother Thomas Wood, 6th Earl (1726-1793); Brother Charles (d.1748); Brother Samuel; Brother Francis.
Service: 28.10.1753 Capt Serv *Cumberland* (66); 10.5.1755 Mid *Winchester* (50); 11.11.1755 Mid *Hampton Court* (64); 23.8.1756 Mid *Prince George* (80); 3.1.1757 Mid *Prince* (90); 1.3.1756/57 Mid *Culloden* (74); 5.4.1757 Action of April 5 1757; 23.8.1757 Mid *Saint George* (90); 6.8.1758-11.10.1758 Mid *Montagu* (60); 11.10.1758 Passed; **Lieutenant**; 27.10.1758 2L *Torrington* (44); 2.12.1758-10.4.1760[†] L. *Bideford* (20).

KNOWLER, CHARLES

Dates: 1789 Died.
Family:
Service: 14.11.1722 Capt Serv *Bedford* (70); 20.7.1724-4.5.1725 Able *Argyll* (50); 5.5.1725 MidO *Argyll* (50); 2.8.1725 Mid *Argyll* (50); 12.7.1728 Passed; **Lieutenant**; 30.3.1734 4L *Orford* (70); 28.7.1738-9.3.1738/39 3L *Chester* (54); 4.3.1739/40 1L *Gloucester* (50); 15.3.1739/40 1L *Adventure* (40); 18.7.1740 2L *Tiger* (50); 6.8.1740 2L *Guernsey* (50); 11.2.1743/44-12.2.1743/44 Battle of Toulon; 14.3.1743/44 1L *Falkland* (50); **Commander**; 2.4.1744-13.4.1744 *Drake*

(14) Sloop; 23.4.1744 *Princess Royal* (24) Storeship; **Captain**; 23.1.1745/46 *Bridgewater* (24); 5.12.1747-17.8.1748[P] *Dover* (44); 5.11.1770 **Superannuated Rear Admiral.**

KNOWLER, THOMAS

Dates: c.1712 Born; 1783 Died.
Family:
Service: 27.6.1732 Mid *Edinburgh* (70); 29.7.1732 Able *Edinburgh* (70); 3.2.1732/33-27.1.1733/34[P] Mid *Suffolk* (70); 6.5.1734 Passed; **Lieutenant**; 14.9.1739 4L *Kent* (70); 7.12.1739 3L *Kent* (70); 8.4.1740 Capture of the Princesa; 27.9.1740 3L *Boyne* (80); 6.10.1740 2L *Boyne* (80); 7.10.1740 1L *Boyne* (80); 8.6.1741[22.1.1741/42]-24.9.1743 1L *Princess Caroline* (80); **Commander**; 19.8.1744[26.6.1745]-28.5.1745 *Nazareth* (8) Fireship; **Captain**; 11.8.1746-13.6.1748[P] *Lys* (24); 16.1.1753-25.2.1756 *Salisbury* (50); 11.1.1756-14.1.1756 Capture of Geriah; 9.4.1763-1.4.1765 *Milford* (28); 1.4.1765[BLI 13.5.1766]-25.1.1766 *Lowestoffe* (32); 10.5.1766 Dismissed; 6.4.1775 **Superannuated Rear Admiral.**

KNOWLES, SIR CHARLES (1ST BARONET KNOWLES)

Dates: 1704 Born; 10.1765 1st Baronet Knowles; 9.12.1777 Died Bulstrode Street, St Marylebone, Middlesex.
Family: Wife Mary Alleyne (d. 1742); Wife Maria-Magdalena Theresa de Bouget; Son Edward, RN (1742-1761); Son Sir Charles Henry (2nd Baronet), RN (1754-1831).
Service: 3.1717/18-4.1718 Capt Serv *Buckingham* (70); 4.1718-3.12.1720[P] Capt Serv *Lennox* (70); 11.8.1718 Battle of Cape Passaro; 6.1721-6.1726 Able *Lyme* (20); 30.1.1728/29 Passed; **Lieutenant**; 29.5.1730[25.3.1731] L. *Trial* (10) Sloop; 15.6.1731 L. *Lion* (60); **Commander**; 24.11.1731-12.3.1734/35[P] *Southampton Hulk*; **Captain**; 4.2.1736/37 *Diamond* (40); 23.3.1739/40 Attack on Chagres; 6.8.1740 *Lichfield* (50); 16.9.1740-8.5.1742[P] *Weymouth* (60); 7.1.1740/41 Action of January 7 1741; 4.3.1740/41-5.1741 Operations against Cartagena; 31.8.1742 *Suffolk* (70); 18.2.1742/43 Attack on La Guaira; 15.4.1743-24.4.1743 Attack on Porto Cabello; 3.10.1743-3.9.1744 *Superb* (60); 8.8.1745-19.1.1745/46 *Devonshire* (80); 1746 Commodore *Canterbury* (60); 22.2.1745/46-21.6.1748[P] *Royal George* (100); 31.3.1746-5.1746 Commodore *Norwich* (50); 10.8.1746 Action of 1746-10-18; 5.1747-11.1747 Commodore *Norwich* (50); 6.6.1747-1749 CinC — Jamaica; **Rear Admiral of the White**; 15.7.1747-9.5.1749[P] *Canterbury* (60); 1748-7.1749 *Cornwall* (80); 9.4.1748 Battle of Santiago de Cuba; 12.5.1748 **Rear Admiral of the Red**; 12.10.1748 Battle of Havana; 28.11.1749-10.4.1752 M.P. for Gatton; 4.2.1755 **Vice Admiral of the Blue**; 13.11.1756 *Essex* (64); 8.12.1756 **Vice Admiral of the White**; 2.1757-1.8.1757 *Neptune* (90); 24.2.1757 **Vice Admiral of the Red**; 31.1.1758 **Admiral of the Blue**; 5.11.1765-10.1770 Rear Admiral of Great Britain; 22.1.1768 **Admiral of the White**; 10.1770-1774 In the service of Russia; 10.1770 Resigned.

KNOWLES, EDWARD

Dates: c.1742 Born; 28.12.1761 Died.
Family: Father Sir Charles Knowles (1st Baronet Knowles), RN (1704-1777); Mother Mary Alleyne (d. 1742); Brother Sir Charles Henry (2nd Baronet), RN (1754-1831).
Service: 2.1759 Mid *Neptune* (90); **Lieutenant**; 22.2.1759[3.3.1760] 6L *Royal William* (84); 3.11.1760 5L *Royal William* (84); **Commander**; 11.2.1761 *Laurel* (12) Sloop; 23.2.1761-28.12.1761 *Peregrine* (20) Sloop.

KNOWLES, JOHN

Dates: 14.3.1801 Died; 26.3.1801 Will Probate.
Family:
Service: **Lieutenant**; 19.1.1759(Africa 16.4.1759) L. *Furnace* (8) Bomb Vessel; 3.7.1759 Bombardment of Le Havre; 2.8.1759-30.3.1764[P] L. *Mercury* (20); 6.6.1762-13.8.1762 Operations against Havana; 29.11.1766-28.12.1770 L. *Scarborough* (20); 9.10.1772 3L *Egmont* (74); 8.11.1773 2L *Egmont* (74); 7.12.1773-9.10.1775 1L *Egmont* (74); **Commander**; 29.9.1778(NA 28.4.1779)-13.1.1779 *Sulphur* (8) Fireship; **Captain**; 1.7.1780(NA 29.12.1780) *Fowey* (24); 22.6.1781-25.11.1782 *Rotterdam* (50); 25.11.1782-17.4.1783[P] *Diligent* (70); 14.2.1799 **Rear Admiral of the Blue**; 1.1.1801 **Rear Admiral of the White**.

KYD, JAMES

Dates: 1793 Died; 9.10.1793 Will Probate.
Family: Wife Hannah Bevis; Wife Anne Eluisal; Daughter Mary Cardenyce; Daughter Helen Marine; Daughter Anna Kyd.
Service: **Lieutenant**; 3.5.1745(MED 15.11.1748) 4L *Russell* (80); 10.8.1745(15.11.1748) 3L *Rupert* (60); 1746 Passed; 11.11.1747(15.11.1748)-7.11.1748[P] 3L *Faversham* (44).

KYRBY, RICHARD

Dates: 1770 Died; 16.6.1770 Will Probate.
Family: Wife Mary; Son Richard; Daughter Mary; Son John; Son Robert; Son George.
Service: **Lieutenant**; 24.5.1744(29.1.1744/45)-19.1.1744/45[P] 4L *Buckingham* (70); 20.3.1744/45-1.9.1745 L. *Winchelsea* (20); 20.1.1745/46-1.8.1746 L. *Rose* (20) Ship; 31.3.1747 L. *Shoreham* (24); 16.11.1747-3.1.1748/49[P] 2L *Salisbury* (50); 11.3.1755-18.3.1757[C] 1L *Greenwich* (50); 26.7.1758 1L *Lion* (4).

Service Records L

LAFOREY, SIR JOHN (1ST BARONET LAFOREY)

Dates: 1729 Born; 2.12.1789 1st Baronet Laforey; 14.6.1796 Died At sea; 21.6.1796 Buried Portsmouth.

Family: Father John Laforey (d. 1753); Mother Mary Clayton (d. c1741); Wife Eleanor Farley (d. 1823) married 1763; Son Francis (2nd Baronet Laforey), RN (1767-1835); Son John (1768-1768); Daughter Juliana Molloy; Daughter Eleanor (1768-1806); Daughter Elizabeth (1772-1772); Brother Jasper (d. 1754); Sister Mary; Brother Francis (d. 1748); Brother Loftus, RN (1739-1769).

Service: 12.4.1748 Passed; **Lieutenant**; 12.4.1748 L. *Viper* (14) Sloop; 26.8.1748-16.9.1752[P] 3L *Centurion* (50); 2.10.1754 3L *Centurion* (50); **Commander**; 24.5.1755-14.8.1756[C] *Ontario* (12) Sloop; 2.12.1756-24.12.1756 *Hunter* (10) Sloop; **Captain**; 26.7.1758 *Echo* (24); 7.2.1762-2.9.1763[P] *Levant* (28); 12.10.1770-23.3.1771 *Pallas* (36); 19.9.1776 *Ocean* (90); 27.7.1778 1st Battle of Ushant; 26.3.1779-9.9.1779 *Invincible* (74); 16.9.1779-26.11.1779 Resident Commissioner at Antigua; 26.11.1779-2.1783 Commissioner of the Navy at Barbados & the Leeward Islands; 2.1783-1789 Resident Commissioner at Plymouth; 11.1789-9.1793 *Trusty* (50); 10.11.1789 **Rear Admiral of the White**; 16.11.1789 CinC — Barbados & the Leeward Islands; 21.9.1790 **Rear Admiral of the Red**; 1.2.1793 **Vice Admiral of the White**; 12.4.1794 **Vice Admiral of the Red**; 1795-1797 *Saturn* (74); 24.2.1795 CinC — Barbados & the Leeward Islands; 5.1795-7.1795 *Aimable* (32); 1.6.1795 **Admiral of the Blue**; 13.7.1795 Battle of Hyeres; 1796-14.6.1796 *Majestic* (74).

LAFOREY, LOFTUS

Dates: c.1739 Born; 1769 Died Portsmouth.

Family: Father John Laforey (d. 1753); Mother Mary Clayton; Brother Sir John (1st Baronet Laforey), RN (1729-1796).

Service: 1752-1758 Merchant Service; 11.1.1755 Ord. *Centurion* (50); 13.6.1755 Able *Centurion* (50); 28.10.1755 Mid *Centurion* (50); 7.3.1756/57 Mid *Torbay* (74); 5.9.1757-6.10.1757 Raid on Rochefort; 18.11.1757-12.3.1759/60 Able *Torbay* (74); 5.6.1758-12.6.1758 Raid on Saint-Malo; 29.12.1758 Capture of Goree; 20.11.1759 Battle of Quiberon Bay; 12.3.1760 Passed; **Lieutenant**; 11.4.1760-6.12.1762[P] 3L *Portland* (50); 24.1.1769 L. *Swan* (14) Sloop.

LAIRD, DAVID

Dates: 1739 Born; 1.1.1815 Died Arbroath, Scotland.

Family: Father Andrew Laird; Mother Ann Graham; Daughter Mary [Warren]; Sister Isabel [Warden].

Service: 1755-1758 Merchant Service; 1.6.1758 Able *Tartar* (28); 5.6.1758-12.6.1758 Raid on Saint-Malo; 7.11.1758 Mid *Tartar* (28); 7.6.1759 Mate *Tartar* (28); 1.7.1761 Passed; **Lieutenant**; 2.7.1762[(EI 28.2.1763)]-25.2.1763[P] L. *Peggy* Hired Transport; **Commander**; 18.5.1778[(NA

21.11.1780)-29.4.1782 *Jersey* (20) Hospital Ship; **Captain**; 1.12.1787 *Inconstant* (36); 3.11.1807 **Superannuated Rear Admiral.**

LAMBERT, HENRY

Dates: c.1730 Born; 1815 Died.
Family:
Service: 1752-1754 Merchant Service; 30.4.1754 Ord. *Worcester* (58); 21.6.1756 Mid *Aldborough* (20); 21.11.1756 Mate *Aldborough* (20); 12.1.1757 Mate *Enterprise* (44); 31.10.1757 Mid *Enterprise* (44); 5.7.1758 Passed; **Lieutenant**; 27.10.1758 L. *Dispatch* (14) Sloop; 9.5.1760 3L *Jersey* (60); 5.4.1762(24.6.1762)-7.7.1762 2L *Lynn* (44); 18.7.1800 **Superannuated Commander.**

LAMBERT, ROBERT

Dates: c.1706 Born; 1767 Died.
Family:
Service: 5.10.1739 Mid *Princess Caroline* (80); 5.11.1739 Mate *Princess Caroline* (80); 11.1.1742 Mid *Somerset* (80); 9.8.1742 Mate *Somerset* (80); 31.8.1742 Master *Gibraltar* (20); 25.2.1743 Master *Adventure* (44); 3.1.1744-15.5.1746 Master *Gloucester* (60); 15.5.1746 Passed; **Lieutenant**; 12.6.1747 6L *Royal Sovereign* (104); 9.10.1747-7.6.1748[P] 6L *Barfleur* (90); 30.1.1753 2L *Yarmouth* (64); 8.11.1756-17.1.1757 1L *Yarmouth* (64); 17.1.1757 3L *Yarmouth* (64); 17.2.1757 2L *Yarmouth* (64); 23.2.1757 3L *Monarch* (74); 23.8.1757 6L *Duke* (90); 22.9.1757-22.11.1757 2L *Harwich* (50); 29.5.1759 5L *Princess Royal* (90); 10.7.1759 4L *Princess Royal* (90); 12.10.1762 3L *Princess Royal* (90); 6.9.1763-27.3.1764 2L *Augusta* (64); 31.7.1765-12.12.1765 1L *Augusta* (64); 26.5.1766-28.10.1767 1L *Yarmouth* (64).

LAMBERT, ROBERT ALEXANDER

Dates: 24.7.1732 Born; 21.12.1801 Died.
Family: Father Sir John Lambert, 2nd Bt. (1690-1772); Mother Anne Holmes; Wife Catherine Byndloss married 19.1.1768; Son Robert Stuart, RN (1771-1836); Son Henry, RN (d.1813); Brother Sir John Lambert, 3rd Bt. (1728-1799).
Service: 8.12.1745 Capt Serv *Edinburgh* (64); 14.10.1747 2nd Battle of Cape Finisterre; 14.2.1747/48 Able *Edinburgh* (64); 3.8.1748 Mid *Edinburgh* (64); 14.9.1748 Able *Shoreham* (24); 21.10.1748 Mid *Centurion* (50); 17.6.1750 Able *Centurion* (50); 2.7.1752-4.10.1752 Mid *Centurion* (50); 4.10.1752 Passed; **Lieutenant**; 3.7.1754(11.11.1757) 2L *Bridgewater* (24); 5.4.1755(11.11.1757) 1L *Bridgewater* (24); 11.1.1756-14.1.1756 Capture of Geriah; 29.1.1757(11.11.1757)-10.5.1757 L. *Racehorse* (18) Sloop; 30.12.1757 2L *Norfolk* (74); 5.6.1758-12.6.1758 Raid on Saint-Malo; 5.10.1758 1L *Norfolk* (74); **Commander**; 10.1.1759 *Jamaica* (10) Sloop; **Captain**; 18.2.1760 *Wager* (24); 1.4.1761(16.12.1763)-1.10.1763[P] *Valeur* (28); 1.10.1766 *Phoenix* (44); 16.9.1767-4.10.1769 *Dorsetshire* (68); 8.10.1777 *Niger* (32); 11.2.1780-27.2.1780 *Leviathan* (50).

LANG, RICHARD

Dates: c.1735 Born; 5.1.1800 Died; 28.5.1800 Will Probate.
Family:
Service: 1753-1755 Merchant Service; 5.6.1755 Gnr Mate *Elizabeth* (70); 10.1.1756 Mid *Elizabeth* (64); 8.6.1757 Mid *Monarch* (74); 28.2.1758 Battle of Cartagena; 23.12.1758 Mid *Conqueror* (68); 25.6.1759 Mate *Raisonnable* (64); 26.10.1759-5.3.1759/60 Mid *Panther* (60); 5.3.1760 Passed; **Lieutenant**; 11.4.1760-6.10.1760[P] 5L *Monarch* (74); 29.3.1762-22.6.1763[P] 2L *Unicorn* (28).

LANGDON, WILLIAM

Dates: 1711 Born; 29.6.1785 Died; 2.7.1785 Will Probate.
Family:
Service: **Lieutenant**; 30.9.1743[4.6.1746]-20.7.1744[P] 3L *Centurion* (60); 4.6.1746 2L *Lark* (44); 18.6.1746 1L *Lark* (44); 4.3.1746/47 5L *Royal Sovereign* (104); 10.5.1747 3L *Royal Sovereign* (104); 9.10.1747 3L *Barfleur* (90); 26.12.1747 3L *Kent* (64); 27.9.1748-6.10.1752[P] 1L *Tavistock* (50); **Commander**; 8.12.1753-25.4.1755 *Swan* (14) Sloop; 16.1.1755 *Albany* (14) Sloop; **Captain**; 5.6.1756-16.1.1761[P] *Edinburgh* (64); 21.10.1757 Forrest's Action; 10.4.1761-21.3.1763[P] *Ocean* (90); 26.9.1780 **Rear Admiral of the White.**

LANGFORD, JOHN

Dates: c.1735 Born; 1781 Died; 27.6.1781 Will Probate.
Family:
Service: 1752-1756 Merchant Service; 31.7.1756 Able *Chichester* (68); 10.11.1756 Mid *Chichester* (68); 5.6.1758-12.6.1758 Raid on Saint-Malo; 26.11.1758 Able *Chichester* (68); 27.1.1759 Mid *Chichester* (68); 20.11.1759 Battle of Quiberon Bay; 30.4.1760 Passed; **Lieutenant**; 10.12.1760-9.2.1763[P] L. *Flamborough Prize* (14) Sloop; 27.3.1764 2L *Dorsetshire* (68); 5.1.1767-7.4.1767 3L *Dorsetshire* (68); 11.8.1768 L. *Favorite* (16) Sloop; 10.6.1770 Capture of Port Egmont; 25.9.1770-10.6.1771[P] 5L *Arrogant* (74); 28.8.1771-15.4.1773[D] L. *Cruizer* (8) Sloop; 15.4.1773 Dismissed; 13.12.1773 Rank restored.

LASH, JOSEPH

Dates: c.1719 Born; 1787 Died; 20.8.1787 Will Probate.
Family:
Service: 1748-1750 Merchant Service; 23.2.1749/50 Able *Defiance* (60); 28.12.1752 Able *Prince of Orange* (60); 26.5.1753 Mate *Solebay* (24); 5.11.1755 Passed; **Lieutenant**; 20.7.1759 5L *Monarch* (74); 23.10.1759-6.10.1760[P] 3L *Monarch* (74); 28.11.1760 3L *Hampton Court* (64); 9.2.1761-3.6.1763[P] 1L *Looe* (44); 2.2.1771 2L *Modeste* (64); 18.3.1771-16.10.1772[P] 1L *Modeste* (64); 4.3.1773 3L *Centaur* (74); 26.1.1774 4L *Centaur* (74); 25.8.1774 3L *Centaur* (74); 6.11.1775-11.5.1776 2L *Centaur* (74); 10.7.1776 3L *Hector* (74); 5.11.1777-13.5.1778 2L *Hector* (74).

LATHAM, THOMAS

Dates: c.1720 Born; 13.2.1762 Died.
Family:
Service: 20.5.1735 Ord. *Torrington* (40); 7.6.1737 Able *Torrington* (40); 21.6.1738 Mid *Jersey* (60); 13.11.1740 Able *Newcastle* (50); 4.6.1741 Passed; **Lieutenant**; 10.8.1741-31.5.1742 3L *Dartmouth* (50); 22.9.1744[MED 2.12.1748] 3L *Boyne* (80); 4.4.1745[MED 2.12.1748]-3.8.1745 6L *Neptune* (90); **Commander**; 15.7.1745[MED 14.12.1747] *Postillon* Xebec; **Captain**; 14.3.1746/47[MED 21.10.1748]-30.3.1747 *Boyne* (80); 10.1.1753-24.1.1754 *Eagle* (60); 24.1.1754 *Bristol* (50); 28.3.1754-3.3.1759 *Tiger* (60); 11.1.1756-14.1.1756 Capture of Geriah; 7.3.1757-1.4.1757 Expedition against Chandernagore; 29.4.1758 Battle of Cuddalore; 3.8.1758 Battle of Negapatam.

LATON, SHELDRAKE

Dates: c.1711 Born; 22.4.1776 Died.
Family:
Service: 12.3.1726/27 Vol-p-O *Prince Frederick* (70); 2.5.1728-30.6.1730[P] MidO *Dover* (40); 16.12.1730 Mid *Fox* (20); 9.12.1732 Able *Suffolk* (70); 18.3.1732/33 Mid *Fly* (8) Sloop;

12.9.1733 Passed; **Lieutenant**; 2.3.1733/34-8.4.1736[P] 6L *Namur* (90); 16.5.1738-2.12.1738[P] 4L *Princess Amelia* (80); 12.6.1739-3.7.1739 6L *Namur* (90); 4.7.1739-2.3.1739/40 3L *Namur* (90); 3.3.1739/40-16.4.1740[P] 1L *Namur* (90); 14.4.1740 1L *Victory* (100); **Captain**; 25.8.1741-21.10.1741 *Flamborough* (20); 24.8.1742-9.10.1743 *Bideford* (20); 14.9.1745-13.10.1747 *Barfleur* (90); 21.7.1756 **Superannuated Rear Admiral**.

LAUGHARNE, THOMAS

Dates: c.1738 Born; 1797 Died; 10.5.1797 Will Probate.
Family: Son Thomas, RN (d.1808).
Service: 1753-1755 Merchant Service; 7.5.1755 Able *Yarmouth* (64); 11.2.1757 Able *Invincible* (74); 1.4.1757 Mid *Lyme* (28); 26.12.1758 Mid *Saint Albans* (60); 18.8.1759-19.8.1759 Battle of Lagos Bay; 10.10.1759 Passed; **Lieutenant**; 7.11.1759 3L *Dover* (44); 23.3.1761 2L *Dover* (44); 3.4.1761-bef.23.12.1762[P] L. *Pluto* (8) Fireship; 28.12.1763-14.11.1768[P] LCmdr *Chaleur* (12) Schooner; 1.2.1770-27.5.1771[P] 3L *Rippon* (60); 24.3.1772 2L *Terrible* (74); 9.9.1773 2L *Ramillies* (74); 21.9.1773 1L *Ramillies* (74); 17.12.1773 4L *Barfleur* (90); 14.7.1774-11.4.1775 3L *Barfleur* (90); **Commander**; 14.9.1783[(NA 30.1.1784)]-19.11.1783[P] *Vulture* (14) Sloop; 16.8.1786-18.12.1787 *Scout* (16) Sloop; 17.10.1788 *Falcon* (14) Sloop; **Captain**; 3.11.1790-22.11.1790 *Thetis* (38).

LAWES, WILLIAM

Dates: c.1728 Born; 1780 Died; 21.10.1780 Will Probate.
Family:
Service: 12.8.1749 Able *Winchelsea* (20); 15.1.1749/50 Mid *Winchelsea* (20); 23.3.1751/52 Mid *Renown* (30); 24.12.1754 Mid *Culloden* (74); 1.10.1755 Passed; **Lieutenant**; 2.2.1757-7.5.1759[P] 2L *Arc-en-Ciel* (50); 6.4.1763-6.6.1766 LCmdr *Goodwill* (4) Cutter; 17.3.1777-30.6.1780[SC] 1L *Cornwall* (74); 6.7.1779 Battle of Grenada; 17.4.1780 Battle of Martinique; 15.5.1780 Action of March 15 1780; 19.5.1780 Action of March 19 1780.

LAWRENCE, PETER

Dates: 17.11.1758 Died.
Family:
Service: **Lieutenant**; 11.2.1726/27[(21.10.1729)] 3L *Nottingham* (60); 16.2.1726/27[(5.8.1729)] 3L *Rippon* (60); 22.5.1728[(5.8.1729)] 2L *Berwick* (70); 6.7.1729[(5.8.1729)]-5.11.1729[P] 1L *Mary Galley* (40); **Commander**; 23.12.1734[(22.8.1735)]-10.4.1738 *Wolf* (8) Sloop; **Captain**; 16.7.1739 *Augusta* (60); 17.9.1740 *Russell* (80); 27.9.1740 *Jersey* (60); 4.3.1740/41-5.1741 Operations against Cartagena; 19.11.1741-22.9.1742 *Tilbury* (60); 15.10.1742[(18.4.1744)] *Cumberland* (80); 11.11.1743[(18.4.1744)]-9.12.1744[P] *Lichfield* (50); 2.10.1744-10.5.1747[P] *Lennox* (70); 3.8.1746 Action of August 3 1746; 25.3.1747 Action of March 25 1747; 5.2.1755 **Superannuated Rear Admiral**.

LAWRIE, THOMAS

Dates: c.1722 Born; 1802 Died.
Family:
Service: 18.10.1749 Ord. *Cumberland* (66); 24.11.1749 Able *Cumberland* (66); 15.11.1754 Able *Badger* (10) Sloop; 5.7.1755 Cox *Badger* (10) Sloop; 1.1.1756 Mid *Badger* (10) Sloop; 27.7.1757 Able *Badger* (10) Sloop; 9.10.1757-14.2.1759 Mate *Nightingale* (22); 6.6.1758-27.7.1758 The Siege of Louisbourg; 14.2.1759 Passed; **Lieutenant**; 10.7.1759-21.7.1762[W] 3L *Chesterfield* (44); 28.6.1770-17.12.1772 L. *Hunter* (10) Sloop; 7.1.1774-1.2.1778 L. *Rose* (20); 2.7.1776-4.7.1776 Staten Island Landings.

LAWRIE, THOMAS

Dates: 1768 Died Bristol; 3.9.1768 Will Probate.
Family:
Service: **Lieutenant**; 14.11.1761[(17.6.1763)] L. *Echo* (24); 7.1.1762-10.2.1762 Operations against Martinique; 6.6.1762-13.8.1762 Operations against Havana; 6.12.1762-4.6.1763[P] L. *Martin* (14) Sloop.

LAWSON, HUGH

Dates: c.1739 Born; 1782 Died; 27.2.1782 Will Probate.
Family:
Service: 1751-1757 Merchant Service; 7.3.1756/57 Able *Tartar* (28); 8.4.1757 Mate *Tartar* (28); 5.6.1758-12.6.1758 Raid on Saint-Malo; 3.11.1758 Mid *Chatham* (50); 19.5.1759-7.5.1760 Able *Chatham* (50); 3.7.1759 Bombardment of Le Havre; 20.11.1759 Battle of Quiberon Bay; 7.5.1760 Passed; **Lieutenant**; 6.11.1762-23.12.1762[P] 3L *Princess Mary* (60); 29.3.1763-4.3.1766 2L *Lark* (32); 2.4.1766-5.12.1768 2L *Adventure* (32); 29.9.1770-3.10.1774[P] 2L *Minerva* (32); 24.1.1777 LCmdr *Kent's Regard* Hired Tender; 6.11.1777 2L *Shrewsbury* (74); 27.7.1778 1st Battle of Ushant; 5.8.1778 1L *Shrewsbury* (74); 13.6.1779-1.2.1780 1L *Royal George* (100); 16.1.1780 Battle of Cape St. Vincent; 1.2.1780 **Commander**; 1.2.1781[(BLI 7.8.1782)]-21.8.1781[SC] *Minorca* (20) Xebec.

LAWSON, JAMES

Dates: c.1725 Born; 29.3.1798 Died.
Family:
Service: 2.6.1739 Mid *Tiger* (50); 10.6.1740 Mid *Guernsey* (50); 21.9.1742 Mid *Norfolk* (80); 11.2.1743/44-12.2.1743/44 Battle of Toulon; 18.8.1744 Mid *Neptune* (90); 4.3.1744/45 Passed; **Lieutenant**; 3.6.1745[(MED 31.10.1748)] L. *Carcass* (8) Bomb Vessel; 18.10.1745[(31.10.1748)]-9.4.1748 4L *Essex* (70); 31.10.1748 3L *Essex* (70); 20.11.1755 L. *Centaur* (20); 24.10.1758-11.7.1763[P] 1L *Alarm* (32); 6.6.1762-13.8.1762 Operations against Havana; 28.6.1765-4.7.1768 LCmdr *Wells* (6) Cutter; 21.9.1796 **Superannuated Commander**.

LE CRAS, EDWARD

Dates: c.1718 Born; 4.4.1784 Died Bishops Teignton.
Family:
Service: 19.2.1732/33 Mid *Otter* (6) Sloop; 11.1.1735/36 Able *Gibraltar* (20); 8.4.1736 MidO *Gibraltar* (20); 28.5.1736 MidO *Leopard* (50); 8.7.1736 Mid *Leopard* (50); 14.5.1737 Able *Centurion* (60); 8.9.1737 Mid *Centurion* (60); 13.12.1737 Mate *Otter* (6) Sloop; 12.4.1739 Passed; **Lieutenant**; 11.12.1739 L. *Scipio* (8) Fireship; 16.9.1740 2L *Rupert* (60); 10.12.1741-12.7.1745 1L *Rupert* (60); 11.2.1743/44-12.2.1743/44 Battle of Toulon; 17.10.1746-13.3.1746/47 1L *Prince Edward* (44); **Commander**; 24.2.1747/48-4.12.1752[P] *Trial* (10) Sloop; 16.5.1753 *Otter* (14) Sloop; **Captain**; 4.2.1755 *Winchester* (50); 16.1.1759-19.1.1759 Attack on Martinique; 20.1.1759-1.5.1759 Capture of Guadeloupe; 23.7.1759[(BLI 19.11.1760)] *Lion* (58); 29.3.1761-11.6.1761 Expedition against Belle-Isle; 31.8.1762-2.3.1763[P] *Buckingham* (68); 19.10.1763-19.4.1766[P] *Kent* (74); 19.11.1767-22.5.1771[P] *Temeraire* (74); 15.9.1773 *Somerset* (68); 31.3.1775-19.9.1776 *Ocean* (90); 23.9.1777-14.1.1778 *Russell* (74).

LE FEBVRE, WILLIAM

Dates: 7.10.1778 Died.

Family:

Service: **Lieutenant**; 22.8.1741$^{(24.5.1742)}$-16.7.1742^{P} 3L *Bristol* (54); 31.7.1742-9.9.1743^{P} 3L *Ruby* (54); 23.9.1743 3L *Northumberland* (64); 29.12.1743-8.5.1744^{C} 3L *Northumberland* (64); 25.3.1745 3L *Gloucester* (50); 30.5.1745 2L *Gloucester* (50); 28.3.1747-5.8.1748^{P} 1L *Gloucester* (50); 14.10.1747 2nd Battle of Cape Finisterre; 9.10.1755-1760^{P} LCmdr *Cornwall* Prison Ship.

LEAK, JOHN

Dates: c.1736 Born; 1764 Died.

Family:

Service: 10.2.1749/50 Capt Serv *Vigilant* (60); 22.5.1754 Mid *Speedwell* (8) Sloop; 22.12.1754 Mid *Norwich* (50); 3.5.1757 Mid *Achilles* (60); 31.7.1757 Mate *Achilles* (60); 5.9.1757-6.10.1757 Raid on Rochefort; 9.8.1758 Passed; **Lieutenant**; 23.10.1759 5L *Monarch* (74); 22.1.1760-8.6.1761 3L *Medway* (60).

LEARY, JOHN

Dates: c.1724 Born; 7.2.1788 Will Probate; 1789 Died.

Family:

Service: 29.7.1749 Able *Guernsey* (50); 14.6.1750 Mid *Guernsey* (50); 30.6.1756 Mate *Sphinx* (24); 1.9.1756 Passed; **Lieutenant**; 30.9.1758 4L *Burford* (68); 20.11.1758 5L *Union* (90); 30.1.1759 5L *Royal William* (84); 7.2.1759 3L *York* (60); 21.2.1759-16.12.1762 4L *Lennox* (74); 24.9.1762-6.10.1762 Battle of Manilla; **Commander**; 10.11.1762$^{(EI\ 13.7.1765)}$-23.8.1763^{P} *Tiger* (74); **Captain**; 13.7.1765-19.7.1765^{P} *Panther* (60).

LEAVER, WILLIAM

Dates: c.1709 Born; 4.2.1764 Died.

Family:

Service: 21.1.1737/38 Mid *Experiment* (20); 12.9.1738 Mate *Phoenix* (20); 4.11.1738 Able *Rose* (20); 9.10.1739 Able *Greyhound* (20); 4.12.1739 Mid *Lancaster* (80); 19.12.1739 Able *Cumberland* (80); 30.3.1740 Mate *Cambridge* (80); 5.6.1740 Passed; **Lieutenant**; 29.8.1740-26.9.1740 L. *Thunder* (8) Bomb Vessel; 27.9.1740 3L *Rupert* (60); 13.10.1740 Able *Dunkirk* (60); 7.1.1740/41 Action of January 7 1741; 4.3.1740/41-5.1741 Operations against Cartagena; 5.10.1741 2L *Sapphire* (44); 27.10.1741-7.9.1742 1L *Sapphire* (44); 27.4.1742 Mid *Chester* (50); 20.9.1742 1L *Assistance* (50); 21.2.1742/43-27.3.1743 L. *Shark* (8) Sloop; 23.9.1743 L. *Sheerness* (20); 21.11.1743-17.9.1744 2L *Burford* (70); 15.2.1744/45 1L *Ludlow Castle* (44); 6.7.1745 1L *Norwich* (50); **Commander**; 10.5.1747$^{(JAM\ 13.12.1748)}$-9.1.1748/49^{P} *Comet* (10) Bomb Vessel; 26.6.1755-2.6.1760 *Wasp* (8) Sloop; 9.7.1763-10.2.1764 *Ranger* (8) Sloop.

LEE, THOMAS

Dates: c.1729 Born; 1.1770 Died Indian Ocean.

Family:

Service: 7.5.1742 Able *Adventure* (44); 19.7.1746 Able *Windsor* (60); 3.5.1747 1st Battle of Cape Finisterre; 5.6.1747 Mid *Windsor* (60); 14.10.1747 2nd Battle of Cape Finisterre; 21.11.1747 Able *Windsor* (60); 22.12.1747 Able *Tartar* (20); 27.12.1747 Mate *Tartar* (20); 10.10.1749-10.5.1750^{P} Mid *Sheerness* (24); 20.6.1750 Passed; **Lieutenant**; 22.4.1755-24.6.1755^{W} 4L *Mars* (64); 2.3.1756 2L *Jersey* (60); 10.8.1757 6L *Royal Anne* (100); 5.9.1757-6.10.1757 Raid on Rochefort; 17.1.1758 5L *Royal Anne* (100); 5.6.1758-12.6.1758 Raid on Saint-Malo; 14.5.1759

5L *Ramillies* (90); 18.10.1759-23.11.1759[P] 4L *Ramillies* (90); 10.3.1760-17.11.1760 1L *Royal George* (100); **Commander**; 21.11.1760-25.3.1763 *Tamar* (16) Sloop; **Captain**; 14.7.1763-16.12.1766[P] *Dreadnought* (60); 5.4.1769 *Achilles* (60); 15.6.1769-1.1770[†] *Aurora* (32).

LEEKE, HENRY SEBASTIAN

Dates: c.1736 Born; 15.9.1776 Died.
Family:
Service: 19.7.1749 Scholar *Royal Naval Academy*; 6.9.1752 MidO *Blandford* (20); 15.1.1754 MidO *Gosport* (44); 14.10.1754 Able *Advice* (50); 4.2.1756 Passed; **Lieutenant**; 27.10.1758-7.11.1758 L. *Saltash* (14) Sloop; 29.9.1770-28.5.1771[P] 2L *Prince of Wales* (74); 29.6.1771 3L *Egmont* (74); 9.10.1772 2L *Egmont* (74); 8.11.1773 1L *Egmont* (74); 7.12.1773-14.7.1774 1L *Barfleur* (90); 9.8.1775-9.10.1776 1L *Roebuck* (44).

LEGEYT, MATTHEW

Dates: c.1728 Born.
Family:
Service: 10.7.1750 Able *Chester* (50); 17.7.1754 Mid *Chester* (50); 1.6.1755 Mate *Bedford* (64); 8.1757-10.1757 Louisbourg Expedition; 5.12.1757 Passed; **Lieutenant**; 1.8.1758[NA 16.11.1759] 3L *Bedford* (64); 21.3.1759[NA 16.11.1759] 4L *Princess Amelia* (80); 29.3.1761-11.6.1761 Expedition against Belle-Isle; 25.3.1762[NA 16.11.1759] 3L *Princess Amelia* (80); 22.6.1762-14.1.1763[P] 3L *Magnanime* (74); 28.8.1778-19.10.1778 3L *Britannia* (100); 27.12.1799 **Superannuated Commander**.

LEGGE, GEORGE

Dates: 1760 Died; 1.4.1760 Will Probate.
Family:
Service: **Lieutenant**; 6.5.1741[9.9.1741] 3L *Shrewsbury* (80); 3.2.1743/44 2L *Shrewsbury* (80); 16.6.1744-10.11.1745 2L *Enterprise* (50); 19.8.1749-17.11.1752[P] 2L *Cumberland* (66); 22.8.1753 2L *Cumberland* (66); 28.3.1754 2L *Eagle* (60); 31.7.1754 2L *Nottingham* (60); **Commander**; 11.3.1755 *Swift* (8) Sloop; 28.2.1756 *Hunter* (10) Sloop; **Captain**; 2.12.1756 *Queenborough* (24); 25.3.1758[EI 6.5.1760]-30.4.1758 *Newcastle* (50); 4.1758 Dismissed; 29.4.1758 Battle of Cuddalore.

LEGGE, JOHN

Dates: c.1716 Born; 9.9.1779 Died; 2.11.1779 Will Probate.
Family:
Service: 1.5.1732 Vol-p-O *Princess Amelia* (80); 23.11.1732 Ord. *Dolphin* (20); 13.11.1733 Able *Dolphin* (20); 10.7.1736 Able *Centurion* (60); 29.8.1736 Mid *Portland* (50); 28.7.1737 Able *Eltham* (40); 23.5.1738 MidO *Romney* (50); 19.7.1739 Passed; **Lieutenant**; 31.8.1739-11.10.1740 3L *Rochester* (54); 12.10.1740 2L *Rochester* (54); 27.3.1741 2L *Elizabeth* (70); 2.6.1741 1L *Elizabeth* (70); 21.3.1742/43[4.7.1744] 3L *Salisbury* (50); 11.2.1743/44-12.2.1743/44 Battle of Toulon; 20.8.1744 1L *Fowey* (40); **Commander**; 19.7.1746-17.8.1747[P] *Pluto* (8) Fireship.

LEGGE, JULIAN

Dates: 29.6.1762 Died.
Family:
Service: **Lieutenant**; 10.4.1744[1.7.1745] 4L *Prince of Orange* (70); 12.4.1744[1.7.1745] 3L *Prince of Orange* (70); 20.3.1744/45[11.6.1745] L. *Experiment* (20); **Commander**; 11.6.1745 *Mediator* (10)

Sloop; 24.6.1745 *Lizard* (10) Sloop; **Captain**; 6.5.1746 *Inverness* (22); 22.1.1746/47-9.8.1748[P] *Fox* (20); 5.12.1751-20.11.1752[P] *Bristol* (50); 1.3.1753-14.8.1754 *Shoreham* (24); 20.8.1756-2.2.1757 *Princess Louisa* (60); 17.8.1757 *Chesterfield* (44); 9.12.1758 *Trident* (64); 1.10.1760[(NA 13.12.1763)] *Sutherland* (50); 3.6.1761-7.6.1761 Occupation of Dominica; 7.1.1762-10.2.1762 Operations against Martinique; 14.3.1762[(13.12.1763)]-29.6.1762 *Temple* (68).

LEIGH, THOMAS

Dates: c.1707 Born; 1765 Died.

Family:

Service: 9.1.1726/27 Vol-p-O *Colchester* (50); 10.1.1729/30 MidO *Colchester* (50); 18.4.1732 Mid *Colchester* (50); 2.8.1732 MidO *Kinsale* (40); 13.11.1732 Able *Success* (20); 16.7.1733 Mate *Dursley Galley* (20); 1.10.1735 Able *Dursley Galley* (20); 25.6.1737 Mate *Dursley Galley* (20); 10.9.1740 Able *Dursley Galley* (20); 12.3.1740/41 Mate *Dursley Galley* (20); 4.6.1741 Passed; **Lieutenant**; 16.9.1741 L. *Grampus* (6) Sloop; 29.7.1742-10.1.1745/46 2L *Cambridge* (80); 11.2.1743/44-12.2.1743/44 Battle of Toulon.

LEIGHTON, EDWARD

Dates: c.1725 Born; 27.3.1750 Died.

Family:

Service: 1738-1740 Merchant Service; 24.7.1740 Able *Elizabeth* (70); 31.5.1741 Mid *Bedford* (70); 6.11.1743 Able *Marlborough* (90); 11.11.1743 Mid *Marlborough* (90); 24.1.1743/44 Mid *Neptune* (90); 11.2.1743/44-12.2.1743/44 Battle of Toulon; 1.6.1745 Passed; **Lieutenant**; 10.6.1747 5L *Royal Sovereign* (104); 9.10.1747-7.6.1748[P] 5L *Barfleur* (90); **Captain**; 9.1.1748/49[(MED 5.5.1749)]-1.5.1749[P] *Superb* (60).

LEITCH, WILLIAM

Dates: c.1717 Born; 1757 Died.

Family:

Service: 15.4.1737-24.10.1737[P] Able *Antelope* (54); 15.12.1737 Able *Falmouth* (50); 17.4.1739 Able *Princess Caroline* (80); 18.1.1739/40 Gnr Mate *Princess Caroline* (80); 5.9.1740 Mid *Princess Caroline* (80); 20.11.1740 Mid *Burford* (70); 7.3.1740/41-2.11.1741[P] Mate *Burford* (70); 30.4.1742 Mid *Nonsuch* (50); 20.8.1743 Mate *Nonsuch* (50); 11.2.1743/44-12.2.1743/44 Battle of Toulon; 27.10.1744 Able *Warwick* (60); 11.1.1744/45 Passed; **Lieutenant**; 18.5.1745 2L *Poole* (44); 4.6.1746-23.6.1749[P] 2L *Lichfield* (50).

LEMOINE, FRANCIS

Dates: c.1731 Born; 1765 Died; 15.11.1765 Will Probate.

Family:

Service: 27.3.1746 Able *Boyne* (80); 18.11.1746-21.12.1746 Able *Nonsuch* (50); 22.12.1746-15.11.1748[P] Mid *Nonsuch* (50); 18.5.1754 Mid *Fowey* (24); 11.8.1754-5.9.1755 Able *Fowey* (24); 5.9.1755 Passed; **Lieutenant**; 1.11.1755 3L *Hampshire* (50); 10.3.1757 2L *Hampshire* (50); 5.4.1758-25.8.1758 2L *Eagle* (60).

LEMPRIERE, THOMAS

Dates: 29.12.1763 Died.

Family:

Service: **Lieutenant**; 11.8.1741[(2.7.1742)] 4L *Grafton* (70); 1.11.1741[(2.7.1742)] 3L *Grafton* (70); 9.2.1741/42[(2.7.1742)]-16.3.1741/42 3L *Chester* (54); 26.7.1742-17.8.1742[P] 2L *Chester* (54);

15.10.1742 3L *Princess Mary* (60); 2.4.1744 2L *Princess Mary* (60); 12.6.1744 1L *Princess Mary* (60); 14.11.1744 2L *Dreadnought* (60); 11.12.1744 2L *Prince Frederick* (70); 25.4.1746 L. *Fox* (20); 20.5.1748 1L *Renown* (30); 3.5.1750[NA 25.7.1753] L. *Ferret* (14) Sloop; 15.11.1752[JAM 25.7.1753]-22.2.1753[P] L. *Viper* (14) Sloop; 6.2.1755 2L *Edinburgh* (64); 16.7.1755 1L *Weymouth* (60); 7.10.1755-10.2.1757 1L *Newark* (80); 12.3.1757 1L *Prince* (90); 19.4.1757 2L *Royal Anne* (100); **Commander**; 10.6.1757 *Canterbury* (6); **Captain**; 22.2.1759-12.3.1762[P] *Port Mahon* (24).

LENDRICK, JOHN

Dates: c.1724 Born; 1780 Died.
Family: Son Richard.
Service: 1740-1742 Merchant Service; 5.12.1742 Able *Furnace* (8) Bomb Vessel; 15.2.1742/43 Steward *Discovery* (18); 13.4.1743 Mid *Furnace* (8) Bomb Vessel; 2.8.1744 Mid *Monmouth* (70); **Lieutenant**; 4.6.1746 L. *Viper* (10) Sloop; 15.3.1746/47 Passed; 19.3.1747/48-25.6.1748[P] 2L *Greenwich* (50); 30.9.1748-11.9.1751[W] L. *Fox* (20); 21.5.1755 1L *Windsor* (60); **Commander**; 30.6.1756 *Charlotte* (8) Yacht; 23.8.1756-11.9.1758 *Swallow* (14) Sloop; 5.6.1758-12.6.1758 Raid on Saint-Malo; **Captain**; 26.12.1758-14.1.1759[P] *Blandford* (20); 14.1.1759-1760 *Nottingham* (60); 19.2.1762-24.3.1762[P] *Echo* (24).

LENOX, JAMES

Dates: 1771 Died.
Family:
Service: **Lieutenant**; 13.6.1760[28.3.1763]-17.7.1761 2L *Hampshire* (50); 18.10.1760 Action off Cuba.

LESINGHAM, THOMAS

Dates: c.1737 Born; 16.1.1787 Died.
Family:
Service: 1753-1756 Merchant Service; 23.4.1756 Able *Stirling Castle* (64); 27.5.1757 Mid *Stirling Castle* (64); 1.7.1759 Mid *Belliqueux* (64); 7.11.1759 Passed; **Lieutenant**; 7.12.1759-28.2.1760 4L *Vanguard* (68); 28.2.1760-25.1.1763[P] 2L *Diana* (32).

LESLIE, CHARLES

Dates: 29.12.1775 Died.
Family:
Service: **Lieutenant**; 24.5.1757[3.2.1758]-27.10.1757 L. *Mediterranean* (12) Xebec; 14.5.1758[21.9.1758]-9.9.1758[P] 5L *Monarch* (74); 13.1.1759 3L *Medway* (60); 22.1.1760 5L *Monarch* (74); 24.3.1760 3L *Thunderer* (74); **Commander**; 7.4.1762-26.4.1763[P] *Cruizer* (8) Sloop; 7.6.1763 *Wasp* (8) Sloop; 12.8.1763 *Cygnet* (18) Sloop; **Captain**; 20.6.1765 *Seahorse* (24); 17.2.1767-30.5.1770 *Ranger* (8) Sloop; 19.2.1771 *Warwick* (50); 10.2.1772[1.11.1773]-1.6.1775[P] *Orford* (68).

LESLIE, LACHLAN

Dates: 31.3.1762 Died.
Family:
Service: **Lieutenant**; 14.4.1733-12.5.1734 3L *Rupert* (60); 12.8.1735 L. *Rye* (20); 30.9.1735-16.2.1735/36[P] 3L *Dorsetshire* (80); 28.7.1738-13.8.1739 1L *Advice* (54); 12.6.1739 2L *Weymouth* (60); 14.3.1739/40-30.10.1740 1L *Weymouth* (60); 8.6.1741[24.5.1743] 4L *Cumberland* (80); 6.2.1741/42[24.5.1743] 4L *Boyne* (80); 26.6.1742[24.5.1743] 3L *Boyne* (80); 23.8.1742[24.5.1743]-1.5.1743 2L *Boyne* (80); **Commander**; 14.10.1742[30.3.1743] *Vulcan* (8) Fireship; 19.12.1743-5.6.1744

Lightning (8) Bomb Vessel; **Captain**; 8.9.1744 *Sandwich* (90); 11.2.1744/45 *Ipswich* (70); 3.5.1745(MED 24.1.1746/47) *Russell* (80); 29.5.1745(MED 24.1.1746/47)-21.11.1746[P] *Cambridge* (80); 1.7.1755 *Bristol* (50); 16.1.1759-19.1.1759 Attack on Martinique; 29.1.1759(BLI 2.7.1759) *Buckingham* (68); 5.7.1759-6.10.1760[P] *Monarch* (74); 31.8.1759 CinC — Thames, Medway and The Nore; 6.7.1761 CinC — Thames, Medway and The Nore.

LESLIE, PATRICK
Dates: c.1733 Born; 1783 Died.
Family:
Service: 21.4.1747 Land. *Terror* (8) Bomb Vessel; 5.9.1748 Mid *Anglesea* (44); 20.6.1750 Able *Shoreham* (24); 26.7.1750 Mid *Invincible* (74); 25.11.1750 Able *Queenborough* (24); 27.11.1750 Mate *Queenborough* (24); 1.5.1754 Passed; **Lieutenant**; 23.6.1755(NA 25.2.1756) 5L *Terrible* (74); 5.7.1756 6L *Marlborough* (80); 12.4.1758(JAM 19.10.1758) 2L *Lynn* (44); 27.10.1758 2L *Temple* (68); 1.12.1758 1L *Trent* (28); 1.7.1760 L. *Cormorant* (8) Fireship; 20.8.1761-10.5.1763[P] 2L *Blenheim* (90); 6.4.1763-6.4.1765 LCmdr *Morning Star* (4) Cutter; 19.6.1769-8.5.1771[P] LCmdr *Meredith* (10) Cutter; 14.2.1777-6.9.1777 1L *Royal Oak* (74); 16.9.1777 1L *Panther* (60); 4.3.1779 **Commander**; 31.3.1779(MED 31.5.1779) *Minorca* (20) Xebec; **Captain**; 26.1.1780(BLI 4.5.1780)-14.8.1781[P] *Enterprise* (28); 6.9.1781-17.3.1783 *Preston* (50); 17.3.1783-9.10.1783[P] *Torbay* (74).

LESLIE, WILLIAM
Dates: 2.12.1766 Died.
Family:
Service: 13.5.1747 Unk *Elizabeth* Mer; 11.7.1748 Able *Centurion* (50); 20.4.1749 Mid *Tavistock* (50); 27.7.1752 Mate *Advice* (50); 4.9.1753 Passed; **Lieutenant**; 16.7.1756(3.8.1757)-8.8.1758 L. *Trial* (10) Sloop; 8.4.1760 1L *Centaur* (74); 6.6.1762-13.8.1762 Operations against Havana; **Captain**; 20.3.1763(JAM 1.11.1763)-29.9.1763[P] *Danae* (38).

LEWIS, HENRY
Dates: 1789 Died; 21.1.1789 Will Probate.
Family:
Service: **Lieutenant**; 1.4.1758(EI 5.1.1761)-6.5.1758 5L *Cumberland* (66); 29.4.1758 Battle of Cuddalore; 16.10.1770-17.12.1773[P] 1L *Diana* (32).

LEWIS, ISAAC
Dates: c.1735 Born; 1762 Died; 18.6.1762 Will Probate.
Family:
Service: 1753-1757 Merchant Service; 19.6.1755 Ord. *Buckingham* (68); 20.5.1756 Battle of Minorca; 20.3.1757 Mid *Prince* (90); 19.8.1757 Mid *Richmond* (32); 31.10.1757 Mid *Diana* (32); 6.6.1758-27.7.1758 The Siege of Louisbourg; 11.4.1759 Passed; **Lieutenant**; 11.1.1760-6.8.1761 L. *Aetna* (8) Fireship; 29.3.1761-11.6.1761 Expedition against Belle-Isle.

LEWIS, JOSHUA
Dates: c.1731 Born; 1773 Died.
Family:
Service: 18.3.1747/48 Capt Serv *Captain* (70); 23.6.1748 Ord. *Captain* (70); 26.7.1748 Capt Serv *Captain* (70); 21.5.1749 Able *Captain* (70); 3.6.1750 Able *Kent* (64); 29.9.1750 Mid *Mermaid* (24); 21.3.1750/51 Mid *Kent* (64); 12.12.1752-24.4.1753[W] Able *Assurance* (44); 1.12.1755 Able *Kent* (64); 11.1.1756-14.1.1756 Capture of Geriah; 25.2.1756 Able *Shoreham*

(24); 28.4.1757-20.10.1757^{P} Mid *Shoreham* (24); 9.8.1758 Passed; **Lieutenant**; 30.3.1759-8.1.1761 L. *Greyhound* (20); 20.8.1763-28.8.1766 L. *Escort* (14) Sloop; 18.5.1768 2L *Arrogant* (74); 26.5.1769 3L *Arrogant* (74); 23.8.1769 2L *Arrogant* (74); 18.1.1771-1773† 3L *Sandwich* (90).

LEWIS, THOMAS

Dates: c.1741 Born; 16.7.1796 Died.
Family:
Service: 21.7.1756 Capt Serv *Berwick* (64); 5.4.1757 Action of April 5 1757; 20.10.1757 Ord. *Berwick* (64); 28.2.1758 Battle of Cartagena; 10.4.1758-19.6.1758^{P} Able *Siren* (20); 22.9.1758 Able *Shrewsbury* (74); 11.2.1759 Mid *Shrewsbury* (74); 6.4.1759 Mid *Thames* (32); 20.4.1760 Able *Thames* (32); 20.6.1760 Mid *Thames* (32); 18.12.1760-1.7.1761 Mate *Thames* (32); 1.7.1761 Passed; **Lieutenant**; 20.11.1761-24.5.1763^{P} 3L *Montagu* (60); 25.6.1779 1L *Formidable* (98); 26.4.1781 1L *Sampson* (64); 16.2.1782 *Pluto* (8) Fireship; 16.5.1782 **Commander**; **Captain**; 7.6.1782 *Romney* (50); 23.12.1782-6.5.1783 *Blenheim* (90); 1.1796-16.7.1796 *Hannibal* (74).

LEY, THOMAS ARTHUR

Dates: 1786 Died; 14.10.1786 Will Probate.
Family:
Service: **Lieutenant**; 21.3.1757$^{(25.8.1764)}$ 4L *Yarmouth* (64); 8.5.1757$^{(25.8.1764)}$ 3L *Yarmouth* (64); 25.3.1758$^{(25.8.1764)}$ 5L *Elizabeth* (64); 29.4.1758 Battle of Cuddalore; 3.8.1758 Battle of Negapatam; 20.2.1759$^{(EI\ 25.8.1764)}$ 5L *Grafton* (68); 3.3.1759$^{(EI\ 25.8.1764)}$ 4L *Grafton* (68); 10.9.1759 Battle of Pondicherry; 17.3.1760$^{(EI\ 25.8.1764)}$ 5L *Grafton* (68); 14.6.1760$^{(25.8.1764)}$ 5L *Norfolk* (74); 27.11.1760$^{(25.8.1764)}$ 4L *Norfolk* (74); 1.2.1761$^{(25.8.1764)}$ 3L *Norfolk* (74); 18.11.1761$^{(EI\ 25.8.1764)}$ 2L *Lennox* (74); 24.9.1762-6.10.1762 Battle of Manilla; 21.10.1762$^{(EI\ 25.8.1764)}$ 5L *Norfolk* (74); 10.11.1762$^{(EI\ 25.8.1764)}$ 4L *Norfolk* (74); 16.12.1762$^{(EI\ 25.8.1764)}$ 3L *Norfolk* (74); 18.7.1763$^{(EI\ 25.8.1764)}$-29.7.1764^{P} 2L *Norfolk* (74); 2.5.1770-1.6.1771^{P} 1L *San Antonio* (64); 22.4.1773 2L *Somerset* (68); 2.11.1773 1L *Resolution* (74); 31.1.1778-4.3.1778 4L *Ardent* (64); 19.6.1781-18.7.1782 1L *Diligent* (70); **Commander**; 29.6.1782 *Prince Edward* (60); 9.7.1782-21.4.1783^{P} *Dragon* (74) Receiving Ship.

LIELL, THOMAS

Dates: 1796 Died.
Family:
Service: **Lieutenant**; 7.4.1761$^{(2.6.1761)}$-7.2.1763^{P} 2L *Shannon* (28).

LINCOLNE, JAMES

Dates: c.1725 Born; 1756 Died.
Family:
Service: 1740-1741 Merchant Service; 19.1.1740/41 Capt Serv *Rose* (20) Ship; 24.1.1743/44 Mid *Rose* (20) Ship; 5.6.1746 Passed; **Lieutenant**; 4.10.1746-24.4.1747 3L *Dragon* (60).

LIND, JOHN

Dates: 1791 Died; 3.9.1791 Will Probate.
Family:
Service: **Lieutenant**; 4.1.1743/44$^{(18.4.1745)}$ 4L *Grafton* (70); 31.5.1744$^{(18.4.1744)}$-20.10.1744^{W} 3L *Greenwich* (50); 1.5.1745-7.11.1748^{P} L. *Scarborough* (20); 17.1.1748/49 L. *Queenborough* (24); 21.3.1748/49-22.6.1752^{P} L. *Unicorn* (24); 20.2.1755-23.1.1758 1L *York* (60); 25.7.1758

1L *Panther* (60); 16.1.1759-19.1.1759 Attack on Martinique; 20.1.1759-1.5.1759 Capture of Guadeloupe; 25.10.1759-16.12.1760[P] 2L *Barfleur* (80); 11.2.1761 3L *Royal Sovereign* (104); 30.4.1762-14.12.1762 1L *Chester* (50); 7.1769-29.6.1771[P] LCmdr *Morning Star* (4) Cutter.

LINDESAY, JOHN

Dates: 1763 Died.

Family:

***Service:* Lieutenant**; 3.4.1757[(21.9.1757)] 4L *Stirling Castle* (64); 13.10.1757 2L *Trent* (28); 6.6.1758-27.7.1758 The Siege of Louisbourg; 1.7.1760-9.9.1763[P] 1L *Trent* (28); 6.6.1762-13.8.1762 Operations against Havana.

LINDSAY, GEORGE

Dates: c.1737 Born; 1798 Died.

Family:

Service: 1752-1755 Merchant Service; 31.10.1755 Mid *Intrepid* (64); 20.5.1756 Battle of Minorca; 23.2.1757 Able *Newark* (80); 11.4.1757 Mid *Newark* (80); 8.1757-10.1757 Louisbourg Expedition; 28.2.1758 Able *Namur* (90); 6.6.1758-27.7.1758 The Siege of Louisbourg; 21.8.1758-13.12.1758 Mid *Namur* (90); 13.12.1758 Passed; **Lieutenant**; 20.8.1759[(MED 24.3.1760)] 4L *Newark* (80); 15.9.1761-15.7.1763[P] 1L *Nottingham* (60); 7.1.1762-10.2.1762 Operations against Martinique; 6.6.1762-13.8.1762 Operations against Havana; 28.4.1773-20.2.1776 2L *Lark* (32); 30.10.1776-24.7.1780 1L *Aeolus* (32); **Commander**; 22.4.1781[(Portugal 27.6.1781)] *Porto* (12) Sloop; 19.6.1783 *Scout* (16) Sloop; 24.6.1790 *Roebuck* (44) Hospital Ship; **Captain**; 21.9.1790-22.11.1790 *Amphitrite* (24).

LINDSAY, LORD JAMES (5TH EARL OF BALCARRES)

Dates: 14.11.1691 Born; 25.7.1736 5th Lord Lindsay and Balneil; 25.7.1736 6th Lord Lindsay of Balcarres; 25.7.1736 5th Earl of Balcarres; 20.2.1768 Died Balcarres, Fife.

Family: Father Colin Lindsay, 3rd Earl of Balcarres (1652-1722); Mother Lady Margaret Campbell (d.1747); Wife Anne Dalrymple (1727-1820) married 24.10.1749; Daughter Margaret Janet [Fordyce/Lamb] (d.1814); Daughter Anne [Barnard] (1750-1825); Son Alexander, 6th Earl of Balcarres (1752-1825); Son Hon. Robert (1754-1836); Son Rt. Rev. Hon. Charles Dalrymple (1760-1846); Son Lt.-Col. Hon. John (1762-1826); Daughter Lady Elizabeth Scot [Yorke] (1763-1858); Son Hon. Hugh (1765-1844); Half-sister Lady Margaret [Fleming]; Half-brother Colin Lindsay, Lord Cumberland (d.1708); Sister Lady Eleanor [Fraser] (d.1735); Brother Alexander, 4th Earl of Balcarres (1690-1736).

Service: 17.10.1705 Vol-p-O *Ipswich* (70); 11.11.1706-6.5.1707 Vol-p-O *Bedford* (70); 18.6.1707 Able *Defiance* (64); 19.12.1707 Mid *Defiance* (64); 27.9.1708 Mid *Burford* (70); 14.4.1710 Passed; **Lieutenant**; 17.5.1711 L. *Lizard* (24); 30.6.1711-31.10.1712[P] 2L *Portland* (54); 1716 Dismissed.

LINDSAY, JOHN

Dates: 1737 Born; 10.2.1764 Knight Bachelor; 28.6.1770 Order of the Bath; 7.6.1788 Died.

Family: Father Sir Alexander Lindsay, 3rd Bt.; Mother Amelia Murray; Wife Mary Milner married 19.9.1768; Mistress Maria Belle; Mistress Mary Vellet; Mistress Sarah Gandwell; Mistress Martha G; Mistress Francis Edwards; Illegitimate Daughter Dido Elizabeth Belle [Davinière] (1761-1804); Illegitimate Son John Edward Vellet (1762-1762); Illegitimate Daughter Ann Gandwell (1766-?); Illegitimate Daughter Elizabeth [Hill] (1766-1842);

Illegitimate Son John Edwards (1767-1821); Brother David, 4th Bt. (c.1732-1797); Sister Margaret [Ramsey]; Brother William; Sister Katherine [Lindsay].
Service: 31.10.1749-18.6.1752 Scholar *Royal Naval Academy*; 4.9.1752 Vol-p-O *Deptford* (50); 27.2.1754 MidO *Deptford* (50); 1.3.1756 Passed; **Lieutenant**; 2.3.1756 3L *Nottingham* (60); 4.3.1756 6L *Royal George* (100); 23.3.1756 2L *Tartar* (24); **Commander**; 4.4.1757 *Pluto* (8) Fireship; **Captain**; 29.9.1757 *Trent* (28); 6.6.1758-27.7.1758 The Siege of Louisbourg; 2.7.1762 *Cambridge* (80); 24.8.1763-9.9.1763ᴾ *Trent* (28); 24.11.1763-5.6.1766ᴾ *Tartar* (28); 9.1.1767-12.4.1768 M.P. for Aberdeen Burghs; 23.8.1769-1772 CinC — East Indies; 23.8.1769-25.4.1772ᴾ Commodore *Stag* (32); 9.3.1778 *Victory* (100); 13.5.1778-14.4.1779 *Prince George* (98); 27.7.1778 1st Battle of Ushant; 10.4.1783-30.12.1783 Lord Commissioner of the Admiralty; 29.8.1783-1784 CinC — The Mediterranean Sea; 29.8.1783-1784 Commodore *Trusty* (50); 24.9.1787 **Rear Admiral of the Red.**

LINZEE, ROBERT

Dates: c.1740 Born; 9.1805 Died.
Family:
Service: 28.10.1754 Scholar *Royal Naval Academy*; 23.5.1756 Mid *Gibraltar* (20); 13.1.1757 Able *Roebuck* (44); 22.1.1757 Mid *Roebuck* (44); 1.7.1757 Mid *Marlborough* (80); 28.8.1757 Mid *Dreadnought* (60); 21.10.1757 Forrest's Action; 23.3.1759 Mate *Dreadnought* (60); 4.1.1760 Mid *Marlborough* (80); 19.8.1760 Passed; **Lieutenant**; 29.1.1761 L. *Carcass* (14) Bomb Vessel; 7.8.1761 3L *Africa* (64); 13.10.1763 3L *Dragon* (74); 13.9.1764 5L *Thunderer* (74); 1.3.1765 3L *Thunderer* (74); 2.5.1766-3.2.1767 3L *Jersey* (60); 24.2.1767 1L *Romney* (50); 17.9.1768 ActM&C *Viper* (10) Sloop; **Commander**; 25.11.1768 *Viper* (10) Sloop; **Captain**; 3.10.1770(12.11.1770)-25.3.1771ᴾ *Romney* (50); 11.2.1775 *Surprise* (28); 16.4.1779-24.8.1779 *Ajax* (74); 21.9.1779-12.5.1781 *Thetis* (32); 14.11.1781-27.6.1783ᴾ *Magnificent* (74); 12.4.1782 Battle of the Saintes; 19.4.1782 Battle of the Mona Passage; 10.5.1790 *Saturn* (74); 5.1.1791-6.9.1791ᴾ *Saturn* (74); 1.12.1792 *Alcide* (74); 9.2.1793-11.4.1794 Commodore *Alcide* (74); **Rear Admiral of the White**; 12.4.1794-8.1794 *Alcide* (74); 4.7.1794 **Rear Admiral of the Red**; 8.1794-12.1795 *Windsor Castle* (98); 14.3.1795 Action off Genoa; 1.6.1795 **Vice Admiral of the White**; 13.7.1795 Battle of Hyeres; 10.1795-11.1795 *Victory* (100); 1.1.1801 **Admiral of the Blue.**

LISLE, TREVELYAN

Dates: c.1723 Born; 1760 Died; 18.12.1760 Will Probate.
Family:
Service: 8.4.1751 Able *Hector* (44); 6.6.1751 Mate *Hector* (44); 21.11.1752 Mid *Hector* (44); 25.3.1754 Mate *Hector* (44); 5.5.1754 Mid *Hector* (44); 4.11.1754 Able *Hector* (44); 18.7.1755 Mate *Windsor* (60); 1.7.1756 Acting Master *Windsor* (60); 22.11.1756 Mate *Windsor* (60); 25.5.1757 ActL *Windsor* (60); 8.1757-10.1757 Louisbourg Expedition; 2.1.1758 Passed; **Lieutenant**; 1.2.1758-26.4.1758ᴾ L. *Cruizer* (8) Sloop; 22.5.1758 2L *Cerberus* (28); 4.12.1758-12.6.1760 1L *Cerberus* (28).

LITTLE, CHARLES

Dates: 1772 Died.
Family:
Service: **Lieutenant**; 3.5.1759-3.3.1762 L. *Badger* (10) Sloop; 5.5.1762-29.9.1766 L. *Hind* (24); 20.6.1770-20.10.1772 L. *Gibraltar* (20).

LITTLEFIELD, JOHN

Dates: c.1724 Born; 17.12.1801 Died.
Family:
Service: 22.11.1749 Able *Princess Royal* (90); 10.4.1751 Able *Strafford* (58); 19.4.1752 Able *Adventure* (44); 15.11.1752 Able *Windsor* (60); 22.4.1753 QM *Windsor* (60); 4.10.1753 Cox *Windsor* (60); 23.12.1753 Mid *Windsor* (60); 26.3.1755 Mid *Weymouth* (60); 31.1.1757 Mid *Invincible* (74); 6.6.1757 Passed; **Lieutenant**; 6.8.1759[(MED 16.9.1761)]-2.4.1763[P] L. *Favorite* (16) Sloop.

LLEWHELLIN, RICHARD

Dates: c.1732 Born; 1768 Died; 28.3.1768 Will Probate.
Family:
Service: 30.5.1746-1.6.1748[P] Ord. *York* (16) Hired Armed vessel; 17.9.1753 Able *Solebay* (24); 20.4.1754 Cpl *Solebay* (24); 16.10.1754 Mid *Solebay* (24); 30.9.1755 QM *Experiment* (24); 14.1.1756 Cox *Experiment* (24); 20.5.1756 Battle of Minorca; 18.9.1756 Mid *Experiment* (24); 12.2.1757 Mate *Chesterfield* (44); 6.12.1758 Passed; **Lieutenant**; 7.12.1758 3L *Chesterfield* (44); 10.7.1759-21.7.1762[W] 2L *Chesterfield* (44).

LLOYD, CHARLES

Dates: c.1715 Born; 1755 Died.
Family:
Service: 20.6.1732 Mid *Edinburgh* (70); 5.3.1732/33 Able *Edinburgh* (70); 6.3.1733/34 Mid *Edinburgh* (70); 23.1.1735/36 Able *Edinburgh* (70); 22.3.1737/38-30.5.1740[P] Mid *Edinburgh* (70); 11.1.1740/41 Mate *Boyne* (80); 4.6.1741 Passed; **Lieutenant**; 17.4.1743[(16.8.1743)]-30.9.1743[P] 3L *Norwich* (50); 14.10.1743-27.2.1744/45 3L *Worcester* (58).

LLOYD, FRANCIS

Dates: 9.8.1759 Will Probate; bef.9.8.1759 Died.
Family:
Service: 10.9.1739 Able *Winchester* (50); 11.7.1741 QGnr *Winchester* (50); 14.9.1742 QGnr *Nassau* (70); 2.10.1743 MidO *Nassau* (70); 3.10.1743-12.2.1745/46 Mid *Nassau* (70); 11.2.1743/44-12.2.1743/44 Battle of Toulon; 3.2.1745/46 Passed; **Lieutenant**; 19.8.1747[(3.1.1748/49)]-5.10.1748[P] L. *Brave* (3) Storeship; 14.10.1755 3L *Falkland* (50); 28.10.1755-11.12.1755 L. *Blandford* (20); 22.7.1756-bef.9.8.1759[†] 2L *Ambuscade* (40).

LLOYD, HENRY

Dates: 15.11.1792 Died; 22.11.1792 Will Probate.
Family:
Service: **Lieutenant**; 13.10.1757[(2.2.1758)] 3L *Portland* (50); 5.6.1758-12.6.1758 Raid on Saint-Malo; 30.11.1758 3L *Lancaster* (66); 26.2.1759-28.8.1765[P] 2L *York* (60); 24.10.1766 2L *Firm* (74); **Commander**; 26.5.1768 *Infernal* (14) Bomb Vessel; 26.7.1769 *Hawk* (10) Sloop; **Captain**; 23.3.1771[(10.4.1772)] *Dolphin* (24); 10.2.1772[(21.6.1774)]-28.2.1775[P] *Warwick* (50); 6.5.1777 *Pelican* (24); 26.11.1779-21.4.1783[P] *Oiseau* (32).

LLOYD, HENRY

Dates: c.1731 Born; 1771 Died.
Family:
Service: 1749-1752 Merchant Service; 15.11.1752 Ord. *Gloucester* (50); 3.5.1754 Mate *Kingfisher* (14) Sloop; 11.1.1756-14.1.1756 Capture of Geriah; 3.1.1758 Passed; **Lieutenant**; 20.5.1758 L. *Infernal* (8) Bomb Vessel; 5.6.1758-12.6.1758 Raid on Saint-Malo; 16.1.1759-19.1.1759 Attack on Martinique; 20.1.1759-1.5.1759 Capture of Guadeloupe; 26.11.1759-10.7.1761 2L *Panther* (60); 9.12.1762[EI 9.8.1764]-30.7.1764[P] 3L *Elizabeth* (64).

LLOYD, HUGH

Dates: c.1738 Born; 9.1.1789 Died.
Family:
Service: 9.2.1755 Able *Prince* (90); 23.11.1755 Able *Prince* (90); 18.4.1756 Mid *Prince* (90); 15.9.1756 Able *Culloden* (74); 19.3.1757 Mid *Saint George* (90); 28.2.1758-4.5.1758 Mid *Orphee* (64); 3.3.1759 Able *Neptune* (90); 21.9.1759 Mid *Neptune* (90); 6.6.1760 Passed; **Lieutenant**; 8.7.1760-9.7.1760 L. *Hound* (14) Sloop; 6.9.1763 3L *Thunderer* (74); 13.9.1764-24.9.1766 3L *Dragon* (74); 19.11.1767 3L *Temeraire* (74); 26.5.1768 2L *Temeraire* (74); 24.9.1770-22.5.1771[P] 4L *Temeraire* (74); 28.6.1771 3L *Torbay* (74); 29.11.1771-2.5.1772 2L *Torbay* (74); 3.11.1773 3L *Ocean* (90); 31.1.1775 4L *Ocean* (90); 7.11.1776-30.8.1777 5L *Ocean* (90); 14.11.1778-4.11.1780 *Vulture* (14) Sloop.

LLOYD, JAMES

Dates: 8.2.1761 Died.
Family:
Service: **Lieutenant**; 13.5.1720[8.12.1720]-8.10.1721[P] 3L *Dunkirk* (50); 24.1.1725/26-8.9.1727[P] 3L *Northumberland* (70); 26.7.1728 1L *Ludlow Castle* (40); 21.2.1728/29 1L *Royal Oak* (70); 20.6.1729 2L *Lion* (60); **Commander**; 31.12.1729[1.7.1735]-18.7.1735[P] *Happy* (10) Sloop; **Captain**; 30.8.1739 *Winchester* (50); 13.9.1742[MED 25.7.1746] *Nassau* (70); 11.2.1743/44-12.2.1743/44 Battle of Toulon; 8.11.1744[MED 25.7.1746]-8.2.1745/46 *Boyne* (80); c.1751-8.2.1761 Captain of Greenwich Hospital.

LLOYD, JOHN

Dates: 8.3.1778 Died.
Family:
Service: c.29.11.1723 Ord. *Advice* (54); c.27.1.1725 Able *Dragon* (54); c.18.4.1725 MidO *Preston* (50); c.22.4.1726 Mid *Preston* (50); c.18.9.1726 MidO *Canterbury* (60); c.19.9.1727-c.1.4.1728[P] Mid *Canterbury* (60); 23.5.1730-27.12.1731[P] Mid *Canterbury* (60); 4.5.1732 Able *Princess Amelia* (80); 21.8.1732 Mid *Princess Amelia* (80); 17.10.1732 Able *Princess Amelia* (80); 9.3.1732/33 Passed; **Lieutenant**; 19.3.1733/34-18.1.1735/36 3L *Roebuck* (40); 15.3.1737/38-27.3.1740[P] 3L *Berwick* (70); 4.11.1740 LCmdr *Blenheim* (96); 30.1.1740/41-20.9.1741 2L *Royal Sovereign* (104); 14.6.1743-28.3.1745 1L *Berwick* (70); 11.2.1743/44-12.2.1743/44 Battle of Toulon; **Commander**; 24.7.1744 *Fly* (8) Sloop; 5.7.1745-27.1.1745/46 *Raven* (10) Sloop; **Captain**; 4.9.1746 *Deal Castle* (20); 9.10.1748[EI 2.8.1750]-12.6.1750[P] *Eltham* (40); 23.4.1753 *Arundel* (24); 11.3.1755-27.1.1757 *Newcastle* (50); 6.5.1763-6.5.1766 *Fame* (74); 6.12.1769-27.5.1771[P] *Cornwall* (74); 31.3.1775 **Rear Admiral of the Blue**; 7.12.1775 **Rear Admiral of the Red**; 29.1.1778 **Vice Admiral of the Blue**.

LLOYD, THOMAS

Dates: c.1731 Born; 1772 Died.
Family:
Service: 4.10.1745 Land. *York* (16) Hired Armed vessel; 9.5.1747-1.6.1748[P] Able *York* (16) Hired Armed vessel; 28.6.1750 Ord. *Solebay* (24); 20.12.1750 Mid *Solebay* (24); 31.1.1750/51 Able *Solebay* (24); 14.4.1751 Mid *Solebay* (24); 14.11.1751 Able *Baltimore* (14) Sloop; 26.4.1752 Mid *Baltimore* (14) Sloop; 7.8.1752 Mid *Peregrine* (20) Sloop; 8.10.1752 Able *Peregrine* (20) Sloop; 1.7.1753 Mid *Peregrine* (20) Sloop; 26.11.1753 Mid *Fowey* (24); 23.9.1754 Able *Fowey* (24); 23.11.1754 Mid *Swan* (14) Sloop; 17.3.1755 Passed; **Lieutenant**; 2.3.1756 L. *Otter* (14) Sloop; 25.2.1758-22.10.1761 1L *Liverpool* (28); 12.4.1762-25.3.1763 1L *Pearl* (32); 14.6.1766-6.1769 LCmdr *Charlotte* (4) Cutter.

LLOYD, WILLIAM

Dates: 1725 Born; 19.7.1796 Died.
Family:
Service: 2.10.1740 Scholar *Royal Naval Academy*; 13.3.1743/44 **Lieutenant**; 13.3.1744/45[BLI 26.12.1746] 3L *Superb* (60); 30.3.1746[BLI 26.12.1746] 1L *Chester* (50); 4.4.1747-29.5.1747 1L *Devonshire* (66); **Commander**; 18.7.1747 *Otter* (14) Sloop; **Captain**; 12.1.1747/48-30.8.1748 *Invincible* (74); 30.9.1748-11.9.1751 *Sphinx* (24); 31.7.1755-20.8.1756 *Chesterfield* (44); 20.5.1756 Battle of Minorca; 6.6.1756[1.2.1757]-20.8.1756 *Princess Louisa* (60); 2.2.1757 *Princess Louisa* (60); 5.4.1757 Action of April 5 1757; 13.8.1759[MED 5.5.1760]-26.10.1760[W] *Conqueror* (68); 18.8.1759-19.8.1759 Battle of Lagos Bay; 23.1.1778 **Rear Admiral of the Blue**; 19.3.1779 **Rear Admiral of the Red**; 26.9.1780 **Vice Admiral of the Blue**; 24.9.1787 **Vice Admiral of the Red**; 1.2.1793 **Admiral of the Blue**; 1.6.1795 **Admiral of the White.**

LLOYD, WILLIAM

Dates: c.1736 Born; 1.11.1758 Died.
Family:
Service: 27.11.1747 L. Serv *Oxford* (50); 12.10.1748 Battle of Havana; 21.3.1748/49-24.4.1753[W] Able *Assurance* (44); 9.8.1754 Mid *Hazard* (14) Sloop; 24.3.1755 Mid *Tiger* (60); 2.4.1755 Able *Tiger* (60); 27.4.1755 Mid *Tiger* (60); 11.1.1756-14.1.1756 Capture of Geriah; 7.2.1757 Passed; 24.6.1757 **Lieutenant**; 27.6.1757 L. *Merlin* (18) Frigate; 29.6.1757-1.11.1758[†] L. *Racehorse* (18) Sloop.

LOBB, JACOB

Dates: 20.2.1773 Died.
Family:
Service: **Lieutenant**; 9.1.1747/48[21.10.1748]-31.8.1748[P] L. *Panzy* Unknown; 5.8.1756 5L *Invincible* (74); 11.11.1756 4L *Invincible* (74); 15.11.1756 3L *Invincible* (74); 17.12.1756 3L *Royal George* (100); 6.5.1757 2L *Royal George* (100); 29.7.1757 1L *Royal George* (100); **Commander**; 23.12.1757-19.4.1758[P] *Cruizer* (8) Sloop; 1.12.1758 *Swan* (14) Sloop; 4.4.1763-1766[P] *Viper* (10) Sloop; 11.9.1772-20.2.1773[†] *Kingfisher* (14) Sloop.

LOCKER, WILLIAM

Dates: 2.1731 Born London; 26.12.1800 Died Greenwich Hospital.
Family: Father John Locker (1693–1760); Mother Elizabeth Stillingfleet (d. 1759); Wife Lucy Parry (1746/7-1780); Son Edward Hawke Locker.

Service: 2.4.1746-14.2.1747/48 Capt Serv *Kent* (64); 3.5.1747 1st Battle of Cape Finisterre; 14.10.1747 2nd Battle of Cape Finisterre; 15.2.1747/48 Mid *Vanqueur* Sloop; 30.5.1748 Able *Vulture* (14) Sloop; 13.7.1748 Mid *Cornwall* (80); 12.10.1748 Battle of Havana; 19.11.1748-18.5.1749 Mid *Elizabeth* (70); 6.1749-1755 HEIC Service; 22.2.1755 Mate *Saint George* (90); 7.1.1756 Passed; 8.1.1756 Mate *Antelope* (50); **Lieutenant**; 4.7.1756[ECH 23.2.1758] L. *Experiment* (24); 17.7.1758 2L *Sapphire* (32); 12.12.1758 1L *Sapphire* (32); 20.11.1759 Battle of Quiberon Bay; 10.3.1760 5L *Royal George* (100); 27.6.1760 4L *Royal George* (100); 17.11.1760 2L *Royal George* (100); 27.7.1761 1L *Royal George* (100); **Commander**; 7.4.1762-23.2.1763[P] *Roman Emperor* (8) Fireship; 21.5.1763-8.3.1768[P] *Nautilus* (16) Sloop; **Captain**; 26.5.1768-22.8.1770 *Mercury* (20); 2.10.1770-14.10.1773 *Thames* (32); 1.3.1777-2.5.1779 *Lowestoffe* (28); 12.5.1790-24.3.1791 *Cambridge* (80); 1792 CinC — River Medway and The Nore; 26.12.1792-8.2.1793 *Sandwich* (90); 15.2.1793-26.12.1800 Lieutenant-governor of Greenwich Hospital at Greenwich Hospital.

LOCKHART, SIR JOHN (6TH BARONET LOCKHART-ROSS OF CARSTAIRS)

Dates: 11.11.1721 Born Lockhart Hall, Lanarkshire; 13.8.1778 6th Baronet Lockhart-Ross of Carstairs; 9.6.1790 Died Balnagown Castle.
Family: Father Sir James Lockhart (d.1755); Mother Grizel Ross; Wife Elizabeth Dundas married 6.9.1762; Son Charles, 7th Bt. (c.1763-1814); Brother James, 4th Bt.; Brother George, 5th Bt. (d.1778).
Service: 2.3.1736/37 Ord. *Portland* (50); 28.1.1737/38 MidO *Diamond* (40); 9.7.1739 Able *Romney* (50); 26.5.1740 Mid *Trial* (8) Sloop; 10.9.1740 Mate *Lively* (20); 12.3.1740/41 Mate *Ruby* (54); 6.4.1743 Mid *Ruby* (54); 28.9.1743 Passed; **Lieutenant**; 9.11.1743-3.6.1744 3L *Dover* (44); 9.2.1746/47 2L *Chester* (50); 4.4.1747-23.12.1747 2L *Devonshire* (66); 14.10.1747 2nd Battle of Cape Finisterre; 12.1.1747/48-15.11.1752[P] 1L *Invincible* (74); 28.1.1755 1L *Prince* (90); **Commander**; 22.4.1755 *Savage* (8) Sloop; **Captain**; 23.3.1756 *Tartar* (24); 13.1.1758 *Chatham* (50); 3.7.1759 Bombardment of Le Havre; 20.11.1759 Battle of Quiberon Bay; 5.3.1760-26.9.1761[P] *Bedford* (64); 29.3.1761-11.6.1761 Expedition against Belle-Isle; 20.4.1761-14.4.1768 M.P. for Linlithgow Burghs; 14.4.1768-28.10.1774 M.P. for Lanarkshire; 19.9.1777-29.1.1779 *Shrewsbury* (74); 27.7.1778 1st Battle of Ushant; 19.3.1779 **Rear Admiral of the Blue**; 5.1779-12.1779 *Romney* (50); 6.1779-1.1780 *Britannia* (100); 8.1779-12.1781 *Royal George* (100); 16.1.1780 Battle of Cape St. Vincent; 26.9.1780 **Rear Admiral of the Red**; 1782-3.1783 *Bienfaisant* (64); 2.4.1782 CinC — North Sea; 20.10.1782 Battle of Cape Spartel; 24.9.1787 **Vice Admiral of the Blue**.

LOCKHART, WILLIAM

Dates: 1800 Died; 16.7.1800 Will Probate.
Family:
Service: **Lieutenant**; 18.12.1760[9.10.1761] 4L *Belliqueux* (64); 21.5.1761[9.10.1761] 3L *Belliqueux* (64); 23.11.1761 4L *Belliqueux* (64); 28.11.1761-13.8.1763[P] 3L *Belliqueux* (64); 11.9.1764-9.5.1765 L. *Hazard* (8) Sloop; 23.9.1766 LCmdr *Ferret* (6) Cutter; 16.10.1770 2L *Diana* (32); 31.10.1770 2L *Terrible* (74); 13.11.1771 3L *Terrible* (74); 9.9.1773-21.9.1773 3L *Ramillies* (74); 26.11.1776 4L *Prince George* (90); 28.8.1777 2L *Sultan* (74); **Commander**; 7.11.1777 *Dromedary* (30) Armed Storeship; **Captain**; 7.10.1779 *Royal George* (100); 26.11.1779-5.1.1780 *Pelican* (24); 1799 **Superannuated Captain.**

LOCKWOOD, DAVID

Dates: 1787 Died.
Family:
Service: **Lieutenant**; 21.12.1758[(BLI 23.7.1762)]-11.8.1762 L. *Barbadoes* (14) Sloop; 7.1.1762-10.2.1762 Operations against Martinique; 17.11.1764-4.12.1764 1L *San Antonio* (64); 27.3.1777-17.12.1778[C] L. *Ceres* (18) Sloop.

LOEFFS, CHARLES

Dates: c.1705 Born; 1757 Died.
Family:
Service: 18.5.1734 Able *Preston* (50); 21.5.1735 Mid *Preston* (50); 27.8.1736 Able *Grafton* (70); 6.10.1736 Mid *Grafton* (70); 1.5.1737 Able *Grafton* (70); 9.9.1738 Able *Seahorse* (20); 11.9.1739 Mid *Seahorse* (20); 11.3.1740/41 Mid *Sandwich* (90); 12.5.1741 Passed; **Lieutenant**; 24.8.1743 L. *Drake* (14) Sloop; 5.7.1745[(14.2.1748/49)]-11.5.1748 L. *Bideford* (20).

LOFTING, SAMUEL

Dates: c.1696 Born London; 1779 Died; 13.12.1779 Will Probate.
Family: Father John Lofting (1659-1742); Mother Hester Basses (1670-1709); Wife Mary Edmonds married 1720; Wife Barbara Whitaker married 9.12.1730; Wife Hester Beckford married 1769; Son Samuel (1721-?); Daughter Charlotte; Son William (1759-?); Daughter Hester; Daughter Matilda (1761-?); Brother Benjamin.
Service: 21.12.1728 Able *Cumberland* (80); 16.8.1729 Mid *Cumberland* (80); 17.5.1730 Mid *Sandwich* (90); 2.8.1731 Mid *Hampton Court* (70); 4.3.1731/32 Mid *Grafton* (70); 23.11.1732 Mate *Romney* (50); 14.9.1733 Mate *King William* HEIC; 13.3.1733/34 **Lieutenant**; 1.3.1734/35 Passed; 13.3.1734/35-27.7.1738 3L *Romney* (50); 28.7.1738-18.6.1739 2L *Advice* (54); 19.6.1739[(11.5.1742)] 2L *Jersey* (60); 4.3.1740/41-5.1741 Operations against Cartagena; 23.5.1741[(11.5.1742)] 2L *Norfolk* (80); **Commander**; 25.2.1741/42 *Wolf* (14) Sloop; **Captain**; 28.6.1744-9.3.1744/45 *Wager* (20); 27.3.1745-16.7.1745 *Kinsale* (44); 16.7.1745 Dismissed.

LOGIE, CHARLES

Dates: 1805 Died; 6.6.1805 Will Probate.
Family:
Service: **Lieutenant**; 13.2.1759 4L *Bienfaisant* (64); 22.2.1759 3L *Bienfaisant* (64); 2.10.1761-15.8.1763[P] 2L *Bienfaisant* (64); 12.10.1770-21.1.1771 1L *Venus* (36).

LOGIE, JAMES

Dates: c.1714 Born; 1.1779 Died; 26.2.1779 Will Probate.
Family: Wife Elizabeth Foster; Daughter Harriott; Daughter Catherine; Daughter Charlotte; Son Charles, RN (1755-1781); Son Edward.
Service: 22.4.1733 Able *Torrington* (40); 11.7.1734 Mid *Medway* (60); 28.12.1735 Mid *Hawk* (8) Sloop; 26.2.1736/37-10.1739[F] Mate *Hawk* (8) Sloop; 12.5.1741 Passed; **Lieutenant**; 29.5.1741 3L *Chester* (54); 2.6.1741 L. *Grampus* (6) Sloop; 16.9.1741 L. *Greyhound* (20); 25.6.1743 L. *Dolphin* (20); 24.12.1743-22.4.1744 L. *Squirrel* (20); 9.6.1744 3L *Harwich* (50); 12.6.1744 2L *Harwich* (50); 16.1.1744/45 2L *Prince George* (90); 16.7.1745 2L *Nottingham* (60); 6.3.1746/47-3.12.1747 1L *Nottingham* (60); 3.5.1747 1st Battle of Cape Finisterre; 14.10.1747 2nd Battle of Cape Finisterre; 31.3.1748-18.11.1752[P] 1L *Vanguard* (68); 16.1.1753-6.11.1754 1L *Vanguard* (68); 6.11.1754 2L *Vanguard* (68); 6.2.1755 1L *Lancaster* (66); **Commander**; 23.3.1756

Peregrine (20) Sloop; **Captain**; 20.4.1758-12.11.1759 *Greyhound* (20); 15.11.1759-19.3.1763[P] *Brilliant* (36); 28.2.1760 Action of February 28 1760; 6.5.1763-6.5.1766 *Burford* (68).

LONG, CHARLES

Dates: c.1711 Born; 1761 Died.
Family:
Service: 3.11.1728 Able *Winchelsea* (20); 27.5.1729 MidO *Torbay* (80); 3.12.1729 Mid *Romney* (50); 5.10.1732 Mid *Namur* (90); 21.5.1733 Able *Namur* (90); 17.6.1733 Mid *Rupert* (60); 26.2.1733/34 Mid *Namur* (90); 17.7.1734 Able *Poole* (32); 1.11.1734 Passed; **Lieutenant**; 18.5.1735[(27.8.1736)]-15.7.1736 L. *Fox* (20); 16.7.1736-2.8.1736[P] 2L *Newcastle* (50); 7.2.1737/38 2L *Anglesea* (40); **Commander**; 4.10.1740 *Saltash* (8) Sloop; **Captain**; 13.5.1741-17.8.1742[P] *Chester* (54); 12.4.1745-17.9.1746 *Royal Oak* (70); 1746 Dismissed.

LONG, ROBERT

Dates: 6.7.1771 Died.
Family:
Service: 7.4.1701 Vol-p-O *Coventry* (54); 31.3.1703-24.7.1704[C] Mid *Coventry* (54); 22.3.1704/5 Able *Cambridge* (80); 19.6.1705 Mid *Sunderland* (60); 14.3.1705/6 Passed; **Lieutenant**; 22.5.1709[(20.9.1710)] 2L *Kingston* (60); 22.10.1712-12.12.1714 L. *Aldborough* (20); 24.2.1715/16 2L *Falmouth* (54); 22.2.1716/17-6.7.1717 5L *Barfleur* (90); 15.3.1717/18 4L *Barfleur* (90); 26.3.1718 3L *Barfleur* (90); 11.8.1718 Battle of Cape Passaro; **Commander**; 3.10.1719[(13.12.1720)] *Thunder* (6) Bomb Vessel; 7.12.1721 *Furnace* (4) Bomb Vessel; 28.12.1721-21.6.1726 *Thunder* (6) Bomb Vessel; **Captain**; 21.3.1726/27 *Shoreham* (8) Bomb Vessel; 5.9.1727-1.4.1731 *Shoreham* (8) Bomb Vessel; 7.2.1731/32-6.1735[P] *Seaford* (20); 14.7.1738 *Portland* (50); 15.8.1738-7.12.1738[P] *Tilbury* (60); 30.8.1739-1.5.1741 *Tilbury* (60); 4.3.1740/41-5.1741 Operations against Cartagena; 2.6.1741[(13.2.1744/45)]-1.12.1741[P] *Hampton Court* (70); 3.4.1742 *Russell* (80); 11.2.1743/44-12.2.1743/44 Battle of Toulon; 18.3.1743/44[(13.2.1744/45)]-31.7.1744 *Marlborough* (90); 21.7.1747 **Superannuated Rear Admiral**.

LONG, WALTER

Dates: c.1735 Born; c.1782 Died; 1.1782 Will Probate.
Family:
Service: 9.7.1750 Capt Serv *Cumberland* (66); 19.12.1751 Able *Vulture* (14) Sloop; 8.8.1752 Able *Wager* (24); 29.3.1754 Mid *Wager* (24); 26.12.1755 Mid *Winchester* (50); 1.12.1756 Passed; **Lieutenant**; 13.6.1757 2L *Lowestoffe* (28); 5.6.1758-12.6.1758 Raid on Saint-Malo; 29.8.1759[(1.11.1759)]-19.5.1760[W] 1L *Lowestoffe* (28); 6.4.1763-13.8.1766 L. *Hunter* (10) Sloop; 2.11.1769-9.1772 LCmdr *Lurcher* (6) Cutter; 27.12.1775-14.10.1778[P] LCmdr *Lurcher* (6) Cutter; 15.10.1778 LCmdr *Expedition* (10) Cutter; **Commander**; 30.8.1779-27.6.1780[P] *Comet* (8) Fireship; 15.7.1780-9.1781[P] *Molly* Hired Armed vessel.

LONG, WILLIAM

Dates: c.1704 Born; 1778 Died; 24.11.1778 Will Probate.
Family:
Service: 4.8.1726 Able *Otter* (6) Sloop; 3.11.1727 Gnr Mate *Otter* (6) Sloop; 23.10.1730 Mate *Swallow* (60); 5.2.1732/33 Mate *Kingston* (60); 28.3.1733 Mid *Kingston* (60); 15.8.1733 Mate *Kingston* (60); 8.5.1734 Passed; **Lieutenant**; 4.3.1739/40-4.8.1741 3L *Saint Albans* (50); 13.2.1741/42[(5.2.1742/43)] 2L *Saint Albans* (50); 23.8.1742[(5.2.1742/43)]-13.10.1742 1L *Saint Albans* (50); 16.6.1743 2L *Berwick* (70); 11.2.1743/44-12.2.1743/44 Battle of Toulon; 29.3.1745[(23.11.1745)]

1L *Berwick* (70); 3.8.1745[23.11.1745]-25.5.1746[P] 6L *Neptune* (90); 11.12.1747-12.7.1748[P] 1L *Launceston* (44); 1.12.1748-14.11.1752[P] 1L *Eagle* (60); 6.11.1754 1L *Vanguard* (68); **Commander**; 15.11.1756 *Portsmouth* (6) Storeship; 20.7.1757 *Raven* (14) Sloop; **Captain**; 22.2.1760 *Bellona* (74); 25.2.1760-9.3.1763[P] *Wolf* (8) Sloop; 13.8.1767-31.3.1769[P] *Gibraltar* (20); 30.8.1769-16.11.1770 *Hind* (24).

LONGUEVILLE, SIR THOMAS (4TH BARONET LONGUEVILLE OF WOLVERTON, BUCKS)

Dates: 28.8.1718 4th Baronet Longueville of Wolverton, Bucks; 1759 Died;
Family: Father Edward Longueville, 3rd Bt. (1662-1718); Mother Mary; Wife Maria Margaretta Conway (d.1731); Daughter Maria Margaretta [Hope]; Daughter Harry [Williams]; Daughter Diana [Wilding];
Service: 1703-1704 Merchant Service; 1.10.1704 Vol-p-O *Pembroke* (60); 10.3.1704/5 Battle of Marbella; 4.3.1706/7 Mid *Weymouth* (50); 17.2.1707/8 Mid *Oxford* (54); 11.3.1708/9 Passed; **Lieutenant**; 3.6.1709-8.9.1710 L. *Diligence* (10); 10.9.1711-2.5.1715[P] 2L *Ruby* (54); 27.7.1715-21.2.1716/17 3L *Royal Oak* (70).

LORING, JOSHUA

Dates: 1725 Born North America; 5.10.1781 Died.
Family:
Service: **Lieutenant**; 23.5.1745[BLI 20.1.1745/46]-21.6.1745 3L *Vigilant* (60); 25.9.1745 Passed; 30.9.1745[22.2.1745/46]-15.10.1746 3L *Canterbury* (60); 27.11.1748[JAM 24.7.1749]-12.7.1749[P] 1L *Cornwall* (80); **Commander**; 13.3.1756-10.8.1756[C] *London* (18) Brigantine; **Captain**; 19.12.1757-21.12.1757 *Squirrel* (20); 1760-8.1760 *Onondaga* (18) Sloop.

LORT, GEORGE

Dates: c.1736 Born; 1764 Died; 1.3.1764 Will Probate.
Family:
Service: 25.9.1749-15.8.1753 Able *Weazle* (16) Sloop; 16.8.1753 Mid *Weazle* (16) Sloop; 30.4.1754 Mid *Invincible* (74); 11.6.1754 Able *Invincible* (74); 23.7.1754 Mid *Sheerness* (24); 7.12.1755 Mid *Tiger* (60); 11.1.1756-14.1.1756 Capture of Geriah; 8.5.1756 Able *Tiger* (60); 12.11.1756 Passed; **Lieutenant**; 12.11.1756-2.5.1758 L. *Wolf* (8) Sloop; 2.5.1758-9.10.1760 L. *Granado* (8) Bomb Vessel; 5.6.1758-12.6.1758 Raid on Saint-Malo; 16.1.1759-19.1.1759 Attack on Martinique; 20.1.1759-1.5.1759 Capture of Guadeloupe; 2.3.1762 L. *Proserpine* (8) Fireship.

LOVELACE, PAUL

Dates: c.1711 Born; 1757 Died; 19.12.1757 Will Probate.
Family:
Service: 1.9.1730 Vol-p-O *Hampshire* (54); 3.3.1731/32 Mid *Hampshire* (54); 30.6.1732 Able *Plymouth* (60); 1.8.1732 Mid *Plymouth* (60); 29.12.1732 Able *Anglesea* (40); 19.5.1733 Able *Southampton Hulk*; 7.10.1733 MidO *Canterbury* (60); 4.4.1734 Mid *Canterbury* (60); 28.6.1734 Mid *Buckingham* (70); 23.10.1736 Passed; **Lieutenant**; 6.3.1740/41-27.8.1743 3L *Bedford* (70); 11.1.1744/45-2.4.1746 1L *Lark* (44); 29.1.1757-14.12.1757 L. *Lightning* (6) Hospital Ship; 8.1757-10.1757 Louisbourg Expedition.

LOVETT, JOHN

Dates: 20.2.1758 Died.
Family:
Service: 10.5.1722 Able *Leopard* (50); 13.5.1724 MidO *Leopard* (50); 30.3.1726 Mid *Union* (90); 11.1.1726/27 Passed; **Lieutenant**; 2.3.1733/34-12.3.1733/34 3L *Princess Louisa* (40); 1.10.1736-29.12.1736 1L *Princess Louisa* (40); 4.2.1736/37-15.8.1740[P] 1L *Diamond* (40); 23.3.1739/40 Attack on Chagres; 16.9.1740 1L *Nassau* (70); **Commander**; 11.6.1741 *Otter* (6) Sloop; **Captain**; 16.11.1741-15.5.1743 *Neptune* (90); 15.5.1743[(MED 6.10.1747)] *Kingston* (60); 11.2.1743/44-12.2.1743/44 Battle of Toulon; 2.4.1745[(MED 29.12.1747)]-9.12.1747[P] *Princess Caroline* (80).

LOVING, JOHN

Dates: c.1709 Born; 1785 Died.
Family:
Service: 12.5.1729-3.1.1729/30 Able *Edinburgh* (70); 4.1.1729/30-23.11.1732 Mid *Salisbury* (50); 24.11.1732-21.1.1732/33 Able *Sunderland* (60); 22.1.1732/33-31.3.1735 Mid *Sunderland* (60); 1.4.1735-6.4.1736 Mate *Sunderland Hulk* (60); 16.4.1736 Passed; **Lieutenant**; 16.11.1739 3L *Bristol* (54); 20.1.1740/41 3L *Cambridge* (80); 27.3.1741 3L *Barfleur* (90); 29.5.1741-21.2.1743/44 2L *Barfleur* (90); 11.2.1743/44-12.2.1743/44 Battle of Toulon; **Commander**; 12.1.1744/45[(MED 7.12.1747)]-4.12.1747[P] *Firedrake* (8) Bomb Vessel.

LOWDER, JOHN

Dates: c.1739 Born; 1813 Died.
Family:
Service: 1754-1756 HEIC Service; 12.7.1756 Mid *Swiftsure* (68); 28.2.1758 Battle of Cartagena; 18.8.1759-19.8.1759 Battle of Lagos Bay; 20.11.1759 Battle of Quiberon Bay; 30.1.1760 Passed; **Lieutenant**; 2.4.1760-13.8.1761 5L *Hercules* (74); 8.3.1763-26.3.1763[P] 4L *Hercules* (74); 9.1768-30.4.1771[P] LCmdr *Laurel* (6) Cutter; 12.10.1807 **Superannuated Commander**.

LOWER, EDWARD

Dates: c.1730 Born; 1802 Died; 18.2.1802 Will Probate.
Family:
Service: 28.3.1749 Able *Vanguard* (68); 13.11.1751-13.8.1752 Cox *Torrington* (44); 14.8.1752 Able *Torrington* (44); 7.12.1753 Mid *Torrington* (44); 12.11.1754 Able *Mars* (64); 30.1.1755 Mid *Mars* (64); 2.5.1755-24.6.1755[W] Mate *Mars* (64); 25.7.1755 Mid *Torbay* (74); 3.3.1756 Passed; **Lieutenant**; 15.11.1756 3L *Saint Albans* (60); 26.2.1757 2L *Saint Albans* (60); 21.2.1759 2L *Hero* (74); 20.8.1759 1L *Hero* (74); 20.11.1759 Battle of Quiberon Bay; 29.3.1761-11.6.1761 Expedition against Belle-Isle; 6.9.1762 1L *Achilles* (60); 11.5.1763-10.5.1766 2L *Burford* (68); 16.10.1767 1L *Fame* (74); 3.11.1770 2L *Fame* (74); 7.11.1771-12.5.1773 2L *Dublin* (74); 1779-9.1783 LCmdr *Pelican* Hired Tender; 21.9.1796 **Superannuated Commander**.

LOWFIELD, WILLIAM

Dates: c.1723 Born; 29.10.1762 Died off Nantucket.
Family:
Service: 21.3.1738/39 Capt Serv *Kent* (70); 8.4.1740 Capture of the Princesa; 9.3.1740/41 Gnr Serv *Dunkirk* (60); 17.10.1741 Gnr Serv *Boyne* (80); 10.7.1742 Able *Hawk* (8) Sloop; 21.2.1742/43 Mid *Kinsale* (44); 9.5.1745 Passed; **Lieutenant**; 19.6.1745 3L *Milford* (44); 21.10.1745-6.8.1748 2L *Milford* (44); 3.8.1746 Action of August 3 1746; 22.7.1755-22.8.1758

3L *Princess Mary* (60); 23.12.1760-17.3.1762 3L *Marlborough* (68); 7.1.1762-10.2.1762 Operations against Martinique; **Commander**; 19.4.1762(8.11.1764)-29.10.1762[C] *Basilisk* (8) Bomb Vessel; 6.6.1762-13.8.1762 Operations against Havana.

LOWNDES, RICHARD

Dates: c.1719 Born; 1761 Died; 20.5.1761 Will Probate.

Family:

Service: 23.8.1741 Mid *Antelope* (50); 14.2.1742/43 Mate *Plymouth* (60); 8.2.1743/44 Able *Plymouth* (60); 14.8.1744 Mate *Blast* (8) Bomb Vessel; 10.10.1744 Mid *Cornwall* (80); 17.1.1744/45 Mate *Cornwall* (80); 22.2.1744/45-11.5.1745 Able *Pembroke* (60); 11.5.1747 Passed; **Lieutenant**; 27.1.1747/48 2L *Fame* (30); 20.5.1748-9.8.1748[P] L. *Fox* (20); 24.1.1756-22.7.1756 2L *Ambuscade* (40); 20.1.1757-24.7.1760 2L *Newcastle* (50); 29.4.1758 Battle of Cuddalore; 3.8.1758 Battle of Negapatam; 10.9.1759 Battle of Pondicherry.

LUCAS, CHARLES

Dates: 23.3.1773 Died.

Family:

Service: 1734-1739 HEIC Service; 17.2.1738/39 Able *Tilbury* (60); 3.3.1738/39 Mid *Tilbury* (60); 16.10.1740 Mate *Tilbury* (60); 4.3.1740/41-5.1741 Operations against Cartagena; 7.1741-10.1741 Operations against Santiago; 22.9.1742 Mid *Cumberland* (80); **Lieutenant**; 20.6.1743(26.2.1744/45) 4L *Kent* (70); 5.7.1743(26.2.1744/45) 3L *Kent* (70); 4.1.1743/44(26.2.1744/45)-15.9.1744[P] 2L *Kent* (70); 27.9.1744 Passed; 21.10.1745 5L *Royal George* (100); 13.11.1745 4L *Royal George* (100); 23.1.1745/46-14.5.1746 2L *Royal George* (100); 9.7.1747-30.8.1748[P] 1L *Augusta* (60); 3.4.1755 1L *Romney* (44); 5.7.1756-29.9.1756 1L *Guernsey* (50); **Commander**; 15.11.1756 *London* (6) Storeship; 25.1.1757-18.10.1758 *Medway* (6) Storeship; **Captain**; 18.10.1758 *Torrington* (44); 1.11.1762-10.11.1762[P] *Saint George* Prison Ship; 26.8.1763 *Prince Edward* (44); 22.11.1764(28.5.1765)-20.6.1765 *Swift* (14) Sloop.

LUCE, JOHN

Dates: 1795 Died.

Family:

Service: **Lieutenant**; 18.10.1758(NA 14.3.1760)-1.5.1759 3L *Prince of Orange* (60).

LUKEY, PATHERICK

Dates: c.1727 Born; 1768 Died.

Family:

Service: 1.12.1746-5.12.1747[P] Able *Grand Turk* (22); 19.12.1747-1.7.1748[P] Able *Ranger* (28); 15.6.1752 Mid *Badger* (10) Sloop; 30.7.1754 Able *Badger* (10) Sloop; 4.6.1755 Passed; **Lieutenant**; 25.11.1757 2L *Tartar* (28); 22.5.1758 2L *Chatham* (50); 30.3.1759 1L *Chatham* (50); 3.7.1759 Bombardment of Le Havre; 20.11.1759 Battle of Quiberon Bay; 9.12.1760 1L *Superb* (74); 23.3.1761-2.3.1763[P] 2L *Superb* (74); 11.5.1763-10.5.1766 3L *Burford* (68).

LURCOCK, WILLIAM

Dates: c.1733 Born; 1786 Died; 9.3.1786 Will Probate.

Family:

Service: 6.5.1748 Ord. *Otter* (14) Sloop; 4.10.1748 Able *Otter* (14) Sloop; 15.11.1748 Cox *Otter* (14) Sloop; 4.10.1749 Mid *Boston* (24); 28.1.1751 Able *Boston* (24); 6.9.1751-16.1.1752[P] Mid *Boston* (24); 17.6.1756 Able *Fowey* (24); 2.9.1756 Mate *Fowey* (24); 14.11.1756 Mate *Namur*

(90); 5.9.1757-6.10.1757 Raid on Rochefort; 6.6.1758-27.7.1758 The Siege of Louisbourg; 31.7.1758 Mate *Royal George* (100); 2.5.1759 Passed; **Lieutenant**; 23.8.1759-23.3.1761 2L *Repulse* (32); 1.4.1762(9.5.1763)-13.5.1763P 3L *Devonshire* (70); 6.6.1762-13.8.1762 Operations against Havana.

LUTTRELL, JOHN

Dates: 17.3.1829 Died Devonshire Place, Middlesex.
Family: Wife Maria Anne (1776/7–1857), daughter of John Morgan married 16.6.1798; Wife Elizabeth Olmius (d. 1797), married 13.6.1765.
Service: 23.1.1751/52-c.1755 Scholar *Royal Naval Academy*; **Lieutenant**; 10.10.1758-12.2.1760 2L *Vestal* (32); 3.7.1759 Bombardment of Le Havre; 7.4.1760 1L *Achilles* (60); 28.11.1760 2L *Hampton Court* (64); **Commander**; 4.3.1761 *Druid* (10) Sloop; 29.3.1761-11.6.1761 Expedition against Belle-Isle; **Captain**; 25.8.1762-25.10.1763P *Mars* (74); 17.5.1765-1.6.1768 *Achilles* (60); 5.11.1778-1.6.1780 *Charon* (44); 15.9.1779-20.10.1779 Capture of Omoa.

LUTWIDGE, SAMUEL

Dates: c.1731 Born.
Family:
Service: 4.1.1747/48 Able *Ferret* (14) Sloop; 15.8.1748 Mid *Ferret* (14) Sloop; 27.10.1752 Able *Assurance* (44); 4.11.1752-24.4.1753W Mate *Assurance* (44); 6.6.1753 Passed; **Lieutenant**; 15.2.1755(16.5.1760)-7.7.1758 2L *Salisbury* (50); 11.1.1756-14.1.1756 Capture of Geriah; 7.3.1757-1.4.1757 Expedition against Chandernagore; 29.4.1758 Battle of Cuddalore.

LUTWIDGE, SKEFFINGTON

Dates: 13.3.1737 Born Whitehaven; 21.8.1814 Died.
Family: Father Thomas Lutwidge; Mother Lucy Hoghton; Wife Catherine Harvey (d.1810).
Service: 28.4.1759-15.8.1759 ActL *Echo* (24); **Lieutenant**; 15.8.1759(24.9.1760)-17.1.1761 L. *Echo* (24); 6.4.1763-6.6.1766 LCmdr *Cholmondley* (4) Cutter; **Commander**; 21.1.1771-14.10.1773P *Carcass* (8) Bomb Vessel; **Captain**; 15.10.1773 *Success* (20); 10.8.1775 *Triton* (28); 16.1.1780 Battle of Cape St. Vincent; 7.11.1780(BLI 5.2.1781) *Yarmouth* (64); 28.3.1781-13.9.1783P *Perseverance* (36); 13.9.1786 *Crown* (64); 4.10.1786 *Scipio* (64); 23.8.1788-21.10.1789 CinC — River Medway and The Nore; 21.10.1789-11.1789 Commodore *Scipio* (64); 22.12.1792 *Terrible* (74); 12.4.1794 **Rear Admiral of the Blue**; 4.7.1794 **Rear Admiral of the White**; 1.6.1795 **Vice Admiral of the Blue**; 21.6.1797-4.1799 CinC — River Medway and The Nore; 7.1797-9.1797 *Sandwich* (90); 10.1797-1799 *Zealand* (64); 14.2.1799 **Vice Admiral of the Red**; 4.1799-1.1802 CinC — The Downs; 4.1799-21.1.1802P *Overyssel* (64); 1.1.1801 **Admiral of the Blue**; 9.11.1805 **Admiral of the White**; 31.7.1810 **Admiral of the Red.**

LUX, JOHN

Dates: c.1720 Born; 23.11.1778 Died.
Family:
Service: 5.12.1739 Able *Deptford* (60); 9.2.1740/41 Able *Mary Galley* (40); 28.7.1741-12.3.1742/43P Cox *Mary Galley* (40); 7.8.1743 Able *Jersey* (60); 4.11.1743 Mid *Jersey* (60); 13.9.1744 Mid *Prince Frederick* (70); 11.9.1746 Passed; **Lieutenant**; 21.9.1757-26.3.1759 L. *Speedwell* (8) Sloop; 5.6.1758-12.6.1758 Raid on Saint-Malo; 26.4.1759 4L *Hercules* (74); 20.11.1759 Battle of Quiberon Bay; 8.3.1763-26.3.1763P 3L *Hercules* (74).

LYELL, DAVID

Dates: c.1719 Born; 1758 Died; 4.1.1758 Will Probate.
Family:
Service: 18.9.1740 Able *Buckingham* (70); 24.12.1740 Mid *Buckingham* (70); 11.2.1743/44-12.2.1743/44 Battle of Toulon; 30.6.1745 Mid *Shrewsbury* (80); 9.8.1745 Passed; **Lieutenant**; 6.2.1745/46-16.4.1746 L. *Dispatch* (10) Sloop; 12.8.1746-30.6.1748[P] 3L *Folkestone* (44); 13.5.1755-21.7.1756 L. *Rye* (20).

LYNCH, STEPHEN

Dates: c.1731 Born; 7.3.1767 Died.
Family: Wife Ann;
Service: 1755-1757 Merchant Service; 4.12.1757 Mid *Augusta* (60); 29.4.1760 Mate *Centaur* (20); 30.11.1761 Passed; **Lieutenant**; 17.7.1762[(EI 21.10.1763)]-23.9.1763[P] 3L *Edgar* (60).

LYNN, FRANCIS

Dates: c.1735 Born; 1810 Died.
Family: Father James Lynn.
Service: 14.8.1747 Able *Lion* (58); 14.10.1747 2nd Battle of Cape Finisterre; 1.3.1747/48 Able *Yarmouth* (64); 19.2.1749/50 Capt Serv *Sheerness* (24); 27.8.1751 Mid *Amazon* (22); 3.5.1753 Able *Saint Albans* (60); 29.3.1754 Mid *Saint Albans* (60); 13.9.1754 Able *Wolf* (8) Sloop; 14.3.1755 Passed; **Lieutenant**; 15.3.1755-29.3.1757 3L *Falmouth* (50); 12.11.1757 3L *Falmouth* (50); 1.12.1757 2L *Falmouth* (50); 7.12.1757 1L *Falmouth* (50); 19.2.1759 6L *Princess Royal* (90); 7.11.1759 LCmdr *Princess Caroline* (80) Hospital Ship; **Commander**; 26.10.1761-9.2.1763[P] *Flamborough Prize* (14) Sloop; 5.9.1763-24.10.1766 *Pomona* (18) Sloop.

LYNN, THOMAS

Dates: 1781 Died.
Family: Wife Jane Seymour married 1750; Son Charles Seymour, RN (d.1790).
Service: **Lieutenant**; 20.1.1746/47[(MED 24.1.1748/49)]-31.7.1748 L. *Cruizer* (12) Brig; 14.3.1750/51-6.9.1753[P] 2L *Glory* (44); 6.2.1755 4L *Ramillies* (90); 7.10.1755-31.12.1755 2L *Colchester* (50); **Commander**; 6.4.1756-3.9.1756[P] *Roehampton* (16) Hired Armed Ship; **Captain**; 10.11.1756 *Aldborough* (20); 1.11.1757 *Roebuck* (44); 16.1.1759-19.1.1759 Attack on Martinique; 20.1.1759-1.5.1759 Capture of Guadeloupe; 7.8.1759 *Royal Sovereign* (104); 27.10.1759 *Dover* (44); 9.4.1760-31.7.1764[P] *Chatham* (50); 11.9.1770-9.10.1773 *Garland* (24); 17.11.1780 **Superannuated Rear Admiral**.

LYON, SCROOP

Dates: 1757 Died.
Family:
Service: 28.12.1707 Vol-p-O *Tiger* (48); 22.1.1710/11 MidO *Southsea Castle* (42); 8.5.1713 Mid *Southsea Castle* (42); 15.5.1716 Able *Exeter* (60); 26.11.1716 Mid *Exeter* (60); 25.7.1717 Mid *Shrewsbury* (80); 8.10.1717 Mid *Superb* (64); 1.5.1718 Passed; **Lieutenant**; 17.9.1718[(16.3.1720/21)]-15.9.1721[P] L. *Garland* (32); 16.3.1725/26 2L *Rippon* (60); 24.12.1726[(22.8.1727)] L. *Winchelsea* (20); 18.1.1727/28-19.6.1729 1L *Adventure* (40); 25.7.1729 2L *Burford* (70); 5.5.1730-4.9.1731[P] 1L *Diamond* (40); 31.1.1733/34-4.2.1734/35 2L *Cornwall* (80).

LYS, JAMES
Dates: c.1739 Born; 1814 Died.
Family:
Service: 23.3.1756 QM *Barfleur* (80); 25.10.1756 Mid *Barfleur* (80); 4.5.1757-19.2.1758[W] Mid *Invincible* (74); 8.1757-10.1757 Louisbourg Expedition; 14.2.1758 Mid *Royal George* (100); 27.8.1758 Mid *Warspite* (74); 18.8.1759-19.8.1759 Battle of Lagos Bay; 20.11.1759 Battle of Quiberon Bay; 6.6.1760 Passed; **Lieutenant**; 7.6.1760-5.5.1763[P] 5L *Warspite* (74); 25.1.1771-22.5.1771[P] 3L *Temeraire* (74); 3.11.1775 2L *Conquestador* (60); **Commander**; 29.4.1778-31.10.1780[P] *Wasp* (8) Sloop.

Service Records M

MACARTNEY, JOHN

Dates: c.1730 Born; 5.8.1781 Died Battle of Dogger Bank; 31.8.1781 Will Probate.

Family:

Service: 9.11.1748 Able *Southsea Castle* (44); 8.5.1749 Able *Superb* (60); 20.10.1749 Able *Anson* (60); 20.1.1749/50 Cox *Anson* (60); 8.11.1750 Mid *Anson* (60); 28.3.1752 Mid *Penzance* (44); 25.10.1752 Mate *Penzance* (44); 10.3.1755 Passed; **Lieutenant**; 20.1.1756-22.5.1758 Lieutenant *Jane and Barbara* Hired Tender; 13.2.1756 3L *Royal George* (100); 12.5.1756 5L *Prince* (90); 29.11.1756 3L *Culloden* (74); 5.4.1757 Action of April 5 1757; 1.6.1757-18.10.1758 3L *Saint George* (90); 15.1.1759 2L *Torbay* (74); **Commander**; 22.9.1759[(31.12.1760)]-3.7.1760 *Porcupine* (16) Sloop; 19.8.1760[(NA 30.6.1763)]-3.6.1763[P] *Racehorse* (16) Sloop; 12.12.1765 *Hound* (14) Sloop; **Captain**; 4.9.1766-1.10.1766[SP] *Phoenix* (44); 10.1.1774-14.11.1775 *Mercury* (20); 31.1.1776-30.1.1779 *Ambuscade* (32); 2.9.1779 *Sandwich* (90); 1.10.1779-5.8.1781 *Princess Amelia* (80); 5.8.1781 Battle of Dogger Bank.

MACBRIDE, JOHN

Dates: c.1735 Born Scotland; 17.2.1800 Died.

Family: Father Robert McBride (1687–1759); Mother ? Boyd; Wife Charlotte Anne Harrison (d.1771) married 1769; Wife Ursula Folkes married 14.7.1774; Daughter Charlotte Anne [Lake); Son John David;

Service: 1751-1754 Merchant Service; 12.7.1754 Able *Garland* (24); 14.4.1756 Mid *Garland* (24); 15.1.1757 Mate *Garland* (24); 5.1.1758 Mate *Norfolk* (6) Mer; 6.10.1758 Passed; **Lieutenant**; 27.10.1758-7.4.1760 2L *Stag* (32); 16.12.1761-29.12.1761 4L *Newark* (80); **Commander**; 7.4.1762 *Grampus* (8) Fireship; 14.10.1762-18.5.1763 *Vulture* (14) Sloop; 27.5.1763 *Cruizer* (8) Sloop; **Captain**; 20.6.1765 *Renown* (30); 30.7.1765 *Cruizer* (8) Sloop; 22.8.1765 *Jason* (32); 1767-1768 Gov. of Falkland Islands; 13.8.1767-15.11.1769 *Seaford* (20); 23.3.1771-25.5.1771 *Arethusa* (32); 1.8.1771 *Southampton* (32); 23.4.1773-9.8.1774[P] *Orpheus* (32); 6.11.1776-23.1.1780 *Bienfaisant* (64); 27.7.1778 1st Battle of Ushant; 16.1.1780 Battle of Cape St. Vincent; 6.3.1780 *Bienfaisant* (64); 8.1.1781-23.4.1783[P] *Artois* (40); 5.8.1781 Battle of Dogger Bank; 10.6.1783 *Druid* (32); 7.4.1784-26.6.1790 M.P. for Plymouth; 13.10.1787-14.9.1791[P] *Cumberland* (74); 1.2.1793 **Rear Admiral of the Blue**; 6.2.1793-6.6.1793 CinC — The Downs; 10.2.1793-4.1793 *Iphigenia* (32); 4.1793-6.6.1793 *Quebec* (32); 14.7.1793-10.8.1793 *Cumberland* (74); 12.1793-1.1794 *Flora* (36); 12.4.1794 **Rear Admiral of the Red**; 1.6.1794 **Vice Admiral of the Blue**; 4.7.1794-1795 *Minotaur* (74); 1795 *Sceptre* (64); 1.6.1795 **Vice Admiral of the White**; 12.1796-4.1797 *Russell* (74); 14.2.1799 **Admiral of the Blue**.

MACCARTHY, LORD ROBERT (VISCOUNT MUSKERRY)

Dates: 1685 Viscount Muskerry; 1685 Born; 19.9.1769 Died Boulogne, Boulogne-sur-Mer.

Family: Father Donogh MacCarty, 4th Earl of Clancarty (c.1668-1734); Mother Lady Elizabeth Spencer (c.1673-1704); Wife Joanna Player (1693-1759) married 14.12.1722; Wife Elizabeth

Farnelly (d.1790) married 1759; Daughter Cecilia [Bayard] (aft.1759-c.1792); Sister Charlotte [West] (d.1735).
Service: 11.9.1713-20.9.1714P Vol-p-O *Ludlow Castle* (42); 23.2.1713/14 Ord. *Ludlow Castle* (42); 20.5.1714 Vol-p-O *Ludlow Castle* (42); 15.6.1715 Able *Anglesea* (50); 12.7.1715 Mid *Anglesea* (50); 6.10.1716 MidO *Argyle* (54); 14.12.1716 MidO *Dragon* (54); 8.5.1718 Passed; **Lieutenant**; 31.5.1718-14.2.1719/20 2L *Dover* (40); 15.2.1719/20-3.4.1720 2L *Saint Albans* (50); **Captain**; 17.3.1721/22-22.1.1722/23 *Solebay* (42); 18.7.1727-1.12.1727P *Hampshire* (54); 11.1.1727/28 *Adventure* (40); 6.3.1732/33-7.1.1734/35 *Romney* (50); 5.4.1733-1734 Gov. of Newfoundland.

MACKAY, HUGH
Dates: 1765 Died.
Family:
Service: **Lieutenant**; 2.1.1745/46 L. *Swift* (8) Sloop; 2.12.1746-20.5.1749P 3L *Adventure* (44).

MACKENZIE, GEORGE
Dates: 1780 Died;
Family: Wife Ann; Son Thomas, RN (1753-1813).
Service: **Lieutenant**; 2.5.1740(14.7.1740) 4L *Prince of Orange* (70); 26.2.1741/42-11.8.1742P 3L *Prince of Orange* (70); 8.10.1742 3L *Princess Mary* (60); 15.10.1742 1L *Hampshire* (50); 19.3.1743/44-10.8.1744 1L *Strafford* (58); 16.10.1744-4.12.1744 1L *Defiance* (60); **Commander**; 20.7.1745 *Amazon* (22); 22.8.1745 *Tavistock* (10) Sloop; 20.9.1746-25.9.1746 Lorient Operations; 1.10.1746 Action of 1746-10-01; **Captain**; 24.1.1746/47-3.5.1748 *Inverness* (22); 5.3.1751/52-17.5.1756P *Fowey* (24); 21.2.1757-31.1.1758 *Sunderland* (60); 8.1757-10.1757 Louisbourg Expedition; 16.5.1758 *Renown* (30); 5.6.1758-12.6.1758 Raid on Saint-Malo; 16.1.1759-19.1.1759 Attack on Martinique; 20.1.1759-1.5.1759 Capture of Guadeloupe; 16.4.1761(1.11.1763)-10.8.1763P *Defiance* (60); 6.6.1762-13.8.1762 Operations against Havana; 1.12.1763-1.12.1766 *Cornwall* (74); 18.5.1768 *Arrogant* (74); 1.8.1770 CinC — Jamaica; 1.8.1770-6.3.1772P Commodore *Dunkirk* (60); 11.1.1774 *Ardent* (64); 12.1.1774 CinC — River Medway and The Nore; 12.1.1774 Commodore *Ardent* (64); 11.3.1775-6.5.1775 *Ramillies* (74); 8.8.1775 CinC — River Medway and The Nore; 8.8.1775-29.4.1777 Commodore *Ramillies* (74); 28.4.1777 **Rear Admiral of the Blue**; 23.1.1778 **Rear Admiral of the White**; 29.1.1778 **Rear Admiral of the Red**; 19.3.1779 **Vice Admiral of the Blue**.

MACKENZIE, GEORGE
Dates: 1773 Died; 1.9.1773 Will Probate.
Family:
Service: **Lieutenant**; 9.11.1756-23.4.1757 L. *Wasp* (8) Sloop; 27.7.1759 3L *Monarch* (74); 23.10.1759-6.10.1760P 2L *Monarch* (74).

MACKENZIE, GEORGE
Dates: c.1723 Born; 5.10.1780 Died.
Family:
Service: 20.12.1743 Able *Duke* (90); 6.2.1744/45 Able *Monmouth* (70); 3.9.1745 Able *John and Anne* (16) Hired Armed vessel; 24.1.1745/46 Mid *Tavistock* (28) Mer; 15.9.1747 Able *Inverness* (22); 5.11.1747-14.11.1748P Mate *Inverness* (22); 23.4.1751 Mate *Seahorse* (24); 10.9.1755 Mate *Crown* (44); 25.1.1757 Mate *Norwich* (50); 6.3.1758 Passed; **Lieutenant**; 18.5.1758 L. *Fly* (8)

Sloop; 15.3.1759 2L *Dover* (44); 7.11.1759-7.10.1760 2L *Niger* (32); 13.4.1761-21.3.1763[P] 4L *Ocean* (90).

MACKENZIE, JAMES

Dates: c.1715 Born; 1789 Died.
Family:
Service: 5.5.1736-31.7.1736 Ord. *Greyhound* (20); 1.8.1736-6.10.1737 Ord. *Captain* (70); 7.10.1737-29.6.1739 Able *Captain*; 30.6.1739-16.10.1740 Gnr *Elizabeth* (70); 17.10.1740-26.4.1742 Gnr *Kent* (70); 27.4.1742 Mid *Kent* (70); 11.10.1744 Passed; **Lieutenant**; 19.12.1744-18.7.1747 L. *Serpent* (10) Bomb Vessel; 18.7.1747-29.5.1752[P] L. *Tartar* (20); 19.2.1755-11.3.1755 4L *Royal George* (100); 11.3.1755 5L *Royal George* (100); 17.1.1756 5L *Royal Anne* (100); **Commander**; 4.4.1757 *Infernal* (8) Bomb Vessel; 5.9.1757-6.10.1757 Raid on Rochefort; 5.6.1758-12.6.1758 Raid on Saint-Malo; 16.1.1759-19.1.1759 Attack on Martinique; 20.1.1759-1.5.1759 Capture of Guadeloupe; 29.3.1761-11.6.1761 Expedition against Belle-Isle; 7.1.1762-10.2.1762 Operations against Martinique; 7.4.1762-24.5.1763[P] *Swallow* (14) Sloop.

MACKERELL, THOMAS

Dates: c.1736 Born; 1778 Died.
Family:
Service: 23.3.1755 Able *Terrible* (74); 9.6.1755 Mid *Terrible* (74); 1.10.1755 Mid *Ramillies* (90); 19.2.1756 Mid *Trident* (64); 20.5.1756 Battle of Minorca; 24.2.1761 Mate *Sutherland* (50); 3.6.1761-7.6.1761 Occupation of Dominica; 4.11.1761 Passed; **Lieutenant**; 24.5.1762-20.12.1762[P] 4L *Bedford* (64); 6.12.1769-25.6.1771 L. *Pomona* (18) Sloop; 18.7.1775-29.8.1775 1L *Niger* (32); 12.2.1776-6.3.1776 LCmdr *Concord* Hired Tender; 5.4.1776-1778 LCmdr *Hunter* Hired Tender; 1777-2.9.1777[D] L. *Cornwall* (74); 2.9.1777 Dismissed.

MACKIE, JAMES

Dates: 1771 Died.
Family:
Service: **Lieutenant**; 29.12.1743 L. *Granado* (8) Bomb Vessel; 20.4.1745-27.6.1748[W] 2L *Fowey* (44); 6.2.1755 2L *Barfleur* (80); 5.9.1757-6.10.1757 Raid on Rochefort; 27.10.1758 1L *Crescent* (32) Frigate; **Commander**; 29.3.1759-1760 *Canterbury* (6).

MACKIE, THOMAS

Dates: 4.3.1790 Died.
Family:
Service: **Lieutenant**; 23.3.1761[NA 6.6.1763]-30.5.1763[P] 2L *Repulse* (32); 3.6.1761-7.6.1761 Occupation of Dominica; 7.1.1762-10.2.1762 Operations against Martinique; 2.1.1776-23.4.1776 1L *Brune* (32); 23.4.1776 5L *Barfleur* (90); 2.8.1776 4L *Barfleur* (90); 6.12.1776 3L *Barfleur* (90); 5.4.1777 3L *Princess Royal* (90); 4.5.1778 3L *Albion* (74); 26.5.1778 3L *Namur* (90); 23.7.1778-9.10.1778 2L *Namur* (90).

MACNAMARA, JAMES

Dates: c.1736 Born; 1802 Died; 10.3.1802 Will Probate.
Family:
Service: 1753-1757 HEIC Service; 14.1.1757 Mid *Royal George* (100); 8.2.1758 Mid *Namur* (90); 6.6.1758-27.7.1758 The Siege of Louisbourg; 18.8.1759-19.8.1759 Battle of Lagos Bay; 20.11.1759 Battle of Quiberon Bay; 10.9.1760 Passed; **Lieutenant**; 25.6.1761-25.12.1762[P]

5L *Hero* (74); 7.4.1767-10.4.1770 3L *Dorsetshire* (68); 10.4.1770-15.2.1772[P] L. *Dolphin* (24); 10.12.1776-3.5.1777 2L *Aeolus* (32); **Commander**; 2.5.1779[JAM 14.7.1781] *Hound* (14) Sloop; **Captain**; 5.2.1781-10.5.1783[P] *Nestor* (26); 30.10.1790 *America* (64).

MAINWARING, THOMAS BORNFORD

Dates: c.1734 Born; c.1780 Died Shoreditch, Middlesex; 30.12.1780 Buried St Leonards, Shoreditch, Middlesex; 11.9.1781 Will Probate.

Family: Father Cavendish Tyrell Manwaring (1703-1775); Mother Catherine Borneford (1700-1772); Wife Ann Bazely (1740-?); Daughter Olivia (1764-?); Daughter Harriet (1768-?); Daughter Catherine (1769-?); Son Cavendish Tyrell (1774-?).

Service: 19.11.1747 Scholar *Royal Naval Academy*; 21.11.1750 Vol-p-O *Prince Henry* (44); 5.3.1753 Able *Penzance* (44); 23.2.1754 Mid *Penzance* (44); 16.2.1755 Mate *Penzance* (44); 3.3.1756 Passed; **Lieutenant**; 1.6.1756 L. *Greyhound* (20); 26.4.1757-11.5.1757 6L *Royal Anne* (100); 12.4.1759-17.3.1763 1L *Tweed* (32); 29.3.1761-11.6.1761 Expedition against Belle-Isle; 11.4.1763-10.6.1766 LCmdr *Endeavour* (4) Cutter; c.8.10.1769-20.3.1773 LCmdr *Anson* (6) Cutter; 5.4.1776 LCmdr *Meredith* (10) Cutter; **Commander**; 13.5.1778-6.2.1779[P] *Speedwell* (8) Sloop; 22.5.1779-1.6.1779 *Fortune* (14) Sloop.

MAINWARING, WILLIAM

Dates: c.1718 Born; 26.10.1763 Died.

Family:

Service: 5.9.1732-16.12.1732[P] Ord. *Rye* (20); 15.1.1732/33-6.2.1734/35 Able *Rye* (20); 7.2.1734/35-1.2.1735/36 Able *Rippon* (60); 2.2.1735/36-5.12.1736 Able *Orford* (70); 6.12.1736-31.5.1737 Mid *Orford* (70); 1.6.1737-27.10.1737 Able *Alderney* (8) Bomb Vessel; 28.10.1737-19.7.1738 Mid *Alderney* (8) Bomb Vessel; 20.7.1738-8.1.1739/40 Mid *Deal Castle* (20); 8.2.1739/40 Passed; **Lieutenant**; 4.3.1739/40 3L *Winchester* (50); 14.8.1741 1L *Winchester* (50); 13.11.1741 2L *Cambridge* (80); 10.12.1741 L. *Flamborough* (20); 6.7.1744-15.2.1744/45 L. *Wager* (20); 13.7.1745 1L *Looe* (44); 2.1.1747/48 1L *Saint Albans* (60); 30.9.1748-16.12.1748 L. *Sphinx* (24); 22.12.1748 1L *Saint Albans* (60); 8.11.1751-20.11.1752[P] 1L *Mars* (64); 16.1.1753-25.2.1756 1L *Salisbury* (50); 11.1.1756-14.1.1756 Capture of Geriah; 10.3.1757 1L *Princess Amelia* (80); 5.9.1757-6.10.1757 Raid on Rochefort; 14.12.1757 LCmdr *Canterbury* (60); **Commander**; 9.1.1760 *Baltimore* (14) Sloop; **Captain**; 6.8.1761-24.11.1763 *Arundel* (24).

MAINWARING, WILLIAM

Dates: 1770 Died.

Family:

Service: **Lieutenant**; 5.4.1756[JAM 4.8.1756] L. *Falcon* (10) Bomb Vessel; 23.4.1756[NA 25.11.1756] L. *Weazle* (16) Sloop; 23.2.1757-26.2.1757 2L *Tilbury* (58); 26.2.1757-25.9.1757[W] 3L *Tilbury* (58); 23.1.1758-1.8.1758 2L *York* (60); 6.6.1758-27.7.1758 The Siege of Louisbourg.

MAISTERSON, SAMUEL

Dates: 10.9.1762 Died.

Family:

Service: 13.4.1714 Vol-p-O *Swiftsure* (64); 7.5.1714 Vol-p-O *Dreadnought* (60); 3.11.1715 Mid *Royal Oak* (70); 3.2.1715/16 Vol-p-O *Kinsale* (36); 31.12.1718 Mid *Kinsale* (40); 24.2.1719/20-30.10.1720 Mid *Kinsale* (36); 10.11.1720 Passed; **Lieutenant**; 20.6.1729-23.8.1730 3L *Adventure* (40); 31.1.1733/34 4L *Lancaster* (80); 27.2.1733/34-17.2.1735/36[P] 6L *Blenheim* (96); 28.2.1737/38 1L *Hector* (40); 4.1740-5.7.1740 Attack on St. Augustine; 20.11.1741 1L

Leopard (50); 11.5.1742 6L *Victory* (100); 13.7.1742 5L *Victory* (100); 8.2.1743/44 3L *Victory* (100); **Commander**; 30.5.1744 *Hawk* (8) Sloop; **Captain**; 26.8.1745 *Squirrel* (20); 1746 *Duke William* Hired Armed Ship; 22.4.1746 *Sapphire* (44); 20.9.1746-25.9.1746 Lorient Operations; 29.12.1747-22.1.1747/48 *Tilbury* (58); 21.3.1747/48-12.8.1750[P] *Hector* (44).

MAITLAND, DAVID

Dates: c.1733 Born; c.1779 Died Alverstoke, Southampton; 30.10.1779 Will Probate.

Family: Wife Edith Marshall married 26.12.1769; Son John James Frederick Maitland (1771-?); Daughter Renira Charlotte (1772-?); Son Henry Topham Harley, RN (1774-?); Daughter Edith Elizabeth Catherine (1776-?).

Service: 28.11.1748 L. Serv *Hector* (44); 15.9.1750 Able *Hector* (44); 8.10.1752 Able *Amazon* (22); 29.3.1754 Able *Port Mahon* (24); 25.5.1755 Mid *Port Mahon* (24); 5.12.1755-21.9.1757 Mid *Anson* (60); 21.9.1757 Passed; **Lieutenant**; 19.10.1757-21.5.1760 3L *Intrepid* (60); 18.8.1759-19.8.1759 Battle of Lagos Bay; 20.11.1759 Battle of Quiberon Bay; 12.12.1760-17.3.1763[P] 1L *Niger* (32); 24.9.1766-11.10.1769 1L *Dragon* (74); 15.11.1769-26.5.1770[P] 1L *Superb* (74); 23.5.1770 2L *Ajax* (74); 17.9.1770 2L *Ajax* (74); 7.11.1770-21.9.1773 1L *Centaur* (74); 15.9.1774 2L *Royal Oak* (74); 14.6.1775-14.2.1777 1L *Royal Oak* (74); 15.4.1778-25.9.1781 1L *Fame* (74); 6.7.1779 Battle of Grenada.

MAITLAND, FREDERICK LEWIS

Dates: 19.1.1729/30 Born Edinburgh; 16.12.1786 Died Rankeillor, Fife.

Family: Father Charles, 6th earl of Lauderdale (d.1744); Mother Lady Elizabeth Ogilvy; Mistress Mary Arnot (d.1782); Wife Margaret Dick (c.1732-1825) married 27.8.1767; Illegitimate Son James Maitland (1758-1760); Illegitimate Son Frederick (c.1760-?); Illegitimate Daughter Elizabeth (1763-?); Illegitimate Son John (1765-?); Daughter Mary Turner [Scrymgeour] (1768-1851); Son Charles (1769-?); Son James Heriot (1774-1848); Daughter Elizabeth (1773-1856); Daughter Isabella [Roy] (1775-?); Son Frederick Lewis, RN (1777-1839).

Service: 20.10.1748 Mid *Tavistock* (50); 14.4.1749 Mid *Speedwell* (10) Sloop; 3.1.1750 Mid *Tavistock* (50); **Lieutenant**; 11.6.1750[(31.7.1751)]-9.8.1751[P] L. *Otter* (14) Sloop; 23.1.1753-31.7.1754 L. *Port Mahon* (24); 11.3.1755 2L *Rochester* (50); **Commander**; 17.1.1757 *Port Royal* (12) Storeship; **Captain**; 9.3.1759[(JAM 15.11.1759)] *Lively* (20); 7.8.1759[(JAM 9.10.1761)] *Lively* (20); 18.10.1760 Action off Cuba; 16.4.1761[(9.10.1761)]-25.8.1764[P] *Renown* (30); 3.1.1778-14.12.1778 *Elizabeth* (74); 27.7.1778 1st Battle of Ushant; 10.2.1779-8.1.1781[P] *Elizabeth* (74); 6.7.1779 Battle of Grenada; 18.12.1779 Combat de la Martinique; 17.4.1780 Battle of Martinique; 15.5.1780 Action of March 15 1780; 19.5.1780 Action of March 19 1780; 2.1.1781-9.9.1782 *Queen* (90); 12.12.1781 2nd Battle of Ushant; 19.9.1782 *Grafton* (74); 20.11.1782-30.6.1785 *Princess Augusta* (6) Yacht.

MAJOR, CHRISTOPHER

Dates: c.1737 Born; 1784 Died; 1.3.1785 Will Probate.

Family:

Service: 27.7.1755 Able *Prince* (90); 2.10.1756 Mid *Prince* (90); 16.12.1756 Mate *Prince* (90); 20.3.1756/57 Mid *Prince* (90); 16.5.1757 Mid *Culloden* (74); 17.11.1757 Mid *Saint George* (90); 31.10.1758-5.1.1759 Able *Montagu* (60); 5.1.1759 Passed; **Lieutenant**; 1.2.1761[(28.9.1763)]-1.10.1763[P] 2L *Valeur* (28); c.6.1775-10.12.1777[P] LCmdr *Esther* (6) Cutter; 18.12.1778-18.8.1780[P] LCmdr *Coureur* (8) Schooner; 1782-4.3.1783[P] LCmdr *Charlotte* Hired Tender.

MALE, THOMAS

Dates: c.1727 Born; 4.8.1769 Died; 6.3.1770 Will Probate.

Family:

Service: 7.3.1739/40-28.4.1740P Ord. *Canterbury* (60); 10.10.1741 Capt Serv *Norfolk* (80); 13.2.1741/42 Surg Serv *Orford* (70); 23.7.1742 L. Serv *Cumberland* (80); 13.1.1743/44-20.10.1744W Capt Serv *Bonetta* (8) Sloop; 23.3.1744/45 Mid *Princess Royal* (90); 6.11.1745 Able *Folkestone* (44); 18.2.1745/46 Mid *Folkestone* (44); 15.4.1746 Mate *Folkestone* (44); 4.2.1746/47 Passed; **Lieutenant**; 4.7.1757 L. *Diligence* (10) Sloop; 26.4.1758 3L *Dorsetshire* (68); 19.6.1759 2L *Dorsetshire* (68); 20.11.1759 Battle of Quiberon Bay; 23.2.1760 2L *Bellona* (74); 23.12.1760 1L *Bellona* (74); **Commander**; 31.12.1761-14.3.1762/63P *George* (30) Hired Armed vessel; 4.4.1763-20.6.1765 *Alderney* (10) Sloop; 17.10.1766-4.8.1769† *Hound* (14) Sloop.

MALTBY, WILLIAM

Dates: c.1725 Born; 26.4.1793 Died; 27.5.1793 Will Probate.

Family:

Service: 1751-1754 Merchant Service; 6.10.1754 Able *Falcon* (10) Bomb Vessel; 4.9.1755 Able *Queenborough* (24); 27.6.1756 Able *Ambuscade* (40); 4.9.1756 Mate *Ambuscade* (40); 9.11.1758 Passed; **Lieutenant**; 22.8.1759-23.8.1759 2L *Repulse* (32); 3.2.1767 1L *Aquilon* (28); 5.3.1767 L. *Gibraltar* (20); 3.2.1768 2L *Bellona* (74); **Commander**; 26.5.1768 *Nautilus* (16) Sloop; 11.8.1768 *Favorite* (16) Sloop; 10.6.1770 Capture of Port Egmont; **Captain**; 10.1.1771 *Aquilon* (28); 12.8.1771-10.1.1775D *Glasgow* (20); 10.1.1775 Dismissed.

MAN, ROBERT

Dates: 1721 Born; 1783 Died.

Family: Father Robert Man, RN (1675-1745).

Service: 7.11.1731 Vol-p-O *Plymouth* (60); 28.4.1733 Vol-p-O *Sunderland* (60); 4.1.1736 Mid *Orford* (70); 4.9.1736 Mid *Somerset* (80); 19.5.1737 MidO *Shoreham* (20); 28.11.1737 MidO *Gloucester* (50); 13.10.1738-12.3.1740 Able *Gloucester* (50); 12.3.1739/40 Passed; **Lieutenant**; 17.9.1740 L. *Deptford* (24) Storeship; 10.1.1740/41 4L *Duke* (90); 7.9.1741 3L *Duke* (90); 26.11.1742 2L *Woolwich* (50); 15.2.1742/43 1L *Woolwich* (50); 23.5.1745(BLI 30.5.1759) 1L *Vigilant* (60); **Captain**; 22.6.1745 *Launceston* (44); 4.6.1746-20.4.1749P *Lynn* (44); 4.2.1755 *Anson* (60); 6.1.1758 *Prince Frederick* (64); 6.6.1758-27.7.1758 The Siege of Louisbourg; 31.7.1758(NA 11.8.1761)-19.8.1761P *Lancaster* (66); 5.8.1761-5.2.1763P *Cornwall* (74); 2.1769-1770 Commodore *Montagu* (60); 16.5.1769 CinC — Barbados & the Leeward Islands; 18.10.1770 **Rear Admiral of the Blue**; 24.10.1770 **Rear Admiral of the Red**; 3.1774-1777 *Medway* (60); 4.6.1774 CinC — The Mediterranean Sea; 31.3.1775 **Vice Admiral of the Blue**; 7.12.1775 **Vice Admiral of the White**; 29.1.1778 **Vice Admiral of the Red**; 23.4.1779-21.9.1780 Lord Commissioner of the Admiralty; 26.9.1780 **Admiral of the Blue**.

MAN, ROBERT

Dates: 1720 Born; 9.3.1762 Died; 22.7.1762 Will Probate.

Family: Daughter Elizabeth; Son William; Son Robert, RN (1745-1813).

Service: 23.3.1738/39 Passed; **Lieutenant**; 6.3.1746/47 3L *Nottingham* (60); 3.5.1747 1st Battle of Cape Finisterre; 14.10.1747 2nd Battle of Cape Finisterre; 3.12.1747-12.10.1748P 2L *Nottingham* (60); 31.1.1747/48 Action of 1748/01/31; 10.2.1755-5.7.1756 4L *Buckingham* (68); 20.5.1756 Battle of Minorca; **Commander**; 10.11.1756 *Charlotte* (8) Yacht; 4.4.1757 *Porcupine* (16) Sloop; **Captain**; 16.11.1757 *Penguin* (20); 30.7.1759-7.4.1762 *Milford* (28).

MANISTRE, FISKE

Dates: c.1740 Born; 1785 Died.
Family: Father John Manistre; Wife Jane Sparrow (1751-1800).
Service: 1753-1755 Merchant Service; 9.12.1755 Ord. *Lancaster* (66); 20.5.1756 Battle of Minorca; 24.9.1757 Mid *Lancaster* (66); 6.6.1758-27.7.1758 The Siege of Louisbourg; 26.4.1759 Mid *Hero* (74); 20.11.1759 Battle of Quiberon Bay; 13.8.1760 Passed; **Lieutenant**; 9.4.1762 3L *Torrington* (44); 17.12.1764-23.12.1767 3L *Cornwall* (74); 8.11.1770-22.4.1773 5L *Egmont* (74).

MANLEY, RICHARD

Dates: 1759 Died.
Family:
Service: 25.11.1738 Capt Serv *Sheerness* (20); 2.6.1740 Mid *Greenwich* (50); 19.11.1741 Mid *Duke* (90); 27.3.1742 Able *Duke* (90); 12.4.1742 Mid *Sandwich* (90); 10.6.1743 Mate *Orford* (70); 17.8.1743 Mid *Orford* (70); 26.12.1743 Mid *Woolwich* (50); **Lieutenant**; 25.5.1744[(BLI 22.4.1746)] 3L *Launceston* (44); 14.2.1744/45[(BLI 22.4.1746)] 2L *Launceston* (44); 27.2.1744/45 Passed; 13.3.1744/45[(BLI 22.4.1746)] 1L *Launceston* (44); 27.6.1745[(BLI 25.4.1746)] 2L *Chester* (50); 30.9.1745[(BLI 25.4.1746)] 1L *Superb* (60); 26.4.1746-10.6.1746[P] 3L *Shrewsbury* (80); 31.8.1747-21.10.1747 3L *Tavistock* (50); 9.10.1755 2L *Falkland* (50); 14.10.1755-6.5.1756 1L *Falkland* (50); 8.5.1759 Dismissed.

MANLEY, WILLIAM

Dates: c.1722 Born.
Family:
Service: 5.12.1741 Capt Serv *Kent* (70); 31.3.1742 Capt Serv *Elizabeth* (70); 14.2.1742/43 Adm Serv *Saint George* (90); 15.3.1742/43 Able *Argyll* (50); 30.6.1743 Mid *Argyll* (50); 26.5.1744 Mid *Dorsetshire* (80); 11.9.1746 Passed; **Lieutenant**; 28.11.1748-19.8.1749 L. *Falcon* (10) Bomb Vessel.

MANN, JOHN HOLLINGBERY

Dates: 1795 Died; 4.5.1795 Will Probate.
Family:
Service: **Lieutenant**; 20.3.1756 L. *Albany* (14) Sloop; 24.8.1757-21.8.1759 1L *Shannon* (28); 6.6.1758-27.7.1758 The Siege of Louisbourg; 9.1.1760 6L *Namur* (90); 2.4.1761-1.2.1762 2L *Namur* (90); 22.2.1762 1L *Lancaster* (66); 23.4.1762-25.1.1763[D] 1L *Ludlow Castle* (44); 25.1.1763 Dismissed; 1.7.1766-c.7.1769 LCmdr *Esther* (6) Cutter.

MANNING, THOMAS

Dates: 1768 Died; 1.7.1768 Will Probate.
Family:
Service: **Lieutenant**; 4.2.1742/43[(20.8.1743)] L. *Pembroke Prize* (8) Sloop; 20.2.1742/43[(20.8.1743)] 3L *Norwich* (50); 17.4.1743[(20.8.1743)]-30.9.1743[P] 2L *Norwich* (50); 10.12.1743-25.6.1744 L. *Phoenix* (20); 7.11.1744-5.5.1746 2L *Sutherland* (50); 1.2.1753 2L *Salisbury* (50); 11.1.1756-14.1.1756 Capture of Geriah; 7.3.1757-1.4.1757 Expedition against Chandernagore; **Captain**; 4.2.1758[(EI 21.11.1759)]-28.4.1758[SC] *Bridgewater* (24).

MANSELL, SAMUEL

Dates: c.1724 Born; 1758 Died; 3.1.1759 Will Probate.
Family:
Service: 1745-1752 Merchant Service; 29.1.1751/52 Mid *Falkland* (50); 18.3.1753/54-2.6.1756 Mate *Falkland* (50); 2.6.1756 Passed; **Lieutenant**; 11.8.1757-22.5.1758[†] L. *Peregrine* (20) Sloop.

MANTELL, WILLIAM

Dates: c.1714 Born; 13.12.1765 Died.
Family:
Service: 12.4.1730-9.12.1731 Vol-p-O *Gosport* (42); 10.12.1731-5.6.1733 Able *Gosport* (42); 6.6.1733-1.9.1733 Mid *Lion* (60); 2.9.1733-17.10.1733 Capt *Captain* (70); 18.10.1733-14.7.1734 MidO *Sunderland Hulk* (60); 15.7.1734-20.11.1734 Mid *Sunderland Hulk* (60); 21.11.1734 Mid *Orford* (70); 16.4.1737 Passed; **Lieutenant**; 12.5.1740 L. *Lyme* (20); 15.6.1744-11.8.1745 2L *Royal George* (100); 22.8.1747 3L *Namur* (74); **Commander**; 1.3.1748/49[(EI 22.11.1750)] *Basilisk* (8) Bomb Vessel; **Captain**; 8.6.1749[(EI 10.6.1752)]-28.5.1752[P] *Siren* (20); 2.10.1754 *Centurion* (50); 6.6.1758-27.7.1758 The Siege of Louisbourg; 19.11.1759-21.3.1760[P] *Captain* (64); 19.10.1761-21.6.1762 *Montagu* (60).

MAPLESDEN, JERVIS

Dates: c.1705 Born; 3.4.1781 Died.
Family:
Service: 1.12.1722 Capt Serv *Prince Frederick* (70); 3.6.1723 Capt Serv *Guernsey* (50); 1.11.1724 Capt Serv *Nassau* (70); 5.6.1725 Ord. *Essex* (70); 19.10.1725 Able *Essex* (70); 30.4.1726 Able *Nottingham* (60); 1.6.1728 Mid *Northumberland* (70); 16.1.1729/30 Able *Nassau* (70); 25.7.1730 Mid *Nassau* (70); 16.4.1731 Able *Nassau* (70); 2.6.1731 Able *Cornwall* (80); 24.10.1731 Mid *Cornwall* (80); 9.11.1731 Mid *Namur* (90); 21.6.1732 Able *Namur* (90); 19.10.1732 Able *Salisbury* (50); 17.8.1733 Mate *Bideford* (20); 4.1.1734/35 Mid *Namur* (90); 11.1.1734/35 Passed; **Lieutenant**; 3.11.1739[(20.5.1741)] 3L *Plymouth* (60); 2.6.1741[(15.4.1743)]-9.10.1743 1L *Plymouth* (60); 10.10.1743 1L *Hector* (44); 20.12.1743 2L *Duke* (90); 19.3.1743/44 L. *Portsmouth* (24) Storeship; 12.8.1745 6L *Royal George* (100); 21.10.1745 4L *Royal George* (100); 13.11.1745 3L *Royal George* (100); 23.1.1745/46 1L *Royal George* (100); **Commander**; 6.10.1746-13.9.1748[P] *Furnace* (8) Bomb Vessel; 29.5.1754 *Fortune* (14) Sloop; 20.5.1756 Battle of Minorca; **Captain**; 21.5.1756 *Phoenix* (24); 26.6.1756[(8.3.1758)]-11.9.1758[C] *Portland* (50); 5.4.1757 Action of April 5 1757; 5.6.1758-12.6.1758 Raid on Saint-Malo; 10.10.1759 *Intrepid* (60); 20.11.1759 Battle of Quiberon Bay; 17.11.1760-12.3.1763[P] *Prince Frederick* (64); 29.3.1761-11.6.1761 Expedition against Belle-Isle.

MARBEUF, DANIEL

Dates: c.1730 Born; 1761 Died.
Family:
Service: 29.11.1751 Capt Serv *Cornwall* (80); 19.2.1755 Able *Cornwall* Prison Ship; 24.6.1755 Mid *Cornwall* Prison Ship; 24.9.1756 Mid *Deal Castle* (20); 21.10.1757 Mid *Shannon* (28); 6.6.1758-27.7.1758 The Siege of Louisbourg; 7.3.1759 Passed; **Lieutenant**; 20.3.1761-18.11.1761[D] 2L *Looe* (44); 18.11.1761 Dismissed.

MARLOW, BENJAMIN

Dates: 1795 Died.

Family:

Service: **Lieutenant**; 25.7.1743(11.10.1746) 4L *Grafton* (70); 2.8.1743(11.10.1746) 3L *Assistance* (50); 22.2.1744/45(11.10.1746)-24.10.1746[P] 1L *Falmouth* (50); 13.2.1746/47 MidE *Princess* (70); 5.9.1747(3.12.1748)-9.1.1747/48 3L *Boyne* (80); 18.3.1756 MidE *Ramillies* (90); 30.3.1756 4L *Ramillies* (90); 20.5.1756 Battle of Minorca; **Commander**; 21.5.1756 *Fortune* (14) Sloop; **Captain**; 6.6.1756-8.6.1756 *Dolphin* (24); 1.2.1757 *Dolphin* (24); 5.8.1761 *Minerva* (32); 18.2.1762-25.1.1763[P] *Prince* (90); 14.1.1775-25.6.1777 *Coventry* (28); 25.10.1778(EI 8.2.1781)-23.1.1780 *Rippon* (60); 26.9.1780 **Rear Admiral of the White**; 24.9.1787 **Vice Admiral of the Blue**; 21.9.1790 **Vice Admiral of the White**; 1.2.1793 **Vice Admiral of the Red**; 12.4.1794 **Admiral of the Blue.**

MARRIOTT, JOHN

Dates: 1809 Died; 29.12.1809 Will Probate.

Family:

Service: **Lieutenant**; 16.12.1758(EI 30.6.1762) 5L *Grafton* (68); 20.2.1759(EI 30.6.1762) 5L *Elizabeth* (64); 3.3.1759(EI 30.6.1762)-17.3.1760 4L *Salisbury* (50); 10.9.1759 Battle of Pondicherry; 28.6.1760(30.6.1762)-28.8.1761[P] 3L *Salisbury* (50).

MARSH, HENRY

Dates: 1772 Died.

Family:

Service: **Lieutenant**; 20.1.1739/40(19.8.1743)-30.9.1741 3L *Pembroke* (60); 24.3.1742/43(MED 10.3.1745/46)-1.6.1743 6L *Namur* (90); 4.8.1743(MED 10.3.1745/46) 5L *Namur* (90); 13.1.1743/44(MED 10.3.1745/46)-19.8.1744 3L *Namur* (90); 11.2.1743/44-12.2.1743/44 Battle of Toulon; **Commander**; 6.3.1743/44(MED 8.2.1745/46) *Nazareth* (8) Fireship; 19.8.1744(MED 8.2.1745/46)-11.1.1744/45 *Terrible* (6) Bomb Vessel; **Captain**; 12.3.1747/48-5.6.1748[P] *Chichester* (80); 23.3.1757 *Katherine* (8) Yacht; 14.12.1763-6.9.1764 *Africa* (64); 14.11.1764-19.11.1767 *San Antonio* (64); 1.6.1768-5.4.1769 *Achilles* (60).

MARSH, JOHN

Dates: 1770 Died.

Family:

Service: **Lieutenant**; 18.10.1758 6L *Saint George* (90); 23.10.1758-27.12.1760[P] 5L *Saint George* (90); 16.1.1759-19.1.1759 Attack on Martinique; 20.1.1759-1.5.1759 Capture of Guadeloupe; 14.5.1762-20.12.1762[P] 3L *Bedford* (64).

MARSH, WILLIAM

Dates: 15.10.1765 Died.

Family:

Service: **Lieutenant**; 18.3.1731/32(6.6.1732)-5.6.1732[P] 3L *Lion* (60); 26.2.1732/33 3L *Dreadnought* (60); 23.2.1733/34-10.3.1736/37 2L *Dreadnought* (60); **Commander**; 25.5.1741(26.12.1741) *Terrible* (6) Bomb Vessel; **Captain**; 25.5.1743(16.1.1743/44)-1.6.1743 *Stirling Castle* (70); 3.1.1743/44(13.2.1744/45)-1.9.1745 *Winchelsea* (20); 11.2.1743/44-12.2.1743/44 Battle of Toulon; 14.8.1754 *Shoreham* (24); 21.9.1757-4.10.1760[W] *Harwich* (50); 9.3.1758-24.5.1758 Capture of Fort Louis; 6.12.1762 **Superannuated Rear Admiral.**

MARSHALL, CHARLES

Dates: 29.12.1803 Died; 27.1.1804 Will Probate.
Family:
Service: 27.6.1753-c.1756 Scholar *Royal Naval Academy*; **Lieutenant**; 10.9.1759-17.5.1763[P] L. *Jamaica* (10) Sloop; 30.8.1764 3L *Bellona* (74); 13.6.1766 2L *Bellona* (74); 12.11.1766-3.2.1768 1L *Bellona* (74); 16.1.1770 2L *Dorsetshire* (68); 9.8.1770-29.5.1771[P] 3L *Dorsetshire* (68); 13.1.1772 2L *Asia* (64); 31.5.1774 3L *Asia* (64); 6.10.1774 4L *Asia* (64); 26.6.1775 3L *Asia* (64); 2.7.1776-4.7.1776 Staten Island Landings; 29.4.1777 2L *Asia* (64); 17.2.1778-26.3.1781 1L *Asia* (64); 3.6.1782-25.3.1783[P] 1L *Atlas* (98); 20.10.1782 Battle of Cape Spartel; 12.1782-3.1783 LCmdr *Seaflower* (16) Cutter; 15.4.1783-22.4.1786[P] 1L *Queen* (90).

MARSHALL, GEORGE

Dates: c.1727 Born; 1759 Died; 5.2.1759 Will Probate.
Family:
Service: 1740-1743 Merchant Service; 31.12.1743 Mate *Fly* (8) Sloop; 2.9.1744-27.11.1744[W] MidO *Rye* (20); 9.3.1744/45 Able *Sandwich* (90); 29.6.1745 Mid *Sandwich* (90); 1.8.1745 Able *Poole* (32); 13.12.1745 Mid *Poole* (44); 11.1.1745/46 Captain's Clerk *Poole* (44); 20.9.1746-25.9.1746 Lorient Operations; 1.10.1746 Action of 1746-10-01; 12.1.1746/47 Mate *Poole* (44); 2.7.1747 ActL *Poole* (44); **Lieutenant**; 27.9.1748[(5.12.1749)]-16.9.1749[P] L. *Centaur* (20); 17.11.1749 Passed; 8.2.1755 4L *Prince George* (80); 14.5.1756-5.7.1756 3L *Prince George* (80); 28.4.1757-23.8.1759 2L *Buckingham* (68); 16.1.1759-19.1.1759 Attack on Martinique; 20.1.1759-1.5.1759 Capture of Guadeloupe.

MARSHALL, JOHN

Dates: c.1733 Born; 1771 Died; 5.8.1771 Will Probate.
Family:
Service: 8.7.1748 Capt Serv *Vanguard* (68); 11.7.1750 Able *Vanguard* (68); 14.1.1751/52 Mid *Saint Albans* (60); 12.4.1754 Mid *Vanguard* (68); 14.2.1757 Passed; **Lieutenant**; 15.2.1759 3L *America* (60); 15.3.1759-29.1.1763[P] 3L *Fame* (74); 29.3.1761-11.6.1761 Expedition against Belle-Isle; 1.6.1766-16.7.1766 2L *Dolphin* (24).

MARSHALL, LEONARD

Dates: 1773 Died.
Family:
Service: **Lieutenant**; 13.1.1739/40 2L *Sunderland* (60); 20.2.1741/42 2L *Antelope* (50); 1.3.1742/43 1L *Antelope* (50); 1.6.1745[(MED 1.2.1745/46)]-26.11.1745[P] 1L *Torbay* (80); **Commander**; 17.4.1746-11.9.1746[P] *Aetna* (8) Fireship.

MARSHALL, SAMUEL

Dates: c.1711 Born; 4.1768 Died Gosport; 7.5.1768 Will Probate.
Family: Wife Edith Pratt (1712-c.1781) married 10.7.1736; Daughter Edith (1744-1809); Daughter Mary (1739-?); Son Sir Samuel, RN (1741-1795).
Service: 22.4.1722 Ord. *Greyhound* (20); 14.2.1724/25 Able *Greyhound* (20); 8.12.1727-9.9.1728[P] Mid *Superb* (64); 25.11.1728 Mid *Ferret* (4) Sloop; 3.5.1729 Mid *Argyll* (50); 19.12.1730 Mid *Hector* (40); 13.9.1731 Mid *Cornwall* (80); 31.1.1731/32 Passed; **Lieutenant**; 26.8.1732[(26.3.1733)] 3L *Kingston* (60); 5.10.1732[(26.3.1733)] 3L *Rupert* (60); 2.1.1732/33[(26.3.1733)]-30.10.1733 L. *Shoreham* (20); 23.11.1733 L. *Blandford* (20); 30.12.1734-16.8.1736 L. *Sheerness* (20); 17.8.1736 L. *Bridgewater* (32); 7.10.1737 L. *Aldborough* (20); 16.5.1738-1.10.1739 2L

Elizabeth (70); 2.2.1740/41 3L *Marlborough* (90); 20.3.1740/41 4L *Royal George* (100); 6.5.1741 3L *Royal George* (100); 21.1.1741/42 2L *Royal George* (100); 10.2.1741/42-2.9.1742[P] 1L *Royal George* (100); 4.4.1743 1L *Captain* (70); **Commander**; 12.9.1743-3.12.1744 *Serpent* (10) Bomb Vessel; 13.8.1744-12.1.1744/45 *Firedrake* (8) Bomb Vessel; **Captain**; 17.7.1747-13.4.1749[W] *Namur* (74); 16.1.1753 *Tiger* (60); 28.3.1754 *Bristol* (50); 31.7.1754-30.6.1756[P] *Nottingham* (60); 1760-25.3.1762 *Nottingham* (60); 7.1.1762-10.2.1762 Operations against Martinique.

MARSHALL, SIR SAMUEL

Dates: 1741 Born; 7.3.1740/41 Baptised Alverstoke, Hampshire; 29.6.1794 Knight Bachelor; 2.10.1795 Died Holles Street, Cavendish Square, London; 10.10.1795 Will Probate.
Family: Father Samuel Marshall, RN (1711-1768); Mother Edith Pratt; Wife Elizabeth Worsley married 10.10.1764.
Service: 5.3.1753 Capt Serv *Tiger* (60); 10.8.1753 Able *Bristol* (50); 6.5.1754 Mid *Bristol* (50); 20.6.1754 Able *Bristol* (50); 14.9.1754 Mid *Nottingham* (60); 26.1.1756 Able *Somerset* (68); 3.5.1757 Mid *Somerset* (68); 27.10.1757 Mid *Nottingham* (60); 8.2.1758 Able *Namur* (90); 24.6.1758 ActL *Terrible* (74); 6.2.1760 Passed; **Lieutenant**; 11.2.1760 5L *Terrible* (74); 7.10.1760 3L *Nottingham* (60); 7.1.1762-10.2.1762 Operations against Martinique; 17.3.1762[(8.9.1763)] 3L *Marlborough* (68); 1.5.1762[(EI 8.9.1763)] 2L *Rochester* (50); 8.6.1762[(8.9.1763)] 1L *Foudroyant* (80); **Commander**; 24.9.1762[(30.8.1763)]-17.7.1763[P] *Antigua* (14) Sloop; 9.10.1770 *Merlin* (18) Frigate; **Captain**; 24.1.1771 *Princess Amelia* (80); 31.5.1773[(29.10.1774)]-29.9.1774[P] *Portland* (50); 26.12.1776 *Arethusa* (32); 27.7.1778 1st Battle of Ushant; 23.7.1779 *Emerald* (32); 31.12.1779 Affair of Fielding and Bylandt; 15.11.1781 *Flora* (36); 12.4.1782 Battle of the Saintes; 15.4.1783-24.9.1787 *Pegase* (74); 1787-1793 Commissioner of the Victualling Board; 12.1793-2.10.1795 Commissioner of the Navy; 10.1794-2.10.1795 Deputy Controller of the Navy.

MARSHALL, THOMAS

Dates: 1809 Died.
Family:
Service: **Lieutenant**; 11.5.1760[(BLI 19.11.1760)] 3L *Lion* (58); 23.12.1760[(BLI 19.11.1760)]-15.12.1762[P] 2L *Lion* (58); 29.3.1761-11.6.1761 Expedition against Belle-Isle; 10.1.1777 3L *Princess Amelia* (80); 8.12.1777 1L *Princess Amelia* (80); **Commander**; 5.5.1778-13.5.1778 *Diligence* (10) Sloop; 24.7.1778 *Atalanta* (14) Sloop; 13.10.1780[(NF 12.6.1781)] *Volcano* (8) Fireship.

MARSHALL, WILLIAM

Dates: 1776 Died; 16.2.1776 Will Probate.
Family:
Service: **Lieutenant**; 14.2.1757 L. *Garland* (24); 1.12.1757 3L *Falmouth* (50); 23.1.1759 3L *Dublin* (74); 12.12.1759 2L *Cambridge* (80); **Commander**; 16.4.1761[(3.5.1762)]-24.7.1761 *Merlin* (18) Frigate.

MARTELL, WILLIAM

Dates: None Known.
Family:
Service: 1.3.1748/49 **Commander**.

MARTIN, SIR HENRY (BARONET MARTIN OF LOCKYNGE)

Dates: 29.8.1733 Born Shroton House, Dorset; 28.7.1791 Baronet Martin of Lockynge; 1.8.1794 Died 51 Upper Harley Street, London.
Family: Father Samuel Martin; Mother Sarah Irish née Wyke; Wife Eliza Anne Gillman, née Parker married 26.11.1761; Son Thomas Byam, RN (1773-1854); Daughter Sarah Catherine Martin (c.1768-1826).
Service: 3.8.1749 Scholar *Royal Naval Academy*; 5.8.1752 Vol-p-O *Phoenix* (24); 21.12.1753 Mid *Phoenix* (24); 5.11.1755 Passed; **Lieutenant**; 18.12.1755-4.6.1756 3L *Jersey* (60); 1756 Impress Service; 6.8.1756 5L *Royal George* (100); 9.11.1756-17.12.1756 3L *Royal George* (100); 24.12.1756 6L *Torbay* (74); **Commander**; 21.1.1757 *Lightning* (6) Hospital Ship; 8.1757-10.1757 Louisbourg Expedition; **Captain**; 19.12.1757-7.2.1758 *Northumberland* (68); 13.5.1758[NA 14.3.1759]-7.5.1759[P] *Arc-en-Ciel* (50); 10.8.1759-20.3.1763 *Danae* (38); 1.11.1770-3.11.1770 *Phoenix* (44); 17.11.1770-17.6.1771 *Intrepid* (64); 30.9.1780-3.1790 Resident Commissioner at Portsmouth Dockyard; 6.11.1780 Gov. of Royal Naval Academy; 29.3.1790-1.8.1794 Comptroller of the Navy; 18.6.1790-1.8.1794 M.P. for Southampton.

MARTIN, JOHN

Dates: c.1724 Born; 1775 Died.
Family:
Service: 29.11.1737 Able *Hound* (8) Sloop; 19.4.1741 Mid *Assistance* (50); 7.9.1742 Mid *Launceston* (44); 27.5.1744 Able *Launceston* (44); 1.12.1744 Passed; **Lieutenant**; 12.12.1744[BLI 18.10.1745]-18.10.1745[P] 3L *Lynn* (44); 6.5.1746 4L *Yarmouth* (64); 11.8.1746 1L *Lion* (58); 21.8.1746 2L *Lion* (58); 14.10.1747 2nd Battle of Cape Finisterre; 2.1.1747/48 6L *Prince George* (90); 5.5.1748-21.6.1748[P] 5L *Prince George* (90); 16.1.1753 2L *Monarch* (74); 6.2.1755 2L *Prince George* (80); 11.3.1755 4L *Royal George* (100); 17.1.1756 4L *Royal Anne* (100); 19.4.1757 3L *Prince* (90); 9.10.1758-18.10.1758 2L *Saint George* (90); **Commander**; 4.10.1759-15.2.1760[P] *Medway* (6) Storeship.

MARTIN, ROGER

Dates: 1779 Died.
Family:
Service: **Lieutenant**; 1.5.1723-31.1.1725/26 2L *Sandwich* (90); 1.2.1725/26-8.2.1725/26 6L *Sandwich* (90); 9.2.1725/26-1.12.1726[P] 6L *Union* (90); 20.12.1726-19.6.1727 3L *Chatham* (50); 2.4.1729-20.2.1733/34 1L *Advice* (54); 21.2.1733/34-25.7.1734 1L *Britannia* (100); **Commander**; 25.7.1734-26.7.1738 *Hound* (8) Sloop; **Captain**; 24.9.1740 *Lichfield* (50); 27.9.1740-8.8.1742 *Assistance* (50); 5.4.1744 *Winchester* (50); 16.4.1744 *Sandwich* (90); 16.6.1744 *Saint George* (90); 20.2.1744/45 *Yarmouth* (64); 11.8.1746-12.3.1747/48 *Chichester* (80); 16.1.1753 *Monarch* (74); 4.2.1755 *Prince George* (80); 14.2.1755 *Royal George* (100); 17.1.1756-30.6.1756 *Royal Anne* (100); 28.6.1756 **Superannuated Rear Admiral.**

MARTIN, WILLIAM

Dates: c.1696 Born; 17.9.1756 Died Twickenham, London.
Family: Wife Mary Atkins married 16.8.1726.
Service: 26.8.1708-5.1710 Vol. *Dragon* (54); 1710 Mid *Ranelagh* (80); **Lieutenant**; 30.7.1710[16.11.1713]-10.1.1710/11 2L *Resolution* (70); 4.1.1711/12[16.11.1713]-31.8.1714[P] 2L *Superb* (64); 5.3.1714/15-14.10.1716 3L *Cumberland* (80); 15.3.1717/18 1L *Rupert* (60); 2.4.1718 1L *Cumberland* (80); **Captain**; 9.10.1718[10.11.1718] *Cumberland* (80); 5.11.1718 *Seahorse* (20); 9.2.1719/20-25.11.1724[P] *Blandford* (20); 13.2.1726/27 *Advice* (54); 11.8.1727-23.5.1728 *Advice*

(54); 3.6.1728 *Grafton* (70); 2.4.1729 *Advice* (54); 29.11.1733-6.5.1737 *Sunderland* (60); 16.5.1738 *Ipswich* (70); 2.3.1742/43 Sinking of the San Isidoro; 7.12.1743 **Rear Admiral of the Blue**; 1744-1745 *Saint George* (90); 19.6.1744 **Vice Admiral of the Blue**; 1745 *Edinburgh* (64); 23.4.1745 **Vice Admiral of the White**; 10.1745-6.1746[P] *Shrewsbury* (80); 1746-7.1746 *Yarmouth* (64); 15.7.1747 **Admiral of the Blue**.

MARTIN, WILLIAM

Dates: c.1724 Born; 28.6.1766 Died; 5.7.1766 Will Probate.
Family:
Service: 21.6.1739 Able *Hound* (8) Sloop; 20.9.1741 Mid *Marlborough* (90); 12.11.1741 Mid *Norwich* (50); 18.2.1742/43 Attack on La Guaira; 15.4.1743-24.4.1743 Attack on Porto Cabello; 27.6.1743 Mid *Barfleur* (90); 11.2.1743/44-12.2.1743/44 Battle of Toulon; 10.3.1744-20.8.1744 Mid *Neptune* (90); 20.8.1744 Passed; **Lieutenant**; 22.9.1744[(MED 9.12.1748)]-8.12.1744 3L *Newcastle* (50); 18.12.1746[(MED 9.12.1748)] *Terrible* (6) Bomb Vessel; **Captain**; 16.8.1748[(9.12.1748)]-15.11.1748[P] *Nonsuch* (50); 20.1.1754 *Bridgewater* (24); 11.1.1756-14.1.1756 Capture of Geriah; 25.2.1756[(6.9.1759)] *Salisbury* (50); 7.3.1757-1.4.1757 Expedition against Chandernagore; 2.3.1758[(EI 6.9.1759)]-7.6.1758 ActCapt *Cumberland* (66); 29.4.1758 Battle of Cuddalore; 14.5.1762-20.12.1762[P] *Bedford* (64.

MARTIN, WILLIAM

Dates: c.1725 Born; 1777 Died; 20.6.1777 Will Probate.
Family:
Service: 27.5.1742 Ord. *Duke* (90); 17.12.1742 Able *Duke* (90); 3.4.1745 Able *Falkland* (50); 26.4.1745 Mid *Falkland* (50); 3.5.1747 1st Battle of Cape Finisterre; 4.5.1749 Passed; **Lieutenant**; 2.4.1757 L. *Proserpine* (8) Fireship; 3.6.1757-30.1.1758 2L *Royal William* (84); 5.9.1757-6.10.1757 Raid on Rochefort; 30.1.1758 3L *Royal William* (84); 25.3.1758 3L *Lennox* (74); 5.6.1758-12.6.1758 Raid on Saint-Malo; 30.1.1759-5.8.1761 3L *Union* (90); 20.11.1759 Battle of Quiberon Bay; 29.3.1761-11.6.1761 Expedition against Belle-Isle; 17.5.1762-20.12.1762[P] 1L *Bedford* (64).

MARTIN, WILLIAM

Dates:
Family:
Service: **Lieutenant**; 22.2.1759 3L *Raisonnable* (64); 11.4.1759-8.1.1762[W] 2L *Raisonnable* (64); 13.6.1759 Passed; 5.5.1762-6.4.1763 1L *Rainbow* (44); 8.11.1770 2L *Egmont* (74); 29.6.1771-8.11.1773 1L *Egmont* (74); 16.3.1776-22.11.1776 1L *Foudroyant* (80).

MARTYN, ROGER

Dates: c.1728 Born; 1763 Died.
Family:
Service: 21.7.1746 Ord. *James and Mary* (16) Hired Sloop; 24.6.1747-2.1.1748/49 Able *Chesterfield* (44); 3.1.1748/49 Mid *Chesterfield* (44); 24.8.1750-5.2.1750/51 Able *Badger* (10) Sloop; 6.2.1750/51 Mid *Badger* (10) Sloop; 6.12.1751 Passed; **Lieutenant**; 10.6.1756 3L *Medway* (60); 9.11.1756 2L *Medway* (60); 5.9.1757-6.10.1757 Raid on Rochefort; 19.1.1758-1763[†] 1L *Medway* (60).

MASCLARY, WILLIAM HENRY

Dates: 1771 Died.
Family:
Service: 14.8.1719-15.6.1720[P] Vol-p-O *Tartar* (32); 27.11.1720 Vol-p-O *Panther* (54); 11.4.1722 MidO *Panther* (54); 11.10.1723 Mid *Sandwich* (90); 25.3.1724 MidO *Argyll* (50); 5.4.1725 Passed; **Lieutenant**; 3.7.1731-11.7.1731 2L *Suffolk* (70).

MASON, CHRISTOPHER

Dates: 26.5.1801 Died.
Family:
Service: **Lieutenant**; 21.11.1762[(10.2.1763)] 4L *Somerset* (68); 2.5.1763-6.8.1765[P] L. *Flamborough* (20); 24.10.1766 2L *Boreas* (28); 1.7.1767 2L *Carysfort* (28); 3.3.1769-9.11.1770 3L *Dunkirk* (60); 25.2.1772-16.12.1774[P] 1L *Panther* (60); 26.7.1775 1L *Chatham* (50); **Commander**; 7.6.1776 *Tamar* (16) Sloop; 4.2.1777 *Dispatch* (14) Sloop; **Captain**; 22.4.1778[(NA 12.12.1780)]-27.2.1781[P] *Delaware* (28) Frigate; 17.5.1781-6.1.1783[P] *Quebec* (32); 20.12.1782 Capture of the South Carolina; 24.5.1794 *Zealous* (74); **Rear Admiral of the White**; 1.6.1795-10.1795 *Zealous* (74); 14.2.1799 **Vice Admiral of the Blue**; 1.1.1801 **Vice Admiral of the White**.

MASON, HOLMAN

Dates: c.1736 Born; 12.6.1798 Died; 20.7.1798 Will Probate.
Family:
Service: 1752-1755 Merchant Service; 16.3.1754/55-20.11.1759[S] Mid *Essex* (64); 5.6.1758-12.6.1758 Raid on Saint-Malo; 20.11.1759 Battle of Quiberon Bay; 13.2.1760 Passed; **Lieutenant**; 25.8.1762-6.9.1762 6L *Saint George* Prison Ship; 26.5.1766 2L *Yarmouth* (64); 4.3.1769-26.5.1769 3L *Yarmouth* (64); 3.11.1770-29.5.1771[P] 4L *Elizabeth* (74); 16.12.1775-24.2.1776[P] 2L *Dublin* (74); 25.2.1776 2L *Raisonable* (64); 31.5.1776 3L *Raisonable* (64); 22.2.1777-24.10.1778 2L *Raisonable* (64).

MASON, ROBERT

Dates: 1761 Died.
Family:
Service: 14.9.1719 Vol-p-O *Hampton Court* (70); 19.6.1721 Vol-p-O *Buckingham* (70); 30.7.1722 Mid *Buckingham* (70); 20.4.1723 MidO *Essex* (70); 30.10.1723 Able *Cumberland* (80); 17.12.1724 QM *Cumberland* (80); 24.7.1726 Mate *Cornwall* (80); 27.3.1728 Passed; **Lieutenant**; 4.3.1739/40 3L *Chichester* (80); 18.9.1741 2L *Chichester* (80); 6.1.1741/42 2L *Looe* (44); 22.4.1742 1L *Looe* (44); 11.5.1742 1L *Leopard* (50); 4.6.1742-30.7.1742 3L *Sandwich* (90); 31.7.1742 4L *Sandwich* (90); 13.9.1742 3L *Sandwich* (90); 14.7.1744-17.5.1745 2L *Duke* (90); 18.5.1745-25.12.1748[P] 1L *Poole* (44); 20.9.1746-25.9.1746 Lorient Operations; 1.10.1746 Action of 1 October 1746.

MASON, THOMAS TUNSTALL

Dates: 1776 Died.
Family:
Service: **Lieutenant**; 18.11.1758 L. *Furnace* (8) Bomb Vessel; 29.12.1758 Capture of Goree; 16.1.1759 3L *Prince Edward* (44); 19.3.1759-24.10.1761 2L *Prince Edward* (44); 29.9.1770-13.10.1772[P] 1L *Portland* (50).

MASTER, HENRY

Dates: c.1735 Born; 1790 Died.
Family:
Service: 1753-1755 Merchant Service; 16.6.1755 Able *Newcastle* (50); 28.9.1755 Mid *Newcastle* (50); 10.2.1756 Mid *Somerset* (68); 6.8.1757 Mid *Barfleur* (80); 5.9.1757-6.10.1757 Raid on Rochefort; 5.6.1758-12.6.1758 Raid on Saint-Malo; 7.2.1759 Mid *Royal Anne* (100); 4.4.1759 Mid *Resolution* (74); 3.10.1759 Passed; **Lieutenant**; 23.6.1761-12.1762[P] L. *Lightning* (6) Hospital Ship; 10.4.1770 3L *Dorsetshire* (68); 9.8.1770-29.5.1771[P] 4L *Dorsetshire* (68); 14.3.1778-21.4.1778 3L *Vengeance* (74).

MATHEWS, DANIEL

Dates: c.1737 Born; 1772 Died; 15.6.1772 Will Probate.
Family:
Service: 13.2.1755 Capt Serv *Otter* (14) Sloop; 15.11.1756 Capt Serv *Winchester* (50); 26.3.1757 Able *Winchester* (50); 14.7.1758 Mid *Winchester* (50); 16.1.1759-19.1.1759 Attack on Martinique; 20.1.1759-1.5.1759 Capture of Guadeloupe; 8.3.1761 Able *Winchester* (50); 1.12.1761 Able *Torbay* (74); 4.8.1762 Passed; **Lieutenant**; 14.10.1762 L. *Vulture* (14) Sloop; 18.4.1763-18.9.1764 3L *Rainbow* (44); 13.11.1770-17.11.1770[P] 3L *Augusta* (64); 1771-1772 Impress Service at King's Lynn.

MATHEWS, GEORGE

Dates: 1782 Died; 3.1.1782 Will Probate.
Family:
Service: 15.6.1740 Able *Dragon* (60); 24.7.1741 Action of 1741-07-24; 11.11.1742 Mid *Dragon* (60); 11.2.1743/44-12.2.1743/44 Battle of Toulon; 15.3.1745-8.7.1745 Mid *Neptune* (90); 8.7.1745 Passed; **Lieutenant**; 18.5.1746[(MED 1.12.1747)]-23.12.1746 4L *Revenge* (70); 3.9.1747[(1.12.1747)]-9.12.1747[P] 4L *Princess Caroline* (80); 24.12.1747 3L *Mars* (64); 4.4.1748 2L *Lion* (58); 13.8.1748[(27.1.1748/49)]-17.2.1748/49[P] 2L *Panther* (50); 24.9.1756 2L *Union* (90); 1.8.1757 2L *Neptune* (90); 5.9.1757-6.10.1757 Raid on Rochefort; 20.2.1759 1L *Anson* (60); 3.7.1760-16.12.1760[P] 3L *Barfleur* (80); 16.1.1761 4L *Duke* (90); 24.5.1762 3L *Duke* (90); 14.6.1762-19.2.1763[P] 2L *Duke* (90); 8.9.1763-6.11.1766 LCmdr *Lurcher* (6) Cutter; 14.2.1771-20.5.1771[P] 1L *Conquestador* (60); 6.1777-20.6.1781 LCmdr *Pheasant* (10) Cutter.

MATHEWS, JOHN

Dates: 1775 Died; 28.2.1775 Will Probate;.
Family:
Service: 21.8.1731 Able *Gosport* (42); 16.11.1732 Able *Princess Amelia* (80); 23.2.1733 Mid *Princess Amelia* (80); 26.5.1733 Able *Princess Amelia* (80); 12.7.1733 Able *Trial* (8) Sloop; 31.10.1733 QM Mate *Trial* (8) Sloop; 29.6.1734 QM Mate *Torbay* (80); 6.8.1736 QM *Falkland* (50); 2.11.1738 Mid *Pembroke* (60); 24.4.1741 Mate *Pembroke* (60); 24.11.1743 Mid *Berwick* (70); 11.2.1743/44-12.2.1743/44 Battle of Toulon; 30.5.1744-21.10.1744 Mate *Namur* (90); 20.10.1744[(MED 31.5.1748)]-18.5.1746 4L *Revenge* (70); 21.10.1744 Passed; 22.10.1744 **Lieutenant**; 21.3.1746/47[(MED 31.5.1748)]-1.6.1748[P] 2L *Diamond* (44).

MATHEWS, JOHN

Dates: c.1738 Born; 19.7.1799 Died.

Family:

Service: 1752-1756 Merchant Service; 26.1.1756 Able *Somerset* (68); 3.2.1756 Mid *Somerset* (68); 6.6.1758-27.7.1758 The Siege of Louisbourg; 23.2.1759 Mid *Royal George* (100); 2.5.1759 Passed; **Lieutenant**; 14.5.1759-2.11.1761 4L *Temple* (68); 20.11.1759 Battle of Quiberon Bay.

MATHIAS, HERBERT

Dates: c.1727 Born; 1773 Died; 25.9.1773 Will Probate.

Family:

Service: 20.2.1745/46 Capt Serv *Jersey* (60); 3.3.1746/47 Mid *Jersey* (60); 30.5.1749 Mid *Queenborough* (24); 27.8.1749 Mid *Garland* (24); 24.12.1750 Able *Prince Henry* (44); 6.6.1753 Passed; **Lieutenant**; 4.6.1756-24.5.1757 3L *Jersey* (60); 20.3.1761-31.12.1762 L. *Siren* (20); 1.6.1764-12.5.1766 LCmdr *Lion* (4) Cutter; 9.1770-20.4.1771[P] LCmdr *Spy* (4) Cutter.

MATHIAS, JOHN

Dates: c.1724 Born; 18.7.1800 Died.

Family:

Service: 27.3.1735 Ord. *Torrington* (40); 21.2.1736/37-18.4.1737 Capt Serv *Torrington* (40); 19.4.1737-15.10.1741[P] Able *Torrington* (40); 7.6.1744 Passed; **Lieutenant**; 17.7.1744-24.5.1745 3L *Jersey* (60); 28.10.1744 Mid *Hampshire* (50); 24.4.1747-7.6.1747 Mid *Princess Amelia* (66); 21.9.1796 **Superannuated Commander**.

MATHISON, JOHN

Dates: c.1721 Born; 4.1.1764 Died; 16.7.1765 Will Probate.

Family: Mistress Thomasina Newton; Illegitimate Daughter Jane Newton; Sister Rose; Brother Gilbert.

Service: 1736-1741 Merchant Service; 11.10.1741 Mid *Drake* (8) Sloop; 14.12.1741-30.9.1744 Mid *Gibraltar* (20); 1.10.1744 Mate *Gibraltar* (20); 11.7.1745 Passed; **Lieutenant**; 17.8.1745 L. *Lizard* (10) Sloop; 14.5.1746 L. *Inverness* (22); 8.12.1747-26.8.1748[P] 3L *Yarmouth* (64); 1.12.1748-18.11.1752[P] 3L *Yarmouth* (64); 24.10.1755 2L *Cambridge* (80); 2.4.1756 1L *Cambridge* (80); 12.5.1757-12.1.1759 2L *Devonshire* (70); 6.6.1758-27.7.1758 The Siege of Louisbourg; 21.2.1759 1L *Lennox* (74); **Commander**; 10.7.1761[(EI 4.9.1765)] *Tiger Hulk*; **Captain**; 25.8.1762[(EI 21.3.1770)]-4.1.1764[†] *Panther* (60); 24.9.1762-6.10.1762 Battle of Manilla.

MATTHEWS, RICHARD

Dates: 1760 Died.

Family:

Service: 8.12.1717-3.12.1720[P] Carp Serv *Lennox* (70); 11.8.1718 Battle of Cape Passaro; 14.4.1722 L. Serv *Hampton Court* (70); 14.11.1722-6.1.1722/23 Able *Berwick* (70); 7.1.1722/23 Able *Rose* (20); 7.6.1724 Gnr Mate *Rose* (20); 13.2.1724/25-23.6.1725 Able *Rose* (20); 24.6.1725 Mid *Rose* (20); 5.12.1725-30.1.1728/29 Mate *Rose* (20); 30.1.1738/39 Passed; **Lieutenant**; 14.9.1739 4L *Buckingham* (70); 4.3.1739/40 3L *Buckingham* (70); 26.3.1740 2L *Eltham* (40); 18.2.1742/43 Attack on La Guaira; 15.4.1743-24.4.1743 Attack on Porto Cabello; 22.6.1743[(JAM 14.5.1747)] 1L *Lynn* (44); 14.5.1745-16.3.1746/47[P] 1L *Kinsale* (44); 21.11.1747 1L *Assistance* (50); 1.12.1748-20.11.1752[P] 1L *Devonshire* (66); 16.1.1753 1L *Cumberland* (66); 28.3.1754 1L *Eagle* (60); 31.7.1754 1L *Nottingham* (60); 2.8.1757[(MED 1.4.1758)] 1L *Sunderland* (60); 22.5.1758-14.7.1758 *Speaker* (10) Sloop; 22.5.1758 **Commander**.

MAURICE, JOHN

Dates: c.1732 Born; 1779 Died; 27.11.1779 Will Probate.
Family:
Service: 6.2.1748/49 Capt Serv *Oxford* (50); 24.10.1749 Mid *America* (44); 6.5.1752-3.9.1753 Able *Glory* (44); 4.9.1753 Able *Dolphin* (24); 21.10.1755 Mid *Romney* (44); 8.4.1756 Passed; **Lieutenant**; 9.11.1756-1.2.1758 L. *Cruizer* (8) Sloop; 7.4.1758 2L *Sapphire* (32); 10.7.1758-23.5.1759[P] L. *Experiment* (24); 29.12.1758 Capture of Goree; 10.8.1759-29.9.1763[P] 1L *Danae* (38); 17.9.1770-7.6.1771[P] 1L *Ajax* (74).

MAY, JOHN

Dates: c.1736 Born; c.1826 Died; 11.2.1826 Will Probate.
Family:
Service: 1753-1756 Merchant Service; 6.2.1756-27.10.1756 Able *Kingston* (60); 20.5.1756 Battle of Minorca; 28.10.1756 Mid *Kingston* (60); 8.1757-10.1757 Louisbourg Expedition; 6.6.1758-27.7.1758 The Siege of Louisbourg; 14.2.1759 Passed; **Lieutenant**; 20.2.1759 3L *Firm* (74); 9.3.1759 2L *Firm* (74); bef.29.12.1760-13.5.1763[P] 1L *Firm* (74); 15.1.1771 3L *Kent* (74); 4.3.1773-22.6.1775 2L *Kent* (74); 19.5.1790 1L *Royal Sovereign* (100); 8.4.1801 **Superannuated Commander**.

MAY, SAMUEL

Dates: c.1731 Born.
Family:
Service: 25.6.1746-10.12.1746[C] Capt Serv *Hinchingbrooke* (10) Sloop; 26.3.1748 Capt Serv *Yarmouth* (64); 11.10.1749 Ord. *Chester* (50); 16.11.1749 Capt Serv *Chester* (50); 24.11.1749 Able *Chester* (50); 3.8.1751 Mid *Chester* (50); 17.6.1752 Able *Kingfisher* (14) Sloop; 13.8.1752 Mid *Kingfisher* (14) Sloop; 20.10.1752 Mid *Wager* (24); 5.6.1754 Passed; **Lieutenant**; 29.10.1755-13.1.1756 L. *Squirrel* (20).

MAYNE, PERRY

Dates: 1697 Baptised St Dunstan's, Stepney, Middlesex; c.1697 Born; 5.8.1761 Died Mortlake.
Family: Father Covill Mayne, RN (1674-1746); Mother Martha Perry.
Service: 27.9.1715 Ord. *Dolphin* (20); 1.5.1716 Mid *Dolphin* (20); 2.7.1716 Able *Dolphin* (20); 23.12.1717 Cox *Dolphin* (20); 5.3.1717/18 Mid *Dolphin* (20); 20.3.1717/18 Mid *Lynn* (42); 6.6.1718 Mid *Prince Frederick* (70); 28.7.1719 Mate *Prince Frederick* (70); 8.10.1719 Mid *Guernsey* (50); 20.10.1719 Mate *Guernsey* (50); 21.6.1720 Passed; **Lieutenant**; 7.7.1720 4L *Ipswich* (70); 29.6.1721-2.12.1724 2L *Falkland* (50); **Commander**; 22.3.1724/25[(11.10.1726)] *Spence* (8) Sloop; **Captain**; 24.9.1725[(11.10.1726)]-22.6.1726 *Dragon* (54); 21.3.1726/27 *Seaford* (20); 5.9.1727 *Seaford* (8) Bomb Vessel; 10.12.1730[(13.6.1732)]-5.6.1732[P] *Lion* (60); 14.7.1738 *Worcester* (60); 21.11.1739 Attack on Puerto Bello; 4.3.1740/41-5.1741 Operations against Cartagena; 5.6.1741[(30.3.1742)] *Orford* (70); 17.7.1742 *Princess* (70); 29.10.1742-13.2.1744/45[W] *Orford* (70); 23.4.1745 **Rear Admiral of the Blue**; 17.6.1745-5.9.1745 CinC — River Medway and The Nore; 14.7.1746 **Rear Admiral of the Red**; 18.7.1746-18.12.1747 CinC — River Medway and The Nore; 15.7.1747 **Vice Admiral of the White**; 12.5.1748 **Vice Admiral of the Red**; 12.5.1757 **Superannuated Vice Admiral**.

MAYNE, ROBERT

Dates: 29.9.1820 Died.
Family:
Service: **Lieutenant**; 26.1.1759 3L *Torrington* (44); 4.6.1759-24.12.1760 L. *Solebay* (24); 22.2.1762 3L *Lancaster* (66); 4.3.1762 2L *Lancaster* (66); 28.4.1762-13.1.1763[P] 1L *Lancaster* (66); 23.2.1776-4.5.1776 1L *Diamond* (32); 9.6.1801 **Superannuated Commander**.

MCCARTIE, ALEXANDER

Dates: 31.1.1761 Died.
Family:
Service: **Lieutenant**; 27.4.1741[(25.6.1745)]-4.6.1741 3L *Superb* (60); 2.8.1743[(24.10.1745)] 3L *York* (60); 31.3.1745[(25.6.1745)] 4L *Cumberland* (80); 18.9.1745 3L *London* (100); 6.5.1757 1L *Falkland* (50); 18.9.1758-13.3.1759[P] 1L *Royal Sovereign* (104); 10.8.1759-31.1.1761† 1L *Royal Sovereign* (104).

MCCLEVERTY, WILLIAM

Dates: 1725 Born; 11.12.1779 Died.
Family:
Service: 11.7.1745 Passed; **Lieutenant**; 13.7.1745 L. *Speedwell* (10) Sloop; 5.4.1746-13.6.1748 L. *Flamborough* (20); 29.5.1755 3L *Revenge* (64); 29.1.1756-23.3.1756 2L *Revenge* (64); **Commander**; 21.6.1756-1.11.1757 *Peggy* (8) Sloop; **Captain**; 1.11.1757 *Gibraltar* (20); 18.8.1759-19.8.1759 Battle of Lagos Bay; 5.3.1760-24.9.1762[P] *Norwich* (50); 3.6.1761-7.6.1761 Occupation of Dominica; 7.1.1762-10.2.1762 Operations against Martinique; 8.12.1762-18.8.1766 *Hind* (24); 16.11.1770-29.11.1773 *Hind* (24).

MCDONALD, COLL

Dates: 8.9.1753 Died.
Family:
Service: **Lieutenant**; 26.6.1741[(1.3.1741/42)] 4L *Grafton* (70); 11.8.1741[(1.3.1741/42)] 3L *Grafton* (70); 24.10.1741[(1.3.1741/42)] 3L *Deptford* (60); 20.4.1742 2L *Deptford* (60); 1.12.1743 2L *Suffolk* (70); 11.4.1744 2L *Hampton Court* (64); 17.7.1744 1L *Hampton Court* (64); 8.1.1744/45 Action of 1745-01-08; **Commander**; 11.6.1750[(10.7.1751)]-9.8.1751[P] *Otter* (14) Sloop; 1.5.1753-3.1.1754 *Baltimore* (14) Sloop.

MCDOUALL, WILLIAM

Dates: c.1725 Born; 1770 Died.
Family:
Service: 23.6.1741 Ord. *Buckingham* (70); 24.8.1741 Ord. *Torbay* (80); 24.11.1741 Able *Torbay* (80); 31.3.1743 Able *Dreadnought* (60); 5.3.1744/45 Mid *Dreadnought* (60); 24.11.1745 Mid *Sandwich* (90); 21.10.1746 Able *Sandwich* (90); 27.12.1746 Mid *Sandwich* (90); 10.7.1747 Passed; **Lieutenant**; 21.5.1756[(21.5.1757)] 4L *Lancaster* (66); 30.3.1757 4L *Saint George* (90); 6.4.1757-4.5.1757 3L *Saint George* (90); 4.5.1757-1.6.1757 5L *Saint George* (90).

MCDOUGALL, ROBERT

Dates: 1729 Born; 16.2.1816 Died.
Family:
Service: 1753-1756 Merchant Service; 31.8.1756 Mid *Berwick* (64); 25.12.1756 Mate *Berwick* (64); 5.4.1757 Action of April 5 1757; 28.2.1758 Battle of Cartagena; 25.10.1758 Master *Racehorse* (8) Bomb Vessel; 22.11.1758 Master *Garland* (24); 14.7.1759-5.9.1759 Master

Phoenix (20); 5.9.1759 Passed; **Lieutenant**; 7.9.1759-9.4.1760 L. *Grampus* (14) Sloop; 31.3.1761 L. *Druid* (10) Sloop; 4.9.1761-5.2.1763[P] 3L *Cornwall* (74); 23.3.1780 **Commander**; 23.11.1780-24.7.1781 *Shark* (16) Sloop; **Captain**; 24.7.1781[(Portugal 31.10.1781)]-22.8.1781[SP] *Romney* (50); 8.1.1782-17.5.1784[P] *Africa* (64); 20.6.1783 2nd Battle of Cuddalore; 2.1795-3.1796 *Scipio* (64); 2.4.1796-30.4.1799[P] *Ganges* (74); 26.4.1796-24.5.1796 Capture of St Lucia; 1.1.1801 **Rear Admiral of the Blue**; 23.4.1804 **Rear Admiral of the Red**; 9.3.1805 **Vice Admiral of the Blue**; 28.4.1808 **Vice Admiral of the White**; 31.7.1810 **Vice Admiral of the Red**; 4.12.1813 **Admiral of the Blue.**

MCINTOSH, JOSEPH

Dates: c.1739 Born; 22.10.1765 Died.
Family:
Service: 1754-1755 Merchant Service; 21.11.1755 Capt Serv *Orford* (68); 10.9.1756 Able *Orford* (68); 28.2.1757 Mid *Orford* (68); 8.1757-10.1757 Louisbourg Expedition; 6.6.1758-27.7.1758 The Siege of Louisbourg; 2.1.1760 Passed; **Lieutenant**; 8.6.1762[(7.9.1763)]-2.9.1763[P] 2L *Levant* (28).

MCKILLOP, DAVID

Dates: 9.7.1805 Died.
Family: Wife Jane; Daughter Mary; Son Richard;
Service: **Lieutenant**; 16.12.1762[(EI 3.9.1764)]-20.6.1764[P] 4L *Lennox* (74); 27.10.1770-3.10.1771 4L *Buckingham* (68).

MCKINLEY, SAMUEL

Dates: c.1719 Baptised; 1777 Died.
Family:
Service: 8.11.1737 Able *Deptford* (60); 4.3.1740-4.12.1740 Able *Princess Louisa* (60); 5.12.1740-20.11.1742[P] Mid *Princess Louisa* (60); 4.3.1740/41-5.1741 Operations against Cartagena; 31.10.1744-13.2.1745 Mate *Princess Louisa* (60); 14.2.1745 Mid *Ludlow Castle Hulk*; **Lieutenant**; 27.8.1745 L. *Amazon* (22); 4.5.1746 6L *Saint George* (90); 26.7.1746-15.8.1746 Master *Ludlow Castle Hulk*; 15.8.1746 Passed; 13.4.1747 5L *Saint George* (90); 5.10.1747-21.6.1748[P] 4L *Saint George* (90); 9.4.1754 1L *Augusta* (60); 16.1.1755-5.8.1755 L. *Dispatch* (14) Sloop; 8.8.1759 Dismissed.

MEAD, JOSEPH

Dates: c.1710 Born; 1799 Died; 11.12.1799 Will Probate.
Family:
Service: 19.12.1739 Mate *Rippon* (60); 20.2.1739/40 Mid *Rippon* (60); 14.9.1740 Mate *Deptford* (60); 4.3.1740/41-5.1741 Operations against Cartagena; 2.3.1743/44 Mate *Suffolk* (70); 25.6.1744 Mate *Hampton Court* (64); 8.1.1744/45 Action of 1745-01-08; 6.3.1745/46 Passed; **Lieutenant**; 19.8.1747-9.12.1748[P] 4L *Hampton Court* (64); 7.1.1757 2L *Weymouth* (60); 11.1.1757-5.4.1757 2L *Preston* (50); **Commander**; 5.4.1757 *Crown* (18) Storeship; **Captain**; 7.7.1761-3.6.1763[P] *Fowey* (24); 7.1.1762-10.2.1762 Operations against Martinique; 6.6.1762-13.8.1762 Operations against Havana.

MEAD, SAMUEL

Dates: 21.10.1776 Died.
Family:
Service: 1.10.1707-6.4.1709 Ord. *Dispatch* (8) Brigantine; 7.4.1709-7.11.1709 Vol-p-O *Margate* (14); 8.11.1709-16.3.1709/10 Capt Serv *Hector* (42); 17.3.1709/10-30.10.1710 Vol-p-O *Sweepstakes* (42); 31.10.1710-26.6.1712 Ord. *Woolwich* (54); 27.6.1712-11.7.1713 Mid *Nonsuch* (54); 12.7.1713-3.6.1714 Mid *Lowestoffe* (32); 4.6.1714-30.6.1714 Able *Success* (24); 1.7.1714 Mid *Success* (24); 20.7.1716 Passed; **Lieutenant**; 13.3.1717/18[(21.6.1720)]-15.6.1720[P] L. *Tartar* (32); 1726-28.8.1727 *Otter* (6) Sloop; **Captain**; 29.8.1727-24.11.1727 *Dolphin* (20); 25.11.1727-12.11.1731[P] *Deal Castle* (20); 16.5.1738-4.12.1738[P] *Deptford* (60); 29.1.1740/41 *Sandwich* (90); 9.6.1741-26.9.1741 *Duke* (90).

MEDOWS, LORD CHARLES (1ST EARL MANVERS)

Dates: 14.11.1737 Born; 23.7.1796 1st Viscount Pierrepont of Holme Pierrepont; 23.7.1796 1st Baron Newark of Newark-on-Trent; 9.4.1806 1st Earl Manvers; 17.6.1816 Died;
Family: Father Philip Medows (1708-1781); Mother Frances Pierrepont; Wife Anne Orton Mills (d.1832) married 14.3.1774; Daughter Frances Augusta Eliza [Bentinck/Stephens] (d.1847); Son Evelyn Henry Frederick (1775-1801); Son Charles Herbert, 2nd Earl (1778-1780); Son Henry Manvers (1780-1851); Son Philip Sydney (1786-1864); Sister Frances (d.1770); Brother Edward, RN (1741-?); Brother Evelyn Philip (1736-1826); Brother Sir William, K.B. (1739-1813).
Service: 13.6.1747 Scholar *Royal Naval Academy*; 17.9.1751 Vol-p-O *Rainbow* (44); 15.2.1751/52 Able *Centurion* (50); 3.10.1752 Able *Garland* (24); 17.12.1752-23.5.1753 Able *Deptford* (50); 24.5.1753 Mid *Deptford* (50); 6.8.1755 Passed; 7.8.1755 **Lieutenant**; 15.1.1756 5L *Torbay* (74); 19.2.1756 4L *Torbay* (74); 20.5.1756-3.1.1757 3L *Torbay* (74); 3.1.1757 4L *Torbay* (74); **Commander**; 5.4.1757-17.8.1757 *Albany* (14) Sloop; **Captain**; 17.8.1757 *Shannon* (28); 6.6.1758-27.7.1758 The Siege of Louisbourg; 6.4.1761[(10.1.1763)]-11.8.1762 *Isis* (50); 1769 Resigned; 9.12.1778-7.6.1796 M.P. for Nottinghamshire.

MEDOWS, EDWARD

Dates: c.1741 Born.
Family: Father Philip Medows (1708-1781); Mother Frances Pierrepont; Wife Mary Brodie married 1785; Sister Frances (d.1770); Brother Evelyn Philip (1736-1826); Brother Lord Charles (1st Earl Manvers), RN (1737-1816); Brother Sir William, K.B. (1739-1813).
Service: 13.4.1756 Scholar *Royal Naval Academy*; 19.11.1757 Mid *Shannon* (28); 6.6.1758-27.7.1758 The Siege of Louisbourg; 2.5.1759 Mid *Hero* (74); 20.11.1759 Battle of Quiberon Bay; 29.3.1761-11.6.1761 Expedition against Belle-Isle; 2.6.1762 Passed; **Lieutenant**; 9.6.1762 5L *Princess Amelia* (80); 22.6.1762 5L *Magnanime* (74); 18.5.1763 3L *Centurion* (50); 20.6.1765-25.9.1766[P] 2L *Centurion* (50); **Commander**; 26.5.1768 *Hornet* (10) Sloop; **Captain**; 10.1.1771 *York* (60); 21.3.1771-16.1.1776 *Tartar* (28); 26.12.1793 Resigned.

MEEKESON, JAMES

Dates: 4.6.1766 Died.
Family:
Service: **Lieutenant**; 3.12.1761[(EI 23.10.1764)] 5L *Medway* (60); 2.6.1762[(EI 23.10.1764)] 4L *Medway* (60); 12.12.1762[(EI 23.10.1764)]-23.8.1765[P] 3L *Medway* (60).

MELDRUM, WILLIAM

Dates: 1762 Died.
Family:
Service: **Lieutenant**; 19.3.1743/44[MED 11.10.1746] L. *Enterprise* Sloop; 1.3.1744/45[MED 11.10.1746] 3L *Cambridge* (80); 11.1.1745/46[MED 11.10.1746]-21.11.1746[P] 2L *Cambridge* (80); 25.8.1747-30.6.1748[P] 1L *Folkestone* (44); 1.12.1748 3L *Intrepid* (64); 22.4.1752-22.11.1752[P] 2L *Intrepid* (64); 20.12.1756 1L *Achilles* (60); 17.1.1757 1L *Achilles* (60); 1.4.1757 1L *Norwich* (50); 3.7.1759 Bombardment of Le Havre; 23.12.1760-1.5.1762 1L *Marlborough* (68); 7.1.1762-10.2.1762 Operations against Martinique.

MELDRUM, WILLIAM

Dates: 1800 Died.
Family:
Service: **Lieutenant**; 29.1.1759[BLI 4.6.1759] L. *Spy* (10) Sloop; 30.4.1760-24.12.1760 1L *Princess Amelia* (80); 23.11.1761 2L *Belliqueux* (64); 25.1.1762-26.1.1764[P] 2L *Enterprise* (44); 24.2.1762-25.2.1762 Capture of Saint Lucia; 6.6.1762-13.8.1762 Operations against Havana; 30.12.1775-2.4.1778 L. *Jersey* (20) Hospital Ship.

MENNELL, GEORGE

Dates: 1781 Died; 2.5.1781 Will Probate.
Family:
Service: **Lieutenant**; 8.12.1759 3L *Antelope* (50); 1.4.1763-4.4.1764[P] 2L *Antelope* (50); 21.9.1770 1L *Centaur* (74); 30.10.1770-21.6.1771[P] 4L *Namur* (90); 13.11.1771 2L *Terrible* (74); 25.2.1772-26.5.1775[P] 3L *Prudent* (64).

MEREDITH, DAVID

Dates: c.1719 Born; 1770 Died; 7.5.1770 Will Probate.
Family:
Service: 23.7.1738-5.10.1739 Able *Grampus* (6) Sloop; 6.10.1739-20.7.1741 Mid *Argyll* (50); 21.7.1741-29.10.1741 Mid *Cambridge* (80); 30.10.1741-30.12.1741 Mid *Norwich* (50); 31.12.1741-14.10.1743 Mate *Norwich* (50); 18.2.1742/43 Attack on La Guaira; 15.4.1743-24.4.1743 Attack on Porto Cabello; 15.10.1743-26.11.1743 Mid *Suffolk* (70); 27.11.1743-10.4.1744 Mid *Deptford* (60); 11.4.1744 Mate *Suffolk* (70); 14.2.1744/45 Passed; **Lieutenant**; 11.4.1746[NA 11.2.1746/47]-13.7.1746[P] 3L *Ipswich* (70); 2.9.1747-30.1.1749/50 L. *Speedwell* (10) Sloop; 21.1.1756-28.5.1756 L. *Saltash* (14) Sloop; 5.7.1756-11.1.1757 5L *Marlborough* (80); 10.2.1757 5L *Newark* (80); 8.1757-10.1757 Louisbourg Expedition; 5.6.1758-12.6.1758 Raid on Saint-Malo; 18.8.1759-19.8.1759 Battle of Lagos Bay; 3.4.1760 3L *Royal Sovereign* (104); 2.2.1761-27.12.1762[P] 2L *Royal Sovereign* (104); 1764-1769 Agent for Transports.

METCALFE, STEPHEN

Dates: c.1737 Born; 20.10.1790 Died.
Family:
Service: 21.8.1755 Able *Hampton Court* (64); 19.6.1756 Mid *Prince George* (80); 30.7.1756 Able *Prince George* (80); 31.10.1756 Mid *Prince* (90); 27.12.1756 Mid *Culloden* (74); 5.4.1757 Action of April 5 1757; 30.6.1757 Mid *Saint George* (90); 13.7.1758 Mid *Prince* (90); 18.8.1759-19.8.1759 Battle of Lagos Bay; 18.7.1760-1.9.1760 Able *Magnanime* (74); 2.9.1760 Mid *Magnanime* (74); 7.10.1761 Passed; **Lieutenant**; 14.10.1761 4L *Burford* (68); 6.4.1763-9.6.1766

LCmdr *Hornet* (6) Cutter; 1.7.1766-18.8.1766 L. *Happy* (8) Sloop; 4.11.1776 5L *Queen* (90); 27.3.1778-20.4.1778 4L *Queen* (90).

MICHELL, ALEXANDER

Dates: 1763 Died.
Family:
Service: **Lieutenant**; 14.6.1731[(25.2.1731/32)]-11.8.1731 3L *Lion* (60); 12.8.1731[(25.2.1731/32)]-5.2.1731/32[P] 2L *Lark* (40); 12.5.1733-26.2.1733/34 3L *York* (60); 27.2.1733/34-3.11.1734 2L *York* (60); 4.11.1734-15.4.1736 1L *York* (60); 16.4.1736[(16.9.1737)]-9.3.1736/37 L. *Gibraltar* (20); 10.3.1736/37[(16.9.1737)]-3.9.1737[P] 2L *Dreadnought* (60); 28.2.1737/38-3.7.1739 1L *Romney* (50); 4.7.1739-2.3.1739/40 4L *Namur* (90); 3.3.1739/40-16.4.1740[P] 2L *Namur* (90); 14.4.1740-11.6.1741 2L *Victory* (100).

MICHELL, REYNELL

Dates: 26.12.1732 Born Dittisham, Devon; 16.1.1732/33 Baptised Dittisham, Devon; 2.1802 Died Totnes, Devon; 6.2.1802 Buried Totnes, Devon; 17.4.1802 Will Probate.
Family: Father John Michell (c.1700-1769); Mother Margaret Narracott (1699-1741); Wife Jane Taylor (1739-1827) married 14.8.1765; Son John Taylor, RN (1777-1833); Son Renold (1767-?); Son William Forord (1766-1826); Daughter Jane (1774-?); Son Walter Taylor (1777-1860); Brother John (1730-?); Sister Mary (1735-?).
Service: 8.7.1753 Able *Jamaica* (10) Sloop; 18.9.1754 Mid *Jamaica* (10) Sloop; 18.1.1755 Mate *Jamaica* (10) Sloop; 8.1757-10.1757 Louisbourg Expedition; 24.12.1757 Supnum *Sapphire* (32); 25.1.1758-19.3.1758 Able *Vestal* (32); 20.3.1758 Mid *Vestal* (32); 3.7.1759 Bombardment of Le Havre; 18.7.1759 Passed; **Lieutenant**; 19.7.1759-23.10.1759 4L *Monarch* (74); 12.2.1760 2L *Vestal* (32); 15.4.1762-1.5.1763[P] 1L *Vestal* (32); 15.1.1771-11.5.1771[P] 2L *Royal William* (84); 1779 Regulating Officer at Dartmouth; 1784 Mayor at Totnes; 1792 Mayor at Totnes; 1800 Mayor at Totnes.

MICHIE, COLIN

Dates: 10.9.1759 Died Battle of Pondicherry.
Family:
Service: **Lieutenant**; 6.9.1757[(EI 17.11.1760)] 4L *Tiger* (60); 1.12.1757[(EI 17.11.1760)] 3L *Tiger* (60); 25.3.1758[(EI 17.11.1760)] 4L *Yarmouth* (64); 29.4.1758 Battle of Cuddalore; 7.7.1758[(EI 17.11.1760)] 2L *Yarmouth* (64); 3.8.1758 Battle of Negapatam; 1.10.1758[(EI 17.11.1760)] 1L *Yarmouth* (64); **Captain**; 23.2.1759[(EI 17.11.1760)]-10.9.1759† *Newcastle* (50); 10.9.1759 Battle of Pondicherry.

MIDDLEHURST, JAMES

Dates: c.1723 Born; bef.8.1762 Died.
Family: Wife Mary.
Service: 1.3.1738/39 Capt Serv *Torrington* (40); 6.9.1740 Ord. *Torrington* (40); 12.6.1744 L. Serv *Seaford* (20) Ship; 9.3.1744/45 Able *Seaford* (20) Ship; 4.6.1747 Able *Chester* (50); 12.12.1748 Mate *Chester* (50); 7.2.1753 Passed; **Lieutenant**; 18.6.1757 L. *Happy* (8) Sloop; 20.7.1757-6.1.1760[W] L. *Mermaid* (24); 24.12.1760-23.11.1761 L. *Solebay* (24).

MIDDLETON, CHARLES (1ST BARON BARHAM)

Dates: 14.10.1726 Born Leith; 23.10.1781 Baronet; 1.5.1805 1st Baron Barham; 17.6.1813 Died.

Family: Father Robert Middleton; Mother Lord Charles Middleton (1st Baron Barham), RN (1726-1813); Wife Margaret Gambier (d.1792) married 21.12.1761; Daughter Diana [Edwards] (d.1823).

Service: 27.5.1738 Unk *Loyal Jane* Mer; 27.6.1741 Capt Serv *Sandwich* (90); 15.8.1741 Capt Serv *Duke* (8) Fireship; 20.1.1741/42 Capt Serv *Flamborough* (20); 25.6.1742 Able *Flamborough* (20); 28.7.1742 Mid *Flamborough* (20); 3.8.1745 Mate *Flamborough* (20); 4.10.1745 Passed; **Lieutenant**; 5.11.1745-16.7.1749[P] 3L *Chesterfield* (44); 3.6.1752-15.11.1752[P] 3L *Culloden* (74); 10.1.1753 2L *Anson* (60); 19.3.1754 3L *Monarch* (74); 23.7.1754-15.7.1756 2L *Anson* (60); **Commander**; 26.2.1757 *Speaker* (10) Sloop; **Captain**; 22.5.1758 *Arundel* (24); 14.7.1758(BLI 10.3.1760)-7.9.1759 *Barbadoes* (14) Sloop; 15.7.1760(19.11.1761)-26.10.1761[P] *Emerald* (28); 22.2.1762-20.3.1763[P] *Adventure* (32); 11.3.1775 *Ardent* (64); 2.11.1776 *Prince George* (90); 26.1.1778 *Royal Oak* (74); 29.4.1778-17.7.1778 *Jupiter* (50); 7.8.1778-29.3.1790 Comptroller of the Navy; 1.4.1784-19.6.1796 M.P. for Rochester; 24.9.1787 **Rear Admiral of the White**; 21.9.1790 **Rear Admiral of the Red**; 1.2.1793 **Vice Admiral of the White**; 12.4.1794 **Vice Admiral of the Red**; 12.5.1794-19.11.1795 Lord Commissioner of the Admiralty; 1.6.1795 **Admiral of the Blue**; 14.2.1799 **Admiral of the White**; 2.5.1805-9.2.1806 1st Lord; 9.11.1805 **Admiral of the Red**.

MIDDLETON, CHRISTOPHER

Dates: 12.2.1770 Died.

Family:

Service: 7.4.1737-1770 FRS; **Commander**; 5.3.1740/41-9.1.1742/43 *Furnace* (8) Bomb Vessel; 29.5.1745-16.6.1748[P] *Shark* (8) Sloop.

MIDDLETON, SIR HUGH (5TH BARONET MIDDLETON OF RUTHIN)

Dates: 2.2.1701 5th Baronet Middleton of Ruthin; 16.11.1756 Died.

Family:

Service: **Lieutenant**; 20.7.1709(14.9.1709)-2.11.1710 2L *Tiger* (48); 3.11.1710-28.6.1711 2L *Romney* (54); **Captain**; 9.8.1712(27.7.1713)-24.5.1713[P] Capt&M *Medway Prize* (28); 14.9.1716-13.1.1717/18[P] *Lowestoffe* (32); 1727 Dismissed; 12.5.1727-10.8.1727 *Pearl* (40); 11.8.1727-10.1727 *Pearl* (22).

MIHELL, BEST

Dates: 2.1755 Died.

Family:

Service: **Lieutenant**; 4.12.1739(10.2.1741/42) 3L *Diamond* (40); 5.2.1739/40(10.2.1741/42)-13.1.1740/41 3L *Strafford* (60); 20.2.1740/41(10.2.1741/42) 2L *Weymouth* (60); 4.3.1740/41-5.1741 Operations against Cartagena; 25.2.1741/42-8.5.1742[P] 1L *Weymouth* (60); 24.6.1742 1L *Falmouth* (50); 10.12.1743(16.4.1744) 1L *Lichfield* (50); 15.6.1744 1L *Gosport* (44); 11.8.1744 1L *Strafford* (58); 30.8.1744-16.5.1746 4L *Cornwall* (80); 19.1.1746/47 1L *Princess* (70); 19.8.1747(30.12.1748) 3L *Boyne* (80); **Commander**; 6.9.1747(9.12.1748)-24.8.1748[P] *Cruizer* (12) Brig; 20.1.1754-17.2.1755 *Kingfisher* (14) Sloop.

MILBANK, WILLIAM

Dates: c.1730 Born; 1766 Died.

Family:

Service: 1753-1759 Merchant Service; 14.5.1755-29.7.1756[P] Able *Romney* (44); 30.8.1756 Mid *Guernsey* (50); 5.4.1757 Action of April 5 1757; 13.6.1758 Mid *Revenge* (64); 7.11.1759 Passed; **Lieutenant**; 1.4.1760-6.7.1762 2L *Brilliant* (36); 11.8.1762 L. *Barbadoes* (14) Sloop; 23.8.1762-4.2.1763[P] 4L *Torbay* (74); 4.3.1766-10.8.1766 2L *Lark* (32).

MILBANKE, MARK

Dates: 4.1724 Born Croft-on-Tees, Yorkshire; 12.4.1724 Baptised; 10.6.1805 Died.

Family: Father Sir Ralph Milbanke, fourth baronet of Halnaby (d. 1748); Mother Anne Delavall; Wife Mary Webber (c.1740-1812) married 16.7.1768; Son Ralph, RN (1761-1823); Daughter Harriet [Tilghman] (1765-1835); Son Mark (1768-1769); Daughter Eliza Emily [Huskisson] (1777-1856).

Service: 23.2.1736/37-17.1.1739/40 Scholar *Royal Naval Academy*; 15.10.1740-20.5.1741 Vol-p-O *Tilbury* (60); 4.3.1740/41-5.1741 Operations against Cartagena; 21.5.1741-11.9.1742 Mid *Romney* (50); 12.9.1742-9.12.1742 Able *Old Portsmouth* (6) Yacht; 10.12.1742-19.4.1744 Mid *Princess Mary* (60); 22.3.1743/44 Passed; **Lieutenant**; 20.4.1744 3L *Anglesea* (44); 19.12.1744 6L *Royal Sovereign* (104); 29.8.1745 5L *Royal Sovereign* (104); 23.1.1745/46 4L *Royal Sovereign* (104); **Commander**; 13.9.1746 *Serpent* (10) Bomb Vessel; **Captain**; 21.5.1748-14.11.1748[P] *Inverness* (22); 3.4.1755-29.7.1756[P] *Romney* (44); 5.7.1756-14.4.1761 *Guernsey* (50); 5.4.1757 Action of April 5 1757; 18.8.1759-19.8.1759 Battle of Lagos Bay; 1.11.1775 *Barfleur* (90); 5.4.1777-4.5.1778 *Princess Royal* (90); 16.5.1778-22.3.1779 *Namur* (90); 19.3.1779 **Rear Admiral of the White**; 26.9.1780 **Vice Admiral of the Blue**; 6.1782-9.4.1783[P] *Fortitude* (74); 6.7.1782-1783 CinC — North Sea; 9.1782-10.1.1783[P] *Ocean* (90); 20.10.1782 Battle of Cape Spartel; 1783-24.4.1783[P] *Panther* (60); 16.5.1783-3.6.1786 CinC — Plymouth; 1785 *Sampson* (64); 24.9.1787 **Vice Admiral of the White**; 6.4.1789-21.9.1790 *Salisbury* (50); 10.4.1789-1791 Gov. of Newfoundland; 10.4.1789-11.4.1792 CinC — Newfoundland; **Vice Admiral of the Red**; 21.9.1790-2.12.1791[P] *Salisbury* (50); c.31.8.1791-1792 *Bedford* (74); 1.2.1793 **Admiral of the Blue**; 1.6.1795 **Admiral of the White**; 14.9.1799-24.3.1803 CinC — Portsmouth; 1800-1801 *Royal William* (84); c.25.4.1802-c.30.5.1802 *Cambrian* (40).

MILLAR, ARCHIBALD

Dates: 16.10.1766 Died; 2.4.1767 Will Probate.

Family:

Service: **Lieutenant**; 21.5.1746[(9.9.1748)] 4L *Suffolk* (70); 22.5.1747[(25.11.1748)] 3L *Sunderland* (60); 21.6.1748[(25.11.1748)]-22.2.1748/49[P] 2L *Sunderland* (60); 16.10.1755-4.11.1755 4L *Royal Sovereign* (104); 4.11.1755 5L *Royal Sovereign* (104); 27.11.1756 4L *Royal Sovereign* (104); **Commander**; 29.9.1757-29.4.1758 *London* (6) Storeship; 12.6.1759 *Thunder* (8) Bomb Vessel; 20.11.1759 Battle of Quiberon Bay; **Captain**; 16.6.1761-15.3.1763[P] *Lynn* (44).

MILLER, DAVID

Dates: bef.1.6.1756 Died; 3.6.1756 Will Probate.

Family:

Service: **Lieutenant**; 18.10.1745[(MED 16.5.1746)] 4L *Stirling Castle* (70); 29.11.1745[(MED 25.10.1748)]-27.1.1745/46 3L *Roebuck* (44); 16.3.1745/46[(MED 25.10.1748)]-27.10.1748[P] 2L *Roebuck* (44); 8.7.1755-bef.1.6.1756[†] L. *Greyhound* (20).

MILLER, GEORGE
Dates: 25.11.1759 Died Quebec.
Family:
Service: **Lieutenant**; 1.3.1758[(21.8.1758)]-28.5.1758 4L *Trident* (64); 28.8.1758-12.12.1758 3L *Penzance* (44); 12.12.1758 2L *Sapphire* (32); 23.1.1759-2.6.1759 4L *Dublin* (74); **Commander**; 2.6.1759-25.11.1759† *Racehorse* (8) Bomb Vessel.

MILLER, ROBERT
Dates: 1758 Died.
Family:
Service: 23.4.1741 **Lieutenant**; 13.3.1741/42 3L *Dunkirk* (60); 25.3.1742-29.11.1745 2L *Dunkirk* (60); 11.2.1743/44-12.2.1743/44 Battle of Toulon; 8.7.1755-16.5.1757[P] 1L *Oxford* (50); 13.9.1757 1L *Royal Sovereign* (104); 20.10.1757-13.4.1758[B] 1L *Prince George* (80).

MILLIGAN, JOHN
Dates: 1788 Died.
Family:
Service: **Lieutenant**; 28.6.1746 L. *Scorpion* (10) Sloop; 5.1.1747/48-5.7.1748[P] 3L *Thetis* (44); 7.5.1755-28.2.1758 2L *Eagle* (60); 7.3.1758-17.1.1759 1L *Shrewsbury* (74); 5.6.1758-12.6.1758 Raid on Saint-Malo; **Commander**; 27.2.1761-2.2.1762 *Laurel* (12) Sloop; 24.9.1762-5.9.1763 *Pomona* (18) Sloop; **Captain**; 26.5.1768-10.1.1771 *Success* (20); 9.1.1777 *Blonde* (32); 8.5.1779-28.4.1783[P] *Dunkirk* (60).

MILNE, ROBERT
Dates: 1796 Died; 27.9.1796 Will Probate.
Family:
Service: **Lieutenant**; 6.9.1760 3L *Liverpool* (28); 13.10.1761-15.9.1762 L. *Wasp* (8) Sloop; 30.11.1770 3L *Orford* (68); 19.1.1771 2L *Orford* (68); 15.2.1775-6.9.1775 L. *Carcass* (8) Bomb Vessel.

MILTON, WILLIAM
Dates: 1764 Died; 9.5.1764 Will Probate.
Family:
Service: **Lieutenant**; 10.2.1746/47[(MED 8.1.1747/48)]-12.9.1747 3L *Bedford* (70); 18.6.1755 L. *Swan* (14) Sloop; 10.7.1755 3L *Stirling Castle* (64); 3.11.1757 2L *Stirling Castle* (64); 24.3.1758-14.9.1762[P] 1L *Stirling Castle* (64); 3.6.1761-7.6.1761 Occupation of Dominica; 7.1.1762-10.2.1762 Operations against Martinique; 6.6.1762-13.8.1762 Operations against Havana.

MILWARD, THOMAS
Dates: 1780 Died.
Family:
Service: **Lieutenant**; 18.10.1759 3L *Jason* (30); 28.1.1762-10.11.1762[P] 5L *Saint George* Prison Ship.

MINISIE, JOHN

Dates: 1772 Died.
Family:
Service: **Lieutenant**; 22.1.1761-2.3.1763[P] 4L *Buckingham* (68); 29.3.1761-11.6.1761 Expedition against Belle-Isle; 7.4.1763-24.10.1766 2L *Boreas* (28); 29.3.1770-22.7.1772[P] 1L *Niger* (32).

MITCHELL, JAMES

Dates: 1773 Died.
Family:
Service: **Lieutenant**; 21.10.1756 L. *Dispatch* (14) Sloop; 27.10.1758 1L *Aurora* (38); 6.2.1761-18.6.1762 L. *Garland* (24); 29.11.1766 1L *Renown* (30); 27.4.1769-8.1.1771[P] 2L *Antelope* (50).

MITHERELL, ANTHONY

Dates: 11.8.1778 Died.
Family:
Service: **Lieutenant**; 22.5.1758 4L *Chichester* (68); 5.6.1758-12.6.1758 Raid on Saint-Malo; 20.11.1759 Battle of Quiberon Bay; 16.6.1760 3L *Chichester* (68); 29.3.1761-11.6.1761 Expedition against Belle-Isle; 22.10.1761-5.4.1763[P] 2L *Chichester* (68); 30.11.1770 3L *Royal Oak* (74); 11.12.1770 2L *Royal Oak* (74); 9.1.1771-10.5.1771 1L *Royal Oak* (74); 20.10.1775-4.1776 LCmdr *Mercury* Hired Tender; 12.3.1776-17.4.1776 LCmdr *Rose* Hired Tender; 17.4.1776-31.5.1778 LCmdr *Fanny* Hired Tender.

MOGG, THOMAS

Dates: 22.10.1756 Died.
Family:
Service: **Lieutenant**; 28.7.1726-8.9.1727[P] 4L *Northumberland* (70); 18.1.1727/28-10.11.1729 2L *Sapphire* (42); 14.6.1732-22.2.1733/34 3L *Norfolk* (80); 23.2.1733/34-8.12.1737 2L *Windsor* (60); 19.6.1739-12.4.1741 1L *Newcastle* (50); **Commander**; 31.7.1741 *Spence* (8) Sloop; 11.2.1743/44-12.2.1743/44 Battle of Toulon; **Captain**; 16.7.1744[(17.1.1744/45)]-19.9.1744[P] *Rochester* (54).

MOLLOY, CHARLES

Dates: 24.8.1760 Died.
Family:
Service: **Lieutenant**; 16.3.1704/5 L. *Bridgewater* (32); 15.5.1711-2.7.1711[P] 5L *Union* (96); **Commander**; 18.4.1719-1727 *Mary* (8) Yacht; 26.3.1728 *Mary* (8) Yacht; **Captain**; 6.4.1742-6.12.1750 *Royal Caroline* (8) Yacht; 26.1.1749/50-7.11.1753 *Royal Caroline* (8) Yacht; 1753 **Superannuated Captain**.

MONAT, GEORGE

Dates: None Known.
Family:
Service: 19.10.1759 **Lieutenant**; 18.6.1805 **Superannuated Commander**.

MONEYPENNY, JAMES

Dates: 19.2.1788 Died.
Family:
Service: **Lieutenant**; 17.10.1735[(30.7.1736)]-19.7.1736[P] 3L *Warwick* (60); 28.7.1738-7.12.1738[P] 3L *Tilbury* (60); 12.6.1739-29.8.1739 4L *Prince of Orange* (70); 30.8.1739 2L *Rippon* (60); 7.1.1740/41 Action of January 7 1741; 20.3.1740/41 1L *Liverpool* (44); 31.8.1742-21.6.1743 1L *Suffolk* (70); 18.2.1742/43 Attack on La Guaira; 15.4.1743-24.4.1743 Attack on Porto Cabello.

MONTAGU, JOHN

Dates: 1719 Born; 7.9.1795 Died.
Family: Father James Montagu (d. 1747); Mother Elizabeth Eyles; Wife Sophia Wroughton married 2.12.1748; Son James, RN (1752-1794); Son George, RN (1750-1829); Son Unknown; Son Unknown; Daughter Unknown.
Service: 14.8.1733 Scholar *Royal Naval Academy*; 5.6.1740 Passed; **Lieutenant**; 22.12.1740 4L *Buckingham* (70); 2.2.1740/41 3L *Buckingham* (70); 11.2.1743/44-12.2.1743/44 Battle of Toulon; 20.8.1744[(11.1.1744/45)]-23.1.1744/45[P] 1L *Namur* (90); **Commander**; 2.3.1744/45-25.8.1745 *Hinchingbrooke* (10) Sloop; **Captain**; 15.1.1745/46 *Rose* (20) Ship; 11.8.1746-27.5.1747 *Ambuscade* (40); 3.5.1747 1st Battle of Cape Finisterre; 10.3.1747/48-15.4.1754 M.P. for Huntingdon; 18.3.1747/48 *Greenwich* (50); 6.4.1748 *Bristol* (50); 13.9.1748 *Kent* (64); 24.7.1749 *Mermaid* (24); 10.1.1749/50-16.11.1752[P] *Kent* (64); 23.1.1753-24.1.1754 *Port Mahon* (24); 4.2.1755 *Elizabeth* (70); 17.1.1757 *Orford* (68); 27.1.1757-9.9.1758[P] *Monarch* (74); 28.2.1758 Battle of Cartagena; 16.2.1759 *Raisonnable* (64); 14.7.1759[(BLI 14.7.1759)] *Panther* (60); 19.11.1759 *Terrible* (74); 14.4.1760 *Newark* (80); 6.4.1761 *Princess Amelia* (80); 22.6.1762-14.1.1763[P] *Magnanime* (74); 6.5.1763-6.5.1766 *Dragon* (74); 26.7.1769-25.10.1770 *Bellona* (74); 18.10.1770 **Rear Admiral of the Blue**; 16.1.1771 CinC — The Downs; 2.1771-1774 *Captain* (64); 3.3.1771-6.1774 CinC — North America; 31.3.1775 **Rear Admiral of the Red**; 7.12.1775 **Vice Admiral of the Blue**; 28.2.1776 CinC — Newfoundland; 4.1776-1.1777 *Romney* (50); 2.4.1776 **Vice Admiral of the White**; 29.1.1778 **Vice Admiral of the Red**; 4.1778-9.1778 *Europe* (64); 8.4.1782 **Admiral of the Blue**; 31.3.1783-1786 CinC — Portsmouth; 4.1783-3.1786 *Queen* (90); 24.9.1787 **Admiral of the White**.

MONTAGUE, THOMAS

Dates: 1786 Died.
Family:
Service: **Lieutenant**; 19.2.1756 4L *Swiftsure* (68); 9.4.1757 2L *Lancaster* (66); 6.6.1758-27.7.1758 The Siege of Louisbourg; 31.7.1758[(NA 5.12.1758)] 1L *Lancaster* (66); 21.8.1759-22.1.1761 1L *Maidstone* (28); 20.11.1759 Battle of Quiberon Bay; 7.8.1761 3L *Blenheim* (90); 17.6.1762[(9.8.1762)]-18.1.1763[P] 2L *Neptune* (90); 13.4.1763-10.6.1766[P] LCmdr *Duke of York* (4) Cutter; 15.1.1771-11.1772 LCmdr *Folkestone* (6) Cutter.

MONTAGUE, HON. WILLIAM

Dates: 1720 Born; 10.2.1757 Died Fareham, Hampshire.
Family: Father Edward Richard Montagu, Viscount Hinchingbrooke (1692–1722); Mother Elizabeth Popham (d. 1761); Wife Charlotte Naylor married 11.3.1748/49; Sister Mary; Sister Elizabeth [Courtenay/Smith] (d.1762); Brother Edward; Brother John Montagu, 4th Earl of Sandwich (1718-1792).
Service: 5.6.1740 Passed; **Lieutenant**; 20.9.1740[(7.9.1741)]-3.6.1741 3L *Defiance* (60); 4.3.1740/41-5.1741 Operations against Cartagena; 21.9.1741-1.12.1741[P] 3L *Hampton Court* (70);

16.1.1741/42 1L *Launceston* (44); 22.3.1741/42-13.4.1742 6L *Namur* (90); **Commander**; 23.5.1744(BLI 21.8.1745) *Mercury* (16) Sloop; **Captain**; 23.5.1745(BLI 21.8.1745) *Mermaid* (44); 21.8.1745 *Prince Edward* (44); 9.11.1745-18.7.1747 M.P. for Huntingdonshire; 2.7.1746-6.4.1748 *Bristol* (50); 3.5.1747 1st Battle of Cape Finisterre; 23.9.1748-13.6.1749 *Bristol* (50); 12.1.1749/50-5.12.1751 *Cumberland* (66); 22.2.1751/52-17.4.1754 M.P. for Bossiney.

MONTRESOR, JAMES

Dates: 1.1770 Died.
Family:
Service: **Lieutenant**; 15.6.1760(3.9.1764)-19.6.1761 4L *Panther* (60); 15.6.1769-1.1770† 2L *Aurora* (32).

MOODIE, JOHN

Dates: 1755 Died.
Family:
Service: 16.5.1731-4.6.1734 Able *Dreadnought* (60); 5.6.1734-31.7.1734 Able *Captain* (70); 1.8.1734-4.12.1735 Able *Dreadnought* (60); 5.12.1735-28.3.1736 Able *Captain* (70); 29.3.1736-6.6.1738 Mid *Captain* (70); 7.6.1738 Able *Edinburgh* (70); 8.5.1740 Passed; **Lieutenant**; 21.2.1740/41 3L *Roebuck* (40); 20.3.1740/41 6L *Marlborough* (90); 11.5.1741 5L *Marlborough* (90); 6.7.1741-23.11.1741 4L *Marlborough* (90); 25.11.1741(17.1.1743/44) 4L *Somerset* (80); 20.2.1741/42(17.1.1743/44) 2L *Bedford* (70); 11.9.1742(17.1.1743/44) 3L *Marlborough* (90); 3.2.1743/44(17.1.1743/44)-24.1.1746/47 2L *Warwick* (60); 11.2.1743/44-12.2.1743/44 Battle of Toulon; 22.5.1755 1L *Revenge* (64); 24.9.1755-17.11.1755 L. *Experiment* (24).

MOODY, THOMAS

Dates: 11.11.1807 Died.
Family:
Service: **Lieutenant**; 29.1.1747/48(JAM 28.8.1751) 3L *Warwick* (60); 9.4.1748 Battle of Santiago de Cuba; 16.4.1748(JAM 28.8.1751)-17.2.1748/49[P] 2L *Warwick* (60); 12.10.1748 Battle of Havana; 4.8.1756 L. *Lively* (20); 24.9.1756 5L *Union* (90); 1.8.1757 5L *Neptune* (90); 5.9.1757-6.10.1757 Raid on Rochefort; 20.10.1757-17.6.1762 4L *Neptune* (90); 21.9.1796 **Superannuated Commander**.

MOORE, SIR JOHN

Dates: 24.3.1717/18 Born; 18.5.1770 Knight Bachelor; 2.2.1779 Died.
Family: Father Henry Moore; Mother Catherine Knatchbull; Wife Penelope Matthews.
Service: 6.4.1738 Passed; **Lieutenant**; 23.5.1738(9.5.1739)-9.3.1738/39 4L *Lancaster* (80); 21.1.1741/42 2L *Newcastle* (50); 14.4.1742-23.7.1742 6L *Namur* (90); **Commander**; 26.2.1742/43-5.5.1743 *Terror* (8) Bomb Vessel; 6.5.1743-1.9.1743 *Ferret* (14) Sloop; **Captain**; 24.12.1743 *Squirrel* (20); 18.4.1744 *Dolphin* (20); 25.2.1744/45-25.9.1746[P] *Deptford* (60); 21.7.1747 *Duke* (90); 29.12.1747-20.12.1748[P] *Saint Albans* (60); 1.12.1748-25.4.1749 *Monarch* (74); 20.2.1753 *William and Mary* (10) Yacht; 31.3.1756 *Devonshire* (66); 5.5.1757 CinC — Barbados & the Leeward Islands; 5.5.1757-1760 Commodore *Cambridge* (80); 16.1.1759-19.1.1759 Attack on Martinique; 20.1.1759-1.5.1759 Capture of Guadeloupe; 2.12.1761 CinC — The Downs; 21.10.1762 **Rear Admiral of the Red**; 1766-1769 CinC — Portsmouth; 18.10.1770 **Vice Admiral of the Blue**; 24.10.1770 **Vice Admiral of the White**; 31.3.1775 **Vice Admiral of the Red**; 29.1.1778 **Admiral of the Blue**.

MOORE, JOHN
Dates: 1803 Died.
Family:
Service: **Lieutenant**; 12.5.1740 3L *Newcastle* (50); 5.10.1742(18.4.1743)-5.4.1744 4L *Lennox* (70); 6.4.1747 2L *Kent* (64); 3.5.1747 1st Battle of Cape Finisterre; 14.10.1747 2nd Battle of Cape Finisterre; 26.12.1747 1L *Kent* (64); 5.12.1748-16.11.1752P 1L *Kent* (64); 6.2.1755 1L *Chichester* (68); 1.6.1756 1L *Saint George* (90); 6.4.1757 1L *Prince of Orange* (60); **Commander**; 2.5.1757 *Bolton* (6) Yacht; 9.9.1772-1803† *Medina* (6) Yacht.

MOORE, JOHN
Dates: 14.4.1792 Died; 28.4.1792 Will Probate.
Family:
Service: **Lieutenant**; 26.7.1762(25.3.1763) L. *Good Intent* Hired Tender; 7.11.1766-2.11.1769 LCmdr *Lurcher* (6) Cutter; 25.11.1776-4.3.1783P LCmdr *Kitty* Hired Tender.

MOORE, MATHEW
Dates: 4.7.1787 Died.
Family:
Service: **Lieutenant**; 15.8.1743(17.1.1743/44)-5.3.1743/44 6L *Namur* (90); 11.2.1743/44-12.2.1743/44 Battle of Toulon; 2.8.1745(MED 8.11.1745)-7.2.1745/46 3L *Neptune* (90); 3.11.1747(JAM 26.8.1748)-24.5.1748 2L *Canterbury* (60); **Commander**; 15.1.1747/48(JAM 13.7.1748)-12.7.1748P *Dreadnought Prize* (12) Sloop; 9.4.1748 Battle of Santiago de Cuba; 25.4.1755 *Granado* (8) Bomb Vessel; **Captain**; 20.8.1756-1.2.1757 *Dolphin* (24); 18.5.1757-19.1.1758 *Sheerness* (24); 10.7.1758 *Adventure* (32); 29.3.1761-11.6.1761 Expedition against Belle-Isle; 22.2.1762-14.7.1763 *Dreadnought* (60); 9.8.1770-10.6.1771P *Arrogant* (74); 1.12.1773 *Lennox* (74); 19.1.1775-9.6.1778 *Exeter* (64); 26.9.1780 **Rear Admiral of the Blue**.

MORGAN, JEREMIAH
Dates: 2.1773 Died.
Family:
Service: **Lieutenant**; 22.11.1746(MED 3.12.1748)-30.10.1748P 3L *Leopard* (50); 23.1.1751/52-14.11.1752P 3L *Monarch* (74); 16.1.1753 3L *Bristol* (50); 19.2.1754 3L *Bristol* (50); 28.3.1754-30.1.1755 3L *Tiger* (60); 9.4.1757(9.11.1757)-6.10.1758 1L *Kingfisher* (14) Sloop; 19.7.1759-28.9.1760P 2L *Princess Mary* (60); **Commander**; 11.8.1762-1.6.1763P *Hornet* (10) Sloop; 3.6.1763-5.3.1768P *Hornet* (10) Sloop; 1.7.1771-2.1773† *Hunter* (10) Sloop.

MORGAN, PROBERT
Dates: 1756 Died.
Family:
Service: 15.2.1745/46 **Lieutenant**; 9.10.1746-5.10.1748P L. *Nightingale* (22); 28.11.1751 L. *Boston* (24); 16.1.1751/52-6.5.1753P L. *Winchelsea* (20).

MORICE, THOMAS
Dates: c.1734 Born; 22.11.1778 Died.
Family:
Service: 4.12.1735-16.2.1736P Able *Tilbury* (60); 27.9.1736-4.5.1737P Able *Captain* (70); 26.11.1738 Capt Serv *Richmond* (24); 7.6.1739 Able *Garland* (20); 7.2.1743-5.8.1743P Mid *Garland* (20); 21.9.1744-8.4.1746 Mid *Gibraltar* (20); 8.4.1756 Passed; **Lieutenant**; 21.6.1756

6L *Marlborough* (80); 14.7.1756 6L *Duke* (90); 17.8.1757 2L *Shannon* (28); 17.1.1758 6L *Royal Anne* (100); 5.6.1758-12.6.1758 Raid on Saint-Malo; 25.7.1758-15.8.1758 2L *Lion* (58); 15.8.1758 3L *Lion* (58); 16.1.1759-19.1.1759 Attack on Martinique; 20.1.1759-1.5.1759 Capture of Guadeloupe; 17.3.1760 2L *Dunkirk* (60); 6.5.1760 1L *Dunkirk* (60); 24.10.1761[(8.3.1762)] 2L *Prince Edward* (44); 8.3.1762-27.1.1763[P] 1L *Prince Edward* (44); 30.8.1764-12.11.1767 1L *Belleisle* (64); 3.11.1770 3L *Ocean* (90); 25.6.1773 2L *Ocean* (90); 14.8.1773-3.11.1773 1L *Ocean* (90); 3.10.1776-3.12.1776 1L *Courageux* (74); 28.2.1778-15.4.1778 1L *Fame* (74).

MORLAND, SAMUEL

Dates: c.1725 Born; c.1758 Died; 18.9.1758 Will Probate.
Family:
Service: 1.4.1741 Capt Serv *Hastings* (44); 12.1.1741/42 Mid *Hastings* (44); 12.12.1743 Able *Hastings* (44); 17.6.1745 Mid *Scarborough* (20); 28.5.1747 Passed; **Lieutenant**; 31.12.1755-16.4.1756 4L *Trident* (64).

MORRICE, THOMAS

Dates: c.1741 Born; 1.1793 Died.
Family:
Service: 18.4.1753 Able *Garland* (24); 29.12.1756 Mid *Garland* (24); 27.6.1757-19.2.1758[W] Able *Invincible* (74); 8.1757-10.1757 Louisbourg Expedition; 8.8.1758 Mid *Royal Sovereign* (104); 7.3.1758/59-4.2.1761 Mid *Warspite* (74); 18.8.1759-19.8.1759 Battle of Lagos Bay; 20.11.1759 Battle of Quiberon Bay; 4.2.1761 Passed; **Lieutenant**; 8.5.1761 6L *Union* (90); 5.8.1761-25.2.1763[P] 5L *Union* (90); 8.2.1766-9.2.1769 L. *Merlin* (18) Frigate.

MORRIS, JOHN

Dates: c.1725 Baptised; 5.7.1776 Died.
Family: Wife Elizabeth; Son James Nicoll, RN (1763-1830).
Service: 27.11.1740 Capt Serv *Bristol* (54); 6.6.1741 Capt Serv *Princess Louisa* (60); 14.6.1741-20.11.1742[P] Clerk *Princess Louisa* (60); 8.8.1743 Mid *Captain* (70); 25.9.1747 Mate *Captain* (70); 23.2.1747/48-9.9.1748[P] Mate *Sutherland* (50); 18.12.1748 Able *Captain* (70); 9.4.1749 Mate *Captain* (70); 14.9.1749 Passed; **Lieutenant**; 10.7.1755[(NA 11.12.1755)] 4L *Somerset* (68); 13.12.1755-22.1.1759 3L *Somerset* (68); 6.6.1758-27.7.1758 The Siege of Louisbourg; 12.2.1759-20.11.1759[S] 3L *Resolution* (74); 20.11.1759 Battle of Quiberon Bay; 3.4.1760-30.7.1762 1L *Sandwich* (90); 29.3.1761-11.6.1761 Expedition against Belle-Isle; 24.6.1768-19.6.1770[P] 1L *Venus* (36); 21.9.1770 1L *Albion* (74); **Commander**; 7.1.1771 *Lynx* (10) Sloop; 10.1.1771-26.11.1773[P] *Otter* (14) Sloop; **Captain**; 13.10.1775-5.7.1776[†] *Bristol* (50).

MORTIMER, ROBERT

Dates: c.1733 Born; 2.5.1799 Died.
Family:
Service: 31.3.1739-22.8.1739[P] Able *Port Mahon* (20); 24.7.1740 Able *Severn* (50); 6.7.1741 Able *Lark* (40); 1.10.1742 Able *Tartar* (20); 24.7.1743 Able *Leopard* (50); 13.3.1743/44 Mid *Leopard* (50); 13.3.1745/46 Passed; **Lieutenant**; 4.4.1746-24.12.1748[P] 3L *Mary Galley* (44); 29.3.1755 2L *Somerset* (68); 8.2.1757-23.5.1763[P] 1L *Somerset* (68); 6.6.1758-27.7.1758 The Siege of Louisbourg; 23.5.1778-3.12.1782[P] LCmdr *Favourite* Hired Tender; 24.3.1790 **Superannuated Lieutenant**; 21.9.1796 **Superannuated Commander.**

MOSTYN, SAVAGE

Dates: 1713 Born; 16.9.1757 Died.
Family: Father Sir Roger Mostyn, 3rd Bt. (1673–1739); Mother Lady Essex Finch (d. 1721); Brother Thomas, MP (1704-58); Brother John, MP (c.1709-79).
Service: 2.2.1733/34 Passed; **Lieutenant**; 2.3.1733/34-12.4.1734 3L *Pembroke* (60); 13.4.1734-28.5.1736 2L *Pembroke* (60); 29.5.1736(12.5.1737)-3.8.1736 6L *Britannia* (100); 4.8.1736(12.5.1737)-4.10.1736 5L *Britannia* (100); 5.10.1736(12.5.1737)-11.3.1736/37 4L *Britannia* (100); 12.3.1736/37(12.5.1737)-11.6.1739 3L *Britannia* (100); 12.6.1739-2.7.1739 2L *Namur* (90); **Commander**; 3.7.1739 *Duke* (8) Fireship; **Captain**; 17.12.1739(6.3.1739/40)-5.5.1740[P] *Seaford* (20); 24.4.1740-12.10.1740 *Winchelsea* (20); 12.10.1740 *Deptford* (60); 4.3.1740/41-5.1741 Operations against Cartagena; 14.12.1743 *Suffolk* (70); 2.4.1744-26.12.1748[P] *Hampton Court* (64); 8.1.1744/45 Action of 1745-01-08; 1.7.1747-16.9.1757 M.P. for Weobley; 23.8.1748 CinC — River Medway and The Nore; 27.3.1749-2.1755 Comptroller of the Navy; **Rear Admiral of the Blue**; 4.2.1755-5.1756 *Monarch* (74); 5.1756-7.1757 *Magnanime* (74); 4.6.1756 **Rear Admiral of the Red**; 24.2.1757 **Vice Admiral of the Blue**; 6.4.1757-1.7.1757 Lord Commissioner of the Admiralty.

MOTLEY, JOHN

Dates: c.1703 Born; 1776 Died.
Family:
Service: 1728-1734 Merchant Service; 12.9.1734-9.5.1735[P] Mid *Kingston* (60); 10.4.1740 Mid *Torbay* (80); 2.9.1740 Able *Torbay* (80); 3.2.1740/41 Mid *Torbay* (80); 11.2.1743/44-12.2.1743/44 Battle of Toulon; 27.2.1744/45-12.6.1745[P] Mid *Newcastle* (50); 19.2.1745/46 Passed; **Lieutenant**; 4.6.1746 3L *Lynn* (44); 7.6.1746-20.4.1749[P] 2L *Lynn* (44).

MOUAT, GEORGE

Dates: 27.2.1822 Died.
Family:
Service: **Lieutenant**; 19.10.1759(EI 20.1.1761)-14.6.1762 4L *York* (60); 18.6.1805 **Superannuated Commander**.

MOUAT, PATRICK

Dates: c.1712 Born Northmavine, Shetland Islands; 5.5.1790 Died Westminster; 20.5.1790 Will Probate.
Family: Father James Mouat; Mother Elizabeth Mackenzie; Wife Margaret; Son Frederick (d.1786); Son Henry, RN (1734-1798); Son James; Son Stephen Peter, RN (1751-1834); Son Alexander, RN (1761-1793); Son Charles (c.1761-1830).
Service: 1734-1740 Merchant Service; 23.10.1740 Mid *Trial* (8) Sloop; 29.1.1740/41-14.5.1741[W] Mid *Wager* (28); 22.11.1742 Mid *Pearl* (40); 8.4.1743 Master *Severn* (50); 12.12.1743 Act3L *Severn* (50); 30.3.1744 Mate *Strafford* (58); 9.7.1745 Mate *Adventure* (44); 9.12.1745 Passed; **Lieutenant**; 20.1.1745/46-23.11.1747 3L *Windsor* (60); 3.5.1747 1st Battle of Cape Finisterre; 14.10.1747 2nd Battle of Cape Finisterre; 6.4.1748-16.11.1752[P] 4L *Fougueux* (64); 11.2.1755-19.1.1758 1L *Medway* (60); 5.9.1757-6.10.1757 Raid on Rochefort; 27.1.1758 1L *Dorsetshire* (68); 26.4.1758 6L *Ramillies* (90); **Commander**; 22.5.1758 *Cormorant* (8) Fireship; 5.6.1758-12.6.1758 Raid on Saint-Malo; 7.4.1762-27.6.1762[C] *Gramont* (18) Sloop; 26.3.1764 *Tamar* (16) Sloop; **Captain**; 28.4.1765(EI 12.6.1766)-19.6.1766 *Dolphin* (24).

MOUBRAY, GEORGE

Dates:

Family:

Service: **Lieutenant**; 29.3.1760-16.12.1761 5L *Newark* (80); 16.12.1761 L. *Hound* (14) Sloop; 24.5.1762 6L *Royal Sovereign* (104); 25.10.1763 2L *Superb* (74); 17.10.1765-12.11.1766 3L *Superb* (74); 21.2.1769 1L *Alarm* (32); 25.6.1771-4.3.1773 1L *Worcester* (64); 24.1.1775 3L *Royal Oak* (74); 14.6.1775 2L *Royal Oak* (74); 21.10.1775 3L *Royal Oak* (74); 3.2.1777 2L *Royal Oak* (74); 6.9.1777-26.1.1778 1L *Royal Oak* (74); 5.2.1782 2L *Diligent* (70); 18.7.1782-17.4.1783[P] 1L *Diligent* (70).

MOULDEN, WILLIAM

Dates: c.1737 Born; 23.12.1778 Died; 3.2.1779 Will Probate.

Family:

Service: 16.3.1755 Able *Torbay* (74); 23.5.1755 Mid *Torbay* (74); 6.6.1755-8.6.1755 Action of 6-8 June 1755; 1.3.1756 Mid *Invincible* (74); 15.1.1757 Mid *Royal George* (100); 22.2.1758 Mid *Namur* (90); 6.6.1758-27.7.1758 The Siege of Louisbourg; 14.2.1759 Passed; **Lieutenant**; 4.3.1760[(ECH 6.5.1760)]-14.10.1761 5L *Culloden* (74); 4.4.1763[(ECH 6.5.1760)]-7.4.1763[P] 4L *Culloden* (74); 12.9.1767 LCmdr *Sir Edward Hawke* (8) Schooner; 28.10.1767 1L *Yarmouth* (64); 4.3.1769 2L *Yarmouth* (64); 15.6.1769-23.11.1769[P] 3L *Yarmouth* (64); 2.11.1776 2L *Invincible* (74); 28.6.1777-20.2.1778 1L *Invincible* (74).

MOUNTFORD, EDWARD

Dates: c.1713 Born; 1772 Died.

Family:

Service: 22.10.1730 Able *Lively* (20); 24.8.1731 Mid *Lively* (20); 27.6.1734-20.11.1738[P] Mate *Lively* (20); 17.11.1739 Mate *Pearl* (40); 27.11.1740 Passed; **Lieutenant**; 2.2.1740/41-2.6.1743 4L *Buckingham* (70); 24.9.1755 1L *Revenge* (64); 20.5.1756 Battle of Minorca; 28.2.1758 Battle of Cartagena; **Commander**; 27.9.1758-1763 *Pelican* (8) Bomb Vessel.

MOUTRAY, JOHN

Dates: 22.11.1785 Died Bath; 26.11.1785 Buried Bath Abbey.

Family: Father James Moutray (b. 1687, d. before 1734); Mother Emelia Malcolm (d. 1762); Wife Mary Pemble (1752 - 1844) married 2.9.1777; Wife Mary Pemble (1752 - 1844).

Service: **Lieutenant**; 12.5.1744-13.2.1744/45[W] 4L *Orford* (70); 13.7.1745 2L *Looe* (44); 29.4.1746 5L *Duke* (90); 18.3.1746/47-28.8.1748[P] 1L *Centurion* (50); 3.5.1747 1st Battle of Cape Finisterre; 6.12.1750-10.5.1753[P] L. *Peregrine* (20) Sloop; 5.2.1754 L. *Mermaid* (24); 22.5.1755-14.6.1755 British attack on Fort Beauséjour; 9.12.1755 1L *Yarmouth* (64); 17.9.1756-11.1.1757 3L *Marlborough* (80); **Commander**; 16.2.1757 *Thetis* (44) Hospital Ship; **Captain**; 28.12.1758[(JAM 24.1.1763)]-17.1.1763[P] *Thetis* (32); 16.8.1769-23.4.1771 *Emerald* (32); 7.12.1773-4.7.1775[P] *Thames* (32); 11.4.1777-25.8.1778 *Warwick* (50); 27.8.1778-22.3.1779 *Britannia* (100); 31.3.1779-27.2.1781 *Ramillies* (74); 2.3.1782 *Edgar* (74); 6.5.1782-23.12.1782 *Vengeance* (74); 20.10.1782 Battle of Cape Spartel.

MOWAT, HENRY

Dates: 1734 Born; 14.4.1798 Died North America; 30.5.1799 Will Probate.

Family: Father Patrick Mouat, RN (1712-1790).

Service: 5.7.1755-16.12.1755 Able *Antelope* (50); 17.12.1755 Mid *Chesterfield* (44); 20.5.1756 Battle of Minorca; 6.7.1756 Mate *Chesterfield* (44); 3.10.1756 Mid *Chesterfield* (44); 4.5.1757

Mate *Chesterfield* (44); 15.12.1757 Mid *Ramillies* (90); 9.5.1758 Passed; **Lieutenant**; 22.1.1759 L. *Baltimore* (8) Bomb Vessel; 14.1.1760-13.4.1763 L. *Aldborough* (20); 29.3.1761-11.6.1761 Expedition against Belle-Isle; 14.3.1764-2.6.1776 LCmdr *Canceaux* (6); **Commander**; 2.6.1776[NA 22.8.1781]-28.12.1781[W] *Albany* (16) Sloop; 7.1776-16.1.1777 *Milford* (28); 10.1776-23.11.1779[P] LCmdr *Halifax* (6) Schooner; 24.7.1779-12.8.1779 Penobscot Expedition; 10.1782-12.1782 *Sophie* (28); 26.10.1782 **Captain**; 5.1795-14.4.1798[†] *Assistance* (50).

MOYLE, HENRY

Dates: 1787 Died.
Family:
Service: 27.5.1740 Able *Suffolk* (70); 4.3.1740/41-5.1741 Operations against Cartagena; 20.12.1742 Mid *Stirling Castle* (70); 26.9.1743 Mid *Duke* (90); 3.4.1744 Mid *Victory* (100); 4.6.1744 Mid *Cornwall* (80); 2.8.1745 Passed; **Lieutenant**; 23.10.1745[19.1.1746/47] 3L *Plymouth* (60); 30.5.1746[19.1.1746/47]-28.7.1748[P] 2L *Plymouth* (60); 3.8.1746 Action of August 3 1746; 25.3.1747 Action of March 25 1747; 1748-1787 Lieutenant of Greenwich Hospital; 9.4.1748 Battle of Santiago de Cuba.

MUNDEN, THOMAS

Dates: c.1715 Born; c.1766 Died; 13.3.1766 Will Probate.
Family:
Service: 1.6.1735-25.5.1737 Ord. *Windsor* (60); 26.5.1737-28.5.1738 Able *Windsor* (60); 29.5.1738 Mid *Flamborough* (20); 30.5.1740 Mate *Flamborough* (20); 6.10.1741 Passed; **Lieutenant**; 2.5.1746-15.9.1748[P] L. *Alderney* (20).

MURRAY, ARCHIBALD

Dates: c.1715 Born; c.1759 Died; 19.4.1759 Will Probate.
Family:
Service: 3.4.1733 Ord. *Kingston* (60); 10.5.1733 Ord. *Rupert* (60); 9.9.1733 Ord. *Wolf* (8) Sloop; 3.4.1734 Able *Garland* (20); 30.6.1734 Mid *Roebuck* (40); 13.4.1736 Able *Roebuck* (40); 11.5.1738 Mid *Roebuck* (40); 28.10.1738-14.3.1738/39 Able *Greenwich* (50); 15.3.1738/39 Able *William and Mary* (10) Yacht; 12.4.1739 Passed; **Lieutenant**; 4.3.1739/40 3L *Chester* (54); 30.9.1740 2L *Chester* (54); 9.2.1741/42[2.7.1742]-17.8.1742[P] 1L *Chester* (54); 29.12.1742 2L *Severn* (50); 29.4.1743-6.6.1745 1L *Sapphire* (44); 1.7.1745 2L *Sandwich* (90); 6.7.1745-5.11.1745 1L *Milford* (44); 13.11.1745 3L *Royal Sovereign* (104); 11.1.1745/46-13.4.1747 2L *Royal Sovereign* (104).

MURRAY, GEORGE

Dates: 11.11.1785 Died.
Family:
Service: 8.1.1721/22 Vol-p-O *Lyme* (20); 9.1.1723/24 Mid *Lyme* (20); 2.2.1725/26 Passed; **Lieutenant**; 5.5.1727-31.7.1728 4L *Orford* (70); 1.8.1728-13.9.1729[P] 2L *Ludlow Castle* (40); 8.7.1730-2.7.1731 3L *Princess Louisa* (40); 3.7.1731-13.6.1732 2L *Captain* (70); 14.6.1732-30.1.1733/34 3L *Captain* (70); 31.1.1733/34-5.3.1735/36 3L *Captain* (70); 6.3.1735/36[25.5.1736]-8.12.1737 3L *Princess Caroline* (80); 9.12.1737-23.7.1740 2L *Hampton Court* (70); 21.11.1739 Attack on Puerto Bello; **Commander**; 24.7.1740 *Trial* (8) Sloop; **Captain**; 3.11.1740[1.2.1742/43] *Wager* (28); 19.2.1740/41[1.2.1742/43] *Pearl* (40); 6.10.1743 *Hampshire* (50); 28.5.1745[MED 10.1.1748/49]-17.11.1748[P] *Revenge* (70); 7.5.1755 *Trident* (64); 23.9.1755-15.6.1756 *Duke* (90); 16.7.1756 **Superannuated Rear Admiral**.

MURRAY, THE HON. GEORGE

Dates: 22.8.1741 Born Tullibardine, Scotland; 17.10.1797 Died Hunton, Kent.
Family: Father Lord George Murray (1694-1760); Mother Amelia (1710-1766); Wife Wilhelmina King (1738-1795) married 13.5.1784.
Service: 23.8.1756 Scholar *Royal Naval Academy*; 8.3.1758 Capt Serv *Newark* (80); 5.6.1758-12.6.1758 Raid on Saint-Malo; 2.1.1759 Able *Newark* (80); 17.2.1759 Mid *Falmouth* (50); 17.5.1760 Mid *York* (60); 23.1.1762 Able *Terpsichore* (24); 17.8.1762 Able *Princess Royal* (90); 1.9.1762 Passed; **Lieutenant**; 14.10.1762-29.3.1763 L. *Swift* (14) Sloop; 18.11.1763 2L *Tartar* (28); **Commander**; 20.6.1765 *Ferret* (14) Sloop; **Captain**; 26.5.1768-20.6.1770 *Kennington* (20); 1.9.1769[JAM 21.2.1770]-13.1.1770[P] *Adventure* (32); 31.3.1775-15.10.1779[P] *Levant* (28); 27.10.1779 *Cleopatra* (32); 5.8.1781 Battle of Dogger Bank; 4.12.1782-20.3.1783 *Irresistible* (74); 28.8.1790-14.12.1790[P] *Defence* (74); 27.10.1792-4.2.1793 CinC — River Medway and The Nore; 27.10.1792 *Vengeance* (74); 1.2.1793-18.3.1793 *Duke* (98); 21.3.1794-1796 CinC — Nova Scotia; **Rear Admiral of the White**; 12.4.1794-1.6.1795 *Resolution* (74); 4.7.1794 **Rear Admiral of the Red**; 1.6.1795 **Vice Admiral of the White.**

MURRAY, JOHN

Dates: c.1710 Born; 1770 Died.
Family:
Service: 1.11.1737-24.3.1737/38 Able *Lively* (20); 25.3.1738 Able *Port Mahon* (20); 12.8.1738-22.8.1739[P] Mid *Port Mahon* (20); 17.4.1740 Mid *Severn* (50); 18.11.1740 Mate *Severn* (50); 7.2.1740/41 Mid *Guernsey* (50); 28.1.1741/42 Mate *Guernsey* (50); 22.3.1742/43 Mate *Norfolk* (80); 11.2.1743/44-12.2.1743/44 Battle of Toulon; 24.3.1744/45 Able *Namur* (96); 11.7.1745 Passed; **Lieutenant**; 13.7.1745 3L *Ruby* (50); 7.3.1745/46-18.6.1747 2L *Ruby* (50); 20.9.1746-25.9.1746 Lorient Operations; 17.12.1747-2.1.1747/48 6L *Prince George* (90); 3.4.1755 3L *Romney* (44); 5.7.1756 3L *Guernsey* (50); 29.9.1756 2L *Guernsey* (50); 25.1.1757-25.4.1757 1L *Gosport* (44); 23.8.1758-19.2.1759 6L *Princess Royal* (90); 3.4.1759 5L *Princess Royal* (90); 29.5.1759 4L *Princess Royal* (90); 10.7.1759 2L *Princess Royal* (90); 12.10.1762-15.1.1763[P] 1L *Princess Royal* (90).

MURRAY, RICHARD

Dates: c.1734 Born; 1789 Died; 10.1.1789 Will Probate.
Family:
Service: 21.5.1749 Able *Prince Henry* (44); 28.6.1753 Mid *Shoreham* (24); 4.8.1756 Passed; **Lieutenant**; 2.2.1757 3L *Arc-en-Ciel* (50); 21.7.1757[8.1.1759] 4L *Bedford* (64); 8.1757-10.1757 Louisbourg Expedition; 6.6.1758-27.7.1758 The Siege of Louisbourg; 3.8.1758[8.1.1758]-25.1.1763[P] 1L *Diana* (32); 18.4.1763-3.7.1765 L. *Merlin* (18) Frigate; 11.9.1768-30.6.1773 LCmdr *Saint John* (6) Schooner; 13.3.1776 LCmdr *Ferret* (6) Cutter; **Commander**; 26.1.1778-13.4.1781[P] *Hawk* (10) Sloop; 31.12.1779 Affair of Fielding and Bylandt; **Captain**; 2.7.1781-20.11.1782 *Princess Augusta* (6) Yacht; 28.11.1782-20.2.1783[P] *Gladiator* (44).

Service Records N

NAILOUR, CHARLES
Dates: None Known.
Family:
Service: 8.2.1749/50-c.1753 Scholar *Royal Naval Academy*; **Lieutenant**; 7.4.1756$^{\text{(8.4.1757)}}$-21.5.1756 4L *Lancaster* (66); 20.5.1756 Battle of Minorca; 5.1.1759-13.3.1759 2L *Minerva* (32).

NAPIER, CHARLES
Dates: c.1730 Born; 1831 Died; 23.4.1831 Will Probate.
Family:
Service: 27.8.1745 Able *Sheerness* (24); 11.11.1745-15.6.1746 Capt Serv *Chesterfield* (44); 16.6.1746 Able *Chesterfield* (44); 17.11.1747 Mid *Assistance* (50); 13.11.1748 Mid *Tavistock* (50); 17.5.1751 Able *Otter* (14) Sloop; 30.7.1751-11.10.1751 NR *Mary* (8) Yacht; 1.11.1751 Passed; **Lieutenant**; 31.7.1754-20.8.1754^{P} 3L *Crown* (44); 21.8.1754-25.5.1755 3L *Norwich* (50); 10.7.1755 3L *Isis* (50); 5.7.1756$^{\text{(ECH 5.1.1757)}}$ 3L *Prince George* (80); 7.10.1756$^{\text{(ECH 5.1.1757)}}$ 2L *Deptford* (50); 5.2.1757 2L *Marlborough* (80); **Commander**; 3.5.1758$^{\text{(JAM 28.8.1759)}}$ *Hornet* (10) Sloop; 17.12.1759 *Cygnet* (18) Sloop; 6.6.1762-13.8.1762 Operations against Havana; **Captain**; 17.8.1762$^{\text{(EI 20.6.1763)}}$-14.9.1762^{SC} *Stirling Castle* (64); 20.9.1762$^{\text{(EI 13.10.1763)}}$ *Richmond* (32); 3.4.1763$^{\text{(JAM 13.10.1763)}}$-2.7.1763^{P} *Glasgow* (20); 16.6.1783-8.8.1783 *Europa* (50).

NASH, EZEKIEL
Dates: c.1730 Born; 16.4.1803 Died; 20.6.1803 Will Probate.
Family:
Service: 1752-1756 Merchant Service; 22.9.1756 CaptP *Caesar Privateer* (20) PMW; 10.1.1757 Able *Prince Edward* (44); 30.3.1757 Mate *Prince Edward* (44); 28.7.1757 Mid *Badger* (10) Sloop; 11.10.1759 Mid *Milford* (28); 30.5.1760 Passed; **Lieutenant**; 2.6.1760 2L *Milford* (28); 8.4.1762-23.3.1763^{P} 1L *Milford* (28); 3.2.1768 3L *San Antonio* (64); 17.9.1770 4L *San Antonio* (64); 3.11.1770-1.6.1771^{P} 2L *San Antonio* (64).

NASMITH, JOHN LOCKHART
Dates: c.1731 Born; 25.8.1792 Died.
Family: Wife Margaret Hamilton married 1788.
Service: 1750-1755 Merchant Service; 12.12.1755 Able *Firedrake* (10) Bomb Vessel; 15.5.1756 Mate *Unicorn* (24); 26.4.1757 Able *Newark* (80); 8.1757-10.1757 Louisbourg Expedition; 10.2.1758 Mid *Newark* (80); 5.6.1758-12.6.1758 Raid on Saint-Malo; 18.8.1759-19.8.1759 Battle of Lagos Bay; 6.11.1759 Mate *Newark* (80); 7.5.1760 Passed; **Lieutenant**; 14.12.1762$^{\text{(7.9.1763)}}$-3.9.1763^{P} L. *Amazon* (22); 31.1.1774 2L *Egmont* (74); 21.10.1775 1L *Egmont* (74); 18.5.1776 2L *Egmont* (74); 2.8.1776 3L *Egmont* (74); 12.11.1776 4L *Egmont* (74); 6.12.1776 4L *Barfleur* (90); 5.4.1777 4L *Princess Royal* (90); 4.5.1778 4L *Albion* (74); 2.10.1778-27.11.1778 2L *Alexander*

(74); **Commander**; 27.2.1779[NA 19.8.1779]-14.6.1779 *Supply* (26) Armed Storeship; 19.10.1780-25.12.1782 *Alderney* (12) Sloop.

NEAL, JAMES

Dates: c.1725 Born; 1782 Died; 22.8.1782 Will Probate.
Family:
Service: 24.12.1745 Able *Suffolk* (70); 9.3.1746/47 Mid *Suffolk* (70); 20.1.1748/49 Mate *Suffolk* (70); 14.9.1749 Mid *Intrepid* (64); 28.8.1750-24.4.1753[W] Mate *Assurance* (44); 13.11.1753 Able *Severn* (50); 20.11.1754 Mid *Severn* (50); 3.9.1755-8.4.1757[P] Mate *Severn* (50); 19.3.1760 Passed; **Lieutenant**; 20.3.1760 L. *Seaford* (20); 23.10.1760-6.12.1762[P] 2L *Portland* (50); 4.1764-12.1765 LCmdr *Pitt* (6) Cutter; 24.9.1770 3L *Temeraire* (74); 25.1.1771-22.5.1771[P] 2L *Temeraire* (74).

NEALE, JOHN

Dates: c.1785 Died; 15.1.1785 Will Probate.
Family:
Service: **Lieutenant**; 15.2.1744/45[BLI 5.5.1749]-21.5.1746 L. *Comet* (10) Bomb Vessel; 21.5.1746[BLI 5.5.1749] L. *Saxon* (16) Ship; 3.1.1746/47 2L *Chichester* (80); 23.2.1746/47-5.6.1748[P] 1L *Chichester* (80); 1.11.1748[BLI 5.5.1749]-1.3.1748/49[P] 2L *Tilbury* (58); 27.5.1755 2L *Antelope* (50); 12.5.1756-1.4.1763 1L *Antelope* (50); 12.12.1778-4.1783 LCmdr *Tiger* (74) Hospital Ship.

NEILSON, THOMAS

Dates: 10.10.1761 Died The Channel.
Family:
Service: **Lieutenant**; 21.7.1741[22.12.1741] 3L *Sunderland* (60); 20.2.1741/42-7.12.1744 3L *Antelope* (50); 8.10.1744[NA 2.5.1747] 2L *Kingston* (60); 10.2.1744/45[NA 2.5.1747]-11.4.1746 1L *Kingston* (60); 11.4.1746[NA 5.2.1746/47] 2L *Kingston* (60); 25.7.1746[NA 5.2.1746/47]-26.2.1746/47[P] 1L *Kingston* (60); 23.3.1749/50-4.12.1752[P] L. *Trial* (10) Sloop; 12.10.1755-1.11.1755 3L *Duke* (90); 18.5.1756 1L *Hampton Court* (64); 28.4.1757 4L *Ramillies* (90); 5.9.1757-6.10.1757 Raid on Rochefort; 26.4.1758 3L *Ramillies* (90); 5.6.1758-12.6.1758 Raid on Saint-Malo; 11.10.1758 2L *Ramillies* (90); 18.10.1759 1L *Ramillies* (90); **Commander**; 1.3.1760 *Raven* (14) Sloop; 8.6.1761-10.10.1761[F] *Pheasant* (14) Sloop.

NEVILLE, JOSEPH

Dates: c.1730 Born.
Family:
Service: 12.9.1739 Mst Serv *Lichfield* (50); 27.9.1740 Mst Serv *Weymouth* (60); 7.1.1740/41 Action of January 7 1741; 29.3.1741-8.5.1742[P] Able *Weymouth* (60); 22.9.1742 Mst Serv *Woolwich* (50); 26.1.1743/44 MidO *Woolwich* (50); 21.4.1746-20.4.1747[P] Mid *Woolwich* (50); 10.8.1746 Action of 1746-10-18; 2.1.1750/51 Mid *Mars* (64); 16.2.1751/52 Able *Mars* (64); 27.2.1751/52 Mate *Saint Albans* (60); 1.5.1754 Passed; **Lieutenant**; 11.4.1759 2L *Tweed* (32); 29.3.1761-11.6.1761 Expedition against Belle-Isle; 31.12.1762-27.4.1763 L. *Siren* (20); 3.1.1765-24.2.1767 LCmdr *Kite* (4) Cutter.

NEWNHAM, THOMAS

Dates: 1795 Died; 3.9.1795 Will Probate.
Family:
Service: **Lieutenant**; 6.12.1760(11.10.1762)-5.6.1762 2L *Boreas* (28); 19.2.1767 3L *Achilles* (60); 1.6.1769-20.4.1771 LCmdr *Hunter* (4) Cutter; 2.8.1776-19.12.1778 1L *Bedford* (74); **Commander**; 24.3.1779(NA 29.11.1779) *Star* (10) Brig; **Captain**; 30.7.1779(NA 10.2.1780)-5.6.1780 *Grafton* (74); 17.4.1780 Battle of Martinique; 15.5.1780 Action of March 15 1780; 19.5.1780 Action of March 19 1780; 25.4.1781 *Africa* (64); 8.1.1782 *Defence* (74); 20.6.1783 2nd Battle of Cuddalore; 23.12.1783(EI 1.9.1784)-30.7.1784[P] *Isis* (50); 21.10.1793-10.6.1794[P] *Saturn* (74).

NEWSON, WILLIAM

Dates: c.1717 Born; 1787 Died; 2.10.1787 Will Probate.
Family:
Service: 7.4.1736 Able *Fly* (8) Sloop; 21.9.1736 Able *Norfolk* (80); 30.8.1738-11.9.1738 Able *Grampus* (6) Sloop; 12.9.1738-29.6.1739 Mid *Grampus* (6) Sloop; 30.6.1739 Able *Grampus* (6) Sloop; 12.8.1739-1.1.1741/42 Mid *Grampus* (6) Sloop; 2.1.1741/42 Mid *Gibraltar* (20); 6.5.1742 Passed; **Lieutenant**; 4.4.1743 L. *Scipio* (8) Fireship; 14.6.1743 L. *Deal Castle* (20); 27.7.1744(JAM 27.2.1746/47)-8.3.1744/45 3L *Woolwich* (50); 11.4.1748-9.1748[P] L. *Granado* (8) Bomb Vessel; 1.11.1755 1L *Nassau* (64); 10.3.1757 2L *Princess Amelia* (80); **Commander**; 15.6.1757-20.4.1758[P] *Roman Emperor* (16) Sloop; 3.5.1758-18.5.1759[P] *Roman Emperor* (8) Fireship; 29.12.1758 Capture of Goree; 13.12.1759 *Southsea Castle* (28) Storeship; **Captain**; 27.11.1760(25.5.1763) *Baleine* (20); 30.4.1761(26.5.1763)-24.8.1762[D] *Panther* (60).

NEWTON, GEORGE

Dates: c.1720 Born; 18.9.1782 Died.
Family:
Service: 28.2.1738/39 Able *Orford* (70); 8.4.1740 Capture of the Princesa; 7.1.1740/41 Action of January 7 1741; 21.5.1741 Able *Namur* (90); 12.2.1741/42 Mate *Endeavour* Tender; 4.6.1744 Mid *Royal Sovereign* (104); 18.5.1745 Mate *Squirrel* (20); 10.10.1745 Passed; **Lieutenant**; 9.5.1746 L. *Vulcan* (16) Sloop; 20.9.1746-25.9.1746 Lorient Operations; 3.5.1747 1st Battle of Cape Finisterre; 31.12.1747-12.8.1750[P] 3L *Hector* (44); 24.7.1755 3L *Lynn* (44); 5.11.1755 2L *Lynn* (44); 15.7.1758 2L *Adventure* (32); 31.7.1758-4.11.1760 1L *Adventure* (32); 5.5.1762-16.9.1762[W] 1L *Humber* (44); 2.11.1762-26.8.1763[P] 1L *Nightingale* (22).

NEWTON, HENRY

Dates: c.1725 Born; c.1758 Died; 21.2.1758 Will Probate.
Family:
Service: 28.12.1747 Capt Serv *Experiment* (24); 20.11.1748 Able *Experiment* (24); 23.11.1748 QGnr *Experiment* (24); 25.12.1749 Mate *Experiment* (24); 20.9.1751 Mid *Norwich* (50); 10.7.1752 Mate *Norwich* (50); 28.6.1753 Mate *Suffolk* (70); 23.7.1753 Mid *Captain* (64); 19.8.1753 Mate *Captain* (64); 30.7.1754 Mid *Sutherland* (50); 4.12.1754 Passed; **Lieutenant**; 31.12.1755-27.4.1757 3L *Assistance* (50).

NEWTON, HENRY

Dates: c.1798 Died; 17.4.1798 Will Probate.
Family:
Service: **Lieutenant**; 2.12.1758(JAM 9.10.1760) 2L *Harwich* (50); 9.2.1759(JAM 9.10.1760) 1L *Harwich* (50); 20.5.1760(JAM 9.10.1760)-30.9.1760[P] 6L *Marlborough* (80); 20.4.1761-17.9.1761 L. *Wolf* (8)

Sloop; 8.1.1762 L. *Carcass* (14) Bomb Vessel; 1.6.1762-26.3.1763[P] 2L *Lark* (32); 12.10.1770-17.12.1773[P] 1L *Lizard* (28); 11.9.1778-29.6.1782[P] LCmdr *Elizabeth and Mary* Hired Tender.

NEWTON, JOHN

Dates: c.1737 Born; 3.2.1803 Died.
Family:
Service: 1752-1756 Merchant Service; 1.2.1756 Able *Ipswich* (64); 24.4.1756 Mate *Ipswich* (64); 22.5.1757 Mid *Ipswich* (70) Hulk; 21.1.1758 Mid *Greyhound* (20); 7.2.1759 Passed; **Lieutenant**; 10.12.1760-24.11.1762 L. *Ferret* (14) Sloop; 7.1.1762-10.2.1762 Operations against Martinique; 6.6.1762-13.8.1762 Operations against Havana; 2.12.1763-1.12.1766 2L *Cornwall* (74); 1775-19.6.1775[D] L. *Kent* (74); 19.6.1775 Dismissed; 4.11.1776 3L *Terrible* (74); 5.3.1778-27.5.1779 2L *Terrible* (74); 27.7.1778 1st Battle of Ushant; 1779-12.1783 LCmdr *Neptune* Hired Tender.

NEWTON, ROBERT

Dates: c.1734 Born; c.1764 Died; 2.7.1764 Will Probate.
Family:
Service: 5.3.1756 Able *Squirrel* (20); 2.1.1757 Mid *Squirrel* (20); 2.6.1757 Mate *Squirrel* (20); 12.11.1757 Mid *Brilliant* (36); 25.4.1758 Mate *Brilliant* (36); 5.6.1758-12.6.1758 Raid on Saint-Malo; 3.7.1759 Bombardment of Le Havre; 5.12.1759 Passed; **Lieutenant**; 19.12.1759 3L *Norfolk* (74); 23.6.1760[(4.6.1763)] 3L *Grafton* (68); 27.11.1760[(4.6.1763)]-24.6.1764[P] 2L *Grafton* (68); 24.9.1762-6.10.1762 Battle of Manilla.

NEWTON, WILLIAM

Dates:
Family:
Service: **Lieutenant**; 4.3.1761 2L *Mars* (74); 29.3.1761-11.6.1761 Expedition against Belle-Isle; 25.8.1762 2L *Prince Frederick* (64); 6.9.1762-25.10.1763[P] 3L *Mars* (74).

NEWTON, WITHAM

Dates: c.1735 Born; 1776 Died; 16.1.1776 Will Probate.
Family:
Service: 28.11.1750 Mate *Lyme* (24); 8.3.1751-7.7.1752[P] Mate *Windsor* (60); 12.12.1756 Mate *Windsor* (60); 8.1757-10.1757 Louisbourg Expedition; 2.1.1758 Passed; **Lieutenant**; 13.1.1758-11.3.1761 L. *Alderney* (10) Sloop; 29.8.1765-13.8.1768 L. *Savage* (8) Sloop; 16.5.1769 2L *Burford* (68); 22.2.1770-29.5.1771[P] 2L *Defence* (74); 25.1.1772-18.12.1775 L. *Aldborough* (20).

NICHOLAS, JAMES

Dates: c.1729 Born.
Family:
Service: 26.12.1743 Mst Serv *Dolphin* (20); 12.6.1744 Mst Serv *Squirrel* (20); 29.7.1745 Mst Serv *York* (60); 5.3.1746/47 Ord. *York* (60); 30.6.1748-14.5.1750[P] Able *York* (60); 24.6.1751 Mid *Torrington* (44); 7.4.1753 Able *Torrington* (44); 6.4.1754 Mid *Torrington* (44); 14.7.1754 Able *Peregrine* (20) Sloop; 10.1.1755 Gnr Mate *Peregrine* (20) Sloop; 2.7.1755 Passed; **Lieutenant**; 25.6.1759[(BLI 19.10.1759)]-5.5.1762 3L *Rippon* (60); 29.3.1761-11.6.1761 Expedition against Belle-Isle; 4.11.1762-26.8.1763[P] 2L *Nightingale* (22); 9.6.1766-19.6.1769 LCmdr *Fly* (4) Cutter; 12.1786-9.1788 LCmdr *Sprightly* (10) Cutter.

NIGHTINGALE, GAMALIEL

Dates: c.1732 Born; 1791 Died.

Family:

Service: 4.10.1744 Scholar *Royal Naval Academy*; 4.12.1746 Vol-p-O *Rippon* (54); 8.2.1747/48-12.12.1749[P] Mid *Rippon* (54); 3.9.1750 Mid *Porcupine* (16) Sloop; 28.2.1751/52 Passed; **Lieutenant**; 8.7.1753(BLI 10.6.1755)-17.4.1754 L. *Hind* (24); 17.4.1754(JAM 10.6.1755) L. *Falcon* (10) Bomb Vessel; 19.1.1755(JAM 10.6.1755) L. *Wager* (24); 30.9.1755 5L *Prince George* (80); 14.5.1756-26.2.1757 4L *Prince George* (80); 26.2.1757 4L *Prince George* (80); 4.4.1757-5.5.1757 2L *Dublin* (74); **Commander**; 3.8.1757 *Badger* (10) Sloop; **Captain**; 18.10.1758-24.5.1761[P] *Vengeance* (28); 20.11.1759 Battle of Quiberon Bay; 6.7.1761-22.1.1763[P] *Flora* (32).

NIXON, ANDERSON

Dates: c.1729 Born; 7.1.1800 Died; 5.2.1800 Will Probate.

Family:

Service: 1752-1755 Merchant Service; 13.7.1755 Mid *Isis* (50); 10.11.1756-5.3.1759/60 Mate *Isis* (50); 3.7.1759 Bombardment of Le Havre; 5.3.1760 Passed; **Lieutenant**; 7.7.1762-4.2.1763[P] 5L *Torbay* (74).

NOBLE, GEORGE

Dates: c.1737 Baptised.

Family:

Service: 1754-1757 Merchant Service; 11.5.1757 Mid *Burford* (68); 5.9.1757-6.10.1757 Raid on Rochefort; 6.6.1758-27.7.1758 The Siege of Louisbourg; 6.12.1758 Mid *Vengeance* (28); 20.11.1759 Battle of Quiberon Bay; 12.11.1760 Passed; **Lieutenant**; 11.6.1761-20.1.1762 6L *Ocean* (90); 11.5.1763 3L *Prince of Orange* (60); 6.6.1763-16.3.1764 3L *Bellona* (74).

NOEL, THOMAS

Dates: c.1718 Born; 5.6.1756 Died.

Family:

Service: 15.11.1731 Vol-p-O *Pearl* (40); 6.11.1732 MidO *Ludlow Castle* (40); 21.4.1734 Mid *Falkland* (50); 20.2.1737/38 Mate *Falkland* (50); 25.9.1738 Mate *Pembroke* (60); 1.3.1738/39 Passed; **Lieutenant**; 27.2.1739/40-20.2.1740/41 L. *Deal Castle* (20); 18.4.1741 2L *Dartmouth* (50); 3.6.1743(21.2.1745/46) 2L *Warwick* (60); 23.1.1743/44 1L *Ruby* (44); 19.3.1743/44 1L *Medway* (60); 29.3.1744 1L *Princess Royal* (90); 1.6.1744 1L *Edinburgh* (64); **Commander**; 16.11.1744 *Furnace* (8) Bomb Vessel; **Captain**; 12.11.1745 *Greyhound* (20); 1.5.1746 Action of 1746-05-01; 9.7.1747-10.6.1749[P] *Severn* (50); 18.6.1755-6.6.1756 *Princess Louisa* (60); 20.5.1756 Battle of Minorca.

NORBURY, CONINGSBY

Dates: 1786 Died; 27.8.1793 Will Probate.

Family:

Service: **Lieutenant**; 10.4.1734(3.9.1734)-12.6.1734 L. *Deal Castle* (20); 4.2.1734/35 L. *Bridgewater* (32); 17.8.1736 L. *Sheerness* (20); 8.7.1738(26.12.1741) 1L *Falmouth* (50); 4.3.1740/41-5.1741 Operations against Cartagena; 2.10.1741 1L *Sutherland* (50); 20.2.1741/42 1L *Antelope* (50); **Commander**; 12.2.1742/43 *Furnace* (8) Bomb Vessel; **Captain**; 17.11.1744 *Gibraltar* (20); 19.9.1745-20.5.1749[P] *Looe* (44); 31.7.1755-6.1.1761 *Hampshire* (50); 18.10.1760 Action off Cuba.

NORBURY, RICHARD

Dates: c.1720 Born; 1800 Died.

Family:

Service: 26.1.1731/32 Able *Berwick* (70); 13.3.1731/32 Vol-p-O *Berwick* (70); 29.8.1732 Able *Berwick* (70); 16.2.1732/33 Vol-p-O *Berwick* (70); 11.4.1733-5.10.1734 Able *Berwick* (70); 6.10.1734 Vol-p-O *Berwick* (70); 20.12.1734-3.5.1737[P] Vol-p-O *Leopard* (50); 22.9.1739 MidO *Blandford* (20); 23.1.1739/40 Mid *Blandford* (20); 16.1.1740/41 Mid *Dover* (44); 16.5.1741 Mid *Royal George* (100); 7.10.1741 Mid *Victory* (100); c.30.11.1741 Passed; **Lieutenant**; 28.5.1742[(MED 7.11.1745)]-23.1.1742/43 4L *Elizabeth* (70); 4.4.1747-23.12.1747 4L *Devonshire* (66); 14.10.1747 2nd Battle of Cape Finisterre; 12.1.1747/48-15.11.1752[P] 3L *Invincible* (74); 19.4.1753 1L *Crown* (44); 21.8.1754-28.4.1755 1L *Norwich* (50); 24.11.1755 2L *Newark* (80); **Commander**; 10.1.1757-18.5.1758 *Fly* (8) Sloop; **Captain**; 4.6.1759-20.11.1759[S] *Resolution* (74); 20.11.1759 Battle of Quiberon Bay; 24.10.1760-22.1.1763[P] *Sandwich* (90); 29.3.1761-11.6.1761 Expedition against Belle-Isle.

NORBURY, THOMAS

Dates: None Known.

Family:

Service: **Lieutenant**; 27.12.1758-26.2.1760 3L *Hampshire* (50).

NORMAN, JAMES

Dates: c.1735 Born; 1806 Died.

Family:

Service: 20.6.1749 Able *Sphinx* (24); 7.7.1753 Mid *Sphinx* (24); 14.2.1755 Mid *Captain* (64); 3.5.1756 Passed; **Lieutenant**; 25.6.1756[(16.2.1757)] 3L *Deptford* (50); 6.4.1757 2L *Pembroke* (60); 6.6.1758-27.7.1758 The Siege of Louisbourg; 4.3.1760-27.12.1760[P] 1L *Saint George* (90); 17.4.1761 2L *Winchester* (50); 19.5.1761-31.7.1761 1L *Winchester* (50); 6.9.1763 2L *Bellona* (74); 13.6.1766-12.11.1766 1L *Bellona* (74); 18.5.1768-23.8.1769 1L *Arrogant* (74); 16.10.1770 LCmdr *Ferret* (6) Cutter; 21.9.1773 1L *Centaur* (74); 25.8.1774 1L *Barfleur* (90); 13.5.1776-29.10.1777[P] LCmdr *Effort* Hired Tender; **Commander**; 27.8.1779 *Spitfire* (8) Fireship; 16.8.1780 *Lynx* (10) Hospital Ship; 7.4.1783 *Ariel* (16) Sloop; 26.8.1788-4.12.1789 *Flirt* (14) Sloop; **Captain**; 21.9.1790-22.11.1790 *Boston* (32); 1.1.1793-12.1795 *Medusa* (50).

NORRIS, HARRY

Dates: 13.6.1764 Died; 7.8.1764 Will Probate.

Family: Father Sir John Norris, RN (1670-1749); Mother Mrs. Elizabeth Moore, née Aylmer; Brother Richard, RN; Brother Mathew, RN (1705-1738); Sister Lucy [Aylmer]; Brother John, MP (1702-67).

Service: **Lieutenant**; 17.12.1739[(14.4.1740)]-30.1.1739/40 3L *Romney* (50); **Captain**; 26.9.1740 *Russell* (80); 8.6.1741[(2.6.1744)]-14.10.1742 *Cumberland* (80); 14.3.1742/43 *Jersey* (60); 30.4.1744-15.4.1748 *Prince Frederick* (70); 3.5.1747 1st Battle of Cape Finisterre; 10.9.1748-6.12.1748[P] *Prince Frederick* (70); 1.12.1748-28.2.1748/49 *Somerset* (68); 30.1.1755-30.6.1756 *Yarmouth* (64); 4.6.1756 **Rear Admiral of the White**; 31.1.1758 **Rear Admiral of the Red**; 14.2.1759 **Vice Admiral of the White.**

NORRIS, JOHN

Dates: c.1728 Born.
Family:
Service: 30.4.1746 Able *Diamond* (44); 20.10.1746 Able *Dunkirk* (60); 1.6.1747 Mid *Dunkirk* (60); 25.3.1748-4.5.1748[P] Able *Dunkirk* (60); 13.12.1754 Mid *Torbay* (74); 6.6.1755-8.6.1755 Action of 6-8 June 1755; 10.7.1755 Able *Torbay* (74); 4.9.1755 Able *Falkland* (50); 24.10.1755 Clerk *Falkland* (50); 22.9.1756 Clerk *Princess Royal* (90); 13.2.1759 Mate *Princess Royal* (90); 14.5.1760 Passed; **Lieutenant**; 8.5.1761-9.8.1762 L. *Epreuve* (14) Sloop; 6.12.1763-20.6.1765 1L *Emerald* (32); 6.11.1775-10.5.1776 3L *Centaur* (74).

NORRIS, STEPHEN

Dates: c.1735 Born.
Family:
Service: 1752-1756 Merchant Service; 8.7.1756 Capt Serv *Raven* (14) Sloop; 9.9.1756 Mid *Barfleur* (80); 5.9.1757-6.10.1757 Raid on Rochefort; 5.6.1758-12.6.1758 Raid on Saint-Malo; 25.7.1760 Passed; **Lieutenant**; 22.10.1761-14.6.1766 L. *Beaver* (14) Sloop; 18.8.1766-14.9.1766[W] L. *Happy* (8) Sloop; 24.10.1766-26.10.1769 L. *Pomona* (18) Sloop; 28.1.1771 3L *Somerset* (68); 22.4.1773-24.2.1774 4L *Somerset* (68); 18.6.1776-5.9.1780[P] LCmdr *Greyhound* (4) Cutter; 1780-19.6.1780[P] LCmdr *Wells* (6) Cutter.

NORTH, ABRAHAM

Dates: c.1712 Born; 1781 Died.
Family:
Service: 23.1.1726/27 Vol-p-O *Chatham* (50); 27.2.1728/29 Able *Flamborough* (20); 1.1.1729/30 Mid *Flamborough* (24); 7.10.1732 Able *Kingston* (60); 6.6.1733 Able *Edinburgh* (70); 12.7.1734 Mid *Edinburgh* (70); 1.11.1734 Passed; **Lieutenant**; 24.2.1738/39[(16.6.1739)] 3L *Chatham* (50); 4.3.1739/40 2L *Chatham* (50); 12.3.1741/42-15.1.1747/48[P] 1L *Chatham* (50); 8.2.1747/48 MidE *Tilbury* (58); **Commander**; 6.5.1748[(28.4.1749)]-13.7.1748 *Speedwell* (10) Sloop; **Captain**; 16.1.1755 *Winchester* (50); 4.2.1755-16.12.1756 *Monarch* (74); 21.11.1780 **Superannuated Rear Admiral**.

NORTON, WILLIAM

Dates: c.1779 Died; 27.4.1779 Will Probate.
Family:
Service: **Lieutenant**; 7.4.1742[(9.12.1745)] L. *Guarland's Prize* Xebec; 24.9.1742[(MED 18.12.1745)] 3L *Guernsey* (50); 16.5.1743[(MED 18.12.1745)] 2L *Guernsey* (50); 11.2.1743/44-12.2.1743/44 Battle of Toulon; 24.5.1744[(MED 18.12.1745)]-3.8.1745 1L *Guernsey* (50); 17.9.1746-26.11.1748[P] 1L *Colchester* (50); 22.4.1755 2L *Prince* (90); 14.10.1755 1L *Prince* (90); **Commander**; 4.11.1755 *Cruizer* (8) Sloop; **Captain**; 15.11.1756-21.1.1757 *Amazon* (22); 21.1.1757-7.1760 *Amazon* (22); 16.1.1759-19.1.1759 Attack on Martinique; 20.1.1759-1.5.1759 Capture of Guadeloupe; 21.11.1760 *Assistance* (50); 17.11.1762-24.12.1762[P] *Guernsey* (50); 5.12.1763 *Africa* (64); 14.12.1763-29.4.1779 *William and Mary* (10) Yacht.

NORWOOD, JOSEPH

Dates: c.1725 Born; 1793 Died; 12.6.1793 Will Probate.
Family:
Service: 21.7.1740 Capt Serv *Experiment* (20); 4.3.1740/41-5.1741 Operations against Cartagena; 24.6.1741 Capt Serv *Rippon* (60); 23.11.1743 Mid *Rippon* (60); 5.8.1745 Mid

Saint George; 13.4.1746 Mid *Surprise* (24); 22.6.1746 Mate *Surprise* (24); 6.11.1746 Passed; **Lieutenant**; 21.1.1747/48(JAM 13.12.1748)-29.1.1747/48 3L *Milford* (44); 6.8.1748(JAM 13.12.1748)-19.1.1748/49[P] 2L *Milford* (44); 16.1.1753 3L *Cumberland* (66); 28.3.1754 3L *Eagle* (60); 31.7.1754 3L *Nottingham* (60); 11.3.1755 2L *Nottingham* (60); 16.7.1755 4L *Trident* (64); 31.12.1755 3L *Trident* (64); 16.4.1756(16.2.1757) 1L *Trident* (64); 20.5.1756 Battle of Minorca; 6.4.1757 1L *Richmond* (32); 30.8.1757-3.8.1758 1L *Diana* (32); 6.6.1758-27.7.1758 The Siege of Louisbourg; 9.1.1760 1L *Namur* (90); **Commander**; 21.11.1760-12.1762[P] *Lightning* (6) Hospital Ship; 11.4.1763 *Wasp* (8) Sloop; **Captain**; 7.6.1763 *Princess Louisa* (60); 23.5.1764(BLI 27.6.1766)-24.6.1766 *Actaeon* (28); 25.1.1766(BLI 19.8.1766)-7.8.1766[P] *Lowestoffe* (32).

NOTT, FRANCIS

Dates: c.1727 Born.

Family:

Service: 10.6.1756 Mid *Bristol* (50); 4.5.1758-20.6.1758 Able *Anson* (60); 21.6.1758 Able *Burford* (68); 29.6.1758 Mid *Prince Edward* (44); 29.12.1758 Capture of Goree; 11.9.1759-5.8.1761 Mid *Saint Florentine* (60); 5.8.1761 Passed; **Lieutenant**; 7.8.1761 6L *Blenheim* (90); 17.6.1762(9.8.1762)-18.1.1763[P] 5L *Neptune* (90); 27.6.1763-20.3.1765 L. *Fly* (8) Sloop; 3.2.1777-24.6.1777 4L *Royal Oak* (74); 28.12.1778-17.4.1782 LCmdr *Security*.

NOTT, JOHN NEALE PLEYDELL

Dates: c.1732 Born; 30.4.1781 Died.

Family: Son George; Son John, RN.

Service: 7.8.1746 Scholar *Royal Naval Academy*; 1.11.1749 Vol-p-O *Sphinx* (24); 16.10.1750 Ord. *Sphinx* (24); 17.11.1750 Mid *Sphinx* (24); 6.5.1752 MidO *Sphinx* (24); 8.10.1752 Mid *Sphinx* (24); 14.11.1753 Passed; **Lieutenant**; 3.7.1756(21.3.1757)-1.3.1757[P] 4L *Ipswich* (64); 20.5.1757 3L *Buckingham* (68); 14.7.1758(BLI 30.7.1760) 4L *Cambridge* (80); 21.12.1758(BLI 30.7.1760) 3L *Cambridge* (80); 16.1.1759-19.1.1759 Attack on Martinique; 31.1.1759(BLI 30.7.1760) 2L *Cambridge* (80); 12.5.1759(BLI 30.7.1760) 1L *Cambridge* (80); 6.7.1759(BLI 30.7.1760) 1L *Lancaster* (66); 1.8.1759(30.7.1760) 1L *Berwick* (64); **Commander**; 7.9.1759(BLI 17.1.1761) *Barbadoes* (14) Sloop; 15.7.1760(17.5.1762) *Antigua* (14) Sloop; **Captain**; 24.9.1761(27.6.1764)-14.5.1764[P] *Rose* (20); 7.1.1762-10.2.1762 Operations against Martinique; 6.6.1762-13.8.1762 Operations against Havana; 9.6.1778-25.1.1779 *Exeter* (64); 27.7.1778 1st Battle of Ushant; 12.4.1779-30.4.1781[†] *Centaur* (74); 31.12.1779 Affair of Fielding and Bylandt; 29.4.1781-30.4.1781 Battle of Fort Royal.

NOURSE, ROBERT

Dates: c.1733 Born.

Family:

Service: 8.4.1747 Land. *Kent* (64); 3.5.1747 1st Battle of Cape Finisterre; 14.10.1747 2nd Battle of Cape Finisterre; 30.10.1748-28.8.1749 Able *Kent* (64); 29.8.1749 Able *Albany* (14) Sloop; 21.4.1751 Mid *Albany* (14) Sloop; 10.8.1753 Mid *Saltash* (14) Sloop; 5.2.1755 Passed; **Lieutenant**; 23.6.1755(NA 6.5.1756) 6L *Terrible* (74); 8.1757-10.1757 Louisbourg Expedition; 6.6.1758-27.7.1758 The Siege of Louisbourg; 19.2.1759-20.8.1759 4L *Newark* (80); 18.8.1759-19.8.1759 Battle of Lagos Bay; 3.4.1760-26.8.1763[P] 2L *Newark* (80); 2.4.1766 1L *Launceston* (44); 6.5.1766 2L *Launceston* (44); 3.11.1766-6.11.1769[P] 1L *Launceston* (44); 12.5.1778-28.11.1778 1L *Suffolk* (74).

NUCELLA, TIMOTHY

Dates: c.1713 Born; 4.4.1756 Died.
Family:
Service: 10.2.1727/28 Mid *Advice* (54); 22.6.1729 Mid *Orford* (70); 30.5.1730 Mid *Winchester* (50); 9.8.1731 Mid *Spence* (8) Sloop; 10.12.1732 Able *Rye* (20); 28.4.1733 Able *Buckingham* (70); 11.6.1733 Mid *Saltash* (8) Sloop; 1.12.1733 Mid *Cornwall* (80); 23.3.1733/34 Passed; **Lieutenant**; 15.7.1740 L. *Port Mahon* (20); 30.7.1741[(20.12.1744)] 2L *Warwick* (60); 28.9.1742[(20.12.1744)] L. *Firedrake* (8) Bomb Vessel; 5.11.1743[(20.12.1744)] 2L *Diamond* (44); 22.1.1743/44[(20.12.1744)] 4L *Marlborough* (90); 3.2.1743/44[(20.12.1744)] 2L *Marlborough* (90); 11.2.1743/44-12.2.1743/44 Battle of Toulon; 6.3.1743/44[(20.12.1744)] 1L *Marlborough* (90); **Commander**; 17.12.1744-10.1.1744/45 *Wolf* (14) Sloop; **Captain**; 12.4.1745-3.7.1746 *Chichester* (80); 22.7.1746-16.1.1749/50 *York* (60); 29.7.1752-4.4.1756[†] *Hind* (24).

NUNN, JOSEPH

Dates: c.1734 Born; c.1813 Died; 3.12.1813 Will Probate.
Family:
Service: 1753-1757 Merchant Service; 16.3.1756/57 QM Mate *Duke* (90); 8.2.1758 Mid *Duke* (90); 5.6.1758-12.6.1758 Raid on Saint-Malo; 1.3.1758/59 Mid *Defiance* (60); 19.7.1759 Mid *Duke* (90); 12.11.1759-3.9.1760 Mid *Barfleur* (80); 3.9.1760 Passed; **Lieutenant**; 23.12.1760 2L *Juno* (32); 3.6.1763-4.4.1766[P] 1L *Juno* (32); 8.4.1771-19.9.1771 2L *Active* (28); 19.4.1774-15.2.1775[W] LCmdr *Halifax* (6) Schooner; 15.8.1775 LCmdr *Magdalen* (6) Schooner; **Commander**; 12.6.1776-5.9.1776 *Beaver* (14) Sloop; 18.7.1777-1.4.1779 *Hound* (14) Sloop; 25.10.1809 **Captain**.

NUTALL, JOHN

Dates: 1757 Died; 23.5.1757 Will Probate.
Family:
Service: **Lieutenant**; 13.11.1746-18.8.1747 3L *Falkland* (50); 3.5.1747 1st Battle of Cape Finisterre.

NUTT, JUSTINIAN

Dates: c.1704 Born; 11.12.1757 Died.
Family: Wife Elizabeth Cooke (1726-?) married 8.8.1749; Son George Anson (1750-c.1793); Son Justinian Saunders Bentley (1754-1811).
Service: 4.12.1728 L. Serv *Bideford* (20); 3.8.1731-17.11.1734 Able *Bideford* (20); 18.11.1734-18.3.1735/36[F] Cpl *Bideford* (20); 12.7.1738 Mate *York* (60); 9.6.1740 Master *Centurion* (60); **Lieutenant**; 21.6.1743 1L *Centurion's Prize* Unknown; 17.11.1743 3L *Centurion* (60); 31.8.1744 Passed; 18.1.1744/45 1L *Prince George* (90); **Commander**; 27.2.1744/45 *Tavistock* (10) Sloop; **Captain**; 12.8.1745 *Grand Turk* (22); 2.7.1746 *Prince Edward* (44); 7.3.1746/47-11.7.1747 *Edinburgh* (64); 19.8.1747 *Tavistock* (50); 23.9.1748-17.11.1752[P] *Anson* (60).

Service Records O

O'BRIEN, CHRISTOPHER
Dates: c.1724 Born; 1771 Died.
Family:
Service: 1.2.1733/34 Able *Rupert* (60); 19.5.1734-3.11.1735[P] Mid *Rupert* (60); 14.7.1739 Able *Dorsetshire* (80); 6.10.1739 Able *Windsor* (60); 26.6.1740 Mid *Princess Louisa* (60); 21.11.1740 Mid *Rupert* (60); 30.8.1741 Mid *Norfolk* (80); 13.10.1741 Mid *Rupert* (60); 25.4.1742-18.10.1743[P] Mid *Panther* (54); 17.11.1743 Passed; **Lieutenant**; 2.7.1746 L. *Blandford* (20); 21.11.1747-5.12.1748[P] 2L *Intrepid* (64); 5.8.1752-14.11.1752[P] 3L *Tiger* (60); 28.9.1756 3L *Berwick* (64); 17.11.1756 1L *Chichester* (68); 15.5.1758-21.9.1759 2L *Warspite* (74); 18.8.1759-19.8.1759 Battle of Lagos Bay; **Commander**; 10.1.1771-19.1.1771 *Tamar* (16) Sloop.

O'BRIEN, LUCIUS
Dates: 13.7.1771 Died.
Family:
Service: **Lieutenant**; 14.2.1737/38-14.3.1737/38 L. *Garland* (20); 1739 In the service of Russia; 29.8.1740-2.10.1740 2L *Grafton* (70); 3.10.1740 2L *Shrewsbury* (80); 31.10.1740[(16.2.1741/42)] 1L *Shrewsbury* (80); **Commander**; 31.3.1744 *Portsmouth* (24) Storeship; **Captain**; 3.12.1745 *Sheerness* (24); 12.5.1746 *Ambuscade* (40); 11.8.1746-26.11.1748[P] *Colchester* (50); 26.7.1749-7.10.1755 *Peggy* (8) Sloop; 23.9.1755 *Colchester* (50); 17.5.1756 Action of 17th May 1756; 4.6.1759-20.11.1759[S] *Essex* (64); 20.11.1759 Battle of Quiberon Bay; 22.2.1760 *Temple* (68); 7.1.1762-10.2.1762 Operations against Martinique; 14.5.1762[(BLI 18.2.1763)] *Stag* (32); 1.7.1762[(BLI 18.2.1763)]-29.11.1762[P] *Woolwich* (44); 6.5.1763 *Essex* (64); 26.12.1763-20.6.1765 *Juno* (32); 3.3.1767 *Gibraltar* (20); 13.8.1767-27.6.1770 *Solebay* (28) Frigate; 24.10.1770 **Rear Admiral of the White.**

O'BRIEN, LUCIUS
Dates: 1780 Died.
Family:
Service: 11.8.1756-c.1759 Scholar *Royal Naval Academy*; **Lieutenant**; 19.9.1761[(11.5.1763)]-8.1.1762[P] 4L *Raisonnable* (64); 17.10.1766-29.10.1767 L. *Hound* (14) Sloop; 24.11.1775-18.1.1776 2L *Emerald* (32).

O'BRYEN, JOHN
Dates: 1789 Died.
Family:
Service: **Lieutenant**; 27.9.1747[(MED 28.10.1748)] 3L *Superb* (60); 9.1.1747/48[(31.10.1748)]-25.11.1748[P] 4L *Burford* (70); 1.12.1748 3L *Culloden* (74); 23.6.1749-16.5.1750 L. *Mermaid* (24); 14.3.1750/51-19.8.1753 3L *Glory* (44); 31.1.1754-4.12.1754 3L *Salisbury* (50); 18.9.1758-29.2.1760 3L *Falkland* (50); 20.11.1759 Battle of Quiberon Bay; 29.9.1762-7.2.1763[P] 1L *Romney* (50).

O'HARA, FRANCIS

Dates: c.1736 Born; 14.6.1769 Died Arguin.
Family:
Service: 2.6.1749-19.8.1752 Scholar *Royal Naval Academy*; 20.8.1752 Vol-p-O *Deptford* (50); 26.2.1754 MidO *Deptford* (50); 19.10.1755 MidO *Lancaster* (66); 5.2.1756 Mid *Prince George* (90); 3.3.1756 Passed; **Lieutenant**; 25.5.1756 6L *Marlborough* (80); 16.6.1756 5L *Marlborough* (80); 21.6.1756 4L *Marlborough* (80); 5.7.1756 4L *Terrible* (74); 20.1.1757 3L *Rochester* (50); 15.2.1758-29.8.1759 1L *Lowestoffe* (28); 5.6.1758-12.6.1758 Raid on Saint-Malo; **Commander**; 28.12.1763 *Ferret* (14) Sloop; **Captain**; 20.6.1765-13.5.1766 *Sheerness* (24); 10.1.1769-14.6.1769[†] *Merlin* (18) Sloop.

O'HARA, JAMES

Dates: 1790 Died.
Family:
Service: **Lieutenant**; 12.4.1748-20.5.1752[P] L. *Grampus* (14) Sloop; 16.5.1753-12.6.1754 L. *Otter* (14) Sloop; 28.8.1754 L. *Dolphin* (6) Fireship; **Commander**; 2.6.1756-29.11.1756 *Polacca* (12) Sloop; 5.5.1757-27.9.1758 *Pelican* (16) Sloop; 30.8.1759-31.12.1761 *George* (30) Hired Armed vessel; 6.6.1763 *Peggy* (8) Sloop; **Captain**; 20.6.1765 *Nightingale* (22); 30.7.1765-18.8.1766 *Peggy* (8) Sloop; 30.8.1769-14.11.1770 *Peggy* (8) Sloop; 18.5.1771-29.3.1774 *Alderney* (10) Sloop; 8.11.1775-2.1.1776 *Pearl* (32).

O'HARA, PATRICK

Dates: c.1710 Born; 18.9.1774 Died London; 31.10.1774 Will Probate.
Family:
Service: **Lieutenant**; 16.5.1727-4.7.1728 3L *Lark* (40); 5.7.1728[(11.10.1728)]-24.10.1728[P] 4L *Berwick* (70); 6.3.1732/33-12.3.1732/33 2L *Romney* (50); 13.3.1733/34-14.3.1737/38 1L *Romney* (50); 15.3.1737/38 2L *Lancaster* (80); 16.7.1739-18.12.1739 1L *Argyll* (50); 19.12.1739-3.3.1739/40 2L *Cumberland* (80); 4.3.1739/40-11.4.1742 1L *Torbay* (80); 23.11.1742 1L *Princess Royal* (90); **Commander**; 10.10.1743-15.1.1743/44 *Scipio* (8) Fireship; **Captain**; 16.11.1744-8.2.1747/48[P] *Gosport* (44); 6.12.1762 **Superannuated Rear Admiral**.

O'HARA, PETER

Dates: 6.1762 Died.
Family: Wife Elizabeth.
Service: 2.6.1749-c.1752 Scholar *Royal Naval Academy*; **Lieutenant**; 27.11.1756 4L *Revenge* (64); 28.2.1758 Battle of Cartagena; 2.4.1759-2.11.1759 3L *Revenge* (64).

OAKLEY, JOHN

Dates: c.1733 Born; 4.6.1790 Died.
Family:
Service: 20.2.1746/47 Clerk *Saltash* (10) Sloop; 7.9.1747 Capt Serv *Lys* (24); 3.11.1748 Capt Serv *Kingfisher* (14) Sloop; 28.1.1748/49 Able *Surprise* (24); 14.5.1749-4.6.1755 Mid *Triton* (20); 4.6.1755 Passed; **Lieutenant**; 13.11.1756 L. *Alderney* (10) Sloop; 2.1.1758 2L *Jason* (30); 5.6.1758-12.6.1758 Raid on Saint-Malo; 28.1.1762-10.11.1762[P] 4L *Saint George* Prison Ship.

OAKLEY, THOMAS

Dates: 1769 Died.
Family:
Service: 6.7.1719 Capt Serv *Dorsetshire* (80); 20.3.1720/21-7.12.1721[W] Trump *Hind* (24); 11.2.1721/22 Able *Panther* (54); 1.9.1724 MidO *Colchester* (50); 2.5.1726 Mid *Lennox* (70); 20.8.1726-21.6.1729 Mate *Lennox* (70); 8.8.1729 Passed; **Lieutenant**; 4.4.1741 6L *Barfleur* (90); 29.5.1741 5L *Barfleur* (90); 5.10.1742[(18.1.1742/43)]-10.11.1743 3L *Plymouth* (60); 8.1.1745/46-5.2.1745/46 L. *Dispatch* (10) Sloop.

OAKLEY, WILLIAM

Dates: c.1740 Born; 1811 Died; 7.3.1811 Will Probate.
Family:
Service: 23.11.1755 MidE *Oxford* (50); 14.2.1756 Adm Ret *Newark* (80); 8.5.1756 Able *Royal Sovereign* (104); 28.7.1756 Mid *Royal Sovereign* (104); 6.9.1757-25.5.1758 Mid *Dover* (44); 26.5.1758 NR *Savage* (8) Sloop; 27.6.1758 NR *Norfolk* (6) Mer; 19.8.1758 NR *Falmouth* (50); 4.9.1758 NR *Revenge* (28); 18.2.1759-13.3.1759 Able *Falkland* (50); 14.3.1759 Mid *Falkland* (50); 20.11.1759 Battle of Quiberon Bay; 20.2.1760 Passed; **Lieutenant**; 13.8.1761-10.10.1761[F] L. *Pheasant* (14) Sloop; 22.10.1761-23.12.1762 2L *Liverpool* (28); 25.10.1809 **Captain.**

OCHTERLONY, ALEXANDER

Dates: c.1760 Died; 21.4.1760 Will Probate.
Family:
Service: **Lieutenant**; 15.10.1757[(16.11.1758)] L. *Hawke* (8) Sloop; 6.6.1758-27.7.1758 The Siege of Louisbourg; 2.8.1758-23.12.1760 2L *Juno* (32); 3.7.1759 Bombardment of Le Havre.

OGILVIE, GEORGE

Dates: 1808 Died.
Family:
Service: **Lieutenant**; 23.5.1745[(BLI 25.5.1747)]-30.11.1746[P] L. *Bien Aime* (18) Armed Storeship; 2.9.1747-12.4.1748 L. *Fly* (8) Sloop.

OGLE, SIR CHALONER

Dates: 1738 Born; 12.3.1816 Knight Bachelor; 27.8.1816 Died.
Family: Father Nathaniel Ogle; Wife Hester Thomas; Son Sir Charles, RN (1775-1858).
Service: 19.11.1740 Able *Cumberland* (80); 11.6.1742 Mid *Defiance* (60); 13.11.1743 Mid *Kent* (70); 10.7.1744 Mid *Falmouth* (50); 3.1.1744/45 Passed; **Lieutenant**; 19.11.1745[(30.10.1746)]-24.10.1746[P] 2L *Falmouth* (50); 18.6.1747-29.5.1752[P] 2L *Ruby* (50); 12.4.1755-8.5.1755 2L *Prince Frederick* (64); 8.5.1755 3L *Prince Frederick* (64); **Commander**; 17.6.1755-30.6.1756 *Swan* (14) Sloop; **Captain**; 30.6.1756 *Yarmouth* (64); 20.8.1756-17.8.1757 *Chesterfield* (44); 22.5.1758-24.12.1761 *Aquilon* (28); 29.3.1761-11.6.1761 Expedition against Belle-Isle; 20.10.1770-29.5.1771[P] *Elizabeth* (74); 15.7.1775-17.1.1780 *Resolution* (74); 16.1.1780 Battle of Cape St. Vincent; 17.1.1780 Commodore *Resolution* (74); 17.4.1780 Battle of Martinique; 26.9.1780 **Rear Admiral of the Blue**; 24.9.1787 **Vice Admiral of the Blue**; 1.2.1793 **Vice Admiral of the Red**; 12.4.1794 **Admiral of the Blue**; 14.2.1799 **Admiral of the White**; 9.11.1805 **Admiral of the Red.**

OGLE, CHALONER

Dates: 1814 Died.
Family:
Service: **Lieutenant**; 31.1.1747/48[JAM 18.11.1748] 4L *Elizabeth* (70); 9.4.1748 Battle of Santiago de Cuba; 1.8.1748[JAM 18.11.1748]-23.3.1748/49[P] 3L *Norwich* (50); 12.5.1749-31.5.1750 L. *Blandford* (20); 30.12.1757 5L *Torbay* (74); 25.5.1758 6L *Ramillies* (90); 5.6.1758-12.6.1758 Raid on Saint-Malo; 11.10.1758 5L *Ramillies* (90); 14.5.1759 4L *Ramillies* (90); 18.10.1759 3L *Ramillies* (90); **Commander**; 27.12.1759-29.3.1762 *Strombolo* (14) Fireship; **Captain**; 29.3.1762[22.4.1763] *Dover* (44); 29.6.1762[EI 18.8.1763] *Temple* (68); 10.9.1762[EI 18.8.1763]-15.7.1763[P] *Nottingham* (60).

OKES, JOHN

Dates: None Known.
Family:
Service: **Lieutenant**; 7.2.1760 2L *Liverpool* (28); 22.10.1761-2.11.1764[P] 1L *Liverpool* (28); 1805 **Superannuated Lieutenant.**

OMMANNEY, CORNTHWAITE

Dates: 1736 Born Portsea; 15.8.1736 Baptised St. Mary's Church, Portsea; 26.3.1801 Died.
Family:
Service: 1751-1755 Merchant Service; 21.8.1755 Mid *Defiance* (60); 1.1.1756-14.5.1756 Mid *Monarch* (74); 15.5.1756 Mid *Magnanime* (74); 6.6.1757 Passed; 22.5.1758 L. *Otter* (14) Sloop; 22.8.1758 **Lieutenant**; 27.6.1760 6L *Royal George* (100); 17.11.1760 4L *Royal George* (100); 27.7.1761 2L *Royal George* (100); 19.5.1762 1L *Royal George* (100); 11.5.1763 2L *Essex* (64); **Commander**; 20.6.1765 *Alderney* (10) Sloop; 8.2.1766-15.12.1767[P] *Zephyr* (10) Sloop; 4.2.1768-24.11.1769 *Otter* (14) Sloop; **Captain**; 22.2.1772-16.12.1774[P] *Panther* (60); 16.1.1776-29.10.1778 *Tartar* (28); 28.4.1794 **Superannuated Rear Admiral.**

OMMANNEY, JOHN

Dates: c.1733 Born; c.1760 Died; 14.4.1760 Will Probate.
Family:
Service: 20.2.1747/48-14.12.1748 Able *Norwich* (50); 15.12.1748-19.1.1748/49[P] Able *Milford* (44); 30.8.1749 Able *Norwich* (50); 14.11.1749 Clerk *Norwich* (50); 14.2.1749/50 Scholar *Royal Naval Academy*; 23.10.1751 Able *Lyme* (24); 9.1.1751/52 Mid *Lyme* (24); 12.12.1753 Mid *Monarch* (74); 19.2.1754-25.5.1754 ActL *Baltimore* (14) Sloop; 26.5.1754 Able *Shoreham* (24); 30.1.1755 ActL *Jamaica* (10) Sloop; 23.6.1755 Act3L *Norwich* (50); 10.3.1757 Passed; **Lieutenant**; 11.3.1757 3L *Norwich* (50); 1.4.1757 3L *Achilles* (60); 5.9.1757-6.10.1757 Raid on Rochefort; 3.7.1759 Bombardment of Le Havre; 7.3.1760-25.3.1760 2L *Achilles* (60).

ONSLOW, RICHARD GCB, (1ST BARONET OF ALTHAIN)

Dates: 23.6.1741 Born; 1797 1st Baronet of Althain; 2.1.1815 Order of the Bath; 27.12.1817 Died.
Family: Father Lieutenant-General Richard Onslow (c.1697–1760); Mother Pooley Walton; Wife Anne Michell, daughter of Commodore Matthew Michell married 1773.
Service: **Lieutenant**; 17.12.1758[EI 14.11.1760] 4L *Sunderland* (60); 3.3.1759[EI 14.11.1760] 5L *Grafton* (68); 10.9.1759 Battle of Pondicherry; 17.3.1760[EI 14.11.1760]-19.12.1760[P] 4L *Yarmouth* (64); **Commander**; 11.2.1761 *Martin* (14) Sloop; **Captain**; 14.4.1762-16.9.1762[W] *Humber* (44); 29.11.1762-22.5.1763[P] *Phoenix* (44); 18.1.1766-13.7.1769[P] *Aquilon* (28); 12.10.1770-18.1.1773 *Diana* (32); 18.1.1773[21.4.1773]-21.4.1773[P] *Achilles* (60); 31.10.1776 *Saint Albans* (64);

14.12.1778-15.12.1778 Battle of St. Lucia; 21.2.1780-7.6.1783[P] *Bellona* (74); 20.10.1782 Battle of Cape Spartel; 23.10.1787 *Triumph* (74); 31.3.1789-5.9.1791[P] *Magnificent* (74); 1.2.1793 **Rear Admiral of the White**; 12.4.1794 **Rear Admiral of the Red**; 4.7.1794 **Vice Admiral of the White**; 1.6.1795 **Vice Admiral of the Red**; 1796-1799 CinC — Plymouth; 7.1797-8.1797 *Nassau* (64); 9.1797-1798 *Monarch* (74); 11.10.1797 Battle of Camperdown; 14.2.1799 **Admiral of the Blue**; 23.4.1804 **Admiral of the White**; 9.11.1805 **Admiral of the Red**.

OPIE, JOHN
Dates: 1758 Died.
Family:
Service: 28.11.1703 Vol-p-O *Bedford* (70); 13.8.1704 Battle of Malaga; 11.10.1705 Mid *Bedford* (70); 12.1.1707/8 Passed; **Lieutenant**; 21.2.1708/9[(12.12.1709)] L. *Drake* (14) Sloop; 1.5.1711-20.11.1714 2L *Moor* (54); 14.12.1714-23.12.1714[P] 2L *Canterbury* (60); 4.3.1714/15-13.6.1718 2L *Centurion* (54); 25.1.1725/26 2L *Swallow* (50); 28.4.1727[(26.4.1728)]-13.5.1728[P] 1L *Swallow* (50); 23.2.1733/34 2L *Montagu* (60); 10.6.1735-12.2.1735/36[P] 1L *Montagu* (60); 1739 In the service of Russia; 30.8.1739-13.9.1739 1L *Rippon* (60); **Commander**; 25.6.1741-25.6.1743 *Sutherland* (54).

ORCHARD, FRANCIS
Dates: c.1720 Born; c.1763 Died; 1.10.1763 Will Probate.
Family:
Service: 5.4.1747 Able *Norfolk* (80); 1.7.1747 Able *Launceston* (44); 4.7.1749 Mid *Launceston* (44); 21.5.1750 Able *Superb* (60); 11.6.1750 Mid *Superb* (60); 24.8.1750 Able *Superb* (60); 5.9.1750 Mate *Superb* (60); 1.12.1750 Master *Mermaid* (24); 2.3.1751/52 Master *Chester* (50); 31.8.1755 Master *Antelope* (54); 7.1.1756 Passed; **Lieutenant**; 11.11.1756 6L *Invincible* (74); 15.11.1756-24.12.1756 5L *Invincible* (74); 28.12.1756 3L *Weymouth* (60); 12.1.1757-29.1.1759 L. *Spy* (10) Sloop; 16.1.1759-19.1.1759 Attack on Martinique; 25.6.1759[(19.10.1759)]-31.7.1762 2L *Rippon* (60); 29.3.1761-11.6.1761 Expedition against Belle-Isle.

ORD, CHRISTOPHER
Dates: 1785 Died.
Family:
Service: **Lieutenant**; 14.7.1758-21.12.1758 L. *Barbadoes* (14) Sloop; 21.12.1758[(2.9.1760)] 4L *Buckingham* (68); 16.1.1759-19.1.1759 Attack on Martinique; 20.1.1759-1.5.1759 Capture of Guadeloupe; 23.8.1759[(2.9.1760)] 3L *Buckingham* (68); 29.1.1761[(2.9.1760)]-2.3.1763[P] 1L *Buckingham* (68); 29.3.1761-11.6.1761 Expedition against Belle-Isle; 10.6.1766-30.11.1768 LCmdr *Winchelsea* (4) Cutter.

ORDE, JOHN
Dates: c.1739 Born; 1819 Died.
Family:
Service: 1753-1755 Merchant Service; 15.5.1755-7.1.1757 Able *Yarmouth* (64); 8.1.1757 Mid *Invincible* (74); 16.5.1757 Mid *Barfleur* (80); 5.9.1757-6.10.1757 Raid on Rochefort; 5.6.1758-12.6.1758 Raid on Saint-Malo; 26.1.1759 Mid *Royal Anne* (100); 7.3.1759 Passed; **Lieutenant**; 23.8.1759 L. *Proserpine* (8) Fireship; 20.11.1759 Battle of Quiberon Bay; 2.4.1760-1.2.1762[D] 1L *Stag* (32); 1.2.1762 Dismissed; 20.3.1762[(18.8.1763)]-15.7.1763[P] 2L *Nottingham* (60); 6.6.1762-13.8.1762 Operations against Havana; 24.1.1805 **Superannuated Commander**.

ORME, JOHN

Dates: 1686 Born; 23.8.1764 Died.
Family: Brother Humphrey, RN (d.1751).
Service: 24.5.1702 YoS *Crown* (50); 22.2.1702/3 Vol-p-O *Worcester* (54); 10.10.1704 Mid *Worcester* (54); 1.1705 Worcester vs Jason; 6.6.1705 Mid *Dorsetshire* (80); 27.1.1706/7 Passed; **Lieutenant**; 5.3.1711/12-25.6.1716 L. *Bideford* (24); 17.3.1717/18-14.2.1718/19[W] 3L *Burford* (70); 11.8.1718 Battle of Cape Passaro; 5.7.1720-4.12.1721 3L *Essex* (70); **Commander**; 12.8.1745 *Tavistock* (10) Sloop; **Captain**; 20.8.1745 *Royal Sovereign* (104); 13.10.1747-7.6.1748[P] *Barfleur* (90).

ORROK, JAMES

Dates: c.1721 Born; c.1763 Died; 23.11.1784 Will Probate.
Family:
Service: 6.4.1736 Capt Serv *Terrible* (6) Bomb Vessel; 27.5.1737 Able *Terrible* (6) Bomb Vessel; 18.12.1738 Able *Falkland* (50); 7.2.1739/40-18.11.1741[P] Mid *Falkland* (50); 18.3.1741/42 Able *Neptune* (90); 13.9.1743 Mid *Neptune* (90); 11.2.1743/44-12.2.1743/44 Battle of Toulon; 5.6.1745 Passed; **Lieutenant**; 19.6.1745 6L *Duke* (90); 29.11.1745 5L *Duke* (90); 29.4.1746-7.4.1748 2L *Looe* (44); 18.6.1757 1L *Intrepid* (60); 5.9.1757-6.10.1757 Raid on Rochefort; **Commander**; 19.10.1757-14.8.1758[W] *Portsmouth* (6) Storeship; 9.3.1758-24.5.1758 Capture of Fort Louis; 15.9.1758-28.2.1763[P] *Firedrake* (10) Bomb Vessel; 29.12.1758 Capture of Goree; 3.7.1759 Bombardment of Le Havre; 29.3.1761-11.6.1761 Expedition against Belle-Isle; 26.10.1769-28.10.1772 *Hazard* (8) Sloop; 21.1.1775-13.9.1775[P] *Racehorse* (16) Sloop; 24.11.1775 *Hazard* (8) Sloop; 20.11.1777 *Leith* (20) Hired Armed Ship; **Captain**; 5.5.1779-29.7.1782[P] *Conquestador* (60); 24.7.1782-22.5.1783[P] *Prince Edward* (60).

ORSBRIDGE, PHILIP

Dates: c.1720 Born; 5.8.1766 Died.
Family:
Service: 7.8.1739 Ord. *Prince of Orange* (70); 3.1.1739/40 Able *Namur* (90); 20.9.1740 Cox *Victory* (100); 16.5.1742 Able *Victory* (100); 3.10.1742 Able *Torbay* (80); 21.2.1742/43 Mid *Torbay* (80); 11.2.1743/44-12.2.1743/44 Battle of Toulon; 26.8.1744 Mid *Barfleur* (90); 11.7.1745 Passed; **Lieutenant**; 13.1.1758 L. *Swan* (14) Sloop; 9.3.1758-24.5.1758 Capture of Fort Louis; 25.10.1758 1L *Stag* (32); 19.2.1759 1L *Torrington* (44); 16.7.1759-5.10.1761 1L *Torrington* (44); 10.12.1761-14.3.1763 3L *Orford* (68); 6.6.1762-13.8.1762 Operations against Havana; 1.1766-5.8.1766 LCmdr *Pitt* (6) Cutter.

OSBORN, WILLIAM

Dates: c.1737 Born; 1781 Died.
Family:
Service: 24.12.1751 L. Serv *Seahorse* (24); 30.6.1753 Able *Crown* (44); 14.11.1754 Able *Norwich* (50); 25.12.1755 Mid *Norwich* (50); 7.7.1757 Mid *Achilles* (60); 5.9.1757-6.10.1757 Raid on Rochefort; 27.11.1757 Able *Ramillies* (90); 14.12.1757-7.3.1758/59 Mid *Ramillies* (90); 5.6.1758-12.6.1758 Raid on Saint-Malo; 7.3.1759 Passed; 10.10.1759 **Lieutenant**; 7.3.1760-15.12.1762[P] 4L *Dragon* (74); 29.3.1761-11.6.1761 Expedition against Belle-Isle; 7.1.1762-10.2.1762 Operations against Martinique; 24.2.1762-25.2.1762 Capture of Saint Lucia; 6.6.1762-13.8.1762 Operations against Havana; 20.8.1763 2L *Solebay* (28) Frigate; 13.10.1770-14.10.1773 1L *Thames* (32); 11.5.1775 L. *Raven* (14) Sloop; 3.8.1780-7.1782 LCmdr *Nabob* (26) Convalescent Ship.

OSBORNE, CHARLES

Dates: c.1731 Born; 14.10.1797 Died; 5.1.1798 Will Probate.
Family:
Service: 29.5.1747 Mid *Prince George* (90); 1748-1755 HEIC Service; 29.7.1755 Mid *Monarch* (74); 24.6.1756 Mid *Dublin* (74); 5.9.1757-6.10.1757 Raid on Rochefort; 17.4.1758 Mid *Thames* (32); 22.1.1759 Mate *Thames* (32); 19.3.1760 Passed; **Lieutenant**; 23.3.1761-26.2.1763[P] 3L *Dover* (44); 7.1.1762-10.2.1762 Operations against Martinique; 24.2.1762-25.2.1762 Capture of Saint Lucia; 6.6.1762-13.8.1762 Operations against Havana; 6.4.1763-4.1766 LCmdr *Duke William* (4) Cutter; 17.3.1777 2L *Conqueror* (74); 16.12.1777-22.8.1780 1L *Conqueror* (74); 6.7.1779 Battle of Grenada; 18.12.1779 Combat de la Martinique; 17.4.1780 Battle of Martinique; 15.5.1780 Action of March 15 1780; 19.5.1780 Action of March 19 1780; 1781-1782 LCmdr *Florida* (12) Schooner.

OSBORNE, FRANCIS

Dates: c.1714 Born; c.1758 Died; 5.5.1758 Will Probate.
Family:
Service: 6.11.1734 Mid *Monmouth* (70); 7.8.1736 Mid *Falkland* (50); 13.11.1736 Mate *Falkland* (50); 21.11.1738 Mate *Pembroke* (60); 12.5.1741 Passed; **Lieutenant**; 27.3.1744 L. *Scipio* (8) Fireship; 1.6.1744 4L *Edinburgh* (64); 20.3.1746/47 3L *Edinburgh* (64); 14.10.1747 2nd Battle of Cape Finisterre; 23.12.1747-9.8.1748[P] 2L *Edinburgh* (64).

OSBORNE, HENRY

Dates: 27.8.1694 Born Campton, Bedfordshire; 4.2.1771 Died London.
Family: Father Sir John Osborn, second baronet (1659–1720); Mother Martha Kelynge (c.1665–1713); Wife Mary Hughes; Brother Peter, RN (d.1753).
Service: 20.12.1710 Vol-p-O *Superb* (64); 25.10.1713 Mid *Superb* (64); 19.5.1715-28.2.1716/17[P] Mid *Lion* (60); 8.3.1716/17 Passed; **Lieutenant**; 7.7.1717(29.7.1717) 4L *Barfleur* (90); 8.1.1717/18-10.1.1717/18 2L *Hampton Court* (70); 4.4.1718 3L *Royal Oak* (70); 11.8.1718 Battle of Cape Passaro; 6.6.1719(23.11.1719) L. *Experiment* (20); 6.9.1720 3L *Nassau* (70); 17.2.1720/21-28.4.1721 3L *Hector* (40); 10.5.1722 2L *Yarmouth* (70); 14.2.1725/26-26.10.1726 1L *Leopard* (50); 22.6.1726 L. *Bredah* (70); **Commander**; 12.10.1727 *Weazle* (8) Sloop; **Captain**; 4.1.1727/28-27.12.1731[P] *Squirrel* (20); 14.5.1729-1730 Gov. of Newfoundland; 22.2.1733/34 *Portland* (50); 16.5.1738 *Salisbury* (50); 24.9.1740 *Prince of Orange* (70); 11.6.1741(3.4.1742) *Chichester* (80); 4.1.1741/42-12.2.1744/45 *Princess Caroline* (80); 11.2.1743/44-12.2.1743/44 Battle of Toulon; 29.4.1746-1748 CinC — Thames, Medway and The Nore; 15.7.1747 **Rear Admiral of the Red**; 5.2.1747/48-12.1748 CinC — Barbados & the Leeward Islands; 5.1748-1749 *Captain* (70); 12.5.1748 **Vice Admiral of the White**; 4.2.1755 **Vice Admiral of the Red**; 1756-30.4.1757 CinC — Portsmouth; 1756 *Somerset* (68); 24.2.1757 **Admiral of the Blue**; 30.4.1757-4.1760 CinC — The Mediterranean Sea; 5.1757-1759 *Prince* (90); 13.12.1758-1.4.1761 M.P. for Bedfordshire; 21.10.1762 **Admiral of the White**; 4.1.1763-11.1765 Vice Admiral of Great Britain.

OSBORNE, JAMES

Dates: c.1730 Born; c.1760 Died; 24.3.1760 Will·Probate.
Family: Father Jospeh Osbourne; Sister Ann; Brother Thomas.
Service: 7.2.1744/45 Ord. *Chichester* (80); 5.12.1745 Able *Chichester* (80); 26.5.1746 Able *Chesterfield* (44); 5.12.1746 Mid *Captain* (70); 7.6.1747 Mid *Kent* (64); 14.10.1747 2nd Battle of Cape Finisterre; 14.4.1749 Able *Rainbow* (44); 2.7.1750 Mid *Rainbow* (44); 3.7.1751

Able *Rainbow* (44); 1.5.1752 Passed; **Lieutenant**; 1.5.1753-3.5.1753 L. *Baltimore* (14) Sloop; 23.10.1754 L. *Nightingale* (22); 5.1.1757 3L *Grafton* (68); 25.1.1757 2L *Grafton* (68); 8.1757-10.1757 Louisbourg Expedition; 2.2.1758-1760† 1L *Grafton* (68); 10.9.1759 Battle of Pondicherry.

OSBORNE, JOHN
Dates: c.1724 Born; 1757 Died.
Family:
Service: 24.9.1737 Capt Serv *Gloucester* (50); 22.8.1740-23.2.1740/41 Able *Prince Frederick* (70); 24.2.1740/41 Mid *Nassau* (70); 11.7.1741 Mid *Barfleur* (90); 11.2.1743/44-12.2.1743/44 Battle of Toulon; 29.4.1744 Mid *Buckingham* (70); 28.7.1744 Able *Namur* (90); 22.1.1744/45 Passed; **Lieutenant**; 22.1.1744/45-17.5.1745 4L *Shrewsbury* (80); 19.6.1745-20.10.1745 2L *Milford* (44); 4.12.1747-30.12.1747 L. *Gibraltar* (20); 23.6.1749-13.6.1751 2L *Culloden* (74).

OSBORNE, THOMAS
Dates: c.1740 Born; 1762 Died.
Family:
Service: 8.5.1755 Able *Nightingale* (22); 17.11.1756 Mid *Nightingale* (22); 18.5.1757 Able *Grafton* (68); 8.1757-10.1757 Louisbourg Expedition; 8.8.1758 Able *Swan* (14) Sloop; 18.4.1759-3.6.1761 Mid *Swan* (14) Sloop; 3.6.1761 Passed; **Lieutenant**; 5.5.1762-1.10.1762 L. *Baltimore* (8) Bomb Vessel.

OSBORNE, WADHAM
Dates: 1768 Died; 21.4.1768 Will Probate.
Family:
Service: **Lieutenant**; 21.12.1758(4.10.1759)-22.1.1760P 3L *Bristol* (50); 16.1.1759-19.1.1759 Attack on Martinique; 20.1.1759-1.5.1759 Capture of Guadeloupe; 24.4.1760-15.5.1763 3L *Centaur* (74); 6.6.1762-13.8.1762 Operations against Havana.

OSBORNE, WILLIAM
Dates: c.1714 Born.
Family:
Service: 13.4.1738 QGnr *Alderney* (8) Bomb Vessel; 23.10.1738 Able *Alderney* (8) Bomb Vessel; 6.4.1739 Cox *Deal Castle* (20); 2.12.1741 Able *Sapphire* (44); 28.1.1741/42 Mid *Dartmouth* (50); 18.3.1743/44 Mid *Warwick* (60); 3.7.1745 Mate *Warwick* (60); 2.11.1745 Mate *Lion* (58); 28.5.1747 Passed; **Lieutenant**; 9.6.1747-5.11.1747 2L *Bellona* (30); 7.12.1747-23.5.1748 2L *Penzance* (44); 4.11.1748-31.3.1753 L. *Seahorse* (24); 3.4.1753-31.7.1754 3L *Crown* (44); 21.8.1754-15.10.1755 2L *Norwich* (50); 1.4.1757 1L *Achilles* (60); 5.9.1757-6.10.1757 Raid on Rochefort; 3.7.1759 Bombardment of Le Havre; **Commander**; 1.3.1760-22.10.1762P *Diligence* (10) Sloop.

OURRY, GEORGE
Dates: 1732 Born; 3.2.1800 Died Bath.
Family: Father Lewis Ourry (d.1771); Mother Anne Louise Beauvais (d.1732); Wife Hon. Amelia Newton (d.1800); Son George Treby; Brother Isaac Florimond, RN (1721-1773); Brother Lewis; Brother Paul Henry, RN (1719-1783).
Service: 20.10.1746 Mid *Kennington* (20); 14.12.1746 Mid *Salisbury* (50); 24.11.1749-21.8.1750 Able *Gloucester* (50); 22.8.1750 Mid *Gloucester* (50); 31.8.1753-14.12.1754 Able

Deptford (50); 15.12.1754 ActL *Unicorn* (24); 2.7.1755 Passed; **Lieutenant**; 9.7.1755-3.4.1757 4L *Stirling Castle* (64); 3.4.1757(13.3.1758) 1L *Winchester* (50); 24.3.1758 2L *Stirling Castle* (64); 21.2.1759 2L *Lennox* (74); **Commander**; 24.8.1761(EI 9.8.1764) *Southsea Castle* (28) Storeship; 1.8.1762-24.8.1762 ActCapt *Panther* (60); **Captain**; 10.11.1762(EI 27.8.1764)-29.7.1764[P] *Norfolk* (74); 1.11.1769-6.5.1771[P] *Belleisle* (64); 8.1.1774 *Worcester* (64); 31.3.1775-2.11.1778[W] *Somerset* (68); 2.9.1779-4.1.1782 *Ocean* (90); 12.12.1781 2nd Battle of Ushant; 19.2.1793 **Superannuated Rear Admiral.**

OURRY, ISAAC FLORIMOND

Dates: 9.4.1721 Born; 6.6.1773 Died Madras; 2.1.1775 Will Probate.
Family: Father Lewis Ourry (d.1771); Mother Anne Louise Beauvais (d.1732); Wife Ann Gouin married 1763; Brother Lewis; Brother Paul Henry, RN (1719-1783); Brother George, RN (1732-1800).
Service: 16.9.1738 Ord. *Burford* (70); 21.11.1739 Attack on Puerto Bello; 6.3.1739/40 Able *Princess Caroline* (80); 4.9.1740 Able *Boyne* (80); 12.9.1741 Mid *Ludlow Castle* (40); 27.2.1742/43 Mid *Superb* (60); 17.7.1743 Vol. *Launceston* (44); 9.4.1744 Able *Rippon* (60); 25.9.1744 Able *Mary Galley* (44); 12.2.1744/45 Passed; **Lieutenant**; 14.2.1744/45(BLI 7.1.1745/46) 3L *Launceston* (44); 13.3.1744/45(BLI 7.1.1745/46) 2L *Launceston* (44); 23.6.1745(BLI 7.1.1745/46) 3L *Mermaid* (44); 26.8.1745(BLI 7.1.1745/46) 3L *Chester* (50); 30.9.1745(BLI 22.11.1746) 2L *Superb* (60); 14.11.1746 1L *Superb* (60); 1.8.1748(18.10.1748)-11.10.1748 1L *Princess* (70); 24.12.1756 1L *Lichfield* (50); 3.2.1757 2L *Elizabeth* (64); 29.4.1758 Battle of Cuddalore; 3.8.1758 Battle of Negapatam; 20.2.1759(EI 26.12.1761) 2L *Grafton* (68); 3.3.1759(EI 26.12.1761) 1L *Queenborough* (24); 10.9.1759 Battle of Pondicherry; 11.9.1759(EI 26.12.1761) 5L *Yarmouth* (64); 17.3.1760(EI 26.12.1761)-23.6.1760 2L *Grafton* (68); **Commander**; 1.2.1761(27.8.1764) *Southsea Castle* (28) Storeship; **Captain**; 6.6.1761(EI 25.8.1764)-30.7.1764[P] *Elizabeth* (64); 24.9.1762-6.10.1762 Battle of Manilla; 19.2.1771-6.6.1773[†] *Buckingham* (68).

OURRY, PAUL HENRY

Dates: 3.10.1719 Born St Helier, Jersey; 31.1.1783 Died; 16.4.1783 Will Probate.
Family: Father Louis Ourry (d.1771); Mother Anne Louise Beauvais (d.1732); Wife Charity Treby (1727-1805) married 26.8.1749; Brother Isaac Florimond, RN (1721-1773); Brother Lewis; Brother George, RN (1732-1800).
Service: **Lieutenant**; 13.11.1742(MED 24.10.1745)-2.2.1743/44 3L *Shrewsbury* (80); 8.3.1743/44(MED 24.10.1745) L. *Kennington* (20); 21.3.1743/44(MED 14.11.1745)-8.3.1744/45 3L *Elizabeth* (70); 23.1.1745/46 1L *Salisbury* (50); 1.12.1748-31.5.1752[P] 1L *Monmouth* (70); 3.6.1752 1L *Deptford* (50); **Commander**; 27.4.1756-11.6.1756[C] *Proserpine* (8) Fireship; **Captain**; 3.2.1757 *Success* (20); 8.1757-10.1757 Louisbourg Expedition; 5.6.1758-12.6.1758 Raid on Saint-Malo; 11.12.1759-29.8.1763 *Actaeon* (28); 29.3.1761-11.6.1761 Expedition against Belle-Isle; 7.1.1762-10.2.1762 Operations against Martinique; 6.10.1763-24.10.1766 *Hero* (74); 24.5.1770 *Firm* (74); 20.10.1770 *Fame* (74); 7.11.1771-1.7.1773 *Dublin* (74); 10.10.1774-7.2.1775 M.P. for Plympton Erle; 1775-31.1.1783 Resident Commissioner at Plymouth Dockyard.

OWEN, JOHN

Dates: c.1733 Born; c.1780 Died; 1.3.1780 Will Probate.
Family:
Service: 4.6.1748-20.2.1749/50 Capt Serv *Elizabeth* (70); 21.2.1749/50-5.4.1751 Capt Serv *Strafford* (58); 6.4.1751 Able *Strafford* (58); 23.4.1751 Mid *Strafford* (58); 10.8.1752-1.8.1753 Able *Baltimore* (14) Sloop; 2.8.1753 Mid *Baltimore* (14) Sloop; 13.12.1753 Mid *Peregrine*

(20) Sloop; 17.3.1755 Passed; **Lieutenant**; 16.6.1756 6L *Marlborough* (80); 21.6.1756 5L *Marlborough* (80); 5.7.1756 5L *Terrible* (74); 29.1.1757 4L *Terrible* (74); 8.1757-10.1757 Louisbourg Expedition; 15.5.1758 1L *Enterprise* (44); 30.8.1760[(23.11.1761)] L. *Viper* (10) Sloop; 6.6.1762-13.8.1762 Operations against Havana; 1.4.1763-14.6.1765 LCmdr *Meredith* (10) Cutter.

OWEN, THOMAS

Dates: c.1718 Born; 1796 Died.
Family:
Service: 15.12.1734-30.4.1735 Capt Serv *Torrington* (40); 30.4.1735-17.9.1735 Ord. *Torrington* (40); 17.9.1735-1.12.1735 Clerk *Torrington* (40); 1.12.1735-7.12.1737 Able *Torrington* (40); 7.12.1737-13.8.1740 Able *Anglesea* (40); 13.8.1740-4.10.1741 Mid *Anglesea* (40); 4.3.1740/41-5.1741 Operations against Cartagena; 4.10.1741-27.4.1742 Mate *Adventure* (44); 27.4.1742 Mid *Royal George* (100); 21.9.1742 Passed; **Lieutenant**; 3.10.1743-24.5.1744 L. *Comet* (10) Bomb Vessel; 3.10.1744-27.6.1747[W] 2L *Maidstone* (50); 2.11.1747 1L *Anson* (60); 26.8.1748-16.9.1752[P] 1L *Centurion* (50); 2.10.1754 1L *Centurion* (50); **Commander**; 28.4.1755[(MED 3.1.1757)]-24.5.1755 *Ontario* (12) Sloop; 12.9.1755[(NA 27.9.1757)]-21.9.1758 *Baltimore* (14) Sloop; **Captain**; 28.9.1758-19.4.1759 *Torbay* (74); 29.12.1758 Capture of Goree.

OWEN, WILLIAM

Dates: 1737 Born; 24.10.1778 Died Madras; 20.5.1779 Will Probate.
Family: Wife Sarah Haslam (housekeeper); Son William Fitzwilliam, RN (1774-1857); Son Sir Edward William Campbell Rich, RN (1771-1849).
Service: **Lieutenant**; 25.3.1758[(EI 28.7.1761)]-1.10.1758 3L *Tiger* (60); 29.4.1758 Battle of Cuddalore; 3.8.1758 Battle of Negapatam; 30.5.1776 1L *Rippon* (60); **Commander**; 7.11.1777[(EI 2.9.1778)]-25.10.1778 *Cormorant* (14) Sloop; 10.8.1778 Second Battle of Pondicherry.

OWEN, WILLIAM

Dates: c.1734 Born; 15.7.1768 Died.
Family:
Service: 24.1.1753 Capt Serv *Royal George* (100); 12.9.1753 Ord. *Colchester* (50); 21.9.1754 Able *Colchester* (50); 17.7.1755 Mate *Revenge* (28); 14.5.1757 Master *Squirrel* (20); 6.6.1758-27.7.1758 The Siege of Louisbourg; 18.12.1758-4.4.1759 Master *Kennington* (20); 4.4.1759 Passed; **Lieutenant**; 22.6.1759 L. *Blast* (8) Bomb Vessel; 3.7.1759 Bombardment of Le Havre; 22.8.1760-30.12.1762[D] 2L *Richmond* (32); 6.6.1762-13.8.1762 Operations against Havana; 30.12.1762 Dismissed.

Service Records P

PADESON, EDMUND

Dates: 1807 Died; 27.2.1807 Will Probate.
Family:
Service: **Lieutenant**; 3.10.1761-16.10.1762 4L *Vanguard* (68); 7.1.1762-10.2.1762 Operations against Martinique; 29.1.1770-30.1.1773 L. *Speedwell* (8) Sloop; 15.7.1776 4L *Hector* (74); 5.11.1777 3L *Hector* (74); 13.5.1778 2L *Hector* (74); 27.7.1778 1st Battle of Ushant; 29.7.1779 LCmdr *Duke* Hired Tender; 3.5.1780 1L *Diligent* (70); 19.6.1781-5.2.1782 2L *Diligent* (70).

PADGET, HENRY

Dates: c.1735 Born; 21.2.1773 Died.
Family:
Service: 5.6.1755 Able *Prince* (90); 4.12.1755 Mid *Prince* (90); 17.7.1756 Mid *Prince George* (80); 19.10.1756 Mate *Prince* (90); 14.11.1756 Mid *Culloden* (74); 5.4.1757 Action of April 5 1757; 18.6.1757 Mid *Saint George* (90); 1.6.1758 Able *Montagu* (60); 7.8.1758 Able *Ramillies* (90); 5.1.1759 Passed; **Lieutenant**; 24.9.1759[(26.6.1760)] 2L *Richmond* (32); 22.8.1760-25.2.1763[P] L. *Blast* (8) Bomb Vessel; 19.5.1763-25.1.1765 2L *Venus* (36).

PAGE, HENRY

Dates: 1777 Died.
Family:
Service: **Lieutenant**; 25.6.1735[(30.3.1736)]-6.4.1736[P] 4L *Hampton Court* (70); 14.7.1738-4.12.1738[P] 3L *Lion* (60); 12.6.1739-13.1.1739/40 3L *Lion* (60); 26.6.1742[(7.10.1742)]-20.11.1742[P] 1L *Princess Louisa* (60); 29.12.1742-9.9.1745 1L *Dorsetshire* (80); 11.2.1743/44-12.2.1743/44 Battle of Toulon; 4.4.1747-23.12.1747 3L *Devonshire* (66); 14.10.1747 2nd Battle of Cape Finisterre; 12.1.1747/48-15.11.1752[P] 2L *Invincible* (74).

PAINE, JOHN

Dates:
Family:
Service: 4.2.1761 **Lieutenant**; 14.6.1762[(21.2.1764)] 4L *York* (60); 1.9.1763[(EI 23.2.1765)]-25.8.1764[P] 3L *Baleine* (20); 24.2.1809 **Superannuated Commander**.

PAKENHAM, EDWARD MICHAEL (2ND BARON LONGFORD)

Dates: 1.4.1743 Born Westmeath; 30.4.1766 2nd Baron Longford; 3.6.1792 Died.
Family: Father Thomas Pakenham, 1st Baron Longford (1713-1766); Mother Elizabeth Cuffe, 1st Countess of Longford (1719-1794); Wife Catherine Rowley; Brother Thomas, RN (1757-1836).
Service: **Lieutenant**; 12.8.1761[(24.11.1762)]-9.7.1762 L. *Terror* (8) Bomb Vessel; 7.6.1763-17.9.1764 3L *Romney* (50); **Commander**; 20.6.1765-16.7.1767 *Bonetta* (10) Sloop; **Captain**; 31.5.1766-

25.5.1768 *Sheerness* (24); 27.12.1777 *America* (64); 27.7.1778 1st Battle of Ushant; 5.4.1779-19.12.1782 *Alexander* (74); 12.12.1781 2nd Battle of Ushant; 20.10.1782 Battle of Cape Spartel.

PALLISER, SIR HUGH (1ST BARONET)

Dates: 26.2.1721/22 Born Kirk Deighton, Yorkshire; 6.8.1773 1st Baronet; 19.3.1796 Died The Vache, Nr. Chalfont St Giles, Buckinghamshire.
Family: Father Hugh Palliser (1671-?); Mother Mary Robinson (1693-?); Wife Anne Thomas; Son George Thomas (d.1829); Sister Rebecca [Walters]; Sister Mary; Sister Alice [Clough]; Sister Ursula [Fletcher] (1725-1796).
Service: 3.5.1735 Mid *Aldborough* (20); 5.11.1735 Able *Aldborough* (20); 27.12.1735 MidO *Aldborough* (20); 21.9.1736 Mid *Aldborough* (20); 5.6.1737 Mid *Kennington* (20); 14.7.1740 Mid *Deptford* (24) Storeship; 16.12.1740 Mid *Tiger* (50); 13.4.1741-12.5.1741 Mid *Essex* (70); 12.5.1741 Passed; **Lieutenant**; 18.9.1741-1.4.1743 4L *Essex* (70); **Captain**; 25.11.1746-5.5.1748 *Captain* (70); 9.1747-6.5.1748 *Sutherland* (50); 20.12.1748-10.5.1750[P] *Sheerness* (24); 30.1.1753 *Yarmouth* (64); 31.3.1753 *Seahorse* (24); 17.9.1755-15.2.1758 *Eagle* (60); 7.3.1758-2.3.1763[P] *Shrewsbury* (74); 5.6.1758-12.6.1758 Raid on Saint-Malo; 13.3.1764-4.3.1766 *Guernsey* (50); 30.4.1764 CinC — Newfoundland; 1765-1769 Gov. of Newfoundland; 5.3.1766 CinC — Newfoundland; 2.4.1766-5.1.1769[P] Commodore *Guernsey* (50); 6.8.1770-12.4.1775 Comptroller of the Navy; 3.10.1774-2.1779 M.P. for Scarborough; 31.3.1775 **Rear Admiral of the Blue**; 12.4.1775-22.4.1779 Lord Commissioner of the Admiralty; 7.12.1775 **Rear Admiral of the White**; 1778-1779 *Ocean* (90); 23.1.1778 **Rear Admiral of the Red**; 29.1.1778 **Vice Admiral of the Blue**; 2.1778-1779 *Formidable* (98); 27.7.1778 1st Battle of Ushant; 1780-19.3.1796 Governor of Greenwich Hospital at Greenwich Hospital; 26.9.1780 **Vice Admiral of the White**; 20.11.1780-31.3.1784 M.P. for Huntingdon; 24.9.1787 **Admiral of the Blue**; 1.2.1793 **Admiral of the White**.

PALMER, EDWARD

Dates: c.1738 Born; 1796 Died; 3.9.1796 Will Probate.
Family:
Service: 31.1.1750/51 Capt Serv *Porcupine* (16) Sloop; 3.11.1753 Able *Porcupine* (16) Sloop; 29.10.1755 Mid *Anson* (60); 9.5.1758 Passed; **Lieutenant**; 27.10.1758-14.5.1759 2L *Vengeance* (28); 21.4.1761 4L *Marlborough* (68); 28.10.1761-1.5.1762 5L *Marlborough* (68); 7.1.1762-10.2.1762 Operations against Martinique; 7.11.1771 4L *Dublin* (74); 16.12.1772 3L *Dublin* (74); 22.4.1773 4L *Dublin* (74); 12.5.1773 3L *Dublin* (74); 12.7.1773-26.3.1774 2L *Dublin* (74).

PALMER, WILLIAM

Dates: c.1727 Born; c.1781 Died; 8.6.1781 Will Probate.
Family:
Service: 13.6.1743-10.5.1747[P] Mid *Lennox* (70); 3.8.1746 Action of August 3 1746; 25.3.1747 Action of March 25 1747; 13.6.1754 Mid *Tiger* (60); 4.12.1754 Mid *Assistance* (50); 13.2.1756 Mate *Newark* (80); 25.5.1756 Mate *Dreadnought* (60); 5.9.1757 Passed; **Lieutenant**; 8.10.1758[(JAM 20.9.1759)] 3L *Jersey* (60); 18.8.1759-19.8.1759 Battle of Lagos Bay; 9.5.1760-12.5.1763[P] 2L *Jersey* (60); 5.12.1776-2.1784 LCmdr *Swan* Hired Tender; 1.8.1778-11.1780 LCmdr *Charlotte* Hired Tender.

PANTON, HENRY GIBSON

Dates: c.1738 Born; c.1769 Died; 20.7.1769 Will Probate.

Family:

Service: 12.4.1755 Ord. *Yarmouth* (64); 13.4.1756 Able *Yarmouth* (64); 7.3.1757 Able *Invincible* (74); 9.6.1757 Mid *Buckingham* (68); 7.8.1757 Mid *Princess Amelia* (80); 6.9.1757 Mid *Dunkirk* (60); 5.6.1758-12.6.1758 Raid on Saint-Malo; 29.12.1758 Capture of Goree; 3.10.1759 Passed; **Lieutenant**; 8.12.1759 L. *Southsea Castle* (28) Storeship; 4.10.1760[(31.7.1765)] 4L *Weymouth* (60); 24.9.1762-6.10.1762 Battle of Manilla; 21.10.1762[(EI 31.7.1765)]-19.7.1765[P] 3L *Weymouth* (60).

PANTON, JOHN ALEXANDER

Dates: 1781 Died.

Family:

Service: **Lieutenant**; 4.11.1762[(JAM 7.9.1763)]-7.9.1763[P] 3L *Alcide* (64); 10.3.1766 L. *Gibraltar* (20); 5.3.1767-2.3.1772[P] 1L *Liverpool* (28); 9.9.1773 1L *Salisbury* (50); **Commander**; 22.2.1776[(EI 5.9.1776)] *Swallow* (14) Sloop; **Captain**; 26.6.1777[(EI 26.7.1780)]-2.1779 *Seahorse* (24); 10.8.1778 Second Battle of Pondicherry.

PARKE, THOMAS

Dates: 1777 Died.

Family:

Service: **Lieutenant**; 7.10.1746[(BLI 19.1.1746/47)]-30.11.1746[P] L. *Bien Aime* (18) Armed Storeship; 28.5.1747 3L *Rainbow* (44); 11.10.1748-10.5.1750[P] L. *Sheerness* (24); 6.2.1755 2L *Chichester* (68); 1.6.1756 1L *Chichester* (68); 17.11.1756 3L *Berwick* (64); 5.4.1757 Action of April 5 1757; 28.2.1758 Battle of Cartagena; 16.1.1759-19.1.1759 Attack on Martinique; 20.1.1759-1.5.1759 Capture of Guadeloupe; 26.11.1759[(26.11.1759)] 2L *Cambridge* (80); 12.12.1759-22.2.1760 1L *Dublin* (74); 15.6.1766-15.6.1769 LCmdr *Mecklenburgh* (6) Cutter.

PARKER, CHRISTOPHER

Dates: c.1682 Born; 1.2.1765 Died Dublin.

Family: Son Sir Peter, RN (1715-1811); Son George.

Service: 15.7.1696 Vol-p-O *Fowey* (32); 25.6.1697 Vol-p-O *Woolwich* (54); 31.1.1697/98 Ord. *Coventry* (54); 27.3.1698 Vol-p-O *Coventry* (54); 30.3.1700 Vol-p-O *Bridgewater* (32); 4.4.1701 Mid *Medway* (60); 10.3.1701/2 Mid *Hampton Court* (70); 17.4.1702 Passed; **Lieutenant**; 21.6.1702 3L *Revenge* (70); 19.5.1704 3L *Mary* (60); 5.12.1705-29.7.1708 1L *Mary* (60); **Commander**; 17.8.1708 *Speedwell Prize* (20); **Captain**; 7.2.1714/15-15.6.1720[P] *Tartar* (32); 28.2.1739/40-26.9.1740 *Torbay* (80); 1.9.1747 **Superannuated Rear Admiral**.

PARKER, EDWARD

Dates: c.1713 Born; 1762 Died; 23.10.1762 Will Probate.

Family:

Service: 16.6.1728 Vol-p-O *Portland* (50); 14.6.1730 Able *Leopard* (50); 24.10.1730 Mid *Leopard* (50); 10.12.1730 Able *Advice* (54); 6.4.1732 Mid *Advice* (54); 14.6.1732 MidO *Bideford* (20); 31.7.1734 Passed; **Lieutenant**; 2.2.1740/41 4L *Lennox* (70); 23.11.1741 6L *Sandwich* (90); 9.2.1742/43 5L *Sandwich* (90); 14.7.1744 3L *Duke* (90); 17.12.1744-17.1.1744/45 1L *Prince George* (90); **Commander**; 28.1.1745/46-1.8.1748[P] *Raven* (10) Sloop.

PARKER, SIR HYDE (5TH BARONET OF MELFORD HALL)

Dates: 25.2.1713/14 Born Tredington, Gloucestershire; 1782 5th Baronet of Melford Hall; 1.1783 Died;

Family: Father Hyde Parker (d. 1726); Mother Mary, daughter of John Reeves; Wife Sarah Smithson married 1734; Son Sir Hyde, RN (1739-1807).

Service: 12.8.1736-24.10.1737[P] Able *Antelope* (54); 26.5.1739 Mid *Argyll* (50); 8.7.1739-7.11.1740[P] Mid *Swift* (6) Sloop; 28.12.1740 Mate *Pearl* (40); 18.5.1741 Able *Centurion* (60); 17.12.1743 Mate *Centurion* (60); 16.1.1744/45 Passed; **Lieutenant**; 16.1.1744/45 3L *Harwich* (50); 20.12.1745[(EI 12.9.1749)] 1L *Preston* (50); 25.6.1746 1st Battle of Negapatam; 5.2.1746/47[(EI 12.9.1749)]-5.4.1747 3L *Princess Mary* (60); **Captain**; 24.3.1747/48-22.8.1749[P] *Lively* (24); 12.11.1751-18.11.1752[P] *Vanguard* (68); 13.2.1753 *Cruizer* (8) Sloop; 28.10.1755 *Squirrel* (20); 20.10.1757 *Brilliant* (36); 5.6.1758-12.6.1758 Raid on Saint-Malo; 3.7.1759 Bombardment of Le Havre; 15.11.1759 *Norfolk* (74); 23.6.1760[(5.7.1764)]-18.7.1763 *Grafton* (68); 24.9.1762-6.10.1762 Battle of Manilla; 9.5.1769-3.10.1770 *Romney* (50); 2.11.1776 *Invincible* (74); 23.1.1778 **Rear Admiral of the Blue**; 4.1778 *Royal Oak* (74); 1779 *Conqueror* (74); 19.3.1779 **Rear Admiral of the Red**; 6.7.1779 Battle of Grenada; 18.12.1779 Combat de la Martinique; 1.1780-5.6.1780 *Princess Royal* (98); 17.4.1780 Battle of Martinique; 15.5.1780 Action of March 15 1780; 19.5.1780 Action of March 19 1780; 26.9.1780 **Vice Admiral of the Blue**; 1781 CinC — North Sea; 21.3.1781 *Victory* (100); 6.1781 *Fortitude* (74); 5.8.1781 Battle of Dogger Bank; 5.1782-1.1783[F] *Cato* (50); 3.7.1782 CinC — East Indies.

PARKER, SIR HYDE

Dates: 1739 Born; 21.4.1779 Knight Bachelor; 16.3.1807 Died London.

Family: Father Sir Hyde Parker (5th Baronet of Melford Hall), RN (1714-1783); Mother Sarah Smithson; Wife Frances Onslow (d.1844) married 23.12.1800; Wife Anne Boteler.

Service: 1751-1752 Merchant Service; 31.3.1752 Able *Vanguard* (68); 9.4.1753 Able *Mars* (64); 10.6.1753 Able *Cruizer* (8) Sloop; 6.1.1754 Mid *Cruizer* (8) Sloop; 14.5.1755 Mid *Medway* (60); 5.9.1757-6.10.1757 Raid on Rochefort; 7.11.1757 Passed; **Lieutenant**; 25.1.1758 2L *Brilliant* (36); 5.6.1758-12.6.1758 Raid on Saint-Malo; 3.7.1759 Bombardment of Le Havre; 20.11.1759 3L *Norfolk* (74); 19.12.1759 2L *Norfolk* (74); 23.6.1760[(16.5.1763)]-27.11.1760 2L *Grafton* (68); 11.7.1761[(16.5.1763)] 5L *Lennox* (74); 24.9.1762-6.10.1762 Battle of Manilla; **Commander**; 16.12.1762[(EI 18.8.1764)] *Manilla* (14) Storeship; **Captain**; 18.7.1763[(EI 18.8.1764)]-25.8.1764[P] *Baleine* (20); 29.11.1766-9.5.1769 *Hussar* (28); 15.9.1770[(2.12.1772)]-9.7.1772[P] *Boston* (32); 4.7.1775-4.10.1780[F] *Phoenix* (44); 2.7.1776-4.7.1776 Staten Island Landings; 22.7.1778 Encounter at Sandy Hook; 19.2.1781 *Latona* (38); 5.8.1781 Battle of Dogger Bank; 16.10.1781-8.4.1783[P] *Goliath* (74); 20.10.1782 Battle of Cape Spartel; 15.4.1783-9.8.1786 *Goliath* (74); 22.9.1787 *Orion* (74); 21.2.1788 *Royal Charlotte* (8) Yacht; 10.5.1790 *Brunswick* (74); 22.10.1790 *Formidable* (98); 11.12.1790 *Royal Charlotte* (8) Yacht; 23.3.1791 1Capt. *Victory* (100); **Rear Admiral of the White**; 1.2.1793-23.4.1793 *Bedford* (74); 24.4.1793 First Captain; 12.4.1794 **Rear Admiral of the Red**; 4.7.1794 **Vice Admiral of the Blue**; 1.3.1795-17.1.1796 *Saint George* (98); 14.3.1795 Action off Genoa; 1.6.1795 **Vice Admiral of the Red**; 13.7.1795 Battle of Hyeres; 1.1796-1797 *Britannia* (100); 28.6.1796-10.1800 *Queen* (90); 24.8.1796-1800 CinC — Jamaica; 14.2.1799 **Admiral of the Blue**; 9.1800-1801 *Royal George* (100); 2.1801-1802 *London* (90); 2.4.1801 Battle of Copenhagen; 23.4.1804 **Admiral of the White**; 9.11.1805 **Admiral of the Red**.

PARKER, SIR PETER (1ST BARONET OF BASSINGBOURN)

Dates: 1715 Born; 10.6.1772 Knight Bachelor; 28.12.1782 1st Baronet of Bassingbourn; 21.12.1811 Died.
Family: Father Christopher Parker, RN (1682-1765); Wife Margaret Nugent (d. 1803); Brother George.
Service: 1743 Passed; **Lieutenant**; 23.11.1743(MED 14.2.1746/47) L. *Firedrake* (8) Bomb Vessel; 18.1.1743/44(MED 14.2.1746/47) 6L *Neptune* (90); 11.2.1743/44-12.2.1743/44 Battle of Toulon; 19.3.1743/44(MED 14.2.1746/47) 6L *Barfleur* (90); **Commander**; 11.3.1744/45(MED 29.11.1746) *Maidstone* (54) Hospital Ship; **Captain**; 6.5.1747-28.4.1749[P] *Margate* (24); 21.5.1755 *Woolwich* (44); 16.1.1759-19.1.1759 Attack on Martinique; 29.1.1759(BLI 14.8.1760) *Bristol* (50); 12.5.1759(BLI 14.8.1760) *Buckingham* (68); 20.1.1761 *Buckingham* (68); 29.3.1761-11.6.1761 Expedition against Belle-Isle; 31.8.1762-23.1.1763[P] *Terrible* (74); 26.10.1773 *Barfleur* (90); c.13.10.1775-28.4.1777 Commodore *Bristol* (50); 1.11.1775-24.10.1776 *Royal Oak* (74); 6.9.1776-28.4.1777 Commodore *Chatham* (50); 6.12.1776-8.12.1776 Occupation of Rhode Island; **Rear Admiral of the Blue**; 28.4.1777-1779 *Bristol* (50); 11.6.1777-19.7.1781 CinC — Jamaica; 23.1.1778 **Rear Admiral of the White**; 29.1.1778 **Rear Admiral of the Red**; 19.3.1779 **Vice Admiral of the Blue**; 1.1780 *Ruby* (64); 26.9.1780 **Vice Admiral of the White**; 1781 *Ruby* (64); 4.1782-8.1782 *Sandwich* (90); 30.3.1784-13.3.1786 M.P. for Seaford; 19.2.1787-16.6.1790 M.P. for Maldon; 24.9.1787 **Admiral of the Blue**; 12.1792-1799 *Royal William* (84); 8.4.1793-14.9.1799 CinC — Portsmouth; 12.4.1794 **Admiral of the White**; 16.9.1799 **Admiral of the Fleet**.

PARKER, SAMUEL

Dates: c.1737 Born; 1775 Died.
Family:
Service: 1753-1755 Merchant Service; 14.4.1755 Mid *Barfleur* (80); 21.4.1757 Mid *Princess Royal* (90); 26.5.1757 Act3L *Dover* (44); 11.11.1757 Mate *Dover* (44); 26.1.1758 Passed; **Lieutenant**; 6.2.1758-19.2.1758[W] 3L *Invincible* (74); 20.3.1761-14.2.1763[P] 1L *Southampton* (32); 29.3.1761-11.6.1761 Expedition against Belle-Isle.

PARKES, JOHN

Dates: c.1736 Born; 1764 Died; 1.6.1764 Will Probate.
Family:
Service: 1753-1755 Merchant Service; 2.7.1755 L. Serv *Revenge* (64); 5.10.1755 Capt Serv *Revenge* (64); 8.4.1756 Ord. *Revenge* (64); 20.5.1756 Battle of Minorca; 11.9.1756 Mid *Revenge* (64); 28.2.1758 Battle of Cartagena; 11.4.1759 Passed; **Lieutenant**; 17.10.1759-20.11.1759[S] 4L *Essex* (64); 20.11.1759 Battle of Quiberon Bay; 14.3.1760 3L *Rochester* (50); 7.1.1762-10.2.1762 Operations against Martinique; 1.5.1762(EI 28.5.1763)-29.11.1762[F] 5L *Marlborough* (68); 6.6.1762-13.8.1762 Operations against Havana.

PARKIN, HENRY

Dates: c.1721 Born; c.1782 Died; 13.7.1782 Will Probate.
Family:
Service: 27.5.1738 Able *Princess Louisa* (60); 10.8.1738 Mid *Princess Louisa* (60); 4.12.1738 Able *Princess Louisa* (60); 8.6.1739 Mid *Princess Louisa* (60); 21.11.1739 Attack on Puerto Bello; 4.3.1740/41-5.1741 Operations against Cartagena; 20.10.1741-16.7.1742[P] Mid *Bristol* (54); 19.3.1742/43 Able *Argyll* (50); 27.6.1743 Mid *Severn* (50); 25.11.1744 Able *Superb* (60); 26.12.1744 Mid *Superb* (60); 5.12.1745 Passed; **Lieutenant**; 17.4.1746-2.9.1747 L. *Speedwell* (10) Sloop; 2.9.1747-3.1.1748/49[P] 3L *Expedition* (44); 8.7.1752 3L *Assistance* (50); 5.6.1755-

13.10.1757 3L *Portland* (50); 20.5.1756 Battle of Minorca; 5.4.1757 Action of April 5 1757; 30.11.1770-28.5.1771 1L *Torbay* (74).

PARKINSON, THOMAS
Dates: c.1726 Born; 20.9.1778 Died.
Family:
Service: 1746-1755 Merchant Service; 13.2.1755 Mate *Medway* (60); 20.11.1756 Mate *Royal George* (100); 27.12.1756 Mate *Namur* (90); 5.9.1757-6.10.1757 Raid on Rochefort; 7.2.1758 Mate *Royal George* (100); 21.5.1758 Mate *Dorsetshire* (68); 7.2.1759 Passed; **Lieutenant**; 19.6.1759 4L *Dorsetshire* (68); 20.11.1759 Battle of Quiberon Bay; 23.2.1760 4L *Bellona* (74); 23.12.1760 3L *Bellona* (74); 11.3.1761 2L *Bellona* (74); 7.1.1762-19.1.1763[P] 3L *Bellona* (74).

PARNELL, JOHN
Dates: c.1741 Born; 1765 Died.
Family:
Service: 26.3.1755 Capt Serv *Intrepid* (64); 20.5.1756 Battle of Minorca; 21.7.1756 Ord. *Burford* (68); 18.9.1757 Able *Echo* (24); 7.1.1758 Mid *Echo* (24); 5.6.1758 Mid *Alarm* (32); 18.11.1758-5.1.1759[P] Mid *Centaur* (20); 15.2.1761 Mid *Royal Sovereign* (104); 3.3.1762 Passed; **Lieutenant**; 8.6.1762-15.11.1762 4L *Saint Ann* (64).

PARREY, ANTHONY
Dates: 11.7.1789 Died; 18.7.1789 Will Probate.
Family:
Service: **Lieutenant**; 12.4.1761[(23.6.1762)] 3L *Preston* (50); 26.8.1765-25.8.1766[P] L. *Carcass* (8) Bomb Vessel; 5.8.1768 3L *Augusta* (64); 20.9.1770 4L *Augusta* (64); 13.11.1770-17.11.1770[P] 2L *Augusta* (64); 9.9.1772 2L *Triumph* (74); 17.12.1773-26.8.1775 2L *Ramillies* (74); **Commander**; 11.5.1776 *Bute* Hired Unknown; 26.2.1777 *Alderney* (10) Sloop; **Captain**; 2.5.1778-26.3.1779 *Invincible* (74); 8.5.1779 *Pandora* (24); 28.3.1781-18.5.1781 *Hannibal* (50); 27.9.1781-13.3.1783 *Yarmouth* (64); 12.4.1782 Battle of the Saintes; 19.4.1782 Battle of the Mona Passage.

PARREY, ROBERT
Dates: c.1739 Born; 24.8.1808 Died; 15.9.1808 Will Probate.
Family: Wife Ann;
Service: 5.12.1752 Capt Serv *Swift* (8) Sloop; 17.2.1753 Able *Peggy* (8) Sloop; 8.11.1753 Capt Serv *Raven* (14) Sloop; 6.7.1754 Capt Serv *Rye* (20); 20.11.1755 Mid *Falmouth* (50); 5.1.1759 Passed; **Lieutenant**; 22.2.1759 4L *Bienfaisant* (64); 2.10.1761-15.8.1763[P] 3L *Bienfaisant* (64); 29.8.1765-18.4.1767 2L *Jason* (32); 13.8.1767-1.12.1768 L. *Seaford* (20); 14.12.1768 2L *Augusta* (64); 20.9.1770 3L *Augusta* (64); 13.11.1770 1L *Augusta* (64); 3.10.1771 3L *Resolution* (74); 30.11.1771-28.8.1772 4L *Resolution* (74); **Commander**; 17.1.1783-19.2.1783[P] *Sulphur* (8) Fireship; **Captain**; 22.11.1790 *Tartar* (28).

PARRY, FRANCIS
Dates: c.1739 Born; 18.12.1803 Died; 4.2.1804 Will Probate.
Family:
Service: 31.12.1752 Able *Norfolk* (6) Mer; 24.11.1753 Able *Peggy* (8) Sloop; 20.10.1754 Able *Nottingham* (60); 11.12.1755 Mid *Barfleur* (80); 27.4.1757 Mid *Invincible* (74); 8.1757-10.1757 Louisbourg Expedition; 6.3.1757/58-7.2.1759 Mid *Dorsetshire* (68); 7.2.1759 Passed; **Lieutenant**; 20.8.1759[(NA 12.5.1760)] 4L *Conqueror* (68); 20.9.1759[(JAM 26.5.1760)]-30.1.1760 3L

Conqueror (68); 12.4.1762 5L *Sandwich* (90); 30.7.1762 4L *Sandwich* (90); 27.9.1762-22.1.1763[P] 3L *Sandwich* (90); 25.5.1763-7.1766[P] L. *Vulture* (14) Sloop; 8.7.1767 1L *Boreas* (28); 16.5.1769 1L *Glory* (32); 30.10.1770-21.6.1771[P] 3L *Namur* (90); 29.6.1771-13.1.1772 4L *Egmont* (74); **Commander**; 11.1.1775[(NA 15.5.1775)]-2.10.1776[B] *Cruizer* (8) Sloop; 10.3.1777 *Lynx* (16) Sloop; **Captain**; 7.4.1778 *Europe* (64); 5.5.1778 *Proserpine* (28); 27.7.1778 1st Battle of Ushant; 8.3.1779 *Lizard* (28); 23.11.1780-19.7.1783[P] *Actaeon* (44); 23.1.1787-19.9.1788 *Adventure* (44); 30.9.1794 *Prince* (98); 1.6.1795 **Rear Admiral of the White**; 14.2.1799 **Vice Admiral of the Blue**; 1.1.1801 **Vice Admiral of the White**.

PARRY, WILLIAM

Dates: c.1699 Born; 29.4.1779 Died.

Family:

Service: 7.8.1728 Able *Adventure* (40); 21.11.1728 Ord. *Adventure* (40); 19.12.1728 Able *Dursley Galley* (20); 16.11.1731 Mid *Dursley Galley* (20); 23.4.1732 Mid *Torrington* (40); 29.5.1734 Mid *Ipswich* (70); 4.9.1734 Passed; **Lieutenant**; 22.7.1738[(24.7.1739)]-11.7.1739 3L *Kinsale* (40); 24.7.1739-8.8.1739 2L *Kinsale* (40); 9.8.1739 2L *Ruby* (54); 16.1.1740/41 1L *Ruby* (54); 31.7.1742 2L *Sandwich* (90); 13.9.1742 1L *Sandwich* (90); 3.11.1743 1L *Suffolk* (70); **Commander**; 29.12.1743 *Granado* (8) Bomb Vessel; **Captain**; 2.10.1744 *Gibraltar* (20); 16.11.1744 *Prince George* (90); 14.9.1745-21.2.1745/46 *Royal George* (100); 21.11.1747-22.11.1752[P] *Intrepid* (64); 22.2.1755-20.8.1756 *Kingston* (60); 20.5.1756 Battle of Minorca; 1.2.1757-4.3.1761[P] *Kingston* (60); 8.1757-10.1757 Louisbourg Expedition; 6.6.1758-27.7.1758 The Siege of Louisbourg; 20.11.1759 Battle of Quiberon Bay; 21.6.1762 *Montagu* (60); 26.9.1762[(27.4.1763)]-23.5.1763[P] *Somerset* (68); 21.10.1762 **Rear Admiral of the Blue**; 7.6.1766-1769 CinC — Jamaica; 1767-1769 *Preston* (50); 18.10.1770 **Rear Admiral of the Red**; 24.10.1770 **Vice Admiral of the Blue**; 3.1772-7.1775 *Chatham* (50); 12.5.1772 CinC — Barbados & the Leeward Islands; 31.3.1775 **Vice Admiral of the White**; 7.12.1775 **Vice Admiral of the Red**; 29.1.1778 **Admiral of the Blue**.

PARTRIDGE, THOMAS

Dates: c.1735 Born.

Family:

Service: 6.3.1750/51 Capt Serv *Saltash* (14) Sloop; 11.2.1755 Able *Saltash* (14) Sloop; 22.12.1755 Able *Barfleur* (80); 24.1.1756 Mid *Barfleur* (80); 5.9.1757-6.10.1757 Raid on Rochefort; 10.1.1758 Mid *Princess Royal* (90); 3.6.1758 ActL *Roman Emperor* (8) Fireship; 4.10.1758 Passed; **Lieutenant**; 30.7.1759-2.8.1759 3L *Launceston* (44).

PASCAL, MICHAEL HENRY

Dates: 1786 Died; 8.5.1786 Will Probate.

Family:

Service: 1736-1742 Merchant Service; 27.11.1742 Mid *Guernsey* (50); 11.2.1743/44-12.2.1743/44 Battle of Toulon; 14.7.1745 Passed; **Lieutenant**; 9.12.1745[(MED 11.12.1747)]-14.8.1746 4L *Stirling Castle* (70); 9.5.1748-29.11.1750[P] 2L *America* (44); 18.6.1755 2L *Roebuck* (44); 13.7.1756 1L *Roebuck* (44); 7.1.1757 1L *Preston* (50); 24.12.1757 6L *Royal George* (100); 27.1.1758 6L *Namur* (90); 6.6.1758-27.7.1758 The Siege of Louisbourg; 18.8.1759-19.8.1759 Battle of Lagos Bay; **Commander**; 21.8.1759[(MED 20.9.1759)]-18.12.1762[P] *Aetna* (8) Fireship; 29.3.1761-11.6.1761 Expedition against Belle-Isle; 12.4.1763-30.4.1764[P] *Dispatch* (14) Sloop; **Captain**; 20.6.1765-29.11.1766 *Scarborough* (20).

PASCOE, RICHARD

Dates: c.1712 Born; 1762 Died.
Family:
Service: 19.1.1731/32 L. Serv *Dreadnought* (60); 24.6.1734 Able *Saltash* (8) Sloop; 31.1.1735/36 Mid *Warwick* (60); 19.4.1738 Mate *Saltash* (8) Sloop; 28.11.1740-8.10.1741[P] Mate *Anglesea* (40); 4.3.1740/41-5.1741 Operations against Cartagena; 11.2.1741/42 Passed; **Lieutenant**; 23.5.1744[(28.6.1745)]-14.4.1745[C] L. *Mercury* (16) Sloop; 23.9.1745 1L *Ludlow Castle* (44); 19.5.1748[(9.9.1748)]-8.9.1748[P] 2L *Dreadnought* (60); 6.11.1755-15.1.1756 L. *Albany* (14) Sloop; 26.1.1757-28.11.1757 L. *Swan* (14) Sloop.

PASLEY, SIR THOMAS (BARONET PASLEY OF CRAIG)

Dates: 2.3.1734 Born; 26.7.1794 Baronet Pasley of Craig; 29.11.1808 Died Winchester.
Family: Father James Pasley (1692/3–1773); Mother Magdalen Elliot; Wife Mary Heywood (d.1788); Daughter Unknown; Daughter Unknown.
Service: 20.10.1751 Able *Garland* (24); 11.4.1753 Mid *Weazle* (16) Sloop; 9.9.1756 Mid *Dreadnought* (60); 4.4.1757 Mid *Bideford* (20); 1.8.1757 Passed; **Lieutenant**; 10.10.1757-20.4.1758[P] L. *Roman Emperor* (16) Sloop; 5.5.1758 2L *Hussar* (28); 26.12.1758 2L *Aeolus* (32); 20.11.1759 Battle of Quiberon Bay; 28.2.1760 Action of February 28 1760; 25.4.1760 1L *Aeolus* (32); **Commander**; 9.8.1762-12.2.1763[P] *Albany* (14) Sloop; 10.2.1764-17.2.1767 *Ranger* (8) Sloop; 14.3.1769 *Weazle* (16) Sloop; 18.9.1770 *Pomona* (18) Sloop; **Captain**; 21.1.1771-23.4.1773 *Seahorse* (24); 6.9.1776 *Glasgow* (20); 30.10.1778-26.9.1780 *Sibyl* (28); 20.9.1780-28.7.1783[P] *Jupiter* (50); 16.4.1781 Battle of Porto Praya; 21.7.1781 Attack in Saldanha Bay; 21.10.1789-8.5.1790 CinC — River Medway and The Nore; 21.10.1789 *Scipio* (64); 17.7.1790-9.9.1791[P] *Bellerophon* (74); 25.12.1790-28.3.1791 CinC — River Medway and The Nore; 10.9.1791-27.10.1792 Commodore *Vengeance* (74); 19.9.1791 CinC — River Medway and The Nore; 12.3.1793 *Bellerophon* (74); 11.9.1793 Commodore *Bellerophon* (74); 9.1.1794 Commodore *Bellerophon* (74); **Rear Admiral of the Blue**; 12.4.1794-1.6.1796 *Bellerophon* (74); 1.6.1794 Glorious 1st of June; 4.7.1794 **Rear Admiral of the Red**; 1.6.1795 **Vice Admiral of the White**; 16.6.1795-17.6.1795 First Battle of Groix; 14.2.1799 **Admiral of the Blue**; 29.3.1799-1802 CinC — Plymouth; 5.1799-1802 *Cambridge* (80); 9.11.1805 **Admiral of the White.**

PASTON, WILLIAM

Dates: 1731 Born; 1774 Died.
Family:
Service: 4.1.1751/52 Passed; **Lieutenant**; 19.9.1755 L. *Swan* (14) Sloop; **Commander**; 8.3.1757 *Crown* (18) Storeship; 4.4.1757 *Alderney* (10) Sloop; 15.6.1757 *Badger* (10) Sloop; **Captain**; 3.8.1757-11.9.1758[C] *Jason* (44); 5.6.1758-12.6.1758 Raid on Saint-Malo; 12.4.1759 *Tweed* (32); 29.3.1761-11.6.1761 Expedition against Belle-Isle; 25.12.1762-27.4.1763 *Siren* (20); 27.4.1763[(JAM 6.9.1764)]-17.5.1764[P] *Deptford* (50).

PATERSON, JAMES

Dates: c.1725 Born; 1761 Died.
Family:
Service: 1735-1739 Merchant Service; 29.6.1739 Mid *Buckingham* (70); 24.10.1741 Mate *Buckingham* (70); 25.10.1742 Mate *Royal Oak* (70); 11.2.1743/44-12.2.1743/44 Battle of Toulon; 9.5.1745 Passed; **Lieutenant**; 10.5.1745[(25.6.1745)] 4L *Dorsetshire* (80); 26.5.1745[(25.6.1745)]-22.7.1745[P] 6L *Barfleur* (90); 30.1.1746/47-4.4.1747 3L *Devonshire* (66); 6.4.1747 5L *Saint George* (90);

13.4.1747-24.4.1747 4L *Elizabeth* (70); 30.1.1747/48[JAM 10.7.1749] 2L *Strafford* (58); 9.4.1748 Battle of Santiago de Cuba; 12.10.1748 Battle of Havana; 1.11.1748[JAM 10.7.1749]-7.7.1749[P] 1L *Strafford* (58); 11.3.1755-19.4.1755 2L *Monmouth* (70); 19.4.1755-5.4.1756 L. *Sphinx* (24); 12.4.1758[JAM 25.5.1761]-30.1.1759 6L *Marlborough* (80).

PATTERSON, FORBES

Dates: 1777 Died.
Family:
Service: 17.11.1746 **Lieutenant.**

PATTISON, MARK

Dates: 1798 Died; 1.3.1798 Will Probate.
Family:
Service: 5.6.1745 Mate *Colchester* (50); 23.10.1747-12.7.1749[P] Mate *Aldborough* (20); 23.6.1755 Master *Jersey* (60); 4.10.1758 Passed; **Lieutenant**; 15.1.1759 6L *Torbay* (74); 20.11.1759 Battle of Quiberon Bay; 29.3.1761-11.6.1761 Expedition against Belle-Isle; **Commander**; 14.10.1762-30.11.1762[P] *Strombolo* (8) Fireship; **Captain**; 21.8.1765 *Jason* (32); 22.8.1765-25.8.1766[P] *Carcass* (8) Bomb Vessel.

PATTON, PHILIP

Dates: 27.10.1739 Born Anstruther, Fife; 31.12.1815 Died Fareham, Hampshire.
Family: Father Philip Patton (d. 1792?); Mother Agnes Loch; Wife Unknown married 1783; Brother Charles, RN (1741-1837); Brother Robert (1742–1812).
Service: 1753-1755 Merchant Service; 21.3.1755 Able *Torbay* (74); 6.6.1755-8.6.1755 Action of 6-8 June 1755; 5.2.1756 Able *Invincible* (74); 21.11.1756 Mid *Invincible* (74); 30.12.1756 Mid *Royal George* (100); 6.2.1758 Mid *Namur* (90); 6.6.1758-27.7.1758 The Siege of Louisbourg; 18.8.1759-19.8.1759 Battle of Lagos Bay; 20.11.1759 Battle of Quiberon Bay; 10.9.1760 Passed; 29.3.1761-11.6.1761 Expedition against Belle-Isle; 6.6.1762-13.8.1762 Operations against Havana; **Lieutenant**; 3.7.1762[EI 24.6.1763]-6.1763[P] L. *Granado* (8) Bomb Vessel; 20.6.1765 2L *Emerald* (32); 6.6.1770 2L *Emerald* (32); 27.6.1771-5.5.1772[P] 1L *Emerald* (32); 21.12.1776 5L *Prince George* (90); 30.8.1777 4L *Prince George* (90); 19.9.1777 3L *Prince George* (90); 1.10.1777 2L *Prince George* (90); 26.1.1778-5.5.1778 1L *Royal Oak* (74); **Commander**; 9.5.1778 *Aetna* (8) Bomb Vessel; 1.2.1779 *Thorn* (16) Sloop; **Captain**; 22.3.1779 *Namur* (90); 14.4.1779-23.5.1780 *Prince George* (98); 16.1.1780 Battle of Cape St. Vincent; 12.7.1780-28.11.1780[P] *Milford* (28); 6.2.1781-28.11.1782[P] *Belle Poule* (36); 5.8.1781 Battle of Dogger Bank; 1.6.1795 **Rear Admiral of the Blue**; 14.2.1799 **Rear Admiral of the Red**; 1.1.1801 **Vice Admiral of the Blue**; 23.4.1804 **Vice Admiral of the Red**; 9.11.1805 **Admiral of the Blue**; 31.7.1810 **Admiral of the White**; 4.6.1814 **Admiral of the Red.**

PAWLETT, EDMUND

Dates: c.1726 Born; c.1759 Died; 2.7.1759 Buried Eccles, Lancashire.
Family: Wife Elizabeth Warburton married 7.8.1748.
Service: 18.12.1741 Capt Serv *Dartmouth* (50); 22.11.1743 Able *Warwick* (60); 11.2.1743/44-12.2.1743/44 Battle of Toulon; 31.1.1744/45 Mid *Warwick* (60); 9.7.1745 Mid *Pembroke* (60); 13.2.1745/46 Able *Pembroke* (60); 4.4.1746 Mid *Pembroke* (60); 16.5.1746-12.8.1746[P] Mid *Argyll* (50); 22.7.1752 Able *Dorsetshire* (68); 25.12.1752 Able *Captain* (70); 3.5.1753 Mid *Captain* (64); 5.6.1754 Able *Vulture* (14) Sloop; 17.3.1755 Able *Phoenix* (24); 14.6.1755

Mate *Phoenix* (24); 3.12.1755 Passed; **Lieutenant**; 29.3.1757-12.11.1757 3L *Falmouth* (50); 28.11.1757-8.5.1758[D] 2L *Roebuck* (44); 8.5.1758 Dismissed.

PEARCE, VINCENT

Dates: 12.1759 Died.

Family:

Service: **Lieutenant**; 19.2.1740/41[11.2.1741/42]-7.6.1741 3L *Worcester* (60); 4.3.1740/41-5.1741 Operations against Cartagena; 8.6.1741[11.2.1741/42] 4L *Orford* (70); 26.5.1742 3L *Revenge* (70); 31.12.1742[23.7.1745] 6L *Barfleur* (90); 11.2.1743/44-12.2.1743/44 Battle of Toulon; 19.3.1743/44[23.7.1745]-22.7.1745[P] 4L *Barfleur* (90); **Commander**; 11.9.1747-9.3.1747/48 *Drake* (14) Sloop; **Captain**; 4.11.1748-28.10.1749[P] *Boston* (24); 7.6.1751-8.6.1754[P] *Blandford* (20); 11.2.1756 *Mercury* (20); 23.3.1757-18.10.1758 *Lizard* (28); 29.1.1759-1.1.1760 *York* (60).

PEARD, GEORGE

Dates: c.1716 Born.

Family:

Service: 22.3.1733/34-3.5.1737[P] Mid *Leopard* (50); 27.5.1740 Mid *Princess Caroline* (80); 18.2.1740/41-2.11.1741[P] Mid *Burford* (70); 20.2.1741/42 Mid *Saint George* (90); 10.10.1743 Passed; **Lieutenant**; 15.6.1744 4L *Captain* (70); 5.5.1746[13.9.1748]-10.4.1747 2L *Sutherland* (50); 23.10.1754-30.4.1755 L. *Seaford* (20); **Commander**; 23.8.1759-22.12.1762 *Savage* (8) Sloop.

PEARSON, SIR RICHARD

Dates: 3.1730/31 Born Langton Hall, Westmorland; 19.4.1780 Knight Bachelor; 26.1.1806 Died Royal Naval Hospital, Greenwich.

Family: Father Richard Pearson; Mother Hannah; Wife Margaret Harrison (1743-1816); Son Richard Harrison, RN.

Service: 20.11.1745 Capt Serv *Dover* (44); 27.1.1745/46 Able *Seaford* (20) Ship; 21.4.1747-14.1.1748/49[P] Mid *Seaford* (20) Ship; 15.1.1748/49 Mid *Amazon* (22); 27.5.1750-1.9.1750 Able *Amazon* (22); 5.11.1755 Passed; **Lieutenant**; 16.12.1755 4L *Elizabeth* (70); 13.11.1756 3L *Elizabeth* (64); 29.4.1758 Battle of Cuddalore; 3.8.1758 Battle of Negapatam; 10.9.1759 Battle of Pondicherry; 10.7.1761-21.10.1762 1L *Lennox* (74); 24.9.1762-6.10.1762 Battle of Manilla; 21.2.1769 1L *Dunkirk* (60); **Commander**; 29.10.1770-26.12.1771[P] *Druid* (10) Sloop; 16.1.1773 *Ferret* (14) Sloop; 26.1.1773 *Speedwell* (8) Sloop; **Captain**; 25.6.1773 *Juno* (32); 26.6.1773-26.1.1776 *Speedwell* (8) Sloop; 30.3.1776 *Garland* (24); 1.3.1779-23.9.1779[C] *Serapis* (44); 23.9.1779 Battle of Flamborough Head; 13.4.1780 *Alarm* (32); 28.3.1781-25.3.1783[P] *Arethusa* (38); 12.12.1781 2nd Battle of Ushant; 1800-1805 Lieutenant-governor of Greenwich Hospital at Greenwich Hospital.

PEAT, GEORGE

Dates: 1772 Died; 30.12.1772 Will Probate.

Family:

Service: **Lieutenant**; 22.3.1762[16.11.1762]-4.11.1762[P] 2L *Crescent* (32) Frigate; 15.7.1763-11.2.1767[P] L. *Jamaica* (10) Sloop; 21.6.1770-27.3.1772 L. *Zephyr* (10) Sloop.

PEERMAN, JOHN

Dates: 6.1758 Died.

Family:

Service: **Lieutenant**; 28.8.1743[MED 30.6.1748] L. *Terrible* (6) Bomb Vessel; 5.10.1747[28.10.1748]-14.11.1748[P] 1L *Nassau* (70); 7.1.1757 2L *Terrible* (74).

PEEVEY, WILLIAM

Dates: c.1714 Born.

Family:

Service: 1737-1739 Merchant Service; 5.6.1739 Able *Adventure* (40); 3.4.1740 Mid *Gloucester* (50); 18.5.1741-16.8.1742[SC] Mate *Gloucester* (50); 30.8.1743 Able *Centurion* (60); 5.8.1745 Mid *Lion* (58); 30.8.1745-6.3.1746 Mate *Lion* (58); 6.3.1745/46 Passed; **Lieutenant**; 7.3.1745/46-19.10.1747 3L *Ruby* (50); 20.9.1746-25.9.1746 Lorient Operations; 1.12.1748-21.1.1752[P] 3L *Somerset* (68); 6.2.1755 3L *Nassau* (64); 18.2.1755 2L *Nassau* (64); 1.11.1755 6L *Duke* (90); 14.7.1756 5L *Duke* (90); 26.5.1757 4L *Duke* (90); 5.6.1758-12.6.1758 Raid on Saint-Malo; 4.9.1759 3L *Duke* (90); 20.11.1759 Battle of Quiberon Bay; 24.5.1762-14.6.1762 2L *Duke* (90).

PEIGHIN, JOHN

Dates: c.1725 Born; 31.7.1785 Died Bath; 31.8.1785 Will Probate.

Family: Wife Mary Hodgson married 16.12.1766.

Service: 1735-1739 Merchant Service; 25.11.1739 Mid *Eltham* (40); 21.1.1741/42 Mid *Burford* (70); 14.5.1743 Mid *Burford* (70); 6.7.1744 Mid *Marlborough* (90); 25.9.1744 Mate *Marlborough* (90); **Lieutenant**; 2.6.1745[MED 8.9.1746]-12.10.1745 3L *Antelope* (50); 4.6.1745 Passed; 8.5.1751-16.11.1752[P] 3L *Fougueux* (64); 16.1.1755 3L *Captain* (64); 20.3.1756 2L *Captain* (64); 20.5.1756 Battle of Minorca; 31.3.1757 6L *Ramillies* (90); 5.9.1757-6.10.1757 Raid on Rochefort; **Commander**; 4.1.1758 *Alderney* (10) Sloop; **Captain**; 1.12.1761[EI 10.6.1762]-28.6.1765[P] *Seaford* (20); 24.9.1762-6.10.1762 Battle of Manilla.

PELL, THOMAS

Dates: c.1713 Born.

Family:

Service: 28.11.1735 Mid *Berwick* (70); 28.3.1736 QM *Berwick* (70); 23.12.1736 Mid *Berwick* (70); 20.2.1736/37 QM *Berwick* (70); 2.9.1737 Able *Lancaster* (80); 26.10.1737 Mid *Lancaster* (80); 29.3.1738 Able *Edinburgh* (70); 19.9.1738-30.5.1740[P] Mid *Edinburgh* (70); 19.4.1745 Mate *Marlborough* (90); 15.12.1745 Mid *Antelope* (50); 6.4.1746 Mate *Antelope* (50); 2.4.1747 Passed; **Lieutenant**; 29.7.1757-13.4.1758[B] 5L *Prince George* (80).

PEMBERTON, HENRY

Dates: c.1735 Born; 1796 Died; 7.5.1796 Will Probate.

Family:

Service: 1753-1755 Merchant Service; 24.7.1755 Able *Winchelsea* (20); 29.12.1755 QGnr *Falkland* (50); 8.11.1757 Mid *Falkland* (50); 30.8.1759 Mate *Goree* (10) Sloop; 1.11.1759 Mid *Chesterfield* (44); 31.12.1760 Passed; **Lieutenant**; 16.3.1761-6.1.1762[P] L. *Grampus* (14) Sloop; 17.2.1762-2.3.1763[P] 5L *Superb* (74); **Commander**; 1.4.1778-2.7.1778 *Pluto* (8) Fireship.

PEMBLE, THOMAS

Dates: c.1724 Born; 22.12.1724 Baptised Greenwich, Kent; c.4.1785 Died; 17.4.1785 Buried Borden, Kent; 26.5.1785 Will Probate.
Family: Father James Pemble; Mother Mary.
Service: 7.1.1737/38 Surg Serv *Lowestoffe* (20); 16.5.1741 Mid *Dartmouth* (50); 28.6.1743 Mid *Warwick* (60); 11.2.1743/44-12.2.1743/44 Battle of Toulon; 7.2.1744/45 Passed; **Lieutenant**; 15.2.1744/45 L. *Trial* (10) Sloop; 1.4.1746-4.6.1755[P] L. *Triton* (20); 5.8.1755 3L *Newark* (80); 7.10.1755 3L *Intrepid* (64); 20.5.1756 Battle of Minorca; 13.4.1757-14.10.1761 1L *Burford* (68); 5.9.1757-6.10.1757 Raid on Rochefort; 6.6.1758-27.7.1758 The Siege of Louisbourg; 16.1.1759-19.1.1759 Attack on Martinique; 20.1.1759-1.5.1759 Capture of Guadeloupe; 20.11.1759 Battle of Quiberon Bay; 29.3.1761-11.6.1761 Expedition against Belle-Isle; 11.5.1763 1L *Prince of Orange* (60); 6.6.1763 1L *Bellona* (74); 6.9.1763 1L *Augusta* (64); **Commander**; 20.6.1765 *Grampus* (8) Fireship; 25.8.1766-24.9.1766 *Lynx* (10) Sloop; 24.10.1766-26.10.1769 *Hazard* (8) Sloop.

PENNY, TAYLOR

Dates: c.1722 Born; 1.3.1722/23 Baptised Melcombe Regis, Dorset; 13.4.1786 Died.
Family: Father John Penny; Mother Elizabeth; Wife Mary Taver married 21.4.1748; Daughter Martha (1749-?); Daughter Elizabeth (1758-?); Son Taver (1770-?).
Service: 25.7.1745 Passed; **Lieutenant**; 6.8.1745 3L *Lion* (58); 14.10.1747 2nd Battle of Cape Finisterre; 1.2.1747/48-4.4.1748 2L *Lion* (58); 3.5.1750-6.1.1756 L. *Porcupine* (16) Sloop; **Commander**; 31.12.1755-17.2.1757[P] *Firebrand* (6) Fireship; **Captain**; 1.11.1757 *Aldborough* (20); 26.11.1759-3.6.1763[P] *Looe* (44); 22.5.1778 *Burford* (68); 25.1.1779 *Arrogant* (74); 7.6.1779-22.7.1783[P] *Marlborough* (74); 16.1.1780 Battle of Cape St. Vincent; 12.4.1782 Battle of the Saintes.

PERCEVAL, PHILIP TUFTON

Dates: 10.3.1740/41 Born Pall Mall, Westminster; 12.3.1741 Baptised St James, Westminster; 21.4.1795 Died.
Family: Father Sir John Perceval, 2nd Earl of Egmont (1710-1770); Mother Catherine Cecil (1719-1752); Wife Catherine Hennesay (d.1834) married 15.5.1790; Son Michael Henry (1779-1829); Son Lt. Col. Philip Joshua (1791-1847); Daughter Sarah Jane [Pownall] (1793-?); Brother Edward (1744-1829); Brother Frederick Augustus (1749-1757); Sister Catherine [Wynn] (1745-1782); Sister Margaret (1748-1749); Half-brother Charles George (1756-1840); Half-sister Mary (1758-1839); Half-sister Anne (1759-1772); Half-brother John Thomas (1760-?); Half-sister Charlotte (1761-1761); Half-brother Spencer, KC PM (1762-1812); Half-sister Elizabeth (1763-1846); Half-brother Henry (1765-1772); Half-sister Frances (1767-1817); Half-sister Margaret (1769-1854).
Service: **Lieutenant**; 5.7.1759[(14.1.1760)] 4L *Stirling Castle* (64); **Commander**; 5.9.1759[(14.1.1760)]-11.4.1760 *Badger* (10) Sloop; 11.4.1760 *Badger* (10) Sloop; **Captain**; 21.7.1760 *Dover* (44); 7.1.1762-10.2.1762 Operations against Martinique; 24.2.1762-25.2.1762 Capture of Saint Lucia; 29.3.1762[(18.11.1763)]-18.9.1763[P] *Aquilon* (28); 6.10.1763 *Ramillies* (74); 19.3.1764 *Tweed* (32); 1.4.1765 *Aquilon* (28); 18.1.1766 *Launceston* (44); 2.4.1766 *Fubbs* (12) Yacht; 7.7.1781 *Mary* (8) Yacht.

PERCIVALL, CREAN
Dates: c.1729 Born; c.1759 Died; 20.12.1759 Will Probate.
Family:
Service: 11.1.1748/49 Ord. *Tartar* (20); 24.5.1751-29.5.1752[P] Able *Tartar* (20); 13.9.1753 Able *Kent* (64); 12.7.1754 Able *Yarmouth* (64); 17.12.1754 Mid *Yarmouth* (64); 17.2.1755 Mid *Winchester* (50); 9.8.1756 Mate *Winchester* (50); 14.12.1757 Passed; **Lieutenant**; 16.12.1757-26.9.1760[P] L. *Squirrel* (20); 6.6.1758-27.7.1758 The Siege of Louisbourg.

PERKINS, WILLIAM
Dates: c.1724 Born; 6.1793 Died.
Family:
Service: c.1.1739-c.6.1740 Merchant Service; 1.6.1740 Able *Hound* (8) Sloop; 2.6.1741 Able *Prince George* (90); 25.11.1741 Mid *Nassau* (70); 13.9.1742-4.3.1742/43[P] Mid *Winchester* (50); 6.3.1742/43 Mid *Torrington* (44); 27.10.1743 Mid *Shrewsbury* (80); 15.12.1743 Mid *Chichester* (80); 11.2.1743/44-12.2.1743/44 Battle of Toulon; 27.10.1744 Mate *Revenge* (64); 15.1.1744/45 Passed; 29.1.1744/45 **Lieutenant**; 23.12.1746[(MED 23.12.1746)]-18.8.1747 4L *Revenge* (70); 19.3.1747/48[(15.11.1748)]-29.7.1748 3L *Princess* (70); 1.8.1748[(12.5.1749)]-1.5.1749[P] 1L *Superb* (60).

PERREAU, SAMUEL
Dates: c.1734 Born; 24.3.1757 Died India; 21.3.1759 Will Probate.
Family: Wife Elizabeth.
Service: 22.12.1747 Capt Serv *Centurion* (50); 22.3.1748/49 Ord. *Centurion* (50); 21.1.1750/51 Able *Centurion* (50); 22.4.1751 Mid *Centurion* (50); 9.10.1752 Able *Saint Albans* (60); 18.10.1752-6.2.1754 Mid *Saint Albans* (50); 6.2.1754 Passed; c.1756 **Lieutenant**; 16.1.1757-24.3.1757[†] 1L *Kent* (64).

PERRY, JOHN
Dates: c.1737 Born.
Family:
Service: 6.9.1752 Capt Serv *Badger* (10) Sloop; 15.1.1753 Able *Badger* (10) Sloop; 12.12.1754 Mid *Badger* (10) Sloop; 3.2.1756 Mid *Falkland* (50); 18.4.1758 Able *Falkland* (50); 25.10.1758 Mid *Richmond* (32); 2.5.1759 Passed; **Lieutenant**; 11.3.1760 5L *Fame* (74); 29.3.1761-11.6.1761 Expedition against Belle-Isle; 8.9.1763-29.10.1763[D] L. *Zephyr* (10) Sloop; 29.10.1763 Dismissed; 18.9.1770 5L *Cornwall* (74); 5.11.1770-27.5.1771[P] 4L *Cornwall* (74); 13.1.1772 4L *Egmont* (74); 16.9.1773-14.9.1774 L. *Hunter* (10) Sloop; 25.10.1775 1L *Fox* (28); 7.6.1777 Action of 7th June 1777; 19.3.1778 1L *Vigilant* (64); 2.4.1778-3.4.1779 3L *Cumberland* (74); 27.7.1778 1st Battle of Ushant; 27.7.1779-26.1.1780 1L *Arrogant* (74).

PETT, ROBERT
Dates: c.2.1775 Died; 19.2.1775 Buried Faversham; 19.12.1776 Will Probate.
Family: Daughter Susanna; Son John.
Service: 31.3.1720 Vol-p-O *Ipswich* (70); 25.7.1721 MidO *Dursley Galley* (20); 3.5.1722-24.7.1724 Mid *Dursley Galley* (20); 24.7.1724 Passed; **Lieutenant**; 19.9.1727-26.5.1728[P] 4L *Revenge* (70); 9.2.1728/29-9.10.1729[P] 2L *Winchester* (50); 27.1.1729/30-14.6.1731 3L *Lark* (40); 15.2.1732/33-14.3.1737/38 3L *Edinburgh* (70); **Captain**; 15.7.1740 *Bridgewater* (20); 2.12.1741 *Diamond* (44); 31.1.1742/43-5.7.1745 *Princess* (70); 11.2.1743/44-12.2.1743/44 Battle of Toulon; 1.3.1745/46 *Norwich* (50); 21.4.1748-25.6.1748[P] *Greenwich* (50); 16.1.1753

Invincible (74); 16.5.1753-10.2.1755 *Terrible* (74); 10.7.1762-c.2.1775 Commissioner of the Victualling Board.

PETTIGREW, WILLIAM

Dates: 24.11.1756 Died Portsmouth.
Family:
Service: **Lieutenant**; 16.3.1743/44(28.5.1746)-19.10.1745[C] L. *Blast* (8) Bomb Vessel; **Commander**; 30.4.1746-6.10.1748[P] *Vulcan* (16) Sloop; 20.9.1746-25.9.1746 Lorient Operations; 3.5.1747 1st Battle of Cape Finisterre; **Captain**; 18.7.1755-24.11.1756† *Queenborough* (24).

PEYTON, JOSEPH

Dates: 1725 Born; 27.9.1804 Died.
Family: Son Joseph, RN.
Service: **Lieutenant**; 4.6.1743(MED 25.1.1745/46)-5.8.1748 4L *Essex* (70); 11.2.1743/44-12.2.1743/44 Battle of Toulon; 15.9.1747(23.8.1748) 1L *Essex* (70); 9.4.1748(23.8.1748)-22.8.1748[P] 3L *Guernsey* (50); 10.7.1755-5.8.1755 L. *Sheerness* (24); **Commander**; 23.3.1756 *Savage* (8) Sloop; **Captain**; 2.12.1757-13.4.1758[B] *Prince George* (80); 14.5.1758(26.10.1758) *Saint George* (90); 13.6.1758(8.4.1760) *Prince* (90); 18.8.1759-19.8.1759 Battle of Lagos Bay; 24.12.1761 *Aquilon* (28); 18.2.1762-3.2.1763[P] *Minerva* (32); 24.10.1766 *Belleisle* (64); 8.1.1771-9.4.1771 *Modeste* (64); 29.12.1777 *Cumberland* (74); 27.7.1778 1st Battle of Ushant; 16.1.1780 Battle of Cape St. Vincent; 11.9.1781-13.3.1783[P] 1Capt. *Britannia* (100); 12.12.1781 2nd Battle of Ushant; 20.10.1782 Battle of Cape Spartel; 24.9.1787 **Rear Admiral of the White**; 28.9.1788-1789 *Leander* (52); 29.9.1788 CinC — The Mediterranean Sea; 1789 *Edgar* (74); 21.9.1790 **Vice Admiral of the Blue**; 1.2.1793 **Vice Admiral of the White**; 6.6.1793-4.1799 CinC — The Downs; 2.1794-2.1796 *Leopard* (50); 12.4.1794 **Vice Admiral of the Red**; 10.1794 *Terror* (8) Bomb Vessel; 1.6.1795 **Admiral of the Blue**; 1796 *Savage* (14) Sloop; 7.1796-1799 *Overyssel* (64); 10.1798 *Wassenar* (66); 14.2.1799 **Admiral of the White**.

PHILIPS, HENRY

Dates: c.1725 Baptised; 22.11.1779 Died; 11.1.1780 Will Probate.
Family:
Service: 28.9.1740 Capt Serv *Winchester* (50); 19.11.1740 Capt Serv *Montagu* (60); 9.2.1741/42-16.7.1742[P] Capt Serv *Bristol* (54); 25.12.1742 Mid *Montagu* (60); **Lieutenant**; 16.5.1746-10.9.1748[P] 3L *Ambuscade* (40); 30.8.1746 Mid *Tilbury* (58); 20.9.1746-25.9.1746 Lorient Operations; 25.2.1746/47 Mid *Sandwich* (90); 15.3.1746/47 Passed; 3.5.1747 1st Battle of Cape Finisterre; 6.2.1755 2L *Weymouth* (60); 7.10.1755-17.1.1757 1L *Weymouth* (60); 16.1.1757-8.2.1757 3L *Weymouth* (60); 11.5.1763-10.5.1766 1L *Burford* (68); **Commander**; 26.5.1768 *Grampus* (8) Fireship.

PHILLIP, ARTHUR

Dates: 11.10.1738 Born Fulham, London, Fulham; 31.8.1814 Died Bath.
Family:
Service: **Lieutenant**; 7.6.1761(24.3.1763)-14.9.1762[P] 4L *Stirling Castle* (64); 7.1.1762-10.2.1762 Operations against Martinique; 6.6.1762-13.8.1762 Operations against Havana; 13.11.1770-29.6.1771 4L *Egmont* (74); 9.10.1778-16.9.1779 1L *Alexander* (74); **Commander**; 2.9.1779-24.7.1781 *Basilisk* (8) Fireship; **Captain**; 30.11.1781 *Ariadne* (20); 23.12.1782-15.5.1784[P] *Europe* (64); 25.10.1786 *Sirius* (10) Armed Storeship; 15.12.1786-15.3.1790[W] Commodore *Sirius* (10) Armed Storeship; 16.3.1796 *Alexander* (74); 20.10.1796-27.9.1797 *Swiftsure* (74);

28.9.1797-8.2.1798 *Blenheim* (98); 1798-1799 Sea Fencibles at Hampshire; 1.1.1801 **Rear Admiral of the Blue**; 23.4.1804 **Rear Admiral of the White**; 9.11.1805 **Rear Admiral of the Red**; 25.10.1809 **Vice Admiral of the White**; 31.7.1810 **Vice Admiral of the Red**; 4.6.1814 **Admiral of the Blue.**

PHILLIPS, GEORGE

Dates: None Known.
Family:
Service: **Lieutenant**; 11.3.1755-2.12.1755 3L *Warwick* (60).

PHILLIPS, GEORGE

Dates: c.1735 Born.
Family:
Service: 9.2.1750/51 Able *Vulture* (14) Sloop; 30.5.1752 Mid *Vulture* (14) Sloop; 8.5.1755 Mate *Vulture* (14) Sloop; 22.1.1756 Mate *Fougueux* (64); 21.10.1756 Mid *Grafton* (68); 7.2.1757 Passed; **Lieutenant**; 10.2.1757 3L *Centurion* (50); 29.3.1757-22.9.1759 2L *Centurion* (50); 6.6.1758-27.7.1758 The Siege of Louisbourg; 3.1.1760-17.6.1762 5L *Neptune* (90).

PHILLIPS, HENRY JOHN

Dates: 1718 Born; 3.9.1762 Died.
Family:
Service: 19.5.1735 Able *Shoreham* (20); 12.5.1737 Mid *Shoreham* (20); 17.3.1737/38 Able *Windsor* (60); 4.11.1740-19.11.1741[P] Mid *Windsor* (60); 4.3.1740/41-5.1741 Operations against Cartagena; 27.11.1741 Mid *Buckingham* (70); 19.1.1741/42 Passed; **Lieutenant**; 6.8.1742[(21.1.1744/45)] L. *Terrible* (6) Bomb Vessel; 27.8.1743[(MED 14.12.1747)]-18.8.1744 4L *Revenge* (70); 11.2.1743/44-12.2.1743/44 Battle of Toulon; 12.7.1745[(MED 21.11.1748)]-26.10.1748[P] 1L *Rupert* (60); 3.6.1752-7.10.1756 2L *Deptford* (50); **Commander**; 27.4.1756-11.6.1756 *Blast* (8) Fireship; 20.5.1756 Battle of Minorca; **Captain**; 17.1.1757 *Fowey* (24); 14.11.1758-3.9.1762[†] *Juno* (32); 3.7.1759 Bombardment of Le Havre.

PHILLIPS, NATHANIEL

Dates: 17.6.1784 Died.
Family:
Service: **Lieutenant**; 5.6.1761[(EI 25.8.1764)]-8.9.1763 4L *America* (60); 24.9.1762-6.10.1762 Battle of Manilla; 31.10.1770 2L *Diana* (32); 21.1.1773[(23.8.1774)]-18.1.1774[P] LCmdr *Earl of Northampton*; 9.11.1776 5L *Monarch* (74); 15.11.1776 4L *Monarch* (74); 10.6.1778 3L *Monarch* (74); 27.7.1778 1st Battle of Ushant; 8.12.1778-13.10.1781[P] 3L *Suffolk* (74); 6.7.1779 Battle of Grenada; 21.12.1779-22.12.1779 Action of 1779-12-21; 17.4.1780 Battle of Martinique; 15.5.1780 Action of March 15 1780; 19.5.1780 Action of March 19 1780; 13.12.1782-16.3.1784[P] *Abondance* (14) Storeship.

PHILLIPS, WILLIAM

Dates: c.1724 Born; 1762 Died; 24.5.1762 Will Probate.
Family:
Service: 22.7.1738 Able *Torrington* (40); 29.4.1739 Able *Saint Albans* (50); 18.7.1739 Trump *Warwick* (60); 23.1.1740/41 Mid *Warwick* (60); 11.2.1743/44-12.2.1743/44 Battle of Toulon; 7.2.1744/45 Passed; **Lieutenant**; 26.6.1745-15.9.1745[W] L. *Sapphire's Prize* (10) Sloop; 31.3.1748 4L *Vanguard* (68); 15.4.1748 3L *Bristol* (50); 23.4.1748-3.5.1748 2L *Bristol* (50);

3.5.1748 3L *Bristol* (50); 27.9.1748 3L *Tavistock* (50); 17.7.1749(30.8.1750) L. *Shark* (8) Sloop; 30.1.1749/50(30.8.1750) L. *Speedwell* (10) Sloop; 18.4.1750(4.10.1752)-22.10.1751 L. *Rose* (24) Ship.

PHILLIPS, WILLIAM

Dates: c.1735 Born; 5.3.1771 Died.
Family:
Service: 14.1.1740/41 Able *Lichfield* (50); 4.3.1740/41-5.1741 Operations against Cartagena; 14.10.1741 Able *Deptford* (24) Storeship; 23.12.1741 Mid *Romney* (50); 11.2.1743/44-12.2.1743/44 Battle of Toulon; 14.10.1745 Able *Royal Sovereign* (104); 25.12.1745 Mid *Royal Sovereign* (104); 7.8.1747 Passed; **Lieutenant**; 21.6.1756 6L *Saint George* (90); 6.4.1757 5L *Saint George* (90); 15.4.1757 2L *Trident* (64); 15.5.1758 2L *Enterprise* (44); 5.7.1758(BLI 8.11.1759)-22.1.1760[P] 1L *Bristol* (50); 16.1.1759-19.1.1759 Attack on Martinique; 20.1.1759-1.5.1759 Capture of Guadeloupe; **Commander**; 24.3.1760-19.11.1761 *Spy* (10) Sloop; 25.3.1763-28.1.1765 *Spy* (10) Sloop; 4.8.1768-5.3.1771† *Trial* (10) Sloop.

PHILPOT, GEORGE

Dates: c.1731 Born.
Family:
Service: 2.12.1745 Able *Aldborough* (20); 31.8.1747 Able *Hampshire* (50); 1.8.1748 Mid *Nottingham* (60); 10.2.1748/49 Mid *Cumberland* (66); 6.5.1749 Mid *Mercury* (20); 21.1.1750/51-16.1.1751/52[P] Able *Boston* (24); 27.1.1751/52-6.5.1753[P] Able *Winchelsea* (20); 6.6.1753 Passed; **Lieutenant**; 9.12.1757-6.8.1759 L. *Favorite* (16) Sloop; 20.8.1759(NA 19.5.1760) 4L *Culloden* (74); 15.8.1760-28.3.1763 3L *Culloden* (74); 6.6.1762-13.8.1762 Operations against Havana; 28.3.1763-7.4.1763[P] 2L *Culloden* (74).

PHIPPS, CONSTANTINE JOHN (1ST BARON OF MULGRAVE IN THE COUNTY OF YORK)

Dates: 3.5.1744 Born; 13.9.1775 2nd Baron Mulgrave; 7.7.1790 1st Baron of Mulgrave in the County of York; 10.10.1792 Died Liège.
Family: Father Constantine Phipps, 1st Baron Mulgrave (d.1775); Mother Lepell Hervey; Wife Anne Elizabeth Cholmley married 20.6.1787; Daughter Unknown; Brother The Hon. Charles, RN (1753-1786); Brother Hon. Henry (1755-1831).
Service: 1.1759 Mid *Monmouth* (70); c.6.3.1760 Mid *Dragon* (74); 29.3.1761-11.6.1761 Expedition against Belle-Isle; 7.1.1762-10.2.1762 Operations against Martinique; 24.2.1762-25.2.1762 Capture of Saint Lucia; **Lieutenant**; 17.3.1762(19.11.1762) 5L *Dragon* (74); 2.7.1762(EI 19.11.1762)-15.12.1762[P] 2L *Dragon* (74); 10.5.1763 L. *Deal Castle* (20); 7.6.1763 1L *Romney* (50); **Commander**; 24.11.1763(NA 19.6.1764) *Diligence* (10) Sloop; **Captain**; 20.6.1765 *Terpsichore* (24); 10.6.1767-3.5.1768 *Boreas* (28); 19.3.1768-12.10.1774 M.P. for Lincoln; 16.4.1773-13.10.1773[P] *Racehorse* (16) Sloop; 31.1.1776-31.3.1784 M.P. for Huntingdon; 6.11.1776-26.1.1778 *Ardent* (64); 1777-3.1782 Lord Commissioner of the Admiralty; 7.2.1778-1.4.1783[P] *Courageux* (74); 27.7.1778 1st Battle of Ushant; 31.12.1779 Affair of Fielding and Bylandt; 12.12.1781 2nd Battle of Ushant; 1.4.1784-21.6.1790 M.P. for Newark-on-Trent; 23.4.1784-23.4.1792 Privy Counsellor; 19.10.1790-10.10.1792† *Leviathan* (74).

PHIPPS, DAVID

Dates: c.1726 Baptised; 1811 Died.
Family:
Service: 1741-1747 Merchant Service; 15.1.1746/47 Mid *Chester* (50); 29.5.1747 Mid *Devonshire* (66); 1.8.1747 ActL *Falkland* (50); 14.1.1747/48 Mid *Saint George* (90); 1.6.1748 ActL *Culloden*

(74); 10.9.1748 Mid *Devonshire* (66); 17.10.1748 Mid *Prince Frederick* (70); 19.1.1748/49 Passed; **Lieutenant**; 24.11.1750[NA 4.4.1751]-15.4.1751[P] 2L *Renown* (30); **Commander**; 1.5.1779[NA 29.6.1780]-6.8.1782[C] *Allegiance* (16) Sloop; 21.7.1781 Action of 1781-07-21; 25.10.1809 **Captain.**

PICKERING, THOMAS WOOLLEY

Dates: c.1728 Born; 1792 Died; 20.10.1792 Will Probate.
Family:
Service: 1.4.1731 Vol-p-O *Shoreham* (20); 29.1.1731/32 Vol-p-O *Winchester* (50); 7.9.1734-7.9.1736 Vol-p-O *Shoreham* (20); 7.9.1739-1.12.1739 Mid *Burford* (70); 21.11.1739 Attack on Puerto Bello; 2.12.1739 Able *Royal Caroline* (8) Yacht; 6.3.1739/40 Passed; **Lieutenant**; 8.5.1740 4L *Prince Frederick* (70); 7.1.1740/41 Action of January 7 1741; 4.3.1740/41-5.1741 Operations against Cartagena; 11.6.1741[27.5.1742]-10.6.1742 2L *Prince Frederick* (70); 11.9.1742 3L *Preston* (50); 24.1.1744/45 Straits of Banca; 26.2.1744/45[4.10.1746] 1L *Preston* (50); 20.12.1745[4.10.1746]-25.9.1746[P] 1L *Deptford* (60).

PIERCY, THOMAS

Dates: c.1732 Born; 22.9.1793 Died; 19.10.1793 Will Probate.
Family:
Service: 11.2.1745 Adm Serv *Ipswich* (70); 3.5.1745 Adm Serv *Russell* (80); 4.10.1746-9.1.1749[P] Able *Enterprise* Sloop; 12.11.1752 Mid *Kent* (64); 10.3.1755 Passed; **Lieutenant**; 14.2.1757-31.7.1761[P] L. *Success* (20); 8.1757-10.1757 Louisbourg Expedition; 5.6.1758-12.6.1758 Raid on Saint-Malo; 24.9.1761-4.4.1763 1L *Maidstone* (28); 15.2.1770-13.3.1772 1L *Carysfort* (28); 7.4.1777 1L *Conquestador* (60); **Commander**; 18.4.1778-23.9.1779[C] *Countess of Scarborough* (20) Hired Armed Ship; 23.9.1779 Battle of Flamborough Head; **Captain**; 19.4.1780 *Squirrel* (20); 23.8.1781-12.1.1782 *Dolphin* (44); 15.1.1782-28.6.1782 *Panther* (60).

PIGOT, HUGH

Dates: 28.5.1722 Born; 15.12.1792 Died.
Family: Father Richard Pigot (bap. 1679, d. 1729); Wife Elizabeth le Neve married c.1749; Wife Frances Wrottesley (d. 1811) married 1768; Son Unknown; Daughter Unknown; Son Unknown; Daughter Unknown; Daughter Unknown.
Service: 9.5.1735-4.5.1737[P] Able *Captain* (70); 10.5.1737 Capt Serv *Seaford* (20); 30.4.1739 Able *Seaford* (20); 18.9.1739-5.5.1740[P] Mid *Seaford* (20); 12.6.1740 Mid *Cumberland* (80); 2.7.1741 Mid *Russell* (80); 5.11.1741 Passed; **Lieutenant**; 9.2.1741/42 L. *Portsmouth* (24) Storeship; 2.8.1742[7.3.1743/44] 3L *Romney* (50); 11.2.1743/44-12.2.1743/44 Battle of Toulon; 14.3.1743/44 2L *Falkland* (50); 5.7.1745 1L *Falkland* (50); **Commander**; 2.11.1745 *Vulcan* (16) Sloop; **Captain**; 22.4.1746 *Centaur* (20); 14.4.1747[BLI 14.4.1749]-18.2.1748/49[P] *Ludlow Castle* (44); 20.2.1755 *York* (60); 6.6.1758-27.7.1758 The Siege of Louisbourg; 30.1.1759-23.2.1763[P] *Royal William* (84); 29.3.1761-11.6.1761 Expedition against Belle-Isle; 2.3.1768-12.10.1774 M.P. for Penryn; 8.1.1771-13.5.1771 *Triumph* (74); 31.3.1775 **Rear Admiral of the White**; 7.12.1775 **Vice Admiral of the Blue**; 29.1.1778 **Vice Admiral of the White**; 16.2.1778-5.4.1784 M.P. for Bridgnorth; 26.9.1780 **Vice Admiral of the Red**; 4.1782-1783 *Formidable* (98); 1.4.1782-30.12.1783 Lord Commissioner of the Admiralty; 12.4.1782 Battle of the Saintes; 24.4.1782 **Admiral of the Blue**; 24.4.1782 CinC — Barbados & the Leeward Islands; 24.9.1787 **Admiral of the White**; 26.9.1787 CinC — English Channel.

PIGOT, ROWLAND

Dates: None Known.
Family:
Service: **Lieutenant**; 26.3.1759[(BLI 8.8.1760)]-5.8.1760[P] 4L *Berwick* (64); 16.1.1762 2L *Assistance* (50); 17.6.1766-19.4.1768 LCmdr *Friendship* (4) Cutter.

PIGOT, THOMAS

Dates: c.1724 Born; 29.9.1782 Died.
Family:
Service: 18.11.1740 Chap Serv *Liverpool* (44); 29.3.1744 Able *Liverpool* (44); 9.7.1745 Mid *Liverpool* (44); 26.8.1745 Mid *Barfleur* (90); 14.9.1745 Mid *Worcester* (58); 21.12.1745 Mid *Looe* (44); 24.4.1746 Mid *Swan* (10) Sloop; 18.9.1747 Passed; **Lieutenant**; 31.12.1747-17.2.1748/49 L. *Ferret* (14) Sloop; 17.1.1757 LCmdr *Hunter* (10) Hired Cutter; 6.6.1758-27.7.1758 The Siege of Louisbourg; 19.7.1759 2L *Monarch* (74); 23.10.1759-6.10.1760[P] 1L *Monarch* (74).

PINFOLD, RICHARD

Dates: c.1721 Born; 4.3.1793 Died.
Family:
Service: 12.3.1746/47 Capt Serv *Elizabeth* (70); 15.2.1747/48 Able *Rupert* (60); 25.4.1749 Mid *Rupert* (60); 20.2.1753 Mate *Rupert* (60); 8.6.1754-7.4.1756 Mid *Rupert* (60); 7.4.1756 Passed; **Lieutenant**; 23.2.1757-25.9.1757[W] 3L *Tilbury* (58); 6.1.1778-11.1779 LCmdr *Spy* Hired Tender.

PITCAIRN, ROBERT

Dates: c.1726 Born Edinburgh; 1.1770 Died.
Family:
Service: 9.2.1748/49 Able *Revenge* (70); 20.5.1755 Mid *Saint George* (90); 3.8.1756 Mid *Namur* (90); 5.9.1757-6.10.1757 Raid on Rochefort; 26.12.1757 Mate *Namur* (90); 16.4.1758 Mate *Royal George* (100); 20.11.1759 Battle of Quiberon Bay; 20.2.1760 Passed; **Lieutenant**; 1.3.1760-6.4.1763 L. *Fortune* (14) Sloop.

PITCHFORD, SAMUEL

Dates: 1739 Born; 3.4.1816 Died.
Family: Father Samuel Pitchford (1705-1756); Mother Susannah Cornish; Wife Mary Gambier married 16.10.1771; Sister Margaret [King].
Service: **Lieutenant**; 6.8.1759 3L *Falmouth* (50); **Commander**; 6.6.1761[(EI 30.8.1764)] *Southsea Castle* (28) Storeship; **Captain**; 24.8.1761[(EI 30.8.1764)]-11.8.1764[P] *America* (60); 24.9.1762-6.10.1762 Battle of Manilla; 12.11.1778 *London* (90); 9.9.1779-21.3.1780 *Invincible* (74); 16.1.1780 Battle of Cape St. Vincent; 9.5.1781-18.7.1783[P] *Arrogant* (74); 12.4.1782 Battle of the Saintes; 10.5.1790 *Marlborough* (74); 21.9.1790 **Rear Admiral of the Blue**; 1.2.1793 **Rear Admiral of the Red**; 21.4.1794 **Vice Admiral of the Blue**; 4.7.1794 **Vice Admiral of the White**; 1.6.1795 **Vice Admiral of the Red**; 14.2.1799 **Admiral of the Blue**; 1.1.1801 **Admiral of the White**; 9.11.1805 **Admiral of the Red.**

PLAYSTOWE, PHILIP

Dates: c.1734 Born.
Family:
Service: 14.9.1748 Capt Serv *Tilbury* (58); 12.10.1748 Battle of Havana; 2.12.1748 Able *Captain* (70); 15.9.1749 Able *Somerset* (68); 18.7.1751 Mid *Somerset* (68); 4.12.1752 Mid *Hind*

(24); 20.8.1753 Mate *Hind* (24); 5.11.1755 Passed; 8.6.1757 **Lieutenant**; 12.1.1759[NA 29.12.1759]-2.4.1760 2L *Devonshire* (70); 5.12.1760-14.4.1761 2L *Assistance* (50); 18.5.1762-22.12.1762[P] 3L *Captain* (64).

PLINT, THOMAS
Dates: c.1730 Born; 1778 Died; 17.12.1778 Will Probate.
Family:
Service: 20.4.1746 Mid *Essex* (70); 7.10.1751 Mate *Gosport* (44); 17.7.1752 Mate *Advice* (50); 18.9.1753-22.5.1756[P] Master *Advice* (50); 2.6.1756 Passed; **Lieutenant**; 9.11.1756 6L *Namur* (90); 5.9.1757-6.10.1757 Raid on Rochefort; 17.1.1758-31.8.1759 1L *Active* (28); 5.6.1758-12.6.1758 Raid on Saint-Malo; 9.1.1760 3L *Namur* (90); 2.4.1761 5L *Namur* (90); 28.10.1761-15.2.1762 4L *Namur* (90); 22.2.1762-15.6.1762 2L *Saint Ann* (64); 5.10.1762-2.11.1762 L. *Nightingale* (22); 7.6.1766-17.6.1769 LCmdr *Goodwill* (4) Cutter; 31.5.1776-31.7.1776 1L *Barfleur* (90).

PLOWDEN, JAMES CHICHLEY
Dates: 29.4.1781 Died.
Family:
Service: **Lieutenant**; 19.7.1762[EI 22.2.1763]-5.10.1763[P] 5L *Dublin* (74); 24.1.1771-24.9.1773[P] 5L *Princess Amelia* (80); 16.11.1776 4L *Centaur* (74); 16.12.1776 3L *Centaur* (74); 13.5.1778 2L *Centaur* (74); 27.7.1778 1st Battle of Ushant; 1779 **Commander**; 22.9.1779 1L *Centaur* (74).

POCKLINGTON, CHRISTOPHER
Dates: 10.1766 Died Dublin.
Family: Father John Pocklington M.P. (c.1658-1731); Mother Elizabeth Hatton; Wife Elizabeth Domvile (c.1700-1774) married 29.9.1722; Daughter Anna Maria [Domville] (1723-1806); Daughter Ann [Gore]; Daughter Elizabeth [Hatton] (1725-1810); Daughter Bridget [Savage] (1726-1814); Son Charles (c.1739-1810).
Service: 13.3.1701/2 Ord. *Ranelagh* (80); 12.10.1702 Battle of Vigo; 30.11.1702 Ord. *Triumph* (90); 10.3.1702/3-27.11.1703[W] Ord. *Mary* (64); 4.3.1703/4 Ord. *Royal Anne* (100); 6.2.1705/6 Able *Royal Anne* (100); 15.3.1706/7 Mid *Royal Anne* (100); 2.12.1707 Mid *Fame* (24); 9.2.1708/9 Mid *Ludlow Castle* (42); 20.8.1710 Passed; **Lieutenant**; 3.7.1716-15.7.1717[P] 2L *Chester* (54); 11.3.1718/19 2L *Plymouth* (60); **Captain**; 14.11.1727-12.11.1730[P] *Port Mahon* (20); 28.9.1739-4.12.1739 *Rippon* (60); 5.12.1739-11.10.1740 *Deptford* (60); 21.8.1747 **Superannuated Rear Admiral**.

POCOCK, GEORGE CB
Dates: 6.3.1705/6 Born Thames Ditton, Surrey; 23.3.1761 Order of the Bath; 3.4.1792 Died Curzon Street, London.
Family: Father Thomas Pocock (1672-1745); Mother Joyce Master (d.1745); Wife Sophia Pitt Drake (d.1767) married 28.11.1763; Daughter Sophia (d. 1811); Son George (1765–1840).
Service: 1.9.1719 Vol-p-O *Looe* (32); 25.5.1720 Vol-p-O *Superb* (64); 12.11.1721-20.9.1722[P] MidO *Looe* (42); 25.5.1723 MidO *Prince Frederick* (70); 14.4.1724 Mid *Argyll* (50); 19.4.1725 Passed; **Lieutenant**; 7.12.1726[14.5.1728] 4L *Burford* (70); 8.10.1727 3L *Burford* (70); 16.7.1728 3L *Romney* (50); 24.5.1730[22.2.1730/31] 3L *Canterbury* (60); 19.5.1731-1.1.1731/32[P] 5L *Namur* (90); 14.6.1732 4L *Namur* (90); 28.6.1732 3L *Namur* (90); 22.8.1732 2L *Namur* (90); 9.5.1733 1L *Namur* (90); **Commander**; 26.2.1733/34-10.10.1737[P] *Bridgewater* (32); **Captain**; 1.8.1738[26.8.1741]-15.12.1741[P] *Aldborough* (20); 16.8.1742 *Suffolk* (70); 20.8.1742 *Woolwich* (50);

31.12.1742 *Shrewsbury* (80); 4.4.1743-9.1747 *Sutherland* (50); 2.11.1744 CinC — Plymouth; 6.5.1748[(18.10.1748)]-9.9.1748[P] *Sutherland* (50); 23.7.1752-17.11.1752[P] *Cumberland* (66); 24.1.1754 *Eagle* (60); 28.3.1754 *Cumberland* (66); 4.2.1755 **Rear Admiral of the White**; 4.7.1755-1757 *Cumberland* (66); 11.1.1756-14.1.1756 Capture of Geriah; 4.6.1756 **Rear Admiral of the Red**; 8.12.1756 **Vice Admiral of the Blue**; 1757-1759 CinC — East Indies; 24.2.1757 **Vice Admiral of the White**; 22.3.1757-23.3.1757 *Tiger* (60); 1758-1760 *Yarmouth* (64); 31.1.1758 **Vice Admiral of the Red**; 29.4.1758 Battle of Cuddalore; 3.8.1758 Battle of Negapatam; 10.9.1759 Battle of Pondicherry; 26.1.1760-18.3.1768 M.P. for Plymouth; 10.2.1761 **Admiral of the Blue**; 1762-21.10.1762 *Namur* (90); 6.6.1762-13.8.1762 Operations against Havana; 21.10.1762-1763 *Namur* (90); 11.9.1766 Resigned; 1786-1790 Master of Trinity House.

POLLARD, GEORGE

Dates: c.1734 Born; 1.7.1797 Died.
Family:
Service: 1751-1755 Merchant Service; 3.4.1755 Mate *Elizabeth* (70); 2.5.1757-29.11.1758[W] Mate *Lichfield* (50); 12.12.1759 Passed; **Lieutenant**; 7.5.1762-11.4.1763 L. *Happy* (8) Sloop; 15.9.1770 4L *Yarmouth* (64); 30.11.1771-1.7.1773 L. *Scorpion* (14) Sloop; 17.3.1777-16.12.1777 3L *Conqueror* (74).

POMEROY, THOMAS

Dates: c.1739 Born.
Family:
Service: 1754-1755 HEIC Service; 9.10.1755 Mid *Isis* (50); 17.8.1758 Mid *Warspite* (74); 18.8.1759-19.8.1759 Battle of Lagos Bay; 6.10.1759 Able *Namur* (90); 20.11.1759 Battle of Quiberon Bay; 1.5.1760 Mid *Namur* (90); 14.10.1760 Passed; 29.3.1761-11.6.1761 Expedition against Belle-Isle; **Lieutenant**; 4.8.1761 3L *Torrington* (44); 9.4.1762-28.3.1763[P] 4L *Kent* (74).

POOLE, ROBERT

Dates: c.1731 Born.
Family:
Service: 4.10.1746 Capt Serv *Augusta* (60); 15.11.1748 Ord. *Augusta* (60); 25.10.1750 Able *Augusta* (60); 12.1.1750/51 Mid *Augusta* (60); 27.11.1751 Able *Augusta* (60); 3.4.1752 Mid *Augusta* (60); 8.5.1752 Able *Saltash* (14) Sloop; 18.3.1753 Mid *Penzance* (44); 4.6.1753 Able *Penzance* (44); 30.1.1755 Mid *Prince* (90); 3.12.1755 Passed; **Lieutenant**; 9.12.1755-14.4.1756 L. *Macclesfield* (16) Hired Armed Ship; 29.9.1756 3L *Guernsey* (50); 25.1.1757 2L *Guernsey* (50); 5.4.1757 Action of April 5 1757; 14.6.1757-24.12.1762[P] 1L *Guernsey* (50); 18.8.1759-19.8.1759 Battle of Lagos Bay.

PORTER, JERVIS HENRY

Dates: c.1717 Born; 31.3.1763 Died.
Family:
Service: 8.3.1731/32 Vol-p-O *Kingston* (60); 8.3.1734/35 MidO *Kingston* (60); 22.6.1735-5.9.1735[P] Mid *Kingston* (60); 4.1.1736/37 Able *Dorsetshire* (80); 14.1.1736/37 Mid *Somerset* (80); 22.5.1737 Mid *Dreadnought* (60); 3.9.1737 Able *Gloucester* (50); 21.8.1738 MidO *Gloucester* (50); 3.12.1738 Mid *Gibraltar* (20); 21.3.1738/39 Mid *Gibraltar* (20); 18.6.1739 Mate *Adventure* (40); 19.7.1739 Passed; **Lieutenant**; 31.8.1739-7.8.1740 4L *Princess Amelia* (80); 9.6.1741[(25.5.1742)] 2L *Orford* (70); 30.6.1742-25.5.1743 L. *Squirrel* (20); 12.1.1743/44 1L *Eltham* (40); 7.7.1744 1L *Princess Amelia* (80); **Commander**; 16.11.1744 *Speedwell* (10)

Sloop; **Captain**; 3.4.1746 *Flamborough* (20); 5.12.1747-18.12.1748[P] *Penzance* (44); 12.4.1755-12.5.1757 *Prince Frederick* (64); 1.6.1758 *Magnanime* (74); 5.6.1758-12.6.1758 Raid on Saint-Malo; 16.3.1759-26.3.1763[P] *Hercules* (74); 20.11.1759 Battle of Quiberon Bay.

PORTER, PETER
Dates: 6.10.1762 Died; 7.11.1764 Will Probate.
Family:
Service: 3.2.1748/49-c.1752 Scholar *Royal Naval Academy*; **Lieutenant**; 23.7.1756(9.10.1761)-2.5.1757[P] L. *Blaze* (10) Fireship; 13.10.1757(EI 9.10.1761) 3L *Tiger* (60); 1.12.1757(EI 9.10.1761) 2L *Tiger* (60); 25.3.1758(EI 9.10.1761) 1L *Tiger* (60); 29.4.1758 Battle of Cuddalore; 3.8.1758 Battle of Negapatam; 1.10.1758(EI 9.10.1761)-3.3.1759 1L *Queenborough* (24); 17.3.1760(EI 15.6.1763) 4L *Grafton* (68); 23.6.1760(15.6.1763) 4L *Norfolk* (74); 27.11.1760(15.6.1763) 3L *Norfolk* (74); 1.2.1761(15.6.1763)-6.10.1762[†] 2L *Norfolk* (74); 24.9.1762-6.10.1762 Battle of Manilla.

PORTER, THOMAS
Dates: c.1732 Born; 1775 Died; 13.10.1775 Will Probate.
Family:
Service: 9.2.1750/51 Able *Assistance* (50); 22.11.1751 Able *Devonshire* (66); 3.8.1752 Mid *Devonshire* (66); 4.4.1754 Able *Blandford* (20); 17.4.1755 Mid *Blandford* (20); 30.9.1755 Able *Experiment* (24); 6.3.1756 Mid *Experiment* (24); 31.3.1756 Mate *Experiment* (24); 20.5.1756 Battle of Minorca; 14.2.1757 Passed; **Lieutenant**; 10.3.1757 4L *Nassau* (64); 25.3.1757 3L *Nassau* (64); 28.9.1757 2L *Nassau* (64); 9.3.1758-24.5.1758 Capture of Fort Louis; 29.12.1758 Capture of Goree; 16.1.1760-12.3.1763[P] 1L *Nassau* (64); 6.9.1763-13.9.1764 1L *Thunderer* (74); 24.2.1767-20.1.1769 3L *Romney* (50); **Commander**; 3.10.1770-12.1771[P] *Viper* (10) Sloop.

POTTS, JOSEPH
Dates: c.1734 Born; 1773 Died; 3.9.1773 Will Probate.
Family:
Service: 1753-1755 Merchant Service; 2.9.1755 Mid *Hampton Court* (64); 3.10.1755 Mate *Hampton Court* (64); 26.6.1756 Mate *Prince George* (80); 10.11.1756 Mate *Prince* (90); 10.1.1757 Mate *Culloden* (74); 5.4.1757 Action of April 5 1757; 11.7.1757 Mate *Saint George* (90); 24.6.1758 Able *Montagu* (60); 3.8.1758 Able *Ramillies* (90); 5.1.1759 Passed; **Lieutenant**; 22.2.1759(29.2.1760)-22.10.1759 L. *Cormorant* (8) Fireship; 22.10.1759(18.12.1760)-4.11.1762 3L *Alcide* (64); 7.1.1762-10.2.1762 Operations against Martinique; 6.6.1762-13.8.1762 Operations against Havana.

POTTS, ROBERT
Dates: c.1739 Born; 1807 Died; 17.7.1807 Will Probate.
Family:
Service: 1754-1755 Merchant Service; 28.12.1755 Able *Colchester* (50); 17.5.1756 Action of 17th May 1756; 16.11.1756-13.2.1760 Mid *Colchester* (50); 13.2.1760 Passed; **Lieutenant**; 9.12.1760(6.7.1762) 5L *Shrewsbury* (74); 17.6.1762(6.7.1762) 4L *Shrewsbury* (74); 7.7.1762(6.7.1762)-2.3.1763[P] 3L *Shrewsbury* (74); 17.6.1763 2L *Phoenix* (44); 27.8.1764-1.10.1766 1L *Phoenix* (44); 19.1.1771-18.11.1772 2L *Saint Albans* (64); 14.5.1778 2L *Suffolk* (74); 28.11.1778 1L *Suffolk* (74); 8.12.1778-26.1.1779 1L *Monarch* (74).

POWELL, SAMUEL

Dates: c.1710 Born; 1775 Died.
Family:
Service: 25.10.1729 Capt Serv *Argyll* (50); 27.9.1731-16.12.1732[P] Able *Rye* (20); 21.3.1735/36 Able *Buckingham* (70); 15.10.1736 Able *Revenge* (70); 18.10.1736 Mid *Revenge* (70); 4.12.1737 Mid *Newark* (80); 9.10.1738 Mid *Aldborough* (20); 28.2.1738/39 Mid *Prince of Orange* (70); 15.8.1739 Able *Buckingham* (70); 11.10.1739 Mid *Buckingham* (70); 18.11.1740 Passed; **Lieutenant**; 13.4.1741 3L *Fowey* (40); 1.5.1741-10.12.1741 6L *Neptune* (90); 18.1.1743/44-18.3.1743/44 4L *Barfleur* (90); 11.2.1743/44-12.2.1743/44 Battle of Toulon; 21.10.1755-14.4.1756 1L *Princess Royal* (90); 4.4.1758-19.10.1759 LCmdr *Princess Caroline* (80) Hospital Ship.

POWLETT, CHARLES

Dates: c.1711 Born; 4.4.1762 Died.
Family:
Service: 28.3.1728 Ord. *Kent* (70); 3.5.1728 Vol-p-O *Dursley Galley* (20); 8.12.1728 MidO *Sapphire* (42); 29.3.1729 Ord. *Sapphire* (42); 21.5.1730 Mid *Sapphire* (42); 7.7.1730 Able *Chatham* (50); 19.11.1730 Mid *Chatham* (50); 4.4.1731 Mid *Salisbury* (50); 5.1.1733/34 Mid *Diamond* (40); 29.3.1734 Mid *Roebuck* (40); 6.5.1734 Passed; **Lieutenant**; 4.4.1735-bef.8.7.1737 L. *Poole* (32); 9.12.1737 3L *Falmouth* (50); 4.7.1738[(25.5.1742)] 3L *Diamond* (40); 22.7.1738[(25.5.1742)] L. *Spence* (8) Sloop; 4.1740-5.7.1740 Attack on St. Augustine; 10.1.1740/41 1L *Folkestone* (44); 11.6.1741 1L *Rupert* (60); **Commander**; 22.10.1741 *Royal Escape* Smack; 18.12.1742 *Aetna* (8) Fireship; **Captain**; 10.10.1743 *Bideford* (20); 2.8.1748[(JAM 19.6.1749)]-1.3.1748/49[P] *Tilbury* (58); 12.10.1748 Battle of Havana.

POWLETT, FRANCIS LASCOE

Dates: c.1732 Born; 1800 Died; 14.1.1800 Will Probate.
Family:
Service: 1751-1755 Merchant Service; 9.6.1755 Mid *Fougueux* (64); 8.7.1755 Mid *Fougueux* (64); 23.6.1757-5.9.1757 Mid *Richmond* (32); 5.9.1757 Passed; **Lieutenant**; 1.12.1757 L. *Furnace* (8) Bomb Vessel; 18.4.1758 3L *Gosport* (44); 4.5.1759-20.5.1761[D] 3L *Belliqueux* (64); 20.5.1761 Dismissed.

POWLETT, HARRY (6TH DUKE OF BOLTON)

Dates: 6.11.1720 Born Berkshire; 28.8.1754 Lord; 5.7.1765 6th Duke of Bolton; 5.7.1765 Marquess of Winchester; 25.12.1794 Died Hackwood House, Hampshire.
Family: Father Harry Powlett, 4th Duke of Bolton (1691–1759); Mother Catherine Parry (d. 1744); Wife Mary Nunn (d.1764) married 13.5.1752; Wife Katherine Lowther (1736?–1809) married 8.4.1765; Daughter Maria Henrietta (1753-1779); Daughter Amelia; Daughter Catharine Margaret (1766-1807); Sister Henrietta (d.1753); Brother Charles, 5th Duke of Bolton (1718-1765); Sister Catherine (d. 1775).
Service: 14.8.1733 Scholar *Royal Naval Academy*; **Lieutenant**; 9.3.1738/39[(4.3.1739/40)] 4L *Berwick* (70); 4.3.1739/40-3.6.1740 4L *Shrewsbury* (80); **Captain**; 15.7.1740 *Port Mahon* (20); 30.7.1741[(19.2.1744/45)]-14.3.1744/45[P] *Oxford* (50); 11.2.1743/44-12.2.1743/44 Battle of Toulon; 26.3.1745-26.6.1745 *Sandwich* (90); 12.7.1745-31.7.1746 *Ruby* (50); 19.11.1746-3.5.1750[P] *Exeter* (60); 26.11.1751-18.4.1754 M.P. for Christchurch; 16.1.1753 *Somerset* (68); 17.1.1755-27.3.1761 M.P. for Lymington; 4.2.1755-12.6.1756 *Barfleur* (80); 4.6.1756 **Rear Admiral of the White**; 31.1.1758 **Rear Admiral of the Red**; 14.2.1759 **Vice Admiral of the Blue**; 9.12.1760

Vice Admiral of the White; 30.3.1761-24.12.1765 M.P. for Winchester; 1766-1770 Gov. of Isle of Wight; 10.12.1766-25.12.1794 Privy Counsellor; 1767-25.12.1794 Vice Admiral of the Coast , Hampshire; 1767-25.12.1794 Vice Admiral of the Coast , Dorset; 5.8.1767 **Vice Admiral of the Red**; 18.10.1770 **Admiral of the Blue**; 31.3.1775 **Admiral of the White**; 1782-1791 Gov. of Isle of Wight; 1782-25.12.1794 Lord Lieutenant of Hampshire.

POWLETT, PERCY

Dates: c.1733 Born.

Family:

Service: 31.12.1746 Able *Ruby* (50); 24.4.1747 Able *Exeter* (60); 22.6.1748 Mid *Exeter* (60); 16.6.1750 Able *Berwick* (70); 31.5.1751 Mid *Swan* (14) Sloop; 2.11.1751 Able *Glory* (44); 28.2.1751/52 Mid *Glory* (44); 26.3.1752 Able *Queenborough* (24); 29.5.1752 Able *Gloucester* (50); 13.1.1753 Able *Penzance* (44); 7.2.1753 Passed; **Lieutenant**; 23.3.1756-20.5.1756 6L *Royal George* (100); 2.6.1756 2L *Rainbow* (44); 8.6.1757 4L *Magnanime* (74); 11.7.1757 3L *Magnanime* (74); 29.7.1757-19.9.1757 3L *Prince of Orange* (60); 10.10.1757 6L *Royal Sovereign* (104); 27.1.1758-22.5.1758 3L *Chatham* (50); 24.9.1759 3L *Barfleur* (80); 19.2.1760 2L *Shrewsbury* (74); 9.12.1760[(9.3.1762)] L. *Hind* (24); 1.12.1761-26.4.1763[P] L. *Cruizer* (8) Sloop; 27.2.1771-13.3.1771 1L *Buckingham* (68).

POWNOLL, PHILIMON

Dates: c.1735 Born; 15.6.1780 Died.

Family:

Service: 20.3.1750/51 Capt Serv *Mars* (64); 11.4.1751 Able *Mars* (64); 28.8.1751 Mid *Mars* (64); 14.1.1751/52 Able *Grampus* (14) Sloop; 21.7.1752 Mid *Assistance* (50); 11.5.1753 Mid *Culloden*; 27.6.1753 Mid *Unicorn* (24); 9.4.1755 Passed; **Lieutenant**; 7.10.1755-28.12.1756 3L *Weymouth* (60); 29.12.1756 L. *Firebrand* (6) Fireship; 17.2.1757 1L *Enterprise* (44); 6.5.1757 6L *Royal George* (100); 29.7.1757 5L *Royal George* (100); 24.12.1757 4L *Royal George* (100); 27.1.1758 4L *Namur* (90); 6.6.1758-27.7.1758 The Siege of Louisbourg; **Commander**; 6.8.1759[(MED 11.6.1762)]-6.8.1762 *Favorite* (16) Sloop; **Captain**; 10.1.1771-21.1.1775 *Argo* (28); 4.12.1775-9.1.1777 *Blonde* (32); 1.1.1777-16.6.1780[P] *Apollo* (32); 16.1.1780 Battle of Cape St. Vincent.

PRATT, WILLIAM

Dates: None Known.

Family:

Service: 21.8.1739 Mid *Augusta* (60); 7.1.1740/41 Action of January 7 1741; 26.6.1741 Mid *Rippon* (60); 12.1.1743/44 Passed; **Lieutenant**; 20.8.1745[(30.10.1746)]-24.10.1746[P] 3L *Falmouth* (50); 7.9.1747-22.7.1752 4L *Culloden* (74); 6.2.1755 3L *Monarch* (74); 7.1.1756 2L *Monarch* (74); 16.4.1756 2L *Magnanime* (74); 26.8.1756 1L *Magnanime* (74); **Commander**; 8.4.1757-23.5.1757 *London* (18) Hired Armed vessel.

PRATTEN, EDWARD

Dates: c.1715 Born; 22.10.1763 Died.

Family:

Service: 2.5.1730 Ord. *Torrington* (40); 15.3.1731/32 Able *Dolphin* (20); 3.9.1734 Mid *Dolphin* (20); 10.10.1735 Mid *Nottingham* (60); 4.11.1736 Passed; **Lieutenant**; 6.12.1739[(27.4.1741)]-4.2.1739/40 3L *Nonsuch* (50); 5.2.1739/40[(27.4.1741)] 2L *Nonsuch* (50); 7.9.1741 1L *Norwich* (50); 4.2.1742/43[(8.8.1743)] 1L *Suffolk* (70); 18.2.1742/43 Attack on La Guaira; **Commander**;

24.2.1742/43[8.8.1743] *Otter* (14) Sloop; 16.4.1743[8.8.1743] *Pembroke Prize* (8) Sloop; **Captain**; 2.6.1743[8.8.1743]-9.9.1743[P] *Eltham* (40); 15.10.1743 *Suffolk* (70); 14.12.1743 *Deptford* (60); 18.4.1744 *Suffolk* (70); 30.1.1748/49-12.5.1749 *Assurance* (44); 12.5.1749-7.6.1751 *Blandford* (20); 17.7.1751 *Charlotte* (8) Yacht; 7.2.1755 *Katherine* (8) Yacht; 7.6.1756-20.5.1757 *Buckingham* (68); 30.5.1757 *Princess Amelia* (80); 18.6.1757-10.10.1759 *Intrepid* (60); 5.9.1757-6.10.1757 Raid on Rochefort; 18.8.1759-19.8.1759 Battle of Lagos Bay.

PRENTICE, NATHANIEL

Dates: c.1730 Born.

Family:

Service: 24.8.1745 Mid *Mermaid* (44); 25.9.1745 Mid *Prince Edward* (44); 28.10.1746 Mid *Bristol* (50); 3.5.1747 1st Battle of Cape Finisterre; 27.1.1747/48 Mate *Bristol* (50); 11.3.1749/50 Able *Cumberland* (66); 3.2.1751/52 Passed; **Lieutenant**; 4.12.1754[26.5.1760] 4L *Salisbury* (50); 4.7.1755[26.5.1760] 5L *Kent* (64); 11.1.1756-14.1.1756 Capture of Geriah; 25.2.1756[26.5.1760] 4L *Kent* (64); 11.3.1756[26.5.1760] 3L *Kent* (64); 23.7.1756[26.5.1760]-1.8.1757 2L *Kent* (64); 7.3.1757-1.4.1757 Expedition against Chandernagore.

PRESCOTT, ISAAC

Dates: c.1737 Born; 1830 Died; 7.5.1830 Will Probate.

Family:

Service: 10.3.1751/52 Scholar *Royal Naval Academy*; 23.2.1755 Mid *Dunkirk* (60); 6.6.1755-8.6.1755 Action of 6-8 June 1755; 6.7.1757 Mid *Magnanime* (74); 5.9.1757-6.10.1757 Raid on Rochefort; 21.4.1758 Passed; **Lieutenant**; 22.5.1758 4L *Dorsetshire* (68); 25.5.1758 3L *Jason* (30); 5.6.1758-12.6.1758 Raid on Saint-Malo; 27.10.1758-24.1.1759 1L *Argo* (28); 24.1.1759 2L *Argo* (28); 9.7.1759 3L *Deptford* (50); 25.3.1760-23.7.1762 4L *Valiant* (74); 29.3.1761-11.6.1761 Expedition against Belle-Isle; 2.11.1776 1L *Valiant* (74); **Commander**; 28.11.1777 *Content* (20) Hired Armed Ship; **Captain**; 8.4.1778 *Duke* (90); 16.4.1778 *Queen* (90); 27.7.1778 1st Battle of Ushant; 19.11.1778 *Seaford* (20); 31.12.1779 Affair of Fielding and Bylandt; 1.1.1780-16.5.1782[P] *Mercury* (28); 4.12.1782-22.3.1783 *Ardent* (64); 1.6.1795 **Rear Admiral of the White**; 14.2.1799 **Vice Admiral of the Blue**; 1.1.1801 **Vice Admiral of the White**; 23.4.1804 **Vice Admiral of the Red**; 9.11.1805 **Admiral of the Blue**; 25.10.1809 **Admiral of the White**; 4.6.1814 **Admiral of the Red**.

PRESCOTT, THOMAS

Dates: c.1718 Born; 1808 Died Southampton; 17.11.1808 Buried Holy Rood Church, Southampton.

Family: Wife Catherine Lort married 7.2.1771.

Service: 3.2.1734/35 Capt Serv *Winchester* (50); 17.8.1736 Ord. *York* (60); 29.7.1737 Gnr Serv *Kent* (70); 28.7.1738 QGnr *Kent* (70); 20.1.1738/39 Able *Kent* (70); 29.7.1739 Mid *Kent* (70); 8.4.1740 Capture of the Princesa; 16.2.1740/41 Mid *Elizabeth* (70); 6.10.1741 Passed; **Lieutenant**; 3.6.1743[28.12.1744] 4L *Buckingham* (70); 11.2.1743/44-12.2.1743/44 Battle of Toulon; 6.3.1743/44[28.12.1744]-19.1.1744/45[P] 3L *Buckingham* (70); 27.1.1745/46 2L *Saint George* (90); 18.12.1746-2.11.1747 2L *Falkland* (50); 3.5.1747 1st Battle of Cape Finisterre; 6.2.1755-2.2.1758 1L *Grafton* (68); 8.1757-10.1757 Louisbourg Expedition; 6.2.1758 1L *Penzance* (44); 15.5.1758 1L *Warspite* (74); 23.1.1759 1L *Dublin* (74); 12.12.1759 1L *Cambridge* (80); **Commander**; 22.7.1761-1763 *Port Royal* (12) Storeship; 6.6.1762-13.8.1762 Operations against Havana.

PRESTON, JAMES

Dates: c.1722 Born.

Family:

Service: 26.10.1746 Able *Royal Sovereign* (104); 16.1.1746/47 Ord. *Folkestone* (44); 1748-1756 Merchant Service; 7.2.1747/48-23.6.1748[P] Able *Terror* (8) Bomb Vessel; 20.7.1756 Mid *Swan* (14) Sloop; 29.6.1757 Mid *Colchester* (50); 27.1.1758 Mid *Antelope* (50); 9.8.1758 Passed; **Lieutenant**; 27.10.1758-13.12.1762[P] 2L *Trident* (64); 29.3.1761-11.6.1761 Expedition against Belle-Isle; 2.2.1771-1.4.1771[P] 2L *Firm* (74); 10.7.1776 2L *Hector* (74); 5.11.1777-23.12.1779 1L *Hector* (74); 27.7.1778 1st Battle of Ushant; 1.8.1800 **Superannuated Commander**.

PRESTON, WILLIAM

Dates: c.1717 Born; 29.9.1756 Died.

Family:

Service: 16.7.1733 Ord. *Lyme* (20); 3.9.1736-14.8.1739[P] Mid *Kinsale* (40); 30.9.1739 Mid *Falkland* (50); 19.6.1740 Passed; **Lieutenant**; 10.11.1740[(12.11.1741)] L. *Aetna* (8) Fireship; 4.3.1740/41-5.1741 Operations against Cartagena; 25.5.1742 2L *Medway* (60); 10.10.1743 1L *Medway* (60); 13.7.1744-4.7.1745 1L *Falkland* (50); **Commander**; 20.10.1746 *Basilisk* (8) Bomb Vessel; **Captain**; 1.3.1748/49-9.5.1750[P] *Deal Castle* (20); 11.2.1756-29.9.1756[†] *Wager* (24).

PRETTIE, HENRY

Dates: 1708 Born Dunalley Castle, Tipperary; 1768 Died Ireland.

Family: Father Henry Prittie (1683-1738).

Service: 19.6.1734 Able *Garland* (20); 1.10.1734 Able *Kingston* (60); 25.2.1734/35 Vol-p-O *Deal Castle* (20); 1.8.1737 Able *Edinburgh* (70); 9.11.1737 Mid *Lowestoffe* (20); 3.9.1741 Passed; **Lieutenant**; 28.9.1741-7.2.1741/42 6L *Royal Sovereign* (104); 16.3.1741/42 4L *Royal Sovereign* (104); 23.11.1742 5L *Princess Royal* (90); 12.2.1742/43 2L *Diamond* (44); 21.2.1742/43 3L *Woolwich* (50); 7.3.1742/43-27.12.1743 4L *Orford* (70); 10.7.1744 Dismissed; 6.4.1745 3L *Prince George* (90); 13.11.1745 6L *Royal George* (100); 23.1.1745/46 4L *Royal George* (100); 7.5.1746 3L *Kent* (64); 3.5.1747 1st Battle of Cape Finisterre; 14.10.1747 2nd Battle of Cape Finisterre; 26.12.1747-5.12.1748 2L *Kent* (64); 7.4.1749-28.12.1750[P] 2L *Humber* (44); 6.4.1763-6.2.1765[W] LCmdr *King of Prussia* (6) Cutter; 24.5.1765-17.8.1768 LCmdr *Swift* (4) Cutter.

PRICE, EDWARD

Dates: c.1728 Born; c.1759 Died; 3.1.1760 Will Probate.

Family:

Service: 11.7.1744-12.6.1745[P] Mid *Newcastle* (50); 7.4.1746 Mid *Torbay* (80); 9.12.1746 Mid *Triton* (20); 21.7.1748 Mid *Rippon* (54); 1.1.1749/50 Mid *Cornwall* (80); 17.9.1750 Able *Devonshire* (66); 20.7.1751 Mid *Devonshire* (66); 21.5.1752 Mate *Glory* (44); 30.7.1753 Mate *Dolphin* (6) Fireship; 29.6.1755-19.12.1755 Mate *Dunkirk* (60); 19.12.1755 Passed; 8.11.1756 4L *Yarmouth* (64); 9.11.1756 **Lieutenant**; 24.12.1756-19.2.1758[W] 4L *Invincible* (74); 8.1757-10.1757 Louisbourg Expedition; 9.3.1758-31.1.1760 2L *Magnanime* (74); 5.6.1758-12.6.1758 Raid on Saint-Malo; 20.11.1759 Battle of Quiberon Bay.

PRICE, RICHARD

Dates: c.1733 Born.

Family:

Service: 1752-1756 Merchant Service; 1.2.1756 Mate *Princess Louisa* (60); 20.5.1756 Battle of Minorca; 5.4.1757 Action of April 5 1757; 9.2.1758 Able *Prince* (90); 1.5.1758 Mid *Prince* (90); 19.11.1758 Mid *Orford* (68); 18.12.1758 Mate *Pelican* (8) Bomb Vessel; 7.2.1759 Passed; **Lieutenant**; 22.2.1759-29.1.1763[P] 4L *Fame* (74); 29.3.1761-11.6.1761 Expedition against Belle-Isle; 11.5.1763-10.10.1763 2L *Dragon* (74).

PRINCE, CHARLES

Dates: 17.8.1799 Died.

Family:

Service: **Lieutenant**; 25.7.1757 L. *Aldborough* (20); 3.1.1760 2L *Looe* (44); 15.9.1760 1L *Looe* (44); 9.2.1761-23.12.1762 3L *Hampton Court* (64); 29.3.1761-11.6.1761 Expedition against Belle-Isle; 6.6.1762-13.8.1762 Operations against Havana; 21.9.1796 **Superannuated Commander.**

PRINGLE, THOMAS

Dates: 9.12.1803 Died.

Family:

Service: **Lieutenant**; 30.11.1760[(22.3.1764)] 3L *Anson* (60); 17.10.1761[(4.4.1764)] L. *Cygnet* (18) Sloop; 6.6.1762-13.8.1762 Operations against Havana; 27.4.1763[(JAM 4.4.1764)] 4L *Centaur* (74); 15.5.1763[(JAM 4.4.1764)]-6.12.1763[P] 3L *Centaur* (74); 20.6.1775-22.6.1776 1L *Lizard* (28); **Commander**; 10.5.1776 *Lord Howe* Hired Armed Ship; **Captain**; 25.11.1776 *Camel* (24); 20.12.1776-6.11.1779 *Ariadne* (20); 14.12.1778-15.12.1778 Battle of St. Lucia; 6.7.1779 Battle of Grenada; 2.5.1780 *Daedalus* (32); 21.4.1783-3.7.1784[P] *Daedalus* (32); 1.10.1787-25.2.1788 *Impregnable* (98); 10.5.1790-31.12.1790[P] *Royal George* (100); 21.10.1793 *Valiant* (74); 1.6.1794 Glorious 1st of June; 4.7.1794 **Rear Admiral of the Blue; Rear Admiral of the Red;** 1.6.1795-1796 *Asia* (64); 1796-7.1796 *Tremendous* (74); 19.1.1797 CinC — Cape of Good Hope; 14.2.1799 **Vice Admiral of the White**; 1.1.1801 **Vice Admiral of the Red.**

PRISSICK, CHRISTOPHER

Dates: c.1724 Born.

Family:

Service: 13.5.1743 Mid *Dorsetshire* (80); 22.1.1743/44 Able *Dorsetshire* (80); 11.2.1743/44-12.2.1743/44 Battle of Toulon; 14.6.1745 Able *Hinchingbrooke* (10) Sloop; 16.8.1746 Mid *Defiance* (60); 3.5.1747 1st Battle of Cape Finisterre; 14.10.1747 2nd Battle of Cape Finisterre; 10.12.1747 Passed; **Lieutenant**; 15.4.1756-4.2.1758 L. *Kennington* (20); 8.1757-10.1757 Louisbourg Expedition; 19.4.1758 2L *Rippon* (60); 16.1.1759-19.1.1759 Attack on Martinique; 20.1.1759-1.5.1759 Capture of Guadeloupe; 25.6.1759[(BLI 31.10.1759)]-13.3.1763[P] 1L *Rippon* (60); 29.3.1761-11.6.1761 Expedition against Belle-Isle; 6.6.1762-13.8.1762 Operations against Havana.

PRITCHARD, JOHN

Dates: 1777 Died.

Family:

Service: **Lieutenant**; 9.4.1723-2.4.1724 3L *Weymouth* (50); 3.4.1724-8.2.1728/29 L. *Sheerness* (20); 9.2.1728/29-30.1.1733/34 2L *Assistance* (50); 31.1.1733/34-23.5.1734 2L *Norfolk* (80);

24.5.1734-2.4.1736[P] 1L *Norfolk* (80); 28.4.1738-18.6.1739 1L *Assistance* (50); 19.6.1739-31.7.1740 1L *Russell* (80); **Commander**; 27.9.1740 *Deptford Prize* (8) Sloop; **Captain**; 5.2.1741/42 *Lyme* (20); 29.12.1742 *Severn* (50); 16.6.1744[(31.8.1744)]-30.4.1745 *Scarborough* (20); 9.5.1746-13.4.1747 *Devonshire* (80); 12.1.1747/48-22.6.1748[P] *Duke* (90); 14.7.1758 **Superannuated Rear Admiral.**

PROBY, CHARLES
Dates: 31.3.1799 Died; 13.4.1799 Will Probate.
Family: Wife Sarah (d.1783) married 1758.
Service: **Lieutenant**; 25.2.1744/45[(MED 26.6.1747)] 4L *Ipswich* (70); 3.5.1745[(MED 26.6.1747)] 1L *Russell* (80); 2.8.1745[(MED 26.6.1747)] 3L *Marlborough* (90); **Commander**; 16.10.1745[(MED 2.12.1748)]-18.12.1746 *Terrible* (6) Bomb Vessel; **Captain**; 17.9.1746[(MED 20.5.1747)] *Royal Oak* (70); 20.11.1746[(MED 15.11.1748)]-8.11.1748[P] *Lowestoffe* (24); 17.1.1748/49-23.1.1753[P] *Lyme* (24); 2.10.1754-22.7.1756 *Siren* (20); 22.5.1755-14.6.1755 British attack on Fort Beauséjour; 24.8.1756-11.11.1756 *Namur* (90); 15.11.1756-28.12.1759 *Medway* (60); 5.9.1757-6.10.1757 Raid on Rochefort; 24.3.1760-4.3.1763[P] *Thunderer* (74); 6.5.1763 *Yarmouth* (64); 17.12.1763 CinC — River Medway and The Nore; 17.12.1763-12.10.1766 Commodore *Yarmouth* (64); 3.1769-1772 Commodore *Pembroke* (60); 8.6.1769 CinC — The Mediterranean Sea; 1771-31.3.1799 Resident Commissioner at Chatham Dockyard.

PROLE, HENRY
Dates: 1762 Died; 30.3.1762 Will Probate.
Family:
Service: 31.7.1748 **Lieutenant**; 31.7.1749[(30.5.1749)]-21.1.1751/52 3L *Severn* (50).

PRYCE, DAVID
Dates: c.1718 Born.
Family:
Service: 1731-1739 Merchant Service; 29.9.1745 Passed; **Lieutenant**; 30.9.1745[(BLI 7.1.1745/46)] 3L *Superb* (60); 26.5.1746 4L *Royal George* (100); 5.5.1747-4.11.1747 2L *Oxford* (50); 21.3.1747/48 3L *Fougueux* (64); 1.12.1748-19.8.1749 3L *Cumberland* (66); 2.9.1755-3.9.1756[P] L. *Roehampton* (16) Hired Armed Ship; 13.7.1757 Agent for Transports; **Commander**; 11.1.1758 *Taylor* (6) Hired Armed Ship; 2.1.1759-18.2.1760[P] *Europa* Hired Unknown; 6.1759-9.1760 Agent for Transports; 26.8.1760 *Lion* Transport; 13.4.1775-15.11.1775 *Viper* (10) Sloop.

PUCKINGHORN, JAMES
Dates: c.1722 Born.
Family:
Service: 20.9.1739 Purs Serv *Deptford* (60); 4.3.1740/41-5.1741 Operations against Cartagena; 14.3.1741/42 Able *Deptford* (2) Lighter; 16.10.1742 Able *Argyll* (50); 21.1.1742/43-18.10.1746[P] Mid *Severn* (50); 10.8.1746 Action of 1746-10-18; 10.7.1747 Passed; **Lieutenant**; 2.8.1755[(NA 29.3.1756)]-25.10.1757 3L *Augusta* (60); 21.10.1757 Forrest's Action; 10.3.1759 6L *Marlborough* (80); 19.10.1759 5L *Marlborough* (80); 23.2.1760 4L *Marlborough* (80); 20.5.1760-30.9.1760[P] 3L *Marlborough* (80); 13.7.1762-7.3.1763[P] 1L *Boulogne* (32).

PUDDICOMBE, STEPHEN
Dates: c.1725 Born.
Family:
Service: 27.6.1744 Mid *Deptford* (24) Storeship; 14.3.1744/45 Mid *Dartmouth* (50); 27.4.1746-11.12.1746[P] Mate *Dartmouth* (50); 31.3.1757 Mate *Deptford* (24) Storeship; 3.1.1758 Passed; **Lieutenant**; 2.2.1758-17.3.1760 4L *Grafton* (68); 10.9.1759 Battle of Pondicherry; 9.10.1775 1L *Egmont* (74); 21.10.1775-3.2.1777 2L *Royal Oak* (74); 23.6.1798 **Superannuated Commander**.

PURCELL, JAMES JOHN
Dates: c.1720 Born; 1759 Died; 14.12.1759 Will Probate.
Family:
Service: 2.10.1732 Ord. *Grafton* (70); 15.10.1732 Vol-p-O *Grafton* (70); 2.6.1733 Ord. *Grafton* (70); 30.10.1733 Vol-p-O *Grafton* (70); 1.1.1733/34 Ord. *Grafton* (70); 19.5.1735 Vol-p-O *Newcastle* (50); 3.1.1736/37 Able *Terrible* (6) Bomb Vessel; 8.9.1737 Able *Gloucester* (50); 11.3.1737/38 Mid *Gloucester* (50); 31.3.1740 Able *Gloucester* (50); 3.7.1740 Passed; **Lieutenant**; 21.2.1740/41 2L *Liverpool* (44); 15.2.1742/43 2L *Woolwich* (50); 21.2.1742/43-4.11.1743 2L *Diamond* (44); 25.2.1744/45-6.8.1747 1L *Saint George* (90); 8.3.1747/48 1L *Humber* (44); 4.4.1749-18.4.1750 L. *Rose* (24) Ship; 20.4.1750[(EI 27.6.1753)]-26.3.1753[P] L. *Hornet* (10) Sloop.

PURCELL, JOHN
Dates: 12.10.1801 Died.
Family:
Service: 4.4.1757 4L *Alcide* (64); 4.4.1757 **Lieutenant**; 20.10.1757-29.8.1759 3L *Alcide* (64); 5.6.1758-12.6.1758 Raid on Saint-Malo; 25.3.1760-18.5.1763 2L *Centurion* (50); 6.6.1762-13.8.1762 Operations against Havana; 25.8.1766-4.9.1766 L. *Glasgow* (20); 21.3.1771-14.5.1771 1L *Active* (28); 21.9.1796 **Superannuated Commander**.

PURVIS, CHARLES WAGER
Dates: c.1714 Born; 15.1.1772 Died.
Family:
Service: 1.5.1729 Able *Monmouth* (70); 12.11.1729 Able *Cornwall* (80); 13.1.1729/30 Able *Sunderland* (60); 24.2.1729/30-5.5.1730 Able *Rose* (20); 6.5.1730 Able *Gibraltar* (20); 17.4.1732 Able *Swift* (6) Sloop; 15.5.1732 Mid *Success* (20); 27.11.1732 Mid *Greyhound* (20); 28.3.1734 Mid *Deptford* (60); 7.5.1735 Passed; **Lieutenant**; 19.6.1735 L. *Salamander* (6) Bomb Vessel; 13.2.1735/36 3L *Oxford* (50); 26.4.1737 2L *Oxford* (50); 16.5.1738 L. *Trial* (8) Sloop; **Commander**; 9.5.1739 *Charlotte* (8) Yacht; **Captain**; 18.7.1740-10.6.1741 *Gibraltar* (20); 1.2.1742/43 *Diamond* (44); 4.8.1743[(MED 10.1.1745/46)] *Dunkirk* (60); 11.2.1743/44-12.2.1743/44 Battle of Toulon; 9.3.1744/45[(MED 10.1.1745/46)]-26.11.1745[P] *Torbay* (80); 5.12.1747-19.6.1748[P] *Prince George* (90); 21.6.1756 **Superannuated Rear Admiral**.

PYE, SIR THOMAS
Dates: 1713 Born; 24.6.1773 Knight Bachelor; 26.12.1785 Died London.
Family: Father Henry Pye (1683-1749); Mother Anne Bathurst; Wife (d.1762); Mistress Mrs. Anna Maria Bennett (d.1808); Daughter Mary; Son Thomas Pye, RN; Daughter Harriet [Esten] (c.1761–1865); Brother Henry, MP (1709-66).
Service: 11.4.1728 Vol-p-O *Lark* (40); 11.4.1730 Mid *Torrington* (40); 18.5.1732 Able *Rose* (20); 10.6.1732 Mid *Rose* (20); 12.6.1734 Passed; **Lieutenant**; 18.4.1735 3L *Preston* (50); 30.8.1739-13.9.1739 2L *Bristol* (54); 11.7.1740 2L *Cumberland* (80); 6.8.1740 4L *Boyne* (80);

2.9.1740 3L *Boyne* (80); 27.9.1740 3L *Kent* (70); 13.10.1740 3L *Elizabeth* (70); 30.1.1740/41 3L *Sandwich* (90); **Captain**; 13.4.1741-16.6.1744 *Seaford* (20) Ship; 19.8.1744[(MED 4.3.1747/48)]-11.12.1747[P] *Norfolk* (80); 6.4.1748 *Greenwich* (50); 21.4.1748-23.3.1748/49[P] *Norwich* (50); 7.4.1749-28.12.1750[P] *Humber* (44); 6.4.1751-1.2.1751/52[P] *Gosport* (44); 4.2.1751/52-22.5.1756[P] Commodore *Advice* (50); 28.3.1752-1756 CinC — Barbados & the Leeward Islands; 5.7.1758 **Rear Admiral of the Blue**; 19.3.1759 **Rear Admiral of the Red**; 21.10.1762 **Vice Admiral of the Blue**; 6.1763-2.1766 CinC — Plymouth; 17.2.1766-1769 CinC — Barbados & the Leeward Islands; 17.2.1766-1767 *Lark* (32); 8.1767-8.1769 *Chatham* (50); 18.10.1770 **Vice Admiral of the Red**; 1771-18.5.1774 CinC — Portsmouth; 9.3.1771-9.10.1774 M.P. for Rochester; 1772 *Royal Oak* (74); 24.6.1773 **Admiral of the Blue**; 10.5.1777-1783 CinC — Portsmouth; 1778 *Princess Amelia* (80); 29.1.1778 **Admiral of the White**; 26.9.1780-3.1783 Lieutenant-general of Marines.

Service Records Q

QUARME, WILLIAM
Dates: c.1732 Born Cornwall; 1802 Died; 9.12.1802 Will Probate.
Family:
Service: 1754-1757 Merchant Service; 14.10.1757 Mid *Wager* (24); 4.1.1760 Mid *Lynn* (44); 14.10.1760 Passed; 15.10.1760-2.2.1761 Mid *Namur* (90); **Lieutenant**; 19.3.1761 L. *Lynx* (10) Sloop; 27.11.1762-28.12.1762[P] L. *Aetna* (8) Fireship; 27.10.1766-10.11.1769 3L *Belleisle* (64); 12.10.1770 1L *Tartar* (28); 23.2.1776-10.1776 LCmdr *Halifax* (6) Schooner; 1.12.1779-10.4.1780[C] LCmdr *Active* (16) Sloop; 6.1790-4.1799 LCmdr *Union* (90).

QUIN, ROBERT
Dates: 1757 Died.
Family:
Service: **Lieutenant**; 8.5.1752-29.5.1752[P] 3L *Ruby* (50); 1.11.1755 L. *Peregrine* (20) Sloop; 10.8.1757-13.4.1758[B] 3L *Prince George* (80).

Service Records R

RAINS, STEPHEN
Dates: c.1728 Born.
Family:
Service: 30.12.1748 Able *Monmouth* (70); 2.3.1749/50 Mid *Ruby* (50); 21.11.1753 Mate *Ruby* (50); 19.12.1755 Passed; 19.6.1760 L. *Laurel* (12) Sloop; 29.6.1760 **Lieutenant**; 16.6.1762-13.1.1763[P] 4L *Lancaster* (66); 4.4.1766 3L *Firm* (74); 26.5.1768-16.5.1769 2L *Firm* (74); 15.6.1769-31.5.1772 LCmdr *Sherborne* (6) Cutter; 14.8.1773 3L *Ocean* (90); 3.11.1773 2L *Ocean* (90); 31.1.1775-6.9.1776 3L *Ocean* (90); 7.11.1776 4L *Ocean* (90); 30.8.1777 3L *Ocean* (90); 25.10.1777 4L *Ocean* (90); 13.5.1778 3L *Ocean* (90); 27.7.1778 1st Battle of Ushant; **Commander**; 12.8.1779-1.6.1780 *Louden* (24) Hired Armed Ship; 30.4.1780 Action of 30th April 1780; 28.5.1781 Dismissed.

RANDELL, JAMES
Dates: c.1705 Born; 1764 Died.
Family: Wife Sarah Maslen married 18.10.1757; Daughter Elizabeth; Son James; Brother John, RN (1708-1766).
Service: 14.2.1714/15-1.4.1716[P] Capt Serv *Tiger* (48); 6.2.1719/20 Capt Serv *Kinsale* (36); 31.3.1723-21.12.1727 Able *Swift* (6) Sloop; 22.12.1727 QM *Kingston* (60); 30.6.1728 Mid *Kingston* (60); 13.1.1728/29 QGnr *Canterbury* (60); 15.9.1730 Cox *Canterbury* (60); 28.7.1731 Mid *Canterbury* (60); 22.6.1732 Able *Royal Oak* (70); 27.9.1732 Mid *Royal Oak* (70); 24.11.1732 Able *Royal Oak* (70); 20.12.1732 Gnr *Shark* (8) Sloop; 8.11.1739 Master *Colchester* (50); 5.1.1740/41 Act3L *Colchester* (50); 20.1.1740/41 Passed; **Lieutenant**; 21.1.1740/41 3L *Colchester* (50); 20.4.1741-10.12.1741[P] 1L *Colchester* (50); 22.4.1742-5.2.1743/44[W] 2L *Looe* (44); 17.7.1744 1L *Exeter* (58); 20.12.1744 1L *Princess Louisa* (60); 5.9.1745 4L *Yarmouth* (64); 6.5.1746-10.8.1746 3L *Yarmouth* (64); 19.3.1747/48-29.7.1748[P] 1L *Berwick* (70); 1.12.1748 2L *Devonshire* (66); 29.7.1752-20.11.1752[P] 1L *Bristol* (50); 19.2.1755 1L *Royal George* (100); 17.1.1756-7.2.1757 1L *Royal Anne* (100); **Commander**; 10.10.1758 *Thomas and Mary* (6) Hired Armed Ship; 8.1759-1762 Agent for Transports; 27.8.1759-8.3.1760[P] *Juline and Elizabeth* (32) Hired Armed Ship; 21.10.1760 *Saint Peter* Hired Armed Ship; 6.3.1761-1.2.1762[P] *Albemarle* Hired Armed Troopship; 2.2.1762-6.2.1762[F] *Laurel* (12) Sloop; **Captain**; 12.3.1762 *Success* (20); 15.4.1762-25.2.1763[P] *Peggy* Hired Transport.

RANDELL, JOHN
Dates: c.1708 Born; 1766 Died; 15.10.1766 Will Probate.
Family: Wife Susannah; Brother James, RN (1705-1764).
Service: 28.12.1722 Capt Serv *Swift* (6) Sloop; 28.5.1725 Ord. *Swift* (6) Sloop; 31.12.1725 Able *Swift* (6) Sloop; 29.9.1730 Gnr Mate *Garland* (20); 23.2.1730/31 QM *Lion* (60); 16.3.1731/32-5.6.1732[P] Mid *Lion* (60); 20.7.1734 Mid *Royal Oak* (70); 12.9.1734 Mid *Shark* (8) Sloop; 1.1.1735/36 Mate *Shark* (8) Sloop; 1.7.1737 Able *Berwick* (70); 12.5.1738 Mid *Garland* (20);

10.3.1739/40 Mate *Garland* (20); 18.8.1741 Able *Plymouth* (60); 24.8.1741 Mate *Plymouth* (60); 18.7.1743 Passed; **Lieutenant**; 6.4.1748[JAM 11.9.1751]-17.5.1751[P] L. *Rye* (20); 31.7.1755-7.7.1756 3L *Chesterfield* (44); 20.5.1756 Battle of Minorca; 29.11.1756[ECH 12.11.1759]-28.4.1760[P] 1L *Princess Louisa* (60); 5.4.1757 Action of April 5 1757; 18.8.1759-19.8.1759 Battle of Lagos Bay; 31.3.1761-18.12.1762[P] LCmdr *Royal Anne* Prison Ship.

RAPER, CHRISTOPHER

Dates: c.1722 Born.
Family:
Service: 6.9.1743 Mid *Squirrel* (20); 6.3.1744/45 Mid *Dolphin* (8) Storeship; 24.5.1745 Mid *Chester* (54); 27.8.1746 Mate *Prince Frederick* (70); 3.5.1747 1st Battle of Cape Finisterre; 28.5.1747 Passed; **Lieutenant**; 13.9.1756 3L *Antelope* (50); 6.11.1756 2L *Antelope* (50); 30.4.1759-20.3.1760 1L *Belliqueux* (64); 3.4.1760 2L *Sandwich* (90); 29.3.1761-11.6.1761 Expedition against Belle-Isle; 30.7.1762-22.1.1763[P] 1L *Sandwich* (90); 1.1.1766-15.6.1769 LCmdr *Sherborne* (6) Cutter; 30.10.1770-21.6.1771[P] 2L *Namur* (90).

RAWE, THOMAS

Dates: c.1740 Born; 1809 Died; 21.11.1809 Will Probate.
Family: Brother Richard.
Service: 1.7.1756 Adm Serv *Newark* (80); 3.7.1757 Adm Ret *Prince* (90); 1.9.1757 Supnum *Royal Anne* (100); 5.9.1757-6.10.1757 Raid on Rochefort; 21.11.1757 Mid *Jersey* (60); 31.10.1758 Mid *Jersey* (60); 18.8.1759-19.8.1759 Battle of Lagos Bay; 8.1.1760 Mid *Culloden* (74); 13.1.1761 Mid *Hero* (74); 3.6.1761 Passed; **Lieutenant**; 7.8.1761 4L *Africa* (64); 14.9.1761-5.2.1763[P] 4L *Cornwall* (74); 24.10.1766-10.11.1769 3L *Hero* (74); 19.9.1770-6.5.1771[P] 4L *Belleisle* (64); 4.7.1771-5.9.1772 L. *Dispatch* (14) Sloop; 3.5.1776 1L *Raisonable* (64); 31.5.1776[BLI 27.9.1776] 5L *Ocean* (90); 7.11.1776 6L *Ocean* (90); 30.8.1777 5L *Ocean* (90); 16.9.1777 4L *Sultan* (74); 14.10.1777 4L *Ocean* (90); 25.10.1777 5L *Ocean* (90); 13.5.1778 4L *Ocean* (90); 27.7.1778 1st Battle of Ushant; 23.3.1779 2L *Victory* (100); **Commander**; 9.9.1779-7.4.1780 *William* (20) Hired Armed Ship; **Captain**; 16.1.1783-18.1.1783 *Panther* (60); 9.3.1786-25.6.1789[P] *Myrmidon* (22); 1.6.1804 **Superannuated Rear Admiral.**

RAWLIN, WILLIAM

Dates: None Known.
Family:
Service: **Lieutenant**; 8.6.1762[JAM 7.9.1763] 5L *Foudroyant* (80); 5.11.1762[26.6.1765] L. *Virgin* (12) Sloop; 18.4.1764[BLI 26.6.1765]-1.4.1765 2L *Actaeon* (28); 1.11.1765[BLI 19.8.1766]-21.11.1765 3L *Princess Louisa* (60); 14.6.1766[BLI 7.1.1768]-28.11.1766 L. *Beaver* (14) Sloop; 18.7.1772[Leeward Antilles 2.6.1774]-26.4.1773[P] L. *Seahorse* (24).

RAWLING, JOHN

Dates: c.1730 Born; 18.5.1757 Died.
Family:
Service: 1744-1750 Merchant Service; 1.3.1748 Able *Anson* (60); 22.6.1748 Mid *Anson* (60); 25.11.1748 Mid *Centurion* (50); 13.5.1749 Mid *Gloucester* (50); 4.10.1749 Act3L *Lark* (44); **Lieutenant**; 29.5.1750[NA 9.8.1750]-23.6.1750[P] 3L *Lark* (44); 23.7.1750 Passed; 4.2.1751/52 3L *Advice* (50); **Commander**; 26.5.1753-28.6.1753[P] *Scorpion* (14) Sloop; 4.12.1753 *Raven* (14) Sloop; **Captain**; 11.3.1755 *Seaford* (20); 24.9.1756-18.5.1757 *Unicorn* (28).

RAWLINGS, HUMPHREY

Dates: c.1712 Born; 1772 Died.
Family:
Service: 26.2.1726/27-17.6.1729 Vol-p-O *Weymouth* (50); 18.6.1729-4.2.1731/32 Mid *Lively* (20); 5.2.1731/32 Able *Dolphin* (20); 28.6.1734 Passed; **Lieutenant**; 28.5.1740-26.12.1743 L. *Scarborough* (20); 7.9.1747-1.12.1748 2L *Culloden* (74); 6.2.1755 L. *Grampus* (14) Sloop; 21.9.1757 1L *Vanguard* (68); 25.3.1758 1L *Lennox* (74); 5.6.1758-12.6.1758 Raid on Saint-Malo; 22.2.1759-20.11.1759[S] 1L *Resolution* (74); 20.11.1759 Battle of Quiberon Bay.

RAWLINGS, JAMES

Dates: c.1735 Born; 1.1.1761 Died.
Family:
Service: 29.3.1751 Able *Surprise* (24); 14.8.1751 Able *Torrington* (44); 31.7.1754 Able *Northumberland* (68); 2.10.1754 Mid *Northumberland* (68); 23.3.1757 Mid *Duke* (90); 4.7.1757 Passed; **Lieutenant**; 10.3.1758 4L *Duc d'Aquitaine* (64); 5.6.1758-12.6.1758 Raid on Saint-Malo; 3.4.1759-1.1.1761[F] 3L *Duc d'Aquitaine* (64).

RAYMENT, THOMAS

Dates: c.1724 Born; 30.3.1791 Died.
Family:
Service: 12.7.1743 Able *Superb* (60); 28.7.1745 Able *Solebay* (42) Hospital Ship; 6.3.1745/46 Mid *Solebay* (42) Hospital Ship; 25.7.1747 Mid *Bristol* (54); 13.9.1747-20.9.1747 Able *Grand Turk* (22); 21.9.1747-5.12.1747[P] Mid *Grand Turk* (22); 17.3.1755/56 Mid *Queenborough* (24); 12.12.1756-27.12.1756 Able *Queenborough* (24); 27.12.1756 Passed; **Lieutenant**; 22.1.1759 3L *Somerset* (68); 31.1.1759 2L *Somerset* (68); 26.1.1761-30.11.1761 2L *Essex* (64); 29.3.1761-11.6.1761 Expedition against Belle-Isle; 11.2.1762-12.3.1763[P] 1L *Sapphire* (32); 5.9.1763 1L *Hussar* (28); 23.12.1767 3L *Cornwall* (74); 8.12.1769 2L *Cornwall* (74); 18.9.1770-17.12.1770 3L *Cornwall* (74); 1.6.1772-4.6.1775 LCmdr *Sherborne* (6) Cutter; 18.4.1777 2L *Belleisle* (64); 12.5.1778-12.11.1783[P] LCmdr *Freedom* Hired Tender; **Commander**; 26.8.1789-5.1790 *Speedwell* (14) Cutter.

RAYNOR, JOHN

Dates: c.1730 Born; 1784 Died.
Family:
Service: 13.11.1747 Able *Elizabeth* (70); 9.4.1748 Battle of Santiago de Cuba; 16.6.1748 Able *Surprise* (24); 13.8.1749 Mid *Renown* (30); 4.7.1752-28.4.1753 Able *Penzance* (44); 29.4.1753 Mate *Swift* (8) Sloop; 16.4.1755-19.12.1755 NR *Arundel* (24); 19.12.1755 Passed; **Lieutenant**; 26.2.1757-8.7.1760 L. *Hound* (14) Sloop; 29.12.1761-26.8.1763[P] 4L *Newark* (80); **Commander**; 1.7.1766-1.6.1769[P] *Swift* (14) Sloop; 1768-1769 Gov. of Falkland Islands; **Captain**; 26.7.1775 *Chatham* (50); 2.7.1776-4.7.1776 Staten Island Landings; 6.9.1776[NA 1.2.1779] *Bristol* (50); 7.12.1777[NA 20.1.1780] *Isis* (50); 14.12.1778-15.12.1778 Battle of St. Lucia; 14.2.1780-28.8.1780 *Inflexible* (64).

READ, JACOB

Dates: c.1717 Born; 1757 Died; 26.1.1757 Will Probate.
Family:
Service: 9.12.1733 Vol-p-O *Portland* (50); 28.2.1733/34-28.8.1735[P] MidO *Winchelsea* (20); 19.8.1736 Mid *Roebuck* (40); 14.9.1738-3.3.1738/39 Able *Roebuck* (40); 4.3.1738/39 Able

Greenwich (50); 19.7.1739 Passed; **Lieutenant**; 2.2.1740/41 3L *Fowey* (40); 13.4.1741-4.11.1742 2L *Fowey* (40); 23.11.1742 4L *Princess Royal* (90); 19.8.1743 L. *Squirrel* (20); 24.12.1743 L. *Dolphin* (20); 14.3.1743/44 1L *Chester* (50); 10.12.1744-28.3.1745[C] 1L *Anglesea* (44); 28.3.1745 Anglesea vs Apollon; 3.7.1746-25.8.1747 1L *Folkestone* (44); 10.7.1755-31.3.1756 1L *Bristol* (50).

READ, JOHN

Dates: c.1733 Born; 15.2.1799 Died Deal.

Family:

Service: 1751-1755 Merchant Service; 28.5.1755 Mate *Ramillies* (90); 21.7.1755 Mid *Terrible* (74); 15.10.1755 Mate *Terrible* (74); 19.9.1756 Mate *Marlborough* (80); 6.4.1757-6.3.1757/58 Mate *Newark* (80); 8.1757-10.1757 Louisbourg Expedition; 6.3.1758 Passed; **Lieutenant**; 5.10.1758 6L *Saint George* (90); 18.10.1758 5L *Saint George* (90); 23.10.1758-27.12.1760[P] 4L *Saint George* (90); 16.1.1759-19.1.1759 Attack on Martinique; 20.1.1759-1.5.1759 Capture of Guadeloupe; 26.5.1769 2L *Arrogant* (74); 23.8.1769-10.6.1771[P] 1L *Arrogant* (74); 24.12.1776-17.4.1781[P] LCmdr *Josepha* Hired Tender.

REDDALL, AMBROSE

Dates: c.1741 Born; 1791 Died.

Family:

Service: 1754-1755 Merchant Service; 17.7.1755 Capt Serv *Newcastle* (50); 18.3.1756/57 Mid *Barbadoes* (14) Sloop; 28.2.1759 Able *Barbadoes* (14) Sloop; 27.4.1759 Mid *Medway* (60); 29.5.1759 Able *Medway* (60); 13.8.1759 Mid *Medway* (60); 30.8.1760 Supnum *Chesterfield* (44); 21.11.1760-1.7.1761 Mate *Pluto* (8) Fireship; 1.7.1761 Passed; **Lieutenant**; 8.7.1762-7.2.1763[P] 3L *Romney* (50); 12.4.1763-30.12.1765[D] 1L *Lowestoffe* (32); 30.12.1765 Dismissed; 3.11.1770-3.6.1773[P] 2L *Pallas* (36); 11.7.1775 1L *Experiment* (50); 6.1776 LCmdr *Buckingham* (68); **Commander**; 23.8.1777 *Grampus* (30) Storeship; 20.10.1778 *Delight* (14) Sloop; 20.2.1779 **Captain**; 24.2.1779-6.2.1783 *Eagle* (64); 17.2.1782 Battle of Sadras; 12.4.1782 Battle of Providien; 6.7.1782 2nd Battle of Negapatam; 3.9.1782 Battle of Trincomalee.

REDDISH, EDWARD

Dates: c.1729 Born; 1800 Died; 23.10.1800 Will Probate.

Family:

Service: 8.3.1741/42 Scholar *Royal Naval Academy*; 9.9.1745 Able *Sutherland* (50); 10.8.1747 Mid *Sutherland* (50); 21.6.1749 Mid *Captain* (70); 25.6.1750 Able *Princess Amelia* (66); 23.3.1750/51 Mid *Humber* (44); 3.2.1751/52 Passed; **Lieutenant**; 14.4.1756 3L *Windsor* (60); 9.7.1756-8.12.1756 2L *Windsor* (60); 27.10.1758 1L *Torrington* (44); 19.2.1759 1L *Stag* (32); 2.4.1760-15.9.1761 1L *Actaeon* (28); 29.3.1761-11.6.1761 Expedition against Belle-Isle; 22.2.1762-14.7.1763 1L *Dreadnought* (60); 21.11.1770-22.4.1775[P] 1L *Intrepid* (64); 28.8.1778-24.3.1779 1L *Britannia* (100).

REDMAN, JOHN

Dates: bef.30.11.1763 Died.

Family:

Service: 20.4.1703 **Lieutenant**; 22.7.1704-10.12.1704 3L *Revenge* (70); 11.12.1704-25.1.1704/5 3L *Royal Oak* (70); 30.3.1709-1.3.1710/11 2L *Revenge* (70); 2.3.1710/11-12.1.1714/15 1L *Oxford* (54).

REDMON, WILLIAM
Dates: c.1739 Born.
Family:
Service: 8.3.1751/52 Clerk *Advice* (50); 30.9.1754-12.8.1755 Able *Advice* (50); 13.8.1755-22.5.1756[P] Mid *Advice* (50); 12.10.1756 Mid *Swiftsure* (68); 28.2.1758 Battle of Cartagena; 4.7.1759 Passed; **Lieutenant**; 11.7.1759-7.5.1762 3L *Penzance* (44); 3.6.1761-7.6.1761 Occupation of Dominica; 7.1.1762-10.2.1762 Operations against Martinique; 24.2.1762-25.2.1762 Capture of Saint Lucia; 20.8.1763 1L *Hussar* (28); 5.9.1763-24.10.1766 L. *Pomona* (18) Sloop; 17.12.1770 3L *Lennox* (74); 28.6.1771 4L *Barfleur* (90); 24.3.1772 5L *Barfleur* (90); 25.6.1773-17.12.1773 4L *Barfleur* (90); 26.7.1775 1L *Orpheus* (32); **Commander**; 16.10.1779-18.2.1783[P] *Heart of Oak* (20) Hired Armed Ship.

REEVE, SAMUEL
Dates: c.1732 Born; 1803 Died; 30.6.1803 Will Probate.
Family:
Service: 6.2.1745/46 Able *Royal George* (100); 22.9.1747 Able *Falkland* (50); 24.1.1748/49 Mid *Queenborough* (24); 7.2.1748/49 Able *Sheerness* (24); 18.3.1748/49 Mid *Unicorn* (24); 1.2.1750/51-22.6.1752[P] Able *Unicorn* (24); 13.7.1752 Mid *Falcon* (10) Bomb Vessel; 2.9.1752 Passed; **Lieutenant**; 4.1.1757[(19.11.1759)]-12.3.1757 2L *Kingfisher* (14) Sloop; 1.4.1757[(26.5.1760)] 3L *Tiger* (60); 1.8.1757[(26.5.1760)] 3L *Kent* (64); 5.9.1757[(EI 26.5.1760)]-28.4.1758[SC] 2L *Bridgewater* (24); 19.4.1760 2L *Modeste* (64); 10.1.1761 1L *Modeste* (64); 8.4.1761 2L *Modeste* (64); 5.10.1761 1L *Modeste* (64); 7.1.1762-10.2.1762 Operations against Martinique; 22.10.1762[(2.2.1764)]-21.9.1763[P] 5L *Foudroyant* (80); 7.4.1767 1L *Achilles* (60); 5.7.1769-10.4.1770 2L *Achilles* (60); 7.12.1770-2.6.1772 1L *Barfleur* (90); 8.11.1775 1L *Pearl* (32); 7.2.1776 1L *Eagle* (64); **Commander**; 16.1.1777[(NA 7.12.1778)]-23.10.1777 *Merlin* (18) Frigate; 25.9.1777 *Scorpion* (14) Sloop; **Captain**; 1.2.1778[(NA 15.12.1778)]-31.8.1779 *Nonsuch* (64); 14.12.1778-15.12.1778 Battle of St. Lucia; 29.1.1779 *Shrewsbury* (74); 16.4.1779 *Surprise* (28); 6.7.1779 Battle of Grenada; 8.3.1782 *Crown* (64); 20.10.1782 Battle of Cape Spartel; 12.4.1783-21.4.1786[P] *Crown* (64); 31.1.1793 *Captain* (74); 14.3.1795 Action off Genoa; 1.6.1795 **Rear Admiral of the White**; 20.2.1797 **Rear Admiral of the Red**; 14.2.1799 **Vice Admiral of the White**.

REEVES, JOHN
Dates: c.1731 Born; 1776 Died; 24.5.1776 Will Probate.
Family:
Service: 8.8.1742 Ord. *Barfleur* (90); 11.2.1743/44-12.2.1743/44 Battle of Toulon; 7.12.1745 Ord. *Neptune* (90); 10.10.1746 Ord. *Monmouth* (70); 8.11.1746-13.6.1748[P] Mid *Lys* (24); 1.3.1754/55-7.4.1756 Mate *Barfleur* (80); 7.4.1756 Passed; **Lieutenant**; 12.8.1757 L. *Savage* (8) Sloop; 20.7.1758-29.5.1759 L. *Raven* (14) Sloop; 4.7.1763-29.8.1765 L. *Savage* (8) Sloop; 2.2.1771-18.3.1771 1L *Modeste* (64).

REID, JAMES
Dates: c.1733 Born; 1798 Died; 17.7.1798 Will Probate.
Family:
Service: 23.4.1750 NR *Royal Sovereign* (104); 31.5.1750 Capt Serv *Queenborough* (24); 23.2.1750/51 Able *Queenborough* (24); 17.5.1751 Able *Garland* (24); 25.11.1751-9.1.1754 Mate *Garland* (24); 9.1.1754 Passed; 16.9.1755 **Lieutenant**; 16.9.1756[(NA 7.12.1756)] L. *Baltimore* (14) Sloop; 24.12.1756-15.8.1758 2L *Lichfield* (50); 15.1.1759 3L *Terrible* (74); 29.4.1760-9.6.1767[P] 1L *Argo* (28); 24.9.1762-6.10.1762 Battle of Manilla; 10.11.1769 1L *Firm* (74); 23.11.1769-

20.5.1771[P] 1L *Hero* (74); 31.1.1772 1L *Dublin* (74); **Commander**; 25.6.1773 *Zephyr* (10) Sloop; 21.1.1775 *Carcass* (8) Bomb Vessel; 24.10.1775 *Thunder* (8) Bomb Vessel; **Captain**; 5.7.1776[(NA 6.6.1777)]-6.7.1776 *Bristol* (50); 6.7.1776[(NA 7.9.1778)]-30.4.1779[P] *Rose* (20); 1.5.1779[(NA 25.10.1781)]-7.10.1781[P] *Galatea* (20); 24.7.1779-12.8.1779 Penobscot Expedition; 7.7.1794 **Superannuated Rear Admiral.**

REID, JOHN

Dates: c.1731 Born.

Family:

Service: 23.12.1749 Able *Yarmouth* (64); 22.9.1751 QGnr *Yarmouth* (64); 27.7.1752 Cox *Yarmouth* (64); 26.3.1753 QM *Yarmouth* (64); 16.7.1753 Mid *Seahorse* (24); 2.8.1756 Mid *Cambridge* (80); 14.2.1757 Passed; **Lieutenant**; 21.12.1758[(BLI 10.8.1759)] L. *Bonetta* (10) Sloop; 16.1.1759-19.1.1759 Attack on Martinique; 20.1.1759-1.5.1759 Capture of Guadeloupe; 10.8.1759 5L *Royal Sovereign* (104); 21.1.1762 2L *Enterprise* (44); 25.1.1762-26.1.1764[P] 1L *Enterprise* (44); 24.2.1762-25.2.1762 Capture of Saint Lucia; 6.6.1762-13.8.1762 Operations against Havana; 24.8.1779 1L *Ajax* (74); 30.8.1779-8.12.1779 1L *Montagu* (74).

REYNOLDS, LORD FRANCIS (3RD BARON DUCIE)

Dates: 28.3.1739 Born; 28.3.1739 Lord Ducie; 11.9.1785 3rd Baron Ducie; 20.8.1808 Died;

Family: Father Francis Reynolds, MP (d.1773); Wife Mary Provis (d.1789); Wife Mrs Sarah Child née Jodrell married 18.1.1791.

Service: 13.4.1752 Scholar *Royal Naval Academy*; 25.4.1755 Mid *Dunkirk* (60); 6.6.1755-8.6.1755 Action of 6-8 June 1755; 12.7.1757-27.4.1758 Mid *Magnanime* (74); 5.9.1757-6.10.1757 Raid on Rochefort; 27.4.1758 Passed; **Lieutenant**; 28.4.1758 2L *Melampe* (36); **Commander**; 21.11.1760 *Weazle* (16) Sloop; **Captain**; 12.4.1762-24.5.1762 *Ludlow Castle* (44); 24.5.1762-12.2.1763[P] *Garland* (24); 13.4.1763-10.4.1765 *Flamborough* (20); 15.6.1769-10.8.1772[P] *Quebec* (32); 29.10.1776-23.10.1777[S] *Augusta* (64); 17.7.1778 *Jupiter* (50); 20.10.1778 Action of 1778-10-20; 20.9.1780-29.6.1783[P] *Monarch* (74); 29.4.1781-30.4.1781 Battle of Fort Royal; 5.9.1781 Battle of the Chesapeake; 25.1.1782-26.1.1782 Battle of Saint Kitts; 12.4.1782 Battle of the Saintes; 19.4.1782 Battle of the Mona Passage; 26.4.1784-11.9.1785 M.P. for Lancaster; 1785 **Superannuated Captain.**

REYNOLDS, JOHN

Dates: c.1713 Born; 1766 Died; 8.1.1766 Will Probate.

Family:

Service: 28.6.1729 Vol-p-O *Aldborough* (20); 29.6.1731-18.7.1734[P] Mid *Aldborough* (20); 31.7.1734 Passed; **Lieutenant**; 14.10.1736[(10.5.1737)]-7.5.1737[P] L. *Griffin* (8); 28.7.1738-27.11.1738[P] 3L *Argyll* (50); 25.6.1739-26.9.1740 2L *Argyll* (50); 27.6.1741[(29.3.1743)] L. *Vulcan* (8) Fireship; 14.3.1742/43-7.2.1743/44 1L *Jersey* (60); 24.9.1746-15.12.1746[P] 2L *Prince of Orange* (70).

REYNOLDS, JOHN

Dates: 3.2.1788 Died.

Family: Wife Maria Catharina; Son George, RN.

Service: **Lieutenant**; 16.7.1740 L. *Kennington* (20); 24.8.1743 4L *Chichester* (80); 8.2.1743/44-9.7.1744 5L *Victory* (100); **Commander**; 23.4.1745-3.1.1745/46 *Scipio* (8) Fireship; **Captain**; 30.10.1746-2.10.1751[P] *Arundel* (24); 2.1759-1763 Commodore *Firm* (74); 7.4.1762-23.3.1763[P] *Milford* (28); 11.4.1763-28.4.1763 *Garland* (24); 6.5.1766-26.2.1768[P] *Fame* (74); 16.5.1769-28.5.1770[P] *Burford* (68); 22.2.1770-29.5.1771[P] *Defence* (74); 1.7.1773 *Dublin* (74); 1.11.1773-

31.3.1775 *Ocean* (90); 31.3.1775 **Rear Admiral of the Blue**; 7.12.1775 **Rear Admiral of the White**; 23.1.1778 **Rear Admiral of the Red**; 29.1.1778 **Vice Admiral of the Blue**; 26.9.1780 **Vice Admiral of the White**; 24.9.1787 **Admiral of the Blue.**

REYNOLDS, JOHN

Dates: 19.6.1793 Died; 10.7.1793 Will Probate.
Family:
Service: **Lieutenant**; 9.5.1758[BLI 10.8.1759] 3L *Roebuck* (44); 16.1.1759-19.1.1759 Attack on Martinique; 20.1.1759-1.5.1759 Capture of Guadeloupe; 10.8.1759 4L *Royal Sovereign* (104); 24.5.1762-27.12.1762[P] 3L *Royal Sovereign* (104); 20.9.1770 2L *Yarmouth* (64); 28.10.1771-16.4.1773 L. *Racehorse* (16) Sloop; 26.1.1774 3L *Centaur* (74); 25.8.1774 2L *Centaur* (74); 6.11.1775 1L *Centaur* (74); 20.4.1778 1L *Queen* (90); **Commander**; 14.5.1778-15.5.1778 *Diligence* (10) Sloop; 18.6.1778 *Ranger* (8) Sloop; 19.5.1781 *Arundel* (74) Hospital Ship; **Captain**; 10.7.1782 *Princess Amelia* (80); 20.10.1782 Battle of Cape Spartel; 16.4.1783-10.4.1784[P] *Leander* (52).

REYNOLDS, WILLIAM

Dates: c.1739 Born; 1810 Died; 28.5.1810 Will Probate.
Family:
Service: 1750-1753 Merchant Service; 25.4.1753 Able *Warwick* (60); 22.6.1753-11.3.1755/56[C] Mid *Warwick* (60); 8.5.1758 Able *Ramillies* (90); 5.6.1758-12.6.1758 Raid on Saint-Malo; 13.8.1758-7.2.1759 Mid *Ramillies* (90); 7.2.1759 Passed; **Lieutenant**; 24.8.1759 L. *Albany* (14) Sloop; 23.2.1760-11.4.1760 L. *Scorpion* (14) Sloop; 25.6.1761-21.6.1762 4L *Hero* (74); 21.6.1762 4L *Magnanime* (74); 22.6.1762-23.1.1763[P] 4L *Princess Amelia* (80); 9.1.1771 4L *Royal Oak* (74); 10.5.1771 3L *Royal Oak* (74); 25.6.1773-10.1.1774 2L *Royal Oak* (74); 2.8.1776 3L *Resolution* (74); 6.12.1776 2L *Resolution* (74); 28.2.1782 7L *Royal George* (100); 8.4.1782 7L *Ocean* (90); 6.5.1782 7L *Britannia* (100); 13.8.1782 6L *Britannia* (100); 30.5.1783-29.8.1786[P] LCmdr *Cockatrice* (14) Cutter.

RICH, SIR THOMAS (5H BARONET RICH)

Dates: 1733 Born Berkshire; 17.7.1762 5th Baronet Rich; 6.4.1803 Died.
Family: Father Sir William Rich, 4th Bt. (d.1762); Mother Elizabeth Royall; Wife Ann Willis; Mistress Elizabeth Burt; Illegitimate Son Sir Henry, MP Bt.; Illegitimate Son Charles, RN; Illegitimate Son George Frederick, RN (d.1863); Illegitimate Daughter Grace [Abdy].
Service: **Lieutenant**; 25.3.1758[EI 27.5.1762] 4L *Salisbury* (50); 29.4.1758 Battle of Cuddalore; 6.5.1758[EI 27.5.1762] 3L *Salisbury* (50); 7.7.1758[EI 27.5.1762]-18.1.1759 2L *Salisbury* (50); 3.8.1758 Battle of Negapatam; 25.3.1761[EI 27.5.1762]-28.8.1761[P] 2L *Salisbury* (50); 1.6.1763-18.6.1765 LCmdr *Anson* (6) Cutter; 24.2.1767 2L *Romney* (50); **Commander**; 1.3.1769 *Senegal* (14) Sloop; **Captain**; 14.2.1771[NA 30.11.1770]-20.9.1773[P] *Gibraltar* (20); 23.5.1775-26.1.1780 *Enterprise* (28); 26.1.1780[BLI 1.4.1780]-30.5.1781 *Princessa* (70); 29.4.1781-30.4.1781 Battle of Fort Royal; 27.7.1781-23.8.1781 *Sandwich* (90); 31.3.1784-16.6.1790 M.P. for Great Marlow; 11.6.1786-25.6.1789 *Culloden* (74); 10.5.1790-10.9.1791 *Vengeance* (74); 22.12.1792 *Culloden* (74); **Rear Admiral of the Blue**; 12.4.1794-1795 *Culloden* (74); 1.6.1794 Glorious 1st of June; 4.7.1794 **Rear Admiral of the Red**; 1.6.1795 **Vice Admiral of the Blue**; 14.2.1799 **Vice Admiral of the Red**; 1.1.1801 **Admiral of the Blue.**

RICHARDS, EDWARD

Dates: c.1739 Born; 17.9.1761 Died.

Family:

Service: 17.8.1756 Capt Serv *Devonshire* (70); 9.6.1757 Able *Cambridge* (80); 3.4.1758 Mid *Cambridge* (80); 16.1.1759-19.1.1759 Attack on Martinique; 20.1.1759-1.5.1759 Capture of Guadeloupe; 5.2.1760 Mid *Bedford* (64); 20.4.1760 Able *Rochester* (50); 5.5.1760-22.10.1760 Mid *Swiftsure* (68); 22.10.1760 Passed; **Lieutenant**; 17.9.1761 L. *Wolf* (8) Sloop; 12.4.1762-28.3.1763[P] 5L *Kent* (74).

RICHARDS, FRANCIS

Dates: c.1719 Born; 1784 Died; 20.8.1784 Will Probate.

Family:

Service: 18.7.1736 Able *Kinsale* (40); 20.9.1737 MidO *Ipswich* (70); 28.4.1738-30.5.1740[P] Mid *Edinburgh* (70); 5.8.1740 Mid *Torbay* (80); 10.9.1741 Mate *Torbay* (80); 8.7.1742 Able *Saint George* (90); 9.12.1742 Passed; **Lieutenant**; 8.6.1744 L. *Furnace* (8) Bomb Vessel; 1.2.1744/45 5L *Saint George* (90); 29.3.1745 4L *Saint George* (90); 23.5.1745 3L *Saint George* (90); 2.7.1745-30.6.1748[P] 2L *Folkestone* (44); 30.1.1748/49-11.9.1751 1L *Assurance* (44); 11.9.1751-24.4.1753[W] 2L *Assurance* (44); 6.2.1755-1.11.1755 1L *Nassau* (64); 1.11.1755 2L *Nassau* (64); 10.3.1757 1L *Nassau* (64); 8.1757-10.1757 Louisbourg Expedition; 9.3.1758-24.5.1758 Capture of Fort Louis; **Commander**; 27.9.1758-2.6.1759 *Racehorse* (8) Bomb Vessel; 12.4.1762-17.1.1764[P] *Weazle* (16) Sloop; 18.5.1768-18.5.1771 *Alderney* (10) Sloop; 29.3.1774-23.5.1775 *Alderney* (10) Sloop.

RICHARDS, WILLIAM

Dates: c.1731 Born; 7.11.1784 Died.

Family:

Service: 14.6.1746 Capt Serv *Stirling Castle* (70); 12.7.1748 Able *Assistance* (50); 20.6.1749 Mid *Assistance* (50); 25.1.1750/51 Able *Culloden*; 12.6.1751 Able *Fortune* (14) Sloop; 24.6.1751 Mid *Fortune* (14) Sloop; 27.7.1752-6.12.1752 Able *Peggy* (8) Sloop; 6.12.1752 Passed; 6.4.1757 **Lieutenant.**

RICHARDSON, JOHN

Dates: c.1737 Born.

Family:

Service: 1.7.1752 Capt Serv *Phoenix* (24); 2.11.1753 Able *Phoenix* (24); 3.1.1755 Mid *Phoenix* (24); 20.5.1756 Battle of Minorca; 27.5.1756 Mid *Ramillies* (90); 8.7.1756 Mid *Hampton Court* (64); 7.2.1757 Passed; **Lieutenant**; 6.4.1757 6L *Princess Royal* (90); 25.5.1757 2L *Unicorn* (28); 3.7.1759 Bombardment of Le Havre; 16.1.1760-29.3.1762 1L *Unicorn* (28); 29.3.1761-11.6.1761 Expedition against Belle-Isle.

RICHARDSON, THOMAS

Dates: c.1734 Born; 14.8.1793 Died.

Family:

Service: 6.2.1754-22.5.1756[P] Land. *Advice* (50); 2.8.1756 Mid *Bedford* (64); 29.9.1756 Able *Ranger* (8) Sloop; 7.10.1757 Mid *Royal Sovereign* (104); 10.1.1759 Mate *Union* (90); 20.11.1759 Battle of Quiberon Bay; 14.5.1760 Passed; **Lieutenant**; 23.12.1760 5L *Bellona* (74); 11.3.1761-4.8.1761 3L *Torrington* (44); 22.3.1777-11.9.1777 3L *Cornwall* (74).

RIGBY, CHRISTOPHER

Dates: 11.1.1795 Died.
Family:
Service: 29.3.1758 **Lieutenant**; 8.12.1758[(EI 8.12.1760)]-21.10.1762 4L *Weymouth* (60); 10.9.1759 Battle of Pondicherry; 24.9.1762-6.10.1762 Battle of Manilla; 11.9.1771-26.5.1775[P] 1L *Prudent* (64); 15.11.1776 2L *Sandwich* (90); **Commander**; 25.10.1777-13.4.1779[P] *Greenwich* (26) Storeship.

RIPLEY, HORATIO

Dates: c.1732 Born; 4.10.1789 Died.
Family:
Service: 25.10.1746 Capt Serv *Princess Mary* (60); 10.9.1749 Able *Princess Mary* (60); 27.1.1749/50 Mid *Princess Mary* (60); 11.4.1750 Able *Prince Henry* (44); 6.6.1750 Mid *Prince Henry* (44); 6.12.1752 Passed; **Lieutenant**; 26.2.1756-4.1.1757 2L *Kingfisher* (14) Sloop; 4.4.1757 3L *Alcide* (64); 20.10.1757-7.9.1763[P] 2L *Alcide* (64); 5.6.1758-12.6.1758 Raid on Saint-Malo; 7.1.1762-10.2.1762 Operations against Martinique; 6.6.1762-13.8.1762 Operations against Havana.

ROBARTS, JOSEPH

Dates: bef.1764 Died.
Family:
Service: 8.5.1740 **Lieutenant**; 29.9.1743-9.6.1746 L. *Port Mahon* (20); 24.6.1755 1L *Princess Louisa* (60); 20.5.1756 Battle of Minorca; 29.11.1756[(ECH 4.4.1757)]-12.3.1757 1L *Prince* (90); 27.6.1757-2.1.1758 1L *Jason* (44); 4.5.1763-20.5.1766 1L *Preston* (50).

ROBBINS, GEORGE

Dates: c.1734 Born.
Family:
Service: 24.10.1748 Able *Fougueux* (64); 6.9.1750 Mid *Fougueux* (64); 6.11.1750 Mid *Prince Henry* (44); 28.1.1753 Mid *Fougueux* (64); 27.3.1753 Able *Savage* (8) Sloop; 3.6.1754 Able *Arundel* (24); 5.2.1755 Passed; **Lieutenant**; 11.3.1755 3L *Newcastle* (50); 30.9.1755-6.1.1757 3L *Kingston* (60); 20.5.1756 Battle of Minorca.

ROBERTS, CHRISTOPHER

Dates: c.1732 Born; 19.8.1815 Died Walworth; 17.10.1815 Will Probate.
Family:
Service: 28.2.1748/49 Able *Gloucester* (50); 7.11.1752-24.4.1753[P] Able *Assurance* (44); 23.1.1757 Mid *Badger* (10) Sloop; 15.8.1757 Mid *Seahorse* (24); 14.11.1757-4.4.1759 Mate *Seahorse* (24); 4.4.1759 Passed; **Lieutenant**; 7.7.1762-2.3.1763[P] 5L *Shrewsbury* (74); 25.10.1809 **Superannuated Commander**.

ROBERTS, EDWARD

Dates: None Known.
Family:
Service: 24.7.1751-c.1754 Scholar *Royal Naval Academy*; **Lieutenant**; 18.1.1759[(EI 27.5.1762)] 2L *Salisbury* (50); 10.9.1759 Battle of Pondicherry; 25.3.1761[(EI 27.5.1762)]-28.8.1761[P] 1L *Salisbury* (50); 9.6.1801 **Superannuated Commander**.

ROBERTS, JOHN

Dates: c.1720 Born; 19.8.1815 Died.

Family:

Service: 18.10.1732 Vol-p-O *York* (60); 16.5.1733 Vol-p-O *Edinburgh* (70); 3.7.1733 Able *Spy* (8) Sloop; 17.3.1734 MidO *Pearl* (40); 27.3.1737 Able *Somerset* (80); 30.4.1738 MidO *Windsor* (60); 9.3.1739 Mid *Kinsale* (40); 14.12.1739 Mid *Ruby* (54); 14.4.1740 Mid *Assistance* (50); 16.8.1740-5.3.1741 Mid *Oxford* (50); 5.3.1740/41 Passed; **Lieutenant**; 20.3.1740/41 3L *Roebuck* (40); 3.11.1743-29.5.1746 2L *Plymouth* (60); 12.4.1755-17.6.1757 1L *Prince Frederick* (64); 21.9.1796 **Superannuated Commander**.

ROBERTSON, GEORGE

Dates: c.1739 Born; 21.11.1791 Died.

Family:

Service: 1755-1757 Merchant Service; 17.9.1757 Mid *Essex* (64); 5.6.1758-12.6.1758 Raid on Saint-Malo; 1.8.1759 Mid *Royal George* (100); 20.11.1759 Battle of Quiberon Bay; 9.4.1760 Mid *Dorsetshire* (68); 7.10.1761 Passed; **Lieutenant**; 5.3.1762[(3.5.1763)] 4L *Dorsetshire* (68); 26.7.1762[(3.5.1763)]-7.5.1763[P] 2L *Dorsetshire* (68); 1.6.1766 3L *Dolphin* (24); 9.6.1767-9.7.1771[P] L. *Fowey* (24); **Commander**; 4.11.1778-13.9.1779 *Incendiary* (8) Fireship; 19.2.1780-15.8.1781 *Firebrand* (8) Fireship; **Captain**; 15.8.1781 *Buffalo* (50); 1.5.1782-18.1.1783 *Danae* (32); 14.4.1783-15.1.1784[P] *Aeolus* (32); 18.12.1783-1.4.1786 *Thisbe* (28).

ROBERTSON, JAMES

Dates: c.1730 Born; c.1815 Died; 19.1.1815 Will Probate.

Family:

Service: 1749-1753 Merchant Service; 1.3.1753 Able *Prince Edward* (44); 25.4.1754 Mid *Princess Royal* (90); 23.11.1754 Mate *Terrible* (74); 28.2.1756-16.9.1757 Master *Medway* (60); 1.8.1759 Passed; **Lieutenant**; 3.8.1759[(BLI 25.7.1760)] 3L *Lion* (58); 13.9.1759[(BLI 11.10.1762)] 2L *Crescent* (32) Frigate; 7.1.1762-10.2.1762 Operations against Martinique; 22.3.1762[(BLI 11.10.1762)]-4.11.1762[P] 1L *Crescent* (32) Frigate; 19.4.1763-5.3.1766 LCmdr *Lord Howe* (6) Cutter; **Commander**; 26.5.1768-18.7.1770 *Spy* (10) Sloop; 10.8.1771-8.1773 *Dispatch* (14) Sloop; 9.3.1776-18.7.1777 *Hound* (14) Sloop; 25.10.1809 **Captain**.

ROBERTSON, WILLIAM

Dates: c.1729 Born; 1813 Died.

Family:

Service: 1750-1755 HEIC Service; 16.7.1755 Mid *Ramillies* (90); 20.5.1756 Battle of Minorca; 5.9.1757-6.10.1757 Raid on Rochefort; 5.6.1758-12.6.1758 Raid on Saint-Malo; 4.4.1759 Passed; **Lieutenant**; 12.3.1760 4L *Swiftsure* (68); 10.12.1760-20.1.1763[P] 2L *Swiftsure* (68); 29.3.1761-11.6.1761 Expedition against Belle-Isle; 13.1.1776-27.8.1781[P] LCmdr *Earl of Inchiquin* Hired Tender; 20.4.1807 **Superannuated Commander**.

ROBINSON, EDWARD

Dates: 1792 Died; 5.9.1792 Will Probate.

Family:

Service: 4.12.1739 **Lieutenant**; 16.2.1741/42 2L *Lark* (40); 14.10.1742[(JAM 5.8.1745)] 1L *Saint Albans* (50); 6.1744 Bombardment of Porto Bello; 24.10.1746-15.3.1747/48 1L *Anglesea* (44); 22.2.1755-30.9.1755 1L *Kingston* (60).

ROBINSON, HUGH

Dates: 17.5.1735 Born; 15.11.1802 Died York; 4.2.1803 Will Probate.

Family: Father Charles Robinson; Mother Hannah Deane; Wife Mary Myers married 24.3.1787; Daughter Elizabeth (d.1832); Son Thomas, RN (d.1838); Son Charles, RN; Brother John Robinson, MP.

Service: 1749-1751 Merchant Service; 28.11.1751 Mid *Nassau* (70); 17.8.1753 Able *Ramillies* (90); 15.6.1754-15.7.1755 Mid *Ramillies* (90); 2.4.1760 Passed; **Lieutenant**; 5.8.1761-25.2.1763[P] 6L *Union* (90); 24.3.1764-24.3.1767 2L *Fame* (74); 29.5.1767-21.1.1771 L. *Glasgow* (20); **Commander**; 10.1.1771-9.1771[P] *Blast* (8) Bomb Vessel; 23.1.1777 *Swift* (14) Sloop; 18.3.1777 *Proteus* (26); **Captain**; 8.5.1777 *Proteus* (26); 18.2.1778-10.10.1781[SC] *Guadeloupe* (28); 1.6.1780-13.9.1780 *Solebay* (28) Frigate; 16.3.1781 Battle of Cape Henry; 16.9.1794 **Superannuated Rear Admiral**.

ROBINSON, JOHN

Dates: c.1733 Born; c.1807 Died; 2.10.1807 Will Probate.

Family:

Service: 29.3.1748 Capt Serv *Warwick* (60); 9.4.1748 Battle of Santiago de Cuba; 21.8.1748 Able *Warwick* (60); 12.10.1748 Battle of Havana; 23.1.1748/49 Mid *Canterbury* (60); 28.9.1749-3.12.1751 Able *Yarmouth* (64); 4.12.1751 Mid *Sphinx* (24); 3.5.1753 Mate *Sphinx* (24); 4.12.1754 Passed; **Lieutenant**; 30.1.1758-24.8.1759 L. *Tamar* (16) Sloop; 2.11.1759-7.8.1761 2L *Revenge* (64); 20.11.1759 Battle of Quiberon Bay; 7.3.1760-2.7.1762 2L *Dragon* (74); 29.3.1761-11.6.1761 Expedition against Belle-Isle; 7.1.1762-10.2.1762 Operations against Martinique; 24.2.1762-25.2.1762 Capture of Saint Lucia; 5.5.1763 1L *Centurion* (50); **Commander**; 20.6.1765-7.1766[P] *Vulture* (14) Sloop; 7.6.1769 *Wolf* (8) Sloop; 24.6.1771-16.1.1773 *Ferret* (14) Sloop; **Captain**; 26.1.1774-8.4.1776 *Preston* (50); 4.11.1776-16.4.1778 *Queen* (90); 14.7.1779-30.6.1780[P] *Cyclops* (28); 26.1.1794 **Superannuated Rear Admiral**.

ROBINSON, JOHN

Dates: c.1727 Born; c.1762 Died; 30.10.1762 Will Probate.

Family:

Service: 1753-1755 Merchant Service; 5.2.1755-14.3.1754/55 Able *Culloden* (74); 15.3.1754/55 Mid *Culloden* (74); 20.5.1756 Battle of Minorca; 12.12.1756 Mid *Prince* (90); 16.5.1757-5.1.1759 Mid *Ramillies* (90); 5.9.1757-6.10.1757 Raid on Rochefort; 5.6.1758-12.6.1758 Raid on Saint-Malo; 5.1.1759 Passed; **Lieutenant**; 4.9.1759 6L *Duke* (90); 20.11.1759 Battle of Quiberon Bay; 24.5.1762-14.6.1762 5L *Duke* (90).

ROBINSON, MARK

Dates: 22.4.1722 Born; 23.11.1799 Died Bath.

Family: Wife Elizabeth Reade married 26.11.1747; Son Mark, RN (1753-1834); Son Charles, RN (d.1853); Son John Reade (c.1750-1781).

Service: 1740-1742 Merchant Service; 11.8.1742 Able *Launceston* (44); 11.11.1744 Mid *Launceston* (44); 13.12.1745 Able *Superb* (60); **Lieutenant**; 30.3.1746[BLI 15.5.1747]-16.10.1747 4L *Vigilant* (60); 14.5.1747 Passed; 19.3.1747/48-29.7.1748[P] 4L *Berwick* (70); 5.12.1748-11.9.1751 3L *Kent* (64); 28.1.1755 2L *Culloden* (74); 20.5.1756 Battle of Minorca; 5.4.1757 Action of April 5 1757; 28.4.1757 2L *Ramillies* (90); 5.9.1757-6.10.1757 Raid on Rochefort; 26.4.1758 1L *Ramillies* (90); 5.6.1758-12.6.1758 Raid on Saint-Malo; **Commander**; 27.9.1758-19.4.1759[W] *Falcon* (8) Bomb Vessel; 16.1.1759-19.1.1759 Attack on Martinique; **Captain**; 13.8.1760 *Vanguard* (68); 7.1.1762-10.2.1762 Operations against Martinique; 7.4.1762-4.4.1763 *Rainbow*

(44); 9.6.1767-9.7.1771[P] *Fowey* (24); 1.4.1775 *Worcester* (64); 27.7.1778 1st Battle of Ushant; 11.1.1779-21.9.1781 *Shrewsbury* (74); 29.4.1781-30.4.1781 Battle of Fort Royal; 5.9.1781 Battle of the Chesapeake; 6.10.1787 **Superannuated Rear Admiral.**

ROBINSON, ROBERT

Dates: 10.9.1785 Died.
Family:
Service: 30.5.1724 Ord. *Spy* (8) Sloop; 10.2.1725/26 Mid *Spy* (8) Sloop; 15.8.1726-13.5.1728[P] Mid *Swallow* (50); 5.8.1728-6.10.1729 Able *Ludlow Castle* (40); 7.10.1729 Able *Looe* (32); 14.12.1730 Mid *Looe* (42); 19.5.1732 Mid *Tiger* (50); 1.8.1733 Passed; **Lieutenant**; 5.5.1735-5.1737[P] 4L *Royal Oak* (70); 14.7.1738-23.11.1738[P] 2L *Superb* (60); 25.5.1739 3L *Adventure* (40); 5.7.1739 2L *Adventure* (40); 15.3.1739/40 2L *Gloucester* (50); 27.8.1740 1L *Roebuck* (40); 27.9.1740 1L *Kingston* (60); 21.2.1740/41 2L *Essex* (70); 27.3.1741-4.2.1742/43 1L *Essex* (70); **Captain**; 22.2.1743/44[MED 29.12.1746]-17.3.1743/44 *Marlborough* (90); 23.8.1744[MED 15.6.1748]-1.6.1748[P] *Diamond* (44); 6.12.1762 **Superannuated Rear Admiral.**

ROBINSON, WILLIAM

Dates: c.1715 Born; 10.1782 Died; 31.5.1783 Will Probate.
Family:
Service: 10.11.1739 Able *Namur* (90); 17.8.1740 QGnr *Victory* (100); 14.4.1743 Gnr Mate *Princess Mary* (60); 28.10.1744 Mid *Princess Mary* (60); 24.3.1744/45 Able *Royal Sovereign* (104); 31.5.1745 Mate *Royal Sovereign* (104); 15.12.1745 Able *Gloucester* (50); 27.1.1745/46 Mid *Gloucester* (50); 5.3.1745/46 ActL *Eltham* (40); 5.9.1746 ActL *Baltimore* (14) Sloop; 14.5.1747 Passed; **Lieutenant**; 18.7.1747-1.9.1748[W] L. *Serpent* (10) Bomb Vessel; 10.7.1755-16.5.1757 2L *Isis* (50); 1.6.1757-29.7.1757 4L *Neptune* (90); 1.8.1757 3L *Union* (90); 5.6.1758-12.6.1758 Raid on Saint-Malo; 20.11.1758 2L *Union* (90); 30.1.1759-26.1.1762 2L *Royal William* (84); 29.3.1761-11.6.1761 Expedition against Belle-Isle.

ROBSON, JOHN

Dates: c.1733 Born.
Family:
Service: 24.1.1749/50 Capt Serv *Canterbury* (60); 4.3.1750/51-3.7.1751[W] Capt Serv *Weymouth* (60); 3.7.1751 Able *Lark* (44); 17.4.1752 Able *Tiger* (60); 13.4.1753 Able *Swan* (14) Sloop; 9.8.1754 Mid *Swan* (14) Sloop; 17.4.1755 Mid *Yarmouth* (64); 3.1.1756-10.3.1756/57 Mate *Yarmouth* (64); 10.3.1757 Passed; **Lieutenant**; 21.8.1758[NA 19.11.1759]-29.3.1759 3L *Pembroke* (60); 10.3.1761-20.2.1764[P] 1L *Pembroke* (60); 6.6.1762-13.8.1762 Operations against Havana; 15.11.1769-26.5.1770[P] 2L *Superb* (74); 23.5.1770 2L *Ajax* (74); 17.9.1770 3L *Ajax* (74); 4.12.1770-7.6.1771[P] 2L *Ajax* (74); 4.9.1771 1L *Montreal* (32); 7.1.1774 2L *Worcester* (64); 29.10.1777-19.1.1779 1L *Worcester* (64); 27.7.1778 1st Battle of Ushant; 10.4.1779 1L *Lennox* (74).

ROCH, HUGH

Dates: c.1730 Born.
Family:
Service: 14.8.1746 Able *John and Anne* (16) Hired Armed vessel; 28.9.1746-31.5.1747[P] Mid *John and Anne* (16) Hired Armed vessel; 4.9.1749-16.7.1750[P] Able *Speedwell* (10) Sloop; 8.5.1751 Capt Serv *Tilbury* (58); 30.7.1751 Able *Captain* (70); 12.5.1752 Mid *Torrington* (44);

24.5.1755 Mid *Grafton* (68); 5.5.1756 Passed; **Lieutenant**; 30.6.1756-2.2.1757 3L *Newcastle* (50); 22.4.1757-27.10.1757 5L *Monarch* (74); 22.7.1765-8.1768 LCmdr *Laurel* (6) Cutter.

ROCH, WILLIAM

Dates: c.1728 Born; c.1767 Died; 10.8.1767 Will Probate.
Family:
Service: 1752-1754 Merchant Service; 30.5.1754 Able *Prince Edward* (44); 8.7.1754 Mid *Prince Edward* (44); 18.6.1755 Able *Dispatch* (14) Sloop; 5.8.1755 Mate *Dispatch* (14) Sloop; 22.7.1756 Mid *Chichester* (68); 15.2.1758 Passed; **Lieutenant**; 22.5.1758-22.8.1759 L. *Proserpine* (8) Fireship; 5.9.1759 2L *Arethusa* (32); 3.10.1759-3.3.1763[P] 3L *Saint Florentine* (60); 27.10.1766-24.3.1767[†] 2L *Belleisle* (64).

ROCHE, CHARLES

Dates: 1768 Died; 8.6.1768 Will Probate.
Family:
Service: **Lieutenant**; 31.5.1755[(MED 14.3.1757)]-16.9.1756 L. *Baltimore* (14) Sloop; 15.9.1755[(NA 14.3.1757)] 3L *Norwich* (50); 15.10.1755[(NA 14.3.1757)] 2L *Norwich* (50); 1.4.1757 2L *Achilles* (60); 5.4.1757-15.1.1759 4L *Torbay* (74); 5.9.1757-6.10.1757 Raid on Rochefort; 5.6.1758-12.6.1758 Raid on Saint-Malo; 29.12.1758 Capture of Goree; 5.1.1760-14.12.1761 1L *Valiant* (74); 29.3.1761-11.6.1761 Expedition against Belle-Isle; **Commander**; 7.4.1762-23.3.1763[P] *Infernal* (14) Bomb Vessel; 21.8.1765 *Cruizer* (8) Sloop; 13.8.1766-16.1.1768 *Diligence* (10) Sloop.

RODDAM, ROBERT

Dates: 1719 Born; 31.3.1808 Died Morpeth.
Family:
Service: **Lieutenant**; 2.11.1741[(19.3.1741/42)]-8.5.1742[P] 3L *Superb* (60); 7.9.1742 3L *Monmouth* (70); 14.7.1744 2L *Monmouth* (70); 29.5.1746 *Viper* (10) Sloop; **Captain**; 9.7.1747-30.9.1751[P] *Greyhound* (20); 30.1.1753-24.1.1754 *Bristol* (50); 13.5.1755-18.3.1757[C] *Greenwich* (50); 4.6.1759-22.12.1760[P] *Colchester* (50); 7.12.1770-1.12.1773 *Lennox* (74); 17.3.1777-23.1.1778 *Cornwall* (74); 23.1.1778 **Rear Admiral of the White**; 29.4.1778-1783 CinC — River Medway and The Nore; 19.3.1779 **Vice Admiral of the Blue**; 26.9.1780 **Vice Admiral of the White**; 24.9.1787 **Vice Admiral of the Red**; 1789-1790 *Barfleur* (98); 20.4.1789-1792 CinC — Portsmouth; 18.5.1790-16.9.1791[P] *Royal William* (84); 8.1791-1792 *Duke* (98); 1.2.1793 **Admiral of the Blue**; 12.4.1794 **Admiral of the White**; 9.11.1805 **Admiral of the Red**.

RODNEY, GEORGE BRYDGES CB (1ST BARON RODNEY)

Dates: 1719 Born; 19.2.1718/19 Baptised Walton-on-Thames, Surrey; 22.1.1764 Baronet; 14.11.1780 Order of the Bath; 19.6.1782 1st Baron Rodney; 24.5.1792 Died.
Family: Father Henry Rodney; Mother Mary Newton; Wife Jane Compton (d.1757) married 31.1.1753; Wife Henrietta Clies married 1764; Son John, RN (1765-1847); Son Sir Edward, RN (d.1828).
Service: **Lieutenant**; 15.2.1739/40 L. *Dolphin* (20); 21.2.1740/41 4L *Essex* (70); 27.3.1741 3L *Essex* (70); 20.2.1741/42 3L *Royal Sovereign* (104); 12.3.1741/42 5L *Namur* (90); 22.3.1741/42 4L *Namur* (90); **Captain**; 9.11.1742 *Plymouth* (60); 22.9.1743 *Sheerness* (20); 4.8.1744 *Ludlow Castle* (44); 3.12.1745-14.8.1748[P] *Eagle* (60); 14.10.1747 2nd Battle of Cape Finisterre; 3.3.1748/49-20.4.1752[P] *Rainbow* (44); 13.5.1751-18.4.1754 M.P. for Saltash; 16.1.1753-20.1.1754 *Kent* (64); 7.4.1754 *Fougueux* (64); 14.2.1755 *Prince George* (80); 3.5.1756 *Monarch* (74); 4.4.1757-23.1.1759 *Dublin* (74); 5.9.1757-6.10.1757 Raid on Rochefort; 1.4.1759-

21.8.1759 *Achilles* (60); 19.5.1759 **Rear Admiral of the Blue**; 3.7.1759 Bombardment of Le Havre; 24.11.1759-27.3.1761 M.P. for Okehampton; 4.4.1761-21.3.1768 M.P. for Penryn; 10.9.1761 *Marlborough* (68); 6.10.1761-7.6.1763 CinC — Barbados & the Leeward Islands; 1762-1763 *Foudroyant* (80); 7.1.1762-10.2.1762 Operations against Martinique; 21.10.1762 **Vice Admiral of the Blue**; 1.4.1768-10.10.1774 M.P. for Northampton; 18.10.1770 **Vice Admiral of the White**; 24.10.1770 **Vice Admiral of the Red**; 1.1771-1773 *Princess Amelia* (80); 23.1.1771 CinC — Jamaica; 17.8.1771-6.11.1781 Rear Admiral of Great Britain; 1774-29.9.1774[P] *Portland* (50); 29.1.1778 **Admiral of the White**; 9.1779-8.1781 *Sandwich* (90); 1.10.1779-24.4.1782 CinC — Barbados & the Leeward Islands; 16.1.1780 Battle of Cape St. Vincent; 17.4.1780 Battle of Martinique; 10.10.1780-12.6.1782 M.P. for Westminster; 10.1781 *Gibraltar* (80); 6.11.1781-24.5.1792 Vice Admiral of Great Britain; 24.11.1781-13.4.1782 *Formidable* (98); 12.4.1782 Battle of the Saintes.

ROGERS, FREDERICK

Dates: c.1716 Born; 1775 Died.
Family:
Service: 22.9.1730 Vol-p-O *Gosport* (42); 21.10.1732 Mid *York* (60); 4.12.1732 Able *York* (60); 11.4.1733 Mid *Falmouth* (50); 20.10.1735 Able *Somerset* (80); 29.12.1735 Mid *Somerset* (80); 11.5.1736-9.10.1736 Able *Exeter* (60); 9.10.1736 Passed; **Lieutenant**; 1.9.1738-15.7.1739 3L *Saint Albans* (50); 3.11.1739-21.1.1739/40 2L *Superb* (60); 22.1.1739/40 2L *Mary Galley* (40); 13.4.1741 1L *Mary Galley* (40); **Commander**; 15.5.1741 *Otter* (6) Sloop; 11.6.1741 *Drake* (8) Sloop; **Captain**; 2.12.1741 *Bridgewater* (20); 31.12.1742 *Woolwich* (50); 28.1.1742/43 *Dover* (44); 2.10.1744-25.10.1745 *Maidstone* (50); 17.7.1747-20.11.1752[P] *Mars* (64); 16.1.1753-17.10.1753 *Vanguard* (68).

ROGERS, JACOB

Dates: c.1729 Born.
Family:
Service: 23.11.1748 Capt Serv *Launceston* (44); 21.11.1751 Capt Serv *Superb* (60); 17.8.1752 Mid *Superb* (60); 11.1.1755 Able *Princess* (70); 6.2.1755 Mid *Princess* (70); 6.5.1755 Able *Centurion* (50); 4.8.1756 Passed; **Lieutenant**; 4.4.1757 1L *Vestal* (32); 19.10.1757-5.7.1759 4L *Stirling Castle* (64); 22.7.1760-7.6.1761 3L *Stirling Castle* (64); 3.6.1761-7.6.1761 Occupation of Dominica; 16.5.1769 L. *Lively* (20); 10.4.1773-18.4.1774[D] LCmdr *Halifax* (6) Schooner; 18.4.1774 Dismissed.

ROGERS, JOHN

Dates: c.1715 Born; c.1764 Died; 7.9.1764 Will Probate.
Family:
Service: 11.3.1735/36-3.10.1737 Able *Edinburgh* (70); 4.10.1737-28.11.1738 Able *Princess Amelia* (80); 29.11.1738-25.9.1739 Able *Augusta* (60); 26.9.1739-22.1.1739/40 Gnr Mate *Portland* (50); 23.1.1739/40-16.1.1741/42 Mid *Sunderland* (60); 17.1.1741/42-1.9.1742 Mate *Sunderland* (60); 2.9.1742-8.9.1742 Able *Sutherland* (50); 9.9.1742-21.10.1743 Mate *Sutherland* (50); 22.10.1743-22.11.1743 Mid *Captain* (70); 23.11.1743-9.6.1744 Mate *Captain* (70); 10.6.1744-25.1.1744/45 Mate *Saint George* (90); 26.1.1744/45-15.2.1744/45 Able *Winchester* (50); 16.2.1744/45 Mate *Winchester* (50); 5.6.1745 Passed; **Lieutenant**; 29.8.1745 6L *Royal Sovereign* (104); 23.1.1745/46 5L *Royal Sovereign* (104); 19.1.1746/47-17.3.1747/48 4L *Princess* (70); 23.7.1755-6.5.1756 2L *Prince Edward* (44); 23.8.1756-31.12.1756[P] L. *Brilliant* (16) Hired Unknown; 8.3.1757 L. *Porcupine* (16) Sloop; 16.5.1758 1L *Sapphire* (32); 12.12.1758

3L *Penzance* (44); 2.7.1759-1.12.1762[P] 1L *Penzance* (44); 3.6.1761-7.6.1761 Occupation of Dominica; 7.1.1762-10.2.1762 Operations against Martinique; 24.2.1762-25.2.1762 Capture of Saint Lucia; 6.6.1762-13.8.1762 Operations against Havana.

ROOKE, NICHOLAS

Dates: c.1730 Born; 1805 Died.
Family:
Service: 20.11.1749-28.3.1750 Able *Ranger* (8) Sloop; 29.3.1750 Mid *Garland* (24); 2.7.1754-7.3.1755 Able *Garland* (24); 8.3.1755 Able *Eagle* (60); 14.5.1755 Mid *Augusta* (60); 5.5.1756 Passed; **Lieutenant**; 23.3.1757 L. *Strombolo* (14) Fireship; 17.1.1758 L. *Adventure* (18) Hired Armed Ship; 8.5.1758-27.10.1758 L. *Seahorse* (24); 19.4.1759 3L *Sandwich* (90); 7.6.1759-3.4.1760 2L *Sandwich* (90); 8.1.1762-5.10.1762 1L *Torrington* (44); 25.2.1767-17.3.1770 LCmdr *Kite* (4) Cutter; 4.3.1773-16.3.1776 1L *Worcester* (64); 24.9.1779-8.10.1783[P] LCmdr *Amy* Hired Tender; 5.1783-6.1786 LCmdr *Spider* (12) Cutter; 21.9.1796 **Superannuated Commander.**

ROOME, CHARLES

Dates: c.1714 Born; 1776 Died; 29.10.1776 Will Probate.
Family:
Service: 25.11.1731 Vol-p-O *Berwick* (70); 12.11.1733 MidO *Berwick* (70); 10.4.1734 Mid *Cornwall* (80); 28.5.1734 Able *York* (60); 1.7.1734 Able *Blandford* (20); 8.5.1737 Able *Revenge* (70); 18.5.1737 Mid *Revenge* (70); 28.5.1737 Mid *Newark* (80); 2.4.1738 Mid *Spence* (8) Sloop; 17.11.1739 Able *Greenwich* (50); 16.4.1740 Passed; **Lieutenant**; 13.7.1745 3L *Southsea Castle* (44); 22.11.1745-19.3.1745/46 2L *Southsea Castle* (44).

ROSCO, JAMES

Dates: None Known.
Family:
Service: **Lieutenant**; 24.9.1759[BLI 20.8.1762] L. *Antigua* (14) Sloop; 7.1.1762-10.2.1762 Operations against Martinique; 3.5.1762[20.8.1762]-24.9.1762[P] 3L *Norwich* (50).

ROSEWELL, HENRY

Dates: c.1716 Born; 9.5.1771 Died.
Family: Father William Rosewell (d.1726); Mother Elizabeth Lake; Brother Benjamin (1714-1782); Brother John (1722-1755); Sister Mary [Hargood]; Sister Elizabeth [Hargood]; Sister Susannah [Freeman];
Service: 25.12.1728 Able *Canterbury* (60); 6.9.1730 Able *Spence* (8) Sloop; 5.4.1731-27.12.1731 Able *Bideford* (20); 28.12.1731 Mid *Bideford* (20); 6.11.1734 Mid *Nottingham* (60); 4.11.1736 Passed; **Lieutenant**; 19.1.1739/40[11.7.1740]-26.9.1740 3L *Superb* (60); 20.3.1740/41-17.5.1742 1L *Hastings* (44); 14.10.1743 2L *Worcester* (58); 25.11.1743-13.4.1744 2L *Cornwall* (80); 18.4.1744 2L *Deptford* (60); 24.1.1744/45 Straits of Banca; **Commander**; 26.2.1744/45 *Dolphin* (8) Storeship; **Captain**; 21.7.1745[29.8.1746]-1.2.1745/46 *Lively* (24); 3.5.1746-5.7.1748 *Medway* (60); 24.1.1771 **Superannuated Rear Admiral.**

ROSS, GEORGE

Dates: c.1731 Born; c.1762 Died; 15.12.1762 Will Probate.
Family:
Service: 13.3.1746/47 Able *Ruby* (50); 3.4.1749 Mid *Ruby* (50); 4.10.1752 Passed; **Lieutenant**; 21.10.1755 L. *Lightning* (8) Fireship; 13.10.1756-20.3.1760 L. *Seaford* (20).

ROUS, JOHN

Dates: 3.4.1760 Died.
Family:
Service: **Lieutenant**; 22.6.1745[NA 29.7.1745]-7.7.1745 3L *Vigilant* (60); 9.8.1745 L. *Shirley* (10) Sloop; **Captain**; 24.9.1745 *Shirley* (10) Sloop; 11.3.1748/49-10.12.1753[P] *Albany* (14) Sloop; 26.3.1754 *Success* (20); 22.5.1755-14.6.1755 British attack on Fort Beauséjour; 2.2.1757-13.5.1758 *Arc-en-Ciel* (50); 12.5.1758[NA 12.3.1760]-3.4.1760† *Sutherland* (50); 6.6.1758-27.7.1758 The Siege of Louisbourg.

ROUTH, ROBERT

Dates: c.1724 Born; 3.10.1760 Died.
Family:
Service: 3.11.1739 Capt Serv *Newcastle* (50); 8.6.1741 Able *Newcastle* (50); 7.12.1742 Mid *Newcastle* (50); 28.3.1745 Mid *Barfleur* (90); 27.8.1745 Mid *Royal George* (100); 6.6.1746 Passed; **Lieutenant**; 7.8.1746 L. *Granado* (8) Bomb Vessel; 9.4.1748 3L *Mars* (64); 4.10.1752 1L *Saint Albans* (60); **Commander**; 27.12.1753[JAM 1.5.1755] *Falcon* (10) Bomb Vessel; **Captain**; 19.1.1755-26.4.1755[P] *Jason* (44); 29.4.1756 *Scarborough* (20); 6.6.1758-27.7.1758 The Siege of Louisbourg; 1.8.1758[NA 24.3.1760]-17.11.1760 *Prince Frederick* (64).

ROWLEY, SIR JOSHUA (1ST BARONET ROWLEY)

Dates: 5.1734 Born Dublin; 27.6.1786 1st Baronet Rowley; 26.2.1790 Died Tendring Hall, Suffolk.
Family: Father William Rowley, RN (1690-1768); Mother Arabella Dawson (d.1784); Son William Rowley (1761–1832), 2nd Baronet; Son Bartholomew Samuel, RN (1763-1811); Son Charles (Baronet of Hill House), RN (1770-1845).
Service: **Lieutenant**; 2.7.1747[MED 30.12.1747]-22.1.1747/48[P] 4L *Bedford* (70); 8.2.1747/48 3L *Tilbury* (58); 5.5.1748[7.2.1748/49]-16.2.1748/49[P] 3L *Captain* (70); 18.2.1751/52 1L *Penzance* (44); 16.1.1753 *Raven* (10) Sloop; 23.1.1753 **Commander**; **Captain**; 4.12.1753 *Rye* (20); 22.3.1755 *Ambuscade* (40); 24.1.1756 *Harwich* (50); 21.9.1757-11.9.1758[C] *Montagu* (60); 28.2.1758 Battle of Cartagena; 28.11.1760-2.3.1763[P] *Superb* (74); 29.10.1776-8.12.1778 *Monarch* (74); 27.7.1778 1st Battle of Ushant; 12.1778-29.3.1779 Commodore *Suffolk* (74); 19.3.1779 **Rear Admiral of the Blue**; 29.3.1779-17.1.1780 *Suffolk* (74); 6.7.1779 Battle of Grenada; 21.12.1779-22.12.1779 Action of 1779-12-21; 3.1780-1781 *Conqueror* (74); 17.4.1780 Battle of Martinique; 15.5.1780 Action of March 15 1780; 19.5.1780 Action of March 19 1780; 5.6.1780-27.7.1781[P] *Princess Royal* (98); 26.9.1780 **Rear Admiral of the Red**; 19.7.1781-1783 CinC — Jamaica; 1782-7.1782 *Ramillies* (74); 10.1782-7.1783 *London* (90); 17.10.1782 Action of 1782-10-17; 18.10.1782 Action of 18 October 1782; 24.9.1787 **Vice Admiral of the White**.

ROWLEY, WILLIAM CB

Dates: 1690 Born; 12.12.1753 Order of the Bath; 1.1.1768 Died.
Family: Father William Rowley (d. 1705); Mother Elizabeth Dawson; Wife Arabella Dawson (d.1784) married bef.1729; Son Sir Joshua (1st Baronet Rowley), RN (1734-1790); Son Clotworthy, MP (c.1731-1805); Son Thomas (c.1734-?); Daughter Arabella [Martin] (1740-?); Son William (c.1745-?);
Service: 13.6.1704 Vol-p-O *Orford* (70); 13.8.1704 Battle of Malaga; 6.9.1706 Mid *Orford* (70); 16.6.1708 Mid *Royal Anne* (100); 15.9.1708 Passed; **Lieutenant**; 7.1.1708/9-12.4.1710 3L *Somerset* (80); 23.3.1713/14-25.6.1716 2L *Woolwich* (54); **Captain**; 26.6.1716-11.3.1718/19 Capt&M *Bideford* (24); 29.9.1719 *Lively* (20); 11.8.1727-5.7.1728[P] *Lively* (20); 5.6.1741 *Barfleur*

(90); **Rear Admiral of the White**; 7.12.1743-1744 *Barfleur* (90); 19.6.1744 **Vice Admiral of the Blue**; 26.6.1744-7.1745 CinC — The Mediterranean Sea; 8.1744-10.1745 *Neptune* (90); 23.4.1745 **Vice Admiral of the White**; 15.7.1747 **Admiral of the Blue**; 12.5.1748 **Admiral of the White**; 12.7.1749-1763 Rear Admiral of Great Britain; 27.2.1749/50-15.4.1754 M.P. for Taunton; 22.6.1751-17.11.1756 Lord Commissioner of the Admiralty; 18.4.1754-17.3.1761 M.P. for Portsmouth; 6.4.1757-1.7.1757 Lord Commissioner of the Admiralty; 17.12.1762 **Admiral of the Fleet**.

ROXBURGH, WILLIAM

Dates: c.1739 Born.
Family:
Service: 9.7.1755 Capt Serv *Nightingale* (22); 5.9.1755 Mid *Nightingale* (22); 25.7.1757 Able *Newark* (80); 30.8.1757 Mid *Newark* (80); 5.6.1758-12.6.1758 Raid on Saint-Malo; 18.8.1759-19.8.1759 Battle of Lagos Bay; 15.2.1760 Passed; **Lieutenant**; 1.12.1760 4L *Stirling Castle* (64); 3.6.1761-7.6.1761 Occupation of Dominica; 7.6.1761-14.9.1762[P] 3L *Stirling Castle* (64); 7.1.1762-10.2.1762 Operations against Martinique; 6.6.1762-13.8.1762 Operations against Havana; 1764-1777 In the service of Russia; 1.5.1764 **Captain of the 2nd Rank** (Imperial Russian Navy); 1.5.1764 Resigned.

ROY, ST ALBAN

Dates: c.1731 Born; 11.1796 Died Hampshire.
Family:
Service: 23.12.1747-1.9.1748[P] Mid *Gibraltar* (20); 3.3.1749/50 Purser *Kingfisher* (14) Sloop; 3.11.1752 Purser *Unicorn* (24); 30.8.1753 ActL *Unicorn* (24); 25.9.1753 Purser *Unicorn* (24); 23.3.1754 ActL *Unicorn* (24); 26.6.1754 Mate *Bideford* (20); 17.11.1754-8.7.1755 Mid *Adventure* (44); 2.5.1759 Passed; **Lieutenant**; 29.5.1759-3.7.1760 L. *Raven* (14) Sloop; 27.8.1760-27.12.1760[P] 6L *Saint George* (90); 26.1.1761-2.3.1763[P] 3L *Buckingham* (68); 29.3.1761-11.6.1761 Expedition against Belle-Isle; 6.4.1763-8.6.1766 LCmdr *Fly* (4) Cutter; 25.9.1770-23.10.1770 3L *Arrogant* (74); 30.11.1770 2L *Raisonable* (64); 1.4.1772-22.4.1775[P] 3L *Intrepid* (64); 1.8.1775 2L *Mars* (74); 11.12.1776-5.2.1778[P] 1L *Mars* (74); 23.1.1778 1L *Elizabeth* (74); **Commander**; 11.4.1778-28.10.1780[P] *Content* (20) Hired Armed Ship; 8.6.1782-15.6.1782 *Pluto* (8) Fireship; **Captain**; 8.7.1782-9.7.1782 *Cato* (50); 21.10.1782-28.3.1783[P] *Perseus* (20); 16.8.1783-31.10.1783 *Unicorn* (20).

RULE, JAMES

Dates: c.1740 Born.
Family:
Service: 20.11.1753 Able *Seahorse* (24); 7.4.1756 Able *Eagle* (60); 10.7.1756 Able *Eagle* (60); 22.3.1757/58 Mid *Shrewsbury* (74); 5.6.1758-12.6.1758 Raid on Saint-Malo; 28.5.1759-2.1.1760 Able *Torbay* (74); 20.11.1759 Battle of Quiberon Bay; 2.1.1760 Passed; **Lieutenant**; 4.4.1760-9.12.1760 5L *Shrewsbury* (74); 9.4.1762[(6.12.1762)]-30.11.1762[P] L. *Strombolo* (8) Fireship; 18.4.1763-18.8.1766 L. *Wasp* (8) Sloop; 24.3.1767 2L *Belleisle* (64); 10.11.1769-29.3.1770 3L *Belleisle* (64).

RUNWA, BENJAMIN

Dates: c.1737 Born; 1807 Died; 4.8.1807 Will Probate.
Family:
Service: 23.8.1750 Capt Serv *Grampus* (14) Sloop; 1.8.1751 Ord. *Grampus* (14) Sloop; 3.5.1752 Able *Grampus* (14) Sloop; 18.7.1752 Mid *Deptford* (50); 10.8.1755 Mate *Deptford* (50); 20.5.1756 Battle of Minorca; 16.6.1756 Mate *Lancaster* (66); 7.7.1756 Mid *Ramillies* (90); 10.1.1757 Passed; **Lieutenant**; 13.6.1757-2.9.1760 L. *Fowey* (24); 11.5.1763-3.1.1765 1L *Dragon* (74); 22.8.1776 1L *Thames* (32); **Commander**; 13.1.1779-30.7.1779 *Sulphur* (8) Fireship; 26.9.1782-21.4.1783[P] *Falcon* (14) Sloop.

RUNWA, JOHN

Dates: c.1721 Born.
Family:
Service: 1740-1743 Merchant Service; 20.1.1742/43 Mid *Princess Royal* (90); 26.1.1743/44 Mate *Royal Sovereign* (104); 5.1.1746/47 Passed; **Lieutenant**; 22.7.1755[NA 14.12.1756] 4L *Fougueux* (64); 7.12.1756[NA 14.12.1756] 3L *Fougueux* (64); 29.12.1756[NA 14.12.1756] 2L *Fougueux* (64); 17.6.1757[NA 14.12.1756]-21.5.1759[P] 1L *Fougueux* (64); 29.12.1758 Capture of Goree.

RUSHWORTH, JOHN

Dates: 1779 Died.
Family:
Service: **Lieutenant**; 12.5.1741[4.9.1741]-30.5.1743 4L *Torbay* (80); 14.2.1746/47-3.5.1750[P] 1L *Exeter* (60); 11.9.1751-24.4.1753[W] 1L *Assurance* (44); 16.1.1755 1L *Augusta* (60); 2.8.1755[NA 9.12.1755] 6L *Torbay* (74); 31.1.1756 6L *Invincible* (74); 5.8.1756 3L *Invincible* (74); 11.11.1756 2L *Invincible* (74); 15.11.1756 1L *Invincible* (74); 17.12.1756 1L *Royal George* (100); **Commander**; 5.5.1757-19.5.1758 *Happy* (8) Sloop; **Captain**; 7.12.1758 *Garland* (24); 19.11.1759 *Centurion* (50); 16.6.1760-9.11.1761 *Alarm* (32); 20.10.1770-1.4.1771[P] *Firm* (74).

RUSSELL, JOHN

Dates: c.1753 Died; 6.7.1753 Will Probate.
Family:
Service: **Lieutenant**; 24.6.1741[6.2.1745/46] 3L *Warwick* (60); 3.6.1743[MED 6.2.1745/46] 3L *Dartmouth* (50); 5.11.1743[MED 6.2.1745/46]-23.11.1743 L. *Firedrake* (8) Bomb Vessel; 7.12.1743[MED 6.2.1745/46] 3L *Rochester* (54); 29.4.1744[MED 6.2.1745/46]-11.12.1746[P] 2L *Dartmouth* (50); 23.12.1746 2L *Captain* (70); 1.11.1748[BLI 2.2.1749/50] 1L *Cornwall* (80); **Commander**; 27.11.1748-17.2.1749/50[P] *Falcon* (10) Bomb Vessel; 13.12.1750-25.1.1753 *Scorpion* (14) Sloop.

RUSSELL, WILLIAM

Dates: 1755 Died; 10.7.1755 Will Probate.
Family:
Service: 2.2.1717/18 Vol-p-O *Dreadnought* (60); 11.8.1718 Battle of Cape Passaro; 13.5.1720-5.8.1720[P] Mid *Dreadnought* (60); 23.3.1720/21 Mid *Lion* (60); 6.6.1721 Mid *Yarmouth* (70); 24.6.1721 Able *Yarmouth* (70); 8.7.1721 Mid *Yarmouth* (70); 22.2.1722/23 Passed; 14.9.1728 **Lieutenant**; 29.5.1730[10.9.1730]-30.9.1730[P] 2L *Anglesea* (40); 19.5.1731 3L *Advice* (54); 14.6.1732 4L *Captain* (70); 23.11.1733 2L *Lancaster* (80); 23.2.1733/34 3L *Lancaster* (80); 5.1.1735/36 2L *Lancaster* (80); 15.3.1737/38 3L *Lancaster* (80); **Commander**; 17.1.1739/40[18.5.1743]-29.11.1740 *Duke* (8) Fireship.

RUTHERFORD, LORD DAVID

Dates: 1760 7th Lord Rutherford of Hunthill; 1785 Died; 23.12.1785 Will Probate.
Family: Father George Durie [Rutherford], 6th Lord Rutherford; Mother Margaret Ogilvy; Sister ?.
***Service:* Lieutenant**; 12.11.1757[17.4.1759]-7.8.1759 4L *Somerset* (68); 6.6.1758-27.7.1758 The Siege of Louisbourg; 21.8.1759 1L *Repulse* (32); 24.12.1760-25.3.1762 3L *Princess Amelia* (80); 29.3.1761-11.6.1761 Expedition against Belle-Isle; 25.3.1763-29.11.1766 1L *Niger* (32); 11.4.1775 2L *Barfleur* (90); 26.5.1775 3L *Barfleur* (90); 2.8.1776 2L *Barfleur* (90); 6.12.1776 1L *Barfleur* (90); 5.4.1777 1L *Princess Royal* (90); 4.5.1778-24.12.1781[P] 1L *Albion* (74); 6.7.1779 Battle of Grenada; 17.4.1780 Battle of Martinique; 15.5.1780 Action of March 15 1780; 19.5.1780 Action of March 19 1780.

RUTHVEN, HON. JOHN

Dates: 29.3.1743 Born Gretna, Dumfriesshire; 7.4.1743 Baptised Perth, Scotland; 14.12.1771 Died.
Family: Father James Johnson Ruthven, Lord Ruthven (1693-1783); Mother Anne Stuart (1709-1786).
Service: 1.4.1756 Adm Ret *Newark* (80); 2.4.1757 Adm Ret *Saint George* (90); 28.4.1757 MidO *Colchester* (50); 12.2.1758 Mid *Colchester* (50); 8.5.1759 Mid *Torbay* (74); 20.11.1759 Battle of Quiberon Bay; 11.2.1760 Mid *Valiant* (74); 3.9.1760 Passed; **Lieutenant**; 23.12.1760 2L *Sapphire* (32); **Commander**; 12.4.1762 *Senegal* (14) Sloop; **Captain**; 24.5.1762-27.2.1764[P] *Terpsichore* (24); 14.3.1764-27.6.1766 *Guadeloupe* (28); 24.5.1770-14.12.1771[†] *Glory* (32).

RYALL, GEORGE

Dates: c.1716 Born; 1769 Died.
Family:
Service: 1.8.1732 Vol-p-O *Norfolk* (80); 6.9.1732 Vol-p-O *Rose* (20); 6.8.1734 Able *Rose* (20); 8.2.1734/35 MidO *Rose* (20); 12.4.1739 Passed; **Lieutenant**; 31.8.1739 3L *York* (60); 4.3.1739/40 2L *York* (60); 8.6.1741-2.11.1741[P] 4L *Burford* (70); 28.12.1741-3.4.1742 2L *Nonsuch* (50); 6.7.1742 1L *Cambridge* (80); 10.7.1742-7.12.1743 1L *Kinsale* (44); 7.5.1746-26.12.1747 1L *Kent* (64); 3.5.1747 1st Battle of Cape Finisterre; 14.10.1747 2nd Battle of Cape Finisterre; 21.9.1757-28.11.1757 1L *Juno* (32).

RYCAULT, JAMES

Dates: 1758 Died.
Family:
Service: 9.5.1703 Vol. *Centurion* (54); 13.8.1704 Battle of Malaga; 6.12.1704 Mid *Kinsale* (36); 19.1.1704/5 Ord. *Crown* (50); 17.2.1704/5 Able *Crown* (50); 18.3.1704/5 Mid *Crown* (50); 10.10.1705 Mid *Northumberland* (70); 20.2.1705/6 Mid *Assurance* (66); 28.4.1706 Mid *Dunkirk* (50); 5.1.1706/7 Mid *Warwick* (54); 21.4.1707 Passed; **Lieutenant**; 4.2.1707/8-14.12.1708 L. *Griffin* (8); 26.12.1710-1.6.1712 2L *Canterbury* (60); 4.3.1714/15-28.11.1717[P] 1L *Hampshire* (54); 10.1.1717/18 1L *Winchester* (50); 15.1.1717/18-18.6.1720[W] L. *Milford* (36); **Commander**; 28.8.1730 *Swift* (6) Sloop; 5.9.1732 *Trial* (8) Sloop; **Captain**; 10.8.1739 *Panther* (54); 6.9.1740-5.2.1741/42 *Grafton* (70).

RYDER, JAMES
Dates: 1776 Died.
Family:
Service: 10.4.1745 Passed; **Lieutenant**; 27.7.1745^(MED 9.12.1748) 3L *Worcester* (58); 8.2.1745/46^(MED 9.12.1748)-27.12.1748^P 2L *Worcester* (58); 3.8.1746 Action of August 3 1746; 25.3.1747 Action of March 25 1747; 9.4.1748 Battle of Santiago de Cuba; 21.10.1755-1.11.1755 4L *Princess Royal* (90); 1.11.1755-27.11.1755 5L *Princess Royal* (90); 19.12.1755-12.1.1757 4L *Princess Royal* (90); 12.1.1757 5L *Princess Royal* (90); 4.4.1757 4L *Princess Royal* (90); 19.9.1757 3L *Princess Royal* (90); 12.10.1762-15.1.1763^P 2L *Princess Royal* (90).

Service Records S

SAINTHILL, HUMPHREY
Dates: c.1718 Born; 1761 Died; 26.8.1761 Buried St Anne, Limehouse, Tower Hamlets, Middlesex.
Family:
Service: 23.7.1739 Mid *Superb* (60); 28.11.1739 Mid *Sunderland* (60); 19.12.1739 Able *Strafford* (60); 24.12.1739 Mid *Strafford* (60); 22.11.1741 Mid *Norfolk* (80); 26.2.1742/43 Mid *Marlborough* (90); 23.10.1743 Mate *Marlborough* (90); 11.2.1743/44-12.2.1743/44 Battle of Toulon; 25.3.1745 Mate *Shrewsbury* (74); 9.8.1745 Passed; **Lieutenant**; 1.1.1745/46-6.3.1745/46 L. *Swallow* (10) Sloop; 24.1.1746/47-29.1.1747/48[P] L. *Glasgow* (20); 18.6.1755 4L *Revenge* (64); 23.3.1756-26.11.1756 3L *Revenge* (64); 20.5.1756 Battle of Minorca; 12.2.1759-10.12.1759 1L *Boreas* (28); 3.7.1759 Bombardment of Le Havre.

SALMON, JOSEPH
Dates: 14.4.1790 Died.
Family:
Service: 26.5.1739 Able *Chatham* (50); 5.3.1740/41 Mid *Chatham* (50); 28.11.1742 Mid *Burford* (70); 26.12.1742 Mid *Nonsuch* (50); 11.2.1743/44-12.2.1743/44 Battle of Toulon; 13.9.1744 Mid *Burford* (70); 12.7.1745 Passed; **Lieutenant**; 13.7.1745[(MED 22.7.1746)]-4.3.1745/46 3L *Princess Caroline* (80); 9.10.1746-21.11.1746[P] 4L *Cambridge* (80); 6.7.1747-26.5.1749[P] 3L *Crown* (44); 28.1.1760-3.10.1761 1L *Vanguard* (68).

SALT, SAMPSON
Dates: c.1710 Born; 27.7.1792 Died.
Family:
Service: 30.8.1733 Mid *Princess Amelia* (80); 26.3.1734 Able *Fox* (20); 19.9.1734 Mid *Diamond* (40); 10.6.1737 Able *Diamond* (40); 4.1.1737/38 Mid *Diamond* (40); 4.6.1739 Mid *Kinsale* (36); 13.11.1739 Passed; **Lieutenant**; 16.11.1739-20.2.1739/40 3L *Pearl* (40); 21.4.1740-24.7.1740 2L *Pearl* (40); 25.7.1740 1L *Pearl* (40); 2.2.1742/43 1L *Prince Frederick* (70); 30.4.1744 1L *Jersey* (60); 24.5.1745[(MED 4.6.1748)] 4L *Princess Caroline* (80); 13.7.1745[(MED 3.6.1748)] 1L *Princess Caroline* (80); 18.3.1746/47[(MED 4.6.1748)]-1.6.1748[P] 1L *Diamond* (44); **Commander**; 13.7.1748-16.7.1750[P] *Speedwell* (10) Sloop; 28.1.1755-3.5.1758 *Hornet* (10) Sloop.

SAMBER, JAMES
Dates: c.1736 Born; 1816 Died; 10.6.1816 Will Probate.
Family:
Service: 1753-1756 HEIC Service; 12.3.1755/56 Mid *Chichester* (68); 9.5.1758 Mate *Chichester* (68); 5.6.1758-12.6.1758 Raid on Saint-Malo; 18.9.1759 ActL *Defiance* (60); 20.11.1759 Battle of Quiberon Bay; 2.4.1760 Passed; **Lieutenant**; 9.4.1760-17.3.1762 5L *Dragon* (74); 29.3.1761-11.6.1761 Expedition against Belle-Isle; 7.1.1762-10.2.1762 Operations against

Martinique; 24.2.1762-25.2.1762 Capture of Saint Lucia; 7.6.1763-24.7.1766[P] L. *Deal Castle* (20); 25.6.1771 2L *Crescent* (32) Frigate; 18.7.1771 1L *Crescent* (32) Frigate; 3.11.1775-15.11.1776 1L *Conquestador* (60); 4.11.1776 2L *Queen* (90); 27.3.1778-20.4.1778 1L *Queen* (90); 17.9.1778 5L *Victory* (100); 20.11.1778 4L *Victory* (100); 16.2.1779-23.3.1779 3L *Victory* (100); **Commander**; 1.2.1780 *Satisfaction* (20) Hired Armed Ship; **Captain**; 26.3.1782-18.6.1782 *Bristol* (50); 15.7.1783[(NA 25.9.1783)]-30.7.1783[P] *Formidable* (98); 1.10.1787-10.12.1787[P] *Royal Sovereign* (100).

SANDHAM, HENRY

Dates: None Known.
Family:
Service: 9.2.1759 **Lieutenant**; 9.2.1761 3L *Harwich* (50); 12.11.1761 L. *Cruizer* (8) Sloop; 1.12.1761-2.3.1762[D] L. *Hind* (24); 2.3.1762 Dismissed.

SANDIVER, PHILIP

Dates: c.1735 Born; 1763 Died; 14.11.1763 Will Probate.
Family:
Service: 1752-1755 Merchant Service; 29.11.1755 Mid *Anson* (60); 6.3.1758 Mate *Anson* (60); 5.7.1758 Passed; **Lieutenant**; 20.11.1758 3L *Ludlow Castle* (44); 2.1.1759 2L *Liverpool* (28); 7.2.1760-5.5.1762 L. *Baltimore* (14) Sloop.

SANDYS, STEPHEN

Dates: 14.9.1739 Born Cork; 13.5.1782 Died at sea.
Family: Father William Sandys (1704-1750); Mother Abigail Gover (1699-1745); Son William (1771-1796); Son Richard (1773-1781); Son Samuel Edwin (1774-1796); Son Stephen Miles (1776-1823); Brother John (1742-1748); Sister Barbara Lloyd; Sister Frances (1744-1748); Brother Samuel (1745-1745).
Service: **Lieutenant**; 4.8.1762[(EI 18.1.1764)]-6.2.1764[P] L. *Bonetta* (10) Sloop; 16.3.1764 3L *Superb* (74); 20.3.1765-29.6.1768 2L *Hussar* (28); 30.11.1770 5L *Torbay* (74); 28.5.1771-28.6.1771 4L *Torbay* (74); 10.4.1776 3L *Exeter* (64); 28.6.1777 1L *Exeter* (64); 10.10.1777 2L *Exeter* (64); 27.7.1778 1st Battle of Ushant; 1.2.1779-13.5.1782[†] 1L *Exeter* (64); 17.2.1782 Battle of Sadras; 12.4.1782 Battle of Providien.

SAUMAREZ, THOMAS

Dates: 4.1720 Born St Peter Port, Guernsey; 21.9.1766 Died Rickmansworth, Hertfordshire.
Family: Father Matthew de Sausmarez; Mother Anne Durell; Wife Katharine Mountstevens; Brother Philip, RN (1710-1747).
Service: 31.3.1731 Ord. *Gibraltar* (20); 7.5.1731 Able *Gibraltar* (20); 29.8.1736-13.8.1737 Able *Leopard* (50); 14.8.1737 Able *Centurion* (60); 14.3.1737/38-24.6.1739 Able *Windsor* (60); 25.6.1739 Mid *Diamond* (40); 23.3.1739/40 Attack on Chagres; 24.9.1740 Mid *Centurion* (60); 6.8.1743 Mate *Centurion's Prize* Unknown; 1.2.1743/44 Mid *Centurion* (60); 6.9.1744 Passed; **Lieutenant**; 15.12.1744 L. *Wolf* (14) Sloop; 2.7.1745 3L *Folkestone* (44); 11.8.1746 4L *Yarmouth* (64); 3.5.1747 1st Battle of Cape Finisterre; 19.5.1747 3L *Yarmouth* (64); 29.5.1747 2L *Yarmouth* (64); 14.10.1747 2nd Battle of Cape Finisterre; **Commander**; 23.11.1747-27.11.1748 *Falcon* (10) Bomb Vessel; **Captain**; 27.11.1748-19.2.1748/49[P] *Bideford* (20); 21.1.1751/52 *Wager* (24); 23.9.1755 *Ludlow Castle* (44); 4.6.1756-10.4.1759 *Antelope* (50); 26.4.1759-5.3.1760 *Belliqueux* (64).

SAUNDERS, CHARLES CB

Dates: 1713 Born; 16.5.1761 Order of the Bath; 7.12.1775 Died Spring Gardens,, London.
Family: Father Ambrose Saunders; Mother Ann Bentley; Wife Miss Buck married 1751; Brother George; Sister Ann [Kinsey]; Brother Ambrose.
Service: 26.11.1727 Ord. *Seahorse* (20); 29.11.1727 Vol-p-O *Seahorse* (20); 1.12.1729 Mid *Seahorse* (20); 15.8.1730 MidO *Hector* (40); 30.9.1731 Mid *Hector* (40); 7.6.1734 Passed; **Lieutenant**; 8.11.1734 3L *Exeter* (60); 28.7.1738-3.12.1738[P] 3L *Norfolk* (80); 12.6.1739 3L *Oxford* (50); 25.6.1739 2L *Sunderland* (60); 14.8.1739-11.11.1739 3L *Centurion* (60); 12.11.1739 2L *Centurion* (60); 3.11.1740[(2.6.1743)] 1L *Centurion* (60); **Commander**; 19.2.1740/41[(1.6.1743)] *Trial* (8) Sloop; **Captain**; 26.9.1741[(1.6.1743)] *Trial Prize* (8); 29.11.1743 *Plymouth* (60); 20.12.1743 *Sapphire* (44); 11.2.1744/45 *Sandwich* (90); 22.3.1744/45-4.2.1746/47 *Gloucester* (50); 26.8.1747-9.11.1747 *Yarmouth* (64); 14.10.1747 2nd Battle of Cape Finisterre; 25.12.1747-29.11.1748[P] *Tiger* (60); 6.4.1750-20.4.1754 M.P. for Plymouth; 2.1752-1754 CinC — Newfoundland; 18.2.1751/52-23.1.1753 Commodore *Penzance* (44); 18.4.1754-7.12.1775 M.P. for Hedon; 16.1.1755 *Yarmouth* (64); 28.1.1755-25.11.1755 *Prince* (90); 25.11.1755-24.6.1756 Comptroller of the Navy; 4.6.1756 **Rear Admiral of the Blue**; 3.12.1756-5.1757 CinC — The Mediterranean Sea; 5.1757-1759 *Saint George* (90); 13.7.1758 **Rear Admiral of the White**; 18.10.1758-26.1.1763[P] *Neptune* (90); 11.1758 *Ramillies* (90); 1759 *Somerset* (68); 14.2.1759 **Vice Admiral of the Blue**; 28.4.1760-1763 CinC — The Mediterranean Sea; 26.9.1762-10.5.1763[P] *Blenheim* (90); 21.10.1762 **Vice Admiral of the White**; 15.9.1765-10.12.1766 Lord Commissioner of the Admiralty; 10.9.1766-7.12.1775 Privy Counsellor; 15.9.1766-11.12.1766 1st Lord; 18.10.1770 **Admiral of the Blue**; 23.4.1773 CinC — The Mediterranean Sea.

SAUNDERS, RICHARD

Dates: None Known.
Family:
Service: **Lieutenant**; 16.10.1759[(JAM 13.4.1763)] 2L *Cerberus* (28); 17.7.1761[(13.4.1763)]-1.4.1763[P] 2L *Hampshire* (50); 6.6.1762-13.8.1762 Operations against Havana; 6.10.1763 2L *Firm* (74); 4.4.1766-28.8.1769[P] 1L *Chatham* (50); 29.9.1770-28.5.1771[P] 3L *Prince of Wales* (74); 4.12.1776-19.2.1777 2L *Boyne* (68); 18.6.1805 **Superannuated Commander**.

SAUNDERS, THOMAS

Dates: c.1724 Born.
Family:
Service: 1751-1756 Merchant Service; 30.9.1756 Mid *Oxford* (50); 26.10.1756 Master *Fly* (8) Sloop; 7.11.1756 Mid *Tilbury* (58); 24.4.1757 Mid *Royal Anne* (100); 18.8.1757 Mate *Union* (90); 1.10.1757-4.10.1758 Mate *Royal Sovereign* (104); 4.10.1758 Passed; **Lieutenant**; 6.10.1758-31.1.1759 L. *Falcon* (8) Bomb Vessel; 16.1.1759-19.1.1759 Attack on Martinique.

SAUTEL, GEORGE

Dates: c.1728 Born.
Family:
Service: 1751-1755 HEIC Service; 27.2.1755 Mid *Medway* (60); 20.11.1756 Mid *Royal George* (100); 26.12.1756 Mid *Namur* (90); 5.9.1757-6.10.1757 Raid on Rochefort; 6.2.1758 Mid *Royal George* (100); 20.5.1758 Mid *Dorsetshire* (68); 3.7.1758 Mate *Dorsetshire* (68); 7.2.1759 Passed; **Lieutenant**; 2.6.1761[(EI 21.8.1764)]-4.6.1761 4L *America* (60); 23.8.1769-27.11.1770 2L *Boston* (32); 4.7.1775-4.10.1780[F] 1L *Phoenix* (44); 2.7.1776-4.7.1776 Staten Island Landings; 22.7.1778 Encounter at Sandy Hook.

SAUVAIRE, THOMAS
Dates: c.1733 Born.
Family:
Service: 26.10.1747 Capt Serv *Nottingham* (60); 31.1.1747/48 Action of 1748/01/31; 13.4.1748 Able *Nottingham* (60); 17.11.1748 Able *Falcon* (10) Bomb Vessel; 12.3.1748/49-12.7.1749 Mid *Falcon* (10) Bomb Vessel; 13.7.1749 Mid *Bideford* (20); 5.10.1749 Able *Anson* (60); 11.7.1750 Able *Surprise* (24); 19.3.1751/52 Mate *Wager* (24); 2.7.1755 Passed; **Lieutenant**; 7.7.1756 3L *Chesterfield* (44); 23.9.1756 2L *Chesterfield* (44); 7.12.1758-21.7.1762[W] 1L *Chesterfield* (44).

SAVAGE, HENRY
Dates: 1823 Died.
Family:
Service: **Lieutenant**; 20.7.1758[EI 25.6.1761]-25.3.1761[P] 4L *Cumberland* (66); 3.8.1758 Battle of Negapatam; 10.9.1759 Battle of Pondicherry; 24.4.1761[5.1762]-10.7.1761[P] 2L *Tiger* (60); 19.5.1762-19.3.1763[P] 2L *Emerald* (32); 6.4.1763 L. *Favorite* (16) Sloop; 31.5.1766 L. *Happy* (8) Sloop; 1.7.1766 2L *Achilles* (60); 6.12.1766 3L *Achilles* (60); 19.2.1767-5.7.1769 2L *Achilles* (60); 28.10.1771-17.1.1773 L. *Fowey* (24); 20.1.1774 1L *Ardent* (64); 28.1.1778 1L *Grafton* (74); 6.7.1779 Battle of Grenada; 17.4.1780 Battle of Martinique; 15.5.1780 Action of March 15 1780; 19.5.1780 Action of March 19 1780; **Commander**; 16.6.1780[BLI 7.8.1781] *Rover* (16) Sloop; **Captain**; 31.1.1781[BLI 29.11.1781] *Russell* (74); 9.5.1781[BLI 29.11.1781] *Boreas* (28); 24.12.1781-13.4.1782 *Hercules* (74); 12.4.1782 Battle of the Saintes; 13.5.1789-21.10.1791[P] *Pomona* (28); 18.3.1794-26.6.1797 *Albion* (22) Floating Battery; 4.1797-5.1799 *Warrior* (74); 14.2.1799 **Rear Admiral of the Blue**; 1.1.1801 **Rear Admiral of the White**; 23.4.1804 **Rear Admiral of the Red**; 9.11.1805 **Vice Admiral of the White**; 25.10.1809 **Vice Admiral of the Red**; 31.7.1810 **Admiral of the Blue**; 4.6.1814 **Admiral of the White**.

SAWYER, HERBERT
Dates: c.1731 Born; 4.6.1798 Died.
Family: Son Herbert, RN (d.1833).
Service: 25.9.1747 Able *Sheerness* (24); 21.2.1747/48 Able *Crown* (44); 4.3.1747/48 Mid *Essex* (70); 21.7.1748 Mid *Superb* (60); 18.4.1749 Able *Gloucester* (50); 21.4.1751 Mid *Gloucester* (50); 6.6.1752 Able *Severn* (50); 4.11.1752-14.11.1752 Able *Assurance* (44); 15.11.1752-24.4.1753[W] Mid *Assurance* (44); 23.6.1753-3.7.1753 Able *Invincible* (74); 4.7.1753-12.9.1753 Able *Terrible* (74); 12.9.1753 Passed; **Lieutenant**; 4.3.1756 3L *Nottingham* (60); 5.1.1757-19.1.1758 4L *Grafton* (68); 8.1757-10.1757 Louisbourg Expedition; 1.2.1758 2L *Rochester* (50); **Commander**; 19.5.1758 *Happy* (8) Sloop; 18.10.1758 *Swallow* (14) Sloop; **Captain**; 26.12.1758 *Chesterfield* (44); 21.2.1759-2.8.1763 *Active* (28); 17.10.1776-10.8.1779 *Boyne* (68); 14.12.1778-15.12.1778 Battle of St. Lucia; 6.7.1779 Battle of Grenada; 8.3.1780-18.12.1781 *Namur* (90); 20.4.1783-26.1.1785 *Bombay Castle* (74); 26.1.1785 CinC — Nova Scotia; 26.1.1785-8.1786 Commodore *Assistance* (50); 1787-30.10.1787[P] Commodore *Ariadne* (20); 24.9.1787 **Rear Admiral of the White**; 1788-c.3.9.1788[P] *Leander* (52); 7.1790-10.1790 *Windsor Castle* (98); 21.9.1790 **Rear Admiral of the Red**; 1.2.1793 **Vice Admiral of the Blue**; 12.4.1794 **Vice Admiral of the White**; 4.7.1794 **Vice Admiral of the Red**; 1.6.1795 **Admiral of the Blue**.

SAX, ROBERT
Dates: c.1726 Born.
Family:
Service: 30.10.1742 Capt Serv *Princess* (70); 21.12.1742 Capt Serv *Orford* (70); 4.2.1742/43

Ord. *Orford* (70); 1.4.1744-13.2.1744/45[W] Able *Orford* (70); 24.10.1747 Mid *Prince George* (90); 24.3.1747/48 Able *Vigilant* (60); 2.4.1748 Mid *Vigilant* (60); 27.7.1748 Able *Vigilant* (60); 20.8.1749 Mid *Vigilant* (60); 6.12.1752 Passed; **Lieutenant**; 6.2.1755 6L *Prince George* (80); 14.5.1756-26.2.1757 5L *Prince George* (80); 31.5.1757 L. *Swallow* (14) Sloop; 27.10.1757-13.3.1759[P] 6L *Royal Sovereign* (104); 9.1760-27.9.1760 LCmdr *John and Thomas* Hired Tender; 21.10.1760 Resigned; 21.1.1771-12.5.1771[P] L. *Glasgow* (20).

SAXTON, SIR CHARLES (1ST BARONET SAXTON OF CIRCOURT)

Dates: c.1732 Born; 19.7.1794 1st Baronet Saxton of Circourt; c.11.1808 Died; 25.11.1808 Will Probate.

Family: Father Edward Saxton; Mother Elizabeth Bush; Wife Mary Bush married 11.5.1771; Son Sir Charles Saxton, 2nd Baronet, MP (1773–1838); Son John; Son Clement; Daughter Philadelphia-Hannah [Oliver]; Daughter Ann; Daughter Mary; Daughter Sophia.

Service: 26.8.1747 Capt Serv *Gloucester* (50); 14.10.1747 2nd Battle of Cape Finisterre; 6.8.1749 Ord. *Gloucester* (50); 24.10.1750-14.11.1752[P] Mid *Eagle* (60); 3.1.1753 Passed; 17.1.1754-26.8.1754[P] Mid *Eagle* (60); 16.1.1755 Mid *Saint Albans* (60); 4.10.1755-3.1.1756 Mid *Eagle* (60); **Lieutenant**; 2.1.1757[(23.11.1758)]-16.1.1757 5L *Kent* (64); 19.4.1759 2L *Sandwich* (90); 7.6.1759-3.4.1760 1L *Sandwich* (90); 19.4.1760 1L *Modeste* (64); **Commander**; 11.10.1760 *Flamborough Prize* (14) Sloop; 10.7.1761 *Senegal* (14) Sloop; **Captain**; 28.1.1762-22.6.1762 *Magnanime* (74); 9.1762-21.2.1763[P] *Monmouth* (70); 9.4.1763-10.4.1766 *Pearl* (32); 3.11.1770 *Phoenix* (44); 9.1.1771-10.10.1771 *Flora* (32); 22.7.1778-10.11.1779 *Winchelsea* (32); 19.4.1780 *Monarca* (68); 2.5.1780-1.8.1783[P] *Invincible* (74); 29.4.1781-30.4.1781 Battle of Fort Royal; 5.9.1781 Battle of the Chesapeake; 25.1.1782-26.1.1782 Battle of Saint Kitts; 13.3.1790-7.1806 Resident Commissioner at Portsmouth Dockyard.

SAYER, JAMES

Dates: 1721 Born; 15.10.1777 Died.

Family:

Service: 14.6.1736 Capt Serv *Northumberland* (70); 8.12.1736 Able *Northumberland* (70); 28.3.1737 Able *Somerset* (68); 11.7.1738 Mid *Romney* (50); 2.9.1740 Able *Romney* (50); 6.5.1741 Mid *Romney* (50); 15.7.1742 Passed; **Lieutenant**; 19.12.1743 L. *Lightning* (8) Bomb Vessel; 20.4.1744-9.9.1745 3L *Lennox* (70); **Captain**; 22.3.1745/46[(NA 23.4.1749)]-28.7.1749[P] *Richmond* (24); 8.5.1756-16.1.1761 *Nassau* (64); 8.1757-10.1757 Louisbourg Expedition; 9.3.1758-24.5.1758 Capture of Fort Louis; 29.12.1758 Capture of Goree; 22.2.1762-13.1.1763[P] *Lancaster* (66); 4.1762-12.3.1763[P] *Nassau* (64); 18.10.1770 **Rear Admiral of the Blue**; 31.3.1775 **Rear Admiral of the Red**; 7.12.1775 **Vice Admiral of the Blue**; 2.4.1776 **Vice Admiral of the White**.

SAYER, JOSHUA

Dates: c.1731 Born.

Family:

Service: 1751-1755 Merchant Service; 14.4.1755 Mid *Yarmouth* (64); 17.2.1757 Mid *Invincible* (74); 25.6.1757 Mate *Barfleur* (80); 5.9.1757-6.10.1757 Raid on Rochefort; 5.6.1758-12.6.1758 Raid on Saint-Malo; 23.9.1758-7.3.1758/59 Mid *Barfleur* (80); 7.3.1759 Passed; **Lieutenant**; 27.9.1759-7.2.1760[P] L. *Broderick* Hired Armed vessel; 27.10.1770-28.10.1773 2L *Boyne* (68).

SBIREL, JOHN

Dates: c.1714 Born Jersey; 5.2.1770 Died.

Family:

Service: 22.1.1728/29 Vol-p-O *Guernsey* (50); 14.11.1729 Vol-p-O *Defiance* (60); 21.1.1731/32 Mid *Defiance* (60); 2.3.1731/32 MidO *Defiance* (60); 15.11.1732 Mid *Nassau* (70); 15.1.1732/33 MidO *Nassau* (70); 26.2.1732/33 Mid *Colchester* (50); 17.3.1733/34 Mid *Pembroke* (60); 4.2.1734/35 Passed; **Lieutenant**; 30.9.1739[(1.10.1740)] L. *Kennington* (20); 3.3.1739/40[(1.10.1740)] 3L *Falkland* (50); 7.7.1740[(1.10.1740)]-19.10.1740 1L *Superb* (60); 10.1.1740/41 2L *Faversham* (44); 2.2.1740/41 3L *Elizabeth* (70); 2.6.1741 2L *Elizabeth* (70); 11.2.1743/44-12.2.1743/44 Battle of Toulon; 12.8.1745 4L *Royal George* (100); 21.10.1745-12.11.1745 3L *Royal George* (100).

SCAIFE, JOHN

Dates: c.1709 Born; 1773 Died; 17.4.1773 Will Probate.

Family:

Service: 11.8.1734 Mate *Swallow* (60); 5.6.1737 Mid *Diamond* (40); 27.1.1739 Able *Dursley Galley* (20); 21.3.1739 Able *Shoreham* (20); 10.6.1739 Mid *Shoreham* (20); 9.2.1740/41-1.4.1742 Master *Shoreham* (20); 7.1741-10.1741 Operations against Santiago; 30.8.1744-19.11.1745 Master *Experiment* (20); 20.11.1745 Master *Montagu* (60); 12.9.1746 Passed; **Lieutenant**; 19.12.1747[(EI 19.4.1750)] 3L *Deptford* (60); 24.1.1748/49[(EI 19.4.1750)] 2L *Deptford* (60); 14.7.1749[(EI 19.4.1750)]-18.5.1750[P] 1L *Deptford* (60); 28.1.1755 1L *Torbay* (74); **Commander**; 10.5.1755[(NA 27.12.1757)] *Vulture* (14) Sloop; 8.1757-10.1757 Louisbourg Expedition; 21.3.1758 *Grampus* (14) Sloop; **Captain**; 22.2.1759-21.7.1762[W] *Chesterfield* (44).

SCARLETT, NATHANIEL

Dates: c.1713 Born; 1757 Died; 5.9.1757 Will Probate.

Family:

Service: 29.4.1731 Able *Spence* (8) Sloop; 21.11.1731 Able *Bideford* (20); 26.8.1733 Mid *Bideford* (20); 25.12.1733 Able *Bideford* (20); 19.6.1734 Mid *Bideford* (20); 12.5.1735 Mate *Bideford* (20); 28.6.1735 Mid *Nottingham* (60); 30.1.1735/36 Able *Nottingham* (60); 16.3.1736/37 Mate *Nottingham* (60); 10.4.1737-31.7.1737[P] Mid *Nottingham* (60); 16.6.1738 Mid *Dragon* (60); 5.1.1738/39-28.1.1738/39 Able *Dragon* (60); 29.1.1738/39-19.3.1738/39[R] Mid *Dragon* (60); 20.3.1738/39 Mate *Dragon* (60); 26.11.1740 Gnr *Grampus* (6) Sloop; 20.6.1741 Gnr *Kennington* (20); 14.8.1744 Gnr *Rupert* (60); 21.11.1745 Passed; **Lieutenant**; 7.6.1746 6L *Royal Sovereign* (104); 18.2.1746/47-28.8.1748[P] 3L *Centurion* (50); 3.5.1747 1st Battle of Cape Finisterre; 6.2.1755 2L *Medway* (60); 24.9.1756 3L *Union* (90); 29.7.1757-20.10.1757 3L *Neptune* (90); 5.9.1757-6.10.1757 Raid on Rochefort.

SCHOMBERG, SIR ALEXANDER

Dates: c.1726 Born; 4.6.1776 Knight Bachelor; 19.3.1804 Died; 27.4.1804 Will Probate.

Family:

Service: 11.12.1743 Ord. *Suffolk* (70); 15.1.1743/44 Ord. *Deptford* (60); 20.5.1744 Ord. *Suffolk* (70); 12.3.1744/45 Mid *Suffolk* (70); 26.9.1747 ActL *Suffolk* (70); 3.12.1747 Passed; **Lieutenant**; 11.12.1747 L. *Hornet* (10) Sloop; 20.4.1750[(19.7.1750)]-16.7.1750[P] L. *Speedwell* (10) Sloop; 6.2.1755-10.6.1756 3L *Medway* (60); **Commander**; 12.2.1757 *Gibraltar's Prize* (14) Sloop; **Captain**; 5.4.1757 *Richmond* (32); 30.8.1757-22.9.1760 *Diana* (32); 6.6.1758-27.7.1758 The Siege of Louisbourg; 21.1.1761-27.1.1763[P] *Essex* (64); 29.3.1761-11.6.1761 Expedition against Belle-Isle; 20.10.1770 *Prudent* (64); 30.11.1771-19.3.1803 *Dorset* Yacht.

SCOTT, ARTHUR

Dates: 27.2.1756 Died.
Family:
Service: 20.12.1739 **Lieutenant**; 5.10.1742-16.3.1742/43 4L *Barfleur* (90); 5.6.1743 1L *Namur* (90); **Captain**; 4.8.1743 *Rochester* (54); 13.7.1744[MED 5.4.1746] *Essex* (70); 18.8.1744 *Antelope* (50); 1.10.1745[MED 30.1.1746/47]-13.6.1746[P] *Marlborough* (90); 4.7.1746 *Chichester* (80); 11.8.1746 *Lion* (58); 14.10.1747 2nd Battle of Cape Finisterre; 19.1.1747/48-25.1.1747/48 CinC — River Medway and The Nore; 25.1.1747/48-2.7.1748[P] *Princess Louisa* (60); 25.11.1748 *Culloden* (74); 9.12.1749 *Assistance* (50); 2.3.1749/50-3.5.1750 *Culloden* (74).

SCOTT, CECIL

Dates: c.1734 Born.
Family:
Service: 22.6.1748 Capt Serv *Advice* (50); 7.6.1749 Able *Cumberland* (66); 19.7.1750 Carp Serv *Rainbow* (44); 26.8.1750 Able *Rainbow* (44); 10.11.1751 Mid *Rainbow* (44); 21.9.1752 Mid *Deptford* (50); 7.12.1754 Able *Deptford* (50); 5.11.1755 Passed; **Lieutenant**; 9.11.1756 L. *Peggy* (8) Sloop; 6.4.1757 2L *Tartar* (28); 25.11.1757 1L *Tartar* (28); 22.5.1758 1L *Chatham* (50); 30.3.1759-20.9.1759 2L *Conqueror* (68); 18.8.1759-19.8.1759 Battle of Lagos Bay; 9.1.1760 5L *Namur* (90); 2.4.1761 3L *Namur* (90); 28.10.1761-17.1.1762 4L *Marlborough* (68); **Commander**; 19.4.1762[9.8.1763]-24.9.1762 *Antigua* (14) Sloop.

SCOTT, HENRY

Dates: c.1724 Born; 24.9.1762 Died Orkneys.
Family:
Service: 30.5.1736 Able *Sunderland* (60); 7.9.1739 Able *Greenwich* (50); 12.5.1741 Mid *Woolwich* (50); 9.10.1742 Mid *Monmouth* (70); 5.7.1744 Passed; **Lieutenant**; 20.2.1744/45 6L *Sandwich* (90); 7.5.1746 4L *Kent* (64); 3.5.1747 1st Battle of Cape Finisterre; 14.10.1747 2nd Battle of Cape Finisterre; 30.9.1748-5.12.1748 3L *Kent* (64); 6.4.1751 2L *Torrington* (44); 9.5.1751-22.11.1752 1L *Torrington* (44); 19.1.1757 L. *Swallow* (14) Sloop; 23.3.1757 **Commander**; 23.5.1757 *London* (18) Hired Armed vessel; 9.3.1758-24.5.1758 Capture of Fort Louis; 24.7.1760-24.9.1762[W] *Badger* (10) Sloop; 7.11.1760[NA 15.5.1765]-8.3.1762 3L *Norwich* (50); 3.6.1761-7.6.1761 Occupation of Dominica; 7.1.1762-10.2.1762 Operations against Martinique.

SCOTT, JAMES

Dates: c.1736 Born.
Family:
Service: 29.6.1752 Able *Deptford* (50); 1.7.1753 Able *Eagle* (60); 17.2.1754 Mid *Eagle* (60); 5.6.1754 Mid *Cumberland* (66); 11.1.1756-14.1.1756 Capture of Geriah; 7.3.1757-1.4.1757 Expedition against Chandernagore; 23.2.1758 Mate *Cumberland* (66); 29.4.1758 Battle of Cuddalore; 8.5.1758-29.12.1760 Mate *Yarmouth* (64); 3.8.1758 Battle of Negapatam; 10.9.1759 Battle of Pondicherry; 29.12.1760 Passed; **Lieutenant**; 17.7.1762[EI 16.3.1763]-29.10.1762[C] L. *Basilisk* (8) Bomb Vessel; 29.9.1770-28.5.1771[P] 4L *Prince of Wales* (74); 9.1.1772-25.4.1772[P] L. *Fly* (8) Sloop; 28.1.1774 2L *Somerset* (68); 25.8.1774-16.6.1775[D] 1L *Somerset* (68); 16.6.1775 Dismissed.

SCOTT, JOHN
Dates: c.1731 Born; 27.2.1790 Died.
Family:
Service: 1753-1756 Merchant Service; 29.12.1756 Mid *Royal Sovereign* (104); 5.1.1758 Mate *Royal Sovereign* (104); 23.2.1758 Mid *Royal Sovereign* (104); 29.9.1758 Mate *Royal Sovereign* (104); 31.12.1758 Mid *Royal Sovereign* (104); 23.5.1759 Mate *Royal Sovereign* (104); 20.3.1760 Passed; **Lieutenant**; 9.7.1762[(14.3.1763)]-6.8.1762 5L *Thunderer* (74); 21.2.1771 2L *Worcester* (64); 25.5.1771 1L *Worcester* (64); 25.6.1771-19.5.1773 2L *Worcester* (64).

SCOTT, ROBERT
Dates: 19.12.1770 Died.
Family:
Service: **Lieutenant**; 15.9.1760[(NA 5.4.1764)]-9.7.1762 3L *Falkland* (50); 3.6.1761-7.6.1761 Occupation of Dominica; 7.1.1762-10.2.1762 Operations against Martinique.

SCOTT, SAMUEL
Dates: c.1718 Born; 28.8.1774 Died; 3.9.1774 Will Probate.
Family:
Service: 1.11.1730 Able *Oxford* (50); 15.6.1731 Able *Salisbury* (50); 11.2.1731/32 Mid *Salisbury* (50); 16.8.1732 Able *Namur* (90); 23.9.1732 Able *Tiger* (48); 15.11.1733 Mid *Antelope* (54); 12.8.1737-24.10.1737[P] Mate *Antelope* (54); 18.12.1737 Mid *Centurion* (60); 27.1.1738/39 Mate *Centurion* (60); 10.4.1740 Passed; **Lieutenant**; 4.11.1740[(19.6.1744)] 3L *Gloucester* (50); 19.2.1740/41[(19.6.1744)]-16.8.1742[SC] 2L *Gloucester* (50); 22.4.1745-5.8.1745 1L *Lion* (58); 9.7.1745 Lion v L'Elizabeth; **Commander**; 26.7.1745 *Badger* (10) Sloop; **Captain**; 29.1.1747/48-30.6.1748[P] *Folkestone* (44); 7.5.1755-5.1.1758[P] *Humber* (44); 17.1.1759-16.1.1761[P] *Aurora* (38).

SCOTT, SAMUEL
Dates: c.1738 Born.
Family:
Service: 16.8.1753 Capt Serv *Crown* (44); 20.9.1754 Able *Norwich* (50); 26.11.1754 Mid *Norwich* (50); 16.5.1757 Mid *Achilles* (60); 5.9.1757-6.10.1757 Raid on Rochefort; 3.7.1759 Bombardment of Le Havre; 3.10.1759 Passed; **Lieutenant**; 5.10.1761-22.10.1762 4L *Modeste* (64); 7.1.1762-10.2.1762 Operations against Martinique; 23.6.1767 L. *Beaver* (14) Sloop; 10.1768-6.11.1770[D] LCmdr *Halifax* (6) Schooner; 6.11.1770 Dismissed.

SCOTT, WILLIAM
Dates: Not Known
Family:
Service: 27.4.1755 Mid *Dolphin* (24); 20.5.1756 Battle of Minorca; 12.11.1757 Mid *America* (60); 12.1.1759 Mid *Norfolk* (74); 16.1.1759-19.1.1759 Attack on Martinique; 13.3.1759 Mid *Lennox* (74); 14.4.1759 Mid *London Buss* Storeship; 14.4.1759-1.10.1760 Merchant Service; 2.10.1760 Mid *Savage* (8) Sloop; **Lieutenant**; 10.7.1761[(EI 17.7.1765)] 2L *Southsea Castle* (28) Storeship; 13.7.1761 Passed; 24.9.1762-6.10.1762 Battle of Manilla; 21.10.1762[(EI 17.7.1765)]-19.7.1765[P] 4L *Weymouth* (60); 30.11.1770 3L *Raisonable* (64); 29.11.1773-18.12.1773 1L *Raisonable* (64); 7.2.1776-13.4.1779[P] 1L *Pearl* (32); 22.7.1778 Encounter at Sandy Hook; 11.8.1778 Howe's encounter with d'Estaing; 27.11.1779 2L *London* (90); 16.3.1781 Battle of Cape Henry; **Commander**; 21.8.1781[(NA 19.6.1782)] *Beaumont* (16) Sloop; **Captain**; 25.9.1781[(NA

(19.6.1782)-17.7.1783[P] *Bedford* (74); 25.1.1782-26.1.1782 Battle of Saint Kitts; 12.4.1782 Battle of the Saintes.

SCREECH, JAMES
Dates: c.1724 Born.
Family:
Service: 27.1.1742/43-11.12.1746[P] Able *Dartmouth* (50); 11.7.1754 Able *Duke* (90); 25.12.1754 Mid *Plymouth* (60); 15.3.1755 Mate *Rainbow* (44); 27.6.1756 Mate *Barfleur* (80); 18.5.1757 Mate *Invincible* (74); 8.1757-10.1757 Louisbourg Expedition; 2.1.1758 Passed; **Lieutenant**; 25.1.1758 4L *Prince Frederick* (64); 1.7.1758(NA 5.12.1758) 3L *Lancaster* (66); 30.11.1758-5.2.1759 4L *Lancaster* (66); 7.8.1761 2L *Cornwall* (74); 3.9.1761-5.2.1763[P] 1L *Cornwall* (74); 20.6.1770-30.9.1773[P] L. *Kennington* (20); 30.4.1777-28.10.1777 LCmdr *Sally* Hired Tender; 24.7.1781-1.3.1783[P] LCmdr *Hinchinbrook* (16) Sloop; 29.3.1798 **Superannuated Commander**.

SCROPE, CARR
Dates: c.1719 Born; 1762 Died.
Family:
Service: 7.5.1733 Vol-p-O *Blandford* (20); 7.7.1737 Mid *Blandford* (20); 19.6.1740 Passed; **Lieutenant**; 19.11.1740 L. *Blast* (8) Bomb Vessel; 2.2.1740/41 4L *Neptune* (90); 27.3.1741 3L *Neptune* (90); 11.2.1743/44-12.2.1743/44 Battle of Toulon; 19.3.1743/44(MED 14.11.1745) 2L *Barfleur* (90); 20.8.1744(MED 21.11.1745)-17.9.1744 5L *Namur* (90); **Commander**; 11.8.1746 *Whitehaven* (18) Hired Ship; 23.10.1747 *Ferret* (14) Sloop; **Captain**; 14.11.1752(JAM 6.6.1753)-24.4.1753[W] *Assurance* (44); 21.8.1754-6.6.1756 *Dolphin* (24); 20.5.1756 Battle of Minorca; 10.2.1757-4.10.1759 *Coventry* (28); 5.6.1758-12.6.1758 Raid on Saint-Malo; 21.11.1760-13.1.1762 *Hampton Court* (64); 29.3.1761-11.6.1761 Expedition against Belle-Isle.

SECCOMBE, AMBROSE
Dates: 1758 Died; 19.12.1758 Will Probate.
Family:
Service: 15.9.1719-18.1.1721/22 Mid *Lynn* (42); 19.1.1721/22-20.8.1722 Able *Plymouth*; 21.8.1722-22.9.1722 Mid *Plymouth*; 23.9.1722-5.7.1724 Mid *Buckingham* (70); 6.7.1724-17.7.1724 Able *Lynn* (42); 18.7.1724-24.10.1725 Mid *Lynn* (42); **Master**; 25.10.1725 Master *Lynn* (42); 26.8.1728 Passed; **Lieutenant**; 2.3.1733/34 L. *Poole* (32); 27.3.1734 L. *Greyhound* (20); 29.5.1736(10.5.1737) 2L *Pembroke* (60); 12.3.1736/37(10.5.1737)-27.7.1738 1L *Pembroke* (60); 1.8.1738 L. *Port Mahon* (20); 14.8.1739-29.6.1740 2L *Severn* (50); 13.8.1742 1L *Orford* (70); 17.12.1742-9.7.1745 1L *Princess* (70); 11.2.1743/44-12.2.1743/44 Battle of Toulon; **Commander**; 23.1.1745/46 *Princess Royal* (24) Storeship; 29.1.1745/46-8.3.1747/48 *Deptford* (24) Storeship.

SELBY, JERRARD
Dates: 1781 Died; 14.2.1781 Will Probate.
Family: Son William, RN (d.1811).
Service: **Lieutenant**; 31.1.1759(BLI 29.12.1760)-19.4.1759[W] L. *Falcon* (8) Bomb Vessel; 1.8.1759(BLI 10.8.1761) 2L *Lancaster* (66); 7.8.1761 3L *Cornwall* (74); 3.9.1761-5.2.1763[P] 2L *Cornwall* (74); 14.6.1765-19.6.1769 LCmdr *Meredith* (10) Cutter; 7.11.1776 1L *Albion* (74); 28.1.1778 3L *Ardent* (64); **Commander**; 14.11.1778(NA 19.5.1780)-12.12.1779[P] *North* Hired Armed Ship.

SENIOR, ABRAHAM

Dates: c.1724 Born.
Family:
Service: 20.8.1744 Able *Mermaid* (44); 20.5.1745 Mid *Mermaid* (44); 9.1.1745/46 Able *Mermaid* (44); 19.3.1745/46 Mid *Vigilant* (60); 20.11.1747 Passed; **Lieutenant**; 16.11.1757-9.5.1758 3L *Roebuck* (44); 10.8.1759 3L *Royal Sovereign* (104); 3.4.1760-16.12.1761 3L *Newark* (80); 16.12.1761 2L *Enterprise* (44); 21.1.1762-27.2.1762 5L *Royal Sovereign* (104); 11.6.1762-16.9.1762[W] 2L *Humber* (44); 12.10.1762-15.1.1763[P] 5L *Princess Royal* (90).

SETON, GEORGE

Dates: 1758 Died.
Family:
Service: **Lieutenant**; 28.10.1741-4.3.1742/43[P] 3L *Winchester* (50); 30.12.1743 L. *Portsmouth* (24) Storeship; 19.3.1743/44 6L *Duke* (90); 23.3.1743/44 5L *Duke* (90); 8.1.1744/45 4L *Duke* (90); 11.5.1745 3L *Duke* (90); 18.5.1745-22.6.1748[P] 2L *Duke* (90).

SEYMOUR, BERKELEY

Dates: c.1714 Born; 1777 Died.
Family:
Service: 21.1.1727/28-30.8.1728[P] Able *Rippon* (60); 19.9.1728-9.10.1729[P] Mid *Winchester* (50); 19.5.1736 Able *Canterbury* (60); 28.2.1737/38 Able *Torrington* (40); 20.9.1738 Mid *Torrington* (40); 31.1.1738/39 Mate *Torrington* (40); 10.2.1740/41 Mate *Norwich* (50); 4.6.1741 Passed; **Lieutenant**; 9.6.1741 L. *Rupert's Prize* (8); 29.1.1742/43-10.5.1744 2L *Dover* (44); 15.8.1744 2L *Shrewsbury* (80); 17.5.1745-25.4.1746 1L *Shrewsbury* (80); 25.8.1747-12.11.1748[P] 1L *Assurance* (44); 7.11.1757 Dismissed.

SHACKERLY, WILLIAM

Dates: c.1710 Born; 1777 Died; 27.10.1777 Will Probate.
Family:
Service: 20.4.1736-31.1.1736/37 Mate *Newcastle* (50); 1.2.1736/37-25.3.1737 Able *Seaford* (20); 25.3.1737-27.3.1740 Mate *Seaford* (20); 28.3.1740 Mate *Winchelsea* (20); 29.3.1740-22.9.1740 Master *Winchelsea* (20); 23.9.1740-29.5.1741 Master *Superb* (60); 30.5.1741-20.6.1741 Master *Falmouth* (50); 21.6.1741 Master *Shrewsbury* (80); 8.5.1743 Passed; **Lieutenant**; 26.6.1744 L. *Phoenix* (20); 2.12.1745[(MED 20.6.1746)]-13.6.1746[P] 5L *Marlborough* (90); 17.9.1746-26.11.1748[P] 2L *Colchester* (50); 1754-9.1756 Agent for Transports; 4.11.1755-7.4.1756 *Macclesfield* (16) Hired Armed Ship; 9.1756-6.1764 Agent for Transports for North America & West Indies; 4.11.1774 **Commander**; 14.2.1776 *Strombolo* (8) Fireship; 10.4.1776-11.10.1776 *Spy* (14) Sloop.

SHADFORTH, JOHN

Dates: c.1721 Born.
Family:
Service: 3.6.1744 Mid *Prince Frederick* (70); 4.4.1745 Able *Prince Frederick* (70); 20.12.1745-6.12.1748[P] Mid *Prince Frederick* (70); 3.5.1747 1st Battle of Cape Finisterre; 26.9.1755 Mate *Yarmouth* (64); 27.12.1756 Passed; **Lieutenant**; 24.8.1757-25.8.1757 L. *Albany* (14) Sloop; 28.4.1758-27.6.1759 5L *Duke* (90); 5.6.1758-12.6.1758 Raid on Saint-Malo; 21.2.1771 3L *Egmont* (74); 29.6.1771-9.10.1772 2L *Egmont* (74).

SHAIRP, JOHN

Dates: c.1729 Born; 15.5.1795 Died.
Family:
Service: 10.8.1746 Able *Folkestone* (44); 19.2.1747/48-30.6.1748[P] Mid *Folkestone* (44); c.7.1748-c.11.1752 Merchant Service; 14.11.1752 Mid *Albany* (14) Sloop; 6.10.1756 Passed; 22.6.1757[(11.9.1758)]-2.8.1758 L. *Hunter* (10) Sloop; 22.7.1757 **Lieutenant**; 8.1757-10.1757 Louisbourg Expedition; 13.2.1759 L. *Echo* (24); 12.6.1759-14.1.1764[P] 2L *Pallas* (36); 28.2.1760 Action of February 28 1760; 14.3.1778-17.8.1781[P] 1L *Vengeance* (74); 27.7.1778 1st Battle of Ushant; 21.12.1779-22.12.1779 Action of 1779-12-21; 17.4.1780 Battle of Martinique; 15.5.1780 Action of March 15 1780; 19.5.1780 Action of March 19 1780; **Commander**; 10.4.1783[(Tonnay-Charentes 13.6.1786)]-14.4.1783 *Duc de Chartres* (18) Sloop.

SHAMMON, WILLIAM

Dates: c.1732 Born; 23.11.1795 Died.
Family:
Service: 23.9.1750 Able *Prince Henry* (44); 24.3.1753 Mid *Dolphin* (24); 27.8.1754 Mid *Experiment* (24); 19.4.1755 Mid *Elizabeth* (70); 1.12.1756 Passed; **Lieutenant**; 5.10.1758 4L *Norfolk* (74); 16.1.1759-19.1.1759 Attack on Martinique; 20.1.1759-1.5.1759 Capture of Guadeloupe; 20.11.1759 2L *Brilliant* (36); 28.2.1760 Action of February 28 1760; 1.4.1760-19.3.1763[P] 1L *Brilliant* (36); 10.7.1777 1L *Proserpine* (28); 22.10.1777 3L *Sandwich* (90); 16.5.1778-9.3.1779[P] 2L *Sandwich* (90); 27.7.1778 1st Battle of Ushant.

SHANK, JOSEPH

Dates: None Known.
Family:
Service: 29.1.1759 **Lieutenant**; 28.11.1771-19.11.1772[P] 1L *Raleigh* (10).

SHARPE, ISAAC

Dates: None Known.
Family:
Service: **Lieutenant**; 23.4.1762[(EI 6.9.1764)]-28.6.1765[P] 2L *Seaford* (20); 24.9.1762-6.10.1762 Battle of Manilla; 12.12.1766-21.12.1769 3L *Rippon* (60); 16.8.1770 1L *Rainbow* (44); **Commander**; 10.1.1771-6.3.1772 *Savage* (8) Sloop.

SHARPE, THOMAS

Dates: 15.2.1760 Died.
Family:
Service: **Lieutenant**; 6.11.1756 3L *Chesterfield* (44); 7.12.1758-10.7.1759 2L *Chesterfield* (44); 18.10.1759-15.2.1760[W] 6L *Ramillies* (90).

SHAUGHNESY, WILLIAM

Dates: c.1730 Born; 1.1770 Died; 18.11.1771 Will Probate.
Family:
Service: 6.5.1749 Able *Grampus* (14) Sloop; 15.5.1753 Cox *Grampus* (14) Sloop; 25.4.1755 Mid *Monarch* (74); 7.5.1756 Mid *Magnanime* (74); 29.6.1756 Mate *Magnanime* (74); 2.5.1757 Passed; **Lieutenant**; 10.5.1757 L. *Pelican* (16) Sloop; 15.6.1757 6L *Royal William* (84); 17.6.1757 5L *Royal William* (84); 5.9.1757-6.10.1757 Raid on Rochefort; 6.6.1758-27.7.1758 The Siege of Louisbourg; 30.1.1759 5L *Union* (90); 20.11.1759 Battle of Quiberon Bay; 8.5.1761 4L

Union (90); 5.8.1761-25.2.1763[P] 3L *Union* (90); 16.4.1763-29.11.1763 L. *Dispatch* (14) Sloop; 17.11.1764-19.11.1767 1L *Temeraire* (74); 15.6.1769-1.1770[†] 1L *Aurora* (32).

SHEALL, ROBERT

Dates: c.1726 Born; c.1760 Died; 13.5.1760 Will Probate.
Family:
Service: 1746-c.2.1748 Merchant Service; 4.2.1747/48-9.8.1751 Master *Otter* (14) Sloop; 1751-1756 Merchant Service; 7.7.1756 Passed; **Lieutenant**; 23.3.1757-10.8.1757[P] L. *Hazard's Prize* (8) Sloop; 23.9.1757-10.12.1759 3L *Vanguard* (68); 6.6.1758-27.7.1758 The Siege of Louisbourg.

SHERWOOD, WILLIAM

Dates: c.1733 Born.
Family:
Service: 26.12.1747 Capt Serv *Adventure* (44); 18.2.1749/50 Mid *Blandford* (20); 20.11.1751 Mid *Blandford* (20); 9.1.1754 Passed; **Lieutenant**; 9.11.1756 L. *Savage* (8) Sloop; 5.8.1757-12.2.1759 2L *Boreas* (28); 6.6.1758-27.7.1758 The Siege of Louisbourg; 21.2.1759 3L *Lennox* (74); **Commander**; 25.8.1762[(EI 28.4.1763)]-1.10.1762 *Southsea Castle* (28) Storeship.

SHEWARD, RIDGWAY

Dates: c.1713 Baptised; 1770 Died; 7.5.1770 Will Probate.
Family:
Service: 30.5.1734-14.6.1737 Able *Windsor* (60); 15.6.1737 QGnr *Gloucester* (50); 2.4.1740 Able *Adventure* (40); 11.4.1740 YoP *Prince Frederick* (70); 7.1.1740/41 Action of January 7 1741; 4.3.1740/41-5.1741 Operations against Cartagena; 5.11.1741 Mid *Prince Frederick* (70); 21.2.1742 Mate *Prince Frederick* (70); 1.7.1742 Mid *Dreadnought* (60) Receiving Ship; 7.2.1744/45 Passed; **Lieutenant**; 4.12.1745 3L *Augusta* (60); 21.4.1746-30.8.1748[P] 2L *Augusta* (60); 6.2.1755 2L *Grafton* (68); 29.3.1756 1L *Elizabeth* (64); 3.2.1757-20.9.1763[P] 1L *Orford* (68); 8.1757-10.1757 Louisbourg Expedition; 6.6.1758-27.7.1758 The Siege of Louisbourg; 6.6.1762-13.8.1762 Operations against Havana.

SHEWEN, RICHARD PHILLIPS

Dates: c.1727 Born; 1805 Died.
Family:
Service: 20.4.1749 Ord. *Lynn* (44); 27.1.1749/50 Able *Lynn* (44); 4.4.1751 Mid *Lynn* (44); 20.12.1751 Mid *Blandford* (20); 15.4.1753 Mate *Blandford* (20); 7.7.1756 Passed; **Lieutenant**; 17.6.1757-27.7.1757 L. *Fly* (8) Sloop; 17.8.1757 2L *Pallas* (36); 5.6.1758-12.6.1758 Raid on Saint-Malo; 7.6.1759-14.1.1764[P] 1L *Pallas* (36); 28.2.1760 Action of February 28 1760; 20.6.1769-9.5.1771[P] LCmdr *Lord Howe* (6) Cutter; 21.9.1796 **Superannuated Commander**.

SHIRLEY, JAMES

Dates: c.1705 Born; 2.4.1774 Died; 12.4.1774 Will Probate.
Family: Son James, RN (1734-1777);
Service: 7.9.1740 Master *Deptford* (60); 4.3.1740/41-5.1741 Operations against Cartagena; 13.1.1744/45 Master *Suffolk* (70); 8.5.1745 Master *Hampton Court* (64); 11.9.1746 Passed; **Lieutenant**; 9.10.1746 L. *Furnace* (8) Bomb Vessel; 25.12.1747-20.12.1748[P] 3L *Assistance* (50); 1749 Impress Service at Chatham; 5.11.1755 3L *Cambridge* (80); 2.4.1756-12.5.1757 2L *Cambridge* (80); 26.5.1757 1L *Prince of Orange* (60); 19.9.1757 5L *Princess Royal* (90);

30.12.1757 1L *Norfolk* (74); 5.6.1758-12.6.1758 Raid on Saint-Malo; 5.10.1758 4L *Royal George* (100); 23.2.1759 3L *Royal George* (100); 19.6.1759 2L *Royal George* (100); 5.9.1759 1L *Royal George* (100); **Commander**; 15.10.1759-14.11.1759 *Fortune* (14) Sloop; 18.2.1760 *Fortune* (14) Sloop; **Captain**; 27.4.1762-23.12.1762[P] *Princess Mary* (60).

SHIRLEY, JAMES

Dates: c.1734 Born; 31.10.1777 Died.
Family: Father James Shirley, RN (1705-1774).
Service: 1.5.1751 Capt Serv *Hampton Court* (64); 11.3.1753 Able *Assistance* (50); 30.11.1753-24.6.1755[W] Able *Mars* (64); 23.10.1755 Mid *Prince Frederick* (64); 6.5.1756 Mate *Prince Frederick* (64); 12.7.1757 Mid *Chichester* (68); 7.11.1757 Passed; **Lieutenant**; 20.12.1757 L. *Strombolo* (14) Fireship; 11.2.1760 2L *Minerva* (32); 26.3.1761 1L *Minerva* (32); 7.8.1761-2.5.1763[P] 2L *Africa* (64); 3.2.1767-15.2.1768[P] 1L *Coventry* (28); **Commander**; 26.5.1768 *Blast* (8) Bomb Vessel; 6.11.1770 *Swallow* (14) Sloop; **Captain**; 10.2.1772[(26.8.1773)]-15.2.1772[P] *Dolphin* (24); 7.5.1777-31.10.1777 *Vestal* (20).

SHIRLEY, THOMAS

Dates: 6.4.1733 Born; 7.4.1814 Died.
Family: Father Laurence Shirley (1693-1743); Mother Anne Clarges (d.1782); Wife Mrs. Mary Anderson née Elsgood (d.1808) married 30.3.1773; Wife Anne Hele married 6.11.1809; Brother Laurence, 4th Earl Ferrers (1720-1760); Brother Washington (5th Earl Ferrers), RN (1722-1778); Brother Robert, 6th Earl Ferrers (1723-1787); Brother Rev. Walter (1726-1786).
Service: **Lieutenant**; 11.10.1755[(JAM 16.7.1756)] L. *Weazle* (16) Sloop; 23.4.1756[(NA 23.8.1756)]-27.8.1756[P] 3L *Severn* (50); 20.12.1756-31.5.1757 4L *Monarch* (74); **Commander**; 22.2.1759 *Grampus* (14) Sloop; **Captain**; 19.11.1759 *Garland* (24); 14.5.1762-26.3.1763[P] *Lark* (32); 21.6.1780 *Leander* (52); 5.1.1783[(20.11.1783)]-17.7.1783[P] *Union* (90); 1.6.1791 **Superannuated Rear Admiral**.

SHIRLEY, WASHINGTON (5TH EARL FERRERS)

Dates: 26.5.1722 Born; 5.5.1760 5th Earl Ferrers; 1.10.1778 Died Chartley Manor Place, Staffordshire; 11.10.1778 Buried Staunton Harold, Leicestershire.
Family: Father Laurence Shirley (1693-1743); Mother Anne Clarges (d.1782); Wife Anne Elliot (1723-1791) married 1.12.1747; Brother Laurence, 4th Earl Ferrers (1720-1760); Brother Robert, 6th Earl Ferrers (1723-1787); Brother Rev. Walter (1726-1786); Brother Thomas, RN (1733-1814).
Service: 10.7.1735 Capt Serv *Falkland* (50); 9.8.1737 Able *Falkland* (50); 12.9.1738 Mid *Pembroke* (60); 17.7.1741 Passed; **Lieutenant**; 6.1.1741/42-14.6.1743 3L *Looe* (44); 15.3.1743/44 3L *Prince Frederick* (70); 9.1.1744/45 1L *Lark* (44); 11.1.1744/45 1L *Pearl* (44); **Commander**; 26.8.1745-4.3.1745/46 *Hawk* (8) Sloop; **Captain**; 19.4.1746 *Fox* (20); 24.1.1746/47-5.12.1747 *Dover* (44); 5.12.1747-22.12.1747 *Gloucester* (50); 27.1.1747/48-15.4.1751[P] *Fame* (30); 3.1.1754 *Bridgewater* (24); 20.1.1754 *Mermaid* (24); 22.5.1755-14.6.1755 British attack on Fort Beauséjour; 8.11.1756-17.2.1757 *Monmouth* (70); 7.3.1758 *Duc d'Aquitaine* (64); 5.6.1758-12.6.1758 Raid on Saint-Malo; 10.1.1759-22.2.1760 *Temple* (68); 20.11.1759 Battle of Quiberon Bay; 14.12.1761-1.10.1778 FRS; 31.3.1775 **Rear Admiral of the White**; 7.12.1775 **Vice Admiral of the Blue**; 29.1.1778 **Vice Admiral of the White**.

SHOREDICHE, RICHARD

Dates: 9.1786 Died.
Family:
Service: **Lieutenant**; 17.3.1760[(EI 29.7.1761)]-28.6.1760 4L *Salisbury* (50); 4.3.1762 3L *Lancaster* (66); 16.6.1762-13.1.1763[P] 2L *Lancaster* (66); 10.5.1766-25.7.1766[P] 3L *Thunderer* (74); 13.8.1766 L. *Hunter* (10) Sloop; 27.10.1770 3L *Buckingham* (68); 2.11.1770-26.5.1775[P] 2L *Buckingham* (68); 6.12.1776 3L *Resolution* (74).

SHORT, JOHN IDES

Dates: c.1732 Born; 1785 Died; 20.12.1785 Will Probate.
Family: Son John Ides, RN.
Service: 1750-1755 Merchant Service; 11.3.1754/55 Mid *Medway* (60); 16.12.1756 Mate *Royal Sovereign* (104); 22.1.1757-11.4.1757 Mid *Namur* (90); 11.4.1757 Passed; **Lieutenant**; 21.9.1757 L. *Grampus* (14) Sloop; 10.9.1759 1L *Arethusa* (32); 3.10.1759-11.12.1760 2L *Arethusa* (32); 14.4.1761 2L *Assistance* (50); 16.1.1762 1L *Assistance* (50); 6.12.1766 2L *Tweed* (32); 25.8.1769-29.1.1770 1L *Tweed* (32); 3.11.1770-29.5.1771[P] 1L *Elizabeth* (74); 29.6.1771-16.5.1772 3L *Lennox* (74); 26.3.1778-5.9.1778[P] LCmdr *Adventure* Hired Tender.

SHORT, JOSEPH

Dates: c.1675 Born; 1770 Died.
Family:
Service: 11.9.1691 L. Serv *Essex* (70); 18.5.1692 L. Serv *Centurion* (54); 19.5.1692 Battle of Barfleur; 30.1.1692/93 Able *Phaeton* (28); 4.4.1693 Able *Phaeton* (28); 19.8.1693 Mid *Nonsuch* (36); 28.7.1694 Mid *Mermaid* (32); 11.9.1694 Able *Owner's Love* (10) Fireship; 16.12.1694 Mid *Ruby* (48); 17.8.1695 Mate *Dover Prize* (32); 4.1.1695/96 Passed; **Lieutenant**; 5.5.1705-3.2.1707/8 L. *Griffin* (8); 21.4.1708-8.3.1712/13 L. *Squirrel* (24); 17.3.1717/18-25.1.1719/20[P] 2L *Captain* (70); 11.8.1718 Battle of Cape Passaro; 25.1.1725/26-27.4.1727 1L *Swallow* (50); 23.2.1733/34-16.2.1735/36[P] 1L *Tilbury* (60).

SHORT, SAMUEL

Dates: c.1724 Born; 1803 Died; 18.7.1803 Will Probate.
Family:
Service: 6.1.1741/42 Able *Sutherland* (50); 20.5.1742 Able *Antelope* (50); 14.2.1743/44 Mid *Antelope* (50); 25.11.1744 Mid *Russell* (80); 30.7.1745 Mid *Ipswich* (70); 8.10.1746 Mid *Yarmouth* (64); 3.5.1747 1st Battle of Cape Finisterre; 11.9.1747 Passed; **Lieutenant**; 21.11.1747-5.12.1748[P] 4L *Intrepid* (64); 16.1.1753 2L *Tiger* (60); 28.3.1754 2L *Bristol* (50); 31.7.1754 2L *Defiance* (60); 13.11.1754-5.5.1755 3L *Anson* (60); 31.7.1755 3L *Hampton Court* (64); 16.4.1756[(16.2.1757)] L. *Phoenix* (24); 20.5.1756 Battle of Minorca; 8.6.1757-20.7.1757 5L *Royal Anne* (100); 3.8.1757 2L *Intrepid* (60); 5.9.1757-6.10.1757 Raid on Rochefort; 19.10.1757-21.5.1760 1L *Intrepid* (60); 18.8.1759-19.8.1759 Battle of Lagos Bay; 20.11.1759 Battle of Quiberon Bay; 6.12.1769-27.10.1770 1L *Ramillies* (74); 4.1791-1792 LCmdr *Vulture* (14) Slop Ship.

SHUCKFORTH, DAVID

Dates: c.1730 Born; 1813 Died.
Family:
Service: 7.1.1747/48 Land. *Advice* (50); 26.1.1748/49 Mid *Advice* (50); 21.3.1748/49 Able *Advice* (50); 14.5.1749 Able *Monarch* (74); 13.7.1749-13.9.1749 Able *Mermaid* (24); 14.9.1749

Mid *Mermaid* (24); 12.8.1750 Able *Mermaid* (24); 21.5.1751 Mid *Mermaid* (24); 8.5.1752 Mate *Mermaid* (24); 21.12.1752 ActL *Scorpion* (14) Sloop; **Lieutenant**; 7.6.1753-28.6.1753[P] L. *Scorpion* (14) Sloop; 1.8.1753 Passed; 6.2.1755 L. *Experiment* (24); 12.8.1755 L. *Albany* (14) Sloop; 19.9.1755 3L *Assistance* (50); 31.12.1755-30.6.1760[P] 2L *Assistance* (50); 5.8.1760-29.3.1763[P] 1L *Anson* (60); 29.8.1763-9.9.1763 1L *Actaeon* (28); 2.2.1771-28.5.1771[P] 1L *Prince of Wales* (74); 16.3.1776-29.10.1777 1L *Worcester* (64); 21.9.1796 **Superannuated Commander**.

SHULDHAM, LEMUEL

Dates: c.1735 Born; 9.3.1766 Died.
Family:
Service: 6.9.1749 Able *Unicorn* (24); 30.3.1750-22.6.1752[P] Mid *Unicorn* (24); 29.5.1753-1.9.1756 Mid *Deptford* (50); 20.5.1756 Battle of Minorca; 1.9.1756 Passed; **Lieutenant**; 29.3.1757 3L *Centurion* (50); 6.6.1758-27.7.1758 The Siege of Louisbourg; 22.9.1759[(13.11.1759)] 2L *Centurion* (50); 4.3.1760 1L *Temple* (68); 7.1.1762-10.2.1762 Operations against Martinique; **Commander**; 26.3.1762[(13.12.1762)]-4.4.1763 *Sardoine* (14) Sloop.

SHULDHAM, MOLYNEAUX (BARON SHULDHAM)

Dates: 1717 Born; 31.7.1776 Baron Shuldham; 21.9.1798 Died.
Family: Father Rev. Lemuel Shuldham; Mother Elizabeth née Molyneux; Wife Mrs Margaret Irene Harcourt née Sarney married 4.10.1790.
Service: 1.11.1732 Capt Serv *Cornwall* (80); 19.12.1732 Vol-p-O *Cornwall* (80); 23.3.1732/33 MidO *Solebay* (6) Bomb Vessel; 26.5.1734 MidO *Falkland* (50); 26.4.1735 Mid *Falkland* (50); 21.9.1738 Mid *Pembroke* (60); 25.1.1738/39 Passed; **Lieutenant**; 31.8.1739-23.2.1740/41 3L *Tilbury* (60); **Commander**; 12.5.1744[(31.5.1746)]-19.10.1745[C] *Blast* (8) Bomb Vessel; **Captain**; 12.5.1746-20.12.1748 *Sheerness* (24); 27.12.1748 *Queenborough* (24); 21.3.1748/49-22.6.1752[P] *Unicorn* (24); 23.10.1754 *Seaford* (20); 11.3.1755-11.3.1756[C] *Warwick* (60); 25.7.1758 *Panther* (60); 16.1.1759-19.1.1759 Attack on Martinique; 20.1.1759-1.5.1759 Capture of Guadeloupe; 14.7.1759[(BLI 23.3.1760)]-8.1.1762[W] *Raisonnable* (64); 27.4.1762-1.5.1762 *Marlborough* (68); 1.5.1762[(EI 14.9.1763)] *Rochester* (50); 8.6.1762[(25.10.1763)]-21.9.1763[P] *Foudroyant* (80); 1.12.1766-6.12.1769 *Cornwall* (74); 17.11.1770 *Royal Oak* (74); 1772-1774 Gov. of Newfoundland; 14.2.1772 CinC — Newfoundland; 14.2.1772-16.12.1774[P] Commodore *Panther* (60); 10.10.1774-7.4.1784 M.P. for Fowey; 31.3.1775 **Rear Admiral of the White**; 9.1775-5.2.1776 *Chatham* (50); 29.9.1775-2.1776 CinC — North America; 7.12.1775 **Vice Admiral of the Blue**; 5.2.1776-6.9.1776 *Chatham* (50); 2.7.1776-4.7.1776 Staten Island Landings; 22.3.1777-10.9.1777 CinC — Plymouth; 10.9.1777 CinC — Barbados & the Leeward Islands; 29.1.1778 **Vice Admiral of the White**; 12.1778-1779 *Foudroyant* (80); 26.9.1780 **Vice Admiral of the Red**; 1782 *Dunkirk* (60); 24.9.1787 **Admiral of the Blue**; 1.2.1793 **Admiral of the White**.

SHURMUR, WILLIAM

Dates: 1721 Born; 13.2.1777 Died; 22.3.1777 Will Probate.
Family:
Service: 5.4.1739 Able *Elizabeth* (70); 22.8.1739 Mid *Boyne* (80); 9.10.1740 Mid *Elizabeth* (70); 17.1.1740/41 Mid *Sandwich* (90); 1.6.1741 Mid *Duke* (90); 21.9.1741 Mate *Duke* (90); 9.12.1741 Able *Neptune* (90); 12.12.1741 Mate *Neptune* (90); 11.2.1743/44-12.2.1743/44 Battle of Toulon; 18.2.1744/45 Supnum *Newcastle* (50); 5.5.1745 NR *Princess Royal* (90); 5.6.1745 Passed; **Lieutenant**; 23.1.1745/46 5L *Royal George* (100); 5.5.1747-21.6.1748[P] 4L *Royal George* (100); 25.9.1755 2L *Assistance* (50); 2.12.1755 2L *Dreadnought* (60); 12.2.1757 **Commander**; 23.2.1757[(JAM 20.10.1758)] 1L *Edinburgh* (64); **Captain**; 12.3.1757[(JAM 21.6.1759)]-7.8.1759 *Wager* (24).

SIDDALL, JOHN
Dates: c.1732 Born.
Family:
Service: 13.12.1747 Able *Port Mahon* (24); 21.5.1748 Able *Royal George* (100); 21.11.1749 Mid *Royal George* (100); 29.6.1750 Mid *Vigilant* (60); 17.3.1755 Passed; **Lieutenant**; 15.1.1756-19.6.1756 4L *Hampton Court* (64); 19.6.1756 LCmdr *Bolton* Hired Tender; 16.5.1758-24.9.1759 2L *Richmond* (32); 5.6.1758-12.6.1758 Raid on Saint-Malo.

SIMCOE, JOHN
Dates: 14.5.1759 Died.
Family:
Service: **Lieutenant**; 7.8.1739 3L *Newcastle* (50); 12.5.1740 2L *Newcastle* (50); 11.10.1740 3L *Princess Caroline* (80); 14.1.1740/41(JAM 16.9.1746) 3L *Burford* (70); 27.4.1741(JAM 16.9.1746) 4L *Russell* (80); 8.6.1741(JAM 16.9.1746) 2L *Cumberland* (80); 2.5.1743(JAM 16.9.1746) 1L *Cumberland* (80); **Commander**; 19.7.1743(16.9.1746) *Thunder* (8) Bomb Vessel; **Captain**; 28.12.1743(16.9.1746) *Kent* (70); 19.2.1743/44(16.9.1746) *Seahorse* (20); 29.1.1744/45(16.9.1746)-24.10.1746[P] *Falmouth* (50); 7.3.1746/47-12.9.1748[P] *Prince Edward* (44); 30.6.1756 *Saint George* (90); 23.3.1757-14.5.1759[†] *Pembroke* (60); 6.6.1758-27.7.1758 The Siege of Louisbourg.

SIMONTON, ROBERT
Dates: c.1737 Born; 1768 Died.
Family:
Service: 19.7.1754 L. Serv *Somerset* (68); 29.8.1754 QGnr *Norwich* (50); 28.5.1755 Mid *Norwich* (50); 25.4.1757 Mid *Achilles* (60); 5.9.1757-6.10.1757 Raid on Rochefort; 3.3.1758 Mate *Achilles* (60); 7.2.1759 Passed; **Lieutenant**; 27.6.1759 6L *Duke* (90); 4.9.1759 5L *Duke* (90); 20.11.1759 Battle of Quiberon Bay; 7.3.1760 3L *Achilles* (60); 25.3.1760 2L *Achilles* (60); 29.3.1761-11.6.1761 Expedition against Belle-Isle; 6.9.1762-25.12.1762[P] 4L *Hero* (74); 11.9.1767-29.6.1770[P] L. *Tamar* (16) Sloop; 21.9.1770 2L *Albion* (74); 15.1.1771-20.9.1773 1L *Albion* (74); 4.11.1776 1L *Prince of Wales* (74); **Commander**; 5.5.1778 *Alderney* (10) Sloop; **Captain**; 9.7.1778 *Superb* (74); 23.10.1780(EI 11.2.1782)-26.11.1780[W] *Sartine* (32); 28.6.1782-16.1.1783 *Panther* (60); 20.10.1782 Battle of Cape Spartel; 6.6.1795 **Superannuated Rear Admiral**.

SINCLAIR, JAMES
Dates: Not Known
Family:
Service: 7.1760 **Lieutenant**; 3.7.1760(NA 9.11.1762)-4.11.1762 4L *Alcide* (64); 7.1.1762-10.2.1762 Operations against Martinique; 6.6.1762-13.8.1762 Operations against Havana.

SINFIELD, WILLIAM
Dates: c.1722 Born.
Family:
Service: 2.6.1745 Capt Serv *Portland* (50); 14.10.1747 2nd Battle of Cape Finisterre; 19.10.1747 Mid *Prince Henry* (44); 9.10.1750 Able *Prince Henry* (44); 9.12.1752 Mate *Prince Henry* (44); 12.4.1753 Mate *Port Mahon* (24); 2.6.1756 Passed; **Lieutenant**; 15.6.1758(5.1.1761)-6.1.1760 6L *Prince* (90); 18.8.1759-19.8.1759 Battle of Lagos Bay.

SKELLY, GORDON

Dates: c.1741 Born.

Family:

Service: 1755-1757 Merchant Service; 28.6.1757 Mid *Devonshire* (70); 6.6.1758-27.7.1758 The Siege of Louisbourg; 5.5.1760 Mid *Magnanime* (74); 5.8.1761 Passed; **Lieutenant**; 1.10.1762-6.12.1762[P] L. *Baltimore* (8) Bomb Vessel; 24.12.1762-4.4.1763[P] 3L *Chester* (50); 25.4.1763-17.11.1764 2L *Lowestoffe* (32); 14.3.1769 1L *Pembroke* (60); **Commander**; 10.1.1771-1.7.1771 *Lynx* (10) Sloop.

SKENE, ALEXANDER

Dates: 1769 Died; 17.4.1769 Will Probate.

Family:

Service: **Lieutenant**; 14.4.1744 3L *Cornwall* (80); 9.6.1744 3L *Enterprise* (50); 10.11.1745[(24.1.1748/49)] 2L *Enterprise* (44); 22.8.1746[(24.1.1748/49)]-13.12.1748[P] 1L *Enterprise* (44).

SKINNER, GEORGE

Dates: c.1720 Born; 1810 Died; 22.10.1810 Will Probate.

Family:

Service: 28.2.1740-12.3.1743[P] Able *Mary Galley* (40); 13.4.1743 Able *Hastings* (44); 25.4.1743 QGnr *Hastings* (44); 22.11.1743 Mid *Hastings* (44); 27.5.1745-14.8.1746 Mid *Prince George* (90); 14.8.1746 Passed; **Lieutenant**; 15.9.1756 L. *Princess of Wales* (18) Hired Armed Ship; 16.8.1758 L. *Escort* (14) Sloop; 26.4.1759-12.6.1760 L. *Port Mahon* (24); 22.12.1761 6L *Sandwich* (90); 30.7.1762 5L *Sandwich* (90); 27.9.1762-22.1.1763[P] 4L *Sandwich* (90).

SKONE, THOMAS

Dates: None Known.

Family:

Service: 9.12.1731-15.6.1733 Vol-p-O *Cruizer* (24); 8.3.1733/34-1.2.1734/35 Mid *Blenheim* (96); 27.11.1741-4.11.1743 Mid *Saint George* (90); 7.12.1743-26.2.1743/44 Mate *Serpent* (10) Bomb Vessel; 17.3.1743/44-26.2.1744/45 Mate *Dolphin* (20); 13.7.1745 Passed; **Lieutenant**; 21.7.1745[(EI 30.11.1747)]-21.8.1749 L. *Lively* (24); 25.6.1746 1st Battle of Negapatam; 15.6.1756 3L *Namur* (90); 1.9.1756 2L *Namur* (90); **Commander**; 15.10.1756-8.1758[P] *Sarah* (16) Hired Armed Ship.

SKYNNER, LANCELOT

Dates: 4.4.1760 Died HMS *Bideford*.

Family:

Service: **Lieutenant**; 23.4.1748 3L *Bristol* (50); 3.5.1748-18.12.1748[P] 3L *Penzance* (44); 26.7.1749 L. *Peggy* (8) Sloop; 26.4.1750-24.1.1751/52[P] L. *Kingfisher* (14) Sloop; 16.1.1753 3L *Mars* (64); 22.4.1755-24.6.1755[W] 3L *Mars* (64); 23.3.1756 1L *Tartar* (24); 6.8.1756 4L *Royal George* (100); 9.11.1756 2L *Royal George* (100); **Commander**; 15.11.1756 *Viper* (10) Sloop; 25.11.1757 *Proserpine* (8) Fireship; **Captain**; 7.2.1758-4.4.1760[†] *Bideford* (20).

SLADE, JOHN

Dates: 1779 Died.

Family:

Service: **Lieutenant**; 29.12.1760[(24.11.1762)]-13.5.1763[P] 3L *Firm* (74); 8.6.1763-14.2.1767[P] L. *Hawk* (10) Sloop; 10.11.1769 2L *Hero* (74); 8.10.1770-20.5.1771[P] 3L *Hero* (74); 29.11.1771 4L *Torbay*

(74); 2.5.1772 3L *Torbay* (74); 7.7.1772 4L *Torbay* (74); 3.11.1773-26.3.1774 3L *Torbay* (74).

SLIFORD, THOMAS

Dates: c.9.1710 Born; 8.9.1710 Baptised St Oswald, Chester; bef.13.12.1756 Died; 23.12.1756 Will Probate.
Family: Father Thomas Sliford; Sister Sarah [Condon].
Service: **Lieutenant**; 17.4.1742 3L *Hector* (40); 10.8.1742-1.8.1743 3L *Assistance* (50); 9.1.1745/46 1L *Exeter* (60); 20.9.1746-25.9.1746 Lorient Operations; 1.10.1746 Action of 1746-10-01; 14.2.1746/47-18.4.1747[P] 4L *Sandwich* (90); 28.7.1747 1L *Severn* (50); 29.7.1748[(18.10.1748)]-22.11.1748[P] 3L *Princess* (70); 16.10.1755 2L *Royal Sovereign* (104); 27.11.1756-13.12.1756[†] 1L *Royal Sovereign* (104).

SLOASS, JAMES

Dates: c.1725 Born; c.1765 Died; 2.1.1766 Will Probate.
Family: Wife Mary Boatswain married 5.7.1753; Son William Benjamin (1755-?).
Service: 28.4.1749 Able *Augusta* (60); 12.8.1750 Able *Revenge* (70); 20.5.1756 Battle of Minorca; 8.2.1757 Mid *Union* (90); 30.3.1757 Mate *Union* (90); 5.6.1758-12.6.1758 Raid on Saint-Malo; 14.2.1759 Passed; **Lieutenant**; 24.9.1759-16.12.1760[P] 6L *Barfleur* (80); 13.3.1761-25.10.1761 3L *Prince Edward* (44).

SLORACH, JAMES

Dates: c.1720 Born; 1764 Died; 27.4.1765 Will Probate.
Family:
Service: 28.7.1738 L. Serv *Romney* (50); 1.8.1739 Able *Romney* (50); 24.6.1741 Mid *Nassau* (70); 11.2.1743/44-12.2.1743/44 Battle of Toulon; 24.8.1744-23.1.1744/45[P] Mid *Namur* (90); 14.2.1744/45 Passed; **Lieutenant**; 30.5.1745 3L *Gloucester* (50); 10.7.1747 2L *Mars* (64); 24.12.1747-8.11.1751 1L *Mars* (64); 11.1.1757 3L *Princess Royal* (90); 19.9.1757 2L *Princess Royal* (90); 20.6.1759-14.3.1760 1L *Foudroyant* (80).

SMELT, CORNELIUS

Dates: c.1719 Born; 2.6.1755 Died; 24.7.1755 Will Probate.
Family: Sister Dorothy.
Service: 6.8.1734 Capt Serv *Lennox* (70); 23.4.1735 Able *Lennox* (70); 10.6.1736 Able *Roebuck* (40); 13.3.1737/38 Mid *Roebuck* (40); 27.11.1740 Passed; **Lieutenant**; 21.2.1740/41 3L *Dover* (44); 28.1.1742/43-9.5.1745 4L *Dorsetshire* (80); 11.2.1743/44-12.2.1743/44 Battle of Toulon; **Commander**; 9.4.1748-9.1748[P] *Granado* (8) Bomb Vessel; 28.10.1748-22.2.1753[P] *Viper* (14) Sloop; 26.4.1755-2.6.1755 Impress Service.

SMITH, ABEL

Dates: 1714 Born Deal; 11.9.1714 Baptised Deal; 12.5.1756 Died; 1.6.1756 Will Probate.
Family: Father Cornelius Smith (d.1769); Mother Elizabeth Bowles; Wife Mary.
Service: 2.5.1733 MidO *Captain* (70); 30.4.1734 Able *Spy* (8) Sloop; 4.1.1734/35-8.2.1739/40 Mid *Spy* (8) Sloop; 9.2.1739/40 Mate *Saint Albans* (50); 20.1.1740/41 Passed; **Lieutenant**; 19.2.1740/41 3L *Eltham* (40); 18.2.1742/43 Attack on La Guaira; 15.4.1743-24.4.1743 Attack on Porto Cabello; 2.6.1743-21.6.1743 *Otter* (14) Sloop; **Captain**; 22.1.1745/46 *Surprise* (24); 13.6.1746-15.1.1747/48[P] *Chatham* (50).

SMITH, ELLIOTT

Dates: 1774 Died; 19.9.1774 Will Probate.
Family: Wife Sarah; Daughter Mary.
Service: **Lieutenant**; 18.9.1726[(14.11.1726)] 4L *Cumberland* (80); 22.11.1726 3L *Portland* (50); 12.10.1727[(11.10.1728)]-23.10.1728[P] 2L *Portland* (50); 22.2.1728/29-6.1.1731/32[P] 2L *Dreadnought* (60); 26.2.1732/33 1L *Dreadnought* (60); 31.1.1733/34 4L *Ipswich* (70); 27.2.1733/34-17.2.1735/36[P] 3L *Blenheim* (96); 16.5.1738 1L *Augusta* (60); 18.8.1738-2.12.1738[P] 1L *Princess Amelia* (80); 12.6.1739 1L *Princess Caroline* (80); **Commander**; 10.8.1739 *Fly* (8) Sloop; **Captain**; 25.2.1741/42-18.4.1744[P] *Advice* (54); 28.9.1744-1.10.1744 *Dover* (44); 5.7.1745-28.2.1745/46 *Norwich* (50); 19.5.1756-4.6.1756 *Prince* (90); 1769-31.3.1769 Captain of Greenwich Hospital.

SMITH, HENRY

Dates: c.1723 Born; c.7.1757 Died; 18.7.1757 Buried St Mary at Hill, London; 17.5.1758 Will Probate;
Family: Father Rev. John Smyth; Brother Rev. John.
Service: 11.6.1738 Able *Rupert* (60); 28.5.1739 Able *Centurion* (60); 12.11.1740 Mid *Rose* (20) Ship.**Lieutenant**; 7.6.1745[(2.12.1746)] 2L *Dragon* (60); 10.10.1745 Passed; 2.11.1745-8.5.1746 L. *Vulcan* (16) Sloop; 24.4.1747[(17.2.1748/49)]-1.11.1747 4L *Elizabeth* (70); 21.3.1748/49 L. *Queenborough* (24); 1.4.1750[(NA 18.4.1751)] 3L *Gloucester* (50); 26.1.1750/51[(NA 18.4.1751)]-15.4.1751[P] 1L *Renown* (30); 5.2.1754 2L *Kent* (64); **Commander**; 4.7.1755-25.2.1756 *Kingfisher* (14) Sloop; 11.1.1756-14.1.1756 Capture of Geriah; **Captain**; 24.8.1756-c.7.1757† *Bridgewater* (24); 7.3.1757-1.4.1757 Expedition against Chandernagore.

SMITH, HENRY

Dates: c.1740 Born; c.2.1801 Died; 27.2.1801 Will Probate.
Family: Wife Maria; Son John Henry; Daughter Frances Elizabeth Ann; Daughter Maria; Daughter Emma.
Service: 1753-1757 Merchant Service; 31.8.1757 Able *Royal George* (100); 7.2.1758 Able *Namur* (90); 6.6.1758-27.7.1758 The Siege of Louisbourg; 4.8.1758 Mid *Namur* (90); 18.8.1759-19.8.1759 Battle of Lagos Bay; 20.11.1759 Battle of Quiberon Bay; **Lieutenant**; 27.8.1760-20.2.1763[P] 2L *Blonde* (32); 10.9.1760 Passed; 1801-c.2.1801 Lieutenant of Greenwich Hospital.

SMITH, JAMES

Dates: c.1725 Born; 1786 Died.
Family:
Service: 24.9.1741 QM Mate *Furnace* (8) Bomb Vessel; 29.9.1741 QM Mate *Discovery* (6); 16.3.1742/43 Able *Princess Royal* (90); 8.8.1743 Mid *Alderney* (20); 11.12.1744 Mid *Princess* (70); 18.8.1745 Mid *Shark* (8) Sloop; 13.10.1745 Mid *Ruby* (50); 20.9.1746-25.9.1746 Lorient Operations; 15.7.1747-12.10.1747 Mid *Royal Sovereign* (104); 10.12.1747 Passed; **Lieutenant**; 17.2.1747/48 3L *Lion* (58); 18.5.1748-25.6.1748[P] 3L *Greenwich* (50); 6.2.1755 3L *Elizabeth* (70); 16.12.1755 2L *Elizabeth* (70); **Commander**; 10.11.1756 *Hazard's Prize* (8) Sloop; 23.3.1757 *Strombolo* (14) Fireship; 18.10.1758 *Seahorse* (24); 28.10.1758 **Captain**; 24.7.1760-17.1.1761 *Seahorse* (24); 14.4.1761 *Guernsey* (50); 17.11.1762-31.8.1763[P] *Assistance* (50); 18.10.1763-29.11.1766 *Hussar* (28); 31.3.1768-16.1.1772[P] *Mermaid* (28).

SMITH, JOHN
Dates: c.1736 Born; 25.6.1762 Died.
Family:
Service: 1751-1755 Merchant Service; 24.2.1755 Mid *Chichester* (68); 5.6.1758-12.6.1758 Raid on Saint-Malo; 11.10.1758 Passed; **Lieutenant**; 23.1.1759-25.6.1762[†] 3L *Sapphire* (32); 20.11.1759 Battle of Quiberon Bay.

SMITH, RICHARD
Dates: c.1734 Born; 7.1811 Died.
Family:
Service: 1754-1757 HEIC Service; 20.4.1757 Mid *Royal George* (100); 8.9.1757 Mate *Royal George* (100); 14.2.1758 Mid *Namur* (90); 6.6.1758-27.7.1758 The Siege of Louisbourg; 9.9.1758 Mate *Namur* (90); 18.8.1759-19.8.1759 Battle of Lagos Bay; 20.11.1759 Battle of Quiberon Bay; 30.4.1760 Passed; **Lieutenant**; 12.6.1760-23.12.1760 L. *Port Mahon* (24); 31.12.1760 4L *Prince Frederick* (64); **Commander**; 4.5.1761 *Hawk* (10) Sloop; **Captain**; 1.11.1762 *Torrington* (44); 18.5.1763-23.7.1767 *Squirrel* (20); 21.2.1769-17.10.1772[P] *Montagu* (60); 20.2.1776-5.8.1778 *Lark* (32).

SMITH, RICHARD
Dates: c.1733 Born.
Family:
Service: 1756-1758 Merchant Service; 26.7.1758 Mid *Saint George* (90); 16.1.1759-19.1.1759 Attack on Martinique; 1.3.1759 Mid *Antelope* (50); 24.8.1759 Mid *Prince* (90); 17.9.1759 Mid *Royal Anne* (100); 11.1.1762 Passed; **Lieutenant**; 25.6.1762 L. *Alderney* (10) Sloop; 7.4.1763-31.12.1767[P] 2L *Mermaid* (28); 26.10.1769-6.12.1769 L. *Pomona* (18) Sloop; 4.12.1775 1L *Flora* (32); 28.3.1776-28.6.1777 2L *Exeter* (64); 16.4.1778-10.3.1783[P] LCmdr *Achilles* Hired Tender.

SMITH, THOMAS
Dates: c.1707 Born; 26.8.1762 Died.
Family: Father Sir Thomas Lyttelton, Bt.; Half-brother George.
Service: **Lieutenant**; 6.2.1727/28[(25.5.1728)] 4L *Royal Oak* (70); 20.6.1728-29.3.1729 3L *Gosport* (42); 12.5.1729 2L *Enterprise* (42); **Captain**; 5.5.1730 *Success* (20); 6.5.1732-23.10.1740 *Dursley Galley* (20); 1741-4.1742 CinC — Newfoundland; 29.1.1740/41-5.4.1742 *Romney* (50); 8.10.1742 *Princess Mary* (60); 1743 CinC — Newfoundland; 7.11.1744-19.8.1745 *Royal Sovereign* (104); 5.9.1745-11.9.1745 CinC — River Medway and The Nore; 11.2.1745/46-12.1.1746/47 CinC — North Sea; 15.7.1747 **Rear Admiral of the Red**; 12.5.1748 **Vice Admiral of the White**; 8.1755-1757 CinC — The Downs; 9.1755-1756 *Ramillies* (90); 1756-5.1757 *Oxford* (50); 5.1756-7.1756 *Newark* (80); 24.9.1756-10.1757 *Union* (90); 8.12.1756 **Vice Admiral of the Red**; 1.1757-5.1757 *Saint George* (90); 24.2.1757 **Admiral of the Blue**; 10.1757-1758 *Royal Sovereign* (104).

SMITH, THOMAS
Dates: c.1724 Born; 2.6.1765 Died.
Family: Father Sir Thomas Lyttelton (1688–1751), illegitimate son of..
Service: 4.7.1738 Scholar *Royal Naval Academy*; 1739-1741 Merchant Service; 19.4.1741 Ord. *Marlborough* (90); 8.9.1741 Able *Fowey* (40); 19.10.1741 Mid *Fowey* (40); 27.4.1743 Mid *Scarborough* (18) Hospital Ship; 18.8.1744-21.10.1744[W] Mid *Colchester* (50); 13.10.1745 NR *Hector* (44); 30.10.1745 NR *Princess Royal* (90); 7.12.1745 Mid *Triton* (20); 5.6.1746

Passed; **Lieutenant**; 6.6.1746-29.10.1747 3L *Lynn* (44); 16.1.1753-6.2.1755 3L *Somerset* (68); 18.6.1757-29.7.1757 3L *Neptune* (90); 1.8.1757 2L *Union* (90); 5.6.1758-12.6.1758 Raid on Saint-Malo; **Commander**; 18.10.1758-27.12.1759 *Strombolo* (14) Fireship.

SMITH, WILLIAM

Dates: c.1674 Born; 23.2.1756 Died.
Family:
Service: 21.8.1691 Vol-p-O *Grafton* (70); 25.11.1691 Vol-p-O *Monck* (58); 19.5.1692 Battle of Barfleur; 12.12.1692 Mid *Expedition* (70); 16.10.1693 Mid *Southampton* (54); 24.4.1695 Passed; **Lieutenant**; 26.6.1695 2L *Bonaventure* (36) Hired Ship; 21.8.1695-6.3.1695/96 1L *Bonaventure* (36) Hired Ship; 6.11.1696-3.11.1698^{P} 1L *Bonaventure* (36) Hired Ship; 2.12.1698-31.1.1699/0 L. *Speedwell* (24); **Commander**; 26.6.1708-6.2.1708/9^{C} *Burchett* (6) Hired Sloop; 14.6.1711-14.1.1711/12^{P} *Whiting* (4) Ship; 21.9.1715 *Swift* (10) Sloop; **Captain**; 10.5.1716 Capt&M *Port Mahon* (20); 29.5.1720$^{(6.3.1730/31)}$-9.11.1721^{P} *Dartmouth* (54); 13.4.1726-26.7.1728 *York* (60); 1729 CinC — Jamaica; 1.2.1728/29-9.9.1729^{P} *Faversham* (42); 21.7.1747 **Superannuated Rear Admiral.**

SMITH, WILLIAM

Dates: 1756 Died.
Family:
Service: 7.9.1713 Ord. *Windsor* (60); 4.11.1714 Vol-p-O *Elizabeth* (70); 15.1.1715/16 Mid *Hampshire* (54); 18.2.1716/17 Mid *Rochester* (54); 7.2.1717/18 Passed; **Lieutenant**; 11.6.1718$^{(19.1.1719/20)}$ 3L *Bredah* (70); 11.8.1718 Battle of Cape Passaro; 28.3.1720 2L *Worcester* (54); 4.4.1720-28.10.1721^{P} 3L *Revenge* (70); 4.12.1721 3L *Ipswich* (70); 15.3.1721/22-31.12.1722^{P} 3L *Chatham* (50); 4.3.1723/24 3L *Ludlow Castle* (40); 13.4.1725 2L *Ludlow Castle* (40); **Commander**; 6.1.1727/28 *Weazle* (8) Sloop; **Captain**; 13.6.1728 *Success* (20); 27.7.1728 *Enterprise* (42); 1729 CinC — Jamaica; 26.5.1730-15.9.1731^{P} *Enterprise* (42); 22.2.1733/34-5.2.1736/37 *Windsor* (60); 12.6.1739-26.8.1740 *Lion* (60); 21.7.1747 **Superannuated Rear Admiral.**

SMITH, WILLIAM

Dates: c.1724 Born.
Family:
Service: 30.8.1745 Mid *Gosport* (44); 2.6.1746 Mid *Roebuck* (44); 23.10.1747-4.5.1748^{P} Mid *Dunkirk* (60); 30.4.1752 Mid *Berwick* (70); 5.8.1752 Able *Russell* (80); 3.10.1753 Mid *Russell* (80); 20.10.1753 Able *Boyne* (80) Prison Ship; 26.4.1755 Able *Gloucester* (50); 18.6.1755 Mid *Gloucester* (50); 22.8.1756 Mate *Gloucester* (50); 4.7.1757 Passed; **Lieutenant**; 17.1.1758 2L *Shannon* (28); 6.6.1758-27.7.1758 The Siege of Louisbourg; 21.8.1759$^{(MED\ 12.6.1761)}$-7.2.1763^{P} 1L *Shannon* (28).

SMITH, WILLIAM

Dates: c.1727 Born; 1814 Died St. Columb, Cornwall.
Family:
Service: 1752-1756 Merchant Service; 8.6.1757 Master *Southampton* (32); 5.6.1758-12.6.1758 Raid on Saint-Malo; 22.10.1760 Passed; 23.10.1760 Mid *Namur* (90); 23.3.1761-31.12.1762 Mid *Valiant* (74); 29.3.1761-11.6.1761 Expedition against Belle-Isle; 6.6.1762-13.8.1762 Operations against Havana; **Lieutenant**; 31.12.1762$^{(JAM\ 19.6.1764)}$-25.6.1764^{P} 2L *Richmond* (32);

26.12.1775-24.6.1778[C] LCmdr *Folkestone* (6) Cutter; **Commander**; 2.4.1781-4.10.1781 *Zephyr* (14) Sloop; 1808-1809 *Hunter* (18) Sloop; 25.10.1809 **Captain**.

SMITHETT, WILLIAM

Dates: c.1734 Born; 23.2.1733/34 Baptised St Mary, Dover.
Family: Father Luke Smithett; Mother Abigail.
Service: 1753-1755 Merchant Service; 10.3.1755 Able *Somerset* (68); 27.4.1755 Mid *Somerset* (68); 19.1.1757 Mate *Somerset* (68); 6.6.1758-27.7.1758 The Siege of Louisbourg; 30.4.1760 Passed; **Lieutenant**; 7.8.1761-3.2.1763[P] 2L *Minerva* (32).

SMYTH, HENRY

Dates: Not Known.
Family:
Service: **Lieutenant**; 25.5.1755[(MED 26.11.1755)]-15.9.1755 3L *Norwich* (50).

SOMERSET, JOHN STUKLEY

Dates: 1805 Died; 7.9.1805 Buried St James, Piccadilly, Westminster.
Family: Wife Elizabeth Preston married 23.11.1771.
Service: **Lieutenant**; 5.4.1755[(17.6.1762)] 2L *Bridgewater* (24); 11.1.1756-14.1.1756 Capture of Geriah; 19.3.1756[(26.7.1762)] 4L *Cumberland* (66); 7.3.1757-1.4.1757 Expedition against Chandernagore; 1.8.1757[(26.7.1762)] 4L *Tiger* (60); 1.9.1757[(EI 26.7.1762)] 2L *Cumberland* (66); 4.2.1758[(EI 26.7.1762)] 1L *Cumberland* (66); **Captain**; 2.3.1758[(EI 17.6.1762)] *Salisbury* (50); 29.4.1758 Battle of Cuddalore; 7.7.1758[(EI 17.6.1762)]-3.3.1759 *Weymouth* (60); 3.8.1758 Battle of Negapatam; 2.11.1760-25.3.1761[P] *Cumberland* (66).

SOMERVILLE, MARK

Dates: c.1736 Born; 14.11.1736 Baptised Wotton under Edge, Gloucestershire; 11.9.1758 Died.
Family: Father George Somerville; Mother Elizabeth Hicks.
Service: 13.7.1750 Able *Surprise* (24); 17.4.1752 Mid *Surprise* (24); 11.9.1754 Able *Gosport* (44); 21.10.1754 Mid *Centurion* (50); 23.7.1755 Able *Seahorse* (24); 7.9.1755 Mid *Swiftsure* (68); 29.2.1756 Mid *Torbay* (74); 26.8.1756 Passed; **Lieutenant**; 26.2.1757 6L *Prince George* (80); 4.4.1757 5L *Prince George* (80); 14.6.1757 3L *Dunkirk* (60); 24.6.1757 L. *Bideford* (20); 22.5.1758 2L *Rochester* (50); 5.6.1758-12.6.1758 Raid on Saint-Malo; 15.8.1758-11.9.1758[†] 1L *Vestal* (32).

SPARKE, HENRY

Dates: c.1737 Born.
Family:
Service: 6.5.1748 Capt Serv *Windsor* (60); 30.1.1749-31.5.1752[P] Capt Serv *Monmouth* (70); 28.9.1752 Able *Deptford* (50); 14.12.1754 Mid *Deptford* (50); 20.5.1756 Battle of Minorca; 21.10.1756 Mid *Duke* (90); 7.2.1757 Passed; **Lieutenant**; 22.3.1757-19.4.1757[C] L. *Merlin* (10) Sloop; 12.5.1757 4L *Swiftsure* (68); 28.2.1758 Battle of Cartagena; 24.1.1759 3L *Swiftsure* (68); 18.8.1759-19.8.1759 Battle of Lagos Bay; 20.11.1759 Battle of Quiberon Bay; 12.3.1760-11.8.1760[D] 2L *Swiftsure* (68); 11.8.1760 Dismissed.

SPEARING, GEORGE

Dates: 1728 Born; c.11.1824 Died Greenwich Hospital; 2.11.1824 Buried Greenwich; 1.12.1824 Will Probate.

Family: Wife Mary Ann Turner married 28.5.1774; Son George Augustus, RN (1779-1808).

Service: 1750-1754 HEIC Service; 1.10.1754 Able *Intrepid* (64); 21.7.1755 Mid *Woolwich* (44); 12.11.1756 Mate *Woolwich* (44); 23.6.1757 Mid *Anson* (60); 5.9.1757 Passed; **Lieutenant**; 8.9.1757-20.7.1758[P] L. *Saint Anne* (18) Hired Armed Ship; 29.9.1758-4.1.1763 L. *Firedrake* (10) Bomb Vessel; 29.12.1758 Capture of Goree; 3.7.1759 Bombardment of Le Havre; 29.3.1761-11.6.1761 Expedition against Belle-Isle; 1780-1825 Lieutenant of Greenwich Hospital.

SPEKE, HENRY

Dates: c.1718 Born; 17.11.1760 Died Lisbon; 10.4.1761 Will Probate.

Family: Wife Elizabeth Meade married 10.1.1738; Daughter Elizabeth; Son Peter (1745-?); Son Edward (1753-?).

Service: 9.4.1732 Adm Ret *Cornwall* (80); 23.10.1732 Ord. *Diamond* (40); 19.12.1732 Able *Diamond* (40); 7.10.1733 Ord. *Shoreham* (20); 5.11.1733 Able *Shoreham* (20); 24.8.1735 Mid *York* (60); 9.11.1735 Mid *Bonetta* (8) Sloop; 5.8.1736 Mid *Hector* (40); 10.7.1737 Mid *Rippon* (60); 22.3.1738 Mid *Oxford* (50); 31.3.1738-5.12.1738 Able *Nottingham* (60); 5.12.1738 Passed; **Lieutenant**; 2.11.1745 L. *Pluto* (16) Sloop; 6.2.1745/46-5.2.1746/47 3L *Princess Mary* (60); 3.8.1747[(EI 6.3.1749/50)] 3L *Winchester* (50); **Commander**; 8.6.1749[(EI 10.5.1750)] *Basilisk* (8) Bomb Vessel; 1.9.1749[(20.6.1753)]-22.1.1753[P] *Swallow* (14) Sloop; 4.12.1753 *Kingfisher* (14) Sloop; **Captain**; 20.1.1754-16.9.1757[P] *Kent* (64); 11.1.1756-14.1.1756 Capture of Geriah; 7.3.1757-1.4.1757 Expedition against Chandernagore; 16.2.1759-20.2.1759 *America* (60); 17.4.1759 *Sandwich* (90); 19.4.1760-17.11.1760[†] *Modeste* (64).

SPENCER, SAMUEL

Dates: c.1717 Born; 1795 Died.

Family:

Service: 19.3.1731/32 L. Serv *Assistance* (50); 29.3.1734 Able *Edinburgh* (70); 16.7.1734 Mid *Kent* (70); 21.5.1736 Able *Shoreham* (20); 13.12.1736 Mid *Shoreham* (20); 7.3.1737/38 Mid *Chatham* (50); 6.4.1738 Passed; **Lieutenant**; 21.1.1741/42 L. *Cumberland* (80); 4.5.1742 L. *Firedrake* (8) Bomb Vessel; 28.9.1742[(12.1.1743/44)]-2.2.1743/44 3L *Warwick* (60); 29.5.1747-23.12.1747 1L *Devonshire* (66); 14.10.1747 2nd Battle of Cape Finisterre; 23.12.1747-1.12.1748 3L *Devonshire* (66); 28.1.1755-7.5.1755 3L *Saint George* (90); **Commander**; 15.10.1756-10.11.1756 *Charlotte* (8) Yacht; **Captain**; 3.6.1757-13.6.1757 *Magnanime* (74).

SPENDELOW, CHARLES

Dates: c.1727 Born; 27.5.1727 Baptised Polesworth, Warwickshire; 9.7.1755 Died Monongahela River.

Family: Father Thomas Spendelow.

Service: 29.5.1742 Able *Deptford* (60); 26.12.1743 Able *Suffolk* (70); 19.4.1744 Able *Hampton Court* (64); 8.1.1744/45 Action of 1745-01-08; 29.4.1746 Mid *Hampton Court* (64); 18.5.1748 Mate *Hampton Court* (64); 16.9.1748 Passed; **Lieutenant**; 1.5.1752 L. *Garland* (24); 12.6.1754-5.4.1755 L. *Gibraltar* (20).

SPENDLOVE, SAMUEL
Dates: c.1712 Born; 12.12.1787 Died.
Family:
Service: 13.3.1733/34 Mid *Yarmouth* (70); 24.8.1734 Mate *Yarmouth* (70); 17.1.1735/36-16.2.1735/36^{P} Mid *Yarmouth* (70); 28.2.1740/41 Mate *Gibraltar* (20); 22.1.1741/42 Mate *Saint George* (90); 12.6.1744 Mate *Captain*; 14.8.1746 Passed; **Lieutenant**; 28.5.1747$^{(9.9.1748)}$-8.9.1748^{P} 3L *Dreadnought* (60); 7.2.1757 3L *Lynn* (44); 15.2.1757 L. *Hazard's Prize* (8) Sloop; 4.3.1757-21.3.1760^{P} 1L *Captain* (64); 8.1757-10.1757 Louisbourg Expedition; 6.6.1758-27.7.1758 The Siege of Louisbourg.

SPICER, JOHN
Dates: c.1728 Born.
Family:
Service: 18.8.1746 Able *Prince Frederick* (70); 3.5.1747 1st Battle of Cape Finisterre; 16.3.1747/48 Able *Hampton Court* (64); 5.9.1748 Mid *Hampton Court* (64); 24.12.1748 Able *Sphinx* (24); 29.5.1751 YoP *Sphinx* (24); 23.9.1751 Able *Sphinx* (24); 13.12.1752 Mate *Sphinx* (24); 2.4.1753 Mid *Sphinx* (24); 24.8.1753 Mid *Sphinx* (24); 30.7.1754-6.11.1754^{P} Mate *Sphinx* (24); 5.2.1755 Passed; **Lieutenant**; 9.4.1760-16.3.1761 L. *Grampus* (14) Sloop; 9.4.1762$^{(5.10.1762)}$-7.7.1762 3L *Shrewsbury* (74).

SPICER, WILLIAM
Dates: c.1730 Born.
Family:
Service: 22.2.1746/47 Cox *Saltash* (10) Sloop; 9.11.1750 Mid *Saltash* (14) Sloop; 16.4.1752 Mate *Phoenix* (24); 20.5.1756 Battle of Minorca; 4.8.1756 Passed; **Lieutenant**; 13.1.1758 3L *Windsor* (60); 9.1.1760-4.2.1763^{P} 1L *Torbay* (74); 29.3.1761-11.6.1761 Expedition against Belle-Isle; 6.10.1763-24.10.1766^{P} 2L *Hero* (74); 1.12.1766-8.12.1769 1L *Cornwall* (74); 24.9.1770 2L *Temeraire* (74); 25.1.1771-22.5.1771^{P} 1L *Temeraire* (74); 19.9.1771-18.6.1774^{P} 1L *Active* (28); 31.5.1776-22.11.1776 2L *Foudroyant* (80); 4.11.1776 3L *Queen* (90); 27.3.1778-20.4.1778 2L *Queen* (90); 24.11.1778-29.5.1779 1L *Foudroyant* (80).

SPRAGGE, EDWARD
Dates: 24.1.1757 Died.
Family:
Service: **Lieutenant**; 12.11.1729$^{(1.7.1730)}$ 3L *Plymouth* (60); 31.12.1729$^{(10.9.1730)}$-30.9.1730^{P} 3L *Anglesea* (40); 29.1.1730/31 L. *Spence* (8) Sloop; 1.5.1732$^{(18.10.1732)}$-24.10.1732 L. *Rye* (20); 31.1.1733/34 4L *Burford* (70); 13.3.1733/34 3L *Burford* (70); 20.5.1735 2L *Burford* (70); 16.5.1738-26.11.1738^{P} 2L *Prince of Orange* (70); 12.6.1739 2L *Prince of Orange* (70); 14.11.1739-6.12.1739 1L *Sunderland* (60); 4.3.1739/40 2L *Chichester* (80); 30.6.1740 3L *Boyne* (80); 2.9.1740 2L *Boyne* (80); 27.9.1740 2L *Kent* (70); 13.10.1740 2L *Elizabeth* (70); 30.1.1740/41-12.9.1742 1L *Sandwich* (90); **Commander**; 28.8.1742 *Peregrine Prize* (8) Sloop; 10.1.1742/43 *Furnace* (8) Bomb Vessel; 12.2.1742/43 *Saltash* (14) Sloop; **Captain**; 11.6.1744-15.2.1744/45^{P} *Princess Amelia* (80); 14.9.1745 *Prince* (90).

SPRY, SIR RICHARD
Dates: 1715 Born; 24.6.1773 Knight Bachelor; 29.11.1775 Died.
Family: Father George Spry (1685-1732); Mother Mary Bullock; Sister Mary [Davey].
Service: 8.7.1733 Vol-p-O *Exeter* (60); 31.8.1733 Able *Exeter* (60); 4.4.1734 Able *Swallow*

(60); 15.1.1734/35 MidO *Swallow* (60); 10.8.1735 Vol-p-O *Swallow* (60); 18.5.1738-28.4.1740[P] Mid *Canterbury* (60); 26.6.1740 Passed; **Lieutenant**; 27.9.1740 L. *Deptford Prize* (8) Sloop; 4.4.1743 2L *Superb* (60); **Commander**; 4.9.1744[(JAM 30.3.1747)]-12.2.1744/45 *Comet* (10) Bomb Vessel; **Captain**; 23.9.1745-14.5.1750[P] *Chester* (50); 17.10.1753-5.6.1754 *Garland* (24); 12.6.1754 *Gibraltar* (20); 25.3.1755 *Fougueux* (64); 6.6.1755-8.6.1755 Action of 6-8 June 1755; 27.1.1757 *Orford* (68); 8.1757-10.1757 Louisbourg Expedition; 6.6.1758-27.7.1758 The Siege of Louisbourg; 11.11.1761 *Mars* (74); 25.8.1762-10.1763 CinC — North America; 25.8.1762-25.10.1763[P] Commodore *Mars* (74); 14.12.1763 *Fubbs* (12) Yacht; 2.4.1766-20.12.1769[P] Commodore *Jersey* (60); 5.5.1766-1769 CinC — The Mediterranean Sea; 18.10.1770 **Rear Admiral of the Blue**; 20.10.1770 *Fame* (74); 24.10.1770 **Rear Admiral of the White**; 1771-2.2.1774 CinC — Plymouth; 1771 *Lively* (20); 1772-1773 *Ocean* (90); 31.3.1775 **Rear Admiral of the Red.**

ST BARBE, JOHN

Dates: 8.10.1741 Born Southampton; 1816 Died.
Family: Father Alexander St Barbe; Mother Eleanor Wyatt; Wife Ann Mambey (d.1791) married 1766; Wife Margaret Galbraith (d.1802) married 6.1792.
Service: **Lieutenant**; 21.1.1761[(24.3.1763)] 3L *Enterprise* (44); 14.4.1761[(24.3.1763)] L. *Port Royal* (12) Storeship; 22.8.1808 **Superannuated Commander**.

ST JOHN, HON. HENRY

Dates: 1.6.1740 Born; 17.4.1780 Died Battle of Martinique.
Family: Father John St. John, the 11th Lord Bletso; Mother Elizabeth Crowley; Wife Mary Schuyler.
Service: 11.8.1754 Scholar *Royal Naval Academy*; 12.8.1757 Vol-p-O *Newark* (80); 5.6.1758-12.6.1758 Raid on Saint-Malo; 13.8.1758 MidO *Newark* (80); 9.7.1759-26.8.1760 MidO *Namur* (90); 18.8.1759-19.8.1759 Battle of Lagos Bay; 20.11.1759 Battle of Quiberon Bay; 26.8.1760 Passed; **Lieutenant**; 15.9.1760-9.2.1761 2L *Looe* (44); 16.2.1761 6L *Royal William* (84); 29.3.1761-11.6.1761 Expedition against Belle-Isle; **Commander**; 28.1.1762 *Hazard* (8) Sloop; **Captain**; 31.8.1762-12.4.1763[P] *Tartar* (28); 28.4.1763-22.2.1768[P] *Garland* (24); 11.1.1770-22.5.1771[P] *Edgar* (60); 13.5.1771-14.1.1773 *Raisonable* (64); 31.3.1775-29.5.1778[P] *Torbay* (74); 15.1.1779-17.4.1780 *Intrepid* (64); 17.4.1780 Battle of Martinique.

ST LOE, EDWARD

Dates: c.1730 Born; 5.1760 Died;.
Family: Father Edward St Lo.
Service: 22.5.1744 Scholar *Royal Naval Academy*; 6.1.1746/47 Able *Princess Amelia* (66); 13.11.1748 Mid *Princess Royal* (90); 9.10.1749 Vol-p-O *Intrepid* (64); 22.6.1750 Able *Mercury* (20); 13.8.1751 Mid *Boston* (24); 8.12.1751 Mid *Katherine* (8) Yacht; 6.6.1753 Passed; **Lieutenant**; 14.10.1755-21.12.1758 3L *Woolwich* (44); 21.12.1758[(BLI 3.6.1761)] 4L *Cambridge* (80); 16.1.1759-19.1.1759 Attack on Martinique; 20.1.1759-1.5.1759 Capture of Guadeloupe; **Commander**; 31.1.1760[(BLI 3.6.1761)]-5.1760 *Virgin* (12) Sloop.

ST LOE, JOHN

Dates: 28.12.1757 Died; 8.1.1758 Buried Northfleet.
Family:
Service: 19.4.1704-20.10.1705[C] Vol-p-O *Pendennis* (54); 22.3.1705/6 Vol-p-O *Assurance* (66); 22.7.1707 Mid *Assurance* (66); 2.3.1708/9 Action of 1709-03-02; 12.10.1709 Passed;

Lieutenant; 2.12.1709-1.1.1710/11 3L *Swiftsure* (64); **Commander**; 2.1.1710/11-16.6.1713 *Valeur* (24); **Captain**; 17.6.1713-1.3.1716/17 Capt&M *Valeur* (24); 1724-26.7.1728 *Ludlow Castle* (40); 26.7.1728-29.1.1730/31 *York* (60); 24.11.1731-26.8.1735[P] *Experiment* (20); 3.7.1742 *Princess Amelia* (80); 6.6.1744-17.2.1746/47[P] *Princess Royal* (90); 15.7.1747 **Superannuated Rear Admiral**.

STACEY, THOMAS

Dates: None Known.
Family:
Service: 18.1.1755 Able *Trident* (64); 6.8.1755 Mid *Prince Frederick* (64); 2.6.1757 Master *Fly* (8) Sloop; 26.8.1758 Master *Bideford* (20); 5.4.1760 ActL *Bideford* (20); 5.11.1760 Passed; **Lieutenant**; 10.11.1760-31.12.1761[W] L. *Bideford* (20).

STAFFORD, ISRAEL

Dates: c.1755 Died; 10.7.1755 Will Probate.
Family:
Service: 1697-1702 Merchant Service; 5.1.1701/2 Capt Serv *Nonsuch* (54); 23.5.1702 Vol-p-O *Nonsuch* (54); 29.7.1704 Mid *Nonsuch* (54); 31.3.1707 Passed; **Lieutenant**; 22.9.1709-12.1.1714/15 L. *Swan* (12); 13.1.1714/15-3.4.1715 3L *Strafford* (54); 4.4.1715-14.4.1715 2L *Strafford* (54); 6.6.1715 MidE *Strafford* (54); 13.4.1726-25.7.1728 2L *York* (60); 23.2.1733/34-19.12.1734 1L *Argyll* (50); 20.12.1734-4.10.1736 1L *Sunderland* (60); bef.1755 **Superannuated Lieutenant**.

STAINFORTH, GEORGE

Dates: c.1741 Born; 1810 Died.
Family:
Service: 15.6.1755 Capt Serv *Medway* (60); 25.11.1756 Capt Serv *Royal George* (100); 2.1.1757 Capt Serv *Namur* (90); 5.9.1757-6.10.1757 Raid on Rochefort; 12.2.1758 Capt Serv *Dorsetshire* (68); 14.9.1758 MidO *Dorsetshire* (68); 5.5.1759 Mid *Dorsetshire* (68); 20.11.1759 Battle of Quiberon Bay; 26.3.1760 Mid *Bellona* (74); 6.5.1761 Passed; **Lieutenant**; 11.9.1761-22.6.1764[P] 2L *Montreal* (32); 25.10.1809 **Superannuated Commander**.

STAINS, ROBERT

Dates: c.1712 Born.
Family:
Service: 8.12.1739 Able *Pearl* (40); 26.11.1740 Mid *Pearl* (40); 29.1.1742/43 Mate *Pearl* (40); 24.7.1743 Mate *Jersey* (60); 13.9.1744 Mate *Prince Frederick* (70); 11.9.1746 Passed; **Lieutenant**; 17.2.1757-5.5.1757 L. *Crown* (18) Storeship; 21.9.1757 3L *Harwich* (50); 22.11.1757 2L *Harwich* (50); 9.3.1758-24.5.1758 Capture of Fort Louis; 29.11.1758-23.9.1763[P] 1L *Edgar* (60); 18.8.1759-19.8.1759 Battle of Lagos Bay; 6.6.1762-13.8.1762 Operations against Havana.

STANCOMBE, GEORGE

Dates: c.1714 Born.
Family:
Service: 28.3.1741 Able *Portland* (50); 28.4.1741 Able *Blenheim* (96); 1.8.1741 QM *Elizabeth* (70); 12.10.1741 Able *Mary Galley* (40); 23.1.1741/42 Mid *Mary Galley* (40); 16.2.1741/42 Able *Mary Galley* (40); 20.3.1741/42 Mid *Drake* (8) Sloop; 19.7.1742 Mate *Bridgewater* (20); 23.8.1743 Mid *Woolwich* (50); 7.9.1743 Mate *Woolwich* (50); 18.9.1743 Mate *Dover* (44);

3.1.1744/45 Mate *Maidstone* (50); 11.7.1745 Passed; **Lieutenant**; 25.7.1745 L. *Whitehaven* (18) Hired Ship; 17.10.1747-17.1.1748/49 L. *Queenborough* (24); **Commander**; 16.11.1757-23.12.1757 *Cruizer* (8) Sloop; 22.2.1759-6.1.1760 *Saltash* (14) Sloop.

STANFORD, WILLIAM

Dates: c.1728 Born; 5.1774 Died; 19.1.1791 Will Probate.
Family:
Service: 1753-1756 HEIC Service; 21.1.1756 Mid *Harwich* (50); 2.4.1757 Able *Harwich* (50); 5.6.1757 Mid *Harwich* (50); 21.6.1757 Able *Harwich* (50); 15.9.1757 Mid *Harwich* (50); 3.10.1757 Mate *Montagu* (60); 28.2.1758 Battle of Cartagena; 2.8.1758 Act3L *Montagu* (60); 21.9.1758 Mate *Montagu* (60); 7.2.1759 Passed; **Lieutenant**; 28.8.1759-3.9.1759 L. *Cygnet* (18) Sloop; 6.6.1763 2L *Pearl* (32); 27.3.1764-14.5.1766 1L *Pearl* (32); 4.10.1765-31.3.1768 LCmdr *Hope* (6) Schooner.

STANHOPE, JOHN

Dates: c.9.1744 Born; 19.9.1744 Baptised St Peter's, Nottingham; 1.12.1800 Died Salisbury.
Family: Father Ferdinand Stanhope; Mother Mary Phillips; Wife Caroline Dent (1763-1830) married 27.9.1784; Daughter Caroline [Rashleigh] (1785–1866); Son Henry, RN (1788-1865); Son Lt.Col Philip John (1787-1830); Son Henry, RN (1788-1865); Son Charles George (1789–1833); Daughter Eliza Sophia [Moor] (1800-1873); Brother Charles (1746–1767); Sister Mary [Moor] (1746–1812); Brother Michael, RN (1750-1790); Brother Arthur, RN (1752-1836).
Service: 2.1.1756 Clerk *Edinburgh* (64); 9.2.1757 Mid *Swiftsure* (68); 28.2.1758 Battle of Cartagena; 18.8.1759-19.8.1759 Battle of Lagos Bay; 20.11.1759 Battle of Quiberon Bay; 29.3.1761-11.6.1761 Expedition against Belle-Isle; 25.8.1762 Passed; **Lieutenant**; 15.10.1762-24.12.1762[P] 3L *Guernsey* (50); 25.3.1763 L. *Tamar* (16) Sloop; 27.3.1764 L. *Spy* (10) Sloop; 14.5.1766-2.1.1767 3L *Guernsey* (50); 23.12.1767-17.3.1769 2L *Montreal* (32); 12.5.1771[MED 28.10.1771] 3L *Pembroke* (60); 3.12.1771[MED 28.10.1771]-6.3.1772[P] 2L *Pembroke* (60); 26.3.1774 1L *Medway* (60); **Commander**; 4.6.1774 *Raven* (14) Sloop; **Captain**; 5.3.1779 *Garland* (24); 20.6.1780-4.1783 *Pegasus* (28); 25.1.1782-26.1.1782 Battle of Saint Kitts; 10.5.1790 *Arethusa* (38); 20.2.1793-28.2.1794 *Vanguard* (74); 1.6.1795 **Rear Admiral of the Blue**; 14.2.1799 **Rear Admiral of the Red**.

STANHOPE, SIR THOMAS

Dates: c.1718 Born Mansfield, Nottinghamshire; 30.3.1718 Baptised Mansfied, Nottingham; 5.10.1759 Knight Bachelor; 7.3.1770 Died London;.
Family: Father Rev. Michael Stanhope (1681–1737); Mother Penelope Lovell (1685–1740); Brother Arthur Charles, MP (1715-1770); Brother Ferdinand (1718-1790).
Service: 19.6.1733 Ord. *Yarmouth* (70); 29.6.1735 Able *Dreadnought* (60); 14.2.1736/37 Able *Shoreham* (20); 11.4.1737 Mate *Shoreham* (20); 10.3.1737/38 Mid *Dragon* (60); 29.12.1739-6.6.1740 Able *Dolphin* (20); 5.6.1740 Passed; **Lieutenant**; 26.8.1740-9.10.1740 3L *Lichfield* (50); 10.10.1740 2L *Assistance* (50); 6.5.1741 4L *Nassau* (70); 12.8.1743[MED 4.10.1745] 3L *Somerset* (80); 11.2.1743/44-12.2.1743/44 Battle of Toulon; **Commander**; 11.1.1744/45 *Wolf* (14) Sloop; **Captain**; 12.7.1745-22.1.1745/46 *Bridgewater* (24); 2.4.1746 *Hector* (44); 21.3.1747/48-16.11.1752[P] *Fougueux* (64); 4.2.1755 *Edinburgh* (64); 15.6.1756 *Namur* (90); 30.6.1756-7.1762 *Swiftsure* (68); 28.2.1758 Battle of Cartagena; 18.8.1759-19.8.1759 Battle of Lagos Bay; 20.11.1759 Battle of Quiberon Bay; 29.3.1761-11.6.1761 Expedition against Belle-Isle; bef.1770-7.3.1770 Colonel of Marines.

STANTON, JOHN

Dates: c.1713 Born; 24.8.1796 Died; 17.9.1796 Will Probate.

Family: Wife Elizabeth married 6.7.1773.

Service: 1731-1740 Merchant Service; 24.7.1740 Mid *Falkland* (50); 17.9.1742 Mate *Sandwich* (90); 13.1.1744/45 Mate *Prince George* (90); 21.11.1745 Passed; **Lieutenant**; 14.2.1745/46-13.12.1747[P] 4L *Devonshire* (80); 9.4.1747 3L *Hastings* (44); 3.5.1747 1st Battle of Cape Finisterre; 7.5.1748-22.1.1748/49[P] 2L *Hastings* (44); 18.6.1755 3L *Roebuck* (44); 13.7.1756 2L *Roebuck* (44); 7.1.1757-16.11.1757 1L *Roebuck* (44); **Captain**; 4.3.1758-28.4.1758[B] *Triton* (20); 25.6.1762-3.3.1763[P] *Saint Florentine* (60); 27.11.1770-29.6.1771 *Crescent* (32) Frigate; 8.5.1779-22.1.1781 *Formidable* (98); 2.2.1788 **Superannuated Rear Admiral**.

STARR, JOHN

Dates: c.1737 Born; 24.7.1801 Died; 6.10.1801 Will Probate.

Family: Wife Sarah Tooth married 9.12.1773; Son Thomas; Daughter Mary (1775-?); Daughter Harriet (1783-?).

Service: 22.5.1755 Able *Falmouth* (50); 2.6.1755 Mid *Falmouth* (50); 11.3.1759 Mate *Falmouth* (50); 31.3.1759 Mate *Active* (28); 22.4.1761 Mid *Shannon* (28); 3.6.1761 Passed; **Lieutenant**; 5.5.1762-26.11.1762[P] L. *Grampus* (8) Fireship; 4.12.1770-25.3.1771[P] 1L *Romney* (50).

STEEDMAN, WILLIAM

Dates: c.1732 Born.

Family:

Service: 1751-1755 Merchant Service; 8.9.1755 Able *Windsor* (60); 17.11.1755 Mid *Windsor* (60); 8.1757-10.1757 Louisbourg Expedition; 11.5.1758 Mate *Windsor* (60); 21.5.1758 Mid *Windsor* (60); 13.8.1758 Mate *Windsor* (60); 6.2.1760 Passed; **Lieutenant**; 30.7.1762 6L *Sandwich* (90); 27.9.1762-22.1.1763[P] 5L *Sandwich* (90).

STEEL, ROBERT

Dates: c.1729 Born.

Family:

Service: 1753-1755 Merchant Service; 25.5.1755 Mate *Essex* (64); 5.6.1758-12.6.1758 Raid on Saint-Malo; 28.9.1759 Mate *Royal George* (100); 20.11.1759 Battle of Quiberon Bay; 13.2.1760 Passed; **Lieutenant**; 5.4.1760-5.2.1762 L. *Basilisk* (8) Bomb Vessel; 7.10.1781-7.12.1782 LCmdr *Keppel* (14) Sloop.

STEEVENS, CHARLES

Dates: 2.1705 Born West Hanningfield, Essex; 17.5.1761 Died; 14.4.1762 Will Probate.

Family: Father John Steevens (Army officer); Mother Elizabeth.

Service: **Lieutenant**; 19.3.1728/29[(17.6.1729)]-3.2.1730/31 L. *Spence* (8) Sloop; 4.2.1730/31-6.6.1734 3L *Salisbury* (50); 7.6.1734-8.12.1737 3L *Salisbury* (50); 9.12.1737-7.7.1738 1L *Falmouth* (50); 7.7.1738-28.5.1741 L. *Sheerness* (20); **Commander**; 25.3.1741 *Cumberland* (8) Fireship; 12.6.1741-14.10.1741 *Phaeton* (8) Fireship; 7.1741-10.1741 Operations against Santiago; **Captain**; 11.1.1741/42[(22.8.1744)] *Ludlow Castle* (40); 2.10.1744-8.7.1748[P] *Portland* (50); 14.10.1747 2nd Battle of Cape Finisterre; 31.1.1747/48 Action of 1748/01/31; 1.12.1748-14.11.1752[P] *Tiger* (60); 16.1.1755 *Lichfield* (50); 7.3.1755 CinC — Barbados & the Leeward Islands; 5.4.1755 *Orford* (68); 17.1.1757-6.7.1758 Commodore *Elizabeth* (64); 29.4.1758 Battle of Cuddalore; **Rear Admiral of the Blue**; 6.7.1758 *Elizabeth* (64); 3.8.1758 Battle of

Negapatam; 20.2.1759 *Grafton* (68); 19.5.1759 **Rear Admiral of the Red**; 10.9.1759 Battle of Pondicherry; 1760-1761 CinC — East Indies; 23.6.1760-17.5.1761 *Norfolk* (74).

STEPHENS, STEPHEN

Dates: c.1741 Born.
Family:
Service: 1755-1758 Merchant Service; 24.5.1758 Capt Serv *Fougueux* (64); 1.8.1758-21.5.1759[P] Able *Fougueux* (64); 29.12.1758 Capture of Goree; 27.4.1760 Mid *Princess Mary* (60); 20.6.1761 Able *Solebay* (24); 27.7.1761 Mid *Winchester* (50); 20.6.1762 Passed; **Lieutenant**; 20.6.1762[9.7.1764]-1.11.1763 3L *Winchester* (50); 17.11.1764 3L *San Antonio* (64); 29.11.1766-2.2.1770 2L *Renown* (30); 25.10.1809 **Commander**.

STEVENS, RICHARD

Dates: c.1727 Born; 5.10.1780 Died.
Family:
Service: 2.1.1739/40 Ord. *Weymouth* (60); 7.1.1740/41 Action of January 7 1741; 4.3.1740/41-5.1741 Operations against Cartagena; 8.4.1742 Ord. *Norfolk* (80); 11.2.1743/44-12.2.1743/44 Battle of Toulon; 30.12.1744 Able *Norfolk* (80); 19.11.1747-11.12.1747[P] Mid *Norfolk* (80); 24.12.1751 Cox *Launceston* (44); 9.3.1751/52 Mid *Launceston* (44) Hulk; 1.6.1752 Mid *Blandford* (20); 5.7.1754 Passed; **Lieutenant**; 12.2.1759 2L *Boreas* (28); 3.7.1759 Bombardment of Le Havre; 10.12.1759-4.3.1760 1L *Boreas* (28); 11.3.1761 2L *Modeste* (64); 8.4.1761 3L *Modeste* (64); 5.10.1761-22.10.1762 2L *Modeste* (64); 7.1.1762-10.2.1762 Operations against Martinique; 23.2.1778 2L *Thunderer* (74); 27.7.1778 1st Battle of Ushant; 24.12.1778-5.10.1780[†] 1L *Thunderer* (74); 31.12.1779 Affair of Fielding and Bylandt.

STEVENS, WILLIAM

Dates: c.1736 Born; 1.3.1782 Died; 27.9.1782 Will Probate.
Family:
Service: 28.11.1750 Capt Serv *Garland* (24); 29.5.1753 Mid *Otter* (14) Sloop; 5.3.1755 Mid *Augusta* (60); 18.9.1755 Mate *Augusta* (60); 2.6.1756-17.12.1756 Mid *Chichester* (68); 14.12.1756 Passed; **Lieutenant**; 11.5.1757-10.8.1757 6L *Royal Anne* (100); 29.3.1758 2L *Duc d'Aquitaine* (64); 5.6.1758-12.6.1758 Raid on Saint-Malo; 4.12.1758-3.4.1759 1L *Duc d'Aquitaine* (64); 30.4.1759 2L *Temple* (68); 14.5.1759-4.3.1760 1L *Temple* (68); 20.11.1759 Battle of Quiberon Bay; 28.8.1760 1L *Essex* (64); 17.1.1761-19.8.1763[P] 4L *Arrogant* (74); 17.12.1770-28.1.1771 1L *Northumberland* (68); 5.3.1771-13.1.1772 1L *Asia* (64); 1.1777 LCmdr *Elizabeth and Mary* Hired Tender; 10.7.1778 2L *Superb* (74); **Commander**; 25.1.1780[EI 5.2.1781] *Nymph* (14) Sloop; **Captain**; 2.1.1782-1.3.1782 *Superb* (74); 17.2.1782 Battle of Sadras.

STEVENSON, JOSEPH

Dates: c.1720 Born; 1799 Died; 31.5.1799 Will Probate.
Family:
Service: 31.8.1744 Able *Mermaid* (44); 4.2.1745/46 Mid *Vigilant* (60); 26.3.1748 Mate *Berwick* (70); 30.12.1748 Able *Fougueux* (64); 3.2.1748/49 Mate *Seahorse* (24); 6.6.1753 Passed; **Lieutenant**; 15.6.1757 L. *Pelican* (16) Sloop; 22.5.1758-12.4.1763[P] 2L *Tartar* (28); 5.6.1758-12.6.1758 Raid on Saint-Malo; 19.11.1775-10.5.1776 LCmdr *Betsey's Friendship* Hired Tender; 30.4.1776-10.12.1776 LCmdr *Prosperity* Hired Tender; 21.9.1796 **Superannuated Commander**.

STEWARD, SAMUEL

Dates: 13.2.1795 Died.
Family:
Service: **Lieutenant**; 18.10.1758(NA 18.1.1760)-3.11.1758 L. *Kennington* (20); 23.11.1758(NA 18.1.1760) 4L *Devonshire* (70); 12.1.1759(NA 18.1.1760) 3L *Devonshire* (70); 2.4.1760(NA 18.1.1760) 2L *Devonshire* (70); 7.1.1762-10.2.1762 Operations against Martinique; 3.4.1762(NA 18.1.1760)-13.5.1763[P] 1L *Devonshire* (70); 6.6.1762-13.8.1762 Operations against Havana.

STEWART, GEORGE

Dates: 3.11.1759 Died.
Family:
Service: 17.10.1704 Able *Bonaventure* (48); 11.7.1705 Able *Montagu* (60); 15.1.1705/6 Mid *Montagu* (60); 6.11.1706 Mid *Suffolk* (70); 1.7.1707 Mid *Portsmouth* (42); 3.8.1708 Mid *Nonsuch* (54); 8.2.1708/9 Passed; **Lieutenant**; 28.2.1708/9-24.4.1710 3L *Burford* (70); **Commander**; 8.11.1710-15.11.1712[P] *Delight* (14).

STEWART, JAMES

Dates: c.1678 Born; 30.3.1757 Died.
Family: Father John Steuart; Wife Mary Taylor married bef.1744.
Service: 13.2.1697/98 Vol-p-O *Fowey* (32); 8.9.1700 Vol-p-O *Mary* (60); 19.9.1700 Vol-p-O *Windsor* (60); 11.10.1700 Mid *Shrewsbury* (80); 17.3.1700/1 Mid *Rochester* (50); 4.12.1701 Passed; **Lieutenant**; 16.1.1701/2 5L *Association* (90); 20.7.1702 4L *Association* (90); 12.10.1702 Battle of Vigo; 12.2.1702/3-26.7.1703 2L *Association* (90); 13.12.1704-12.1.1704/5 1L *Ranelagh* (80); 24.1.1704/5-19.2.1704/5 1L *Dunkirk* (50); 9.3.1704/5-19.12.1705 2L *Royal Anne* (100); 29.12.1705-5.9.1706 1L *Saint George* (96); **Commander**; 29.1.1706/7(2.5.1707) *Hunter* (8); 18.8.1707 *Dunwich* (24); **Captain**; 14.1.1708/9-26.8.1711[W] *Greyhound* (40); 26.7.1715 *Royal Anne Galley* (42); 5.11.1718-16.4.1723[P] *Winchester* (50); 22.2.1733/34-16.2.1735/36[P] *Devonshire* (80); 30.8.1739 *Cumberland* (80); 8.5.1741(8.4.1742)-2.4.1742 *Russell* (80); 11.5.1741-4.7.1747 M.P. for Weymouth and Melcombe Regis; 6.4.1742 **Rear Admiral of the Blue**; 7.9.1742-16.9.1742 CinC — Portsmouth; 28.4.1743-15.12.1743 CinC — Portsmouth; 9.8.1743 **Rear Admiral of the White**; 7.12.1743 **Vice Admiral of the Blue**; 19.6.1744 **Vice Admiral of the Red**; 9.1744-1745 *Duke* (90); 15.7.1747 **Admiral of the White**; 22.11.1750 **Admiral of the Fleet**.

STEWART, JAMES

Dates: c.1729 Born.
Family:
Service: 1.5.1744 Capt Serv *Hind* (10) Sloop; 4.9.1746 Able *Aldborough* (20); 14.10.1747-12.7.1749[P] Mid *Aldborough* (20); 11.12.1751 Able *Gosport* (44); 14.8.1752 Able *Cumberland* (66); 22.2.1753 Mid *Cumberland* (66); 6.6.1753 Passed; **Lieutenant**; 9.11.1756 3L *Medway* (60); 5.9.1757-6.10.1757 Raid on Rochefort; 19.1.1758 2L *Medway* (60); 11.1.1760 6L *Royal Anne* (100); 24.3.1760-14.2.1763 2L *Thunderer* (74).

STEWART, JOHN

Dates: c.1730 Born.
Family:
Service: 6.10.1749 Capt Serv *Basilisk* (8) Bomb Vessel; 7.1.1749/50 Able *Defiance* (60); 14.6.1751 Able *Success* (20); 16.2.1751/52 Mid *Success* (20); 28.2.1755 Able *Porcupine* (16)

Sloop; 5.11.1755 Passed; **Lieutenant**; 20.10.1757 4L *Alcide* (64); 5.6.1758-12.6.1758 Raid on Saint-Malo; 31.8.1759(14.4.1762)-29.9.1761 L. *Zephyr* (10) Sloop.

STEWART, JOHN (7TH EARL OF GALLOWAY)

Dates: 13.3.1735/36 Born; 1747 Viscount Garlies; 24.9.1773 7th Earl of Galloway; 13.11.1806 Died.
Family: Father Alexander Stewart, 6th Earl of Galloway (c. 1694–1773); Mother Catherine Cochrane; Wife Charlotte Greville (d. 1763) married 14.8.1762; Wife Anne Dashwood (1743–1830) married 13.6.1764; Daughter Catherine [Graham] (1765–1836); Son Alexander (1766–1766); Daughter Susan [Spencer-Churchill] (1767–1841); Son Sir George (8th Earl of Galloway), RN (1768-1834); Daughter Anne Harriet [Chichester] (1769–1850); Daughter Elizabeth Euphemia [Inge] (1771–1855); Son Leveson Keith (1772–1780); Daughter Georgiana Frances (1776–1804); Son Lt.-Gen. Sir William (1774–1827); Son Rev. Charles James (1775–1837); Daughter Charlotte [Crofton] (1777–1842); Daughter Caroline [Rushout-Bowles] (1778–1818); Son Montgomery Granville John (1780–1860); Son Edward Richard (1782–1851); Son Lt.-Col. James Henry Keith (1783–1836); Daughter Georgiana Charlotte Sophia [Bligh] (1785–1809); Half-sister Mary [Mackenzie] (1720-1751); Sister Susanna [Leveson-Gower] (1742-1805); Brother The Hon. Keith, RN (1739-1795); Brother James Edward (1743–1812); Sister Margaret [Gordon] (d.1762); Sister Catherine [Murray]; Sister Charlotte [Murray] (d.1818); Sister Harriet [Hamilton] (d.1788).
Service: 1753-1755 Merchant Service; 28.7.1755 Able *Success* (20); 1.8.1757-3.10.1759 Mid *Success* (20); 5.6.1758-12.6.1758 Raid on Saint-Malo; 3.10.1759 Passed; **Lieutenant**; 10.12.1759-6.12.1760 2L *Boreas* (28); 18.10.1760 Action off Cuba.

STEWART, JOHN

Dates: c.1736 Born.
Family:
Service: 24.8.1753 Ord. *Shoreham* (24); 13.5.1755 Able *Shoreham* (24); 2.3.1756 Mid *Shoreham* (24); 24.3.1758 Mid *Harwich* (50); 5.12.1759 Passed; **Lieutenant**; 1.4.1760(27.8.1761)-30.3.1761 5L *Foudroyant* (80); 26.11.1762-8.3.1768P L. *Nautilus* (16) Sloop.

STEWART, HON. KEITH

Dates: 1739 Born; 1795 Died.
Family: Father Alexander, 6th Earl of Galloway; Mother Lady Catherine Cochrane (d.1786); Wife Georgina Isabella D'Aguilar married 13.5.1782; Son James Alexander (1784-1843); Son Leveson Douglas (1786-1819); Son Unknown; Son Unknown; Half-sister Mary [Mackenzie] (1720-1751); Sister Susanna [Leveson-Gower] (d.1805); Brother James Edward (1743–1812); Sister Margaret [Gordon] (d.1762); Sister Catherine [Murray]; Sister Charlotte [Murray] (d.1818); Sister Harriet [Hamilton] (d.1788); Brother Lord John (7th Earl of Galloway), RN (1736-1806).
Service: **Lieutenant**; 2.1.1759(Africa 5.4.1759)-25.8.1759 4L *Nassau* (64); **Commander**; 11.2.1761 *Speedwell* (8) Sloop; 4.3.1761-15.3.1762 *Lynx* (10) Sloop; 19.2.1762-3.1762 M.P. for Wigtown Burghs; **Captain**; 7.4.1762-21.2.1765P *Lively* (20); 16.3.1765-6.3.1766 *Montreal* (32); 22.4.1768-9.1784 M.P. for Wigtownshire; 27.12.1777-21.3.1781 *Berwick* (74); 27.7.1778 1st Battle of Ushant; 27.3.1781-1782 CinC — North Sea; 17.6.1782-30.12.1782 *Cambridge* (80); 20.10.1782 Battle of Cape Spartel; 10.5.1790 *Formidable* (98); 21.9.1790 **Rear Admiral of the Blue**; 1.2.1793 **Rear Admiral of the Red**; 12.4.1794 **Vice Admiral of the Blue**; 4.7.1794 **Vice Admiral of the White**.

STIRLING, SIR WALTER

Dates: 18.5.1718 Born; 1781 Knight Bachelor; 24.11.1786 Died.
Family: Father Walter Stirling (1686–1732); Mother Janet Ruthven; Wife Dorothy Willing (d.1782) of Philadelphia; Son Walter, 1st Bt. (1758–1832); Daughter Anne Dorothea; Son Charles, RN (1760-1833).
Service: 1732-1743 Merchant Service; 7.12.1743-11.2.1745/46 Mid *Princess Amelia* (80); 18.2.1745/46 Passed; **Lieutenant**; 18.2.1745/46-19.5.1747 3L *Ludlow Castle* (44); 20.6.1748[(7.2.1748/49)]-16.2.1748/49[P] 4L *Captain* (70); 22.7.1755 2L *Hampton Court* (64); 6.8.1755-22.10.1755 2L *Winchester* (50); 15.7.1756[(5.9.1757)] 2L *Anson* (60); **Commander**; 9.12.1756[(22.11.1757)] *Speaker* (10) Sloop; 25.10.1757 *Saltash* (14) Sloop; 5.6.1758-12.6.1758 Raid on Saint-Malo; 29.12.1758 Capture of Goree; **Captain**; 10.1.1759 *Lynn* (44); 29.3.1761-11.6.1761 Expedition against Belle-Isle; 16.6.1761-11.4.1763 *Lowestoffe* (32); 4.4.1763-3.10.1766[P] *Rainbow* (44); 21.2.1769-21.11.1770 *Dunkirk* (60); 17.11.1770[(JAM 4.9.1771)]-7.8.1771 *Seaford* (20); 7.8.1771-13.10.1772[P] *Portland* (50); 13.10.1780-7.2.1781 *Gibraltar* (80); 24.11.1781-24.12.1781 *Duke* (90); 12.12.1781 2nd Battle of Ushant; 1783-1785 CinC — River Medway and The Nore.

STONEY, GEORGE

Dates: c.1740 Born; 1786 Died; 5.9.1786 Will Probate.
Family:
Service: 1754-1757 Merchant Service; 24.6.1757 Able *Assistance* (50); 6.6.1758 Able *Marlborough* (80); 9.8.1758 Mid *Dreadnought* (60); 5.11.1760 Passed; **Lieutenant**; 13.4.1761-23.7.1762 2L *Mermaid* (28); 18.4.1763 2L *Coventry* (28); 3.2.1767-15.2.1768[P] 2L *Coventry* (28); 14.7.1768-25.7.1771 LCmdr *Wells* (6) Cutter; 4.12.1776 3L *Monarch* (74); 26.1.1778 4L *Prince George* (98); 13.5.1778 3L *Victory* (100); 2.7.1778 2L *Victory* (100); 27.7.1778 1st Battle of Ushant; 17.9.1778 1L *Victory* (100); **Commander**; 19.11.1778 *Furnace* (8) Fireship; 30.5.1780-27.2.1781 *Duguay Trouin* (18) Sloop; **Captain**; 27.2.1781[(JAM 27.12.1781)] *Hinchingbrooke* (28); 20.5.1781[(JAM 15.8.1782)] *Lowestoffe* (28); 1.2.1782[(JAM 23.11.1784)] *Fox* (32); 1.4.1784[(NA 10.11.1785)]-9.1786 *Flora* (36).

STORR, JOHN

Dates: c.1709 Born; 1.1783 Died.
Family: Wife Mrs. Gordon married 5.1773.
Service: 6.10.1726 MidO *Leopard* (50); 22.9.1728 Mid *Leopard* (50); 9.10.1728 MidO *Leopard* (50); 9.5.1730 Mid *Leopard* (50); 6.5.1731 Mid *Lion* (60); 24.7.1731 Mid *Rupert* (60); 25.6.1732 Mid *Gibraltar* (20); 15.5.1733 Able *Gibraltar* (20); 11.1.1734/35 Passed; **Lieutenant**; 30.10.1739[(23.5.1743)] 3L *Strafford* (60); 21.11.1739 Attack on Puerto Bello; 5.1.1739/40[(23.5.1743)] 2L *Strafford* (60); 14.1.1740/41[(23.5.1743)]-5.1.1741/42 1L *Strafford* (60); 14.10.1743 1L *Worcester* (58); 27.2.1744/45[(8.7.1745)]-22.7.1745[P] 5L *Barfleur* (90); 3.7.1746 **Commander**; **Captain**; 1.11.1748-23.12.1752[P] *Gloucester* (50); 28.1.1755-19.5.1756 *Saint George* (90); 11.8.1756 *Revenge* (64); 28.2.1758 Battle of Cartagena; 20.11.1759 Battle of Quiberon Bay; 23.6.1760-9.1762 *Monmouth* (70); 29.3.1761-11.6.1761 Expedition against Belle-Isle; 19.3.1779 **Rear Admiral of the White**; 26.9.1780 **Rear Admiral of the Red**.

STOTT, JOHN

Dates: c.1729 Born; 22.8.1778 Died.
Family:
Service: 28.12.1747 Able *Folkestone* (44); 29.2.1748-30.6.1748[P] Mid *Folkestone* (44); c.7.1748-1755 Merchant Service; 7.4.1755 Master *Jamaica* (10) Sloop; 13.4.1756 Master *Grafton* (70);

17.2.1757 Passed; **Lieutenant**; 17.2.1757 L. *Gibraltar's Prize* (14) Sloop; 14.6.1757 **Commander**; 15.6.1757 *Gibraltar's Prize* (14) Tender; 8.1757-10.1757 Louisbourg Expedition; 6.1.1758-1.8.1758 *Gramont* (18) Sloop; 6.6.1758-27.7.1758 The Siege of Louisbourg; **Captain**; 3.8.1758-23.10.1764[P] *Scarborough* (20); 20.10.1770-20.2.1772[P] *Juno* (32); 29.6.1772-31.5.1776 *Alarm* (32); 22.1.1775-23.6.1775 *Zephyr* (10) Sloop; 19.9.1777-22.8.1778[†] *Minerva* (32); 22.8.1778 Minerva vs Concorde.

STRACHAN, JOHN

Dates: 28.12.1777 Died Bath.

Family: Father Sir Patrick Strachan; Wife Elizabeth, daughter of Robert Lovelace; Wife ? Gregory.

Service: 1.1747 Passed; **Lieutenant**; 5.2.1746/47[EI 2.12.1748]-5.1747[P] L. *Fogo* Fireship; 7.2.1748/49-21.5.1753[P] L. *Dispatch* (14) Sloop; 28.1.1755 4L *Saint George* (90); 7.5.1755 3L *Saint George* (90); 11.11.1755 2L *Saint George* (90); 24.5.1756 2L *Namur* (90); 5.6.1756 2L *Ramillies* (90); **Captain**; 9.9.1756[ECH 30.1.1758] *Experiment* (24); 29.11.1756[ECH 22.1.1759] *Experiment* (24); 21.3.1758-12.3.1763[P] *Sapphire* (32); 20.11.1759 Battle of Quiberon Bay; 20.8.1763-18.10.1763 *Hussar* (28); 17.11.1770-27.2.1771 *Orford* (68); 13.3.1771-10.2.1772 *Orford* (68).

STRACHAN, PATRICK

Dates: c.1734 Born.

Family:

Service: 22.12.1749 Ord. *Dispatch* (14) Sloop; 9.3.1750/51 Able *Dispatch* (14) Sloop; 2.9.1751 Able *Kent* (64); 7.11.1751 Mid *Glory* (44); 6.1.1753 Mid *Dolphin* (24); 8.3.1755 Mid *Siren* (20); 22.5.1755-14.6.1755 British attack on Fort Beauséjour; 27.12.1756 Mid *Ramillies* (90); 10.3.1757 Passed; **Lieutenant**; 6.4.1757 3L *Prince of Orange* (60); 29.7.1757 4L *Magnanime* (74); 5.9.1757-6.10.1757 Raid on Rochefort; 5.6.1758-12.6.1758 Raid on Saint-Malo; 26.9.1759 3L *Magnanime* (74); 20.11.1759 Battle of Quiberon Bay; 31.1.1760 2L *Magnanime* (74); 14.6.1762 1L *Magnanime* (74); 22.6.1762-23.1.1763[P] 1L *Princess Amelia* (80); 4.5.1763-13.6.1766 LCmdr *Friendship* (4) Cutter; 22.11.1770 1L *Orford* (68); 22.4.1773 3L *Lennox* (74); 27.5.1773 2L *Lennox* (74); 10.1.1774 L. *Mercury* (20); 27.10.1774-29.4.1777 1L *Asia* (64); 2.7.1776-4.7.1776 Staten Island Landings.

STRANGE, EDMUND

Dates: 10.12.1756 Died Rochester.

Family: Wife Mary married 16.12.1741; Daughter Mary (1742-?); Son Robert (1744-?); Daughter Elizabeth (1740-?).

Service: 15.11.1715 Mid *Weymouth* (50); 31.7.1717 Mid *Panther* (54); 28.9.1717 Mate *Panther* (54); 17.6.1718 Able *Superb* (64); 11.8.1718 Battle of Cape Passaro; 29.8.1718 Mid *Superb* (64); 19.11.1719 Mate *Superb* (64); 21.6.1720 Passed; **Lieutenant**; 22.3.1726/27 L. *Shoreham* (8) Bomb Vessel; 5.9.1727-31.3.1731 L. *Shoreham* (8) Bomb Vessel; 5.7.1731-13.6.1732 3L *Princess Louisa* (40); 14.6.1732-4.9.1732 2L *Grafton* (70); 5.9.1732-4.5.1735 2L *Grafton* (70); 5.5.1735-13.4.1736[P] 1L *Grafton* (70); 15.3.1737/38-13.4.1738 3L *Somerset* (80); 14.4.1738-1.5.1740 1L *Somerset* (80); **Captain**; 24.2.1738/39[13.6.1739] *Chatham* (50); 2.12.1741 *Burford* (70); 29.12.1741-18.8.1744 *Nonsuch* (50); 11.2.1743/44-12.2.1743/44 Battle of Toulon; 19.8.1744[MED 27.1.1718/19]-25.11.1748[P] *Burford* (70); 15.2.1755 **Superannuated Rear Admiral.**

STREET, JOHN

Dates: c.1731 Born; 8.8.1767 Died; 10.8.1767 Buried St George the Martyr, Camden, London; 24.11.1767 Will Probate.
Family: Wife Elizabeth Bull.
Service: 1749-1751 HEIC Service; 2.2.1750/51 Capt Serv *Exeter* (60); 12.8.1752 Ord. *Exeter* (60); 2.10.1752 Able *Exeter* (60); 12.11.1752 Mid *Exeter* (60); 3.3.1753 MidO *Ambuscade* (40); 31.7.1753 Mid *Deptford* (50); 7.4.1756 Passed; **Lieutenant**; 14.5.1756 5L *Monarch* (74); 2.6.1756 4L *Monarch* (74); 20.12.1756 L. *Mermaid* (24); 20.7.1757 L. *Happy* (8) Sloop; 21.4.1758 2L *Melampe* (36); 28.4.1758 2L *Emerald* (28); 17.6.1760-26.10.1761[P] 1L *Emerald* (28).

STUART, HON. ARCHIBALD

Dates: c.1717 Born; 20.2.1795 Died.
Family: Father Francis Stuart, 7th Earl of Moray (c.1674-1739); Mother Jean Elphinstone (d.1739); Sister Anne [Steuart] (c.1703-1783); Brother James, 8th Earl (1708-1767); Brother John, MP (c.1708-1796); Brother Francis (d.1760); Brother Henry; Sister Amelia [Halkett] (c.1717-d.1781).
Service: 1.4.1733 Able *Dreadnought* (60); 12.11.1734-4.5.1737[P] Mid *Captain* (70); 11.7.1737 Able *Terrible* (6) Bomb Vessel; 30.5.1738 Mid *Edinburgh* (64); 8.5.1740 Passed; **Lieutenant**; 20.1.1740/41 3L *Dover* (44); 5.2.1740/41 2L *Dover* (44); 20.2.1740/41 L. *Dolphin* (20); 25.6.1743 3L *Argyll* (50); 19.7.1743 6L *Saint George* (90); 3.2.1743/44 5L *Saint George* (90); 29.3.1744-11.4.1744 4L *Saint George* (90); 5.4.1744 **Commander**; 4.5.1744 *Scipio* (8) Fireship; **Captain**; 20.2.1744/45 *Squirrel* (20); 26.8.1745-23.12.1746 *Hastings* (44); 20.9.1746-25.9.1746 Lorient Operations.

STUART, ARCHIBALD

Dates: Not Known.
Family:
Service: 24.9.1761[(19.3.1764)] 5L *Dublin* (74); 7.1.1762-10.2.1762 Operations against Martinique; 17.3.1762[(19.3.1764)] 3L *Modeste* (64); 24.9.1762 **Lieutenant**; 22.10.1762[(19.3.1764)]-14.3.1764[P] 2L *Modeste* (64); **Commander**; 26.5.1768 *Escort* (14) Sloop.

STUART, HON. DAVID

Dates: c.1745 Baptised; 12.6.1784 Died Budleigh Salterton, Devon; 27.10.1784 Will Probate.
Family: Father James Stuart, 8th Earl of Moray KT (1708–1767); Mother Margaret Wemyss; Brother James (d. 1808); Brother Francis, 9th Earl of Moray (1737–1810).
Service: **Lieutenant**; 15.4.1761[(7.6.1763)]-17.1.1763[P] 2L *Thetis* (32); 8.11.1770-21.2.1771 3L *Egmont* (74).

STUART, NATHANIEL

Dates: c.1725 Born; 11.9.1759 Died Cowes; 1.8.1760 Will Probate.
Family: Illegitimate Daughter Sarah Kaytes; Sister Elizabeth [Madox].
Service: 3.2.1738/39 Mid *Boyne* (80); 12.6.1741 Mid *Sandwich* (90); 8.2.1744/45 Mid *Ipswich* (70); 10.5.1745 Passed; **Lieutenant**; 19.5.1745[(MED 15.11.1748)] 3L *Royal Oak* (70); 3.5.1746[(MED 15.11.1748)]-6.11.1748[P] 3L *Antelope* (50); 19.5.1756 3L *Prince* (90); 22.6.1756-29.11.1756 2L *Prince* (90); 28.4.1757 5L *Ramillies* (90); 5.9.1757-6.10.1757 Raid on Rochefort; 26.4.1758 4L *Ramillies* (90); 5.6.1758-12.6.1758 Raid on Saint-Malo; 11.10.1758 3L *Ramillies* (90); 18.10.1759 2L *Ramillies* (90); 14.11.1759-19.11.1759[†] *Fortune* (14) Sloop.

STUART, PATRICK

Dates: c.1734 Born; 4.12.1797 Died; 12.12.1797 Will Probate.
Family:
Service: 25.11.1747 Mid *Bellona* (30); 1.4.1748-7.10.1748[P] Cpl *Bellona* (30); c.10.1748-1753 Merchant Service; 22.4.1753 Able *Mermaid* (24); 21.1.1754 Mid *Baltimore* (14) Sloop; 30.10.1755 Able *Torbay* (74); 19.12.1755 Passed; **Lieutenant**; 25.8.1758[NA 24.1.1759] 3L *Nottingham* (60); 31.1.1760[MED 24.1.1759] 2L *Nottingham* (60); 7.10.1760-17.3.1763[P] 2L *Niger* (32); 8.5.1766 2L *Dragon* (74); 24.9.1766-21.3.1769 3L *Dragon* (74); 7.11.1770-9.9.1773 2L *Centaur* (74); 14.11.1776 1L *Burford* (68); 5.5.1778-20.5.1778[P] 1L *Royal Oak* (74); bef.1797 Lieutenant of Greenwich Hospital.

STUTEVILLE, CHARLES

Dates: c.1708 Born; 26.6.1740 Baptised Holborn, London; 24.7.1773 Will Probate; 24.7.1773 Died Greenwich Hospital.
Family: Father Sir Martin Stuteville (1688-1743); Mother Angell Payne (1690-1737); Wife Susannah Christmas married 21.7.1772; Brother Ricahrd Martin (1749-?).
Service: 13.2.1734/35 Ord. *Burford* (70); 1.1.1737/38 Able *Burford* (70); 7.5.1738 Mid *Ipswich* (70); 16.7.1741 Passed; **Lieutenant**; 12.4.1744[19.10.1747]-20.3.1744/45 4L *Prince of Orange* (70); 1749-1773 Lieutenant of Greenwich Hospital.

SUCKLING, MAURICE

Dates: 4.5.1726 Born Barsham, Suffolk; 17.7.1778 Died.
Family: Father Rev. Maurice Suckling (1676-1730); Mother Mary Anne Turner (1693-1768); Wife Mary Walpole (d. 1766) married 20.6.1764; Brother Robert (1724-?); Sister Catherine [Nelson] (1725-1767); Brother John (1728-1728); Brother William (1730-?).
Service: 22.1.1739/40 Ord. *Newcastle* (50); 7.4.1741 Able *Newcastle* (50); 7.9.1741 Mid *Newcastle* (50); 16.6.1744-20.6.1745 Mid *Chichester* (80); 8.3.1744/45 Passed; **Lieutenant**; 8.3.1744/45[MED 22.3.1745/46] 4L *Burford* (70); 7.2.1746/47[MED 2.12.1748] 4L *Russell* (80); 6.5.1747[28.10.1748] 4L *Boyne* (80); 9.1.1747/48[28.10.1748] 3L *Boyne* (80); 16.8.1748[28.10.1748] 2L *Boyne* (80); 1.11.1748-23.12.1752[P] 1L *Gloucester* (50); 16.1.1753 2L *Somerset* (68); 19.4.1753 1L *Somerset* (68); **Commander**; 3.1.1754 *Baltimore* (14) Sloop; 1.7.1755-9.9.1755[P] *Lys* (64); **Captain**; 2.12.1755-19.11.1760[P] *Dreadnought* (60); 21.10.1757 Forrest's Action; 16.1.1761-4.1762 *Nassau* (64); 2.1762-22.2.1762 *Lancaster* (66); 17.11.1770 *Raisonable* (64); 13.5.1771-1.12.1773 *Triumph* (74); 12.4.1775-17.7.1778 Comptroller of the Navy; 18.5.1776-14.7.1778 M.P. for Portsmouth.

SUMMERS, THOMAS

Dates: 1715 Born; 1755 Died; 25.10.1755 Will Probate.
Family:
Service: 29.4.1737 Cox *Seaford* (20); 25.7.1737 Mid *Seaford* (20); 17.12.1739 Able *Seaford* (20); 5.2.1739/40-5.5.1740[P] Mid *Seaford* (20); 22.4.1741 Mid *Centurion* (60); 18.11.1741 Mate *Centurion* (60); **Lieutenant**; 21.6.1743[6.7.1744]-20.7.1744[P] 2L *Centurion* (60); 5.7.1744 Passed; 13.7.1745-31.7.1746 1L *Ruby* (50).

SURTEES, GEORGE

Dates: c.1739 Born; 7.1.1800 Died.
Family:
Service: 1754-1757 Merchant Service; 22.5.1757 Mid *Dublin* (74); 5.9.1757-6.10.1757 Raid on Rochefort; 1.4.1760 Able *Royal Sovereign* (104); 16.6.1760 Mid *Deptford* (50); 20.8.1760

Passed; **Lieutenant**; 17.3.1762[(14.7.1763)]-15.7.1763[P] 3L *Nottingham* (60); 6.6.1762-13.8.1762 Operations against Havana; 17.3.1777 2L *Stirling Castle* (64).

SUTHERLAND, JAMES

Dates: c.1733 Born; 1793 Died.
Family:
Service: 10.12.1746 Capt Serv *Eltham* (40); 9.1748-10.1748 Siege of Pondicherry; 12.5.1749 Capt Serv *Harwich* (50); 15.5.1749 Able *Harwich* (50); 20.12.1750-11.9.1751[W] Able *Fox* (20); 16.1.1751/52 Able *Ferret* (14) Sloop; 6.2.1753 Mid *Ferret* (14) Sloop; 9.10.1753 Mid *Anson* (60); 14.4.1754 Mid *Mermaid* (24); 22.5.1755-14.6.1755 British attack on Fort Beauséjour; 11.11.1755 Able *Torbay* (74); 19.12.1755 Passed; **Lieutenant**; 15.6.1757 L. *Escort* (14) Sloop; 15.8.1758-29.11.1758[W] 3L *Lichfield* (50); 9.10.1760-17.8.1762 2L *Temeraire* (74); 29.3.1761-11.6.1761 Expedition against Belle-Isle; 7.1.1762-10.2.1762 Operations against Martinique; 6.6.1762-13.8.1762 Operations against Havana; 2.8.1763-8.6.1767[P] 1L *Active* (28); 21.9.1796 **Superannuated Commander**.

SWANTON, ROBERT

Dates: 11.7.1765 Died.
Family: Wife Emma (d.1822); Daughter Frances (d.1841).
Service: 8.9.1724 Vol-p-O *Plymouth* (60); 2.7.1725 MidO *Tartar* (32); 17.7.1726 Mid *Tartar* (32); 23.12.1728 Passed; **Lieutenant**; 17.1.1734/35 L. *Rye* (20); 28.3.1735 3L *Rippon* (60); 13.2.1735/36 2L *Oxford* (50); 26.4.1737 1L *Oxford* (50); 28.2.1737/38 L. *Flamborough* (20); 4.1740-5.7.1740 Attack on St. Augustine; 17.9.1740 1L *Defiance* (60); 29.5.1741 3L *Princess Caroline* (80); 8.6.1741 1L *Boyne* (80); **Commander**; 6.10.1741[(22.8.1744)] *Scarborough* (18) Hospital Ship; 1.5.1743-17.1.1743/44[B] *Astrea* (20) Armed Storeship; **Captain**; 27.8.1744-24.12.1748[P] *Mary Galley* (44); 15.6.1756 *Saint George* (90); 30.6.1756-3.10.1756 *Prince* (90); 29.11.1756[(ECH 23.9.1757)] *Hampton Court* (64); 21.9.1757-13.8.1760 *Vanguard* (68); 6.6.1758-27.7.1758 The Siege of Louisbourg; 13.8.1760-20.10.1762 Commodore *Vanguard* (68); 7.1.1762-10.2.1762 Operations against Martinique; **Rear Admiral of the Blue**; 21.10.1762-1764 *Vanguard* (68).

SWAYSLAND, HENRY

Dates: 19.11.1757 Died.
Family:
Service: **Lieutenant**; 27.4.1718[(4.11.1718)]-5.10.1719 3L *Hampton Court* (70); 11.1.1719/20-4.4.1720 2L *Buckingham* (70); 5.4.1720-19.1.1720/21 3L *Buckingham* (70); 20.1.1720/21-20.5.1721 4L *Buckingham* (70); 4.3.1723/24 2L *Argyll* (50); 21.11.1727[(28.5.1728)] 3L *Orford* (70); 9.2.1728/29 3L *Nassau* (70); 5.7.1731 1L *Suffolk* (70); 23.2.1733/34-8.4.1736[P] 2L *Namur* (90); 28.7.1738-7.12.1738[P] 1L *Tilbury* (60); 7.8.1739 1L *Dunkirk* (60); **Commander**; 11.7.1740 *Shark* (8) Sloop; **Captain**; 22.1.1740/41-10.5.1742 *Lively* (20); 3.6.1746-12.7.1748[P] *Launceston* (44); 9.8.1756 **Superannuated Rear Admiral**.

SYMES, THOMAS

Dates: 8.2.1795 Died.
Family:
Service: **Lieutenant**; 28.4.1757 4L *Buckingham* (68); 20.5.1757 3L *Dover* (44); 1.2.1758 2L *Dover* (44); 19.7.1758 3L *Dover* (44); 1.2.1759-15.3.1759 2L *Dover* (44); 26.1.1761 2L

Launceston (44); 29.3.1761-11.6.1761 Expedition against Belle-Isle; 7.8.1761-12.5.1763^{P} 1L *Launceston* (44).

SYMONDS, THOMAS

Dates: c.1720 Born; 15.5.1792 Will Probate; 25.5.1792 Died.

Family:

Service: 23.11.1744 Adm Serv *Cornwall* (80); 25.12.1746 Mid *Lennox* (70); 25.3.1747 Action of March 25 1747; 21.8.1747 Mid *Cornwall* (80); 9.4.1748 Battle of Santiago de Cuba; 12.10.1748 Battle of Havana; 14.11.1748 Mid *Lennox* (70); 24.4.1749 Able *Fougueux* (64); 30.6.1749 Mid *Monarch* (74); 17.5.1750 Able *Rainbow* (44); 13.2.1750/51 Passed; **Lieutenant**; 22.1.1755 L. *Unicorn* (24); 6.2.1755 4L *Elizabeth* (70); 16.12.1755-13.11.1756 3L *Elizabeth* (70); 15.11.1756-17.12.1756 2L *Royal George* (100); 25.1.1757-19.1.1758 3L *Grafton* (68); 8.1757-10.1757 Louisbourg Expedition; 17.4.1758 1L *Emerald* (28); 19.2.1760$^{(BLI\ 22.7.1760)}$-5.8.1760^{P} 4L *Berwick* (64); **Commander**; 18.2.1762-9.8.1762 *Albany* (14) Sloop; **Captain**; 18.1.1771 *Sandwich* (90); 22.2.1771 *Captain* (64); 25.7.1775 *Solebay* (28); 1.6.1780-10.10.1781^{S} *Charon* (44); 28.11.1782 *Diadem* (64); 28.3.1783-17.3.1786^{P} *Diadem* (64).

SYMONS, JOHN

Dates: c.1732 Born; 16.12.1799 Died.

Family:

Service: 23.9.1747 Able *Expedition* (44); 10.4.1749 Ord. *Culloden* (74); 11.5.1750 Able *Rainbow* (44); 31.7.1751 Mid *Rainbow* (44); 12.5.1752 Mid *Jason* (44); 14.11.1753 Passed; **Lieutenant**; 24.4.1755 3L *Defiance* (60); 7.5.1755 L. *Otter* (14) Sloop; 19.2.1756 3L *Swiftsure* (68); 25.5.1757 1L *Unicorn* (28); 3.7.1759 Bombardment of Le Havre; **Commander**; 15.1.1761-12.5.1763^{P} *Mortar* (14) Bomb Vessel; 24.10.1766-26.10.1769 *Pomona* (18) Sloop; **Captain**; 28.1.1771 *Northumberland* (68); 25.8.1773$^{(1.6.1775)}$-26.5.1775^{P} *Buckingham* (68); 25.7.1775-5.8.1778^{B} *Cerberus* (28); 6.12.1776-8.12.1776 Occupation of Rhode Island; 20.10.1779 *Brune* (32); 23.5.1780$^{(BLI\ 22.8.1781)}$ *Ajax* (74); 29.4.1781-30.4.1781 Battle of Fort Royal; 3.5.1781$^{(BLI\ 17.10.1781)}$ *Sandwich* (90); 27.7.1781$^{(BLI\ 24.1.1782)}$ *Gibraltar* (80); 9.11.1781-15.7.1783 *Formidable* (98); 12.4.1782 Battle of the Saintes; 12.4.1782$^{(BLI\ 2.12.1782)}$ *Resolution* (74); 12.7.1782$^{(BLI\ 9.7.1783)}$-28.6.1783^{P} *Warrior* (74); 12.4.1794 **Rear Admiral of the Blue**; 4.7.1794 **Rear Admiral of the Red**; 1.6.1795 **Vice Admiral of the Blue**; 14.2.1799 **Vice Admiral of the Red.**

Service Records T

TAAFF, JOHN
Dates: c.1719 Born; 19.9.1773 Died.
Family:
Service: 5.1.1737/38 Able *Gloucester* (50); 17.12.1740 Able *Adventure* (40); 26.12.1740 Able *Prince Frederick* (70); 7.1.1740/41 Action of January 7 1741; 4.3.1740/41-5.1741 Operations against Cartagena; 31.7.1741 Able *Victory* (100); 25.4.1742 Mid *Victory* (100); 7.4.1743 Mid *Princess Mary* (60); 26.6.1743 Mid *Victory* (100); 7.6.1744 Passed; **Lieutenant**; 23.11.1744 6L *Royal Sovereign* (104); 19.12.1744-28.3.1745[C] 3L *Anglesea* (44); 28.3.1745 Anglesea vs Apollon; 16.8.1748[(13.12.1748)]-14.11.1748[P] 2L *Nassau* (70); 18.4.1755-9.1755 LCmdr *Elizabeth* Hired Tender; 1.4.1756-12.1756 Lieutenant *Providence* Hired Tender; 22.5.1758-2.12.1758 L. *Bideford* (20); 17.6.1762-25.1.1763[P] 1L *Prince* (90).

TAITE, PETER
Dates: c.1733 Born; 27.3.1830 Died.
Family:
Service: 1751-1755 Merchant Service; 20.7.1755 Mid *Gibraltar* (20); 20.12.1756 Mate *Gibraltar* (20); 10.3.1757 Master *Gibraltar* (20); 3.10.1757 Mate *Pallas* (36); 5.6.1758-12.6.1758 Raid on Saint-Malo; 9.8.1758 Passed; **Lieutenant**; 27.10.1758 L. *Seahorse* (24); 29.8.1759[(16.6.1760)] 3L *Alcide* (64); 22.10.1759[(16.6.1760)] L. *Cormorant* (8) Fireship; 22.2.1760-14.1.1763[P] 2L *Windsor* (60); 6.12.1763-12.12.1766 1L *Rippon* (60); 7.5.1782-20.1.1784[P] LCmdr *Bountiful* (24) Storeship; 1.8.1800 **Superannuated Commander**.

TALBOT, GEORGE
Dates: c.1730 Born; 1787 Died.
Family: Wife Mary (c.1732-1819); Son Francis (d.1738).
Service: 25.10.1744-26.11.1745[P] Able *Torbay* (80); 22.1.1746/47 Able *Lichfield* (50); 16.8.1747 Mid *Lichfield* (50); 27.1.1749/50 Able *Hazard* (8) Sloop; 17.2.1750/51 Mid *Hazard* (8) Sloop; 16.5.1751 Able *Hazard* (8) Sloop; 7.2.1751/52 Able *Bristol* (50); 12.10.1752 Mid *Assistance* (50); 1.5.1754 Passed; **Lieutenant**; 19.2.1756 3L *Bristol* (50); 31.3.1756 2L *Bristol* (50); 5.9.1757[(2.3.1758)] 2L *Winchester* (50); 16.1.1759-19.1.1759 Attack on Martinique; 20.1.1759-1.5.1759 Capture of Guadeloupe; 17.4.1761[(2.3.1758)] 1L *Winchester* (50); **Commander**; 19.5.1761 *Proserpine* (8) Fireship; 12.8.1763-25.8.1766 *Wasp* (8) Sloop; 20.1.1768-27.1.1770[W] *Jamaica* (10) Sloop; **Captain**; 26.5.1768-1.3.1770 *Aldborough* (20); 10.12.1770 *Lively* (20); 11.10.1773[(29.6.1774)]-18.4.1774[P] *Active* (28); 14.7.1775-8.10.1777 *Niger* (32); 11.1.1779-19.5.1782 *Worcester* (64); 17.2.1782 Battle of Sadras; 12.4.1782 Battle of Providien.

TATHAM, THOMAS
Dates: c.1734 Born; c.1781 Died; 6.2.1781 Will Probate.
Family:

Service: 1750-1756 Merchant Service; 13.7.1756 Mid *Lowestoffe* (24); 12.1.1757 Able *Lowestoffe* (28); 6.2.1757 Mid *Lowestoffe* (28); 27.10.1757 Mate *Lowestoffe* (28); 5.6.1758-12.6.1758 Raid on Saint-Malo; 5.9.1759 Passed; **Lieutenant**; 10.9.1759-4.7.1763 L. *Savage* (8) Sloop; 24.8.1779-31.8.1781[P] 1L *Endymion* (44).

TATHWELL, JOSEPH

Dates: 1788 Died; 8.5.1788 Will Probate.

Family:

Service: **Lieutenant**; 19.6.1756-29.1.1757 L. *Dolphin* (24); 23.4.1757 L. *Wasp* (8) Sloop; 10.4.1758-11.1.1759 3L *Shrewsbury* (74); 5.6.1758-12.6.1758 Raid on Saint-Malo; 4.3.1760 1L *Boreas* (28); 26.4.1760[(18.6.1762)]-16.12.1762[P] 5L *Cambridge* (80); 6.6.1762-13.8.1762 Operations against Havana; 11.5.1763 1L *Essex* (64); 23.5.1763-26.5.1766 1L *Yarmouth* (64); 18.4.1771 2L *Cambridge* (80); 10.5.1771 1L *Royal Oak* (74); **Commander**; 25.6.1773 *Spy* (10) Sloop; 25.9.1776-20.9.1777[P] *Kent* (20) Hired Armed Ship; 8.10.1777 *Leviathan* (68); 13.10.1778-24.11.1778 *Swift* (14) Sloop.

TATTUM, JOHN

Dates: 24.9.1762 Died.

Family:

Service: **Lieutenant**; 27.10.1757[(25.8.1758)] L. *Mediterranean* (12) Xebec; 1.4.1758[(25.8.1758)]-5.3.1759[P] 3L *Hampton Court* (64); 20.6.1759 4L *Foudroyant* (80); 27.7.1759 5L *Foudroyant* (80); 21.3.1760 4L *Foudroyant* (80); 1.4.1760 3L *Foudroyant* (80); 7.1.1762-10.2.1762 Operations against Martinique; 3.3.1762-24.9.1762[W] L. *Badger* (10) Sloop.

TAYLOR, JOHN

Dates: c.1731 Born.

Family:

Service: 1749-1750 HEIC Service; 26.11.1750 Capt Serv *Devonshire* (66); 26.1.1750/51 Able *Devonshire* (66); 28.9.1751 Able *Monmouth* (70); 15.3.1753 Able *Intrepid* (64); 18.8.1753 Mid *Ruby* (50); 8.10.1754 Able *Culloden* (74); 28.10.1754 Mid *Culloden* (74); 4.2.1755 Mid *Yarmouth* (64); 5.5.1756 Passed; **Lieutenant**; 2.5.1759 L. *Rose* (20); 15.5.1759-4.4.1760 6L *Sandwich* (90); 9.11.1759-24.11.1760[P] LCmdr *Barrington* Tender; 14.6.1762-6.9.1762 4L *Duke* (90); 6.9.1762-25.1.1763[P] 5L *Prince* (90).

TAYLOR, MICHAEL

Dates: 30.10.1758 Died.

Family:

Service: **Lieutenant**; 10.1.1740/41 L. *Deptford* (24) Storeship; 1.12.1748-22.4.1752 2L *Intrepid* (64).

TAYLOR, POLYCARPUS

Dates: 1780 Died Durham.

Family:

Service: **Lieutenant**; 4.5.1733[(26.8.1735)]-10.4.1738 L. *Wolf* (8) Sloop; 21.6.1739-26.7.1740 2L *Augusta* (60); 3.10.1740 1L *Russell* (80); 19.6.1741[(12.7.1743)] 4L *Boyne* (80); 6.10.1741[(12.7.1743)] 3L *Boyne* (80); 6.2.1741/42[(12.7.1743)]-25.6.1742 1L *Boyne* (80); **Captain**; 2.5.1743[(20.7.1744)] *Fowey* (40); 23.6.1743[(JAM 9.6.1749)]-29.7.1744[P] *Basilisk* (8) Bomb Vessel; 27.8.1744 *Fowey* (44); 3.11.1747[(JAM 23.3.1749/50)] *Warwick* (60); 29.1.1747/48[(JAM 23.3.1749/50)]-23.6.1748 *Elizabeth* (70); 9.4.1748 Battle of

Santiago de Cuba; 29.10.1748[JAM 23.3.1749/50]-12.12.1749[P] *Rippon* (54); 7.6.1756 *Culloden* (74); 3.10.1756[ECH 25.1.1757]-25.1.1758 *Deptford* (50); 6.12.1762 **Superannuated Rear Admiral**.

TAYLOR, ROBERT

Dates: c.1714 Born.
Family:
Service: 23.12.1730 Vol-p-O *Bideford* (20); 26.9.1733 Able *Flamborough* (20); 8.8.1736 Mid *Monmouth* (70); 15.8.1737 Mid *Windsor* (60); 21.8.1738 Able *Lennox* (70); 25.8.1738 Mate *Lennox* (70); 4.10.1739 Passed; **Lieutenant**; 13.3.1739/40 4L *Orford* (70); 8.4.1740 Capture of the Princesa; 7.1.1740/41 Action of January 7 1741; 1.6.1742 2L *Leopard* (50); 7.12.1747-18.12.1748[P] 1L *Penzance* (44); 2.1.1755-4.3.1757 1L *Captain* (64); 20.5.1756 Battle of Minorca; 28.4.1757 3L *Ramillies* (90); 5.9.1757-6.10.1757 Raid on Rochefort; 26.4.1758 2L *Ramillies* (90); 5.6.1758-12.6.1758 Raid on Saint-Malo; 11.10.1758 1L *Ramillies* (90); **Commander**; 21.9.1759-27.12.1759[P] *Arthur* Hired Unknown.

TAYLOR, SAMUEL

Dates: 17.2.1790 Died.
Family:
Service: **Lieutenant**; 7.7.1745[MED 11.11.1747] 4L *Dorsetshire* (80); 9.9.1745[MED 11.11.1747]-10.5.1747[P] 4L *Lennox* (70); 3.8.1746 Action of August 3 1746; 25.3.1747 Action of March 25 1747; 13.12.1756 3L *Royal Sovereign* (104); **Commander**; 2.3.1759-14.3.1760 *Speedwell* (8) Sloop.

TAYLOR, THOMAS

Dates: 1721 Born; 21.4.1797 Died.
Family: Son Thomas, RN.
Service: 22.7.1745 Passed; **Lieutenant**; 29.11.1745 L. *Fly* (8) Sloop; 15.10.1746[NA 12.5.1749] 3L *Canterbury* (60); 28.11.1746-18.4.1747[P] 6L *Sandwich* (90); 30.6.1747[JAM 12.5.1749] 2L *Canterbury* (60); 3.11.1747[JAM 12.5.1749] 3L *Warwick* (60); 23.12.1747-23.9.1748 3L *Anson* (60); **Commander**; 17.8.1756-8.3.1757 *Badger* (10) Sloop; **Captain**; 2.5.1757 *Seahorse* (24); 18.10.1758-27.10.1761 *Griffin* (28); 27.2.1771-13.3.1771 *Orford* (68).

TAYLOR, WITTEWRONGE

Dates: c.1719 Born; 15.2.1760 Died Bolt Head.
Family: Father Revd Thomas Taylor; Mother Mary Wittewronge; Wife Catherine Vincent (1737-1803) married 28.9.1756.
Service: 3.9.1741 Passed; **Lieutenant**; 7.9.1741-16.12.1743 6L *Duke* (90); 3.2.1743/44 6L *Saint George* (90); 29.3.1744 5L *Saint George* (90); 12.4.1744 4L *Saint George* (90); 21.6.1744-6.12.1744 3L *Saint George* (90); 6.12.1744 MidE *Cornwall* (80); 16.5.1746[25.4.1749] 4L *Cornwall* (80); 9.4.1748 Battle of Santiago de Cuba; 12.10.1748 Battle of Havana; **Commander**; 1.11.1748-6.5.1749[P] *Weazle* (16) Sloop; 11.3.1755 *Raven* (14) Sloop; **Captain**; 16.12.1755 *Monarch* (74); 16.4.1756 *Magnanime* (74); 3.6.1757-30.1.1758 *Royal William* (84); 5.9.1757-6.10.1757 Raid on Rochefort; 15.2.1758-15.2.1760[W] *Ramillies* (90); 5.6.1758-12.6.1758 Raid on Saint-Malo.

TEAGUE, WILLIAM

Dates: c.1728 Born.
Family:
Service: 15.8.1749 Able *Lion* (58); 28.9.1751 Cox *Swan* (14) Sloop; 9.7.1752 Able *Swan* (14) Sloop; 24.11.1754 Mate *Centaur* (20); 1.3.1755 Mate *Nightingale* (22); 20.1.1756 Mid *Somerset*

(68); 9.4.1756 Mate *Somerset* (68); 6.6.1757 Passed; 16.4.1759 L. *Penquin* (20); 26.4.1759 **Lieutenant**; 9.6.1760-27.4.1763 4L *Centaur* (74); 6.6.1762-13.8.1762 Operations against Havana.

TEALE, RICHARD

Dates: c.1719 Born; 4.11.1798 Died.
Family:
Service: 28.2.1733/34 Scholar *Royal Naval Academy*; 14.7.1736 Able *Blandford* (20); 14.11.1738-13.12.1740[P] Mid *Blandford* (20); 28.10.1741 Mid *Dover* (44); 22.10.1742 Mate *Squirrel* (20); 18.7.1743 Passed; **Lieutenant**; 7.12.1743 L. *Fly* (8) Sloop; 14.3.1743/44-26.3.1745 3L *Chester* (50); 19.2.1756 1L *Swiftsure* (68); 28.2.1758 Battle of Cartagena; 18.8.1759-19.8.1759 Battle of Lagos Bay; 20.11.1759 Battle of Quiberon Bay; **Commander**; 5.3.1760-7.4.1762 *Gramont* (18) Sloop; **Captain**; 7.1762-20.1.1763[P] *Swiftsure* (68).

TEAPE, JAMES

Dates: c.1723 Born; c.1755 Died; 15.5.1755 Will Probate.
Family:
Service: 11.10.1739 Mid *York* (60); 10.7.1740 Mid *Buckingham* (70); 29.9.1740 Mid *Torbay* (80); 19.4.1742 Mate *Torbay* (80); 15.1.1743/44 Able *Namur* (90); 11.2.1743/44-12.2.1743/44 Battle of Toulon; 19.10.1744-23.1.1744/45[P] Mid *Namur* (90); 8.5.1745 Mid *Sandwich* (90); 7.10.1745 Mid *Glasgow* (20); 10.1.1745/46 Passed; **Lieutenant**; 12.2.1745/46-15.8.1748[P] 3L *Advice* (50); 11.5.1754[(JAM 9.10.1754)]-6.11.1754[P] L. *Sphinx* (24).

TEMPLE, HENRY

Dates: c.1740 Born.
Family:
Service: 19.10.1755 Able *Ludlow Castle* (44); 22.8.1756 Mid *Ludlow Castle* (44); 2.10.1758 Able *Brilliant* (36); 10.4.1759 Mid *Brilliant* (36); 3.7.1759 Bombardment of Le Havre; 28.2.1760 Action of February 28 1760; 9.12.1761 Passed; **Lieutenant**; 14.6.1762-19.2.1763[P] 6L *Duke* (90).

TEMPLE, WILLIAM THOMAS

Dates: 15.7.1768 Died.
Family:
Service: **Lieutenant**; 4.4.1720-28.5.1720 3L *Defiance* (60).

THOMAS, JAMES

Dates: c.1714 Born; 1772 Died; 18.4.1772 Will Probate.
Family:
Service: 1.6.1737 Ord. *Norfolk* (80); 29.8.1737 Able *Exeter* (60); 27.10.1737 Able *Newcastle* (50); 30.9.1739 Mid *Saint Albans* (50); 27.5.1740 Mate *Saint Albans* (50); 10.10.1741 Mid *Rupert* (60); 10.1.1742 Mate *Hound* (8) Sloop; 26.3.1742-18.9.1743[W] Master *Bridgewater* (20); 7.6.1744 Passed; **Lieutenant**; 12.5.1759[(BLI 27.11.1759)]-14.7.1759 3L *Panther* (60); 30.11.1770 4L *Royal Oak* (74); 11.12.1770 3L *Royal Oak* (74); 9.1.1771-10.5.1771 2L *Royal Oak* (74).

THOMAS, RICHARD

Dates: 5.9.1758 Died.
Family:
Service: 4.4.1700-27.11.1703[W] Vol-p-O *Eagle* (10) Advice Boat; **Lieutenant**; 20.1.1708/9[(15.11.1709)]-29.1.1710/11 3L *Essex* (70); **Commander**; 11.1.1727/28-18.9.1731[P] *Hawk* (8) Sloop.

THOMAS, RICHARD

Dates: Not Known.
Family:
Service: **Lieutenant**; 1.10.1756-3.5.1759 L. *Badger* (10) Sloop; 14.5.1759-24.5.1761[P] 1L *Vengeance* (28); 20.11.1759 Battle of Quiberon Bay.

THOMAS, WILLIAM

Dates: c.1737 Born; 2.10.1800 Died; 10.8.1801 Will Probate.
Family: Wife Ann.
Service: 27.11.1754 Able *Gibraltar* (20); 7.1.1756 Mid *Gibraltar* (20); 5.11.1756 Able *Vanguard* (68); 14.12.1756 Mid *Vanguard* (68); 10.6.1757 Mid *America* (60); 5.9.1757-6.10.1757 Raid on Rochefort; 18.8.1759-19.8.1759 Battle of Lagos Bay; 1.5.1760 Mate *Swiftsure* (68); 3.12.1760 Passed; **Lieutenant**; 2.2.1762[(24.4.1764)]-14.5.1764[P] 2L *Stag* (32); 8.11.1770 4L *Terrible* (74); 9.9.1773-21.9.1773 4L *Ramillies* (74); 8.4.1776-19.9.1777 L. *Wolf* (8) Sloop; 17.7.1778 2L *Royal George* (100); 19.11.1778 2L *Queen* (90); 22.2.1779 4L *Europe* (64); **Commander**; 8.3.1780[(NA 21.5.1781)]-7.10.1780[W] *Hope* (14) Sloop; 21.12.1782-25.4.1783[P] *Fairy* (14) Sloop; 1.5.1783-13.5.1786[P] *Fairy* (14) Sloop.

THOMPSON, BRADWARDEN

Dates: 15.2.1756 Died.
Family:
Service: **Lieutenant**; 22.6.1728[(8.10.1728)] 3L *Diamond* (40); 21.2.1728/29-29.7.1730 3L *Argyll* (50); 30.1.1730/31 3L *York* (60); 24.1.1731/32-4.10.1732 3L *Rupert* (60); 13.4.1733[(4.9.1735)]-5.9.1735[P] 2L *Kingston* (60); 23.2.1737/38 1L *Chatham* (50); 14.4.1738 3L *Somerset* (80); **Commander**; 1.11.1739[(10.3.1743/44)] *Mercury* (8) Fireship; 17.12.1739[(10.3.1743/44)]-16.1.1739/40 *Duke* (8) Fireship; **Captain**; 15.7.1740-31.10.1742 *Success* (20).

THOMPSON, SIR CHARLES (1ST BARONET VIRKEES)

Dates: 1740 Born; 23.6.1797 1st Baronet Virkees; 17.3.1799 Died Fareham.
Family: Father? Norborne Berkeley; Mother Margaret Thompson; Wife Jane Selby; Son Norborne Charles (1785–1826); Son Charles Robert (1788–1801); Daughter Elizabeth (1790-?); Daughter Jane (1794–1815); Son Henry (1796–1868); Sister Elizabeth.
Service: 1754-1755 Merchant Service; 13.6.1755 Capt Serv *Nassau* (64); 22.6.1756 Capt Serv *Prince Frederick* (64); 12.3.1757 Mid *Prince Frederick* (64); 22.3.1758 Mid *Achilles* (60); 3.7.1759 Bombardment of Le Havre; 3.12.1760 Passed; **Lieutenant**; 16.1.1761 5L *Arrogant* (74); 12.8.1763-14.7.1768[P] L. *Cygnet* (18) Sloop; 31.5.1770 1L *Salisbury* (50); **Commander**; 14.2.1771[(NA 30.11.1770)]-28.5.1771[P] *Senegal* (14) Sloop; **Captain**; 7.3.1772 *Chatham* (50); 2.11.1772[(Leeward Islands 31.3.1774)]-23.8.1774[P] *Crescent* (32) Frigate; 25.8.1775 *Boreas* (28); 6.7.1779 Battle of Grenada; 20.10.1780[(BLI 14.10.1782)]-14.7.1783[P] *Alcide* (74); 29.4.1781-30.4.1781 Battle of Fort Royal; 5.9.1781 Battle of the Chesapeake; 25.1.1782-26.1.1782 Battle of Saint Kitts; 12.4.1782 Battle of the Saintes; 23.1.1787 *Edgar* (74); 14.6.1790-1.12.1790[P] *Elephant* (74); 1.2.1793-9.1.1794 *Vengeance* (74); 12.4.1794 **Rear Admiral of the Blue**; 14.5.1794-6.11.1794

Vanguard (74); 4.7.1794 **Rear Admiral of the White**; 1.6.1795 **Vice Admiral of the Blue**; 1796 *London* (90); 18.1.1796-9.3.1798 *Saint George* (98); 1797-2.1798 *Britannia* (100); 14.2.1797 2nd Battle of Cape St Vincent; 10.1797-12.1798 *Prince George* (98); 14.2.1799 **Vice Admiral of the Red.**

THOMPSON, EDWARD

Dates: c.1737 Born; 1787 Died.
Family:
Service: 1751-1755 Merchant Service; 16.11.1755 Mid *Stirling Castle* (64); 16.11.1757 Passed; **Lieutenant**; 26.11.1757 3L *Jason* (30); 25.5.1758 4L *Dorsetshire* (68); 19.6.1759 3L *Dorsetshire* (68); 20.11.1759 Battle of Quiberon Bay; 23.2.1760 3L *Bellona* (74); 23.12.1760-11.3.1761 2L *Bellona* (74); 7.1.1762-19.1.1763[P] 1L *Bellona* (74); 2.8.1766-10.6.1769 LCmdr *Tartuffe* (6) Cutter; **Commander**; 10.1.1771-24.6.1771 *Kingfisher* (14) Sloop; 29.8.1771 *Raven* (14) Sloop; **Captain**; 7.4.1772[(MED 6.6.1772)]-22.7.1772[P] *Niger* (32); 13.1.1778-17.5.1782[P] *Hyaena* (24); 19.7.1783-27.3.1786 *Grampus* (50).

THOMPSON, EDWARD

Dates: c.1737 Born.
Family:
Service: 18.6.1751 Capt Serv *Seahorse* (24); 13.8.1751 Able *Seahorse* (24); 14.11.1753 Mid *Seahorse* (24); 9.12.1755 Mate *Seahorse* (24); 9.7.1756 Able *Chatham* (6) Yacht; 6.8.1756 Mid *Chatham* (6) Yacht; 15.6.1757-4.7.1757 Mid *Royal Anne* (100); 4.7.1759 Passed; **Lieutenant**; 13.8.1762[(EI 29.7.1763)]-22.7.1763[P] 4L *Belleisle* (64).

THOMPSON, SAMUEL

Dates: 13.8.1718 Born; 13.8.1813 Died Titchfield, Hampshire; 9.12.1813 Will Probate.
Family:
Service: 1739 Able *Cumberland* (8) Fireship; **Lieutenant**; 25.7.1744[(14.2.1748/49)] L. *Experiment* (20); 20.3.1744/45[(11.4.1749)] 4L *Prince of Orange* (70); 25.5.1745[(11.4.1749)]-10.7.1745 3L *Prince of Orange* (70); 29.1.1746/47[(JAM 11.4.1749)]-29.1.1747/48 3L *Strafford* (58); 6.2.1755 2L *Elizabeth* (70); 16.12.1755 1L *Elizabeth* (70); 29.3.1756-5.1.1757 2L *Grafton* (68); **Commander**; 14.2.1757-9.12.1757[P] *Jamaica* (10) Sloop; 8.1757-10.1757 Louisbourg Expedition; 1758-1760 Regulating Officer at Southampton; **Captain**; 4.11.1760-6.1.1763[P] *Flamborough* (20); 29.3.1761-11.6.1761 Expedition against Belle-Isle; 27.3.1763-17.2.1766 *Lark* (32); 5.1766-12.12.1766 *Triumph* (74); 12.12.1766-9.1.1770 *Rippon* (60); 10.10.1771-31.3.1775 *Levant* (28); 13.2.1776 *Conquestador* (60); 5.5.1779-30.7.1783[P] *America* (64); 16.3.1781 Battle of Cape Henry; 5.9.1781 Battle of the Chesapeake; 25.1.1782-26.1.1782 Battle of Saint Kitts; 12.4.1782 Battle of the Saintes; 23.5.1788 **Superannuated Rear Admiral.**

THORNBROUGH, EDWARD

Dates: c.1712 Born; 1784 Died.
Family: Wife Mary; Son Sir Edward, RN (1754-1834).
Service: **Lieutenant**; 6.6.1744-22.10.1744 L. *Hawk* (8) Sloop; 7.11.1744-21.9.1749[P] 1L *Winchester* (50); 25.6.1746 1st Battle of Negapatam; 13.6.1751-15.11.1752[P] 2L *Culloden* (74); 16.1.1753 2L *Augusta* (60); 29.3.1753-29.1.1759 1L *Northumberland* (68); 8.1757-10.1757 Louisbourg Expedition; 6.6.1758-27.7.1758 The Siege of Louisbourg; 16.1.1761-19.8.1763[P] 1L *Arrogant* (74); 6.10.1763 1L *Firm* (74); 19.11.1767-25.1.1771 1L *Temeraire* (74); 18.1.1771 1L

Sandwich (90); 25.2.1771 2L *Captain* (64); **Commander**; 15.4.1774[1.8.1775]-7.6.1776 *Tamar* (16) Sloop; 13.10.1774 L. *Falcon* (14) Sloop.

THOROWGOOD, DYNES

Dates: c.1737 Baptised.
Family: Father Thomas Thorowgood; Mother Elizabeth.
Service: 8.11.1752 Able *Sphinx* (24); 24.8.1754 Able *Wager* (24); 5.2.1755 Mid *Hind* (24); 11.6.1756 Mid *Sphinx* (24); 29.3.1757 Mate *Sphinx* (24); 22.10.1757-3.10.1759 Mid *Augusta* (60); 3.10.1759 Passed; **Lieutenant**; 18.10.1759-11.8.1764[P] 3L *America* (60); 24.9.1762-6.10.1762 Battle of Manilla.

THOROWGOOD, SELBY

Dates: c.1728 Born.
Family:
Service: 18.9.1742 Capt Serv *Worcester* (60); 27.5.1744 Ord. *Stirling Castle* (70); 15.8.1747 Able *Stirling Castle* (70); 8.6.1748 Mid *Burford* (70); 13.3.1749/50 Mid *Unicorn* (24); 13.2.1750/51 Passed; **Lieutenant**; 30.1.1759[JAM 16.4.1760] 3L *Assistance* (50); 28.6.1759[JAM 11.12.1760] 4L *Edinburgh* (64); 19.10.1759[JAM 11.12.1760] 3L *Edinburgh* (64); 19.11.1760-20.3.1763[P] 1L *Adventure* (32); 29.3.1761-11.6.1761 Expedition against Belle-Isle.

THORPE, JAMES

Dates: c.1722 Born; 22.1.1798 Died.
Family:
Service: 1739-1744 Merchant Service; 19.8.1744 Mid *Monmouth* (70); 6.11.1746 Passed; **Lieutenant**; 15.1.1746/47-17.8.1748[P] 3L *Dover* (44); 3.3.1748/49 3L *Rainbow* (44); 6.2.1755 3L *Chichester* (68); 1.6.1756 2L *Chichester* (68); 22.5.1758-22.10.1761 1L *Chichester* (68); 5.6.1758-12.6.1758 Raid on Saint-Malo; 20.11.1759 Battle of Quiberon Bay; 29.3.1761-11.6.1761 Expedition against Belle-Isle; 8.1762-1763 Agent for Transports; **Commander**; 26.8.1762-7.6.1763[P] *Esk* Hired Transport.

TIDDEMAN, MARK

Dates: c.1698 Born; 1772 Died; 29.1.1773 Will Probate.
Family:
Service: 20.1.1710/11 Vol-p-O *Nassau* (70); 18.8.1712 Ord. *Severn* (54); 28.9.1712 Vol-p-O *Severn* (54); 1.7.1713 Ord. *Greenwich* (54); 15.1.1713/14-15.3.1714/15 Able *Greenwich* (54); 16.3.1714/15-15.4.1716[P] Mid *Greenwich* (54); 13.4.1721-12.2.1721/22[P] Mid *Worcester* (54); 12.9.1725-21.1.1726/27[P] Mate *Cumberland* (80); 17.6.1735 Passed; **Lieutenant**; 27.3.1741-9.9.1741 L. *Drake* (8) Sloop; 26.5.1742-31.12.1742 4L *Revenge* (70).

TIDDEMAN, RICHARD

Dates: 7.10.1762 Died Manila.
Family: Wife Rebecca.
Service: 19.4.1721-7.12.1721 Vol-p-O *Cumberland* (80); 8.12.1721-2.9.1723 Vol-p-O *Elizabeth* (70); 3.9.1723 Mid *Lyme* (20); 3.8.1728 Mid *Advice* (54); 16.4.1729 Passed; **Lieutenant**; 21.7.1732[30.10.1733]-3.5.1734 L. *Wolf* (8) Sloop; 31.5.1734-10.8.1735 4L *Princess Amelia* (80); 11.8.1735[21.7.1736]-20.11.1737 3L *Revenge* (70); 21.11.1737-23.4.1742[P] L. *Phoenix* (20); 4.1740-5.7.1740 Attack on St. Augustine; 23.3.1742/43 1L *Superb* (60); **Commander**; 1.7.1744[JAM 2.11.1745] *Fame* (12) Sloop; 4.9.1744[JAM 2.11.1745] *Ludlow Castle* (44); **Captain**; 9.3.1744/45[BLI 2.11.1745]

Superb (60); 24.6.1745(BLI 2.11.1745) *Eltham* (40); 9.1748-10.1748 Siege of Pondicherry; 9.10.1748(EI 11.5.1750)-16.5.1750[P] *Harwich* (50); 18.1.1758 *Grafton* (68); 20.2.1759(EI 1.3.1763)-6.6.1761 *Elizabeth* (64); 10.9.1759 Battle of Pondicherry; 1761-7.10.1762 Commodore *Elizabeth* (64); 24.9.1762-6.10.1762 Battle of Manilla.

TILLY, THOMAS
Dates: None Known.
Family:
Service: **Lieutenant**; 29.8.1759-10.9.1759 L. *Savage* (8) Sloop; 19.2.1771-28.8.1771 L. *Cruizer* (8) Sloop; 15.11.1776-7.4.1777 1L *Conquestador* (60); 11.9.1779-7.10.1779 1L *Ajax* (74).

TINDALL, GEORGE
Dates: 1777 Died.
Family:
Service: 23.4.1741 **Lieutenant**; 25.4.1741 L. *Success* (8) Fireship; 7.9.1742 3L *Woolwich* (50); 21.2.1742/43 2L *Woolwich* (50); 27.7.1744(JAM 2.9.1746) L. *Deal Castle* (20); 4.9.1744(JAM 2.9.1746) 2L *Superb* (60); 28.10.1744(JAM 2.9.1746)-13.3.1744/45 1L *Superb* (60); **Commander**; 11.3.1744/45(BLI 6.9.1746) *Ludlow Castle* (44); 24.12.1746-23.5.1748 *Porcupine* (16) Sloop; 13.2.1753 *Ranger* (8) Sloop; **Captain**; 18.10.1758-2.2.1763[P] *Deal Castle* (20).

TINKER, JOHN BLADEN
Dates: c.1725 Born; 19.7.1767 Died.
Family:
Service: 15.6.1741 Ord. *Barfleur* (90); 7.5.1743 Mid *Dartmouth* (50); 10.3.1743/44 Mid *Berwick* (70); 24.3.1744/45 Mid *Roebuck* (44); 12.8.1745 Mid *Marlborough* (90); 3.12.1745 Mid *Russell* (80); 2.3.1745/46 Passed; 4.3.1745/46-10.8.1746 4L *Royal Oak* (70); 29.4.1747-14.9.1747 Vol. *Adventure* (44); 10.12.1747-11.3.1747/48 Mate *Gore* Mer; **Lieutenant**; 25.12.1748(JAM 21.4.1749)-9.5.1749[P] 3L *Canterbury* (60); 10.6.1752-17.4.1754 L. *Falcon* (10) Bomb Vessel; 28.1.1755 2L *Saint George* (90); 11.11.1755 1L *Saint George* (90); 24.5.1756 1L *Namur* (90); 5.6.1756 1L *Ramillies* (90); **Captain**; 4.7.1756(ECH 5.4.1757)-9.9.1756 *Experiment* (24); 28.11.1756(21.3.1757)-1.2.1757 *Trident* (64); 23.4.1757 *Dover* (44); 18.10.1758 *Argo* (28); 28.12.1759-23.8.1765[P] *Medway* (60).

TOBY, RICHARD
Dates: c.1717 Born; c.5.1773 Died; 26.5.1773 Will Probate.
Family: Son Richard James Walter, RN.
Service: 16.4.1739 Able *Dragon* (60); 24.4.1741 Mid *Dragon* (60); 24.7.1741 Action of 1741-07-24; 11.2.1743/44-12.2.1743/44 Battle of Toulon; 21.1.1744/45 Mid *Dragon* (60); 11.2.1745/46 Passed; **Lieutenant**; 23.7.1748(24.3.1748/49)-1.8.1748 3L *Norwich* (50); 22.7.1752-15.11.1752[P] 4L *Culloden* (74); 19.2.1754-25.2.1756 4L *Kent* (64); 11.1.1756-14.1.1756 Capture of Geriah; **Commander**; 11.3.1756(19.10.1757)-23.7.1756 *Kingfisher* (14) Sloop; 14.11.1770-20.12.1770 *Peggy* (8) Sloop; 21.10.1772-4.4.1773[P] *Wasp* (8) Sloop.

TODD, ALEXANDER
Dates: c.1736 Born.
Family:
Service: 1752-1755 HEIC Service; 19.6.1755 Able *Nassau* (64); 12.8.1755 Mid *Nassau* (64); 26.2.1757 Mid *Colchester* (50); 23.4.1757 Mid *Marlborough* (80); 21.4.1758 Passed; **Lieutenant**;

6.10.1758 3L *Dunkirk* (60); 29.12.1758 Capture of Goree; 20.11.1759 Battle of Quiberon Bay; 1.4.1763-11.4.1763[P] 2L *Dunkirk* (60); 1.2.1800 **Superannuated Commander**.

TOLL, EDMUND

Dates: 1705 Born; 1.7.1767 Died; 8.4.1768 Will Probate.
Family: Father Ashburnham Toll; Mother Anne Newman; Son Ashburnham (d.1800); Daughter Mary [Bulley]; Daughter Jane [Aldridge]; Brother Ashburnham.
Service: 14.4.1728 Mid *Orford* (70); 11.12.1728 Mid *Lion* (60); 31.5.1729 Mid *Rippon* (60); 4.8.1729 Mid *Monmouth* (70); 5.4.1730 Able *Monmouth* (70); 26.5.1730 Mid *Looe* (42); 6.8.1732 Able *Dreadnought* (60); 11.2.1733/34 Mid *Pembroke* (60); 6.5.1734 Passed; **Lieutenant**; 24.5.1734-16.2.1735/36[P] 4L *Dorsetshire* (80); 16.5.1738-11.6.1739 2L *Oxford* (50); 12.6.1739-10.9.1739 4L *Princess Caroline* (80); 11.9.1739-20.4.1740 3L *Princess Caroline* (80); 21.4.1740-26.9.1740 2L *Princess Caroline* (80); 27.9.1740 2L *Lennox* (70); 16.1.1740/41 2L *Saint George* (90); 25.5.1742 1L *Saint George* (90); **Commander**; 20.3.1743/44 *Portsmouth* (24) Storeship; 31.3.1744-17.5.1744 *Grampus* (14) Sloop; **Captain**; 14.6.1744 *Phoenix* (20); 18.7.1744-27.9.1744 *Shoreham* (20); 12.4.1745-1.9.1746[P] *Dorsetshire* (80); 18.12.1747-4.3.1748/49[P] *Oxford* (50); 12.10.1748 Battle of Havana; 6.12.1762 **Superannuated Rear Admiral**.

TOMKINS, CHRISTOPHER

Dates: 1759 Died.
Family:
Service: **Lieutenant**; 18.10.1757[NA 10.2.1758]-1759[†] L. *Vulture* (14) Sloop.

TOMKYS, HOPE

Dates: c.1739 Born; 6.1766 Died; 12.6.1766 Buried Staffordshire.
Family: Wife Rachel Quartermain married 15.6.1765; Son Hope Dancastle (1766-1766).
Service: 1753-1757 Merchant Service; 28.4.1757 Able *Duke* (90); 24.4.1758 Mid *Chatham* (50); 17.11.1758 Mate *Chatham* (50); 3.7.1759 Bombardment of Le Havre; 20.11.1759 Battle of Quiberon Bay; 30.5.1760 Passed; **Lieutenant**; 23.12.1760-15.12.1762[P] 3L *Lion* (58); 29.3.1761-11.6.1761 Expedition against Belle-Isle.

TOMLINSON, ROBERT

Dates: c.1735 Born; 1813 Died; 20.12.1813 Will Probate.
Family: Son Robert, RN (d.1844); Son Philip, RN (d.1839); Son Nicholas, RN (1765-1847).
Service: 1751-1755 Merchant Service; 25.3.1755 Mid *Saint George* (90); 28.5.1756 Mid *Namur* (90); 12.6.1756 Able *Ramillies* (90); 12.7.1756 Mate *Ramillies* (90); 2.5.1757 Passed; **Lieutenant**; 19.1.1758-13.1.1759 3L *Medway* (60); 19.2.1760-15.3.1763[P] 1L *Lynn* (44); 29.3.1761-11.6.1761 Expedition against Belle-Isle; 23.1.1767-17.1.1770 LCmdr *Boscawen* (4) Cutter; 17.3.1770-19.4.1771[P] LCmdr *Kite* (4) Cutter; 30.11.1771 3L *Resolution* (74); 28.8.1772-3.12.1774 2L *Resolution* (74); 2.10.1782 1L *Standard* (64); **Commander**; 15.11.1782-25.2.1783[P] *Furnace* (8) Fireship; 25.10.1809 **Captain**.

TOMS, PETER

Dates: 20.2.1763 Died.
Family:
Service: 10.2.1709/10-27.6.1711[C] Vol-p-O *Advice* (48); 6.6.1712 Vol-p-O *Southsea Castle* (42); 18.8.1714 MidO *Southsea Castle* (42); 11.10.1715-5.9.1719[P] Mid *Scarborough* (32); 10.2.1720/21 Passed; **Lieutenant**; 5.10.1727 3L *Faversham* (42); 11.11.1727-9.9.1729[P] 2L

Faversham (42); 31.1.1733/34-3.4.1736[P] 3L *Torbay* (80); 28.7.1738 2L *Norwich* (50); 21.11.1739 Attack on Puerto Bello; 6.12.1739[(20.7.1742)] 1L *Anglesea* (40); 4.3.1740/41-5.1741 Operations against Cartagena; **Commander**; 27.7.1741-4.9.1741[P] *Saltash* (8) Sloop; 18.12.1742 *Saltash* (8) Sloop; **Captain**; 12.2.1742/43-4.9.1748[P] *Alderney* (20); 6.12.1762 **Superannuated Rear Admiral.**

TONGE, WILLIAM NORRIS

Dates: None Known.
Family:
Service: 3.8.1759 **Lieutenant.**

TONKEN, THOMAS

Dates: c.1732 Born; 9.1791 Died; 11.9.1791 Will Probate.
Family: Son Thomas, RN.
Service: 7.12.1749 Mid *Saint Albans* (60); 10.3.1751/52 Mate *Severn* (50); 7.11.1754 Master *Wager* (24); 4.9.1755 Master *Isis* (50); 4.2.1756 Passed; **Lieutenant**; 6.4.1757-3.6.1757 4L *Royal William* (84); 16.5.1757-15.3.1763 3L *Isis* (50); 3.7.1759 Bombardment of Le Havre; 11.5.1763-26.5.1766 2L *Yarmouth* (64); 6.12.1766 2L *Achilles* (60); 19.2.1767 1L *Achilles* (60); 7.4.1767-6.12.1769 1L *Ramillies* (74); 15.9.1770 2L *Ramillies* (74); 27.10.1770-17.6.1771[P] 1L *Ramillies* (74); 28.8.1771-15.9.1774 1L *Triumph* (74); 9.6.1775-12.8.1775 1L *Mars* (74); **Commander**; 25.12.1778[(NA 21.6.1779)] *Otter* (14) Sloop; 26.12.1778-1782 Principal Agent of Transports at New York; **Captain**; 15.5.1780[(NA 1.8.1780)]-12.7.1781 *Charlestown* (28); 25.9.1787-20.2.1788[P] *Sandwich* (90); 10.5.1790-24.2.1791[P] *Sandwich* (90); 24.3.1791-5.9.1791[P] *Dictator* (64).

TONYN, GEORGE ANTHONY

Dates: c.1735 Born; 17.10.1770 Died.
Family:
Service: 13.12.1747 Scholar *Royal Naval Academy*; 15.12.1750 Capt Serv *Elizabeth* (70); 6.11.1751 Capt Serv *Strafford* (58); 31.12.1752-16.1.1753 Able *Strafford* (58); 17.1.1753 Mid *Strafford* (58); 6.5.1753 Mid *Port Mahon* (24); 28.8.1755 Able *Port Mahon* (24); 7.1.1756 Passed; **Lieutenant**; 13.1.1756 L. *Squirrel* (20); **Commander**; 2.12.1757 *Savage* (8) Sloop; **Captain**; 14.11.1758 *Fowey* (24); 6.7.1761-15.11.1763[P] *Brune* (32); 19.11.1767 *San Antonio* (64); 7.10.1768-17.10.1770 *Phoenix* (44).

TOPPING, WILLIAM

Dates: c.1733 Born.
Family:
Service: 12.7.1752 Mid *Fowey* (24); 14.7.1754 Able *Fowey* (24); 6.9.1756 Mid *Royal George* (100); 4.1.1757 Mid *Yarmouth* (64); 5.4.1758-21.9.1759 Able *Yarmouth* (64); 29.4.1758 Battle of Cuddalore; 3.8.1758 Battle of Negapatam; 10.9.1759 Battle of Pondicherry; 22.9.1759-12.11.1760 Mid *Yarmouth* (64); 12.11.1760 Passed; **Lieutenant**; 29.1.1761-8.4.1761 4L *Modeste* (64); 22.2.1762 4L *Saint Ann* (64); 8.6.1762-3.6.1763[P] 3L *Saint Ann* (64).

TOULMIN, JOHN

Dates: c.1737 Born; 17.2.1780 Died.
Family:
Service: 1754-1756 Merchant Service; 29.1.1756 Able *Gosport* (44); 7.2.1756 Mid *Gosport* (44); 12.5.1758 Mid *Sapphire* (32); 1.8.1758 Mid *Experiment* (24); 29.12.1758 Capture of

Goree; 1.2.1759 Mid *Torbay* (74); 20.11.1759 Battle of Quiberon Bay; 20.2.1760 Passed; **Lieutenant**; 4.11.1762[JAM 30.8.1763]-7.9.1763[P] 4L *Alcide* (64); 1.10.1766-28.10.1767 3L *Phoenix* (44); 29.9.1770-28.5.1771[P] 5L *Prince of Wales* (74).

TOWERS, GEORGE

Dates: c.1732 Born; 5.6.1767 Died.
Family:
Service: 6.7.1751 Able *Glory* (44); 2.1.1754-22.8.1754 Able *Fougueux* (64); 23.8.1754 Able *Experiment* (24); 6.2.1755-8.6.1755 Able *Yarmouth* (64); 9.6.1755 Mid *Yarmouth* (64); 3.1.1757 Mid *Invincible* (74); 11.5.1757 Mid *Barfleur* (80); 5.9.1757-6.10.1757 Raid on Rochefort; 7.2.1758 Passed; **Lieutenant**; 28.10.1758-24.1.1759 2L *Argo* (28); 1.2.1759 3L *Dover* (44); 7.11.1759 2L *Dover* (44); 23.3.1761-26.2.1763[P] 1L *Dover* (44); 7.1.1762-10.2.1762 Operations against Martinique; 24.2.1762-25.2.1762 Capture of Saint Lucia; 6.6.1762-13.8.1762 Operations against Havana; 6.4.1763-5.6.1767[†] L. *Sardoine* (14) Sloop.

TOWERS, THOMAS

Dates: None Known.
Family:
Service: **Lieutenant**; 21.12.1758[BLI 21.6.1759] 3L *Woolwich* (44); 16.1.1759-19.1.1759 Attack on Martinique; 20.1.1759-1.5.1759 Capture of Guadeloupe; 24.7.1759[BLI 21.6.1759] 2L *Woolwich* (44); 19.9.1760 L. *Lightning* (6) Hospital Ship; 10.3.1761-20.2.1764[P] 2L *Pembroke* (60); 6.6.1762-13.8.1762 Operations against Havana.

TOWNLEY, EDMUND

Dates: c.1714 Born; 1759 Died.
Family:
Service: 6.7.1725 Able *Weazle* (8) Sloop; 8.12.1727-9.9.1728[P] Vol-p-O *Superb* (64); 20.5.1728 Able *Greyhound* (20); 20.2.1731/32 MidO *Pearl* (40); 26.8.1733 Able *Pearl* (40); 12.4.1735 QGnr *Blenheim* (96); 7.6.1736 Mate *Aldborough* (20); 21.5.1738 Mate *Kennington* (20); 13.11.1739 Passed; **Lieutenant**; 16.11.1739 3L *Southsea Castle* (40); 3.9.1741-6.12.1743[P] 2L *Southsea Castle* (40); 24.1.1743/44 1L *Plymouth* (60); 6.2.1743/44 2L *Saint George* (90); 29.3.1744-13.7.1744 1L *Saint George* (90); 17.7.1744 2L *Saint George* (90); 5.2.1744/45 1L *Saint George* (90); 22.2.1744/45 1L *Yarmouth* (64); **Commander**; 26.8.1745-10.12.1746[C] *Hinchingbrooke* (10) Sloop; 30.9.1755-15.6.1756 *Ferret* (14) Sloop; **Captain**; 21.6.1756-4.3.1758 *Triton* (20).

TOWNLEY, THOMAS

Dates: c.1723 Born; 15.8.1803 Died.
Family:
Service: 11.2.1741 Able *Essex* (70); 23.12.1741 Mid *Essex* (70); 11.2.1743/44-12.2.1743/44 Battle of Toulon; 11.5.1747-25.10.1748[P] Mate *Essex* (70); 18.3.1750-10.5.1750[P] Mate *Sheerness* (24); 17.3.1753 Mate *Sheerness* (24); 16.1.1754 Mate *Seahorse* (24); 5.1.1757 Passed; **Lieutenant**; 25.8.1757-24.8.1759 L. *Albany* (14) Sloop; 21.9.1796 **Superannuated Commander**.

TOWNSEND, HENRY

Dates: c.1733 Born.
Family:
Service: 1.4.1750 Scholar *Royal Naval Academy*; 3.4.1753 Able *Ambuscade* (40); 19.11.1753 Clerk *Ambuscade* (40); 16.12.1753 MidO *Ambuscade* (40); 10.4.1754 Mid *Winchelsea* (20);

1.7.1755 Mid *Captain* (64); 30.7.1755 Mid *Winchester* (50); 9.1.1756 Mid *Hampton Court* (64); 7.7.1756 Passed; **Lieutenant**; 30.11.1756-15.6.1758 6L *Prince* (90); 9.10.1758 5L *Saint George* (90); 18.10.1758 4L *Saint George* (90); 23.10.1758-27.12.1760[P] 3L *Saint George* (90); 16.1.1759-19.1.1759 Attack on Martinique; 20.1.1759-1.5.1759 Capture of Guadeloupe; 12.5.1766-13.10.1768 LCmdr *Lion* (4) Cutter; 1770-9.1770 LCmdr *Spy* (4) Cutter.

TOWNSEND, ISAAC

Dates: 1684 Born; 21.11.1765 Died.
Family: Wife Elizabeth Larcum (1699-1754).
Service: 15.1.1705/6 Passed; **Lieutenant**; 21.7.1706[(29.7.1707)] 3L *Shrewsbury* (80); 31.8.1706[(29.7.1707)]-20.3.1706/7 3L *Resolution* (70); 19.3.1706/7-20.3.1706/7 Loss of the Resolution; 24.9.1707-29.1.1707/8 L. *Hastings* (42); 3.3.1717/18-21.5.1718 2L *Dorsetshire* (80); 7.3.1718/19-21.11.1721[P] 2L *Dorsetshire* (80); **Commander**; 30.6.1719 *Poole* (32); **Captain**; 9.2.1719/20-1721 *Success* (20); 22.2.1733/34 *Plymouth* (60); 24.6.1739[(26.8.1740)] *Berwick* (70); 4.3.1739/40-25.8.1740 *Shrewsbury* (80); 19.6.1744 **Rear Admiral of the Red**; 27.10.1744-1.12.1744 CinC — River Medway and The Nore; 28.12.1744-1754 M.P. for Portsmouth; 2.1745-1.9.1746[P] *Dorsetshire* (80); 23.4.1745 **Vice Admiral of the Blue**; 1746 *Pembroke* (60); 14.7.1746 **Vice Admiral of the White**; 15.7.1747 **Admiral of the Blue**; 1754-21.11.1765 Governor of Greenwich Hospital; 24.2.1757 **Admiral of the White**; 28.3.1757-21.11.1765 M.P. for Rochester.

TOWNSEND, JAMES

Dates: c.1714 Born; 25.9.1757 Died.
Family:
Service: 17.9.1733-18.7.1735[P] Mid *Happy* (10) Sloop; 2.5.1742 Mid *Namur* (90); 11.2.1743/44-12.2.1743/44 Battle of Toulon; 22.9.1744 Mate *Burford* (70); 16.12.1745 Mid *Russell* (80); 2.3.1745/46 Passed; **Lieutenant**; 4.3.1745/46[(MED 21.11.1748)]-22.11.1746 3L *Leopard* (50); 18.11.1755-2.3.1756 2L *Jersey* (60); 25.5.1756 3L *Tilbury* (58); 18.12.1756 2L *Tilbury* (58); 23.2.1757-26.2.1757 1L *Tilbury* (58); 26.2.1757-25.9.1757[W] 2L *Tilbury* (58); 15.11.1758-4.4.1762[P] L. *Princess*.

TOWNSEND, THOMAS

Dates: Not Known.
Family:
Service: **Lieutenant**; 4.3.1759[(EI 26.11.1761)] 4L *Tiger* (60); 4.9.1759[(EI 26.11.1761)] 3L *Tiger* (60); 10.9.1759 Battle of Pondicherry; 1.2.1761[(26.11.1761)]-24.4.1761 2L *Tiger* (60); 21.4.1762-12.3.1763[P] 2L *Sapphire* (32); 14.7.1763-7.2.1766 3L *Dreadnought* (60); 12.10.1801 **Superannuated Commander**.

TOWNSHEND, HON. GEORGE

Dates: 29.10.1716 Born; 8.1769 Died.
Family: Father Charles Townshend, 2nd Viscount Townshend (1674–1738); Mother Dorothy Walpole (d. 1726); Half-sister Hon. Elizabeth Townshend (d. 1785); Half-brother Charles Townshend, 3rd Viscount Townshend (1700–1764); Half-brother Hon. Thomas Townshend (1701-1780); Half-brother Hon. William Townshend (1702-1738); Half-brother Hon. Roger Townshend (1708-1760); Brother Hon. Augustus Townshend (1716-1746); Brother Hon. Horatio Townshend (1718-1764); Brother Very Rev. Hon. Edward Townshend (1719-1765); Brother Hon. Richard Townshend (1721-1721); Sister Hon. Dorothy Townshend (1722-1779); Sister Hon. Mary Townshend (1724–1776).

Service: 17.7.1729 Vol-p-O *Rose* (20); 25.7.1731 Mid *Rose* (20); 3.3.1731/32 Able *Namur* (90); 30.3.1732 Mid *Scarborough* (20); 16.6.1736 Mate *Scarborough* (20); 23.10.1736 Passed; **Lieutenant**; 12.11.1736-24.6.1739 3L *Greenwich* (50); **Captain**; 30.1.1738/39 *Tartar* (20); 4.1740-5.7.1740 Attack on St. Augustine; 2.12.1741-31.3.1743 *Chatham* (50); 12.1.1743/44[MED 18.12.1747]-22.1.1747/48[P] *Bedford* (70); 11.2.1743/44-12.2.1743/44 Battle of Toulon; 18.12.1747-27.2.1747/48 CinC — River Medway and The Nore; 4.1748-6.1748 Commodore *Folkestone* (44); 3.6.1748-19.1.1749 CinC — River Medway and The Nore; 4.11.1748-1752 CinC — Jamaica; 1749-11.1752 Commodore *Gloucester* (50); 1755-7.1757 CinC — Jamaica; 4.2.1755 **Rear Admiral of the White**; 7.1755-7.1757 *Dreadnought* (60); 4.6.1756 **Rear Admiral of the Red**; 24.2.1757 **Vice Admiral of the Blue**; 31.1.1758 **Vice Admiral of the White**; 14.2.1759 **Vice Admiral of the Red**; 10.12.1765 **Admiral of the Blue**.

TOWRY, GEORGE PHILLIPS

Dates: c.1729 Born; 1817 Died; 26.4.1817 Will Probate.
Family: Wife Elizabeth More (d. bef. 1770) married 6.6.1766; Wife Susanna Haywood; Son George Henry, RN (1767-1809); Son Charles George, RN; Daughter Anne [Law] (1769-1843).
Service: 10.2.1757 **Lieutenant**; 2.10.1784-9.1817 Commissioner of the Victualling Board.

TOWRY, JOHN

Dates: 20.3.1757 Died.
Family:
Service: **Lieutenant**; 9.10.1718[5.11.1718] 3L *Prince Frederick* (70); 1.5.1723 2L *Prince Frederick* (70); 14.3.1726/27-13.4.1728[P] 1L *Prince Frederick* (70); 26.7.1728-24.10.1728 1L *Monmouth* (70); 2.4.1729 3L *Princess Amelia* (80); 12.4.1729 3L *Cornwall* (80); 29.4.1730 1L *Cornwall* (80); 19.5.1731 1L *Namur* (90); 2.1.1731/32 1L *Namur* (90); **Commander**; 28.6.1732-8.8.1732[P] *Griffin* (8); **Captain**; 7.11.1732 *Success* (20); 30.10.1733-12.6.1738 *Shoreham* (20); 30.8.1739 *Lichfield* (50); 11.7.1740-17.7.1740 *York* (60); 29.10.1740 *Kent* (70); 17.11.1740-19.1.1744/45[P] *Buckingham* (70); 11.2.1743/44-12.2.1743/44 Battle of Toulon; 12.1.1746/47 CinC — North Sea; 7.6.1749 **Superannuated Rear Admiral**.

TRAILL, WILLIAM

Dates: None Known.
Family:
Service: **Lieutenant**; 2.5.1759-28.11.1760[D] L. *Happy* (8) Sloop; 28.11.1760 Dismissed.

TRANT, HENRY

Dates: c.1703 Born; 1760 Died; 23.4.1760 Will Probate.
Family:
Service: 9.6.1723 Able *Superb* (64); 24.4.1725 Able *Sandwich* (90); 5.1.1726/27 Able *Nottingham* (60); 9.3.1726/27-15.2.1728/29[P] Mid *Nottingham* (60); 18.5.1729 Mid *Advice* (54); 12.8.1731 Mate *Advice* (54); 27.10.1731-10.5.1732 Able *Berwick* (70); 11.5.1732 Mate *Success* (20); 25.11.1732 Mate *Greyhound* (20); 28.3.1734-19.7.1736[P] Mate *Deptford* (60); 22.3.1736/37 Mate *Greenwich* (50); 14.3.1738/39 Mate *Tartar* (20); 4.1740-5.7.1740 Attack on St. Augustine; 19.1.1741/42 Passed; **Lieutenant**; 20.4.1742 3L *Deptford* (60); 14.12.1743 3L *Suffolk* (70); 11.4.1744 3L *Hampton Court* (64); 17.7.1744-30.5.1745 2L *Hampton Court* (64); 8.1.1744/45 Action of 1745-01-08; 28.2.1745/46-9.12.1748[P] 2L *Hampton Court* (64).

TREHEARNE, JOHN

Dates: c.1719 Born; 1785 Died Saltash, Cornwall; 13.5.1785 Will Probate.
Family:
Service: 4.6.1735 Capt Serv *Orford* (70); 26.12.1736 Able *Windsor* (60); 16.2.1736/37 QGnr *Windsor* (60); 12.6.1738 Able *Hector* (40); 10.9.1738 Mid *Hector* (40); 4.1740-5.7.1740 Attack on St. Augustine; 20.8.1741-13.4.1742[P] Mate *Hector* (40); 15.7.1742 Passed; **Lieutenant**; 17.9.1744(11.10.1744) 4L *Monmouth* (70); 13.5.1746-20.5.1746 2L *Ambuscade* (40); 30.9.1748 2L *Saint Albans* (60); 21.12.1748-8.7.1752 3L *Assistance* (50); 16.1.1753-1.2.1753 2L *Salisbury* (50); 19.2.1754 L. *Arundel* (24); 18.11.1757-6.2.1758 1L *Penzance* (44); 22.5.1758 1L *Tartar* (28); 5.6.1758-12.6.1758 Raid on Saint-Malo; 6.9.1763-19.4.1766[P] 1L *Kent* (74); 16.10.1766 2L *Firm* (74); 24.10.1766-10.11.1769 1L *Firm* (74); 29.3.1770-6.5.1771[P] 1L *Belleisle* (64); 7.7.1772 1L *Torbay* (74); 3.11.1773-7.7.1775 1L *Ocean* (90); 10.3.1777-5.2.1780[P] 1L *Blenheim* (90).

TRELAWNY, SIR WILLIAM

Dates: c.1722 Born; 11.12.1772 Died.
Family: Father William Trelawny, RN; Mother Mary Bisset; Wife Laetitia Trelawny married bef.1755; Son Unknown; Daughter Laetitia Anne [Ourry].
Service: **Lieutenant**; 25.9.1743(MED 23.8.1748) 3L *Faversham* (44); 11.2.1743/44-12.2.1743/44 Battle of Toulon; 16.1.1753-9.4.1754 1L *Augusta* (60); **Commander**; 10.5.1754 *Peregrine* (20) Sloop; **Captain**; 9.4.1756-4.4.1757 *Port Mahon* (24); 16.5.1757-6.1767 M.P. for West Looe; 10.6.1757-7.2.1758 *Vestal* (32); 25.7.1758 *Lion* (58); 16.1.1759-19.1.1759 Attack on Martinique; 20.1.1759-1.5.1759 Capture of Guadeloupe; 23.7.1759-3.4.1760 *Winchester* (50); 15.12.1760-25.6.1762 *Saint Florentine* (60); 1767-11.12.1772 Gov. of Jamaica.

TRENWITH, THOMAS

Dates: 1798 Died.
Family:
Service: **Lieutenant**; 15.2.1739/40(9.11.1744) L. *Astrea* (20) Armed Storeship; 4.3.1740/41-5.1741 Operations against Cartagena; 28.6.1742(21.11.1744) L. *Spy* (8) Sloop; 20.4.1745-6.8.1746 L. *Granado* (8) Bomb Vessel; 29.9.1746-8.9.1748[P] 1L *Dragon* (60); 21.9.1796 **Superannuated Commander**.

TRESILLIAN, NICHOLAS

Dates: 13.9.1767 Died.
Family:
Service: **Lieutenant**; 28.3.1743(MED 18.10.1745) L. *Shark* (8) Sloop; 8.12.1744(25.11.1745) 3L *Newcastle* (50); 22.1.1744/45(25.11.1745)-26.11.1745[P] 2L *Torbay* (80); 30.4.1746 3L *Duke* (90); 14.2.1746/47-1.2.1747/48 1L *Princess Louisa* (60); 3.5.1747 1st Battle of Cape Finisterre; 14.10.1747 2nd Battle of Cape Finisterre; 3.1.1754 1L *Somerset* (68); 6.2.1755-6.9.1759 1L *Barfleur* (80); 5.9.1757-6.10.1757 Raid on Rochefort; 5.6.1758-12.6.1758 Raid on Saint-Malo.

TRISTRAM, LAWRENCE

Dates: 1765 Died; 18.5.1765 Will Probate.
Family:
Service: **Lieutenant**; 3.3.1759(EI 11.12.1760)-30.7.1764[P] 5L *Elizabeth* (64); 10.9.1759 Battle of Pondicherry; 24.9.1762-6.10.1762 Battle of Manilla.

TROTTEN, RICHARD
Dates: c.1731 Born; 1800 Died Portsea; 14.5.1800 Will Probate.
Family: Wife Sarah Godman married 20.1.1785.
Service: 9.9.1746-25.9.1749 Scholar *Royal Naval Academy*; 26.9.1749 MidO *Blandford* (20); 4.6.1752 Able *Penzance* (44); 5.4.1754 Mate *Experiment* (24); 11.9.1754 Passed; **Lieutenant**; 8.4.1757 4L *Somerset* (68); 1.6.1757-29.7.1757 6L *Neptune* (90); 1.8.1757 5L *Union* (90); 5.6.1758-12.6.1758 Raid on Saint-Malo; 11.10.1758 4L *Union* (90); 20.11.1758 3L *Union* (90); 30.1.1759-23.2.1763[P] 3L *Royal William* (84); 29.3.1761-11.6.1761 Expedition against Belle-Isle; 10.4.1770 2L *Achilles* (60); 26.4.1771 1L *Achilles* (60); 8.6.1772[(JAM 1.12.1772)]-22.9.1772[P] LCmdr *Sir Edward Hawke* (8) Schooner; 7.11.1776 1L *Sandwich* (90); **Commander**; 16.5.1778-17.5.1778 *Diligence* (10) Sloop; 12.6.1778-3.6.1780 *Queen* (20) Hired Armed Ship.

TROTTER, SAVAGE
Dates: c.1735 Born.
Family:
Service: 7.12.1746 Ord. *Ferret* (14) Sloop; 29.3.1747 Ord. *Squirrel* (20); 29.7.1747 Capt Serv *Dolphin* (6) Fireship; 1.3.1747/48-26.5.1748[P] Able *Dolphin* (6) Fireship; 25.3.1751 Mid *Deptford* (60); 12.9.1752 Mid *Captain* (70); 29.1.1754 Mid *Speedwell* (8) Sloop; 12.1.1755 Able *Speedwell* (8) Sloop; 6.2.1755 Mid *Speedwell* (8) Sloop; 7.4.1756 Passed; **Lieutenant**; 15.11.1756 L. *Vesuvius* (14) Fireship; 27.4.1758 2L *Lennox* (74); 5.6.1758-12.6.1758 Raid on Saint-Malo; 22.2.1759 2L *Raisonnable* (64); 2.4.1759-8.1.1762[W] 1L *Raisonnable* (64); 24.5.1762-22.12.1762[P] 2L *Captain* (64); 8.6.1763-16.9.1766[P] L. *Speedwell* (8) Sloop.

TROUGHTON, ELLIS
Dates: c.1730 Born.
Family:
Service: 14.5.1747 Able *Sandwich* (90); 18.12.1747 Able *Superb* (60); 18.4.1748-5.6.1748[P] Able *Chichester* (80); 10.1.1751/52-6.7.1752 Able *Monmouth* (70); 7.7.1752 Mid *Weymouth* (60); 15.8.1752 Able *Lively* (20); 15.4.1753 Mid *Lively* (20); 2.2.1754 QM Mate *Lively* (20); 25.8.1757 Able *Dunkirk* (60); 5.9.1757-6.10.1757 Raid on Rochefort; 8.10.1757 Mid *Dunkirk* (60); 5.6.1758-12.6.1758 Raid on Saint-Malo; 29.12.1758 Capture of Goree; 4.4.1759 Passed; 25.7.1762 **Lieutenant**; 25.7.1763[(EI 13.9.1763)]-5.10.1763[P] 5L *Dublin* (74); 17.3.1777 4L *Conqueror* (74); 16.12.1777-6.2.1781[P] 2L *Conqueror* (74); 6.7.1779 Battle of Grenada; 18.12.1779 Combat de la Martinique; 17.4.1780 Battle of Martinique; 15.5.1780 Action of March 15 1780; 19.5.1780 Action of March 19 1780.

TRUSCOTT, WILLIAM
Dates: 25.11.1734 Born; 31.1.1798 Died.
Family:
Service: 4.1.1749/50 Capt Serv *Chester* (50); 28.7.1752 Able *Weazle* (16) Sloop; 26.2.1753 Mid *Weazle* (16) Sloop; 28.2.1755 Mate *Weazle* (16) Sloop; 26.8.1756 Able *Falcon* (10) Bomb Vessel; 19.11.1756 Passed; **Lieutenant**; 8.2.1757 3L *Newcastle* (50); 29.4.1758 Battle of Cuddalore; 3.8.1758 Battle of Negapatam; 10.9.1759 Battle of Pondicherry; 17.3.1760[(EI 20.4.1761)]-19.12.1760[P] 5L *Yarmouth* (64); 1.2.1762-25.2.1763[P] 4L *Namur* (90); 6.6.1762-13.8.1762 Operations against Havana; **Commander**; 17.8.1762[(EI 21.6.1763)]-13.4.1763[P] *Lurcher* (6) Cutter; 29.1.1777 *Grasshopper* (14) Sloop; 15.1.1778[(BLI 9.1.1779)] *Beaver* (14) Sloop; **Captain**; 14.12.1778-10.2.1779 *Elizabeth* (74); 10.2.1779 *Vengeance* (74); 28.7.1779[(NA 10.11.1780)]-23.10.1780[P] *Preston* (50); 27.1.1781 *Buffalo* (50); 5.8.1781 Battle of Dogger Bank; 15.8.1781-30.8.1783[P] *Nonsuch*

(64); 12.4.1782 Battle of the Saintes; 15.10.1790-11.1.1791^{P} *Fame* (74); 21.1.1794-9.1.1795 *Ganges* (74); 1.6.1795 **Rear Admiral of the Blue**; 20.2.1797 **Rear Admiral of the White.**

TRUSSELL, GEORGE

Dates: 30.6.1798 Died.
Family:
Service: **Lieutenant**; 22.12.1761-21.1.1763^{P} L. *Spy* (10) Sloop; 2.2.1771-22.4.1773 4L *Somerset* (68).

TUCKER, THOMAS

Dates: 8.8.1766 Died.
Family:
Service: 19.12.1708 Ord. *Faversham* (32); 13.1.1709/10 Ord. *Falmouth* (54); 28.5.1711 Able *Cornwall* (80); 13.8.1711 YoS *Cornwall* (80); 31.8.1711 Mid *Cornwall* (80); 11.5.1712 Mid *Speedwell* (24); 8.11.1715-11.4.1716^{P} Mate *Speedwell* (24); 13.12.1718 Mid *Orford* (70); 9.5.1719 Able *Pearl* (42); 12.6.1719 Mate *Pearl* (42); 15.1.1719/20 Passed; **Lieutenant**; 4.4.1720-15.6.1721 3L *Saint Albans* (50); 23.2.1724/25-24.10.1728 L. *Tartar* (32); 5.7.1731-4.5.1737^{P} 1L *Captain* (70); 16.5.1738-15.7.1739 1L *Strafford* (60); 14.8.1739-19.8.1740 1L *Panther* (54); **Commander**; 8.8.1740 *Bonetta* (8) Sloop; **Captain**; 17.7.1741 *Fowey* (40); 2.5.1743$^{(22.8.1744)}$-22.8.1744^{P} *Scarborough* (18) Hospital Ship; 23.7.1756 **Superannuated Rear Admiral.**

TUCKER, WILLIAM

Dates: c.1729 Born; 31.1.1772 Died.
Family:
Service: 18.2.1744/45 Scholar *Royal Naval Academy*; 13.2.1747/48 Able *Triton* (20); 16.5.1749 Mid *Triton* (20); 2.4.1750-23.8.1751 Mid *Nightingale* (22); 23.8.1751 Passed; 11.5.1754 **Lieutenant**; 25.2.1755 4L *Terrible* (74); 13.5.1755 3L *Terrible* (74); **Commander**; 1.7.1756-1.11.1756 *Otter* (14) Sloop; **Captain**; 11.1.1757 *Sphinx* (24); 18.10.1758-7.2.1762 *Levant* (28).

TUITE, HENRY

Dates: c.1739 Born; 26.8.1805 Died.
Family:
Service: 20.12.1755 Capt Serv *Swiftsure* (68); 5.3.1756 Capt Serv *Torbay* (74); 5.9.1757-6.10.1757 Raid on Rochefort; 8.4.1758 Mid *Torbay* (74); 5.6.1758-12.6.1758 Raid on Saint-Malo; 29.12.1758 Capture of Goree; 20.11.1759 Battle of Quiberon Bay; 6.2.1760 Mid *Valiant* (74); 12.1.1761 Passed; **Lieutenant**; 15.12.1761$^{(5.7.1763)}$-17.1.1762 5L *Temeraire* (74); 2.8.1763-8.9.1763 2L *Shannon* (28).

TUNSTALL, MATHEW

Dates: c.1734 Born; 10.1771 Died.
Family:
Service: 1751-1755 Merchant Service; 4.5.1755 Mid *Prince* (90); 17.7.1756 Mate *Prince* (90); 19.10.1756 Mid *Prince* (90); 15.12.1756 Mid *Culloden* (74); 5.4.1757 Action of April 5 1757; 18.6.1757 Mid *Saint George* (90); 1.6.1758 Able *Montagu* (60); 7.8.1758 Able *Ramillies* (90); 5.1.1759 Passed; 13.8.1761 **Lieutenant**; 17.6.1762$^{(17.6.1762)}$ 5L *Shrewsbury* (74); 7.7.1762$^{(17.6.1762)}$-2.3.1763^{P} 4L *Shrewsbury* (74); 30.11.1770-10.1771† 4L *Orford* (68).

TWISDEN, WILLIAM

Dates: c.1740 Born.
Family:
Service: 1754-1755 Merchant Service; 19.5.1755 Mid *Somerset* (68); 6.6.1758-27.7.1758 The Siege of Louisbourg; 22.2.1759 Able *Lennox* (74); 17.4.1759 Able *Resolution* PMW; 8.8.1759 Able *Ramillies* (90); 17.10.1759 Act3L *Montagu* (60); 20.11.1759 Battle of Quiberon Bay; 13.2.1760 Passed; **Lieutenant**; 4.4.1760-23.11.1761 6L *Sandwich* (90); 29.3.1761-11.6.1761 Expedition against Belle-Isle; 23.11.1761-28.11.1761 3L *Belliqueux* (64); 1.6.1762 1L *Boston* (32); 4.11.1762 4L *Torbay* (74); 4.2.1763-28.12.1763 2L *Tweed* (32); 26.10.1768-8.11.1769 2L *Phoenix* (44).

TWYMAN, ARTHUR

Dates: c.1738 Born; 1780 Died; 10.2.1780 Will Probate.
Family:
Service: 1753-1755 Merchant Service; 21.10.1755 Able *Prince* (90); 13.5.1756 Mid *Prince* (90); 15.6.1757 Mid *Culloden* (74); 13.12.1757 Mid *Saint George* (90); 26.11.1758 Able *Montagu* (60); 31.1.1759 Passed; **Lieutenant**; 27.9.1759-8.3.1760[P] L. *Juline and Elizabeth* (32) Hired Armed Ship; 11.4.1760-7.11.1760 3L *Norwich* (50); 28.12.1763-16.9.1765 1L *Boreas* (28); 11.11.1776-28.6.1777 1L *Invincible* (74); 17.9.1777 LCmdr *Sherborne* (6) Cutter; **Commander**; 17.5.1778 *Diligence* (10) Sloop; 15.10.1778-9.9.1779 *William* (20) Hired Armed Ship.

TYLER, CHARLES

Dates: c.1728 Born; 1.1.1761 Died Pondicherry; 3.9.1762 Will Probate.
Family:
Service: 24.1.1745/46 Able *Prince Edward* (44); 18.1.1746/47 Able *Bristol* (50); 3.5.1747 1st Battle of Cape Finisterre; 3.3.1747/48 Mid *Bristol* (50); 9.7.1750 Able *Fly* (8) Sloop; 28.3.1751 Able *Vulture* (14) Sloop; 3.2.1751/52 Passed; **Lieutenant**; 26.9.1757 L. *Baltimore* (14) Sloop; 19.1.1758-1.1.1761† 2L *Sunderland* (60); 10.9.1759 Battle of Pondicherry.

TYRRELL, RICHARD

Dates: Buried at Sea; 1691 Born Dublin; 26.6.1766 Died West Indies; 5.8.1766 Will Probate.
Family: Father James Tyrrell; Mother Mary; Wife Russell Tankard; Daughter Ann Barnes; Son Richard Tyrrell; Daughter Catherine Reily.
Service: **Lieutenant**; 29.11.1740(13.1.1741/42) 3L *Ludlow Castle* (40); 27.5.1741(13.1.1741/42) L. *Squirrel* (20); 16.1.1741/42 3L *Launceston* (44); 11.3.1741/42 2L *Launceston* (44); **Commander**; 5.3.1742/43(17.6.1743) *Comet* (8) Bomb Vessel; **Captain**; 26.12.1743(BLI 18.8.1746) *Launceston* (44); 4.9.1744(BLI 2.2.1749/50)-21.2.1744/45 *Deal Castle* (20); 7.6.1745(BLI 27.2.1749/50) *Lyme* (20); 28.4.1747(BLI 30.1.1749/50)-16.9.1749[P] *Centaur* (20); 4.2.1755-1.3.1757[P] *Ipswich* (64); 20.5.1757-29.1.1759 *Buckingham* (68); 16.1.1759-19.1.1759 Attack on Martinique; 25.6.1759-5.3.1760 *Foudroyant* (80); 21.10.1762 **Rear Admiral of the White**; 7.6.1763-26.6.1766 CinC — Barbados & the Leeward Islands; 6.1765-26.6.1766† *Princess Louisa* (60).

TYRWHITT, JOHN

Dates: 1813 Died.
Family: Son John.
Service: **Lieutenant**; 24.9.1759(10.3.1760) 4L *Orford* (68); 16.11.1761(10.3.1760) 3L *Orford* (68); 27.11.1761-25.10.1763[P] 5L *Mars* (74); 6.5.1805 **Superannuated Commander**.

Service Records U

UNDERDOWN, THOMAS

Dates: 27.12.1734 Born Ticehurst, Sussex; 1803 Died Loose, Kent.

Family: Father William Underdown (1709-1785); Mother Jane Yeomans (1710-1785); Wife Sarah Mercer (1736-1771) married 12.10.1758.

Service: 5.9.1751 Able *Port Royal* (12) Storeship; 21.4.1753 Able *Bridgewater* (24); 22.4.1754 Mid *Bridgewater* (24); 3.6.1755-9.5.1758 Mate *Falmouth* (50); 9.5.1758 Passed; **Lieutenant**; 30.9.1758 3L *Ludlow Castle* (44); 2.11.1758-3.3.1761 3L *Defiance* (60); 20.11.1759 Battle of Quiberon Bay; 24.3.1761[(28.7.1761)]-16.12.1761 2L *Enterprise* (44); 7.8.1782-22.5.1783[P] 1L *Prince Edward* (60).

UPPLEBY, SAMUEL

Dates: c.1733 Born; 11.10.1780 Died at Sea; 2.8.1781 Will Probate.

Family: Illegitimate Daughter Elizabeth Jury Yates; Brother John; Half-sister Elizabeth Howorth; Sister Jury [Sostin?].

Service: 7.2.1746/47 Capt Serv *Poole* (44); 1.2.1749/50 Able *Gloucester* (50); 18.11.1750 Mid *Gloucester* (50); 16.1.1754 Passed; **Lieutenant**; 9.11.1756 L. *Swift* (8) Sloop; 24.12.1756 3L *Lichfield* (50); 15.8.1758-29.11.1758[W] 2L *Lichfield* (50); 9.10.1760 1L *Temeraire* (74); 29.3.1761-11.6.1761 Expedition against Belle-Isle; 7.1.1762-10.2.1762 Operations against Martinique; 6.6.1762-13.8.1762 Operations against Havana; 2.7.1763-12.7.1764[P] L. *Valiant* (74); 12.11.1766-15.11.1769[P] 2L *Superb* (74); 29.1.1771 2L *Northumberland* (68); **Commander**; 2.6.1772[(EI 1.6.1773)]-8.4.1775[P] *Hawk* (10) Sloop; **Captain**; 8.4.1776 *Preston* (50); 6.12.1776-8.12.1776 Occupation of Rhode Island; 14.12.1778-15.12.1778 Battle of St. Lucia; 28.7.1779[(NA 22.8.1781)] *Vengeance* (74); 21.12.1779-22.12.1779 Action of 1779-12-21; 17.1.1780[(NA 9.10.1781)]-11.10.1780[†] *Blanche* (36).

UPTON, FRANCIS

Dates: c.1720 Born; 24.9.1757 Died off Louisbourg.

Family: Father Col. John Upton (1671-?); Mother Mary Upton; Brother Arthur (1715-1768); Brother Clotworthy, 1st Baron Templetown (1721-1785).

Service: 7.6.1742 Ord. *Norfolk* (80); 2.4.1743 Invalid *Plymouth* (60); 22.6.1743 MidO *Mortar* (10) Bomb Vessel; 23.11.1743 Mid *Mortar* (10) Bomb Vessel; 20.8.1744 Mid *Shoreham* (20); 13.10.1744 Mid *Royal Sovereign* (104); 17.9.1745 Mid *Milford* (44); 29.4.1746 Mid *Windsor* (60); 3.5.1747 1st Battle of Cape Finisterre; 14.10.1747 2nd Battle of Cape Finisterre; 17.2.1747/48 Mid *Tilbury* (58); 6.5.1748 Mid *Captain* (70); **Lieutenant**; 21.6.1748[(8.5.1749)]-22.2.1748/49[P] 3L *Sunderland* (60); 4.5.1749 Passed; 22.4.1752-3.1.1754 3L *Jason* (44); 27.5.1755 3L *Colchester* (50); 7.10.1755-30.3.1756 4L *Ramillies* (90); 19.5.1756 1L *Prince* (90); **Commander**; 15.6.1756-24.9.1757[†] *Ferret* (14) Sloop.

URRY, JOHN

Dates: c.1730 Born; 1801 Died Yarmouth IOW.
Family: Father David Urry, RN (d.1748); Wife Mary Stone married 12.12.1771; Daughter Sarah [Gregory];
Service: 29.5.1744 Clerk *Gibraltar* (20); 21.9.1744 Able *Cornwall* (80); 14.12.1746 Mid *Cornwall* (80); 9.4.1748 Battle of Santiago de Cuba; 12.10.1748 Battle of Havana; 24.9.1749 Able *Monarch* (74); 20.7.1750 Passed; **Lieutenant**; 12.11.1755(JAM 6.9.1756) L. *Hind* (24); 24.9.1756 6L *Union* (90); 1.8.1757 6L *Neptune* (90); 5.9.1757-6.10.1757 Raid on Rochefort; 21.9.1758-18.11.1758 5L *Torbay* (74); 23.1.1759-12.12.1759 2L *Dublin* (74); **Commander**; 6.8.1761-4.4.1763 *Viper* (10) Sloop; 6.6.1762-13.8.1762 Operations against Havana; **Captain**; 26.5.1768-23.4.1773 *Milford* (28); 1794 **Superannuated Captain**.

USHER, ARTHUR

Dates: 6.5.1763 Died.
Family:
Service: 1739-1740 Merchant Service; 26.11.1740 Able *Rippon* (60); 7.1.1740/41 Action of January 7 1741; 4.3.1740/41-5.1741 Operations against Cartagena; 23.3.1741/42 Mid *Rippon* (60); 18.11.1743 QGnr *Chichester* (80); 11.2.1743/44-12.2.1743/44 Battle of Toulon; 8.2.1744/45 Mid *Neptune* (90); 5.5.1745 Mid *Marlborough* (90); 7.9.1745 Passed; **Lieutenant**; 1.12.1745(MED 5.5.1749)-28.8.1746 3L *Liverpool* (44); 3.1.1748/49(5.5.1749)-1.5.1749[P] 3L *Superb* (60); 11.3.1755-14.5.1756 3L *Orford* (68); **Commander**; 17.1.1757-20.3.1759 *Port Antonio* (12) Storeship; 30.1.1759(JAM 16.12.1763) *Viper* (10) Sloop; **Captain**; 6.1.1761(16.12.1763) *Cambridge* (80); 22.1.1761-1.4.1763[P] *Hampshire* (50); 6.6.1762-13.8.1762 Operations against Havana.

USSHER, CHRISTOPHER

Dates: c.1733 Born; c.1775 Died; 25.2.1775 Will Probate.
Family: Wife Margaret; Daughter Jane; Daughter Elizabeth; Daughter Sarah; Brother William.
Service: 28.9.1749 Able *Amazon* (22); 14.7.1750 Ord. *Amazon* (22); 1.10.1750 Capt Serv *Amazon* (22); 19.12.1750 Ord. *Amazon* (22); 8.5.1751 Able *Amazon* (22); 10.12.1751 Mid *Amazon* (22); 12.4.1754 Able *Rye* (20); 20.5.1755 Mid *Ambuscade* (40); 4.2.1756 Passed; **Lieutenant**; 8.2.1757-23.2.1757 3L *Weymouth* (60); 26.2.1757 3L *Saint Albans* (60); 18.8.1759-19.8.1759 Battle of Lagos Bay; 6.1.1760(JAM 14.5.1760) 5L *Prince* (90); 20.10.1761(JAM 14.5.1760)-25.1.1763[P] 2L *Prince* (90).

UVEDALE, SAMUEL

Dates: 7.6.1729 Born Suffolk; 14.12.1808 Died; 7.2.1809 Will Probate.
Family: Father Rev. Samuel Uvedale; Mother Sophia Spragge; Wife Margaret Cooke married 18.1.1763.
Service: 30.10.1740 Capt Serv *Bideford* (20); 22.3.1740/41 Capt Serv *Rochester* (54); 28.7.1741 Capt Serv *Royal Sovereign* (104); 12.11.1741 Ord. *Royal Sovereign* (104); 6.10.1742 Capt Serv *Charlotte* (8) Yacht; 18.10.1743 Able *Prince of Orange* (70); 6.2.1743/44 Mid *Prince of Orange* (70); 17.7.1746 Mid *Elizabeth* (70); 9.3.1746/47 Passed; **Lieutenant**; 5.5.1747 6L *Royal George* (100); 29.7.1747-14.5.1750[P] 2L *Chester* (50); 6.2.1755 4L *Chichester* (68); 1.6.1756 3L *Chichester* (68); **Commander**; 16.1.1758 *Granado* (8) Bomb Vessel; 5.6.1758-12.6.1758 Raid on Saint-Malo; 16.1.1759-19.1.1759 Attack on Martinique; 20.1.1759-1.5.1759 Capture of Guadeloupe; **Captain**; 18.2.1760-22.11.1762[P] *Boreas* (28); 18.10.1760 Action off Cuba; 6.6.1762-13.8.1762 Operations against Havana; 24.8.1779-23.5.1780 *Ajax* (74); 16.1.1780 Battle of Cape St.

Vincent; 17.4.1780 Battle of Martinique; 15.5.1780 Action of March 15 1780; 19.5.1780 Action of March 19 1780; 4.10.1780-2.1.1781 *Dublin* (74); 15.10.1790 **Superannuated Rear-Admiral**.

Service Records V

VAILLANT, ISAAC
Dates: c.1741 Born; 27.9.1804 Buried Warfield, Berkshire; bef.27.9.1804 Died; 17.12.1804 Will Probate.
Family:
Service: 27.3.1755 Scholar *Royal Naval Academy*; 23.6.1758 Able *Deptford* (50); 3.7.1759 Bombardment of Le Havre; 6.10.1759 Mid *Deptford* (50); 25.12.1760 Mid *Essex* (64); 29.3.1761-11.6.1761 Expedition against Belle-Isle; 18.11.1761 Passed; **Lieutenant**; 25.11.1761 2L *Looe* (44); 6.4.1763-30.8.1764 L. *Wolf* (8) Sloop; 23.4.1766 2L *Guernsey* (50); 10.5.1766 3L *Renown* (30); 3.11.1770-1.5.1771 4L *Boyne* (68); 22.7.1774 3L *Torbay* (74); 2.8.1774 2L *Torbay* (74); 17.3.1777 3L *Torbay* (74); 15.8.1777 2L *Torbay* (74); **Commander**; 8.10.1777-13.4.1779[P] *Nabob* (26) Storeship; 15.2.1780-23.11.1780 *Shark* (16) Sloop; **Captain**; 23.11.1780-26.1.1781[W] *Siren* (24); 20.2.1781 Dismissed; 3.12.1781-25.3.1782 *Seaford* (22); 25.3.1782 *Nemesis* (28); 25.4.1783[(JAM 23.11.1784)]-31.8.1783[P] *Endymion* (44).

VALENTINE, JOHN
Dates: c.1725 Born; 1.1.1761 Died.
Family:
Service: 26.5.1746 Able *Cambridge* (80); 23.11.1746 Mid *Cambridge* (80); 14.2.1746/47 Master *Saltash* (10) Sloop; 26.11.1747 Master *Queenborough* (24); 23.10.1748 Master *Garland* (24); 5.12.1757 Passed; **Lieutenant**; 6.12.1757-20.12.1757[P] L. *Garland* (24); 14.3.1758 3L *Duc d'Aquitaine* (64); 5.6.1758-12.6.1758 Raid on Saint-Malo; 3.4.1759-1.1.1761[F] 2L *Duc d'Aquitaine* (64).

VAN COURT, PETER
Dates: 24.9.1807 Died.
Family:
Service: **Lieutenant**; 25.12.1747-13.9.1748[P] L. *Furnace* (8) Bomb Vessel; 22.2.1755 3L *Kingston* (60); 30.9.1755-4.3.1761[P] 2L *Kingston* (60); 20.5.1756 Battle of Minorca; 8.1757-10.1757 Louisbourg Expedition; 6.6.1758-27.7.1758 The Siege of Louisbourg; 20.11.1759 Battle of Quiberon Bay; 19.5.1762-26.3.1763[P] 1L *Lark* (32); 17.5.1763-4.3.1766 1L *Lark* (32); 23.6.1780 1L *Leander* (52); 17.4.1783 1L *Carnatic* (74); 26.9.1787-20.2.1788[P] 1L *Sandwich* (90).

VANDEPUT, GEORGE
Dates: 14.3.1800 Died Halifax; 19.8.1800 Will Probate.
Family: Father Sir George Vandeput, 2nd Bt. (c.1717-1784); Wife Emily; Illegitimate Son George; Half-sister Philadelphia [Smyth].
Service: 1759 Mid *Torbay* (74); **Lieutenant**; 24.9.1759[(3.3.1760)] 4L *Shrewsbury* (74); 9.4.1762-28.3.1763[P] 3L *Kent* (74); 17.6.1763 1L *Phoenix* (44); **Commander**; 17.4.1764-26.4.1764[P] *Goree* (10); **Captain**; 20.6.1765 *Surprise* (24); 25.8.1766 *Boreas* (28); 10.6.1767-24.1.1770 *Carysfort*

(28); 27.6.1770 *Solebay* (28) Frigate; 23.4.1773-15.6.1773[P] *Southampton* (32); 14.10.1773 *Thames* (32); 7.12.1773-30.6.1781[P] *Asia* (64); 2.7.1776-4.7.1776 Staten Island Landings; 18.2.1782 *Atlas* (98); 20.10.1782 Battle of Cape Spartel; 16.12.1782 *Ganges* (74); 27.1.1783 *William and Mary* (10) Yacht; 22.12.1786 *Princess Augusta* (6) Yacht; 1791 Regulating Officer; 1.2.1793 **Rear Admiral of the Blue**; 12.4.1794 **Rear Admiral of the Red**; 4.7.1794 **Vice Admiral of the Blue**; 25.8.1794 *Saturn* (74); 5.1795 *Jupiter* (50); 1.6.1795 **Vice Admiral of the White**; 16.2.1796 *Saint Albans* (64); 4.4.1796 CinC — Portugal; 30.11.1796-14.3.1800 CinC — Nova Scotia; 25.5.1797 *Resolution* (74); 10.1798-14.3.1800[†] *Asia* (64); 14.2.1799 **Admiral of the Blue**.

VANE, THE HON. RABY

Dates: 2.1.1736 Born; 23.10.1769 Died.
Family: Father Henry Vane, 1st Earl of Darlington, PC (1705-1758); Mother Grace Fitzroy (1697-1763); Wife Elizabeth Sayer married 15.4.1768; Daughter Mary [Carr]; Brother Henry, 2nd Earl (1726-1792); Sister Anne [Hope] (1726-1776); Sister Harriet (d.1758); Brother Frederick (1732-?).
Service: **Lieutenant**; 18.7.1757(13.1.1759) L. *Fortune* (14) Sloop; 27.10.1757(12.2.1758) 5L *Monarch* (74); 28.2.1758 Battle of Cartagena; 22.3.1758-31.3.1761 M.P. for Durham; 14.5.1758(12.2.1758)-9.9.1758[P] 4L *Monarch* (74); **Commander**; 14.1.1759 *Proserpine* (8) Fireship; **Captain**; 4.9.1759-19.2.1763[P] *Arethusa* (32); 31.3.1761-23.3.1768 M.P. for Carlisle; 5.12.1763 *Achilles* (60); 19.3.1764-19.11.1764 *Ramillies* (74).

VARLO, WESTON

Dates: 1789 Died.
Family:
Service: **Lieutenant**; 16.5.1743(MED 30.1.1744/45) L. *Enterprise* Sloop; 19.3.1743/44(MED 5.7.1746) 3L *Torbay* (80); 28.11.1744(MED 13.5.1748)-4.5.1748[P] 3L *Dunkirk* (60); 31.3.1756 2L *Devonshire* (66); 12.5.1757 2L *Cambridge* (80); 18.11.1758(BLI 27.9.1759) *Antigua* (14) Sloop; 16.1.1759-19.1.1759 Attack on Martinique; 20.1.1759-1.5.1759 Capture of Guadeloupe; **Captain**; 12.5.1759(BLI 21.9.1759) *Rye* (20); 5.8.1761-4.4.1763 *Maidstone* (28); 25.10.1770-14.3.1771[P] *Yarmouth* (64); 19.9.1776-10.4.1778 *Bedford* (74); 20.10.1787 **Superannuated Commander**.

VASSMER, HENRY

Dates: c.1740 Born; 8.11.1766 Died.
Family:
Service: 20.6.1753 Capt Serv *Jason* (44); 22.8.1753 Ord. *Jason* (44); 6.2.1754 Able *Jason* (44); 21.3.1756 Mid *Newark* (80); 1.5.1756 Mid *Intrepid* (64); 20.5.1756 Battle of Minorca; 21.5.1757 Mid *Deptford* (50); 27.6.1757 Mid *Invincible* (74); 8.1757-10.1757 Louisbourg Expedition; 2.11.1757 Mid *Barfleur* (80); 13.12.1757 Mid *Aeolus* (32); 27.1.1759 Mid *Neptune* (90); 9.1.1760 Passed; **Lieutenant**; 7.2.1760-20.5.1763[P] 2L *Lizard* (28); 3.6.1761-7.6.1761 Occupation of Dominica; 7.1.1762-10.2.1762 Operations against Martinique; 6.6.1762-13.8.1762 Operations against Havana; 6.10.1763 3L *Firm* (74); 4.4.1766 2L *Firm* (74); 29.9.1766-8.11.1766[†] 1L *Levant* (28).

VAUGHAN, ARTHUR

Dates: c.1715 Born; 1785 Died; 4.5.1785 Will Probate.
Family:
Service: 15.5.1730 Vol-p-O *Captain* (70); 1.5.1731 MidO *Chatham* (50); 30.10.1731 Able

Portland (50); 3.12.1731 Mid *Portland* (50); 1.9.1732 MidO *Portland* (50); 5.10.1732 MidO *Kingston* (60); 22.12.1732 Able *Gibraltar* (20); 6.12.1734 Mid *Gibraltar* (20); 9.6.1735 Able *Royal Oak* (70); 2.10.1735-13.3.1736 Able *Swift* (6) Sloop; 13.3.1735/36 Passed; **Lieutenant**; 1.3.1739/40 4L *Boyne* (80); 4.3.1739/40 3L *Boyne* (80); 8.4.1740 2L *Boyne* (80); 30.6.1740 3L *Suffolk* (70); 19.1.1740/41[(25.5.1743)] 2L *Princess Amelia* (80); 24.12.1742 2L *Diamond* (44); 12.2.1742/43 1L *Diamond* (44); 31.1.1743/44[(MED 6.12.1745)]-21.1.1744/45 2L *Torbay* (80); 11.2.1743/44-12.2.1743/44 Battle of Toulon; 15.6.1747-24.8.1747 1L *Crown* (44); 19.2.1756-13.3.1756 L. *Mercury* (20).

VAUGHAN, HUGH

Dates: c.1727 Born.
Family:
Service: 1749-1753 Merchant Service; 5.7.1753 Mid *Solebay* (24); 15.6.1755 Master *Macclesfield* (16) Hired Armed Ship; 22.9.1755 Mid *Charlotte* (8) Yacht; 5.11.1755 Passed; **Lieutenant**; 31.12.1755-12.3.1757 4L *Edinburgh* (64); 16.11.1757-21.12.1758 1L *Roebuck* (44).

VAUGHAN, JOHN

Dates: c.1715 Born; 2.11.1789 Died.
Family:
Service: 27.10.1729 Vol-p-O *York* (60); 4.6.1730 Ord. *Torrington* (40); 1.10.1731 Vol-p-O *Torrington* (40); 19.4.1732 MidO *Dolphin* (20); 1.8.1734 Mid *Dolphin* (20); 28.11.1735 Mid *Portland* (50); 14.12.1736 Able *Greenwich* (50); 3.5.1737 Mid *Greenwich* (50); 5.12.1738 Passed; **Lieutenant**; 17.4.1740-7.6.1741 4L *Cumberland* (80); 13.10.1741 3L *Russell* (80); 7.1.1741/42 L. *Deal Castle* (20); 30.1.1741/42 L. *Tartar* (20); 13.9.1742-7.9.1744 4L *Sandwich* (90); **Commander**; 12.7.1745 *Whitehaven* (18) Hired Ship; **Captain**; 11.8.1746-19.2.1748/49[P] *Solebay* (24); 26.7.1749 *Baltimore* (14) Sloop; 6.12.1750-4.5.1753[P] *Peregrine* (20) Sloop; 20.8.1756-1.2.1757 *Kingston* (60); 30.9.1757-14.11.1758 *Juno* (32); 6.6.1758-27.7.1758 The Siege of Louisbourg; 31.3.1775 **Rear Admiral of the White**; 7.12.1775 **Rear Admiral of the Red**; 29.1.1778 **Vice Admiral of the White**; 26.9.1780 **Vice Admiral of the Red**; 24.9.1787 **Admiral of the Blue**.

VAVASOR, RICHARD

Dates: c.1721 Born; 1803 Died; 2.6.1803 Will Probate.
Family:
Service: 23.1.1739/40 Mid *Fly* (8) Sloop; 13.6.1742 Mate *Portsmouth* (24) Storeship; 29.2.1743/44 Mate *Torrington* (44); 6.9.1744 Mid *Saint George* (90); 14.2.1744/45 Mate *Saint George* (90); 9.5.1745 Passed; **Lieutenant**; 30.1.1745/46 L. *Princess Royal* (24) Storeship; 22.8.1746[(MED 30.1.1748/49)]-9.4.1748 L. *Phoenix* (24); 29.7.1748[(6.6.1749)]-9.1.1751/52 1L *Severn* (50); 16.1.1755 L. *Lyme* (24); 17.5.1756 Action of 17th May 1756; 15.10.1756 1L *Lyme* (28); 10.8.1759[(MED 27.10.1760)]-22.12.1760[P] 1L *Rainbow* (44); 15.6.1769-23.11.1769[P] 1L *Yarmouth* (64); 12.8.1775-11.12.1776 1L *Mars* (74); 13.2.1777-25.6.1782 LCmdr *Orford* (68) Hospital Ship; 17.4.1782-25.2.1783[P] LCmdr *Security*; 21.9.1796 **Superannuated Commander**.

VEALE, JOSEPH

Dates: 10.4.1718 Baptised Charles, Plymouth; bef.10.4.1718 Born Plymouth; bef.1783 Died.
Family: Father John Veale (d.1763); Mother Abigail Robins (d.1769); Wife Eleanor Melhuish (d.1783) married 30.11.1752; Son Joseph (1753-?).

Service: **Lieutenant**; 30.9.1740(28.3.1743) 3L *Tilbury* (60); 24.2.1740/41(28.1.1742/43)-22.9.1742[B] 2L *Tilbury* (60); 4.3.1740/41-5.1741 Operations against Cartagena; 7.1741-10.1741 Operations against Santiago; 3.5.1743 4L *Chichester* (80); 24.8.1743 3L *Chichester* (80); 11.11.1743 3L *Torrington* (44); 8.9.1744 2L *Torrington* (44); 11.1.1744/45 1L *Torrington* (44); 6.9.1745(MED 11.4.1749) 2L *Boyne* (80); 19.12.1745(MED 24.3.1748/49)-14.8.1746 3L *Diamond* (44); **Commander**; 30.8.1746(MED 31.10.1747)-26.8.1747[P] *Guernsey's Prize* Unknown; 17.1.1748/49-21.5.1753[P] *Dispatch* (14) Sloop.

VERNON, EDWARD
Dates: 12.11.1684 Born; 30.10.1757 Died.
Family: Father Rt. Hon. James Vernon, MP; Mother Mary Buck; Wife Sarah Best married c.1729; Son Unknown; Son Unknown; Son Unknown; Brother James, MP (1677–1756).
Service: **Lieutenant**; 16.9.1702 3L *Lennox* (70); 12.10.1702 Battle of Vigo; 28.2.1703/4 5L *Barfleur* (90); 13.8.1704 Battle of Malaga; 18.12.1704 4L *Britannia* (100); 27.12.1704-14.1.1705/6 3L *Britannia* (100); **Captain**; 22.1.1705/6 *Dolphin* (24); 2.2.1705/6 *Rye* (32); 21.11.1707-29.8.1712[P] *Jersey* (54); 17.7.1711 Action off Cartagena; 7.8.1711 Capture of the San Joaquín; 2.3.1714/15-14.10.1717[P] *Assistance* (54); 11.3.1718/19-20.8.1721[P] *Mary* (60); 18.5.1719-1720 CinC — Jamaica; 12.4.1722-3.5.1734 M.P. for Penryn; 4.4.1726-19.6.1727 *Grafton* (70); 1739-1742 CinC — Jamaica; 9.7.1739 **Vice Admiral of the Blue**; 24.7.1739-1741 *Burford* (70); 21.11.1739 Attack on Puerto Bello; 2.1740-4.1740 *Strafford* (60); 1741-1742 *Princess Caroline* (80); 21.2.1740/41-27.4.1741 M.P. for Portsmouth; 8.5.1741-30.10.1757 M.P. for Ipswich; 6.1741-11.1742 *Boyne* (80); 12.3.1741/42 **Vice Admiral of the White**; 9.8.1743 **Vice Admiral of the Red**; 23.4.1745 **Admiral of the White**; 10.1745-6.1748 *Royal George* (100).

VERNON, SIR EDWARD
Dates: 30.10.1723 Born; 24.6.1773 Knight Bachelor; 16.6.1794 Died.
Family: Father Henry Vernon (1663-1732); Mother Penelope Phillips (d. 1726); Wife Hannah; Brother Henry Vernon (1718–1765); Brother Richard Vernon (1726–1800).
Service: 4.11.1735-18.5.1739 Scholar *Royal Naval Academy*; 19.5.1739 Vol-p-O *Portland* (50); 4.9.1739 Vol. *Sunderland* (60); 3.10.1740-19.2.1741/42[P] Mid *Sunderland* (60); 4.3.1741/42 Able *Sutherland* (50); 11.3.1741/42 Mid *Sutherland* (50); 3.3.1742/43 Passed; **Lieutenant**; 4.4.1743 L. *Granado* (8) Bomb Vessel; 16.6.1743-17.3.1743/44 4L *Berwick* (70); 11.2.1743/44-12.2.1743/44 Battle of Toulon; **Commander**; 5.12.1747-29.12.1748 *Baltimore* (14) Sloop; **Captain**; 3.4.1753-30.6.1753 *Mermaid* (24); 21.5.1755 *Lyme* (24); 17.5.1756 Action of 17th May 1756; 6.11.1758(JAM 19.4.1760)-31.5.1760[P] *Saint Albans* (60); 18.8.1759-19.8.1759 Battle of Lagos Bay; 30.6.1760-18.10.1760[W] *Lyme* (28); 5.8.1761-8.2.1763[P] *Revenge* (64); 6.9.1763-19.10.1763 *Kent* (74); 3.1.1770 *Yarmouth* (64); 25.10.1770-24.5.1771[P] *Bellona* (74); 25.5.1771-26.10.1773 *Barfleur* (90); 6.5.1775-8.8.1775 CinC — River Medway and The Nore; 6.5.1775-8.8.1775 Commodore *Ramillies* (74); 30.5.1776-1780 CinC — East Indies; 30.5.1776 Commodore *Rippon* (60); 10.8.1778 Second Battle of Pondicherry; **Rear Admiral of the White**; 19.3.1779-26.9.1780 *Rippon* (60); **Rear Admiral of the Red**; 26.9.1780-3.5.1782 *Rippon* (60); 24.9.1787 **Vice Admiral of the White**; 1.2.1793 **Vice Admiral of the Red**; 12.4.1794 **Admiral of the Blue**.

VEYSEY, JOHN

Dates: 1813 Died.
Family:
Service: 27.2.1760 Passed; **Lieutenant**; 28.2.1760 4L *Vanguard* (68); 3.10.1761-16.10.1762 3L *Vanguard* (68); 7.1.1762-10.2.1762 Operations against Martinique; 28.1.1806 **Superannuated Commander.**

VINCENT, JOHN

Dates: c.1734 Born.
Family:
Service: 15.2.1747/48 Able *Mars* (64); 18.12.1749 Mid *Trial* (10) Sloop; 20.10.1750 Able *Sphinx* (24); 8.12.1751 Mid *Sphinx* (24); 30.4.1752 Able *Badger* (10) Sloop; 21.7.1752 Able *Surprise* (24); 25.7.1752 Mid *Surprise* (24); 20.11.1752 Mid *Vanguard* (68); 27.12.1752 Mid *Assistance* (50); 1.3.1754 Passed; **Lieutenant**; 16.6.1756 4L *Chichester* (68); 20.3.1758 3L *Chichester* (68); 22.5.1758 2L *Chichester* (68); 5.6.1758-12.6.1758 Raid on Saint-Malo; 20.11.1759 Battle of Quiberon Bay; 3.4.1760-25.3.1762 5L *Sandwich* (90); 29.3.1761-11.6.1761 Expedition against Belle-Isle; 25.3.1762 5L *Duke* (90); 24.5.1762 4L *Duke* (90); 14.6.1762-19.2.1763[P] 3L *Duke* (90).

VINCENT, NATHANIEL

Dates: c.1734 Born; 1779 Died.
Family:
Service: 10.8.1748 Able *Baltimore* (14) Sloop; 17.12.1748 Able *Bridgewater* (24); 29.4.1749 Ord. *Seahorse* (24); 11.9.1749 Able *Seahorse* (24); 24.6.1753 Mid *Seahorse* (24); 19.7.1753 Able *Saltash* (14) Sloop; 18.9.1753 Mid *Saltash* (14) Sloop; 26.1.1756 Mate *Dover* (44); 4.7.1757 Passed; **Lieutenant**; 28.7.1757 L. *Pluto* (8) Fireship; 5.6.1758-12.6.1758 Raid on Saint-Malo; 27.10.1758 3L *Temple* (68); 14.5.1759-18.12.1762[F] 2L *Temple* (68); 20.11.1759 Battle of Quiberon Bay; 7.1.1762-10.2.1762 Operations against Martinique; 6.6.1762-13.8.1762 Operations against Havana.

VINCENT, NICHOLAS

Dates: c.1723 Born; 1809 Died.
Family: Wife Martha Boscawen Evelyn.
Service: 14.9.1737 Able *Exeter* (60); 30.12.1737 Able *Jersey* (60); 8.2.1739/40 Mid *Jersey* (60); 19.2.1740/41 Mid *Duke* (90); 16.6.1741 Mid *Sandwich* (90); 22.12.1741 Able *Neptune* (90); 28.12.1741 Mid *Neptune* (90); 11.10.1742 Mid *Preston* (50); 11.10.1743 Passed; **Lieutenant**; 3.2.1743/44 3L *Warwick* (60); 11.2.1743/44-12.2.1743/44 Battle of Toulon; 9.6.1744-15.6.1744 2L *Enterprise* (50); 16.1.1744/45 2L *Harwich* (50); 25.6.1746 1st Battle of Negapatam; 5.4.1747[(EI 17.8.1749)] 3L *Princess Mary* (60); 30.8.1747[(EI 17.8.1749)] 2L *Princess Mary* (60); 24.3.1747/48[(EI 17.8.1749)] 1L *Princess Mary* (60); **Captain**; 5.7.1748[(EI 17.8.1749)] *Medway Prize* (30); 28.7.1749[(EI 7.11.1749)]-21.8.1749[P] *Winchester* (50); 24.6.1755 *Greyhound* (20); 17.1.1757-7.7.1758 *Weymouth* (60); 29.4.1758 Battle of Cuddalore; 6.1758 Dismissed; 25.8.1766-14.5.1767 *Glasgow* (20); 1.11.1769-20.5.1771[P] *Hero* (74); 3.4.1777-22.7.1778 *Yarmouth* (64); 7.3.1778 Action of 1778-03-07; 28.12.1778-26.3.1779 *Union* (90); 19.3.1779 **Rear Admiral of the White**; 26.9.1780 **Rear Admiral of the Red**; 24.9.1787 **Vice Admiral of the White**; 1.2.1793 **Vice Admiral of the Red**; 12.4.1794 **Admiral of the Blue**; 1.6.1795 **Admiral of the White**; 9.11.1805 **Admiral of the Red.**

VITU, JOHN

Dates: c.1723 Born; 1770 Died; 12.5.1770 Will Probate.

Family:

Service: 21.8.1743 Able *Anglesea* (44); 13.7.1744 Able *Sunderland* (60); 12.8.1746 Mid *Sunderland* (60); 22.3.1746/47 Mate *Deal Castle* (20); 31.12.1748 Mate *Eltham* (40); 10.1.1749/50-2.9.1752 Mid *Ruby* (50); 2.9.1752 Passed; **Lieutenant**; 16.6.1756 6L *Saint George* (90); 21.6.1756 5L *Saint George* (90); 6.4.1757-4.5.1757 4L *Saint George* (90); 31.5.1757(22.9.1758) 4L *Monarch* (74); 28.2.1758 Battle of Cartagena; 14.5.1758(22.9.1758)-9.9.1758P 3L *Monarch* (74); 2.9.1760-3.6.1763P L. *Fowey* (24); 7.1.1762-10.2.1762 Operations against Martinique; 6.6.1762-13.8.1762 Operations against Havana; 15.6.1769-28.6.1769 1L *Lowestoffe* (32); 12.10.1770-3.11.1770 1L *Pallas* (36).

Service Records W

WADMAN, JOHN
Dates: c.1731 Born; 9.12.1793 Died.
Family:
Service: 28.9.1745 Able&Mid *Prince George* (90); 3.5.1747 1st Battle of Cape Finisterre; 3.9.1755 Able *Intrepid* (64); 20.5.1756 Battle of Minorca; 29.8.1756 Mid *Bideford* (20); 3.12.1757 Mid *Dunkirk* (60); 5.6.1758-12.6.1758 Raid on Saint-Malo; 29.12.1758 Capture of Goree; 7.3.1759 Passed; **Lieutenant**; 6.8.1759-17.2.1763[P] L. *Postillion* (18) Sloop.

WAGHORN, MARTIN
Dates: 1788 Died; 7.1.1788 Will Probate.
Family: Wife Ann Marriottt.
Service: **Lieutenant**; 16.12.1762[EI 30.10.1764] L. *Manilla* (14) Storeship; 2.8.1763[EI 30.10.1764]-2.11.1764[P] 2L *Liverpool* (28); 19.3.1778 3L *Victory* (100); 29.4.1778 2L *Victory* (100); 13.5.1778 2L *Prince George* (98); 27.7.1778 1st Battle of Ushant; 16.2.1779-13.9.1779 6L *Victory* (100); 27.5.1780-28.8.1780 8L *Victory* (100); 30.1.1781 1L *Victory* (100); **Commander**; 15.8.1781-16.3.1782 *Fly* (14) Sloop; **Captain**; 6.4.1782-29.8.1782 *Royal George* (100); 5.9.1783-22.7.1785 *Trusty* (50).

WAINWRIGHT, JOHN
Dates: c.1734 Born; 22.7.1810 Died; 15.8.1810 Will Probate.
Family: Wife Mary.
Service: 1752-1756 HEIC Service; 19.5.1756 Mate *Mercury* (20); 19.7.1757 Mid *Lizard* (28); 19.3.1760 Passed; **Lieutenant**; 19.6.1760 L. *Cruizer* (8) Sloop; 11.6.1761-21.3.1763[P] 5L *Ocean* (90); 4.4.1766-28.8.1769[P] 2L *Chatham* (50); 5.10.1770 L. *Tamar* (16) Sloop; 4.3.1776-7.4.1777 2L *Ramillies* (74); 7.4.1778 2L *Europe* (64); **Commander**; 16.10.1778[NF 30.11.1778]-24.7.1781 *Hinchinbrook* (16) Sloop; **Captain**; 28.11.1782 *Camilla* (20); 6.3.1783 *Camilla* (20); 15.4.1783-22.4.1786[P] *Queen* (90); 23.4.1804 **Superannuated Captain**.

WALKER, JAMES
Dates: c.1730 Born; 13.6.1762 Died.
Family:
Service: 29.10.1745 Able *Glasgow* (20); 9.4.1748 Mid *Glasgow* (20); 4.1.1750-25.6.1752[P] Mate *Glasgow* (20); 20.11.1755 Able *Culloden* (74); 20.5.1756 Battle of Minorca; 26.5.1756 Mid *Culloden* (74); 1.9.1756 Passed; **Lieutenant**; 11.10.1756 L. *Sheerness* (24); 28.5.1760 6L *Saint George* (90); 27.8.1760-27.12.1760[P] 2L *Saint George* (90); 13.4.1761 2L *Ocean* (90); **Commander**; 4.5.1761-14.6.1762 *Lurcher* (6) Cutter.

WALL, JAMES

Dates: None Known.

Family:

Service: **Lieutenant**; 30.7.1758[NA 7.12.1759]-26.9.1761[P] 4L *Bedford* (64); 29.3.1761-11.6.1761 Expedition against Belle-Isle; 23.10.1761-22.10.1762[P] L. *Diligence* (10) Sloop; 8.12.1769 1L *Cornwall* (74); 18.9.1770-27.5.1771[P] 2L *Cornwall* (74); 20.9.1773-6.12.1776 5L *Albion* (74).

WALLACE, SIR JAMES

Dates: c.1732 Born; 12.2.1777 Knight Bachelor; 6.3.1803 Died.

Family:

Service: 24.6.1746 Scholar *Royal Naval Academy*; 11.11.1748 MidO *Siren* (20); 22.4.1751 Able *Vigilant* (60); 5.10.1751 Mid *Vigilant* (60); 6.9.1752 Able *Intrepid* (64); 3.1.1753 Passed; **Lieutenant**; 11.3.1755-18.3.1757[C] 3L *Greenwich* (50); 28.2.1758 2L *Eagle* (60); 4.4.1758-25.6.1759 1L *Rippon* (60); 16.1.1759-19.1.1759 Attack on Martinique; 20.1.1759-1.5.1759 Capture of Guadeloupe; 3.1.1760-17.6.1762 6L *Neptune* (90); **Commander**; 3.11.1762 *Alderney* (10) Sloop; 4.4.1763 *Trial* (10) Sloop; 6.8.1767 *Bonetta* (10) Sloop; **Captain**; 10.1.1771 *Unicorn* (28); 15.11.1771 *Rose* (20); 25.4.1776-24.9.1779[C] *Experiment* (50); 6.12.1776-8.12.1776 Occupation of Rhode Island; 27.9.1778 Capture of the Raleigh; 23.3.1780-15.8.1781 *Nonsuch* (64); 16.10.1781 *Warrior* (74); 12.4.1782 Battle of the Saintes; 19.4.1782 Battle of the Mona Passage; 12.7.1782[BLI 25.2.1783]-27.11.1782[P] *Resolution* (74); 24.6.1790-13.9.1791[P] *Swiftsure* (74); 3.12.1792-11.12.1793 *Monarch* (74); **Rear Admiral of the White**; 12.4.1794-4.1795 *Monarch* (74); 21.5.1794 CinC — Newfoundland; 4.7.1794 **Rear Admiral of the Red**; 6.1795-6.1797 *Romney* (50); 1.6.1795 **Vice Admiral of the White**; 14.2.1799 **Admiral of the Blue**.

WALLIS, MATTHEW

Dates: c.1712 Born; 29.5.1788 Died.

Family:

Service: 8.3.1732/33 Ord. *Nassau* (70); 29.4.1733-22.11.1733[P] Able *Nassau* (70); 12.7.1736 Able *Sunderland* (60); 29.8.1739 Able *Strafford* (60); 18.9.1739 Mid *Strafford* (60); 21.11.1739 Attack on Puerto Bello; 31.7.1740 Mate *Strafford* (60); 18.7.1743 Passed; **Lieutenant**; 16.3.1743/44-15.9.1744[P] 4L *Kent* (70); 22.10.1744-12.7.1749[P] L. *Aldborough* (20); 16.1.1753-5.2.1754 1L *Bristol* (50).

WALLIS, SAMUEL

Dates: 4.1728 Born Fentenwoon, Cornwall; 23.4.1728 Baptised Lanteglos; 21.1.1795 Died.

Family: Father John Wallis (1680–1768); Mother Sarah Barrett (d.1731); Wife Betty Hearle (d.1804).

Service: **Lieutenant**; 19.10.1748[EI 12.7.1750]-12.6.1750[P] 3L *Eltham* (40); 10.1.1753 3L *Anson* (60); 9.10.1754 L. *Jamaica* (10) Sloop; 5.4.1755 2L *Torbay* (74); 6.6.1755-8.6.1755 Action of 6-8 June 1755; 2.8.1755[NA 9.12.1755] 1L *Torbay* (74); 31.1.1756 1L *Invincible* (74); **Commander**; 30.6.1756 *Swan* (14) Sloop; **Captain**; 8.4.1757-30.9.1758 *Port Mahon* (24); 8.1757-10.1757 Louisbourg Expedition; 6.6.1758-27.7.1758 The Siege of Louisbourg; 18.12.1760-10.3.1763[P] *Prince of Orange* (60); 29.3.1761-11.6.1761 Expedition against Belle-Isle; 19.6.1766-19.5.1768[P] *Dolphin* (24); 17.11.1770-4.4.1772 *Torbay* (74); 6.10.1779 *Dublin* (74); 3.10.1780-1.1.1781 *Queen* (90).

WALSH, JOHN

Dates: c.1723 Born; 15.12.1798 Died Kentish Town.
Family:
Service: 25.5.1737 Capt Serv *Grampus* (6) Sloop; 21.8.1738-15.12.1741[P] Mid *Aldborough* (20); 6.4.1742 Able *Sutherland* (50); 10.4.1742 Mid *Sutherland* (50); 11.10.1744 Passed; **Lieutenant**; 23.11.1744 L. *Hazard* (10) Sloop; 11.2.1744/45 3L *Princess Louisa* (60); 7.9.1745-29.5.1747 2L *Princess Louisa* (60); 3.5.1747 1st Battle of Cape Finisterre; 27.5.1747 6L *Saint George* (90); 5.10.1747-21.6.1748[P] 5L *Saint George* (90); 21.9.1796 **Superannuated Commander**.

WALSH, PHILIP

Dates: c.1733 Born; 1789 Died; 6.10.1789 Will Probate.
Family:
Service: 5.9.1755 Mid *York* (60); 1.5.1757 Mate *York* (60); 6.6.1758-27.7.1758 The Siege of Louisbourg; 11.7.1759 Able *Achilles* (60); 9.1.1760 Passed; **Lieutenant**; 16.6.1760-18.1.1762[P] L. *Ranger* (8) Sloop; 14.11.1776 2L *Augusta* (64); 17.3.1777-20.6.1777 2L *Torbay* (74); **Commander**; 9.7.1778-16.10.1778 *Alderney* (10) Sloop; 25.8.1779-14.2.1781 *Harpy* (18) Sloop; 1.5.1783-16.11.1784 *Fortune* (16) Sloop.

WALTER, ROBERT

Dates: c.1731 Born; 1784 Died; 5.1.1785 Will Probate.
Family:
Service: 16.1.1745/46 Capt Serv *Princess Mary* (60); 22.1.1745/46 Able *Royal Sovereign* (104); 16.4.1747 Capt Serv *Triton* (20); 19.5.1747-12.12.1749[P] Able *Rippon* (54); 30.6.1750 Able *Wasp* (8) Sloop; 4.8.1750 Able *Prince Henry* (44); 8.3.1751/52 Mid *Prince Henry* (44); 19.1.1753 Mate *Wasp* (8) Sloop; 4.12.1754 Passed; **Lieutenant**; 4.11.1755-24.11.1755 4L *Newark* (80); 22.1.1759-31.1.1759 2L *Somerset* (68); 30.3.1759 2L *Hercules* (74); 20.11.1759 Battle of Quiberon Bay; 17.6.1762[(9.8.1762)]-18.1.1763[P] 4L *Neptune* (90); 4.11.1762-26.3.1763[P] 1L *Boston* (32); **Commander**; 10.5.1781[(NA 13.2.1782)]-14.5.1781 *Beaumont* (16) Sloop.

WALTERS, GEORGE ROBINSON

Dates: c.1742 Born; 16.12.1789 Died Greenwich Hospital; 8.1.1790 Will Probate.
Family:
Service: 11.8.1756 Able *Eagle* (60); 15.3.1756/57 Scholar *Royal Naval Academy*; 31.10.1760 Mid *Shrewsbury* (74); 21.8.1762 Mid *Launceston* (44); 21.12.1762-25.12.1762 Mid *Blenheim* (96); 25.12.1762 Passed; **Lieutenant**; 27.12.1762[(31.3.1763)]-10.5.1763[P] 5L *Blenheim* (90); 20.8.1763 2L *Hussar* (28); 20.3.1765 3L *Guernsey* (50); 14.5.1766-5.1.1769[P] 2L *Guernsey* (50); 6.11.1770-7.12.1770 3L *Barfleur* (90); 31.12.1770-24.3.1772 5L *Barfleur* (90); **Commander**; 25.6.1773 *Martin* (14) Sloop; **Captain**; 2.9.1773 *Salisbury* (50); 3.12.1778-1.10.1779 *Princess Amelia* (80).

WALTON, SAMUEL

Dates: c.1729 Born; 1795 Died; 12.6.1795 Will Probate.
Family: Son John Bentley, RN.
Service: 12.8.1747 Mid *Duke* (90); 13.6.1748 Mid *Defiance* (60); 21.9.1749 Mid *Triton* (20); 4.6.1750 Able *Invincible* (74); 31.7.1750 Mid *Invincible* (74); 9.2.1753 Mid *Mars* (64); 31.1.1755-24.6.1755[W] Mate *Mars* (64); 17.1.1756 Passed; **Lieutenant**; 18.5.1756 L. *Granado* (8) Bomb Vessel; 25.11.1757-21.3.1760[P] 3L *Captain* (64); 6.6.1758-27.7.1758 The Siege of Louisbourg; 3.7.1760-5.5.1763[P] 1L *Warspite* (74); 17.12.1770-22.2.1772 2L *Lennox* (74); 25.6.1773-23.4.1774[P] LCmdr *Anson* (6) Cutter; 12.7.1774-27.6.1775 LCmdr *Wells* (6) Cutter.

WALTON, WILLIAM
Dates: c.1715 Born; 16.7.1787 Died.
Family:
Service: 6.10.1732 Able *Seahorse* (20); 19.5.1733 Mid *Seahorse* (20); 22.5.1735 Mid *Windsor* (60); 24.6.1738 Mate *Newcastle* (50); 19.7.1739 Passed; **Lieutenant**; 31.8.1739 3L *Ludlow Castle* (40); 19.9.1739 2L *Ludlow Castle* (40); 4.3.1739/40-27.7.1743 1L *Ludlow Castle* (40).

WANDBY, DANIEL
Dates: c.1721 Born; 12.3.1779 Died; 5.5.1779 Will Probate.
Family:
Service: 21.10.1739 Able *Lennox* (70); 1.12.1739 Able *Sunderland* (60); 5.7.1740-19.2.1741/42[P] Mid *Sunderland* (60); 12.3.1741/42 Mid *Sutherland* (50); 28.4.1743 Mid *Captain*; 14.8.1746 Passed; **Lieutenant**; 18.8.1747(18.10.1748) 4L *Revenge* (70); 17.3.1747/48(18.10.1748) 4L *Princess* (70); 31.7.1748(18.10.1748)-24.8.1748[P] L. *Cruizer* (12) Brig; 29.5.1755 2L *Colchester* (50); 7.10.1755-5.6.1756 3L *Ramillies* (90); 20.5.1756 Battle of Minorca; 6.4.1757 2L *Burford* (68); 5.9.1757-6.10.1757 Raid on Rochefort; 6.6.1758-27.7.1758 The Siege of Louisbourg; 16.1.1759-19.1.1759 Attack on Martinique; 20.1.1759-1.5.1759 Capture of Guadeloupe; 20.11.1759 Battle of Quiberon Bay; 29.3.1761-11.6.1761 Expedition against Belle-Isle; 14.10.1761 1L *Burford* (68); 11.5.1763 1L *Yarmouth* (64); 23.5.1763-22.7.1766[P] 1L *Essex* (64); 9.10.1778(NA 16.6.1779)-10.3.1779[†] 2L *Raleigh* (32).

WAPLE, EDWARD
Dates: c.1731 Born.
Family:
Service: 1754-1757 HEIC Service; 14.10.1757 Mate *Juno* (32); 6.6.1758-27.7.1758 The Siege of Louisbourg; 3.7.1759 Bombardment of Le Havre; 29.12.1759-22.10.1760 ActL *Juno* (32); 22.10.1760 Passed; **Lieutenant**; 2.7.1762(EI 28.2.1763)-15.12.1762[P] 5L *Dragon* (74).

WARBURTON, CHARLES
Dates: None Known.
Family:
Service: **Lieutenant**; 5.3.1762(4.2.1763)-5.4.1763[P] 4L *Chichester* (68); 2.4.1766-13.1.1770[P] 1L *Adventure* (32); 22.10.1767(21.4.1773)-11.3.1771 LCmdr *Sir Edward Hawke* (8) Schooner.

WARD, ARCHIBALD
Dates: None Known.
Family:
Service: 1761 **Lieutenant**.

WARD, HENRY
Dates: c.1713 Born; 4.12.1766 Died.
Family:
Service: 23.10.1727 Able *Spy* (8) Sloop; 5.12.1728 QGnr *Spy* (8) Sloop; 30.4.1729 Able *Cornwall* (80); 27.6.1729 Ord. *Grafton* (70); 30.7.1729 Able *Grafton* (70); 24.10.1730 MidO *Hector* (40); 17.4.1732 Able *Suffolk* (70); 20.6.1732 Mid *Success* (20); 9.12.1732 Mid *Greyhound* (20); 1.4.1734 Mid *Britannia* (100); 11.1.1734/35 Passed; **Lieutenant**; 26.3.1737(9.5.1737)-15.5.1738 3L *Sunderland* (60); 28.7.1738-6.6.1739 4L *Burford* (70); 7.6.1739-10.2.1739/40 4L *Burford* (70); 21.11.1739 Attack on Puerto Bello; 13.12.1740 **Commander**; 13.12.1740(11.11.1742) *Alderney* (8)

Bomb Vessel; 4.3.1740/41-5.1741 Operations against Cartagena; **Captain**; 25.5.1741[11.11.1742]-25.11.1742[P] *Sheerness* (20); 7.1741-10.1741 Operations against Santiago; 26.8.1743-18.7.1747 *Tartar* (20); 10.1.1753-7.6.1756 *Culloden* (74); 20.5.1756 Battle of Minorca; 30.9.1757 **Superannuated Rear Admiral.**

WARD, THOMAS

Dates: 1774 Died.
Family:
Service: **Lieutenant**; 14.7.1740 2L *Salisbury* (50); 9.6.1741[23.7.1745] L. *Winchelsea* (20); 1.6.1742[23.7.1745] 3L *Dartmouth* (50); 3.6.1743[20.7.1745] 2L *Dartmouth* (50); 29.4.1744[23.7.1745] 1L *Dartmouth* (50); 22.12.1744[23.7.1745] L. *Princess Royal* (24) Storeship; 4.1.1745/46 3L *Prince George* (90); 3.2.1745/46 2L *Prince George* (90); **Commander**; 15.1.1746/47 *Swift* (8) Sloop; 21.4.1748-8.10.1749[P] *Swift* (8) Sloop; **Captain**; 22.7.1756 *Siren* (20); 19.1.1758-31.8.1758 *Penzance* (44).

WARD, WILLIAM

Dates: 4.7.1806 Died.
Family:
Service: **Lieutenant**; 21.11.1762[19.4.1763]-15.8.1763[P] 4L *Bienfaisant* (64); 12.6.1778-10.4.1779 1L *Defence* (74).

WARDEN, JAMES

Dates: c.1736 Born; 28.4.1792 Died.
Family:
Service: 1753-1756 HEIC Service; 28.4.1756 Mate *Tartar* (24); 22.12.1757 Able *Tartar* (28); 22.1.1758 Mate *Chatham* (50); 13.4.1759 Supnum *Royal Anne* (100); 2.5.1759 Passed; **Lieutenant**; 27.8.1760-27.6.1763 L. *Fly* (8) Sloop; 29.3.1761-11.6.1761 Expedition against Belle-Isle; 27.9.1764-30.9.1767 LCmdr *Adventure* (6) Cutter; 25.11.1775-5.7.1779[P] 1L *Emerald* (32); 1.6.1779 LCmdr *Wells* (6) Cutter; 18.7.1782-17.4.1783[P] 2L *Diligent* (70).

WARDEN, JOHN

Dates: bef.23.3.1767 Died.
Family:
Service: 12.7.1719 Vol-p-O *Royal Oak* (70); 26.8.1719 Vol-p-O *Royal Oak* (70); 9.1.1719/20 Mid *Royal Oak* (70); 3.2.1720/21 Mid *Nassau* (70); 4.5.1721 Mid *Guernsey* (50); 29.3.1722 Able *Torbay* (80); 19.4.1722 MidO *Torbay* (80); 28.6.1722 MidO *Torbay* (80); 13.8.1722 Mid *Leopard* (50); 16.10.1722 Mid *Torbay* (80); 6.5.1723 Passed; **Lieutenant**; 28.10.1726[10.11.1726]-10.6.1727 4L *Nassau* (70); 16.1.1727/28-1.8.1728 1L *Dover* (40); 11.4.1729 L. *Lively* (20); 12.4.1729-31.1.1730/31[P] 2L *Severn* (54); 30.8.1739-13.9.1739 2L *Cumberland* (80); 2.2.1740/41-26.3.1741 3L *Neptune* (90).

WARREN, SAMUEL

Dates: 1792 Died; 15.8.1792 Will Probate.
Family:
Service: **Lieutenant**; 25.8.1759[BLI 28.7.1760] 4L *Nassau* (64); 7.9.1759[BLI 28.7.1760] 3L *Nassau* (64); 27.2.1761-10.5.1763 L. *Senegal* (14) Sloop; 17.12.1770-10.1.1771 3L *Northumberland* (68); 25.1.1771-23.9.1772[P] LCmdr *Grace* (6) Cutter; **Commander**; 25.6.1773 *Beaver* (14) Sloop;

20.9.1773-17.10.1776 *Weazle* (16) Sloop; 27.3.1777 *Ceres* (18) Sloop; **Captain**; 5.9.1777-29.11.1777 *Hind* (24); 18.2.1778-28.10.1778 *Proteus* (26).

WARRINER, GEORGE

Dates: c.1725 Born; 1769 Died; 3.6.1769 Will Probate.
Family:
Service: 3.4.1740-13.11.1740[P] Vol-p-O *Greyhound* (20); 3.7.1741 Mate *Rupert* (60); 30.1.1743/44 Able *Namur* (90); 11.2.1743/44-12.2.1743/44 Battle of Toulon; 20.10.1744 Mid *Essex* (70); 18.2.1744/45 Passed; **Lieutenant**; 24.2.1744/45[(MED 29.11.1748)]-11.1.1745/46 L. *Duke* (8) Fireship; 19.12.1746[(MED 13.12.1748)] 4L *Russell* (80); 19.8.1747[(13.12.1748)]-21.8.1747 3L *Princess* (70); 19.12.1747[(MED 13.12.1748)] 3L *Boyne* (80); 17.3.1747/48[(13.12.1748)]-17.11.1748[P] 4L *Revenge* (70).

WARWICK, THOMAS

Dates: c.1721 Born; 1775 Died.
Family:
Service: 29.5.1738 Able *Shrewsbury* (80); 6.8.1739 Able *Weymouth* (60); 7.1.1740/41 Action of January 7 1741; 4.3.1740/41-5.1741 Operations against Cartagena; 28.10.1741-8.5.1742[P] Mid *Weymouth* (60); 23.9.1742 Mid *Dreadnought* (60) Receiving Ship; 11.1.1744/45 Passed; **Lieutenant**; 18.5.1745 L. *Weazle* (16) Sloop; 12.2.1745/46-6.4.1748 L. *Rye* (20); 10.1.1753-28.3.1754 2L *Eagle* (60); 2.4.1754 2L *Cumberland* (66); 11.1.1756-14.1.1756 Capture of Geriah; **Commander**; 4.1.1757[(19.9.1757)]-5.5.1757 *Racehorse* (18) Sloop; 23.2.1758 *Proserpine* (8) Fireship; **Captain**; 1.12.1758 *Jason* (30); 28.1.1762 *Saint George* Prison Ship; 1.11.1762-19.2.1763[P] *Duke* (90).

WASTELL, JAMES

Dates: c.1736 Born.
Family:
Service: 28.6.1750 Scholar *Royal Naval Academy*; 31.7.1752 Vol-p-O *Hind* (24); 13.9.1753 Mid *Severn* (50); 4.8.1756 Passed; **Lieutenant**; 9.11.1756 L. *Hazard* (8) Sloop; 19.7.1757 3L *Intrepid* (60); 5.9.1757-6.10.1757 Raid on Rochefort; 19.10.1757-3.8.1763[P] 2L *Intrepid* (60); 18.8.1759-19.8.1759 Battle of Lagos Bay; 20.11.1759 Battle of Quiberon Bay; 14.3.1764-23.4.1766 2L *Guernsey* (50); 20.5.1766 1L *Preston* (50); **Commander**; 16.1.1768[(3.8.1768)]-20.5.1769[P] *Diligence* (10) Sloop.

WATERFALL, MATTHEW

Dates: c.1762 Died; 9.9.1762 Will Probate.
Family:
Service: **Lieutenant**; 13.9.1748[(EI 5.9.1749)]-1.9.1749[P] 3L *Pearl* (44); 6.2.1755-20.5.1755 5L *Ramillies* (90); 20.5.1755-5.6.1755 6L *Ramillies* (90); 29.1.1757-6.8.1758[C] L. *Stork* (10) Sloop; 22.12.1758 2L *Lynn* (44); 15.3.1759-18.10.1759 2L *America* (60); 18.8.1759-19.8.1759 Battle of Lagos Bay.

WATHERSTON, ALEXANDER

Dates: c.1739 Born; c.1776 Died; 15.8.1776 Will Probate.
Family:
Service: 1754-1755 Merchant Service; 5.4.1755 Able *Prince* (90); 18.6.1756 Mid *Royal George* (100); 11.1.1757 Mid *Yarmouth* (64); 29.1.1757 Able *Essex* (64); 27.4.1757 Gnr Serv *Tartar* (28); 16.2.1758 Mid *Chatham* (50); 3.7.1759 Bombardment of Le Havre; 20.11.1759 Battle of Quiberon Bay; 14.5.1760 Passed; **Lieutenant**; 8.5.1761-12.3.1763[P] 4L *Prince Frederick* (64);

6.12.1766-4.5.1768 L. *Hazard* (8) Sloop; 10.8.1768 2L *Rippon* (60); 21.12.1769 3L *Rippon* (60); 1.2.1770 3L *Edgar* (60); 19.3.1771 2L *Warwick* (50); 21.9.1773 3L *Ramillies* (74); 26.8.1775 2L *Ramillies* (74); 4.3.1776-9.10.1776 3L *Ramillies* (74).

WATKINS, JOHN
Dates: 24.4.1757 Died.
Family:
Service: 17.10.1721 Vol-p-O *Blandford* (20); 21.10.1723 MidO *Blandford* (20); 27.8.1725 MidO *Yarmouth* (70); 20.9.1725 Able *Yarmouth* (70); 16.10.1725 Mid *Port Mahon* (20); 16.12.1726 MidO *Superb* (64); 28.8.1727 Passed; **Lieutenant**; 7.9.1727-2.12.1727 4L *Monmouth* (70); 26.7.1728 2L *Ludlow Castle* (40); 31.1.1733/34 2L *Lennox* (70); 31.5.1735-1.8.1738 L. *Port Mahon* (20); 14.8.1739 2L *Boyne* (80); 4.9.1739-11.11.1739 2L *Lichfield* (50); 20.12.1739 1L *Argyll* (50); 20.10.1740-13.3.1740/41 L. *Blaze* (8) Fireship; 21.9.1741 5L *Victory* (100); 12.3.1741/42-21.3.1741/42 1L *Namur* (90); **Commander**; 7.4.1742 *Carcass* (8) Bomb Vessel; **Captain**; 4.8.1743$^{(27.5.1745)}$ *Dursley Galley* (20); 13.1.1743/44$^{(11.6.1745)}$ *Faversham* (44); 11.2.1743/44-12.2.1743/44 Battle of Toulon; 6.3.1743/44$^{(11.6.1745)}$-12.6.1745^{P} *Newcastle* (50).

WATKINS, RICHARD
Dates: 4.1770 Died.
Family: Wife Mary.
Service: **Lieutenant**; 7.8.1735$^{(24.12.1736)}$-3.3.1735/36 4L *Norfolk* (80); 29.5.1736$^{(19.2.1740/41)}$-15.9.1741 L. *Greyhound* (20); **Commander**; 19.2.1740/41 *Pembroke Prize* (8) Sloop; 24.10.1742 *Lively* (20); 14.2.1742/43$^{(8.8.1743)}$ *Eltham* (40); 18.2.1742/43 Attack on La Guaira; 24.2.1742/43 **Captain**; 15.4.1743-24.4.1743 Attack on Porto Cabello; 2.6.1743$^{(8.8.1743)}$ *Burford* (70); 1.8.1744$^{(MED\ 30.9.1745)}$ *Marlborough* (90); 3.8.1745$^{(MED\ 30.9.1745)}$-19.11.1745^{P} *Elizabeth* (70); 30.1.1755-25.2.1757 *Blandford* (20); 3.1757 Dismissed; 15.3.1763 **Superannuated Rear Admiral**.

WATSON, CHARLES
Dates: 1714 Born; 8.1757 Buried St John's Church, Calcutta; 16.8.1757 Died; 2.12.1758 Will Probate.
Family: Father John Watson, prebendary of Westminster (d1724).
Service: **Lieutenant**; 2.8.1734 3L *Deptford* (60); 31.1.1734/35 Passed; 5.5.1735 2L *Falkland* (50); 27.5.1737 2L *Berwick* (70); **Captain**; 14.2.1737/38 *Garland* (20); 25.5.1741 *Plymouth* (60); 9.11.1742$^{(MED\ 9.1.1745/46)}$-17.11.1745^{P} *Dragon* (60); 11.2.1743/44-12.2.1743/44 Battle of Toulon; 28.12.1745 *Princess Mary* (60); 7.2.1745/46 *Advice* (50); 14.3.1745/46 *Princess Louisa* (60); 3.5.1747 1st Battle of Cape Finisterre; 14.10.1747 2nd Battle of Cape Finisterre; 25.1.1747/48-5.3.1747/48 *Lion* (58); 16.3.1747/48 CinC — Newfoundland; **Rear Admiral of the Blue**; 12.5.1748-23.12.1748^{P} *Lion* (58); 1754-16.8.1757 CinC — East Indies; 20.1.1754-16.9.1757^{P} *Kent* (64); 4.2.1755 **Rear Admiral of the Red**; 11.1.1756-14.1.1756 Capture of Geriah; 17.3.1756 **Vice Admiral of the Blue**; 24.2.1757 **Vice Admiral of the White**; 7.3.1757-1.4.1757 Expedition against Chandernagore; 31.1.1758 **Vice Admiral of the Red**.

WATSON, GEORGE
Dates: c.1729 Born; 16.6.1774 Died.
Family:
Service: 5.2.1745 Capt Serv *Harwich* (50); 20.5.1746 Able *Harwich* (50); 25.6.1746 1st Battle of Negapatam; 9.6.1748 Mid *Harwich* (50); 8.6.1750-20.6.1750 Mid *Porcupine* (16) Sloop;

20.6.1750 Passed; **Lieutenant**; 6.8.1755[JAM 13.4.1757]-8.2.1756 L. *Falcon* (10) Bomb Vessel; 19.5.1757 L. *Shoreham* (24); 20.9.1757 1L *Pallas* (36); 22.5.1758 4L *Royal George* (100); 5.10.1758 1L *Royal George* (100); **Commander**; 23.12.1758 *Hawke* (8) Sloop; 4.9.1759 *Cygnet* (18) Sloop; **Captain**; 11.12.1759 *Success* (20); 19.5.1761-7.4.1763 *Mermaid* (28); 5.9.1763-7.5.1764 *Alarm* (32); 10.4.1765-6.8.1765[P] *Flamborough* (20); 18.8.1766-30.8.1769 *Hind* (24); 9.1.1771 *Arethusa* (32); 23.3.1771-18.9.1772 *Pallas* (36).

WATSON, NATHANIEL
Dates: 17.2.1766 Died.
Family:
Service: 8.1.1703/4 Ord. *Winchester* (54); 24.1.1704/5 Vol-p-O *Somerset* (80); 18.2.1705/6 Ord. *Somerset* (80); 30.4.1706-9.6.1709[P] Able *Assistance* (50); 13.7.1709 Mid *Kent* (70); 19.10.1711 Passed; **Lieutenant**; 19.5.1731-10.1.1733/34[P] L. *Seahorse* (20); 31.1.1733/34-31.3.1736[P] 4L *Kent* (70); 9.12.1737-7.2.1737/38 2L *Anglesea* (40); 30.8.1739 **Commander**; 30.8.1739-17.12.1740 *Deptford* (24) Storeship; **Captain**; 16.1.1740/41-24.7.1742 *Faversham* (44); 24.7.1741 Action of 1741-07-24.

WATSON, THOMAS
Dates: 1781 Died; 28.11.1781 Will Probate.
Family:
Service: 6.9.1759 **Lieutenant**; 29.9.1766-16.1.1770 1L *Solebay* (28) Frigate; 5.11.1776 1L *Monarch* (74); 27.7.1778 1st Battle of Ushant; 8.12.1778 1L *Suffolk* (74); 28.8.1779[NA 25.12.1780] 2L *Princess Royal* (98); **Captain**; 17.1.1780[North Sea 5.5.1780]-16.6.1780 *Conqueror* (74); 17.4.1780 Battle of Martinique; 15.5.1780 Action of March 15 1780; 19.5.1780 Action of March 19 1780.

WATT, JAMES
Dates: c.1733 Born; 3.9.1782 Died Battle of Trincomalee.
Family:
Service: 5.4.1755 Able *Dunkirk* (60); 6.6.1755-8.6.1755 Action of 6-8 June 1755; 13.2.1756 Mid *Dunkirk* (60); 11.11.1756 Able *Dunkirk* (60); 15.7.1757 Mid *Magnanime* (74); 5.9.1757-6.10.1757 Raid on Rochefort; 5.6.1758-12.6.1758 Raid on Saint-Malo; 11.4.1759 Passed; **Lieutenant**; 24.6.1762-23.1.1763[P] 5L *Princess Amelia* (80); 2.4.1764 2L *Pearl* (32); 14.5.1766-3.2.1768 2L *Pearl* (32); 30.11.1770-1.6.1771[P] 4L *San Antonio* (64); 29.8.1771-29.11.1773[P] 1L *Arethusa* (32); 25.8.1774 4L *Lennox* (74); 28.2.1775-10.4.1776 3L *Exeter* (64); 10.5.1776[NA 22.12.1778]-11.5.1777 5L *Eagle* (64); **Commander**; 23.11.1777[NA 10.2.1779]-22.4.1778 *Delaware* (28) Frigate; 25.7.1778[NA 10.2.1779]-29.9.1778 *Sulphur* (8) Fireship; 11.8.1778 Howe's encounter with d'Estaing; 13.9.1779-19.4.1780[P] *Worsley* Hired Unknown; **Captain**; 9.5.1781-3.9.1782[†] *Sultan* (74); 12.4.1782 Battle of Providien; 6.7.1782 2nd Battle of Negapatam; 3.9.1782 Battle of Trincomalee.

WATTS, WALTER
Dates: 24.5.1814 Died.
Family:
Service: **Lieutenant**; 3.7.1760-9.5.1763[P] 2L *Quebec* (32); 30.11.1807 **Superannuated Commander**.

WAYMAN, JOHN

Dates: c.1738 Born.
Family:
Service: 5.11.1753 Able *Culloden* (74); 20.5.1756 Battle of Minorca; 16.2.1757 Mid *Prince* (90); 22.8.1757 Mid *Burford* (68); 5.9.1757-6.10.1757 Raid on Rochefort; 6.6.1758-27.7.1758 The Siege of Louisbourg; 16.1.1759-19.1.1759 Attack on Martinique; 20.1.1759-1.5.1759 Capture of Guadeloupe; 20.11.1759 Battle of Quiberon Bay; 27.2.1760 **Lieutenant**; 13.8.1760 Passed; 27.2.1761-22.10.1761 L. *Beaver* (14) Sloop; 18.11.1761-3.3.1762 L. *Weazle* (16) Sloop; 1762 Impress Service.

WEBB, JAMES

Dates: 14.5.1761 Died Plymouth Sound.
Family:
Service: **Lieutenant**; 14.9.1744[(6.2.1744/45)]-29.9.1744 3L *Liverpool* (44); **Commander**; 1.5.1745 *Jamaica* (10) Sloop; **Captain**; 25.6.1746-3.2.1748/49[P] *Surprise* (24); 13.2.1753-6.8.1756 *Speedwell* (8) Sloop; 9.11.1756-21.2.1757 *Sunderland* (60); 10.3.1757 *Saint Albans* (60); 1.3.1758[(3.10.1758)]-5.3.1759[P] *Hampton Court* (64); 10.4.1759-14.5.1761 *Antelope* (50).

WEBB, JOHN

Dates: 8.11.1786 Died.
Family:
Service: **Lieutenant**; 18.1.1761[(16.10.1764)] 3L *Chatham* (50); 18.7.1763[(EI 16.10.1764)]-31.7.1764[P] 2L *Chatham* (50); 3.11.1770-20.9.1773 L. *Wolf* (8) Sloop; 10.8.1776 3L *Belleisle* (64); 30.5.1778-31.8.1781[P] 1L *Belleisle* (64).

WEBBER, CHARLES

Dates: 1783 Died.
Family:
Service: **Lieutenant**; 23.1.1743/44[(MED 25.11.1748)] 4L *Elizabeth* (70); 11.2.1743/44-12.2.1743/44 Battle of Toulon; 8.11.1744[(MED 25.11.1748)]-17.12.1745 4L *Nassau* (70); 16.8.1748[(25.11.1748)]-10.11.1748[P] 4L *Boyne* (80); 7.4.1749-28.12.1750[P] 3L *Humber* (44); 21.1.1751/52 2L *Severn* (50); **Commander**; 19.1.1755[(JAM 6.10.1759)] *Falcon* (10) Bomb Vessel; **Captain**; 5.4.1756[(JAM 30.8.1756)]-10.11.1756 *Hind* (24); 15.11.1756 *Rose* (20); 21.1.1757 *Rose* (20); 22.5.1758 *Cerberus* (28); 6.6.1762-13.8.1762 Operations against Havana; 13.9.1763-27.9.1763[P] *Cerberus* (28); 26.9.1780 **Rear Admiral of the White.**

WEBSTER, WILLIAM

Dates: c.1727 Born; c.1777 Died; 22.3.1777 Will Probate.
Family:
Service: 1.12.1739 Able *Greenwich* (50); 1.4.1741 Mid *Deptford* (24) Storeship; 25.2.1742 Able *Prince George* (90); 6.12.1742 Mid *Prince George* (90); 2.6.1745 Mid *Warwick* (60); 23.9.1746 NR *Lennox* (70); 14.2.1757 Passed; **Lieutenant**; 15.2.1757-19.7.1757 L. *Scorpion* (14) Sloop; 22.5.1758 1L *Aquilon* (28); 28.2.1759 L. *Fortune* (14) Sloop; 21.5.1759-28.12.1759 LCmdr *Experiment* Tender; **Commander**; 14.10.1762-20.2.1763[P] *Wasp* (8) Sloop; 19.5.1763-24.10.1766 *Hazard* (8) Sloop; 29.11.1766-18.1.1770 *Speedwell* (8) Sloop; 13.3.1776-26.2.1777 *Alderney* (10) Sloop.

WELDON, JOHN

Dates: bef.19.2.1760 Died.
Family:
Service: **Lieutenant**; 22.6.1726(30.8.1728) 3L *Leopard* (50); 27.10.1726(30.8.1728) 4L *Bredah* (70); 26.7.1727(30.8.1728) 3L *Bredah* (70); 12.11.1727(30.8.1728)-4.6.1728 1L *Bredah* (70).

WELLARD, ROBERT

Dates: 15.4.1776 Died.
Family:
Service: **Lieutenant**; 12.3.1739/40 4L *Cambridge* (80); 27.3.1741 3L *Cambridge* (80); 5.10.1741 2L *Cambridge* (80); 13.11.1741-4.3.1742/43[P] 1L *Winchester* (50); 2.5.1743 1L *Severn* (50); 1.7.1744(JAM 9.6.1749) 3L *Superb* (60); **Commander**; 28.10.1744(28.6.0501)-14.4.1745[C] *Mercury* (16) Sloop; **Captain**; 31.5.1746-3.9.1746 *Namur* (74); 23.12.1746-22.1.1748/49[P] *Hastings* (44).

WELLER, JOHN

Dates: c.1717 Born; 7.9.1772 Died.
Family:
Service: 20.1.1730/31 Vol-p-O *Falmouth* (50); 2.3.1731/32 MidO *Falmouth* (50); 15.9.1734-7.7.1735 Mid *Falmouth* (50); 8.7.1735 Mid *Dublin* (12) Yacht; 18.7.1737 Passed; **Lieutenant**; 15.9.1739(9.6.1740) 3L *Canterbury* (60); 7.1.1739/40 L. *Mercury* (8) Fireship; 28.5.1741 4L *Ipswich* (70); 21.9.1741 4L *Royal Sovereign* (104); 8.2.1741/42 3L *Royal Sovereign* (104); 20.2.1741/42 2L *Royal Sovereign* (104); 23.7.1742 6L *Saint George* (90); 19.7.1743 5L *Saint George* (90); 24.8.1743-2.2.1743/44 6L *Sandwich* (90); **Commander**; 8.11.1744(MED 7.4.1749)-16.10.1745 *Carcass* (8) Bomb Vessel; **Captain**; 29.11.1745-27.10.1748[P] *Roebuck* (44); 18.4.1751-26.9.1752[P] *Dublin* (12) Yacht; 18.7.1753 *Dorset* Yacht; 25.11.1755-5.5.1758 *Assistance* (50); 6.6.1758(JAM 30.10.1760)-30.9.1760[P] *Marlborough* (80); 19.5.1763-16.5.1765[P] *Venus* (36); 5.11.1770 **Superannuated Rear Admiral**.

WELLS, THOMAS

Dates: c.1760 Died; 26.11.1760 Will Probate.
Family:
Service: 4.4.1722 Vol-p-O *Faversham* (42); 4.3.1723/24 MidO *Faversham* (42); 13.7.1724 Mid *Faversham* (42); 19.10.1724 MidO *Prince Frederick* (70); 9.1.1725/26 MidO *Kinsale* (40); 20.1.1726/27 MidO *Dragon* (54); 19.12.1727-5.10.1728[P] Mid *Dragon* (54); 13.2.1728/29 Passed; **Lieutenant**; 3.3.1739/40-4.5.1742[P] L. *Firebrand* (8) Fireship; 4.3.1740/41-5.1741 Operations against Cartagena; 22.7.1742 2L *Princess* (70); 20.12.1742-14.12.1744 L. *Success* (20); **Commander**; 27.9.1745-11.2.1745/46 *Saint Quentin* (16) Hired Armed vessel.

WEMYSS, HON. JAMES

Dates: 23.2.1725/26 Born; 10.5.1786 Died.
Family: Father James, 5th Earl of Wemyss; Mother Janet Charteris; Wife Elizabeth Sutherland married 29.8.1757; Son Gen. William Wemyss, MP (1760–); Brother Lord Elcho; Brother Francis.
Service: 24.7.1745 Passed; **Lieutenant**; 26.9.1745(EI 1.12.1747) 2L *Medway* (60); 5.2.1746/47(EI 29.8.1749) 2L *Preston* (50); 24.3.1747/48(EI 29.8.1749)-23.11.1749[SC] 1L *Preston* (50); 7.3.1755-21.4.1756 2L *Orford* (68); 12.1.1757 Resigned; 7.1.1763-31.3.1768 M.P. for Fife; 14.4.1768-10.5.1786 M.P. for Sutherland.

WENTWORTH, THOMAS

Dates: c.1706 Born; 4.1756 Died; 30.4.1756 Buried St Leonard, Shoreditch, Middlesex; 13.11.1756 Will Probate.
Family: Son Thomas.
Service: 2.3.1725/26 Able *Bredah* (70); 6.6.1727-22.8.1728^{P} Vol-p-O *Bredah* (70); 5.9.1730 Vol-p-O *Hector* (40); 8.2.1730/31 MidO *Hector* (40); 14.5.1732 Able *Hector* (40); 3.4.1734 Mid *Nottingham* (60); 12.9.1734 Mid *Bideford* (20); 11.7.1735 Passed; **Lieutenant**; 30.5.1741$^{\text{(4.9.1741)}}$ 2L *Torrington* (40); 16.10.1741-5.2.1744/45 2L *Hampshire* (50); 27.5.1755-29.1.1756 2L *Revenge* (64).

WEST, JOHN

Dates: c.1714 Born; 14.1.1759 Died; 23.7.1759 Will Probate.
Family:
Service: 2.8.1738-15.10.1740 Able *Augusta* (60); 16.10.1740-23.10.1740 Able *Russell* (80); 24.10.1740-6.6.1741 Able *Jersey* (60); 4.3.1740/41-5.1741 Operations against Cartagena; 7.6.1741-27.8.1742 Mate *Jersey* (60); 28.8.1742-3.10.1742 Mate *Solebay* (42) Hospital Ship; 4.10.1742-5.3.1742/43 Mid *Monmouth* (70); 6.3.1742/43 Mate *Monmouth* (70); 11.10.1744 Passed; **Lieutenant**; 18.5.1745-16.11.1746 L. *Hound* (10) Sloop; 8.6.1747 2L *Expedition* (44); 15.6.1747-26.5.1749^{P} 2L *Crown* (44); 29.7.1755 L. *Queenborough* (24); 1.1.1756-14.1.1759† 1L *Prince Edward* (44); 29.12.1758 Capture of Goree.

WEST, JOHN

Dates: c.1783 Died; 30.7.1783 Will Probate.
Family:
Service: **Lieutenant**; 21.5.1761$^{\text{(5.10.1761)}}$-23.11.1761 4L *Belliqueux* (64); 7.4.1763 L. *Trial* (10) Sloop; 10.11.1765$^{\text{(NA 5.8.1766)}}$-23.7.1766^{P} L. *Aldborough* (20).

WEST, TEMPLE

Dates: 1713 Born; 9.8.1757 Died.
Family: Father Rev. Richard West; Mother Maria Temple; Wife Frances Balchen; Son Unknown; Son Unknown; Son Unknown.
Service: 11.12.1727 Vol-p-O *Revenge* (70); 19.8.1728 Vol-p-O *Canterbury* (60); 20.2.1729/30 MidO *Canterbury* (60); 2.7.1731 Mid *Canterbury* (60); 27.1.1731/32 Able *Berwick* (70); 9.6.1732 Mid *Dursley Galley* (20); 15.11.1733 Mid *Sheerness* (20); 21.12.1733 Passed; **Lieutenant**; 23.2.1733/34 3L *Dorsetshire* (80); 24.5.1734-2.4.1736^{P} 3L *Norfolk* (80); **Commander**; 7.4.1737 *Grampus* (6) Sloop; 14.5.1737 *Alderney* (8) Bomb Vessel; **Captain**; 13.6.1738 *Deal Castle* (20); 19.2.1740/41 *Sapphire* (44); 16.4.1741 *Dartmouth* (50); 3.6.1743$^{\text{(16.4.1745)}}$-13.7.1745 *Warwick* (60); 11.2.1743/44-12.2.1743/44 Battle of Toulon; 11.2.1743/44 Dismissed; 1.4.1747-13.4.1747 *Saint George* (90); 13.4.1747-13.12.1747^{P} *Devonshire* (80); 3.5.1747 1st Battle of Cape Finisterre; 27.2.1747/48-3.6.1748 CinC — Ribadeo; 17.1.1753-15.4.1754 M.P. for Buckingham; 4.2.1755 **Rear Admiral of the Red**; 8.2.1755-3.7.1756 *Buckingham* (68); 20.5.1756 Battle of Minorca; 17.11.1756-5.4.1757 Lord Commissioner of the Admiralty; 8.12.1756 **Vice Admiral of the Blue**; 1.5.1757 **Vice Admiral of the White**; 2.7.1757-9.8.1757 Lord Commissioner of the Admiralty.

WEST, THOMAS
Dates: c.1736 Born.
Family:
Service: 1753-1755 Merchant Service; 7.4.1755 Mid *York* (60); 6.6.1758-27.7.1758 The Siege of Louisbourg; 14.8.1758 Able *Namur* (90); 3.1.1759 Passed; **Lieutenant**; 22.2.1759 L. *Pluto* (8) Fireship; 20.11.1759 Battle of Quiberon Bay; 3.4.1761-26.2.1763[P] 2L *Dover* (44); 7.1.1762-10.2.1762 Operations against Martinique; 24.2.1762-25.2.1762 Capture of Saint Lucia; 6.6.1762-13.8.1762 Operations against Havana.

WESTLAKE, BERNARD
Dates: c.1739 Born.
Family:
Service: 1753-1755 HEIC Service; 1.3.1755 Purs Serv *Solebay* (24); 20.4.1756-11.6.1756[P] Able *Blast* (8) Fireship; 28.6.1757 Mid *Devonshire* (70); 9.10.1757 Mid *Cambridge* (80); 16.1.1759-19.1.1759 Attack on Martinique; 20.1.1759-1.5.1759 Capture of Guadeloupe; 4.6.1759 Mate *Cambridge* (80); 4.7.1759 Passed; **Lieutenant**; 10.8.1759 6L *Royal Sovereign* (104); 24.5.1762-27.12.1762[P] 5L *Royal Sovereign* (104).

WHEELER, EDWARD
Dates: 1.4.1761 Died.
Family:
Service: **Lieutenant**; 23.1.1741/42[(2.5.1744)] L. *Lightning* (8) Bomb Vessel; 29.10.1742[(3.5.1744)] 4L *Grafton* (70); 25.7.1743[(3.5.1744)]-17.12.1743[D] 2L *Grafton* (70); 17.12.1743 Dismissed; 14.8.1744-6.3.1745/46 2L *Mary Galley* (44); 4.4.1748 1L *Lion* (58); 5.7.1748 **Captain**; 23.7.1748[(3.7.1749)]-4.11.1748 *Boston* (24); 11.9.1751-6.11.1754[P] *Sphinx* (24); 1.7.1755-1.4.1761[†] *Isis* (50); 3.7.1759 Bombardment of Le Havre.

WHEELOCK, JOHN
Dates: 1779 Died.
Family:
Service: 18.2.1732/33 Scholar *Royal Naval Academy*; **Lieutenant**; 26.6.1741[(6.11.1742)] 3L *Princess Louisa* (60); 26.5.1743 L. *Squirrel* (20); 19.9.1743-15.7.1744[P] 3L *Liverpool* (44); 7.2.1746/47[(MED 22.7.1748)] 1L *Russell* (80); 6.5.1747[(MED 22.7.1748)] 1L *Boyne* (80); 20.8.1747[(MED 22.7.1748)]-4.6.1748[P] 1L *Russell* (80); 7.10.1747 Action of 1747-10-07; 1.11.1748-1.4.1750 3L *Gloucester* (50); 27.3.1755 1L *Bedford* (64); **Commander**; 19.2.1756 *Fly* (8) Sloop; 10.1.1757-5.5.1757 *Stork* (10) Sloop; **Captain**; 21.12.1757-12.5.1759 *Squirrel* (20); 6.6.1758-27.7.1758 The Siege of Louisbourg; 15.5.1759[(27.1.1760)]-20.2.1764[P] *Pembroke* (60); 6.6.1762-13.8.1762 Operations against Havana; 16.8.1770 *Achilles* (60); 9.4.1771-16.10.1772[P] *Modeste* (64); 24.10.1777-14.11.1778 *Sultan* (74).

WHISTON, JOHN
Dates: c.1735 Born.
Family:
Service: 1753-1757 HEIC Service; 4.3.1757 Mid *Bridgewater* (24); 7.3.1757-1.4.1757 Expedition against Chandernagore; 21.10.1757 Mate *Gibraltar* (20); 18.8.1759-19.8.1759 Battle of Lagos Bay; 5.3.1760 Passed; **Lieutenant**; 19.6.1760-13.10.1761 L. *Wasp* (8) Sloop; 18.8.1766-1.2.1770 L. *Ranger* (8) Sloop; 10.8.1771-13.10.1772[P] 2L *Portland* (50); 25.10.1775-26.10.1776 L. *Wasp* (8) Sloop; 18.12.1776-23.10.1783[P] LCmdr *Fanny* Hired Tender.

WHITAKER, THOMAS

Dates: 1767 Died.
Family:
***Service:* Lieutenant**; 19.1.1704/5[(22.7.1706)]-9.5.1705 2L *Monck* (64); 10.5.1705[(22.7.1706)]-28.9.1706[P] 2L *Gloucester* (60); 22.10.1706-10.1.1706/7 3L *Ranelagh* (80); 11.1.1706/7-2.6.1709 2L *Portland* (54); 28.5.1708 Wager's Action.

WHITE, DAVID

Dates: c.1735 Born; c.1762 Died; 22.4.1762 Will Probate.
Family:
Service: 21.6.1752 Capt Serv *Rainbow* (44); 12.11.1754 Able *Rainbow* (44); 14.6.1755 Able *Deptford* (50); 20.5.1756 Battle of Minorca; 4.6.1756 Mid *Prince George* (80); 17.12.1756 Mid *Monarch* (74); 13.11.1757 Mate *Dublin* (74); 9.8.1758 Passed; **Lieutenant**; 27.10.1758 3L *Lynn* (44); 8.3.1759 2L *America* (60); 15.3.1759 3L *America* (60); 18.10.1759-11.8.1764[P] 1L *America* (60); 24.9.1762-6.10.1762 Battle of Manilla.

WHITE, GEORGE

Dates: 11.1778 Died.
Family:
Service: 12.2.1756-8.4.1759 Mid *Monmouth* (70); 28.2.1758 Battle of Cartagena; 9.4.1759 Mid *Montagu* (60); 13.6.1759 Passed; **Lieutenant**; 16.7.1759-24.2.1763[P] L. *Thunder* (8) Bomb Vessel; 20.11.1759 Battle of Quiberon Bay; 7.1.1762-10.2.1762 Operations against Martinique; 6.6.1762-13.8.1762 Operations against Havana; 4.12.1770-4.7.1771 L. *Dispatch* (14) Sloop.

WHITE, JAMES

Dates: c.1735 Born; 1790 Died.
Family:
Service: 3.10.1750 Mst Serv *Sphinx* (24); 22.1.1753 Able *Sphinx* (24); 17.11.1753 Mid *Sphinx* (24); 7.11.1754 Able *Sphinx* (24); 10.11.1755 Mid *Sphinx* (24); 10.3.1756 Able *Sphinx* (24); 12.3.1756 Mid *Sphinx* (24); 20.6.1756 Mid *Seaford* (20); 27.11.1756 Mate *Seaford* (20); 4.4.1757 Passed; **Lieutenant**; 27.10.1758-17.10.1761[W] 1L *Griffin* (28).

WHITE, OLIVER

Dates: c.1731 Born.
Family:
Service: 14.5.1748 Able *Intrepid* (64); 8.3.1748/49 Able *Amazon* (22); 6.8.1750 Mid *Amazon* (22); 24.3.1754 Able *Rye* (20); 2.5.1755 Mid *Saint George* (90); 1.9.1755 Mate *Saint George* (90); 3.12.1755 Passed; **Lieutenant**; 7.7.1756[(ECH 6.4.1757)] 4L *Intrepid* (64); 2.2.1757-8.2.1757 3L *Newcastle* (50); 6.4.1757 4L *Burford* (68); 5.9.1757-6.10.1757 Raid on Rochefort; 6.6.1758-27.7.1758 The Siege of Louisbourg; 29.9.1758 3L *Burford* (68); 16.1.1759-19.1.1759 Attack on Martinique; 20.1.1759-1.5.1759 Capture of Guadeloupe; 20.11.1759 Battle of Quiberon Bay; 29.3.1761-11.6.1761 Expedition against Belle-Isle; 14.10.1761-11.5.1763 2L *Burford* (68).

WHITEHURST, THOMAS

Dates: c.1730 Born; 1766 Died; 7.10.1766 Will Probate.
Family:
Service: 1753-1755 Merchant Service; 4.11.1755 Able *Otter* (14) Sloop; 23.7.1756 Cox *Otter* (14) Sloop; 17.2.1757 Cpl *Greyhound* (20); 5.5.1757 Mid *Greyhound* (20); 10.5.1758 Mid *Venus*

(36); 16.6.1759 Able *Venus* (36); 1.8.1759 Passed; 11.10.1759 **Lieutenant**; 8.4.1760 1L *Sapphire* (32); 7.1.1761 3L *Lynn* (44); 29.3.1761-11.6.1761 Expedition against Belle-Isle; 7.7.1762-15.3.1763P 2L *Lynn* (44); 18.4.1763-26.6.1765 L. *Viper* (10) Sloop.

WHITTLE, PRICE WARREN

Dates: c.1739 Born; 15.8.1778 Died.
Family:
Service: 27.10.1753 Able *Otter* (14) Sloop; 4.12.1753 Mid *Experiment* (24); 19.4.1754 Able *Experiment* (24); 19.7.1755 Mid *Prince Edward* (44); 27.2.1757 Mid *Preston* (50); 22.4.1758 Mate *Preston* (50); 2.4.1760 Passed; **Lieutenant**; 5.1.1762(6.7.1762)-21.11.1762 4L *Somerset* (68).

WHITWELL, MATTHEW

Dates: c.1720 Born; 15.2.1789 Died.
Family:
Service: 5.11.1733-29.8.1734 Ord. *Blenheim* (96); 30.8.1734-31.1.1734/35 Able *Blenheim* (96); 1.2.1734/35-2.10.1736 Able *Shoreham* (20); 3.10.1736-29.10.1737 Mid *Shoreham* (20); 30.10.1737-19.1.1739/40 Mid *Romney* (50); 19.6.1740 Passed; **Lieutenant**; 10.1.1740/41 5L *Duke* (90); 7.9.1741 4L *Duke* (90); 26.11.1742-16.12.1743 3L *Duke* (90); 3.2.1743/44 4L *Saint George* (90); 29.3.1744 3L *Saint George* (90); 15.6.1744 4L *Cornwall* (80); 30.8.1744-26.8.1746 3L *Cornwall* (80); 12.6.1747-9.10.1747 1L *Deptford* (60); 23.11.1747 1L *Intrepid* (64); **Commander**; 5.12.1747 *Speedwell* (10) Sloop; **Captain**; 6.5.1748-23.12.1748P *Poole* (44); 12.10.1749-4.6.1755P *Triton* (20); 4.6.1755 *Roebuck* (44); 5.11.1756-10.3.1757 *Saint Albans* (60); 15.2.1759-1.11.1762 *Anson* (60); 6.9.1763-24.10.1766 *Augusta* (64); 6.11.1770-3.1.1771 *Egmont* (74); 26.4.1779 **Superannuated Rear Admiral**.

WHYTE, MARK

Dates: c.1732 Born.
Family:
Service: 20.12.1749 Scholar *Royal Naval Academy*; 3.1.1753 Vol-p-O *Blandford* (20); 13.4.1753 Mid *Raven* (14) Sloop; 21.1.1754 Mid *Rye* (20); 7.6.1755 Mid *Ambuscade* (40); 3.12.1755 Passed; **Lieutenant**; 24.1.1756 3L *Harwich* (50); 21.9.1757 2L *Montagu* (60); 28.2.1758 Battle of Cartagena; 22.2.1759-2.10.1761 1L *Montagu* (60); 20.11.1759 Battle of Quiberon Bay.

WICKHAM, JOHN

Dates: 21.10.1763 Died.
Family:
Service: 16.11.1719 Vol-p-O *Norwich* (50); 14.2.1720/21-31.10.1721P Vol-p-O *Gloucester* (54); 14.8.1723 Able *Essex* (70); 24.9.1723 Able *Guernsey* (50); 19.7.1724 Mid *Guernsey* (50); 12.4.1725 Able *Elizabeth* (70); 6.2.1725/26 Mid *Elizabeth* (70); 13.4.1727 Mid *Medway* (60); 17.11.1727 Passed; **Lieutenant**; 24.11.1731-16.12.1732 L. *Experiment* (20); 31.1.1733/34-30.5.1734 4L *Princess Amelia* (80); 31.5.1734-9.7.1736P 3L *Princess Amelia* (80); 15.3.1737/38 3L *Ipswich* (70); 12.5.1738 2L *Ipswich* (70); 9.3.1739/40(2.11.1742) 1L *Ipswich* (70); 2.5.1740(2.11.1742) 1L *Somerset* (80); **Commander**; 2.9.1740(2.11.1742) *Mercury* (8) Fireship; 17.5.1741(10.4.1742)-26.5.1742 *Salamander* (6) Bomb Vessel; **Captain**; 1.11.1742 *Success* (20); 11.5.1744 *Lark* (44); 29.5.1746-17.2.1748/49P *Panther* (50); 1.7.1755-2.12.1755 *Dreadnought* (60); 19.5.1756-13.4.1757 *Augusta* (60); 30.4.1757(NA 27.2.1758)-25.10.1757 *Rye* (20); 13.6.1759 **Superannuated Rear Admiral**.

WIGHTMAN, WILLIAM
Dates: c.1731 Born.
Family:
Service: 6.3.1749/50 Ord. *Roebuck* (44); 13.6.1750 Able *Dragon* (60); 13.11.1751 Able *Princess Louisa* (60); 24.5.1753 Mid *Princess Louisa* (60); 20.10.1753 Mid *Lion* (58); 6.4.1754 Mid *Panther Hulk* Hulk; 29.5.1754 Mid *America* (44); 24.7.1754 Mate *America* (44); 31.12.1754 Able *Humber* (44); 20.4.1755 Mid *Humber* (44); 2.6.1756 Passed; **Lieutenant**; 8.10.1756 3L *Ludlow Castle* (44); 15.3.1757-30.9.1758 2L *Ludlow Castle* (44).

WILDING, PETER MANWARING
Dates: 2.5.1766 Died.
Family:
Service: **Lieutenant**; 17.1.1748/49[EI 6.10.1749]-23.8.1749[P] 2L *Medway Prize* (30); 25.10.1759 1L *Panther* (60); 7.5.1761[11.9.1764]-25.8.1764[P] 1L *Baleine* (20).

WILIS, JOHN
Dates: 8.4.1804 Died.
Family:
Service: 23.2.1757 **Lieutenant**.

WILKIE, ALEXANDER
Dates: c.1708 Born; 1759 Died; 20.3.1759 Will Probate.
Family:
Service: 2.9.1733 Able *Griffin* (8); 28.2.1733/34-10.10.1737[P] Mate *Bridgewater* (32); 11.11.1737 Mate *Aldborough* (20); 6.10.1741 Passed; **Lieutenant**; 16.2.1741/42 L. *Fly* (8) Sloop; 7.12.1743 3L *Anglesea* (44); 20.4.1744-16.5.1746 3L *Sunderland* (60); 22.7.1755-2.12.1755 2L *Dreadnought* (60); 1.6.1756 1L *Augusta* (60); 30.4.1757[NA 9.3.1758]-27.10.1757 L. *Rye* (20).

WILKIE, JAMES
Dates: c.1726 Baptised.
Family:
Service: 25.6.1742 Capt Serv *Sapphire* (44); 18.1.1743/44 Able *Cornwall* (80); 13.6.1744 Capt Serv *Enterprise* Sloop; 15.12.1745 Able *Enterprise* Sloop; 20.11.1746 Mid *Enterprise* Sloop; 24.5.1747 Mid *Lennox* (70); 9.4.1748 Battle of Santiago de Cuba; 12.10.1748 Battle of Havana; 14.11.1748 ActL *Lennox* (70); 8.12.1748 Passed; 9.12.1748 **Lieutenant**; 21.12.1748-29.12.1748[P] 4L *Lennox* (70); 6.2.1755 5L *Prince George* (80); 20.3.1755 L. *Albany* (14) Sloop; 19.8.1755-19.9.1755 L. *Experiment* (24); 12.8.1756 L. *Spy* (10) Sloop; 11.1.1757 3L *Preston* (50); 15.3.1757-21.10.1757 3L *Prince Edward* (44); 21.10.1757 Dismissed.

WILKINS, WILLIAM
Dates: c.1730 Born.
Family:
Service: 14.8.1747 Able *Defiance* (60); 14.10.1747 2nd Battle of Cape Finisterre; 13.9.1748 Able *Mars* (64); 14.4.1749 Able *Hornet* (10) Sloop; 19.7.1750 Mid *Hornet* (10) Sloop; **Lieutenant**; 3.12.1751 L. *Scorpion* (14) Sloop; 25.1.1753-1.8.1753 LCmdr *Scorpion* (14) Sloop; 1.8.1753 Passed; 6.3.1755 4L *Orford* (68); 21.3.1755-2.8.1755 6L *Torbay* (74); 6.6.1755-8.6.1755 Action of 6-8 June 1755.

WILKINSON, ANDREW

Dates: 24.5.1787 Died.

Family:

Service: **Lieutenant**; 22.8.1747(MED 13.5.1748)-31.5.1748[P] 3L *Jersey* (60); 18.2.1751/52 2L *Penzance* (44); 28.1.1755 5L *Prince* (90); 14.10.1755 4L *Prince* (90); 12.11.1755 3L *Prince* (90); 7.4.1756 2L *Prince* (90); 12.5.1756 2L *Royal George* (100); **Commander**; 2.8.1756 *Diligence* (10) Sloop; **Captain**; 23.3.1757-21.8.1759 *Glasgow* (20); 20.8.1759(MED 21.4.1760)-12.5.1763[P] *Jersey* (60); 29.11.1766-6.12.1769 *Niger* (32); 2.10.1777-14.7.1779 *Grafton* (74); 6.7.1779 Battle of Grenada.

WILKINSON, GEORGE

Dates: c.1729 Born; 19.9.1782 Died; 30.10.1783 Will Probate.

Family:

Service: 1752-1755 Merchant Service; 1.9.1755 Mid *Windsor* (60); 27.6.1756 Mate *Windsor* (60); 11.12.1756 Mid *Windsor* (60); 21.5.1757 Mate *Windsor* (60); 19.8.1757 Mid *Windsor* (60); 30.1.1758 Mate *Windsor* (60); 9.11.1758 Passed; **Lieutenant**; 9.1.1760-14.1.1763[P] 3L *Windsor* (60); 24.1.1771-24.9.1773[P] 3L *Princess Amelia* (80); 19.10.1778 4L *Britannia* (100); 10.3.1779 1L *Berwick* (74); 1.10.1779 5L *Sandwich* (90); 16.1.1780 Battle of Cape St. Vincent; 17.4.1780 Battle of Martinique; **Commander**; 27.5.1780(BLI 4.7.1781)-13.2.1781 *Saint Vincent* (14) Sloop; **Captain**; 14.5.1781(BLI 7.5.1782) *Prince William* (64); 25.1.1782-26.1.1782 Battle of Saint Kitts; 12.4.1782 Battle of the Saintes; 13.4.1782-19.9.1782 *Ville de Paris* (104).

WILKINSON, MATTHEW

Dates: Not Known.

Family:

Service: **Lieutenant**; 2.1.1759(22.2.1763)-11.6.1763[P] L. *Goree* (10) Sloop; 22.3.1777 3L *Trident* (64); 29.4.1777-5.9.1781[P] 2L *Trident* (64); 6.7.1779 Battle of Grenada; 17.4.1780 Battle of Martinique; 15.5.1780 Action of March 15 1780; 19.5.1780 Action of March 19 1780.

WILKINSON, THOMAS

Dates: c.1736 Born; c.12.1776 Died.

Family: Wife Millicent Howe; Son Philip, RN.

Service: 17.5.1747 Capt Serv *Warwick* (60); 20.6.1747 Able *Warwick* (60); 30.11.1747 Capt Serv *Canterbury* (60); 9.4.1748 Battle of Santiago de Cuba; 2.8.1748-19.1.1748/49[P] Capt Serv *Milford* (44); 5.2.1748/49 L. Serv *Assurance* (44); 21.10.1752-24.4.1753[W] Able *Assurance* (44); 29.1.1757 Mid *Prince Frederick* (64); 6.6.1758-27.7.1758 The Siege of Louisbourg; 5.10.1758 Mid *Boreas* (28); 31.1.1759 Passed; **Lieutenant**; 22.8.1759-12.7.1762[P] L. *Furnace* (8) Bomb Vessel; 29.3.1761-11.6.1761 Expedition against Belle-Isle; 27.5.1763 L. *Cruizer* (8) Sloop; 18.10.1764 L. *Hound* (14) Sloop; **Commander**; 4.9.1766-17.10.1766 *Hound* (14) Sloop; 23.2.1768 *Swan* (14) Sloop; **Captain**; 10.1.1771 *Boulogne* (32); 28.10.1771-7.7.1772 *Fowey* (24); 17.4.1772-21.6.1775[P] *Winchelsea* (32); 2.1.1776-c.12.1776[†] *Pearl* (32).

WILLES, JOHN

Dates: None Known.

Family:

Service: **Lieutenant**; 1.3.1748/49(EI 19.11.1751)-8.5.1752 3L *Ruby* (50); 21.9.1796 **Superannuated Commander.**

WILLETT, WILLIAM SALTERN

Dates: 8.12.1769 Died.

Family:

Service: **Lieutenant**; 23.7.1741[27.8.1741]-27.5.1742 4L *Elizabeth* (70); 17.9.1742 3L *Royal Oak* (70); 11.2.1743/44-12.2.1743/44 Battle of Toulon; 22.9.1744[16.1.1743/44]-14.3.1744/45[P] 3L *Oxford* (50); 4.12.1744-14.12.1744 1L *Pembroke* (60); 14.12.1744 LCmdr *John and Anne* (16) Hired Armed vessel; **Commander**; 27.12.1745-3.8.1747 *Kingfisher* (10) Sloop; **Captain**; 1.10.1747 *Queenborough* (24); 16.9.1748 *Garland* (24); 17.10.1753-19.5.1756 *Augusta* (60); 31.5.1756 *Chichester* (68); 5.6.1758-12.6.1758 Raid on Saint-Malo; 20.11.1759 Battle of Quiberon Bay; 10.5.1761-5.5.1763[P] *Warspite* (74); 19.11.1764-19.11.1767 *Ramillies* (74); 28.11.1766 CinC — River Medway and The Nore; 15.11.1769-3.1.1770 Commodore *Yarmouth* (64); 16.11.1769 CinC — River Medway and The Nore.

WILLIAMS, BOSVILLE

Dates: c.1692 Born; bef.27.5.1757 Died.

Family:

Service: 28.10.1726 Mid *Suffolk* (70); 14.1.1729 Able *Suffolk* (70); 7.4.1729 QM *Hawk* (8) Sloop; 3.7.1729 Mid *Hawk* (8) Sloop; 14.9.1729 Mate *Hawk* (8) Sloop; 20.10.1729 Mid *Hawk* (8) Sloop; 4.9.1730-16.9.1730 Able *Hawk* (8) Sloop; 17.9.1730-8.6.1732[P] Mate *Gosport* (42); 26.11.1732 Master *Fox* (20); 30.11.1734 Master *Poole* (32); 11.4.1735 Act3L *Newcastle* (50); 5.6.1735 ActL *Fox* (20); **Lieutenant**; 27.7.1736-12.8.1736[P] L. *Fox* (20); 23.10.1736 Passed; 31.3.1737 L. *Seaford* (20); 12.5.1737 3L *Torrington* (40); 16.5.1737 L. *Grampus* (6) Sloop; 27.9.1740 2L *Kingston* (60); 21.2.1740/41 1L *Kingston* (60); 21.8.1741 1L *Royal Oak* (70); 27.7.1742[15.3.1744/45] L. *Spence* (8) Sloop; 25.9.1743[15.3.1744/45]-25.10.1744 1L *Princess Caroline* (80); 11.2.1743/44-12.2.1743/44 Battle of Toulon; 9.5.1745 2L *Sandwich* (90); 20.5.1745 1L *Sandwich* (90); 1.7.1745-10.6.1748[P] LCmdr *Britannia* (100).

WILLIAMS, COURTNAY

Dates: c.1736 Born.

Family:

Service: 10.10.1753 Able *Penzance* (44); 18.6.1754 Mid *Penzance* (44); 19.6.1755 Mid *Elizabeth* (70); 30.7.1756 Mid *Seaford* (20); 29.7.1757 Mid *Duke* (90); 9.2.1758 Able *Lowestoffe* (28); 5.6.1758-12.6.1758 Raid on Saint-Malo; 28.12.1758 Mid *Lowestoffe* (28); 7.11.1759 Passed; **Lieutenant**; 8.4.1760-23.12.1760 2L *Sapphire* (32).

WILLIAMS, JOHN

Dates: 1768 Died.

Family:

Service: 11.3.1721/22 Ord. *Warwick* (54); 5.6.1722-1.12.1722 Vol-p-O *Buckingham* (70); 2.12.1722 Ord. *Deptford* (50); 14.12.1722 Vol-p-O *Deptford* (50); 19.3.1723/24-15.4.1724[P] Mid *Deptford* (50); 12.11.1726 Mid *Lennox* (70); 28.5.1727 MidO *Chatham* (50); 29.7.1727 Mid *Chatham* (50); 29.12.1727 Mid *Medway* (60); 10.4.1728 Mid *Medway* (60); 25.6.1728 MidO *Dursley Galley* (20); 30.8.1728 MidO *Looe* (42); 13.2.1728/29 Passed; **Lieutenant**; 14.9.1732 L. *Saltash* (8) Sloop; 28.3.1735-14.4.1735 2L *Rippon* (60); 28.3.1737 1L *Exeter* (60); 19.8.1737 1L *Jersey* (60); 15.3.1737/38 2L *Jersey* (60); 19.6.1739-13.2.1739/40 4L *Russell* (80); **Commander**; 18.7.1740 *Charlotte* (8) Yacht; 6.4.1742-29.6.1744[P] *Katherine* (8) Yacht; 6.8.1745-7.2.1755 *Katherine* (8) Yacht.

WILLIAMS, JONATHON

Dates: c.1713 Born; 1773 Died.

Family:

Service: 29.8.1729 Vol-p-O *York* (60); 8.5.1730 Vol-p-O *Gosport* (42); 29.8.1731 MidO *Gosport* (42); 11.3.1731/32-8.6.1732[P] Mid *Gosport* (42); 7.8.1732 QM *Exeter* (60); 5.10.1732 Mid *Saltash* (8) Sloop; 7.11.1735 Passed; **Lieutenant**; 29.11.1738 2L *Roebuck* (40); 27.12.1740-26.3.1741 1L *Roebuck* (40); 27.3.1741 1L *Dartmouth* (50); 29.4.1744[(10.12.1744)]-19.9.1744[P] 3L *Rochester* (54); 30.7.1746 1L *Royal Sovereign* (104); 13.10.1747-7.6.1748[P] 1L *Barfleur* (90).

WILLIAMS, RICHARD

Dates: c.1725 Born; 1814 Died; 19.10.1814 Will Probate.

Family:

Service: 5.10.1739 Capt Serv *York* (60); 20.8.1740 Capt Serv *Buckingham* (70); 8.11.1740 Capt Serv *Torbay* (80); 28.7.1741 Ord. *Torbay* (80); 3.8.1741 Able *Torbay* (80); 13.8.1741 Mid *Torbay* (80); 11.2.1743/44-12.2.1743/44 Battle of Toulon; 30.4.1744 Mid *Barfleur* (90); 24.3.1744/45 Mid *Newcastle* (50); 30.5.1745 Supnum *Princess Royal* (24) Storeship; 16.5.1746 Passed; 15.8.1746 **Lieutenant**; 7.3.1746/47 3L *Panther* (50); 13.8.1748[(3.12.1748)]-23.12.1748[P] 3L *Lion* (58); 19.2.1755-11.3.1755 5L *Royal George* (100); 11.3.1755 6L *Royal George* (100); 14.10.1755-29.11.1756 3L *Culloden* (74); 20.5.1756 Battle of Minorca; 4.4.1757 2L *Alcide* (64); 20.10.1757 1L *Alcide* (64); 5.6.1758-12.6.1758 Raid on Saint-Malo; 12.9.1759[(17.4.1761)]-1763[P] L. *Pelican* (8) Bomb Vessel; 17.1.1770-22.5.1771[P] 1L *Edgar* (60); 7.11.1776-18.7.1777 1L *Bienfaisant* (64); 26.5.1779[(NA 14.11.1781)] 5L *Russell* (74); **Commander**; 5.5.1781-30.7.1781[C] *Loyalist* (14) Sloop; 18.2.1783 *Otter* (14) Sloop; 18.4.1783-19.4.1783 *Otter* (14) Sloop; 24.10.1783 Dismissed; 14.9.1797-30.6.1799 *Gorgon* (20) Storeship; 27.6.1799 **Captain**.

WILLIAMS, ROGER

Dates: c.1731 Born; 1762 Died; 23.11.1762 Will Probate.

Family:

Service: 3.10.1747 Able *Edinburgh* (64); 14.10.1747 2nd Battle of Cape Finisterre; 31.1.1747/48 Able *Chester* (50); 17.3.1749/50 Mid *Chester* (50); 11.10.1750 Able *Berwick* (70); 29.4.1751 Mid *Blandford* (20); 15.6.1751 Mate *Blandford* (20); 5.7.1754 Passed; **Lieutenant**; 7.10.1756 4L *Essex* (64); 13.1.1757 3L *Essex* (64); 5.6.1758-12.6.1758 Raid on Saint-Malo; 5.9.1759 2L *Essex* (64); 17.10.1759-10.3.1760 6L *Royal George* (100); 20.11.1759 Battle of Quiberon Bay; 17.6.1760 2L *Saint George* (90); **Commander**; 27.8.1760-19.4.1762 *Guadaloupe* Sloop.

WILLIAMS, VINCENT

Dates: bef.1752 Died.

Family:

Service: **Lieutenant**; 22.10.1751[(1.7.1752)]-25.6.1752[P] L. *Rose* (24) Ship; 28.5.1756-22.11.1757 L. *Saltash* (14) Sloop.

WILLIAMS, WILLIAM

Dates: c.1735 Born; 10.1778 Died; 29.7.1779 Will Probate.

Family: Son Sir Thomas, RN (1761-1841); Son Edward, RN.

Service: 10.5.1750-14.10.1752 Able *Wasp* (8) Sloop; 15.10.1752 Mid *Wasp* (8) Sloop; 22.4.1755 Supnum *Seaford* (20); 3.5.1755 Mid *Dunkirk* (60); 6.6.1755-8.6.1755 Action of 6-8 June 1755; 9.4.1756-2.6.1756 Mid *Newark* (80); 2.6.1756 Passed; **Lieutenant**; 10.2.1757 L. *Antigua* (14) Sloop; 16.1.1759-19.1.1759 Attack on Martinique; **Commander**; 2.3.1759-3.12.1762[P]

Salamander (8) Fireship; 18.8.1766-30.8.1769 *Peggy* (8) Sloop; 24.11.1769-10.1.1771 *Otter* (14) Sloop; **Captain**; 10.1.1771 *Enterprise* (44); 8.7.1771-3.6.1774 *Wolf* (8) Sloop; 6.10.1775-1.9.1778 *Active* (28).

WILLIAMSON, WILLIAM

Dates: c.1720 Born; 13.6.1771 Died.
Family:
Service: 16.5.1735 Ord. *Edinburgh* (70); 20.1.1737/38 Ord. *Phoenix* (20); 3.1.1738/39-23.4.1742[P] Mid *Phoenix* (20); 4.1740-5.7.1740 Attack on St. Augustine; 15.7.1742 Passed; **Lieutenant**; 6.10.1744-8.7.1748[P] 3L *Portland* (50); 14.10.1747 2nd Battle of Cape Finisterre; 31.1.1747/48 Action of 1748/01/31; 1.12.1748 3L *Tiger* (60); 16.5.1750-14.11.1752[P] 2L *Tiger* (60); 16.1.1755 2L *Lichfield* (50); **Commander**; 15.11.1756-28.9.1758 *Furnace* (8) Bomb Vessel; 8.1757-10.1757 Louisbourg Expedition; **Captain**; 18.10.1758 *Sphinx* (24); 10.1.1759-30.5.1759 *Defiance* (60); 10.3.1760-19.10.1761 *Montagu* (60); 4.6.1762-13.6.1771 *Dorset* Yacht.

WILLIS, THOMAS

Dates: c.1725 Born; 1766 Died.
Family:
Service: 27.6.1739 Ord. *Pembroke* (60); 24.7.1739-8.5.1742[P] Able *Superb* (60); 23.11.1742 Able *Deptford* (60); 22.5.1744 Able *Suffolk* (70); 19.7.1744 Mid *Suffolk* (70); 15.9.1744 Mid *Hampton Court* (64); 8.1.1744/45 Action of 1745-01-08; 1.2.1745/46 Mid *Chesterfield* (44); 4.10.1746 Passed; **Lieutenant**; 11.7.1747-31.7.1749 3L *Severn* (50); 2.4.1754-19.3.1756[SP] 4L *Cumberland* (66); 11.1.1756-14.1.1756 Capture of Geriah; 1.8.1757[(29.5.1759)]-16.9.1757[P] 2L *Kent* (64); 19.4.1759 1L *Sandwich* (90); **Commander**; 5.6.1759 *Blast* (8) Bomb Vessel; 3.7.1759 Bombardment of Le Havre; **Captain**; 4.5.1761-27.1.1763[P] *Prince Edward* (44).

WILLS, JOHN

Dates: c.1735 Born; 8.4.1804 Died.
Family:
Service: 4.5.1749 Capt Serv *Chester* (50); 14.2.1751/52 Ord. *Kingfisher* (14) Sloop; 19.6.1752 Able *Kingfisher* (14) Sloop; 29.12.1752 Able *Garland* (24); 23.1.1753 Mid *Garland* (24); 25.6.1753 Mid *Gibraltar* (20); 31.3.1755 Mid *Fougueux* (64); 9.5.1755 Mid *Torbay* (74); 6.6.1755-8.6.1755 Action of 6-8 June 1755; 7.2.1756-19.11.1756 Mid *Invincible* (74); 19.11.1756 Passed; **Lieutenant**; 23.2.1757 3L *Dunkirk* (60); 8.6.1757 5L *Magnanime* (74); 11.7.1757 4L *Magnanime* (74); 29.7.1757 3L *Magnanime* (74); 5.9.1757-6.10.1757 Raid on Rochefort; 5.6.1758-12.6.1758 Raid on Saint-Malo; 26.9.1759 2L *Saint Florentine* (60); 25.8.1762-25.10.1763[P] 2L *Mars* (74); 20.9.1779 4L *Formidable* (98); 10.2.1780 3L *Formidable* (98); 12.7.1781-19.11.1781 2L *Formidable* (98); 23.3.1782-8.4.1782 2L *Ocean* (90).

WILLS, ROGER

Dates: c.1722 Born; 1789 Died; 8.8.1789 Will Probate.
Family:
Service: 23.8.1733 Capt Serv *Deal Castle* (20); 19.4.1735 Mst Serv *Deal Castle* (20); 5.9.1735 Mst Serv *Orford* (70); 8.1.1737/38 Ord. *Fly* (8) Sloop; 7.3.1738/39 Ord. *Worcester* (60); 3.4.1739 Able *Deptford* (60); 18.8.1739 Able *Tartar* (20); 28.5.1740 Cox *Tartar* (20); 22.6.1742 Mate *Tartar* (20); 17.3.1743/44 Mate *Hector* (44); 7.2.1744/45 Passed; **Lieutenant**; 12.10.1745 3L *Exeter* (60); 20.9.1746-25.9.1746 Lorient Operations; 1.10.1746 Action of 1746-10-01; 16.2.1746/47-3.5.1750[P] 2L *Exeter* (60); 29.8.1754 1L *Gosport* (44); 7.1.1756 3L *Monarch* (74);

16.4.1756 3L *Magnanime* (74); 26.8.1756 2L *Magnanime* (74); 8.4.1757 1L *Magnanime* (74); 3.6.1757-30.1.1758 1L *Royal William* (84); 5.9.1757-6.10.1757 Raid on Rochefort; 30.1.1758 2L *Royal William* (84); 6.6.1758-27.7.1758 The Siege of Louisbourg; 30.1.1759-25.2.1763[P] 2L *Union* (90); 20.11.1759 Battle of Quiberon Bay; 29.3.1761-11.6.1761 Expedition against Belle-Isle; 3.11.1770 1L *Ocean* (90); **Commander**; 25.6.1773-13.4.1775 *Viper* (10) Sloop; 8.3.1776-12.9.1776 *Ranger* (8) Sloop; 24.4.1777-25.8.1779 *Harpy* (18) Sloop.

WILSON, JOHN

Dates: c.1728 Born; 1795 Died; 15.12.1795 Will Probate.
Family:
Service: 29.6.1743 Chap Serv *Nonsuch* (50); 4.12.1743 Chap Serv *Namur* (90); 22.12.1743 Adm Serv *Namur* (90); 11.2.1743/44-12.2.1743/44 Battle of Toulon; 19.6.1744-30.9.1744 Able *Captain* (70); 1.10.1744 Mid *Captain* (70); 21.5.1748 Able *Rainbow* (44); 6.3.1750/51 Passed; **Lieutenant**; 23.4.1752-6.9.1753[P] 1L *Glory* (44); **Commander**; 15.11.1756 *Medway* (6) Storeship; 25.1.1757 *London* (6) Storeship; 8.4.1757-1.12.1758 *Swan* (14) Sloop; 9.3.1758-24.5.1758 Capture of Fort Louis; **Captain**; 3.7.1761-7.2.1763[P] *Solebay* (24.

WILSON, ROBERT

Dates: 14.6.1787 Died.
Family:
Service: **Lieutenant**; 6.4.1758[(31.3.1760)]-23.6.1758 3L *Saint Albans* (60); 30.11.1759[(JAM 31.3.1760)]-31.5.1760[P] 1L *Saint Albans* (60); 7.8.1761-8.2.1763[P] 2L *Revenge* (64); 9.7.1763-18.8.1766 L. *Ranger* (8) Sloop; 1.3.1779-8.2.1780[P] LCmdr *Union* Hired Tender.

WILSON, WILLIAM

Dates: c.1734 Born.
Family:
Service: 27.4.1755 Mid *Prince* (90); 27.3.1756 Mate *Prince* (90); 27.7.1756 Mid *Prince George* (80); 28.10.1756 Mid *Prince* (90); 24.12.1756 Mate *Culloden* (74); 5.4.1757 Action of April 5 1757; 27.6.1757 Mate *Saint George* (90); 10.6.1758 Able *Montagu* (60); 16.8.1758 Able *Ramillies* (90); 5.1.1759 Passed; **Lieutenant**; 10.8.1759[(5.8.1761)]-17.11.1763 L. *Scarborough* (20).

WINGATE, JOHN

Dates: 19.5.1760 Died.
Family:
Service: 1700-1703 Merchant Service; 19.4.1703 Vol-p-O *Mary* (64); 3.7.1703 Vol. *Boyne* (80); 25.9.1703 Vol-p-O *Mary* (64); 20.11.1703 Vol-p-O *Chichester* (80); 31.12.1705 Mid *Reserve* (54); 14.11.1706 Able *Portland* (54); 11.4.1707-29.8.1707[F] Mid *Winchelsey* (26); 14.2.1707/8 Able *Bristol* (50); 5.2.1708/9 Mid *Guernsey* (54); 30.6.1709 Mid *Lancaster* (80); 5.12.1709 Passed; **Lieutenant**; 10.11.1722 3L *Faversham* (42); 25.1.1725/26-20.12.1726 3L *Chatham* (50); **Captain**; 6.4.1732-18.4.1732 *Torrington* (40).

WINNIETT, EDWARD

Dates: c.1732 Born.
Family:
Service: 24.2.1755 Capt Serv *Canterbury* (60); 12.7.1755 Ord. *Canterbury* (60); 22.9.1756 Able *Squirrel* (20); 28.11.1756 Mid *Squirrel* (20); 18.7.1757 Mate *Squirrel* (20); 16.12.1757 Mid *Dublin* (74); 9.9.1759 Mate *Dublin* (74); 6.8.1760 Supnum *Deptford* (50); 20.12.1760 Mid

Nottingham (60); 1.4.1761 Passed; **Lieutenant**; 15.12.1761(2.8.1762)-29.8.1763 2L *Actaeon* (28); 7.1.1762-10.2.1762 Operations against Martinique.

WINTER, THOMAS
Dates: c.1708 Born; 16.10.1755 Died; 26.11.1757 Will Probate.
Family:
Service: 7.3.1729/30 Able *Northumberland* (70); 20.7.1731 Able *Winchester* (50); 30.7.1731 Mid *Winchester* (50); 31.5.1732 Mid *Sheerness* (20); 15.7.1734 Mate *Lichfield* (50); 2.12.1736 Passed; **Lieutenant**; 17.4.1742 2L *Hector* (40); 13.8.1742-1.11.1742P L. *Galgo* (8) Sloop; 26.1.1742/43 L. *Bridgewater* (20); 9.5.1743-13.4.1744 3L *Cornwall* (80); 15.6.1744-21.7.1746 2L *Gosport* (44); 2.10.1754 L. *Siren* (20); 22.5.1755-14.6.1755 British attack on Fort Beauséjour; 16.8.1755-16.10.1755† 3L *Fougueux* (64).

WINZAR, DAVID
Dates: Not Known.
Family:
Service: **Lieutenant**; 14.2.1757-6.11.1757P 4L *Monmouth* (70); 10.1.1761-21.2.1763P 3L *Monmouth* (70); 29.3.1761-11.6.1761 Expedition against Belle-Isle.

WITHERSPOON, DAVID
Dates: c.1726 Born.
Family:
Service: 1750-1752 HEIC Service; 20.2.1751/52 Mid *Terror* (8) Bomb Vessel; 25.7.1753 Mate *Anglesea* (44); 24.10.1754 Able *Anglesea* (44); 30.4.1755 NR *Bedford* (64); 3.3.1756 Passed; **Lieutenant**; 20.3.1761-10.8.1761 3L *Pembroke* (60).

WITHY, JOHN
Dates: c.1725 Born.
Family:
Service: 26.2.1743/44 Ord. *Woolwich* (50); 5.2.1744/45-2.4.1747P Able *Woolwich* (50); 10.8.1746 Action of 1746-10-18; 15.2.1748/49-1.5.1749P Able *Superb* (60); 6.7.1756 Mid *Prince Edward* (44); 21.8.1757-3.10.1759 Mid *Bristol* (50); 16.1.1759-19.1.1759 Attack on Martinique; 20.1.1759-1.5.1759 Capture of Guadeloupe; 3.10.1759 Passed; 12.10.1759 **Lieutenant**; 2.4.1762-9.2.1763P L. *Rye* (20).

WOLFE, WILLIAM
Dates: None Known.
Family:
Service: **Lieutenant**; 23.8.1759(BLI 8.8.1760) 4L *Buckingham* (68); 4.11.1760-20.3.1763P 2L *Adventure* (32); 29.3.1761-11.6.1761 Expedition against Belle-Isle.

WOLLASTON, ROBERT
Dates: c.1738 Born; 14.6.1774 Died.
Family:
Service: 16.8.1752 Scholar *Royal Naval Academy*; 6.7.1755 Mid *Prince* (90); 14.12.1755 Mid *Lancaster* (66); 20.5.1756 Battle of Minorca; 30.6.1756 Mid *Deptford* (50); 13.11.1756-15.11.1756 Able *Prince George* (80); 16.11.1756 Mid *Prince George* (80); 2.12.1756 Mid *Prince* (90); 28.1.1757 Mid *Culloden* (74); 5.4.1757 Action of April 5 1757; 1.8.1757 Mid *Saint George*

(90); 15.7.1758 Mid *Montagu* (60); 6.9.1758 Passed; **Lieutenant**; 23.10.1758 6L *Saint George* (90); 16.1.1759-19.1.1759 Attack on Martinique; 20.1.1759-1.5.1759 Capture of Guadeloupe; 28.5.1760-17.12.1763[P] L. *Sheerness* (24).

WOLSELEY, CHARLES

Dates: 24.10.1741 Born; 10.4.1808 Died.
Family: Father Sir William Wolseley, 5th Bt.; Mother Ann Fieldhouse.
Service: **Lieutenant**; 25.1.1759(BLI 29.7.1760) 4L *Burford* (68); 5.7.1759(BLI 29.9.1760) 3L *Lion* (58); 2.8.1759(BLI 29.9.1760) 2L *Lion* (58); 11.5.1760(BLI 29.9.1760) 1L *Lion* (58); **Commander**; 21.11.1760 *Ferret* (14) Sloop; **Captain**; 9.11.1761-25.7.1762 *Alarm* (32); 10.2.1775-9.9.1780 M.P. for Milborne Port; 28.8.1780 *Saint Albans* (64); 7.10.1780-1.1.1783 *Magnanime* (64); 12.4.1782 Battle of Providien; 6.7.1782 2nd Battle of Negapatam; 3.9.1782 Battle of Trincomalee; 21.9.1790 **Rear Admiral of the Blue**; 1.2.1793 **Rear Admiral of the Red**; 12.4.1794 **Vice Admiral of the Blue**; 4.7.1794 **Vice Admiral of the White**; 1.6.1795 **Vice Admiral of the Red**; 14.2.1799 **Admiral of the Blue**; 1.1.1801 **Admiral of the White**; 9.11.1805 **Admiral of the Red.**

WOOD, CHARLES

Dates: c.1732 Born; 3.9.1782 Died Battle of Trincomalee; 19.5.1783 Will Probate.
Family:
Service: 2.10.1748 Capt Serv *Tiger* (60); 9.6.1749 Capt Serv *Queenborough* (24); 11.7.1749 Capt Serv *Garland* (32); 20.7.1751 Able *Garland* (24); 10.6.1752 Mid *Garland* (24); 23.7.1754 Able *Monarch* (74); 13.11.1754 Passed; 18.6.1756 3L *Dover* (44); 15.10.1756 **Lieutenant**; 23.4.1757-4.8.1757 2L *Dover* (44); 28.11.1757 1L *Juno* (32); 6.6.1758-27.7.1758 The Siege of Louisbourg; 3.7.1759 Bombardment of Le Havre; 7.2.1760-20.5.1763[P] 1L *Lizard* (28); 3.6.1761-7.6.1761 Occupation of Dominica; 7.1.1762-10.2.1762 Operations against Martinique; 6.6.1762-13.8.1762 Operations against Havana; **Commander**; 4.6.1779 *Terror* (8) Bomb Vessel; 16.4.1781 Battle of Porto Praya; 16.4.1781(Portugal 5.12.1781) *San Carlos* (22) Storeship; **Captain**; 23.7.1781(EI 16.11.1781) *Hero* (74); 17.2.1782 Battle of Sadras; 12.4.1782 Battle of Providien; 19.5.1782(EI 6.6.1783)-9.10.1782 *Worcester* (64); 6.7.1782 2nd Battle of Negapatam; 3.9.1782 Battle of Trincomalee.

WOOD, JOHN

Dates: 31.1.1778 Died.
Family:
Service: **Lieutenant**; 30.3.1758(EI 21.6.1763)-3.3.1759 4L *Salisbury* (50); 29.4.1758 Battle of Cuddalore; 3.8.1758 Battle of Negapatam.

WOODWARD, JOHN

Dates: c.1717 Born; 1794 Died; 14.8.1794 Will Probate.
Family:
Service: 21.5.1733 Able *Gibraltar* (20); 17.8.1735-16.2.1735/36 Able *Dreadnought* (60); 17.2.1735/36 QGnr *Dreadnought* (60); 8.6.1738 QGnr *Romney* (50); 22.9.1739 QM *Romney* (50); 30.4.1741 Mate *Romney* (50); 7.5.1742 Mid *Romney* (50); 7.1.1742/43 Mate *Romney* (50); 11.2.1743/44-12.2.1743/44 Battle of Toulon; 25.3.1745 Passed; **Lieutenant**; 25.4.1746 3L *Sapphire* (44); 20.9.1746-25.9.1746 Lorient Operations; 2.4.1748 6L *Duke* (90); 5.5.1748-22.6.1748[P] 5L *Duke* (90); 16.1.1753-5.2.1754 3L *Kent* (64); 26.11.1755-1.3.1757[P] 2L *Ipswich* (64); 19.7.1757-3.5.1758[P] L. *Hazard* (8) Sloop; 3.6.1758-6.9.1758 1L *Penzance* (44); 22.6.1768-3.10.1770 1L *Bellona* (74).

WOOLRIDGE, FRANCIS

Dates: c.1734 Born; 1805 Died.

Family:

Service: 1751-1755 Merchant Service; 2.3.1755 Mid *Vanguard* (68); 10.3.1757 Passed; **Lieutenant**; 24.1.1760 4L *Swiftsure* (68); 12.3.1760 3L *Swiftsure* (68); 10.12.1760-20.1.1763[P] 1L *Swiftsure* (68); 29.3.1761-11.6.1761 Expedition against Belle-Isle; 23.1.1778-15.4.1778 2L *America* (64); 1781 L. *Southampton* (32); 14.4.1782(BLI 27.10.1783) 1L *Ville de Paris* (104); **Commander**; 29.6.1782(BLI 8.5.1783)-15.8.1782 *Porcupine* (16) Sloop; 14.6.1783(JAM 17.10.1783)-16.7.1783[P] *Jamaica* (16) Sloop; 13.11.1792-12.9.1793[P] *Fortune* (16) Sloop; 4.11.1793-11.1796 *Fortune* (16) Sloop.

WORTH, JAMES

Dates: c.1722 Born.

Family: Wife Margaret; Son James Andrew, RN (d.1841); Son Edward John (1797-?).

Service: 31.1.1731/32 Capt Serv *Falmouth* (50); 6.12.1732 Capt Serv *Deal Castle* (20); 12.2.1732/33 Mst Serv *Deal Castle* (20); 18.2.1733/34-3.11.1735[P] Vol-p-O *Rupert* (60); 12.5.1737-15.4.1738 Able *Lowestoffe* (20); 16.4.1738 MidO *Lowestoffe* (20); 7.2.1739/40-4.9.1741[P] MidO *Saltash* (8) Sloop; 18.9.1741-8.11.1741 Able *Lowestoffe* (20); 9.11.1741 Mid *Lowestoffe* (20); 31.12.1741 YoP *Aetna* (8) Fireship; 22.1.1741/42 Mate *Diamond* (40); 25.3.1743 Mid *Medway* Receiving Ship; 10.10.1743 Passed; **Lieutenant**; 20.4.1744-8.4.1746 L. *Hind* (10) Sloop; 27.10.1746-1.7.1752[P] L. *Saltash* (10) Sloop; 16.1.1753 2L *Invincible* (74); 20.2.1753 2L *Culloden* (74); 6.11.1754 1L *Culloden* (74); 20.5.1756 Battle of Minorca; 29.11.1756(ECH 1.2.1757)-12.3.1757 2L *Prince* (90); 4.4.1757 1L *Dublin* (74); 5.9.1757-6.10.1757 Raid on Rochefort; 23.1.1759 1L *Warspite* (74); 18.8.1759-19.8.1759 Battle of Lagos Bay; 20.11.1759 Battle of Quiberon Bay; **Commander**; 1.7.1760-17.3.1763[P] *Kingfisher* (14) Sloop; 1.8.1765-3.8.1768 *Dispatch* (14) Sloop; 18.7.1770 *Spy* (10) Sloop; **Captain**; 2.11.1772(Leeward Islands 1.6.1773)-26.7.1775 *Chatham* (50); 18.10.1775-12.12.1776[P] *Deal Castle* (20); 3.1777-1779 Regulating Officer at Liverpool; 24.1.1781-6.8.1783 *Assistance* (50); 21.4.1794 **Superannuated Rear Admiral**.

WRAY, CHARLES

Dates: 1773 Died.

Family: Son Henry, RN.

Service: **Lieutenant**; 24.6.1739(8.8.1743) L. *Solebay* (20); 1.11.1739(8.8.1743) 3L *Pembroke* (60); 17.1.1739/40(8.8.1743) 2L *Pembroke* (60); 2.9.1740(8.8.1743)-24.10.1741 1L *Pembroke* (60); 29.3.1744-26.9.1745 1L *Medway* (60); **Commander**; 1.2.1745/46(24.9.1746) *Dolphin* (8) Storeship; **Captain**; 9.12.1746-17.5.1751[P] *Rye* (20); 20.8.1756 *Captain* (64); 1.2.1757-4.4.1757 *Trident* (64); 4.4.1757 *Charlotte* (8) Yacht; 29.7.1761-6.4.1771[P] *Augusta* (8) Yacht; 23.7.1773-1.11.1774 *Princess Augusta* (6) Yacht.

WYATT, FRANCIS

Dates: 1777 Died.

Family:

Service: **Lieutenant**; 4.4.1740(28.9.1741) 3L *Windsor* (60); 4.9.1740(28.9.1741) 2L *Windsor* (60); 4.3.1740/41-5.1741 Operations against Cartagena; 28.12.1741 1L *Kinsale* (44); 4.2.1742/43-10.11.1743 2L *Torrington* (44); 21.8.1745 1L *Prince Edward* (44); 3.7.1746-23.4.1748 1L *Bristol* (50); 3.5.1747 1st Battle of Cape Finisterre; **Commander**; 7.5.1748-18.8.1748[P] *Dispatch* (14) Sloop; 11.3.1748/49-4.2.1750/51[P] *Fly* (8) Sloop; 24.1.1750/51-10.12.1751 *Vulture* (14) Sloop; **Captain**; 17.8.1756-9.3.1759 *Lively* (20); 7.8.1759(JAM 15.6.1763)-18.2.1760 *Wager* (24).

WYBORN, HERCULES

Dates: c.1742 Born; 1782 Died; 28.8.1782 Will Probate.

Family:

Service: 16.1.1756 Capt Serv *Royal Sovereign* (104); 16.6.1756 Able *Barfleur* (80); 15.4.1757-19.2.1758[W] Able *Invincible* (74); 8.1757-10.1757 Louisbourg Expedition; 19.3.1758 Capt Serv *Essex* (64); 5.6.1758-12.6.1758 Raid on Saint-Malo; 16.10.1758 Mid *Warspite* (74); 18.8.1759-19.8.1759 Battle of Lagos Bay; 20.11.1759 Battle of Quiberon Bay; 9.4.1761 Able *Antelope* (50); 7.4.1762 Passed; **Lieutenant**; 23.7.1762-7.4.1763 2L *Mermaid* (28); 11.1.1770-13.3.1772 2L *Carysfort* (28); 22.4.1773 5L *Torbay* (74); 22.11.1776 4L *Invincible* (74); 28.6.1777 3L *Invincible* (74); **Commander**; 19.11.1777 *Three Sisters* (20) Hired Armed Ship; 23.11.1780 *Martin* (14) Sloop; **Captain**; 29.1.1781-14.9.1781 *Ranger* (30) Hired Armed Ship.

WYNNELL, JOHN

Dates: c.1674 Born; 1759 Died.

Family:

Service: 29.8.1690 Vol-p-O *Kingfisher* (46); 7.6.1694 Able *Humber* (80); 14.5.1695 Mid *Humber* (80); 22.7.1696 Mid *Mary* (60); 22.3.1696/97 Passed; **Lieutenant**; 16.3.1701/2 L. *Phoenix* (28); 12.10.1702 Battle of Vigo; 14.1.1702/3-9.12.1703 L. *Phoenix* (28); 6.12.1705 1L *Monck* (64); 2.2.1710/11 2L *Union* (96); 12.2.1710/11-13.2.1710/11 1L *Kingston* (60); **Commander**; 30.3.1727-31.8.1727[P] *Portsmouth* (42) Hospital Ship; 14.9.1732-15.2.1737/38 *Saltash* (8) Sloop; **Captain**; 14.6.1739-5.12.1739 *Assistance* (50).

Service Records XYZ

YATES, EDWARD VERNON

Dates: c.1729 Born; 20.4.1801 Died; 27.8.1801 Will Probate.

Family: Father Charles Yates; Mother Catherine Vernon; Wife Mary Legall; Son Thomas Legall Yates (1753-1832).

Service: **Lieutenant**; 29.10.1755 3L *Dover* (44); 15.10.1756 2L *Lyme* (28); 6.11.1758(JAM 7.3.1760)-30.11.1759 1L *Saint Albans* (60); 18.8.1759-19.8.1759 Battle of Lagos Bay; 24.3.1760 1L *Thunderer* (74); **Commander**; 2.6.1760-6.8.1761 *Wasp* (8) Sloop; 12.9.1776-18.6.1778 *Ranger* (8) Sloop.

YEAMAN, SHERWOOD

Dates: c.1720 Born.

Family: Wife Ann Hinton married 2.9.1746.

Service: 16.1.1738/39 Able *Shoreham* (20); 9.2.1740/41 Mid *Shoreham* (20); 7.1741-10.1741 Operations against Santiago; 2.4.1742 Mate *Shoreham* (20); 11.7.1742-11.5.1743[P] Mid *Shoreham* (20); 9.6.1743 NR *Ferret* (14) Sloop; 10.9.1743 Mid *Phoenix* (20); 1.5.1744 Mate *Exeter* (58); 24.3.1744/45 Mate *Hector* (44); 11.9.1746 Passed; **Lieutenant**; 6.2.1755 6L *Barfleur* (80); 19.8.1757-13.10.1757 4L *Barfleur* (80); 5.9.1757-6.10.1757 Raid on Rochefort; 13.10.1757-9.1.1759[P] 5L *Barfleur* (80); 5.6.1758-12.6.1758 Raid on Saint-Malo.

YEO, JOHN

Dates: 16.5.1681 Born; 3.12.1756 Died.

Family: Wife Emblin (d.1724); Wife Lucretia Harris married 11.11.1724; Daughter Catherine [Jemmat] (1714 – 1766); Son William (1716-?); Daughter Emblin [Drake] (1718-?); Son John (1725-?); Daughter Joanna (1727-?); Daughter Susanna (1733-?); Daughter Lucretia (1735-?).

Service: **Lieutenant**; 25.7.1706(23.3.1712/13)-22.10.1707[W] 3L *Eagle* (70); 3.11.1707-14.9.1708 4L *Saint George* (96); 9.5.1709(6.6.1709)-5.1.1712/13[P] 2L *Kent* (70); **Commander**; 22.8.1717 *Ferret* (10) Sloop; **Captain**; 27.6.1718(5.1.1718/19)-1.9.1718[C] *Greyhound* (20); 11.3.1718/19-23.5.1719[P] *Lowestoffe* (32); 18.5.1719 *Mermaid* (36); 17.7.1719-30.11.1720[P] *Lynn* (42); 24.12.1720-15.10.1724[P] *Enterprise* (42); 18.4.1727 *Mary Galley* (40); 16.11.1727-5.11.1729[P] *Mary Galley* (40); 22.2.1733/34 *Exeter* (60); 19.8.1737 *Jersey* (60); 14.6.1739-5.12.1739 *Deptford* (60); 25.7.1747 **Superannuated Rear Admiral.**

YETTS, JOHN

Dates: 1820 Died; 17.4.1820 Will Probate.

Family: Wife Elizabeth Mitchelhill; Wife Chrsitian White; Daughter Elizabeth [Windgate]; Daughter Isabella.

Service: **Lieutenant**; 19.1.1761(6.8.1764)-31.7.1764[P] 4L *Chatham* (50); 1.1.1773-1.1.1776 L. *Hazard* (8) Sloop; 22.3.1777 4L *Trident* (64); 29.4.1777-5.9.1781[P] 3L *Trident* (64); 6.7.1779 Battle of Grenada; 17.4.1780 Battle of Martinique; 15.5.1780 Action of March 15 1780;

19.5.1780 Action of March 19 1780; 31.10.1781-5.7.1782[P] L. *Leith* (20) Hired Armed Ship; 17.7.1782-29.1.1783 1L *Egmont* (74); 20.10.1782 Battle of Cape Spartel; 23.1.787 1L Edgar (74); 1.1.1798-10.6.1803 LCmdr *Enterprise* (28).

YONGE, WILLIAM

Dates: c.1724 Born.
Family:
Service: 27.5.1741 Scholar *Royal Naval Academy*; 8.7.1742 Mid *Squirrel* (20); 1743 Mid *Dolphin* (20); 17.2.1743/44 Mid *Chester* (50); 9.4.1745 Mid *Ipswich* (70); c.1.6.1745 Mid *Russell* (80); 30.7.1745-12.12.1745 ActL *Cambridge* (80); 13.12.1745 Passed; **Lieutenant**; 8.7.1748[(4.11.1748)] 2L *Burford* (70); 15.11.1748 3L *Bristol* (50); 21.1.1751/52-29.10.1752 3L *Severn* (50); **Commander**; 5.8.1755-11.10.1755 *Weazle* (16) Sloop.

YONGE, WILLIAM HERNE

Dates: 1770 Died; 3.11.1770 Will Probate.
Family: Wife Margrett Freeman married 3.12.1764.
Service: **Lieutenant**; 3.8.1759[(JAM 27.10.1762)] L. *Lightning* (6) Hospital Ship; 12.6.1760[(15.11.1762)] 1L *Cerberus* (28); 17.7.1762[(EI 15.11.1762)]-16.12.1762[P] 2L *Cambridge* (80); 4.5.1768 L. *Hazard* (8) Sloop; 29.11.1768-14.3.1769 L. *Peggy* (8) Sloop; 23.2.1769-bef.3.11.1770[†] 1L *Winchelsea* (32).

YOUNG, BENJAMIN

Dates: 1777 Died; 13.6.1777 Will Probate.
Family: Father Benjamin Young, RN (d.1754); Wife Ursula Wynell married 10.10.1749.
Service: 20.11.1741 **Lieutenant**; 13.2.1741/42[(JAM 29.7.1745)] 3L *Saint Albans* (50); 23.8.1742[(29.7.1745)]-20.10.1744[W] 2L *Saint Albans* (50); 6.1744 Bombardment of Porto Bello; 14.8.1745 1L *York* (60); 5.2.1745/46 3L *Sandwich* (90); 14.2.1746/47-18.4.1747[P] 2L *Sandwich* (90); 21.12.1747-20.5.1749[P] 1L *Looe* (44).

YOUNG, DAVID

Dates: c.1712 Born.
Family:
Service: 3.10.1740 Mid *Hampton Court* (70); 28.2.1741 Able *Hampton Court* (70); 7.4.1741 Able *Lancaster* (80); 25.8.1741 Able *Eltham* (40); 15.10.1741 QM *Eltham* (40); 23.8.1742 Mid *Eltham* (40); 18.2.1742/43 Attack on La Guaira; 15.4.1743-24.4.1743 Attack on Porto Cabello; 6.5.1745 Mid *Defiance* (60); 13.1.1746-3.10.1746 Mate *Defiance* (60); 3.10.1746 Passed; **Lieutenant**; 7.1.1746/47 4L *Chichester* (80); 25.5.1747-23.6.1748 3L *Lark* (44); 27.3.1755-6.12.1756[P] L. *Firedrake* (8) Bomb Vessel; 8.6.1757-7.3.1759 L. *Swallow* (14) Sloop; 5.6.1758-12.6.1758 Raid on Saint-Malo.

YOUNG, SIR GEORGE

Dates: 17.6.1732 Born; 24.8.1781 Knight Bachelor; 28.1810 Died Formosa Place, Berkshire.
Family: Father Rev. George Young; Mother Eleanor Knowles; Wife Elizabeth Bradshaw (d.1779) married 1763; Wife Anne Battie married 1779; Daughter Lucia (1764-?); Son Sir Samuel, 1st Bt. (1766–1826); Son George Forbes Freeman, RN (1767-1799); Daughter Maria (1768-?); Brother Thomas Young; Sister Elisabeth [Broughton]; Brother Robert, RN (1734-1797); Brother James Young.
Service: 1747-1756 HEIC Service; 24.12.1756-6.2.1757 Able *York* (60); 7.2.1757 Mid *York* (60); 6.6.1758-27.7.1758 The Siege of Louisbourg; 23.2.1759 Mid *Royal William* (84); 3.9.1760

Passed; **Lieutenant**; 16.11.1761-14.3.1763 4L *Orford* (68); 6.6.1762-13.8.1762 Operations against Havana; 1.10.1766 2L *Phoenix* (44); **Commander**; 29.9.1768 *Ferret* (14) Sloop; 18.9.1770-20.9.1773 *Weazle* (16) Sloop; 23.5.1775 *Alderney* (10) Sloop; 14.3.1776 *Vulture* (14) Sloop; 13.6.1776 *Cormorant* (14) Sloop; **Captain**; 7.11.1777-25.10.1778 *Rippon* (60); 10.8.1778 Second Battle of Pondicherry; 29.4.1779 *William and Mary* (10) Yacht; 15.2.1781 FRS; 27.1.1783 *Katherine* (8) Yacht; 23.10.1794 **Rear Admiral of the Blue**; 1.6.1795 **Rear Admiral of the Red**; 14.2.1799 **Vice Admiral of the White**; 1.1.1801 **Vice Admiral of the Red**; 23.4.1804 **Admiral of the Blue**; 28.4.1808 **Admiral of the White.**

YOUNG, GILBERT

Dates: c.1718 Born; 5.4.1755 Died.
Family:
Service: 1.6.1734 Capt Serv *Britannia* (100); 24.6.1735 Ord. *Dunkirk* (60); 21.1.1736 Able *Dunkirk* (60); 24.12.1736 Able *Argyll* (50); 19.3.1737 Able *Bridgewater* (32); 2.11.1737 Mid *Gloucester* (50); 5.11.1739-9.1.1740 Able *Solebay* (20); 10.1.1740-25.2.1740 Supnum *Gloucester* (50); 26.2.1740-15.4.1740 Able *Gloucester* (50); 15.4.1740 Passed; **Lieutenant**; 25.11.1740-19.6.1743 4L *Kent* (70); 8.10.1744-16.5.1746 1L *Portland* (50); 3.7.1746 **Commander**; 20.10.1746 *Happy Jennet* (20) Hired Ship; 24.1.1746/47 *Tavistock* (10) Sloop; 20.8.1747-11.3.1748/49 *Albany* (10) Sloop.

YOUNG, JAMES

Dates: 15.11.1717 Born; 29.11.1717 Baptised St Martin in the Fields, Westminster; 24.1.1789 Died; 2.2.1789 Buried St Anne's Church, Soho, London.
Family: Father William Young; Mother Susannah Walker; Wife Elizabeth Bolton married 1747; Wife Sophia Vasmer married 1762; Son William, RN (1751-1821); Daughter Elizabeth; Daughter Susan; Daughter Philippa; Daughter Sophia; Daughter Sophia; Son James, RN (1762-1833); Daughter Charlotte; Son Thomas.
Service: 1737-1738 Mid *Gloucester* (50); 1738-8.3.1738/39 Mid *Lancaster* (80); **Lieutenant**; 9.3.1738/39(15.2.1739/40)-17.11.1741 4L *Lancaster* (80); **Commander**; 13.11.1742(19.3.1744/45) *Salamander* (6) Bomb Vessel; **Captain**; 16.5.1743-18.8.1744 *Kennington* (20); 18.8.1744(MED 1.5.1747) *Chatham* (50); 2.1.1745/46(MED 27.4.1747)-4.5.1748[P] *Dunkirk* (60); 13.2.1751/52-13.12.1753 *Jason* (44); 31.7.1755 *Newark* (80); 23.9.1755 *Intrepid* (64); 20.5.1756 Battle of Minorca; 4.4.1757-4.2.1758 *Burford* (68); 5.9.1757-6.10.1757 Raid on Rochefort; 16.3.1759-11.11.1761 *Mars* (74); 20.11.1759 Battle of Quiberon Bay; 29.3.1761-11.6.1761 Expedition against Belle-Isle; 11.11.1761 CinC — Le Havre; 11.11.1761 Commodore *Guernsey* (50); **Rear Admiral of the Red**; 21.10.1762-24.12.1762[P] *Guernsey* (50); 18.10.1770 **Vice Admiral of the White**; 31.3.1775 **Vice Admiral of the Red**; 3.4.1775 CinC — Barbados & the Leeward Islands; 26.4.1775-29.1.1778 *Portland* (50); 29.1.1778 **Admiral of the White.**

YOUNG, JOHN

Dates: c.1739 Born; 9.11.1797 Died Deal; 13.12.1797 Will Probate.
Family: Wife Frances; Daughter Sarah [Stephens]; Daughter Ann; Son Robert; Daughter Frances; Daughter Susan.
Service: **Lieutenant**; 2.9.1762-31.12.1763[P] L. *Crown* (18) Storeship; **Commander**; 9.12.1780(BLI 28.6.1781)-14.5.1781 *Carcass* (8) Bomb Vessel; 6.7.1782-20.5.1783 *Speedy* (14) Sloop; 2.11.1795 *Spy* (16) Sloop; **Captain**; 3.10.1796-16.10.1797[P] *Overyssel* (64).

YOUNG, PATRICK

Dates: c.1724 Born.
Family: Father Robert Young;.
Service: 1739-1741 Merchant Service; 19.6.1741 Able *Duke* (90); 9.2.1741/42 Mid *Duke* (90); 6.3.1745/46 Passed; **Lieutenant**; 14.4.1746-9.5.1749[P] L. *Squirrel* (20); 20.5.1755 4L *Bedford* (64); 23.2.1756-23.2.1757 3L *Bedford* (64); 4.4.1757 1L *Alcide* (64); 20.10.1757-13.4.1758[B] 2L *Prince George* (80).

YOUNG, ROBERT

Dates: c.1734 Born; 3.10.1797 Died Deal; 6.10.1797 Buried Deal.
Family: Father Rev. George Young; Mother Eleanor Knowles; Wife Sarah; Sister Elisabeth [Broughton]; Brother Sir George, RN (1732-1810); Brother James; Brother Thomas.
Service: 1754-3.1757 Merchant Service; 26.3.1757 Mid *Burford* (68); 5.9.1757-6.10.1757 Raid on Rochefort; 6.6.1758-27.7.1758 The Siege of Louisbourg; 16.1.1759-19.1.1759 Attack on Martinique; 20.1.1759-1.5.1759 Capture of Guadeloupe; 20.11.1759 Battle of Quiberon Bay; 21.11.1759 Mid *Barfleur* (80); 30.4.1760 Passed; **Lieutenant**; 28.8.1760 4L *Essex* (64); 2.9.1760 3L *Essex* (64); 29.3.1761-11.6.1761 Expedition against Belle-Isle; 14.9.1762-27.1.1763[P] 2L *Essex* (64).

YOUNG, STEWART

Dates: c.1731 Born; 1767 Died; 7.5.1767 Will Probate.
Family:
Service: 1748-6.1751 Merchant Service; 18.6.1751 Able *Lichfield* (50); 21.12.1751 Mid *Lichfield* (50); 2.6.1754 Able *Prince Henry* (44); 13.11.1754 Passed; **Lieutenant**; 6.2.1755-21.5.1756 4L *Lancaster* (66); 20.5.1756 Battle of Minorca; 9.4.1757-12.5.1757 4L *Swiftsure* (68); 12.3.1760-25.3.1762 5L *Duke* (90).

YOUNGHUSBAND, GEORGE

Dates: c.1732 Born; 1792 Died; 25.8.1792 Buried Berwick-upon-Tweed.
Family: Father George Younghusband; Mother Elizabeth Leighondee (1702-?); Wife Anne Hall (1748-1816) married 10.7.1763; Son George, RN (1776-1806); Son Charles (1778 - 1843); Daughter Frances Elizabeth [Elers/Napier] (c.1785 - 1857); Brother Arm Younghusband (1727-1807).
Service: 1752-8.1756 Merchant Service; 5.8.1756 Able *Somerset* (68); 24.8.1757 Mid *Somerset* (68); 6.6.1758-27.7.1758 The Siege of Louisbourg; 8.6.1759 Mid *Renown* (30); 26.8.1759 Mid *Sandwich* (90); 13.2.1760 Passed; **Lieutenant**; 17.6.1761-31.8.1762 L. *Speedwell* (8) Sloop; 1.10.1767-30.1.1768[P] LCmdr *Adventure* (6) Cutter; 28.6.1770-6.5.1771[P] LCmdr *Alarm* (6) Cutter; 31.12.1776-3.5.1780[P] LCmdr *Africa* (4) Hired Tender; 22.5.1791-15.5.1792 LCmdr *Expedition* (10) Cutter.

Appendix I

Strength of the Royal Navy 1750–1769

The numbers given are for all vessels in service, not just those in commission. Where a ship's rating was changed during a year, only its rating on 1 January is used.

The count of unrated vessels excludes those which, while technically unrated, were not intended for naval use. These include such ships as the *Chatham*, sheer hulk, as well as various barges, store hulks etc. but does include active vessels such as store ships.

The hired count includes only those identified as hired armed vessels; it excludes those hired as tenders or transports. Where the distinction is not clear caution has prevailed and the vessel has been excluded from the number.

Year	1st Rates	2nd Rates	3rd Rates	4th Rates	5th Rates	6th Rates	Unrated	Hired
1750	4	11	56	62	38	43	56	0
1751	3	11	54	61	38	41	52	0
1752	3	11	55	60	38	40	56	0
1753	3	10	54	61	38	39	56	0
1754	3	10	54	62	37	40	58	0
1755	3	10	59	62	37	39	65	5
1756	4	11	57	63	37	47	103	15
1757	3	11	63	64	45	57	90	14
1758	3	11	72	63	50	68	94	17
1759	3	12	79	63	57	67	106	31
1760	3	12	81	60	57	67	113	33
1761	3	13	82	59	62	62	117	14
1762	4	13	89	58	67	59	106	8
1763	4	13	87	57	62	58	136	3
1764	4	11	89	54	52	51	126	0
1765	5	11	92	52	47	48	123	0
1766	5	12	91	46	46	48	119	0
1768	4	13	94	37	42	44	122	1
1769	3	14	96	33	41	42	115	1

Appendix II

Royal Navy Vessels during the Seven Years War

Vessels are shown with the name, rating and nominal number of guns they held at the beginning of the Seven Years War in 1756 or when first commissioned if after that date. The name is followed by any name changes during the Seven Years War (indicated by the year and '⇒' symbol), the nominal number of guns carried and the years of acquisition and end of service. Name changes after the end of the Seven Years War are not indicated.

Where a vessel had undergone a rebuild prior to 1756 the year of acquisition given is that of the rebuild, not that of the original acquisition.

The list for Hired Vessels includes only some of the more significant vessels. It does not include all of the multitude of hired transports, supply vessels, and tenders that were used during the war.

First Rates (4 vessels)
Royal Anne (100) (1715-1767), *Royal Sovereign* (104) (1729-1768), *Royal George* (100) (1756-1782), *Britannia* (100) (1762-1825).

Second Rates (13 Vessels)
Blenheim (96) (1709-1763), *Princess Royal* (90) (1711-1763), *Duke* (90) (1739-1769), *Saint George* (90) (1740-1774), *Ramillies* (90) (1749-1760), *Prince* (90) (1750-1775), *Namur* (90) (1756-1804), *Union* (90) (1756-1816), *Neptune* (90) (1756-1816), *Royal William* (84) (1757-1813), *Sandwich* (90) (1759-1810), *Ocean* (90) (1761-1791), *Blenheim* (90) (1761-1801).

Third Rates (96 vessels)
Ipswich (64) 1757⇒*Ipswich Hulk* (1730-1764), *Russell* (80) (1735-1762), *Elizabeth* (64) (1737-1766), *Suffolk* (70) (1739-1765), *Prince Frederick* (64) (1740-1784), *Princess* (70) (1740-1784), *Nassau* (64) (1740-1770), *Essex* (64) (1741-1759), *Bedford* (64) (1741-1787), *Royal Oak* (70) (1741-1764), *Stirling Castle* (64) (1742-1762), *Revenge* (64) (1742-1787), *Monmouth* (70) (1742-1767), *Captain* (64) (1743-1777), *Berwick* (64) (1743-1760), *Hampton Court* (64) (1744-1774), *Edinburgh* (64) (1744-1771), *Yarmouth* (64) (1745-1811), *Kent* (64) (1746-1757), *Devonshire* (66) (1747-1772), *Invincible* (74) (1747-1758), *Intrepid* (64) (1747-1765), *Newark* (80) (1747-1787), *Culloden* (74) (1747-1770), *Fougueux* (64) (1747-1759), *Monarch* (74) (1747-1760), *Terrible* (74) (1747-1763), *Trident* (64) (1747-1763), *Magnanime* (74) (1748-1775), *Vanguard* (68) (1748-1774), *Somerset* (68) (1748-1778), *Cumberland* (66) (1748-1760), *Torbay* (74) (1749-1784), *Lancaster* (66) (1749-1773), *Orford* (68) (1749-1783), *Grafton* (68) (1750-1767), *Swiftsure* (68) (1750-1773), *Northumberland* (68) (1750-1780), *Buckingham* (68) (1751-1779), *Chichester* (68) (1753-1803), *Barfleur* (80) (1755-1783), *Prince George* (80) (1755-1758), *Alcide* (64) (1755-1772), *Cambridge* (80) (1755-1808), *Marlborough* (80) (1756-

1762), *Burford* (68) (1757-1785), *Princess Amelia* (80) (1757-1788), *Dublin* (74) (1757-1784), *Duc d'Aquitaine* (64) (1757-1761), *Dorsetshire* (68) (1757-1775), *Norfolk* (74) (1757-1774), *Shrewsbury* (74) (1758-1783), *Lennox* (74) (1758-1789), *Foudroyant* (80) (1758-1787), *Orphee* (64) (1758-1758), *Warspite* (74) (1758-1801), *Raisonnable* (64) (1758-1762), *Conqueror* (68) (1758-1760), *Bienfaisant* (64) (1758-1814), *Belliqueux* (64) (1758-1772), *Temple* (68) (1758-1762), *Resolution* (74) (1758-1759), *Fame* (74) (1759-1814), *Mars* (74) (1759-1784), *Hercules* (74) (1759-1784), *Hero* (74) (1759-1810), *Valiant* (74) (1759-1826), *Modeste* (64) (1759-1800), *Centaur* (74) (1759-1782), *Temeraire* (74) (1759-1784), *Formidable* (80) (1759-1768), *Bellona* (74) (1760-1814), *Dragon* (74) (1760-1784), *Thunderer* (74) (1760-1780), *Essex* (64) (1760-1799), *Superb* (74) (1760-1783), *Arrogant* (74) (1761-1810), *Belleisle* (64) (1761-1784), *Cornwall* (74) (1761-1780), *Saint Ann* (64) (1761-1784), *Africa* (64) (1761-1774), *Courageux* (74) (1761-1796), *Kent* (74) (1762-1784), *Defence* (74) (1762-1811), *Infanta* (74) (1762-1775), *Moro* (74) (1762-1770), *Reyna* (74) (1762-1772), *San Antonio* (64) (1762-1775), *San Genaro* (64) (1762-1763), *Soverano* (74) (1762-1770), *Tiger* (74) (1762-1784), *Terrible* (74) (1762-1781).

Fourth Rates (70 vessels)

Plymouth (60) (1722-1764), *Oxford* (50) (1727-1758), *Deptford* (50) (1732-1767), *Centurion* (50) (1733-1769), *Prince of Orange* (60) (1734-1810), *Strafford* (58) (1735-1756), *Worcester* (58) (1735-1765), *Jersey* (60) (1736-1783), *Augusta* (60) (1736-1765), *Superb* (60) (1736-1757), *Dragon* (60) (1736-1757), *Lion* (58) (1738-1765), *Guernsey* (50) (1740-1786), *Kingston* (60) (1740-1762), *Sutherland* (50) (1741-1770), *Leopard* (50) (1741-1761), *Hampshire* (50) (1741-1766), *Nonsuch* (50) (1741-1766), *Antelope* (50) (1742-1783), *Dreadnought* (60) (1742-1784), *Princess Mary* (60) (1742-1766), *Harwich* (50) (1743-1760), *Canterbury* (60) (1744-1770), *Chester* (50) (1744-1767), *Falkland* (50) (1744-1768), *Exeter* (60) (1744-1763), *Gloucester* (50) (1744-1764), *Sunderland* (60) (1744-1761), *Winchester* (50) (1744-1769), *Princess Louisa* (60) (1744-1766), *Portland* (50) (1744-1763), *Defiance* (60) (1744-1766), *Advice* (50) (1745-1756), *Windsor* (60) (1745-1777), *Vigilant* (60) (1745-1759), *Norwich* (50) (1745-1768), *Tilbury* (58) (1745-1757), *Ruby* (50) (1745-1765), *Nottingham* (60) (1745-1773), *Eagle* (60) (1745-1767), *Assistance* (50) (1745-1773), *Salisbury* (50) (1746-1761), *Panther* (50) (1746-1756), *Lichfield* (50) (1746-1758), *Bristol* (50) (1746-1768), *Colchester* (50) (1746-1773), *Anson* (60) (1747-1773), *Tiger* (60) 1761⇒*Tiger Hulk* (1747-1765), *Isis* (50) (1747-1766), *Severn* (50) (1747-1759), *Tavistock* (50) (1747-1768), *Saint Albans* (60) (1747-1765), *Greenwich* (50) (1748-1757), *Rochester* (50) (1749-1770), *Newcastle* (50) (1750-1761), *Weymouth* (60) (1752-1772), *Falmouth* (50) (1752-1765), *York* (60) (1753-1772), *Dunkirk* (60) (1754-1792), *Medway* (60) (1755-1811), *Arc-en-Ciel* (50) (1756-1759), *Preston* (50) (1757-1815), *America* (60) (1757-1771), *Pembroke* (60) (1757-1793), *Achilles* (60) (1757-1784), *Montagu* (60) (1757-1774), *Rippon* (60) (1758-1808), *Chatham* (50) (1758-1814), *Panther* (60) (1758-1813), *Edgar* (60) (1758-1774), *Firm* (74) (1759-1791), *Saint Florentine* (60) (1759-1771), *Romney* (50) (1762-1804), *Conquestador* (60) (1762-1782).

Fifth Rates (74 vessels)

Enterprise (44) (1718-1771), *Romney* (44) (1726-1757), *Eltham* (40) (1736-1763), *Dover* (44) (1740-1763), *Gosport* (44) (1741-1768), *Sapphire* (44) (1741-1756), *Hastings* (44) (1741-1763), *Lynn* (44) (1741-1763), *Liverpool* (44) (1741-1756), *Diamond* (44) (1741-1756), *Kinsale* (44) (1741-1762), *Torrington* (44) (1743-1763), *Hector* (44) (1743-1762), *Roebuck* (44) (1743-1764), *Mary Galley* (44) (1744-1764), *Pearl* (44) (1744-1759), *Lark* (44) (1744-1757), *Ludlow Castle* (44) (1744-1771), *Poole* (44) (1745-1765), *Southsea Castle* (44) (1745-1762), *Prince Edward*

(44) (1745-1766), *Chesterfield* (44) (1745-1762), *Ambuscade* (40) (1746-1762), *Anglesea* (44) (1746-1764), *Thetis* (44) (1747-1767), *Glory* (44) (1747-1763), *Jason* (44) (1747-1763), *Rainbow* (44) (1747-1802), *Expedition* (44) (1747-1764), *Prince Henry* (44) (1747-1766), *Crown* (44) (1747-1770), *Penzance* (44) (1747-1766), *Humber* (44) (1748-1762), *Boston* (44) (1748-1757), *Woolwich* (44) (1749-1762), *Southampton* (32) (1757-1812), *Vestal* (32) (1757-1775), *Shannon* (28) (1757-1765), *Diana* (32) (1757-1793), *Pallas* (36) (1757-1783), *Juno* (32) (1757-1778), *Brilliant* (36) (1757-1776), *Melampe* (36) (1757-1764), *Unicorns Prize* (26) (1757-1758), *Richmond* (32) (1757-1781), *Aurora* (38) (1757-1763), *Venus* (36) (1758-1828), *Thames* (32) (1758-1793), *Sapphire* (32) (1758-1784), *Adventure* (32) (1758-1770), *Stag* (32) (1758-1783), *Alarm* (32) (1758-1812), *Aeolus* (32) (1758-1801), *Minerva* (32) (1759-1778), *Repulse* (32) (1759-1776), *Danae* (38) (1759-1771), *Tweed* (32) (1759-1776), *Arethusa* (32) (1759-1779), *Phoenix* (44) (1759-1780), *Looe* (44) (1759-1763), *Niger* (32) (1759-1814), *Blonde* (32) (1760-1782), *Quebec* (32) (1760-1779), *Flora* (32) (1761-1778), *Brune* (32) (1761-1792), *Comet* (32) (1761-1763), *Lowestoffe* (32) (1761-1801), *Montreal* (32) (1761-1779), *Boulogne* (32) (1762-1784), *Pearl* (32) (1762-1832), *Lark* (32) (1762-1778), *Boston* (32) (1762-1811), *Emerald* (32) (1762-1793).

Sixth Rate (73 vessels)
Bombay (24) (1739-1789), *Experiment* (24) (1740-1763), *Winchelsea* (20) (1740-1758), *Success* (20) (1740-1779), *Port Mahon* (24) (1740-1763), *Greyhound* (20) (1741-1768), *Blandford* (20) (1741-1763), *Phoenix* (24) (1743-1762), *Sheerness* (24) (1743-1768), *Shoreham* (24) (1744-1759), *Wager* (24) (1744-1763), *Bridgewater* (24) (1744-1758), *Amazon* (22) (1745-1763), *Triton* (20) (1745-1758), *Siren* (20) (1745-1764), *Surprise* (24) (1746-1770), *Rye* (20) (1746-1763), *Solebay* (24) (1746-1763), *Centaur* (20) (1746-1761), *Nightingale* (22) (1746-1783), *Arundel* (24) (1746-1765), *Queenborough* (24) (1747-1761), *Renown* (30) (1747-1771), *Garland* (24) (1748-1783), *Seahorse* (24) (1748-1784), *Unicorn* (24) (1748-1771), *Lyme* (24) (1748-1760), *Sphinx* (24) (1748-1770), *Mermaid* (24) (1749-1760), *Fowey* (24) (1749-1781), *Hind* (24) (1749-1784), *Dolphin* (24) (1751-1777), *Gibraltar* (20) (1754-1773), *Seaford* (20) (1754-1784), *Revenge* (28) (1755-1782), *Squirrel* (20) (1755-1783), *Deal Castle* (20) (1756-1780), *Bideford* (20) (1756-1761), *Mercury* (20) (1756-1777), *Tartar* (24) (1756-1797), *Scarborough* (20) (1756-1780), *Kennington* (20) (1756-1774), *Flamborough* (20) (1756-1772), *Aldborough* (20) (1756-1777), *Lowestoffe* (24) (1756-1760), *Lively* (20) (1756-1778), *Rose* (20) (1757-1779), *Tartar's Prize* (24) (1757-1760), *Lizard* (28) (1757-1828), *Coventry* (28) (1757-1783), *Hussar* (28) (1757-1762), *Boreas* (28) (1757-1770), *Glasgow* (20) (1757-1779), *Emerald* (28) (1757-1761), *Actaeon* (28) (1757-1766), *Trent* (28) (1757-1764), *Eurus* (24) (1757-1760), *Sun Prize* (6) (1758-1759), *Vengeance* (28) (1758-1766), *Active* (28) (1758-1778), *Maidstone* (28) (1758-1794), *Liverpool* (28) (1758-1778), *Echo* (24) (1758-1770), *Aquilon* (28) (1758-1776), *Levant* (28) (1758-1780), *Argo* (28) (1758-1776), *Cerberus* (28) (1758-1778), *Griffin* (28) (1758-1761), *Milford* (28) (1759-1785), *Valeur* (28) (1759-1764), *Terpsichore* (24) (1760-1766), *Baleine* (20) (1760-1767), *Mermaid* (28) (1761-1778), *Oiseau* (26) (1762-1762).

UNRATED (192 VESSELS)

Sloops (101 vessels)
Peregrine (20) (1733-1761), *Swift* (8) (1741-1756), *Otter* (14) (1742-1763), *Baltimore* (14) (1742-1762), *Ferret* (14) (1743-1757), *Vulture* (14) (1744-1761), *Jamaica* (10) (1744-1770), *Trial* (10) (1744-1776), *Albany* (14) (1745-1763), *Hound* (14) (1745-1773), *Weazle* (16) (1745-1779), *Raven* (14) (1745-1763), *Badger* (10) (1745-1762), *Kingfisher* (14) (1745-1763), *Swallow* (14) (1745-1769), *Swan* (14) (1745-1763), *Dispatch* (14) (1745-1773), *Fortune* (14)

(1746-1770), *Scorpion* (14) (1746-1762), *Porcupine* (16) (1746-1763), *Grampus* (14) (1746-1780), *Saltash* (14) (1746-1763), *Hornet* (10) (1747-1770), *Wasp* (8) (1749-1781), *Peggy* (8) (1749-1770), *Hazard* (8) (1749-1783), *Savage* (8) (1750-1776), *Fly* (8) (1752-1772), *Cruizer* (8) (1752-1776), *Ranger* (8) (1752-1783), *Speedwell* (8) (1752-1780), *Wolf* (8) (1754-1781), *Happy* (8) (1754-1766), *Ontario* (12) (1755-1756), *Oswego* (5) (1755-1756), *Earl of Loudoun* (1755-1757), *Polacca* (12) (1756-1762), *Spy* (10) (1756-1773), *Bonetta* (10) (1756-1776), *Hunter* (10) (1756-1780), *Merlin* (10) (1756-1757), *Viper* (10) (1756-1779), *Hawke* (8) (1756-1759), *London* (18) (1756-1756), *Mohawk* (12) (1756-1756), *Diligence* (10) (1756-1780), *Halifax* (18) (1756-1756), *Hazard's Prize* (8) (1756-1759), *Beaver* (18) (1756-1761), *Speaker* (10) (1756-1758), *Stork* (10) (1756-1758), *Barbadoes* (14) (1756-1763), *Alderney* (10) (1757-1783), *Gibraltar's Prize* (14) (1757-1761), *Escort* (14) (1757-1768), *Cormorant* (18) (1757-1762), *Flamborough Prize* (14) (1757-1763), *Postillion* (18) (1757-1763), *Pelican* (16) (1757-1763), *Racehorse* (18) (1757-1778), *Dolphins Prize* (12) (1757-1760), *Roman Emperor* (16) (1757-1763), *Antigua* (14) (1757-1763), *Merlin* (18) (1757-1777), *Merlin* (10) 1757⇒*Zephyr* (1757-1778), *Gramont* (18) (1757-1762), *Favorite* (16) (1757-1784), *Comet* (10) (1758-1758), *Earl of Halifax* (14) (1758-1760), *Tamar* (16) (1758-1780), *Cygnet* (18) (1758-1768), *Goree* (10) (1758-1763), *Mohawk* (18) (1759-1764), *Onandaga* (22) (1759-1764), *Mississauga* (1759-1759), *Duke of Cumberland* (20) (1759-1761), *Boscawen* (16) (1759-1761), *Musquelongy* (1759-1771), *Laurel* (12) (1759-1763), *Virgin* (12) (1760-1760), *Onondaga* (18) (1760-1760), *Mississauga* (10) (1760-1765), *Guadaloupe* (1760-1762), *Virgin* (12) (1760-1764), *Johnson* (10) (1760-1764), *Williamson* (10) (1760-1761), *Epreuve* (14) (1760-1764), *Ferret* (14) (1760-1776), *Senegal* (14) (1760-1778), *Sardoine* (14) (1761-1768), *Pomona* (18) (1761-1776), *Beaver* (14) (1761-1783), *Hawk* (10) (1761-1781), *Martin* (14) (1761-1784), *Druid* (10) (1761-1773), *Lynx* (10) (1761-1777), *Pheasant* (14) (1761-1761), *Michigan* (6) (1762-1763), *Nautilus* (16) (1762-1780), *Endeavour* (14) (1763-1780), *Vulture* (14) (1763-1771)

Cutters (17 vessels)
Lurcher (6) (1760-1765), *Swift* (10) (1761-1761), *Hornet* (6) (1763-1772), *Esther* (6) (1763-1779), *Fly* (4) (1763-1771), *Goodwill* (4) (1763-1786), *Grace* (6) (1763-1772), *Alarm* (6) (1763-1780), *Pitt* (6) (1763-1766), *Anson* (6) (1763-1774), *Boscawen* (4) (1763-1773), *Duke of York* (4) (1763-1766), *Duke William* (4) (1763-1768), *Charlotte* (4) (1763-1770), *Mecklenburgh* (6) (1763-1773), *Morning Star* (4) (1763-1773), *Cholmondley* (4) (1763-1771).

Bomb Vessels (11 vessels)
Furnace (8) (1740-1763), *Firedrake* (10) (1742-1763), *Granado* (8) (1742-1763), *Falcon* (10) (1745-1759), *Infernal* (8) (1757-1774), *Terror* (8) (1759-1774), *Carcass* (8) (1759-1784), *Basilisk* (8) (1759-1762), *Blast* (8) (1759-1771), *Mortar* (8) (1759-1774), *Thunder* (8) (1759-1774).

Fireships (13 vessels)
Firebrand (6) (1732-1760), *Lightning* (8) (1746-1762), *Maryland Planter* (16) (1755-1757), *Proserpine* (8) (1756-1756), *Blast* (8) (1756-1756), *Blaze* (10) (1756-1759), *Aetna* (8) (1756-1763), *Vesuvius* (8) (1756-1763), *Pluto* (8) (1756-1762), *Strombolo* (8) (1756-1768), *Proserpine* (8) (1757-1763), *Salamander* (8) (1757-1762), *Protector* (8) (1760-1761).

Hulks & Sheer Hulks (12 vessels)
Chatham, Sheer Hulk (1694-1813), *Jersey* (1698-1763), *Southampton* (1700-1771), *Yarmouth* (1709-1769), *Devonshire* (1710-1760), *Panther* (1716-1768), *Winchester* (50) (1717-1781),

Captain (1722-1762), *Stirling Castle* (1723-1771), *Berwick* (1723-1783), *Launceston* (1741-1784), *Looe* (1745-1759).

Hospital Ships (2 ships)
Princess Caroline (1731-1764), *Rupert* (1740-1767).

Prison Ships (2 vessels)
Cornwall (1726-1761), *Boyne* (1739-1763).

Schooners (6 vessels)
George (8) (1755-1756), *Valiant* (1755-1756), *Farquhar* (1759-1759), *Mercury* (4) (1760-1765), *Anson* (10) (1760-1761), *Huron* (4) (1761-1763).

Smacks (3 vessels)
Betty (1728-1813), *Minorca* (2) (1740-1756), *Culloden* (1746-1765).

Storeships, Hoys & Transports (21 vessels)
Unity (4) (1707-1773), *Old Truelove* (1720-1830), *Supply* (4) (1725-1757), *Woolwich* (2) (1726-1767), *Hayling* (10) 1759⇒*Goree* (1729-1764), *Plymouth* (4) (1742-1806), *Portsmouth* (4) (1747-1767), *Forester* (4) (1748-1828), *Navy Transport* (1752-1791), *Lion* (1753-1775), *Canterbury* (6) (1756-1764), *London* (6) (1756-1758), *Medway* (6) (1756-1764), *Portsmouth* (6) (1756-1758), *Saltash* (1756-1775), *Port Antonio* (12) (1757-1763), *Port Royal* (12) (1757-1763), *London Buss* (1758-1762), *Hayling* (4) (1760-1782), *Supply* (4) (1759-1792), *Manilla* (14) (1762-1763).

Yachts (13 vessels)
William and Mary (10) (1694-1765), *Old Portsmouth* (6) (1703-1772), *Bolton* (6) (1709-1817), *Princess Charlotte* (8) 1761⇒*Augusta* (1711-1771), *Queenborough* (6) (1718-1777), *Katherine* (8) (1721-1801), *Fubbs* (12) (1724-1781), *Mary* (8) (1728-1816), *Mary* (1728-1778), *Chatham* (6) (1741-1793), *Royal Caroline* (8) 1761⇒*Royal Charlotte* (1750-1820), *Dorset* (1753-1815), *Plymouth* (6) (1755-1793).

Xebec (1 vessel)
Mediterranean (12) (1756-1758).

Hired Vessels (21 Vessels)
Experiment (1755-1760), *Bolton* (1755-1759), *Providence* (1755-1763), *Adventure* (6) (1755-1756), *Brilliant* (16) (1755-1757), *Macclesfield* (16) (1755-1758), *Roehampton* (16) (1755-1756), *Hunter* (10) (1755-1760), *Halifax* (12) (1756-1757), *Delight* (1756-1763), *Parnassus* (1756-1757), *Jane and Barbara* (1756-1762), *Success* (1756-1759), *Saint Anne* (18) (1756-1758), *Cumberland* (1756-1759), *Hawk* (1756-1760), *Two Brothers* (1756-1757), *Devonshire* (1756-1763), *Princess of Wales* (18) (1756-1758), *Sarah* (16) (1756-1758), *Industry* (1757-1766), *Adventure* (18) (1757-1758), *London* (18) (1757-1758), *William and Ann* (20) (1757-1758), *Fox* (12) (1757-1759), *Friendship* (6) (1758-1759), *Europa* (1758-1760), *Lydia* (1758-1758), *Somerset* (1758-1758), *Pretty Betsey* (1758-1759), *Samuel and John* (1758-1759), *Taylor* (6) (1758-1759), *Grace* (10) (1758-1759), *Cleveland* (8) (1758-1762), *Thomas and Mary* (6) (1758-1760), *Hawke* (1758-1760), *Cybella* (1758-1759), *Cruizer* (1759-1759), *Union* (1759-1760), *Charming Polly* (1759-1759), *Rodney* (1759-1759), *Broderick* (1759-1760), *Arthur*

(1759-1760), *Britannia* (32) (1759-1760), *Experiment* (22) (1759-1760), *Duke of Marlborough* (26) (1759-1760), *Hussar* (22) (1759-1762), *George* (30) (1759-1763), *Juline and Elizabeth* (32) (1759-1760), *Mary* (22) (1759-1763), *Royal Exchange* (22) (1759-1760), *Lion* (18) (1759-1760), *Marquis of Granby* (14) (1759-1760), *Reynolds* (1759-1760), *Scourge* (12) (1759-1760), *Prince Ferdinand* (18) (1759-1760), *Wolf* (14) (1759-1759), *Prince of Wales* (6) (1759-1760), *Boscawen* (6) (1759-1760), *Sarah* (16) (1759-1758), *Drake* (10) (1760-1761), *Cypress* (1760-1760), *Esther* (6) (1760-1763), *Duke* (1760-1761), *John and Thomas* (1760-1760), *Queenborough* (1760-1762), *Albemarle* (1760-1762), *Roast Beef* (12) (1760-1761), *Speedwell* (8) (1760-1761), *Swift* (8) (1760-1761), *Saint Peter* (1760-1761), *Good Intent* (1761-1762), *Hay* (6) (1761-1762), *Charlotte* (10) (1761-1763), *Esk* (1762-1763), *Charming Polly* (1762-1763), *Peggy* (1762-1762).

Appendix III

Royal Navy Deployment, May 1 1756

Extracted from the Admiralty disposition book ADM 8/30 1755-1756. 'The present disposal of his Majesty's ships and vessels in sea pay'.

East Indies

Rate	Number	Ships
Third	2	*Kent* (70), Flag of R.A. Watson *Cumberland* (66), Flag of R.A. Pocock
Fourth	2	*Tiger* (60) *Salisbury* (50)
Sixth	1	*Bridgewater* (20)
Sloops	1	*Kingfisher* (10)

Plantations – Jamaica

Rate	Number	Ships
Fourth	3	*Dreadnought* (60), Flag of R.A. Townshend *Princess Mary* (60) *Greenwich* (50)
Fifth	1	*Humber* (44)
Sixth	3	*Shoreham* (24) *Sphinx* (24) *Rye* (24)
Sloops	1	*Weazle* (16)

Plantations – Leeward Islands

Rate	Number	Ships
Fourth	3	*Winchester* (50), Flag of R.A. Frankland *Warwick* (60) *Advice* (50)
Fifth	1	*Woolwich* (44), In transit via Boston
Sixth	1	*Blandford* (24) *Siren* (24), in South Carolina *Winchelsea* (20), in South Carolina *Garland* (24), in Virginia *Mermaid* (28), in New England
Sloops	1	*Trial* (10) *Jamaica* (10), in the Bahamas *Baltimore* (14), in North Carolina

Plantations – Lake Ontario

Rate	Number	Ships
Sloops	2	*Ontario* (12) *Oswego* (5)
Brigantines	2	*Earl of Loudoun* *Halifax*

Plantations – Nova Scotia

Rate	Number	Ships
Third	1	*Fougueux* (64)
Fourth	3	*Norwich* (50) *Lichfield* (50) *Centurion* (60)
Sixth	1	*Success* (20)
Sloop	1	*Vulture* (14)

Plantations – Coast of Africa

Rate	Number	Ships
Fourth	1	*Assistance* (50)

Plantations – In Transit

Rate	Number	Ships
Third	1	*Grafton* (68), for North America
Fourth	1	*Nottingham* (60), for North America
Fifth	1	*Woolwich* (44), via Boston for the Leeward Islands *Lynn* (44), convoy and carrying arms to Boston

Plantations – Ordered Home

Rate	Number	Ships
Fourth	1	*Severn* (50), Flag of R.A. Cotes from Jamaica
Sixth	1	*Hind* (24) from Jamaica
Sloops	1	*Falcon* (10) from Jamaica *Hornet* (10) from Boston

The Mediterranean

Rate	Number	Ships
Second	1	*Ramillies* (90), Flag of Adm Byng
Third	7	*Buckingham* (70), Flag of R.A. West *Culloden* (74) *Captain* (70) *Revenge* (70) *Trident* (64) *Lancaster* (66) *Intrepid* (64)

Fourth	5	*Kingston* (60) *Defiance* (60) *Princess Louisa* (60) *Deptford* (50) *Portland* (50)
Fifth	1	*Chesterfield* (44)
Sixth	3	*Dolphin* (24) *Phoenix* (24) *Experiment* (24)
Sloops	1	*Fortune* (14)
Fireships	2	*Blast* *Proserpine*

Convoys and Cruisers

Rate	Number	Ships
Fourth	3	*Hampshire* (50) *Anson* (60) *Bristol* (50)

The Western Squadron (Hawke's command)

Rate	Number	Ships
Second	1	*Saint George* (90), Flag of Sir Edward Hawke
Third	9	*Terrible* (70), Flag of R.A. Holburne *Torbay* (70) *Northumberland* (70) *Somerset* (70) *Vanguard* (70) *Chichester* (70) *Edinburgh* (70) *Essex* (70) *Monmouth* (70)
Fourth	7	*Eagle* (60) *Dunkirk* (60) *York* (60) *Medway* (60) *Newcastle* (50) *Rochester* (50) *Warwick* (50)
Sixth	3	*Lyme* (24) *Sheerness* (24) *Unicorn* (24), at Plymouth
Sloops	2	*Swan* (10), at Plymouth

The Western Squadron (Boscawen's command)

Rate	Number	Ships
Third	7	*Invincible* (74), Flag of V.A. Boscawen *Cambridge* (80) *Yarmouth* (70) *Bedford* (70) *Elizabeth* (70) *Prince Frederick* (70) *Swiftsure* (70)

The Western Squadron (Boscawen's command)

Fourth	6	*Saint Albans* (60) *Colchester* (50) *Weymouth* (60), between Scilly and Cape Clear *Windsor* (60), between Scilly and Ushant *Falmouth* (50), off the Isle of Bass *Antelope* (50), off Cape Barfleur
Fifth	2	*Romney* (44) *Gosport* (44), at Plymouth
Sixth	3	*Gibraltar* (24), off the Isle of Bass *Greyhound* (24), off the Isle of Bass *Deal Castle* (24), off Cape Barfleur
Sloops	3	*Ferret* (10), off the Isle of Bass *Hazard* (10), off Cape Barfleur *Savage* (10), off Cape Barfleur
Armed Vessel	1	*Maryland Planter* (16), off Cape Barfleur

The Downs Squadron

Rate	Number	Ships
Third	1	*Newark* (80), Flag of V.A. Smith
Fourth	2	*Oxford* (50) *Tilbury* (60), at Cork
Fifth	3	*Ambuscade* (44) *Roebuck* (44), convoy from Stade *Prince Edward* (44), in King's Road
Sixth	4	*Centaur* (24) *Queenborough* (24), convoy from Stade *Arundel* (24), at Liverpool *Solebay* (24), at Leith
Sloops	23	*Peregrine* (12) *Granado* (14) *Spy* (14) *Cruizer* (10) *Dispatch* (14) *Fly* (12) *Wasp* (10) *Wolf* (10) *Hunter* (14), Iceland fishery *Grampus* (14), convoy to the Baltic *Swallow* (14), convoy from Stade *Otter* (14), at Dublin *Firedrake* (14), at Plymouth *Saltash* (14), at Whitehaven *Albany* (14), at King's Road *Raven* (14), at Bideford *Happy* (10), at Falmouth *Speedwell* (10), at Exmouth *Hound* (14), at Yarmouth *Ranger* (10), at Lynn *Scorpion* (14), in the Humber *Peggy* (10), at Newcastle *Porcupine* (14), at Leith
Armed Vessel	3	*Brilliant* (16) *Rockhampton* (16) *Macclesfield* (16), in Galleon's Reach nr. Plymouth

At Home

Rate	Number	Ships
First	3	*Royal George* (100), at Longreach *Royal Sovereign* (100), at Chatham
Second	3	*Royal Anne* (90), at Portsmouth *Prince* (90), at Spithead *Duke* (90), at Portsmouth
Third	10	*Prince George* (80), at Spithead, flag of V.A. Osborn *Barfleur* (80), at Portsmouth *Magnanime* (74), at Plymouth, flag of R.A. Mostyn *Monarch* (74), at Plymouth *Orford* (70), at Plymouth *Ipswich* (70), at Plymouth *Hampton Court* (70), at Portsmouth *Nassau* (70), at Portsmouth *Devonshire* (66), at Chatham *Sterling Castle* (70), at Spithead
Fourth	3	*Augusta* (60), at Portsmouth *Falkland* (50), at Plymouth *Isis* (50), at Portsmouth
Fifth	2	*Dover* (44), in Cowes Road *Ludlow Castle* (44), order to clean
Sixth	14	*Port Mahon* (24), at Plymouth *Nightingale* (24), at Spithead *Surprise* (24), at the Nore *Mercury* (24), at Harwich *Triton* (24), in Longreach *Bideford* (24), in Longreach *Wager* (24), at Deptford *Tartar* (28), at Deptford *Kennington* (24), at Bewly *Seaford* (24), at Plymouth *Scarborough* (24), at Hull fitting *Aldborough* (24), at Blackwall fitting *Seahorse* (24), at Portsmouth *Squirrel* (24), at Sheerness
Sloop	3	*Merlin* (14), in Galleon's Reach *Viper* (14), at Deptford *Bonetta* (14), coming from Holland
Fireship	2	*Firebrand* (8), at Portsmouth *Lightning* (8), at Plymouth
Yacht		*Charlotte* (8), at Deptford *Katherine* (8), at Deptford *Fubbs* (8), at Deptford *Dorset* (4), in Ireland

Harbour Service

Rate	Number	Ships
Second	1	*Princess Royal* (90), Seareach near Gravesend
Hospital Ships	3	*Princess Caroline*, at Sheerness *Blenheim*, at Portsmouth *Rupert*, at Plymouth

Appendix IV

Naval Operations 1755 - 1763

This section list only those engagements that are referenced in the service records of officers. As such it does not include single ship or other smaller engagements. The major actions noted in the service records that occurred outside the period of the Seven Years War are not included.

Battle of Fort Beauséjour, 22 May 1755 (North America)
Three Royal Navy vessels, Success (20), Mermaid (24) and Siren (20) escorted 31 transports carrying 2,000 provincial troops. The fort surrendered on 8 June.

Action of 8 June 1755 (North America)
Four Royal Navy vessels, *Torbay* (74), *Fougueux* (64), *Dunkirk* (60), and *Defiance* (60) under Edward Boscawen chased three French Ships of the line, two of them armed *en-flute*, near the entrance to the Gulf of St. Lawrence, taking two of them.

Capture of Geriah, 11-14 January 1756 (Asia)
A mixed squadron of six Royal Naval vessels and eight Company vessels landed troops of the East India Company under Clive and destroyed a large part of the Maratha Indian Navy.

Action of 17 May 1756 (Europe)
The *Colchester* (50) and the *Lyme* (26) engaged two French vessels escorting a convoy into Rochefort. After a six-hour engagement both sides withdrew heavily damaged.

Battle of Minorca, 20 May 1756 (Mediterranean)
The first major naval action of war. Admiral Hon. John Byng, with 12 ships of the line, failed to closely engage twelve French ships, with the result that the garrison of Minorca surrendered on June 29 to a French force landed after Byng withdrew to Gibraltar. Byng was later executed for his failure.

Expedition against Chandernagore, 7 March – 1 April 1757 (Asia)
A combined arms British force consisting of 2,500 men under Clive, supported by four ships of the line and 3 frigates, two of them company vessels, under Vice Admiral Watson, besieged and, on 23 March, took the French settlement of Chandernagore on the Hugli river, 50 miles upstream of Calcutta.

Action of 5 April 1757 (Mediterranean)
An inconclusive skirmish between five British ships under Rear Admiral Saunders and six French ships. The French evaded the British at night, passed the Straits of Gibraltar and later arrived in Louisbourg.

Louisbourg Expedition, August 1757 – October 1757 (North America)
A failed British attempt to take Louisbourg. The intended landing operation was abandoned in August after the true strength of the French at Louisbourg, 18 ships of the line, was established. The 16 battalions of troops intended to land were twice embarked in transports only to be quickly disembarked, and the expedition finally abandoned after Vice Admiral Holbourne's fleet of 21 ships of the line plus supporting vessels intending to blockade Louisbourg was scattered by gales in late September.

Raid on Rochefort, 5 September – 6 October 1757 (North Atlantic)
The first of William Pitt's 'Descents' on the French coast, a British fleet under Admiral Hawke with 16 ships of the line and 18 supporting vessels escorted 45 transports carrying 7,000 troops in an ineffective and slightly chaotic attempt to take Rochefort. Despite initial success the British failed to land their main force.

Forrest's Action, 21 October 1757 (West Indies)
Three British ships of the line engaged four French ships of the line supported by three other vessels off Cap-Français, Haiti in a bloody but indecisive action.

Battle of Cartagena, 28 February 1758 (Mediterranean)
Three French ships of the line attempted to pass the British blockade of Cartagena to join the French fleet there. Two were taken and the third run aground to avoid the same fate.

Capture of Fort Louis, 9 March – 24 May 1758 (Africa)
A British expedition of two ships of the line, *Harwich* (50) and *Nassau* (64), with 13 supporting vessels and transports attacked and took Fort Louis in Sénégal which surrendered on 1 May, but failed in their attempt to also capture Gorée.

Battle of Cuddalore, 29 April 1758 (Asia)
This was the first in a series of three actions between the British with 7 ships of the line under Vice Admiral George Pocock and the French under Comte d'Aché with 8 ships of the line, all but one vessels of the Compagnie des Indes, in the Indian Ocean. One of the French ships was wrecked due to damage sustained.

Raid on Saint-Malo, 5 – 12 June 1758 (Europe)
Another of Pitt's 'descents'. The Channel Fleet under Lord Anson, totalling 24 ships of the line with support vessels and including an escort squadron under Commodore Howe escorted 130 transports carrying 13,000 troops. The target was Saint Malo and the expedition anchored in Cancale Bay and landed the troops. Saint Malo was not taken, although much other damage, including the destruction of 20 privateers, was inflicted. The fleet then spent the rest of June looking at other possible landing places including Le Havre, Caen and Cherbourg, but no landings were undertaken due to poor weather and French resistance and the whole enterprise abandoned in early July.

The Siege of Louisbourg, 6 June – 27 July 1758 (North America)
Following the failed attempt in 1757, the British sent a fleet with 22 ships of the line and 18 other vessels under Admiral Boscawen escorting 150 transports carrying 11,000 soldiers. The British landed on 6 June and the fortress capitulated on the 26 July. This pivotal success opened the way for the British to take control of North America by allowing uncontested access to the St Lawrence.

Battle of Negapatam, 3 August 1758 (Asia)
The second action between George Pocock with seven ships of the line and Comte d'Aché with eight, seven of which were vessels of the Compagnie des Indes. Another indecisive, but bloody, action which ended when the French withdrew to Pondicherry.

Capture of Gorée, 29 December 1758 (Africa)
A British expedition of six small ships of the line and five smaller vessels escorted transports carrying a regiment of troops to the West coast of Africa. On 11 November 1758 the expedition departed from Kinsale and arrived in off Gorée in Sénégal on 28 December, and took the island on 29 December, having lost the *Litchfield* (50) and a transport on route.

Attack on Martinique, 16 – 19 January 1759 (West Indies)
A British force of 11 ships of the line and 14 other vessels under the command of Commodore Hughes sailed from Barbados on 3 January, escorting 5,000 men in 60 transports, the expedition arrived off Martinique on 15 January. An unopposed landing was performed on the 16 January, but French opposition forced the expedition to re-embark on 19 January. It was decided to attempt an attack on Guadeloupe instead.

Capture of Guadeloupe, 20 January – 1 May 1759 (West Indies)
Following the failed attempt on Martinique the British force arrived off Basse Terre on 22 January. Landings on the same day led to the occupation of Basse Terre and Port Royal but it was not until 1 May that the island finally capitulated.

Bombardment of Le Havre, 3 July 1759 (Europe)
A squadron under Rear Admiral Rodney sailed from St. Helen's five small ships of the line, six frigates and sloops and 6 bomb vessels on a mission to destroy French invasion barges. Arriving off Le Havre on 3 July he took position and, on 4 July, began a 52-hour bombardment. The town was set fire and many of the French invasion barges were destroyed. Rodney then started a blockade which was to last for the remainder of the year.

Battle of Lagos, 18 – 19 August 1759 (Europe)
On 5 August, French Admiral Comte de la Clue, with 12 ships of the line and three frigates escaped from Toulon while the British blockading fleet, under Admiral Boscawen, was off station re-supplying at Gibraltar. De la Clue passed the straits on the night of 17/18 August, when he was spotted by Boscawen's scouts. In the morning only seven French ships were under de la Clue's command, the rest having separated during the night. Pursued by the British three were taken and two driven ashore and destroyed. The remainder escaped to Cadiz where they were blockaded.

Battle of Pondicherry, 10 September 1759 (Asia)
The third and final engagement between George Pocock, with 9 ships of the line, and d'Ache with 11. Another indecisive action notable for the extremely heavy casualties on both sides, the French had more than 1,500 including two captains killed and the British with nearly 600 including Captain Colin Michie killed.

Battle of Quiberon Bay, 20 November 1759 (Europe)
The major fleet engagement of the war which ended French hopes of an invasion of the British Isles. The French under the Comte de Conflans, with 21 ships of the line and five frigates, had put to sea on 14 November, in the hope of catching the observation squadron of Captain Robert Duff, with four 50-gunners, off-guard. Admiral Edward Hawke's channel fleet, with 24 ships of the line and 10 frigates and sloops, on hearing that the Brest fleet had sailed immediately sailed for Quiberon Bay seeing a chance to bring Conflans to battle. While Conflans was chasing Duff out of Quiberon Bay on 19 November, Duff sighted Hawke's fleet approaching, the British reversed course and the French, realising their danger did the same. The hunter had become the hunted. The battle on 20 November, was a confused affair, fought in a variable wind, including heavy squalls and reaching storm force at time, which often prevented the lower gun decks from opening their ports, the French *Thésée* being lost by foundering for this reason. By the end of the day the French fleet had been scattered to several different ports and had lost six ships sunk and one captured. Six ships and four frigates escaped into the Vilaine, where they remained under blockade until 1761. The British lost two ships, *Resolution* (74) and *Essex* (64), both wrecked.

Operations against Quebec, 1 June – 18 September 1759 (North America)
On 1 June, a British expedition commanded by Vice Admiral Charles Saunders and Rear Admiral Charles Holmes began to sail from Louisbourg for the Saint-Laurent where they joined forces with a squadron under Rear Admiral Philip Durell. This fleet, consisting of 22 ships of the line, 13 frigates and 14 other ships of war was escorting transports carrying 9,000 British troops under Major General James Wolfe. By 26 June the entire British fleet was anchored a few miles downriver of Quebec and on 27 June the British Army was landed. After weeks of stand-off, the British landed a part of their forces on the Plains of Abraham below Quebec and decisively defeated the French who withdrew the next day, On 18 September the British occupied Quebec.

Action of 28 February 1760 (Europe)
Three British frigates, *Aeolus* (32), *Pallas* (36), and *Brilliant* (36), under the command of Captain John Elliot intercepted and took three French frigates as they put to sea from Carrickfergus in Ireland. The French had sailed with 1,300 troops, which they had briefly landed at Carrickfergus but were now back on board.

Action off Cuba, 18-19 October 1760 (West Indies)
Three British vessels, *Hampshire* (50), *Boreas* (28), and *Lively* (20) commanded by Captain Coningsby Norbury chased five French frigates that has sailed from Cap-Francois on 16 October. The French were engaged in a series of single ship actions which resulted in two being taken and two being run aground and burnt by their crews.

Expedition against Belle-Isle, 29 March – 11 June 1761 (Europe)
A British force of 7,000 men, escorted by a fleet of 15 ships of the line, eight frigates and eight smaller vessels under Commodore Augustus Keppel was sent to occupy Belle-Isle in the Bay of Biscay. The expedition was supported by a second squadron of 13 sail of the line and three frigates under Captain Matthew Buckle sent to cruise of Brest and prevent interference from there. After delays caused by bad weather the British landed on 22 April, and after a lengthy siege of the fortress of Palais secured the island on 11 June. Belle-Isle was held by the British until the end of the war. As part of these operations a squadron of seven ships of the line with one frigate and three smaller vessels was detached on 31 April under Captain sir Thomas Stanhope to blockade Rochefort and Bordeaux and destroy the defensive works on Isle d'Aix.

Occupation of Dominica, 3 – 7 June 1761 (West Indies)
A British squadron of four ships of the line and three frigates under Commodore James Douglas escorted transports carrying 1,500 troops transferred from North America left Guadeloupe on 3 June. The troops were landed on 6 June and the following day the island surrendered.

Operations against Martinique, 5 January – 16 February 1762 (West Indies)
On 5 January, a British Fleet of 17 ships of the line, 14 frigates, five sloops and four bomb vessels commanded by Rear Admiral George Brydges Rodney escorting transports carrying 14,000 troops sailed from Barbados. They arrived off Martinique on 7 January and anchored in Saint-Pierre's Bay on 8 January, losing the *Raisonnable* (64) when she ran aground. After a couple of abortive landing attempts, the main force was landed on 16/17 January, and by 25 January was in position to attack Fort Royal. Fort Royal surrendered on 3 February and was occupied the next day. The whole of Martinique was in British hands by 16 February.

Capture of Saint Lucia, 24/25 February 1762 (West Indies)
A squadron of 5 vessels, *Dragon* (74), *Norwich* (50), *Penzance* (44), *Dover* (44), and *Basilisk* bomb (8), under Captain Augustus John Hervey were detached from Martinique against Saint Lucia. Unsure of the strength of the French defences Hervey landed in disguise to reconnoitre. Having determined it feasible he brought his squadron into position to bombard the fortress defending the harbour on 25 February, upon which the French surrendered.

Operations against Havana, 6 June 1762 – 13 August 1762 (West Indies)
On 6 June 1762, the British Jamaica fleet with 21 ships of the line, 14 frigates and 11 support vessels under Admiral George Pocock escorting transports carrying 14,000 troops approached Havana on the island of Cuba. Troops began to land in the afternoon and by 12 June, the British began to bombard the outlying forts which were suppressed by combined land and naval artillery on1 July. Attention then switched to Havana itself which capitulated on 13 August, the British occupied the city the next day. The British took possession of nine Spanish ships of the line, three frigates and nine smaller vessels.

Operations against Manilla, 23 September – 5 October 1762 (Asia)
A British fleet under Rear Admiral Samuel Cornish with seven ships of the line, three frigates and a store ship escorted 3,000 troops from India to Manilla in the Philippines via Malacca. The fleet arrived off Manilla on 23 September, and troops were landed on 24 and 25 September. On 4 October the land batteries and the fleet began a bombardment and on 6 October the breach that had been created was stormed and the city surrendered.

Appendix V

Crew Establishments 1757

Extracted from the 'Regulations and Instructions relating to His Majesty's Service as Sea'. ninth edition Published in 1757.

In each table cell the top number indicates the number of men carried at that rank or rating, the lower their pay in the format Pounds-Shillings-Pence. There are 20 shillings to a Pound and 12 pence to a shilling. Commissioned officers are paid the amount given per day, all other ranks and ratings for a lunar month of 28 days.

Flag officers were paid the following rates

- Admiral and Commander in Chief £5-0-0 per day
- Admiral £3-10-0 per day
- Vice-Admiral £2-10-0 per day
- Rear-Admiral £1-15-0 per day

Where a chaplain was included on the vessel's books they received £0-19-0 per lunar month irrespective of the vessels rate.

The following ratings are not included in the tables below. The first group were all paid £1.4.0 per lunar month.

- Midshipman Ordinary
- Cook's Mate
- Coxswain's Mate
- Yeoman of the Boatswain's Store Room
- Swabber
- Cooper
- Captain's Cook
- Ordinary Trumpeter

The following ratings were all paid £0.19.0 per lunar month.

- Ordinary Seaman
- Landsman
- Shifter
- Barber
- Gunner's Taylor

Table of Establishments and Pay by Rate

	Rated Vessels Commanded by a Post Captain						Unrated Vessels Commanded by a Commander or Lieutenant					
	1st 100+ guns	2nd 90+ guns	3rd 70+ guns	4th 50+ guns	5th 30+ guns	6th 20+ guns	Fire ships	Hospital ships	Store Ships	Sloops 60+ men	Bombs & smaller sloops	Yachts
Captain	1 £1-0-0	1 £0-16-0	1 £0-13-6	1 £0-10-0	1 £0-8-0	1 £0-6-0	1 £0-8-0	1 £0-8-0	1 £0-8-0	1 £0-6-0	1 £0-6-0	1 £0-6-0
Lieutenant	6 £0-5-0	6 £0-5-0	4 £0-4-0	3 £0-4-0	3 £0-4-0	1 £0-4-0	1 £0-4-0	-	1 £0-4-0	1 £0-4-0	-	-
Master	1 £9-2-0	1 £8-8-0	1 £6-6-0	1 £5-12-0	1 £5-2-8	1 £4-0-0	-	1 £5-2-8	1 £5-2-8	-	-	-
Master's Mate	6 £3-6-0	4 £3-0-0	3 £2-16-2	2 £2-7-10	2 £2-2-0	2 £2-2-0	1 £2-2-0	1 £2-2-0	1 £2-2-0	1 £2-2-0	1 £2-2-0	-
Midshipman	24 £2-5-0	24 £2-0-0	16 £1-17-6	10	6	4	2	2	2	2	1	1
Schoolmaster	-	-	1 £1-17-6	1 £1-13-9	1 £1-10-0	-	-	-	-	-	-	-
Captain's Clerk	1 £2-5-0	1 £2-0-0	1 £1-17-6	1 £1-13-9	1 £1-10-0	1 £1-10-0	1 £1-10-0	1 £1-10-0	1 £1-10-0	1 £1-10-0	1 £1-10-0	1 £1-10-0
Quartermaster	8 £1-15-0	8 £1-15-0	6 £1-12-0	4 £1-10-0	3 £1-8-0	2 £1-6-0	2 £1-8-0	2 £1-8-0	2 £1-8-0	2 £1-6-0	1 £1-6-0	1 £1-6-0
Quartermaster's Mate	6 £1-10-0	6 £1-10-0	4 £1-8-0	4 £1-8-0	3 £1-6-0	2 £1-5-0	1 £1-6-0	1 £1-6-0	1 £1-6-0	1 £1-5-0	-	1 £1-5-0
Boatswain	1 £4-0-0	1 £3-10-0	1 £3-0-0	1 £2-10-0	1 £2-5-0	1 £2-0-0	1 £2-5-0	1 £2-5-0	1 £2-5-0	1 £2-0-0	1 £2-0-0	1 £2-0-0
Boatswain's Mate	4 £1-15-0	4 £1-15-0	2 £1-12-0	2 £1-12-0	1 £1-10-0	1 £1-8-0	1 £1-10-0	1 £1-10-0	1 £1-10-0	1 £1-8-0	1 £1-8-0	1 £1-8-0

	Rated Vessels Commanded by a Post Captain						Unrated Vessels Commanded by a Commander or Lieutenant					
	1st 100+ guns	2nd 90+ guns	3rd 70+ guns	4th 50+ guns	5th 30+ guns	6th 20+ guns	Fire ships	Hospital ships	Store Ships	Sloops 60+ men	Bombs & smaller sloops	Yachts
Yeoman of the Sheets	4 £1-12-0	4 £1-10-0	4 £1-8-0	2 £1-8-0	2 £1-6-0	1 £1-6-0	-	-	-	-	-	-
Coxswain	1 £1-12-0	1 £1-10-0	1 £1-8-0	1 £1-8-0	1 £1-6-0	1 £1-6-0	1 £1-6-0	1 £1-6-0	1 £1-6-0	-	-	-
Master Sailmaker	1 £1-15-0	1 £1-15-0	1 £1-15-0	1 £1-14-0	1 £1-12-0	1 £1-10-0	1 £1-12-0	1 £1-12-0	1 £1-12-0	1 £1-10-0	-	-
Sailmaker's Mate	1 £1-8-0	1 £1-8-0	1 £1-8-0	1 £1-8-0	1 £1-8-0	1 £1-8-0	-	-	-	-	-	-
Sailmaker's Crew	2 £1-5-0	2 £1-5-0	2 £1-5-0	2 £1-5-0	1 £1-5-0	1 £1-5-0	1 £1-5-0	1 £1-5-0	1 £1-5-0	1 £1-5-0	-	-
Gunner	1 £4-0-0	1 £3-10-0	1 £3-0-0	1 £2-10-0	1 £2-5-0	1 £2-0-0	1 £2-5-0	1 £2-5-0	1 £2-5-0	1 £2-0-0	1 £2-0-0	1 £2-0-0
Gunner's Mate	4 £1-15-0	4 £1-15-0	2 £1-12-0	1 £1-10-0	1 £1-8-0	1 £1-6-0	1 £1-8-0	1 £1-8-0	1 £1-8-0	1 £1-6-0	1 £1-6-0	1 £1-6-0
Yeoman of the Powder Room	2 £1-15-0	2 £1-15-0	2 £1-12-0	1 £1-10-0	1 £1-8-0	1 £1-6-0	1 £1-8-0	1 £1-8-0	1 £1-8-0	1 £1-6-0	-	1 £1-6-0
Quarter Gunner	* £1-6-0	* £1-6-0	* £1-5-0	* £1-5-0	* £1-5-0	* £1-5-0	* £1-5-0	* £1-5-0	* £1-5-0	* £1-5-0	* £1-5-0	* £1-5-0
Armourer	1 £1-5-0	1 £1-5-0	1 £1-5-0	1 £1-5-0	1 £1-5-0	1 £1-5-0	1 £1-5-0	1 £1-5-0	1 £1-5-0	1 £1-5-0	-	-
Gunsmith	1 £1-5-0	1 £1-5-0	-	-	-	-	-	-	-	-	-	-

	Rated Vessels Commanded by a Post Captain						Unrated Vessels Commanded by a Commander or Lieutenant					
	1st 100+ guns	2nd 90+ guns	3rd 70+ guns	4th 50+ guns	5th 30+ guns	6th 20+ guns	Fire ships	Hospital ships	Store Ships	Sloops 60+ men	Bombs & smaller sloops	Yachts
Carpenter	1 £4-0-0	1 £3-10-0	1 £3-0-0	1 £2-10-0	1 £2-5-0	1 £2-0-0	1 £2-5-0	1 £2-5-0	1 £2-5-0	1 £2-0-0	1 £2-0-0	1 £2-0-0
Carpenter's Mate	2 £2-0-0	2 £2-0-0	1 £1-16-0	1 £1-14-0	1 £1-12-0	1 £1-10-0	1 £1-12-0	1 £1-12-0	1 £1-12-0	1 £1-10-0	1 £1-10-0	1 £1-10-0
Carpenter's Crew	12 £1-6-0	10 £1-6-0	8 £1-5-0	6 £1-5-0	5 £1-5-0	4 £1-5-0	1 £1-5-0	1 £1-5-0	2 £1-5-0	2 £1-5-0	1 £1-5-0	-
Purser	1 £4-0-0	1 £3-10-0	1 £3-0-0	1 £2-10-0	1 £2-5-0	1 £2-0-0	-	-	-	1 £2-0-0	-	-
Steward	1 £1-5-0	1 £1-5-0	1 £1-5-0	1 £1-3-4	1 £1-0-8	1 £1-0-0	1 £1-0-8	1 £1-0-8	1 £1-0-8	1 £1-0-0	1 £1-0-0	-
Stewards Mate	1 £1-0-8	1 £1-0-8	1 £1-0-8	1 £1-0-8	-	-	-	-	-	-	-	-
Cook	1 £1-5-0	1 £1-5-0	1 £1-5-0	1 £1-5-0	1 £1-5-0	1 £1-4-0	-	1 £1-5-0	1 £1-5-0	1 £1-4-0	-	-
Surgeon	1 £5-0-0	1 £5-0-0	1 £5-0-0	1 £5-0-0	1 £5-0-0	1 £5-0-0	1 £5-0-0	1 £5-0-0	1 £5-0-0	1 £5-0-0	1 £5-0-0	1 £5-0-0
Surgeon's 1st Mate	1 £2-10-0	1 £2-10-0	1 £2-10-0	1 £2-10-0	1 £2-10-0	1 £2-10-0	-	1 £2-10-0	1 £2-10-0	1 £2-10-0	-	-
Surgeon's 2nd Mate	1 £2-0-0	1 £2-0-0	1 £2-0-0	1 £2-0-0	1 £2-0-0	1 £2-0-0	-	1 £2-0-0	-	-	-	-
Surgeon's 3rd, 4th, 5th Mate	3 £1-10-0	2 £1-10-0	1 £1-10-0	-	-	-	-	2 £1-10-0	-	-	-	-

	Rated Vessels Commanded by a Post Captain						Unrated Vessels Commanded by a Commander or Lieutenant					
	1st 100+ guns	2nd 90+ guns	3rd 70+ guns	4th 50+ guns	5th 30+ guns	6th 20+ guns	Fire ships	Hospital ships	Store Ships	Sloops 60+ men	Bombs & smaller sloops	Yachts
Master at Arms	1 £2-5-0	1 £2-0-0	1 £1-17-6	1 £1-13-9	1 £1-10-0	1 £1-10-0	-	-	-	-	-	-
Corporal	2 £1-15-0	2 £1-12-0	2 £1-10-0	2 £1-10-0	2 £1-8-0	1 £1-6-0	1 £1-8-0	-	1 £1-8-0	1 £1-6-0	-	-
Trumpeter	1 £1-10-0	1 £1-8-0	1 £1-5-0	1 £1-5-0	1 £1-5-0	1 £1-4-0	-	-	-	-	-	-

* Quarter gunners were carried at the rate of one per four guns of the ships establishment.

Appendix VI

List of Officers by Date of First Commission

1693
Hughes, Richard

1695
Smith, William

1696
Gunman, James

1701
Hemmington, John

1702
Stewart, James
Wynnell, John
Parker, Christopher
Falkingham, Edward
Vernon, Edward
Graves, Thomas

1703
Redman, John

1705
Forbes, Lord George (3rd Earl of Granard)
Whitaker, Thomas
Molloy, Charles
Short, Joseph

1706
Fenwick, Benjamin
Harrison, Henry
Dumaresque, Philip
Townsend, Isaac
Yeo, John
Gideon, Solomon

1707
Brand, Ellis
Davies, William
Blackett, Sir Edward (3rd Baronet Blackett of Newcastle)
Hildesley, John

1708
Rycault, James
Bargrave, Charles
Kennedy, Silvester

1709
Rowley, William
Atkins, Samuel
Thomas, Richard
Opie, John
Stewart, George
Hamilton, James
Long, Robert
Longueville, Sir Thomas (4th Baronet Longueville of Wolverton,Bucks)
Middleton, Sir Hugh (5th Baronet Middleton of Ruthin)
Fleming, William Henry
Stafford, Israel
St Loe, John

1710
Martin, William

1711
Lindsay, Lord James (5th Earl of Balcarres)
Drummond, Charles
Gwyn, Richard

1712
Orme, John
Clinton, Hon. George

1714
Ellerker, William

1716
Anson, Lord George (1st Baron Anson)
Pocklington, Christopher

1717
Dilke, William
Osborne, Henry
Beauclerk, Lord Vere (1st Baron Vere, of Hanworth)

1718
Mead, Samuel
Swaysland, Henry
MacCarthy, Lord Robert (Viscount Muskerry)
Smith, William
Lyon, Scroop
Towry, John
Griffin, Thomas

1720
Dawnay, George
Barnard, Isaac
Dodd, Edward
Temple, William Thomas
Tucker, Thomas
Duncomb, Abraham
Lloyd, James
Mayne, Perry
Fanshawe, Charles

1722
Wingate, John

1723
Byng, Hon. John
Pritchard, John
Chaloner, Edward
Martin, Roger

1724
Fielding, William

1726
Burrish, George
Weldon, John
Hughes, Sir Richard (1st Baronet of East Bergholt)
Mogg, Thomas
Smith, Elliott
Warden, John
Pocock, George

1727
Lawrence, Peter
Strange, Edmund
Coe, Fyfield
Murray, George
O'Hara, Patrick
Colby, Charles
Catford, Charles
Dennis, Henry
Watkins, John
Pett, Robert
Toms, Peter
Bladwell, William Clement
Edwards, Richard
Holburne, Francis
Dove, Thomas
Gascoigne, James
Goddard, Samuel

1728
Brodrick, Thomas
Gould, Abraham
Smith, Thomas
Campbell, William
Cooke, John
Fox, Thomas
Ambrose, John
Thompson, Bradwarden
Barber, Edward
Russell, William

1729
Edwards, Rice
Steevens, Charles
Erskine, Robert

Hawke, Lord Edward (1st Baron Hawke of Towton)
Hore, Daniel
Maisterson, Samuel
Collins, Richard
Spragge, Edward

1730
Holcombe, Essex
Knowles, Sir Charles (1st Baronet Knowles)
Douglas, John
Fowke, Thorpe

1731
Forbes, John
Watson, Nathaniel
Michell, Alexander
Bedford, Thomas
Durell, Philip
Masclary, William Henry
Callis, Smith
Wickham, John

1732
Hume, John
Marsh, William
Boscawen, Hon. Edward
Douglas, Sir James (1st Baronet Douglas)
Tiddeman, Richard
Marshall, Samuel
Williams, John
Burnaby, Sir William (1st Baronet Burnaby of Broughton Hall)

1733
Leslie, Lachlan
Taylor, Polycarpus

1734
West, Temple
Brett, John
Coates, Thomas
Collins, William
Crookshanks, John
Dent, Digby
Galloway, William
Hill, Thomas
Laton, Sheldrake
Lovett, John
Mostyn, Savage
Seccombe, Ambrose
Cornewall, Frederick
Fawler, John
Jefferys, Robert
Lofting, Samuel
Geary, Sir Francis (1st Baronet of Oxenheath)
Lloyd, John
Bentley, Sir John
Kerr, Robert
Knowler, Charles
Norbury, Coningsby
Dyve, Henry
Toll, Edmund
Falkingham, Edward
Holmes, Charles
Watson, Charles
Saunders, Charles
Brett, Sir Piercy

1735
Swanton, Robert
Powlett, Charles
Clarke, Edward
Hill, John
Pye, Sir Thomas
Gordon, William
Barker, John
Boys, William
Cooper, Thomas
Hamar, Joseph
Huish, Henry
Robinson, Robert
Dent, Cotton
Long, Charles
Aylmer, Lord Henry (3rd Baron Aylmer)
Purvis, Charles Wager
Page, Henry
Watkins, Richard
Jelfe, Andrew
Cleland, Thomas
Moneypenny, James

1736
Hamilton, Hon. John

Williams, Bosville
Brodie, David
Reynolds, John
Townshend, Hon. George

1737
Hardy, Sir Charles
Ward, Henry
Carnegie, Lord George (6th Earl of Northesk)
Brand, John

1738
O'Brien, Lucius
Frankland, Sir Thomas (5th Baronet)
Cockburne, George
Baker, William
Baker, Thomas
Godsalve, Henry
Moore, Sir John
Gardiner, Arthur
Hughes, Robert
Parry, William
Rogers, Frederick
Bonfoy, Hugh
Baird, Patrick
Williams, Jonathon
Knackston, Thomas

1739
North, Abraham
Jasper, Richard
Powlett, Lord Harry (6th Duke of Bolton)
Young, James
Duff, Robert
Buckle, Mathew
Wray, Charles
Angel, Henry
Hill, George
Calmady, Warwick
Herne, Hanover
Amherst, John
Innes, Alexander
Simcoe, John
Davids, Charles
Eeles, John
Gwynn, Richard
Hanway, Thomas
Arbuthnot, Marriot
Arundell, Francis
Baynes, Robert
Brown, John
Colville, Lord Alexander (7th Viscount Colville of Culross)
Davis, Richard
Legge, John
Porter, Jervis Henry
Ryall, George
Shuldham, Lord Molyneaux (Baron Shuldham)
Walton, William
Dorrill, Richard
Knowler, Thomas
Matthews, Richard
Weller, John
Sbirel, John
Ferguson, John
Edgcumbe, Lord George (1st Earl of Mount Edgcumbe)
Donkley, John
Storr, John
Cowe, Peter
Maplesden, Jervis
Cornish, Sir Samuel (1st Baronet of Sharnbrook)
Denis, Sir Peter (1st Baronet of St Mary's)
Holburne, William
Cookson, Thomas
Loving, John
Salt, Sampson
Townley, Edmund
Craven, Thomas
Mihell, Best
Robinson, Edward
Pratten, Edward
Le Cras, Sir Edward
Norris, Harry
Scott, Arthur

1740
Barton, Matthew
Marshall, Leonard
Rosewell, Henry
Marsh, Henry
Hebden, Baker
Knight, Sir Joseph

Rodney, Lord George Brydges (1st Baron Rodney)
Trenwith, Thomas
Hackman, William
Noel, Thomas
Vaughan, Arthur
Brett, William
Graves, Samuel
Hudson, George
Wells, Thomas
Askew, Robert
Hardy, John
Jones, Roger
Long, William
Mainwaring, William
Mason, Robert
Murray, Archibald
Wellard, Robert
Hill, Christopher
Wyatt, Francis
Arnott, Robert
Vaughan, John
Belitha, Warren
Mackenzie, George
Pickering, Thomas Woolley
Robarts, Joseph
Mantell, William
Moore, John
Rawlings, Humphrey
Elwall, Eber
Faulknor, Samuel
Cooper, William
Cumming, James
Ward, Thomas
Nucella, Timothy
Allison, Thomas
Reynolds, John
Knight, John
Hume, James
Barnsley, Henry
Hemmington, Henry
Campbell, Alexander
Hughes, Edward
Stanhope, Sir Thomas
Leaver, William
Donaldson, James
Evans, John
Man, Robert
Montague, Hon. William
Barry, Hon. Richard
Hutchenson, Thomas Howard
Spry, Sir Richard
Veale, Joseph
Elliott, George
Horne, Edmund
Crickett, Edward
Hervey, Lord Augustus John (3rd Earl of Bristol)
Scott, Samuel
Fortescue, William
Preston, William
Scrope, Carr
Young, Gilbert
Tyrrell, Richard
Edwards, Richard
Kerly, Joseph
Galbraith, James
Montagu, John

1741

Taylor, Michael
Whitwell, Matthew
Kempenfelt, Richard
Hobbs, James
Armiger, John
Stuart, Hon. Archibald
Randell, James
Edwards, David
Harman, William
Harrison, John
Mountford, Edward
Parker, Edward
Read, Jacob
Foley, Thomas
Pearce, Vincent
Smith, Abel
Brown, Richard
Burr, William
Clark, John
Hackman, James
Hankerson, Thomas
Hatch, John
Moodie, John
Purcell, James John
Smelt, Cornelius
Craig, Robert

Middleton, Christopher
Chads, William
Fraser, Thomas
Lovelace, Paul
Churchill, Thomas
Brooking, Peter Franklin
Roberts, John
Bennett, William
Byron, Lord William (5th Baron Byron)
Ericks, James
Tiddeman, Mark
Oakley, Thomas
Cocks, Reginald
Grant, Robert
Jacobs, William
Powell, Samuel
Andrews, Thomas
Miller, Robert
Tindall, George
McCartie, Alexander
Legge, George
Rushworth, John
Forrest, Arthur
Haldane, Robert
Bromfield, George
Hale, John
Kinsey, William
Logie, James
Wentworth, Thomas
Kerly, Anthony
Seymour, Berkeley
Cockburne, Andrew
Hartwell, Broderick
Foley, Thomas
Wheelock, John
Neilson, Thomas
Willett, William Saltern
Latham, Thomas
Lempriere, Thomas
Le Febvre, William
Gilchrist, James
Every, Dennis
Bonnyman, Jonas
Taylor, Wittewronge
Darrock, Archibald
Leigh, Thomas
Palliser, Sir Hugh (1st Baronet)
Prettie, Henry
Faulknor, Robert
Elmy, Benjamin
Garencieres, Charles
Seton, George
Gaines, Francis
Dudley, O'Brien
Roddam, Robert
Blair, James
Facey, John
Young, Benjamin
Atkinson, Anthony

1742

Hallum, Thomas
Shirley, Lord Washington (5th Earl Ferrers)
Washington, Shirley
Dalston, Sir George (4th Baronet Dalston of Dalston)
Spencer, Samuel
Wheeler, Edward
Hinxman, John
Brady, Matteate
Pigot, Hugh
Wilkie, Alexander
Coard, William
Butler, James
Gordon, Alexander
Harland, Sir Robert (1st Baronet of Sproughton)
Johnston, Sir William
Carkett, John
Colby, Stephen
Gayton, Clark
Hunt, Edmund
Brewse, John
Blanckley, George
Gascoigne, Edward
Norton, William
Sliford, Thomas
Winter, Thomas
Trant, Henry
Bollard, Robert
Gugelman, Charles
Cozentine, Ezekiel
Knight, Richard
Norbury, Richard
Gardiner, John
Davis, Francis

Dunkley, John
Phillips, Henry John
Farmer, Hon. William
Botterell, John
Darby, George
Bargus, Richard
Jekyll, Edward
Ourry, Paul Henry

1743
Bucknall, Joseph
Kirk, James
Manning, Thomas
Falkingham, John
Guilliard, John
Tresillian, Nicholas
Gore, Hamilton
Hay, David
Newson, William
Vernon, Sir Edward
Lloyd, Charles
Harmer, Jeremiah
Eastwood, Joseph
Varlo, Weston
Bladen, John
Prescott, Thomas
Peyton, Joseph
Clarke, Francis
Lucas, Charles
Nutt, Justinian
Summers, Thomas
Blyte, George
Gage, Joseph
Graves, Thomas (1st Baron of Gravesend in the County of Londonderry)
Marlow, Benjamin
Moore, Mathew
Loeffs, Charles
Bray, John
Hanbury, Thomas
Peerman, John
Burslem, Francis
Evans, Thomas
Trelawny, Sir William
Langdon, William
Heron, Benjamin
Owen, Thomas
Jarvis, Daniel
Higgs, Richard
Lockhart, Sir John (6th Baronet Lockhart-Ross of Carstairs)
Parker, Sir Peter
Teale, Richard
Sayer, James
Cock, William
Crispo, John
Gordon, Thomas
Mackie, James

1744
Lind, John
Grant, Charles Cathcart
Allan, James
Hinde, Richard
Bastard, John
Webber, Charles
Bateman, Hon. William
Harris, William
Hyde, Frederick
Vincent, Nicholas
Hamilton, William
Kearny, Michael
Cunningham, James
Carey, John
Gambier, James
Gayton, George
Lloyd, William
Edwards, Owen
Jones, James
Pettigrew, William
Wallis, Matthew
Meldrum, William
Keppel, Lord Augustus (1st Viscount Keppel)
Osborne, Francis
Dumaresque, William
Coles, Christopher
Farmar, Robert
Acton, John
Legge, Julian
Clements, Richard
Stuteville, Charles
Haven, Arthur
Skene, Alexander
Byng, Henry
French, Wildy

Carteret, Peter
Hollwall, John
Jones, Thomas
Milbanke, Mark
Moutray, John
Dundas, Robert
Pascoe, Richard
Kyrby, Richard
Manley, Richard
Davis, Nathaniel
Cowell, Henry
Barker, Thomas
Goostrey, William
Fortye, Anthony
Thornbrough, Edward
Gardner, James
Richards, Francis
Candler, John
Everitt, Michael
Irvine, Alexander
Shackerly, William
Dubois, Henry Richard
Haswell, Robert
Gough, William
Mathias, John
Johnston, James
Thompson, Samuel
Coode, Nicholas
Bagster, John
Beamish, William
Burnett, Thomas
Bryant, George
Clark, Edward
Baker, James
Drummond, Patrick
Hammond, Thomas
Hodges, John
Webb, James
Binks, William
Trehearne, John
Bover, John
Martin, William
Cunningham, Thomas
Gordon, John
Hoy, Isaac
Williamson, William
Furneaux, James
Mathews, John
Cary, John
Chaplen, James
Carteret, Richard
Cormack, John
Taaff, John
Walsh, John
Fortescue, John
Martin, John
Saumarez, Thomas
Kennedy, Lord Archibald (11th Earl of Cassilis)
Gillis, John
Mackenzie, James

1745

Boles, John
Campbell, John
Downing, Dennis
Goard, John
Parker, Sir Hyde (5th Baronet of Melford Hall)
Osborne, John
Perkins, William
Hovell, James
Cleland, John
Falconer, George
Ourry, Isaac Florimond
Neale, John
Pemble, Thomas
Scott, Henry
Warriner, George
Proby, Charles
Ansell, William
Carkett, Robert
Hallam, John
Gordon, Robert
Gideon, Henry
Clapp, John
Suckling, Maurice
Boucher, James
Baillie, Thomas
Foulkes, Peter
Hughes, Sir Richard (2nd Baronet of East Bergholt)
Forster, William
Kyd, James
Paterson, James
Gentil, George

Broadley, Housman
Frankland, Robert
Leitch, William
Warwick, Thomas
West, John
Stuart, Nathaniel
Jones, Morgan
Loring, Joshua
Ogilvie, George
Slorach, James
Peighin, John
Lawson, James
Edwards, Charles Turner
Coultas, Jeremiah
Hughes, John
Smith, Henry
Allen, John Carter
Lowfield, William
Orrok, James
Rous, John
Phillips, William
Hathorn, Robert
Balfour, George
Holburne, James
Taylor, Samuel
Cave, Joseph
Digges, Dudley
McCleverty, William
Murray, John
Roome, Charles
Salmon, Joseph
Brent, Robert
Hyde, Boyle
Affleck, Sir Edmund (1st Baronet of Dalham Hall)
Henley, Charles
Ryder, James
Penny, Taylor
Dod, Thomas
Howe, Lord Richard (1st Earl Howe)
Mathison, John
Francis, Thomas
Mckinley, Samuel
Rogers, John
Brock, John
Greenwood, William
Wemyss, Hon. James
Hooper, Edward
Atkins, John
Wills, Roger
Barrington, Hon. Samuel
Miller, David
Moyle, Henry
Hammick, Stephen
Speke, Henry
Dishington, Andrew
Middleton, Lord Charles (1st Baron Barham)
Hurt, Christopher Jarvis
Ogle, Sir Chaloner
Basset, Christopher
How, John
Atkinson, John
Taylor, Thomas
Usher, Arthur
Fraine, Joseph
Sheward, Ridgway
Pascal, Michael Henry
Hewett, Sir William (5th Baronet of Headley Hall)

1746

Sainthill, Humphrey
Deacon, Sabine
Mackay, Hugh
Mouat, Patrick
Shurmur, William
Drake, Francis William
Hall, John
Innes, James
Jones, Ambrose
Hawford, John
Vavasor, Richard
King, Sir Richard (1st Baronet of Bellevue)
Lyell, David
Foss, Joseph
Bickerton, Sir Richard (1st Baronet Bickerton of Upwood)
Teape, James
Stanton, John
Boyd, John
Morgan, Probert
Stirling, Sir Walter
Cock, William
Cobby, Thomas
Townsend, James

Kite, William
Clive, Benjamin
Grigg, Arthur
Byron, John
Baker, Samuel
Robinson, Mark
Davies, Lewis
Boog, David
Mortimer, Robert
Meredith, David
Evans, John
Parkin, Henry
Hall, William
Woodward, John
Dunn, George
Munden, Thomas
Newton, George
Froude, James
Philips, Henry
Chads, James
Mathews, George
Millar, Archibald
Brown, William
Covell, Isaac
Lendrick, John
Motley, John
Smith, Thomas
Scarlett, Nathaniel
Hickes, John
Griffies, Samuel
Hood, Samuel (1st Viscount Hood of Whitley)
Milligan, John
O'Brien, Christopher
Deards, John
Baker, Henry
Jocelyn, Robert
Routh, Robert
Crowcher, James
Williams, Richard
Elphinstone, John
Foster, William
Jurd, William
Allen, Nathaniel
Lincolne, James
Parke, Thomas
Shirley, James
Grape, Samuel
Hamilton, George
Burrows, Richard
Nutall, John
Cook, Andrew
Patterson, Forbes
Morgan, Jeremiah
Hood, Lord Alexander Arthur (1st Viscount Bridport)

1747

Brett, Charles
Hamilton, Sir John (1st Baronet of Trebinshun House)
Thorpe, James
Humphris, Thomas
Lynn, Thomas
Crouch, Isaac
Strachan, John
Milton, William
Cunningham, Thomas
Man, Robert
Bond, Robert
Dugdale, Robert
Hammond, William
Hay, Robert
Christian, John
Uvedale, Samuel
Edgcombe, Robert
Andrews, Robert
Spendlove, Samuel
Lambert, Robert
Barker, William
Rowley, Sir Joshua (1st Baronet Rowley)
Brookes, John
Willis, Thomas
Robinson, William
Wandby, Daniel
Lloyd, Francis
Mead, Joseph
Wilkinson, Andrew
Harmood, James
Ellery, George
O'Bryen, John
Haldane, James
Calder, Patrick
Crooke, Peter Thomas
Short, Samuel
Combs, James

Douthwaite, George
Doake, James
Farr, Walker
Harrison, Thomas
Allwright, Thomas
Hutchings, Edward
Schomberg, Sir Alexander
Scaife, John
Van Court, Peter
Bishop, Thomas
Pigot, Thomas

1748
Kerr, Robert
Lobb, Jacob
Archer, John
Norwood, Joseph
Lowndes, Richard
Brown, Alexander
Forford, William
Grant, Murdo
Moody, Thomas
Ogle, Chaloner
Smith, James
Freno, Zachariah
Randell, John
Essington, Claphamson
Laforey, Sir John (1st Baronet Laforey)
O'Hara, James
Bowerbank, John
Crow, William
Cope, John
Gresley, Sir Nigel (6th Baronet Gresley)
Fletcher, Lowther
Skynner, Lancelot
Keith, Alexander
Hamilton, Lord Richard (4th Viscount Boyne)
Upton, Francis
Carre, Robert
Toby, Richard
Prole, Henry
Bulteele, James
Fraser, John
Crymble, Murray
Waterfall, Matthew
Marshall, George
Wallis, Samuel
Russell, John
Manley, William
Wilkie, James
Tinker, John Bladen

1749
Bunyan, William
Hervey, Pynsent
Leighton, Edward
Wilding, Peter Manwaring
Campbell, James
Kestell, John
Martell, William
Willes, John
Bayne, William
Alms, James
Brewse, Hobart
Cornwall, Thomas
Hope, Sir William (3rd Baronet Hope of Kirkliston)
Burton, John
Christian, Edward
Drake, Sir Francis Samuel (1st Baronet Drake)
Gillam, Thomas

1750
Adams, William
Rawling, John
Maitland, Frederick Lewis
McDonald, Coll
Collingwood, Thomas
Hudson, Thomas
Phipps, David
Bate, Elias

1751
Williams, Vincent
Cary, Ebenezer
Wilkins, William

1752
Wilson, John
Spendelow, Charles
Quin, Robert
Digby, Robert
Jacobs, Maximilian

1753
Ellys, Charles
Graham, Mitchell
Osborne, James
Shuckforth, David
Grant, Francis
Nightingale, Gamaliel
Brograve, William
Faulknor, Jonathon
Kirby, Mathew
Douglas, Sir Charles (1st Baronet Carr)

1754
Becher, Michael
Gambier, Samuel
Collins, Henry
Tucker, William
Collier, Sir George
Harris, John
Lambert, Robert Alexander
Napier, Charles
Fielding, Basil
Prentice, Nathaniel

1755
Duncan, Lord Adam (1st Viscount Duncan of Camperdown)
Gidoin, John Lewis
Symonds, Thomas
Cosby, Philips
Hotham, Sir William (1st Baron Hotham)
Edwards, Timothy
Griffiths, Joseph
Inglis, Charles
Sax, Robert
Yeaman, Sherwood
Young, Stewart
Eastwood, Jennings
Kirk, Robert
Lutwidge, Samuel
Jervis, John (1st Earl St. Vincent)
Fitzherbert, Thomas
Carteret, John
Collins, Richard
Phillips, George
Robbins, George
Wallace, Sir James
Lynn, Francis
Cranston, James
Somerset, John Stukley
Lee, Thomas
Symons, John
Carpenter, Robert
Cleveland, Archibald
Deane, Joseph
Brown, John
Affleck, Philip
Daniel, Thomas
I'Anson, Henry
Braithwaite, Richard
Griffith, Walter
Howorth, Edward
Smyth, Henry
Roche, Charles
Leslie, Patrick
Nourse, Robert
Brereton, William
Ourry, George
Allen, William
Morris, John
Runwa, John
Runwa, William
Codrington, Christopher
Puckinghorn, James
Yonge, William
Watson, George
Medows, Lord Charles (1st Earl Manvers)
Barnsley, John
Reid, James
Paston, William
Pownoll, Philimon
Johnston, George
Shirley, Thomas
St Loe, Edward
Chapman, John
Cumming, William
Ross, George
Deane, Edward
Dumaresq, Thomas
Bremer, James
May, Samuel
Yates, Edward Vernon
Haynes, Thomas
Lemoine, Francis
Walter, Robert
Child, Smith

Urry, John
Campbell, Duncan
Clements, Michael
Clark, William
Poole, Robert
Pearson, Sir Richard
Martin, Sir Henry (Baronet Martin of Lockynge)
Dickson, William
Hawker, James
Morland, Samuel
Newton, Henry
Vaughan, Hugh

1756

Perreau, Samuel
Tonyn, George Anthony
Gill, Thomas
Siddall, John
Macartney, John
Whyte, Mark
Burr, Daniel
Franks, Jacob
Gordon, James
Gregory, Robert
Montague, Thomas
Talbot, George
Barber, Robert
Boteler, Philip
Ripley, Horatio
Dalrymple, Hugh
Dalrymple, John
Lindsay, John
Lloyd, Thomas
Sawyer, Herbert
Hill, Edward
Joass, John
Clerke, Sir John
Birt, John
Mann, John Hollingbery
Boyle, Hon. Robert
Graham, Edmund
Powlett, Percy
Banks, Francis
Chenoweth, Michael
Keating, Christopher
Forrester, Lord William
Mainwaring, William
Collins, Richard
Nailour, Charles
Hoey, William Parsons
Reddish, Edward
Prissick, Christopher
Caesar, Charles
Duff, William
Bensley, John
Brown, James
Brice, Robert
Elliot, John
Barker, Thomas
Burdon, George
Gyde, James
Hanby, Joseph
Street, John
Allen, William
Walton, Samuel
Halstead, William Anthony
McDouall, William
O'Hara, Francis
Denne, William
Hay, William
Mainwaring, Thomas Bornford
Davers, Henry
Hunt, Joseph
Mathias, Herbert
Buckner, Charles
Heslopp, Robert
Martyn, Roger
Owen, John
Vincent, John
Vitu, John
Chinnery, Saint John
Tathwell, Joseph
Morice, Thomas
Phillips, William
Bellew, Henry
Norman, James
Holmes, Lancelot
Holton, Frederick
Houlton, John
Roch, Hugh
Borwick, Halley
Nott, John Neale Pleydell
Collingwood, George
Locker, William
Bateman, Nathaniel

Henderson, John
Sauvaire, Thomas
White, Oliver
Cockfield, Samuel
Brustis, Paul
Leslie, William
Cundall, George
Porter, Peter
Jackson, John
Cuming, Penhallow
Keeler, Robert
Goodall, Samuel Granston
Colmer, John
Raper, Christopher
Skinner, George
Ferguson, John
Bromedge, Hugh
Davis, Henry
Jones, William
Thomas, Richard
Williams, Roger
Wightman, William
Walker, James
Hodder, Edward
Skone, Thomas
Wood, Charles
Mitchell, James
Hollingworth, Thomas
Sharpe, Thomas
Curry, Robert
Baillie, Alexander
Baron, James
Bradshaw, Thomas
Brome, Henry
Brown, William
Eastwood, Thomas
French, George
Gellie, Lewis
Grant, William
Horne, Charles
Mackenzie, George
Maurice, John
Plint, Thomas
Price, Edward
Scott, Cecil
Sherwood, William
Stewart, James
Uppleby, Samuel
Wastell, James
Caldwell, Charles
Orchard, Francis
Howe, William
Lort, George
Crews, John
Ellis, Thomas
Hart, Henry Hare
Keith, Sir Basil
Oakley, John
Antrobus, Charles
Bloom, William
Collins, David
Crosby, Nathaniel
Ferguson, James
Lower, Edward
Trotter, Savage
Champernowne, Rawlin
Dickens, William
Hulke, Benjamin
Duane, Abraham
O'Hara, Peter
Beale, Richard
Clayton, Samuel Wittewronge
Townsend, Henry
Haswell, William
Kerswell, Edward
Douglas, Stair

1757

Saxton, Sir Charles (1st Baronet Saxton of Circourt)
Howorth, John
Reeve, Samuel
Drummond, John
Hansford, William
Becher, John
Dering, Daniel
Lawes, William
Murray, Richard
Truscott, William
Ussher, Christopher
Grenfell, William
Ayscough, James
Fabian, William
Phillips, George
Towry, George Phillips
Williams, William

Marshall, William
Piercy, Thomas
Winzar, David
Baird, Sir William (5th Baronet of Saughton Hall)
Corner, John
Webster, William
Stains, Robert
Stott, John
Clark, Archibald
Fenwick, Barnabas
Hodgson, Connolly
Pinfold, Richard
Wilis, John
Wills, John
Raynor, John
Somerville, Mark
Brudenell, Richard
Gauntlett, John
Harvey, Henry
Porter, Thomas
Hey, Rawlins
Ommanney, John
Blomer, Charles
Burnett, James
Godfrey, John
Ley, Thomas Arthur
Butler, Daniel
Sparke, Henry
Feattus, James
Rooke, Nicholas
Sheall, Robert
Gascoigne, James
Pawlett, Edmund
Shuldham, Lemuel
Hoskins, Henry
Barter, James
Columbine, Edward
Hunt, Anthony
Martin, William
Lindesay, John
Forbes, Peter
Rogers, Jacob
Purcell, John
Buckingham, James
Ford, Thomas
Atkins, Christopher
Bensley, Sir William (1st Baronet of St Marylebone)
Brenton, Jahleel
Brown, John
Charley, Isaac
Dalrymple, Robert
Gaven, William
Haygarth, William
Jarden, John
Jardine, George
Richards, William
Richardson, John
Strachan, Patrick
Tonken, Thomas
Pratt, William
Trotten, Richard
Brown, John
Bell, George
Henry, John
Symes, Thomas
Arrowsmith, Joseph
Cole, Martin
Doherty, John
Hawkins, John
Shaughnesy, William
Stevens, William
Fielding, Charles
Leslie, Charles
Adams, Sir Thomas (6th Baronet of London)
Bodledge, John
Playstowe, Philip
Long, Walter
Runwa, Benjamin
Carteret, Philip
Collins, Sir John
Gordon, Lewis
Stevenson, Joseph
Sutherland, James
Cowe, John
Daws, John
Shewen, Richard Phillips
Durell, Philip
Middlehurst, James
Glover, John
Cuckow, Trevor
Lloyd, William
Hudson, Charles
Greenfield, John
Male, Thomas

Braithwaite, Thomas Patrickson
Vane, Hon. Raby
Bower, Robert
Holburne, Sir Alexander (3rd Baronet of Menstrie)
Bentinck, John Albert
Shairp, John
Prince, Charles
King, Isaac
Vincent, Nathaniel
Clarke, Peter
Pell, Thomas
Brisbane, John
Mansell, Samuel
Baird, John
Johnston, Samuel
Reeves, John
Elliot, Benjamin
Shadforth, John
Townley, Thomas
Disher, James
Michie, Colin
Spearing, George
Blake, Peter
Lux, John
Short, John Ides
Garner, William
Dring, Robert
Jackson, Joseph
Tyler, Charles
Durell, Thomas Pike
Hammett, John
Bligh, Sir Richard Rodney
Pasley, Sir Thomas (Baronet Pasley of Craig)
Hopkins, Benjamin
Lloyd, Henry
Ochterlony, Alexander
Tomkins, Christopher
Maitland, David
Stewart, John
Fleming, William
Eliot, John
Bacon, William
Tattum, John
Dundas, Ralph
Rutherford, Lord David
Day, Thomas
Senior, Abraham
Stancombe, George
Adston, James
Corbett, Walter
Hayne, Arthur
Hooper, Edward
Lukey, Patherick
Thompson, Edward
Bone, John
Powlett, Francis Lascoe
Jones, William
Valentine, John
Philpot, George
Ashington, Henry
Percivall, Crean
Edgar, Alexander
Fairfax, Sir William George
Shirley, James

1758

Pryce, David
Baskerville, Peter
Newton, Witham
Orsbridge, Philip
Spicer, William
Collins, John
Smith, William
Tomlinson, Robert
Brisbane, Stewart
Gordon, James
Parker, Sir Hyde
Screech, James
Robinson, John
Abdy, Sir William (6th Baronet of Felix Hall, Essex)
Lisle, Trevelyan
Puddicombe, Stephen
Dent, Sir Digby
Parker, Samuel
Bowyer, Sir George (5th Baronet of Denham Court)
Bowen, Essex
Miller, George
Brand, Andrew
Rawlings, James
Chandler, David
Crosbe, William
Owen, William
Rich, Sir Thomas (5th Baronet Rich)

Hayward, Thomas
Carteret, James
Rigby, Christopher
Hayes, Frederick
Wood, John
Dundas, Charles
Henshaw, John
Knight, George
Lewis, Henry
Hilgrove, James
Wilson, Robert
Cumming, James
Bruce, Alexander
Haven, John
Reynolds, Lord Francis (3rd Baron Ducie)
Hickes, Thomas
Couchman, Thomas
Reynolds, John
Groat, Robert
Anderson, Mathew
James, John
Exton, Francis
Heathcote, George
Mackenzie, George
Lloyd, Henry
Clear, Henry
Crowley, William
Dodd, Henry
Harris, George
Kinloch, David
Mitherell, Anthony
Prescott, Isaac
Roch, William
Coalke, William
Curle, Nicholas Wilson
Bourke, William Francis
Barnsley, Samuel
Brown, Johnson
Sinfield, William
Curtiss, Hyde
Burr, John
Edgcumbe, Robert
Ord, Christopher
Savage, Henry
Dobson, Charles
Wall, James
Legeyt, Matthew
Don, William
Ferrior, Samuel
Furneaux, Abraham
Robson, John
Ommanney, Cornthwaite
Cannon, Richard
Stuart, Patrick
Cowling, John
Galbraith, John
Bradby, James
Leary, John
Underdown, Thomas
Glasford, James
Balfour, David
Read, John
Shammon, William
Baker, James
Home, George
Saunders, Thomas
Todd, Alexander
Palmer, William
Brabazon, Lambert
Luttrell, John
Arthur, David
Frodsham, John
Colville, James
Luce, John
Marsh, John
Steward, Samuel
Wollaston, Robert
Coltheart, Walter
Arnold, Sampson
Barkley, Andrew
Besson, Charles
Boyd, James
Boys, Pearson
Buckworth, Francis
Burrows, John
Burstall, William
Daniel, William
Feild, Thomas
Ferguson, Patrick
Field, John
Grey, Henry
Jordan, Thomas
Knollys, Hon. Cyprian
Lambert, Henry
Leeke, Henry Sebastian
Macbride, John

Palmer, Edward
Preston, James
Taite, Peter
White, David
White, James
Towers, George
Cox, Henry
Gower, Hon. John Leveson
Mason, Thomas Tunstall
Sandiver, Philip
Newton, Henry
Llewhellin, Richard
Marriott, John
Onslow, Richard (1st Baronet of Althain)
Lockwood, David
Osborne, Wadham
Reid, John
Towers, Thomas
Johnstone, Gideon
Norbury, Thomas
Jackson, Henry

1759
Dewey, Thomas
Stewart, Hon. Keith
Wilkinson, Matthew
Gaborian, Thomas
de Havilland, James
Pattison, Mark
Roberts, Edward
Knowles, John
Cam, Joseph
Mowat, Henry
Rayment, Thomas
Smith, John
Wolseley, Charles
Mayne, Robert
Meldrum, William
Shank, Joseph
Breton, John
Thorowgood, Selby
Hill, Lionel
Selby, Jerrard
Downs, Jonathon
Sandham, Henry
Stevens, Richard
Hay, John
Logie, Charles
Marshall, John
Harmood, Harry
Judd, William
May, John
Herbert, Thomas
Allen, Thomas
Collingwood, John Trevor
Dare, William
Knowles, Edward
Martin, William
Parrey, Robert
Potts, Joseph
Price, Richard
West, Thomas
Gaborian, James
Hill, James
Tristram, Lawrence
Townsend, Thomas
Chads, Henry
Clarke, Arthur
Colton, Caleb
Green, John
Debat, Peter
Hay, Charles
Katon, Edward
Jones, William
Clark, William
Campbell, William
Allen, James
Allen, Thomas
Hayes, Matthew
Pigot, Rowland
Bechinoe, Benjamin
Elliston, Edmund
Lewis, Joshua
Cumine, John
Deacon, Richard
Cunningham, Alexander
Hawker, Thomas
Kidd, Dandy
Neville, Joseph
Baillie, Alexander Francis
Teague, William
Dowson, Charles
Clarke, Charles
Dupre, Michael
Burford, Samuel
Taylor, John

Traill, William
Little, Charles
Davis, Henry
Atkinson, Edward
Thomas, James
Mathews, John
Henderson, William
Farmer, George
Roy, St Alban
Gibbes, Anthony
Edwards, Arthur
Augustus, Lord Edward (Prince Edward)
Fairlie, Gilbert
Hamond, Sir Andrew Snape (1st Baronet of Holly Grove)
Parkinson, Thomas
Owen, William
Nicholas, James
Simonton, Robert
Perceval, Philip Tufton
Lawrie, Thomas
Redmon, William
Ford, Francis
White, George
Michell, Reynell
Caulfield, Tobias
Cocks, Thomas
Lash, Joseph
Partridge, Thomas
Babb, William
Robertson, James
Tonge, William Norris
Yonge, William Herne
Forth, John
Clifford, Nicholas
Kemp, Richard
Littlefield, John
Pitchford, Samuel
Wadman, John
Kinneer, James
Westlake, Bernard
Wilson, William
Fowler, Andrew
Lutwidge, Skeffington
Elletson, William
Lindsay, George
Parry, Francis
Anningson, Joseph
Buchanan, John
Dalyell, Thomas
Fox, William
Maltby, William
Wilkinson, Thomas
Bourn, George
Lurcock, William
Orde, John
Peard, George
Wolfe, William
Dickenson, James
Reynolds, William
Warren, Samuel
Chubb, John Fhoedra
Stanford, William
Tilly, Thomas
Bowers, John Hope
Bromedge, John
Jarvis, John
Robinson, John
Boswell, Robert
Watson, Thomas
Edwards, Edward
McDougall, Robert
Marshall, Charles
Tatham, Thomas
Bligh, John
Fanshawe, Robert
Bandinel, Thomas
Harvey, John
Dickson, Sir Archibald (1st Baronet of Hardingham Hall)
Edwards, Thomas
Broughton, Francis
Duncan, Henry
Hills, William
Taylor, Robert
Hue, Philip
Cumby, David Pryce
Dyson, Thomas
Padget, Henry
Rosco, James
Sloass, James
Tyrwhitt, John
Vandeput, George
Forrest, Digory
Sayer, Joshua
Twyman, Arthur

Ardesoif, John Plummer
Duddingston, William
Hemmings, William
Osborn, William
Whitehurst, Thomas
Hawker, Edmund
Withy, John
Saunders, Richard
Parkes, John
Gaspey, William
Milward, Thomas
Thorowgood, Dynes
Bourmaster, John
Furneaux, Tobias
Monat, George
Mouat, George
Leak, John
Laugharne, Thomas
Kelly, Charles
Gooding, Nathaniel
Home, Sir George (7th Baronet of Blackadder)
Girling, John
Lesingham, Thomas
Mennell, George
Panton, Henry Gibson
Stewart, Lord John (7th Earl of Galloway)
Bertie, Hon. Peregrine
Newton, Robert

1760

Hamilton, James
Gell, John
Bracey, Jay
Knight, James
Wilkinson, George
Evans, Robert
Lewis, Isaac
Hunter, William
Woolridge, Francis
Bradshaw, John
Cotton, Rowland
Okes, John
Vassmer, Henry
Marshall, Sir Samuel
Dodd, Edmund
Keir, Francis
Wayman, John
Veysey, John
Osborne, William
Pitcairn, Robert
Adamson, Cuthbert
Moulden, William
Gardner, Lord Alan (1st Baron Gardner of Uttoxeter)
Perry, John
Robertson, William
Alexander, John
Shorediche, Richard
Neal, James
Caldwell, Sir Benjamin
Dalrymple, Primrose
Moubray, George
Hill, Benjamin
Kcr, William
Colley, William
Cook, James
Horton, William
Milbank, William
Stewart, John
Burstall, John
Lowder, John
Brady, James
Breedon, Joseph
Brooke, William
Gillingham, Robert
Hawkins, Joseph
Knight, James
Rule, James
Twisden, William
Steel, Robert
Bazely, John
Williams, Courtnay
Berrow, Edward
Samber, James
Spicer, John
Crooks, William
Gooding, John
Laforey, Loftus
Lang, Richard
Friend, Bravil
Jefferson, David
Marshall, Thomas
Duckitt, Peter
Ged, Dougaldus
Johnston, William

Nash, Ezekiel
Lys, James
Geary, Thomas
Smith, Richard
Cotes, John
Lenox, James
Brown, David
Montresor, James
Walsh, Philip
Douglas, John Leigh
Grierson, James
Hasleden, Thomas
Hopkins, Timothy
Wainwright, John
Whiston, John
Day, Bunbury
Hamilton, James
Rains, Stephen
Sinclair, James
Worth, James
Holl, James
Collier, Thomas
Watts, Walter
Lloyd, Hugh
Brown, Annesley
Graeme, Alexander
Bindloss, Edward
Carter, Robert
Smith, Henry
Warden, James
Young, Robert
Barford, Francis
Butchart, John
Bell, William
Gwennap, Walter
Milne, Robert
Scott, Robert
St John, Hon. Henry
Baynes, Henry
Blair, William
Disney, Daniel
Hill, Thomas
Stacey, Thomas
Bourgeois, Louis Freeman
Douglas, Richard
Jones, James Howell
Pringle, Thomas
Roxburgh, William
Campbell, Lord William
Clark, Henry
Heron, William
Newnham, Thomas
Glover, Bonovier
Potts, Robert
Gibson, John
John, Samuel
Langford, John
Newton, John
Henderson, Robert
Fotheringham, Patrick
Lockhart, William
Jolliffe, John
Nunn, Joseph
Richardson, Thomas
Ruthven, Hon. John
Tomkys, Hope
Slade, John

1761

Ward, Archibald
Bell, Thomas
Fletcher, Philip
Thompson, Sir Charles (1st Baronet Virkees)
Webb, John
Yetts, John
St Barbe, John
Baikie, Hugh
Minisie, John
Linzee, Robert
Topping, William
Major, Christopher
Bird, Timothy
Paine, John
Newton, William
Baines, Cuthbert
Pemberton, Henry
Harris, Stephen
Quarme, William
Marbeuf, Daniel
Witherspoon, David
Mackie, Thomas
Osborne, Charles
Fordyce, Alexander
Cornwallis, William
Ford, John
Liell, Thomas

Parrey, Anthony
Grant, William
Stoney, George
Stuart, Hon. David
Blankett, John
Boger, Richard
Morrice, Thomas
Norris, John
Watherston, Alexander
Harrington, Joseph
Cross, John
Jones, John
West, John
Sautel, George
Phillips, Nathaniel
Iggulden, Edward
Phillip, Arthur
Clerk, John
Fielding, William Carr
Noble, George
Younghusband, George
Garrow, Joseph
Master, Henry
George, James
Godfrey, Andrew
Macnamara, James
Jones, Anthony
Cromwell, Henry
Hunter, Charles
Scott, William
Barlow, George
Kirby, Anthony
Boyce, Crawford
Campbell, Andrew
Pomeroy, Thomas
Robinson, Hugh
Kempthorne, James
Agnew, Alexander
Biggs, Robert
Brooks, John
Case, James
Gaydon, John
Inglis, John
Nott, Francis
Rawe, Thomas
Smithett, William
Bandinel, Francois
Pakenham, Lord Edward Michael (2nd Baron Longford)
Hooley, Joseph
Oakley, William
Tunstall, Mathew
Hayter, Samuel
Dove, Jonathan
Herbert, Charles
Stainforth, George
Richards, Edward
O'Brien, Lucius
Irwin, John
Edwards, Charles
Padeson, Edmund
Scott, Samuel
Down, Edward
Bower, Edmund
Metcalfe, Stephen
Inglis, John
Norris, Stephen
Affleck, William
Hindman, Michael
Forster, John
Colins, Henry
Appleby, Thomas
Lawrie, Thomas
Young, Sir George
Lewis, Thomas
Dundas, Adam
Vaillant, Isaac
Emery, Charles
Meekeson, James
Crooke, Charles Cunningham
Tuite, Henry
Winniett, Edward
Dumaresq, George
Trussell, George

1762

Heron, Harry
Whittle, Price Warren
Brown, Joseph
Dalrymple, James
Crespin, Abraham
Dow, Archibald
Thomas, William
Greig, Samuel
Robertson, George
Warburton, Charles

Bradby, Daniel
Phipps, Lord Constantine John (1st Baron of Mulgrave in the County of York)
Surtees, George
Grieve, William
Peat, George
Carr, John
Manistre, Fiske
Sharpe, Isaac
Burnett, William
Osborne, Thomas
Starr, John
Pollard, George
Burrows, John
Fortescue, Faithful Adrian
Griffiths, Delanoy
Jackson, Michael
Mackerell, Thomas
Kent, John
Cunningham, William
McIntosh, Joseph
Parnell, John
Rawlin, William
Boston, Thomas
Medows, Edward
Temple, Henry
Harmer, Burward
Guillaume, Peter
Stephens, Stephen
Hardy, Thomas
Watt, James
Smith, Richard
Laird, David
Waple, Edward
Patton, Philip
Abbs, William
Good, John
Hallum, John
Nixon, Anderson
Roberts, Christopher
Reddall, Ambrose
Cauldwell, Edward
Day, George
Harrison, James
Scott, John
Graves, John
Kelly, Timothy
Lynch, Stephen
Scott, James
Plowden, James Chichley
Wyborn, Hercules
Troughton, Ellis
Brandreth, William Alston
Cayley, William
Kirkwood, Alexander
Moore, John
Steedman, William
Dilkes, John
Sandys, Stephen
Jenkins, William
Budworth, William
Dawson, George
Thompson, Edward
Cole, John Sutton
Mason, Holman
Butler, Jacob
Calder, Sir Robert (1st Baronet of Southwick)
Young, John
Bryne, Henry
Cartwright, John
Stuart, Archibald
Evans, Henry Francis
Gough, John
Fowler, Richard
Skelly, Gordon
Day, Christopher
Godwin, James
Mathews, Daniel
Murray, Hon. George
Stanhope, John
Davidson, William
Colpoys, John
Byam, Edward
Panton, John Alexander
Toulmin, John
Hayward, Thomas
Jago, Richard
Lawson, Hugh
Dickson, William
Grove, Thomas Saunders
Mason, Christopher
Ward, William
Bowen, John
Nasmith, John Lockhart
McKillop, David

Waghorn, Martin
Howard, Phillip
Epworth, Farmery
Ashbury, Francis
Gest, James
Walters, George Robinson
Smith, William

1763
Cartwright, Charles
Kendall, Charles

Selected Bibliography and Sources

Books

Anon., *Regulations and Instructions relating to His Majesty's Service at Sea*, Ninth Edition (London: Privy Council, 1757).

Charnock, John, *Biographia Navalis* (London: Naval & Military Press, 2002; Reprint of 1797 Original Edition).

Colledge, James J, *Ships of the Royal Navy Vol. 1* (London: Greenhill Books, 1987).

Derrick, Charles, *Memoirs of the Rise and Progress of the Royal Navy* (London: Kessinger Publishing, 2010; Reprint of 1806 Original Edition).

James, William, *Naval History of Great Britain* (London: Richard Bentley, 1837).

Laird Clowes, William, *The Royal Navy – A History from the Earliest Times to 1900* (London: Chatham Publishing, 1996).

Lindsay, John, *A Voyage to the Coast of Africa in 1758* (London: S. Paterson, 1759).

Malcolmson, Robert, *Warships of the Great Lakes* (London: Chatham Publishing, 2001).

Marsh, A.J., "The taking of Gorée, 1758", *The Mariner's Mirror*, Volume 51 (1965), pp.117-130.

Marshall, John, Royal Navy Biography (London: W. Pople, 1823-1835).

McLynn, Frank, *1759* (London: Vintage, 2008)

Pappalardo, Bruno, *Royal Navy Lieutenant's Passing Certificates 1691-1902* (Chippenham: List and Index Society, 2001).

Pawlin, Tony, *The Falmouth Packets 1689-1851* (Truro: Truran, 2003).

Robson, Martin, *The Seven Years War* (London: I.B. Tauris & Co Ltd., 2017).

Rodger, N.A.M., *The Wooden World: An Anatomy of the Georgian Navy* (Glasgow: Fontana Press, 1986).

Rodger, N.A.M., *The Safeguard of the Seas: A Naval History of Britain Vol.I 660-1649* (London: Harper Collins, 1997).

Rodger, N.A.M., *The Command of the Ocean: A Naval History of Britain, Vol. 2 1649-1815* (London: Allen Lane, 2004).

Rodger, N.A.M., *Naval Records for Genealogists* (London: Her Majesty's Stationery Office, 1988).

Schomberg, Isaac, *Naval Chronology* (London: C. Roworth, 1802).

Syrett, David and DoNardo, R.L. *The Commissioned Sea Officers of the Royal Navy 1660-1815* (Aldershot: Navy Records Society, 1994).

Tracey, Nicholas, *The Battle of Quiberon Bay: Hawke and the Defeat of the French Invasion,* (Barnsley: Pen & Sword, 2010).

Winfield, Rif, *British Warships in the Age of Sail, 1603-1714* (Barnsley: Seaforth Publishing, 2009).

Winfield, Rif, *British Warships in the Age of Sail, 1714-1792* (Barnsley: Seaforth Publishing, 2007).

Winfield, Rif, *British Warships in the Age of Sail, 1793-1817* (Barnsley: Seaforth Publishing, 2005).

Primary Sources

The National Archives

ADM 1 Admiralty: Correspondence and Papers.

ADM 106 Navy Board Letters.
ADM 107 Lieutenants' passing certificates, Volumes 1-6.
ADM 12/27 1741-1793 'Black Book Vol I', Volumes B-D.
ADM 181 Navy Estimates, Volumes 1-6.
ADM 32 1755- 1811 Ships' pay books.
ADM 33 – Navy Board: Navy Pay Office: Ships' Pay Books, Series I.
ADM 34 – Navy Board: Navy Pay Office: Ships' Pay Books, Series II.
ADM 35 – Navy Board: Navy Pay Office: Ships' Pay Books, Series III.
ADM 354 – Navy Board Out Letters.
ADM 36 Admiralty: Ships' Musters (Series I) 1688-1808.
ADM 37 Admiralty: Ships' Musters (Series II) 1757-1842.
ADM 51 1669-1853 Admiralty: Captains' Logs.
ADM 52 1672-1840 Admiralty: Masters' Logs.
ADM 6 Admiralty: Service Records, Registers, Returns and Certificates, 1673-1960, Volumes 3-26.
ADM 6/86 Lieutenants' Passing Certificates 1744-1747.
ADM 6/87 Lieutenants' Passing Certificates 1753-1776.
ADM 8 Admiralty: List Books, 1673-1909, Volumes 26-39.

Online Resources

English Wikipedia <https://en.wikipedia.org>
French Wikipedia <https://fr.wikipedia.org>
Google Books <https://books.google.co.uk/>
Internet Archive <https://archive.org/>
Oxford Dictionary of National Biography (online) <http://www.oxforddnb.com/>
Project Seven Years War <http://www.kronoskaf.com/syw/index.php>
The National Archives, Discovery <https://discovery.nationalarchives.gov.uk/>
Three Decks – Warships in the Age of Sail <https://threedecks.org/>
Wikisource <https://en.wikisource.org>

Index of Ships

This is an index of warships that were in active service during the Seven Years War, to enable easy cross-referencing. It does not include ships that were extant 1754-1763 but had no commissioned officers assigned to them; nor does it cover ships on which officers listed in the book may have served upon at earlier or later stages of their careers.

FROM REASON TO REVOLUTION – WARFARE 1721-1815

http://www.helion.co.uk/published-by-helion/reason-to-revolution-1721-1815.html

The 'From Reason to Revolution' series covers the period of military history 1721–1815, an era in which fortress-based strategy and linear battles gave way to the nation-in-arms and the beginnings of total war.

This era saw the evolution and growth of light troops of all arms, and of increasingly flexible command systems to cope with the growing armies fielded by nations able to mobilise far greater proportions of their manpower than ever before. Many of these developments were fired by the great political upheavals of the era, with revolutions in America and France bringing about social change which in turn fed back into the military sphere as whole nations readied themselves for war. Only in the closing years of the period, as the reactionary powers began to regain the upper hand, did a military synthesis of the best of the old and the new become possible.

The series will examine the military and naval history of the period in a greater degree of detail than has hitherto been attempted, and has a very wide brief, with the intention of covering all aspects from the battles, campaigns, logistics, and tactics, to the personalities, armies, uniforms, and equipment.

Submissions

The publishers would be pleased to receive submissions for this series. Please contact series editor Andrew Bamford via email (andrewbamford18@gmail.com), or in writing to Helion & Company Limited, Unit 8 Amherst Business Centre, Budbrooke Road, Warwick, CV34 5WE

Titles

No 1 *Lobositz to Leuthen. Horace St Paul and the Campaigns of the Austrian Army in the Seven Years War 1756-57* Translated with additional materials by Neil Cogswell (ISBN 978-1-911096-67-2)

No 2 *Glories to Useless Heroism. The Seven Years War in North America from the French journals of Comte Maurés de Malartic, 1755-1760* William Raffle (ISBN 978-1-1911512-19-6) (paperback)

No 3 *Reminiscences 1808-1815 Under Wellington. The Peninsular and Waterloo Memoirs of William Hay* William Hay, with notes and commentary by Andrew Bamford (ISBN 978-1-1911512-32-5)

No 4 *Far Distant Ships. The Royal Navy and the Blockade of Brest 1793-1815* Quintin Barry (ISBN 978-1-1911512-14-1)

No 5 *Godoy's Army. Spanish Regiments and Uniforms from the Estado Militar of 1800* Charles Esdaile and Alan Perry (ISBN 978-1-911512-65-3) (paperback)

No 6 *On Gladsmuir Shall the Battle Be! The Battle of Prestonpans 1745* Arran Johnston (ISBN 978-1-911512-83-7)

No 7 *The French Army of the Orient 1798-1801. Napoleon's Beloved 'Egyptians'* Yves Martin (ISBN 978-1-911512-71-4)*

No 8 *The Autobiography, or Narrative of a Soldier. The Peninsular War Memoirs of William Brown of the 45th Foot* William Brown, with notes and commentary by Steve Brown (ISBN 978-1-911512-94-3) (paperback)

No 9 *Recollections from the Ranks. Three Russian Soldiers' Autobiographies from the Napoleonic Wars* Translated and annotated by Darrin Boland (ISBN 978-1-912174-18-8) (paperback)

No 10 *By Fire and Bayonet. Grey's West Indies Campaign of 1794* Steve Brown (ISBN 978-1-911512-60-8)

No 11 *Olmütz to Torgau. Horace St Paul and the Campaigns of the Austrian Army in the Seven Years War 1758-60* Translated with additional materials by Neil Cogswell (ISBN 978-1-911512-72-1)

No 12 *Murat's Army. The Army of the Kingdom of Naples 1806-1815* Digby Smith (ISBN 978-1-912390-09-0) (paperback)

No 13 *The Veteran or 40 Years' Service in the British Army. The Scurrilous Recollections of Paymaster John Harley 47th Foot – 1798-1838* John Harley, with notes and commentary by Gareth Glover (ISBN 978-1-912390-25-0) (paperback)

No 14 *Narrative of the Eventful Life of Thomas Jackson. Militiaman and Coldstream Sergeant, 1803-15* Thomas Jackson, with notes and commentary by Eamonn O'Keeffe (ISBN 978-1-912390-12-0) (paperback)

No 15 *For Orange and the States! The Army of the Dutch Republic 1713-1772. Part I: Infantry* Marc Geerdinck-Schaftenaar (ISBN 978-1-911512-15-8)*

No.16 *'Men who are Determined to be Free': The American Assault on Stony Point 15 July 1779* David Bonk (ISBN 978-1-912174-84-3)*

No 17 *Next to Wellington. General Sir George Murray. The Story of a Scottish Soldier and Statesman, Wellington's Quartermaster General* John Harding-Edgar (ISBN 978-1-912390-13-7)

No 18 *Between Scylla and Charybdis: The Army of Friedrich August II of Saxony, 1733-1763. Part I: Staff and Cavalry* Marco Pagan (ISBN 978-1-912174-89-8)*

No 19 *The Secret Expedition: The Anglo-Russian Invasion of Holland 1799* Geert van Uythoven (ISBN 978-1-912390-20-5)

No 20 *'We Are Accustomed to do our Duty' German Auxiliaries with the British Army 1793-95* Paul Demet (ISBN 978-1-912174-96-6)

No 21 *With the Guards in Flanders. The Diary of Captain Roger Morris 1793-95* Peter Harington (ISBN 978-1-911628-15-6) (paperback)

No 22 *The British Army in Egypt 1801. An Underrated Army Comes of Age* Carole Divall (ISBN 978-1-911628-17-0)*

No 23 *Better is the Proud Plaid. The Clothing, Weapons, and Accoutrements of the Jacobites in 1745* Jenn Scott (ISBN 978-1-911628-16-3)*

No 24 *The Lilies and the Thistle. French Troops in the Jacobite '45* Andrew Bamford (ISBN 978-1-911628-17-0)*

No 25 *A Light Infantryman With Wellington* Gareth Glover (ed.) (ISBN 978-1-911628-10-1) (paperback)

No 26 *Swiss Regiments in the Service of France 1798-1815. Uniforms, Organisation, Campaigns* Stephen Ede-Borrett (ISBN 978-1-911628-12-5)*

No 27 *For Orange and the States! The Army of the Dutch Republic 1713-1772. Part II: Cavalry and Specialist Troops* Marc Geerdinck-Schaftenaar (ISBN 978-1-911628-13-2)*

No 28 *Fashioning Regulation, Regulating Fashion. Uniforms and Dress of the British Army 1800-1815 Volume I* Ben Townsend (ISBN 978-1-911628-09-5)

No 29 *Riflemen. The History of the 5th Battalion 60th (Royal American) Regiment, 1797-1818* Robert Griffith (ISBN 978-1-911628-46-0)

No 30 *The Key to Lisbon. The Third French Invasion of Portugal, 1810-11* Kenton White (ISBN 978-1-911628-52-1)

No 31 *Command and Leadership. Proceedings of the 2018 Helion & Company 'From Reason to Revolution' Conference* Andrew Bamford (ed.) (ISBN 978-1-911628-53-8)

No 32 *Waterloo After the Glory. Hospital Sketches and Reports on the Wounded After the Battle* Michael Crumplin and Gareth Glover (ISBN 978-1-911628-48-4)

No 33 *Fluxes, Fevers, and Fighting Men. War and Disease in Ancien Regime Europe 1648-1789* Pádraig Lenihan (ISBN 978-1-911628-51-4)

No 34 *'They Were Good Soldiers'. African-Americans Serving in the Continental Army, 1775-1783* John U. Rees (ISBN 978-1-911628-54-5)*

No 35 *A Redcoat in America. The Diaries of Lieutenant William Bamford, 1757-1765 and 1776* Edited and Annotated by John B. Hattendorf (ISBN 978-1-911628-47-7) (paperback)

No 36 *Between Scylla and Charybdis: The Army of Friedrich August II of Saxony, 1733-1763. Part II: Infantry and Artillery* Marco Pagan (ISBN 978-1-911628-08-8)*

No 37 *Québec Under Siege: French Eye-Witness Accounts from the Campaign of 1759* Translated and Annotated by Charles A. Mayhood (ISBN 978-1-912866-73-1) (paperback)

No 38 *King George's Hangman: Henry Hawley and the Battle of Falkirk 1746* Jonathan D. Oates (ISBN 978-1-912866-64-9)

No 39 *Zweybruken in Command: The Reichsarmee in the Campaign of 1758* Translated with additional materials by Neil Cogswell (ISBN 978-1-911628-55-2)*

No 40 *So Bloody a Day: The 16th Light Dragoons in the Waterloo Campaign* David J. Blackmore (ISBN 978-1-912866-66-3)

No 41 *Northern Tars in Southern Waters: The Russian Fleet in the Mediterranean 1806-1810* Vladimir Bogdanovich Bronevskiy, translated and annotated by Darrin Boland (ISBN 978-1-912866-71-7) (paperback)

No 42 *Royal Navy Officers of the Seven Years War: A Biographical Dictionary of Commissioned Officers 1748-1763* Cy Harrison (ISBN 978-1-912866-68-7) (paperback)

* indicates 'Falconet' format paperbacks, page size 248mm x 180 mm, with high visual content including colour plates; other titles are hardback monographs unless otherwise noted.